FROMMER'S

FAMILY
TRAVEL GUIDE

California
with Kids

4th Edition

by Carey Simon and
Charlene Marmer Solomon

MACMILLAN • USA

ABOUT THE AUTHORS

Carey Simon has been writing books and articles on family travel and activities for more than twelve years. She is joined on her family trips by her husband, Danny, and eleven-year-old daughter Janey.

Charlene Marmer Solomon, mother of fourteen-year-old Andrew and eight-year-old Elizabeth, has been writing articles and books on parenting, travel, and psychology for more than fifteen years. She and her husband, Alan, have traveled extensively with their children. The L.A.–based writers have appeared on television and radio to share their knowledge of family travel.

MACMILLAN TRAVEL

A Simon & Schuster Macmillan Company
15 Columbus Circle
New York, NY 10023

ISBN 0-02860460-1
ISSN 1040-9386

Editors: Peter Katucki, Robin Michaelson
Map Editor: Douglas Stallings
Design by Michele Laseau
Cover design by Michael Freeland
Maps by Ortelius Design

SPECIAL SALES

Bulk purchases (10 or more copies) of Frommer's Travel Guides are available to corporations at special discounts. The Special Sales Department can produce custom editions to be used as premiums and/or for sales promotion to suit individual needs. Existing editions can be produced with custom cover imprints such as corporate logos. For more information write to: Special Sales, Simon & Schuster, 1230 Avenue of the Americas, New York, NY 10020.

Manufactured in the United States of America

Contents

List of Maps

To my family, who travel with me on all my creative journeys: Alan, whose support and love allow me to try new adventures; and Andrew and Elizabeth, who enrich my life by their very existence.

—Charlene

To Danny, with gratitude for your unfailing sense of humor; and to Janey, with thanks for allowing me to see the world through your eyes.

—Carey

Acknowledgments

This fourth edition of *Frommer's California with Kids* has been as rewarding to prepare as the first. If anything, we've gained an even better appreciation of what it means to travel with our families. Once again the book was completed with the love and encouragement of many friends. My thanks also go to Janey's friends who helped us research so many activities. And of course my appreciation goes to Charlene, with whom I share all the ups and downs of traveling with our kids.

—C.S.

No book is written by the authors alone, but a travel book about parents and kids requires the support of lots of people. The glamour and excitement of traveling around the state of California with children quickly pales when a working mother faces up to the stark realities of research and writing on the road—with children in tow. Tape recorder, transcriber, and steno pads lay side by side in hotel rooms with sand pails, coloring books, and Gameboys. Work must go on even when one child is carsick; plans can't be scrapped when a child sprains his toe. My family and friends were of enormous support in this endeavor. Shirley Solomon, Melinda Marmer, and Michele Alonge and David Marmer continue to be a boundless source of support and enthusiasm; Terry Paule and Samuel Greengard always help me think things through. Finally, Barbara and Irving Marmer taught me that traveling with children—no matter how many and how far—is a glorious way to create treasured memories. And, to Carey, thank you for continuing to teach me things, and for keeping a sense of humor.

—C.M.S.

OUR THANKS GO TO: Among the scores of gracious people who have supported our efforts, special thanks go to Jody Welborn, Steve Dolainski, Davida Skigen, Dorothy Jordan, and Susan Tenner.

We won't forget the assistance of Fred Sater of the California Office of Tourism and the special help of many other people in the convention and visitors bureaus around the state, including Gary Sherwin (Los Angeles), Tracey Vaughan (Monterey Peninsula), Helen Chang (San Jose), Laurie Allison (San Diego), Janna Nichols (San Luis Obispo County), Elaine Cali and Barbara McClelland (Anaheim), Jeff Irons (Mammoth Lakes), Cammie Conlon (Fort Bragg), Dawn Strawne and Sharon Rooney (San Francisco), Lucy Steffens (Sacramento), John Reginato (Shasta Cascade Wonderland), Laurie Armstrong (Lake Tahoe Visitors Authority), Debra Wager (Tahoe North), Tami Bissell (Palm Springs), and Terri Shore (Sonoma).

And a special thank you to our many readers who have taken the time to write us with their family travel experiences and suggestions.

An Invitation to the Reader

In researching this book, we discovered many wonderful places—hotels, restaurants, shops, and more. We're sure you'll find others. Please tell us about them, so we can share the information with your fellow travelers in upcoming editions. If you were disappointed with a recommendation, we'd love to know that, too. Please write to:

Carey Simon and Charlene Marmer Solomon
Frommer's California with Kids, 4th Edition
c/o Macmillan Travel
15 Columbus Circle
New York, NY 10023

An Additional Note

Please be advised that travel information is subject to change at any time—and this is especially true of prices. We therefore suggest that you write or call ahead for confirmation when making your travel plans. The authors, editors, and publisher cannot be held responsible for the experiences of readers while traveling. Your safety is important to us, however, so we encourage you to stay alert and be aware of your surroundings. Keep a close eye on cameras, purses, and wallets, all favorite targets of thieves and pickpockets.

A Family Guide to California

1

FAMILY VACATIONS MEAN DIFFERENT THINGS TO DIFFERENT PEOPLE. SOME PARENTS take their children with them whenever and wherever they go. Others believe that children do well only in certain places—Grandma's cabin in the country or Disneyland. Whichever you choose, or if you're somewhere in the middle, we're here to share with you what we've learned—through experience and research—about traveling with children.

For the best-humored, adventurous, flexible parent, family travel is a kick. For the faint-of-heart or those who like complete predictability, we warn you—hold on to your hat! You're about to embark on a wonderful adventure.

1 California with Kids

A BEGINNING

How did this book start? It began when one of us, Carey Simon, took (then) 1-year-old Jane to Paris and found herself ordering pâté (it was closest to chopped liver) and consommé ("It's chicken soup, honey") off the room-service menu because she didn't know where to buy baby food at 9pm. It continued when the other, Charlene Solomon, wrestled with changing baby Elizabeth's dirty diapers in an airplane seat while trying to enjoy 7-year-old Andrew's exuberance about being 30,000 feet above the ground.

It crystallized when we agreed that in spite of all the apparatus we had to carry, all the advance planning required, all the early mornings in hotel rooms when we worried about television cartoons being too loud for the people next door, we loved traveling with our children—and intended to keep enjoying it as they grew.

We weren't alone.

We shared long, funny stories with friends about which child did the "best" in first-class restaurants and which toddler was carried the most on hikes. We watched frustrated parents on airline flights trying to get food to their child before the designated mealtime. We shared experiences about rude hotel desk clerks who eyed our kids as if they were fleas, and about restaurant personnel who made us feel like lepers when we arrived with young children.

That's how the book began.

We were constantly asked by new parents what they should take on weekend trips with their baby. We were asked which fine restaurants and hotels were cordial to children, and which moderately priced and inexpensive places adults would enjoy too. It became clear that there were lots of people just like us who wanted to take their kids with them to places not always considered "family" establishments. It became apparent that this book had to be written.

There is no other comprehensive travel guide like this one, which has activities, accommodations, and restaurants tested by parents and their children. That's not to say that our three little wayfarers tried everything you find in this book. But their perspectives, and those of their friends, older cousins, and acquaintances, have always been the guidelines we've followed.

For example, restaurant and hotel staffs had to be friendly to children to be included. We point out cases where we feel a restaurant or hotel would be a good experience for older kids. Our descriptions of sightseeing attractions are also written with children in mind. You'll notice we don't catalog a museum's collection. Instead, we often tell you which exhibits excite the kids. We don't give a step-by-step guide to the theme parks, but we do tell you if you can buy diapers there, or if you should bring along your own apple juice.

In the years since we began this book we continue to travel with our children. Jane is now 11, Andrew is 14, and Elizabeth is 8 years old. We have all become quite seasoned travelers, adding to our repertoire of knowledge such goodies as adventure travel, skiing, camping, and dude-ranch experiences. You'll see our new knowledge reflected in these pages.

WHY CALIFORNIA?

We chose California because it's the perfect family travel destination. It presents so many opportunities for different vacations. You can take ocean, desert, mountain, and city trips. There are scores of children's activities and all sorts of places to stay, from resorts and first-class hotels to houseboats, cabins, condos, and campgrounds.

2   How to Travel with Kids

When you travel with your children, the whole world opens up. Everyday events become adventures—wanted and unwanted. It's a chance to share activities in a way that makes them lifelong memories. You can't duplicate the astonishment in children's eyes when they catch their first glimpse of the Golden Gate Bridge. You can't anticipate the joy they'll have playing tag with the ocean waves. And you'll never believe the excitement they feel the first time they see Disneyland.

And then there's the unexpected: for us, an evening swim with the kids in a hotel pool on a warm California night; a flight attendant who had (then) 7-year-old Andrew help pass out candies at the end of the flight; a hike in Yosemite that brought us face-to-face with a coyote; a powerful friendship that sprouted up between two 4-year-olds in a Palm Springs resort; two 10-year-olds racing their remote-control cars in the airport lounge. Or your daughter holding her first starfish or climbing her first "mountain." And there are the delightful adult experiences—the people you meet because their kids and yours are playing in the hotel swimming pool together; the fellow parents traveling by air with their encumbrance of diapers, formula, and baby toys with whom you commiserate while walking a fussy baby.

And of course there are the experiences that you're sure will ruin your vacation at the time, but make you laugh later when you reminisce—like the baby who couldn't get used to the new crib and cried for the first four nights of a seven-day vacation, or the toddler who became carsick every time you got in the car to continue your trip, the hotel reservations that weren't honored, and the room-service menus that listed only spinach quiche and médaillons of veal.

Lifetime travelers ourselves, and now with our families, it is our hope to open the world of travel and fun to other families. Prepare to laugh and be surprised, and be sure to get out the scrapbooks because there'll be lots to remember!

SOME ADVICE

The best advice we can give you is threefold: First, plan ahead. Most children want to know how long it takes to get where you're going and what they'll be doing once they arrive. With kids, it's not much fun just to arrive in town without knowing what there is to do as a family. That's not to say that you can't have spontaneity, but be sure to have some game plan in mind, even if it changes as you go along.

Second, don't expect too much from your kids. On a short holiday you can't cover every sightseeing attraction, every historical monument, and every activity with children. You'll just end up with cranky, unhappy kids and a horrible vacation. So either plan a longer trip or a second visit another time. But whatever you do, make lots of rest stops and take lots of energy breaks.

Third, and possibly most important, be sure to approach your family vacation with a grand sense of humor. It won't all be perfect, but some of it will be fabulous. In any event, you'll be spending treasured time together as a family.

PREPARATION

It may be that you used to be the kind of people who took spontaneous weekend trips, threw a bathing suit in the car and just went. Obviously you can't do that anymore. Although some spontaneity is still possible, now you have to plan ahead—where to go, when to go, what forms of transportation to use, and what to pack.

Planning Your Trip

When you conjure up visions of a perfect family vacation, what do you see? Are you enjoying the outdoors—hiking, boating, waterskiing—or are you visiting museums, art galleries, and cultural attractions? Do you want a city sightseeing vacation, or a seaside, mountain, or desert excursion? Are you planning to camp, stay in a hotel, or rent a condo or home?

Consider it all. Then take into account the age of your children, what they're capable of doing, and what they enjoy most. If you love museums but your kids can barely tolerate them, it's fruitless to plan a vacation filled with gallery-hopping. The kids will be restless and frustrated—and so will you, in the end.

Good family vacations balance everyone's likes. We like to include our kids in part of the planning. Experienced travelers advise that after you, as adults, have determined the expense and length of the vacation, you discuss with the kids the options that are available. Take them with you to get travel brochures and maps. Write the visitors' bureaus or chambers of commerce of the places you intend to visit for details of current happenings. Get a good guidebook for further source material. Everyone will get excited about some aspect of the trip.

A Few Tips

Be realistic about your expectations. Remember that when your kids are at home, they follow a routine and know what to expect. Consider how your children will react when they're taken out of that routine, and plan accordingly. Remember, too, that travel requires a lot of waiting around. The relief you may feel when you finally reach your hotel room may not be felt by a youngster who has just experienced a wait in the hotel lobby, preceded by waits at the airport, on the plane, and in the taxi. Remember that *you* can anticipate the great thrills you'll have on the special rides and attractions at theme parks—even when you're standing in a 20-minute-long line. Most children, even very sophisticated ones, have trouble with that.

Many child-development experts will tell you that brothers and sisters may bicker even more than usual when they're traveling. Of course, it depends on the kind of traveling you do, but the discomfort of an eight-hour car trip is felt by all, especially those little munchkins in the back seat who are tucked in with the extra luggage.

Also, remember that kids can get homesick for familiar surroundings. We've always been amazed how happy our children are to get home to their own rooms—even when they enjoyed their trip and continually talk fondly about the vacation. To help with that, be sure to bring favorite cuddlies, blankets, and familiar music cassette tapes for evening relaxation and bedtime.

Toddlers seem to be the ones who have the toughest time adapting to the changes inherent in traveling. If you're on a five-hour coast-to-coast flight, your infant will often sleep through much of it, and your school-age kids and teens may occupy themselves with movies, games, books, and thoughts. Your toddler, however, is a different breed. He or she may sleep for a while, but then wake up disoriented and cranky; may love visiting with people or become shy and clingy. And in the hotel room, you never know what awaits at nap and sleep time, especially if you've made a big jump in clock time.

We always think about traveling from a toddler's point of view because he or she can make or break the trip. We divide up long sightseeing days with lots of activity breaks where a toddler can run around. It's surprising how we forget that while children, even those as young as kindergarten age, get absorbed in many of the joys of traveling, as we do, a 2-, 3-, or 4-year-old just doesn't appreciate the same things. Take this into consideration.

Some people suggest that a way to help your young child prepare for a time change is to start before you leave on your trip. Slightly shift your schedule to start altering the child's internal clock.

We suggest you request that the crib be in the hotel room *before* you arrive. (By the way, most hotel cribs do not come with bumper guards—we have used towels in their place.) We recommend spending some time in the room and having the little one take a nap in the new surroundings before it's time to go to sleep for the night. In fact, we spend time in the room so that all the kids get used to it. Our 8-year-old takes out her toys and arranges them, just so, in a place she wants as her play area.

Also, plan to go at a slower pace than you might do alone. And always have extra snacks and juice along, no matter where you travel—in a car, airplane, or train. We keep a stash in the hotel room and, for emergencies, in Mom's purse.

Packing

Before we had children, packing for a trip was a simple and fairly painless exercise. We could pack at the last minute, and not think too much beyond packing a warm enough sweater, several books, and a hairdryer.

Packing when you travel with kids is an entirely different matter—that is, if you want to stay sane. First of all, you can forget the magazines and novels for yourselves (unless you have children who are older or remarkably self-sufficient), and your own wardrobe becomes considerably less important. (But remember that teething infants can soil almost as many of your shirts as their own.)

Sure, you can wait until the last minute and throw things into several suitcases, but you'll pay for it over and over again. And remember, too, that the younger the child, the greater the need for a plan.

We know now that when we travel with our kids, packing is an experiment in wizardry. How do you pack the contents of half a home into a tiny suitcase? We allow each child one suitcase for clothes and a backpack for toys and books. No matter how we limit the number of things each child can take, there's always the extra stuffed animal and favorite game that has to be included at the last minute.

Before we pack, we first decide whether we're going to use coin-operated laundries or hotel cleaning services, or whether we're going to bring all the soiled laundry home. Once this is decided, we still try to take as little as we think we can get away with, and then think about it again to see if we can cut back. Naturally, this requires planning, actually laying out clothes a few days ahead and writing things down.

Depending on the vacation—time of year and length—we start thinking about the kids' clothes at least a week or two in advance. We make a list for each child, including the type of clothing and the amount we'll need.

Need we tell you that kids get dirty, wet, and messy? We've learned that we need an extra outfit per day for most children over the age of 3 (excluding teens, of course). For children under 3, pack at least three outfits, or plan ahead which ones can be hand-washed and used again.

We also pack a set of clothes that we keep in a carry-on bag for the plane or a car bag, in case we can't get to the suitcases right away (or in case the luggage gets lost!). If you're going to a different climate, don't forget to put that coat or sundress where you can get to it easily.

Consider in advance how many diapers you'll need before you have to get to a market again, and what kind of toys you'll want with you, and which cassette tapes to bring.

And don't forget to write down the names of the medications your kids will need. This is a good time to check on the quantity of such items as prescription cough medicine, Tylenol, and other potential middle-of-the-night necessities. Be sure to pack a thermometer, and if you have a tot in diapers, pack lots of baby wipes and diaper-rash medications. We always include towelettes for all our kids.

For younger children, it doesn't hurt to bring flexible straws and a small plastic cup with a lid. We found too often that glasses in restaurants were too tall and cups on airlines too fat, or that only bottled drinks were available. We also bring a cheap nightlight to ease little ones' fears at night. If you have curious toddlers, you'll find outlet covers handy to bring along, too. And we pack a box of plastic bags, which come in handy for loose toys, wet bathing suits, horribly soiled clothes, and crackers from demolished boxes. The new stain-remover sticks are invaluable if you choose to take soiled clothes back home.

Toys

People have different opinions about the number of toys you should take on a trip. We bring some new toys and some old favorites. The kids each gets his or her own backpack, or small toy box in the back seat of the car, for the toys and books they especially want. We stash new playthings in our suitcase or bag and dole them out when the kids tire of what they've brought. When the trip is a long one, we actually wrap the new toys and distribute them to the kids at key moments—timed to hold their interest. We'll alternate creative-type toys, such as crayons, with toys and games that require some concentration and thinking. We always include items that we enjoy playing with, too, since we'll be doing lots of that. There are so many toys and travel accessories available on the market today that it's no problem finding great ones. Disney and Rand-McNally offer some good possibilities.

Once your child is old enough to enjoy cassette tape stories and songs, you've found a real treasure. These keep Andrew, Janey, and Elizabeth occupied for hours at a time, long enough so that they—and their parents—can endure very long car trips.

When you're traveling, be sure to leave the messy, noisy toys and projects at home. Puzzles and games with little pieces can also give you grief. Our least-favorite words on a cross-country flight were "Oh, I dropped some again!" Picture yourself picking up little game pieces in a crowded, baggage-filled row of airline seats. There are better ways to have fun and meet your neighbors.

Here are some ideas of what to take along: packages of stickers and sticker books, magnetic drawing boards and alphabet boards, magnetic games, hand puppets, write-and-wipe boards, Colorforms™, crayons that don't melt, coloring books, tracing paper and things to trace, self-inking stamps and paper. For older kids, you might want to bring small cars, decks of cards, and a journal or a cassette recorder in which they can describe their experiences. Check the earphones before you purchase the recorder. After surprising Jane with a set on the plane, we spent the next hour trying to make them fit her small head. We often put together a craft box with lots of goodies that the kids can use to create artistic treasures. Try it! If your child will need scissors, purchase safety scissors at a specialty shop. On car trips, you can bring song books and music cassettes. If you're renting a car, check ahead as to whether there's a tape deck.

Precautions

When visiting crowded sightseeing attractions, dress kids in bright clothing so it's easy for you to keep an eye on them, but also decide what your children should do if you should get separated while sightseeing—and talk with them about it.

Every time you check into a new hotel room, it's a good idea to consider what you would do if there's a fire. Where are the exits? Which adult is responsible for which child or children? If you have toddlers, you might want to bring covers for electrical outlets.

In medical matters, be prepared. Be sure to pack all the medications your children may need, and take along your doctors' phone numbers so you can call your personal physician if you have a serious problem—even if it's long distance. If you're flying, be sure that any signs of congestion or a cold are seen by your doctor before departure. He or she can tell you what to do to prevent inner-ear injury. You might also ask about nasal sprays and oral decongestants for your kids for takeoff and landing.

Be prepared for motion sickness. Kids who never get motion sickness in a car can get it on a boat, in a stuffy airplane, or on a train. Those of you who have tried to get a pill down the throat of an uncooperative child will appreciate the joys of liquid Dramamine, which you can give to kids over 2. (We mixed it with soda before getting on the boat from Catalina.) Ask your pediatrician about other remedies. And avoid sweet, gooey snacks before the trip.

And on a less threatening note, we always have all reservation confirmations sent to us in writing. Whenever possible, it's best to have something written down—and with you—to show in the event of a problem.

If you're planning to register your kids for children's programs at hotels, or in day-care or ski schools, be sure to find out whether you need to make reservations in advance. Policies change, and you don't want to make big vacation plans which include children's programs only to get there and find out your kids can't get in. Also remember to check out these programs thoroughly.

AIR TRAVEL

Flying is always an unpredictable adventure. Too bad you can't predict if it's going to be a good one or bad one.

The kids, especially young ones who need to be confined to a small area, get very antsy. You don't have the control you do in a car where you can stop when you want to let the kids run around. And some young children may become frightened.

To ward off negative experiences, talk with your young children before the trip about what will happen. If your children are flying for the first time, some people think it helps if you take them to an airport to look at the planes before your trip. Bringing a favorite blanket or stuffed animal will help a lot in the cabin.

Once on board, remember that cabin temperature can vary. Bring extra clothes for each child and make sure that what they wear is layered, loose, and comfortable.

Waiting in airports can be the torment of many a parent. Although we try to time our arrival so we won't be too early but won't have to run for the plane, it's impossible to predict when a plane will leave late. In the event of a delayed departure, we take our children for walks, try to find video arcades, and look for other kids their age in the waiting area for them to play with. When all else fails, we attempt to find a corner area where we can spread out and play on the floor (ugh!). A few U.S. airports have children's play areas. Ask—they're a blessing.

Warning: Whatever you do, don't leave the terminal. We were once assured by airline officials that we had a three-hour delay, so we took a long walk. When we returned, the plane had already departed. The airline officials said they had paged and paged, but all passengers who didn't return to the flight had to rebook.

A car seat helps to protect the youngster, and in some cases it's useful for keeping the child where you want him or her. Your child may be more likely to sit for a longer period of time in a familiar car seat than in a large seat with a lap belt. You can bring along and use a car seat for a very young child if there are empty seats on the flight. Naturally, purchasing a separate ticket on any airline assures seating for the youngster.

Your kids should always wear their seat belts when seated. And although kids need to move around, don't let them crawl on the floors or in aisles where they could get their fingers pinched or stepped on. Don't let them loose, especially in galleys where there are hot liquids and all kinds of things that are dangerous in little hands.

Request special seating if necessary. Seats facing the bulkhead, with no seat in front, can be comfortable, but because of the fold-in trays, they don't have retractable armrests. Parents should know that kids can't sit next to exit doors, so it's important to tell the reservationist when you book seats that you're bringing children, so that they don't inadvertently put you there. Some airlines have cardboard infant beds with tiny pads that you can put at your feet if you're in the bulkhead seats. Ask in advance.

There's nothing worse than trying to change a baby in an airplane restroom. Some international carriers have pull-down diaper-changing tables; most domestic airlines don't. (In the past, we've taken the airline blanket and a plastic changing pad into the bathroom and spread the blanket on the toilet seat and put the pad on top.) Some flight attendants will offer to let you use the jump seat—ask. If there's an area not occupied, you can go there. In the cabin, you can fold up the armrest and use the seats, but some nonparents are offended and complain. Remember to be discreet and considerate. Take the diaper and dispose of it in the restroom in an in-flight sick bag or plastic bag.

Most airlines warm bottles and baby food, but if you have babies on bottles, ask when booking flights. All airlines carry milk and a selection of juices. Some airlines even carry emergency diapers.

Most airlines serve special kids' meals upon request—usually hamburgers or hot dogs, and sometimes spaghetti. But believe us, you don't want to order spaghetti for your young child on an airplane! Place your meal requests with the reservationist at least 24 hours in advance.

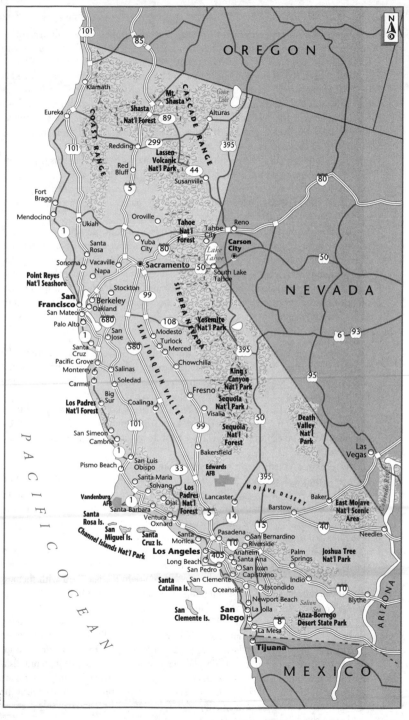

California

Another helpful hint is to carry on a small umbrella stroller that will fit in an overhead bin. This is good for layovers or delays, and is especially helpful for a parent who is carrying many things and is traveling alone with a child.

And always, always bring along snacks and beverages in a carry-on bag. The kids may not always be able to wait for the scheduled meals and you don't even know if they will actually eat the airline food. We pack a full goodie bag, complete with fresh fruit, bread, raisins, crackers and cheese, pretzels, and lots of individual boxes of juice. Kids get very thirsty on flights. In that goodie bag, include several flexible straws, and for little ones, drinking cups with lids.

Finally, airlines will allow you to board in advance with children. This is wonderful if you're carrying on tons of things and/or have more than one child to settle. If you feel your kid needs to expend that last bit of energy, try talking the flight attendant into letting one adult get on board with all the paraphernalia and the other one stay with the child until the last minutes of boarding.

As we mentioned in the "Precautions" section, call your physician if your child has the slightest cold, because there can be long-term damage to ears as a result of the changes in cabin pressurization. You might also want to find out about nose drops for kids who don't have cold symptoms. Swallowing is what helps to equalize the pressure in one's head, so small children should always have something to drink or suck on during ascent or descent—a bottle or pacifier—and older kids can chew gum or suck on a hard candy.

CAR TRAVEL

Traveling in a car with children is unlike any other experience. It's one that cannot be adequately described. You have to experience it to understand it. Remember that you'll all be enclosed in a very small space for an extended period of time. Good humor and lots to do—and eat and drink—are the order of the day.

The main rule is plan to stop every few hours to break up the monotony and allow the kids time to get out and move around. Your stops don't always have to be at restaurants to eat. You can stop when you see a lovely park or where you know there's a special attraction.

Seating arrangements in the car are important too. One parent might get into the back seat along with the kids to ward off trouble. This helps especially if one child is having a hard time, or if your kids tend to bicker or get rowdy when you're on the road. It's better than constantly having to turn around and lean over the front seat, getting nauseated as you look backward. It also protects you from running the risk of being ticketed for not wearing a seatbelt—a law in California.

Also, be sure to bring along an adequate supply of pacifiers, bottles, and snacks. If you want kids to fall asleep, sometimes stroking their heads, along with soft music and the motion of the car, will do the trick. If you're in the back seat with them, it helps if you prevent their heads from flopping around. Prop little kids' heads up with pillows in the car seat. Pack enough pillows and blankets for everyone.

To deal with "When will we get there?" we get a road map and a yellow marking pen before we leave on the trip and plot out the route, circling different points of interest or particular milestones. When we pass those points, or a few minutes before we approach them, we talk about them. This not only gives children a sense of accomplishing the miles, but also tends to make them take a more active interest in the landmarks of the trip. Of course, this takes a little preparation on your part. But the game plan can be as simple as calculating where you'll stop for gas and roadside stretches and letting the kids know these details.

When driving during the day, anticipate where the sun will be. If you can't keep the kids out of the sun, use a visor. Children really get uncomfortable with sun in their eyes, and they may complain unmercifully if they're hot and sweaty. Driving through the California desert can be a grueling experience. Without our knowing it until later, one of our children actually got sunburned from it. You can get a dark cellophanelike material that sticks to the window and can be moved around depending on where the sun is.

To combat motion sickness, experts suggest eating lemon drops, lemon cookies, or peppermint; also foods high in carbohydrates, and salt-covered foods such as crackers or pretzels, which cut down the production of what causes nausea. Again, ask your pediatrician for advice. Also, if your children are susceptible to nausea, don't allow them to read while the car is in motion.

Now for the problem of preventing boredom. Some of the games we play are especially well suited for automobile travel. For kids over 6, try the geography game, where one player chooses a place, country, city, or region, and the next player has to name a place whose first letter begins with the last letter of the previous place name.

Another fun way to pass the time is to make up a game using the license plates of passing vehicles. Young kids can look for the letters of the alphabet in sequence. Older children can try to spell words or find cars from every state in the union. Very little children can name the colors of passing cars or look for particular colors.

There are complete books of road games available, which provide enough games even for very extensive trips.

And an all-time favorite is a group sing.

RENTAL CARS

One of your first decisions will be whether or not you need to rent a car. If you are renting, be sure the agency has car seats for children 4 years old and younger—they're required by law in California. Be sure to specify that you need one—and reserve it.

Often you'll get better rates from smaller companies. Check around and ask about discounts. If you're in a large city, you might consider renting from a company that's located near your hotel, since some rates are higher if you rent at airports. Always ask about discounts.

If you're used to the ease of getting kids in and out of a four-door car at home, be sure to request such a model. And if you're accustomed to electric windows so you're not always reaching back to open the window for your toddler (usually they demand it when you're on the freeway!), ask for a car with that feature. Air conditioning, too, is important during the summer in California. All this sounds elementary, but if you've ever arrived in a town ready to use a rental car for a week only to find you hadn't requested the conveniences you and the kids are used to, you'll realize how important it is to ask for these things in advance.

TRAINS

Train travel, although not the luxurious form of transportation it used to be, is still one way to see the scenery without having to constantly stop for gas, or find a restaurant or hotel. Kids can move around, play easier than in a car, and often learn a lot about this mode of transportation.

For overnight travelers, **Amtrak** (☎ toll free **800/USA-RAIL**) offers family bedrooms on some of its trains. You'll have to check your individual route for information on what accommodations are available.

Short trips, such as those from Los Angeles to San Diego or Santa Barbara, can be fun experiences for children, and the journey itself can be the adventure rather than the destination. You can take a morning train from L.A. to San Diego, for instance, take a trolley to the Embarcadero, have lunch, and then return that evening.

BOATS

There are boats—and then there are ships. Cruising with kids has become big business, and most cruise lines have gotten in on the act. Most family cruises offer children's programs (often all-day activities), babysitting, children's meals, and family-style accommodations. Many lines offer these cruises during summer or holidays. Some have programs year round. Check with individual cruise lines, depending on where you plan to embark. Ask about special prices for children.

You might want to contact **TWYCH (Travel with Your Children),** 45 W. 18th St., New York, NY 10011 (☎ **212/206-0688**), for a copy of their cruise and airline guide.

Boating, especially in California, is a very common activity. As a visitor, you'll more than likely take a harbor cruise of some sort, or a whale-watching or fishing trip. Note the time of year and water conditions if you have a child prone to motion sickness. Even in California you can get cold on the high seas, so wear layers of clothing. Rubber-soled shoes will help you and the children keep your balance. Short trips are best with young children. If you're going on a longer journey, check whether the boat has food and restroom facilities. You might even ask if one of the boats has stabilizers for a smoother ride.

PREPARING CHILDREN FOR THE OUTDOORS

You may have exceptional children, but ours need to be prepared to enjoy outdoor vacationing. Many city kids do. They need to be told how much fun they're going to have without video games nearby. We also find it helpful to mention before we leave home that television won't be an important part of the vacation (of course, unless that isn't true). In fact, the first time Andrew entered a forest, he noticed there were no TV antennas and was convinced his vacation was ruined. That was when he was 7. At 14, it's an entirely different story. He now anticipates the delights that await him—even in an environment sans television.

While parents who have hiked with their youngsters at an early age may not have any problems, most kids need a little advance help from you so they can really enjoy what's in store for them. The first, and most important, way to help your kids love the outdoors is to let them feel your excitement and enjoyment. Even the most jaded, citified child looks in wonder when parents convey their awe at towering peaks or their pleasure at walking on soft pine needles in a dense forest.

We start talking to our group early about the animals we might see, the wildlife in the forest, the environment, and the weather. We use books about the area and about wildlife in general to illustrate some of the wonders we might encounter. Kids relate easily to animals—from Bambi to butterflies—so use that awareness as a bridge to help them become sensitive to the wooded, wild environment. Let little children know that they'll be seeing some big things and hearing some loud noises—huge trees, surging waterfalls, mammoth mountains and cliffs. A case in point: When Janey was 3, she got her first look at the colossal redwood trees. She was so terrified of "the giants" we had to cut the trip short. We hadn't prepared her for what she was about to see, never dreaming that the size of those trees could be overwhelming to a little person. Now, at 11, she's a "pro."

You know your children and what sparks their imaginations. Maybe it's the idea of collecting autumn leaves for a school project or anticipating how many different kinds of animals they'll encounter. You might want to play a game with them, like trying to find camouflaged insects and other creatures. If you're planning special activities, such as horseback riding or bicycling, talk about them. Share your natural enthusiasm. Some children just need a little encouragement when Disneyland isn't the destination.

Remember two more important things about the mountain areas. First, there's lots of dust and pollen and "interesting" blooming foliage around. Be sure to bring medication for children who suffer from such allergies. Second, the altitude is higher. Be conscious of changes in children's behavior because of possible reactions to the change in altitude. Ask your pediatrician for advice.

Cautions

Park rangers are the "wise men" of the national park system. They are fully aware of the dangers for kids within these pristine areas, and they've shared their wisdom with us. Their suggestions are as follows:

SCRAMBLING   Kids are natural scramblers. They love to scurry up one rock and scramble to the next one above it. Scrambling can be dangerous, say the rangers, and parents must be responsible for where their kids scramble. Teach them about safe climbing. Only let your kids scramble if the area is completely safe—no perched rock, no slick or wet areas on which they can slip and fall.

WILDLIFE   Don't attempt to feed the wild animals. Wild animals that become too tame because of feeding by humans are in grave danger during the winter months when there's no one to feed them and they no longer know how to forage for food. Heed all bear warnings, and follow advice about where to store food.

Remember that wild animals are just that—wild. Deer can be more dangerous to little children than bears. Parents, who would never dream of putting their child within reach of a bear, have been known to put their toddlers too close to the "cute" little fawn to grab a great photo, only to have an angry male deer (antlers and all) charge the child.

SWIMMING AND WATER ACTIVITIES   Rivers and lakes are especially enticing, but in general, avoid wading into water that's rushing and swirling. Generally the spring and early summer pose the greatest threat because melting snow swells rivers and streams. If signs aren't posted for swimming (and they usually aren't), ask a passing ranger or stop at a visitor center to inquire about the conditions. Most important, *avoid rocks that are near misty, foggy, and wet areas.* Don't rely on your visual senses to determine if they are safe or not. Rocks near the water have been made slick by years of water agitation that has smoothed them down. A beckoning large rock that's too close to a waterfall or is receiving mist from fast-running water is a treacherous place to be—for you or your kids—and can turn into disaster. Always avoid ledges near waterfalls, no matter how enticing and safe they look.

Speaking about water, it's safest not to drink water unless you know that it's pure. Unfortunately, the wilderness is not always blessed with clean water, so be sure to ask a park ranger about which places have pure water before letting the kids drink from streams and little pools.

HIKING   Remind your kids to stay on trails, to stay with the group, and to be careful when they pick up rocks. It's best for them to move a big rock with their feet first to be sure it isn't protecting a snake's home. Also, caution young children not to put their hands down holes in the ground. Try to find out if there is poison oak or poison ivy in the area, and show your children what it looks like. Finally, always stay *close* to your toddler or preschooler on the trail.

RIVER RAFTING AND CANOEING These are wonderful adventures with school-age children as long as you're prepared and choose a reputable company. Thankfully, several associations offer trips specifically for families with young children, some with storytelling and games.

Rivers are classified from I to V, a Class I river (or section of the river) being the easiest. Trips vary in length of time from overnight to many days, and are offered in several different locations throughout the state. When you consider these adventurous vacations, remember that safety is the primary concern, and keep that in mind when asking questions.

To obtain rafting information for all California rivers, you can contact **California Outdoors** (☎ toll free **800/552-3625** in California). This group offers a free directory of dozens of river-rafting companies operating in California, including a brief description of the trips and the minimum ages for children.

Friends of the River (☎ **415/771-0400**) is another group that offers river-rafting information and booking. When you book your trip through this organization, part of the fee goes toward river preservation.

CLOTHING Typically, mountain areas have a range of climates and temperatures because of the terrain. During the summer it can reach the mid-90s, and during the winter it can fall below 30°. It varies throughout Yosemite, for instance, because the elevation ranges from 2,000 to over 12,000 feet. During the summer months, thunderstorms occur with great frequency.

As a general rule, the best way to pack for the mountains and the rugged Northern California coast is to bring layers of clothing. The air trapped between the layers acts as an insulator. A lot of people bring just one heavy jacket and a sweater. You can't do much with this gear—you either have it on or off. It's much wiser to wear several light layers, so you can remove clothes layer by layer and still not have too much to carry. Many people have found that jogging gear is good hiking gear.

During the summer, wear shorts and a light shirt with a jogging outfit on top of that, and carry a rain jacket that you can roll up and keep in your daypack. That's usually more than adequate for summer hiking, even if a sudden storm hits. You also might want a hat or sun visor.

In fall and winter, add a heavier jacket, a turtleneck, a sweater, and a water-repellent parka. It's critical to wear a hat because you lose a lot of heat through an exposed head.

Small children might insist on taking their favorite backpack. If you want to let them, have them practice carrying it *packed* before you leave home. Be sure they can handle it all the way, or guess who'll end up carrying the extra gear!

CAMPING Avid adult campers agree that you can take children of almost any age camping. Infants certainly aren't a problem. If there's any questionable age group, it's the toddlers, because this group is more apt to walk away from a campsite or stick their hands in a bright, inviting campfire. If there's a perfect age, it's over five. This seems to be the time children are willing to help at camp chores and are genuinely curious about what they're seeing and doing. Remember, no matter what the age, always keep an eye on your children. If they're old enough, have them wear whistles every day and establish a code so you'll know it's them. If there's a problem—they're hurt, lost, or confused—the whistle will help you find them.

Any camping-equipment store will have lists of items you should take. Add to it a potty chair to put outside your tent, even for older kids, so you don't have to forage in the woods in the middle of the night. If there's room in the car, bring along a playpen or corral for crawlers and even toddlers. Then you can relax at your campsite without always having to run after them.

Don't take lots of toys. *Do* take lots of clothes. Don't make this the trip where you attempt to cook food the kids have never eaten before. Do think about making your first trip a short one if you're not an experienced camper, and consider renting camping equipment rather than buying it. Be sure to take a first-aid kit that includes any necessary medications, such as children's Tylenol, insect repellent, sunscreen, and a snakebite kit. Include lots of diapers, and take books and indoor games, in case you're rained in.

If you're unsure of how you'll feel about sleeping in a tent, try renting a camper the first time. No matter what you decide, tent or vehicle, be sure to make reservations if you're traveling during prime season or on holiday weekends. Ask whether the campground is next to a river (if you have curious toddlers), in a hilly area (how perfect for them to get hurt rolling down hills!), and for the less rugged among you, ask whether there are showers and, of course, flush toilets.

For reservations within the California State Park System, you can call the **Department of Parks and Recreation** (☎ toll free **800/444-PARK**). Or write for a family camping reservation application to **MISTIX,** P.O. Box 85705, San Diego, CA 92138.

SNOW SKIING   Even if your kids have never seen snow before, they all know what skiing is, and most of them are eager to give it a try. If it's your first time going downhill or cross-country skiing, there are some things to remember. First, rent your skis. Purchasing skis, boots, and poles can be a big mistake if the kids end up not taking to the sport. And kids grow quickly, so be sure they'll get enough use out of any equipment you purchase. It's suggested that you rent equipment at your ski destination so that if the bindings, boots, or poles need adjustment or have to be changed, you can have it done right there. But be sure to contact a ski-rental shop or the rental office at the slopes first, to find out whether they carry children's equipment and if it can be reserved in advance. After you get into the sport, you may want to find a local shop you like to rent from each time. Whatever you do, *don't* borrow equipment from friends for your children. The bindings may not be right for your kids, and the skis themselves may be geared for a different level skier.

It's a different thing when it comes to ski clothes. You *should* borrow them. It just doesn't make sense to buy expensive ski clothes for the kids the first time out. Some shops rent ski togs for youngsters, but they are few and far between. When in doubt, call the visitors bureaus in the California ski areas for help in that area. Another option is to put together an outfit from what you have at home. As long as the pieces are comfortable, you can combine whatever your kids would ordinarily wear in outdoor winter weather. The key is layering, which will offset changes in temperature. Essential items are a hat, warm gloves, and possibly sunglasses or goggles. Your skin is very vulnerable to the sun when skiing, so be sure to protect yourselves and the children with sunscreen.

Be sure that the ski area you choose has a good ski school for children, and find out at what age they start giving lessons. Downhill lessons might be offered at one age and cross-country at another. Even if you are an excellent skier, consider having your children taught by the experts who know how to combine lessons with an appropriate amount of playtime. Call ahead to find out whether you can reserve a space in advance, or whether it's first-come, first-served. Also inquire as to whether any lesson packages can be combined with your hotel room choice.

HOUSEBOATING   Houseboating is like a rich person's form of camping. Where else can you sit on the prow of a boat watching exquisite scenery, while you can have, if you want, a microwave, television, videocassette player, barbecue, and all the comforts of home while you're outdoors? (Remember, though, that they don't have phones.)

Houseboating gives you the opportunity to fall asleep with water lapping against your boat. Even when a lake is crowded you can find a secluded spot where you don't hear anyone else's noise. Often, you can pull up and dock somewhere and hike in beautiful countryside. The kids can run around and collect shells, or they can fish, climb rocks, swim, snorkel, or laze on a raft.

Think of it as camping out, when determining what you're going to carry on. While your accommodations can be very luxurious and your food can be of any variety (you can even cook gourmet meals), remember that you'll be using lake water to shower and your fresh water will be somewhat limited, although you can always restock.

Keep in mind that you won't need a lot of different kinds of clothes on your houseboat. However, bring lots of sunscreen, zori or flip-flops, and extra pairs of beat-up tennis shoes. Check ahead for what household supplies you'll need to bring. You will usually need your own linens, but that varies. We roll them up into the sleeping bags so they don't take any additional space in our luggage.

Depending on the operation, checking into a houseboat can require a lot of patience. There may be ten people coming in at around the same time, and they all have to be taken to their boat and shown how to use it, which is called giving a shakedown. The boat is checked out, similarly to a rental car, so that if something is not working or is damaged when you are shown the boat, you won't be responsible for it upon your return.

While we've been lucky with a check-in that only took an hour, others have taken as long as six hours to check in. Delays can be caused by arriving before you are scheduled, having many people arrive at the same time, or because others are checking out simultaneously.

The size of the operation can determine the ease of checking in. The larger ones have amenities that make it easier. For example, you pull your car up to a parking lot, just as you would in a hotel, check in, and wait in line as you would in a hotel if there were several people in front of you. Soon they will tell you which boat is yours. Then you take your car down a ramp—the level of the lake will determine how far you need to go. Ask about the procedure before you rent the boat so you know what you're getting into.

BED-AND-BREAKFASTS WITH KIDS   B&Bs are unique places to stay on a vacation. Some are cozy and make you feel as if you're truly staying in someone's home. Some have historical significance or are architecturally interesting. Some are decorated whimsically; some are stuffed to the rafters with antiques and collectibles.

No matter what their decor, B&Bs are usually smaller than hotels, with paper-thin walls. They're geared to people who want to meet other people on an informal basis, such as over breakfast or an evening glass of sherry, and for those who don't want the impersonal feeling of a hotel.

If you have a child who sits politely through breakfast and is willing to live without, in most cases, TV in the room, then a bed-and-breakfast establishment will be a fun place to stay. We don't recommend these places for families with infants or very young children. And in fact, many B&Bs discourage children under a certain age.

Some parents are immune to the noise their kids make. A 3-year-old throwing a temper tantrum in the lobby of any hotel is going to be difficult for everyone to deal with. But in a bed-and-breakfast establishment, it's impossible. When you're sitting at the same table with a number of strangers and your child becomes difficult, you'll feel very uncomfortable. Bring only children who respect the privacy of others.

RENTING CONDOS AND CABINS   When you book a hotel room, you usually don't have much choice about your room configuration. When renting a condo or even a cabin, you often do have a choice, and this becomes an important consideration when you're staying for at least a week.

When you're planning to rent such an accommodation with kids, it's especially important to ask in advance about certain things. Is the unit one or two stories? (We once inadvertently rented a two-story condo when Janey was crawling. Without a safety gate, we were in constant fear that she'd fall down the steps.) What comes with the unit? Be sure to ask if the unit has linens, towels, dishes, a toaster, pots, silverware, and a coffee pot. Does it open up right to a pool or to mountains, streams, a freeway, or a street? Can you get cribs and a highchair? Are there twin beds, bunk beds, etc.? How many bathrooms are there (important if you're sharing the condo with another family)? Is there a working TV? Can you get a VCR? Is there daily maid service, or is it up to you to make your beds and wash the dishes every day?

Can you park close to your unit? Who wants to carry gobs of stuff—and the baby—a distance to the car for every day's outing. Are there places outdoors for the kids to play? Are there markets nearby? Is there a phone in the unit, and if not, can installation be arranged? (You don't want to be without a phone in the event of an emergency.)

If you're staying in a winter resort, how far are you from the slopes? (Stay toward the bottom of the mountain, not the top—it will be easier to get to the lifts, and you won't have to face slick winter roads uphill with a car full of kids.) Is there a covered garage? Is wood provided for the fireplace?

And finally, try to use a rental service with a lenient cancellation policy. Sometimes you can find a service that will allow you to cancel as late as 48 hours in advance. You are giving a substantial deposit for a condo—it could be $500 to $1,000 for a week's rental. You certainly don't want to have your kids come down with the flu just before leaving and be faced with losing that deposit.

3   Traveling to California

Before you start on your journey, you might want to contact the **California Office of Tourism,** P.O. Box 9278, Dept. A-1003, Van Nuys, CA 91409 (☎ toll free **800/TO-CALIF**). They'll provide you with plenty of information about the state. If you have specific questions they can't answer, they'll tell you who can.

When you travel with children, transportation is a major consideration.

BY AIR

Most major airlines fly into Los Angeles International (LAX) and San Francisco International (SFO) Airports. Many carriers also fly directly to several smaller airports within California.

Consider your vacation destinations first, then see if you can fly to the city closest to your destination. For example, don't assume that LAX is the best place to arrive. You might be better off flying into one of the Los Angeles area's other airports, such as Burbank-Glendale-Pasadena or Ontario International, or to Orange County's John Wayne Airport. The same applies to Northern California. Oakland and Sacramento airports are easy to navigate and are served by many major carriers.

Talk with a travel agent to check out the best fares. Especially when traveling with children, costs can mount, and in some cases, lower children's fares are available.

BY TRAIN

You'll find that **Amtrak** (☎ toll free **800/USA-RAIL**) offers transportation to California from many cities. The *California Zephyr* runs from Chicago to San Francisco via Denver and Salt Lake City. The *Southwest Chief* offers service between Los Angeles and Chicago via Albuquerque. The *Desert Wind* services Los Angeles, Denver, and Chicago. The *Sunset Limited* services Los Angeles and New Orleans via San Antonio. And if you're coming from the Northeast, the *Cardinal* runs from New York to Chicago, where you can connect with either the *Southwest Chief* or the *California Zephyr*.

Some of the trains have complete dining cars with full-service restaurants; others have snack bars. Some have bedrooms with sleeping berths; others have family bedrooms—rooms that are the full width of the train, with windows on both sides.

When you consider train travel, ask about family fares and package tours. They make such options considerably more affordable.

4 Traveling Within California

BY CAR

Although California is more than 350 miles wide, and has more than 1,200 miles of coastline, driving through the state at your own pace, stopping whenever you and the kids feel the urge to explore, is one of the lovelier ways to vacation as a family.

Be sure to get a good map before you start. If you're a member of the American Automobile Association, you can get all kinds of wonderful, detailed information from your nearest office. *America on Wheels: California and Nevada* is a good resource when driving within the state. Each chapter of this book will also give you specific driving instructions to get you where you want to go.

BY AIR

Many national and international carriers have service between Los Angeles and San Francisco. Don't automatically rule them out in favor of the smaller airlines—they sometimes offer better fares. In addition: **Alaska Air** has convenient service from Los Angeles area airports to San Francisco and Oakland (call toll free **800/555-1212** to find your local toll-free number); **American Airlines** (☎ toll free **800/433-7300**) services many of the smaller airports such as Fresno, Monterey, Palm Springs, Redding, San Jose, and San Luis Obispo, as well as the larger airports in the Bay Area (San Francisco/Oakland) and in Southern California (LAX, Burbank, Ontario, Long Beach, and Orange County–John Wayne, San Diego); **America West** (☎ toll free **800/235-9292**) has over 100 daily flights between nine state airports; **United Express** (☎ toll free **800/241-6522**) also covers many of the small cities; and **USAir** (formerly PSA) services many smaller cities too, such as Burbank, Concord, Fresno, Long Beach, Monterey, Ontario, and Anaheim (Orange County–John Wayne), in addition to the major airports in the state (call toll free **800/428-4322** to find your local toll-free number); **Reno Air** (☎ toll free **800/RENO-AIR**) services the Tahoe area from L.A. and San Diego.

Airline routes and schedules change often, so be sure to check this information close to the time of your planned trip.

BY TRAIN

There are several **Amtrak** routes within California. Its *Coast Starlight* runs the length of California. Originating in Los Angeles, it stops in Santa Barbara, San Luis Obispo, Salinas, San Jose, Oakland (with a shuttle to San Francisco), Sacramento, Redding, and other cities, and continues north to Seattle. The *San Diegan* connects San Diego to Los Angeles via Orange County. This very popular line is a fun way to travel, and the trips are so short that it's pleasant with almost any child.

Did you know you can take the train to Yosemite? Well, most of the way, anyway. The *San Joaquin* runs the length of the San Joaquin Valley, connecting Bakersfield, Fresno, Merced, and Stockton with San Francisco/Oakland. With bus connections, you can really get off the beaten path without a car.

For more information, call toll free **800/USA-RAIL.**

BUSES AND TOURS

Within California, you might want to consider **Greyhound/Trailways Bus Lines** (no toll-free number; call **555-1212** to find your local number). And be sure to check out touring bus companies, such as **California Parlor Car Tours** and the **Gray Line, Inc.** (call toll free **800/555-1212** for your local toll-free numbers).

2

San Francisco

ONE OF THE MOST BREATHTAKINGLY BEAUTIFUL CITIES IN THE WORLD, San Francisco is at once quaint and cosmopolitan. It is a city of contrasts. Shiny, stunning steel bridges and pinnacle-like skyscrapers sit within minutes of Victorian dwellings and classic cathedrals. Authentic Chinese herb shops with their ancient remedies are found within blocks of bawdy strip joints. The city can be thick with fog or crystalline bright. Or it can be both—in different parts of town.

While San Francisco is known as a sophisticated international city, it also has the largest planned park in the world, it sits within part of the most popular national park in the country, and it's minutes away from spectacular ocean scenery.

It's no wonder that San Francisco charms almost three million visitors a year. It will charm you too, and delight your kids. And unless you're very unusual, there are so many sights to see and things to do that your family will never be bored.

Known as one of the great cities of the world, it's surprisingly small. San Francisco has 730,000 people, although the entire Bay Area has six million. It's located at the very tip of a 32-mile-long peninsula. In an area of less than 47 square miles, there are over 40 hills, 11 islands, 200 parks and playgrounds, 65 museums, 200 buildings that have been designated historical landmarks, 14,000 Victorian homes, 3,300 restaurants, and 37 foreign-language newspapers.

Many people think of San Francisco as an adult city, and indeed it is—but not exclusively. It's a cosmopolitan city that offers abundant things to do for both parents and children together. It's a chance for children to experience the excitement of an urban community like New York, London, and Tokyo, with the advantage of easy escape to the beautiful outdoors when they're tired of the intellectual and sophisticated.

San Francisco's rich history is a mixture of cultures—Spanish and American Old West. A Spanish settlement called Yerba Buena was established here in 1776 by Juan Bautista de Anza; in 1847, under the United States flag, its name was changed to San Francisco. The discovery of gold in the California foothills some 140 miles away brought tens of thousands of people to the area, so that by the height of the Gold Rush in 1849 and 1850, the little town had become quite a city. By 1869 the transcontinental railroad had completed its link to San Francisco, and with it came even more people.

Possibly the one event that everyone knows in San Francisco's history is the Great Earthquake and Fire of April 1906. The quake was 8.25 on the Richter scale, and destroyed more than 25,000 buildings! Surprisingly, the quake only did part of the damage; the greatest part of the disaster is attributable to the fire.

The city began to rebuild immediately, and by 1915 San Francisco rejoiced and celebrated at the Panama-Pacific International Exposition.

1 Getting There

IF YOU'RE DRIVING

There are several routes to San Francisco. From Los Angeles, take I-405 north to I-5 north through the San Joaquin Valley. Check a map first, since you may be located close enough to I-5 to link up with it and avoid I-405 altogether. Hook up with I-580 west to I-80 west (San Francisco–Oakland Bay Bridge) into the city. This is the fastest but most boring route. Or you can take I-405 north to U.S. 101 west, and north, to San Luis Obispo. At San Luis, take either U.S. 101 or Calif. 1 north to San

Francisco. These routes, especially Calif. 1, are slower but very picturesque and interesting. From Sacramento, take I-80 west.

A Stop Along the Way

I-5 is the fastest way to get north and south, but it's one of the most boring highways you'll ever take. There are very few towns (or even gas stations) on this stretch of road. On our treks north, we stop for a stretch and run-around at the junction of Calif. 58 and I-5, near Buttonwillow (about 110 miles north of Los Angeles). There's a Carl's Jr. with a playground at 2640 Tracey Ave. (☎ 805/764-6302). Then we have a real rest and activity break at Harris Ranch, and finally we stop at one of the towns in the north end of the valley.

Harris Ranch (☎ 209/935-0717, or toll free **800/942-2333**) is midway between Los Angeles and San Francisco on I-5 near Coalinga. Harris Ranch is actually a full-service rest area that includes a restaurant, bakery, country store, gas station, convenience store, hotel, even a private airstrip. The early California–style buildings have large rooms and open hallways; the ranch is an inviting place to stop for a meal and run-around. Allow about 1¹/₂ hours.

Clearly a family-oriented spot, Harris Ranch even has a ladies' rest room with a little girls' stall, as well as a vanity area that's good for changing diapers. *Sesame Street* dolls and Disney toys are available for youngsters who may be in need of diversions after the long stretch of nonstop driving.

Even though this is basically a highway rest stop, the food is good and the service attentive. Busboys offer boosters and highchairs even before you ask. Breakfasts range from waffles to huevos rancheros (priced at $4.75–$10). Lunch and dinner are served from 11am to 11pm, and include salads, sandwiches, burgers, Mexican specialties, and steaks (priced at $8–$20). Harris Ranch also serves special complete dinners starting at 5pm in their Fountain Court room that include roast lamb, sweetbreads, and prime rib among the entrees (priced at $23–$28). The children's menu for kids ten and under features hamburgers, grilled cheese sandwiches, and barbecued beef ribs for $3–$6. Open from 6am to 11pm, but call, as there are seasonal hours. Reservations accepted only for the Fountain Court. Most major credit cards are honored.

IF YOU WANT TO TAKE THE TRAIN

The train is an especially fun way to get to San Francisco, and **Amtrak,** with its San Francisco office in the Transbay Terminal, at First and Mission Streets (toll free **800/USA-RAIL**), is the way to go. Amtrak's *Coast Starlight,* originating in Los Angeles, runs the length of the California coast and goes inland up to Portland and Seattle. More accurately, the train disembarks in Oakland and a shuttle takes you to the Transbay Terminal in San Francisco.

The *California Zephyr* comes into Oakland from parts east, originating in Chicago and stopping in Omaha, Denver, and other major cities.

IF YOU TAKE THE BUS

The major transcontinental bus line servicing the Bay Area is **Greyhound/Trailways Bus Lines;** the main terminal at First and Mission Sts. (☎ 415/558-6789).

IF YOU'RE FLYING

These are some of the airlines that fly into **San Francisco International Airport** (☎ 415/761-0800), located 14 miles south of San Francisco: Air Canada (☎ toll free **800/776-3000**), Air France (☎ toll free **800/237-2623**), Alaska Airlines

(☎ toll free **800/426-0333**), American Airlines (☎ toll free **800/433-7300**), America West Airlines (☎ toll free **800/247-5692**), British Airways (☎ toll free **800/247-9297**), Canadian Airlines International (☎ toll free **800/426-7000**), Cathay Pacific Airways (☎ toll free **800/233-2742**), China Airlines (☎ toll free **800/227-5118**), Continental Airlines (☎ toll free **800/435-0040**), Delta Airlines (☎ toll free **800/221-1212**), Hawaiian Airlines (☎ toll free **800/367-5320**), Japan Air Lines (☎ toll free **800/525-3663**), Korean Airlines (☎ toll free **800/438-5000**), Lufthansa (☎ toll free **800/645-3880**), Mexicana Airlines (☎ toll free **800/531-7921**), Northwest (☎ toll free **800/225-2525**), Philippine Airlines (☎ toll free **800/435-9725**), Qantas Airlines (☎ toll free **800/227-4500**), Scandinavian Airlines System (SAS) (☎ toll free **800/221-2350**), Singapore Airlines (☎ toll free **800/742-3333**), Southwest Airlines (☎ toll free **800/531-5601**), TWA (☎ toll free **800/221-2000**), United Airlines and United Express (☎ toll free **800/241-6522**), USAir (☎ toll free **800/428-4322**), and UTA French Airlines (☎ toll free **800/237-2623**). There are also charters that fly into San Francisco.

You might choose to fly into **Oakland International Airport,** a smaller airport that's easier to navigate. It's easy to get into San Francisco from there. The following airlines service Oakland International Airport: Alaska Airlines (☎ toll free **800/426-0333**), America West Airlines (☎ toll free **800/247-5692**), American Airlines (☎ toll free **800/433-7300**), Continental Airlines (☎ toll free **800/435-0040**), Delta Airlines (☎ toll free **800/221-1212**), USAir (☎ toll free **800/428-4322**), and United Airlines and United Express (☎ toll free **800/241-6522**).

GROUND TRANSPORTATION TO THE CITY

You can do quite well in San Francisco without a car; in fact, in many ways it's preferable not to have one. Because of this, there are many companies that take you from the airport to a central location in the city or directly to your hotel.

From San Francisco International Airport

The **SuperShuttle,** 700 16th St. (☎ 415/558-8500), takes you door to door, 24 hours a day. When you land at SFO and have gathered your bags, go upstairs to the departure level and to the outer curb where you'll find the shuttles. Reservations are not essential from the airport to the city, but they are strongly advised when you're going from the city to the airport. General fare: $10 to or from San Francisco hotels; $11 for the first person to or from all other San Francisco locations, $8 for each additional person; free for children under 2.

The **SFO Airporter Bus,** 923 Folsom St. (☎ 415/495-8404), offers transportation between SFO and downtown hotels. It also has regular stops at the Hyatt Regency in the financial district. Service is every 20 minutes. Fare: $8 one way, $12 round-trip, for adults, and $4 each way for children.

Associated Limousines of San Francisco, 1398 Bryant St. (☎ **415/431-7000,** or toll free **800/255-2660**). Door-to-door transportation. Fare: $8 per person, $4 for children under 5. Two bags per person, then extra charges apply.

Taxis are plentiful in this city. A trip from the airport to downtown will cost approximately $25. Taxi fares in San Francisco are approximately $2.90 for the first mile, $1.50 for each additional mile. You can pick up a cab anywhere, but if you need to call, here are two to choose from: **Luxor Cab** (☎ 415/282-4141) and **Veteran's Taxicab Company** (☎ 415/552-1300).

All the major car-rental agencies are represented in San Francisco. Among them, you'll find: **Avis Rent-A-Car** (☎ 415/885-5011, or toll free **800/331-1212**),

Budget Rent-A-Car (☎ **415/875-6850,** or toll free **800/527-0700**), **Dollar Rent-A-Car** (☎ 415/771-5300, or toll free **800/800-4000**), **Hertz Rent-A-Car** (☎ **415/771-2200,** or toll free **800/654-3131**), and **Thrifty Rent-A-Car** (☎ 415/928-6666, or toll free **800/367-2277**).

From Oakland International Airport

If you're flying into Oakland International Airport, you can get into San Francisco, Oakland, and Berkeley using a variety of transportation methods. **AC Transit** (☎ 510/839-2882) will take you to different locations in Oakland. You can then transfer and take a bus to the San Francisco Transbay Terminal, where BART (Bay Area Rapid Transit; ☎ **415/788-BART**) will take you directly under the bay and into the city. An **AIR BART van** (☎ toll free **800/545-2700**) will take you from the airport to the nearest BART station. Ask at the airport information booth for directions.

Possibly the easiest way for you and your family (although the most expensive of the three) is to take a limousine. **569-LIMO, Inc.,** is a good choice. It will take you door to door—from the airport to your destination. It's best to call ahead, but if you can't, just call from an airport phone and you'll have a short wait.

There are major **car-rental agencies** at Oakland International Airport.

You may wish to contact the **Oakland Convention and Visitors Bureau**, 1000 Broadway, Suite 200, Oakland, CA 94607 (☎ **510/839-9000,** or toll free **800/262-5526**).

2 Getting Your Bearings

San Francisco is located at the tip of a peninsula, with Fisherman's Wharf at the northernmost tip and the Golden Gate Bridge on the northwest side.

Created in a traditional gridlike pattern (although it's sometimes hard to tell because the grid is laid over some steep terrain), the city's major sightseeing spots are easy to find. Market Street and Van Ness Avenue are the major thoroughfares. With a good map, you can easily find your way almost anywhere you want to go.

One of your first moves should be to contact the **San Francisco Convention and Visitors Bureau Information Center** at Hallidie Plaza, 900 Market St. at Powell Street (☎ **415/391-2000**). There is a multilingual staff to help you. Hours are 9am to 5:30pm Monday through Friday, 9am to 3pm on Saturday, and 10am to 2pm on Sunday. If you want to plan your trip in advance, you can write to the San Francisco Convention and Visitors Bureau, P.O. Box 429097, San Francisco, CA 94142-9097, and they'll send you a packet of invaluable information, including maps. Request the Visitor's Kit and send $2 for postage and handling.

Another good place is the **Visitors Information Center** of the Redwood Empire Association, 785 Market St., 15th Floor, San Francisco, CA 94103 (☎ 415/543-8334). There are loads of brochures and maps here, covering San Francisco and parts north. Ask for the *Redwood Empire Visitor's Guide.* It's free if you stop by, but if you write ahead, send $3 for postage and handling. The center is open Monday through Friday from 9am to 5pm.

Once you're in town, you can get **recorded tourist information** by dialing **415/391-2001.** Look for the small weekly publications that give you up-to-date information about many of the current happenings in the city.

GOLDEN GATE BRIDGE

The Golden Gate Bridge is one of the most famous—and beautiful—landmarks in the world. Painted bright red-orange, it towers vibrantly above the white-flecked, brilliant aquamarine waters where the Pacific Ocean meets San Francisco Bay. It looms up, almost as if it comes out of nowhere, and is framed by dark-green rolling hills and crystal waters.

Because of the enormous engineering challenges involved in constructing a bridge of this nature over water 318 ft. deep in some places, the project was originally nicknamed "The Bridge That Couldn't Be Built." But on May 27, 1937, at a cost of $35 million, the Golden Gate Bridge was completed.

It's majestic from any angle: You can enjoy the bridge by sailing under it, driving across it, viewing it from distant points in the city . . . even walking on it. Like millions of people, you'll find yourself looking for views of it as you roam the city, and finding reasons to cross it. Breathtaking when it stands bathed in full sunlight, it's also wondrous to see shrouded in mist or partially covered by cumulus clouds.

The 1.7-mile-long bridge also serves as a commuter passageway between San Francisco and Marin Counties. There's a toll booth for southbound traffic ($2 toll); the pedestrian walkway is free.

SAN FRANCISCO–OAKLAND BAY BRIDGE

Linking San Francisco with the East Bay cities of Oakland and Berkeley, the Bay Bridge is 8^1/$_2$ miles long, one of the world's longest steel bridges. The attractive double-decker bridge is a major commuter route, with five lanes in both directions. There is no pedestrian walkway. A $1 toll is collected westbound.

PARTS OF TOWN

San Francisco, like many other large metropolitan areas, is a cluster of diverse neighborhoods. Here are brief descriptions of the ones you're most likely to visit.

Union Square is a lovely shopping district whose heart (the Square) is bordered by Powell, Stockton, Post, and Geary Streets. This bustling, colorful neighborhood of fashionable shops and luxury hotels is in many ways the hub of the city, and there are hundreds of restaurants in the streets adjoining Union Square. Note, however, that during peak hours this delightful area becomes a bit difficult with strollers and children in tow. Nearby is famous **Nob Hill,** the area around California and Mason Streets that was called "the hill of palaces" by Robert Louis Stevenson. Today it's home to magnificent hotels, beautiful Grace Cathedral, and charming Huntington Park. **Chinatown** is the 24-square-block area that surrounds Grant Avenue between Bush and Columbus, the most densely populated Chinese community outside Asia. Adjacent to Chinatown is **North Beach,** the northeastern area of the city, whose main street is Columbus Avenue. Although not really a tourist section for children (especially in the evening when its bars, jazz clubs, and topless cabarets come alive), it's home to some of the city's best family restaurants.

San Francisco features 24 miles of waterfront, with more than 40 deep-water piers for commercial and passenger ships. The area of interest is the **Embarcadero,** which starts at the Ferry Building (at the foot of Market Street; you'll spot it immediately—it's the charming clock tower) and continues toward the Northern Waterfront. The **Northern Waterfront** is roughly the area from Pier 39 to Ghirardelli Square, which also includes Fisherman's Wharf, The Cannery, and the Hyde Street Pier. Nearby are the Marina District and Union Street. The **Marina District** offers many moderately priced accommodations and has some of the best small parks in the city. Union Street between the 1600 and 2200 blocks is the area known as **Cow Hollow,** a trendy, upscale shopping and restaurant area with restored Victorian buildings and quaint little courtyards.

Japantown (Nihonmachi) is San Francisco's Tokyo-like quarter for things Japanese; Post and Buchanan Streets border the five-acre complex called Japan Center. Some 3¹/₂ miles from downtown, the **Richmond District and Clement Street** offer a wonderful international mixture of ethnic groups and their shopping, restaurants, and cultural buildings. Chinese, Indonesian, Thai, Korean, Vietnamese, Russian, Greek, Jewish, and other nationalities are represented here; be sure to go for a delightful—and educational—stroll before you partake of one of the area's good restaurants. Nearby, **Golden Gate Park,** the largest planned park in the world, encompasses well over 1,000 acres. There are band concerts on Sunday (weather permitting), as well as museums, an aquarium, a planetarium, gardens, lakes, and other recreational features. And finally, we go back again to the center—this time, the **Civic Center,** an area made up of government buildings and performing arts centers, all of which are quite lovely. While the area doesn't offer much in the way of family sightseeing, a brief walk around affords an opportunity to look at some wonderful architecture: For example, San Francisco City Hall is a spectacular French Renaissance structure with a dome taller than the Capitol building in Washington, D.C.

If you're driving, one of the best ways to orient yourself is to take the **49-Mile Drive,** which takes you through the city's main areas of interest. Pick up a free *San Francisco Visitor Map* at the Visitor Information Center, and follow the blue-and-white seagull signs as the route takes you past most of the places you'll want to visit, as well as other scenic and historical points. Plan to spend several hours.

3 Getting Around

Once you're settled in, you'll find that this compact city is easy to navigate. For starters, pick up a good map. You'll find that it's most fun to walk, and you can walk almost anywhere (especially if you've brought comfortable shoes). Leave your car behind and when you get tired of walking, there's convenient—and affordable—public and private transportation.

PUBLIC TRANSPORTATION

San Francisco provides wonderful transportation facilities at bargain prices.

Muni (San Francisco Municipal Railway)

Headquartered at 949 Presidio Ave. (☎ 415/673-MUNI), Muni is the general name of San Francisco's 700-mile public transportation system. It includes more than 1,000 buses on some 70 lines, cable cars, trolley coaches, and light rail vehicles which operate underground downtown and on the streets in outer areas of town. And fares are a deal: $1 for adults and 35¢ for children 5–17; except on cable cars, where it's $2 one-way for everyone; children under 5 ride free. Free transfers are good for two changes of vehicle within 90 minutes. **Note:** Exact change is required on all Muni vehicles.

You might want to get *The Official San Francisco Street and Transit Guide,* a map of the Muni routes and transit connections, available at most bookstores for $1.50. You can also get information by writing Muni Map, 949 Presidio Ave., Room 238, San Francisco, CA 94115. Enclose a check or money order for $2.50 (includes 50¢ postage) payable to San Francisco City and County.

There are self-service ticket machines at all major stops and terminals on the cable-car lines. These are located at Powell and Market Streets, California and Drumm Streets, California Street and Van Ness Avenue, Bay and Taylor Streets, Beach and Hyde Streets, and California Street and Grant Avenue. At these machines you can purchase a one-, three-, or seven-day "Passport" ($6, $10, and $15, respectively) that entitles you to unlimited riding on all Muni lines, including cable cars, underground, and buses. The pass entitles you to discounts at some of San Francisco's favorite attractions. Call **415/673-MUNI** for information.

CABLE CARS   There are three cable-car routes. The Powell-Hyde Line starts at Powell and Market Streets, runs by Union Square down to Victorian Park at the Maritime Museum and Aquatic Park, and ends near Ghirardelli Square. The Powell-Mason Line also starts at Powell and Market Streets and runs by Union Square, but its route takes it to Bay Street, near Pier 39 and Fisherman's Wharf. The California Street Line runs from the foot of Market Street at Drumm Street, in front of the Hyatt Regency, up over Nob Hill to Van Ness Avenue.

For more on the cable cars, see the "What to See and Do" section in this chapter.

BART (Bay Area Rapid Transit)

BART, headquartered at 800 Madison St., Oakland (☎ **510/464-6000**), is the 71-mile underground transportation system that links San Francisco with Daly City and the East Bay cities of Oakland and Berkeley. BART is clean, space age in design, and a treat for kids. We found ourselves riding around the city just so our children could experience the exhilarating sensation of subway travel. The fast trains speeding through their underground tunnels are an activity in themselves. BART stations are conveniently located throughout the city, so you can plan your sightseeing with that in mind. BART operates from 4am to midnight Monday through Friday, 6am to midnight on Saturday, and 8am to midnight on Sunday.

Each person over four years old must have a ticket, and ticket prices depend on your destination. Your kids will love the automated ticket machines (which accept nickels, dimes, quarters, and $1 and $5 bills) and the automatic ticket takers at the fare gate. Be sure to save your tickets because you'll need them when you exit. Some people even purchase a round-trip excursion ticket—for $2.60 you can ride anywhere in the system for three hours (note that you must enter and exit at the same station). Children 5–12 can obtain a 90% discount ticket ($1.60 for $16 worth of rides) from an outside vendor. The brochure that lists all vendor locations is called "Tickets to Go" and can be picked up at any BART station.

AC Transit

This is how to get to the East Bay via the San Francisco–Oakland Bay Bridge. AC Transit is located in Transbay Terminal, First and Mission Streets (☎ **510/839-2882**).

Golden Gate Transit

This is the system that gets you to Marin County via the Golden Gate Bridge. Golden Gate Transit's home base is also in the Transbay Terminal, First and Mission Streets (☎ **415/332-6600**).

SAM Trans (San Mateo County Transit District)

This system connects you to the peninsula cities, and is also located in the Transbay Terminal, First and Mission Streets (☎ **415/508-6200**).

OTHER WAYS TO GO

There are taxis, private limousines, and van services that will take you door to door. Limousines can be chartered for a group or for an individual (see the "Getting There" section, above).

When You're Driving

San Francisco is a unique city when it comes to driving. Nowhere else do you find such steep hills in such densely crowded neighborhoods. Possibly the most important tip for driving the hills may have to do with parking on them. Always use your parking brake and curb your wheels. This means, when you're parking uphill, turn the tires toward the street, and when facing downhill, turn the tires toward the curb. In San Francisco, this is the law. Another rule is that cable cars and streetcars *always* have the right-of-way, as do pedestrians.

Finally, don't be embarrassed to use your parking brake if you have to stop in the middle of a steep hill.

Tours

Although we rarely take our kids on tour buses because of their limited attention spans and their need to get up and move around, we know people who've taken their older children along and have found it enjoyable. The **Gray Line of San Francisco,** 350 Eighth St. (☎ **415/558-9400**), offers an array of tours in comfortable buses. Currently, Gray Line offers many tours of San Francisco and the Bay Area that range from a few hours to a full day. Prices for a half-day tour are $26 for adults and $13 for children 5–11; children under 5 are free. Full-day tours vary in price. Reservations are required.

Ferry Service

The **Red-and-White Fleet** (☎ **415/546-2628,** or toll free **800/229-2784** in California) leaves for Sausalito, Tiburon, Muir Woods, and Angel Island from Pier 43¹/₂. Ferries for Alcatraz operate from Pier 41. Tickets can be purchased in advance. Call for schedules that vary with the time of year.

Golden Gate Ferries, leaving from the Ferry Building at the foot of Market Street (☎ **415/332-6600**), has service to Sausalito and Larkspur. The crossing to Sausalito takes 30 minutes; to Larkspur, 45–50 minutes. The one-way adult fare on the Sausalito ferry is $4.25; on the Larkspur ferry it's $2.50 weekdays, $4.25 weekends and holidays. A 25% discount is available to children 6–12; children under 6 travel free when accompanied by a full-fare-paying adult. A family fare is available on weekends and holidays: children 12 and under ride free when accompanied by a full-fare-paying adult; there's a limit of two children per adult.

4   Where to Stay

San Francisco is the visitor's and conventioneer's mecca. It has more hotels, and excellent ones too, than you can imagine. Many warmly welcome children. We've divided the hotels first by area, because when traveling with kids, location is as important as amenities and price. We've listed hotels within neighborhoods by price: deluxe, expensive, moderate, and budget. San Francisco hotels tend to be more expensive than those in other cities, so what we term "moderate" might be considered expensive elsewhere; you must judge by the listed prices.

Tip: Check the parking situation if you've brought a car. It can add substantially to your hotel bill.

UNION SQUARE

Many families like staying in the Union Square area. It is quintessential San Francisco—clanging cable cars, elegant shopping, bustling crowds. Centrally located, it's an easy bus ride, cable-car jaunt, or taxi getaway to almost everything the city has to offer. It's one of our favorite places in the city, and offers a simply fabulous array of choice hotel accommodations. If you have a car, however, the above advice about hotel parking fees certainly applies: They can be astronomical.

There are two little parks in this area for children to expend energy. One is the Square at Union Square. It's pleasant, but can be very crowded. The other is Huntington Park, a beautiful pocket park at the top of Nob Hill. There are several small markets in this area, and a Walgreen's Drugstore (which stocks milk, diapers, formula, etc.) at 500 Geary St. at Taylor Street (☎ **415/673-8411**), open from 8am to midnight daily.

Deluxe

The *crème de la crème* is the **Four Seasons Clift Hotel,** 495 Geary St. (at Taylor Street), San Francisco, CA 94102 (☎ **415/775-4700,** or toll free **800/332-3442**). Imagine this: you want to stay in a first-class hotel; you call to make a reservation; not only does the reservationist take your name, but the names and ages of your kids, and information about their interests!

One of San Francisco's landmarks, the Clift Hotel is known for its luxurious rooms and superb service. The staff treats you as an honored guest; nothing is too much trouble for them. They even learn your name! Because the hotel lobby is rather small, you feel as though you're visiting a beautiful mansion, with people there to serve you but not intrude. Although it has 329 rooms spread over 17 floors, its feel is a far cry from the usual commercial hotel.

When you go out for dinner and come back in the evening, the room is straightened up, the bed covers are turned down, a shoeshine bag for complimentary overnight shoeshine and a door hanger for newspaper delivery are laid out on your bed. As if 24-hour room service isn't enough, the room-service trays are always adorned with a perfect rose. There is also 24-hour valet service, twice-daily maid service, and an exercise room with weights, treadmills, bicycles, and stairmasters.

The Clift also boasts a concierge who knows almost everything about San Francisco, and who honors all requests with ease. Not only has the concierge been known to meet guests at the airport and have their bags delivered and unpacked, but he also offers parents a list of activities and restaurants that cater to children.

The Clift has catered to traveling families for years. It's our kids' special treat! The hotel is gracious and wonderful to children, providing for their every need. Parents will be happy to know that in addition to cribs and refrigerators, available upon request, the hotel can provide bibs, diapers, bottles, strollers, humidifiers, and baby bathtubs. There's even a pediatrician on call 24 hours a day. There are magazines for teenagers, toys for tots, and even bedtime snacks of freshly baked cookies and milk. In fact, parents can arrive empty-handed and within a short time have the basic necessities to make their stay a pleasant one. Other special things the hotel does for children: sends up a packet of baseball cards and comic books, provides kids with their own plush terrycloth minirobes, and sends up popcorn in a basket with balloons flying. For little Nintendo addicts, you can ask for a portable Nintendo unit sent to your room. They even have pocket-size electronic games!

Those unfamiliar with the Clift's two world-famous dining and drinking rooms—the French Room and the Redwood Room—are in for a treat (you should make a point of seeing the hotel even if you can't stay there). Even the French Room (with its wine list of over 20,000 bottles of fine wine) serves breakfast, lunch, and dinner and has its share of highchairs and a children's menu. (See the "Where to Eat" section, below, for details.)

The Redwood Room is acclaimed as one of San Francisco's cultural and architectural traditions. It is entirely paneled in aged redwood burl polished to a shining luster, and the 20-foot ceilings make you feel as if you're sitting in a redwood forest. Designed in classic art deco style, it's an experience not to be missed.

A San Francisco tradition is tea in the lobby of the Clift. Served Monday through Saturday, full high tea costs $13 per person. Reservations are suggested. A special treat is the Children's Christmas Tea, held in conjunction with the American Conservatory Theater presentation of *A Christmas Carol* (call ahead for details).

The 329 rooms of the Clift are elegantly furnished in quiet, understated tones with fine fabrics and Georgian-reproduction furniture, some with satinwood inlays. Oversize rooms are standard. There are telephones in each room and each bath—some phones even have two lines and a hold button. In addition, there's a dataport for computer access. We had a small television in the armoire; other rooms have large-console TVs—all have remote control. Several rooms feature two bathrooms.

Superior and deluxe rooms with queen- or king-size beds range from $215 to $260 single and $215 to $290 double. We like the theater rooms the best. These are bedroom–sitting room combinations that range from $330 to $360. Executive Suites have French doors separating the sitting area from the bedroom, two baths, and cost $365, single or double. Suites run $490 to $1,050.

The Family Plan at the Clift, for children 18 and under, offers two rooms with connecting doors, each room charged at the single-occupancy rate. Children sleep free. Rates are lower on some weekends, so ask about specials. Cribs and rollaways are free. Parking costs $22 per day, with in-and-out privileges.

The **Grand Hyatt San Francisco** (formerly the Hyatt on Union Square), 345 Stockton St. (at Post Street), San Francisco, CA 94108 (☎ **415/398-1234,** or toll free **800/233-1234**) surprised us. Though it's perfectly situated in the heart of Union Square, and generally thought to cater to businesspeople, the hotel's staff and management go out of their way to encourage families to stay here.

Complete with all the usual Hyatt touches (room service, including a Camp Hyatt menu for children even with pizza, full concierge service, nightly turndown, and complimentary fruit at the front desk), this one has an added benefit if you're taking youngsters. The lovely lobby is much smaller than you'd expect for such a large hotel, and you can keep track of your children more easily than in the enormous (though breathtaking) sister hotel, the Hyatt Regency San Francisco. Standing in the lobby, it's hard to believe that the hotel has 36 floors with 693 rooms (all have views). This is a friendly place where the staff smiles and talks with children. The emphasis here is on personalized care.

The hotel offers Camp Hyatt for children 3 to 15 on weekends and during summers and holidays. For approximately $5 per child per hour (or $25 per day), children participate in supervised activities. Children also receive a Frequent Stay

Passport that is validated every time they stay at a Hyatt. After a given number of days, they can redeem the passport for a Camp Hyatt carry pack.

The Plaza Restaurant is a great place to take the kids. Its high ceilings, stained-glass dome, and giant picture windows that look out onto Union Square provide an open feeling for dining. The children's menu offers great kid-meals for $1.50–$3.50, accompanied by helium balloons. All regular menu items (which run $3.75–$12.75) are available for children in half portions for half price. It's open from 6:30am to 10pm every day.

Napper's, is another moderately priced restaurant good for families. Deli-style Napper's features homemade soups, salads, and sandwiches.

The hotel has had a multi-million-dollar renovation. Earth tones and woods predominate in these spacious rooms, which have minibars, televisions with remote control, two phones (one in the bathroom), and small game tables perfect for eating or for children's games. And surprise—the bathrooms have tiny televisions.

Rates for singles are $195; for doubles, $220 (with a king-size bed or two double beds). Cribs and rollaways are free. Adjoining rooms are available. Children under 18 stay free in their parents' room. There's a Camp Hyatt special half-price room rate for children when traveling with their parents. The fee for indoor valet parking (with no in-and-out charges) is $20.

If you want to stay at one of the truly grand old hotels, the **Westin St. Francis,** located at 335 Powell St. (on Union Square, between Post and Geary Streets), San Francisco, CA 94102 (☎ **415/397-7000,** or toll free **800/228-3000**), is one that treats families nicely. The enormous 6,000-square-foot lobby is a stunning picture of old-world opulence. This huge hotel boasts 1,200 rooms (600 of which were added with the new 32-story tower), five outdoor glass elevators (the kids love them), distinctive shops, and one of the busiest lobbies you'll see.

You have to keep a close eye on the little ones—this is a place where kids are just absorbed into the tumult. All children 12 and under are welcomed to the Westin Kids Club with a special check-in procedure: a special room registration card, map of the hotel, a family information sheet, a children's laundry bag (with special kids' prices), and a safety kit for parents. During Christmas and Easter holidays there are decorations all around, and a "Kiddie Concierge" provides families with information on fun holiday activities in the city. Many schoolchildren come here on class outings.

Other amenities include concierge service, 24-hour room service, complimentary fitness center, business services, doctor on-call, and laundry service. Babysitting can be arranged through the concierge. Cribs, high chairs, potty seats, strollers, and step-stools are available.

The St. Francis is known for several of its restaurants. All of the restaurants have highchairs, boosters, a children's menu, coloring book and crayons, and very friendly waitresses. The Compass Rose restaurant is like an English drawing room that opens onto the lobby. It serves lunch and afternoon tea: Lunch entrees cost $9.50–$13.50; tea, $13.75.

The St. Francis Grill is open for dinner daily. Dewey's serves a do-it-yourself soup, salad, and sandwich bar for lunch with Dewey burgers, sandwiches, and California-style pizzas from 4pm nightly. Both have a children's menu. If you stand in Victor's, the restaurant on the 32nd floor, it's like having all of San Francisco at your feet. Although Victor's is open daily for dinner, it's probably best to take the kids here for Sunday brunch. The brunch costs $32.50 for adults, $16 for kids under 12, and if you need either a highchair or booster, just say so when you make reservations.

We suggest that you ask for rooms in the main building (unless you prefer ultra-modern rooms); they're large and very quiet. Hallways of the original building are wide-corridored spaces with beautiful rugs, and the rooms are high-ceilinged and elegant. Some of them are enormous, with love seats and plenty of room for cribs and rollaways. Bathrooms have large sink and counter areas. Suites are two rooms with a connecting door, each with love seat or couch and loads of space. Tower rooms, all of which have bay windows, are large with small entry halls. In-room amenities for all rooms include bathroom scales, turndown service upon request, and Spectra Vision; tower rooms have remote-control TV.

Rates are as follows: in the main building, standard rooms are $150 single and $180 double, medium-size rooms are $175 single and $205 double, and deluxe rooms are $200 single and $230 double; in the tower, medium-size rooms are $215 single and $245 double, and deluxe rooms are $245 single and $275 double. Children under 18 stay free if additional beds are not needed. Ask about weekend specials, as they can offer quite a savings. Family Plan means that when two rooms are booked, each room is billed at the single-occupancy rate. Cribs are free; rollaways cost $30 per stay for adults; children under 18 stay free if additional beds are not needed. There's limited parking on premises for $22 per 24 hours, with in-and-out privileges.

We always feel comfortable taking our offspring to a Hilton hotel since we know that the chain has a welcome policy toward kids. The **San Francisco Hilton and Towers,** San Francisco, CA 94102 (☎ **415/771-1400,** or toll free **800/HILTONS**), offers the chain's usual high level of service and amenities. The hotel is made up of three towers of differing heights, over 1,900 rooms (1,600 have been renovated; 300 are new), a large swimming pool area, a health center, a promenade of shops, and four restaurants. It's the largest hotel on the West Coast.

The main lobby is grand indeed, completely done in marble with accents of beige and light-rose hues that accentuate the color of the stone. Two giant crystal chandeliers and enormously high ceilings make for a spectacular entry into the hotel.

The hotel has two very attractive features for traveling families: the large, heated outdoor pool, which is protected on all sides to block the wind; and indoor self-parking (additional charge) on the same floor as your room, so that you have immediate access to your car. Tell the reservationist you're interested when you book, since only certain floors in certain buildings have this feature. We found this helpful on occasions when we didn't need to bring every toy into the room at once, but could exchange items as we used the car to go sightseeing.

Other hotel amenities include 18-hour room service, same-day laundry and dry cleaning, café, business center, concierge service, and car-rental agencies located within the hotel complex. The concierge will arrange babysitting.

For a charming place to eat breakfast, lunch, or dinner, you might want to try the Café on the Square. It's open from 6am to 12pm, and re-creates the ambience of a sidewalk café. Prices are typical for hotel coffee shops. In addition to regular menu items, the Café on the Square offers tempting buffets for breakfast, lunch, and dinner. Intermezzo offers a great variety of Mediterranean snacks. Prices $7–$10; open 6am to 1am. Kiku restaurant serves authentic Japanese food for lunch and dinner. Cityscape, the rooftop restaurant, open for Sunday brunch and daily dinner has a fabulous panoramic view; and during the holidays they have special activities for the kids.

The Hilton offers king-, queen-, and double-bedded rooms, all tastefully decorated, many with views of the city. All rooms have tub/shower combinations, minibars, remote-control color TVs, and Spectra Vision. Many rooms have a desk and chair. Rooms with two queen-size beds are very large, and the suites are huge.

Rates are $175–$240 single (depending on location and type of room), and $200–$265 double; suites start at $450. Children sleep free in the same room as adults. No charge for cribs.

Expensive

If you're looking for a charming bed-and-breakfast–style accommodation, the **White Swan Inn** is just the place. Located on the Nob Hill slope of Union Square at 845 Bush St., San Francisco, CA 94108 (☎ **415/775-1755**), this delightful 40-room inn welcomes families.

This traditional English-style hotel has many period antiques and English accents—hunting prints, black-and-white granite sinks and tabletops—set off by mahogany woods and beautiful hunter-green and burgundy wallpaper. Glass doors open to the lobby in which many little teddy bears greet you: Some sit on the stairs; others are on the floor next to the restored carousel horse. There are fireplaces in three public areas—the upstairs lobby where you enter from the street, the library, and the lounge—and a fireplace and bathroom in every room.

While the White Swan is bed-and-breakfast style, it's a little easier than a traditional bed-and-breakfast if you're traveling with kids. This isn't someone's home, so rather than worry about inconveniencing your host, you can feel assured that the 24-hour front-desk staff caters to guests' needs. There's also a concierge.

The White Swan, as well as the hotels Petite Auberge and Marina Inn, are owned by Four Sisters Inns. Kimberley Watson, one of the four sisters, suggests that when you book your reservation at any bed-and-breakfast, you tell the clerk the ages of your children. Ask if there are extra charges. Ask which are the best rooms. If your kids might have problems at mealtime, ask if special arrangements can be made; for example, at the White Swan you can take breakfast to your room or to the library. If it's available, the small conference room can be set up so the kids will have more space. During the day the children can bring toys and games into the library to play. When kids are staying at the inn you may see blocks set up in a corner, coloring books laid out on the table, and tots curled up on the floor with a teddy bear. Of course, if there's a business executive making a phone call or honeymooners snuggling, you want to remind your kids to be considerate.

Amenities include terrycloth robes, a wonderful breakfast (croissants, cereal, juices, eggs, potatoes, fruit, and choice of teas or coffee), full afternoon tea (which includes breads, cakes, vegetables and dips, sweets), and wine or sherry service. Breakfast is served in the dining room from 7 to 10am (8 to 11am on weekends)—highchairs are available, or it can be brought to your room. For an extra fee, there is room service 6 to 11pm, from an outside service; and the kitchen will heat anything on request.

If you'll require babysitting services during your stay, mention this to the receptionist when you reserve your room.

Rates are $145 for a room with a queen-size bed, $160 for a king-size bed, and $250 for the suite (which consists of a sitting room with a sofa bed, a bedroom, two baths, and an adjoining hallway). There's a $15-per-day additional charge for children over 2 years old to cover the cost of food. Valet parking is available from 7am to 11pm for $17 per day, with in-and-out privileges.

Just a few doors away is the sister **Petite Auberge,** 863 Bush St., San Francisco, CA 94108 (☎ **415/928-6000**), a cozy inn. This lovely little place with 26 rooms is probably better for small families with older children. Decorated like a French country inn, with straw hats, bouquets of fresh flowers, and colored baskets all around, it's done in subtle tones of peach and French country blues. This inn also has a small eating area for breakfast—on a smaller scale than at the White Swan—and a fireplace in the lobby. Concierge service is available. The staff will arrange babysitting, but they ask you to request it when you reserve your room.

Eighteen of the 26 delightful rooms have fireplaces. Other amenities include a full breakfast available from 7 to 10am weekdays, 8 to 11am on weekends; English tea in the afternoon with crudités, breads, and sweets, and wine or sherry. Room service is available from 6 to 11pm (from an outside service). You'll also be given fluffy terry robes.

While cribs are available at no charge, the small rooms and ambience of the inn are more apropos to an older child. If you're bringing young children, let the reservations clerks know when you book, and they will help with arrangements.

Rates range from $110–$220, but the only rooms appropriate for families start at $140. There's a $17-per-day additional charge for children over 2 years old to cover the cost of food. Valet parking is available from 7am to 11pm for $17 per day, with in-and-out privileges.

Moderate

There's a lovely type of hotel in San Francisco. Called boutique hotels, they are generally small, European-style accommodations that have been renovated. We think they have lots of advantages for traveling families. The first is obviously price: These hotels cost 40% less than the majors, and the savings are even greater when compared with many of the new hotels. Some guests also like staying in smaller hotels because of the increased interaction with the staff: They get to know the kids, and help the parents keep them happy. However, there are two drawbacks. Many small hotels have very small bathrooms, some with virtually no counter space. Most have dressing areas with space, but they may not be near the bath. The second drawback is the street noise, which can be a problem in this city in all but the largest, most modern hotels.

It may seem surprising that one of the small European-style hotels that clearly caters to businesspeople also welcomes families. The **Hotel Bedford,** 761 Post St. (between Jones and Leavenworth Streets), San Francisco, CA 94109 (☎ **415/673-6040,** or toll free **800/227-5642**), not only has a staff that's friendly and warm to children, but because of the 144-room size and the philosophy of the management, it makes even grownups feel like special guests.

This newly renovated 1929-vintage hotel is three blocks from Union Square, near many restaurants and shopping. A charming place, its standard rooms are beautifully decorated, and many of them have panoramic views of the city. Our kids were particularly enchanted with the VCRs in every room (you can rent movies in the lobby), and adults love the complimentary wine served every evening in the lovely English-style lobby. Parlor suites consist of a bedroom (with a double or queen-size bed) and an adjoining parlor that has two overstuffed chairs and a sleeper sofa. The family suites consist of two bedrooms, one with twin beds; there is one small bathroom with bath and shower, one large walk-in closet, and a small counter perfect for a changing table. There are refrigerators (honor bars) in every room, and room service is available from 7 to 10am for breakfast. There is same-day laundry service, and valet parking available at $15 per day, with in-and-out privileges.

Rates at the Hotel Bedford are $99–$119; suites start at $155. There is no charge for children under 14 in their parents' room; cribs are free, but there's a $10 charge for rollaways.

If you seek a hotel that really understands families and kids, **Villa Florence** may be just the place. It's located right on Union Square at 225 Powell St. (near Geary Street), San Francisco, CA 94102 (☎ 415/397-7700, or toll free **800/553-4411, 800/243-5700** in California), on the Powell Street cable-car line which goes to Fisherman's Wharf. It's a place where you know they've seen it all.

The spacious lobby may be deceptive, though: it's 16th-century Italian Renaissance style with a wood-burning fireplace and colonnaded entrance. At first you might not think that this is a place for children; however, the staff knows how to handle families, and will be glad to help you in whatever ways they can. Babysitting can be arranged through the front-desk staff.

While the hotel doesn't have a restaurant of its own, Kuleto's Italian Restaurant (☎ 415/397-7720) opens into the lobby. Open from 7am to 11pm, it has been rated as one of the top three restaurants by *San Francisco Focus* magazine. The restaurant has an antipasto bar, serves full breakfasts, lunches, and dinners, and offers highchairs and boosters.

The 180 inviting guest rooms, decorated with pastels and floral prints, are soundproof. They all have honor-bar/refrigerators, color televisions with remote control, and VCRs. Room service is available from 6:30 to 10:30am and 4pm to midnight. There are many different kinds of rooms here, so be sure to specify what you want when you make your reservations. As a sample, rates are $119, single or double and could have a king-size or queen-size bed, but might have a double; $139 for one of the 30 junior suites with one bedroom, all with king-size beds; and $189 for a deluxe suite of two bedrooms. Children stay free in their parents' room; cribs are free, but rollaways cost $15.

Another delightful European-style inn is the **Hotel Juliana,** 590 Bush St. (at Stockton Street), San Francisco, CA 94108 (☎ 415/392-2540, or toll free **800/328-3880, 800/372-8800** in California). This newly renovated little hotel is meticulously kept and delightful to look at. Amenities include hair dryers, honor-bar/refrigerator, and remote-control color television in each room, and VCR service available. Babysitting can be arranged through the front desk. You can also request use of an ironing board, and even a lint roller.

The 106 guest rooms range in price from $124 for regular size to $170 for junior suites to $150 for executive suites. Rates are per room, not per guest, and include complimentary tea and coffee throughout the day and complimentary wines served in the evening. Cribs are free; rollaways cost $10.

Hotel Diva, 440 Geary St., San Francisco, CA 94102 (☎ 415/885-0200, or toll free **800/553-1900**), between Mason and Taylor Streets in the heart of the theater district, across the street from the A.C.T. and Curran Theaters, is a kick—and a delight to the teens we know, who adore it. Architecturally and design wise, it's as far from the traditional European-style hotel as you can get, and a surprise find in San Francisco. It's hi-tech, Italian style, and futuristic—you feel as if you're entering another age. The Diva has its own little gallery of celebrity handprints on the sidewalk in front of the hotel, including those of Gina Lollobrigida, Carol Channing, Leontyne Price, and Talia Shire. As you enter the lobby via the large chrome doors, you'll be struck by the circular chrome reception desk, the floor-to-ceiling mirrors, and the four large video-playing televisions suspended high on the wall behind the front desk.

This hotel is a deceiver—the staff likes children. An unusual convenience is that each floor has a small room with a table that can be used as a playroom or reading room for youngsters or parents trying to flee the din of television or bickering brothers and sisters. There is room service from 11:30am to 10pm from the California Pizza Kitchen, which is located in the hotel.

Each guest room has a videocassette player, and there is a library of 300 tapes to choose from at $3 each. Highly polished lacquer furniture, down comforters, and contemporary-style pillow shams adorn the rooms. Each of the 108 rooms has an honor-bar/refrigerator, two telephones, luxury toiletries. Other touches include free newspapers, complimentary continental breakfast delivered to the room, a fitness center, and business center.

Rates are $109–$139, single or double, depending on the size of the room; suites cost up to $300. The smaller rooms are large enough to include a crib but would be cramped with a rollaway. For families, we recommend the $119–$139 mini-suites called "executive kings"; ask for the ones that have two rooms. These consist of a bedroom with a queen-size bed and VCR unit, a little hall that's actually part of the vanity area, and a sitting area that's more like a small living room. The sitting room also has a VCR, a closet, and a Sico bed (a Murphy bed) that pulls out of the wall. There is also a table and chairs, and room for a crib and an additional rollaway. It might be crowded for a family of more than five, but it can accommodate them. No charge for cribs or for children under 12 in their parents' room, but rollaways cost $10. Maximum of two children per room at no charge; for each additional child there's a $10 charge. Additional adults also pay $10 each. Complimentary continental breakfast includes croissants, orange juice, coffee, and tea. There's 24-hour valet parking for $16 per day.

The **Kensington Park Hotel,** 450 Post St. (near Powell Street), San Francisco, CA 94102 (☎ **415/788-6400,** or toll free **800/553-1900**), is another small recently renovated hotel in Union Square. European in flavor, this 86-room hotel has a small lobby area in which complimentary tea and sherry are served. The decor and Spanish Gothic architecture in the lobby arrest attention.

Interestingly, this is a multiuse building: the lobby for the hotel is on the first floor, hotel rooms are on the 5th through 12th floors, the Theater on the Square is on the second floor, and the Elks Club is on the third and fourth floors.

The rooms are fairly good size. They have television, radio, toiletries, and such extra touches as pillow shams in the rooms on upper floors. Bathrooms have phones, and refrigerators are available. Each floor has three or four connecting rooms that can be added. They are corner rooms, which we especially liked since it allowed us peace of mind when the kids were a little noisy.

Room service is available from 6:30 to 9:30am and 4pm to midnight. Complimentary continental breakfast of coffee, croissants, and juice is served daily. Every floor has a small eating area or serving area in which coffee and tea are available. While there is no restaurant on the premises, there's a deli next door, and the Dutch Kitchen, part of the Westin St. Francis, is across the street. Room service is available from 11am to 11pm, and includes cold sandwiches.

Rooms cost $115. Ask for specials. No charge for cribs. Children under 12 (maximum of two) stay free if additional beds are not needed. Children 12 and older are charged $10, as is each additional younger child. Valet parking is available for $16 per day.

The **Monticello Inn,** 127 Ellis St., San Francisco, CA 94102 (☎ **415/392-8800,** or toll free **800/669-7777**), is like taking a step back to colonial days. Another hostelry we recommend for older children and teens, this is a delight for anyone who likes Federal-period furniture (Chippendale reproductions, plus a grandfather clock with a brass face in the lobby) and history.

The gracious lobby with its wood-burning fireplace beckons you to sit and relax, and the separate parlor, where wine is served, has a game table and writing desk. It's a find, but only for those parents with quiet, well-behaved children. The prices are great, the location is good, and the ambience is like stepping into Thomas Jefferson's sitting room.

With only 91 rooms, there's a personal hospitality to the place. This feeling is carried out in the guest-room decor with canopied beds and pine furniture. Services and amenities include a stocked honor-bar/refrigerator and remote-control color television, with VCRs available. There's an on-site garage that charges $15 per weekdays and $25 weekend with in-and-out privileges.

Rates include complimentary continental breakfast, and complimentary tea and coffee served throughout the day, plus wine service in the evening. Adjacent to the hotel is the Abiquiu (☎ **415/392-5500**), which serves lunch and dinner. There is a health club across the street that guests can use for an additional fee.

Guest rooms are $109 single and $119 double for rooms with either twin beds or a queen-size bed, junior suites consisting one bedroom with either a king-size or queen-size bed, and executive suites consisting of two bedrooms with either a king-size or queen-size bed rent for $139–$259. No charge for children sleeping in their parents' room; cribs are free, but rollaways cost $15.

Hotel Vintage Court, 650 Bush St., San Francisco, CA 94108 (☎ **415/ 392-4666,** or toll free **800/654-1100**), between Powell and Stockton Streets on the Nob Hill side of Union Square, has a lovely, warm ambience that we think is charming for families with older children. Step down into a cozy lobby with a wood-burning fireplace.

Amenities include complimentary coffee and tea available in the lobby throughout the day and complimentary wine from area wineries every evening in the lobby. The concierge service can arrange babysitting. The desk clerks boast a thorough knowledge of the Napa Valley area and will be delighted to map out a great trip to the vineyards for you.

There is no hotel dining room, which can be a problem with youngsters. However, Masa's Restaurant, a nationally acclaimed French restaurant, is adjacent to the hotel, with an entrance in the lobby. Hotel guests may partake of a complimentary continental breakfast buffet that includes fruit, juices, croissants, muffins, cereals, and coffee.

The hotel is smallish, only 106 rooms, and cozy and very attractive. The wine-country theme is carried throughout. Not only is the decor in burgundy, but many guest rooms and suites are named for individual California wineries. Rooms have refrigerators with honor bar, color televisions, and pay-per-view movies. Some rooms have window seats covered with floral-print pillows that coordinate with country chintz bedspreads.

Rates are $119–$149 for all rooms. Ask for the larger rooms that have bath/shower combinations. Cribs are free; rollaways cost $10. Some adjoining rooms are available.

Located in the financial district near Union Square is the **Galleria Park Hotel,** 191 Sutter St., San Francisco, CA 94104 (☎ **415/781-3060,** or toll free **800/792-9639**), a historic 1911 building that was completely renovated in 1985. The atrium lobby has a working fireplace and a fabulous restored 1907 skylight. Although the hotel bills itself as a businessperson's hotel, it's one of the few hotels that has an outside area in which kids can play.

One of the best things about this hotel is the marvelous outdoor jogging track with wood benches and trees. In this downtown area with little space for children, this is a wonderful, safe haven where kids can play and really run around. The track is located next to the Crocker Galleria shopping area. There is an on-site fitness center and a full-time concierge.

The 177 bright and smartly decorated rooms look less like a commercial hotel than many, are good sized, and come with stocked honor-bar/refrigerator, color television with remote control, air conditioning (unusual here), and a writing desk. One of the most important features in a downtown hotel, the rooms are thoroughly soundproofed, helping to keep out the noise and keep you relaxed about the noise your youngsters might make. Some bathrooms have showers only, so request a tub if you desire one. Junior suites have a small wet bar and refrigerator, plus a king-size bed and sofa; others have queen-size beds with stereo units.

Room service is provided from 6:30am to 9:30pm daily. There are two award-winning restaurants, Bentley's Seafood & Oyster Bar and Brassen Chambord.

All rates are per room, regardless of the number of people in them. Guest rooms rent for $149; suites go for $185–$300. Connecting rooms are available. No charge for cribs; rollaways cost $15. There's an on-site garage, which charges $16 per day.

The **Handlery Union Square Hotel,** 351 Geary St. (between Mason and Powell Streets), San Francisco, CA 94102 (☎ **415/781-7800,** or toll free **800/223-0888**), is another moderately priced accommodation in Union Square, and used to be known as the Handlery Motor Inn. In fact, this is a completely renovated 1988 version of two hotels: the Handlery Motor Inn and the Hotel Stewart. Both these hotels were owned by the Handlery family, who decided to put $10 million into a renovation project, then gave it a new name. What used to be the Handlery has been completely upgraded and is now called the Handlery Club, which features rooms that are a little bigger, decorated more elegantly, and have more amenities than the rooms in the main building.

The guest rooms and common rooms are bright and tastefully decorated in mauve and mint green with complementary print fabrics. Polished wood banisters adorn the hallways. Endearing acquisitions in the main lobby are the commissioned oil paintings that depict the scene in front of the Hotel Stewart in old San Francisco.

But the real surprise is the heated outdoor swimming pool. It's a good-size one too, with plenty of lounge chairs.

Another surprise is the parking. At $12.50 a day, with in-and-out privileges, it represents a real bargain in downtown San Francisco. If you need babysitting, it can be arranged by the concierge.

All 376 good-size rooms open to an inner hallway. They have color TVs and in-room movies, video games, little makeup mirrors in the bathrooms, and custom amenities. A "deluxe king" is a very large room; some have bay windows that look out toward Union Square. A standard double room can be small though, so you should request a large room when you reserve. Also request a tub/shower combination if you prefer. Complimentary morning coffee and tea in every room.

Rates are $115–$125. Suites (two large rooms with a king-size bed and a sofa sleeper that opens to a double bed) run $140–$220. The upgraded rooms in the Handlery Club cost $140–$150. Children 14 and under are free in same room with their parents. Cribs are free, but there are no rollaways. Connecting rooms are available.

Location is everything at **The Raphael,** 386 Geary St. (at Mason Street), San Francisco, CA 94102 (☎ **415/986-2000,** or toll free **800/821-5343;** fax 415/397-2447), a hotel modeled after the "little" hotels of Europe. Guests are within walking distance of Union Square, trolleys, and buses. The hotel is just minutes from Chinatown, and there are numerous restaurants close by. The European-style hotel is perfectly comfortable for families. There is complimentary coffee and tea in the cozy lobby each day, and the adjacent restaurant is directly accessible from the hotel and offers room service. Breakfasts are delicious!

While you probably won't hear street noise, unfortunately the rooms aren't soundproof from each other. Families might request corner rooms, which offer space to spread out. In addition to the queen-size beds, there's a small seating area with a pull-out bed. Rooms are furnished tastefully and include desks or table and chairs, full-length mirror, phone in the bathroom, remote-control color TV and movie channels, AM/FM radio, individually controlled heating and air conditioning, and plenty of lighting. The corner rooms have an additional vanity with a sink and makeup area. Other rooms have king-size or twin beds. Laundry and valet service can be requested; no-smoking rooms are available. Rooms differ by size.

Standard rooms cost $99 single, $109 double. Moderate rooms (corner rooms) are $109 single and $119 double; deluxe units let for $124 single and $134 double. The penthouse suite rents for $195. Be sure to ask about the special Family Package: Two connecting rooms are charged at *one* single-room rate, any time of the year. There are also winter and weekend packages. Children 18 and under are not charged if they stay in their parents' room; additional adults are charged $10. Cribs and rollaways are complimentary.

Budget

Hotel Union Square, 114 Powell St. (at Ellis Street), San Francisco, CA 94102 (☎ **415/397-3000**), standing in the midst of tourist shops and traffic, was built in 1913 and was known as the Golden State Hotel. In this art deco hotel, Dashiell Hammett wrote *The Maltese Falcon.* The Powell Street cable-car line runs right in front of the hotel.

The Union Square's smallish 131 rooms all have color TV, toiletries, turndown service, and complimentary continental breakfast. Rates run $99–$129. Some rooms have two queen-size beds; these rooms are large, with plenty of room for a rollaway or crib. Two-room suites are $180–$280. Children under 12 are free. There's parking in a lot on the premises for $16 a day.

THE EMBARCADERO

Many people like this area, located at the foot of Market Street, because it's extremely convenient.

When you need diapers and sundries, you can try Russell's, at Four Embarcadero Center (☎ **415/397-9565**). Want to let the kids run off some of their energy? The plaza area at the Embarcadero Center is one place. Another nice little grassy park borders Davis, Front, Jackson, and Pacific Streets.

The **Hyatt Regency San Francisco,** 5 Embarcadero Center, San Francisco, CA 94111 (☎ 415/788-1234, or toll free **800/233-1234**), has one of the most dramatic—and popular—lobbies in all of San Francisco (maybe California). Designed by architect John Portman, who originated the atrium-court lobby, the 20-story, pyramid-like building has seven sides and a 300-foot-long skylight in the roof.

You'll catch your breath as you enter the lobby, even if you're not a big fan of contemporary architecture. This is the center of activity in the hotel and, we suspect, the neighborhood! There's no "shh, shh," here. Instead there's movement, life, sounds. Regularly scheduled musicians perform in the atrium lobby. You'll even see groups of children on field trips with their teachers.

There are full-size trees, thousands of plants and shrubs, a running stream, and the wonderful *Eclipse* sculpture fountain. As the water drapes down around the fountain's sides, it looks like plastic wrap. Kids stand at the edge of the fountain, carefully running their fingers around the edge to be sure it *is* water and not plastic wrap. This is a fun place for kids, who enjoy exploring the park-like atmosphere. During holiday season they might spot the Easter Bunny or Santa's helpers. Or they might see the gingerbread-house display (made of real gingerbread).

Then there are the five glass elevators that are edged with tiny lights, a real treat to children who "oooh!" and "ahhh!" as they glide up and down. Probably the only drawback here is that your children can get so caught up in everything they see that they wander off.

The hotel's location is another plus, with a BART station next door, the Ferry Building across the street, and the California Street cable-car line originating outside the hotel's doorsteps. The hotel is adjacent to the Embarcadero Center (the enormous shopping complex of over 140 shops and restaurants) and opens onto the Embarcadero Plaza. The huge plaza is host to lots of skateboarders, who love to ride on the smooth concrete—great for watching.

There is full concierge service whose staff will arrange for babysitting, 24-hour room service, doctor and dentist on call, valet parking with in-and-out privileges, same-day dry cleaning and laundry, retail shops (gift shop, beauty salon, jewelry and women's clothes boutiques), and guest privileges at a nearby health club.

The Market Place Bar and Restaurant has an outdoor and indoor eating area and offers a nice selection of lighter fare. It's open daily for lunch. Prices range from $8–$12.50. Mrs. Candy's is a café located in the atrium lobby, serving breakfast, lunch, and dinner as well as light pastries and snacks. Breakfasts cost $3.50–$11; lunches are $4.75–$11; dinners are $8–$19. The Equinox is the hotel's beautiful rooftop restaurant and lounge that makes a 360º rotation every 45 minutes. It's open for lunch and dinner daily. Highchairs and boosters are available in all restaurants, and children's plates are half price. Sunday brunch (with more than 100 different dishes) is served in the atrium lobby from 10am to 2pm on special days throughout the year. If you're looking for other restaurants nearby, you might try Salamagundi, or MacArthur Park (see "Where to Eat," below).

Each of the 803 guest rooms has a view of either the bay or the city. Many of the rooms have balconies with little tables and chairs, and sliding glass doors. There are a number of one- and two-bedroom suites, as well as the regular rooms that have king- or queen-size beds with small sitting areas. All have mini-bars, Spectra Vision TV, and tub/shower combinations as well as in-room amenities.

Room rates are $185–$218 single and $215–$268 double (depending on location). Suites start at $350. Kids under 18 stay free when they occupy the same room as their parents. Cribs are free. The Family Plan means that if two rooms are occupied, the single rate is charged for each. Additional adults pay $25 per night. Weekend rates start at $149 per room per night. Connecting rooms are available.

NOB HILL AREA

Nob Hill is the crossroads for the Powell, California, and Hyde Street cable cars. It's a beautiful location with charming Huntington Park at its crest.

You'll find several neighborhood markets if you head down toward Union Square. Walgreen's Drugstore, 500 Geary St. (☎ 415/673-8411), is open daily from 8am to midnight and stocks milk, diapers, formula, and other necessities.

The **Fairmont Hotel,** 950 Mason St. (at California Street, atop Nob Hill), San Francisco, CA 94106 (☎ **415/772-5000,** or toll free **800/527-4727**), is as ornate a hotel as you'll find. The 87-year-old grande dame has an enormous lobby done in red velvet with black accents. The formal carriage entrance leads you into the huge room with crystal chandeliers, where massive Corinthian columns support the lavishly carved gilt ceiling.

The Fairmont, with more than 600 rooms, has been called a city within a city. It has six restaurants, a barbershop, beauty shop, drugstore, florist, gift shop, exercise club, and an ATM machine. In addition to 24-hour room service, it offers concierge service, parking, babysitting, and a doctor on call. The concierge will make arrangements for you if you want to use tennis courts, a gym, or a swimming pool.

One of the six restaurants is the Tonga Room (☎ 415/772-5278), a tropical paradise. If you don't want to eat pricey Polynesian food with the kids, come for drinks and a look-around.

The Tonga Room is built around the hotel's transformed Olympic swimming pool. The decor is totally South Seas, with grass-thatched huts and masts of large sailing vessels. There's a large boat floating on the pool, and it "rains" about every 30 minutes! Flowers and plants surround the pool and the dining tables. You can imagine what a thrill the kids get from this place.

The Tonga Special dinner (for two or more people) is a special recommendation. For $19.50 per person, you can dine on Imperial eggroll, soup, almond chicken, beef chop suey, sweet-and-sour pork, rice, and dessert. Other entrees available.

Many of the spacious rooms have high ceilings and huge picture windows. All rooms are air-conditioned and have cable color TVs. The baths have shower/tub combinations and the amenity baskets we've come to rely on. You have a choice of king-size, queen-size, double, or single beds.

Rates in the main building start at $179. Rates in the tower start at $239. Suites start at $500 (in the main building). Children under 18 are free. Connecting rooms are available, and cribs are free. Each additional person is charged $30 per night. Parking is $25 per day.

FISHERMAN'S WHARF

Many traveling families love to stay at Fisherman's Wharf—and there are several advantages to staying here when you're with the kids. The Wharf abounds in things for children to do—Pier 39, the attractions on the Wharf itself, boat rides, the Cannery, the Hyde Street Pier, and Ghirardelli Square (see the "What to See and Do" section for details). It's a tourist area, so kids are just part of the general scene. In addition, there's a little more open space than downtown, making it a little easier to meander and stroll and let the children run around. In fact, you'd be hard-pressed to find a restaurant in the area that isn't well prepared for kids, regardless of the price bracket.

Like other parts of the city, parking is a problem here too. But many hotels at the Wharf anticipate the family vacationer and offer free or lower-cost parking (always ask if you have in-and-out-privileges). You can leave your car at the hotel for the vast majority of excursions you take. In fact, it will be much easier if you don't have the car to worry about.

Waterfront Park (near Pier 39) and Aquatic Park (across from Ghirardelli Square) are wonderful places where you can let the kids play. If you need a 24-hour pharmacy, there's a Walgreen's at 3201 Divisadero St., near Lombard (☎ 415/931-6415).

Note: Once in a while, we find ourselves scouting the territory for reliable fast food. If you find yourself in the same position, you might breathe a sigh of relief to know there's a McDonald's here, located at 2739 Taylor St. between Beach and Jefferson (☎ 415/776-1562). There's also a Burger King at 360 Bay (☎ 415/421-6940), and a Wendy's located in the Anchorage Shopping Center at 2800 Leavenworth (☎ 415/775-7735).

Deluxe

If you prefer to stay in elegantly appointed accommodations, you might choose the **San Francisco Marriott Fisherman's Wharf,** 1250 Columbus Ave., San Francisco, CA 94133 (☎ 415/775-7555, or toll free **800/228-9290**). Polished brass, overstuffed chairs, and chandeliers grace the spacious lobby, which is decorated like a large living room with lots of small conversation areas. Spada's Restaurant and the Lobby Lounge open into it.

Amenities include complimentary morning newspaper and nightly turndown service with a little sweet just for fun. Room service is available from 6:30am to 11pm. The front desk will give you referrals to a babysitting agency. Other amenities include complimentary limo service to the financial district on weekday mornings, valet parking, 24-hour movies, and free HBO, ESPN, and CNN.

Spada—A California Seafood Grill—is open daily from 6:30am to 12pm. Breakfasts average $6, and dinners range from $8.95 to $19.50. It has boosters, highchairs, and a varied children's menu (prices under $3). The Lobby Lounge has complimentary hors d'oeuvres from 5 to 7pm.

The 256 handsomely decorated rooms have beautiful wood furniture. All rooms have two telephones, shower and bath, and such amenities as complimentary shampoo, bubblebath, and lotions. Refrigerators are available upon request for $10 per day. Suites consist of a parlor (with a sofabed), kitchen area (with refrigerator, dining table, and bath), plus the one or two bedrooms that connect. Each bedroom has its own bath, so the two-bedroom suite has three baths. Each floor has an inviting little sitting area lobby off the elevator.

Rates are $119–$189 single, $20 for each additional person; junior suites are $235 single and $250 double. One-bedroom suites rent for $370 and two-bedroom suites start at $495. Be sure to ask about special packages and seasonal rates. Connecting rooms are available. Cribs are free; rollaways cost $10. Children under 18 stay free in their parents' room. Parking is $16 a day, with in-and-out privileges.

Expensive

The entrance to the **Sheraton at Fisherman's Wharf,** 2500 Mason St., San Francisco, CA 94133 (☎ 415/362-5500, or toll free **800/325-3535**), is wide and open, bringing the outdoor wharf motif into the hotel style. This isn't a high-rise hotel, but rather one with four floors that takes up an entire city block, giving the hostelry a resort ambience. There are three buildings, but you never have to go outside to cross to another building.

The heated outdoor swimming pool has a large, shallow area that's good for kids. Lots of families stay at this hotel since it's conveniently situated—just a few blocks from Pier 39 and Ghirardelli Square. Babysitting can be arranged by the concierge, who will also help with tours and sightseeing needs. There's 24-hour room service, and also an express checkout that can be done with your credit card, using the television monitor.

Kid's Koncierge, the hotel's family traveler program, offered June through August, provides guides, maps, and referrals tailored to children and young adults. The Kid's Koncierge desk is staffed by a junior concierge who is an authority on the vast number of activities, restaurants, places to go, and things to do in the San Francisco Bay Area for families.

For food, the Mason Beach Grill serves breakfast, lunch, and dinner in a contemporary eatery, with varied menus for all meals. In the evening there's also an all-you-can-eat seafood buffet at $17.50 for adults and $9.95 for children under 12. Breakfast costs $5–$10; lunch, $5–$12.50; dinners run $7.75–$18. A children's menu is available. For a drink, try Chanen's Lounge, an old San Francisco–style lounge.

The 525 attractive rooms are done in muted tones of gray and peach. Each has a TV with free HBO and Sports Channel. The large rooms (with two double beds) have enough space for a crib. Bathrooms feature tubs and showers and lots of counter space. Complete in-room amenities are provided. Refrigerators can be requested for the length of your stay for a flat charge of $20.

Rooms rent for $149 to $159 double (with two double beds). Ask if there are any special packages available; they can be significantly less expensive. Children under 17 stay free in their parents' room if a rollaway bed is not needed. Cribs are free; rollaways cost $20. Connecting rooms are available. Parking costs $12 per day, with in-and-out privileges for registered guests.

One block up from Fisherman's Wharf, but still in the midst of all the activity is the **Holiday Inn Fisherman's Wharf,** 1300 Columbus Ave., San Francisco, CA 94133 (☎ **415/771-9000,** or toll free **800/HOLIDAY**). It's located across the street from the Cannery and Anchorage Shopping Centers near the cable-car turnaround. Traditionally a family place, this contemporary-style hotel consists of two buildings across the street from each other (the Columbus building and the Beach building). There's a van to shuttle people from one to the other when it's raining.

The swimming pool area is nice and large, and is surrounded by umbrella-shaded tables. There's a coin-operated laundry (washer and dryer) in each of the two buildings for guest use. Babysitting may be arranged by guests through an agency. The Columbus building houses Charley's Restaurant and Lounge, which specializes in buffets for breakfast, lunch, and dinner. There is also a 24-hour Denny's restaurant.

All 580 comfortable rooms have bath/shower combinations, table and chairs, and televisions offering free Showtime as well as pay channels. The large one- and two-bedroom suites have a living room with a sofa bed, television, eating area, voice mail, wet bar with mini-refrigerator, coffee maker, and large dining table and chairs, with plenty of room for a crib or rollaway.

Room rates vary seasonally, with the highest prices in summer, from $94–$175, single or double. A one-bedroom suite rents for $300; a two-bedroom suite is $400.

Connecting rooms are available. Cribs are free; rollaways cost $10 per night. Children under 19 stay free when sharing a room with a parent, and children under 12 eat free if a family plan is available. Additional adults are charged $15 per night. Parking is available at a reduced charge for registered guests.

Located just off the Wharf, the **Ramada Hotel at Fisherman's Wharf,** 590 Bay St. (at Columbus Street), San Francisco, CA 94133 (☎ **415/885-4700,** or toll free **800/228-8408**), gives good value for the money and has a great location. But we think the nicest features are the sun deck and the jogging track (10 times around is a mile). Moms and dads can lounge in the sun while little ones play nearby. Kids need to be supervised, but only hotel guests can use the area, so it's secure. Guests may arrange babysitting through a referral service. Room service is available from 6am to 10pm (the kitchen is closed from 11am to 5pm).

The Conch Pearl Restaurant on premises serves breakfast ($5–$10), and dinner ($7–$19). A very reasonably priced children's breakfast menu is provided. Highchairs and boosters are available. There's a lobby bar called Pecan's Lounge.

The 232 spacious, bright rooms have either a king-size bed or two double beds, plus small game tables, and can accommodate two children, including a baby crib or rollaway. All bathrooms have vanity areas, showers, and tubs. Rooms, decorated in light mauve and brown or burgundy and blues, face either an open courtyard or the street.

"Superior" rooms with king-size beds have sofa beds and coffee tables—and can sleep four or five people. Master suites are huge, and also have refrigerators.

Rooms with two double beds cost $112–$163 single and $127–$178 double; "superior" rooms with one king-size bed are $132–$183 single and $147–$198 double; "superior" rooms with one king-size bed and a sofa bed rent for $140–$200 single and $155–$215 double. A master suite (two-room suite with a king-size bed, a sofa bed, refrigerator and a wet bar) is priced at $190–$275 single and $200–$295 double. Cribs are free; rollaways cost $15. Children under 18 stay free in their parents' room if an extra bed is not needed. Connecting rooms are available. Parking is available in an adjacent garage.

The only bayfront hotel at Fisherman's Wharf is the **Travelodge Hotel at Fisherman's Wharf,** 250 Beach St., San Francisco, CA 94133 (☎ **415/392-6700,** or toll free **800/578-7878**). This nicely landscaped hotel has a swimming pool with a large three-foot-deep wading area. Some rooms have outdoor balconies with views of the bay and the swimming pool.

The 250 rooms have views either of the bay or of the city (Coit Tower and the Pyramid). You can choose from two double beds or one king-size bed. The bathrooms have been completely redecorated and modernized. Not all bathrooms have tubs, so request one in advance if it's important to you. Refrigerators are free upon request. The concierge will arrange for babysitting.

Family rooms have two double beds and a sofa bed that opens into a double bed. In theory, you could sleep six people in one of these large rooms.

Rates change seasonally and vary according to location in the hotel: Singles and doubles range from $105 to $170; suites, from $200 per night. Connecting rooms and no-smoking rooms are available. Cribs are free; rollaways cost $10 per night. Children 18 and under stay free when sharing their parents' room. The hotel will try to upgrade whenever possible, so be sure to tell the clerk at the time you make your reservations that you're bringing your family. There's free parking for registered hotel guests.

Moderate

Located on the Hyde Street cable-car line, just a little off the main area of the Wharf (near Ghirardelli Square and the Cannery) is **Hyde Park Suites,** 2655 Hyde St. (at North Point Street), San Francisco, CA 94109 (☎ **415/771-0200,** or toll free **800/227-3608**).

The hotel itself is pretty and only four floors high (unusual in this high-rise city). The guest suites are built around a contemporary, early California–style atrium, which gives the hotel an open feeling. The courtyard, with its terracotta tiles, wicker furniture, fountain, lots of plants, and small trees that reach up to the skylight, give it an out-of-doors feel. Children love playing in the atrium, and are welcome to do so as long as a parent is with them. A complimentary glass of wine is served every evening in the courtyard.

Each room has a stocked honor bar. Babysitting can be arranged through the concierge. A coin-operated washer/dryer is available. Other touches include 24-hour concierge service, free limo service to downtown, nightly turndown service, free coffee and tea in your room, and complimentary morning newspaper.

Free continental breakfast is served every morning in the lobby. Grocery delivery service is available, and an outside service will provide room service from noon to 8pm. It offers a large assortment of meals from a variety of well-known restaurants throughout the city.

More like a home away from home, these suites come with fully equipped kitchens, including microwave and dishwasher. Although they tend to be a bit on the small side, the suites can function like an apartment and have enough space in the living room for a crib and rollaway. Some have private patios. Each suite has two televisions, tub/shower combinations, and a small dining table. The bedroom is completely separate. Guests also receive such amenities as shampoo, conditioner, and body lotion, as well as terrycloth bathrobes to use during their visit.

Rates range $160–$220 (single or double). Suites with bay views are $190. Two-bedroom suites are $220 and can accommodate up to six people. All suites are furnished with a queen-size sofabed in the sitting room. Children under 12 stay free, those 12 and over are $10 each per night. There is no charge for a crib, rollaway beds are available for $10 per night. Parking is available at $12 per day with in and out privileges.

Budget

A budget-priced alternative is the **Columbus Motor Inn,** 1075 Columbus Ave., San Francisco, CA 94133 (☎ **415/885-1492**), located between Fisherman's Wharf and North Beach. The 45 rooms have king-size, queen-size, or extra-long double beds, separate vanity areas, color televisions, and in-room coffee.

This is a simple place—no lobby, just a front desk. But it's pleasant and less expensive than hostelries with more elaborate facilities. Free parking is available on the premises, and babysitting may be arranged by guests through a bonded babysitting service.

Rooms with a king-size bed rent for $73–$92 single, $78–$97 double. Rooms with two double beds cost $78, single or double, plus $7 each for a third or fourth person. Rooms with two queen-size beds and a sofa bed are $86, single or double, plus $10 for each additional person (up to a total of six). A two-room suite with king- and queen-size beds (accommodating one to four people) costs $108. A two-room suite with two double beds and a queen-size bed (accommodating up to six) rents for $108 for one to four people, plus $7 for each additional person (up to six). Cribs are free; rollaways cost $5 per night. Children under five stay free in their parents' room.

LOMBARD STREET/MARINA AREA

The Marina area is a good choice for families because you can find more moderately priced accommodations here. In fact, if you're looking for budget lodgings, this is the area we recommend. Conveniently located near Fisherman's Wharf (and surrounding Ghirardelli Square, the Cannery, Pier 39, Maritime Museum), Union Street, and not too far from downtown, it's less congested here than in most of the other areas of town—certainly less than Fisherman's Wharf and the Union Square area.

There's a neighborhood park at Chestnut and Laguna, which features playground equipment, a community center, and tennis courts—and you're close to Aquatic Park as well. There's a 24-hour pharmacy, Walgreen's, at 3201 Divisadero St. (☎ 415/931-6415), and a 24-hour Marina Safeway market at 15 Marina Blvd. (☎ 415/563-4946).

Six blocks from Fisherman's Wharf at Union Street is the **Vagabond Inn,** 2550 Van Ness Ave., San Francisco, CA 94109 (☎ **415/776-7500,** or toll free **800/522-1555**), a place so centrally located that it's claimed you can get anywhere in the city without ever using your car. But the biggest draw here is price. These nice rooms come with complimentary continental breakfast (fruit, doughnuts, and coffee), all-day coffee and tea, and apples in the lobby.

Management here is extremely accommodating to families and will give you referrals for babysitters. The nice-size pool area has a little patio and gazebo. Continental breakfast is served from 6:30 to 9am. The inn is adjacent to the Midnite Café, which is open 24 hours and has a full coffee-shop menu. Boosters only available.

Since the 132 rooms vary considerably in size, be sure to tell the reservationist that you're bringing a couple of kids and you want a larger room. Some accommodations are large enough to sleep six people and even have room for a crib. These layouts have large sitting areas in addition to a small game table and chair. Request a bathtub if you have a preference.

Room rates are seasonal. In high season (June 15 to September 30), singles cost $99; doubles, $104. The rest of the year the prices range from $75 single and $90 to $109 double. Family rooms are available and cost $90–$120. Children under 18 stay free in the same room as their parents. No charge for cribs. Free parking.

Best Bet for the Money

A wonderful bed-and-breakfast–style place, the **Marina Inn,** 3110 Octavia St. (at Lombard Street), San Francisco, CA 94123 (☎ **415/928-1000,** toll free **800/274-1420**), is definitely the best buy in this area if you don't mind a small space. This budget-priced accommodation, owned by the same management as the White Swan and Petite Auberge, was designed for the "price-sensitive" traveler. You enter the four-story Victorian hotel created to feel like an English country-style inn, and walk into a small foyer that has vaulted ceilings and is light with color. The inn is bright and fresh, with lots of pink marble, brass fixtures, and simple pine furniture.

The management says that people are so happy to have comfortable rooms at this price that many take a second room for their kids—exactly what we would suggest (if you can afford it), given that many of the rooms are very small. There are no adjoining rooms, but you can get two next door to each other. Since some of the rooms are very small, be sure to indicate that you're bringing your family when you make reservations. The staff wants to accommodate families and encourages people to ask if they need special arrangements. Ask if there are special rates because they will upgrade your room at certain times.

The tasteful English country-inn theme is carried on throughout. If you're lucky, you'll get a room with a charming bay window and seat. All 40 rooms have pine furniture, queen-size poster beds, and comforter that are set off by the pretty pastel-flowered wallpaper and forest-green carpet. Rooms have private baths with showers and tubs, plus phones and TV.

There's a small common room that has a microwave, an ice machine, and all-day coffee and tea service. This is where complimentary continental breakfast (juice, fresh muffins, choice of hot beverage) is served. Guests are encouraged to take their breakfast back to their rooms, however, since there is limited seating. When breakfast is not being served, you're welcome to let the kids play their board games here. Other amenities include turndown service. The front desk will help you make babysitting and sightseeing reservations.

Rates range from $65 to $85, single or double (depending on size and location of room), and include a free continental breakfast and afternoon sherry. Cribs are provided free, but there's a $10 daily charge for a third person 5 years and older.

Budget

Cow Hollow Motor Inn & Suites, 2190 Lombard St. (at Steiner Street), San Francisco, CA 94123 (☎ **415/921-5800**), has 117 spacious, newly decorated and some newly constructed rooms. While some of the inside rooms are dark, the decor—light pink and blue pastels with flowered wallpaper—makes even these rooms acceptable. Ask for an outside room. They're bright and quite lovely.

Rooms are tastefully decorated, and some are so large that even with a king-size bed there's space for a crib and a rollaway and you'll still have plenty of room to move around. Most of the rooms have two extra-long double beds, however, and are quite nice. Rooms have tubs and showers, large sink areas in the bathroom, and a vanity area with a mirror. Each room has a coffee maker.

First Watch restaurant is located on the premises (see the "Where to Eat" section for details), and serves breakfast and lunch. Hours are 7am to 2:30pm. Although there is no children's menu, the restaurant offers an array of items for kids in half-portions.

Rooms with a king-size bed rent for $73 single and $78 double. Those with two double beds cost $78, single or double, plus $7 for each additional occupant up to four. Rooms with two queen-size beds and a sofa rent for $86, single or double, plus $7 for each additional occupant up to four. Connecting rooms are available.

Cow Hollow has newly constructed one- and two-bedroom suites. These are not budget accommodations. Indeed, each has a beautifully furnished living room with wood-burning fireplaces and hardwood floors, fully equipped kitchens, and cable television. The largest suite has two double beds and a king-size bed, and can accommodate one rollaway or crib. Three-room suites with one bath are $175, single or double; four-room suites with two baths are $225, single or double. Each additional person is $10.

In both types of rooms, cribs are free, but rollaways cost $10 per night. Children under five stay free in their parents' room. Free parking.

Owned by the same folks as Cow Hollow, the **Chelsea Motor Inn,** 2095 Lombard St. (at Fillmore Street), San Francisco, CA 94123 (☎ **415/563-5600**), is another attractive budget-priced alternative. Somewhat surprising are the extra touches here:

a no-smoking floor, a security elevator that opens only with a room key, king- and queen-size beds or extra-long double beds, queen-size sofa beds, and coffee and tea in the room.

These are large, comfortable rooms (60 of them). Each is equipped with shower and cast-iron tub, and a vanity area with mirror. Some third-floor rooms have a view.

Rooms with a king-size bed cost $73 single, $78 double. Rooms with two double beds are $78 single or double, plus $7 each for a third or fourth occupant. Rooms with two queen-size beds and a sofa bed rent for $86, single or double; additional occupants (to a total of four) are charged $7 each. Connecting rooms are available. No charge for cribs; rollaways cost $5. Children under five stay free in their parents' room. Free parking.

The **Coventry Motor Inn,** 1901 Lombard St. (at Buchanan Street), San Francisco, CA 94123 (☎ 415/567-1200), is another small (69 rooms) motor inn that offers families good value and pleasant surroundings. Also owned by the same people who own Cow Hollow Motor Inn, this hostelry opened in 1984. The simple rooms are attractively furnished and have either king-size or extra-long double beds, small game tables with chairs, and a convenient bath/vanity area. There is in-room coffee and complimentary indoor parking.

Rates are $73 single and $78 double in rooms with king-size beds; those with two double beds are $78, single or double; $85 triple; and $92 quad. Family rooms consisting of two queen-size beds and a sofa cost $86, single or double; additional occupants (up to a total of five) pay $5 each per night. Cribs are free; rollaways cost $5. Children five and under stay free in their parents' room; children over 5 are charged $5 per night.

The **Comfort Inn by the Bay,** 2775 Van Ness Ave. (at Lombard Street), San Francisco, CA 94109 (☎ 415/928-5000, or toll free **800/221-2222**), is an excellent choice in the budget-price bracket. The rooms are clean and attractive, and you can't beat the location—seven blocks to Ghirardelli Square.

The hotel's 134 guest rooms are divided into two types. On one side of the hotel are "cityside" rooms with one queen-size bed, a table and chairs, and a desk. The bathrooms are small, but do have tub/shower combinations. These rooms can accommodate a crib or rollaway, but may seem cramped.

On the other side are larger "Bayside" rooms, which have a beautiful view of the bay and the Golden Gate Bridge. These have two double beds, a game table and chairs, and a desk, as well as a good-size bathroom.

All rooms have color television and in-room movies.

Rates change seasonally. Bayside rooms start at $79 single and double; cityside rooms start at $69. No charge for cribs; rollaways cost $10. Children under 18 stay free when occupying the same room as a parent. Each additional person pays $10. Parking costs $5.

The best thing about the **Lombard Motor Inn,** 1475 Lombard St. (at Franklin Street, near Van Ness Avenue), San Francisco, CA 94123 (☎ 415/441-6000, or toll free **800/835-3639**), is its convenient location. It has been newly remodeled, yet rates are very reasonable and you'll find it clean and pleasant.

Standard rooms include in-room coffee and a king-size or extra-long double bed. No-smoking rooms are available. If you want a bath with a tub/shower, you need to request it at the time you make your reservations. There's no charge for local telephone calls. Free indoor parking on the premises.

Rooms with a king-size bed rent for $59–$73 single and $64–$78 double. Additional guests pay $5–$7 each per night. Connecting rooms are available. No charge for cribs; rollaways cost $5. Children under five stay free in their parents' room.

Buena Vista Motor Inn, 1599 Lombard St. (at Gough), San Francisco, CA 94123 (☎ 415/923-9600), is another good choice. Built in early 1989, this hostelry offers lovely guest rooms that are quite spacious. They come with either king- or queen-size beds. Free parking, in-room coffee, and cable TV.

Rooms with king- or queen-size beds are $78–$85 for two; $6 for each additional person. Children under 11 are free, as are cribs. Rollaways are $6.

JAPANTOWN AND VAN NESS AVENUE

This area of the city is a bit off-the-beaten-hotel path, but many people like the unusual ambience of Japantown. The Plaza area is a good one for energetic children, and there's a 24-hour Safeway market at 1335 Webster St. (☎ 415/921-4557), near Japan Center.

Moderate

The **Queen Anne Hotel,** 1590 Sutter St., San Francisco, CA 94109 (☎ 415/441-2828), is a stately Victorian building of the 1890s that has been elegantly restored to make guests feel as if they're stepping into another era. Dark, traditional woods set off the other antique pieces—some of polished brass, others of shining silver. And the restored Victorian grand staircase is exquisite. The lobby has a large parlor area separated from the registration desk and has several conversation groups. There's another small room, called the library (which can be closed off), where there is a fireplace, card table and chairs, and upholstered chairs that offer a comfortable place for reading.

The atmosphere of the hotel is somewhat quiet, even hushed, but it's a great place to experience the beauty of the city in a lovely setting. Families are encouraged to visit but older, more reserved children will fit in better.

This graceful, handsome hotel offers a free continental breakfast in the parlor each morning and offers tea, coffee, and sherry service in the parlor in the afternoon.

Each of the 49 guest rooms and suites is unique and decorated in antiques. Some rooms have beautiful bay windows, fireplaces, wet bars, and parlors. Most have tall windows set off by sheer curtains behind richly colored side drapes and other authentic Victorian detailings. Armoires are found in some of the rooms instead of closets, and most rooms are large enough to comfortably accommodate a rollaway or crib. All rooms have remote-control color TV, AM/FM radio, hair dryers, and phones in bedroom and bathroom. All the bathrooms have been completely modernized and include a tub/shower combination.

Rates are from $99 to $175, single or double occupancy and include complimentary continental breakfast and afternoon sherry. There are three one-bedroom suites in which the parlor has a queen-size sofa bed and these cost $175 per night. Children under 12 stay free when sharing a room with an adult, and there's a $10 charge for each additional person over the age of 12.

Budget

If you'd like to stay in Japantown, the **Best Western Miyako Inn,** 1800 Sutter St. (at Buchanan Street), San Francisco, CA 94115 (☎ 415/921-4000, or toll free 800/528-1234), is a small, quiet hotel with 125 accommodations. The rooms are

Western style. It's located in a quiet neighborhood, with public transportation to downtown and other areas available every five or ten minutes. Step down into the sunken lobby with its polished brass doors.

Mum's Bar & Grill, located on the first floor, is open from 7am to 10pm. Breakfasts cost $3.75–$10.75, lunches are $4.25–$8.50, and dinners run $7–$13.50. Japanese specialties are available.

As for the accommodations, the recently renovated rooms with two double beds are fair-sized and open onto interior hallways. The one- and two-bedroom suites have a parlor with a couch that turns into a queen-size bed, a small eating table and chairs, television, coffee table, and easy chairs. Each suite bedroom comes with two double beds and has its own bathroom with steambath. There's plenty of room for a crib in the parlor. A one-bedroom suite could comfortably sleep a family of five or six.

Rooms rent for $81–$83 single ($87–$89 with steambath) and $91–$93 double ($97–$99 with steambath). One- and two-bedroom suites range $158–$258 per night. Connecting rooms are available. No charge for cribs; rollaways cost $10. Children 18 and under stay free when sharing their parents' room. If a family needs more than one room, each room will be charged at the single rate regardless of the number of occupants. Parking is $6.50 per night.

A great buy for a family with two-plus kids, the no-frills, clean, comfortable, and congenial **Holiday Lodge and Garden Hotel** is centrally located at 1901 Van Ness Ave., San Francisco, CA 94109 (☎ **415/776-4469,** or toll free **800/367-8504**). There is no restaurant, but two blocks away is the Hard Rock Café, a hop away from the cable car to nearby Fisherman's Wharf and Chinatown.

In '60ish decor, these 77 modest rooms overlook a landscaped courtyard with lots of running room for kids and seating area for adults to oversee the tots in the swimming pool (there is no wading pool). Room service is available 11am to 10pm in conjunction with "Waiters on Wheels," with selections from 30 area restaurants. Plenty of free parking space is provided.

Children 12 and under stay free. Rates start at $89 for single or double occupancy. The weekly rate is $325 ($550 in summer). Choose from 13 studio apartments with kitchenettes for larger families or family rooms with a queen-size bed and two twin-bed sofas (no kitchenette). Cribs are free; for rollaways, add an extra $10.

5 Where to Eat

It's been said that San Francisco has so many restaurants that if you ate in a different one for every meal, it would take you four years to try them all. And new ones open all the time!

San Francisco is an epicurean's dream—even if that food lover has kids and wants to dine with them. Hundreds of restaurants welcome families. We've chosen many of them, listed them by neighborhood first and price second. And we've limited cuisine to the types that children are most likely to eat. Enjoy!

UNION SQUARE

One of the great things about the Union Square area is that it's packed with restaurants, many of them in hotels. You can walk down almost any block and find at least three restaurants. These are the ones we liked best.

Remember, though, that parking in this area can be a major headache. Unless we so specify, parking is on the street. There's one main parking lot under Union Square and others on side streets, but the rates are high. If at all possible, take a taxi or use public transportation. And remember that distances are short, so walking is often the best way to get from one place to another.

Expensive

The **French Room,** in the Four Seasons Clift Hotel, 495 Geary St. (☎ 415/775-4700), is a spectacularly ornate restaurant. The 18th-century French decor (complete with relief-style paneled walls) is set off by tall tapestry-framed windows and elegant crystal chandeliers. There are Louis XV petit-point chairs, Queen Anne–style love seats, and mahogany console servers. But this award-winning French/California restaurant features more than just beautiful surroundings. And to our delight, it welcomes children!

Open for breakfast and dinner, the restaurant is famous for its evening meals and its collection of over 20,000 bottles of fine French and California wines. Sea scallops in a potato and bacon crust on a bed of marinated lentils or grilled rack of lamb and braised lamb shank with sun-dried–tomato risotto are two of the many dinner specialties. The menu also boasts alternative cuisine items—lower in calories, cholesterol, sodium, and fat. The average check per person, including beverage, is $15 at breakfast, $40 at dinner, and $23 for Sunday brunch.

The children's menu features macaroni and cheese, junior beef or cheeseburger, chicken fingers and jumbo hot dogs, with prices from $2.50 to $6. The restaurant is also willing to serve children smaller portions of most items on the regular menu. Highchairs and boosters are available and the staff greets children with a small trinket, coloring book, comic book or the like.

The French Room is open daily. Breakfast is served from 6:30 to 11am and lunch is served in the Redwood Room located adjacent to the French Room, from noon to 2:30pm, Monday through Saturday. Sunday brunch is offered from 10am to 2pm. Dinner is served from 6 to 10:30pm, Tuesday through Saturday. Reservations are suggested. All major credit cards accepted. Valet parking.

Tucked away behind the chic shops of Union Square at 19 Maiden Lane, the **Iron Horse Restaurant** (☎ 415/362-8133) makes you feel as if you stepped into an old San Francisco establishment. The restaurant has a British air about it—dimly lit, sconces on the wall, white linen cloths. It's a lovely place to enjoy an out-of-the-ordinary Italian dinner.

When we were there, the staff was exceptionally nice to kids (several of whom dined there at 9pm), bringing three cherries in the Shirley Temple, but the wait for dinner was a bit long, so be prepared. The dim light makes it difficult for kids to read; the tablecloths make bringing crayons questionable. Although we saw a toddler there, we'd suggest this place for well-behaved youngsters or older kids. These folks welcome children, and will warm baby bottles and baby food, and make a wide array of children's drinks. We'd suggest that you go early to avoid the romantic diners and businesspeople.

The food is good and the menu is printed daily to feature all the specials. The lunch menu is extensive, offering the likes of 15 different salads, sandwiches, omelets, pasta, seafood, and hot entrees. Prices range from $3 for mixed garden greens to $16 for New York Angus sirloin steak.

For dinner, we loved the marinated rack of lamb and the cannelloni della casa. The artichoke-and-seafood salad was a special treat, and the above-mentioned steak was tender and large. You might split an order of luscious, rich gnocchi. Prices run $9–$21.

Request a highchair when you make your reservation. Boosters are also available. No children's menu here, but the staff is extremely helpful in offering ideas to kids about what to eat and will prepare half-orders whenever possible (for half price). Reservations are accepted. Street parking available.

Open Monday through Saturday for lunch from 11:30am to 4pm, and for dinner daily from 4 to 10:30pm. Major credit cards accepted.

Moderate

The **Dutch Kitchen** is located in the Westin St. Francis Hotel, 335 Powell St. (☎ 415/397-7000 or 774-0264). We were surprised that this café in the ultra-luxurious St. Francis would be as gracious to children as they are. Andrew thinks of this place as one of the truly great breakfast spots in the world. Crayons and the Westin Premier Kid Club menu (which doubles as a coloring page) are handed to each child as quickly as steaming coffee is brought to the table for the grownups. While the adults fill up on fresh berries, melons, and croissants at the Continental Breakfast Buffet ($9.50), the children delight in French toast, Mickey Mouse waffles, silver-dollar pancakes with strawberries at $3, or 1 egg, hash browns, and toast for $3.50, or a variety of other treats. Other adult breakfast items include buttermilk pancakes ($5.85) and full egg breakfasts that range from $8.50 to $11.50; Golden Gate Buffet $14.50.

Breakfast is served every day from 6 to 11:30am. You can park in the hotel lot— but it's costly. **Note:** If you have a stroller, don't enter the restaurant via Post Street— the stairs will do you in. Enter through the hotel lobby, which is located on Powell Street, or the carriage entrance on Geary Street. Major credit cards are accepted.

Looking for a great place for your teens and preteens? **Lori's Diner,** 336 Mason St., near Geary Street (☎ 415/392-8646), a fun, trendy eatery, may just be the place. There's lots of polished chrome and 1950s memorabilia (Elvis and James Dean posters everywhere), but what really grabs the kids is the '50s jukebox filled with Baby Boomer music.

While there are no highchairs, booster seats fit easily in the high-gloss red booths. Our kids loved the place. They watched the cook make the burgers and shakes— always a treat. This place is so trendy they even sell Lori's Diner T-shirts.

The staff is friendly, and the food is good American fare—a palate pleaser for youngsters of all ages. Although there's no children's menu, two children (or an adult and one child) can split one of the enormous burgers, which the cook will cut in half in the kitchen. The staff will be glad to warm bottles and baby food as well.

This restaurant is a real treat at any time. It's open 24 hours a day, seven days a week. That's unusual, even in San Francisco. Breakfasts are priced from $3.50 (pancakes) to $8.95 (steak and eggs). Hot dogs run $4–$6, and terrific burgers start at $4.95 (with fries). Dinners go to $11.95 (for steak). No credit cards or reservations. Another location: 500 Sutter St., at Powell (☎ 415/981-1950).

Mama's of San Francisco, 398 Geary St., near Mason Street (☎ 415/788-1004), is another great eatery at Union Square—and an excellent alternative to pricey hotel coffee shops. Good American fare for breakfast and lunch, and Italian food for dinner. Mama's has a reputation for originality and quality food among the locals.

For breakfast (served all day), munch on fresh-baked muffins, sweet rolls, or croissants while you wait for a truly original omelet. We had the Californian omelet (fresh vegetables and herbs, with home fries and sourdough toast) and Swedish cinnamon French toast. Another great egg dish is the eggs Union Square (scrambled eggs with tomato, green onion, and ham). If you're in the mood for something different, try the kugelhopf brioche (made fresh daily with thick swirls of cinnamon, dates, raisins, and toasted almonds served up as French toast) or the apple pan doré (thin slices of French toast topped with Granny Smith and Red Delicious apples, butter, and cinnamon).

Lunch served from 11am to 5pm consists of an array of salads and Mama's original sandwiches. Nob Hill Salad is chicken, avocado, and fresh fruit with mixed greens. Slim Joe is ground chuck with grilled onion and jack cheese on a French bread baguette.

The dinner menu is quite extensive. Good sandwiches, hamburgers, and daily specials are offered, including pastas and fresh fish. Prime rib, veal, and pasta dinners range from $8.75 to $22. All include fresh vegetable and pasta or potatoes. Breakfast and lunch range from $5–$8.

The children's menu features pasta, chicken, and sandwiches, and ranges in price from $4.50 to $6.50. For breakfast, the kids may have smaller portions or adult orders may be split in the kitchen for two children. Your server will warm bottles and baby food. The service here is very fast, and highchairs and boosters are available. Open from 7am to midnight Sunday through Thursday, and on Friday and Saturday till 1am, every day except Christmas. All major credit cards accepted. Full bar. A simpler version is **Mama's on Washington Square,** at 1701 Stockton St., near Filbert Street (☎ 415/362-6421). No credit cards. Only breakfast and lunch are served, Tuesday through Sunday from 7am to 3pm.

Inexpensive

Salamagundi, 442 Geary St., near Mason Street (☎ 415/441-0894), is across the street from the A.C.T. and Curran Theaters. This soup-and-sandwich place is probably the best casual, inexpensive place to take kids before or after an outing— the theater, cable-car rides, walking through Union Square. The food is very good and the prices are reasonable.

There are 50 different homemade soups, five of them offered daily (favorites include lentil, country chicken with biscuits, and burgundy beef with noodles). For the price of a bowl you get a refill, and believe me you'll want it because it's delicious. Salads, quiche, and unusual sandwiches round out the bill of fare in this buffet-style restaurant. Prices range from $2.95 for a slice of quiche or soup to $7.95 for soup, salad, and a roll or drink. Boosters and highchairs are available. Children can easily split adult orders.

Hours are 11am to midnight Monday through Saturday and 11am to 9pm on Sunday.

Sears Fine Food, 439 Powell St., on Union Square (☎ 415/986-1160), is about as famous as any coffee shop can get. World renowned for its sourdough French toast ($5.40), dollar-size Swedish pancakes—you get 18 of them per serving, for $4.50— and crisp waffles ($4.50–$5.50), this family-oriented restaurant is as popular with the locals as with the tourists. We loved the apple dumpling ($5.50), and the turkey sandwich ($7) is always a big winner with our family.

There's often a line out the door because the food is scrumptious—but we were assured that it always moves quickly, only a 10-minute wait. And with Union Square and all the fascinating shops nearby, Dad could wait in line while Mom and the kids browse.

Open for breakfast or lunch from 6:30am to 3:30 pm Wednesday through Sunday. There are booster seats and highchairs. There is no children's menu, but they'll split adult portions and warm baby bottles and food. No credit cards. Reservations taken for six or more.

If your family is into baseball, **Lefty O'Doul's,** 333 Geary St. (☎ 415/982-8900), is a legendary old-time sports bar, and is known for serving good family-style fare. Baseball memorabilia surrounds you, and it's a fun place (once your eyes get used to the dim light) for children, who can spend lots of time looking at the mementos. The big-screen televisions are always tuned to "the game." Even little ones get caught up in the activity. The noise level is such that any noise your kids make will be absorbed.

Choose from delicious hot fresh turkey, roast beef, ham, pastrami, and more. Sandwiches are $4.59; full meals (which include salad, vegetable, and bread) are $7.75. Typical breakfast fare is priced equally appealingly at $4.25–$4.95. For children, there is a child's plate for $3.50. Lunch and dinner are hofbrau style.

There are highchairs but no boosters, and the staff will warm baby bottles or baby food in the kitchen. Open for breakfast from 7 to 11am; lunch and dinner, from 11am to 12:30am. No reservations accepted; some credit cards accepted. There are family sing-alongs every night at the piano bar (but children are only allowed in areas where food is served).

EMBARCADERO

You'll probably spend a little time in this general area.

MacArthur Park Restaurant, 607 Front St. at Jackson (☎ 415/398-5700), is a restaurant you don't want to miss if you're anywhere near this area. Located across the street from little Jackson Park, in a beautiful brick building that recalls the late 1800s and the sensational Barbary Coast days, it has fabulous food and extremely amicable servers. This place is slightly off the beaten path and is a good one to plan for lunch and either let the children run around before or after across the street. (There's a fabulous travel store, called Travel Market, located nearby at Golden Gateway Commons, 130 Pacific Avenue Mall, ☎ 415/421-4080, if you want to immerse yourself in books, maps, and other travel paraphernalia.)

Specialties are baby back ribs, mesquite-grilled fresh fish and steaks, and excellent salads. Desserts are a real treat. (And most foods can be boxed "to go.") Prices range from $7.25 for a hamburger to $18.95 for a 16-ounce New York steak with yummy onion strings. A full slab of baby back ribs is $16.50, a half is $11.95. We split a combination chicken-and-ribs dinner ($16.50) between the two kids. Waiters will split adult portions for you in the kitchen. Crayons and paper are at the table, which Andrew and Elizabeth put to good use drawing pictures as we wait for the food.

Don't miss the hot fudge or caramel ice-cream sundae—on luscious brownies. For those whose sweet tooth is less extreme, a plate of cookies is another good choice.

Boosters and highchairs are provided. Reservations are accepted and honored. The restaurant does a big cocktail-hour business, but don't let that bother you as the dinner hour doesn't start to get crowded until after 7pm, so try to make it in earlier and you'll have less of a wait. Lunch is best after 1pm, so you miss the business crowd. All major credit cards are accepted. Open for lunch Monday through Friday from 11:30am to 3:30pm, and dinner Monday through Thursday from 5 to 10:30pm, Friday and Saturday until 11pm, and Sunday from 4:30 to 10pm.

Another restaurant is **Chevy's Mexican Restaurant,** Two Embarcadero, podium level (☎ 415/391-2323), part of this Northern California chain. It's a lively, colorful place with simply wonderful chips and guacamole, and a place to stop if you're looking for Mexican food and you're in the Embarcadero. Other locations are at 4th and Howard Streets (☎ 415/543-8060) and in the Stonestown Galleria (☎ 415/665-8705).

Children have their own menu that consists of tacos, enchiladas, burritos, tamales, and quesadillas, with prices ranging from $1.95 to $3.95. Boosters and highchairs are provided. Open Sunday through Thursday from 11am to 10pm, until 11pm on Friday and Saturday.

A restaurant that has created a lot of excitement recently in the city is **Square One,** at 190 Pacific Mall, at Front Street (☎ 415/788-1110). Opposite Walton Park, and minutes from the financial district, this restaurant is the creation of chef and food writer Joyce Goldstein, who has written four cookbooks. Here's a place where quality and quantity go hand-in-hand, and where the joy of cooking is apparent. Most impressive is the innovative, wholesome menu that changes daily. It's international, with a Mediterranean flair.

You and your kids will love the homemade breads prepared on the premises. For lunch there are reasonably priced salads, hearty pastas, and light entrees ($4.75–$10). And for dinner you might try grilled salmon, pork, or veal with vegetables and rice or potato pancakes ($12–$21). The desserts are to die for: seasonal fruits dressed up in pies, sorbets, and ice creams. There is no children's menu, but they'll be glad to split the generous portions. Booster seats, but no highchairs. Open for lunch Monday through Friday from 11:30am to 2:30pm, and for dinner every night from 5:30 to 10pm. Reservations accepted. Valet parking or use the neighborhood lot.

NORTH BEACH

Famed for beatniks, coffeehouses, and strip joints, North Beach also offers a tantalizing array of restaurants everywhere you turn. If standard sit-down meals aren't your style, let the kids enjoy one of the many cafés or gelato places during your stroll through the area. But beware—parking is among the worst in the city, especially on Friday and Saturday nights.

You may want to avoid the area anyway on Friday and Saturday nights. Not only is the parking impossible, but on weekend nights, even the action on the sidewalks may be difficult to take with kids in tow. The barkers in front of the cabarets and shows on Broadway may make you—and the kids—uncomfortable.

We start with **Mara's Bakery,** 503 Columbus Ave. (☎ 415/397-9435), not really a restaurant but possibly one of the best places in North Beach for Italian pastry and cookies. Some say you rarely see these kinds of pastries outside Italy. The tempting goodies are so plentiful that our ten-year-old took 15 minutes trying to pick which pastry he wanted. There are only a few tables, so plan to take the sweets out (you might wander to nearby Washington Square to eat your treats). Espresso, tea, and coffee are also served. Open Sunday through Thursday from 7am to 10:30pm, on Friday and Saturday until midnight.

Expensive

North Beach Restaurant, 1512 Stockton St. (☎ 415/392-1700), serves award-winning northern Italian cuisine—and serves it up to loads of families. They make their own pasta every day, hang and cure their own prosciutto hams, cut and prepare the veal in their own kitchen, and vow to serve the finest food they can. Choose from almost 30 different fish entrees (for example, petrale stuffed with shrimp and crab, abalone, or crab puff au gratin), 20 different veal entrees (veal piccata, veal with marsala wine, veal cutlets parmigiana, veal portafoglio with Grand Marnier sauce), as well as pasta, lamb, chicken, and steak. Full dinners come with antipasto, salad, soup, pasta, fresh vegetable, dessert, and coffee. Lunches range in price from $8.95 to $27.95; seven-course dinners average $22.95 (à la carte prices, from $10.50 to $27.95).

While there is no children's menu, kids can choose from a large part of the menu and can split orders. Owner Lorenzo Petroni says that orders are so large that many parents just share with the children. Highchairs and boosters are available, and your server will gladly get the kids specialty drinks from the full bar. Bottles and baby food will be warmed.

Open daily for lunch and dinner from 11:30am to 11:45pm. All major credit cards accepted. Valet parking $5 lunch; $6 dinner.

Moderate

Capp's Corner, 1600 Powell St., at Green Street (☎ 415/989-2589), is one of those authentic North Beach family restaurants that people associate with San Francisco. Andrew and Elizabeth both love this place—something not always easy to accomplish. Opened more than 30 years ago, the walls are lined with photos of politicians, celebrities, and sports figures who have visited. Pictures of the pennant-winning San Francisco Giants cover the walls. And the colors of the Italian flag line the windows.

The tables are set up for traditional family-style dining. Entrees range from roast beef and leg of lamb to veal in marsala sauce and eggplant parmigiana. They serve clams, mussels, and homemade sausage. All entrees come with soup and salad, pasta, dessert, and coffee. Lunch costs $6.50–$8.50; dinner runs $10–$12. Children's portions are available: lunch, $6.50; dinner, $8.50.

Highchairs and boosters are available, and they'll warm bottles and baby food. Open seven nights for dinner: 4:30 to 10:30pm Sunday through Thursday, to 11pm on Friday and Saturday. Open Monday through Friday for lunch from 11:30am to 2:30pm. Reservations are recommended. Most credit cards are accepted. There's a parking lot across the street.

North Beach Pizza, 1499 Grant Ave., at Union Street (☎ 415/433-2444), is known for some of the best pizza in all San Francisco. This is a warm family place where waitresses laugh and joke with kid-customers. Small and cozy, with traditional red-checked cloths, candles in wine bottles, and garlic ropes hanging along the walls, this restaurant serves up over 20 kinds of pizza—from the tame to the exotic. Some of our favorite combinations are clams with garlic and cheese, and the Coit Tower special, which has mushrooms, sausage, salami, and pepperoni. There are vegetarian and seafood pizzas, as well as a wide selection of pastas, submarine sandwiches, and hot entrees. Reasonably priced full-course dinners ($7–$10) of veal, poultry, seafood, or barbecued ribs include vegetables, spaghetti, soup or salad, and bread and butter.

Boosters are available, but there's no children's menu. The staff will gladly split meals in the kitchen or bring an extra plate for the little ones. Ask for crackers for the kids to munch on while waiting for dinner. One drawback is that no reservations are accepted and you may have to wait if you come during the prime dinner hours.

Open Sunday through Thursday from 11am to 1am, on Friday and Saturday to 3am. Most major credit cards are accepted. Street parking. Also delivers pizzas (in moisture-controlled ovens) to hotels, and bills itself as the city's fastest delivery service.

There are three other locations: **North Beach Pizza, Too,** 1310 Grant Ave., at Vallejo Street (☎ 415/433-2444); **North Beach Pizza at Mission,** 4787 Mission

St., near Ocean Avenue (☎ 415/586-1400; **North Beach Pizza at Haight,** 800 Stanyan St., near Haight (☎ 415/751-2300).

The Gold Spike, 527 Columbus Ave., between Union and Green Streets (☎ 415/986-9747), has been serving huge, six-course family-style meals since 1920. Although the place is small, the walls are filled with business cards, postcards, pictures, signs—it's almost like being in a fantastic old junk store. The kids love to inspect the old treasures everywhere.

Dinners include antipasto, minestrone soup, salad, pasta, dessert, and a choice of entree for $12.95. A la carte and side orders are also available. Children can choose from many of the same items as adults. Portions and prices are adjusted.

No highchairs here, but boosters are available. Weekends tend to be busy, and because they don't take reservations there's often a long wait. The staff tries to be helpful with kids, but warns that Friday and Saturday nights are difficult because of the crowds. Open for dinner only, every day but Wednesday: weekdays from 5 to 10pm, on Friday and Saturday until 10:30pm.

New Pisa Restaurant, 550 Green St. (☎ 415/362-4726 or 415/989-2289), is an institution in North Beach. The restaurant opened in 1921 by the Benedetti family, who came to San Francisco from Torre del Lago, a town near Pisa, Italy. It has been serving family-style American and Italian food ever since. Prices have changed since then, however, when lunch was 25¢ and dinner was 35¢! Today lunch is $8.50 and dinner runs $12.50; children's meals are $6.50 at lunch and $8.50 at dinner.

The choice of entrees is straightforward: roast beef, roast veal, roast pork, breast of lamb, chicken dishes, fresh fish, and daily specials. All meals include soup, salad, pasta, and dessert.

There are highchairs and boosters here, and they'll warm bottles and baby food in the kitchen. Reservations are recommended and all major credit cards are accepted. If you have to wait for a table, the kids can amuse themselves with the baseball exhibit in the waiting area. Open daily except Wednesday from 11:30am to 3pm for lunch and 3 to 10:30pm for dinner.

If you're not taking young kids, the famed **Washington Square Bar & Grill,** 1707 Powell St., North Beach (☎ 415/982-8123), is a fun place to watch local and visiting celebrities. It has a bustling, comfortable, almost clubby ambience, especially for journalists and visiting literary figures. Almost everyone is a regular. People talk back and forth from table to table, and everyone seems to know everyone else, but they make you feel like a local yourself.

Opened in 1973, it was the first bar and grill in the Bay Area. The food is good, and while there aren't any special services for children, the staff loves kids and will use telephone books and cushions to fashion makeshift booster seats. If you do decide to bring your little one they'll split adult portions for children, serve quarter-size pasta dishes, and warm bottles or baby food. They'll even concoct special children's drinks.

There is jazz at night, at which time "The Washbag" acquires a more romantic tone. The place is really best for older kids and teens. The modern Italian cuisine ranges from pasta, veal, and chicken to a good choice of seafood. There are hamburgers and daily specials too. Prices range from $8 to $19.

Open weekdays from 11:30am to 3pm for lunch, 3 to 5pm for light snacks, and 5:30 to 11pm for dinner, on Friday and Saturday until 11:30pm. Open Sunday from 4 to 10pm for dinner. Reservations are recommended. Most major credit cards accepted. Validated parking nearby.

Ed Moose, well-known San Francisco restaurateur, opened up another winner in the heart of North Beach. **Mooses,** 1652 Stockton St. (☎ 415/989-7800), is opposite Washington Square Park, a great play space for kids. This popular, bustling restaurant is spacious with a high noise and energy level and is a great place to take older children. The food is creative, and this lively, happening place also offers piano music nightly.

There's no children's menu, but adult dishes can easily be split. The wide-ranging lunch and dinner menus include a half-pound Mooseburger with fries, a chewy smoked-chicken pizza, or grilled salmon with potato purée. Prices are $5–$12. They'll help you improvise since there are no highchairs or boosters. Open daily from 11:30am to 11:30pm. Reservations are recommended. Valet parking available.

Best Bet for the Money

With a motto like "Rain or shine there's always a line" for **Little Joe's on Broadway,** 523 Broadway (☎ 415/433-4343), you'd expect good food at reasonable prices. And that's what you'll get. You might find that hard to believe when you first walk into the place because it's not much to look at. The restaurant consists of one large room: part of it is a counter area, part a dining room. The dining room has a mural of old San Francisco with the Golden Gate Bridge outlined in tiny white Christmas lights.

The story goes that at the first Joe's location on Columbus, the line got so long it went out the door and around the corner. They then opened a second location next door called Baby Joe's, but the line continued to grow, so they moved to their present location, a large storefront on Broadway.

Mounds of cooked spaghetti are in a tray waiting to be smothered with the sauce and used for hungry diners. Fresh French bread is served as soon as you sit down. Daily specials include beef stew, caciucco (fish stew), and calamari, and come with a choice of vegetables, spaghetti, rigatoni, or beans. The diverse menu includes sandwiches, omelets, pastas, and entrees such as New York steak, pot roast, lamb chops, and all manner of veal. While there's no children's menu, a side order of Joe's spaghetti marinara is so large that it's a meal itself, and certainly enough for a child. Or your waitress will be happy to bring you an extra plate so that junior can have samples from all the adults. Kids roll up their sleeves for Joe's ravioli, minestrone soup, and spaghetti and meatballs. Prices for entrees range from $8.95 to $13.95.

Highchairs and boosters are available. Kids may share their parents' orders at no extra charge. Of course, this family place will also split one adult portion between two kids, as well as warm baby bottles.

The restaurant is open daily for lunch and dinner from 11am to 10:30pm, 11pm on Friday and Saturday. There is no wait between 2 and 5pm. Between 5:30 and 6pm there may be a short line. But then the crowds come. People have been known to stand on line as long as two hours. Call ahead to find out the best time to come. Credit cards accepted. There's a parking lot across the street on Broadway.

You may be confused by the number of restaurants with the name "Joe" in the title. There's Old Joe's, Original Joe's, Little Joe's, New Joe's. At first we thought they were all connected, and became very confused when the type of cuisine changed from place to place. We discovered that "Joe" refers to an open kitchen with an open flame and food made to order. The restaurants usually aren't related, so when you get a recommendation to a restaurant with "Joe" in the title, be sure to get the exact name and location so you don't end up at a completely different place.

CHINATOWN

We had our most potent lesson about parking in San Francisco when we went to a restaurant in Chinatown. To start off, the valet service at our hotel was extremely slow in delivering our car, making us late for our dinner reservation. When we arrived at the restaurant we couldn't find a parking space, so the kids and Grandma went into the restaurant to let them know we had arrived. After ten minutes of no luck at street parking, we tried the parking lot, only to find that it was full—of course, it was a Saturday night at 8:15pm. We continued to try to find street parking. After ten more minutes of frustration, we decided on a drastic measure: Return the car to the hotel— and take a cab. So learn a lesson from us. Don't drive in Chinatown.

There are so many restaurants in Chinatown catering to the family trade that you really could try almost any place that catches your fancy. But here are the ones we like the best.

Moderate

Don't let the lack of decor fool you. The **Canton Tea House and Restaurant,** 1108 Stockton St. (☎ **415/982-1030**), is a wonderful and fun place to go for breakfast, lunch, dim sum, afternoon tea, or dinner. Delectable, reasonably priced food is served by people who are attentive and helpful.

We told our waiter that Andrew was very hungry, and in an instant he was served wonton soup. We saw other children deep in conversation with one waiter. Our waiter asked Andrew if he liked cashew nuts and picked out several especially for him with his chopsticks before he served the rest of the party.

More than 20 kinds of dim sum are made, ranging from barbecued pork bun to sweet Lotus buns. If your kids like soup, the chicken wonton soup is the one to choose, whatever the time of day—the soup base is tasty and rich (not thick, though), with large chunks of chicken and vegetables. It's served piping hot, perfect for everyone in the party on a chilly day or evening.

Entrees range from $7 to $15. Try the sweet-and-sour prawns for a real treat. The shrimp are presented in a very light batter that remains slightly crunchy in the savory sauce. The cashew chicken had lots of nuts and was unusual because it also included mini-ears of corn and Chinese mushrooms. The vegetable chow mein, chicken chow mein, and mild (not spicy) vegetarian dishes are also good for children with less adventurous tastebuds.

This would be a great place to go for dim sum or for a full Chinese meal after wandering around Chinatown. Highchairs and boosters are available. Open daily from 7am to 4pm for dim sum and 5 to 10pm for dinner (kitchen closes at 9pm). Reservations accepted. Some credit cards accepted.

Want Peking-style Mandarin food? Small and cozy, **The Pot Sticker,** 150 Waverly Place, at Washington Street (☎ **415/397-9985**), enjoys serving children (yes, we did say "enjoys"). This lovely place has very good food and a friendly staff who delight in making suggestions about what the kids might like to eat. Although small, the restaurant feels spacious, and while rather subdued, it's not the kind of quiet in which you have to worry about your kids disturbing anyone. The Pot Sticker is so used to serving large groups, primarily families, that the appetizers and soups come with an estimate of the number of servings you'll get per order.

We all loved the hot-and-sour soup, but try the soup of the day, which can be a treat. Pot Sticker dinners, which include soup and pot stickers (Mandarin-style dumplings) or another appetizer, as well as luscious entrees, range from $7.95 to $9.95 per person. The mid-priced dinner includes lemon chicken, Mongolian beef, and Mandarin pork (for three people). Highchairs and boosters are available, and the kitchen staff will gladly warm baby bottles and baby food.

Open from 11:30am to 4pm for lunch and 4:30 to 9:45pm for dinner, seven days a week. Most credit cards honored, and reservations are accepted. Parking in a garage on Washington Street.

The **Golden Phoenix,** 728 Washington St. (☎ **415/989-4400**), is what Sunday-night family-Chinese-dinner restaurants should all be like. Bustling, lots of families (from all over the world—see how many languages you can identify among the other diners), fast service, and good food. Even the decor—phoenix wallpaper and hanging red Chinese lanterns with tassels—lends a certain ambience to the place. This restaurant offers Cantonese, Mandarin, Szechuan, and Hunan dishes.

If you like sweet-and-sour, don't miss the fried wonton appetizers, which come with a side dish of yummy sauce—the best we've ever gobbled down. Soups are fabulous too, and include a wide variety (sizzling rice, hot-and-sour, plus chicken with winter-melon soup); all soups can serve two to four people. The entrees are equally good and cost $6–$9.

Highchairs and boosters are available, and the server will gladly warm bottles and baby food. Children's drinks are available (Shirley Temples, Darth Vaders, etc.). Open from 11:30am to 10:30pm Monday through Friday, 2:30 to 10:30pm on Saturday and Sunday. Reservations and major credit cards are accepted. **Very Important:** There's a municipal parking lot across the street between Clay and Washington Streets—enter on Washington Street.

JAPANTOWN

For another real taste of the Pacific Rim, we love Japantown. You can stroll the area and see which restaurants entice you. Here are some of the ones we like best.

Moderate

One of our favorite restaurants in San Francisco is **Iroha,** 1728 Buchanan St., across the way from Japan Center (☎ **415/922-0321**). This part of Buchanan Street is a continuation of the Japan Center shopping area. The plaza area is closed to cars, and the cobblestone walkways are filled with Japanese shops and restaurants. You'll see two huge windows displaying the food specialties in the usual plastic renditions. Enter a tiny courtyard that has a hint of a Japanese garden, complete with bamboo, and walk up a flight of wooden stairs. Walk through the little slats of cloth that greet visitors and you'll be in the mood for a Japanese lunch or dinner. Lots of little booths give the suggestion of privacy, and a painting of Mount Fuji and hanging paper lanterns complete the mood.

For a treat that the kids as well as you will love, try the gyoza, little dough pockets filled with minced pork or beef and shredded vegetables. Other specialties include hot noodles, ramen, and yakitori (chicken, pork, or beef chunks basted and grilled on little skewers). Entrees range $4.50–$8.50. Dinners—with soup, salad, rice, and pickles—offer a more varied Japanese menu, including tempura, sashimi, and teriyaki, with prices ranging from $8.80 to $12.50. The child's plate is a replica of a U.S. spacecraft and arrives with a combination of deep-fried chicken and sushi ($4.80). But if two kids want to split an adult order, the server will bring an extra plate at no charge. Although the waiters are attentive to children, management will not warm baby bottles or baby food in the kitchen.

Open daily from 11:30am to 9:30pm. Highchairs and boosters are available. Reservations only for parties over six, but if you come between 2 and 7pm there shouldn't be much of a crowd. All major credit cards accepted.

Specializing in homemade Japanese noodles (udon and soba), **Mifune,** 1737 Post St., in the Kintetsu Building restaurant mall (☎ **415/922-0337**), is an extremely popular eatery with families. White Japanese lanterns hang from the ceilings. The interior is red with black latticework, and there are booths. The story goes that the Miwa family has been serving homemade noodles in Japan for more than 50 years. Mifune, with locations in both San Francisco and Los Angeles, is their outpost in the United States.

Be sure to spend time looking at the plastic models of food in the window before you enter the restaurant. The display is fun to look at, and great for kids who get a kick out of seeing the realistic-looking samples on display. A Papa-san doll is in the display case, beckoning you inside.

All manner of noodles can be sampled. Hot noodles (served in a seasoned broth) are accompanied by chicken, tempura, shrimp, and even fishcake. Cold noodles are served with different garnishes ranging from Japanese potato to shrimp and vegetable tempura. For those who prefer something other than noodles, there are hearty rice dishes, and after 4pm a choice of tempura or sashimi. Prices range from $3.50 to $8.50 for noodle and rice dishes, and from $9.30 to $14.50 for dinners.

For kids under 12, order the "Bullet Train," a replica of the famous superspeed transport filled with noodles or rice topped with shrimp and vegetable tempura, a good value at $4.80.

Open daily from 11am to 9:30pm. No reservations. All major credit cards accepted.

Inexpensive

Located across the street from the Peace Plaza, **Sanppo,** 1702 Post St. (☎ **415/346-3486**), is a small, simple Japanese restaurant that has good, standard fare at reasonable prices. We love the different donburi here (rice with a sweetened sauce with different toppings—eggs and vegetables, beef and vegetables, chicken, pork cutlet, even lobster tempura). The kids love the tempura and the ramen (Japanese-style noodles in broth).

The restaurant also offers several kinds of sushi and an unusually wide range of entrees for a Japanese restaurant (ranging from sliced beef cooked in a ginger sauce to lemon steak). The prices are reasonable: $5.95–$14.25 at lunch, $6.95–$17.25 at dinner.

Highchairs and boosters are available. The children's plate ($6.25) is sushi, tempura, or yakitori.

Open Tuesday through Saturday from 11:45am to 9:45pm and on Sunday from 3 to 10pm; closed Monday. Validated parking for Japan Center parking lot. Some credit cards.

CIVIC CENTER AND VAN NESS AVENUE

While these two areas of the city aren't high on our list for tourist attractions, they offer some great restaurants.

Expensive

Ruth's Chris Steak House, 1700 California St., at Van Ness Avenue (☎ 415/673-0557), is another fine eatery that you can enjoy with your older, well-behaved children. Ruth's Chris was founded 30 years ago in New Orleans by Ruth Fertel. The atmosphere is intimate and cozy. White tablecloths, mahogany walls, tuxedoed servers, and soft lighting make this a first-class atmosphere.

The portions are large, the menu is à la carte. Sharing entrees and side dishes is encouraged. There is no charge for splitting items or extra plate charge. Dinner choices include several cuts of beef, fresh salmon and tuna, free-range chicken, lamb and veal chops, and succulent live Maine lobster ($16.50–$25).

Booster seats and highchairs are available, and the bar will happily make kids nonalcoholic beverages. Special birthday treats, balloons for the children, and a family photograph are all free for the asking. Open daily from 5 to 10:30pm. Reservations are recommended. Most major credit cards accepted. Complimentary valet parking.

Here's something different for you and your teens. Perfect for after-theater or a night on the town, **Stars** is at 150 Redwood Alley (☎ 415/861-7827), near the Civic Center. You can enjoy a light supper, piano music, and a star-studded ambience. Stars is a theater event itself. As you are surrounded by colorful wall-to-wall posters from around the world, San Francisco socialites and celebrities will parade by you in their glitter and designer wear.

Dinner ranges from $18.50 to $28.50 with such items as roast salmon, grilled ahi tuna, and sautéed chicken breasts. The supper menu may be better for your kids, with chicken tacos ($4.50), grilled hot dog ($4.25), and individual oven-fired pizza ($7.75); or try the house half-pound burger ($8.50).

Open daily for dinner from 5:30 to 10:30pm, and for lunch Monday through Friday from 11:30am to 2:30pm; the supper menu continues until 11:30pm. Major credit cards accepted, and reservations are highly recommended.

Moderate

Two blocks away from the Museum of Modern Art, the Opera House, Davies Symphony Hall, and City Hall, **Bull's,** 25 Van Ness Ave., at Market Street (☎ 415/864-4288), is a place to go if your family likes Texas-style barbecue and southwestern cuisine. Big and bright, the place is permeated with rustic Texas atmosphere, and kids can move around and make noise while parents can still feel comfortable.

Choose from such favorites as deluxe nachos (chips with pit-smoked brisket of beef, black beans, and jalapeños, baked with cheddar and Monterey Jack cheese), barbecue combo plates (choice of two of four items is $10.25), or steak fajitas. Prices range from $5 to $14. Kids will enjoy the half order of nachos and barbecue sampler appetizer ($7.25). Sassy seats and boosters are available, and the waiters will split adult portions in the kitchen for two kids, as well as warm baby bottles or baby food.

Open Monday through Thursday from 11:30am to 10pm, on Friday and Saturday from 11:30am to 11pm. Reservations accepted for six or more, but on weekends there's only about a 15-minute wait. Street parking. Some credit cards accepted.

Spuntino, 524 Van Ness Ave. near McAllister (☎ 415/861-7772), a casual Italian café, has simply delicious food, and is a good choice whenever you're in the vicinity of the Civic Center. Think about it when you go to the Museum of Modern Art, or for late-night after-opera fare.

The menu is quite varied (try the buttery scones for breakfast) including waffles, French toast, and different types of eggs (you might want to try the poached eggs on a bed of focaccia with different toppings) and coffee cakes. Everything under $10. For lunches and dinners, treat yourselves to salads, pastas, pizzettes (individual pizza), and Italian sandwiches.

Open Monday through Friday at 7am and on Saturday and Sunday at 10am; the restaurant closes on Monday at 10pm, on Tuesday, Wednesday, and Thursday at 11pm, on Friday and Saturday at midnight, and on Sunday at 9pm. Booster seats are available. All major credit cards are accepted; reservations are not.

Inexpensive

Don't pass up **Tommy's Joynt,** 1101 Geary St. (at Van Ness) (☎ **415/775-4216**), just because of appearances. This long-standing, funky tavern is an inexpensive, fast place to have lunch or dinner, and is an institution in San Francisco. As you stand in line waiting to choose between such specialties as buffalo stew (yes, real buffalo meat), chili, hand-carved barbecued beef, pastrami, turkey, or corned beef, the kids will be fascinated by the "decor." All sorts of artifacts, signs, photos, and plates hang on the wall in the large room that is part bar, part eating area. This is a fun, very casual place to go, and is especially popular with preteens, but don't expect a quiet, pristine environment. Go to have a quick, inexpensive lunch in a lively, noisy place. (One note, though: The bathroom is up a narrow, winding flight of stairs—not the best for young kids, toddlers, or infants.)

Prices range from $3.75 for sandwiches and $4.45 for chili to $5.45 for dinner plates that include ham, turkey, pastrami, and the like.

For beer-loving parents, Tommy's has over 150 different kinds of beer and the bar will prepare special kids' drinks from Shirley Temples to Roy Rogerses.

Boosters are available. Management will split adult portions for children, and will warm baby bottles and baby food. Open daily from 11am to 2am. Parking in an adjacent lot and on the street. No credit cards accepted; no reservations, and they're usually busy, but the wait is only a few minutes in this cafeteria-style place.

If you're with teenagers, a meal at the **Hard Rock Café,** 1699 Van Ness Ave. (☎ **415/885-1699**), is likely to be a must with at least one of them. The Hard Rock (like its sister restaurants worldwide) is a loud, hard-driving restaurant that serves up rock music (continuous tapes of blues, surf music, golden oldies, and rock 'n' roll) with its standard American fare. Don't expect to carry on a conversation once you're inside, but sit back and enjoy watching your teens do the "people-watch." Don't forget—you're really coming here for the atmosphere (yes, there really is a Cadillac suspended from the wall) and to satisfy the curiosity of your kids. Most teenagers have heard of the Hard Rock at least once and will love to go back home saying that they've been here. (They can even buy Hard Rock Café T-shirts.)

The menu includes such goodies as burgers ($6–$7), chicken and ribs ($8–$12), salads ($5–$7), and steak or swordfish ($15). Boosters and highchairs here. Reservations for parties of seven or more (they add 15%), except summer. For dinner and peak times on weekends you can expect to wait at least a half hour, so come prepared or come before the rush. Most major credit cards accepted. Open daily from 11:30am to 11:30pm. Valet parking.

THE RICHMOND DISTRICT/CLEMENT STREET

Clement Street, part of the Richmond District, is a panoply of shops, restaurants, and markets (see the description at the beginning of this chapter). It's a wonderful place to park the car, mosey around, and enjoy a meal or snacks. Street parking here is easier than in some other parts of the city, although not that easy. One public lot is at Clement Street and Eighth Avenue—metered parking. Head there first. You might be lucky enough to get a spot.

Moderate

Yet Wah, 2140 Clement St. (☎ 415/387-8056), is the kind of conventional Mandarin Chinese restaurant that children love. In fact, it's so popular that it has grown from a small, single operation to several locations around the area.

This location offers some room for kids to move around, and to have highchairs at the table without causing problems. The staff is very experienced with children (and large families), and make it easy for parents.

Choose from such standards as chicken in plum sauce, egg foo yung, and other specialties like Mongolian lamb, almond pressed duck, and a wide variety of fish and shellfish (prawns cooked 17 different ways). For children—and parents as well— there are many kinds of chow mein and noodles. Entrees range in price from $3.50 to over $10.

Shirley Temples are served with little umbrellas, a treat for all the kids, and the friendly service is terrific. Highchairs and boosters are available.

Open daily from 10am to 10pm. Most major credit cards accepted. Reservations taken on weekends for parties of more than five, otherwise not needed. Another location in San Francisco: Pier 39 (☎ 415/434-4430).

Inexpensive

Where do the locals go when they want pizza? **Giorgio's Pizzeria,** 151 Clement St., at Third Avenue (☎ 415/668-1266). In fact, some locals claim that you'll see *only* families here—possibly because the staff is very experienced with kids and the pizza is terrific. Giorgio's features 18 scrumptious pizza varieties (extra-large size, $13.50–$17.90), calzone, and pastas (average price, $7). If your kids don't eat pizza (is there a child who doesn't?), the staff will split adult pasta portions and of course bring extra plates. Half-orders are available for children under 12. They'll also warm baby bottles and baby food.

Highchairs and boosters are available. No reservations accepted, and on typically busy weekend hours between 6 and 8pm you should expect to wait about 20 minutes. Open Monday through Thursday from 11:30am to 11:30pm, on Friday and Saturday till 12:30am, and on Sunday till 11pm. Some credit cards accepted.

When you're finished with your meal and you want a treat, go to the **Toy Boat Dessert Café,** Clement Street and Fifth Avenue (☎ 415/751-7505), a really fun place for desserts. Toys for sale decorate the entire place. There are robots, pandas, dinosaurs, toys and dolls—Barbies, "Sesame Street" characters. This place has great floats (colas and root beer as well as others), smoothies and sundaes, natural ice creams, frozen yogurts, cakes, and espressos. And in the morning, you can grab a scone or muffin and great bagels! There's a mechanical horse for kids to ride.

Open weekdays from 7am to 11:30pm; Friday and Saturday to midnight; Saturday and Sunday open at 8:30am. No credit cards.

Why would you go all the way to 24th Avenue and Clement Street for a restaurant? **Bill's Place,** 2315 Clement St. (☎ 415/221-5262), has fabulous hamburgers (a third of a pound of freshly ground choice chuck) and thick milkshakes—so good that many San Franciscans believe that this is the best hamburger place in town. (They like to remind you that they're geared for families and that they've been owned by the same family for more than 35 years.)

Unpretentious, with an open grill at which two cooks race to make sure those burgers keep pace with the customers, this place is a treat—and is very popular, so expect a brief wait if you come during peak hours. While you're waiting—or while you're eating—be sure not to miss the collection of presidential china that lines the wall.

The service is fast and very casual and friendly. Kids are everywhere. For hardy souls who like to eat outdoors even in the Richmond District (which is cooler and foggier than other parts of the city), there is a lovely garden patio. Bring sweaters.

Burgers range from $3.95 for a plain hamburger to $5.85 for Celebrity burgers (with fries), to $4.65 for a Herb Caen burger (with Jack cheese), to $5.15 for a Red Skelton burger (made to look like a clown face). There are lots of great sandwiches (grilled cheese for $3.25) and hot dogs (starting at $2.55), and a child's burger (called a Pearl Burger) that's half the adult size and is served with fries for $2.95. Highchairs and boosters are available.

Open daily from 11am to 10pm (to 11pm on Friday and Saturday); closed Christmas and Thanksgiving. Reservations accepted but no credit cards.

You might be surprised that kids would like authentic Vietnamese food, but at **Mai's Vietnamese Restaurant,** 316 Clement St., between Fourth and Fifth Avenues (☎ 415/221-3046), you'll see large families digging into soft-shell crab, Imperial rolls (similar to eggrolls), and coconut chicken. This little storefront isn't much to look at, but it has wonderful food. The kids love the Vietnamese rolls, which are like Imperial rolls but aren't fried. Hanoi soup is a tempting mixture of sliced beef and noodles in a broth flavored with cilantro and lemon. Ask your server to suggest the least spicy dishes.

Prices range from $3.95 (for Imperial rolls or Hanoi soup for two) to $5.95 (for coconut chicken and lemon-grass–barbecued beef).

Mai's has highchairs and boosters. No children's menu is necessary because everyone shares entrees. They'll warm baby bottles or baby food, and will make special drinks for kids. Reservations are accepted—and advisable during the crowded weekend times from 1 to 3pm and 7 to 10pm. Open daily from 11 to 10pm (on Friday and Saturday until 11pm). Most major credit cards honored.

There's another branch at 1838 Union St., Cow Hollow (☎ 415/921-2861).

FISHERMAN'S WHARF AND PIER 39

The Wharf area has an assortment of restaurants to choose from, as well as a number of small cafés and open-air stands that serve walk-away seafood cocktails. We've selected a few of the full-service restaurants we like.

Expensive

Located in the heart of the original Fisherman's Wharf, overlooking the fishing fleet, **Tarantino's,** 206 Jefferson St. (☎ 415/775-5600), has been a Wharf landmark for almost 45 years. Manager Gary Burns, who has kids of his own, says, "Fisherman's Wharf is a family destination. We want to take care of kids." White linen cloths on tables and candles at night provide ambience. While Mom and Dad are enjoying the splendid view, servers take care of the children with little oyster crackers and sourdough French bread. As further proof, the restaurant provides child-size portions as well as an interesting children's menu. (From your table, you'll be able to see the harbor lights at night, the Golden Gate Bridge, and in the distance, Sausalito.)

For lunch or dinner, the darlings can choose from fish and chips, seafood plate, fettuccine, and ravioli, as well as a hamburger for $3.75 to $7. The bar will serve up Shirley Temples, virgin strawberry daiquiris, and whatever else you can think of.

The adult daytime menu (available from 11am to 3pm) consists of pasta (such as seafood fettuccine Tarantino—scallops, shrimp, and baby clams in a sauce of garlic, herbs, cream, and parmesan cheese), seafood (including calamari, baby salmon, and oysters), soups, salads, and sandwiches. Lunch is priced at $6–$11.

For dinner, you might try a swordfish steak ($16.95) or New York steak with potato and vegetables ($16.95). There are salads, sandwiches, sautés, and specials as well, ranging from $9 to $20.

Highchairs and boosters are available. Open from 11am to 11pm daily. Reservations are accepted, and suggested during the busy dinner hours of 7 to 9:30pm. Two-hour free validated parking is available at the lot on Jefferson and Taylor Streets. Major credit cards accepted.

If you've ever been to San Francisco before, you're probably already familiar with **Lolli's Castagnola,** 286 Jefferson St. (☎ **415/776-5015** or **415/775-2446**), a landmark on Fisherman's Wharf since 1916. Located on the water at Pier 45 overlooking the fishing fleet, this restaurant serves breakfast, lunch, and dinner in a simple setting with a view of the Wharf. Kids get balloons. "Our waiters take such good care of children here that they'll do just about anything," says owner Andrew Lolli. During most of the fall, winter, and spring, kids can watch the sea lions that have come to feed in the bay; often there will be ten or more. Sometimes you can watch fishermen docking their boats and unloading their catch. Simple decor, white tablecloths, and floor-to-ceiling windows—you'll feel like you're sitting on the water. Things are generally fast-paced here, with tables turning over as many as three times during dinner. You set your own pace, though—your waiter will accommodate.

Standard breakfasts range from $4 to $9.75. A few pasta, meat, and poultry entrees are also offered. Luncheon specials are available from 11am to 6pm, but items from the entree menu may be chosen for lunch or dinner. Dinners range from $7 to $27 (lobster). The enormous seafood menu is great and the variety of shellfish and calamari specials is delightful.

Kids can choose from the old standbys on the children's menu—grilled cheese and tuna sandwiches—or order spaghetti or filet of sole. Many of these selections are served with fries and most range from $3 to $6.

Moderate

Lolli's Castagnola Upper Deck (located upstairs in Lolli's Castagnola restaurant) is a moderately priced self-service light-lunch alternative with soups, seafood salads, sandwiches, fish and chips, and beverage service. The huge room with big windows is bright and overlooks the water. The patio overlooks the Wharf, a good place for Mom and Dad to have a bite while the kids watch the fishing boats unload (any time between 11am and 4pm, depending on conditions). The Upper Deck is open from 11am to 5pm daily.

At Lolli's Castagnola, highchairs and boosters are available. Reservations are advised, especially in the summer when you can wait up to an hour if you don't reserve ahead. (If you arrive without a reservation, walk in, give your name, and wander the Wharf while you wait.) Open daily for breakfast, lunch, and dinner from 9am to 11pm. Validated parking is available all day at a lot located at the corner of Jefferson and Taylor Streets; valet parking is offered from 10am to 4pm only. All major credit cards accepted.

A. Sabella's Restaurant, 2766 Taylor St., third floor (☎ **415/771-6776**), has good food, excellent service, and a wonderful view. Large arched windows face across

Jefferson Street (the main walkway of the wharf) onto the bay so you and the kids can watch as tankers and ferries come and go, and tourists bustle on the street below. Don't let the white linen tablecloths worry you. The restaurant is very spacious and open, so your children (if they're fairly well behaved) are unlikely to disturb other diners. (You should be advised that the restaurant takes on a decidedly more sophisticated ambience when it's dark outside and the tables are graced with candlelight.)

The waiters are attentive. Ours was so friendly that he insisted on helping Andrew with his lobster—a good thing since this was his first time, and we needed help negotiating with the nutcracker and pick to get the best meat out of the claws.

Luncheon is a variety: from taco salad ($9.75) to red snapper ($10.25). The dinner menu is tempting, with seafood, pasta, and chops. Try the crab cioppino ($23) or the linguine with crab ($18.25). As you might guess, crab is a specialty, and you can have it in a variety of ways—from cold cracked to sautéed with black-bean sauce.

Children will love the extensive "small fry" menu. Choose from fried prawns ($7.75), salmon ($7.25), and other fish (between $5.50 and $7), or hamburger ($3.50) or spaghetti ($3.25). All entrees come with potatoes, vegetable, and a beverage.

The restaurant has plenty of highchairs and boosters, and the management loves children. Open daily from 11am to 11pm. Reservations are advised, and most major credit cards are accepted. There's two-hour validated indoor parking around corner at 350 Beach St.

One of our favorite places, and a really fun restaurant for the kids, is **Alcatraz Bar and Grill,** Pier 39 (at the end of the pier) (☎ 415/434-1818). Straightforward American cuisine like barbecued ribs and chicken, burgers, and sandwiches (turkey, chicken, sausage, and barbecued beef) are a sure bet with any child. And the kid's plate is terrific for those who want grilled cheese, a hot dog, or a little burger.

What makes this place fun? For starters, the back room offers wonderful views of the Golden Gate Bridge, Marin County, and the bay; and on a clear day, you can almost touch Alcatraz Island. Everything in the place recalls the U.S. Penitentiary in the middle of the bay. Placemats are black-and-white photographs detailing the prison or pictures of infamous inmates such as Al Capone and the Birdman of Alcatraz, even the daily prison routine. There's a "rogues' gallery" and an intricate model of Alcatraz. After spending many minutes marveling at the model, Elizabeth and Andrew joined other fascinated children in the authentically styled and sized prison cell. Watch those little fingers as they close the cell door! Our kids had more fun inside that tiny space than we could ever have imagined.

Boosters and highchairs are available. Reservations are accepted, as are most major credit cards. Open Sunday through Thursday from 11:30am to 9:30pm, on Friday and Saturday until 10pm.

In addition to these, you'll find seaside dining at **Alioto's**—Number 8 Fisherman's Wharf (☎ 415/673-0183), for seafood; **Pompeii's Grotto,** 340 Jefferson St. (☎ 415/776-9265), for seafood; and **Scoma's,** Pier 47 (☎ 415/771-4383), for Italian-style seafood. At Pier 39, you'll find **Swiss Louis** (☎ 415/421-2913), with Italian food; the **Eagle Café** (☎ 415/433-3689), with American food; and **Neptune's Palace** (☎ 415/434-2260), with seafood. Also located here is a branch of **Yet Wah's** (☎ 415/434-4430), with more than 200 items on the menu.

THE CANNERY

For a great view and a good children's menu, **Charley Brown's,** 2801 Leavenworth St. (☎ 415/776-3838), is a tempting choice. Window tables look out at the Golden

Gate Bridge, and we were lucky enough to be there when a ship passed by to dock for the night (6pm). Andrew spent the entire time watching the passing scene out the window—endlessly fascinated—first looking in the distance, then looking down on the streets that lead to the Wharf.

The adult food here is good (it's known for prime rib), but the place really rates high for the children's plates, which include extremely generous portions of hamburger with thick-cut fries, sliced tomatoes, soup or salad, beverage, and dessert ($3–$5). Kids can also choose from prime rib, white-meat chicken, and "Popeye-style" green noodles in a cream sauce. Adults can choose from several fish entrees (all fresh), prime-rib cuts, steaks, pastas, and shellfish. Entrees include soup or salad, freshly baked sourdough bread, vegetable, and rice pilaf or potato ($10–$24 for lobster and prime rib).

Boosters and highchairs are available. Two-hour validated parking can be obtained at the Anchorage parking lot, located at Jefferson and Leavenworth Streets. Open for lunch every day from 11:30am to 3pm; and for dinner Sunday through Thursday from 3:30 to 10pm, on Friday and Saturday till 11pm. This is one of the few places that serves lunch on Sunday—no brunch. Reservations are accepted. Most major credit cards are honored.

GHIRARDELLI SQUARE

We love Ghirardelli Square because there are so many dining places to choose from. **Compadres Mexican Bar and Grill,** located on the second floor of the Mustard Building, 900 North Point St. (☎ 415/885-2266), is a lively cantina with good food, a beautiful view, and very friendly, accommodating service. We thoroughly enjoyed our food. The children's menu offers a choice of taco, burrito, enchilada, nachos, quesedilla, or a burger or corn dog with fries ($2.95–$3.95). Andrew had one of the large chicken tacos ($5.50, with beans, rice, and salad). Watch out for the fresh corn tortilla shell—it tends to crumble (we wrapped it with a napkin). Elizabeth downed a quesedilla. We all enjoyed the delicious guacamole with chips and our Mexican dinners (ranging in price from $7.95 for a beef enchilada to $15.95 for New York steak). Sandwiches, burgers, and ribs are offered as well. Try a fresh-fruit smoothie for a treat.

It was one of those nights—baby cranky and needing to be entertained—and this place was terrific. The boisterous cantina atmosphere inside (we dined on the enclosed patio) was perfect—the adults didn't have to worry about the noise the children created. Watching passersby was a treat, and when all the kids got restless (although service was fast), we simply picked them up and went for a walk on the terrace.

Boosters and highchairs are available. Open Sunday through Thursday from 11am to 10pm, and on Friday and Saturday from 11am to 11pm. Reservations are accepted. Most major credit cards honored. Validated parking in the Ghirardelli lot (beneath Ghirardelli Square).

In addition, at Ghirardelli Square you'll find these fine restaurants: **The Mandarin** (☎ 415/673-8812), for Chinese cuisine, and **Paprika's Fono** (☎ 415/441-1223), for Hungarian cuisine. You might want to get a babysitter so you can enjoy a night out on the town.

And for families, there's also **Boudin Bakery** (☎ 415/928-7404), for great San Francisco sourdough bread and sandwiches; **Ghirardelli's Too!** (☎ 415/474-1414), for gelato and espresso.

UNION STREET (COW HOLLOW)

This is a great area to wander through, with lots of boutiques and little courtyards. You'll find many different places to eat here as well.

Moderate

If you're looking for a great breakfast or lunch, consider **Doidge's Kitchen,** 2217 Union St. (☎ **415/921-2149**). This little gem of about 13 tables and a counter area facing an open kitchen is so popular that they turn away as many people as they serve.

This really isn't a place for babies, they don't have highchairs and it's a little cramped, but boosters are available and it's a good place for slightly older children. The food is excellent, and the service is fast.

The waiters are chatty and love to talk with you about what you're doing and tourist attractions you might find interesting. It's a good place to have breakfast if you're staying on Lombard Street or if you're at the Wharf and planning a day of sightseeing elsewhere. You might try it as a starting place for a walk down Union Street (in the Cow Hollow area).

Adults will love the elaborate breakfast menu, with prices ranging from a low of $4.25 for French toast to $8.25 for an omelet stuffed with avocado, ham, or bacon, cheese, and tomato. As if the omelets themselves weren't filling enough, you get toast and a choice of potatoes, salad, tomatoes, cottage cheese, even fruit or steamed veggies (extra charge) to accompany your meal. Lunches include homemade soups, salads, and a wide choice of sandwiches (averaging $6). Kids generally request side orders.

Boosters are available. Reservations are a must on weekends and are accepted at all times. (Even if you're lucky enough to get seated without a reservation, you'd wait 45 minutes.) Open Monday through Friday from 8am to 1:45pm, and on Saturday and Sunday from 8am to 2:45pm. Some credit cards accepted.

Many of you are already familiar with the northern Italian food created at **Prego,** 2000 Union St., at Buchanan Street (☎ **415/563-3305**), through sister restaurants in Los Angeles, and the San Francisco version is another good one. A huge bar greets you in this spare, contemporary-style restaurant with wooden floors, white tablecloths, and linen napkins.

We love the calzone and always have that hot crusty, stuffed little pie when we come here. Pizza in general is good at Prego, and ranges from the tame (tomato and cheese) to the exotic (truffle oil and fontina cheese), with prices from $8.25 to $11.95. Other items include chicken pasta, and fresh fish daily.

Highchairs and boosters are available. There's no children's menu, but the servers will split adult portions. They'll be glad to warm bottles and baby food, and will cheerfully bring breadsticks for the ravenous little ones. You can request paper and pencil. They serve from 11:30am to midnight daily, except Thanksgiving and Christmas. Reservations are accepted for lunch and dinner. Most major credit cards accepted.

Inexpensive

We like bakeries, and **La Nouvelle Pâtisserie,** 2184 Union St. (☎ **415/931-7655**), is a good one. It has 15 tables and a variety of coffee selections, and hot cocoa for the kids: There are mouth-watering displays of tarts, pastries, muffins, croissants, and chocolates. It's a good place to stop for energy renewal while wandering in the Union Street area. Plan to stop in for a quick treat. No boosters or highchairs here, however. Open Monday through Thursday from 6:30am to 8pm, on Friday and Saturday to 11pm, and on Sunday from 8am to 7pm.

Another branch is at Market and 5th streets in San Francisco Center (☎ **415/979-0553**).

MARINA DISTRICT

One of the distinct neighborhoods in San Francisco, the often sun-drenched Marina fronts Marina Green. A lovely area for a stroll, it also offers a few great restaurants.

Expensive

Scott's Seafood Grill and Bar, 2400 Lombard St. (☎ **415/563-8988**), may not be the best place for young kids, but it's a winner with older children or those with sophisticated enough palates that they can choose from the almost strictly seafood menu.

There are no highchairs, nor is there a children's menu, and the place doesn't cater to young ones, but the line out the door will tell you that there's great fresh seafood here.

Scott's Caesar salad is good for starters, and our resident expert on fresh oysters on the half shell swears to their appeal. For parents (and other adults), the cioppino with fresh local crab is excellent, as is the fettuccine with shucked Willapa Bay oysters in a spicy Cajun beer-butter sauce. For less adventurous appetites, the Hawaiian albacore tuna or local snapper or petrale sole doré might be best. When we go, someone always orders (and shares) the seafood sauté. New York strip steak and filet mignon are available, as are hamburgers and cheeseburgers. Prices are $6.50–$19.

Open Sunday through Thursday from 11:30am to 10:30pm, on Friday and Saturday to 11pm. Most major credit cards are honored. The most difficult thing about Scott's with a child is the wait for a table during the prime dinner hours. Early reservations are accepted, and we suggest that you go before 6:30pm to avoid the crowds.

There's a second branch at Three Embarcadero Center (☎ **415/981-0622**).

Greens at Fort Mason, Building A, Fort Mason (☎ **415/771-6222**), may be one of the busiest restaurants in town. The food is so good and the place so well known that it operates at capacity almost every night. Owned by the San Francisco Zen Center, Greens may change your opinion about vegetarian dining. The San Francisco Zen Center also owns the famous Tassajara Zen Center in Carmel, which is known for its food and Tassajara cookbooks.

Not only is the food good, much of which is organically grown at Greens Gulch, but the view is spectacular. The restaurant is housed in an old World War II army barracks. There is a full wall of windows that overlooks the marina filled with sailboats and the Golden Gate Bridge. The restaurant is open and airy, and the wooden tables, many of them redwood burl, and high ceilings make you feel as if you're part of the outdoors. It's breathtaking on a clear day.

The gourmet vegetarian cuisine is quite varied. You can get pizza with sautéed spinach and feta cheese or with eggplant and provolone, or fettuccine and vegetables. There are brochettes (tofu takes the place of meat) with marinated vegetables and a wide array of delicious salads. One favorite is the Gujrati dahl (mushrooms, carrots, zucchini, and other vegetables stewed with tomatoes, ginger, chilies, and curry served on rice). Prices range from $7.50 to $12.75.

On Friday and Saturday nights there is a fixed-price dinner for $36 per person. This luscious combination of vegetarian delights will probably not appeal to your kids, no matter what their age. But if you can, attempt it without them. There's also a fabulous Sunday brunch which appeals to everyone.

Highchairs and boosters are available. There is no children's menu, but they'll gladly split portions. They're quite accommodating folk.

Open Tuesday through Thursday from 11:30am to 2pm and 5:30pm to 9:30pm; Friday and Saturday from 11:30am to 2pm and from 6pm to 9:30pm. Sunday brunch is served from 10am to 2pm. Reservations are highly recommended; make them up to two weeks ahead for Saturday and Sunday. There is a parking lot. They accept major credit cards.

Inexpensive

One of our favorite restaurants in Monterey has opened in San Francisco. **First Watch,** 2150 Lombard St. (part of Cow Hollow Motor Inn) (☎ 415/775-9673), is clean, no frills. The American-style food is very good—and there's lots of it.

For breakfast there are all kinds of egg specialties—omelets, frittatas, eggs Benedict (also egg substitutes). Then there's French toast, gourmet pancakes (such as raisin-walnut and wheatberry), and an array of fruit, cereal, and the like. For lunch, they have the expected salads and sandwiches, but even these are a little different. There's the "Chicken Little" sandwich—chicken salad with water chestnuts, raisins, and celery on an English muffin, or the "BLTE"—bacon, lettuce, tomato, *and* fried egg with melted cheese. And, how about a Caesar salad with grilled chicken? Not what you'd expect. And, they make everything to go, so you can pack yourselves a whopping good picnic. Prices range from $3 to $7.

There are boosters and highchairs, and all kinds of smaller portions for children. The restaurant serves breakfast and lunch. Open daily from 7am to 2:30pm. Some major credit cards. Reservations are taken for parties of 5 or more.

If you remember the movie *American Graffiti,* you'll feel right at home in **Mel's Drive-in,** 2165 Lombard St., at Fillmore Street (☎ 415/921-3039). Even if you don't remember the movie, you'll love this place. This is an original—not a trendy re-creation of a 1950s drive-in. Waiters and waitresses wear white shirts and black bow ties and soda-jerk-style hats. There are giant black-and-white blowups of the early days on the walls and loud music, although not too loud, coming from the jukeboxes. Dine to Dion's "The Wanderer" and Neil Sedaka's "Calendar Girl."

You'll know you're there by the black-and-white checkerboard-tile building with neon lights. Groups of kids with one or two adults wander in and wait for tables. There are boosters, but no highchairs and very small booths, but don't let that stop you from bringing your toddlers and little babies. During the day you'll see all manner of kids crawling on their parents while the folks dig into their delicious one-third-pound burgers, chili, salads, or specials such as chicken pot pie, meatloaf, spaghetti and meatballs, chicken, fish and chips, New York steak, fried egg sandwich, or tuna melt. Prices range from $4.50 to about $11.95 for New York steak. The hot dogs are terrific, and our 8-year-old wanted seconds of Colton's Lunch (a kid's hot dog for $2.75). There is a kid's menu, and children's meals are served in a '50s-style car!

Then there are the fountain items—milkshakes, malts, sundaes, and flavored Cokes—which everyone loves. Desserts and other beverages are also available.

Mel's is also open for breakfast, and offers the usual and unusual omelets, pancakes, French toast, and eggs. Prices range from $3.60 for buttermilk pancakes to $6.50 for an elaborate omelet.

Open Sunday through Thursday from 6am to 1am, on Friday and Saturday till 3am. You can also call ahead for orders to go. No credit cards or reservations accepted. At peak hours you might wait 15 minutes. A parking lot is adjacent; if it's full, try to find street parking.

There's another branch at 3355 Geary St., next to the Coronet Theater (☎ **415/387-2244**).

You'll be surprised by **Original Joe's No. 2,** 2001 Chestnut St., at Fillmore Street (☎ **415/346-3233**). Totally renovated, this Italian restaurant has been serving lunch and dinner to the locals since 1938.

The waitresses bring fresh French bread and butter to the table as soon as you sit down. There is a huge variety of food, from Italian meatloaf to corned beef and cabbage to pastas and veal entrees. The lunch menu is so extensive that it runs the gamut from special omelets to sandwiches and burgers (priced at $3.25–$11.95, most in the $6–9 range). The dinner menu includes pasta and other specialties such as veal, and prime rib, roast lamb, and New York steak ($7–$16).

Many portions are so large that children can share the adult's meal. Boosters are available and highchairs.

Open daily from 11:30am to 1am. Children's menu includes pizza, hamburger or spaghetti, $4.25. Reservations are accepted. Major credit cards. There's street parking and a city parking lot on Lombard Street between Fillmore and Webster Streets. A valet is available evenings.

OCEAN BEACH

Sitting off by itself, perched on the cliff overlooking Seal Rock, is the Cliff House restaurant, the only San Francisco restaurant overlooking the ocean. This tourist attraction is also popular among the locals, since the view is amazing on clear days. These are really two restaurants in one location, the **Cliff House Seafood and Beverage Company** (☎ **415/386-3330**) and **Upstairs at the Cliff House** (☎ **415/387-5847**)—both at 1090 Point Lobos Ave.

This is one attraction that many first-time visitors to San Francisco want to see. There's also a giftshop, a hot-dog stand, and an arcade, called the Musée Mechanique, which has amusements from the turn of the century as well as modern video games. Kids and adults love the place. (For more about the Cliff House, see the "What to See and Do" section, below.)

The Seafood and Beverage Company (located at street level) is a large area, dimly lit with nice atmosphere, where you can sit with your food and drinks and watch the waves and seals. Although the menu is very limited, it's fast-food style and consequently service is very quick.

Lunch and dinner features seafood, chicken, pasta and salads, as well as hamburgers, chicken sandwiches, and a crab sandwich with melted cheese. Prices are $8.95–$17.75.

Open Sunday through Thursday from 11am to 10:30pm, on Friday to 11pm, and on Saturday from 10am to 11pm; Sunday brunch from 9am to 2pm ($7.95–$14.75). They have boosters and highchairs and accept most major credit cards.

Upstairs at the Cliff House is a lovely restaurant with huge picture windows so guests can enjoy the view. You'll see dozens of families here at any given time—little ones watching for seals, older ones looking at the waves breaking on the rocks. Expect leisurely dining and a long wait for tables on weekends (approximately 30 minutes).

The breakfast and lunch menu offers omelets, french toast, waffles, hot and cold sandwiches, chowder, and salads. Prices range from $6.75 to $12. Dinner entrees (which are accompanied by potatoes and fresh vegetable) include chicken, veal, steaks, fresh pastas, and seafood, and cost $11.75–$20. Highchairs and boosters are available. There is no children's menu.

Open for breakfast and lunch daily from 7:30am to 3:30pm (on Sunday from 8am). Dinner is served Sunday through Thursday from 5 to 10:30pm and on Friday and Saturday to 11pm. Most major credit cards are honored. Street parking available.

RESTAURANTS BY CUISINE

You may find that you want to use the restaurant guide by cuisine instead of by location. The following list is alphabetical by type of food. Where applicable, we include locations other than the main one we previewed.

American

Alcatraz Bar and Grill, Pier 39 (p. 67).

Bill's Place, 2315 Clement St., Richmond District (p. 64); another branch near the San Francisco Zoo.

Bull's, 25 Van Ness Ave., Van Ness (p. 62).

Charley Brown's, 2801 Leavenworth St., The Cannery (p. 67).

Doidge's Kitchen, 2217 Union St., Cow Hollow (p. 69).

The Dutch Kitchen, located in the Westin St. Francis Hotel, 335 Powell St., Union Square (p. 52).

First Watch, 2150 Lombard St., Marina District (p. 71).

Hard Rock Café, 1699 Van Ness Ave., Van Ness (p. 63).

Lefty O'Doul's, 333 Geary St., Union Square (p. 54).

Lori's Diner, 336 Mason St., near Geary Street, Union Square (p. 52).

MacArthur Park, 607 Front St., Embarcadero (p. 54).

Mama's of San Francisco, 398 Geary St., near Mason Street, Union Square (p. 52); another branch at Washington Square.

Mel's Drive-in, 2165 Lombard St., Marina District (p. 71); another branch at 3355 Geary St.

Mooses, 1652 Stockton St., North Beach (p. 58).

New Pisa Restaurant, 550 Green St., North Beach (p. 57).

Original Joe's No. 2, 2001 Chestnut St., Marina District (p. 72).

Ruth's Chris Steak House, 1700 California St., Van Ness (p. 61).

Salamagundi, 442 Geary St., near Mason Street, Union Square (p. 53); other branches at Two Embarcadero Center and the Civic Center, 39 Grove St.

Sears Fine Food, 439 Powell St., Union Square (p. 53).

Stars, 150 Redwood Alley, Civic Center (p. 62).

Tommy's Joynt, 1101 Geary St., at Van Ness (p. 63).

Chinese

Canton Tea House and Restaurant, 1108 Stockton St., Chinatown (p. 59).

The Golden Phoenix, 728 Washington St., Chinatown (p. 60).

The Pot Sticker, 150 Waverly Place, at Washington Street, Chinatown (p. 59).

Yet Wah, 2140 Clement St., Richmond District (p. 64) and Pier 39.

Continental

The French Room, at the Four Seasons Clift Hotel, 495 Geary St., Union Square (p. 51).

Spuntino, 524 Van Ness Ave., Van Ness (p. 62).

Italian

Capp's Corner, 1600 Powell St., North Beach (p. 56).

Giorgio's Pizzeria, 151 Clement St., at Third Avenue (p. 64).

The Gold Spike, 527 Columbus Ave., North Beach (p. 57).

The Iron Horse Restaurant, 19 Maiden Lane, Union Square (p. 51).

Little Joe's on Broadway, 523 Broadway, North Beach (p. 58).

Mama's of San Francisco, 398 Geary St., near Mason Street, Union Square (p.52).

New Pisa Restaurant, 550 Green St., North Beach (p. 57).

North Beach Pizza, 1499 Grant Ave., North Beach (p. 56). Other locations at: 1310 Grant Ave; 4787 Mission St.; and 800 Stanyan St.

North Beach Restaurant, 1512 Stockton St., North Beach (p. 55).

Prego, 2000 Union St., Cow Hollow (p. 69).

Spuntino, 524 Van Ness Ave., Van Ness (p. 62).

Washington Square Bar & Grill, 1707 Powell St., North Beach (p. 57).

Japanese

Iroha, 1728 Buchanan St., across from Japan Center (p. 60).

Mifune, 1737 Post St., Japantown (p. 61).

Sanppo, 1702 Post St., Japantown (p. 61).

Mexican

Chevy's, Two Embarcadero, podium level (p. 54).

Compadres Mexican Bar and Grill, 900 North Point St. on the second floor, Ghirardelli Square (p. 68).

Seafood

A. Sabella's, 2766 Taylor St. on the third floor (p. 66).

Cliff House Seafood and Beverage Company (p. 72), and **Upstairs at the Cliff House,** both at 1090 Point Lobos Ave.

Lolli's Castagnola, 286 Jefferson St., Fisherman's Wharf (p. 66).

Scott's Seafood Grill and Bar, 2400 Lombard St., Marina District (p. 70); another branch at Three Embarcadero Center.

Tarantino's, 206 Jefferson St., Fisherman's Wharf (p. 65).

Other Types of Cuisine

Greens at Fort Mason, Building A, Fort Mason (p. 70). Gourmet vegetarian food.

Mai's Vietnamese Restaurant, 316 Clement St., Richmond District (p. 65); another branch at 1838 Union St.

Square One, 190 Pacific Mall, at Front Street (p. 55). Mediterranean food.

---

6   What to See and Do

Many people think of San Francisco as an adult paradise—which it is—but children love it too. This exciting city offers more than simple sightseeing. Its international flavor and its historical buildings permeate your daily adventures, making even the mundane a lively—often educational—experience.

Just getting from one place to another can be exhilarating. In fact that's what we start with—a one-of-a-kind form of transportation.

CABLE CARS

San Francisco is synonymous with cable cars. Proclaimed a national historic landmark, these are the only vehicles of their kind in the world. These delightful, clattering, almost-musical open-air cars run up and down the steep San Francisco terrain at speeds of up to $9^1/_2$ miles per hour, creating roller-coaster fun out of going from one point to another. Kids love these motorless cars that have been gracing San Francisco streets since 1873. The bracing wind in your face, the close fit when cable cars pass going in opposite directions, the conductors so reminiscent of old America—it's all part of the thrill! At one time there were over 600 cars traveling 100 miles of track; today fewer than 40 cars ride the remaining 12 miles of track, offering passengers grand vistas of the city and the bay.

The **Powell-Hyde Line** offers what some people think is the most thrilling and scenic ride. It runs from Powell and Market Streets through Union Square to Victorian Park near Ghirardelli Square. During the course of its ride to the Wharf, it passes Lombard Street (the crookedest street in the world), where you can see the towers of downtown beyond. This car goes down the steepest grade of all, presenting spectacular views of Alcatraz, Angel Island, and Marin County. The **Powell-Mason Line** also starts at Powell and Market Streets, but it goes to the other end of the Wharf, near

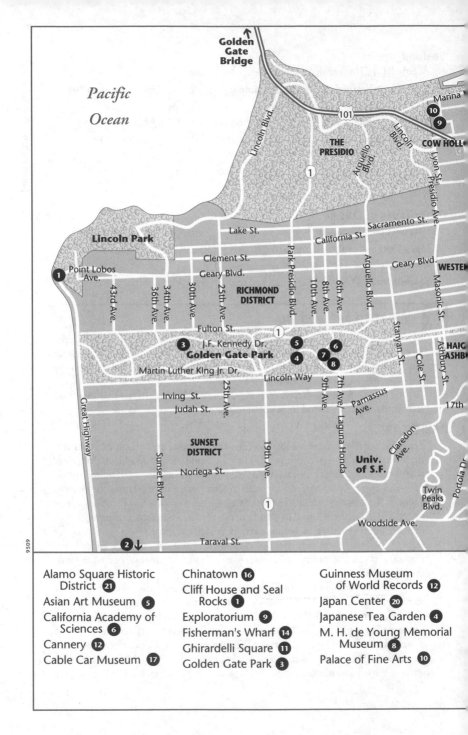

Pacific
Ocean

Golden
Gate
Bridge

Marina

101

THE
PRESIDIO

COW HOLL

1

Lincoln Blvd.

Arguello Blvd.

Lincoln Blvd.

Lyon St.

Presidio Ave.

Sacramento St.

Lake St.

California St.

Geary Blvd.

WESTE

Lincoln Park

Clement St.

Geary Blvd.

Masonic St.

Point Lobos
Ave.

RICHMOND
DISTRICT

Park Presidio Blvd.

10th Ave.

8th Ave.

6th Ave.

Arguello Blvd.

Stanyan St.

ASHB

43rd Ave.

36th Ave.

34th Ave.

30th Ave.

25th Ave.

Fulton St.

1

HAIG
ASHB

3 J.F. Kennedy Dr.

Golden Gate Park

5

6

7

8

Cole St.

17th

Martin Luther King Jr. Dr.

Lincoln Way

4

7th Ave./Laguna Honda

9th Ave.

Parnassus
Ave.

Irving St.

Judah St.

25th Ave.

SUNSET
DISTRICT

19th Ave.

Univ.
of S.F.

Claredon
Ave.

Portola Dr.

Noriega St.

Twin
Peaks
Blvd.

1

Woodside Ave.

Great Highway

Sunset Blvd.

2 ↓

Taraval St.

9509

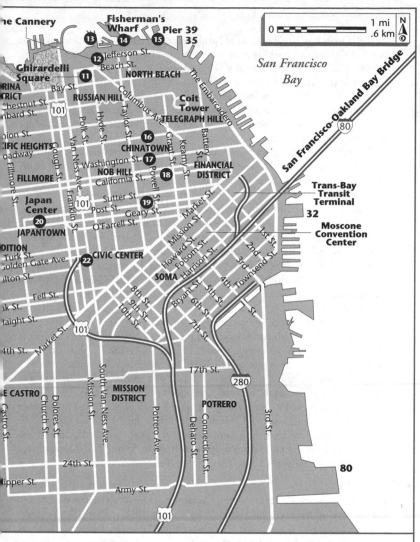

The Cannery

Fisherman's
Wharf
Pier 39
35
15
13
14
12 Jefferson St.
Ghirardelli
Square
11
Beach St.
NORTH BEACH
MARINA
DISTRICT
Chestnut St.
Lombard St.
Bay St.
RUSSIAN HILL
101
Columbus Ave.
Coit
Tower
TELEGRAPH HILL
The Embarcadero
San Francisco
Bay
San Francisco-Oakland Bay Bridge
80
Union St.
PACIFIC HEIGHTS
Broadway
Fillmore St.
FILLMORE
Polk St.
Hyde St.
Taylor St.
16
CHINATOWN
17
NOB HILL
Washington St.
California St.
18
Grant St.
Kearny St.
Battery St.
FINANCIAL
DISTRICT
Trans-Bay
Transit
Terminal
32
Moscone
Convention
Center
Japan
Center
20
JAPANTOWN
Van Ness Ave.
Franklin St.
Gough St.
101
Sutter St.
Post St.
Geary St.
O'Farrell St.
19
Powell St.
Mason St.
Market St.
Mission St.
1st St.
2nd St.
3rd St.
4th St.
Townsend St.
WESTERN
ADDITION
Turk St.
Golden Gate Ave.
Fulton St.
22
CIVIC CENTER
SOMA
Howard St.
Folsom St.
Harrison St.
Fell St.
Oak St.
Haight St.
8th St.
9th St.
10th St.
Bryant St.
5th St.
6th St.
7th St.
Brannan St.
101
4th St.
Market St.
THE CASTRO
Castro St.
Church St.
Dolores St.
Mission St.
South Van Ness Ave.
MISSION
DISTRICT
17th St.
280
Potrero Ave.
Deharo St.
Connecticut St.
POTRERO
3rd St.
80
24th St.
Clipper St.
Army St.
101
0   1 mi
.6 km
N

Pier 39. On its run, you'll see part of North Beach, Coit Tower, and glimpses of the bay. The **California Street Line** starts at Market and Drumm Streets, near the Hyatt Regency San Francisco and ends at Van Ness Avenue. You ride through the towering canyons of the financial district and then through Chinatown and Nob Hill, where you'll see the Mark Hopkins and Fairmont Hotels and beautiful Grace Cathedral.

Once we were "lucky" enough to have the cables go out on us. Imagine what it's like to back down one of those steep hills. What a thrill! Great America and Magic Mountain could do no better.

Here are some tips on riding cable cars with kids. Cable cars can be crowded, so travel as light as you can. We looked pretty funny catching a ride with a huge diaper bag, a collapsible stroller, a large purse, and two children in tow. With that much of an entourage it's difficult to get off and on except at the turnarounds. People are polite, but it's more difficult to find adequate seating or standing space if you're carrying armloads of stuff. Also, remember that you'll be buying souvenirs, which will take up room. Remember to hang onto the kids around those curves, and be sure they don't lean out while standing on the running boards.

Rides cost $2 for adults, 35¢ for children 5–17, and 35¢ for seniors. The cable-car system operates daily from 6:30am to 12:30a.m. Call **415/673-MUNI** for more information. You can purchase day and weekly passes. (see the "Getting Around" section, above).

If your kids are especially fascinated with cable cars, they'll enjoy the **San Francisco Cable Car Museum,** located in the Cable Car Barn and Powerhouse at 1201 Mason St., near Washington Street (☎ **415/474-1887**). This is the only operating street-cable powerhouse in the world, and here you can view the machinery that powers the cables and makes the cars run. Don't miss seeing the collection of early cable cars, including the first one, developed by Andrew Hallidie. To get to the museum—you guessed it—take any of the cable cars, all of which pass within three blocks. (The Powell-Mason and Powell-Hyde Lines stop one block away, and the California Street Line leaves you three blocks away. Buses nos. 1, 30, and 83 also stop nearby. The museum is open daily: from 10am to 5pm (closed Thanksgiving, Christmas, and New Year's Days). Admission is free. Stroller-accessible.

CHINATOWN

Heralding its presence, the Gateway to Chinatown, on Grant Avenue at Bush Street, is a two-level structure crowned with a dragon and guard dogs that tells you you're entering a city within a city. San Francisco boasts the largest number of Chinese Americans outside Asia, and once you see Chinatown, you can believe it. In fact, figures put the Chinese population at around 120,000. In recent years North Beach and the Richmond District have become similar enclaves.

The Chinese settled this area just after the Gold Rush of 1849, but the "Great City of the Golden Hill" was almost completely destroyed in the earthquake and fire of 1906. Rebuilt entirely in the Chinese style, it's a neighborhood where you'll see pagoda-style roofs, Chinese-style filigreed balconies, and lots of bright-red paint.

This bustling section of town is one of the most popular tourist destinations in San Francisco. And no wonder . . . it's like stepping into another world of sights, sounds, and smells! The exotic shops, grocery stores, fruit markets, herb stands, fish markets, souvenir vendors, tea rooms, and streams of people make you feel as if you're part of a parade that's spilling out onto the street. Kids love it here. Have them look for the dragons on the street lamps.

You can get to Chinatown via the California Street cable car or bus nos. 1, 15, 30, 41, or 83; or check with Muni.

The **Chinese Culture Center,** at 750 Kearny St., on the third floor of the Holiday Inn (☎ **415/986-1822**), offers educational and cultural programs, including lectures, art exhibits, films, and festivals. The organization's main objectives are to promote the Chinese cultural heritage and provide an understanding of the Chinese to the surrounding English-speaking community. Changing exhibits are presented year round, but you should call for schedules. The center is open Tuesday through Saturday from 10am to 4pm. Admission is free.

You might also want to stop at the **Chinese Historical Society of America,** 650 Commercial St. between Kearny and Montgomery (☎ **415/391-1188**), where you'll see the important role Chinese immigrants played in the Gold Rush and railroad eras. Open Tuesday through Saturday from noon to 4pm. Admission is free, but a donation is appreciated.

Strolling Around Chinatown

The best way to see this city within a city is to take a walk or two here. In fact, the first rule is to leave your car at the hotel and take public transportation or a taxi to this area. If you're stuck with the car, two parking lots are available, but they're likely to be filled.

Walk down Grant Avenue or Stockton Street at a leisurely pace. Sample the authentic Chinese markets. Look into some of the herb shops. Be sure your stroll includes the **Bank of Canton** at the corner of Grant Avenue and Washington Street. Designed like a pagoda, it's a cultural treat for kids—even if it's not the real thing. Walking tours of the area are very popular.

Culinary Walks

Definitely for older children and those with an avid interest in food or in cultural delights, these tours include markets, food stores, sweet shops, a fortune-cookie factory, and a Chinese herb store. Afterward you might plan to stop for a dim sum lunch.

Two outfits offer these tours. **Wok Wiz Chinatown Walking Tours and Cooking Company** (☎ **415/355-9657**) delights in introducing Chinatown to youngsters and adults alike. There are educational tours for families at special prices. Reservations are necessary. One tour, with a complete lunch, costs $35 for adults, $10 for children 5–12. You may also tour without a meal for a lesser charge. The **Chinese Cultural Center** (☎ **415/986-1822**) also sponsors culinary walks. Reservations are required at least a week ahead. If you have a group of six or more, you can schedule a tour on Wednesday at 10:30am. Otherwise you can call to see if you can join an already-scheduled Wednesday tour. The price is $30 for adults, $15 for children under 12.

Heritage Walks

This guided walking tour is a wonderful way to experience Chinatown's cultural, historical, and social achievements. Visit a newspaper, a fortune-cookie factory, a Chinese temple, the historical society, and other places you request. If you have a group, you can schedule a tour for a weekday. For you and your family only, tours are held on Saturday at 2pm, and reservations are required. The cost is $15 for adults, $5 for children under 12. There is also a **Chinese New Year Walk** given during this special season. Call early for details: (☎ **415/982-3000**).

All walks begin at the **Chinese Culture Center,** 750 Kearny St., on the third floor of the Holiday Inn (☎ **415/986-1822**).

Chinese New Year, which occurs every year between mid-January and late February, is a week in which Chinatown comes alive with folk dancing, pageants, and the Miss Chinatown USA Beauty Contest. There are Chinatown festival walks, exhibits, and displays, all culminating in a spectacular finale called the Chinese New Year Carnival. The Chinese Culture Foundation sponsors special activities. Usually 450,000 spectators line the Chinese New Year Parade route. For information about tickets to the pageant—and the exact dates each year—call **415/982-3071.**

THE NORTHERN WATERFRONT

No matter how often we go to San Francisco, and it can never be often enough(!), we head to this area as soon as we can. Composed of **Ghirardelli Square, Aquatic Park,** the **San Francisco Maritime National Historical Park** with **Hyde Street Pier** (and its historic ships), **The Cannery,** and **Fisherman's Wharf** all the way to **Pier 39,** this is a children's playland and well-known tourist mecca. In fact, we find ourselves in the general area several times during the same trip either because we don't have enough time to do everything in one day, or because we want a meal down by the Wharf.

We think of this area as having three sections: eastern, Pier 39; central, the heart of Fisherman's Wharf; and western, which takes you to the Hyde Street Pier and Ghirardelli Square. You'll want to purchase a map of the area available through Muni (☎ 415/673-MUNI).

One good way to see the area is to start at one end and work your way to the other. Wherever you start, plan to spend all day. If you have little kids, break it into two shorter trips. If you choose to do that, you can start at Pier 39 and work your way to Fisherman's Wharf. The next time, start at the Wharf and work your way west to the Cannery and Ghirardelli Square.

Don't bother to eat lunch or dinner elsewhere; there's more than enough to choose from here. Remember that this is the home of the famous San Francisco walk-around seafood cocktail. And leave your diet plans at home too. The sweets and breads you'll find here are out of this world. To get to Pier 39 and Fisherman's Wharf, take a Powell-Mason cable car to the last stop, Taylor and Bay Streets. Walk three blocks north to Jefferson Street for the Wharf; or for Pier 39, walk two blocks north to Beach Street and go east until you see the colorful flags beckoning you to the pier.

You can also take bus no. 15, 19, 30, 32, 39, 42, 47, or 49 from almost anywhere in town.

To get to Ghirardelli Square and the Cannery, take the Powell-Hyde cable car to Victorian Square. You'll be right there. You can also get there on any of the following buses: nos. 19, 30, 32, 39, 42, 47, or 49.

If you choose to drive to the area, we're here to dispel a myth. There are several all-day parking lots that are not as costly as you might think, especially with validations. But be sure to park and walk. Wear walking shoes and be sure to bring a stroller. This isn't the place to keep moving your car. Street parking is scarce and expensive. However, at Ghirardelli Square there are several affordable lots. If you're willing to walk one more block, it's usually possible to park in the residential neighborhood up the hill from Ghirardelli Square, even on Saturday. There is validated parking at Pier 39.

We usually like to start our northern waterfront tour at Pier 39.

Pier 39

Pier 39 (☎ 415/981-PIER) is a festive and inviting two-tiered marketplace of more than 100 specialty shops, video arcades, and restaurants—and special treats for kids. Named the favorite place in San Francisco in a survey of 45,000 San Francisco schoolchildren, Pier 39 is like getting a taste of all San Francisco in one spot. Located at the northernmost point of the San Francisco peninsula, you can see all the major landmarks from here: the two bridges, Alcatraz, Angel Island, Coit Tower, the TransAmerican Pyramid, and the skyline.

You'll know you're there when you see the banners waving in the breeze. At the entrance you'll see **Waterfront Park,** a fabulous little park stretching between Piers 35 and 41. There's sand, play equipment, and large wooden benches for lounging.

Whether your little ones love the two-tiered Venetian carousel, or enjoy the street performers—mimes, dancers, musicians, and jugglers—who entertain daily, or they're older and are wild about video games, this is a place where you'll want to spend several hours. In addition, there are more than 100 shops (some of the most innovative ones you'll see) that parents will adore; and the exquisite panoramic views of both the East Bay and Marin County which will take your breath away. Pier 39 is also an ideal place to watch the playful sea lions. There's a free program where docents teach children and adults about the California sea lion. The program is held on weekends from noon to 4pm (☎ 415/705-5500).

Constructed of weathered wood from old piers, Pier 39 is a 1,043-foot pier with a 350-berth marina that is home to the Blue and Gold Bay Cruise Fleet. While there is stroller (and wheelchair) access to almost everything, you might want to tuck along a Snuggly or child carrier for greater ease. Several elevators are located on either side of the pier. Most shops are open daily from 10:30am to 8:30pm; restaurants, from 11:30am to 10pm. Most major credit cards are accepted.

One of the attractions is the **San Francisco Experience** (☎ 415/982-7394), a 25-minute multimedia show (35 computerized projectors are used) that covers the history of San Francisco. Learn about the city's Barbary Coast origins and how the cable cars came into existence. Experience the 1906 and 1989 earthquakes and learn about the '60s and the flower children. The huge 50-foot screen wraps partially around a wall, really bringing the images to you. Although children over five shouldn't have any problems, here are a few things to tell your young kids about the three-dimensional effects. During the Chinese New Year scenes, a dragon will pop out of one of the walls; during the Barbary Coast scenes, two bodies will drop out of the ceiling; and during the earthquake, the seats will rumble. Open from 10am to 9:30pm daily, with hours extended in summer. Tickets are $6 for adults, $3 for children 5–16; children under five are free. Show times are very half hour.

As you exit the theater, take some time to look at the earthquake exhibit. The educational display of the 1989 and 1906 earthquakes combines stunning photographs, instructive material about the quakes, and safety information. You and your children will find it fascinating.

One of the most exciting innovations at the pier is the opening of **Underwater World,** scheduled for spring 1996. Designed to be a "dry journey through the sea," it will let visitors travel on a moving footpath through a clear, acrylic 400-foot-long underwater tunnel. It will give guests the chance to feel surrounded by the sea and the species of aquatic life indigenous to Northern California and the San Francisco Bay

Area, including sharks, rays, and sea turtles. There will also be interactive displays and exhibits. Tickets are estimated to be $11 for adults, $5.50 for children and seniors. Hours are 10am to 10pm daily.

FOR OLDER KIDS AND TEENS   For the uninhibited in your crowd, head for **Music Tracks,** where your favorite 13-year-olds can sing and record their favorite hit songs. You simply walk into the sound booth and sing along with the lead singer. After your track is recorded, technicians knock out the lead singer's voice so it's only you singing with the backup group. You get to bring home a cassette recording.

We don't know if there is a magnetic field that draws children over 6 to video arcades, but even if you can't find **Namco Cyber Station Family Games Arcade,** your children will. This place is a large, clean video arcade with wide aisles and lots of room between games so that children don't elbow each other as they're playing. This state-of-the-art experience is open Sunday through Thursday from 10am to 10pm, on Friday and Saturday from 9am to midnight.

FOR YOUNGER KIDS   Especially good for little children is the double-decker **carousel,** where the music isn't too loud and the carousel isn't too big. Kids also love **Puppets on the Pier** (☎ 415/781-4435). This shop brings the puppets out in the open to show kids how they work. You'll see groups of children intently watching the puppeteers as their little dolls dance.

SHOPS AND RESTAURANTS   Some of the unique shops we love are **Left-Hand World** (☎ 415/433-3547), where we buy gifts for those hard-to-shop-for left-handers; **Cartoon Junction** (☎ 415/392-2220), for all kinds of stuff from all kinds of cartoon characters (our favorite is the Betty Boop collection); and **Animal Country** (☎ 415/989-2104) and **Kite Flite** (☎ 415/956-3181), with a wide se-lection of the best. Another favorite for cute, packable gift items and souvenirs is **Magnet P.I.** (☎ 415/989-2361), for the largest selection of fanciful magnets we've ever seen. Even if you have no intention of buying a magnet, go into the shop to see the display. Finally, for wonderfully full evenings back at the hotel when you want the television off and the kids entertained, **Stamp*A*Teria** (☎ 415/989-6103) has a nice selection of kids' stamps and stamp accessories.

There is a wide variety of restaurants and fast-food places to choose from. (See the "Where to Eat" section, above.) Restaurants here are generally open from 11:30am until 9pm. For lighter, walkaway food, don't miss **Chowders** (☎ 415/391-4737). We love the clam chowder in the scooped-out sourdough bread. It's delicious. For a quick snack, there's always **Blue Chip Cookies** and **Vlaho's Fruit Orchard** (May through September).

Fisherman's Wharf

World-famous Fisherman's Wharf is a panorama of sights, smells, and sounds, from souvenir vendors who sell T-shirts, cable-car renditions, posters, and books to side-walk seafood stands with their bubbling cauldrons of crab and inviting sourdough bread. This is where you'll see fishermen working on their vessels alongside mimes, jugglers, and street performers plying their trades. You'll see gulls snatching at pieces of food, plus pelicans and an occasional sea lion.

We love the general hubbub, although during the weekends and busy summer days it gets a bit much to navigate a stroller through the crowds. We recommend a baby carrier.

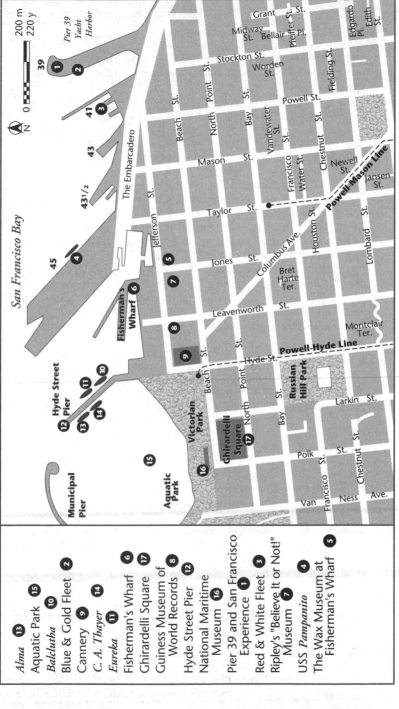

The Northern Waterfront

Cable Car - - - - -

Alma **13**
Aquatic Park **15**
Balclutha **10**
Blue & Gold Fleet **2**
Canney **9**
C. A. Thayer **14**
Eureka **11**
Fisherman's Wharf **6**
Ghirardelli Square **17**
Guiness Museum of World Records **8**
Hyde Street Pier **12**
National Maritime Museum **16**
Pier 39 and San Francisco Experience **1**
Red & White Fleet **3**
Ripley's "Believe It or Not!" Museum **7**
USS Pampanito **4**
The Wax Museum at Fisherman's Wharf **5**

Alcatraz

Only 1¹/₂ miles from Fisherman's Wharf, a trip to ominous Alcatraz Island (☎ 415/546-BOAT for tour information)—known as The Rock—seems as if you're days away from friendly civilization. Once a notorious prison that housed the likes of Al Capone, Machine Gun Kelly, and Doc Barker, a trip to the prison island makes you feel as if they cleared the place of inmates just moments before your arrival.

You can explore Alcatraz with the about 1¹/₂-mile self-guided tour, which takes you through the buildings, cellhouse, and grounds. There is a slide presentation that gives you more background about the grim prison. You can also rent an audiotape program that brings the tour to life; the charge is $9 for adults and $4.50 for children 5–11. National Park Service rangers offer free outdoor walking tours of Alcatraz; the tours leave from outside the cellhouse at regular intervals during the day.

The trip involves stairs and some steep climbs. Be sure to wear walking shoes and bring warm sweaters. (Ask your personal physician for advice in advance if any member of your group has a heart or respiratory condition.) The National Park Service offers some cautions when you're on the Rock. Be sure to follow them. The round trip, including the tour, takes about 2¹/₂ hours.

The **Red and White Fleet** (☎ **415/546-2700**, or toll free **800/229-2784** in California) offers transportation to the island from Pier 41. Departures are at 9:30am, 10:15am, and then every 30 minutes until 4:15pm. These times change occasionally, so call first to be sure. Tickets cost $8.75 for adults, $8 for seniors, and $4.50 for children. These prices include a recorded cassette for the walking tour. Reservations are recommended.

U.S.S. *Pampanito*

This World War II submarine (☎ **415/929-0202**), is exhibited by the National Maritime Museum Association. Docked at Pier 45, this is a special treat for children who are interested in ships, torpedoes, and maritime war duty. Most 8- and 9-year-olds are enchanted with the idea of living underwater in those tiny quarters for a period of time.

For a small fee you get an audio tour; $8 for adults, $3 for children and seniors; children under 6, free. Walk the deck and go below on this submarine, taking a step back in time to World War II.

Be careful of toddlers and babies too old to carry in a Snuggly. The steps from the deck that go into the main part of the sub are steep ladders, and the doors from room to room are like windows, forcing you to bend down while lifting each leg. There is no way to take a stroller, and it's tough to carry a baby. Open Sunday through Thursday from 9am to 6pm (until 9pm during the summer months) and on Friday and Saturday from 9am to 8pm.

Active naval vessels occasionally make port calls at Pier 45. While no schedule is available, you may still be lucky enough to be here on a weekend when a navy ship is here and holding an open house. On clear days this location also affords great views of Alcatraz Island, Sausalito, and the East Bay. Try looking at Alcatraz through the powerful telescopes at the foot of the pier.

Bay Cruises

There are other kinds of boats in the area, too.

On Pier 39 you'll find the **Blue and Gold Fleet** (☎ **415/705-5555**). They offer 1³/₄ hour bay cruises that take you under both the San Francisco–Oakland Bay Bridge and the Golden Gate Bridge, and come within yards of Alcatraz Island. Other points of interest along the way are Sausalito, Tiburon, and Angel Island.

Departures are year round; call to verify since schedules vary throughout the year. Tickets cost $14 for adults, $7 for seniors and children 5–18, free for children under 5.

Piers 41 and 43¹/₂ are home to the **Red and White Fleet** (☎ **415/546-2628,** or toll free **800/229-2784** in California). San Francisco Bay cruises depart daily from Pier 41. This hour-long narrated cruise goes past Alcatraz and Angel Islands and under the Golden Gate Bridge. Tickets are $15 for adults, $12 for seniors and children 12–18, $8 for children 5–11; under 5, free. Call for schedules.

This company also offers ferry service to Sausalito, Tiburon, Muir Woods, and Angel Island, Alcatraz, and Marine World Africa USA (a one-hour cruise on a highspeed catamaran). It offers walking tours of Alcatraz; schedules vary depending on the time of year; call for specific information. If you're planning to take bicycles to Angel Island, be sure there's room for them on the ferry since space is limited.

Other Treats in the Area

You might take a horse-drawn carriage ride around the area, offered by **Carriage Charter** (☎ **415/398-0857**). A ride around Fisherman's Wharf, North Beach, and the Waterfront is $10–$17 for two to five people and takes about 10–15 minutes; and a ride through the Wharf and Ghirardelli Square area costs $25–$32 for two to five people and lasts about 30 minutes. There is a one-hour tour ($60–$75) for two to five people that includes the Wharf, Ghirardelli Square, Aquatic Park, and the North Beach area. The first ride is at about 1pm; the last is at 10pm on weeknights and midnight on weekends. Reservations are accepted but not necessary.

Our kids' favorite among the amusement areas (and we mean amusement) is **Ripley's Believe It or Not! Museum,** located at 175 Jefferson St. at Fisherman's Wharf (☎ **415/771-6188**). Not only did they like it, but because they couldn't believe many of the 2,000-plus exhibits, they begged us to return. Not surprisingly, when Andrew was a 7-year-old he was entranced by the child who grew a beard at the age of four and died of "old age" when he was seven! (That was food for thought for many hours.) The two-headed animals were also a real treat.

The adults in the group, on the other hand, were taken by the miniatures—the smallest violin ever made, the tiniest gold tea set, and itsy-bitsy roller skates that actually work. Don't go there with a smirk . . . people take this place seriously. There's even an official guidebook with a short biography of the founder, Robert LeRoy Ripley.

Open Sunday through Thursday from 10am to 10pm and on Friday and Saturday until midnight. Admission is $6.50 for adults, $5.50 for kids 13–17 and seniors, $3.50 for children 5–12; under 5, free.

The **Wax Museum at Fisherman's Wharf,** 145 Jefferson St. (☎ **415/885-4975**), fascinated and frightened our youngsters. The 270 wax figures are well organized—sports figures, political celebrities, and movie stars together—on four floors. Some of them appear startlingly real.

For sensitive children under nine, we would avoid the Chamber of Horrors, or at least warn them that it's coming. This room was the basis for several evenings of night frights. At the fork, don't go downstairs to the Horrors; instead, go up to the left to the Gallery of Stars.

The museum is open daily in summer from 9am to 11pm; in winter, from 10am to 10pm (on Friday and Saturday from 9am to midnight). Admission is $8.95 for adults, $6.95 for seniors, $4.95 for children 6–12; under 6, free. Stroller access.

Of particular interest to kids over nine is the **Guinness Museum of World Records,** 235 Jefferson St. (☎ 415/771-9890), which makes visual the astounding phenomena in the *Guinness Book of World Records.* See the shoes worn by the world's smallest woman and the world's tallest man. While Andrew (then age 7) was a bit young, he enjoyed the ESP machine, where two people face each other with a partition between them; one person chooses a symbol and the other person has to show his powers of ESP by guessing the correct one. There is stroller access. In summer it's open daily from 10am to midnight; the rest of the year, Saturday through Thursday from 10am to 10pm, on Friday till midnight. Admission is $6.50 for adults, $5 for students and seniors, $3.50 for children 5–12; under 5, free.

Be sure not to miss the area filled with commercial and charter fishing boats between Lolli's Castagnola and Tarantino's restaurants. Walk out to the **Finger Pier** for a better look. If you're lucky, you'll see pelicans, sea lions, lots of gulls, and at the right time of day, fishermen unloading their catch.

The Cannery

While many people think of the Cannery, 2801 Leavenworth St. at Jefferson Street (☎ 415/771-3112), as an architecturally award-winning place to shop, we think of this old Del Monte Fruit Cannery as a terrific place to walk around. We enjoy the street performers—mimes, magicians, musicians—in the lovely courtyard while we partake of al fresco dining.

This brick landmark withstood the earthquake and fire of 1906, and has been transformed to a three-level complex of shops and restaurants.

The stores in the Cannery are open generally Monday through Saturday from 10am to 6pm and on Sunday from 11am. Summer and Christmas hours are longer, and the restaurants have longer hours. The elevator is located near the South building, and restrooms are located in the South building on the mezzanine, and in the North building on the second floor.

Next there's **Confetti Le Chocolatier** (☎ 415/474-7377), not to be missed by the chocoholics in your crowd. You'll find milk-chocolate, hand-dipped candied fruit, handmade Swiss chocolates, and chocolate truffles, among other goodies.

Nearby is the **Cannery Wine Cellar/California** (☎ 415/673-0400), also on the first floor of the North building. This shop offers a wide selection of California wines and hundreds of different kinds of beer. You can buy cheeses and salami and have fresh coffee ground for you. Another great place to put together picnic fixings or find gifts to take home with you.

Hyde Street Pier

Don't miss the Hyde Street Pier (☎ 415/556-3002), a fabulous place many visitors aren't aware of. Part of the **San Francisco Maritime National Historical Park,** this floating museum is a wonderful place to spend an hour or so. Home of the Historic Ships Collection, there are currently six merchant ships docked at the pier—several of which can be boarded. If it's warm, you can enjoy the sun and the view of Angel Island, Marin, the Golden Gate Bridge, and other sights. If it's a foggy, cool day, you'll feel like part of the seagoing community. Visitors may raise the sail and watch rangers climb aloft or demonstrate the rigging or hands-on crafts such as knot tying. The park has a "living history" program where you and the kids can hear old mariners' tales, watch shipboard dancing, hear some of the sailer's songs.

The *Eureka* is a sidewheel ferry built in 1890.

Although it's under construction for part of 1995, usually you and the kids can wander throughout. The kids can pretend they're captains on what was once the largest passenger ferry in the world. There are tours, but check ahead because times vary. And below, on the garage level, is an exceptional exhibit of restored classic cars—a 1924 Dodge Express wagon, a 1931 Model A Ford for the U.S. Mail, and the like.

The *Balclutha* is a square-rigged Cape Horn sailing ship that is done in the traditional black-and-gray and red-and-white colors. Launched in 1886, this impressive ship has three main masts and a several decks. Kids love to see the crew's quarters, the captain's cabin, the charthouse, and the holds where the cargo was stored.

There are other historic ships docked here too. The *C.A. Thayer* is a vessel (one of only two surviving from a group of 900) that carried lumber from the Pacific Northwest to California. Each day there is a tour around the schooner. The *Hercules* is an oceangoing tugboat that once towed ships through the Strait of Magellan. *Eppleton Hall* is a 1914 side-wheeled tugboat reminiscent of ships used during the California Gold Rush. The *Alma* is a tiny two-masted flat-bottomed schooner built in 1891.

You'll love the **Maritime Book Store** (☎ 415/775-2665)—devoted to books, ship models, posters, cards, and gifts on sailing and maritime history. We loved the boats-in-a-bottle kits for children. There's also a small-boat shop on the pier that gives boatbuilding classes.

The pier is open daily from 10am to 6pm in summer, and 9:30am to 5pm in winter. Admission is $3 for adults, $1 for children 12–17, free for seniors over 62 and children 11 and under.

Across from the pier is **Aquatic Park,** where our kids love to romp on the grass, an area we also love because of the bayside scenery. The lagoon offers a sand beach and swimming too. Restrooms are located in the park.

The Maritime Museum

Part of the San Francisco Maritime National Historical Park, the Maritime Museum is located in a white art deco building at the foot of Polk Street, across from Ghirardelli Square (☎ 415/556-3002). Considered very fine by serious nautical enthusiasts, the collection includes a changing exhibition of photographs, ship models and other seafaring memorabilia, a small rowboat, and whaling artifacts. Call for information about all kinds of interesting events—there are work parties on the historic ships, Christmas at Sea festivities, and special children's programs. Open daily from 10am to 5pm. Admission is free.

Ghirardelli Square

That famous red-brick chocolate factory with the 15-foot-high illuminated sign has greeted millions of tourists and delighted the kid in all of us. In fact, we never miss a trip to Ghirardelli's when we're in San Francisco. Sometimes we make it part of a half-day trek from the Wharf to the Cannery to the square, then a cable-car ride back to the hotel. Other times, we make it a quick stop via auto for an Emperor Norton at the Ghirardelli Chocolate Manufactory. Either way, this is one of our enduring favorites.

Bordered by Beach, Larkin, Polk, and North Point Streets, Ghirardelli Square, 900 North Point St. (☎ 415/775-5500), is a great place to end a walk from the Wharf. Plan to have dinner here so you can watch the sun set over the Golden Gate Bridge. By day, you can see Alcatraz Island, Sausalito, and the East Bay.

Ghirardelli Square, named for Italian merchant and chocolate maker Domingo Ghirardelli, was built between 1900 and 1916. For the last 20 years the square, which consists of 14 buildings and eight levels, has undergone extensive restoration. Today it twinkles with a fresh open-air quality that continues to beckon tourists and locals alike.

In addition to numerous clothing stores (such as **Ann Taylor**), there are craft and art galleries, gift stores, and import shops. We love to stroll in the specialty shops— **Sports Fantasy** (second floor of the Clock Tower Building), and the **Kite Shop** (Beach Street). Don't miss the **Nature Company** (West Plaza) and **Brentano's Bookstore** (first floor, Mustard Bldg.).

When you get hungry, there are any number of good restaurants to choose from (see the "Where to Eat" section, above). Then there's the **Ghirardelli Chocolate Manufactory,** on the plaza level of the Clock Tower Building (☎ **415/474-3938**) in Ghirardelli Square, worth the trip in itself. It's the ultimate ice-cream shop, and you can get sodas, ice-cream sundaes, and Ghirardelli chocolate of all kinds there— even smaller, one-scoop sundaes for children. If you're going to be in San Francisco for a birthday, call ahead and ask the manager about their special party program.

If you stop here for a treat, be prepared to wait in line at peak times in the busy season. You present your order to the cashier and when it's ready, your number will be called.

Our kids love to watch the goings-on at the small chocolate manufactory at the back of the store while they wait for their treats. Adults will enjoy browsing in the giftshop. How about a long-stemmed chocolate rose or a milk-chocolate teddy bear? Open daily, 10am to 11pm. Booster seats are available.

A Warning: This delightfully constructed set of buildings is tricky to navigate with a stroller unless you know where you're going. If you have a stroller, don't attempt the stairs from Beach Street. Enter at Larkin or North Point Street and ask at the information desk (fountain level) for directions to ramps and elevator access.

In addition to strolling, browsing, and snacking, Ghirardelli Square boasts some of the city's great restaurants. See the "Where to Eat" section, above, or get a copy of the free *Shop, Dine, Enjoy . . . Ghirardelli Square* guide at the information booth in the courtyard.

If you come by car, use the underground lot with validated free parking. If you come or go by cable car, get on or off at the Hyde Street turnaround at **Victorian Square,** also a lovely place to sit and watch the world go by.

THE EXPLORATORIUM

Don't miss this children's delight. Located at 3601 Lyon St., at Marina Boulevard, in the Palace of Fine Arts, the Exploratorium (☎ **415/563-7337** for information or **415/561-0360** for a recorded message) is like nothing you've ever seen. Also called the Playful Museum, this innovative, hands-on museum was designed so that everyone would gain an understanding of nature and science. There are over 700 exhibit pieces for children to fiddle with and explore. If you walk into the massive 86,000-square-foot structure, you and your kids will immediately be drawn into ingenious exhibits that will help you learn about light, color, sound, motion, language, touch, and electricity. Throughout the museum, exhibit "explainers" work with children to encourage their explorations.

Younger kids will especially enjoy the following exhibits: the Balancing Ball (a traffic cone standing up with a column of air blowing through, and a beach ball that levitates from the air, which kids chase after), the Shadow Box (a walk-in box where a strobe light catches kids' shadows on a phosphorescent wall), the Distorted Room (with a slanted floor that has no right angles; when someone outside looks into the room, people inside look like dwarves or giants), and the Duck Into Kaleidoscope (where children duck under partitions and then see an infinite number of reflections in the three mirrors set up).

Older kids will enjoy Light Strokes (a converted Macintosh computer that offers a sensitive, sophisticated finger-painting experience) and "Everyone Is You and Me" (a two-way mirror that both reflects and can be seen through, so that by adjusting knobs, two kids can superimpose their images one on the other).

Tactile Dome is another great exhibit—adults and kids crawl through this darkened area using their sense of touch to experience another dimension. You must make a reservation several days in advance (☎ 415/561-0362 between 10am and 2pm) and pay an extra fee to enjoy this experience, recommended for children over 7.

Yes, we have our favorite exhibits too. Andrew couldn't get enough of the Momentum Machine, where he—and five other school-agers—pushed off on a scooter-like structure that kept him spinning as long as he balanced evenly. Then we discovered "Viewing the Golden Gate," an interactive video disk where, by moving a rotary control ball, you "fly" over the Golden Gate Bridge. Children (and, we confess, adults too) read radar and see the corresponding environment at the same time. While moving the steering wheel you see the blips on the radar screen, and if you look over that small air-traffic-controller–like screen, you can see a larger screen of the scenery you'd be flying over. This was such a big hit that it was difficult to get kids to take turns. Once on, they wanted to stay.

If you know ahead when you'll be there, call for information on special events, workshops, and field trips. The museum is completely stroller-accessible. It's open Tuesday through Sunday from 10am to 5pm (on Wednesday until 9:30pm).

Admission is $8 for adults, $6 for seniors and stud, and $4 for children 6–17; children under 6 and members enter free.

As if the Exploratorium isn't enough, the view of the **Palace of Fine Arts** is worth the trip by itself. This ornate Greco-Roman fantasy composition rises out of a lagoon, and is the last remaining structure from the 1915 Panama-Pacific Exposition. You can bring a picnic lunch and enjoy the lagoon and lawn area.

The Exploratorium is near the Golden Gate Bridge. Free parking is available. It's a short bus ride from Fisherman's Wharf on the no. 30 bus. Buses nos. 28, 41, 43, and 45 stop within walking distance.

GOLDEN GATE PARK

With park headquarters at McLaren Lodge (☎ 415/666-7200), this is one of the places that makes San Francisco special, and a must-see for anyone visiting the city. There are so many faces to the park, so many things to see and do—fabulous museums, a planetarium and aquarium, a buffalo-grazing paddock, a lake with boats, an antique carousel, great playground equipment, and of course the famous authentic Japanese Tea Garden—that it's hard to know where to start.

Plan to spend lots of time here. We usually try to get to the park at least once, sometimes twice, each trip. Allow at least a half day—a few hours for the planetarium or aquarium, some time to meander, and some time at the playground or Stow Lake. If you want to hike, roller skate, or bike ride, you can do that too.

If you've never been to Golden Gate Park, you're in for a wondrous treat. If you have already been there, you know some of the joys of this park—the largest manmade park in the world—that stretches from the ocean three miles inland and 1½ miles wide. You can go back repeatedly for new adventures.

If you want to get an overview of the park, you can drive west on John F. Kennedy Drive toward the ocean. Be sure to drive to the ocean just to see the Dutch windmill welcoming visitors to San Francisco. At the Great Highway, take a left, and another left onto Martin Luther King Drive, which will bring you back into the park heading east.

You may be surprised (as we were) to learn that Golden Gate Park wasn't always the beautifully wooded haven it is today. In fact when the land was purchased in 1868 it was considered a vast wasteland of sand dunes, a white elephant that the city would later regret. Undaunted by public opinion, William Hammond Hall, the first park engineer, laid out the basic plan of the park. In 1887 John McLaren, who later became affectionately known as Uncle John, was appointed park superintendent. McLaren consulted with botanists around the world to find plants that were suited for the area and set out to create one of the most beautiful parks in the world.

Today Golden Gate Park is a 1,017-acre wonderland of trees, meadows, lakes, and gardens. It is a recreation area par excellence for families. It's more a matter of finding out what you want to do here . . . because there's so much you can do. The area that most families consider the hub is near the **De Young Compound,** also called the Music Concourse. The **Music Concourse** is considered the heart of the park. On Sunday (weather permitting) you can hear everything from opera to Irish folk bands. There are lots of picnic areas here, museums too. This is where you'll find roller skaters and bicyclists.

Japanese Tea Garden

One of the most popular, and possibly the most unique, of the attractions of the park is the Japanese Tea Garden (☎ 415/752-1171), located at the Band Concourse Area. The handsome and delicate garden is a delightful step into a world halfway around the globe. Pathways meander through Japanese greenery, koi-filled ponds, and bonsai.

Kids particularly love the arched drum bridge and the elaborate five-tiered dark-red pagoda. The hand-carved red gateway entrance and the wonderful bronze Buddha intrigue them. If you're in the city during March and early April, you'll find the Japanese cherry trees blossoming. There is a lovely little teahouse in which kimono-clad women serve Japanese tea and cookies. Stroller access is to the left of the main-gate entrance on Tea Garden Drive (marked "Exit"), but be prepared to carry little children, as certain areas are not open to strollers. The garden is open daily from 9am to 5:30pm. Admission is $2 for adults, $1 for children 6–12 and seniors.

California Academy of Sciences

Located on the Music Concourse, the California Academy of Sciences (☎ 415/221-5100) is one of the finest natural science museums in the country. The complex bills itself as the "lively museum of adventure," and includes the Steinhart Aquarium, the Fish Roundabout, the Morrison Planetarium, Life Through Time, Wild California, African Safari, Gem and Mineral Hall, the SafeQuake Ride, and the Discovery Room. It's a place where every member of the family will find something of delight and interest.

There is stroller access throughout the exhibits, and an elevator can be taken to the cafeteria (salad bar, sandwich bar, hot dogs, and other snacks), on the lower floor. The complex is open daily from 10am to 5pm (from July 4 through Labor Day until 7pm). Admission is $7 for adults, $4 for seniors and youths 12–17, $1.50 for children 6–11; those under 6, free. There is free admission for all on the first Wednesday

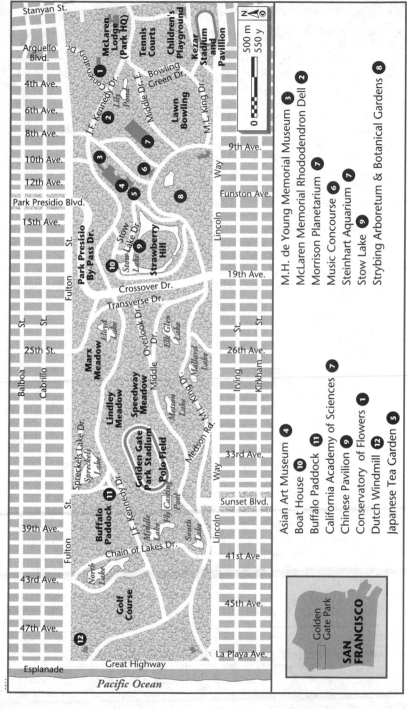

Golden Gate Park

M.H. de Young Memorial Museum **3**
McLaren Memorial Rhododendron Dell **2**
Morrison Planetarium **7**
Music Concourse **6**
Steinhart Aquarium **7**
Stow Lake **9**
Strybing Arboretum & Botanical Gardens **8**

Asian Art Museum **4**
Boat House **10**
Buffalo Paddock **11**
California Academy of Sciences **7**
Chinese Pavilion **9**
Conservatory of Flowers **1**
Dutch Windmill **12**
Japanese Tea Garden **5**

SAN FRANCISCO
Golden Gate Park

of the month. **Note:** The planetarium has a separate admission charge and different hours of operation.

The **Steinhart Aquarium** (☎ 415/750-7145) gives kids the chance to see what it feels like to be surrounded by fish. Be sure to walk up to the top of the Fish Roundabout and take a few moments to sit down (even if it's on the floor). You'll hear oohs and ahs as other people catch their first views of the circular fish tank around you. Our kids love to choose one fish and follow it on its journey around the huge round tank. There's always lots of laughter as we all try to keep track of the fish. (Of course, we lose it and have to start over again and again!) On your way up to the Roundabout, don't miss the California tidepool, where the kids can handle starfish, anemones, and other sea creatures. The docent will explain whatever the children want to know, and is sure to keep the kids gentle with the sea life. (If you can take available-light photos, this is the place to capture priceless expressions on the kids' faces.) You'll also love the dolphins and seals.

Morrison Planetarium (☎ 415/750-7141 for recorded information) is well known for its high-quality shows and is Northern California's largest planetarium. School-age children and those older love to spend the hour gazing up at the "night sky," learning about the celestial bodies. Our only qualifer which applies to all planetarium shows, is that children under 6 find the shows very long, and the darkness seems to scare many of them. The planetarium staff agrees.

Shows change, so call ahead. Shows are presented Monday through Friday at 2pm, and on Saturday and Sunday at noon and 1, 2, 3, and 4pm. From July 4 through early September there are extra shows; call for information. Admission is $2.50 for adults, $1.25 for seniors and children 6–17, free for children under 6 if they're seated on a parent's lap. These charges are in addition to the museum admission fee.

Morrison presents **Laserium shows** (☎ 415/750-7138), which offer a fabulous, colorful lightshow that plays in synch with the planetarium's state-of-the-art sound crowd. The Laserium staff says that the shows are not recommended for infants and children under 6. Shows are presented on Thursday, Friday, Saturday, and Sunday evenings. From July 1 through Labor Day there are also shows Wednesdays. Call ahead. Tickets are available at BASS Ticketing or at the Academy a half hour before show time. Admission is $7 for ages 13–64, $5 for seniors (65+) and children 6–12; the charge is $1 less at the 5pm show, free for children under 6 if seated on a parent's lap.

Life Through Time is a 3.5-billion-year journey through life on Earth. At 10 years old, Andrew was able to appreciate evolution in a new way, while 4-year-old Elizabeth squealed when she saw the life-size dinosaurs. It's a good exhibit for all ages.

A really grand way to appreciate the state is a visit to **Wild California,** an exhibit hall devoted to the vastness and diversity of this amazing region.

For another adventure, the **African Safari** has a lifelike African watering hole exhibit that has realistic sound and lighting effects.

If you have a budding gemologist as we do—and I don't know many kids who don't exclaim over stones that glimmer—take at least a brief look-see at the **Gem and Mineral Hall.** We had missed it on our first few trips with the children, and found that once they knew it was there, they asked to see it again and again. Imagine a child's delight at the 1,350-pound quartz crystal! It is a treat.

You'll want to see the **Discovery Room,** a small, quiet area (designed for family interaction) with lots to see and touch. "Please Touch!" are the words you'll hear. Children are invited to handle such things as shark jaws, dinosaur bones, and birds' nests.

This is where your six-year-old might want to sort through a box of shells, where your eight-year-old can examine different phases of the moon or search for shy Pacific Coast newts and frogs. Even though your toddler won't be able to participate fully, this is a good place to calm him down if he's overstimulated. The Discovery Room is open—free—Sunday 10am to 4. Braille available for sight-impaired; wheelchair accessible. The room is staffed by volunteers, so call ahead for exact hours.

The **SafeQuake Ride** is part of a large exhibit on earthquakes. Elbow your way through the large crowd of kids who stand around waiting to participate in this exhibit. Here you stand on a platform and watch a video about earthquakes. At the same time, the platform is programmed to simulate the vibrations of quakes of different strengths. This is a great favorite of the 8- through 11-year-old set.

When the kids need a break from indoor activities, there's a courtyard with a fountain and statues. On warm days, you'll see lots of families sunning themselves, and children throwing pennies in the fountain. The preschoolers enjoy climbing on the statues and all the kids enjoy running in the plaza area.

The M. H. De Young Memorial Museum

The De Young Museum collection (☎ 415/863-3330) is the most comprehensive in the city. The collection includes one of the most comprehensive presentations of American art—from colonial times into the 20th century, including works from Africa and the Americas.

This is where you can take the kids to sample Winslow Homer, Grant Wood, and Georgia O'Keeffe. There are also Saturday workshops for children 7–12, called "Doing and Viewing Art." The children visit a different museum gallery each week, and then participate in an artistic experience in which they create their own art. These occur every Saturday at 10:30am, and no reservations are necessary.

The museum is open Wednesday through Sunday from 10am to 5pm. Admission is $5 for adults, $3 for seniors, and $2 for children 12–17, free for children 12 and under. Admission is free to all on the first Wednesday of each month.

Located adjacent to the De Young Museum is the **Asian Art Museum** (☎ 415/668-8921), an internationally acclaimed collection with almost 12,000 objets d'art from Asia. There are films and storytelling for children. Call for information.

Stow Lake

This is a delightful little retreat—a place where you can rent boats or hike. Stow Lake comes complete with an island. You can see the **Chinese Pavilion.** Visitors are allowed inside. Wander to the top of the hill to the reservoir that feeds **Huntington Falls,** a lovely artificial waterfall with hand-sculpted rocks. There is stroller access all around the lake, although it can get muddy, and to the top of the falls. Plan to spend about an hour if you're going to walk around the lake and up to the top. You can picnic, but carry out what you bring in. Electric motorboats can be rented by the hour, as can rowboats and pedal boats. A deposit is required for all rentals. The boathouse is open Tuesday through Sunday from 9am to 4pm.

You can picnic anywhere around this area or on the top of the hill. There's a nearby playground that's very good for toddlers. It has a couple of small slides and swings, designed for little ones.

Nearby **Spreckels Lake** is the delight of hobbyists, who bring out their remote-controlled model sailboats and powerboats on weekends. Even our 8-year-old Elizabeth squealed when she saw the buffalo feeding nearby at the **Buffalo Paddock.**

Carousel

This magnificent merry-go-round has a wonderful menagerie of animals. Recently restored at a cost of $800,000, it's one of the last complete Hershell Spillman carousels still operating. A ride costs $1 for adults, 25¢ for children over three feet tall; children under three feet are free. Open daily June through September from 10am to 5pm; October through May, Wednesday to Sunday from 10am to 4pm.

The nearby **Children's Playground** can rightfully be called a young one's exercise complex. Several huge slides, tires for swinging, and huge wooden climbing structures beckon kids from all over the city . . . and all over the world. Outside the playground are lots of meadows for picnicking. And for the babies, there's a tiny elephant slide and low swings. This is where the **Petting Zoo** is located.

If You Have Time

You might want to visit the glass-paneled **Conservatory of Flowers** (☎ 415/666-7017), located on John F. Kennedy Drive. It's an exquisite example of Victorian architecture housing rare tropical plants. Open daily, daily 9am to 5pm. Admission is $1.50 for adults, 75¢ for seniors and children over 6; under 6, free.

You can also visit **Shakespeare's Garden,** in which all the flowers mentioned in Shakespeare's plays have a home, and the **Strybing Arboretum and Botanical Gardens,** on Martin Luther King Drive at Ninth Avenue, where plants from all over the world reside. Open weekdays from 8am to 4:30pm and weekends from 10am to 5pm. Admission is free.

Note: Weather permitting, there are also open-air performances of Shakespeare, etc., in the park. Check with the park office (☎ 415/666-7035) for details.

The **Polo Field** is a weekend haven for rugby and soccer matches. There's a track and a paved bicycle path for serious bicyclists. Polo matches can even be seen during the summer (call the park for information). **Jogging trails** and **nature trails** are located throughout the park.

In addition to the roadway, one of the best ways to see the park is to take the scenic, well-marked **bike trail.** You can start at Fell and Stanyan Streets, and wind your way down John F. Kennedy Drive, across Speedway Meadow, past the polo field to Martin Luther King Drive. The path takes you all the way to the Great Highway. (This is a good way to see the windmill.) Each Sunday John F. Kennedy Drive is closed to automobiles. This is a great area to bicycle and roller skate.

For bicycle rentals near the park, you might try **Lincoln Cyclery,** 772 Stanyan St. (☎ 415/221-2415), which rents mountain bikes and hybrid bikes at $5 per hour. They also rent children's bicycles for $3 per hour. They'll rent you a bike with a toddler carrier only if you have your own helmet. Open on Wednesday through Monday from 9am to 5pm, and on Sunday from 11:30am to 5pm; closed Tuesday.

There are free 1^1/₂-to 2-hour guided **walking tours** (☎ 415/221-1311) of specific areas of the park on weekends from May through October. See the "Family Walks" section, below, for information.

There are a few concessionaires in the park, but not many. Pack a picnic lunch or plan to eat at one of the few eateries in the De Young or Academy of Sciences compounds. Or try one of the restaurants that borders the park. There's a McDonald's on Stanyan Street at Haight Street. You're not too far from the Richmond District where there are plenty of restaurants.

How to Get There

Parking in the park is a problem. Park authorities suggest that the best place to park for the Academy of Sciences, the children's playground, Music Concourse, and Japanese Tea Garden is outside the park between 7th and 11th Avenues along Fulton Street. Then walk into the park, following directions to the Music Concourse. On Sunday, John F. Kennedy Drive is closed as far as Crossover Drive, about a mile.

You can go by bus to the park. From Market Street, take the no. 5 Fulton or the no. 21 Hayes, which runs along the north side of the park; the no. 71 Noriega runs along the south side of the park on Lincoln Avenue; or the no. 7 Haight goes to the east end of the park, from which you'll have to walk a block or two. The no. 44 O'Shaughnessy stops in the Music Concourse. Always call Muni (☎ 415/673-MUNI) to double check bus information before you go.

THE SAN FRANCISCO ZOO

If you have kids, you've probably seen more zoos than you care to count. But when you enter the San Francisco Zoo (☎ 415/753-7061, or 415/753-7083 for recorded information), you're likely to realize (as we did) that this one is really for children. Located at Sloat Boulevard and 45th Avenue, the zoo actually has places for people to roam around and enjoy themselves. A large bank of children's swings greet you as you enter the 45th Avenue entrance. Our children took off to play on the equipment, and were so content to amuse themselves that animal viewing took a back seat.

This zoo boasts more than 1,000 animals and birds, and is considered one of the best in the country. But, you say, "A zoo is a zoo." Ah, that's where you're wrong. One little innovation is the Zoo Key. You purchase a key for $1.50. At exhibits throughout the zoo there are boxes with locks. The keys slip into the locks, and with a turn, you hear an audio explanation of the animals. Children are delighted with this key, and scramble to be the one to unlock the information.

The **Children's Zoo** is a four-acre park within a park that lets your boys and girls get close to little animals. The Barnyard is the place to pet and feed the domestic barnyard animals (it's worth going in just to watch the toddlers chase the chickens and see the four- and five-year-olds feed the sheep and goats—get your camera ready!). But beware of the goats—some of them can get kind of pushy if you have food.

Our little ones love the insect zoo, and talk about it for days afterward. There is also a Baby Nursery, nature trail, and duck pond.

There's a wooden carousel near the entrance to the Children's Zoo. The restored hand-carved horses, giraffes, ostriches, and cats are works of art.

Among the major exhibits is the **Doelger Primate Discovery Center,** considered one of the most sophisticated zoological exhibits ever built. This naturalistic setting provides outdoor atriums, lush meadows, and a nocturnal gallery of 15 species of rare and endangered monkeys and prosimians. Monkeys come within touching distance behind glass walls. You see kids nose to nose with the primates. At one point, Andrew, Elizabeth, and other young children were entertained by (and were entertaining to) a group of monkeys, interacting as if they were in a dance together. This is not only a delight, but it makes the animals more real—and the term "endangered species" becomes more ominous. Included in this area is the **Phoebe Hearst Discovery Hall** of interactive exhibits, where visitors explore the fascinating world of the primates.

The cute little koalas of Australia have a home at **Koala Crossing,** one of only five United States zoos to have koalas. The exhibit is patterned after an Australian outback station. There are videotapes and graphics that help both parents and kids learn more about these likeable characters.

One of the world's largest natural gorilla exhibits, **Gorilla World** is a large stretch of outdoor area for the huge animals to roam and play in. Other exhibits include **Penguin Island, Musk Ox Meadow,** and the **Lion House** where the feedings are a *big* attraction; the trainers get all the big cats "talking" before they're fed. The **Insect Zoo** is one of four insectariums in the U.S. and includes more than 40 species. Your kids will never forget the honey bees, scorpions, and cockroaches housed here. Try to see *Incredible Insects in Action* presented daily in the summer, weekends throughout the year.

The zoo is dedicated to breeding several endangered species: gorillas, orangutans, black rhinos, snow leopards, musk oxen, and many rare insects.

A free informal walking tour of the zoo leaves from Koala Crossing at 1pm on weekends. The *Zebra Zephyr* train takes visitors on 20-minute excursions daily, except in winter when it runs only on weekends. The train tours cost $2.50 for adults and $1.50 for children. Be sure to bring clothing that can be layered; the weather can turn very chilly.

The zoo is open daily from 10am to 5pm; admission is $6.50 for adults, $3 for seniors and children 12–15, $1 for 6–11; and free for children under 5. The children's zoo is open daily in summer, and weekends year round, from 11am to 4pm; admission is $1 for everyone over age 3; children 3 and under are free.

JAPANTOWN

Entering Japantown's core, the Japan Center is like stepping into the Far East. It's a five-acre complex of restaurants, shops, and hotels. **Peace Plaza,** with its five-tiered pagoda, is a lovely spot to stop for a few minutes. Many exhibitions and festivals take place in this open-air arena.

We love Japantown on rainy days because of the huge indoor malls bordered by Post, Geary, Fillmore, and Laguna Streets. We wander around the **Japan Center** (☎ 415/922-6776), looking at Japanese arts, going into the **Kinokuniya bookstore** (☎ 415/567-7625), with a huge selection of Japanese books, or sampling the gift stores while we wait for a movie at the **AMC Kabuki 8 Theatres,** 1881 Post St., at Fillmore Street (☎ 415/931-9800). If your family likes to bowl, there's **Japantown Bowl,** 1790 Post St., at Webster Street (☎ 415/921-6200), a two-story bowling alley with 40 lanes, shoe rental, video games, coffee shop, and two bars.

GOLDEN GATE NATIONAL RECREATION AREA (GGNRA)

Not to be confused with Golden Gate Park, GGNRA is a U.S. National Park, an enormous urban coastal preserve of over 114 square miles that stretches from San Mateo County in the south, through parts of the city's waterfront including the San Francisco Maritime National Historical Park, across the Golden Gate Bridge, and north to include parts of Marin County.

Think of the entrance to San Francisco Harbor at the Golden Gate Bridge. This is part of GGNRA, and is probably the one park landmark most people know best.

Headquartered at Fort Mason (☎ 415/556-0560), this most popular of the U.S. National Parks attracts upward of 20 million visitors a year (more than twice the combined total of the Grand Canyon, Yosemite, and Cape Cod). Within its boundaries are abundant adventures for families. It offers miles of trails, ranger-conducted walks, and historical tours, all within minutes of downtown San Francisco. (Because it spans San Francisco and Marin Counties, many of the park's attractions are covered in the Sausalito Section of Chapter 3, "The Bay Area and Vicinity.") The following are the sights in San Francisco itself.

Fort Mason Center

The headquarters of the GGNRA (☎ 415/556-0560) is located here. This is where you'll want to pick up maps and other information about the GGNRA. (Public transportation is available; if you drive, parking is available.) Open weekdays from 9:30am to 4:30pm.

Anchored at Pier 3 in Fort Mason is the last unchanged ship of the fleet of 2,751 Liberty ships built for World War II. The *Jeremiah O'Brien* (☎ 415/441-3101) took only six to eight weeks to build so that it was operational during World War II. Children (and adults) are stunned by the magnitude of the vessel. You can go through the engine room and the crew's quarters, and see the captain's cabin. It's open from 9am to 3pm on weekdays, to 4pm on weekends, but call to confirm the schedule.

Fort Mason also offers beautiful picnic facilities and is a favored spot of hikers, joggers, and bicyclists. It's a link in the Golden Gate Promenade. You'll find Greens Restaurant here (see the "Where to Eat" section, above, for details).

Golden Gate Promenade

This spectacular four-mile walk is a footpath along the shoreline that takes you from Aquatic Park to Fort Point at the foot of the Golden Gate Bridge. The promenade passes Marina Green (great for kite flying), the yacht harbor, and Fort Mason, offering lovely views through the trees. You can start at Aquatic Park or Fort Point. There is parking at Fort Point, and the walk toward the city provides very dramatic views.

Fort Point (☎ 415/556-1693) is an old brick fort built between 1853 to 1861 and used during the Civil War. It's open Wednesday through Sunday from 10am to 5pm. But the best thing about Fort Point is the views of the Golden Gate Bridge and San Francisco. Be sure to go all the way out to the fort itself. If you're driving, get out of the car, even if it's cold and blustery, because it gives you fantastic views of the city and the Bay Bridge as it crosses over to the East Bay. Dress warmly, and wear comfortable walking shoes.

Cliff House and Seal Rocks

Located above Ocean Beach, the **Cliff House,** 1090 Point Lobos (☎ 415/386-3330), has some of the best views of the Golden Gate National Recreation Area. Cliff House was originally built in 1896 by one-time San Francisco mayor Adolph Sutro, a few years after he had built the Sutro Baths. The baths, which burned down in the 1960s, was a swimming/bathing complex that could accommodate 24,000 people in either saltwater or freshwater pools. The first Cliff House also burned down, but much earlier, in 1907. This is the third structure to be built on this site. The present one, opened in 1909, houses several restaurants (see the "Where to Eat" section, above), a musical museum, restrooms, and a gift shop. To get to the Cliff House, you can take Muni metro no. 18, 38, or 38L.

One of the more interesting aspects of the Cliff House is its proximity to the **Sutro Baths** ruins. Before you enter the building, look to the north and you'll see the empty shells that used to be the famous Sutro Baths. While it may be a little obscure for children to find interesting, parents can envision what it must have been like. If you can get your kids to stand still long enough, you can watch the waves rush in and out of the ruins until the motion becomes almost mesmerizing.

Cliff House is the place to view the **Seal Rocks.** This group of rocks in the ocean is home to sea lions and many birds. It's a great place to bring binoculars and watch the scenery.

Ocean Beach is a three-mile shoreline that gives you a real flavor of a San Francisco beach. You may get lots of fog, and you'll almost always get lots of wind. Although it looks lovely, the water is dangerous.

Bay Area Discovery Museum

Targeted for children from 2 to 12, the **Bay Area Discovery Museum,** 557 East Fort Baker, Sausalito (☎ 415/332-7674) is a wonderful excursion if you have children under 12. Although it's within the borders of Sausalito, we choose to put it here so that visitors who don't plan to go to Sausalito might decide to go to the museum anyway. For one thing, the location is spectacular, on the north side of the Golden Gate Bridge at historic Fort Baker, which is being restored to house the exhibitions. This museum is a *must-see.* A good children's museum is one in which learning takes place through participation, and where there are no right or wrong answers. This place, with its myriad exhibits, all of which offer alternatives and exciting ways to stretch your child's mind, is designed so that every child, no matter what his learning style is, no matter what age, will be enticed into learning—and, of course, having fun.

Some of the hands-on exhibits are "Building the City" (an architectural exhibit that allows children to build and experiment) and "San Francisco Bay" (which focuses on the interaction between people and the natural environment, including sea life, commerce, and industry connected to the sea, such as fishing and navigation, and the city high-rises that ring the bay). There is also a media center, science lab, and a walk-through maze. The museum has indoor and outdoor activities. It's open from 10am to 5pm on Tuesday through Sunday during the summer and Wednesday to Sunday during the winter.

. . . AND MORE SIGHTS

We never have enough time in the Bay Area, so we return again and again. Most often, we like to return to many of the same places. But sometimes we look for new sights. Here are some suggestions:

The **Randall (Children's) Museum,** 199 Museum Way, near Buena Vista Park (☎ 415/554-9600), has ravens, hawks, raccoons, opossum, lizards, and lots of snakes that the kids can interact with. There are a working seismograph and a dinosaur exhibit. The museum also offers special classes after school, on Saturday, and during the summer. There are special classes or programs every Saturday for free or for a small fee. Call for information.

Hours are Tuesday through Saturday from 10am to 5pm, the animal room is open from 10am to 1pm and 2 to 5pm. Admission is free.

Located in the Wells Fargo Bank, 420 Montgomery St., at California Street, the **Wells Fargo History Museum** (☎ 415/396-2619) is a large 6,000-square-foot space devoted to the Old West and the Gold Rush. Youngsters love to climb in the reproduction of the Wells Fargo Overland Stage Coach—and pretend they're back in the Old West. They can work with the telegraph and learn how to drive a team of horses. This is a fun exhibit with lots of pictures and items kids love. Open Monday through Friday from 9am to 5pm (closed bank holidays). Admission is free. You'll be surprised how much time you'll spend here.

The **Old Mint** is located at 88 5th St., at Mission Street (☎ **415/744-6830**). The museum focuses on the turn of the century, the Gold Rush, and the San Francisco earthquake. The building, built in 1874, survived the earthquake and fire, and there's a dramatic documentary film about why it survived. You'll find restored rooms and exciting displays as well as galleries with exhibits. The vaults are used like exhibit space.

The museum is open from 10am to 4pm Monday through Friday; closed weekends and holidays. Tours available. Admission is free.

The **San Francisco Fire Department Museum,** 655 Presidio Ave., at Bush Street (☎ **415/861-8000,** ext. 365), is for kids who are really into fire engines. They can see old uniforms, hand-pumps, and even fire engines (the firehouse is next door). Good for children 6 and up. Stroller-accessible. Open Thursday through Sunday from 1 to 4pm. Admission is free.

Perched on a hill in Lincoln Park is the **California Palace of the Legion of Honor,** 34th Avenue and Clement Street (☎ **415/750-3600**). It houses a collection with works from painters of the 16th through the 20th century, including such masters as Degas, Manet, Monet, and Renoir. Fans of the sculptor Rodin will delight in the extensive collection of his work here—*The Thinker,* for instance. A trip to the park is worthwhile in itself, rewarding you with a fantastic view.

The museum is under construction through 1995.

The **San Francisco Museum of Modern Art,** 151 Third St., adjacent to Yerba Buena Gardens (☎ **415/357-4000**). Although the museum's rotating exhibits of 20th-century art are low on the list of activities with young children, older ones may find the collection interesting. We saw many teens (decked out in the artiest fashions) wandering around and enjoying the exhibits, which include Matisse, Klee, Motherwell, and Pollock. The museum has a terrific book- and giftshop with a great section for children. It's open daily 11am to 6pm, until 9pm on Thursday. Closed Monday and major holidays. Admission is $7 for adults and $3.50 for seniors and students with ID; children under 13, free. It's free on the first Tuesday of each month.

PERFORMING ARTS

San Francisco offers some treats to families interested in the performing arts. If your family is culturally minded, you can take part in some of the fabulous theater and dance available here. The **San Francisco Ballet** performs at the War Memorial Opera House, Van Ness Avenue and Grove Street (☎ **415/703-9400**). Regarded as one of the country's finest ballet companies (and the oldest), the company schedules its regular season from January to May, with such classic performances as *The Sleeping Beauty* and *Romeo and Juliet.* Matinees are on Saturday and Sunday at 2pm. The price of tickets ranges from $7 to $80. During December there are 34 performances of *The Nutcracker,* followed by Sugar Plum Parties after selected matinee performances.

The **American Conservatory Theater (A.C.T.),** performing at the Stage Door Theater, Marines Memorial Theatre, and the Orpheum Theatre (☎ **415/749-2228**), is a nationally known repertory company and winner of a 1979 Tony Award. Productions range from the classics (Shakespeare and Shaw) to modern dramatists (Coward and Shepard). Matinees are on Wednesday and Saturday at 2pm, and on Sunday at 3pm. During the months of November and December, *A Christmas Carol* is presented. There are more matinees for the Dickens classic.

The **Curran Theater,** at 445 Geary St. (☎ **415/474-3800**), the **Golden Gate Theater,** at 25 Taylor St. (☎ **415/474-3800**), and the **Orpheum,** at 1192 Market

St., at Hyde Street (☎ 415/474-3800), are three other theaters that run Broadway productions such as *Cats, H.M.S. Pinafore,* and feature such leading entertainers as Linda Ronstadt. Matinees are held on Wednesday, Saturday, and Sunday. Prices vary dramatically. Call for information.

Beach Blanket Babylon, at Club Fugazi, 678 Green St., near Columbus Avenue (☎ 415/421-4222), is a 90-minute fantasy-filled mini-extravaganza. This upbeat colorful show is San Francisco's longest-running legitimate musical revue. Minors are welcome at Sunday matinees at 3pm. A good entertainment for kids over 13. At all other shows the minimum age is 21. Prices range from $17 to $40 per ticket. Reservations are advised.

And for comedy, there's **Cobb's Comedy Club,** at the Cannery (☎ 415/928-4320), a place we love to come with our teens, though no one under 16 is allowed. The comedy here is rarely off-color, although you should call ahead to see what the program includes. Tell them you're bringing your teenager and ask them if they think the act is appropriate. The cover charge is $5–$12; there's a two-drink minimum.

Children also love the **Young Performers Theater,** at Fort Mason Center (☎ 415/346-5550). Professional adult actors and children who come from the theater's conservatory program perform six main stage shows throughout the year. In the past they've done such variety as *Mother Goose, Inc.* (a young people's version of *The Tempest*), *Peter and the Wolf,* and an adapted version of Chaucer called *Chaucer in a Mud Pit.* Performances take place at Fort Mason, Building C, third floor. Prices are $7 for adults, $5 for children under 13.

SPORTING EVENTS

San Francisco is home to several national sports teams. Will the **San Francisco Giants** baseball team continue to play at Candlestick Park? At this point they're still negotiating, so call to be sure. The **San Francisco 49ers** football team plays its home games in Candlestick Park (☎ 415/468-2249). Across the bay, Oakland is the home of the **Oakland A's** baseball team; they play at the Oakland Coliseum (☎ 510/638-0500). The **Golden State Warriors** basketball team plays at the Oakland Coliseum (☎ 510/638-6300).

SPECIAL ACTIVITIES

In a city with so much to do, we love to combine activities so we can do more.

Family Walks

Walking anywhere in the city is a treat, but we especially love the following walks. A walk across the **Golden Gate Bridge** is an outing you'll never forget. On the 1.7-mile bridge you'll be able to see the area around Fisherman's Wharf and the skyline, as well as Angel Island and Alcatraz. Looking north, you can see Marin County and much of the Golden Gate National Recreation Area. Looking back to the city, you'll get incredibly beautiful vistas at the north edge of the bridge.

There are vista points on both sides of the bridge. The one on the Marin side is where you take the spectacular photos of the bridge with the city in the background. There are also barbecue tables and drinking fountains here.

If you're going to walk on the Golden Gate Bridge, bundle up because it's always windy and often very cold. In fact, you should be sure to bring layers of clothing—the best way to keep warm. We love to take this walk on overcast, drizzly days because it seems more scenic. Even on dismal days, you see fathers and mothers holding their children's hands as they walk across the pedestrianway. This is a good time to bring your slickers, because the rain and wind make an umbrella useless.

Another of our favorite places to walk is **Clement Street** in the Richmond District. Clement Street is known for the many shops, restaurants, and diverse cultural influences that characterize it. From Arguello Boulevard, the north or lower end of Clement Street, all the way to 15th Avenue, you'll find some of the best toy stores, book stores, antiques shops, produce markets, and restaurants in San Francisco.

In just the first ten blocks, from Arguello Boulevard to Tenth Avenue, on Clement Street, there are Chinese, Indonesian, Vietnamese, Thai, Persian, Italian, and French restaurants. In fact, it's becoming known as the second Chinatown. This neighborhood is very family oriented—you'll see children on the streets, in the stores, and in most restaurants throughout early evening.

The parking situation is bad, but traffic is not downtown-like heavy and fast. A midwesterner should be at home here—and might want to come out to the Richmond District on a Saturday in order to get away from the downtown congestion.

Golden Gate Park is an easy six blocks east of Clement Street. Anyone who is hungry or still restless after a day there should come here. Beware of the daytime weather, though. Even when it's warm and sunny elsewhere, it can be cooler and foggy here. At night, everywhere in San Francisco is chilly.

Green Apple Books, 506 Clement St., at Sixth Avenue (☎ 415/387-2272), is one of those places we like as much as the kids do. It's a book lover's dream that welcomes browsers and readers into the stacks of new and used books. There's a terrific children's section too. Plan to stay a while. Open Sunday through Thursday from 10am to 10pm, on Friday and Saturday till midnight.

If for some reason you don't have a meal while you're on Clement Street, at least don't miss the treats at the **Toy Boat** (see the "Where to Eat" section, above).

WALKING TOURS   The **Friends of Recreation and Parks** in Golden Gate Park (☎ 415/221-1311) lead free guided walking, bike, and bus tours on Saturday and Sunday. Call for specific times. May through October, rain or shine. The walks include the Strawberry Hill Tour; Huntington Falls, Stow Lake, the Chinese Pavilion, and a walk up to the top of Strawberry Hill; the East End Tour: Conservatory Valley, Children's Playground, Hippie Hill, the Rhododendron Garden, and the Music Concourse.

City Guides (☎ 415/557-4266) offers a wide variety of free guided walking tours. Tours include the Gold Rush City Tour, City Hall Tour, Fire Department Museum, North Beach Walk, Japantown, the Presidio, Coit Tower, and various mansions and Victorian homes in the city.

Swimming Beaches

Although the area is surrounded by an enticing seashore, San Francisco has only two swimming beaches that you might try. **Aquatic Park,** located at the foot of Polk Street, offers lagoon swimming and fishing. There are restrooms and showers, and lifeguards are on duty from mid-April to mid-October. **China Beach,** located near Seacliff (☎ 415/556-8371), is a small sandy area with showers and restrooms.

Skyrooms

Brunch is a good time to enjoy some of the famous skyrooms that are a little too pricey for dinner, while drinking in fabulous views at the same time. Children are allowed in the skyrooms as long as food is served there, so don't be shy. If you don't want to go for brunch, you and the kids can go for an early-evening nonalcoholic cocktail hour, too. Here are some of the skyrooms we like.

Victor's, in the Westin St. Francis Hotel, Powell Street at Geary Street (☎ 415/956-7777), serves a Sunday champagne brunch from 10am to 3pm.

Cityscape, on the 46th floor of the San Francisco Hilton & Tower, 333 O'Farrell St. (☎ 415/776-0215), serves a Sunday champagne-and-orange-juice brunch with a live band, and an à la carte dinner nightly from 5:30pm. Children under 12 pay half price.

Equinox, in the Hyatt Regency Hotel, Five Embarcadero Center (☎ 415/788-1234), serves brunch, lunch, dinner, and cocktails, and the revolving platform offers a wondrous 360° view.

And Something Really Special

Another fun special activity is a **Hornblower Dining Yacht Champagne Brunch** at Pier 33, on the Embarcadero (☎ 415/394-8900, ext. 7), a two-hour cruise on San Francisco Bay with a champagne brunch, live music, and glorious views from every table.

The sights and natural beauty of the bay are really enhanced by the casual, leisurely atmosphere of the activities on board. The ship is a three-level yacht, with outside decks and indoor dining rooms and bar on each. The Pilot House is at the top. Each dining room has its own staff, live music, and buffet tables. And brunch is a gourmet affair, served the entire trip. There's something for everybody: green salads, pasta salads, eggs Benedict, loads of fresh fruit slices, and beautiful tiny custard tarts with fresh strawberries on top. Our ten-year-old couldn't stay away from the five or six different kinds of pastries and cakes and the all-you-can-eat idea.

The captain and crew are friendly, knowledgeable, and caring. A trip upstairs to the pilot house, where the boat is steered, reveals lots of kids waiting patiently for their turn to navigate the ship's course. A crew member reminded us of possibly the only kid-type hazard aboard: wear rubber-soled shoes, not patent leather!

The weekend brunch cruise sails on Saturday and Sunday from 11am to 1pm, at a cost of $31 (on Saturday) or $36 (on Sunday) for adults; children under 12 are half price. Reservations are required. Dinner and luncheon cruises also available.

Shopping

Yes, we consider shopping for books and toys an essential activity! And there are many places to get great toys while the kids have a good time looking.

Embarcadero Center (☎ 415/772-0500) is a five-block shopping-center complex that has more than 140 retail shops, restaurants, and galleries. The Hyatt Regency is part of the complex. What we love most about this place is the huge open-air plaza. Birds flock there; skateboarders congregate. Here is the famous Vaillancourt Fountain, a strange-looking concrete jumble that fascinates children and parents alike. It's a wonderful place to romp and spend time. There are often midday performances or concerts. We make a few hours of it by also walking into the Hyatt Regency and wandering through the spectacular 17-story atrium lobby.

F.A.O. Schwarz Fifth Avenue, 48 Stockton St., at Stockton and O'Farrell Streets (☎ 415/394-8700), is a branch of the famous New York toy store. This large shop has a great array of toys and games from around the world. It's open Monday through Saturday 10am to 7pm; and on Sunday from 11am to 6pm.

Another delightful place is **Quinby's,** 3411 California St., in the Laurel Village Shopping Center (☎ 415/751-7727). It features one of the largest selections of children's books and educational materials in the Bay Area. Calling itself a place "for the curious child," Quinby's specializes in books and products designed to make family travel easier—items like cassette tapes, sticker books, magnetic games, Mad Libs, and maze and puzzle books for the plane, train, or car journey. Other available products are arts-and-crafts supplies, puzzles, activity items, and educational material.

Quinby's also has workshops and arts-and-crafts activities on Saturday. Call for their schedule of special events. Hours are 9:30am to 6pm Monday through Saturday and 11am to 5pm on Sunday.

INDOOR ACTIVITIES

Rain or fog got you down? There are plenty of indoor activities in the San Francisco area. In addition to the major indoor attractions, the California Academy of Science, the De Young and Asian Art Museums, and the Exploratorium, you can spend some time in these places:

Libraries

The **Main Children's Room,** Civic Center Library, at the corner of Larkin and McAllister Streets (☎ **415/557-4554**), is open on Monday, Wednesday, Thursday, and Saturday from 10am to 6pm, on Tuesday from noon to 9pm, and on Friday from noon to 6pm. Family storytime is on Saturday at 10:30am and the chess club for children meets on Friday from 3 to 6pm. The **Marina Branch,** 1890 Chestnut St. (☎ **415/346-9336**), and the **Richmond Branch,** 351 Ninth Ave. (☎ **415/752-1240**), also have children's reading rooms. Call for hours.

Unusual Hotel Lobbies

For children who are interested in architecture, or if you're interested in heightening their awareness, you can spend a delightful couple of hours in three outstanding hotel lobbies, and enjoy this unusual indoor activity.

We start off with the **Hyatt Regency San Francisco,** Five Embarcadero Center (☎ **415/788-1234**), and let the kids wander through the futuristic lobby. This is a place they can enjoy even if they're active because it's like a little city. Be sure they go for a ride in the elevators up to the top and catch the great view.

Next we head for the **Westin St. Francis Hotel,** 335 Powell St. (☎ **415/397-7000**). Or if you have quiet children, we also love the **Mark Hopkins,** 1 Nob Hill (☎ **415/392-3434,** or toll free **800/327-0200**), where the children can see splendid examples of ornate, stately decor. The Mark Hopkins is much smaller and intimate, with blazing crystal chandeliers and palatial furnishings.

Finally, we head for the understated elegance of the **Four Seasons Clift,** 495 Geary St. (☎ **415/775-4700,** or toll free **800/332-3442**), by which time the children have spent most of their energy and are ready to sit for a little while. Most often, we take tea in the small lobby, nibbling on cucumber sandwiches or scones and people-watching—always pretending that we're actually in London. Occasionally we sit in the art deco Redwood Room. If we're lucky, we've timed it so we can have high tea, served Monday through Saturday.

NEIGHBORHOOD PARKS

San Francisco has hundreds of acres of parks to enjoy. Here are a few we like:

Huntington Park is a few blocks from Union Square—in a beautiful setting atop Nob Hill. The kids can play on the equipment while you look at the city skyline, lavish hotels, and the beautiful facade of Grace Cathedral.

Marina Green has acres for running and Frisbee throwing. And it's a good place to watch some top-notch windsurfers. From the park, you can watch flocks of seagulls swooping down and see the boats cross the bay to Larkspur and Sausalito. It's certainly beautiful, even if a bit overcast and gray. At those times you can watch birds lighting on white-capped water. When it's very windy, the surf splashes up on the parking lot and kite acrobatics decorate the sky.

Alta Plaza is a gorgeous, quiet little park at Clay and Scott Streets. Pathways lead up to the top of a steep hill, giving a crisscross effect. You get fabulous views of the bay and Marin County as you come over the hill on Scott. This is a great park to walk through.

ANNUAL EVENTS AND FESTIVALS

You might say that every day there is a special event or festival in San Francisco. The city is alive with street performers, vendors, and all manner of ethnic pride celebrations. Here are some of the highlights of the year:

Chinese New Year Celebration (January or February). There are all kinds of festivities, culminating with the Chinese New Year Carnival. (Call **415/982-3071** for details.)

St. Patrick's Day Celebration (March). A Sunday parade kicks off the event, which includes flag-raising ceremonies at the Civic Center and festivities at the United Irish Cultural Center. (For more information call **415/467-8218**).

Cherry Blossom Festival (April) in Japantown. This annual event includes Japanese performers and a wonderful parade. (Call **415/922-6776** for details.)

Cinco de Mayo Parade and Celebration (May) in the Mission District. There are two days of cultural activities and entertainment. The fiesta queen is crowned. (Call **415/826-1401** for details.)

Carnaval (May) in the Mission District. This Mardi Gras–like street festival includes a parade, music, dance, and costume contest. (Call **415/826-1401**).

Renaissance Pleasure Faire (August) in Novato. (Call **415/892-0937** for details.)

Columbus Day Celebration (October). See "Queen Isabella's" coronation, civic ceremonies, a landing pageant, Sunday parade, and the blessing of the fishing fleet. (Call **415/434-1492**).

Fleet Week (October). This festival honors the U.S. Navy. There are aerial performances and a parade of naval vessels through the Golden Gate. (Call **415/765-6056.**)

For information on any of these events, you can write for a copy of *The San Francisco Book*. Send $1 to the San Francisco Visitor Information Center, P.O. Box 6977, San Francisco, CA 94101. Or you can call **415/391-2000** for a recorded description of current events.

ACTIVITIES BY AGE GROUP

The following listings suggest activities divided into specific age brackets. Refer back to the individual descriptions for details and any age restrictions.

Teens and Preteens

Alcatraz Island
American Conservatory Theater
Bay Area Discovery Museum

Bay Cruises
Beach Blanket Babylon
Cable Car Museum
California Palace of the Legion of Honor
The Cannery
Chinatown (including the Chinese Culture Center, Chinese Historical Society,
   the Chinese New Year festivities, Culinary Walks, and Heritage Walks)
Cobb's Comedy Club
Curran Theater
Exploratorium
Fire Department Museum
Fisherman's Wharf
Ghirardelli Square
Golden Gate National Recreation Area (including the Cliff House, Fort Point,
   and the World War II ship *Jeremiah O'Brien*)
Golden Gate Park (including the Asian Art Museum, California Academy of
   Sciences, Conservatory of Flowers, De Young Museum, Japanese Tea Garden,
   Morrison Planetarium and Laserium, Spreckles Lake, Steinhart Aquarium,
   Stow Lake, and Strybing Arboretum)
Golden Gate Theater
Guinness Museum of World Records
The Old Mint
Pier 39
Ripley's Believe It or Not! Museum
San Francisco Ballet
San Francisco Museum of Modern Art
San Francisco Maritime National Historical Park
U.S.S. *Pampanito*
Wax Museum
Wells Fargo History Museum

School-Age Kids

Alcatraz Island
Aquatic Park
Bay Area Discovery Museum
Bay Cruises
Cable Car Museum
The Cannery
Chinatown (including the Chinese Culture Center, Chinese Historical Society,
   Chinese New Year festivities, Culinary Walks, and Heritage Walks)
Curran Theater
Exploratorium
Fire Department Museum
Fisherman's Wharf
Ghirardelli Square (including the Chocolate Manufactory)
Golden Gate National Recreation Area (including the Cliff House, Fort Point, and
   the World War II ship *Jeremiah O'Brien*)

Golden Gate Park (including the California Academy of Sciences, Children's Playground, Japanese Tea Garden, Morrison Planetarium and Laserium, Spreckles Lake, Steinhart Aquarium, and Stow Lake)
Guinness Museum of World Records
The Old Mint
Pier 39
Randall (Children's) Museum
Ripley's Believe It or Not! Museum
San Francisco Ballet
San Francisco Maritime National Historical Park
San Francisco Zoo (including the Children's Zoo)
U.S.S. *Pampanito*
Wax Museum
Wells Fargo History Museum
Young Performers Theater

Preschoolers

Aquatic Park
Bay Area Discovery Museum
The Cannery
Chinatown
Fire Department Museum
Fisherman's Wharf
Ghirardelli Square (including the Chocolate Manufactory)
Golden Gate Park (including the California Academy of Sciences, the Children's Playground, Steinhart Aquarium, and Stow Lake)
Pier 39
Randall (Children's) Museum
San Francisco Maritime National Historical Park
San Francisco Zoo (including the Children's Zoo)
Wells Fargo History Museum
Young Performers Theater

In Case of Emergency

Just in case of trouble, here are a few resources you might need to know about:

Police, Fire, Ambulance

For the police, fire department, or medical emergencies, call **911.**

Hospitals

The **Medical Center at the University of California,** 505 Parnassus Ave., at Third Avenue (☎ **415/476-1000** or **415/476-1037),** for 24-hour emergency care; **San Francisco General Hospital Medical Center,** 1001 Potrero Ave. (☎ **415/206-8000**), for 24-hour emergency service and trauma facilities; **St. Francis Memorial Hospital,** 900 Hyde St., on Nob Hill (☎ **415/775-4321**), for 24-hour emergency service; **Mount Zion Hospital and Medical Center,** 1600 Divisadero St. (☎ **415/885-7520**), for 24-hour emergency service; and **Pacific Presbyterian Medical Center,** 2300 Sacramento St., at Buchanan Street (☎ **415/923-3333**), for 24-hour emergency service.

24-Hour Pharmacies

The following pharmacies are open 24 hours daily: **Walgreen's Drugstore,** 500 Geary St., Union Square (☎ **415/673-8411** or **415/673-8413**); open Monday through Friday from 9am to 9pm, on Saturday from 9am to 5pm, and on Sunday from 10am to 6pm; and **Walgreen's Drugstore,** 3201 Divisadero St., near the Marina (☎ **415/931-6415**).

3

The Bay Area and Vicinity

THE BAY AREA TOWNS THAT RADIATE FROM SAN FRANCISCO ARE AS DIVERSE AS THE cosmopolitan city itself. Within 30 minutes of San Francisco you can choose from a rainbow of activities.

To the east is the college town of Berkeley, home of the world-renowned University of California. Well worth a day trip, this colorful community reflects the youthful intellectual life at its center. It has some wonderful family outings as well. Neighboring Oakland, the largest city in the East Bay, is a major industrial port.

To the north, Marin County offers a completely different atmosphere. Known for some of the most expensive real estate in the country, it has exquisite oceanfront scenery, charming villages, majestic woods, and unparalleled views of San Francisco and the bay.

1 Berkeley

The city of Berkeley grew up around the University of California. While the town is an old, established community, it has an intellectual, innovative core that is youthful and forward-looking. In fact, some people say that if everything happens first in California, it gets its start in Berkeley. Think of hippies and the Free Speech Movement, and you automatically think of Berkeley. When bare feet, long hair, and women in "men's jobs" were creating controversy in other places, people here were blasé.

Even today a day in Berkeley is like spending time in a small, almost foreign, enclave where much of the population is under 30, and vestiges of the counterculture movement of the 1960s are still evident. Street vendors selling candles and jewelry line Telegraph Avenue. Musicians play on street corners and at lower Sproul Plaza. Political activism is still evident in the rallies and speeches given at the entrance to the university. And you might happen upon an impromptu jazz concert.

Coffeehouses, bookstores, and cafés dot the community around the campus, reflecting the student environment. And while you shouldn't miss the glorious campus, save a little time for some of the other family activities.

To get to Berkeley, take the San Francisco–Oakland Bay Bridge to I-80 east. Exit at University Avenue and go all the way to Oxford Avenue. Locals refer to parts of town as Northside and Southside. This refers to north and south of University Avenue near the campus.

If you're coming from San Francisco, you can take **BART** (☎ **415/788-BART**) or **AC Transit** (☎ **415/839-2882**).

WHAT TO SEE AND DO

Let's start with the probable reason you've crossed the bridge.

The University of California at Berkeley

Nestled at the foot of the Berkeley hills at Bancroft and Telegraph Avenues, the University of California at Berkeley (☎ **510/642-6000**) is one of the finest universities in the world. With an enrollment of over 30,000 students, it's also one of the largest. The University of California charter was signed in 1868, and this, the first campus of the U.C. system, opened in 1873.

The campus itself is beautiful, filled with distinguished-looking buildings, redwood and oak trees, a delightful creek, and views of the San Francisco Bay. A walking tour is the best way to see it. We'll start our tour on Southside. There is street or meter parking, and some parking lots are available.

Take a little while to wander along Telegraph Avenue. Some people refer to it as a sideshow at the circus complete with hippie-looking characters, vendors, and street people. Whatever your impressions, it's certainly unusual. Then make your way north to the intersection of Telegraph and Bancroft Avenues.

Just past the entrance is **Sproul Plaza,** the most famous area of campus, home of many demonstrations in years past. To your left (west) is the **Martin Luther King Jr. Student Union.** The building to your right (east) is **Sproul Hall,** the administration building. This is the place where the Free Speech Movement began in 1964. Even today this is a center for political and social activities. Rallies occur on a regular basis, and more than 20 tables are set up by organizations and political groups on campus, offering information and conversation. On any given day you'll see such diversity of interests as the Indian Students Group, the Christian Fellowship Society, the Peace Corps, the Young Republicans, the Jewish Student Union, even the Society for Creative Anachronisms.

At the foot of Sproul Steps is **Ludwig's Fountain,** a place where students dangle their feet in the water on hot days. If you look north, you'll see a white stone gate with baroque grillwork. This is **Sather Gate,** a traditional symbol of the university, and still one of the most popular meeting spots on campus.

Just before you get to Sather Gate, there's a path that runs east-west along Sproul Hall. Take that toward the hills (heading east). As you continue, you'll see several interesting buildings.

Along the left, redwoods, oaks, and pines grace your walk. You're now at **Strawberry Creek.** There's a trail along the creek if you wish to walk there. The large, grassy hill called **Faculty Glade** is a great place for the kids to play. You'll see **Stephens Hall,** a Tudor Gothic, built in 1923. The **Faculty Club** is to your east, built by world-famous architect Bernard Maybeck in 1903.

Take the bridge to the north over Strawberry Creek (watch the kids over this bridge—it's a high drop) and keep walking toward Sather Tower, better known as the **Campanile.** This is the most famous landmark of the university. Modeled after St. Mark's Campanile in Venice, it was built in 1914. For 50¢ you get a great ride to the top, where a heart-stopping view greets you. Kids love to ride to the top of the bell tower, and you can see San Francisco, the Golden Gate Bridge, and Marin County. The bells strike every hour, and are played every day at 7:50am, noon, and 6pm. The four clock faces can be seen everywhere in town.

If you look to the west, you'll see the oldest building on campus, **South Hall.** Built in 1873, it is, in fact, the oldest building in the entire University of California system.

Keep walking north to University Drive. Turn right (east). Soon you'll come to the Mining Circle. There is a lily pond and a grassy area. On the north is the **Hearst Mining Building,** built in 1907 in the Italian Renaissance style. Inside are pictures of the California Gold Rush.

Go back to University Drive and walk down to the large white building on your left (south). There are large, sweeping marble stairs to the entrance. This is the **Main Library,** built in 1911, and you'll want to walk inside. You can see the rounding of the marble steps from the thousands of students moving in and out of this entrance. The Berkeley campus has over seven million books—and this library houses many of them.

Take the stairs up to the circulation and reference room. Look up. This has to be the most beautiful room on campus. Three-story windows flank the entire north wall, and four-story arched windows adorn the west and east walls. The card catalog, made of oak, looks as if it spans a football field.

Leave the library by the same sweeping steps. The street in front of you is University Drive. Take it west, over the bridge, and keep walking until you find yourself at West Circle. From here, walk south past the **Life Science Building.** You'll find yourself in the eucalyptus grove as well as at the south fork of Strawberry Creek. Kids love this area.

Cross over the creek again and there'll be a fork in the walk area. Veer to your left and you should see the **Alumni House** on your right. Keep walking and you'll be at Lower Sproul Plaza, back where you started. You might want to talk with someone at the Visitor Information Center, 101 University Hall, 2200 University Ave. (☎ **510/642-5215**). They offer tours and booklets for self-guided tours.

Lawrence Hall of Science (☎ **510/642-5133**) is a hands-on science center located in the hills above the university on Centennial Drive south of Grizzly Peak Boulevard. Part of the University of California, it is dedicated to educating children (and adults) about science, and serves as a resource for public schools.

Kids of all ages are intrigued by the many unusual, imaginative exhibits. For example, there's an exhibit that shows how lasers are used. Kids can control the laser beam and create their own light shows. Another popular exhibit is about holograms, with information about how they are made. Visitors from out-of-state are fascinated by the earthquake exhibit, which maps out the earthquake faults and includes a working seismic recorder. Other displays offer colorful computer-activated games on many different scientific topics. A permanent exhibit is "Within the Human Brain." It includes a giant-size brain model and a color brain imager that lets visitors view the biochemical activity of the brain.

There's an ongoing schedule of temporary participatory exhibits, including a popular animated life-size dinosaur exhibit that has *Triceratops* babies and a huge *Tyrannosaurus rex.*

The hall presents special events during the summer and on weekends and holidays. There are biology labs where children can touch frogs, chinchillas, rabbits, tarantulas, and other animals. The Wizard's Lab has physics gadgets and gizmos so children can learn more about magnetism, electricity, motion. There are daily planetarium shows during the summer and on weekends and holidays. The Discovery Corner sells science kits, games, and books that are difficult to find elsewhere. The shop also has science-oriented cassette tapes.

Lawrence Hall is open from 10am to 5 daily. Admission is $5 for adults. Seniors and children are $3; students are $4. There is complete stroller access. Labs are available on a drop-in basis. Call for information about one-hour workshops and planetarium shows.

At the head of Strawberry Canyon is the **University of California Botanical Gardens.** This 30-acre garden was started in 1890, and serves as a laboratory as well as a garden. It contains more than 8,000 species, totaling more than 50,000 plants, including rare rhododendrons, cacti and succulents, and a rain forest house. Open daily from 9am to 4:45pm. Guided tours are offered on the weekend. For more information about these docent-led tours, call **510/642-3343.** There is no admission charge.

Charles Lee Tilden Regional Park

Located in the rolling hills behind Berkeley, 2,078-acre Charles Lee Tilden Regional Park is a favorite with local East Bay families, and the lucky visitors who know about it. Known for good hiking trails (beware of poison ivy, though), lake swimming, a golf course, equestrian trails, pony rides, a Hershell Spillman merry-go-round (with antique hand-carved animals), a botanic garden, several playgrounds, and a nature area

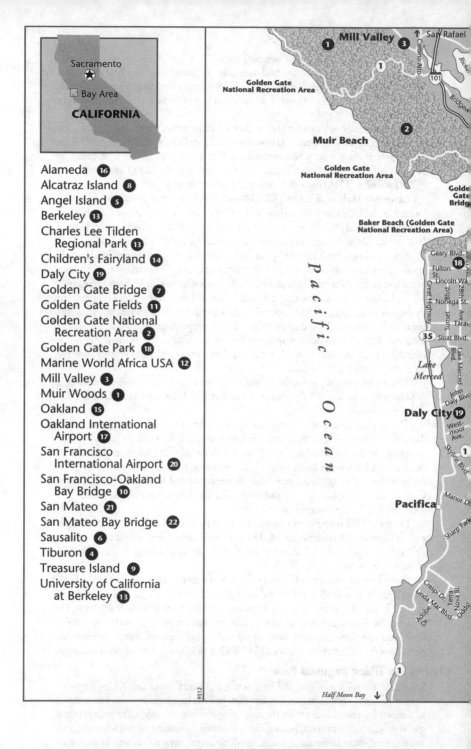

Sacramento

Bay Area

CALIFORNIA

Mill Valley

San Rafael

Golden Gate
National Recreation Area

Muir Beach

Golden Gate
National Recreation Area

Golden
Gate
Bridge

Baker Beach (Golden Gate
National Recreation Area)

Geary Blvd.

Fulton
St.
Lincoln Way

Noriega St.

Taraval

Sloat Blvd.

Lake
Merced

Daly City

West-
moor
Ave.

Pacifica

Half Moon Bay

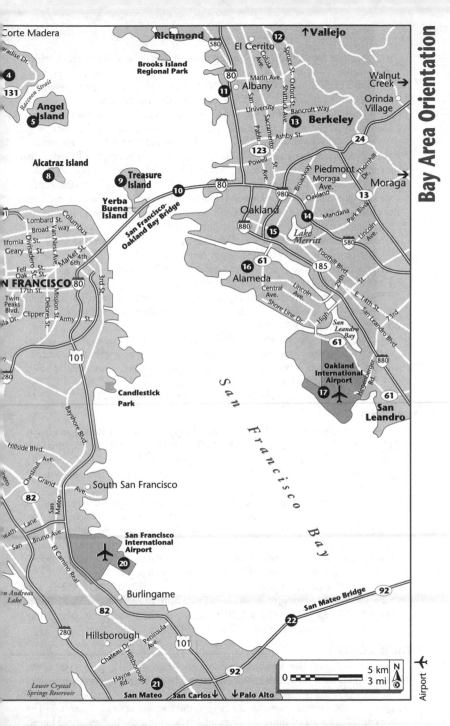

with a petting farm. Tilden also has an Environmental Education Center, which offers naturalist-led programs.

Tilden's **Lake Anza** (☎ 510/848-3385) offers beach sunbathing and swimming from May through October. There is a shallow area that's roped off for children, which offers great swimming even for toddlers. Lifeguards are on duty in summer daily from 11am to 6pm. The admission fee is $2 for adults, $1 for children and seniors.

One of our favorite areas is the **Nature Area,** where the **Little Farm** is located. Here, kids can see cows, pigs, goats, donkeys, and a variety of bunnies. Periodic programs have children come to the early-morning barnyard feed where they can get out there with the animals. **Jewel Lake** is a small area that has a self-guiding trail, perfect for little ones, and the **Environmental Education Center** holds at least one interpretive program each Saturday and Sunday. Naturalists will often bring out animals (a big favorite are the snakes) for the children to see and learn about. Hikes are frequently offered. Most of the events are free. For program information, call **510/525-2233.**

The **pony rides** are within walking distance from the Nature Area, and the **merry-go-round** is about five minutes away by car. The pony rides are open from 11am to 5pm daily during spring and summer vacation. Rides are $2. Call **510/527-0421** for more information. The merry-go-round operates from 10am to 5pm weekends and some holidays, and daily during spring and summer vacation. The charge is $1 per ride (☎ 510/524-6773).

Little Train is another favorite. This miniature version of a steam train is located at the southern end of the park. It operates from 11am to 6pm weekends and holidays all year, as well as weekdays during spring and summer vacation. A ride costs $1.50 (☎ **510/548-6100**).

For park information and directions to Tilden, call **510/525-2233.**

For a Treat

For an incredible children's bookstore, **Mr. Mopps' Children's Books and Toys,** 1405 Martin Luther King Jr. Way (☎ **510/525-9633**), is a delight for inspiring children to read. The huge bookstore has books for infants to 12th-graders, arranged in a room away from the toys. Open from 9:30am to 5:30pm Monday through Saturday; closed Sunday.

If you're looking for a good little toy store, **Sweet Dreams Toy Store,** at 2921 College Ave., and **Sweet Dreams Candy Shop,** at 2901 College Ave. (☎ **510/548-TOYS**), have large, colorful stuffed animals and rows and rows of delicious candies. The stores don't have a lot of traditional toys: They're more like a kid's heaven with tiny trinkets and barrels of trendy little goodies. Open Monday through Saturday from 10am to 6pm and on Sunday from noon to 6pm.

Cody's Bookstore, located at 2454 Telegraph Ave. (☎ **510/845-7852**), is also a delight; it is one of the great bookstores. Open daily 10am to 10pm. **Moe's Bookstore,** 2476 Telegraph Ave. (☎ **510/849-2087**), is another treasure. A multilevel store that's amazingly complete, it's open daily from 10am to 11pm.

WHERE TO STAY

Some visitors to the Bay Area prefer to stay in Berkeley, where the pace is slower and there is more open space than in San Francisco. The 20-minute ride (without traffic) on the San Francisco–Oakland Bay Bridge into the city makes sightseeing in San Francisco very convenient. Generally, the rates in the East Bay are a bit lower, too. The accommodations are all conveniently located. There are many budget-priced motels

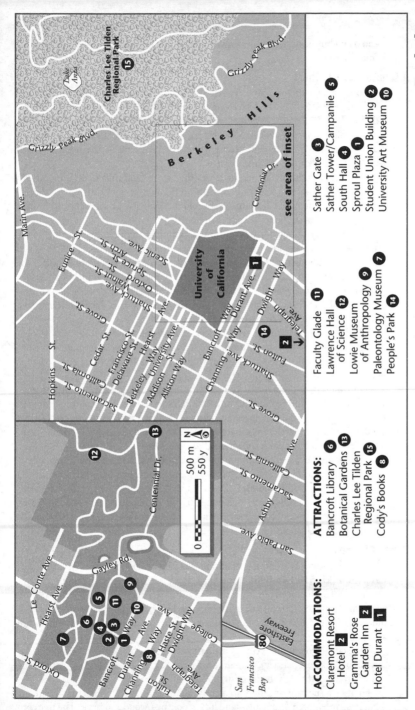

Berkeley

ACCOMMODATIONS:
Claremont Resort Hotel **2**
Gramma's Rose Garden Inn **2**
Hotel Durant **1**

ATTRACTIONS:
Bancroft Library **6**
Botanical Gardens **13**
Charles Lee Tilden Regional Park **15**
Cody's Books **8**

Faculty Glade **11**
Lawrence Hall of Science **12**
Lowie Museum of Anthropology **9**
Paleontology Museum **7**
People's Park **14**

Sather Gate **3**
Sather Tower/Campanile **5**
South Hall **4**
Sproul Plaza **1**
Student Union Building **2**
University Art Museum **10**

located on University Avenue, but we suggest that you personally inspect them before booking a room.

A Grand Resort Hotel

The only resort in the San Francisco Bay area is located at the foot of the Oakland-Berkeley hills. The **Claremont Resort and Spa,** 41 Tunnel Rd., Berkeley (☎ **510/843-3000;** for reservations, write to P.O. Box 23363, Oakland, CA 94623), is a classically beautiful Victorian hotel that has hosted the likes of Cornelius Vanderbilt and Eleanor Roosevelt. The imposing white structure with its lavish grounds and facilities has quite a colorful history.

In the 1870s a former farmer made wealthy by the California Gold Rush bought 40 acres of land on which he built a mansion (known as the Castle) and elaborate gardens for his wife. When his wife died he sold the property, which eventually burned to the ground, leaving only the stables and barn.

The property changed hands and was sold to a group of entrepreneurs, whose vision included development of a line on the electric rail system that would end at a grand hotel. Although construction was started, severe financial problems beset the partners. Local gossip says that the three owners decided that the winner of a checkers (or dominoes) match would take possession of the hotel! One owner emerged, and was finally able to finish the hotel just before the 1915 Panama-Pacific International Exposition held in San Francisco.

The hotel has had several owners and many changes since that time. In 1971 it underwent a $20-million renovation, and in 1982 guest room renovation was completed. In 1988 complete spa facilities were added, and a renovation program is ongoing.

This full-service hotel offers room service from 6am to midnight, and there are several snack bars and restaurants with children's selections. For sporting activities, there are 10 tennis courts, a gorgeous outdoor Olympic-size swimming pool with a children's area, a Jacuzzi, exercise parcourse, and complete spa facilities. Nightly turndown service is offered, with fruit instead of chocolates.

The rooms are tastefully appointed; all are spacious, and have hill views, televisions with Spectra Vision, and individual coffee makers. Suites have refrigerators; you can request one for other rooms.

Rooms rent for $149–$219 single and $169–$229 double. Suites run $235–$800. Children under 18 stay free in their parents' room. Cribs are free, but rollaways cost $10 per night. Ask about specials.

Other Choices

The **Hotel Durant** is a Berkeley tradition. Located at 2600 Durant Ave., Berkeley, CA 94704 (☎ **510/845-8981**), one block from the University of California campus, the Durant has been hosting visitors to the area for more than 60 years. It is *the* accommodation to the south side of the campus. This European-style hotel has a small, quiet lobby and is a good place to stay if your children don't need a lot of room to run around.

The stately Durant offers complimentary continental breakfast, valet and laundry service, parking ($5 per day), and airport service (for an additional fee). Babysitting can be arranged through the front desk.

Henry's restaurant and pub are similar to a San Francisco fern bar. There are Tiffany-style lamps, cluster tables, and lots of polished wood and brass. The free continental breakfast is served from 7 to 10am. Henry's has highchairs and booster seats, but no children's menu; it's best for kids during the breakfast period. As the day wears on, college students frequent the eatery and bar, making it smoky and noisy.

The Hotel Durant has 140 rooms, each of which has a color television, free Showtime and pay-per-view, and AM/FM radio, but no air conditioning. Many of the rooms have a view of the University of California campus or the bay.

Rooms cost $87–$107 single and $102–$127 double. Suites run $112–$240. Children under 12 stay free in their parents' room; children 12 and over and additional adults pay $15 each per night. No charge for cribs.

Gramma's Rose Garden Inn, 2740 Telegraph Ave., Berkeley, CA 94705 (☎ 510/549-2145; fax 510/549-1085), is a lovely alternative to a regular hotel, and many of the rooms are suitable for families. The inn consists of two restored mansions totaling 30 rooms. Decorated with antiques, and loaded with country charm, each room has a television and its own bath or shower. Many have fireplaces. There's a huge grassy lawn in front of the inn, and a large redwood deck in the back where the kids can play.

Rooms range from $85 to $175 double (many with fireplaces). The more expensive rooms can handle families. If your child needs a futon, there's a $10 additional charge per night. Breakfast and evening wine and cheese or cookies and milk are included in the room price.

WHERE TO EAT

For a small town, Berkeley has a surprisingly wide array of excellent eateries. North Berkeley is known in some Northern California circles as the Gourmet Ghetto. Crowned by Chez Panisse, whose owner, Alice Waters, is credited with having started California cuisine, Berkeley's eateries run the gamut. Even the poorest student in Berkeley talks lovingly about some of the specialty food stores—the Cheese Board, Cocolat, and Peet's Coffee—all within a block of Chez Panisse.

Expensive

Internationally acclaimed, **Chez Panisse Café and Restaurant,** 1517 Shattuck Ave., between Cedar and Vine (☎ 510/548-5049 or 510/548-5525), is the place where California cuisine got its start in 1971. Many famous chefs have worked here with Alice Waters and later opened their own successful restaurants. The award-winning restaurant emphasizes freshness and creativity in its nouvelle cuisine.

Naturally, we don't take our kids to the prix-fixe dinner (at $35–$65), which might consist of caviar; pigeon sausage with cabbage, bacon, and mustard; roasted red onion and garlic soup; grilled rack of veal with green beans and sautéed potatoes; garden salad; and baked figs. Instead, we enjoy the same kitchen (with lighter fare) at the upstairs café, but the menu is simpler and à la carte.

Alice Waters opened the café in 1980 because she wanted a place where her friends, family, and neighbors could eat in a casual setting. Often you'll see Alice with daughter Fanny in the café. The pizza comes from the brick oven, and the pizza maker will show the kids how he does it, and will even create a pizza in the child's initials. You can also get pasta, salads, and fish. The "tamest" item is the pizza with tomato sauce and sausage, but our kids will share our grilled swordfish and calzone with goat cheese, mozzarella, prosciutto, and garlic. If you ordered only according to the menu, you'd think your kids would have to have refined taste, but we always tell our server to hold some of the items that seem too "gourmet." To our delight, the food is consistently excellent. Lunch entrees average $14; dinner entrees are about $16.

Booster seats are available. They give crayons to the kids to use on the white paper table coverings.

The café is open Monday through Saturday, for lunch from 11:30am to 3pm and for dinner from 5 to 11:30pm; same-day reservations are accepted for lunch only. In the downstairs restaurant, dinner is served Tuesday through Saturday in four sittings—at 6, 6:30, 8:30, and 9:15pm; and people make reservations weeks in advance. Most major credit cards are accepted, and street parking is available.

"Warehouse modern" is how we describe the inside of the trendy, upbeat **Skates by the Bay,** 100 Seawell Dr. (☎ **510/547-1900**). Large picture windows on three sides allow the light to stream in and give a wonderful bayside view.

Specialties are seafood and pasta dishes, and include such favorites as Hawaiian swordfish, king salmon, fish and chips, and linguine with basil and pinenuts; prices range from $6.95 to $25.95. There's also an assortment of beef and chicken dishes. Children order off the regular menu, but are served child-size portions; some dishes are specially prepared for kids.

Skates is open for lunch Monday through Friday from 11:15am to 3pm and on Saturday from noon to 3:30pm; Sunday brunch is from 10:15am to 3:30pm. It's open for dinner Monday through Friday from 5 to 10pm and on Saturday and Sunday from 4 to 10pm. Highchairs and boosters are available. Reservations are recommended, and most major credit cards are accepted.

Moderate

Blake's has been a tradition in Berkeley since 1940. Located at 2367 Telegraph Ave., off Durant Avenue (☎ **510/848-0886**), one block south of the university campus, Blake's has been a student gathering spot for many years. It's a lively place where children fit right in.

It specializes in barbecued chicken and ribs, burgers, salads, pastas, and steaks. There are daily dinner specials, 4pm to 6pm, which cost $5–$8; lunch prices are $4–$7.

Highchairs and boosters are available.

Open Monday through Friday from 11am to 1:30am and on Saturday and Sunday from 10am to 1:30am. All major credit cards accepted. Street parking is difficult to find.

Inexpensive

If you want to see your kids wolf down a whole order of French toast, the **Homemade Café,** 2454 Dwight Way (☎ **510/845-1940**), is where it's likely to happen. The place is nothing fancy and somewhat crowded, but the best breakfasts in town are said to be served here. Since it's bursting with locals—and their kids—the restaurant staff knows how to handle youngsters, and the food is served quickly.

Besides the great French toast, you might like to try the homemade corned-beef hash or the lox and eggs scrambled with onions. Creative sandwiches are also a specialty: How about guacamole, cheese, lettuce, and tomato? And you can also get the standard simple ones. Prices for breakfast and lunch start at $3 and go as high as $6.75.

In Case of Emergency

If a medical emergency arises during your stay in Berkeley, there's an emergency room at **Alta Bates Medical Center,** 2450 Ashby Ave. (☎ 510/540-4444, or 510/540-1303 for the emergency room).

There are no children's menus, but the servers will split adult portions and warm bottles or baby food; highchairs and boosters are provided.

Open Monday through Friday from 7am to 2pm and on Saturday and Sunday from 8am to 3pm. No reservations or credit cards accepted.

And you wouldn't want to leave town without having tasted one of the great muffins or pies from **Fatapples,** 1346 Martin Luther King Jr. Way (☎ **510/526-2260**). Simple dishes made from scratch, using quality ingredients, is the way they do things here. While they're known for their baked goods, the burgers, fries, soups, and coffee are also excellent. Prices range from $4.50 to $9 for breakfast, and lunch and dinner items. Highchairs and boosters are available. There's no children's menu, but they'll split portions or bring whatever the kids might like.

Open Monday through Friday from 6am to 11pm and on Saturday and Sunday from 7am to 11pm. No reservations or credit cards accepted. Street parking.

Café Intermezzo, 2442 Telegraph Ave. (☎ **510/849-4592**), has humungous portions of fresh salads and delicious sandwiches on freshly baked bread, which cost $3–$5 (plan to split the full-size orders). Don't miss it for lunch or dinner when you're visiting the university or walking down Telegraph Avenue browsing in the bookstores nearby. This bustling place also has highchairs and boosters. Open daily from 7:30am, for breakfast breads and espresso, to 10pm.

Chester's is another café that specializes in terrific breakfasts and lunches. Located at 1508B Walnut St. in the Walnut Square shopping area (☎ **510/849-9995**), this casual eatery with wooden benches and chairs offers both indoor and outdoor service. The owners actively promote children coming to the café by presenting a nice children's (and seniors') menu ($2.75–$3.50) and friendly servers who bring fruit and crackers for little ones. If you prefer to have the children split an adult order, there's no charge if you do it at the table ($1 extra if you request it done in the kitchen). They'll warm baby food and bottles, provide highchairs and boosters.

Egg specialties, omelets, crêpes, seven kinds of burgers, sandwiches, and salads round out the adult menu. Prices are $3.75–$7.50. There are daily pasta specials and weekend brunches with such items as smoked salmon and eggs Benedict.

Open daily from 8am to 5pm. Some credit cards accepted, but no reservations. Street parking is available.

2 Oakland

The city of Oakland, with some 350,000 people, is the largest city in the East Bay. It is a culturally and ethnically diverse city, and qualifies as the quintessential melting pot. In fact, in a recent survey, Oakland was rated the most integrated city in the country. It is also a major world port: Oakland's waterfront is 19 miles long, and has 28 deep-water berths.

To get the full story about what to do and where to go, you'll want to contact the **Oakland Convention and Visitors Bureau,** 1000 Broadway, Suite 200, Oakland, CA 94607 (☎ **510/839-9000,** or toll free **800/262-5526**). For information on upcoming events, telephone **510/444-2489** for a recorded message.

WHAT TO SEE AND DO

The city is quite diverse, with dozens of parks, quaint Victorian neighborhoods, and a variety of museums. Outdoor activities rank high on the list of things to do. Let's start with the heart of the city.

Lake Merritt

At the center of Oakland is a lovely 155-acre saltwater lake (☎ 510/444-3807). Originally a swampy area, it was transformed in 1870 by the then-mayor, Samuel Merritt. Now the area is a haven for joggers, walkers, and picnickers, as well as boaters. If your family likes to be on the water, you can rent sailboats, canoes, and paddleboats. If you like to watch birds or feed the ducks, you can do that too.

Lakeside Park (☎ 510/238-3494) is considered one of the most beautiful city parks around. The 122-acre park is located between Bellevue and Grand avenues. Bordering Lake Merritt, it not only offers sailing and canoeing, but it also has free musical entertainment on summer weekends. If you love horticultural displays, you can see a wide variety at the **Garden Center.**

In Lakeside Park is the fun-for-smallfry **Children's Fairyland,** located at 1520 Lakeside Dr. (☎ 510/832-3609). Great for toddlers and young school-children, Fairyland is a world of make-believe and fantasy that has over 60 three-dimensional nursery-rhyme sets. There are farm animals, a merry-go-round (just right for little kids), and the Jolly Trolley train ride. Kids can roam around and climb on and in the storybook attractions. The Puppet Theater is well known and has daily shows at 11am, 2, and 4pm.

We were delighted to find that the proprietors of Fairyland are ever-careful about the children. Adults are not allowed inside if they don't have children with them. It is completely stroller-accessible.

Hours vary. Admission is $2.50 for adults, $2 for children 12 and under. Completely stroller-accessible.

The Oakland Museum

Unique in its focus, the Oakland Museum, 1000 Oak St. (☎ 510/834-2413 for recorded information), is a regional museum showcasing the art, natural sciences, and history of the state of California. Sometimes referred to as the California Smithsonian, it is a microcosm of California. There is one gallery devoted strictly to California art, from the earliest explorers to today. The Cowell Hall of California History is the largest collection of artifacts relating to California. There are objects from the Gold Rush and 1906 earthquake, back to the Spanish-American colonization and further. Another gallery is devoted to California ecology.

There is a museum café, a rental gallery, and a museum store. Open Wednesday through Saturday from 10am to 5pm and on Sunday from noon to 7pm; closed Monday, Tuesday, New Year's, Thanksgiving, and Christmas Days, and the Fourth of July. Suggested donation: $4 adults; $2 children.

Jack London Square and Jack London Village

Jack London was only one of the literary figures who lived in Oakland. Others are Bret Harte and Robert Louis Stevenson. This picturesque area, comprised of Jack London Square and Jack London Village, has dozens of restaurants and shops. It's located on the waterfront at the Embarcadero where Broadway and Jackson Street end. Jack London Village is a nice place to windowshop with the kids and find a good place to eat.

To get to Jack London Square from San Francisco, take the San Francisco— Oakland Bay Bridge to I-880 south. Exit at Broadway and take a right on Broadway to the Embarcadero (☎ 510/814-6000).

When you're there, you can see **Jack London's Yukon Cabin.** This tiny cabin with a sod roof is where London spent an entire winter.

The Oakland Zoo in Knowland Park

Knowland Park, located at 9777 Golf Links Rd. (☎ **510/632-9525**), is 525 acres of rolling green hills that has picnic and barbecue facilities, and is home to the **Oakland Zoo.** The zoo sits on 100 acres, and has more than 330 birds, reptiles, and mammals.

The children's petting zoo, miniature train, and skyride are the main attractions. The park is open daily from 9am to sunset; closed Thanksgiving and Christmas Days. The Oakland Zoo is open daily from 10am to 4pm. Admission is $4.50 for adults, $2 for children 2–14 and seniors.

Sports

A big draw in Oakland is the **Oakland Athletics,** who play baseball at the Oakland Coliseum (☎ **510/638-0500**) during the season (April through September). The **Golden State Warriors** play basketball at the Coliseum (☎ **510/638-6300**) during their season (October through April).

IF YOU'RE LOOKING FOR SOMETHING TO EAT

With its large selection of restaurants, Jack London Square is probably the best place to find something good to eat.

One of the places we like is **Shenanigans Restaurant,** 30 Jack London Sq. (☎ **510/839-8333**). Located on the water, this attractive rustic restaurant has stained-glass windows and antiques. It serves such standard fare as sandwiches, burgers, and fresh fish for lunch; and chicken, prime rib, and seafood for dinner. Lunch runs $6–$14, dinner prices are $12–$25. There's a children's menu with chicken, hamburger, or fried shrimp for $7.95.

Highchairs and boosters are available, and the servers will warm bottles and baby food. Open for lunch Monday through Saturday from 11am to 3pm. Dinner is served Sunday through Thursday from 5 to 10pm, on Friday and Saturday until 11pm. Sunday brunch is from 9am to 3pm. For children under 10 accompanied by an adult the price is 99¢. Second child is $6.95. Early Bird Brunch from 9am to 10am is $11.95 per adult. Reservations are recommended. There is ample validated parking, and most major credit cards are accepted.

Scott's Jack London Square, on the waterfront at no. 2 Broadway, Jack London Square (☎ **510/444-3456**). Its wide range of seafood dinner entrees, as well as chicken and steaks, are priced from $10.95 to $26.95. Lunch costs a little less. Children tend to prefer the pastas and burgers.

This location has booster seats. Reservations are recommended. Open Monday through Thursday from 11am to 10pm, on Friday and Saturday till 11pm, and on Sunday till 9pm. Most major credit cards are accepted, and there's lots of parking.

In an Emergency

If a medical emergency arises while you're visiting Oakland, you should contact one of the following local emergency rooms: **Kaiser Permanente,** 3801 Howe St. (☎ **510/596-1000**, or **510/596-7600** for the emergency room); or the **Summit Medical Center,** Hawthorne and Webster avenues (☎ **510/869-6600**).

3 Angel Island

Angel Island State Park (☎ 415/435-1915) is like a jewel of 740 thickly forested acres sitting in the middle of San Francisco Bay. It offers good hiking trails, bicycle paths, and wonderful picnic spots. On warm summer days the coves are lovely spots to sit with the kids and do some serious work on elaborate sandcastles.

The treat begins even before you set foot on the island. Take the **Red and White Fleet** from Fisherman's Wharf, Pier 41, or from Tiburon (☎ 415/546-2896) for a short cruise. Call ahead because schedules vary depending on place of departure. The bracing air usually prevents seasickness, but be sure to bring windbreakers even when it's warm. If you plan to bicycle, you can rent bicycles and take them with you on the ferry. But you should call the ferry service ahead of time because bicycle space is limited.

The island has more than 17 miles of paved trails for easy walking; even if you must lug a stroller with you, it may be the best way to go if you have a preschooler who tires easily.

Ayala Cove, which is the closer beach and near the place where the ferry docks, and **Quarry Point Beach** both have nice, protected sandy areas. However, neither beach has lifeguards and there are strong currents, so swimming may not be safe. Throughout the area you'll find lovely picnic sites. Fires are allowed at Ayala Cove and East Garrison.

If you want to venture out of Ayala Cove, **North Garrison** has an old Immigration Station where tours are given on weekends. At **East Garrison** (Fort McDowell) there's a large army fort that was in operation from the Spanish-American War through World War II. There are docent tours of the grounds upon request from 11am to 4pm on weekends April through October. At **West Garrison/Camp Reynolds** you'll find a Civil War camp that you can tour. Our kids love the cannon firings, which take place at approximately 1 and 2pm on weekends, April through October.

Walking the island is possible with children. Most kids (even those under 5) can walk the easy one-mile to West Garrison to the cannon firings without any trouble. Park officials suggest that you bring a wagon (or stroller) for little tykes, if you want to see more. Older children will love bicycling through the island, and if you decide to take bikes, the hills are slight enough so that toddler carriers won't present a problem.

The one main road around the island is five miles and is completely suitable for walking or bicycling. The trek up the hill is steep, but once there, it's a very pleasant, easy walk. This main road is the best for young children. This is where you'll see kids with little red wagons or furiously pedaling tricycles.

The snack bar is open daily during the summer, and on weekends. But we always take a picnic lunch because the selection of food is very limited.

4 Tiburon

If you want to know why people love living in the Bay Area, grab the kids and go to Tiburon, one of the most spectacular settings on the bay. This tiny village, much smaller and less crowded than Sausalito, is surrounded by picturesque Richardson Bay. Any way you get there, you'll discover incredible sights. You'll see Mount Tamalpais emerge on the Marin side, all three bridges across the bay (the Golden Gate, the Bay Bridge, and the San Rafael), and spectacular views of San Francisco, Alcatraz, and Angel Island. Enjoy a meal at bayside, bike-ride, or just wander.

Possibly the most pleasant way to get to Tiburon is to cross the bay on a **Red and White Fleet** ferry (☎ 415/546-2896). Boats leave from Pier 43¹/₂ at Fisherman's Wharf several times a day for the 15-minute ride. The crossing costs $11 round-trip for adults, $5.50 for children 5–11, free for under-5s. If you're driving, take the Tiburon exit off U.S. 101. If you prefer to go by bus, **Golden Gate Transit** (☎ 415/332-6600) offers service from downtown San Francisco. Many families make a full day of it by spending part of the time in Tiburon and then taking the ferry to Angel Island (☎ 415/435-2131) for the remainder of the day.

Before you start, you might want to contact the **Tiburon Peninsula Chamber of Commerce,** 96B Main St., Tiburon, CA 94920 (☎ 415/435-5633). They'll send you free brochures about the downtown shopping area and maps that show various activities in the peninsula region.

WHAT TO SEE AND DO

Plan to spend a few hours in the Tiburon area so you can enjoy the beautiful surroundings and get a flavor of the town.

Wandering Around

Tiburon was once the hub of the Bay Area, with heavy ferry and railroad traffic; people used it as a main link in their trip to San Francisco. Today the best way to enjoy the quaint village is to walk the main streets and the area called Ark Row. Many of the alluring-looking shops are housed in what used to be summer cottages and old arks (houseboats) built in the 1800s.

Blackie's Pasture

Just before you enter town, you'll come across a lovely large green pasture. We often stop here since it's a great place for a picnic. We used to wonder at its name, and we learned that Blackie was a horse born in Kansas in 1926. He began his career as a rodeo horse, then worked in Yosemite and at the San Francisco Presidio. He came to Tiburon in 1938 and grazed in this pasture until his death in 1966. When he died, he was buried in the pasture he loved so well. You can see his grave here, marked by the white cross. He's a legend in Tiburon.

National Audubon Society's Richardson Bay Audubon Center

Located at 376 Greenwood Beach Rd. (☎ 415/388-2524), this sanctuary for thousands of waterfowl is sometimes called a window on the bay. It has several different habitats that reflect the bay's environment. The center offers programs about the environment for both children and adults. Here you'll find the **Book Nest** bookstore, an outstanding natural-history bookstore. Call for current program information.

Walks and Bike Paths

Tiburon is a place to explore on foot or by bike. One of our favorite bike paths runs all along Richardson Bay. Unfortunately, hordes of bicyclists, joggers, and walkers agree. Known as the best bike path in Marin County, it passes the Audubon Society's bird reserve and historic Lyford House. You'll also ride by beautiful McKegney Green, which faces Sausalito across Richardson Bay, and offers wonderful picnicking. You might want to pack that lunch before you hop on the bicycles.

You can start at Tiburon Boulevard. Take Tiburon Boulevard to Blackie's Pasture for the entrance to the Tiburon Bike Path. The path leads into town, and is level for about five miles. Once you get into the village, you'll see one of the most spectacular views of San Francisco there is. The city jumps out at you, making you think you could touch it.

WHERE TO EAT

Al fresco dining is *the* thing in Tiburon—weather permitting. The following are but a few of the choice places to eat.

Our favorite restaurant in Tiburon, and a great place for kids, is **Sam's Anchor Café,** 27 Main St. (☎ 415/435-4527). The view is special, the service is good, and the food is tasty. The deck is the place to eat during the day. You get a spectacular view of San Francisco, the Bay Bridge, Alcatraz, and Angel Island. Although the deck sways, you do get used to it. The friendly sea gulls are entertaining for the kids, but don't let the kids feed them or they'll pull food off your plate before you know it.

The café has its own bit of folk history. It was built in 1920 during Prohibition. Ever-clever entrepreneurs are said to have built a trap door under the building so boats could pull up under the pilings and pass crates of liquor. Amusing as the story is, today's café is a wholesome place, offering savory food. And the deck where they smuggled liquor is where you'll prefer to dine.

If you're outside, watch the little ones. There are railings all around the deck, but the restaurant does sit over the water. Servers keep an ever-watchful eye after the kids, and they say they've *never* had one go overboard. But be careful just the same!

This very casual restaurant offers two indoor rooms in addition to the outdoor deck. The bar, which is located in front, has a large television and serves free popcorn. Known for their delectable swordfish and salmon, they also have daily seafood specials. Cioppino, steamed clams, and sautéed or deep-fried local oysters are other treats. The burgers here are very good. Other fare includes sandwiches (the Dungeness crab on a toasted English muffin is yummy), omelets, chicken, and steak. Prices run $5.50-$13. The children's "color-in" menu includes a Samburger, spaghetti, fish and chips, and a hot dog for $2.75–$4.25 and comes with crayons.

Highchairs and boosters are available. Reservations accepted. We usually put our name on the waiting list and then wander around Tiburon.

The restaurant's hours are a little unusual. It's open Monday through Friday at 11am for lunch; in summer Monday through Thursday it stays open till 10:30pm and on Friday till 11pm. On Saturday it's open from 10am to 11pm, and on Sunday from 9:30am to 10:30pm. During Pacific Standard Time the restaurant closes a half hour earlier. Parking on Main Street. Most major credit cards accepted.

Another local favorite, though more expensive, is **Guaymas,** 5 Main St. (☎ 415/435-6300). This open, airy, traditional Mexican restaurant boasts the best unimpeded view of San Francisco and Angel Island in Tiburon. This colorful restaurant has floor-to-ceiling glass windows, brightly tinted walls, and is adorned by traditional Mexican paper-lace placemats hanging from the ceiling. Even the serving dishes have a Mexican motif.

Guaymas is a seaport in Mexico, and the staff pride themselves on serving mouth-watering traditional cuisine from that locale. The open kitchen affords you the chance to watch the chefs cook the food from scratch and the local women make fresh tortillas.

Mexican delicacies are abundant here, and the kitchen has a special flare. Have you ever tried chicken with chocolate, chiles, fruit, and spices? There are giant shrimp marinated in lime and cilantro, and butterflied baby chicken with tomatillo-jalapeño chile sauce. We find that good choices for the kids include tamales, guacamole and chips, and banana-wrapped red snapper or banderillos de torero (two skewers of beef done over mesquite). Prices range from $8.50–$17.50.

They have highchairs and boosters, but no kids' menu. They'll split adult portions at the table, and will bring chips and tortillas to the table as soon as you're seated.

Guaymas is open Monday through Friday from 11:30am to 10pm, Saturday until 11pm, and on Sunday from 10:30am to 10pm. They accept most major credit cards and recommend reservations; without them, the wait can be extremely long, especially during peak times. Parking is available.

5   Sausalito

Located on the north side of the Golden Gate Bridge, this picturesque village is built into a steep hillside and is surrounded by the bay. Known as an artists' colony, Sausalito has about 7,200 residents. This is a place most first-time visitors to the Bay Area want to see. We find there's enough to do in town to keep the kids busy for a few hours. Then we hightail it to some of the other nearby attractions.

To get to Sausalito from San Francisco, you can drive along Calif. 1 to the Sausalito exit and follow the signs, or you can take the children's favorite way, the ferry. If you go by ferry, choose the 30-minute ride on the **Golden Gate Transit ferry** (☎ **415/332-6600**), which leaves from the San Francisco Ferry Building; one-way fare is $4.25 for adults, $3.20 for children 6–12. Or ride the **Red and White Fleet** (☎ **415/546-2628**), which leaves from Pier 43½ at Fisherman's Wharf. Numerous tour buses include Sausalito in their tours, including **Greyhound** (☎ toll free **800/231-2222**). **Golden Gate Buses** (☎ **415/332-6600**) also come here. Some people who come by ferry use taxi service to get to places outside Sausalito. You can reach **local taxi** service in Sausalito by calling **415/332-2200.**

Before you leave San Francisco on your Sausalito outing, you might want to first get information from the **Sausalito Chamber of Commerce,** 333 Caledonia St. (P.O. Box 566), Sausalito, CA 94966 (☎ **415/332-0505**). Open Tuesday through Sunday, 11:30am to 4pm.

WHAT TO SEE AND DO

Sausalito is just a little over two square miles, and is a place to wander, watch the boats, and do some shopping. Sausalito's main street, **Bridgeway,** is sometimes referred to as Old Town; it's a long line of shops, restaurants, and sailing masts. All the attractions on Bridgeway are conveniently located.

Near the north entrance to town is the **San Francisco Bay and Delta Model,** 2100 Bridgeway (☎ **415/332-3871**). This working scale model of the entire San Francisco Bay and delta area is actually a scientific tool that scientists and engineers use to analyze and solve problems affecting the region. It's a model of currents, tides, and rivers, and visually helps you begin to understand the estuary where Pacific Ocean salt water mixes with fresh water.

You'll see a layout of a 17-mile ocean, several bays, and the delta, 1½ acres in size. It looks as if someone took a map and cut out the bay. When it's in operation, there is water inside and you get an idea of how tides go back and forth. We recommend it for kids 8 and up.

Because this is a testing facility, the model doesn't always operate. It's open Tuesday through Saturday from 9am to 4pm, except from Memorial Day through Labor Day when it's also open on Saturday and Sunday from 10am to 6pm. Call ahead for the operation schedule. No admission charge.

For children over 12, meet at the bay model for a tour of the steam schooner *Wapama* (part of the National Maritime Museum). Built in 1915, this is the last wooden steam vessel of the approximately 225 that were built. Guided tours are conducted on Saturday at 11am. Be sure to wear flat shoes. No charge. Reservations are required (☎ 415/332-3871).

Shopping

Located in the center of town is the **Village Fair,** a group of 30 shops featuring everything from candles to crafts. We like the **Holiday Shop,** on the third floor (☎ 415/332-7432), and **Pet Pixie Children's Shop** (☎ 415/332-5666). Outside the Village Fair you'll find other pleasant shops. And there's **Games People Play** at 695 Bridgeway (☎ 415/332-4151), which has lots of preschool items as well as imported toys for children and their parents. Meander through **High as a Kite,** 34 Princess (☎ 415/332-8944), to see all colors, styles, and sizes of kites, from the most basic to the most elaborate.

And Other Places to See Nearby

In the cliffs just west of Sausalito are the **Marin Headlands** (☎ 415/331-1540), part of Golden Gate National Recreation Area. Some of the cliffs are sandstone, and provide a dramatic setting with the ocean below. It's spectacular scenery. The **Marin Headlands Visitor Center,** located in the historic chapel at Fort Barry, is open from 9:30am to 4:30pm daily. A fine little one-mile trail is located behind the visitor center. **Lagoon Loop** is a fairly level walk that gives you a good idea of the scope of the headlands. From the top of the trail you can see the ocean, and all along the way there are quiet areas where you can hear the birds. This is an area where one of the park's bobcats hangs out, so you might be "lucky" enough to see him.

The visitor center offers guided family walks and special art programs in which children learn about the wildlife and habitat of the region.

The **Marine Mammal Center,** Marin Headlands (☎ 415/289-7325), is dedicated to rescuing and treating orphaned and injured sea mammals. When recovered, the animals are released back to the wild. Children will enjoy a visit to the center, where they will see recovering seals, sea lions, and otters, and talk with animal caretakers, who will gladly share their expertise and love of the animals with the kids.

For special programs, call **415/289-7330.** Open daily from 10am to 4pm. Admission is free.

Don't miss the **Bay Area Discovery Museum** at Fort Baker (☎ 415/289-7268). For a complete description, see "What to See and Do" in Chapter 2 on San Francisco.

WHERE TO EAT

Although restaurants in Sausalito are quite pricey because they cater to tourists, they are numerous.

A little off the beaten tourist path is **Caffè Trieste,** 1000 Bridgeway (☎ 415/332-7770), a good alternative for a quick, fairly reasonably priced bite to eat if you don't need a highchair or booster. This little cafeteria-style bistro is one place you could keep your child in a stroller. Frequented by locals, Caffè Trieste has a changing assortment of sandwiches, pizza, muffins, and delicious specialty coffees, caffè latte, and teas. Open daily from 7am to midnight.

We also like **Flynn's Landing,** 303 Johnson St., just off Bridgeway (☎ 415/332-0131). This restaurant reflects the nautical ambience of Sausalito. The natural-wood and paneled walls offer a casual atmosphere, while colorful sea flags, white tablecloths, and blue napkins add to the authentic flair of seaside dining. Your server will bring the kids crackers, and offer paper and crayons. The menu has a wide variety of seafood, pasta, soups, salads, sandwiches, and half-pound burgers—something for everyone. Items range from $8 to $25. While there's no children's menu, they'll be glad to split orders in the kitchen, and of course warm bottles and baby food. Highchairs and boosters are available.

Reservations are accepted, and you may expect a 20-minute wait at peak hours. Flynn's is open daily from 11:30am to 10:30pm. Most major credit cards are accepted. Metered street parking is available.

For a more formal dining event, we like **Scoma's,** 588 Bridgeway (☎ 415/332-9551). This attractive bayside restaurant has one of the most beautiful views in Sausalito. Overlooking the water, Scoma's has a relaxed atmosphere but a sophisticated seafood menu. A medium-size dining room and comfortable yet intimate seating arrangements encourage leisurely dining. The appeal of the white-walled entrance with blooming flowers in wooden boxes is evident to all passersby. All this attention tends to gather a crowd, so be prepared to wait for about 30 minutes for a table. Reservations are accepted for lunch Monday through Friday, and for parties of six or more, also on Saturday and Sunday. You can drop by, leave your name, and continue your seaside stroll for a few minutes.

Booster seats are available. The children's menu ($6–$7) includes hamburgers, spaghetti, fried prawns, filet of sole, and fish and chips. Or servers will split portions. Their special children's drinks have come into the present as Darth Vaders, taking their place alongside the ever-popular Shirley Temples and Roy Rogerses. Menu prices range from $12 to $26.

Open Monday and Thursday through Saturday from 11:30am to 10:30pm, on Sunday from 11:30am to 9:30pm, and on Tuesday and Wednesday for dinner only, from 5:30.

Winship, 670 Bridgeway (☎ 415/332-1454) is a good California-style seafood restaurant that has been owned by the same family for 28 years—you'll know that owner Bill Charles is an avid sailor by the restaurant decor. One cute touch is the replica of a tugboat wheelhouse called Nellie, when you walk in.

Everything is made from scratch, including their own pastas. Specialties are seafood (don't miss the cioppino if you like that dish), burgers, pasta, and veal. There are a lot of salads and hot and cold sandwiches for lunch.

Although there isn't a children's menu, they'll be glad to split adult portions in the kitchen. They'll warm baby food and bottles. Ask for crayons so the kids can draw on the paper tablecloths. Highchairs and boosters are available.

Open daily from 7:30am to 4:30pm for breakfast and lunch; for dinner Wednesday through Sunday, from 5 to 9:30pm. Reservations aren't necessary, but they are accepted; and they take most major credit cards.

Houlihan's is another good choice for American food. This smallish restaurant with a glassed-in deck is located at 660 Bridgeway (☎ 415/332-8512) and is quite nice.

They have highchairs and boosters, and a good children's menu that comes with crayons. Two nice features are the tray of carrots and celery before the entree, and cookies after the meal. The children's menu offers burgers, hot dogs, grilled cheese, chicken fingers, and spaghetti, all of which come with fries or veggies, beverage, and ice cream for dessert. They'll also warm baby food and bottles.

Open Monday through Thursday from 11am to 10pm, on Friday to 11pm, on Saturday from 10am to 11pm, and on Sunday from 10am to 10pm. Saturday and Sunday brunch is served. Reservations are accepted—and because there tends to be a long wait, we recommend them.

6   Muir Woods

Less than 20 miles from San Francisco via U.S. 101 and Calif. 1, **Muir Woods National Monument** (☎ 415/388-2595) feels like a million miles from civilization. To get to the woods, you drive on winding two-lane roads through the coastal hills that take you through groves of eucalyptus.

There's something about the huge grove of giant redwoods (*Sequoia semper virens*)—this monument to nature—that is at once exhilarating and calming to the kids. The towering redwoods that have stood for hundreds of years, the fern thickets, and the moss that covers the barks of some of the trees are simply beautiful . . . and the forest is peaceful. Our kids love to run along the paved pathway, but they, too, seem to revere these natural giants. You may purchase a trail guide for the self-guided walk for $1.

The tallest trees here are in **Bohemian Grove.** Some stand 250 feet tall. The widest is 13¹/₂ feet. Most of the main trails are level and paved, easy for strollers and young children.

A wonderful feature in Muir Woods is the Junior Ranger program. It's designed to heighten children's enjoyment and skills of observation. Kids are encouraged to pick up a Junior Ranger Pack at the visitor center. The pack comes equipped with cards that correspond to a map and activities to be done in certain areas of the park. Included also are bug boxes, a dip net, a magnifying lens, a clipboard, and a trash bag. The cards present many different ideas for the kids to try. It's a wonderful introduction for the children to be involved with nature.

Muir Woods National Monument has a snack counter, a giftshop, a bookstore, and a visitor center. No picnicking or camping is allowed. Bring warm clothing because the forest is cool. Open daily from 8am to sunset. Admission is free. For further information, write Muir Woods National Monument, Mill Valley, CA 94941 (☎ 415/388-2595).

Side Trips from the Bay Area

4

AY AND WEEKEND JAUNTS FROM THE GREATER SAN FRANCISCO AREA ARE RICH WITH excitement and diversity. Within an hour of San Francisco, there are two theme parks, a water park, lovely swimming beaches, and attractions from before the turn of the century. Santa Cruz, a picturesque seaside community, and San Jose, one of the largest cities in California, each offer family fun. As if that's not enough, Napa Valley and Sonoma County offer lush scenery, winery tours, and other natural wonders.

1 Great America

Paramount's Great America, well known for the Grizzly, its classic and huge wooden roller coaster, is a 100-acre theme park that caters to children of all ages. It's located 45 minutes south of San Francisco in Santa Clara on U.S. 101 at the Great America Parkway exit (☎ 408/988-1776). Youngsters and teens who delight in wild rides, thrilling roller coasters, and lots of action will love this park and its 33 rides. Designed around North America's past, there are **six theme areas,** each with rides, shows, shops, and restaurants—Carousel Plaza, Hometown Square, County Fair, Yukon Territory, Yankee Harbor, and Orleans Place.

A park spokesman said that they try to be particularly sensitive to the needs of small children and offer many attractions and services geared to kids under 12.

RIDES AND ATTRACTIONS

The double-decker **Hanna-Barbera Carousel,** denoting Carousel Plaza, is the entrance to Fort Fun, the action area for little ones. Other rides include **L'il Dodge Em, Yakki Doodle's Lady Bugs,** and **Boo Boo's Biplanes.** Favorite Hanna-Barbera cartoon characters roam the area. Our kids went wild over Scooby Doo.

The **Grizzly** and the **Revolution** are probably the favorite rides of teenage parkgoers. The Grizzly, a classic wooden roller coaster, the largest ever built in Northern California, speeds up to 50 m.p.h. for almost three minutes. Another attraction, the Revolution, is a 360° swinging ship that works like a pendulum. As it goes higher, passengers are suspended upside down; two complete loops are made during the ride. The **Demon** and **Tidal Wave** roller coasters, and the free-fall ride, the **Edge,** will keep you and your teens shook up for hours. **Skyhawk** is a flight ride where riders use a control stick to regulate the angle of flight and rotate the cabin. These, as well as the **Yankee Clipper** and **Logger's Run,** are the most popular rides in the park and are the busiest between noon and 5pm. The newest addition, **Days of Thunder,** is a motion simulator of race car driving.

When you tire of the thrill rides, or want to experience something different, there are musical productions, puppet shows, and other shows to enjoy. Don't miss the **Pictorium Theatre,** which uses the IMAX projection process and gives spectators the feeling of being right inside the action. Inquire about the specific show and seating arrangements if you're taking little ones—it may be very loud, very huge, and overwhelming to them. Teens will think it's fabulous.

Another place very appealing to young teens is the recording studio, where you can record your voice singing over the sound track of a favorite song; an extra fee is required.

FACILITIES

Stroller rentals are available inside the front gate. In Fort Fun is a **Baby Care Center** for changing and nursing. It is roomy and carpeted, has rocking chairs, and provides free diapers, tissues, and baby lotion and there's even an attendant on duty. The **Lost Parent's Center** is a large carpeted area filled with toys, and kids are supervised by a caring attendant until lost parents arrive.

For a sit-down meal, three of the **restaurants** feature children's menus: Maggie Brown's Wings and Preston T. Tucker Roadside Cafe. And, of course, snackstands with hamburgers, hot dogs, fries, and soft drinks abound around the park.

There's a large **picnic area** in front of the main gate. This is where we go to enjoy a healthy, less expensive lunch than we would have inside the park. We bring along all our favorite goodies. Remember to get your hand stamped if you leave the park for a picnic. We also suggest that you bring lots of liquids for the little ones; it gets hot and only a few places sell milk. Bring sun hats, sunscreen, and cool clothing if you come in summer.

HOURS AND PRICES

Open daily from early June through early September and during Easter Week and Memorial Day weekend from 10am; closing times vary. Open weekends from March through May and September through mid-October. The park is closed from mid-October to March. For exact opening and closing dates, call **408/988-1776** or contact the Santa Clara Chamber of Commerce and Convention and Visitors' Bureau, P.O. Box 387, Santa Clara, CA 95052 (☎ **408/296-7111**); or write Paramount's Great America, P.O. Box 1776, Santa Clara, CA 95052. The admission fee, which includes all rides and attractions, is $25.95 for adults, $18.95 for seniors, $12.95 for children 3–6, free for children under 2. Parking costs $5.

2   San Jose

San Jose, the capital of Silicon Valley, is at the southern end of the San Francisco Bay, just 50 miles south of San Francisco. A population of more than 800,000 ranks it as California's third-largest city. It boasts 70 parks, more than 50 wineries, the largest children's museum on the West Coast, and many other attractions, which make it a wonderful day trip with children. For information, contact the **San Jose Convention and Visitors' Bureau,** 333 W. San Carlos St., Suite 1000, San Jose, CA 95110 (☎ **408/295-9600,** or **408/295-2265** for a recorded message); or stop by the **San Jose Visitors' Information Center** located in the lobby of the San Jose McEnery Convention Center, 408 Almaden Blvd, San Jose 95111 (☎ **408/283-8833**).

WHAT TO SEE AND DO

Winchester Mystery House

This is the strangest house you'll ever see: It has 160 rooms, 10,000 windows, 47 fireplaces, 13 bathrooms, and countless spiritual symbols throughout the mansion. It's located at 525 S. Winchester Blvd., between Stevens Creek and I-280 (☎ **408/247-2101**). The story goes that Sarah L. Winchester, heiress to the Winchester rifle estate, was convinced by a spiritualist that the untimely deaths of her husband and baby daughter were caused by the spirits of the people killed with Winchester rifles. She was told that she, too, would be killed, unless she built a home for the spirits. As long as construction continued, she would not die.

Sarah kept a crew of carpenters working 24 hours a day from 1884 until her death in 1922, ultimately spending over $5 million on the bizarre mansion. Even today tour guides refer to her as if she is still their employer.

Winchester House is at once strange and splendid. It's strange because Sarah's dread of and fascination with the spirits motivated her to construct ways to foil ghosts who might come to kill her. There are several staircases that lead nowhere, a switchback stairway that has 7 turns and 44 steps but rises only 9 feet, and several doors that open to blank walls. Sarah was obsessed with the occult, and the number 13 comes up again and again. She even had 13 sections to her last will and testament and signed it 13 times.

Winchester House is splendid because it's filled with fabulous furniture, art, accessories, and other articles of Victorian culture. The **Victorian Gardens** are impressive—don't miss them. And the **Winchester Historical Museum** is located here too, and features a huge collection of Winchester rifles and antique firearms.

The frequency of tours depends on the season. Open daily (except Christmas Day) year round from 9am, closing between 4pm (in winter) and 5:30pm (in summer); closing times vary both by day of the week (weekdays, weekends, and holidays) and seasonally. Admission is $12.50 for adults, $9.50 for seniors, $6.50 for children 6–12, free for children 5 and under. You can rent cameras and backpacks (to carry babies).

Children's Discovery Museum of San Jose

Designed for children between 3 and 13, the Children's Discovery Museum is the largest children's museum in the West. It is housed in a purple high-tech–looking building located at 180 Woz Way (☎ 408/298-5437). The interactive exhibits teach science and technology, the arts and humanities in creative ways that encourage exploration. Your kids will have a great time here, and so will you! It's a place of joy and energy. Children are eagerly engaged in learning and play at this wonderland of childhood learning. There are so many sections that you should plan to spend a couple of hours.

Our kids especially loved **Waterworks,** a place where kids use pumps, siphons, and valves to move water through a water system and learn about kinetic energy. **Doodad Dump** offers kids the chance to create artwork from recycled materials. **Gilliland Global Communications** allows children the opportunity to discover different modes of communication. The museum store has a wonderful array of items.

The museum is open Tuesday through Saturday from 10am to 5pm; Sunday noon to 5; closed New Year's, Thanksgiving, and Christmas Days. Admission is $6 for adults, $4 for seniors and children 6–18, free for children under 6.

Tech Museum of Innovation

Nearby is a museum that packs a technological wallop! **The Tech Museum of Innovation** is a small museum at 145 W. San Carlos St. (☎ 408/279-7150) in downtown San Jose. The exhibits are fascinating. Learn about robotics, biotechnology, computer microchips, and lots more in six areas of interactive exhibits. Open Tuesday through Sunday from 10am to 5pm. Admission is $6 for adults, $4 for seniors and children 6–18, free for children under 6.

Kelley Park

Kelley Park (on Senter Road between Story and Phelan Avenues) is next on our itinerary because at this point our kids are usually ready to run off energy and rollick in the park. It is easy to spend more than a few hours here. This 176-acre family-oriented park complex has large grassy areas, picnic tables and barbecues, a Japanese Friendship Garden, and an historical museum.

Youngsters love the **Happy Hollow Park and Zoo,** 1300 Senter Rd. (☎ **408/292-8188**), a tiny theme park and zoo. The park and rides—Danny the Dragon, Granny Bug Ride, Merry-Go-Round, Mini Putt Putt Car Ride, and King Neptune's Carousel—are perfect for both young children and their parents. Kids can run around here and just play with a minimum of supervision. The zoo is small but interesting and makes viewing the animals easy for the very young, the very short, and the handicapped. There are some interactive informational displays that add a nice touch. Admission, which includes the zoo, all rides, and puppet shows, is $3.50 for adults, $3 for seniors and the disabled, free for children under 2 and seniors over 75. Parking is $3 per car on weekends and in summer. Call for hours as they vary.

The **Kelley Park Express** miniature train is our mode of transportation between different areas of the park.

The **Japanese Friendship Garden,** located at 1300 Senter Rd. (☎ **408/277-4192**), is a lovely traditional Japanese stroll garden. It's patterned after Korakuen Park in Okayama, Japan. Most kids especially enjoy the rare koi fish, the giant brilliantly colored Japanese goldfish. The garden, open daily from 10am to sunset, is a nice place to wander. Free.

The **San Jose Historical Museum,** located in Kelley Park at 1600 Senter Rd., past the Happy Hollow Park and Zoo (☎ **408/287-2290**), is a collection of restored turn-of-the-century buildings. There's an original post office, doctor's and dentist's offices, bank, stables, print shop, candy shop, hotel, and homes.

Older children, especially those interested in history, will enjoy this museum. Our young ones had a great time at the firehouse, which displays old fire engines and photos of San Jose's biggest fires. The Trolley Barn houses the San Jose's trolleys, which are being beautifully restored, even hand-painted, by volunteers. We climbed on them, sat in them, walked through them. Adults like the post office, which is set up as a gathering place for those waiting for news.

There's lots of space surrounding the museum, perfect for picnics and playing on the grass. It's an easy place to take strollers, and diaper changing can be done on the outdoor tables in the park. There's an abundance of special events, so call for the program schedule.

The museum is open Monday through Friday from 10am to 4:30pm and on Saturday and Sunday from noon to 4:30pm. Closed New Year's, Thanksgiving, and Christmas Days. Admission is $2 for adults, $1.50 for seniors, $1 for children 6–17.

Raging Waters

A 14-acre theme park with more than 30 waterslides and many other aquatic activities, Raging Waters is located in **Lake Cunningham Regional Park,** 2333 S. White Rd., at Capitol Expressway and Tully Road (☎ **408/270-8000**).

There are slides of different speeds and heights for children of various age levels. For little dippers, there's a small slide area and two wading pools, with a large sandy area and picnic areas; and also an area that offers colorful jungle gym activities.

The park is open daily in summer and on weekends in May and September from 10am to 7pm. Admission is $15.50, $11.50 for children under 42 inches, and includes all-day use of rides.

Rosicrucian Egyptian Museum and Planetarium

This unusual attraction houses the West Coast's largest collection of Egyptian, Assyrian, and Babylonian artifacts. There are mummies, ornate coffins, jewelry, and sculpture.

The museum, located in Rosicrucian Park at Park and Naglee Avenues (☎ 408/947-3636), is open daily from 9am to 5pm. Admission to the Egyptian Museum is $6 for adults, $4 for seniors and students, $3.50 for children 7–15, and free for children under 7. The planetarium next door will delight children. It is open daily from 9am to 4:15pm; check for the changing planetarium show times. Admission to the planetarium is $4 for adults, $3 for seniors and students, $3 for children 7–15, free for 5- and 6-year-olds, children under 5 are not admitted. Admission to the Science Center is free. Closed New Year's, Thanksgiving, and Christmas Days.

WHERE TO EAT IN THE DOWNTOWN AREA

Scott's Seafood Grill and Bar, 185 Park Ave. (☎ 408/971-1700), is a good choice when you're visiting downtown. Prices range from $9.95 to $24.95 for entrees, $4.25 to $14.75 for salads; burgers are $6.95. Servers will provide boosters and highchairs and warm baby bottles. Open Monday through Saturday from 11:30am to 10pm and on Sunday from 4 to 9pm. Reservations and major credit cards are accepted.

A nice restaurant for breakfast, lunch, or dinner is the **Parrot at the Holiday Inn/ Park Center Plaza** (☎ 408/998-0400). Breakfast is $4.50–$9.75, lunch costs $5.25–$7.75, and dinner goes for $8.95–$17.95. A children's menu has burgers, chicken salad, fish, grilled cheese, and other treats for $4–$5.25. Boosters and highchairs are available. Most credit cards accepted. Open daily from 6am to 10pm.

IF YOU'RE STAYING OVERNIGHT

The Holiday Inn/Park Center Plaza, 282 Almaden Blvd., San Jose, CA 95113 (☎ 408/998-0400), is located in a lovely area of downtown. A typical, clean Holiday Inn, the hotel has 231 nice-sized, air-conditioned rooms. Dining facilities include the Parrot Restaurant (described above), a nice hotel coffee shop, and room service during meal hours. Rooms are $92–$97. Children under 18 stay free in their parents' room.

---

3 Santa Cruz

Santa Cruz is a picture-perfect seaside town hugging the shoreline of Monterey Bay. With good swimming beaches, an old-fashioned boardwalk, and the historical Roaring Camp Steam Railroad, Santa Cruz is a favorite family fun spot. From San Francisco, you can take Calif. 1 right into Santa Cruz. You can contact the **Santa Cruz County Conference & Visitors Council,** 701 Front St., Santa Cruz, CA 95060 (☎ 408/425-1234), for information about the area.

THINGS TO SEE AND DO

Santa Cruz Beach Boardwalk

Dating back to the early 1900s, the **Santa Cruz Beach Boardwalk** (☎ 408/423-5590) is everything a boardwalk should be—colorful and exciting. The boardwalk has 20 major rides and 7 kiddie rides, the most popular being the **Giant Dipper,** which is rated one of the world's top 10 roller coasters. The oldest ride is the classic Looff **merry-go-round** (a treat for all ages), and there are lots and lots of good, old-fashioned boardwalk-type games.

The most exciting addition is **Neptune's Kingdom Adventure Amusement Center** (☎ 408/423-5590). A cross between *Treasure Island* and *20,000 Leagues Under the Sea,* this arcade/miniature-golf course/play center is state-of-the-art. The two-story miniature-golf course will remind you of Disney's Pirates of the Caribbean, complete with life-size pirates, sound effects, and visual displays. (Watch out for those pretend exploding cannons—you'll think they're real!) The arcade has the newest video and pinball games, so good that even the adults in our group didn't want to leave. There are also full-size pool tables and air hockey.

While there is lots of boardwalk-style food, it's hard to find juice and milk, so you might want to bring those or any other healthy snacks you desire. Bring sunscreen, as sunburn is a major health hazard here. Rest rooms are huge (located in the middle of the boardwalk), but have no changing counter. Although you can make room for yourself, you'll have to improvise.

Along the boardwalk are benches for crowd-watching and resting. Infants and toddlers can sometimes be overwhelmed by the crowds here, so it's a good idea to bring your stroller. Youngsters might get worn out from having to manage the crowds.

The boardwalk is open every day during the summer; holidays and weekends the rest of the year. Admission is free.

The sandy beach is popular with swimmers, surfers, and sunbathers. It's a terrific place to play for a while. Located just off the boardwalk, it has rest rooms, parking, and a lifeguard.

Santa Cruz City Museum

You'll recognize this museum by the full-size statue of a whale in front of it (and probably five little kids climbing on it). Located at 1305 E. Cliff Dr. (☎ 408/429-3773), this little museum has a great Ohlone Native American exhibit and a few wonderful hands-on exhibits, including a tidepool where kids can touch sea creatures. If you haven't been to the Monterey Bay Aquarium, this will be a real treat. It is open Tuesday through Saturday from 10am to 5pm. and Sunday from noon to 5pm. Admission is $1.50 for adults, 50¢ for seniors; children free. While the beach across the street is inviting, it can be a bit windy for picnicking. We use the picnic tables and lawns behind the museum instead.

Another treat is the **Santa Cruz Surfing Museum,** located in the Abbott Memorial Lighthouse on Lighthouse Point (☎ 408/429-3429). Exhibits trace more than 100 years of local surfing history with photographs and surfing videos. (And for those of you who just love to watch surfers riding the waves, you can watch them near the museum at Steamer Lane, an internationally known surfing site.)

Open Thursday through Monday, noon to 4pm. Admission is free; donations appreciated.

Four blocks away is the **Santa Cruz Yacht Harbor,** a good place to stroll, with fine beaches on either side of the harbor. Beach-loving teenagers will find great shops nearby. The original **O'Neal's Surf Shop** (☎ 408/475-4151) is the place our teens go to browse for bikinis, surfboards, and skateboards (they rarely buy anything, but love to browse).

Roaring Camp and the Big Trees Narrow-Gauge Railroad

This is billed as a way to relive the excitement of the 1880 pioneer days. Located in Felton, six miles north of Santa Cruz via Graham Hill Road (☎ 408/335-4484), on land covered with remarkable redwoods, the authentic **steam logging train** recalls a time when locomotives took giant logs from the forest to the mills to be made into lumber. This is one of our kids' favorite places. It's the site of an original steam/narrow-gauge railroad, and the site of Bret Harte's short story "The Pride of Roaring

Camp." It has been wonderfully restored. As you cross from the parking lot through a covered bridge, to your right is a pond full of geese. Up to the left is an old schoolhouse. Wander down the dirt road until you come to the station, where you will buy tickets from a man dressed in 1800s garb. Departures are frequent, but if you have to wait, you can sit on a bench in the shade or amble to the general store, which has the required glass jars of peppermint sticks and is filled with memorabilia about trains and the camp. There's a snack shop next door.

The camp also has good bathroom facilities plus a stationary set of train cars that kids adore playing on, plus picnic tables, barbecue pits, and lots of grassy areas where you can plunk down a blanket and enjoy your lunch while lazing in the sun. Sometimes country-and-western musicians perform, and during the summer there are a few volleyball nets set up. What a lovely spot to spend the afternoon!

- The glorious ride up the mountain in the open cars takes about an hour and 15 minutes, and goes in and out of sun and cool forest (bring hats, light sweaters, and sunscreen). It's said that these are the steepest railroad grades in North America. You might want to bring along a snack and juice, and be sure your kids use the bathroom *before you board,* as there are no facilities on the train or at the top of the mountain. The conductor narrates the trip with wonderful stories, dropping in jokes and relating history. The train stops at the top, among the elegant grove of redwoods, and everyone gets a chance to stretch. When we have gone with only our older kids, we've actually disembarked and hiked down the mountain. Some people picnic at the top of the mountain and try to catch a later train. However, check with the conductor and the ticket seller before you do that (or be prepared to hike down), since you will only be let back on a train if there are seats available, and during the summer months trains tend to be crowded.

The fare is $12 for adults, $8.75 for ages 3 to 15; under 3, free.

There is also a train that runs from the camp to Santa Cruz (round trip takes 2 ½ hours), the **Santa Cruz, Big Trees & Pacific.** We have some friends who split up, one parent taking the train with the kids, the other one meeting them with the car in town. The fare is $14 for adults, $8.95 for ages 3 to 15; under 3, free.

Another option is the Moonlight Steam Train Party (June through October on Saturday night at 7pm). Call for reservations—a must—and fares. Also from May through October on Saturday and Sunday from noon to 3p.m., there is a chuck-wagon barbecue. Menu items range from quarter-pound burgers (with all the trimmings) to Gold Rush steak (12-ounce top sirloin), and include salad, western-style beans, sourdough roll, beverages, and marshmallows for roasting.

You might be lucky enough to visit on a special-event day. If you do, be prepared to witness a train robbery or participate in an egg hunt or autumn harvest fair. If you'll be in Santa Cruz on Memorial Day weekend, you'll enjoy the Roaring Camp Annual Civil War Memorial. This reenactment of Civil War battles and camp life is played out by hundreds of soldiers in Union and Confederate uniforms.

You might want to visit the picturesque **Santa Cruz Harbor,** East Cliff Drive and 5th Ave. (☎ **408/475-6161**). You'll find restaurants, shops, boat rentals, and fishing equipment, and you can feed the sea lions.

Natural Bridges State Beach, 2513 West Cliff Drive (☎ **408/688-3241**) is a beautiful rocky beach that you'll want to see if you have time. Home of one of the largest Monarch butterfly colonies in the U.S., it is a great place to ponder the ocean, investigate tidepools, and watch wildlife. Guided tours can be arranged.

If you are interested in pick-your-own fruit, try **Gizdich Ranch,** 55 Peckham Rd., in nearby Watsonville (☎ **408/722-1056**). You can try for apples or berries. Call ahead as hours and fruit vary with the seasons.

Bike Paths

There is lovely bicycling in this town. The **San Lorenzo River Bike Path** is one good route. It follows the river from Santa Cruz Beach.

Above Santa Cruz Wharf is **West Cliff Drive,** where you can rollerskate and bicycle. The path hugs the ocean and goes past Lighthouse Point to Natural Bridges State Beach. On good days there are lots of seals just past the lighthouse. From the wharf up to the top is the only hill—but what a hill! Then it's flat and easy bicycling and rollerskating.

South of the Yacht Harbor is **East Cliff Drive,** another spectacular bicycle route. It stretches from the harbor into Capitola, a hilly two-lane road that goes through residential areas and the beaches.

You can rent bikes at **Bicycle Rental & Tour Center,** 415 Pacific Ave. (☎ **408/426-8687**).

A Day at Capitola by the Sea

Picture this: You're sitting on a charming little beach with children romping in the calm ocean or wading in the water of nearby Soquel Creek. The sun is warm, the kids are enjoying themselves, and you are relaxing. Yes, that's a day at Capitola, just a bit south of Santa Cruz.

Here's how we suggest you "do" Capitola.

Start out at **Gayle's Bakery & Rosticceria,** 504 Bay Ave. (☎ **408/462-1200**). Gayle studied in France as a baker's apprentice. The bakery is full of wonderful pastries, cookies, cakes, and breads. Eight-year-old Elizabeth used to spend a very long time examining the choices before she made up her mind. The Rosticceria, with a huge wood-fired barbecue spit, has everything one would want for a gourmet picnic or casual dinner. Our favorites are the twice-cooked baked potatoes with cheese, roast chicken, salads, and pastas. Open daily 6:30am to 8:30pm.

Picnic in hand, head down to the beach in Capitola Village. It's a good one for kids (there's a lifeguard here during the summer), and has a changing room, rest rooms, and outdoor showers for rinsing off sand. Soquel Creek runs into the beach. There is an espresso/wine bar with indoor as well as outdoor heated patios.

During the summer you can rent paddleboats (a favorite of all the kids). Open daily 6:30am to 7pm.

If you need a break from the beach, Capitola Village is loaded with boutiques and craft galleries, restaurants, and even coffeehouses.

For a real treat, you'll want to be sure to stop in at **Shadowbrook Restaurant,** 1750 Wharf Road, Capitola (☎ **408/475-1511**). Nestled among the trees and hilly terrain, this multilevel eatery is a treat as visual as it is culinary. You can either walk down the pathway or ride the quaint cable car to the entrance. Once inside, lush greenery and a wonderful view of the waterway await.

Specialties include prime rib, scampi, and a variety of fresh seafood. Sunday brunch is also served. Prices for dinner range $13.95–$24.95; Sunday brunch is $7.95–$13.50. The children's menu is $4.95–$7.95, and the kids are treated to a magic hat full of delights.

Highchairs and boosters are available. Reservations are recommended. Open for dinner Monday through Friday from 5:30pm; and Saturday and Sunday from 4:30pm. Sunday brunch is from 10:00am to 2:30pm.

A nearby eatery is **Zachary's,** 819 Pacific Ave. (☎ **408/427-0646**), a fine place to begin the day with a great brunch or breakfast (they're open for lunch too). We love their homemade breads; but for a special treat, be sure not to miss the jalapeño cornbread. And nothing on the menu costs over $6! A basic breakfast of eggs, potatoes, and toast runs $3.50, and a basic burger, $4.25.

This casual restaurant is bright—full of natural light—and the servers are great with kids. Boosters and highchairs are available but there's no children's menu (although they'll split adult portions for two kids). No reservations are accepted. Ample parking nearby. Some major credit cards honored.

Stagnaro Bros. (☎ **408/423-2180**), on the Santa Cruz Municipal Wharf, is a good choice for lunch or dinner. The view is lovely. The seafood louies are very good (and they have small sizes for smaller appetites), and there is a wide variety of seafood, pasta, steak and lobster and sandwiches. Prices range $3.95–$24.95.

Stagnaro's has a children's menu (fish and chicken entrees from $4.95 to $8.95), and has highchairs and boosters. Most credit cards accepted.

4 Marine World Africa USA

A must-see for families who love animals and marine life, a day at this state-of-the-art oceanarium promises an adventure to remember. Picturesque Marine World Africa USA (☎ **707/643-ORCA** for a recorded announcement) is situated in the rolling hills of Vallejo, 30 miles northeast of San Francisco and 10 miles south of the Napa Valley. Take I-80 East and exit at Marine World Parkway; or take Calif. 37; or take U.S. 101 north to Calif. 37 and then east to Marine World Parkway. The **Red and White Fleet** offers daily service to Marine World from San Francisco; it departs from Pier 41 at Fisherman's Wharf (☎ toll free **800/229-2784**).

This 160-acre wildlife park features hundreds of animals, both exotic and familiar, from land, sea, and air. The philosophy of the park is that because there are strong bonds of respect and affection between the animals and their trainers, visitors are able to enjoy close interaction with the animals. Animals such as chimps, snow leopards, orangutans, and camels roam the park with their trainers, giving visitors a close view. At Tiger Island, Bengal tigers swim, wrestle, and relax with their trainers. People and animals are also brought together via inventive activities and themed shows, fulfilling the objectives of delighting parents and thrilling children with both learning experiences and wonderful entertainment.

We try to arrive at opening time. We get a show schedule at the Clock Tower and select those we intend to see. Next we go to the storage lockers, situated at the left of the admission gate, to stow the extra sweaters, baby food, and other items we don't want to carry around. We lather sunscreen on the kids at this time, just in case we can't grab a wiggly, excited kid later on. We choose a meeting place in case someone gets lost. We remind the kids not to feed the animals. We load our cameras, and we're off.

Everyone loves the **scheduled shows,** which include the Killer Whale and Dolphin Show; the Waterski and Boat Show; the Jungle Theater with tigers, lions, and chimps; and the Bird Show. Our family favorite is the **Killer Whale and Dolphin**

Show, in which 9,000- and 6,000-pound killer whales swim and breach (leap) effortlessly through the water. A word of caution: be prepared to be splashed with salt water if you sit in the front area wet zone during a marine show. Remember, salt water stings the eyes. We were drenched sitting in front at a whale show during our first trip to the park.

Marine World's newest attraction, **Shark Experience** explores the fascinating world of the ocean's most feared predators. Shark Experience begins "underwater" as visitors are transported by a moving walkway through a tropical reef habitat, a 300,000-gallon clear acrylic tunnel. The sharks, some up to nine feet long, swim just inches overhead and alongside the tunnel. Fifteen species, including lemons, sand tigers, black tips, and wobbegongs, are represented throughout the entire exhibit. Outside the tunnel, the Discovery Gallery displays more about shark attacks, anatomy, breeding, reproduction, and mythology. Directly outside, Shark Shallows exhibits smaller sharks and shark pups. They can be viewed from underwater and above the pool.

Elephant Encounter is a very exciting attraction where people can enjoy these endangered animals. There's a tug-of-war and other safe encounters. Rides are $3.

The **Gentle Jungle** is a great area where toddlers can hang out with the llamas, goats, prairie dogs, wallabies, and others. During the summer, they can meet tiger cubs and other baby animals in Safari Stroll.

Whale of a Time World Playground is an innovative active play area for children under 90 pounds. The ball crawls, rope games, and net climbs are a treat for preschoolers to preteens. This is a favorite place for kids to spend a good hour. It is well supervised by park attendants.

The small but adequate **Aquarium** is arranged to compare different habitats: the Tropics, the Caribbean, and the California Coast. There are tidepools where youngsters can touch anemones, hermit crabs, sea stars, and other favorite creatures. Staff assistants in the Learning Center next to the Aquarium explain environmental adaptations and answer questions.

Family evening programs are held in the park from 7 to 9pm. **Sunrise and moonlight tours,** which coincide with the full moon, give an opportunity to see animals at different times of day. A variety of educational workshops for school-age children help them to learn about habitats, what animals eat, what their tracks look like. Programs are offered year round, and vary from season to season. For information, call **707/644-4000,** ext. **433.**

Various food concessions are located close together at Lakeside Plaza. The food offerings are remarkably diverse, which enables everyone to choose a different kind of food. Pushcart food vendors are positioned throughout the park. And there are also public barbecue grills located throughout the park. A tip: eat while one of the shows is going on because it's much less crowded. We enjoyed our lunch overlooking scenic Lake Chabot.

Strollers that look like dolphins can be rented for $5, and cameras, too, at the Main Gift Shop. The first-aid station is also located here. There are diaper-changing facilities in each restroom.

Marine World Africa USA is open daily in summer from 9:30am to 6:15pm; the rest of the year, Wednesday through Sunday from 9:30am to 5pm; there's also a special winter holiday schedule. Admission is $24.95 for adults, $20.95 for seniors, $16.95 for children 4–12, free for children 3 and under. Family evening programs cost $11. Credit cards are accepted.

5 The Napa Valley

Robert Louis Stevenson called it "The Valley of Plenty." You'll call it beautiful.

Tucked in among the California coastal mountains about an hour northeast of San Francisco, the tranquil Napa Valley awaits, ready to unfold all its gardenlike splendor to families. Each season brings its own delights. Just before spring, yellow mustard plants cover the ground. In summer you see lush green vines, rich dark soil, and verdant green hills. In late August and September grapes cluster on the vines, awaiting harvest. And in autumn the changing colors and dark clouds present a dramatic, sometimes stormy canvas. The countryside is dotted with cattle ranches and is becoming an important breeding ground for thoroughbred horses.

Known simply as "The Wine Country," the 30-mile-long Napa Valley includes the towns of Napa, Yountville, Oakville, St. Helena, Rutherford, and Calistoga. It is a full-day trip or a good one-night stay. Be prepared for your trip to be pricey, though, since this is a place that attracts wine lovers. Realistically, to truly enjoy the area, the older the children the better.

While visiting wineries and wine tasting have become a tradition, there are other, more family-oriented ways to spend time together. On clear mornings, brilliantly colored hot-air balloons grace the sky. Soaring and gliding are other air adventure possibilities. There is golf and tennis, and the area is an exquisite place to picnic. Or maybe you'd like to go horseback riding. Near Calistoga, you can see one of the world's three "Old Faithful" geysers and visit a petrified forest.

The Napa region is an interesting blend of traditions. The Gold Rush was the initial impetus for building up the area. Enticed from the goldfields into the small towns in Napa Valley when it was too cold in the hills (or when they needed paid work), the miners created a need for services and goods. At the time, cattle ranching and lumbering were the main industries.

In the mid-1880s Napa (among others) was host to the Great Silver Rush. The most famous mine was the Silverado, made immortal by Robert Louis Stevenson's *The Silverado Squatters.* In 1865 a railroad line was completed, linking Napa city with Vallejo to the south, and stagecoaches were already making regular trips as far north as Calistoga.

To the mining ambience, add a dash of early California mission influence. The Spanish settlers brought with them vine cuttings from the nearby missions, where wine was made for sacramental uses. Because of Napa's perfect wine-growing climate, these plantings took hold and blossomed into the Napa Valley of today, known throughout the world for its excellent California wines.

GETTING THERE

We suggest that you visit the wine country by car. From San Francisco, cross the Golden Gate Bridge and continue on U.S. 101 to Calif. 29 and 37. From the east, take I-80 past Sacramento to the Napa exit. From Sonoma, be prepared for a hilly narrow road.

Although half a dozen towns dot the Napa Valley, it's so small we'll treat it as a region. The Napa Valley southern boundary starts at the city of Napa, which is the southern tip of Calif. 29 and 37, a two-lane road. The other Napa Valley towns are easily reached going north on Calif. 29 and 37, or by the Silverado Trail.

Gray Line Tours (☎ 415/558-9400) offers a nine-hour wine country tour with stops for wine tasting. It originates in San Francisco and takes you through Napa and

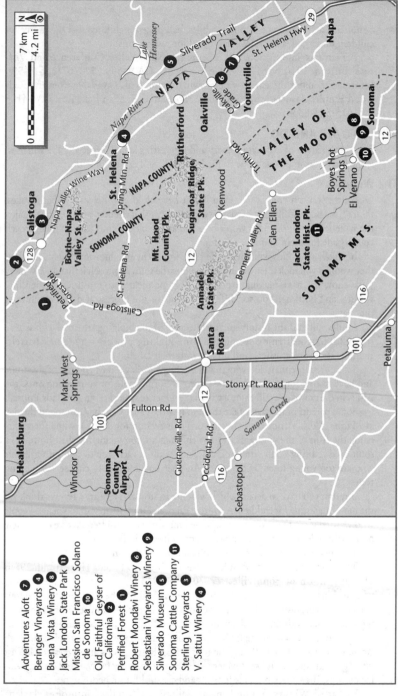

The Wine Country

Legend:

- Adventures Aloft **7**
- Beringer Vineyards **4**
- Buena Vista Winery **8**
- Jack London State Park **11**
- Mission San Francisco Solano de Sonoma **10**
- Old Faithful Geyser of California **2**
- Petrified Forest **1**
- Robert Mondavi Winery **6**
- Sebastiani Vineyards Winery **9**
- Silverado Museum **5**
- Sonoma Cattle Company **11**
- Sterling Vineyards **3**
- V. Sattui Winery **4**

Sonoma. The tour costs $37.50 for adults, half price for children 5–11, and free for children under 5. Call at least a day ahead for reservations.

For advance information, call or write the **Napa Valley Conference and Visitors' Bureau,** 1310 Napa Town Center, Napa, CA 94559 (☎ **707/226-7459**). Information about the entire wine-growing region is also available from the **Redwood Empire Association,** 15th Floor, 785 Market St., San Francisco, CA 94103 (☎ 415/543-8334).

WHAT TO SEE AND DO

The combination of exquisite scenery and interesting sights (especially the wineries) is the main reason people come to the Napa Valley. Let's begin with . . .

The Wineries

Of course you can enjoy them even if you have children with you. What it takes, though, is a slightly different perspective. Remember that children aren't going to enjoy the wineries as you do. This won't be a romantic sojourn into transplanted French countryside for them, but it can be fun.

It's likely your kids will appreciate the wineries in an educational light, much as they would if you took them on any other industrial tour. Approach it that way. Winery tours show the wine-making process from grape picking to crushing, fermenting, storing, and bottling. You see different aspects of the process at different times of the year.

Adults will find the history and architecture of the buildings themselves fascinating. Children will enjoy seeing the wine-making process—huge oak barrels, stainless-steel vats, crushers, and bottles with their labels.

There are more than 200 wineries in the Napa Valley today, and many give tours and have tasting rooms. While wine tasting is not possible for your young ones, the adults in the crowd can still enjoy a trip to the wineries while keeping the kids amused.

Some parents of teenagers take them to nearby Vallejo, so they can spend the day at Marine World Africa USA (see the previous section for details), while the adults enjoy the fruit of the vineyards. If your children are too young for that, however, a solution is to bring a babysitter or choose one adult at each stop to stay with toddlers who are too young to enjoy the tours. Another possibility is to choose self-guiding tours.

But first you have to decide which wineries to stop at. Here are a few we think are the most interesting for children. A word of caution: Don't try to visit too many. People who've tried it say that two wineries is the limit for most children. We've done a few more with older kids, but with several activity breaks in between.

You might want to start at the south end and work north.

The tour at the **Robert Mondavi Winery,** 7801 St. Helena Hwy. (Calif. 29) in Oakville, north of Yountville (☎ **707/963-9611**), gives an overview of the wine-making process in a modern, state-of-the-art facility. The 60-minute guided tour ends with a wine tasting. There's a large lawn with stylized sculptures outside the tasting room where kids can wander while Mom and Dad sample the vintages. The winery is open daily: May through October, from 9am to 5:30pm; November through April, from 9:30am to 4:30pm. The tour is free. Reservations are suggested, at least one day in advance. In July the winery holds an outdoor jazz festival, and during winter months, the winery presents festivals and classical music performances.

V. Sattui Winery, White Lane at Calif. 29, 1¹/₂ miles south of St. Helena (☎ 707/963-7774), may be the best winery to take the kids to. We love to time it so we "do lunch" in the beautiful tree-shaded picnic area, complete with tables. There's a large gourmet cheese shop and deli right there. Tasting hours are daily from 9am to 6pm in summer and 9am to 5pm in winter. Tours are by appointment.

The **Beringer Vineyards,** just north of St. Helena at 2000 Main St. (☎ 707/963-4812), is unique. The family home, called the Rhine House, built in 1883, is an example of old German architecture and is a California National Landmark. You can view the house and take a walking tour of the aging cellars where barrels of wine are stored in hand-dug tunnels carved out of the mountainside. The winery is open daily from 9:30am to 5pm.

Sterling Vineyards, 1111 Dunaweal Lane (☎ 707/942-3300), is a good family place located two miles south of Calistoga. Board the four-seat aerial tram for a fun ride up the mountain to the hilltop winery; the steep climb may be scary for those afraid of heights. You see a sweeping view of the surrounding mountaintops, valley, and vineyards. The stark white monastic building is also a visual treat. The tour is at your own pace with signs to guide. There is no stroller access, so be prepared to carry infants and toddlers. There is a large giftshop and lots of open spaces for children to wander. Tasting times and sales hours are daily from 10:30am to 4:30pm. The visitors' fee is $6 per person over age 16.

Nature's Wonders

At the northern end of the valley near Calistoga, **Old Faithful Geyser of California** is one of three "Old Faithful" geysers in the world. To merit the name "old faithful," a geyser must have a regular interval pattern. Old Faithful Geyser of California erupts approximately every 40 minutes on a yearly average. The eruptions vary with the barometric pressure, moon, tides, and tectonic stresses of the earth. There is an exhibit hall that explains many of these topics. About 45 minutes from Napa, at 1299 Tubbs Lane (☎ 707/942-6463), it can be reached from either Calif. 29 or Calif. 128.

There's a picnic area, a snack bar, and a giftshop. Strollers can navigate the area. Admission is $5 for adults, $4 for seniors over 60, $2 for children 6–12, free for children under 6. The area is open daily: from 9am to 6pm in summer and from 9am to 5pm in winter.

The **Petrified Forest** is of interest to young and old alike. It is located between Calistoga and Santa Rosa, at 4100 Petrified Forest Rd. (☎ 707/942-6667), about 50 minutes from Napa City. Here giant redwoods, covered with volcanic ash, have been turned into stone, permanently preserving them. Kids marvel at the petrified specimens and enjoy touching the stonelike redwoods. The museum describes the processes of fossilization and petrification. Strollers are fine on the trail, and there are picnic areas. Admission is $3 for adults, $1 for children 4–11, and free for children under 4. Open daily from 10am to 5:30pm in summer and from 10am to 4:30pm the rest of the year.

BICYCLE RIDING   Bicycling along the **Silverado Trail** or the **Solano Bicycle Path** is a popular way to experience the lushness and beauty of the vineyards. Parents need to be especially careful, though. Traffic races by on both roads and is especially treacherous on the Silverado Trail. Kids need to be experienced bicyclists.

You can rent bikes at **Napa Valley Cyclery,** 4080 Byway East, in Napa (☎ 707/255-3377), and also little trailers that attach behind the bicycle to carry children up to 125 pounds (they don't rent ordinary bicycle seats). Rates are $6 for the first hour to a maximum of $20 for a business day; overnight or 24 hours is $28;

one-way rentals are based on where you go. They will supply maps. Open Monday through Saturday year round, from 9am to 6pm; in summer, on Sunday from 10am to 4pm, and in winter from 10am to 4pm. You can also rent bikes from **Bicycle Trax,** 796A Soscal Ave., Napa (☎ 707/258-8729).

HORSEBACK RIDING   Wild Horse Valley Ranch, on Wild Horse Valley Road in Napa (☎ 707/224-0727) has guided trail trips that cost $35 for a two-hour ride through 3,000 acres of gorgeous countryside. Children must be 8 years old. For groups of 25 or more, there are breakfast, lunch, and dinner trail rides.

HOT-AIR BALLOONING   Hot-air ballooning is an expensive adventure for those who want a once-in-a-lifetime experience. The balloons take off in early morning when the air is cool and the winds are gentle.

Adventures Aloft, at the Vintage 1870 complex (P.O. Box 2500), Yountville, CA 94599 (☎ 707/944-4400), is the oldest outfit in the valley. Rates are $165 per person; kids 8–12 are half price the minimum age is 8.

Other choices are **Napa Valley Balloons, Inc.,** P.O. Box 2860, Yountville, CA 94599 (☎ 707/253-2224, or toll free **800/253-2224** in California); **Balloon Aviation of Napa Valley,** 2299 3rd St., Napa, CA 94558 (☎ 707/252-7067); and **Once in a Lifetime,** P.O. Box 795, Calistoga, CA 94515 (☎ 707/942-6541, or toll free **800/722-6665**).

Indoor Activities

The **Silverado Museum,** located at 1490 Library Lane in St. Helena (☎ 707/963-3757), is devoted to the life and works of Robert Louis Stevenson. This distinguished museum is the fulfillment of a lifetime dream of Norman Strouse, who started collecting Robert Louis Stevenson memorabilia at the age of 24.

Robert Louis Stevenson spent only two months here, but he has become a part of the region's folklore. In 1880, Stevenson honeymooned with his bride, Fanny Osbourne, in an abandoned bunkhouse near the old Silverado Mine. Here he wrote *The Silverado Squatters.*

More than 160,000 people have visited the museum with its 8,000 objects, including original manuscripts, letters, photographs, and first editions. To prepare your kids, the curator suggests reading something by the author to them before your arrival. A *Child's Garden of Verse, Treasure Island,* and *Dr. Jekyll and Mr. Hyde* top the list. The museum is open Tuesday through Sunday from noon to 4pm; closed holidays. Admission is free; children are welcome and each child receives a free postcard.

WHERE TO EAT

One of our favorite places is **Jonesy's Famous Steak House,** 2044 Airport Rd., Napa (☎ 707/255-2003), at the Napa Airport off Calif. 29 and Calif. 12 as you drive south toward Vallejo. Kids love to watch the planes take off and we love the hearty fare. There's a wonderful dessert selection. A family dinner favorite is the juicy top sirloin steak for two, which includes soup or salad, special or baked potatoes, and a roll, for $18.75. Salads, sandwiches, broasted chicken, and a sampling of seafood specialties complete the menu; prices range from $4.75 to $12.75. The children's menu has steak, a portion ample for two children, for $4.75, and chicken or hamburger for $4.25. The children's dinner comes with a cup of soup or tossed salad and french-fried potatoes; the real favorite is the block of Jell-O on the plate.

The staff will warm baby food and bottles, and provide booster seats and highchairs. Open Tuesday through Sunday from 11:30am to 9pm; winter weeknights, closing is at 8pm. Reservations recommended. Major credit cards accepted. Plenty of parking nearby.

River City, at 505 Lincoln Ave., just north of downtown Napa (☎ 707/ 253-1111), is a good, casual place with an outdoor deck overlooking the Napa River and a big fish pond that children love. Prices for lunch start at $5.75, going up to $8.50. Dinner prices start at $9.75–$14.75. They'll split adult portions and warm baby food and bottles; highchairs and boosters are provided. Reservations are strongly recommended. Open daily from 11am to 5pm for lunch and from 5 to 10pm for dinner.

A Mexican restaurant that locals frequent, is **Red Hen Cantina** at 5091 St. Helena Hwy. (☎ 707/255-8125), between Napa and Yountville. It has a lovely deck with outdoor seating. Fajitas are the house specialty at $10.95, and enchiladas suizas are $8.50. A children's menu offers hamburger, taco, burrito, or enchilada for $4.95. Kids are given Red Hen coloring books and balloons; baby food and bottles are warmed, highchairs and boosters are provided. Open Sunday through Thursday from 11am to 9:30pm and on Friday and Saturday from 11am to 10:30pm. Reservations are accepted for parties of five or more. In the peak of summer, there may be a 30- to 40-minute wait.

Downtown Joe's, 902 Main St., Napa (☎ 707/258-2337), is a casual, American-style restaurant that overlooks the river. The outdoor patio is a fun place to sit and enjoy the city. Prices run $4.95–$12.95. Children can order breast of chicken wings or hamburger or pizza for $4.95 which includes a drink. They make their own root beer. Children are given markers and paper for drawing, booster seats, and highchairs; adult portions will be split. Open Monday daily 11am to 10pm. Thursday through Saturday there is a late-night menu to midnight. Reservations and major credit cards are accepted. There's a nearby parking lot.

The **Vintage Red Rock Café,** 6525 Washington St., Yountville (☎ 707/944-2614), has a pleasant outdoor eating area on the deck. Omelets, salads, sandwiches, fish and chips, and burgers are $3.85 to $7.50. They will warm baby bottles and provide highchairs and boosters. Open daily from 9am to 8pm. Credit cards are accepted, but reservations are not.

WHERE TO STAY

The **Silverado Country Club,** 1600 Atlas Peak Rd., Napa, CA 94558 (☎ 707/ 257-0200, or toll free **800/532-0500**), is a large, 1,200-acre resort surrounded by lush foliage, golf courses and jogging trails. The 280-unit condominium complex has tennis courts, swimming pools, and golf courses. There are children's tennis lessons, bicycle rentals, and acres of grass for playing. Nearby horseback riding is available.

Children are welcome at all three on-premises dining facilities, and booster seats and highchairs are available at all. Babysitting can be arranged through the concierge.

In Case of Emergency

If a medical emergency occurs during your visit to the Napa Valley, there's an emergency room at **Queen of the Valley Hospital,** 1000 Trancas St., Napa (☎ 707/252-4411).

Room service, available from 7am to 10pm, offers good items for children. Most accommodations have fully equipped kitchens, and some cottage suites have fireplaces.

Reservations are taken two weeks prior to your stay. Rates are seasonal, but ask for specials. Studios rent for $175, single or double occupancy; a one-bedroom suite for one or two costs $235, a two-bedroom suite for up to four people rents for $340, and a three-bedroom suite for up to six is $465. Children under 12 stay free in their parents' room. There's no charge for cribs. Each additional person is charged $15 per night.

The **Sheraton Inn, Napa Valley,** 3425 Solano Ave., Napa, CA 94558 (☎ 707/253-7433, or toll free **800/325-3535**) is a good, moderately priced hotel in the heart of the valley. The grass-bordered pool is shallow enough and shaped so that kids can navigate easily. There are two lighted tennis courts. The staff is congenial and very helpful. Babysitting service requires 24 hours' advance notice. The country-style Harvest Cafe is open daily and has a complete children's menu. Room service is available from 7am to 10pm.

Each room is furnished with a king-size bed or two double beds; remote-control TV with HBO and in-room movies. A refrigerator must be requested in advance, at $10 per night. Room rates are seasonal, ranging from $79 to $159, single or double. Children under 17 stay free in the same room with their parents; each additional person over 17 is charged $10 per night. Cribs are free.

The **Inn at Napa Valley/Crown Sterling Suites,** 1075 California Blvd., Napa, CA 94559 (☎ 707/253-9540, or toll free **800/433-4600**), has a large millpond with a working paddlewheel. The Spanish-style hotel has a spacious lobby, a pool, and a Jacuzzi. Bicycles can be rented. Babysitting can be arranged. The Café 1991 restaurant is a three-story atrium-style room, open to guests from 11am to 11pm. Room service is available from 11am to 10pm.

All 205 accommodations are two-room suites, though they're a bit small. The full kitchens have microwaves, wet bars, and coffee makers. The suite rates include a full cooked-to-order breakfast in the restaurant and evening cocktails in the Atrium. Rates in spring, summer, and fall are $99–$179; winter rates are $99–$149. Children under 12 stay free in their parents' suite; those 12 and over are charged $15 per night. Cribs are free; rollaways are not available.

The **Best Western Inn,** a clean and basic motel with a swimming pool and a 24-hour Denny's restaurant next door, is located at 100 Soscol Ave., Napa, CA 94559 (☎ 707/257-1930, or toll free **800/528-1234**). Suites, which have refrigerators, cost $99–$149. Deluxe rooms with one king-size bed are $69–$99; with two queen-size beds, $79–$99. Standard rooms with one king-size bed are $95, single or double occupancy; with two double beds, $69–$95.

6 Sonoma County

Sonoma County is a combination of beaches, rugged coast, redwoods, quaint towns, and the "big city" of Santa Rosa. It also includes the Valley of the Moon, once home to Jack London, and is California's oldest winery and grape-growing region.

The town of Sonoma, like most early California towns once governed by Mexico, has a plaza that forms the center of the town.

U.S. 101 north from San Francisco leads you to Calif. 37, then to Calif. 121. From there, take Hwy. 12 (Broadway) directly to the Plaza.

WHAT TO SEE AND DO

The **Sonoma Valley Visitors Bureau,** 453 1st St., in the Plaza (☎ **707/996-1090**), is open seven days a week from 9am to 5pm; it's closed New Year's, Thanksgiving, and Christmas Days. Call or write in advance for a free visitors' guide. And request the children's activities listing.

On warm summer days you'll see families taking advantage of the Plaza's park. Swings, picnic tables, and a duck pond beckon you, and you can drop by the **Sonoma Cheese Factory,** 2 Spain St. (☎ **707/996-1931**), to watch their famous Sonoma Jack cheese being made. The Cheese Factory and the deli are open from 9:30am to 5:30pm daily.

Historic Sites

You can get a walking tour map of the Plaza area at the Visitors Bureau for $2.25 and a *Visitors Guide* with key historic sights for $1.50. There are a number of key historic sites surrounding the Plaza, but we'll just mention those the kids might enjoy.

One ticket is good within the same day at Sonoma Barracks, Vallejo's home, and the Petaluma Adobe (a 20-minute drive from Sonoma). The charge is $2 for adults, $1 for children 6 to 17. The mission, barracks, and Vallejo's home are all open daily from 10am to 5pm. All these sites have stroller accessibility, but there are stairs in Vallejo's home. Rest rooms can be found in the Plaza, near the mission.

It was Gen. Mariano Vallejo who was given the responsibility of creating a fort and a town here, and who was put in charge of the mission by the Mexican government. His grand rule ended when American settlers captured the region in 1846. Some of the buildings that Vallejo had built for the town are still standing.

Vallejo's home, called **Lachryma Montis,** was built in 1851. His first home, **Casa Grande,** was built in 1836 and is on Spain Street. At the time it was built it was considered one of the grandest homes in all of California. You'll see only the servants' quarters, as the main wing burned down 30 years after it was built.

The **Toscano Hotel** is next door at 20 E. Spain St. Built to be a general store and library, in 1886 it was converted into a hotel. No longer in use, the rooms are still furnished with original items. Free docent-guided tours are given on Saturday and Sunday from 1 to 4 p.m., and on Monday from 11 am to 1 pm.

The **Sonoma Barracks,** at the corner of Spain Street and 1st Street East (☎ **707/938-1519**), which was built in 1836 by Vallejo, displays Sonoma's Native American, Mexican, and American historical periods.

Across the street is the **Mission San Francisco Solano de Sonoma** (☎ **707/938-1519**). This was the last of the 21 missions built in California.

Kitty-corner to the mission is the **Bear Flag Monument,** which marks the revolt that took place in the Plaza between a band of 30 Americans and General Vallejo, who was captured by the raiders in the early-morning hours. The Americans claimed Sonoma as part of the California Republic, and raised the Bear Flag, which later became the official flag of California. A month later an American naval officer claimed the area for the United States, and raised the Stars and Stripes.

Jack London State Park

Any kid (or adult) who has wept through *Call of the Wild,* been mesmerized by *The Sea Wolf,* and impressed by the simplicity of *To Build a Fire,* knows the name

Jack London. (Take Calif. 12 toward Santa Rosa, left on Madrone Road to Arnold, right to London Ranch Road, and then left into the park.) Just seven miles out of Sonoma in Glen Ellen (☎ 707/938-5216), this is part of London's original 1,400-acre Beauty Ranch. Now over 800 acres, the park includes the ruins of London's house, his grave, his wife Charmian's house, and the cottage in which he wrote much of his later works.

At the entrance is **Happy Walls,** Charmian's house, which is now used as a museum for London's photographs and other mementos. At **Wolf House,** you'll see the remains of the house they planned so carefully, but which burned before they could move in. It is reachable by a half-mile trail, and takes approximately one hour round trip. London's ashes are buried next to the marked graves of two pioneer children, and this hike is a half mile. You might have to carry the toddlers on the way back, as the trail is fairly steep.

There's a rest room near the parking lot (and not another one until Wolf House, half a mile away), and picnic facilities in the area. Beware of a few rattlesnakes and poison oak. The park is open daily from 9:30am to 7pm in summer, and until sundown in winter; the museum is open daily from 10am to 5pm. There's a $5-per-car entrance fee.

Horseback Riding

The **Sonoma Cattle Company** (☎ 707/996-8566) accommodates beginners and experts with guided rides on the 20 miles of horse trails in Jack London State Park and in Sugarloaf Ridge State Park, 20 minutes north of Sonoma. The minimum age for riding is 8. Rides in both parks depart at 9am, noon, and 3pm during spring and summer; check ahead for fall hours. Rates for both adults and children are $20 for one hour, $30 for two hours. Reservations are strongly advised during summer and on weekends. When you call, ask for directions to the stables. There's a $5 vehicle cover charge.

Miniature Train Ride

Train Town is located on Broadway, one mile south of the Plaza (☎ 707/938-3912). Little kids especially will love the miniature train ride. The train stops midway on its 1½-mile route so that the passengers can feed the goats and peek through the windows of the miniature buildings. Open weekends throughout the year and daily in summer through Labor Day from 10:30am to 5pm. The fare is $2.60 for adults, $1.90 for children 2–16, free for those under 2.

Wineries

Several famous wineries in the area offer tours. Be sure to call ahead, because tour times change and picnic facilities may not be open. The **Wine Institute,** Suite 1000, 425 Market St., San Francisco, CA 94105 (☎ 415/512-0151), will send a list of wineries; or you can contact the Sonoma Valley Visitors' Bureau.

Buena Vista Winery–Haraszthy Cellars, 18000 Old Winery Rd., one mile east of the Sonoma Plaza (☎ 707/938-1266), is California's oldest premium winery and has been declared an historic landmark. Open daily (except New Year's, Thanksgiving, and Christmas Days) from 10am to 5pm. A 20-minute guided tour leaves at 11am and 2pm in summer, and at 2pm in winter. There's no charge for the tour and tasting.

Sebastiani Vineyards, at 389 4th St. E. (☎ 707/938-5532), has guided tours daily from 10:20am to 4pm. There's also a picnic area.

WHERE TO STAY

The **Sonoma Valley Inn,** is a block from the Plaza at 550 2nd St. W., Sonoma, CA 95476 (☎ **707/938-9200,** or toll free **800/334-5784;** fax 707/938-0935). This Best Western Inn is built in a turn-of-the-century design. There's a courtyard with a large whirlpool and a heated pool. The inn offers rooms with either fireplaces or with kitchenettes and some adjoining rooms. Rooms have either one king-size or two queen-size beds; all have TVs with movie channels.

Rates, including a complimentary continental breakfast and a bottle of wine, are $79–$159. Children under 12 stay free in the same room with their parents; children over 12 are charged $10 per night. Cribs and rollaways are free. Ask about midweek specials.

WHERE TO EAT

Sonoma is dotted with intimate gourmet restaurants, but many are either adult-oriented or higher priced; call restaurants in advance to ask if they welcome children.

One place satisfactory for both children and wallet is **La Casa Restaurant,** 121 E. Spain St. (☎ **707/996-3406**). There's outdoor seating on a deck, the service is excellent and quick, the prices are reasonable, and children love the wonderful tortilla chips, which are brought immediately; parents appreciate the advice about how hot or spicy the different dishes are. A children's combination plate of taco or enchilada with beans and rice is $4.50. The lunch menu has a school-kids' burrito for $3.50. House specials cost $7.50. Portions will be split for two children; baby food and bottles are warmed; highchairs and booster seats are provided.

Open for lunch and dinner daily from 11:30am to 10pm. Major credit cards accepted. Parking is available.

Café at the Feed Store, at 529 First St. W. (☎ **707/938-2122**), announces on its children's menu that The Feed Store loves well-behaved children. The servers provide activity menus, crayons and paper, highchairs and booster seats, and warm baby food and bottles.

The children's menu lists pancakes, eggs, or homemade French toast for breakfast at $3.25; and chicken wings, grilled cheese, or hot dogs with fries for lunch at $3.25. The adult lunch menu offers such items as grilled flank steak, hamburgers, grilled chicken breast, pasta, salads, and club sandwiches. Lunch costs $6–$8.50.

The café is open daily from 7am to 5pm for breakfast and lunch. Reservations accepted. Major credit cards accepted.

SIDE TRIPS

Petaluma, a small town of Victorian homes and 19th-century buildings, is located approximately 20 minutes from Sonoma. Once a leading river town that shipped food downriver to the gold-seeking '49ers, its 20th-century claim to fame is its rank as one of California's leading dairy centers.

Stop by or write the **Petaluma Visitors Center,** 799 Baywood Dr., Ste. 1 (Hwy. 116 exit off Hwy. 101), Petaluma, CA 94954 (☎ **707/769-0429**) for free visitors' guides, maps, and information about walking tours. If you plan on a longer stay, they'll give you ideas for additional family-friendly activities in the area.

Stop here to see the **Petaluma Adobe State Historic Park,** 3325 Adobe Rd., at Casa Grande (☎ **707/762-4871**), home of California's largest adobe. Originally this was General Vallejo's estate. You and the kids can explore the old ranch headquarters building and see the tools and weaving displays, brickmaking, blacksmithing, and the huge pots used to make tallow. There's a picnic area on the grounds, and sheep, goats, and roosters roam free.

Open daily from 10am to 5pm. Guided tours are available by reservation only, on Monday, Wednesday, Thursday, and Friday (☎ 707/938-1519). If you don't use your ticket from Sonoma, the fee is $2 for adults, $1 for children.

Throughout the area, all sorts of farms let you enjoy a look at what they make or grow, including fruits, vegetables, flowers, dairy products, trees, and animals. The **Sonoma County Farm Trails** map points out locations and gives phone numbers. It is available from the Petaluma Visitors Program, the Sonoma Valley Visitors Bureau, and at some hotels and businesses, or write Sonoma County Farm Trails, P.O. Box 6032, Santa Rosa, CA 95406 (include a self-addressed envelope and 52¢ postage).

A highlight of the Farm Trails is **Pet-A-Llama Ranch,** 5505 Lone Pine Rd., Sebastopol (☎ 707/823-9395 after 4 p.m.). Tours by appointment only. The kids and adults can pet and feed actual llamas here. There are also hand-woven goods for sale and spinning demonstrations, along with llama demonstrations and instructional talk for a small fee. Free Saturday and Sunday 10am to 4pm, but no demonstration is given. Feed is 25¢ a cup if you wish to hand-feed the llamas.

The North Coast

5

THE CALIFORNIA COAST IS KNOWN THROUGHOUT THE WORLD FOR ITS BEAUTY. THE northern portion (especially the drive from San Francisco to the border of Oregon) is unparalleled for its extraordinary scenery—a dramatic, ever-changing landscape. North of San Francisco the view might be bleak and foggy on the ocean side and lush and sunny on the other. Curving roads hug cliffs that lead to sheer drop-offs and the raging ocean below. Just 15 minutes farther on, the road may become a narrow forest lane framed by giant redwoods and filled with the fragrance of pine and wildflowers. There's a different sight around every curve—and there are curves! Parts of the drive are straight and easily negotiated, while others take all your driving skills and concentration. Some areas will tempt you to grab the kids' hands and walk along a beach or hike a certain trail. Other places will entice you to find a cozy family cabin with a fireplace and flannel sheets.

You'll drive through artists' colonies, fishing villages, and historic settlements. One village is even a former outpost of Russian fur traders! You'll hear ocean waves pounding against massive rocks and follow the glorious Russian River's smooth trip from Sonoma County to Mendocino County.

Besides viewing exquisite scenery, you and your family can hike, camp, fish, clam, explore, whale-watch, or just enjoy the outdoors.

We will take you on a trip from San Francisco north to Fort Bragg—approximately 450 miles round trip. If you choose to continue farther north, you'll be swept away by the beauty of the northern California giant redwoods, the biggest in the state. If you want to detour inland at various points, you can visit the wine country.

But back to Calif. 1, the coastal road. For all of this beauty, your ride will probably be one of the most rugged you've ever had! The road curves and twists. There are few places to stop between towns, and no rest stops to speak of. Children (and parents) who suffer from motion sickness might want to consider taking U.S. 101. Or perhaps take the coast route partway, then change over to 101 (which can also be pretty trying—it frequently changes from freeway to a two-lane, curvy, slow highway).

As unappealing as it might sound, just throw a roll of paper towels and some plastic bags in the car, take a change of clothes out of the suitcase for each child just in case, and put some crackers and even a can of soda in the front seat. Also, eat something earlier, or bring food along in the car. The first nine miles out of San Francisco seemed like 20 with our hungry daughter in tow. Speaking from the experience, these little items would have helped us out on that trip!

Take Calif. 1 (the coastal road) north from San Francisco to **Stinson Beach,** nine miles from the Golden Gate Bridge. We like to stop here, as it's the first place that offers a good rest stop and somewhere to eat, and it's a good introduction to the coast. The large beach is rugged and bordered by dense foliage. There's a big parking lot and no admission fee. The picnic area near the parking lot is nice, and there's a snackbar right on the beach and clean rest rooms. The beach is open for swimming from May to mid-September. The park is open daily from 9am to sunset.

First-time surfers might want to try their skill here, as the waves are good and the lifeguards are considered to be some of the best. You can rent wetsuits, flippers, boogie boards, and skimboards from **The Live Water,** 3450 Shoreline Hwy., in the town of Stinson Beach (☎ 415/868-0333).

We find that a 30- or 45-minute break here is perfect before continuing up the coast.

1 Point Reyes

Located approximately 40 miles north of San Francisco, **Point Reyes National Seashore** is 65,000 acres of rugged, windswept beaches, marshland and grassland, estuaries, forests, and ranges. It's land ripe for exploration by car, on foot, or on bicycle. It is a wilderness area filled with things to see, from whales and sea lions to tule elk and bobcats, and it offers trails for hiking, plantlife to admire, tidepools to explore, and paths for horseback riding.

The seashore is a series of surprises. Everywhere you turn the terrain—and weather—seems to change from hour to hour and place to place. One minute you're in a parklike setting with gentle grassy hills and a forest nearby. Suddenly you reach a portion of the seashore that is hauntingly bleak, not unlike the marshes of northern England. Then there's sun again, and a bay calm enough for swimming.

ORIENTATION

The best way to learn all you can do here is to begin at the **National Seashore Visitor Center,** located at Bear Valley, just off Calif. 1 at Olema (☎ **415/663-1092**). From this point, there are several sites that can be reached on foot. Right near the Visitor Center are picnic tables and rest rooms. The center has maps and a good driving tour, which may be your best bet with toddlers. In general, Point Reyes is a great place for ages six and up.

The weather can change from hour to hour and place to place. Heavy fog can roll in without warning. Even though it's sunny in one spot (like Bear Valley), this doesn't mean it will be like that throughout the area. So if you decide to hike or walk along one of the beaches, be sure to take water and layers of clothing. Always check with the Visitor Center first for weather and tide information, and ask first which beaches are safe.

Summers can be foggy and windy; very early fall is a good time for a visit. Or come in early February (through July) when the wildflowers bloom. No matter what time of the year you visit, bring jackets in order to be prepared for the unpredictable weather.

WHAT TO SEE AND DO

Directly behind the Visitor Center and up the hill is the **Morgan Horse Ranch** (☎ **415/663-1763**), which is open year-round. Learn about the history of the Morgan Horse via interpretive exhibits; you can watch the horses graze in the fields. These horses are bred and trained here and used by the rangers.

Nearby is **Kule Loklo,** a replica of a Coast Miwok Indian village. The tribe is thought to have lived on Point Reyes Peninsula for thousands of years. Take the half-mile walk to the village to see the reconstructed sweathouse, ceremonial areas, **kotchas** (dwellings), and graneries. The Big Time Festival, held usually the third Saturday in July, is a good time to see a variety of demonstrations and Native American dancers. Call the Visitor Center for information.

Hiking

The 140 miles of trails through Point Reyes offer both the novice and ardent hiker a choice of terrain and level of difficulty. Trails can be reached from four trailheads. The visitor center has trail maps; ask the rangers about the difficulty level and weather conditions.

The **Earthquake Trail,** which begins close to the visitor center parking lot, is a half-hour loop trail (0.7-mile hike) along the San Andreas Fault. It's fascinating, not only for Californians, to see how damage caused by the quake of 1906 affected the Point Reyes Peninsula. There are interpretive signs describing earthquakes along the trail. The paved trail is no problem for children and is stroller and wheelchair accessible.

Our troop enjoys the short, self-guided **Woodpecker Nature Trail** (0.7-mile hike), which takes us into the mixed evergreen forest. There are lots of varieties of birds to accompany us on our hike. The kids like to point out the wild mushrooms (be careful—don't let them touch), mosses, and ferns.

You might also take a drive to **Pierce Ranch,** at the end of Pierce Point Road on the way to Tomales Bay, and take the self-guided walking trail through the old dairy ranch. Call the rangers at **415/669-1534** for more information on the ranch and Dairy Days held in spring. Pierce Point is also home to the area's more than 200 **tule elk.** You can hike in and hope for a look.

Beaches and Ocean Activities

Most of the beaches are rugged, dangerous, and usually unswimmable on the ocean side. The visitor center will give you specific information about each beach. Remember that even at the swimmable beaches you swim at your own risk—there are no lifeguards on duty. The water in the area stays very cold year-round—50° to 55°. Be sure to have plenty of warm clothes available for when you get out of the water, and don't forget how fast the temperature can drop.

Limantour Beach, on the Drakes Bay side, is fine for swimming and picnicking. There's also great birdwatching nearby.

This is the time to check the kids' history knowledge. Ask them what they know about Sir Francis Drake, since this is the bay historians argue that Drake arrived at in 1579, making him the first English explorer to land on this continent.

Drakes Beach, on Drakes Bay, is a good swimming beach. It's the only spot on the seashore with food service, and it has its own information center open weekends and holidays only, yearround.

Several beaches on the Tomales Bay side, including **Tomales Bay State Beach,** are good for swimming and collecting seashells. Although not part of the national seashore, **Tomales Bay State Park,** just north of Iverness, is within easy driving distance. The bay water is warmer, and buoys are set out for swimmers. There's a picnic area and restrooms.

From December to April the **lighthouse observation platform** above the Point Reyes Lighthouse is a wonderful place to watch the migration of the California gray whales. It's a half mile walk from the parking lot to the observation deck. A visitor center is open from 10am to 5pm Thursday through Monday. The lighthouse (which is 300 steps down from the observation deck) is open the same days until 4:30pm. **Note:** The lighthouse closes if winds reach 40 mph or more. During whale-watching season (which peaks January through March), a shuttle bus runs from South Beach or Drakes Beach to the lighthouse (weekends and holidays only). Be sure to call the lighthouse Thursday through Monday at **415/669-1534** for shuttle information.

Horseback Riding

Another good way to see the area is on horseback. **Five Brooks Stables** (☎ **415/663-1570**) offers trips of various lengths with prices ranging $20–$85 per person. The minimum age to ride is 12 years old. Be sure to call for reservations, or write P.O. Box 567, Point Reyes Station, CA 94956.

... and More

The kids might also enjoy a look at the **Johnson Oyster Company** on Drakes Estero. It's an authentic old oyster company—still selling them fresh—where children will be fascinated at seeing how these highly valued oysters are grown on wire strings on wooden platforms, and are fed by the nutrients carried in by the tide. There are mounds of empty oyster shells everywhere.

Guided experiences that can be enjoyed by the whole family are offered by **Point Reyes Field Seminars,** mailing address: Pt. Reyes, CA 94956 (☎ **415/663-1200**). Ask to be put on the mailing list—brochures will be sent three times per year.

There are approximately 15 one-day classes per year. One class, led by a well-known naturalist, is called Family Nature Experience. It consists of short walks (totaling about three miles) exploring the sounds, sights, and smells of the various plants and animals ($45 for a family of three, plus $15-per each additional family member). Family Tidepooling explores the intertidal region of the area. The family will get a good look at scuttling crabs, burrowing clams, and brightly colored sea stars (same price). The suggested age for children participating in the regular family classes is 4 to 12. Classes last from 10am to approximately 4pm.

WHERE TO STAY

Although the seashore is primarily a day-use area, there are several campsites accessible by hiking in. Find out from the visitor center what's available since the sites are not very big.

If you don't want to camp, but choose to stay overnight, we suggest two tiny inns that welcome families.

One is **Jasmine Cottage,** 11561 State Route #1 (P.O. Box 56), Point Reyes Station, CA 94956 (☎ **415/663-1166;** fax 415/663-9565).

Owner Karen Gray converted this carriage house into a guest cottage that sleeps four because many of her friends who had always enjoyed bed-and-breakfast inns were no longer welcome at them with their children. It has a queen-size bed and two twin beds, a wood stove, a fully equipped kitchen, private patio, and garden hot tub. Kids have the run of the pasture in back or can play at the school playground across the street. There are eggs to collect from the resident chickens and a donkey in the next pasture.

She has also built a second cottage called **Gray's Retreat,** a cozy, cheery place, furnished elegantly. It sleeps six and has a fully equipped kitchen, full bath and two furnished patios and a hot tub.

Jasmine Cottage or Gray's Retreat is $115 per night for two people, with a two-night minimum stay on weekends. There are special weekly rates. Additional guests are charged $15 per night. Breakfast is included in Jasmine only. A highchair and portacrib are available.

Be sure to call for reservations; they are booked far in advance.

The Carriage House, 325 Mesa Rd. (P.O. Box 1239), Point Reyes Station, CA 94956 (☎ **415/663-8627;** fax 415/663-8431), is situated about 10 minutes from the Tomales Bay beaches and 15 minutes from the ocean beaches. Innkeeper Felicity Kirsch remodeled a 1920s carriage house into two private units: each has a bedroom with queen-size bed, a living room with a fireplace, a full kitchen, and a full bathroom. Although furnished with antiques, both units offer a comfortable and casual atmosphere.

The Carriage House is a popular spot for families for a weekend away with the kids. There are fabulous gardens and lush green spaces to explore, plus TVs, games, and an outside barbecue, too. Request cribs and highchairs in advance. Babysitting can also be arranged with advance notice.

Rooms cost $120 for two, $150 for four, plus $15 for each additional adult and $10 for each additional child. Inquire about midweek and weekly rates. From November through April, midweek, guests can stay three nights for the price of two. Rates include full breakfasts of eggs, waffles, fruit, and yogurt.

The **Inns of Point Reyes** (☎ 415/663-1420) is a referral service that can advise you about accommodations in seven area homes and bed-and-breakfast establishments in the West Marin/Point Reyes area. Call anytime.

WHERE TO EAT

Because the area is so popular with visitors, nearly every restaurant is suitable for kids. But don't miss enjoying a great meal at the **Station House Café,** on Main Street in Point Reyes Station (☎ 415/663-1515). The food is innovative and fresh, and the selections will appeal to even the most finicky eater. There's an extensive breakfast menu, plus a long list of coffees and teas. Breakfast and lunch can be enjoyed outdoors in the garden. Lunch selections range from your basic grilled cheese or burger to a grilled eggplant sandwich, an outstanding Reuben on rye, chicken sausage pot pie, omelets (served until 2:30pm), Johnson's oysters breaded and deep-fried, and weekly and seasonal specials such as warm barley salad or penne pasta with roasted eggplant and tomatoes. Lunch will run you $4–$8.

Dinner is a cornucopia of delicious selections. There are new specials, old favorites, heart-healthy choices, and numerous starters. Some samples: Niman-Schell sirloin steak, a vegetarian plate, turkey and black bean chili, cornbread-stuffed chicken breast, local shellfish. Dinners run about $7–$17.50.

In addition to ordering off the regular menu, children can have a three-ounce burger and fries for $3.75, or ask your server about the smaller portions at smaller prices.

There are boosters and highchairs. During the busy season, the best time to come for lunch is between 11:30 and 12:30pm; for dinner, between 5 and 6pm. After 6:30 the wait without a reservation can be a half hour to an hour, especially on holiday weekends.

Open Sunday through Thursday from 8am to 9pm, and on Friday and Saturday from 8am to 10pm. Reservations and major credit cards accepted. A parking lot is available.

2 Mendocino

A bit of Cape Cod on the Pacific Coast, Mendocino is a small artists' colony and a picturesque stop as a destination itself or as a place to stay overnight on the way to the giant redwoods farther north. It was settled in the 1850s, and you can still see the original homes of the wealthy lumber barons who made this their town during the great logging boom. Mendocino became a haven for the artists of the 1960s and 1970s who wanted to drop out and move to the country. The entire town has been declared a historic monument. It retains its weathered, noncommercial personality while still hosting some great artists.

After you've exhausted the interesting art galleries and charming boutiques in town, take the children to the nearby state parks, ride bikes, play at the beach, or walk through the Mendocino Coast Botanical Gardens.

WHAT TO SEE AND DO IN TOWN

Although the town is tiny, there are many activities families can participate in, depending on the time of year.

Festivals

Contact the **Fort Bragg–Mendocino Coast Chamber of Commerce,** P.O. Box 1141, Fort Bragg, CA 95437 (☎ 707/961-6300), for specific dates and other details about the following festivals: the Whale Festivals in March, the Mendocino Music Festival in July, and the Fourth of July Salmon Barbecue, the largest in the world.

History

The historic **Ford House,** at 735 Main St. (☎ 707/937-5397), was originally the home of one of the co-owners of the first sawmill in Mendocino, and it also serves as the local visitor center. Tour the house and see the changing exhibits that reflect the seasons. Admission to the house is a $1 donation. The Ford House is open daily from 11am to 4pm.

WHAT TO SEE AND DO IN THE AREA

Outdoor activities are abundant in places within driving distance of Mendocino or Fort Bragg.

Gardens

The **Mendocino Coast Botanical Gardens,** 18220 N. Calif. 1, Fort Bragg (☎ 707/964-4352), are seven miles north of Mendocino and two miles south of Fort Bragg. There are several thousand types of plants here, including heathers, succulents, ivies, roses, perennials, and rhododendrons. It's a peaceful and beautiful place for a walk with the family, and there are picnic areas. Most paths are stroller- and wheelchair-accessible. Open daily: March through October from 9am to 5pm, November through February from 9am to 4pm. Admission is $5 for adults, $4 for seniors, $3 for children 12–17, free for children under 12 accompanied by their parents.

Parks and Beaches

The state parks in this area are wonderful and unique. You'll see headlands, canyons, forests, meadows, dunes. And each park usually offers a view of or accessibility to the ocean at some point. There are lots of picnic areas and camping sites. For information, call **California State Parks** (☎ 707/937-5804).

Two miles south of Mendocino on Calif. 1 is **Van Damme State Park,** which has 74 campsites, a beach, and hiking trails. The beach is relatively safe for ocean swimming, but has no lifeguards and is *very* cold.

The big attraction at Van Damme State Park is the scenic **Fern Canyon Trail.** You can also walk the **Pygmy Forest Discovery Trail,** which has decades–old trees only a few feet tall, stunted because of poor soil conditions.

To see just the trails, drive south on Calif. 1 past the Van Damme State Park entrance to Little River Airport Road and go east 3¹/₂ miles to the intersection with Albion Road. A sign notes the entrance to the Pygmy Forest parking lot. There's a $5 charge per car to enter the parking area at Fern Canyon; the Pygmy Forest area is free. The Pygmy Forest trail is stroller- and wheelchair-accessible and has a trail guide at the entrance.

For reservations at the park's campgrounds, call **MISTIX** (☎ toll free 800/444-7275). The fee is $12–$14, depending on the time of year.

Nearby **Mendocino Headlands State Park,** which horseshoes around the town of Mendocino, is a mecca for activities ranging from fishing and sport diving to surfing and hiking. You can reach the public fishing area via Hesser Drive. **Big River Beach** is accessible on the south side of Mendocino, and can be reached by car from Calif. 1 or by hiking down the bluffs. The park, and its restrooms, are open free for day use.

Russian Gulch State Park is two miles north of Mendocino on the west side of Calif. 1. Families can camp (there are 30 family campsites, plus hot showers and flush toilet facilities), or just hike one of the many trails. The **Falls Loop Trail,** $3^{1}/_{2}$ miles long, is accessible to hikers and is found at the end of 1.6-mile scenic Fern Canyon, which is also accessible to bikes.

North of Mendocino and Caspar is **Jughandle State Reserve,** just north of the north entrance to Caspar on Calif. 1, five miles south of Fort Bragg. There are a number of trails, but the most interesting is the **Ecological Staircase Trail,** where changes in the ocean's level over hundreds of thousands of years, along with other geologic activity, created a series of terraces. Kids should be able to make this hike. There are self-guiding brochures near the entrance to the trail. (There are chemical toilets in the parking lot, north of Caspar on Calif. 1.)

Canoeing

Catch a Canoe and Bicycles, Too! rents a complete line of fine Wenonah canoes and open-top kayaks for paddling down the Big River. Find them at Stanford Inn by the Sea, Coast Hwy. 1 (Calif. 1) and Comptche-Ukiah Road (☎ 707/937-0273), at the mouth of the Big River, just below the bridge on the south shore. A trip up the river by canoe is a trip through still-undeveloped wilderness. Pack a lunch and picnic at a sandy beach. Kids 7 and older can handle the scramblers, which are kayaks just perfect for their size; they rent for $7.50–$10 per hour. Adult-size kayaks are $25–$30 for the day. Canoes run $10–$14 per hour, or $35–$42 for the day. Mountain bikes (helmets included) rent for $7.50–$14.50 per hour, or $25–$45 per day. Open daily from 9:30am to 5pm year round. Call ahead for reservations for holidays.

WHERE TO STAY

The **Little River Inn,** Little River, CA 95456 (☎ 707/937-5942; fax 707/937-3944), should be at the top of your list of places to stay in this part of the state. The 19th-century inn sits on 225 acres adjacent to Van Damme State Park, two miles from Mendocino and ten miles from Fort Bragg. This lovely family-oriented hotel is exceptionally accommodating to children and the staff will make your stay wonderful. Outdoor amenities include a nine-hole golf course, a driving range, and a putting green. Two night-lighted tennis courts can be used free by guests.

The inn's restaurant is open for breakfast, dinner, and Sunday brunch. A children's menu would make the Little River Inn perfect, but items on the regular menu are half price for children. There is no room service, but you may call the restaurant and they'll prepare food-to-go.

The charming country French rooms are spacious and most have ocean views. Rooms come with one king-size bed, or two queen-size beds, or two double beds. Some also have hideabeds. Some rooms have fireplaces; all have TVs; with VCRs and movies.

During most of the year, room rates for double occupancy are $80–$115 without a fireplace, $125–$190 with a fireplace; larger rooms, some with Jacuzzis, rent for $190–$255. Children under 12 sleep free in their parents' room; children over 12 and additional adults are charged $10. Rollaways cost $10; cribs are $5. Ask about special winter rates. Babysitting can be arranged.

Still another fine family lodge is the **Stanford Inn by the Sea,** Calif. 1 and Comptche-Ukiah Road (P.O. Box 487), Mendocino, CA 95460 (☎ **707/937-5615,** or toll free **800/331-8884;** fax 707/937-0305). You'll find beautiful gardens, large grassy playing areas, a pond with resident swans, curious rabbits, llamas, dogs, and cats. Many families return here year after year. This family-owned and -run 10-acre property has the only pool in Mendocino (kids need a key to enter) which is enclosed in a greenhouse along with a sauna and spa. Bikes and bike racks are available free. Canoes can be rented from Catch A Canoe & Bicycles, Too!

No two rooms are identical in the 24-room inn, but they all have ocean views, porches, and fireplaces. Two rooms have views of the meadow and full kitchens; some rooms have sitting areas. Rooms may have a four-poster bed, or sleigh beds; some have trundle beds or hideabeds. There are playpens for babies to sleep in, but no rollaways. You may want to bring your own portacrib. All rooms have telephones, remote-control color TVs plus movie channels, VCRs and videotapes, individual heaters, mini-refrigerators, and coffee makers. Additional touches such as fresh flowers, wine for adults and juice for kids, and dog biscuits for your dog are placed in your room. And a complimentary champagne breakfast is included in the room price. They will provide phone numbers of babysitters.

Rooms with one queen-size bed and one or two twin beds go for $170 to $185. A large one-bedroom suite costs $255; other suites are $200–$255. The extra-person charge is $10 for ages 2–11 and $15 for anyone over 11.

Located right in the heart of town, the **MacCallum House,** 45020 Albion St. (P.O. Box 206), Mendocino, CA 95460 (☎ **707/937-0289**), is a grand inn, comfortable and cozy with a perpetual aura of cheerfulness. This rambling Victorian mansion, whose roots date back to 1882, has retained its authenticity and charm. Children are welcome, and you and they will feel like you're staying in someone's private home.

The well-regarded MacCallum House Restaurant (☎ **707/937-5763**) is on the premises and open for dinner daily. Although children are welcome, prepare for an intimate setting with a menu that offers such adult fare as seared duck breast and bouillabaisse. A complimentary continental breakfast is included in the room price.

There are 20 accommodations at the inn. When you call to reserve, tell them you have children with you and they'll advise you about which room will best meet your needs. All rooms are individually decorated, many with authentic pieces dating from the original owners. Remember, no TVs here. The Watertower is a split-level accommodation with an ocean view, two queen-size beds and a private bath; it costs $140. The Barn Suites are ideal for families; they sleep two to six people and rent for $180 and $240. The Barn Apartment is a full-size apartment, perfect to rent by the week; it costs $165. The Greenhouse is a separate cottage with a Franklin fireplace, two double beds and a private bath; it rents for $125. Rollaways, futons, or cribs are available for a charge of $15 extra per person. A two-night minimum is required on weekends from May through December; a three-night minimum is required on holiday weekends.

WHERE TO EAT

One great family-friendly restaurant in town is **Restaurant 955,** 955 Ukiah St. (☎ 707/937-1955). Owners Peggy and Jamie Griffith, parents of four children, go out of their way to make families feel welcome. Children get crayons to draw with and small toys to play with while waiting for their food.

The staff will warm baby food and bottles; there are booster seats and highchairs. Although there is no printed children's menu, they will prepare just about anything your child wants from the kitchen.

Mom's and Dad's dinner orders will include steamed vegetables and the chef's choice of rice, polenta, or potatoes along with their crispy duck, range chicken, or New York steak. Seafood lovers can order a seafood menagerie of prawns, clams, oysters, mussels, snapper, and other fish selections. Light dishes can be ordered as appetizers or for a meal.

Dinners cost $10.50–$18. Save room for desserts such as bread pudding or mango mousse. Open for dinner beginning at 6pm Wednesday through Sunday, July through October. Open Thursday through Sunday the remainder of the year. Reservations and credit cards accepted.

Stop at the **Mendocino Bakery & Café,** 10483 Lansing St. (☎ 707/937-0836), for a morning pastry or afternoon snack. Pastries are hand-rolled; the cappuccino is great. At lunch you can get pizza by the slice, stuffed potatoes, burritos, and sandwiches. Be sure to treat the kids to a Cowboy Cookie (chocolate chip, walnut, and oats) or a chocolate chip cupcake. The bakery is open daily from 8am to 6pm Monday through Thursday; to 8pm Friday through Sunday.

For a casual lunch or early dinner, stop by **Mendo Burgers,** in the same building as the Mendocino Bakery (☎ 707/937-1111). They serve up all sorts of burgers, including chicken, fish and veggie variations, plus fish and chips. Prices begin at $3.75. There's a kid-size burger or hot dog with French fries for $3. There are highchairs. Open Monday through Saturday, 11am to 7pm, Sunday to 5pm. No reservations. Credit cards are accepted.

You can't miss this place because they're lined up out the door on weekends—some folks say they have the best Black Forest ice cream anywhere. The **Mendocino Ice Cream Company,** on Main Street (☎ 707/937-5884), is open daily: from 9am to 10pm in summer, from 9am to 6pm the rest of the year.

MENDOCINO SHOPS

Bébé Lapin, 551 Ukiah St. (☎ 707/937-0261), features gifts and apparel for children; open daily from 10am to 5pm. The **Golden Goose,** 45094 Main St. (☎ 707/937-4655), also has great clothing for infants and children; open Monday through Friday from 10am to 5pm and on Saturday from 10am to 6pm. A wonderful children's bookstore, **Bookwinkle,** at Main and Kasten Streets (☎ 707/937-2665), is open daily from 10am to 6pm. **Out of This World,** at 45100 Main St. (☎ 707/937-3335), carries games, maps, and other items related to planets, stars and science; open daily from 10am to 5:30pm year round. **The Collector,** on Main Street (☎ 707/937-0888), will entice kids with its wonderful selection of shells, rocks, and fossils at affordable prices; open daily from 10:30am to 5pm. Try the **Village Toy Store,** 10450 Lansing St. (☎ 707/937-4633), for kites, toys, Frisbees; open Monday through Sunday from 10am to 6pm.

3 Fort Bragg

The actual fort was built in 1857 by the army to maintain order for the Mendocino County Indian Reservation. The fort was abandoned in 1864, but in 1885 the first sawmill opened, reinstating the town once more. Now Fort Bragg is home to one of the world's largest redwood sawmills and to the California Western Railroad.

WHAT TO SEE AND DO

The **Skunk Railroad** is known throughout the West. You'll find the depot between Pine Street and Laurel Avenue off Main Street (☎ 707/964-6371). The Skunk line was originally a logging railroad in the late 1800s, hauling lumber inland. After steam service was discontinued in 1925, the trains were powered by gas engines, and picked up their classy name from the perfume of the gas fumes. Now the California Western Railroad operates two passenger trains called Super Skunks, which are powered by historic diesel logging locomotives. Each has open observation cars.

The half-day trip stops in Northspur, a former logging town. It runs along Pudding Creek and then follows the Noyo River and the ubiquitous redwoods over tracks 100 years old. The full-day journey, which takes $7^{1}/_{2}$ hours round-trip, stops in Willits, and climbs the rolling hills on the way back to Fort Bragg, reaching 1,700 feet at the summit. You'll travel over bridges, through tunnels, and past breathtaking scenery. Kids who love trains will adore this trip.

"Know thy child" definitely applies here, because the shortest trip can seem forever with a toddler who wants "off."

The Super Skunks run daily from the third Saturday in June through the second Saturday in September. Check schedules for departure times. While reservations are not required, they are advised, because the trains are filled during tourist season. Arrive a half hour early to secure your reservation.

A round-trip ticket for the full-day run is $26 for adults, $12 for children 5–11, free for children under 5; tickets for the half-day run cost $21 for adults, $10 for children 5–11, and free for children under 5. A parking lot is available.

Turn off Calif. 1 onto North Harbor Drive and you can't miss **Noyo Harbor,** Fort Bragg's tiny fishing village, where you have the choice of chartering a party boat, whale-watching, or fishing. **Anchor Charter Boats,** in the Harbor (☎ 707/964-4550), offers full- and half-day arrangements. Call for prices and schedules.

Take a break from sightseeing at **Bainbridge Park,** at E. Laurel at N. Harrison Streets, a tiny public park in a residential area of town, not far off Calif. 1 and near the Skunk Railroad. Turn east on Laurel Street and go about six blocks. It's open to the public during daylight hours, is stroller-accessible, and has restroom facilities. It's a perfect break for toddlers or older children who may get restless from sightseeing; they can expend some energy on the neat "climber," two slides, and two swings.

Mackerricher State Park is located about four miles north of Fort Bragg. Here are seven miles of beaches, campgrounds, and a lake—Cleone Lake, the only freshwater lake on the north coast. The California gray whales can be viewed from the bluffs—December through April is a good time to spot them. Seals can also be seen from this point.

Nearby **Richochet Ridge Ranch,** 24201 N. Calif. 1 (☎ 707/964-PONY), welcomes riders of all skill levels, including beginners, and provides ponies for younger children. Riders are professionally guided into Jackson State Forest (a full-day ride) or over Fort Bragg's Ten Mile Beach. Children 6 and older can accompany their parents on the $1^{1}/_{2}$-hour rides. The fee is $26 per adult or child. Advance reservations are advised.

A few options for inclement weather: check the marquee at the **Coast Twin Cinemas,** at South Franklin Street and Madrone St. (☎ 707/964-2019), or bowl at **Noyo Bowl,** 900 N. Main St. (☎ 707/964-4051).

For information about festivals and seasonal events, contact the **Fort Bragg— Mendocino Coast Chamber of Commerce,** 332 N. Main St., Fort Bragg, CA 95437 (☎ 707/961-6300, or toll free **800/726-2780;** fax 707/964-2056).

WHERE TO STAY

Most of the bed-and-breakfast establishments in Fort Bragg don't encourage children under 12. But if you have a well-traveled child, reserve a room at the homey and spacious **Grey Whale Inn,** 615 N. Main St., Fort Bragg, CA 95437 (☎ **707/964-0640,** or toll free **800/382-7244;** fax 707/964-4408). This lovely 1915 redwood mansion was once the local hospital; it was converted in 1971 and has been maintained with loving care ever since by owners John and Colette Bailey.

The inn features 14 rooms with private baths, large windows, and plenty of sunlight. The two rooms with kitchen are particularly spacious and comfortable for families. Another accommodation offers a mini-kitchen with microwave and refrigerator. If you want a kitchen, be sure to request it when making a reservation. All rooms have phones; some rooms have TVs. In the downstairs recreation center, there's a fireside lounge, a billiards table, a TV and VCR, and board games. There's no pool.

A yummy full breakfast buffet consisting of homemade coffee breads, a main dish such as waffles or a tasty casserole, fresh fruit, juice, cereal, and beverage is included in the room rate.

Room prices are $60–$160 single and $80–$180 double. Kitchen units cost $100–$140 for two people. Additional guests sharing a room, including children and infants, are charged $25 each. There are no rollaways or cribs. A minimum two- to three-night stay is required on most weekends and during holiday periods. There is a no smoking policy inside the inn.

The **Seabird Lodge,** conveniently located at 191 South St., Fort Bragg, CA 95437 (☎ 707/964-4731, or toll free **800/345-0022** in California; fax 707/961-1779), has large, clean rooms and a particularly friendly and helpful staff. Some rooms have small patios while others have balconies. Three rooms have kitchenettes, and all rooms have refrigerators and real coffee. Connecting rooms are available. There's an indoor pool, a whirlpool, and coin-operated laundry facilities.

Rates vary seasonally: $80–$90 for standard rooms (double occupancy), $95 for kitchenette units which have one queen-size bed and room for a crib or rollaway. Children 12 and older are charged $5 per night; kids under 12 sleep free in their parents' room. Rollaways are $10 per night; cribs are $5. The motel provides free shuttle service to the Skunk train.

WHERE TO EAT

The **Home Style Café,** on South Street next door to the Seabird Lodge (☎ 707/964-6106), serves breakfast and lunch at very reasonable prices. Boosters and highchairs are available. Open daily from 5am to 2pm; closed Monday. Some credit cards accepted. Parking is available.

For a pleasant view of the fishing harbor, the **Wharf Restaurant,** located at 780 N. Harbor Dr., at Noyo Fishing Village (☎ 707/964-4283), is a perfect choice. This large, casual restaurant serves fish selections caught locally.

Adult fare features seafood, as well as steaks, prime rib, and salads. Complete lunches run $6–$8, and dinners go for $13–$20. There is no children's menu at lunch, but there are many sandwiches to choose from. At dinner, the children's menu includes petite New York steak, chicken, fish, and burgers; main dishes cost $5.75–$14. Seafood can be ordered from the regular menu and costs $3 less.

Open daily for lunch from 11am to 4pm and for dinner from 4 to 10pm, to 11pm in summer. Reservations and some credit cards are accepted. Parking is available.

Next door is the very popular and comfortable **Cap'n Flints** (☎ 707/964-9447). Selections include seafood, fried fish, chowder, hamburgers, and salads. The menu stays the same for lunch or dinner; prices are reasonable, from $3.50–$8. Smaller portions for children are served at reduced prices. Boosters and highchairs are available.

Open daily, except Thanksgiving and Christmas Days, from 11am to 9pm. Reservations are accepted. Arrive before 6:30pm or after 7:30pm for a shorter wait. No credit cards accepted. Parking is available.

For Sunday brunch try the family-run **Redwood Cookhouse,** at Redwood and Main Streets (☎ 707/964-1517). There's an all-you-can-eat buffet for $5 which includes ham, eggs, French toast, pancakes, biscuits and gravy, rolls, and other items.

Dinner buffets include roast beef, ham, red snapper, and fried chicken, with all the accompaniments. There are specials on Tuesday, Wednesday, and Saturday, when adults pay $9; children pay 30¢ per year of their age, up to 12. The prices include drinks and dessert. Boosters and highchairs are available.

Sunday brunch is served from 8am to 1pm. Sunday-night dinner, starting at 4pm, features barbecued ribs. Tuesday through Saturday, dinner is served from 4:30 to 8:30pm. There may be a 15-minute wait on Friday night, which is seafood night. Reservations are accepted for seven or more people. Major credit cards are honored. There is street parking.

6

Northern California

Pᴇᴏᴘʟᴇ ᴄᴏᴍᴇ ᴛᴏ ᴛʜɪs ᴘᴀʀᴛ ᴏғ Cᴀʟɪғᴏʀɴɪᴀ ʙᴇᴄᴀᴜsᴇ ᴛʜᴇʏ ᴡᴀɴᴛ ᴛᴏ ɢᴇᴛ ᴀᴡᴀʏ ғʀᴏᴍ crowds and enjoy the out-of-doors. Some have called it the California of the Wild West, with its enormous open spaces, volcanoes, and huge, snow-covered peaks. If elegant accommodations, fine dining, and a fast pace are what you and your family enjoy on vacation, you might prefer elsewhere. But if you want to introduce your kids to an outdoor wonderland of open blue skies, clean azure-blue lakes, and rushing streams, where you can hike with them in dense forests and fish with them in peace and quiet, this is one area you'll love.

1 Redding: Gateway to Lassen and Shasta Cascade

Lassen Peak, a dormant volcano that erupted as recently as 1921, rises 10,457 feet and reigns over the national park bearing its name. Mount Shasta, with its five gla-ciers and majestic stature of over 14,000 feet, towers to the north. Beautiful Shasta Lake is an outdoor-lover's dream.

Be sure to devote your evenings to stargazing. Bundle up the kids and watch a blanket of stars cover the vast night sky. We had fun helping ours pick out the Big Dipper and the Milky Way. This, for city adults, is as big a treat as it is for the kids. Sunrise in the mountains is special too. It's a time to watch and listen. Observe how the dark, shadowy fir trees become outlines against the sky. Then in a matter of min-utes the light reveals stately pines with green and brown needles. Listen as the dark-ness gives way to sunlight, and the sounds of animals and birds start to emerge from the silence.

HOW TO GET THERE

This area requires a bit of time. It's 212 miles northeast of San Francisco, 165 miles north of Sacramento. The Shasta Cascade area is reached most easily by automobile. However, if you're coming from southern or central California, you might consider flying into Sacramento Metropolitan Airport and getting a rental car. This will shave hours off the trip.

By car from Los Angeles and Sacramento, take I-5 all the way to Redding. From San Francisco, take I-80 to Sacramento; then continue north on I-5 past Red Bluff to Redding. For road conditions and information, call **916/445-7623.**

Located just 15 minutes from Shasta Lake and an hour from both Mount Shasta and Lassen Volcanic National Park, Redding is a good starting point for trips to these Northern California wonderlands. It's a good place to stay, buy supplies, and rent equipment. However, if you're going to Lassen Volcanic National Park, you can also drive from Sacramento straight to Lassen. To do so, take Calif. 36 at Red Bluff all the way to the park entrance.

A Stop Along the Way

Red Bluff itself is an interesting little town with neighborhoods of Victorian-style homes and other areas with great views of the Sacramento River. The road from Red Bluff to Redding in summer and early autumn is typical California countryside with California black oaks dotting the brown rolling hills. In spring, it is rich green. Since the trip to Redding is a long one, we were pleased to find a few nice places to stop along the way.

William B. Ide Adobe State Historic Park (☎ **916/529-8599**) is a lovely little stop. Located two miles northeast of Red Bluff on Adobe Road, it's a small park bordered by the Sacramento River, at a spot where the river is very gentle and lazy. We spent a few hours watching the sun play on the slow-moving river. There are lots of places to sit and read a book, or play a game of catch. There are a couple of grassy areas with huge oak trees, as well as an original 1850s homestead memorializing William B. Ide (who was the first, and only, president of California).

There is a picnic area with a few barbecues and several picnic tables. The short, easy walk along the Sacramento River, and the walk to the top of the hill where there are old Native American campgrounds, are worth taking.

The park is open daily from 8am to sunset. There is a posted warning not to swim in the river because the bottom is uneven and the drop-offs are severe. The water is also very cold—about 60°F!

Try **Perko's Café** if you want good coffeeshop food. It's hard to find anything open here late and on Sunday. Perko's is located just off I-5 at the Red Bluff exit; take a left and drive to 201 Antelope Blvd. (☎ **916/527-6565**). We found that we very much liked this chain, which has many locations in Northern California. We enjoyed creating our own omelets. There are also half-pound burgers and charcoal-broiled steaks. Prices for lunch are $3.50–$5; full dinners, with soup or salad bar, vegetable, and potato, run $5–$8. The cute children's menu has favorites like chicken and grilled-cheese sandwiches; prices average $1.50–$2.25. Highchairs and boosters are available. It's open daily from 5:30am to 11pm. Some credit cards accepted.

GETTING ORIENTED

The town of Redding is located just off I-5, in a beautiful setting where you can see regal, snow-covered Mount Shasta in the distance. Throughout Redding there are beautiful views of the Sacramento River. It's easy to find your way around town, with Hilltop, Cypress, Pine, and Market as the major streets.

You might want to stop first at the **Shasta Cascade Wonderland Association,** located at 14250 Holiday Rd., Redding, CA 96001 (☎ **916/275-5555,** or toll free **800/326-6944**). You'll never see a larger assortment of brochures and visitor information, and we dare you to find friendlier people. They really try to make your trip to the Shasta Cascade area one that you'll never forget. In fact, you can tell them what you have in mind and they'll offer lots of helpful information. Be sure to write them if you're interested in camping or houseboating because houseboats require a reservation far in advance. There is rafting, canoeing, hiking, golf, water and snow skiing, mountain climbing, backpacking, cycling, and spelunking.

The **Redding Convention and Visitors Bureau,** 777 Auditorium Dr. (☎ toll free **800/874-7562**), is open daily from April through October, and Monday through Friday from November through March. Call them also for road information.

WHAT TO SEE AND DO AROUND SHASTA LAKE

Located 15 miles north of Redding, Shasta Lake is known for its myriad watersport opportunities. It's a haven for houseboaters.

There are two other attractions as well: the caverns and the dam.

Created by the construction of the Shasta Dam in the 1940s, Shasta Lake has 370 miles of shoreline and a maximum depth of 515 feet. Because it was created by damming up the Sacramento, Pit, and McCloud rivers (and two smaller creeks), Shasta Lake is virtually like a hand with several finger lakes to explore. These smaller areas provide secluded inlets to venture into—on foot or by boat—making Shasta Lake a perfect place for houseboating and other water sports. It's great for fishing and swimming, and it also offers campgrounds in the thick forests surrounding the lake.

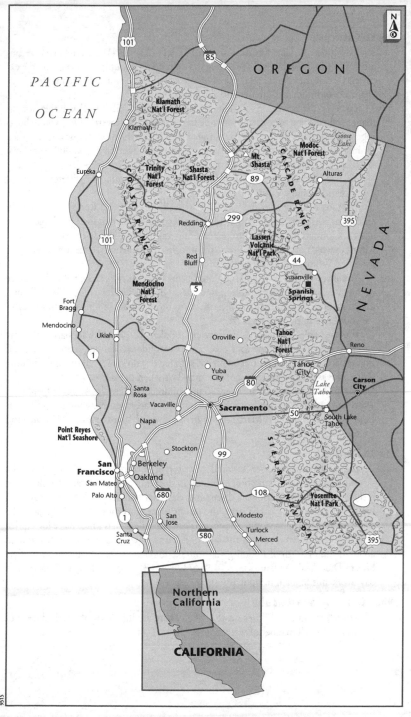

Northern California

N

PACIFIC OCEAN

OREGON

101

85

Klamath Nat'l Forest

Klamath

Goose Lake

Modoc Nat'l Forest

Eureka

Trinity Nat'l Forest

Shasta Nat'l Forest

Mt. Shasta

89

Alturas

CASCADE RANGE

299

Redding

395

COAST RANGE

101

Lassen Volcanic Nat'l Park

Red Bluff

44

Susanville

Spanish Springs

Mendocino Nat'l Forest

5

NEVADA

Fort Bragg

Mendocino

Ukiah

Oroville

Tahoe Nat'l Forest

Reno

1

Yuba City

Tahoe City

Lake Tahoe

Carson City

Santa Rosa

80

Vacaville

Sacramento

50

South Lake Tahoe

Napa

Point Reyes Nat'l Seashore

Stockton

99

San Francisco

Berkeley

Oakland

SIERRA NEVADA

San Mateo

Palo Alto

680

108

Yosemite Nat'l Park

1

San Jose

Santa Cruz

Modesto

580

Turlock

Merced

395

Northern California

CALIFORNIA

9515

Shasta Caverns

Located above the lake, **Shasta Caverns** (☎ 916/238-2341) are a relatively recent attraction for tourists. Until 1964 they were closed to all but spelunkers, who are experienced cave explorers. Today the caverns are open to everyone, displaying their large chambers of brilliant stalactites and stalagmites.

To get to the caverns by car, take I-5 north to Shasta Caverns Road; then a catamaran will take you on a 15-minute ride to the foot of the caverns. Or if you're boating, you can dock at the ferry landing. From the ferry drop-off point, there's a 10-minute bus ride up a very winding, one-lane road that takes you 800 feet above the lake with very pretty views as you ascend.

A guide takes you through the caverns, carefully explaining the different geological formations, and creating stories for the kids.

We took Andrew when he was 10. He loved the Cathedral Room, which has an enormous 100-foot-high ceiling with all kinds of stalactites that look like huge icicles and rock formations. The guide created a fairy tale about a king, a queen, and an evil wizard in which the formations were the imaginary characters. There were even parts for Snow White and the Seven Dwarfs.

You'll see where the original explorers came through, where the natural entrance to the cave is, and where they often find bats. The kids just love it! And like all good cave tours, there's a time when the guide turns off the lights and it's so dark you can't see your hand in front of your face.

We saw babies in backpack carriers and toddlers who would walk part of the way and be carried the rest. The tour takes about two hours including the bus ride, and isn't too long for a toddler. But be prepared to have to do some walking and climbing stairs. This is a cool retreat on hot summer days when the lake can be 90°. Entrance fees are $12 for anyone 13 or older, $6 for children 4–12; under 4, free. Open April 1 through October 1, daily from 9am to 5pm; tours are given every hour on the hour. From October 2 through March 31, tours are given at 10am, noon, and 2pm, wind conditions permitting.

Shasta Dam

People say that once you see it, you'll never forget it. Completed in 1945, this is the second-largest concrete structure ever built in the United States (Grand Coulee Dam is the first), and it has a spillway three times the height of Niagara Falls. Nearby, on a knoll, you can see the entire dam, the power plant, gorgeous Shasta Lake, and the snow-covered volcano, Mount Shasta, to the north. The dam is a nice place for a quick stop as you're on your way to the lake or caverns. There are free tours. It's located about 12 miles north of Redding via I-5; take the Shasta Dam Boulevard exit. The **Shasta Dam Visitors Building** (☎ 916/275-4463) is open Monday through Friday; weekends 8:30am to 5pm.

What to Do on Shasta Lake

There are myriad possibilities on this lake. There are hundreds of coves, dozens of campsites, and all manner of water sports.

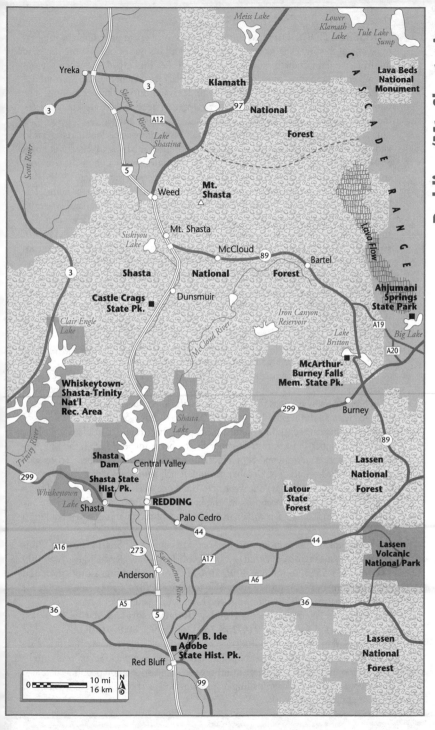

Redding/Mt. Shasta Area

HOUSEBOATING   Definitely the aristocracy's form of camping, houseboating has to be one of the best experiences in the world. And it's one of our favorite things to do. In fact, even Elizabeth, now 8, clearly recalls her first experience when she was 3¹/₂. Where else can you cruise along at a gentle speed on a vibrant blue lake, surrounded by forest-capped, red-brown hills that are under water during the wet months? The houseboat is like a luxury hotel room, but almost nicer because there are separate sleeping areas for adults and kids, and a completely equipped kitchen (even better than ours at home) with a dishwasher, microwave, trash compactor, double refrigerator, and gas barbecue. On the lake, you can travel without ever having to repack your bags and change rooms. The only drawback we found is not having a phone. If you need contact with the outside world, you'll have to make special arrangements.

It's heaven to dock in a secluded cove where you won't see anyone for hours. The kids can play on the banks, swim, fish, or entertain themselves on the boat. Bring extra shoes for walking on the rocky lake bed. We always kept Elizabeth in a life jacket at all times even though she is always under the watchful eye of an adult who knows how to swim. We suggest others do the same. Adults can enjoy the same activities or do absolutely nothing. A great idea, if you can afford it, is to rent a little powerboat and pull it along. That way you can travel around the lake without having to move the houseboat for short jaunts.

During the summer of dry years, Lake Shasta can be very low. This means that the banks of the lake are graded, almost stair-steps to what is normally the top of the lake. These dirt banks are ideal places for shell collecting. The low water can also have negative effects, though; it makes it somewhat more difficult to dock in the designated harbors, because there's much less maneuvering room.

For more details on houseboating, see the "How to Travel with Kids" section in Chapter 1.

There are many marinas that rent houseboats on Shasta Lake, but if you're planning to be there during the high season, be sure to book far in advance. Prices of houseboats fluctuate depending on the time of year. "In-season" is considered mid-June to mid-September; "mid-season" is generally the beginning of May till the June season begins, and again from mid-September through the end of September; "off-season" is generally the beginning of October through April. Some companies also have pre- and post-season rates that are one week before and one week after the season. All companies require substantial deposits for the houseboats. Check to see if there are any special discounts and get a complete run-down on all the amenities when booking a houseboat.

For complete information, your best bet is to contact the **Shasta Cascade Wonderland Association,** located 12450 Holiday Road, Redding, CA 96003 (☎ **916/275-5555,** or toll free **800/326-6944**), or the **Redding Convention and Visitors Bureau,** 777 Auditorium Dr. (☎ toll free **800/874-7562**). Also contact the individual marina with any questions you have before you book.

One of our favorite marinas is **Holiday Harbor Resort and Marina,** P.O. Box 112, O'Brien, CA 96070 (☎ **916/238-2383,** or toll free **800/776-BOAT**). We like Holiday Harbor because it's full service, with a grocery store, restaurant, gift and ski shop, and complete boat-rental shop. Holiday Harbor even includes pillows with its boats. Most impressive is the large number of staff and orientation people available to make your boarding and unloading as pleasant and as speedy as possible. Holiday Harbor also has an RV park.

We also like **Seven Crown Resorts,** which rents houseboats from both Digger Bay Marina, P.O. Box 1516, Central Valley, CA 96019 (☎ **916/275-3072**), and Bridge Bay Resort, 10300 Bridge Bay Rd., Redding, CA 96003 (☎ **916/275-3021**). We like this outfit because you can rent boats during the high season for three- and four-day excursions as well as for a full week. All boats have fully equipped kitchens, a bathroom with shower or tub, and stereo cassettes. Not all have air conditioning and generators, so check if those are important to you. They also offer a linen service upon request. The peak season is mid-June through mid-September; low season, from mid-September through mid-June.

Bridge Bay is a full-service resort with a lovely restaurant, market, giftshop, swimming pool, and hotel. Several different kinds of houseboats can be rented from this marina. Rates vary considerably depending on the boat and number of people it sleeps. Three-day weekends start at $490, four-day midweek specials start at $610, and a week-long stay starts at $1,150.

Lakeview Marina Resort, P.O. Box 992272, Redding, CA 96099-2272 (☎ **916/223-3003**), offers 15- by 56-foot houseboats for rent. All have two bathrooms, two refrigerators, a microwave, and air cooler, and will sleep 10–14 people. All the boats also have double "penthouses" on the upper level. Boats are leased only by the week during the season. Other times of the year, boats can be rented for three and four days, and there are special holiday packages. Lakeview does not provide pillows. Prices vary tremendously depending on the boat you want and the time you want it. Write for a current brochure. As an example, a 56-foot "Royal deluxe" houseboat that accommodates 14 people rents for $2,125 per week. It costs $235 per day midseason and $195 per day off-season; a minimum number of days applies. You can also rent aluminum fishing boats here.

Silverthorn Resort, P.O. Box 4205, Redding, CA 96099 (☎ **916/275-1571,** or toll free **800/332-3044**), has houseboats that accommodate 10–16 passengers, with fully equipped kitchenettes, two bathrooms, two showers, two refrigerators, microwave, and two air conditioners. Prices for boats run $1,750–$2,690 per week in-season, $1,390–$2,300 weekly in pre- and post-season, $1,290–$2,090 in mid-season, and $1,090–$1,750 off-season. Mid- and off-season, you can rent houseboats for shorter periods of time. You can also rent fishing, patio, and ski boats here. **Note:** Even if you don't rent from Silverthorn, be sure to find out if the waterski show will be presented when you're on the lake. It's renowned throughout northern California.

Located at Packer's Bay Marina, **Holiday Flotels, Inc.,** P.O. Box 336-B, Redding, CA 96099 (☎ **916/275-5570**), is another houseboat-rental outfit. Houseboats have two bathrooms, two refrigerators, coolers, and a microwave oven. Bring your own linens and pillows. The larger boats sleep 12 and range from $1,695 to $2,495 per week in high season and $150 to $280 per night in low season. Closed from early October through April.

The **Jones Valley Resort,** 22300 Jones Valley, Marina Drive, Redding, CA 96003 (☎ **916/275-7950,** or toll free **800/223-7950**), is another place that rents luxury houseboats and other boats.

OTHER WATER SPORTS   Don't miss the "adult toys" here. We had loads of fun at the **Toy Box Fun Rental Center** at Holiday Harbor, P.O. Box 112, O'Brien, CA 96070 (☎ **916/238-2383,** or toll free **800/776-BOAT**). This rental center bills itself as Shasta Lake's entertainment hot spot. You only have to try a little addictor boat (a tiny two-seater speedboat) once to know what water-sports entertainment is all about. It beats sunning by the water's edge, hands down.

Ever try a full-size speedboat? And how about waterskiing? People here say that if the kids want to learn, and they're comfortable in the water, they can enjoy the sport. The Toy Box has ski boats, fishing boats, patio boats, and canoes to rent, jet skis (a tremendous hit with teenagers), paddleboats, windsurfers, even fishing poles and parasailing. One unique feature about the Toy Box is that they'll actually work with you till you know how to use the equipment. Rates vary widely depending on what you want, for how long, and when you want it. Advance reservations are recommended. If you're renting your houseboat from Holiday Harbor (see above) they'll give you a 15% "tag-along" discount.

Mike Suyderhoud Water Ski Center, located at the Jones Valley Resort and Marina (☎ 916/275-8419), is a good place for kids to learn how to waterski. Mike teaches children of all ages. The main criterion is that they feel comfortable in the water and know how to swim. He starts with a special training boom that has a solid bar that allows the kids to hold on while they're getting used to the skis. They have enough support so they're pulled without having all the falls. He teaches all skill levels. The waterski lessons cost $35 for a 20-minute session. You can also get group instruction at $79 per hour. There's a fully stocked pro shop that has waterskis, wet suits, life jackets, and the like. It's open daily during the summer from 8am to 5pm. Reservations for rentals are advised.

John Steiner's International Water Ski Center, 19821 Califontana Way (☎ 916/275-6744), at Holiday Harbor on Shasta Lake, is another ski school and pro shop. The shop has waterskis, wet suits, vests, ropes, etc., and sportswear for men and women. A one-hour lesson for 2–3 persons is $60; a package of three half-day lessons is $70; a package of five full-day lessons is $110; and one week of full-day lessons is $395. The center is open mid-May through mid-Sept., Monday through Friday from 8am to 6pm and on Saturday and Sunday from 9am to 5pm.

HIKING AROUND THE LAKE   Shasta Lake has several good family trails. They're relatively short and don't climb in elevation. Some of the trails are rocky, so be sure to wear hiking shoes. Also carry sunscreen, bring lots of water to drink, and watch out for poison oak. For information about good trails for your family, stop at the **Shasta Lake Ranger District and Visitor Center,** located about 10 miles north of Redding on I-5 at 14225 Holiday Rd., Redding, CA 96003 (☎ 916/275-1587).

Here are a few easy walks to get you started. For information call **916/275-1589.**

Waters Gulch Trail is a $3^1/_2$-mile trail. Even though long, it's an easy, lovely wide trail that winds through oak trees. There are benches halfway up, affording beautiful vistas of the Sacramento arm of the lake. The trailhead is located at Packer's Bay Road, a quarter mile before the boat ramp.

Eastside Trail at Packer's Bay is a short half mile to a good swimming and fishing hole. The trailhead is marked.

Bailey Cove Trail is a $2^3/_4$-mile loop that takes off from the Bailey Cove parking lot and winds around an island-type area that has beautiful views of the McCloud arm of the lake. There are some ups and downs, but it's fairly level. There's a picnic area and restrooms at the start. Kids can swim anywhere along the cove.

WHAT TO DO IN REDDING

If you find yourself with some time in Redding proper, there are pleasant ways to pass the time.

Caldwell Park, on Quartz Hill Road, is next to the Sacramento River in a beautiful location with lots of oak trees and small rolling hills. There's a public swimming pool, swings and slides, and a full playground for little kids. There are picnic tables and barbecues. It's beautiful, especially when the sun is setting.

The **Redding Museum of Art and History,** 56 Quartz Hill Rd. (☎ 916/225-4155), is also located in the park. It has a good collection of Native American artifacts, relics of the Gold Rush, and rotating exhibits of contemporary art. In April there's a children's lawn festival which recalls the days of covered wagons. The children get to bake bread in wood-burning stoves, do fence painting, and grind cornmeal. The museum is open in winter, Tuesday through Friday and on Sunday from noon to 5pm, Saturday from 10am; in summer, Tuesday through Sunday from 10am to 5pm; closed major holidays. Admission to the museum is free.

Also located here is the **Carter House Natural Science Museum** (☎ 916/225-4125). There's an animal discovery room with live animals, many of which are native to the Northern California area (screech owls, great horned owls, yellow-billed magpies), and some domestic animals (rabbits and guinea pigs) for kids to pet. There's also a greenhouse solarium and another area with rotating exhibits of the natural history of the region. The museum is open Tuesday through Sunday from 10am to 5pm. Admission is $1 for adults, 50¢ for children.

The **Sacramento River Trail** is a wonderful place to walk, jog, and bicycle. This recreational trail is on both sides of the river. To get there, find the intersection of North Market Street and Riverside Drive, and proceed west for almost half a mile, before you cross the Calif. 273 bridge. There's a parking lot, plus more parking and facilities on the other side of the river. For directions, call the visitors' bureau.

Waterworks Park, 151 N. Boulder Dr. (☎ **916/246-9550**), is one of the cooler ways to spend a hot day in Redding. This water park has three giant water slides, a kiddie water playground, beach volleyball, and a white-water-river inner tube ride. Lifeguards and first-aid staff are always on duty. The park is open Memorial Day to Labor Day, daily from 10am to 8pm. Admission is $12.50 for adults, $10.50 for children 4–11, free for children under 4 and seniors over 65. To get there, take the Burney/Alturas exit (Calif. 299 East) off I-5 at North Redding.

South Redding Park, located at the corner of South Market Street and Parkview Avenue, is a park with children's equipment, baseball and softball fields, and tennis courts.

For another type of entertainment, **Miss Q's Family Billiards,** 2990 Churn Creek Rd. (☎ **916/223-5243**), is a fun place, too. There are 12 pool tables and a video arcade. Tables rent two ways: either 50¢ a game or $6 per hour for two or more people. Open Sunday through Thursday from 1pm to 1am, on Friday and Saturday from 6 to 2am.

A Great Little Store

Learning Country, 3286 Bechelli Lane (☎ **916/223-0596**), is a delightful educational store. Located next to the Holiday Market, it's a small store with a nice assortment of workbooks and paperback books, and some unusual toys and discovery items. Science toys and wonderful coloring kits on Native Americans, different species of fish, and animals are also available. There's a table in the middle where children can sit down and work with some of the materials. Open in summer, Monday through Friday from noon to 6pm and on Saturday from noon to 4pm. Take the Bechelli Lane offramp from I-5—games, math manipulative, travel activities. Free bookmarks to visitors.

DAY TRIPS AND OTHER OUTDOOR ADVENTURES

Mount Shasta

Mount Shasta is not only beautiful from a distance, but offers many adventures as well. Write or call the **Mount Shasta Ranger District and Visitor Center,** 204 W. Alma, Mount Shasta, CA 96067 (☎ **916/926-4511**). The rangers will give you information and suggestions tailormade for your family's abilities and interests. In summer, some of the ski lifts on the mountain are operating, and naturalists give guided tours. There's a volcano exhibit open all summer, daily from 10am to 4pm.

There are trails in the nearby **Castle Crags Wilderness Area** that offer spectacular views of Mount Shasta. In summer, a scenic chairlift ride will take you up the slopes of Mt. Shasta Ski Park (☎ **916/926-8600**). There's a self-guided interpretive trail and volcano exhibit. It's open all summer, Wednesday through Sunday from 10am to 4pm.

Castle Crags State Park (☎ **916/235-2684**) is a 4,000-acre park that's just off I-5 on the way to Mount Shasta. The fantastic granite spires soar to 6,000 feet—a sight well worth the drive. The park is near the Sacramento River and affords some beautiful views. You can camp and picnic. There are 64 campsites, hot showers, picnic facilities, and lots of hiking, fishing, and swimming. The park is open year round, although there may be snow. Day use is $4 per vehicle; camping is $8 from October through May 14, and $12 from May 15 through September.

Castle Crags is just six miles south of the quaint town of **Dunsmuir,** another place you'll want to drive through as you're heading up to Mount Shasta. Dunsmuir is the home of a unique Old West resort called **Railroad Park,** 100 Railroad Park Rd., Dunsmuir, CA 96025 (☎ **916/235-4440**). This charming site has a motel, in which all the guest rooms are converted railroad cars. There is also an RV park and a restaurant where you can dine in antique dining cars. Full dinners range in price from $9.50 to $17.95, and there's a nice little kid's menu. All the restaurant's rooms are really train cars, and you should see what they do with them—really a treat! Even if you don't stay overnight, you'll want to stop by, have a snack or meal, and let the children see the place. It's really an unusual experience.

For something else unusual, you might want to try **Shasta Llamas,** P.O. Box 1088, Mount Shasta, CA 96067 (☎ **916/926-4107**). These folks offer three-day family hiking trips with special hiking and exploration designed with each age group in mind. Llamas carry all the equipment; participants walk. Minimum age is 5. Adults are charged $355 each; children 8–14, $300 for three-day trips. Five-day trips also available.

RIVER RAFTING AND CANOEING   River rafting and canoeing will be some of the most exciting times you share with your kids: Expect to get wet, do some work, and have lots of fun. The entire Shasta Cascade area is perfect for rafting because the river terrain varies, offering everything from gentle waters to raging rapids. River rafting is rapidly gaining in popularity for families.

Rivers are classified by levels of difficulty—from I to V. The river classification can change depending on the time of year. Class I is the easiest. Trip lengths vary from an afternoon outing to several days. Many rafting companies run trips on different rivers; all will send you brochures about their trips and the rivers they run.

Of course, the primary safety consideration is how well your children can swim. Most rafting expeditions will not take children under 8, but a few will. Those are designed especially for families. If you go with your kids, rafting experts suggest that the trip be designed with children's comfort in mind. If everyone knows that kids will be along, the trip will be planned with enough time for the kids to play on the banks and enjoy the trip at a kid's pace. But don't assume anything; always get details!

To obtain rafting information for 45 California river-rafting outfitters, contact **California Outdoors** (☎ toll free **800/552-3625**). This group offers a free directory of dozens of river-rafting companies operating in California, including a brief description of the trips and the minimum ages for children.

Friends of the River (☎ **415/771-0400**) is another group that offers river-rafting information and booking. When you book your trip through this organization, part of the fee goes toward river preservation.

Turtle River Rafting Co., P.O. Box 313, Mount Shasta, CA 96067 (☎ toll free **800/726-3223**), runs guided trips for families with children as young as 4 on very gentle sections of the Klamath River. The Klamath River is treasured for its scenic beauty and was one of the first rivers in California to be granted National Wild and Scenic status. These special family trips are from one- to five-days. The focus is on allowing children to gain confidence and have fun being outdoors and on the river. The rapids are small, yet exciting. There are side creeks to explore, deer, otter, and turtles to watch for, and the warm river to swim or float in. In addition to the rafts, small inflatable kayaks are available on every trip. A two-day "Kid's Klamath" river trip is $122 per child, $196 per adult. A three-day wilderness trip is $252 per child, $296 per adult. Meals, river equipment, and guides are included. The season is May through September.

Wilderness Adventures, 19504 Statton Acres Rd., Lakehead, CA 96051 (☎ **916/238-8121**, or toll free **800/323-RAFT**), is another outfit that takes children. Owned and operated by Dean Munroe, a professional river guide, Wilderness Adventures runs raft trips on the California, Salmon, Scott, Lower Klamath, Sacramento, Trinity, and Upper Klamath Rivers. Several trips welcome children.

The Trinity River and Lower Klamath River are both Class II+ to III rivers, which means that they have long stretches of mellow water, nice beaches, and good places to hike. They're perfect for family rafting. The minimum age for both is 10. There are one- and two-day trips on the Trinity. Trips on the Lower Klamath range from one day to four days.

The trip through the Sacramento Canyon has more than 45 rapids and is a Class III+ trip. There are one- and two-day trips, and the minimum age is 10. The Upper Klamath/Hell's Corner Gorge is the biggest summertime white water on the West Coast, and is considered a Class IV–V trip. Minimum age is 12 for the two-day trips. **Adventure Connection,** P.O. Box 475, Coloma, CA 95613 (☎ toll free **800/556-6060**), is a very reasonably priced river-rafting company. Children and parents can pan for gold, learn about local fauna and play creative and educational games. It offers one- and two-day trips for families with *young* children as well as *older* children, plus special half-price family vacations and family canoe trips for kids over 5. Prices start at $70.

If you already know what you're doing, you can also rent your own raft or canoe at **Park Marina Water Sports,** 2515 Park Marina Dr. in Redding (☎ **916/246-8388**). The rental rate for a two-passenger raft is $29; for a four-passenger raft, $39; for a six-passenger raft, $49. Two-passenger canoes for one or two days are $34 per day; for three or more days, $30 per day. Reservations are required. Open Memorial Day through mid-October, daily from 8:30am to 6:30pm.

For a historical outing, you might want to try **Kimtu Outdoor Adventures** (see "The Trinity Scenic Byway," below).

WINTER SPORTS Mount Shasta is a beautiful area with different terrain that offers wonderful downhill and cross-country skiing. The **Mount Shasta Cross Country Area** has three miles of marked, not groomed, trails for beginning, intermediate, and advanced cross-country skiers. To get to the area, take I-5 north to Everitt Memorial Hwy., past Calif. 89. For information, call the Mount Shasta Ranger District (☎ **916/926-3781**).

The Bunny Flat Trail begins about 12 miles up the highway. This three-quarter-mile trail has gentle, open terrain, and is intended for beginners. The Sand Flat Trail is a level, beautiful, 1¼-mile trail that's designed for beginners. The Overlook Loop Trail is a 1-mile trail for intermediate skiers that begins at Sand Flat. The trail heads west, where you get wonderful views.

There are also two snow-play areas, located at Snowman's Hill and Bunny Flat. The season runs from Thanksgiving to Easter, and is most crowded on holidays and weekends.

Mount Shasta Ski Park, 104 Siskiyou Ave., Mount Shasta, CA 96067 (☎ **916/926-8610,** or **916/926-8686** for snow conditions), is a family ski area that offers alpine and Nordic skiing. There's a lodge with food service and a bar, a ski school, retail and rental shops, and a first-aid station. The Powder Pups program is a ski school for children 3–7. For one 1½-hour session the charge is $30; for two sessions, $40. This is a learn-to-ski package that includes equipment and lift ticket. Older children attend the regular ski school and are grouped by ability level. For one 1½-hour session the charge is $18; for two sessions, $28 (not including rentals). Lifts operate daily from 9am to 4pm; night skiing is available Wednesday through Saturday from 4 to 10pm. Adult lift tickets cost $26; junior (8–12) tickets cost $17; and Powder Pups, $3. Night skiing is $17 for adults, $12 for kids 8–12, and Powder Pups, $3.

McArthur-Burney Falls

With all of this outdoor paradise, there are still other adventures.

Don't miss this one! An absolutely magnificent day trip is the one to **McArthur-Burney Falls Memorial State Park** (☎ **916/335-2777**), located 11 miles northeast of Burney off Calif. 89, in Shasta County. Take Calif. 299 east from Redding to Calif. 89; then go north about five miles. Burney Falls is a spectacular waterfall located between Mount Shasta and Lassen Peak. Known as one of the wonders of the world, the falls thunder down a 129-foot drop to form emerald pools below, sometimes shrouded with misted rainbows. It's a gorgeous spectacle. The falls remain constant throughout the year, with a temperature of 48°. The park is forested with Ponderosa pine, as well as a wide variety of firs, cedars, black oaks, and dogwood. It's an unbelievable show of nature's majestic color schemes in the autumn.

The best way to enjoy the show is the self-guiding nature trail. We prefer our children Elizabeth and Andrew to hike, though we saw a pair of hardy grandparents wheeling a stroller for the first half of the walk. You'll never be able to use a stroller once you cross the bridge, but try to go the whole distance if you can. Bring lots of film, and be sure to get the kids involved in the walk—they'll learn a lot of botany. During the summer there are naturalist walks and campfire programs conducted by rangers. Excellent camping facilities are available with 128 campsites, rest rooms, hot and cold water, showers, stoves, tables, and food lockers. A boat ramp is also available at nearby Lake Britton. Reservations are a must in summer: call MISTIX (☎ toll free **800/444-7275**).

Don't miss nearby **Lake Britton** when you're at Burney Falls. We packed a large lunch, with lots of juice and extra water, for our afternoon in the sun. The lake is shallow and just perfect for wading. It has a nice sandy beach.

Our final junket of the day is a stop at **Crystal Lake Fish Hatchery** (☎ **916/335-4111**), located 12 miles from McArthur-Burney Falls Memorial State Park. This is an interesting 20- to 30-minute side trip. (To get to the hatchery from Redding, take Calif. 299 past Burney about nine miles toward Alturas. The road sign says CASSEL ROAD. Take a right to the sign that indicates the hatchery.) The hatchery is open daily from 8am to 5pm; 7am to 4pm during Daylight Savings Time.

We had never seen a hatchery before, and the thousands of fish were a sight to behold! This hatchery has 66 rearing ponds (each is 100 feet long) that have a variety of sizes and kinds of fish—different strains of rainbow trout, brook trout, and Eagle Lake trout. The sizes vary from catchable trout (about two fish to the pound) to little ones that are as small as 1¹/₂ inches. In one year's time the hatchery will raise more than 1.5 million fish! The fish-and-wildlife assistant feeds the fish four times a day, and if you time it right, you can watch the fish being fed. Even if you don't get to see a feeding, it's fascinating just to watch the groups of different fish swim in their ponds. If they get startled, they all change direction at once.

The Trinity Scenic Byway

Taking a drive down Calif. 299 West out of Redding is a great way to spend a day. If you wish, you can even take a Native American river-rafting tour. For information, contact the **Trinity Scenic Byway Association,** P.O. Box 517, Weaverville, CA 96093 (☎ **916/623-6101** or toll free **800/421-7259**).

Shasta State Historic Park (☎ **916/243-8194**), just four miles west of Redding on Calif. 299, is the remains of the old town of Shasta. Once considered the "Queen" of the Gold Rush towns in the region, it now consists of a small group of restored brick buildings. The museum in the old Courthouse is a good one, with lots of paintings done in the 1800s and displays depicting Shasta County's history back to the beginning of the 1800s. The General Store is restored to its 1880s style with authentically arranged counters that have many antique items and some cleverly designed reproductions. This is a lovely area for picnicking. The park is open Thursday through Monday from 10am to 5pm; and November 1 to March 1, Friday, Saturday and Sunday 10am to 5pm; closed New Year's, Thanksgiving, and Christmas Days. Admission is $2 for adults, $1 for children 6–12, free for children under 6.

Nearby **Whiskeytown Lake,** managed by the U.S. National Park Service, is one of the most popular recreation lakes in the area for waterskiing, sailing, fishing, swimming, and camping. For information, call **916/359-2269** or **916/241-6584.**

Don't miss the **Weaverville Joss House State Historic Park** (☎ **916/623-5284**), a Chinese Taoist temple built in 1874 and still used as a place of worship. The Joss House has ornately carved altars, beautiful tapestries and paintings, and other works of art. Tours are conducted on the hour from 10am to 4pm Thursday through Monday; and November 1 through March 31 open Friday, Saturday, and Sunday. It's closed New Year's, Thanksgiving, and Christmas Days. Admission is $2 for adults, $1 for children 6–13, free for children under 6.

The town displays Gold Rush and pioneer-era artifacts. The historic downtown also has the oldest drugstore and the oldest hardware store in California.

If you continue on to the **Hoopa Valley Indian Reservation** (☎ **916/625-4110**), the largest Indian reservation in California, you'll find exhibits and interesting artifacts.

We like to book a family rafting adventure with **Kimtu Outdoor Adventures,** P.O. Box 938, Willow Creek, CA 95573 (☎ toll free **800/562-8475**). Kimtu offers a wide range of raft tours, from very easy one-day treks to challenging six-day tours. They even offer environmental education camps for the entire family. The minimum age ranges from 3 to 7, depending on the activity, but all activities are geared for children as well as their parents. Costs vary depending on the trip, but all include food and equipment. The one-day Native American river-rafting tour is a wonderful way to learn a tremendous amount about the area.

WHERE TO STAY

Accommodations are simple in this neck of the woods. Don't expect luxury, but you'll be comfortable and you'll meet some of the nicest people around.

Moderate

The best bet for the money are the rooms at the **Best Western Hilltop Inn,** at 2300 Hilltop Dr., Redding, CA 96002 (☎ **916/221-6100,** or toll free **800/336-4880**)— they're simple but adequate and very comfortable. And the people at the Hilltop Inn couldn't be nicer. There's a children's swimming pool, and a wading pool for babies. It's a gated area, away from the parking lot. There's also a small grassy area for children's play.

One of the best features of this inn is the complimentary full continental breakfast featuring a variety of rolls, sweet rolls and muffins, fruit, orange juice and cranberry juice, granola and raisin bran cereals, as well as coffee, tea, and milk. Though there's no room service, if anyone in your party is feeling under the weather the staff will very graciously provide a tray so that you may select as complete a breakfast as you wish and take it to your room. Sometimes the older kids will come to the pub by themselves in the morning and have their continental breakfast there. After you're finished with the free continental breakfast, you may choose to buy lunch or dinner at C. R. Gibbs Alehouse, a traditional English-style pub that has sandwiches, soups, and the like. (See the "Where to Eat," below.)

A room features either a king-size bed, a queen-size bed, two double beds, or two queen-size beds, a game table and two high-back armchairs, and a desk. There is a separate vanity area with a large counter, and all rooms have shower/bath combinations. There is free Showtime. Rooms cost $65–$80 for singles, $75–$90 for doubles. Request a king- or queen-size bed if you prefer. Adjoining rooms are available, and children under 12 stay free in the same room with their parents. No charge for cribs, but rollaways cost $12 per night.

Also lovely is the **Red Lion Motor Hotel,** at 1830 Hilltop Dr., Redding, CA 96002 (☎ **916/221-8700,** or toll free **800/547-8010**), in a very convenient location. Even though the hotel is surrounded by a parking lot and lots of asphalt, the inside rooms overlooking the pool have a view that is wooded and quiet. The courtyard around the pool is lovely, large, with green indoor-outdoor carpeting. Tables, lots of lounge chairs, and many trees complete the inviting picture. In addition to the full-size swimming pool and the Jacuzzi, there's a wading pool. Pool hours are 10am to 10pm. Kids also love to amble around the putting green with their complimentary clubs and balls.

There is a fine-dining restaurant and a reasonably priced coffee shop, both of which have highchairs and boosters, and will make special menu accommodations for children. Other amenities include room service from 6am to 10pm, dry cleaning, and laundry.

The 195 very pretty rooms are good-sized and comfortable, some with balconies. Most have a table with two chairs, a desk and chair, free HBO, and complimentary sundries. Rates run $59–$85 for singles, $85 for two double beds, $85–$95 for a king-size bed. Suites (a large sitting room with a bar and refrigerator and a king-size bed) cost $225. Children under 18 stay free if they use existing bedding, but cribs cost $5. Each other additional person pays $15 per night.

Budget

You'll find many inexpensive places to stay in this area. The **Redding Lodge,** 1135 Market St., Redding, CA 96001 (☎ **916/243-5141**), near Calif. 299, is a step up from a really inexpensive motel. Although it's located downtown, it borders a residential area and there are lots of trees around the parking lot. There's a little grassy area in a corner with a gazebo where children can play in pretty surroundings.

You have a choice of single-bedded rooms or deluxe rooms, all quite lovely. The rooms feature hairdryers and fresh-brewed coffee. Rates range from $36 to $42. Children under 12 sleep free in their parents' room; additional guests pay $4 per night. Cribs are free.

The **Best Western Ponderosa Inn,** 2220 Pine St., Redding, CA 96001 (☎ **916/241-6300**), is a typical two-story motel. In the center is a nice-size swimming pool and a little wading pool. The motel is located on the south end of downtown, two blocks away from Redding City Park. Lulu's Coffee Shop is on the premises and serves breakfast, lunch, and dinner. There's also a nice lounge.

The units are pleasant. The double-bed rooms are good-sized and have a bathtub. The singles are slightly smaller. All rooms have a table for meals or card playing, two chairs, and instant coffee makers. Adjoining rooms are available. Rates range from $45 to $56; single or double. Kids under 12 stay free in the same room with their parents. There's a $5 charge for cribs, and additional adults pay $6 per night.

Camping Facilities at Shasta Lake

There are 28 campgrounds at Shasta Lake, which vary from walk-in sites to trailer sites. There are even boat-in campgrounds, and campgrounds where you can choose a site on the shore of Shasta Lake. Most of them are on a first-come, first-served basis. Contact the **Shasta Lake Ranger District,** 14225 Holiday Rd., Redding, CA 96003 (☎ **916/275-1587**), for information.

Contact the **Shasta Cascade Wonderland Association,** 14250 Holiday Rd., Redding, CA 96003 (☎ **916/275-5555,** or toll free **800/326-6944**), which will send you brochures about several private campgrounds in the area.

WHERE TO EAT

Redding is a small city with a population of about 60,000. We were surprised to find so many good restaurants.

Expensive

The restaurant we like is **C. R. Gibbs,** at the Best Western Hilltop Inn, 2300 Hilltop Dr. (☎ **916/221-2335**), a dimly lit dinner house great for a leisurely meal with kids who don't have to eat "hurry-up" style. A huge iced shrimp bowl to share and scrumptious beer muffins accompany the entrees, which include fresh catch of the day, pasta, blackened redfish, and prime rib. Prices range from $9 to $25. For kids, they'll make up hamburgers, cheeseburgers, and fish and chips, for under $7. There are highchairs and boosters available, and the management will gladly warm baby food and bottles.

C. R. Gibbs is open daily from 5:30 to 10pm. Reservations and most major credit cards are accepted. Parking is easy.

Moderate

Located at the back of Shasta Center Plaza is **Sweetriver Saloon,** 1800 Churn Creek Rd. (☎ **916/223-2797**). You'll feel like you've been transported to a turn-of-the-century San Francisco-style saloon with Victorian decor, two-story high ceilings, and lots of plants and brass. The place has an outdoorsy atmosphere. This is a family-oriented restaurant; you'll know that as soon as you see the children's menu, complete with crayons and a coloring page. The children's menu includes a junior burger, hot dog, and other selections. Meals come with either fries or fruit, and prices range from $2 to $4. Best yet, on Saturday from 11am to 6pm, kids eat free. It's open Monday through Thursday from 11am to 11pm, on Friday and Saturday from 11am to midnight, and on Sunday from 9am (for brunch) to 10pm. Most major credit cards are welcome, but reservations are accepted for eight or more. Parking is easy.

Inexpensive

Here's a little gem. **Lim's Café,** 592 N. Market St. (☎ **916/241-9747** or **916/243-2991**), will remind you of Sunday Chinese dinners when you were a kid. Nothing fancy, but the food and prices are good. The dining room is decorated in 1950s-style vinyl booths and Formica tabletops, and red Chinese lanterns hang from the ceiling. In the front room is a counter and coffee shop–type tables.

The friendly waitresses assured us that kids like the chicken-noodle soup more than the egg-flower soup. If you order individual entrees, a dinner for four will cost just over $25. Chinese entrees are priced at $3–$13 (for lobster Cantonese). The full dinner for three, including soup, pork chow mein, pork fried rice, fried shrimp, sweet-and-sour pork, or sweet-pea chow yuke, eggroll, cookies, and tea, is $18.75 total. Lim's is also open for breakfast. Standard breakfast fare goes for $2.70–$4.60.

Lim's is open Monday through Thursday from 7am to 11pm and on Friday and Saturday from 7am to midnight. A favorite of locals, this place gets hectic on weekends but accepts reservations. It's best to come after 1pm for lunch and between 5:30 and 6pm for dinner. Highchairs and boosters are available. Some credit cards accepted. There's a parking lot behind the restaurant.

Set back from the street in the North Market Square Shopping Center is **Le Chamois Restaurant,** 630 N. Market St. (☎ **916/241-7720**). The atmosphere is rustic: round wood tables, lots of plants in ceramic vases, and rough-hewn wood. There's outdoor seating and take-out orders.

The owners pride themselves on serving wholesome American food without preservatives, what they like to call "old-fashioned family food." Choose from such favorites as French dip, tuna melt, or shrimp salad sandwich; the soup-and-salad combination; or one of the daily specials. Prices range from $4.95 to $7. Kids can have grilled cheese or peanut butter and jelly for $2.75. If you ask, they'll split adult portions and warm bottles or baby food.

Open Monday through Saturday from 7am to 3pm; closed Sunday. There are boosters and highchairs. Reservations are accepted for parties of five or more, but the service is so fast it probably won't be longer than 15 to 25 minutes. They accept some credit cards, and parking is available.

2 Lassen Volcanic National Park

Lassen Volcanic National Park is a quiet, lesser-known park of 165 square miles, located in the southern part of the Cascade Range in northern California. While it may not have the same kind of breathtaking beauty as its cousin to the south, Yosemite, it has beautiful pine forests, exquisite lakes, and awe-inspiring views of Lassen and other nearby peaks.

Its recent volcanic activity has created interesting geologic formations. It is alive with hydrothermal activity and presents an ever-changing landscape, providing all kinds of opportunities for the kids to learn about geology. Forests give way to twisted manzanita bushes with green leaves and red berries. In small sections of the park where a swath of lava once made its way, plant life stops altogether; here the products of the eruptions that occurred in 1914 and 1915 take over—rocks and rock fields.

We think Lassen is perfect for families because kids can enjoy much of the park's natural wonders without having to be expert hikers or geologists. Lassen Park Road takes you through some of this uncommon scenery, allowing you to see almost all the interesting geological formations with very little effort. The park road also offers great views of Lassen Peak. If your kids are good car travelers, you can actually drive from one end of the park to the other (from Mineral at the south to Manzanita Lake in the north, or vice versa), enjoy a few, brief nature walks, and still be back in Redding for the evening. And many of the trails in the park are easy enough for novice hikers to enjoy.

The Devastated Area is fascinating—not for its beauty, but because you see nature in progress. Here, on ground covered with a fine white-gray dust left from the mud flow, there are a few pine trees and little saplings, evidence of the forest starting to come back.

At turnouts, the National Park Service has provided photographs and descriptions of the mid-May 1915 eruption. The last great eruption sent a cloud of steam five miles into the air.

While the park is open all year, Lassen Park Road is closed during the winter. The two seasons that beckon tourists are summer, when hiking, fishing, camping, and backpacking are the outdoor adventures; and winter, when cross-country skiing, mainly in the Lassen Winter Sports area in the southwest, are enjoyed.

HOW TO GET THERE

From Redding, take Calif. 44. From Sacramento, take I-5, which goes through Red Bluff, and then continue on Calif. 36.

Visitor centers are located at the southwest entrance near Mineral and the museum near the northwest entrance near Manzanita Lake. Be sure to pick up *The Road Guide to Lassen National Park* (less than $5). Write ahead for information: Superintendent, Lassen Volcanic National Park, P.O. Box 100, Mineral, CA 96063 (☎ 916/595-4444).

WHAT TO SEE AND DO

The park is dominated by summer outdoors lovers—hikers, fishermen, and campers.

Lassen Park Road

This road through the park is much more than a way to get around. From the road you can see much of the scenery that makes Lassen special. Road markers with corresponding numbers listed in guidebooks inform you about the geologic activity of the area. The *Road Guide to Lassen National Park* is a thorough guide that gives you a basic understanding of the highlights that can be seen from the park road.

Bumpass Hell Self-Guiding Nature Trail

Park rangers describe Bumpass Hell as a window to the middle of the earth. The trail starts at the road, and in a little more than $1^1/_2$ miles, takes you to the largest active hydrothermal area in the park. You'll see fumaroles, which are holes in the ground that spew forth hot gases and vapors; mudpots; bubbling hot springs; and steam vents coming from the earth.

This trail is well marked and completely safe. It's a good trail for children, but there are several dropoffs in places, so be forewarned. Kids should be old enough to either keep on the inside part of the trail by themselves or be small enough to be carried.

The trail changes from heavily forested areas, where you get fabulous views of Lassen Peak, to areas devastated by past volcanic activity. Possibly the most stunning view is the one of Lake Helen, a gorgeous little glacial lake 110 feet deep that's so cold it often has snow patches into the summer. The color of the lake, carved by a glacier, is vibrant sapphire blue. Even if you don't want to take the entire $1^1/_2$-mile trail, one-way, to the thermal area, try to walk as far as the first vista of Lake Helen, which isn't too far. You'll be rewarded.

The descent into the hydrothermal area is fairly steep, but very easy. A boardwalk has been constructed so you can get close enough to feel the heat and see the bubbling pots. And the sulfur smell greets you well before your descent. Heed the warnings and don't go off the trail, as the earth's crust is thin in spots and not at all safe to walk on. You can get badly burned.

Be sure to carry water with you! We didn't, and were so thirsty by the time we got to the bottom that it hurt—and there was no drinking water there either. A kind hiker took pity on the kids and offered them her canteen water, but we adults stayed parched and dry until we got back to the trail head.

Other Sights

Want to see another active hydrothermal area without much effort? **Sulphur Works,** also off Lassen Park Road, is a little boardwalk (less than a half mile) where you can see fumaroles, mud pots, and hot springs. Because of mineral deposits from the geologic activity, the ground, in spots, is colored yellow, green, or orange. Be sure your children stay on the marked path, since the earth's crust is thin and not safe to walk on.

Centrally located in the park, at an altitude of almost 7,000 feet, **Summit Lake** is a beautiful area with two campgrounds, picnic sites, swimming, and good views of the surrounding mountains. Many trails start at Summit Lake. Our kids love to take the easy trail around the lake itself.

Geologically speaking, **Manzanita Lake** is a new one. It formed during the mid-1600s, when rockslides in the area dammed up the nearby creek. We fondly remember this large and beautiful lake because we saw several families of deer grazing within a few yards of our picnic spot. There are lots of deer in the park—if you can keep the kids quiet and at a distance, the deer will continue to graze while you watch. Manzanita Lake has another good loop that circles the lake. With picnic tables, restrooms, and a parking lot, this is a favored spot.

Lassen Volcanic National Park

Although it's a bit of a drive, **Bathtub Lake,** in the northeastern corner of the park, near Butte Lake, is a lot of fun because you can actually swim in it without freezing. This is where you'll find the warmest swimming in the park, and the drive to the Butte Lake trailhead is a scenic one. This drive is not on Lassen Park Road; you have to go outside the park and come back in again. Bathtub Lake is an excellent day trip if you're staying in the park. We pack a lunch and swimsuits, and the kids have a great time.

Summer Activities

Lassen is a hiker's paradise. Much of the 160 miles of **hiking trails** are easy. Children can enjoy walking the trails because so many of them offer good scenery even if you don't reach the end. Many trailheads start right near the road, and there are a lot of lakes where you can just pull your car up, spread out a blanket, and have a picnic at turnouts or picnic areas.

Be careful, though, until you're acclimated to the altitude. Much of the park is at a high elevation that may cause headaches and shortness of breath if you're not used to it.

Yes, you can go **fishing** using artificial lures and single barbless hooks and maybe catch rainbow, brook, or brown trout; and also **boating** in many of the park's beautiful lakes. California fishing regulations are in force, which means that adults need a license. Only nonpowered boats are allowed; however, there are no boat rentals in the park. All waterborne crafts are prohibited on Boiling Springs Lake, Emerald Lake, Lake Helen, and Reflection Lake.

Educational events are held throughout the park. Park naturalists lead these free programs that discuss the area's geology, history, animals, Native Americans, and the like.

Winter Activities

Lassen Park Road is closed from early November until mid- to late June. The road to Lassen Chalet at the southern end of the park is open, as is the road from Calif. 44 to Manzanita Lake Ranger Station.

WHERE TO STAY

Of course, we think the way to enjoy the park is to camp out.

Campgrounds

There are seven campgrounds in the park, all on a first-come, first-served basis. Here are the ones we like.

Manzanita Lake has 179 sites and offers swimming, fireplaces, tables, laundrette, flush toilets, showers, and with electrical outlets in the bath area. Trailers up to 35 feet can camp here. There is a small grocery store. Naturalist programs are also offered.

Summit Lake has 94 sites, divided between the north and south parts of the lake. The campground has swimming, fireplaces, tables, and flush toilets at north Summit and pit toilets at south Summit. There are naturalist programs here.

Other campgrounds are: **Crags Campground** (45 sites for overflow from Manzanita), **Southwest Campground** (21 sites), **Warner Valley** (15 sites), and **Juniper Lake Campground** (18 sites). These campgrounds have only pit toilets, and no drinking water at Juniper Lake.

Fees range $6–$10 per night per site. *All campsites are on a first-come, first-served basis;* maximum stay is 7 or 14 days. For information, contact Lassen Volcanic National Park, P.O. Box 100, Mineral, CA 96063 (☎ **916/595-4444**).

Motels and Other Accommodations

The only accommodation within the park is **Drakesbad Guest Ranch,** Chester, CA 96020 (☎ 916/529-1512), a 100-year-old ranch that's completely off the beaten track. Drakesbad has a trout stream, horseback riding, horse pack trips, and a swimming pool. However, the accommodations are very modest and most don't have electricity. You use kerosene lamps. Some have only half-baths with a sink and toilet. Accommodations are on the American Plan, which includes three meals per day. Rates vary depending on the location and type of bathroom. The charge for one adult in a room is $110–$125; for two adults, $82–$98 per person. Each additional adult pays $70–$75 extra per night. Children over 12 pay full price; children 2–11 are charged $56; free for children under 2. The guest ranch is open from early June to early October.

Or You Can Stay . . .

If you want to stay in a nearby motel or hotel, you have just a few choices. The **Lassen Mineral Lodge,** on Calif. 36 (P.O. Box 160), Mineral, CA 96063 (☎ 916/595-4422), just a few minutes from the park's southern border, is one possibility. This lodge, nestled in a pretty mountain valley, is surrounded by grassy areas, some of which are fenced off and great for young children. It has a lovely swimming pool with a large area that's one to two feet deep. The facilities include a reasonably priced restaurant (see below), a bar with a pool table and video games, a giftshop, grocery store, post office, and nearby tennis courts. There's a loan library for indoor and outdoor lawn games and books. We also enjoyed the neighborhood school playground; just ask a local to tell you where it is.

The rooms are quite modest—in fact, almost bare. There are no televisions or phones, and there are only showers. Rooms rent for $40 single, $50 for two people/two beds, $55 triple, and $60 quad. Kitchenettes, cribs, and rollaways cost $5 extra per night, but there's no additional charge for children. For holidays, reserve six weeks in advance.

If you want to rent a three- or four-bedroom chalet in the town of Mineral, **McGovern's Mt. Lassen Vacation Chalets,** adjacent to Calif. 36 about 20 minutes from the ski slopes at Lassen (mailing address: 563 McClay Rd., Novato, CA 94947; ☎ 415/897-8377), may be the place for you. These vacation homes are completely furnished, for summer or winter use, and will sleep 10–16 people. In the winter, all wood is furnished. Rates are $225–$250 for a weekend, $450 for the week. A nonrefundable deposit of $50 is necessary when reserving.

A DINING POSSIBILITY

The **Lassen Mineral Lodge Restaurant,** located at the lodge (☎ 916/595-4422), is one of the few restaurants in the Lassen area. If you choose the right dinner, the food is very tasty. We loved the locally raised Ruby trout, and you'll lick your fingers from the cinnamon-covered deep-dish apple pie. Full dinners are priced from $7 to $13. Breakfasts and lunches run $4–$8.

This homey restaurant has a surprisingly extensive wine and beer list, and a wonderful children's menu that includes hamburgers, corn dogs, and barbecued ribs. Children's lunches and dinners include fries and fruit, and are priced at $2.50–$4. Breakfast costs $4.35 for bacon, eggs, pancakes, and beverage. They have highchairs and boosters, and they'll warm bottles and baby food.

Open for breakfast, lunch, and dinner: from Memorial Day to September 15, generally daily from 8am to 8pm; the rest of the year hours vary, so call ahead. Some major credit cards are accepted.

3 Spanish Springs

You may feel as if you had to go to the ends of the earth to get there, but **Spanish Springs Ranch** (☎ toll free **800/282-0279, 800/272-8282** in California) is well worth the trek. Located in Lassen County, near the California-Nevada border just north of Susanville, this guest ranch is actually a series of working cattle and horse ranches that invite you and the kids to participate to whatever extent you want. Wrangle horses? Watch a summer rodeo? Or join in daily trail rides, barbecues, and fishing trips. If you're lazy, you can simply swim, play tennis, and relax.

The ranches are on 70,000 acres of grazing land where antelope, mule deer, and even wild mustangs roam. It's one of the most exciting experiences you're likely to have with your children, regardless of their age. Elizabeth became a serious cowhand when she was 6, practicing her horseback riding in the arena and on the trails every day. And, at 12, Andrew drove the huge hay wagon, helped pile the bales of hay, and then threw them out to feed the dozens of waiting horses in the meadow. The cowboys and cowgirls are the friendliest people you'll meet, and they encourage the kids to feed and play with the young barnyard animals. The kids love to watch and feed the menagerie of lambs, piglets, goats, calves, bunnies, and puppies. There is also a swimming pool, tennis courts, volleyball, a horseshoe pit, an archery range, and a children's playground. And there are more planned daily activities than you can imagine. Because the ranch is also open in winter, the activities include sleigh rides, cross-country skiing, ice fishing, ice skating, and an annual winter carnival in February.

The rooms vary in size, but all are rustic and quite comfortable. The bathrooms have showers, and most of the rooms have fireplaces. We had a two-bedroom cottage that had a large living room and front porch—more space than we really needed— with a view to forever.

Meals are terrific and plentiful. Some are served family style; others are not. You can elect to take a board plan (including the meals in the room rate) or pay for your room only, eating at the ranch restaurant whenever you choose and paying separately for your meals.

Prices vary extensively depending on your selection of a board plan, so talk with the reservationist about your family's needs. You can also get driving directions, or arrange to be picked up at the Reno Airport. For information and reservations about all Spanish Springs facilities, write to 1102 2nd St., San Rafael, CA 94901, or call the toll-free numbers above.

Gold Rush Country

7

THERE'S A SECRET UP IN NORTHERN CALIFORNIA AND IT'S CALLED THE GOLD RUSH Country. This is an area where history is alive on a daily basis, where the buildings that housed the adventurous '49ers are as well preserved as the legends that surrounded them. Up and down Calif. 49 are precious pockets of history just waiting to be explored. Bring your school-age children, especially the ones who are studying California history. They'll get a special glimpse back to the time when the sound of "gold" was heard throughout the state.

Sacramento makes a good base from which to explore much of the area, and is a popular stopping-off point for people on their way to Tahoe, Reno, and the Gold Rush Country. Not only does its history relate to the mad years of the Gold Rush, but it has current significance as the capital of one of the largest states in the Union. Sacramento's best-kept secret is that it is rich with outdoor spring and summer family activities.

Lake Tahoe, while it isn't linked historically to the Gold Rush, lies between the two main roads used by the pioneers, now major highways. Its true significance is as a wonderful year-round family resort area, and an especially great place for skiing.

1 Sacramento

While the Gold Rush was probably Sacramento's most important claim to fame, its history actually began with one John Sutter. Sutter arrived in Sacramento in 1839 to establish a farming community, and ultimately opened it up to the pioneers who flocked there in droves with dreams about discovering the bright yellow rock. Sacramento—or Sutter's Fort, as it was first called—was in fact the first place in the West to become a town.

But Sacramento has other claims to fame. It was the western terminus for the short-lived Pony Express, for instance. And railroad buffs will tell you that Sacramento was important as the home of the Central Pacific Railway which, through engineering feats that were considered incredible for that time, was able to climb the steep grades of the Sierras. And it was important as the western terminus for the transcontinental railway. As a matter of fact, the West's very first railroad, the Sacramento Valley Railroad, was based here.

In its efforts to keep time with the 20th century, Sacramento hasn't lost its positive connections to the past. And it hasn't lost its quiet charm either, although it's the capital of one of the country's most powerful states. It remains a city of Victorian houses, blooming camellias (it's called the Camellia Capital of the World), and lush trees (over 200,000 in the city of Sacramento). Most of its modernity is found in the suburbs, where you'll also find Cal Expo, home of the California State Fair.

If you're planning a trip to Sacramento, depending on what you like to do and what time of year it is, your average stay will probably be two to three days.

GETTING THERE

By car from Los Angeles, Orange County, or San Diego, take I-5 north all the way. From San Francisco, take I-80. Most major domestic and many international airlines land at Sacramento Metropolitan Airport. Amtrak services Sacramento direct from Los Angeles and Oakland.

ORIENTATION

There are two offices to assist you with questions about what to see and do in Sacramento. The **Sacramento Convention & Visitors Bureau** is located at 1421 K St.,

Sacramento, CA 95814 (☎ **916/264-7777**). The office is open weekdays from 8am to 5pm. The **Old Sacramento Visitor Information Center** is on Front Street near the foot of K Street (☎ **916/442-7644** or **916/443-6223** for the **Events Hotline**), and is open daily 9am to 5pm.

Information is available by mail from the **California Dept. of Commerce Office of Tourism,** P.O. Box 9278, Van Nuys, CA 91409 (☎ toll free **800/862-2543**, ext. A1003).

We've arranged our Sacramento sightseeing, dining, and overnight stays by area: Old Sacramento, Downtown/Capitol, and Cal Expo. You'll find information about rafting on the American River in the "Outdoor Activities" section.

GETTING AROUND

Downtown Sacramento is a series of one-way streets, but it's easy to find your way around. Numbered streets go north and south; lettered streets go east and west. Just remember that autos are not allowed on the K Street Mall. There's a light rail system, and Regional Transit buses that stop at every historical location (call **916/321-BUSS** for route and schedule information).

Major car-rental agencies such as Hertz (☎ toll free **800/654-3131**), Budget (☎ toll free **800/527-0700**), Dollar (☎ toll free **800/800-4000**), and National (☎ toll free **800/328-4567**) service the area. Check the *Yellow Pages* for local addresses and phone numbers.

WHAT TO SEE AND DO

Sacramento is small enough that you'll be able to visit several areas in a day. Old Sacramento is at the edge of downtown, for instance, and the Capitol area is just 10 minutes away by car. If you're in good shape, you can even walk from Old Sacramento to the Capitol via the K Street Mall. It's approximately 10 blocks.

Old Sacramento

Old Sacramento was the original riverboat landing for Sutter's Fort. As the city grew and spread out, Old Sacramento, which by the 1950s had become a skid-row area, was almost lost to modern freeways. Luckily, some prominent citizens did not want to see the destruction of what was once the pulse of Sacramento, and they were able to convince authorities to save it. It's now a 28-acre historical park. Many of its original buildings have been meticulously renovated, and it is considered one of the best restoration projects in the country.

You will probably want to allow about a day for a look at Old Sacramento. You can make a circle, touring the area on foot. The borders of the park are the Sacramento River and 2nd Street, and I Street and the Capitol Mall. Either come via the pedestrian walkway from the K Street Mall, or park under the freeway at I Street. (A caution to the women in the group: The slatted wooden walkways covering the cobblestone streets love to catch hold of high heels—leave them in your hotel and wear sensible walking shoes instead.)

Begin your tour at the **California State Railroad Museum,** 2nd and I Streets (☎ **916/448-4466**), the largest railroad museum of its kind in the country. The 35 magnificently restored locomotives and train cars on display in this 100,000-square-foot museum are examples of the massive "iron horses" that helped connect the West to the East, and helped to build California. A brief movie explaining the history of the railroads begins your self-guiding tour. As you move through the museum the mournful sound of the whistle of the steam engine follows you. It's a sound that hasn't been heard since trains changed to diesel.

Kids love being able to enter an authentic 1929 Pullman passenger car, which simulates a moving train, complete with railroad noises. The lifelike displays of passengers sleeping in their compartments produces endless conversation for the kids. You'll also be able to enter an actual mail-sorting car, which was retired as recently as the 1970s. It's amazing to see how millions of letters and packages were transported before our postal service was modernized.

You'll also see the first engine of the Central Pacific Railroad, which was used to help build the transcontinental railroad. There's lots of chronological information on nearby displays explaining the history behind the building of the railroad. You—and the kids—will marvel at the huge locomotives, which have been beautifully restored to show off their artistic workmanship. You can also introduce the kids to the history behind the lavishly decorated private railroad cars. The first view of the giant one-million-pound locomotive of the Southern Pacific Railroad is awesome. And these are just some of the locomotives on display.

"Dinner at the Diner" offers a look at the glamorous and romantic era of train travel, highlighted by a walk-through exhibition of the Cochite dining car, complete with 36 place settings of rare railroad china and crystal.

You can all test your skill at an electronic question-and-answer game that asks which style locomotive belongs to what railroad line. There are re-creations of little passenger waiting rooms and a toy train exhibit displaying original cars.

The museum is open daily from 10am to 5pm, except New Year's, Thanksgiving, and Christmas Days. It's stroller-accessible except for the two train cars you can enter. The same ticket is good for entrance to the Central Pacific Passenger Depot (see below). Admission for adults is $5; children 6–12, $2; kids 5 and under free.

Next door to the Railroad Museum, on your way to the History Center, is the **Huntington Hopkins Hardware Store** exhibit, 113 I St. (☎ **916/323-7234**). Over 400 hardware items dating from the 19th century are on display here. You can point out to your kids the housewares and tools used by our great-grandparents. Old-fashioned toys, which the kids love, are for sale. Admission is free. Call for hours and information.

Next you'll come to the new **Discovery Museum,** 101 I St. (☎ **916/264-7057**), formerly the Sacramento History Museum. Now that the museum has merged with the Science Center, the focus is broader. Five thematic exhibition areas present history, science, and technology via original artifacts and hands-on, interactive devices. Exhibition areas include gold (with gold panning and $1 million worth of mother lode gold specimens); an historic, working print shop; agricultural technology (with a variety of machines whirring overhead); and regional history (including a Maidu reed house, dresses, carriages and autos, dolls, sports equipment, and more). There are also hands-on science exhibitions and thematic historical displays. Regularly scheduled science and craft demonstrations are held on the central stage. A self-guiding tour takes about one-and-a-half hours.

Summer hours, Memorial Day to Labor Day, are Tuesday through Sunday 10am to 5pm. Closed Mondays. In winter, the museum is open Wednesday through Friday, noon to 5pm; Saturday and Sunday, 10am to 5pm. Closed Mondays and Tuesdays. Call for hours on Monday holidays. Adult admission is $3.50, children ages 6–17, $2, members and children under 6 enter free.

One look at the **Central Pacific Passenger Depot,** 930 Front St. (☎ **916/322-7626**), and you'll think it's the real thing. This is a well-done reconstruction of the depot of 1876, with several exhibits depicting activities of the time when train travel was so popular. On weekends from May until Labor Day (except July 4th weekend), there are 45-minute steam-train rides that leave every hour on the hour. Open from 10am to 5pm. The fare is $4 for adults, $2 for children 6–12, free for kids under 6. Admission to the depot is $5 for adults, $2 for children 6–12, free for kids under 6. One ticket will allow you in the depot *and* the California State Railroad Museum on the same day.

The **Old Sacramento Schoolhouse Museum** is at Front and L Streets (☎ **916/371-0813**). One look at this replicated one-room schoolhouse from the 1800s and your kids will know they never had it so good. It's set up with the little desks of that period and displays the original readers. Open daily from 10am to 4pm volunteer staff permitting, but call first; even if it's closed, you can peek in the windows and see most of it. Free admission.

The historical **B. F. Hastings Building** is located at 2nd and J Streets (☎ **916/323-7234** or **916/445-4209**). Once a bank housing the Alta California and California State Telegraph Companies, the California Supreme Court, and the Wells Fargo Bank, it's now a museum. You'll see displays from the Wells Fargo Bank, the reconstructed Supreme Court, and the Pony Express. A plaque on the wall outside gives the destinations for the Pony Express when the building was originally a stage stop. Open Tuesday through Sunday from 10am to 5pm. Wells Fargo is open daily. Call ahead. Free admission.

At this point you're almost back at the Railroad Museum. Before you leave Old Sacramento, you might want to explore two other places, besides the myriad souvenir, candy, and specialty shops. One is **Mike's Puzzle Shop,** 1009 2nd St. (☎ **916/444-0446**). The store is full of nothing but—you guessed it—puzzles! There are whimsical and educational puzzles for kids and aficionados alike. Open daily in summer, Monday to Wednesday 10:30am to 5:30pm, Thursday to 9pm, Friday and Saturday 10 to 9, Sunday 11 am to 7pm; 10:30am to 5:30pm the rest of the year. The other interesting store is **Two Crows,** 1003 2nd St. (☎ **916/444-3616**). It's an adventure just to walk through the little store, which is crammed with all sorts of gifts and toys that relate to nature and science: books, science projects, jewelry, games, experiments, figurines, and stuffed animals. Open Monday through Wednesday from 10am to 6pm and Thursday through Saturday from 10am to 9pm.

The historic paddlewheeler *Spirit of Sacramento* embarks from the landing on Front and L Streets (☎ **916/552-2933,** or toll free **800/433-0263**). The 110-foot riverboat has decks for dining, dancing, and just plain watching. Best for families are the one-hour narrated sightseeing tours. Kids 5 years and up will probably enjoy this the most. Snacks and cocktails can be purchased on board, and the boat is stroller- and handicapped-accessible. There are also lunch, dinner, and Saturday and Sunday brunch cruises.

Sightseeing tours depart April through October, twice a day Friday through Sunday; from June through August, the boat sails Wednesday through Sunday. It's best to phone in reservations far in advance, especially for holiday weekends. You can also purchase tickets at the office, 110 L St., in Old Sacramento. Your reservation guarantees you a place on the 350-passenger riverboat. If you have no reservation, check at the ticket booth to see if there's space available.

Adults pay $10; children under 12, $5. Lunch and buffet dinner cruises range $22.50–$34 per person, adult or child. Buffet brunch runs $25. You can purchase the cruise without the meal, or if the child won't be eating, purchase your own ticket with meal and a regular ticket for the child.

Kids get a kick out of the horse-drawn **wagon and carriage rides** through Old Sacramento. There are seven stops in the area, including one at 2nd and K Streets. A 10- to 15-minute ride can range from $2 per person on the covered wagon to $10 per carriage ride.

Downtown and the Capitol Area

You can't miss the **State Capitol** at 10th and L Streets (☎ 916/324-0333), because of its glorious gold dome. Some 50 years after its birth, the Capitol building was in a state of major disrepair—so drastic was its condition that it was almost torn down. Fortunately, the building was gutted, reinforced, and then painstakingly restored to its original glory over a period of six years.

The **California State Capitol Tour** gives you a good look at this elegant monument to government. The one-hour **General Tour** is most suitable for fourth-graders and above. Kids younger than that often get bored. While some children won't be able to appreciate the work that went into the restoration of the grand building, adults will be able to stop and look at the faux marble and the delicate detail work on the ceilings and walls. The Senate and Assembly chambers are included in the tour, but usually anyone can view those proceedings without taking the tour provided the chambers are in use.

The tour gets filled in summer, so be sure to be there a half hour ahead. Thirty tickets per tour are distributed on a first-come, first-served basis. If you don't want a docent-guided tour, you can take a self-guiding one. Brochures are available in the tour office. If you don't have time for the entire tour, there are films shown in the basement museum theater that will take you through the Capitol's history and the restoration of the building in 10 minutes.

The **Capitol Tour** leaves daily, year-round, every hour on the hour from 9am to 4pm. Pick up tickets a half hour before tour time. The tour office is open daily from 8:30am to 5pm (closed New Year's, Thanksgiving, and Christmas Days). Street parking is limited; park in the lot on 10th and L Streets, and enter the Capitol on L Street.

Children or teenagers studying history will be most interested in the **Historic Tour,** which goes into detail about individual government offices. It includes a look at the original offices of the governor, attorney-general, and others, from the early 1900s. A maximum of 10 people are allowed. Young children may become fidgety on this walk. You could manage it with a sleeping infant. The tour leaves every hour on the half hour.

There's also a **Park Tour** daily, weather permitting, from mid-June to Labor Day at 10:30am, or by special arrangement. Each tree in the 40-acre park, adjacent to the Capitol building, represents a different part of the world. Signs specify the origin of each tree. On a pleasant day, this is a nice outdoors tour to take with the family. Free.

Five minutes by car from the Capitol is the **Historic Governor's Mansion,** at 16th and H Streets (☎ 916/323-3047). This grand Victorian mansion was home to 13 California governors. Ronald Reagan was the last to live here—Nancy declared it a firetrap. It's a look at what tastes were in vogue at the time of each governor.

Open daily from 10am to 5pm. Tours are given daily on the hour from 10am to 4pm; the last tour begins at 4pm. The charge is $2 for adults, $1 for children 6–12, free for kids under 6. Fees are higher on Living History Days. Young children below fourth grade may fidget during the one-hour tour; take infants in carriers.

It seems strange to see **Sutter's Fort** in downtown Sacramento, flanked by office buildings and private residences. It's located at 27th and L Streets (☎ 916/445-4422). Dating back to 1839, Sutter's Fort was the first settlement in Sacramento. Listening wands, cordless devices with a recorded narrative, enable you to follow the history of the reconstructed fort. You'll see the blacksmith's shop, Sutter's quarters, and hearth kitchen, among other sights, and hear the history behind them.

Check ahead for Living History Days when volunteers appear in costumes of 1846 and re-create the daily life of the fort. There are also Demonstration Days which feature spinners, weavers, candlemakers, and bakers practicing their crafts.

The fort is open daily from 10am to 5pm. Stroller-accessible. Admission is $2 for adults, $1 for children. Fees are slightly higher on Living History Days.

Californian Native American artifacts from prehistoric times to the present are displayed at the **State Indian Museum** (☎ 916/445-4209). This museum is on the same grounds as Sutter's Fort, but has a separate entrance at 2618 K St. It's open daily from 10am to 5pm. Admission is $2 for adults, $1 for children 6–12, and free for children under 6.

And If You Have Time . . .

Automobile aficionados love to visit the **Towe Ford Museum,** at 2200 Front St. (☎ 916/442-6802). There are more than 180 cars and trucks at this museum dedicated to preserving antique and classic automobiles. Moms, dads, and grandparents can talk about which models they remember because there's an example of almost every Ford car from 1903 to 1953 displayed here.

The museum is stroller-accessible and open daily year round from 10am to 6pm. Admission is $5 for adults, $4.50 for seniors, $2.50 for high school students, $1 for grade school students, and free for younger children. There's free parking available.

The **Crocker Art Museum,** 216 O St., at the corner of 3rd and O Streets (☎ 916/264-5423), is housed in a grand Victorian building named after its founder, Judge Edwin Bryant Crocker. It's the oldest public art museum in the West. The museum contains collections of early Californian and European paintings, old master drawings, and contemporary art.

Family programs are offered throughout the year. There are festivals workshops, family afternoons, and other activities on Saturday and Sunday. Call the museum for the current schedule. In addition, hands-on art activities for children are available year round on Saturday from 1 to 3pm and on the first and third Thursdays in the summer from 7 to 8:30pm. You can arrange by phone for a guided tour. The museum is stroller- and wheelchair-accessible.

It's open Wednesday through Sunday from 10am to 5pm (on Thursday to 9pm). Closed Monday, Tuesday, and major holidays. Admission is $4.50 for adults and seniors, $2 for children 7–17, free for children 6 and under. Check for special admission charges for Family Festivals.

Almonds, if you didn't already know, are California's largest export crop. The **Blue Diamond Visitor's Center,** at 1701 C St. (☎ 916/446-8409 or 916/325-2854), shows a free 20-minute video giving a quick lesson in almond production. Fine for children of all ages. Almond-tasting takes place in the giftshop. Monday through Friday at 10am to 5pm, Saturday 10am to 4pm.

The **Visionarium,** on the second floor of the Sutter Square Galleria, 2901 K St. (☎ 916/443-7476), is Sacramento's hands-on children's museum. Concepts rather than "things" are the key here. Exhibits are created to arouse the curiosity of children of any age, but kids 12 and under will appreciate the displays the most. Education is through active participation. "Watch Me Grow" is meant for the littlest children, infants through 4 years old, and gives them a safe play environment in which to stimulate their senses. Things to touch here are soft, noisy, fuzzy, and squishy. The exhibit on disabilities is great. Entitled "What If I Couldn't," it gives kids the chance to see what the world would be like for them if they had physical limitations.

These and other permanent exhibits, plus special programs and entertainment, are open to the public Tuesday through Saturday from 10am to 5pm and on Sunday from noon to 5pm. Adult admission is $2.50, children 2 years and older pay $4; free for those 6 months to 2 years. The Visionarium is stroller-accessible. Parking is validated.

Cal Expo Area

You can get to the Cal Expo area via Calif. 160, a 10-minute drive from downtown Sacramento, or you can take Bus. 80.

Kids of all ages will love **Waterworld USA,** a 14-acre family water park located at Cal Expo, 1600 Exposition Blvd., at I-80 (☎ 916/924-0555). It boasts the largest wave pool in Northern California, a 25,000-square-foot area called Breaker Beach. The four-foot waves make for great bodysurfing, and there are lifeguards everywhere. Tom Sawyer's Landing is great fun for children 11 and under who have their very own Super Surf Hill, a 100-foot slippery slide for kids 3–6. Teens and adults alike get their thrills on the Cliff Hanger, with its 65-foot near-vertical drop. In addition to Cliff Hanger, there's a six-slide complex called the California Scream Machine, with one pool for adults and another for children. Tubing takes place on an 800-foot-long, 3-foot-deep river called the Calypso Cooler. Sand volleyball courts, picnic areas, lockers, and food concessions complete the picture.

Safety is of primary concern here. In addition to their certification through the National Pool and Waterpark Lifeguard Training, lifeguards at Waterworld go through continuous weekly training.

The park is open daily from Memorial Day weekend to Labor Day weekend from 10:30am to 6pm. The admission price covers all attractions. Anyone over four feet tall pays $14.95; children 48 inches tall and under, $9.95; children under 3, free.

Not far from Cal Expo is the **Iceland Ice Skating Rink,** at 1430 Del Paso Blvd. (☎ 916/925-3121). Sunday and Monday nights and Tuesday and Thursday afternoons are discounted sessions, when admission is $3 with skate rental included. Other nights, admission is $4.50 per adult, $3.50 per child 12 and under, and $3 for seniors 55 and over; skate rental is $1 per person. Call for hours.

Surrounding Sacramento

The **Sacramento Zoo** is located in lush William Land Park, at the corner of Sutterville Road and Land Park Drive (☎ 916/264-5885), a quarter mile off the Sutterville exit on I-5. The 15-acre park is only 10 minutes from downtown Sacramento in a lovely setting. It's open daily (except Christmas Day) from 10am to 4pm. Admission costs $4 for anyone over 12, $2.50 for children 3–12, and free for children under 3. Add 50¢ per person on weekends and holidays.

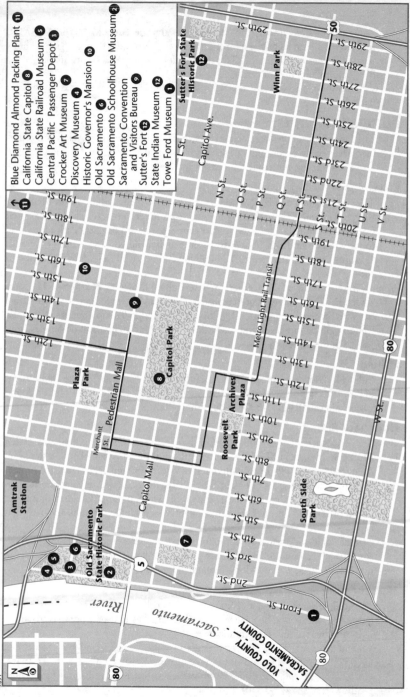

Downtown Sacramento

Blue Diamond Almond Packing Plant **11**
California State Capitol **8**
California State Railroad Museum **5**
Central Pacific Passenger Depot **3**
Crocker Art Museum **7**
Discovery Museum **4**
Historic Governor's Mansion **10**
Old Sacramento **6**
Old Sacramento Schoolhouse Museum **2**
Sacramento Convention and Visitors Bureau **9**
Sutter's Fort **12**
State Indian Museum **12**
Towe Ford Museum **1**

Sutter's Fort State Historic Park

Old Sacramento State Historic Park

Amtrak Station

Sacramento River

YOLO COUNTY
SACRAMENTO COUNTY

Winn Park

Capitol Ave.

L St.
N St.
O St.
P St.
Q St.
R St.
S St.
T St.
U St.
V St.

29th St.
28th St.
27th St.
26th St.
25th St.
24th St.
23rd St.
22nd St.
21st St.
20th St.
19th St.
18th St.
17th St.
16th St.
15th St.
14th St.
13th St.
12th St.

Metro Light Rail Transit

Capitol Park

Plaza Park

Pedestrian Mall

Merchant St.

Capitol Mall

Roosevelt Park

Archives Plaza

South Side Park

11th St.
10th St.
9th St.
8th St.
7th St.
6th St.
5th St.
4th St.
3rd St.
2nd St.
Front St.

80
50
80
W St.

N

9091

Across the street from the zoo entrance is **Fairytale Town** (☎ 916/264-5233), which is a trip into fantasyland for the short set. Kids wander through King Arthur's Castle and Sherwood Forest. Call for information about special events. It's open daily from 9am to 5pm in summer.

Admission is $3 for adults, 50¢ for seniors and children 3–12, free for children under 3.

OUTDOOR ACTIVITIES

The American and the Sacramento Rivers beckon thousands of travelers every summer. The two rivers converge at Discovery Park, which is right off I-5 and Calif. 99.

Families enjoy numerous activities in and around these rivers.

Bicycling

The city's exciting and famous bicycle trail is called the **Jedediah Smith Memorial Bicycle Trail** and is located along the **American River Parkway.** The parkway itself is also a beautiful place for a walk. Start your bike ride at Discovery Park and ride all the way to Folsom Lake. It's a great family activity, and you'll see some of the most beautiful parts of Sacramento. The trail is a little over 30 miles long, with various cut-offs along the way.

American River Bike Centers, at 9203 Folsom Blvd. (☎ 916/363-6271), rents adult bikes for $4 per hour, or $20 per day. Child carriers are $15 per day; helmets are free with the rental. Open Monday through Friday from 9am to 7pm in summer and 9am to 6:30pm in winter, and on Saturday from 9am to 5pm and on Sunday from 9am to 5pm year round.

Fishing

Fishing locations are numerous and the fish are abundant. Contact the **Department of Fish and Game** (☎ 916/355-7090) for information on what type of fish are found where, and call **916/355-0978** about fishing licenses.

Horseback Riding

A way to experience yet another side of Sacramento is on horseback. **Shadow Glen Riding Stables,** 4854 Main Ave. in Fair Oaks, at the intersection of Sunset and Main Avenues (☎ 916/989-1826), offers guided rides in Folsom Lake State Park. Guides lead you along the shore of Lake Natoma, over ridges, down canyons, and up hills where you spot deer, coyotes, wild turkeys, and scores of birds. Children must be at least 6 years old to ride. Ask about moonlight rides beginning at 7pm, and overnight trips.

The stables are open daily year round from 9am. Reservations are necessary. Rides cost $16.50 per hour, or $31.50 for two hours, adult or child. Children under 6 can ride double for $19.50 (we don't recommend this). Closed Thanksgiving Day.

Houseboating

An excellent way to spend a vacation is on a houseboat (see Chapter 1 for more details). The Sacramento Delta area offers a pleasant way to experience that adventure in its hundreds of miles of gentle waters.

You can contact **Herman & Helen's Marina,** Venice Island Ferry, Stockton, CA 95219 (☎ 209/951-4634); and **Seven Crown Resorts,** P.O. Box 16247, Irvine, CA 92713 (☎ toll free 800/752-9669). Or call the **Delta Rental Houseboat Hotline** (☎ 209/477-1840).

You can write for brochures to **Houseboats,** 6333 Pacific Ave., Suite 152, Stockton, CA 95207.

Parks

Sacramento is a mecca for park enthusiasts. You can get to some parks off the bike trail or by river raft. Admission to the parks is $4 per vehicle. Visit or call the **Sacramento County Department of Parks and Recreation,** 3711 Branch Center Rd., Sacramento, CA 95827 (☎ **916/366-2066**), for specific information on directions, hours, and activities, and for a map showing riverfront access for the following county parks:

Discovery Park, located at Jibboom Street and Richards Boulevard, the confluence of the Sacramento and American rivers, has 275 acres. It offers boat launching, picnic areas, horseshoes and archery ranges. Begin the Jedediah Smith Bike Trail here.

Ancil Hoffman Park is in nearby Carmichael at California Avenue and Tarshes Drive. There's golf, walking trails, a nature center with special programs and exhibits.

C. M. Goethe Park is off Folsom Boulevard in Rancho Cordova. This wooded park is a great place to picnic, hike, or to access the bike trail.

Gibson Ranch is a small farmlike facility off Elverta Road East to Gibson Ranch Road. Kids can watch and feed various farm animals, families can picnic or go horseback riding here, and there's an eight-acre pond stocked with fish.

River Rafting

Almost every kind of boat imaginable is found up and down the American River. But rafting remains the river sport of choice in this area. White-water rafting can be energizing, enervating, hard work, exciting, and sometimes dangerous. Rafting on the Lower American River, in the Sacramento area, takes you floating leisurely down the river, making it a perfect family activity. The river is rated Class I, meaning that the water is flat, has small waves, and no serious obstacles. (For information on white-water rafting, see the "Other Outdoor Activities" section in "The Gold Country," below.)

With **American River Raft Rentals,** 11257 S. Bridge St., Rancho Cordova, CA 95670 (☎ **916/635-6400**), the family can raft on a Class I (flat water) float on the lower American River. For $2.50 per person, shuttle buses will pick you up at Goethe Park between 3 and 6pm each day after Memorial Day to take you back to the starting point. The season runs from mid-April through mid-October, with hours daily from 9am to 9pm. Reservations are recommended on weekends. Rentals include the raft, paddles, and life vests. The minimum weight is 30 lbs., and they do have life vests for that size child. Rates are for all day: A four-person raft is $28; six-person, $38, 10-person raft, $70; 12-person, $75, 14-person, $80. Identification and a deposit are required for all raft rentals.

ANNUAL EVENTS

The **Dixieland Jubilee** is held every Memorial Day weekend. Attracting more than 150,000 people, the festival lets 100 jazz bands loose in locations all over the city. Transportation is usually available at all major hotels (make hotel reservations far in advance). You can purchase one pass for all events. Teens love this festival.

For 2 ¹/₂ weeks ending Labor Day each year, the **California State Fair** is held on the grounds of Cal Expo, 1600 Exposition Blvd. (☎ **916/263-3000**). The one-price admission covers most attractions including Kids' Park, which has entertainment by and for children, and many hands-on activities such as face paintings, mask making, and clay sculpting. What would a state fair be without agricultural and animal exhibits? There's also horseracing, continuous live music, nightly fireworks, a carnival, other celebrations, and more than 100 food stands. Nursing and diaper-changing facilities are provided, and strollers are available for rent. Call for current admission prices and special events.

ACTIVITIES BY AGE GROUP

The following listings suggest activities divided into specific age brackets. Refer back to the individual descriptions for details.

Teens and Preteens

Bicycling
Blue Diamond Visitor's Center
B. F. Hastings Building
California State Fair
California State Railroad Museum
Central Pacific Passenger Depot
Crocker Art Museum
Discovery Museum
Dixieland Jubilee
Historic Governor's Mansion
Horseback Riding

Houseboating
Huntington Hopkins Hardware Store
Iceland Ice Skating Rink
Parks
River Rafting
Sacramento Zoo
State Capitol
State Indian Museum
Sutter's Fort
Towe Ford Museum
Waterworld USA

School-Age Children

Bicycling
Blue Diamond Visitor's Center
B. F. Hastings Building
California State Fair
California State Railroad Museum
Central Pacific Passenger Depot
Crocker Art Museum
Discovery Museum
Historic Governor's Mansion
Horseback Riding
Houseboating

Huntington Hopkins Hardware Store
Iceland Ice Skating Rink
Old Sacramento Schoolhouse
Parks
River Rafting
Sacramento Zoo
State Capitol
State Indian Museum
Sutter's Fort
Visionarium
Waterworld USA

Preschoolers and Toddlers

California State Fair
California State Railroad Museum
Central Pacific Passenger Depot
Crocker Art Museum
Discovery Museum
Fairytale Town
Iceland Ice Skating Rink

Parks
River Rafting
Sacramento Zoo
Sutter's Fort
Visionarium
Waterworld USA

WHERE TO STAY

No matter where you choose to stay, you'll be only 15 minutes away from any sightseeing venue. Weekends are when you'll find the best hotel rates. Be sure to ask if there's a weekend rate or special when you make your reservation. Also remember that rates are often higher during the Jazz Festival in May.

Downtown and Capitol Area

Directly across the street from the Capitol and within walking distance of several Sacramento sights is the **Hyatt Regency Sacramento at Capitol Park,** 1209 L St.,

Sacramento, CA 95814 (☎ **916/443-1234,** or toll free **800/233-1234;** fax 916/321-6699). This elegant high-rise hotel has all the usual Hyatt amenities.

The large art-filled lobby makes a fine stroll with a restless toddler. The outdoor pool affords a welcome retreat after a day of sightseeing. Babysitting can be arranged.

The hotel has several restaurants and each has a children's menu. At Ciao-Yama, children under 12 can have smaller portions at half price. Dawson's, the dinner restaurant, features grilled steaks, chops, and fish. There's also a rooftop nightclub and a lobby lounge.

Rooms are quite spacious and nicely appointed. Request a king-size bed or two doubles. In a king-bed unit you'll find a small sofa, chair, and desk in the sitting area, with plenty of room for a rollaway or crib. The armoire houses the TV. Air conditioning, mirrored closets, and an honor bar are standard.

Rooms rent for $150 single, $175 double. Regency Club rooms, with extra amenities, cost $175 single, $200 double. The Business Plan, at $165 single, $190 double, is a special floor equipped with extra amenities for the business traveler. Suites range from $180 to $850. Ask about discounted weekend flat rates. Children under 18 sleep free in their parents' room. Or, a second room can be rented at half the price of the parents' room. Extra adults are charged $25. Cribs and rollaways are complimentary. Self-parking is $6 per night.

The **Best Western Ponderosa,** at 1100 H St., Sacramento, CA 95814 (☎ **916/441-1314,** or toll free **800/528-1234;** fax 916/441-5961), is run practically like someone's home. Owner operated, this comfortable 98-room hotel is immaculate and quite family-friendly.

Complimentary continental breakfast is served daily in the lobby or take it to your room. The pool area is large and clean, and equipped with chaises longues, tables, and chairs.

Many families are repeat customers, attesting to the popularity of this hotel. Tell the reservationist you are bringing your family when you reserve your room. The hotel even provides rubber sheets upon request, and extra towels for lots of little hands are no problem. Although there are no refrigerators in the rooms, you can use the one behind the front desk or request one for your room ($2). Babysitting arrangements can usually be made with advance notice. There is airport shuttle service for $8.

The nice-sized rooms are furnished with dark-mahogany furniture reminiscent of the '40s. The deluxe room with a king-size bed will hold a crib and a rollaway. Amenities include Select TV and cable stations, full-length mirrors, and hairdryers in the bathrooms. There are connecting rooms and non-smoking floors.

Rates are $70–$84 single and $78–$92 double. Kids under 12 stay free in their parents' room; children 12 and over, and additional adults, pay $8 per night. Cribs are free; rollaways cost $8 per night.

The **Travelodge,** at 1111 H St., Sacramento, CA 95814 (☎ **916/444-8880,** or toll free **800/578-7878;** fax 916/447-7540), consists of two buildings across the street from each other and across the street from the Ponderosa. There is no pool, but the location is good and the prices are reasonable.

The standard rooms are small, but clean and fresh. The contemporary decor is light and cheerful. King-size beds are standard, and some rooms have two beds. Adjoining rooms are available. Family rooms are quite large, with a king-size bed, queen-size sleeper sofa, and room for a crib. All rooms have an easy chair, a desk, air conditioning, reading lights, cable TV, and a coffee maker with complimentary coffee.

Single rooms cost $46, doubles and family rooms are $60, and rooms with two beds are $54. Rollaways cost $4. Kids up to age 18 sleep free in their parents' room. Additional adults, add $4.

The Discovery Park Area

The location of the **Fountain Suites Hotel,** 321 Bercut Dr., Sacramento, CA 95814 (☎ 916/441-1444, or toll free **800/767-1777;** fax 916/441-6530), is great for those who want to be near Discovery Park and just off the freeway, one exit from downtown Sacramento.

This apartment-style complex consists of three-story buildings, all with suitelike accommodations, and parking near each building. A nice fenced-in pool area accommodates lots of kids. The pool itself is from three to five feet deep. Airport transportation is complimentary, and shuttle service to the Capitol or Old Sacramento is arranged on request.

Complimentary continental breakfast is served in the lounge and room service is available from 6am to 11pm. The 24-hour Buttercup Pantry is on the grounds and offers take-out service; you can charge your food to your room.

Each suite has a small living area with plenty of room for a rollaway or crib and a desk and chairs set off from the sleeping quarters. Two phones with a voice-mail message system, a separate vanity/dressing area, hairdryer, and a remote-control swivel TV with pay-per-view movies complete the picture. Executive level rooms add cathedral ceilings, robes, complimentary morning newspaper, and a coffee maker. One step above that are the Executive Plus rooms, which include a microwave and refrigerator along with the other amenities.

Standard rooms on the first and second floors cost $89 single, $104 double. Executive Level rooms are $99 single, $114 double; Executive Plus units go for $109 single, $124 double. On weekends rooms cost $69, single or double. Cribs and rollaways can be requested for no charge. Kids 12 and under sleep free in their parents' room; older children and extra adults are charged $15. There are some adjoining rooms. Ask about special promotional rates.

La Quinta Inn (formerly Days Inn), 200 Jibboom St., Sacramento, CA 95814 (☎ **916/448-8100,** or toll free **800/531-5900;** fax 916/447-3621), is just on the outskirts of downtown, off Calif. 5, 10 minutes from the airport, one mile from the Capitol, half a mile from Old Sacramento, and adjacent to Discovery Park and the Sacramento and American Rivers. You can get free airport transportation and there's a shuttle that can drop you at the Amtrak or bus station, putting you practically in the heart of Old Sacramento or downtown. There is no room service, but a free continental breakfast is provided. Local calls are free.

There's a large fenced-in pool area, as well as in-room movies that can be turned off in the front office.

The rooms are furnished with reading lights and have little bathrooms and vanity areas. Request a room with one double bed and a small sofa if you need a crib in the room; a limited number of these rooms are available. There are also a few connecting rooms and non-smoking rooms. If you're noise-sensitive, request a room away from the freeway side. Reserve far in advance if you plan to come during the Jazz Festival.

Rates run $55 to $57 single, $60–$67 double, and $65–$67 for three to four people, depending on the season. There's no charge for cribs or rollaways (request rollaways when you reserve your room), or for kids under 18 staying in their parents' room.

Cal Expo Area

On the deluxe end of the scale in this part of town is the **Red Lion Hotel,** at 2001 Point West Way, Sacramento, CA 95815 (**☎ 916/929-8855,** or toll free **800/547-8010;** fax 916/924-0719). Situated in a suburban setting, the Red Lion is across the street from the Arden Fair Mall and is within walking distance of two movie theaters and several restaurants. It's also five minutes from Cal Expo and Waterworld USA.

There is one pool and Jacuzzi and a fitness room for adults. The pool is fenced in and surrounded by artificial turf, and poolside food service is available. The front desk will give a referral for babysitters. Parking is accessible to the rooms.

The hotel has two restaurants, the Coffee Garden coffee shop and Maxi's–An American Cafe. Both welcome children and provide booster seats and highchairs, and both have Early Bird Specials, a convenient and affordable choice for many families. Sunday brunch in Maxi's is a favorite of parents and children alike. Kids get balloons and everyone selects from a mouth-watering buffet, offered at $14.95 for adults and $8.95 for children under 12. Room service is available Sunday through Thursday from 6am to 11pm and on Friday and Saturday from 6am to midnight.

This is a large hotel with 448 rooms and suites, 219 of which have two double beds. The rooms are larger than average and have space for a crib and a rollaway. They come with double vanities, small bathrooms, full-length mirrors, desks, and cable TVs (in-room movies can be turned off at the front desk). Upper rooms have balconies (but watch your toddlers on the narrow balconies). Hairdryers, curling irons, extra towels, ironing boards, and irons are available for the asking. Family suites, consisting of a room with a king-size bed and a connecting room with two double beds, are perfect for larger families. You can request non-smoking rooms.

Weekday rates for singles are $109–$129, doubles cost $124–$144, and suites (including family suites) begin at $200. The weekend rate is $79 for a queen-bedded unit, $89 for one with a king-size bed. Rates are higher at Jazz Festival time. Rollaways cost $15 and cribs are free. Kids under 18 stay free in existing bedding; older children and extra adults are charged $15 per night. Ask about special promotions or discounts.

Across the street is the Red Lion's sister hotel, **Red Lion's Sacramento Inn,** 1401 Arden Way, Sacramento, CA 95815 (**☎ 916/922-8041,** or toll free **800/547-8010;** fax 916/922-0386). You get to the hotel by driving through the Arden Fair Mall parking lot. The hotel features 376 recently renovated rooms. On the premises are two small pools and one large pool, each surrounded by Astro-turf. There's also a wading pool, a putting green, and a state-of-the-art fitness center for guest use.

The Coffee Garden restaurant, open from 6am to midnight, serves salad, burgers, and sandwiches priced from $6 to $9 at lunch. The children's menu, with its Lil' Lion Trackers Map, gives youngsters chocolate-chip pancakes, batter-dipped fish and chips, floats, and milkshakes, priced at $1.75–$3.75. Sunday brunch has a special children's price. Savannah Jazz Club is the hotel's comfortable lounge, featuring a happy hour from 5 to 7pm, and serving an extensive list of appetizers. Room service can be ordered from 6am to 10pm. There are lots of food outlets at the nearby Arden Fair Mall, as well as sit-down restaurants within easy driving distance of the hotel.

Red Lions are known for their oversize guest rooms, but for extra space, families might want to ask about those rooms with two queen-size beds or family suites. Accommodations in the "700" building are the largest. The family suites have a room with a king-size bed connecting to one with two queen-size beds. Mini-parlor suites have a bedroom with a king-size or double bed connected to a parlor with a wet bar. Rooms come with two sinks, tub/shower combinations or showers only, and full-length mirrors. Rooms with king-size beds are a nice size and the bathrooms are large. Double-bedded rooms, while smaller, still have separate vanities and large bathrooms. Adjoining, no-smoking, and handicapped-accessible rooms are also available. Hairdryers are free upon request, and refrigerators are available at $15 per day. There is hotel laundry service and a coin-operated laundry room. Movies can be turned on— or off—at the front desk.

Room rates vary depending on location. Standard rooms with two double beds rent for $89–$104, and those with one king-size bed cost $89–$104. Deluxe rooms with patios or balconies are $99–$114. Rooms with two queen-size beds and "superior" rooms with king-size beds in the "700" building both rent for $119–$134. Family suites cost $150, and mini-parlor suites are $150. Children under 18 stay free in their parents' room. Cribs are free, but rollaways cost $15 per night.

The **Residence Inn,** at 1530 Howe Ave., Sacramento, CA 95825 (☎ **916/920-9111,** or toll free **800/331-3131;** fax 916/921-5664), close to Cal Expo and the Arden Fair Mall, features apartmentlike accommodations with private entrances, full kitchens, and daily maid service—perfect for longer stays. Guests are treated like family, with special arrangements made for special needs. There's a free shuttle to the airport, and even a shopping service that will pick up groceries for you.

There's a pool, three spas, and barbecues for guest use, and a self-service guest laundry, and hotel laundry service. Be sure to request a room away from Howe Street, a noisy thoroughfare; in summer, you may wish to avoid rooms near the three spas for the same reason. Unfortunately there are no grassy areas or patios, which would make the Residence Inn perfect.

A deluxe complimentary breakfast consisting of waffles, cereals, danish, fruit, and muffins is served daily in the club room, or you can take it back to your suite. Highchairs are available. Five nights a week a complimentary food function offers the opportunity to get to know other people. One night chili dogs are served; another, baked potatoes; yet another, hot hors d'oeuvres. On Friday nights, cookies and juice are on tap. Monday through Thursday there is complimentary beer, wine, and soft drinks.

Studios, which measure 550 square feet, feature one or two queen-size beds, a dressing area, a full-length mirror, a makeup stool, and a nice-size sitting room area, plus good closet space. *Real* Kleenex and complimentary bags of popping corn are special touches that make this choice homey. Studios will sleep four comfortably. There are also penthouse suites—two-story lofts with two beds, two bathrooms, and two TVs; most have wood-burning fireplaces as well.

Rates decrease with longer stays. Studios start at $99 and go down to $89 for a stay of 30 days or more. Penthouses start at $119 and decrease to $109. Cribs and rollaways incur a non-time charge of $5. Kids under 18 stay free in their parents' room.

Between Downtown and Cal Expo

The **Radisson Hotel Sacramento,** 500 Leisure Lane, Sacramento, CA 95815, (☎ **916/922-2020,** or toll free **800/333-3333;** fax 916/649-9463), is a full-scale resort hotel with 314 rooms. It's one of our kids' favorites. Why? Because it's set in a big open area, with lots of grassy space to run around, it has a wonderful swimming pool area, and it has a lovely three-acre lake that the children adore.

Located just off Calif. 160 at Canterbury Road, it's only five or ten minutes from important places in the city. There is a fitness center, a jogging trail, bike paths, and places to stroll. Bike rentals with children's bikes are available, and paddleboats can be rented for a nominal fee. A complimentary shuttle takes guests to various attractions in the area, including the Arden Fair Mall, and transports guests to and from the airport. Summer activities include cash barbecues around the pool, and jazz concerts presented on Friday and Saturday evenings through Labor Day. The spacious Palm Court restaurant serves breakfast, lunch, and dinner, and there is a children's menu. Babysitting can be arranged through the housekeeping department. You can request down pillows, and irons and ironing boards, and there's one-day valet service.

Standard rooms are moderate in size; those around the lake are a little larger. Beamed ceilings, full-length mirrors, hairdryers, and a dressing area are features of these larger rooms. There isn't much space for a crib in rooms with two double beds—it's better to request a room with a king-size bed and add the crib. One- and two-bedroom suites around the pool and lake sleep up to six, with a sleeper sofa in the living room. Lakeside units feature private patios or balconies, and have vaulted ceilings on the second floor. If you need larger accommodations, they can connect enough rooms to give you what you need.

Rates for single or double occupancy are $77 for off-lake units, $107 for lakeside units. Each additional person pays $10. One- and two-bedroom suites go for $184–$369. No charge for cribs and rollaways. Children 17 and under stay free in their parents' room. Be sure to ask whether the "Supersaver" rates, beginning at $72, are available.

The other find in this neighborhood is the **Canterbury Inn,** across the highway from the Radisson Hotel at 1900 Canterbury Rd., Sacramento, CA 95815 (☎ **916/927-3492,** or toll free **800/932-3492;** fax 916/641-8594). This charming motor inn is a good place to stay in summer. There's a large grassy area in the middle of the grounds, perfect for playing, and a large fenced-in pool area and spa with lots of lounge chairs, and tables and chairs for eating outside. Bikes are available for rent, and a shuttle van can whisk you off to Arden Fair Mall, Old Sacramento or the State Capitol. A complimentary continental breakfast is served in the lobby. The adjacent restaurant, Shanley's Bar and Grill, is open for lunch and dinner.

The rooms are clean and adorable, furnished with comfortable beds and lacy curtains. Bathrooms and vanities are small but clean. Cable TV, a hairdryer, coffee maker, a radio, and a table and two chairs complete the picture. If you need to fit a crib or rollaway in the room, request one of the larger poolside rooms with double beds. There are non-smoking rooms, some connecting rooms and a mini-suite, with a refrigerator, that adjoins rooms with two double beds.

Rooms rent for $55 single, $65 double, $75 triple or quad. No charge for cribs, but rollaways cost $10. Children under 17 stay free in their parents' room; extra adults pay $10 each. Ask about special promotional rates and AAA discounts.

WHERE TO EAT

When in Sacramento, you'll probably find yourself eating either in your hotel, in Old Sacramento or nearby, or in North Sacramento near Cal Expo. There are a number of interesting choices in the city. Here are some.

Downtown/Capitol Area

Especially good for breakfast is the **Fox & Goose Public House,** 1001 R St. (☎ **916/443-8825**). Housed in an old factory building, this is a roomy and comfortable British-style restaurant. The staff is particularly pleasant, the coffee great, and the food fresh and natural. The owners pride themselves on not using flavor enhancers or additives. Soups, dressings, and baked goods are prepared from scratch daily, and the potatoes are fresh, never frozen.

There are full English breakfasts, lots of omelets, French toast, homemade granola without sugar, and muffins. The waffles are thin, crispy, and delicious. Breakfast prices range from $2.25 to $6.75. Lunch includes lots of traditional pub fare and vegetarian selections at $2.95–$6.65. There are plenty of choices suitable for kids, and servers will split orders. There are highchairs and booster seats, and bottles and baby food will be warmed in the kitchen, providing they aren't too busy. Try to be there on Friday from noon to 1pm when the magician usually comes; he might choose your child as a participant in his act.

Open weekdays for breakfast and lunch from 7am to 2pm, and on Saturday and Sunday, breakfast only from 9am. No reservations or credit cards accepted. You'll find parking right in front, or on the street.

It seems that Italian restaurants are popular with families who have children of all ages. One modern version of a neighborhood Italian restaurant is **Americo's Trattoria Italiana,** within walking distance of the Capitol building at 2000 Capitol Ave. (☎ **916/442-8119**). The emphasis here is on fresh spices and homemade pastas and sauces. Set in a renovated factory building, this cheerful restaurant has lots of windows hung with cute red-checked café curtains. The noise level is just right here for young-uns. Even with a large clientele of young singles and couples, the staff is friendly to kids, and you'll see a lot of families here for dinner.

The bread comes quickly, but the entrees not so quickly, probably because so many dishes are individually prepared. There's a small children's selection, offering spaghetti or ravioli and soup or salad for $6. Adult à la carte and complete dinners range from $8.50 to $18.50. Selections include numerous pasta dishes, veal, chicken, steak, and fish. There are fewer choices for lunch. Items off the à la carte menu can be split for $2 extra; bottles and baby food will be warmed.

Highchairs and booster seats are available.

Open Tuesday through Friday for lunch from 11:30am to 2pm. Dinner is served weekdays from 5 to 9:30pm, on Friday and Saturday till 10pm, and on Sunday till 9pm; closed Monday. Reservations can be made for six or more. All major credit cards accepted. There's street parking and a small parking lot.

Yet another Italian restaurant, a member of a family-oriented chain, is the **Old Spaghetti Factory,** 1910 J St. (☎ **916/443-2862**). They serve pasta dishes, with several different choices of noodles and sauces. Selections also include baked chicken, and sausage, all served with spaghetti. Adult fare is priced at $4.25–$8.10. Selections come with salad, bread, a beverage, and dessert. Kids get to choose between spaghetti with tomato sauce or a meatball, each served on a special plate with applesauce, an animal cookie, a beverage, and a frozen dessert ($3 and $3.35). The Junior Meal offers a smaller version of an adult meal of spaghetti with a salad, bread, a drink, and ice cream for $5.10. They'll also warm baby bottles or baby food and will make special children's drinks. Since they only take reservations for banquets, come early. On weekends families start lining up at 4pm and by 5 it's often packed.

Open for lunch Monday through Friday from 11:15am to 2:30pm, and for dinner Monday through Thursday from 5 to 10pm, on Friday from 4:30 to 10:30pm, and on Saturday and Sunday from noon to 10:30pm. Major credit cards accepted. Parking lot and street parking available.

One special way to introduce the whole family to formally served, traditional Japanese food is at **Fuji,** located in an Asian neighborhood just outside downtown at

2422 13th St. (☎ **916/446-4135**). At this popular and accommodating family-owned and-run restaurant, owner Julie Fujitue will try to make dining here comfortable for families, and the staff will bring plain rice and chopsticks right away to occupy the little ones. The bar offers a large selection of special nonalcoholic drinks that are nice, festive touches for kids.

Be sure that the children will at least try tempura or sukiyaki or sesame chicken before you commit, because there aren't any American selections on either the lunch or dinner menu. The staff recommends you order an à la carte selection for your child, from $6.95–$12.50, full dinners go for $11–$15. They will warm bottles and baby food. Highchairs and booster seats are available.

Open for lunch Monday through Friday from 11:30am to 2pm. Dinner is served Monday through Friday from 5 to 9:45pm and on Saturday and Sunday from 4:30 to 9:45pm. Reservations are recommended. All major credit cards accepted. There's a small restaurant parking lot and plenty of street parking.

If you crave Mexican food, you'll enjoy the good, homemade fare at **Luis's,** 1218 Alhambra Blvd. (☎ **916/451-7852** or **916/453-9871**), the restaurant that has welcomed everyone from "babies to grandparents" since 1965. Everything is prepared fresh daily and from scratch. The traditional menu selections will please all tastes. Prices at dinner average around $8; large combination plates are slightly higher at $11.

Niños and niñas under 12 can have a burrito, a quesadilla, or chicken with gravy and beans, rice, salad, and tortillas for $3. Or they can order off the lunch menu all day for $5.50. The helpful staff will try to make anything within reason for the kids, will warm bottles and baby food, and will make special nonalcoholic drinks. There are highchairs and boosters.

Open Sunday through Thursday from 11am to midnight, on Friday and Saturday till 1am. Reservations accepted for five or more. Major credit cards accepted. There is a parking lot.

Old Sacramento

We wish we could tell you that there are many great family restaurants in Old Sacramento. Here are a couple of possibilities.

The **Union Restaurant,** 117 J St. (☎ **916/44-UNION**), is set in the original *Sacramento Union* building, home of the West's oldest newspaper. Bentwood chairs and oak tables, and needlepoint-covered paddles converted into ceiling fans now take the place of printing presses. The specialty here is fondue, but you can get almost anything. There are salads, super sandwiches, burgers, barbecued ribs, seafood specialties, chicken, and steak. Fondue runs $10–$15, while the other offerings will cost you $4.50–$13.95. Chocolate fondue will finish your order.

For children 10 and under, the menu offers grilled cheese, ribs and fries, barbecued chicken, burgers, and a hot dog. The prices are $2.45–$4. There are highchairs and booster seats.

Open daily from 11am to 10pm. Reservations are necessary only on weekends; the wait is about 10 minutes without one. Major credit cards are accepted. It's best to park in the parking garage nearby.

For fast food, try **Carl's Jr.,** at the corner of 2nd and L Streets, which is open weekdays from 9am to 9pm and on Saturday and Sunday from 9am to midnight.

Barnum's Ice Cream Parlor & Sandwich Shop, 916 2nd St., makes a cool stop on a hot day.

Discovery Park Area

A real find in this area is **Chevy's**, 1369 Garden Hwy. (☎ **916/649-0390**), on the edge of the river. It's a simple, open, light restaurant with rough wood floors, the green red, and white official colors of Mexico, and tables covered in oilcloth; it's just "rustic" enough not to appear to imitate a typical slick, Americanized Mexican restaurant. The focal point of Chevy's is "El Machino"—not a monster, but a big tortilla-maker, and a big favorite with the kids. The servers give each youngster a ball of *masa,* the flour used for the tortillas: They can feel it, play with it, even turn it into soft sculptures! Each child is also given a balloon on arrival; on Saturday and Sunday evenings (and most evenings in summer), a balloon sculptor mesmerizes kids by creating animal shapes. The children's menus have a variety of activities, but all come with crayons, and sometimes the finished product is even entered in holiday coloring contests. Kids can ask for their own avocado pit to transplant at home! If the restaurant isn't busy, a youngster might even get a tour of the kitchen.

Chevy's prides itself on "fresh-Mex"™ food: No MSG, no preservatives, and frying is done in cholesterol-free canola oil. Choose from traditional combinations and platters, fajitas, and unusual offerings like broiled fresh quail and vegetable fajitas; prices range from $7 to $14.

Children eat for $2.95. The selection includes kiddie cheese quesadillas, tacos, flautas, cheeseburgers, bean and cheese burritos, chicken bites, fruit juices, and the usual sodas. An ice-cream cone comes free. The staff will warm bottles and baby food, and split meals in the kitchen. Special drinks are prepared (the favorite seems to be a virgin strawberry margarita). Highchairs and booster seats are provided. Smoking is permitted only on the outdoor patio.

The restaurant is open Sunday through Thursday from 11am to 10pm, until 11pm on Friday and Saturday. Major credit cards are accepted. There's a parking lot, and free valet parking in the evening. Another branch of Chevy's is located at 1234 Howe Ave. (☎ **916/923-6574**).

Just next door to Chevy's is **Woody's**, 1379 Garden Hwy. (☎ **916/924-3434**). Enter Woody's and you'll think you've traveled to the Caribbean. It's funky, it's wild—the colors are bold and bright. There's a huge parrot chomping on a banana and wearing a Spanish hat. A diving kangaroo, which looks like a cousin to Denver Dinosaur, plays on the walls in purple, pink, and turquoise. The kids will love it!

The kids' menu offers chicken strips, burgers, a corn dog, hot dog, or grilled cheese, for $2–$3.50. The grownup menu has lots of salads, Mexican specialties, pasta, burgers, and "gourmet" sandwiches. Prices begin at $5 and go up to $8. The list of exotic drinks is extensive, and all soft drinks come with free refills. The kids get exotic virgin drinks, too. The Sunday buffet brunch costs $9.95 for adults with champagne, 50¢ per year of age (up to 12) for the kids. Woody's will get you anything you need for the kids. There are booster seats and highchairs, and bottles and baby food can be warmed. The restaurant is no-smoking, except for the outdoor patio.

Open Monday through Saturday from 11am to 11pm, Sunday brunch is served from 9:30am to 2pm, and lunch and dinner go to 10pm. Call about reservations—the policy changes. Without a reservation, arrive before 7pm on summer weekends. All credit cards are accepted. Park in the lot; free valet parking evenings.

Open 24 hours daily, the **Buttercup Pantry,** 455 Bercut Dr., at I-5 and Richards Boulevard (☎ **916/448-0643**), next to the Fountain Suites Hotel, is light, bright, clean, and spacious. And it's very close to Discovery Park. There are too many selections to name, but they include all the usual coffeeshop items. They make their own yummy baked goods, also available for take-out. Complete breakfasts go for $3.65–$6.95. Lunch prices are $4.65–$7, and full dinners cost $7.95–$10.95. Seniors 55 and over are served specials at a discount. The children's menu is for those 12 and under. It includes breakfast items, hamburgers, sandwiches, tacos, hot dogs, chicken strips, and fish and chips, at $2.50–$2.85 each. All drinks are 75¢ and include free refills. Highchairs and booster seats are provided. Servers will warm your baby's bottle or baby food. No reservations are necessary. Major credit cards are accepted. There's a parking lot.

Cal Expo Area

This part of town offers an abundance of restaurants.

Carlos Murphy's is a wonderful surprise. It's located across from the entrance to Cal Expo and Waterworld at 1801 Exposition Blvd. (☎ **916/924-3447**). This is a great place to take kids because there's so much for them to look at. At the glassed-in tortillería in the front of the restaurant, they can watch tortillas being made. Huge pulleys on the ceiling lead to rotating bamboo fans. Soft-sculpture figures hang from the ceiling, and all sorts of old signs and orange-crate–type art line the walls—it all combines to make a sort of vintage '70s California look. The cheerful apple-green decor blends with the pleasant atmosphere to make this a fun place to eat.

Many Mexican dishes are served here. You can choose from burritos, chimichangas, and enchiladas, or combinations; carne asada tacos; marinated chicken burritos; or fajitas. On the other side of the menu are barbecued ribs and chicken, burgers, salads, and sandwiches. Adult prices are reasonable, ranging from $5 to $10 at lunch; dinner tops out at $14, but most selections run between $5.50 and $10. There is a full bar.

There are kids' selections at $1.95 to $3, which include hamburgers, hot dogs, quesadillas, grilled cheese, chicken bits, tacos, and mini-burritos. Leave room for dessert. Ask about their Sunday through Thursday "Kids pay what they weigh" special. They have boosters and highchairs, will split portions, and will warm bottles and baby food. A balloon-maker comes nightly around 5:30pm.

Open Sunday through Thursday from 11am to 10pm, on Friday and Saturday till 11pm. Reservations are accepted. From 5 to 8pm there's not much of a wait, but on weekend evenings it can be 35–40 minutes without a reservation. Major credit cards are accepted. There's a parking lot.

Tony Roma's, 1441 Howe Ave. (☎ **916/922-8787**), is another dependable restaurant. The food is good and the service is fast. The Tony Roma's kids' menu features ribs, chicken, a burger, a hot dog, or a grilled-cheese sandwich with fries and ice cream, for $2.95–$3.95. There are also three interesting drinks made with juice. You can choose from Tony Roma's famous ribs, barbecued chicken or shrimp, grilled selections, and salads and sandwiches. Ribs cost $6.95–$14 at lunch and $12–$15 at dinner; other lunch choices range from $4 to $14. Dinner starts at $5.95. If you've never tried the onion rings here, at least order a half loaf.

They have highchairs and boosters, will warm bottles and baby food, and make special nonalcoholic drinks. A magician "appears" on Friday and Saturday from 6:30 to 9pm.

Open Monday through Thursday from 11am to 9:30pm, on Friday from 11am to 10:30pm, on Saturday from noon to 10:30pm, and on Sunday from noon to 9:30pm. Reservations accepted only for parties of eight or more. Weekdays the wait averages 10–15 minutes; on weekends, come before 6:30pm or you'll have a 30- to 45-minute wait. All major credit cards are accepted. Park in the lot.

Emergency Services

If the need arises, there's a 24-hour emergency room at **Mercy General Hospital,** 4001 J St. in downtown Sacramento (☎ **916/453-4424**).

Consult the local *Yellow Pages* for a list of pharmacies that are open around the clock.

You can always trust **The Good Earth,** 2024 Arden Way (☎ **916/920-5544**), to have natural, fresh food. It has the same bright atmosphere and comfortable feeling typical of the Good Earth chain members. There are all sorts of natural foods to choose from, including vegetarian and chicken dishes, hot and cold sandwiches, and lots of breakfast selections. Anything on the menu can be made vegetarian. Desserts are yummy. Breakfast will run $3–$5.65; entrees go for $7–$9.65; sandwiches, $4.25–$6. Specially made muffins and breads are for sale at the register.

The menu for children 12 and under seems to have something for everyone. Miss Piggy's pancakes and E.T.'s favorite French toast, at $2, are made with 10-grain flour. Lunch and dinner selections include Big Bird's burrito, Alf's teriyake chicken dinner, Batman's super burger, and Charlie's tuna, all reasonably priced at $2–$3. There are highchairs and boosters, and they will warm bottles and baby food. The entire restaurant is designated no-smoking.

Open Monday through Thursday from 7am to 10pm, on Friday from 7am to 11pm, and on Saturday and Sunday from 8am to 10pm. Reservations accepted for seven or more. Some credit cards are accepted. Parking is in a lot.

If you're really desperate for a restaurant where the kids can get rid of excess energy, take them to **Chuck E. Cheese's,** 1690 Arden Way (☎ **916/920-9181**), a chain restaurant specializing in serving kids. Here, there are tons of things to keep them occupied. The big, barnlike restaurant is filled with video games, Skee-Ball machines, small coin-operated rides, and lots of other quarter-gobbling machines kids love to play. Look hard for the restaurant—it's not easy to spot. It's directly across the street from the Arden Fair Mall.

The food specialty here is pizza, which costs from $3 for an individual pizza to $16 for one large one. You can also order a few sandwiches and salads costing $2–$4. All drinks are $1, with unlimited refills. You can order beer and wine. The place is packed with birthday parties on Saturday afternoons. There are highchairs and booster seats. Management thoughtfully provides a changing station in the women's and men's restrooms.

Open Sunday through Thursday from 10am to 10pm and on Friday and Saturday from 10am to 11pm. Major credit cards are accepted. There's a parking lot.

2 The Gold Country

Gold is what brought people to this part of the country in the mid-1800s, and the legends surrounding that gold are what continue to lure people here year in and year out.

James Marshall was the catalyst for the rush to this glorious part of the state. It was while Marshall was building a sawmill for entrepreneur John Sutter that he made his gold discovery. This find sent a shout throughout the United States and all the way to Europe that changed California forever. It proclaimed a quick and easy opportunity for anyone to become wealthy just by finding this heavy, lustrous rock.

But it was no easy task to conquer the rough country. The challenge attracted an eclectic group of adventurers. Towns appeared and disappeared faster than an ice cube in summer. Today, walking through the remains of that golden era is a fascinating trip through a history book—and not a dull history book. There is adventure and romance, legends and ghost stories. Each town has its own story. It's lucky for us that many of the Gold Country towns have been so well preserved that we can submerge ourselves in history, not just study it from afar.

Though it survives on tourism, the Gold Country is not a tourist trap. The well-preserved towns for the most part are real, not like movie sets with their false-front buildings. In fact, many of these buildings are still in use today. But don't worry—a family trip to the Gold Country isn't only about seeing old buildings. You can still pan for gold, check out a working mine, ride a stagecoach, explore ancient caves, attend a melodrama performance, sleep in a room once occupied by Mark Twain, and taste homemade ice cream in an old ice-cream parlor.

GETTING THERE

From Los Angeles, drive I-5 or Calif. 99 to Sacramento and take I-80 through Sacramento to Auburn or Placerville, about a half-hour drive; or go about 20 minutes farther north to Nevada City.

If you want to begin from the southern route, take I-5 to Calif. 99 to Calif. 120 to Sonora. This will take you approximately eight hours. You may want to stop in Fresno overnight and then continue on to the Gold Country.

From San Francisco, take I-80 through Sacramento to Auburn (or up to Nevada City as suggested above). Or you can cut from Sacramento to U.S. 50 to Placerville, the central gateway to the Gold Country.

From Oakland, take I-580 to I-205 to I-5 to Manteca to Calif. 120 and on to Calif. 108 to Sonora, to the south.

If you're combining the Gold Country with a trip to Lake Tahoe, you can reach the Gold Country by taking U.S. 50 from South Lake Tahoe; or Calif. 108, Calif. 4, and Calif. 88 heading west from U.S. 395. From Yosemite, take Calif. 120 west.

If you choose to fly and then rent a car, the closest airports are **Reno International, Stockton Metropolitan, and Sacramento Metropolitan Airports,** each approximately 50 miles from Calif. 49. There is **Greyhound** bus service between San Francisco and Auburn (call toll free **800/231-2222**).

Warning: Winter can mean road closures, so be sure to carry chains, and call the Caltrans Highway information (☎ **213/628-7623** from Touch-Tone phones only, **916/445-1534** from others) for all the latest road conditions and closures.

ORIENTATION

The Gold Country route covers about 300 miles beginning south at Oakhurst and running north along Calif. 49 as far as Vinton. Although it seems like another world, the Gold Country is only 120 miles from San Francisco, 35 miles from Sacramento, 60 miles west of Lake Tahoe, and 50 miles northwest of Yosemite.

Remember that gold was not found only on the Calif. 49 route—there were gold discoveries in numerous places off the highway, others as far east as Bodie, near Mammoth, and still other discoveries in many other places in the Sierra foothills. But it's the golden chain of Calif. 49 that takes us through some of the best-preserved and most interesting spots, and it's the roads that branch off Calif. 49 that offer us the most adventures.

We will take you from Nevada City in the north to Jamestown in the south. This 130-mile strip of Calif. 49 is the most traveled of the Gold Country areas, and affords you lots of opportunities to detour off it to explore towns and sites. We have taken this trip in four nights and five days. You could spend more time, or you can actually drive the 130 miles in one day—but why would you? With kids in tow, you'll find yourselves wanting to stop to see the sites and enjoy the outdoors.

Ideally, this is a trip best understood by children in the fourth grade or older who have had, or are currently studying, American history. But that doesn't mean your younger children won't have fun; it just means they may not understand the historical significance of what they're seeing or hearing.

Our last trip to the Gold Country was in early fall when daytime temperatures were warm and evenings cool, leaning toward crisp. The leaves were beginning to change, and the entire area was aglow, appropriately enough, in gold. This is obviously a more difficult time to take children unless they have a school holiday. Spring bursts with magnificent wildflowers; summer is hot, but not usually humid; winter can bring snow to the foothills.

Each of the nine counties connected by Calif. 49 have active, close-knit communities, which sponsor many seasonal celebrations, music festivals, and live theater presentations. The melodramas may be especially appealing to children. It's best to check with the visitors bureaus of the areas you're interested in for event schedules.

Getting Around Calif. 49

Much to our surprise, we found that some stretches of Calif. 49 aren't very picturesque. But it's the best way to see the area, and there are plenty of delightful roads leading to interesting places off the highway. Take water and snacks in the car. Although you're never very far from a town, you never know when you might want to just pull off the road for a rest and drinks. Speaking of rests, there aren't many rest stops along the road, but many of the towns themselves have convenient public restrooms.

NEVADA CITY

This gem of a Gold Rush town sits in the hills, just off the intrusive freeway that leads to Grass Valley. Arriving in Nevada City is at first like finding yourself on a movie set—until you realize that the buildings don't have false fronts.

Placer mines (surface mining) were being worked here as early as 1849. Like many other Gold Rush–era towns, this one began with tents, moved on to wooden buildings, and then burned down—twice! Needless to say, you'll see a lot of brick and stone edifices.

During the off-season, the town is peaceful and easy to get around. Summers can be crowded; translated, that means it's hard to park.

What to See and Do

Begin your visit at the **Nevada City Chamber of Commerce,** 132 Main St., Nevada City, CA 95959 (☎ **916/265-2692**), to pick up a free self-guided walking-tour map. The office, which has a courtesy restroom, is open weekdays from 9am to 5pm and on Saturday from 11am to 4pm. Occasionally open Sundays, 11am to 4pm. The map is also available at the **Brass Shop,** 225 Broad St. (☎ **916/265-6631**), which is open daily from 10am to 5pm.

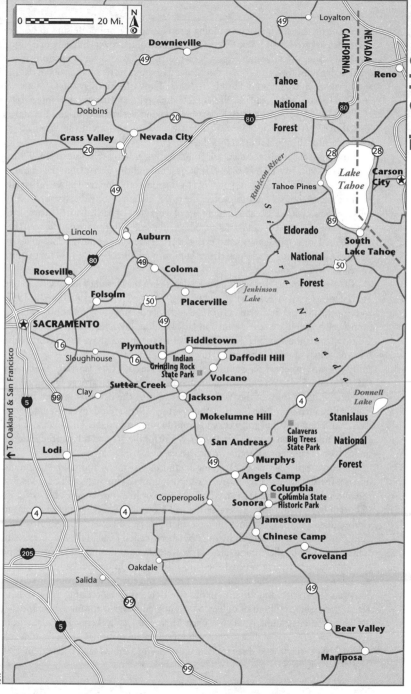

Exploring this town and its winding streets is an adventure. Be sure to wander down the back streets off Broad Street. This is not a tourist town with gobs of figurine and T-shirt shops. Your wanderings will lead you past theaters with live performances, cafés, herb shops, rock and crystal shops, and numerous stores specializing in natural and/or environmentally sound products. **Small Time Clothiers,** at 246 Commercial St. (☎ **916/265-3611**), carries some cute children's gifts and clothes and is open daily.

You'll see white-bearded town locals, some looking just as you'd imagine the miners looked over 140 years ago. If you really try, you can conjure up images of their forebears, probably gold prospectors themselves.

Some special spots we should tell you about include the **Firehouse No. 1 Museum,** 214 Main St. (☎ **916/265-5468**), just around the corner from the chamber of commerce office, a *must* on your list. In this tiny building, which was originally one of three firehouses built to protect the town, are fascinating displays of relics of the Gold Rush period. Ox shoes, examples of variations of barbed-wire fencing, crocheted baby clothes, Chinese cooking pots, and a magnificent ornate Chinese altar from a Joss House (a religious temple) of the 1860s are some of the precious items on display. The firehouse stays open daily, April through October, from 11am to 4pm. Check for winter hours.

Take your budding thespians in for a quick look at the **Nevada Theatre,** 401 Broad St., California's oldest existing theater building—opened in 1865, shut down in 1957, and reopened via public donations in 1968 and still operating today. The original stage hosted celebrities like Mark Twain and Jack London. Look for the art deco **Nevada County Courthouse,** which rises almost like an apparition above the Victorian and brick buildings of this 19th-century town.

If you wish to cheat on the hilly streets, the **Nevada City Carriage Company** (☎ **916/265-5348**) provides an old-fashioned horse-drawn carriage for your comfort. Pick it up in front of the National Hotel during the day, and in front of Friar Tuck's Restaurant on Pine Street in the evening. There are rides year round, weekdays from 11am to 10pm and weekends from 11am to midnight. The town tour lasts about 15 minutes and costs $15 for adults, $2.50 for the 5th and 6th person; children under 10 ride free. Longer tours are also available.

Children easily get weary of going in and out of shops and trudging up and down streets. Perhaps a more interesting experience for them will be a visit to **Malakoff Diggins State Historic Park,** about 26 miles northeast of Nevada City (☎ **916/265-2740**). Take Tyler-Foote Road off Calif. 49. Follow the pavement to Derbec Road and turn right into the park. In its "glory," this was the largest hydraulic gold mine anywhere. The sight of it has been called "cosmic" and "eery" and "ethereal." In hydraulic mining, giant hoses were aimed at the mountainsides and the pressure of such a spray washed the gold-filled gravel loose. Luckily this form of mining was banned in the late 1800s to protect the environment from the silt that was ruining the rivers and the erosion this type of blasting was creating. Now you can see the spot where millions of dollars' worth of gold was taken from the ground.

There's a museum here which is open Memorial Day to Labor Day, daily from 10am to 5pm; the rest of the year, weekends from 10am to 4pm. Campsites are available at $10 per night, and three replicated prospector's cabins can be rented for $20. The day-use fee is $5.

Where to Stay

The **Northern Queen Inn,** 400 Railroad Ave., Nevada City, CA 95959 (☎ 916/265-5824; fax 916/265-3720), tucked just off the freeway at the exit to Nevada City, is a great place for families. There's a wonderful restaurant (see "Where to Eat," below) from which to look at the giant waterwheel that churns the water of the little creek. On the grounds, just adjacent to the parking lot, are restored train cars, including Engine No. 5 from the area's narrow-gauge railroad of the 1800s.

The motel-style rooms are surprisingly spacious. Each neat-and-clean unit comes equipped with a coffee/tea maker, little refrigerator, color TV, table and two chairs, a tub/shower combination, and one or two queen-size beds. No room service available.

Detached cottages offer even more room. These very private accommodations have a separate bedroom with a queen-size bed and a kitchenette with two burners, a refrigerator, a coffee maker, and a toaster, plus an eating area for four. There's a wood-burning stove in the living room and a trundle bed. A private balcony looks into the woods.

Chalets overlook Gold Run Creek and have lots of room for families. The loft houses a large bedroom with a queen-size bed and a full bathroom. The main level has a full kitchen, a separate eating area, a trundle bed in the living room, and a half bathroom.

Room rates for two people in the motel rooms run $50; each additional person over age 5 pays $3. Cottages go for $75, and chalets cost $85, plus $5 per additional person. Rollaways and cribs can be rented for $5 per night. Parking is close to the rooms.

Just at the beginning of downtown Nevada City is the historic **National Hotel,** 211 Broad St., Nevada City, CA 95959 (☎ **916/265-4551**), which has the honor—at 150 years—of being the oldest continuously operating hotel in the West. Its Victorian richness has faded with the years; furniture and rugs are a bit shabby, floors creak and dip; but the flavor of the period remains. Surprisingly, there is a swimming pool on the premises. A cocktail lounge can be found on the ground floor; the hotel lobby is on the second floor.

The Victorian dining room is elegant, not garish, and it's a fun spot for families to have breakfast, lunch, and dinner. The chef will try to accommodate young diners, and will serve half portions of regular entrees for half the price. Breakfast and lunch prices are moderate; dinner ranges from $9 to $14.

Although this is a fun and unusual place to stay, parents should note that while families are encouraged, management insists that parents take charge of their kids at all times. Cribs are not provided nor are babysitting referrals.

All 42 rooms are different, and some share bathrooms. An ideal set-up for families are the rooms with one double bed and full bathroom connecting to a room with two twin beds. There are mini-suites too, with large antique beds and a living area big enough for a rollaway.

The price of a twin- or double-bedded room with a shared bath is $42; with a private bath it costs $68. The mini-suites, two of which have kitchenettes, rent for $96; full suites cost $113. Children under 12 sleep free in the same room with their parents; those 12 and over pay $11 per night. Rollaways are free. There are two parking lots.

Downey House, 517 W. Broad St., Nevada City, CA 95959 (☎ **916/265-2815,** or toll free **800/258-2815**), is a small, charming 1860s bed-and-breakfast inn within walking distance of Nevada City's historic district. Despite its literature to the contrary, Downey House will accept children as long as they're well behaved. The inn is filled with restful nooks and crannies in which to chat or curl up with a book. (When was the last time any parent actually got to curl up with a book?) The upstairs sun porch (with TV) and a downstairs garden entrance room are for guest use. A little lily pond beckons young explorers to the backyard garden. A breakfast buffet can be eaten in one of several rooms or on the outdoor patio.

Whimsical stuffed fabric fish and turned-down pastel sheets welcome guests to the immaculate cozy rooms. Each of the six bedrooms is soundproof and has a private bathroom, but there are no TVs or phones in the rooms.

One small double room costs $75, one a little larger rents for $90, and the four rooms with queen-size beds are larger and cost $100. Children staying in the same room with their parents are not charged extra, although some folks rent one of the small bedrooms for their kids. Sometimes entire families rent out all the rooms. Parents with infants should plan to bring their own porta-crib; there are no rollaways. There's a two-night minimum stay on weekends. Request a 10% discount if you are staying midweek (except holidays and in December).

Where to Eat

The **Trolley Junction Café,** in the Northern Queen Inn, 400 Railroad Ave. (☎ 916/265-5259), was named for the trolley that used to run through Nevada City. Plans are in the works to bring it back, but as of this writing, there is no trolley. This is certainly not a typical motel restaurant. Even the colorful menu covers show that care is taken at this establishment. The café serves up fabulous food for breakfast, lunch, and dinner in a cheerful room surrounded by large windows ideal for viewing the wooded outdoors. Everyone in the restaurant is pleasant and helpful.

The breakfast menu lists pancakes, French toast, and a variety of omelets and egg dishes. (If you like seafood, try the Cable Car Omelet, which is served all day.) You'll pay $3.50–$7 for your breakfast choice. Among the lunch specialties are chicken enchiladas ($5.95) and fried calamari ($6.25). Salads, hamburgers, and sandwiches complete the offerings, and they average $6.

The dinner selections are quite extensive: simple sandwiches (chicken croissants, roast beef), salads, pasta, barbecued pork ribs, prawns, calamari, and steak. Dinner goes for $5–$14. Cocktails, wine, and beer are served, and there are lots of dessert choices.

They haven't ignored the kids. A child's portion of French toast goes for $3. Lunch choices are the typical burgers, grilled cheese, and peanut butter and jelly pegged at $3.25. Dinner gets more sophisticated, with pasta, barbecued ribs or chicken, and prawns. Dinner costs $4.25–$6. There are highchairs and booster seats available. The restaurant is open Friday through Sunday from 7am to 9pm. Monday through Thursday it is open for breakfast and lunch from 7am to 2pm. All credit cards are accepted.

GRASS VALLEY

Grass Valley almost seems like a metropolitan hub after little Nevada City. And in fact its former importance as a gold-mining center lay in its enterprising way of mining: large efficiently run quarries taking in millions of dollars in gold, as opposed to individual prospectors mining individual claims.

But it didn't start out that way. Every Gold Rush–era town has a story, and Grass Valley has its. George Knight, who had come to find gold, supposedly tripped over an outcropping of quartz only to find out it yielded the glittery gold. Deep quartz mining was begun. So much gold was found in the area, mainly from the Empire Mine, that gold from the tailings of the mine was used to pave the streets in 1874—the streets were literally "paved with gold"!

Grass Valley was also known for two famous, albeit different, women. Lotta Crabtree, who was the Shirley Temple of her time, and Lola Montez, whose questionable reputation and fame as an entertainer kept her in the public's eye.

What to See and Do

Grass Valley's main street has plenty of history. The **Grass Valley & Nevada County Chamber of Commerce,** 248 Mill St., Grass Valley, CA 95945 (☎ **916/273-4667,** or toll free **800/655-4667** in California), has lots of information about the area. It's open daily from 9:30am to 4:30pm and on Saturday from 10am to 3pm.

We were given a great suggestion for a way to spend the day with the kids "in the mines." We stopped for sandwiches-to-go at **Grannies Gourmet Deli & Grocery,** 128 Mill St. (☎ **916/272-6409**). They stay open Monday through Saturday from 8:30am to 8pm and on Sunday from 11am to 5pm. Or you could stop for Cornish pasties (the traditional food of the Cornish miners who came to this area to share their expertise) at **Mrs. Dubblebee's,** 251 S. Auburn St. The first pasty can be sampled at 10:15am. Then we continued down Mill Street to the North Star Mining Museum and Pelton Wheel Exhibit. The plan was to walk across the aqueduct over Wolf Creek to the little picnic area within sight of the powerhouse for our picnic lunch, then to drive to Empire Mine State Historic Park. (Please keep little tykes in tow on the aqueduct—there are large open spaces in the railing, and the creek really rages below!)

At the **North Star Mining Museum and Pelton Wheel Exhibit,** at Mill Street and Allison Ranch Road (☎ **916/273-4255**), we saw an array of mining and power displays that date from the mid-1800s. Outside the museum is an actual Cornish pump, the technology of which was brought over by Cornish miners who came here to show the Americans how to pump water out of the tunnels in order to be able to deep-mine. For $1 in quarters you can turn on the huge pump. A fascinating sight are the ore cars and a 20-man skip, the long narrow car that transported the argonauts in and out of the shafts. Inside what was the actual powerhouse for the now-defunct mine is the world's largest Pelton Wheel, the deceptively simple mechanism used to create and force in the compressed air that ran the machinery and produced ventilation inside the mines. There are also displays of different types of drilling and the various equipment that was used.

There are restrooms, but no concessions. The museum is fairly stroller-accessible. The display is open from the first of May to the end of October, daily, weather permitting, from 10am to 5pm. Donations are requested.

The visit to the **Empire Mine,** at 10791 E. Empire St., about two or three miles from North Star (☎ **916/273-8522**), was fascinating, and we discovered we could have picnicked there, too. In its heyday, Empire, now part of a 784-acre state park, was one of the largest and richest hard-rock mines in all of California. It also had a reputation as being the best-managed and most progressive mine in America. You can easily tour the mine area on your own, or docents will guide you. The cottage of owner William Bourn can only be toured with a guide.

With concentration and a little imagination, you can picture men swarming over the area, working the machinery, and preparing to go down in the mine. In its 100+

years of operation, these miners pulled out gold whose value in the 1970s was equal to more than $960 million! Original stone-and-wood outbuildings remain, and there's equipment scattered throughout the grounds. By far one of the eeriest visits is to the actual main Empire shaft. Once you enter, you get a terrific sense of what it must have been like for those argonauts, stuffed like sardines into those skips and zipping up and down the mine shaft. The skips moved at 600 feet a minute, and the ore cars at 1,200. Tunnels branched off for more than two miles from the viewing point and reached 5,000 feet below the surface.

Plans are on hand to create an underground tour that will take visitors on a genuine mining tram through a 730-foot horizontal mine entrance, which will then intersect with the existing mine shaft.

There are restrooms and picnic areas, but no food concessions. The mine area is rough for strollers, but it is accessible. Strollers must be left outside the mansion, but it's accessible to wheelchairs. Empire is open every day from 10am to 5pm. Guided-tour hours run June through September. Adults pay $2; children 6–12, $1; under-6s, free.

Where to Stay

At one time, the venerable **Holbrooke Hotel,** 212 W. Main St., Grass Valley, CA 95945 (☎ **916/273-1353,** or toll free **800/933-7077;** fax 916/273-0434), did not accept children as guests. Happily that is no longer the case, as this charming, refurbished hotel–cum–bed-and-breakfast inn is a real slice of the Gold Country.

At just over 140 years old, the Holbrooke has seen its share of famous boarders. The guest book in the lobby substantiates the fact that President Grover Cleveland, Ulysses Grant, Benjamin Harrison, and Mark Twain stayed there. Gentleman Jim Corbett, Lotta Crabtree, and the town's infamous Lola Montez were also visitors. With all these famous names, it's no surprise that there is said to be a "happy" ghost roaming the hallways.

A complimentary continental breakfast is served in the library, a comfy lobby-level room with wing-backed chairs, a leather sofa, and TV. The elegant restaurant, open for lunch and dinner, is a bit pricey. Full continental dinners run $11–$19. There are several pasta dishes, but on the whole, not many choices that will appeal to unsophisticated children's palates. Plans are on tap to add children's selections. Children are charged half price at Sunday brunch.

All 17 rooms at the Holbrooke evoke the bygone era of saloons, gold mining, and jumping western towns. Each room is decorated differently: Some have exposed-brick walls; some rooms contain Victorian antiques and others have good reproductions. Comforters, ruffled pillow shams, and dust ruffles dress brass canopied and iron beds, and lacy curtains cover the windows. Armoires house the TV. Pictures and framed narrative about the famous person the room is named after hang on the walls. Phones are standard in each room. Almost all of the bathrooms have clawfoot tubs with showers.

For families, there are several rooms called "king verandas," with a king-size bed and a sofa bed in one room. A door leads to a private veranda. An annex building located behind the hotel, the Purcell House, holds 10 additional rooms.

From April through December, midweek, rooms begin at $66 and go to $86 for a veranda room; suites are $120. On weekends and holidays, rooms go for $76–$145. Off-season (January through March), midweek room rates are $55–$120. Weekends and holidays, the rooms are $60–$96; suites are $120. There are cribs and rollaways available.

Where to Eat

The cute little **Railroad Café,** 111 W. Main St. (☎ **916/274-CAFE**), is a good stop for breakfast, lunch, or dinner. Right away the kids will notice the model electric trains and the electric trolley that run overhead on tracks that cover nearly the whole restaurant. Once in a while, the distinct "moo" of a cow in the cattle car on a train can be heard above the conversation. You can eat on the enclosed patio or in the spiffy dining room of exposed rock walls. On the wall near the entrance is a rack of mugs with personalized plaques for the regulars who dine here.

Breakfast items include the standard fare: eggs and omelets, pancakes, French toast, waffles, and biscuits and gravy, priced at $2.70–$5. Children 10 and under can order either one pancake, egg, and bacon, or two halves of French toast and bacon for $2.65. Some lunch and dinner items are named for train routes, train cars, or famous western characters: the "Union Pacific" is a burger with cheese and onions on rye; the "Cattle Car" is a roast beef sandwich with lettuce, tomato, and mayo; and the "Billy the Kid" is a grilled-cheese sandwich. These items run $4–$5. There are also soups, chili, and salads. Youngsters can order the usual children's selections of hamburgers or grilled cheese for $2.75, or chicken nuggets with fries and a beverage for $2.95. There are also sundaes, cakes, and pies for dessert. Highchairs and boosters are available. The Railroad Café opens daily at 8am, closing Monday through Thursday at 3pm, on Friday at 8pm, on Saturday at 6pm, and on Sunday at 4:30pm. Cash only. Street parking.

AUBURN

Auburn makes a good stop before continuing your journey north or south on Calif. 49.

What to See and Do

As you drive into Auburn, signs will lead you to Old Town Auburn, just a small section of Gold Rush–era buildings. Walking-tour maps are available from the **Auburn Chamber of Commerce,** 601 Lincoln Way, Auburn, CA 95603 (☎ **916/885-5616**), open weekdays from 9am to 5pm, Saturday 10am to 2pm.

Take a few minutes to look at the **Gold Country Museum,** 1273 High St., at the Gold Country Fairgrounds (☎ **916/889-4134**). There are exhibits of the lives of the '49ers, a walk through a mine shaft, hands-on gold panning, and a working stamp mill model. The museum is open Tuesday through Sunday from 10am to 4pm. Adults pay $1; seniors and children 6–16, 50¢, free for children under 6.

Where to Eat

Awful Annie's, 160 Sacramento St., Old Town Auburn (☎ **916/888-9857**), is a misnomer for this cute second-story restaurant. It's surrounded by lots of trees and flower boxes, and you can eat indoors or out.

Breakfast is delicious and filling. (Hurray! Finally a place that makes *two*-egg omelets!) Omelets and other egg dishes include potatoes or fresh fruit and toast, at $4.50–$6.50. Lunchtime offerings include whole and half sandwiches, salads, fruit bowls, homemade soups, and daily specials, which are usually sandwiches and salads. Lunch prices are around $5. The 20 different types of beer plus "sinful" desserts complete the picture. Dinner is served in summer (chicken pot pies, meatloaf) and prices are $5–$10.

The children's menu has a few games and a limited but adequate food selection: breakfast specials, pizza bagel, grilled cheese, PB&J, or a quesadilla ($2.95 and $3.25). High chairs and booster seats are provided.

The restaurant is open June through October, daily from 8am to 4pm; the rest of the year, Monday through Thursday from 8:30am to 3pm and Friday through Sunday 8am to 4pm. Reservations are not accepted (except for six people or more). Major credit cards are welcome. Park in the lot.

COLOMA

If you continue south on Calif. 49 about a half hour from Auburn, you'll come to Coloma. You can't miss the **Marshall Gold Discovery State Historic Park,** at Main and Bridge Streets (☎ **916/622-3470**). This is the spot, folks, where gold was first discovered! You may want to spend the day here.

James Marshall, who was busy building a sawmill with partner John Sutter, discovered the glittery flakes and announced it to the world. Thus began an enormous migration of people whose findings ultimately changed the history and the economy of the world.

As the population of the state swelled with the argonauts (and everyone else who was catering to the miners' needs), so did Coloma's population grow. At one time the small area hosted more than 10,000 people, who didn't waste any time in taking out most of the gold there was in a few short years.

Today the park has much to look at in remembrance of that era. Sutter's Mill has been replicated near the river, and there is Marshall's cabin to explore, along with many other buildings. Don't miss Marshall's monument (and gravesite), which has him pointing to the exact spot where the gold was found. The museum and visitor center across the street is the place to start. Ask for the brochure which details the hikes through the park. The visitor center is open daily from 10am to 5pm. The park itself is open from 8am to dusk; closed on major holidays. The park-use fee is $5 per automobile.

PLACERVILLE

Placerville was—and still is—a crossroads between the northern and southern mines. It was formerly called Hangtown, for its reputation as the site of numerous hangings. Locals also describe an oyster-and-bacon omelet as a Hangtown omelet—a dish your kids probably won't want to try!

What to See and Do

If you've had enough of Gold Country hotels and Victorian-fronted buildings, Placerville is a good stop. You can take your first gold-mining expedition with **Gold Country Prospecting,** 3119 Turner St. (☎ **916/622-2484**), and sign up for a three-hour gold-panning trip on the river. The cost is $40 for adults, $20 for children 5–12; free for kids under 5. They supply the equipment and you supply your own lunches. Call ahead for a reservation or brochure. Open year round, weather permitting.

Where to Stay

The 105 rooms at the **Best Western Placerville Inn,** 6850 Greenleaf Dr. (U.S. 50 at the Missouri Flat Road exit), Placerville, CA 95667 (☎ **916/622-9100,** or toll free **800/528-1234;** fax 916/622-9376), are spacious, clean, and light. A small pool and Jacuzzi, plus tables and chairs and a soda machine, are fenced in, although some rooms open directly to the pool. There's no room service, but Eppie's Restaurant, on the grounds, is open 24 hours.

Rooms are simple, with either one king- or two queen-size beds, and all have patios or balconies. Some rooms are adjoining. A table and chairs, reading lights, digital radio, coffee maker, and free HBO are standard. There are vending machines in the hallways, one-day laundry service is available.

Rooms rent from May through September for $58 single, $64 double, $71 triple, and $78 quad. The rest of the year, rooms range in price from $56 to $80. Cribs are no charge; rollaways will cost you $14.

Eppies Restaurant (☎ **916/622-2303**) is adjacent to the Best Western and is open 24 hours daily. The usual coffeeshop breakfasts are offered with four-egg omelets (around $5), country breakfasts such as pork chops and eggs ($4–$6), and such griddle standards as pancakes ($3 and up). A good deal is the Create Your Own Breakfast, available weekdays only: you select four breakfast items for $3.80. The lunch and dinner menu is large: sandwiches, salads, steaks, chops, seafood, chicken, and nightly specials from about $4 to $8.25. There are plenty of desserts.

Children 10 and younger eat for $2. There's shrimp, a hot turkey sandwich, chicken strips, pancakes, and French toast. Every meal comes with a beverage and a junior-size ice-cream cone. There are boosters and highchairs. Credit cards are accepted, and you can charge to your motel room.

A DETOUR OFF CALIF. 49

Part of the lure of the Gold Country is the idea of adventure. Take some back roads off Calif. 49 and go exploring. There's lots of driving on this trip, but if you have good travelers, you can take the time to find some intriguing places.

Fiddletown

As we drove off Calif. 49 and made our way to Fiddletown, the first thing we spotted was the sign claiming a population of 100, then the incongruity of the public tennis court in this decidedly Gold Rush–era town. First settled by Missourians in 1849, it hasn't changed much. The general store, dating from the 1850s, is everything a general store should be—a little of this, a little of that. And smack dab in the middle sits a fiddler with his Amish-like beard, coveralls, and hat. Each Sunday afternoon after church, at around 3pm, musicians play for anyone who wants to listen.

The former home of a Chinese herb doctor is an example of one of the few rammed-earth adobes in California. It's located right near the tennis courts. Built in 1850, it was the store, office, and home of one Dr. Yee.

It's hard to believe, standing on Fiddletown's main street in this day and age, that this hamlet is said to have had the largest Chinese settlement in California outside of San Francisco.

Volcano

Noteworthy along the drive between Fiddletown and Volcano is Daffodil Hill. If you're here in spring around the time when daffodils bloom, you'll catch this amazing sight at Ram's Horn Grade and Shake Ridge Road. We should also note that between Fiddletown and Volcano there aren't any restaurants, there's nowhere to stop for a picnic, and there's no gasoline until Pine Grove. If you continue your drive past Daffodil Hill, you'll come to a true jewel of a town called Volcano.

Time stood still in the little town of Volcano, which dates from 1848. The kids were amazed that the bucolic few blocks they were looking at were once home to dance halls, breweries, and two theaters. Volcano also boasts the first California rental library and the first little theater group, founded by the Volcano Thespian Society in 1854. There's a great park, perfect for a picnic and conversation. The park's Angel Lace Rock was probably formed from a volcanic flow that was suddenly cooled by past river waters—so says the sign. And right nearby is "Old Abe," the Civil War vintage cannon that was smuggled into town to quell rebels who, the Union volunteers thought, were on their way to "get the gold."

Just outside Volcano, on our way to find gasoline in Pine Grove, we happened on **Indian Grinding Rock State Historic Park and Chaw'se Regional Indian Museum,** 14881 Pine Grove–Volcano Rd. (☎ **209/296-7488**). This was one of those discoveries you come upon without planning that turn into such great days.

The 135-acre park offers camping and hiking, but even more fun is the museum and Indian village. Naturally the kids will be jumping to know what a grinding rock is. Start first, though, in the museum, which begins to tell the story of California's Native Americans through displays and interactive exhibits, concentrating on the people of the Sierra Nevada. The collection of baskets, tools, jewelry, and feathers is impressive. Children are encouraged to handle some items to give them a better sense of what they're seeing. Oftentimes on weekends during the summer there are interpretive programs. On the second Saturday of each month, year round, members come from the Sierra Native American council to tell stories. There are animal pelts to touch; a wooden pump drill that would have been used by the native peoples to drill into obsidian or wood, which you can actually use; match-up boards to teach the process of turning acorn into flour; and a quiz board. If you've got the time, ask for the Chaw'se Museum Treasure Hunt list that's given to schoolchildren on tour. Your family can use it to learn lots about the Miwoks and other tribes.

Once you get outside, you'll learn why the acorns and grinding rocks are so important. The grinding rocks are the limestone outcroppings you'll see framed by the log fence. The holes, or cups, were created over years of use as a system for grinding acorns, seeds, and berries. These date from 2,000–3,000 years ago. They were not only utilitarian, they became social centers for the tribe's women. By now you've seen the reconstructed Miwok village set in the beautiful meadow filled with oak trees. You can actually walk into the bark houses to get a sense of how the tribespeople lived. A giant football field is defined by log benches and goal posts. This is where the Miwoks played a game very much like soccer. A peek into the Hung'E (ceremonial roundhouse) is fascinating. This was the central gathering place of the villagers, where ceremonies were performed and still are today, prayers were said, and the dead were mourned.

As you begin your walk down the self-guiding nature trail, you come upon a second village. Stand perfectly still, and if no one else is around, you'll hear the acorns dropping off the trees. If you're around the area in September, call about the festival for the annual acorn harvest when local Native Americans gather for dancing and games.

There are actually two trails to follow, one less than a half mile and the other two miles long (children can handle it). The museum has prepared a wonderful guidebook for the short trail which will introduce you to what you'll see, and how the plants were used by the Miwoks.

Everything except the nature trails is wheelchair- and stroller-accessible. There are restrooms; no concession stands, but picnicking is permitted in the park, which is open from sunrise to sunset daily. The day-use fee is $5 per car. The museum is open weekdays from 11am to 3pm and weekends from 10am to 4pm, year round.

If you need to stop for food or gas, Pine Grove is just minutes away. **Sierra House** offers coffeeshop fare, and there are several faster food spots to the left and right of the turnoff.

Sutter Creek

This is the town that grew up named after Capt. John Sutter. It was used as a camping spot by Sutter's scouts who were seeking timber for his fort in what is now Sacramento. This is considered one of the prettiest and best-preserved Gold Country towns. And, indeed, there are lovely, immaculately groomed homes and cute little stores now housed in the 19th-century buildings.

But it gets quite crowded during peak season. If the children get bored being dragged from one boutique to the other, give them an ice-cream break at **The Chatter Box,** 39 Main St. (☎ **209/267-5935**). This cute little restaurant/soda fountain may not be much to look at, and it gets crowded in summer, but it's perfectly comfortable for breakfast or lunch. Breakfast main dishes come with homemade biscuits "while they last," and range in price from $2 to $5.25. At lunch there are traditional burgers, sandwiches, salads, and french fries. Your youngsters have plenty of choices. The prices are reasonable—nothing is over $6 except steak. The best reason to come here, though, is for the ice-cream cones, sodas, milkshakes, and sundaes. On a hot Gold Country day, there's nothing better. Open weekdays (except Thursdays) from 6am to 3pm, and on Saturday, Sunday, and holidays from 8am to 4pm. Cash only. There's street parking and a public lot nearby.

The other place to take the kids is the well-stocked **Bubble Gum Bookstore,** 48 Main St. (☎ **209/267-5680**). We found books we were unable to locate elsewhere, plus some new finds. This is the place to find books on gold prospecting, and Gold Country history and folklore. There are book titles appealing to everyone. If you haven't already done so, you can pick up a walking-tour map here.

Amador City

If you blink you'll have driven through nearby Amador City. If the Chatter Box is too crowded, make a stop at the **Buffalo Chips Emporium,** Calif. 49 (☎ **209/267-0570**). The kids had trouble deciding between all the different colorful candies on the counter. We went for the ice cream. You can also get simple lunches and drinks here. Open Wednesday through Sunday, 9am to 5pm.

Jackson

As you make your way back to Calif. 49 from your detour to Volcano, you could stop at **Kennedy Tailing Wheels Park,** on Jackson Gate Road, north of Jackson. You can't miss the two giant wheels (whose pictures you've seen everywhere by now) left from the original four that were used at the Kennedy Mine to carry away waste gravel. Information in the park details the way these ingenious wheels worked. The mine itself was important because it was the deepest mine in North America.

MOKE HILL

Keep your eyes open for the sign on Calif. 49 that leads to Mokelumne—it doesn't give you much time to change your mind! It's said that this little tiny area you see today was once one of the largest and most violent towns in the Mother Lode.

Where to Stay

If you really insist on staying in this area, the only hotel in town is the Hotel Leger, and it's about the only place to eat. The hotel is reserved mostly by couples looking for a quiet Gold Country retreat. But now having said that, we'll tell you about the hotel and let you make up your own mind.

The **Hotel Leger,** 8304 Main St. (P.O. Box 50), Mokelumne Hill, CA 95245 (☎ 209/286-1401), has been around since the 1850s when George Leger took it over and gave it his name. The newest owners have sunk a ton of money into it redoing the outside and the public areas. But upstairs, where the accommodations are, the floors dip and creak, and the paint appears to be on the 100th coat. The room decor hasn't quite succeeded at the "Laura Ashley look," and the floors are somewhat shabby, but rooms are neat and clean and full of character. If you're into teeny-weeny towns, and ghosts, this is the place. It's said there are spirits—nice spirits—floating around the hotel. But who knows! In spite of the lack of modern amenities, this is a very popular destination. The hotel has a swimming pool outdoors.

Continental breakfast is included in the room price. Nonno's is the hotel restaurant serving Italian dishes family style, open for dinner only. Children's plates are limited to spaghetti or ravioli with soup and salad, a beverage, and ice cream for $4.95 and $6.95.

There are only 13 accommodations, and each is different. Most of the rooms have double beds and are furnished with a mishmash of Victorian antiques and reproductions. Large families might do well by requesting Rooms 11 and 12, which connect and have a private bath. Parlor suites come with fireplaces and small sitting areas, so you can fit a crib or rollaway.

Rates, double occupancy, are $65–$99, depending on whether you choose a shared or private bath. The family suite with its two rooms and private bath is discounted. Cribs and rollaways are $20 a night.

SAN ANDREAS

San Andreas's historical area consists of one tiny main street. One of its claims to fame is that this is where the infamous stagecoach robber Black Bart was tried. You can see the courtroom and the jail where he awaited trial.

What to See and Do

Only about 15 minutes away by way of winding roads are the **California Caverns,** P.O. Box 78, Vallecito, CA 95251 (☎ 209/736-2708); take Calif. 4 east from Angels Camp. There are three cave systems in the Gold Country. California Caverns and Moaning Caverns near Angels Camp (see below) share the same ownership. These tours seem to be the most spontaneous and unstructured of the cave tours, and are customized to the individual tour group.

The caverns are one of nature's amazing creations. The limestone caverns were discovered back in the mid-1800s by—of course—a prospector. John Muir toured them and considered them to be a "fairyland." Numerous chambers and lakes have been discovered since Muir's visit, and today you'll explore crystal chambers and view stalactites and stalagmites at subterranean levels.

But cave exploring isn't for everyone. You need to be prepared for walking, stooping, and wiggling through narrow passageways. Probably the best tour to start with, and the one appropriate for most of the family, is the 60- to 90-minute Trail of Lights tour. This half-mile route will give you a good sense of the original caves, as well as another room that was found in 1962. You'll explore 10 rooms, connected by different sized passageways. There are handrails, and you'll be provided with a "bump cap" for low ceilings. Youngsters can handle this tour as long as they can walk and don't need to be held, and as long as they have a pretty decent attention span. The tour is limited to 25 people at a time, so reserve in advance.

A number of other spelunking adventures are possible, some more appropriate to older kids and physically fit adults. These are every person's "playing in the mud" fantasy. There are 2¹/₂- and 3¹/₂-hour tours that will take you through chambers with exotic-sounding names like Middle Earth, Cave of the Quills, and Bubble Gum Hall. In some cases you'll walk through knee-deep sticky cave clay or raft across cavern lakes. Most children age 12 and older can handle the introductory spelunking trip; the downstream circuit is for age 12 and over. There's also rappeling for those folks 17 and older who either complete the 3¹/₂-hour Downstream Circuit tour, or who earn a Rappel Card from Moaning Cavern. It's said you could do these caves and those at Moaning Cavern all in one day. Don't ask us how!

Needless to say, high-top shoes or boots are a must. You'll be provided with coveralls, gloves, and a helmet and light. Note, though, that coveralls begin at size 36 adult, so kids have to compensate. There are showers and a hot tub, but bring along a change of clothes, shower items, and a plastic bag for your grimy clothes. Kids have to be at least 12 for these tours.

California Caverns is open mid-May to October seven days a week. The Trail of Lights tour can be taken from 10am to 5pm in summer, to 4pm in fall. It stays open occasional weekends past November. Winter and spring often bring high water levels, so be sure to call ahead to find out if it's open. Call for times of other tours and rappeling. The Trail of Lights tour costs $6.25 for adults, $3 for children 6–12. The introductory spelunking tour is $45; the Downstream Circuit tour and rappeling is $64. You must either pay in full in advance, or reserve by phone with a credit card.

Where to Stay and Eat

The **Black Bart Inn,** Main Street (P.O. Box 216), San Andreas, CA 95249 (☎ 209/754-3808), has motel rooms with all the basics: a bed, color TV, bath-and-shower combination, plus ice and soda machines in the hallways. The Inn also has the only decent restaurant in town, plus a coffee shop that opens at 6am. Rates Sunday through Thursday are $43 single, $46 double, $49 triple, $53 quad; on Friday and Saturday, add about $5 per room. Children are included in the room count. Rollaways or cribs cost $5.

ANGELS CAMP

While you may never have heard of Angels Camp, you may have heard of Mark Twain's *The Celebrated Jumping Frog of Calaveras County,* for which Angels Camp was the setting. Frog-jumping competitions didn't begin in this area until the 1920s; however, frogs continue to play a big part here, even while the charm of the Victorian era has been slowly disappearing. Today you can celebrate the frog and its amazing jumping prowess during the Calaveras County Fair in May, held at the nearby Frogtown fairgrounds. Anyone can rent a frog or bring their own to enter the competition.

The folks at the **Calaveras Lodging & Visitors Association,** P.O. Box 637 (1211 S. Main St.), Angels Camp, CA 95222 (☎ 209/736-0049, or toll free 800/225-3764), can provide information.

You may want to stop at the **Angels Camp Museum,** 753 S. Main St. (☎ 209/736-2963), to see the operating stamp mill and the rock and mineral displays. The museum is open daily 10am to 3pm, April through November; December through March, Wednesday through Sunday from 10am to 3pm. Admission is $1 for adults, 25¢ for kids 6–12, free for children under 6.

Moaning Cavern, Parrot's Ferry Road off Calif. 4 (P.O. Box 78, Vallecito, CA 95251; ☎ 209/736-2708), is on the way to Calaveras Big Trees State Park. Like its counterpart, California Caverns, Moaning Cavern has a 45-minute Traditional Tour suitable for the family. The main chamber is so big it could hold the Statue of Liberty! It is filled with crystal formations in myriad shapes and sizes. Adventurous family members ages 12 and older can opt for the 180-foot rope descent into the chamber. A three-hour Adventure Tour takes you through the lower portions of the cavern and includes rappel.

Moaning Cavern is open daily from 9am to 6pm in summer, from 10am to 5pm the rest of the year. The Traditional Tour costs $6.25 for adults, $3 for children 6–12, free for kids under 6; rappel costs $26.50, and subsequent rappels are half price. The Adventure Tour costs $45.

Calaveras Big Trees State Park lies about 20 miles northeast of Murphys, P.O. Box 120, Arnold, CA 95223 (☎ **209/795-2334**). It was in 1852 when the public first became aware of the giant redwoods in this gorgeous setting. Trees as tall as 325 feet have been living here for between 2,000 and 4,000 years. There is an interpretive center, and there are hiking trails. You can picnic, swim, fish, and camp in the park, and in winter, you can cross-country ski. The North Grove is the most popular section, but you can hike to the South Grove for a more solitary experience.

MURPHYS

On the way to Big Trees, you'll pass through Murphys, a charming village which has stood still in time.

What to See and Do

Its shady Main Street just begs a stroll and will take you to art galleries, boutiques, a toy store, and **The Dolls Castle** (☎ **209/728-8755**), small but brimming with dolls. This might be just the time to get rid of some excess energy at the little, old park behind the main street. You can even picnic near the fast-moving creek complete with footbridge. There's a small playground with swings, a slide, and plenty of sand. On your way to the park, keep your eyes open for the little **Murphys Pokey,** the old tiny town jail—I guess they didn't anticipate a lot of inmates!

The **Old Timers Museum,** on Main Street (☎ **209/728-1160**), is housed in the town's oldest building. Rusty Gold Rush relics look untouched. It's worth a look; admission is by donation. Open Friday through Sunday from 11am to 4pm.

Where to Stay

Once you look around **Murphys Historic Hotel & Lodge,** 457 Main St. (P.O. Box 329), Murphys, CA 95247 (☎ **209/728-3444,** or toll free **800/532-7684;** fax 209/728-1590), you might consider booking a room. This beautifully preserved hotel, dating from 1856, survived numerous fires and lots of different owners. In its heyday, luminaries such as J. P. Morgan, President Ulysses S. Grant, Horatio Alger, Jr., and Mark Twain—who seems to have visited everywhere in the Gold Country— were guests of the hotel. Today the public can go upstairs to see Grant's Presidential Suite through a glass viewing window. Grant's suite and a connecting room can be rented for $95.

Although there are nine rooms in the historic building, most families opt for the adjacent lodge rooms, which are even more charming on the inside than the outside. The immaculate rooms are furnished simply in rich hunter green and white, with dark wood colonial-style furniture. Some rooms come with two double beds; there are two units with two queen-size beds. Each has a private bathroom, and modern conveniences such as TV and phone are included.

Lodge rooms go for $70 midweek and $80 on weekends, single or double occupancy. The rate includes a continental breakfast. Children 12 and under stay free; those over 12 pay $6 per night extra. Rollaways and cribs are $6.

Where to Eat

Whether or not you stay at the hotel, the **Murphys Historic Hotel Restaurant** (☎ **209/728-3444**) is a pleasant stop for breakfast, lunch, or dinner. Lots of local families take meals here; the food is good and reasonably priced. Stop in for a breakfast of eggs, pancakes, or omelets priced $4.25–$7. Lunch sandwiches and salads average around $6. At dinnertime, the continental selections are numerous: pasta, several chicken entrees, prime rib, steak, lamb, and seafood for $7.95–$16.95.

Children under 10 have their own menu with kid-friendly choices such as pancakes and eggs for breakfast ($1.25 and $2.75), sandwiches and hamburgers at lunch ($1.50–$3.95), and spaghetti and steak at dinner ($1.95–$6.95). Special children's drinks are made, too. Seniors get a 10% discount on their menu selections.

The restaurant is open daily from 7am to 11:30am for breakfast, 11:30am to 3pm for lunch, and weeknights for dinner from 5pm to 9pm (until 9:30 on weekends). Reservations are accepted as are major credit cards.

COLUMBIA

Drive west from Murphys on Calif. 4 to Parrotts Ferry Road. Drive South about 10 miles to Columbia.

You must plan to spend at least a full day in **Columbia State Historical Park,** P.O. Box 151, Columbia, CA 95310 (☎ **209/532-0150** weekdays, **532-4301** weekends). Even today, Columbia richly deserves its title "Gem of the Southern Mines." We are all lucky that this once-prosperous gold-mining town, at one point the largest town in the Southern Mines, was preserved in such a manner. The town was never completely deserted, probably because so much gold was discovered here in 1850.

Parts of the well-preserved gold-mining town—bigger than most of the Gold Rush towns in terms of historical buildings—were declared a state park. While it's geared to tourists and more "perfect" than some of the other towns, it's not a theme park. This is a living museum, and almost everything in the park is real. Many of the former businesses are today working stores, some still purveying the wares they did in the 19th century.

Pick up a guide at the museum; it will identify most of the buildings.

In the **pharmacy** are displays of the old bottles of cure-alls, and sundries. There's Dr. Thatcher's Liver & Blood Syrup along with remedies for everything that might ail you. Next door at the old **dentist's office,** one look at the dental instruments and drills that were turned manually with a socket handle and you may never go to the dentist again. At the **Daguerreotype studio,** the old-time sepia photos are some of the best we've seen. The **blacksmith shop** is just as dusty and crammed with "stuff" as it probably was back in the 1800s. If you want, you can get your name stamped on a real horseshoe. There has been a **dry-goods store** on the site of the current one since 1855. In the window are the rules that were laid down by the former proprietor: "Any employee who is in the habit of smoking Spanish cigarettes, getting shaved at the barber shop, going to dances . . . has most surely given his employer reason to be suspicious of his integrity . . ."

Near the giant boulders is the **Matelot Gulch Mine Supply Store,** at the corner of Main and Washington Streets (mailing address for reservations: P.O. Box 28, Columbia, CA 95310; ☎ **209/532-9693**), where you can learn to pan for gold. From here, tours leave daily for the **Hidden Treasure Gold Mine,** the only active hard-rock mine open to the public, and one which still produces pockets of gold today. These tours, which run just over an hour, operate in summer, daily from 10am to 5pm; from October through April, hours vary. Tours cost $7 for adults, $6 for children 5–12, free for children under 5. The tour can be combined with gold panning for an additional fee.

A series of 10-minute **stagecoach rides** leave from the Wells Fargo Express Station daily. The kids love this short ride for the surprises it offers—we promised we wouldn't tell. Eight children or six adults can ride "shotgun" up on top, and that's where most of the kids like to go. When you're finished, walk around the block to the **Fallon Hotel's Ice Cream Parlor** for a homemade wafflecone and ice cream. In the same vicinity are **pony rides** and **horseback riding.**

At the other end of town is the **Franco cabin.** It's really fascinating to peer into this small cabin and see the far-from-glamorous way in which the '49ers lived. The other important site is the **schoolhouse** (save it for the end because you'll probably want to drive there). It was originally built in 1860, and managed to remain in use until it was condemned in 1937. The building you see was restored in 1960 with funds partially raised by California schoolchildren. It's a neat glimpse at the schools and children of that time. Their desks alone are enough to make you feel uncomfortable! And how about that dunce cap?

The park displays open at 8am every day except Thanksgiving and Christmas. The businesses are open from 10am to 5pm (to 6pm in summer). Admission and parking is free. A map of the park is available for $1 in the museum at State and Main Streets.

SONORA

Just a few miles from Columbia lies Sonora, called "The Queen of the Southern Mines" because it was so big and lively. Most of the downtown buildings have been modernized. You might want to make Sonora a base for travels to Jamestown, Columbia, Angels Camp, and areas even farther south. Once there, you may recognize parts of the surrounding areas from the hundreds of westerns that have been filmed on location here throughout the years.

What to See and Do

Sonka's Apple Ranch, 19200 Cherokee Rd., Tuolumne (☎ **209/928-4689**), is a cute place to stop during apple season. There's a little miniature train that takes the kids past the orchard, the farm animals, and the horse pasture. It's just $1.25 per person, and the ride lasts 10 minutes. Youngsters can also feed the farm animals. In the fall you can watch the apple picking and cider making, and can purchase tree-ripened apples, pies, jams, and syrups. They make the best apple coffeecake we've ever eaten! Sonka's is open daily, year round, from 8am to 5:30pm. The train runs weekends and holidays from 10am to 5pm.

Where to Stay

The **Sonora Inn,** 160 S. Washington St., Sonora, CA 95370 (☎ **209/532-2400,** or toll free **800/321-5261** in California; fax 209/532-4542), is a historic building dating from 1896, where you could once sleep and eat for 75¢. Unfortunately, it shows its age inside the main building. The hotel does have a fascinating story: It seems that there are tunnels underneath the building leading to—who knows where? Were they used as escape routes during Prohibition, and/or escape routes for straying husbands who had used the rooms for illicit purposes? No one seems to know for sure. Maybe, by the time you read this, some of the tunnels will be open for public viewing. In the basement is a darkroom used by the Hollywood cameramen and women who shot the great old westerns. Their names and dates of their visits appear in their handwriting on the walls.

There is a pool and a patio in back of the main building. The hotel's restaurant is open for breakfast, lunch, and dinner 24 hours, but there is no room service.

Families yearning to stay in a historic Gold Rush–era building should check out the accommodations in the main building of the Sonora Inn, which is currently undergoing renovation. There are some large rooms with two double beds that have plenty of space for a family. Inquire whether the refurbishing has included soundproofing the front rooms; if your family is easily disturbed, opt for another room.

The rooms in the adjacent motel, however, are perfectly adequate for families. Rooms are furnished with modern furniture and have cable TV, phones, and shower stalls (no tubs). Some rooms are big enough to fit a rollaway or crib. One room has a king-size bed and a hide-a-bed. You can request a refrigerator.

Rooms in the motel cost $49, and in the main building, $59, single or double. During holidays, add $20 per room; on weekends add an extra $10. Suites run $129–$169. Children 10 and under sleep free in their parents' room; those over 10 are charged $5. Rollaways cost $5 and cribs are free.

For a more traditional motel stay, you might consider the **Best Western Sonora Oaks Motor Hotel,** 19551 Hess Ave., Sonora, CA 95370 (☎ **209/533-4400,** or toll free **800/532-1944;** fax 209/532-1964). The motel is conveniently located just off Calif. 108. The outdoor pool and spa in the courtyard are fenced in. The comfortable Oak Tree Restaurant on the premises offers a limited children's menu. There is no room service, but you can order take-out meals from the restaurant, which is open daily from 7am to 11pm.

Rooms at the Sonora Oaks are quite comfortable. They're not huge, but you can fit a rollaway or crib in a room with two double beds, although it would be snug. It would be best to request a deluxe king room if you have a larger family; it comes with a king-size bed and a queen-size hide-a-bed. There are also some adjoining rooms. All accommodations come with a coffee maker, remote-control color TV, a table and two chairs, a desk, phone, and separate vanity.

Rates for standard rooms are $62 for a single, $67 for a double with one bed, and $72–$77 for a double with two queen-size beds. Deluxe rooms cost $90 and suites rent for $115. Children under 12 sleep free in their parents' room; for those over 12 the charge is $5. Rollaways cost $10; cribs are complimentary. Cribs and rollaways are not guaranteed to be available when you check in, so although management assures us it isn't a problem, it would be best to bring along a porta-crib if you have one, just in case.

JAMESTOWN

"Jimtown," as it's known, has a mixed history. Its founder, Col. George James, had a bad reputation and was soon thrown out of town by the townsfolk. Plenty of gold came out of the nearby creek, making it a pretty rich town to settle in. But like most Mother Lode towns, its fame was short-lived. Today, however, it's one of the few places that still has active placer mines.

What to See and Do

Jamestown is a nice stop for a short visit, and there are more family-oriented restaurants in Jamestown than in Sonora. There's also a little public park with playground equipment almost in the middle of the historic area. The clip-clop of horses is heard on weekend evenings when the horse-drawn carriages take folks for rides through the town.

Gold Prospecting Expeditions, 18170 Main St. (P.O. Box 1040, Jamestown, CA 95327; ☎ 209/984-4653), is a good place to try your hand at this alluring "sport." Professionals teach the technique and you do the work. In front of the store are wooden troughs filled with water and gold dust. This is a good place to start. Panning costs $2 if you have your own pan, or rent one for $3. Once you've mastered the technique, you can take one of the special trips to a nearby creek.

GPE prospectors made a find of their own. Receding water at the usual creek site led to the discovery of relics such as rifles, shovels, and pans from an 1849 miners' camp. GPE lost no time in fixing up the site with other historically accurate elements— a donkey, a goat, an ore cart, and such—and even had some tents made from the same period. Today you can visit **Jimtown 1849 Gold Mining Camp** for yourself as part of one of your gold panning excursions. You can choose from half-hour to five-hour trips for two adults and three children which will take you to the camp and give you the chance to pan (or sluice) for your own nugget.

A two- ($60) or three-hour ($85) trip is the most fun for kids. A full day (five hours) will cost $140 for the family. Gold Prospecting is open every day, except Christmas, from 9:30am to 5pm.

Just outside Jamestown is a train-lover's heaven. **Railtown 1897,** Sierra Railway Depot, Fifth Avenue (☎ 209/984-3953), has the country's only operating steam roundhouse open to the public. Fifty-minute tours are given of this 26-acre round-house. Tours run daily in summer and spring: weekdays from 9:30 to 4:30pm, week-ends until 5pm. The fee is $2.50 for adults, $1.25 for children 3–12, free for kids under 3.

Your children might like the train rides, too. There's a one-hour ride from Jamestown to Chinese Station with a 1922 No. 28 engine. In the round house, your kids may recognize an 1891 engine used in the film *Back to the Future III,* and on the TV show "Little House on the Prairie."

The train has restrooms. Bring a picnic lunch. The train rides can be taken from March through November only, on weekends and holidays from 10am to 5pm. The tickets are $9 for adults, $4.50 for children 3–12, free for children under 3. There's a combination ticket for the roundhouse tour and the train ride at $10.50 for adults, $5.50 for children 3–12, free for children under 3. The family plan offers fares of $28 for two adults and two children; each extra child is $4.75.

Where to Eat

Despite its efforts to maintain its 19th-century look, Jamestown sports two restaurants which have made their way to the 1950s and 1990s, respectively. **Boomer's American Diner,** 18141 Main St. (☎ 209/984-5000), serves up basic hamburgers and hot dogs. You may find yourself explaining who Frankie and Annette are, and waxing nostalgic about Marilyn Monroe and James Dean.

There are "Lil" corn dogs and fries for $2 and standard burgers with all sorts of toppings for $4.65–$6. The under-12 set can get a fried chicken dinner for $3.75 or Baby Boomers (burgers and fries) for $2.50. Leave room for luscious desserts at around $4.

Open daily for lunch and dinner, weekdays from 11am to 8pm, on weekends from 11am to 9pm. Credit cards are accepted. Park in the lot.

The **Smoke Café,** nearby on Main Street (☎ **209/984-3733**), looks totally out of place in this Victorian town, but the food is good. The modern Mexican restaurant has a big, airy inside dining room and a front room that opens to the street. There's a children's menu of a taco, enchilada, hamburger, or bean burrito with rice and beans or fries for $3.75. Adults get their choice of combination plates at $7–$9, seafood specials for $8–$11, and other selections such as enchiladas, tamales, chimichangas, and specials of the day. There are no à la carte items, just what they call "small plates."

There is a full bar. Highchairs and booster seats can be requested. The restaurant is open Tuesday through Saturday from 5 to 10pm and on Sunday from 4 to 9pm. Lunch is served year-round on Saturday and Sunday. Reservations are taken for parties of six or more, and some credit cards are accepted. Park on the street.

OTHER OUTDOOR ACTIVITIES

Camping

Tuolumne County alone offers more than 1,000 campsites. For information, contact the **U.S. Forest Service Stanislaus National Forest** c/o Mary Hale, 19777 Greenley Rd., Sonora, CA 95370 (☎ **209/532-3671**), or the **Ranger District offices:** Mi-Wok (☎ **209/586-3234**), Groveland (☎ **209/962-7825**), and Calaveras (☎ **209/795-1381**). Campgrounds are on a first-come, first-served basis.

River Rafting

White-water rafting is exceptional along all three forks of the American River, as well as on the Stanislaus River, and offers varying degrees of difficulty. Some trips are suitable for children, while others may be too dangerous or frightening. The best way to judge is to inquire at individual outfitters, most of which offer both one- and two-day trips, at costs ranging from $50 per person and up.

American River Recreation, 11257 S. Bridge St., Rancho Cordova, CA 95670 (☎ **916/635-4479**), offers challenging white-water rafting as well as family floats and introductory rafting trips perfect for Mom, Dad, and the kids. The minimum age for white-water rafting is 8.

There are a number of other outfitters you can call or write to, as well: **Ahwahnee Whitewater Expeditions,** P.O. Box 1161, Columbia, CA 95310 (☎ **209/533-1401,** or toll free **800/359-9790**); **Wild River Tours, Inc.,** 1295 Rexford Ave., Pasadena, CA 91107 (☎ **310/453-9079,** or toll free **800/821-0183**); **OARS,** P.O. Box 67, Angels Camp, CA 95222 (☎ **209/736-4677,** or toll free **800/446-RAFT**); or **Zephyr River Expeditions,** P.O. Box 510, Columbia, CA 95310 (☎ **209/532-6249,** or toll free **800/431-3636** in California). Also ask about the discounted children's fees for a variety of trips with **Whitewater Voyages,** P.O. Box 20400, El Sobrante, CA 94820 (☎ **501/222-5994,** or toll free **800/488-RAFT**).

Adventurous families may also want to learn white-water kayaking. **California Canoe & Kayak** has its Sacramento location at 11257 S. Bridge St., Rancho Cordova, CA 95670 (☎ **916/631-1400,** or toll free **800/366-9804**). Ask about the other two locations.

Skiing

You may not be aware that there are ski areas nearby. A family-oriented one is **Dodge Ridge Ski Area,** P.O. Box 1188, Pinecrest, CA 95364 (☎ **209/965-3474**), only 30 miles east of Sonora. Its SKIwee program, for ages 3 to 10, has been rated the best in California. Be sure to ask about the midweek specials. Call **209/965-4444** for snow conditions.

3 Lake Tahoe

Lake Tahoe, at 12 miles wide, 22 miles long, and 989 feet deep is the third-deepest lake in North America. Did you know that the water in the lake is 99.9% pure? It's said that if you dropped a dinner plate in the lake, it could be seen at a depth of at least 75 feet.

The lake takes on a number of personalities as you approach it from the highway, or when you catch a glimpse of it as you come around a mountain bend. The winter view is of the snow-capped peaks that surround the lake shimmering in the perpetual sunshine. In summer, the dense green forests framing the blue-blue water makes the perfect alpine picture postcard.

Lake Tahoe is a resort area of many possibilities. In winter, it offers some of the best skiing in the country and has superb children's ski schools; in summer, there's nearly every outdoor activity you can think of. And if you still seek excitement, the casinos on the Nevada side are just waiting to make change. The casino-hotels, realizing the worth of soliciting family travelers, are making a point of providing amenities suitable for children.

It is the south shore of Lake Tahoe that gets the most visitors, along with its neighbor Stateline, Nevada, home of the casinos. The north end is a bit more rustic. There you'll discover numerous ski areas branching off from the main road. The west side of the lake is one of our favorites—it's peaceful and less crowded, there are woods for exploring, and accommodations are often in cabins. The east shore is the least developed area around the lake.

GETTING THERE

If you decide to come by air, your best bet is to fly to the **Reno Cannon International Airport,** which is just less than an hour from North Lake Tahoe. Many of the commercial airlines have flights to and from this airport.

Renting a car is simple. The **Budget Rent-A-Car** rental desk is right in the terminal (☎ **702/785-2545,** or toll free **800/527-0700**). Also in the terminal, near the baggage-claim area, are **Alamo** (☎ toll free **800/327-9633**), **Avis** (☎ toll free **800/331-1212**), **Hertz** (☎ toll free **800/654-3131**), **Dollar** (☎ toll free **800/800-4000**), and **National** (☎ toll free **800/328-4567**).

Alpha Air is the only airline that flies in to the **Lake Tahoe Airport** (☎ **310/322-9882**). Rental cars, bus, and limousine service is handy. Call for the **Greyhound** bus schedule (☎ **800/231-2222**). **Amtrak** (☎ toll free **800/USA-RAIL, 800/872-7245** in California) stops at the Truckee rail station, about 15 miles north of Tahoe City.

If you're driving in from San Francisco, take I-80 to Sacramento. From there it depends on which part of the lake is your destination: take U.S. 50 to the south shore, or stay on I-80 to Calif. 89 for Tahoe City, or take Calif. 267 right to King's Beach.

The drive from Los Angeles also leads to Sacramento. Take I-5 all the way, then follow the directions above into Lake Tahoe. If you have the time, try a drive through parts of the Gold Country by leaving I-5 at Stockton and taking Calif. 88. This will eventually get you to South Lake Tahoe. You can take U.S. 395 to Gardnerville, Nevada, and head west on Nev. 207, which will also take you to the south shore.

Winter Driving Warning: Roads can be treacherous in winter, and some may even close in bad weather. Carry chains in winter. Call **Caltrans Highway information** when in doubt (☎ **916/445-7623,** or **445-1534**) for recorded information.

ORIENTATION

Lake Tahoe is a popular destination for Northern Californians. San Francisco is only 200 miles away; Tahoe lies a mere 100 miles northeast of Sacramento; and Reno, Nevada, is only 55 miles away. Even Yosemite National Park is only 100 miles away. In a funny stroke of geography, the Lake Tahoe area straddles the border between California and Nevada.

One way to get your bearings is to take the 72-mile drive around the lake. If you drive it without many stops, and if it's not a holiday weekend, it should take you no more than three hours. A better plan is to make the drive a day's activity. Grab some sandwiches, bring along a swimsuit, and stop at the various beaches and parks along the way.

Follow Calif. 28, also called North Lake Boulevard, from Kings Beach west to Tahoe City. Then catch Calif. 89 and continue along the west shore to South Lake Tahoe. Or start in Crystal Bay on the north shore on Nev. 28 and drive along the east shore, parallel to the lake, until you connect with U.S. 50, also called Lake Tahoe Boulevard, which will take you into South Lake Tahoe.

On the north is little Kings Beach, a funky town of pine trees, bakeries, ice cream and T-shirt shops, and inexpensive lodging. Many of the ski areas, such as Squaw Valley, Northstar, and Alpine Meadows, are in the vicinity. Moving west is Tahoe City, the "metropolitan" hub of the area. The west shore is glorious and has lots of places to stop along the way: state parks, beaches, and Emerald Bay. There are hiking trails and stables for horseback riding along this route, too.

South Lake Tahoe fills up with visitors who come to play on the beaches, rent bicycles, hike, take a cruise on the lake, or visit the casinos. There are alpine and Nordic ski areas closeby.

Winter skiing means lots of people staying at the ski lodges. If you don't mind the drive to the ski resort every day, you might find better prices lodging near the lake. The opposite happens in summer: everyone is staying near the lake, so you can get some good deals at the ski lodges. Fall and spring—exquisite times of the year to visit—also offer affordable lodging, although some of the attractions may be closing down. Horseback riding, hiking, or mountain biking in spring or fall when there's just a nip in the air is an exhilarating experience.

Nights can be chilly to cold year around, so come prepared. Winter days, while cold enough for snow, can actually be quite pleasant, even warm. Tahoe gets an average of about 300 days of sunshine annually, so you may even be able to remove those parkas in January.

There are excellent visitors bureaus to help you out. For the north shore, contact the **Tahoe North Visitors and Convention Bureau,** P.O. Box 5578, Tahoe City, CA 96145 (☎ **916/583-3494,** or toll free **800/824-6348**). Once in Tahoe City, you can pick up information from the North Lake Tahoe Chamber of Commerce, 245 North Lake Blvd. (☎ **916/581-6900**). In South Lake Tahoe, call the **South Lake Tahoe Visitors Authority,** 1156 Ski Run Blvd., South Lake Tahoe, CA 96150 (☎ **916/544-5050,** or toll free **800/288-2463**). In South Lake Tahoe, pick up information from the South Lake Chamber of Commerce, 3066 Lake Tahoe Blvd. (☎ **916/541-5255**).

Hint: Pick up those "throw-away" newspapers you find in various stores and hotel lobbies in town. Many of them have coupons discounting boat rides, equipment rentals, and sometimes even food.

GETTING AROUND

Most likely you will use a car when you visit Lake Tahoe. But you *can* get around South Lake Tahoe without a car. If you choose to stay in a casino, you'll find several across the street from each other in Stateline, Nevada. Some ski resorts provide **shuttle-bus service** to and from lodgings and other ski areas, and some casinos also offer shuttle service.

In winter and spring the *Tahoe Queen* (☎ **916/541-3363,** or toll free **800/23-TAHOE**), a Mississippi paddlewheeler, takes you to the north shore in about 2¹/₂ hours for bus transfer to Squaw Valley, Alpine Meadows, or Homewood. The 8am departure from the south shore offers a breakfast buffet. Adults pay $18 for the ride, an extra $9 for the buffet; children 11 and under pay $9 to ride, an extra $9 to eat.

If you stay on the west or north shore, you will definitely need your own transportation. Wherever you stay, nothing is that far away from something else. In winter, the north shore ski resorts are accessible from the south, usually within an hour.

WHAT TO SEE AND DO IN WINTER

Tahoe is a winter wonderland for skiers, both downhill and cross country, and for snowmobilers. The ski areas are so family oriented that you'll never have a problem finding a resort to fit your family's needs. Most of the resorts offer child care, children's ski schools, and special rates for kids. With good snow or up-to-date snow-making equipment, nary a day goes by that isn't perfect for shushing down a mountain.

There are snow-play areas just begging for sleds, stables offering old-fashioned sleigh rides, and ice rinks waiting for the next Dorothy Hamill. The scent of burning logs drifts from the fireplaces of cozy accommodations.

A Note on Parking: For information on permit parking while participating in snow recreation, contact **Sno-Park,** a service of the California Department of Parks and Recreation (☎ **916/653-8569**), or the U.S. Forest Service (☎ **916/573-2600**). Permits are required from November 1 through May 30.

Skiing

Usually, you can ski Tahoe from around mid-November to April, though sometimes the season runs as late as May. Because each ski area has different dates of operation, it's best to call the resort direct. The two visitors bureaus report on conditions, openings, and closings, and can make lodging reservations. For the South Lake Tahoe area, call toll free **800/288-2463;** for reservations in North Lake Tahoe, call toll free **800/824-6348.**

You can sometimes make lodging plans and ski-school and child-care arrangements and purchase lift tickets, with one phone call. Sometimes one area's lift tickets are interchangeable with other ski slopes, so be sure to inquire when you make your plans.

Warning: Don't be misled by the fact that it's winter—you need sunscreen just as you do in summer. Not only are you in high altitudes with the sun bouncing off the snow, but Tahoe's nearly year-round sunshine can be strong. Short of a broken leg, few things will ruin your ski vacation more than a bad burn.

NORTH SHORE SKI AREAS Located between Truckee and Kings Beach in North Lake Tahoe, **Northstar-at-Tahoe,** P.O. Box 129, Truckee, CA 96160 (☎ **916/562-1010** for ski information; or toll free **800/GO NORTH** for lodging information), is about a 45-minute drive from Reno. It has a variety of services and events for families in summer and winter (see "Ski Areas in Summer" in "What to

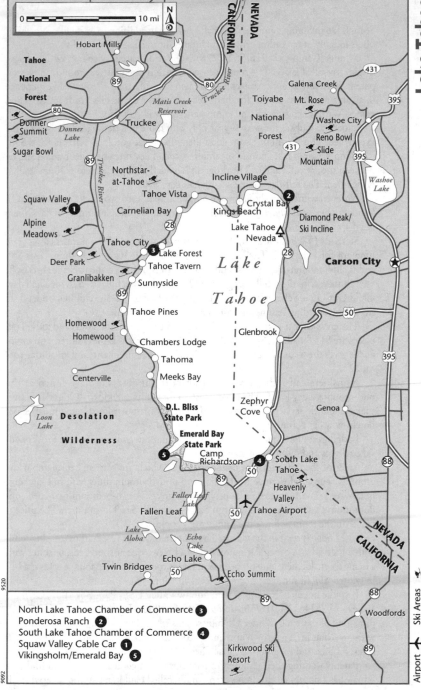

Lake Tahoe

Tahoe National Forest

Hobart Mills

Donner Summit
Sugar Bowl

Donner Lake

Truckee

Matis Creek Reservoir

Truckee River

Northstar-at-Tahoe

Squaw Valley ❶

Alpine Meadows

Tahoe Vista
Carnelian Bay

Tahoe City

Deer Park

Granlibakken

Lake Forest ❸
Tahoe Tavern
Sunnyside

Homewood
Homewood

Tahoe Pines

Chambers Lodge

Tahoma

Centerville

Meeks Bay

Loon Lake

Desolation

Wilderness

D.L. Bliss State Park

Emerald Bay State Park ❺
Camp Richardson

Fallen Leaf Lake

Fallen Leaf

Lake Aloha

Echo Lake

Twin Bridges

Echo Lake

Echo Summit

Galena Creek
Toiyabe
Mt. Rose
Washoe City
National
Reno Bowl
Forest
Slide Mountain

Incline Village

Crystal Bay ❷
Kings Beach
Lake Tahoe Nevada

Diamond Peak/Ski Incline

Washoe Lake

Carson City ★

Glenbrook

Zephyr Cove

Genoa

South Lake Tahoe ❹

Heavenly Valley
Tahoe Airport

NEVADA
CALIFORNIA

Woodfords

Kirkwood Ski Resort

0 ——————— 10 mi

NEVADA
CALIFORNIA

L a k e

T a h o e

| North Lake Tahoe Chamber of Commerce ❸ |
| Ponderosa Ranch ❷ |
| South Lake Tahoe Chamber of Commerce ❹ |
| Squaw Valley Cable Car ❶ |
| Vikingsholm/Emerald Bay ❺ |

Airport ✈   Ski Areas ⛷

9520

9092

See and Do in Spring, Summer, and Fall," below). In addition to its ski lifts, Northstar offers lodging, a recreation center, restaurants, horseback riding, and shops.

Minors' Camp (☎ **916/562-2278**) is the child-care service housed in a large, bright, toy-filled space. The state-licensed service is open all year round. In winter, parents have several options: ages 3–6 can join Ski Cubs for a 1¹/₂-hour ski experience in an area nearby set up just for them. The rest of the day is filled with activities and games. With lunch, snacks, and equipment, this will cost $51.

Super Ski Cubs is for 4- to 6-year-olds with more of a desire to ski or with some experience. This 2¹/₂-hour lesson takes them up on the gondola. This choice is $58.

Minors' Camp takes nonskiing children, too. They must be toilet trained and be between the ages of 2 and 6. The program is open daily from 8am to 4:30pm. Lunch is included. The full-day charge is $40; half day, $30.

Note: In winter you should make reservations at least two weeks in advance. On holidays, they're *absolutely* required. If you're staying a multiple number of days, there is a discount.

StarKids (☎ **916/562-2470**), which is part of the Ski School, offers a separate program for kids 5–12. The full-day program, from 9:30am to 3:30pm, costs $55 and includes lessons, lift tickets, and lunch; with equipment, the package costs $65.

Lift tickets for downhill skiing cost $42 for adults for a full day, $28 for a half day. Children 5–12 are charged $18 for a full day, $12 for a half day; children under 5 ski free. Snowboarding lessons and equipment are also available.

The cross-country ski area offers lessons and equipment for adults and kids. Trail passes are $15 for adults, $8 for children 5–12. First Tracks is the children's program, and it gives the 5- to 12-year-olds a 1¹/₂-hour lesson, equipment, and an all-day pass for $25.

Nonskiers can sightsee via the transport gondola and have lunch at the mid-mountain day lodge. The tickets cost $5 for adults and kids 5–12; under 5, free. Free ski-shuttle services are provided daily to Northstar from selected north-shore hotels, weather permitting.

Lodgings at Northstar are a variety of configurations and rates. Be sure to ask about ski packages and multi-night stay discounts.

Most of the 250 units are condominiums, which are scattered throughout the grounds. The condos range from studios to four-bedroom units with full kitchens, microwaves, and fireplaces or wood-burning stoves. A two-bedroom/two-bath con-dominium that can sleep six will run $265 in winter, $169 in summer. The price is based on the room and not the number of people.

The Lodge is right in the village. The units in the Lodge are studios (one big room with a hide-a-bed), or regular motel rooms with two queen-sized beds, or suites with a living room, kitchen, and loft bedroom. Lodge rooms that sleep four people are $149 in winter, $99 in summer; suites are $211 in winter, $125 in summer.

If you're not already familiar with **Squaw Valley USA,** P.O. Box 2007, Olympic Valley, CA 96146 (☎ **916/583-6985,** or toll free **800/545-4350;** fax 916/583-8184), just think of the 1960 Winter Olympics. This small ski area, which opened in 1949 with one chair lift, has grown and improved since those games, today boasting 4,200 acres, 33 lifts, and 22 grooming machines.

Parents wanting their children to participate in a good ski school will find that Squaw has a simplified children's ski program, called Children's World. Everything is under one roof, in the brown building at the base of Red Dog. Sign up the kids for lessons, get their equipment, and purchase your own lift tickets all in one place. Then hop on a nearby chair lift and take off for your day of skiing. No longer do you have to run in several directions to get the kids set up.

First the children (ages 7 to 12 in the all day program) are tested to determine their skill level. If they qualify for high intermediates, they are taken to the upper mountain for lessons on the adult beginner runs.

An instructional program for 3- to 6-year-olds includes activities on a nearby slope using pony tows. Children 7–12 years learn with the use of a new pulley system on more difficult terrain. Children's World is Squaw's licensed daycare facility. Children 6 months to 2 year olds get outdoor snow-play in a program called 10 Little Indians held at the Olympic Village Inn. The cost of the all-day ski program is $50 per child and includes lunch, snacks, lift tickets, lessons, and activities. It's $40 for each additional sibling. You can opt for a half day at $35, or a discount book of five days for $210. The charge is the same for infants and toddlers. The program is available on weekdays from 9am to 4pm and on weekends from 8am to 4pm.

An innovative new skill-specific ski-school program is available to adults and teens 13 and over. Videos shown at base areas and at the top and bottom of the gondola display in detail the different ski-school lessons being offered that day. The classes are geared to very specific needs and experience levels so that students won't be over- or underrated. For instance, there will be some sessions for beginners, one class advancing to wedge turns, wedge christies, and an introduction to parallel skiing. The video shows exactly what the class will be doing and which lift to take to each class. You decide what best suits your needs. When you reach the top of the lift, an instructor will come around to the station every 20 minutes or so to pick up the students for the next class. There are also two-hour workshops for more advanced skiers with specific needs such as skiing moguls or skiing powder. The regular classes and the two-hour workshops each cost $25 for the day, excluding lift tickets. Private lessons for adults and children are available at $50 per hour.

Squaw Valley is still one of the most affordable family ski destinations. Skiers under 12 years old, or 65 and older, can ski for $5 per day. Adult full-day lift tickets cost $43, or $28 for a half day. First-time skiers 13 and older can get a one-time free introductory lesson, lift ticket, and ski equipment rental, available every weekday, excluding holidays. Make arrangements for special ski and lodging packages through a central reservations number (☎ toll free **800/545-4350**). A shuttle takes you throughout the small valley.

Ski equipment rentals are available in the valley, and only during big holidays is there ever the possibility that the stores might be sold out. Snowboards are also for rent. You can ice skate year round at the outdoor rink in High Camp, at the top of the cable car. Cross-country skiing can be set up at the nearby Resort at Squaw Creek.

See "Ski Areas in Summer" in "What to See and Do in Spring, Summer, and Fall," below, for information on warm-weather activities.

Boreal, on I-80 (Donner Summit) at the Castle Peak exit (mailing address: Boreal/Soda Springs Ski Areas, P.O. Box 39, Truckee, CA 96160; ☎ **916/426-3666;** fax 916/426-3173), has a good children's ski program, too. Animal Crackers is the name of its ski school for kids 4–10. For a full-day program, from 8:30am to 3pm, the charge is $49 and includes lunch, lesson, lift ticket, and equipment rental. There are also $3^{1}/_{2}$-hour morning and afternoon programs for $37. These prices include lunch, lift tickets, and equipment. **Note:** This is not daycare—kids must participate in the ski lessons. They don't accept reservations so come early; call for registration information.

For anyone new to moguls and mountains, a first-time-skiers' package is available. There's also a Family Savings Book of coupons, giving you $101 in savings on lift tickets, equipment rentals, group ski workshops, and Animal Crackers. Midweek discounts are in force; night skiing runs to 9pm. Lodging packages are available in midweek, and children under 12 stay free. Adult lift tickets for a full day will cost $31, $24 for a half day; children 5–12 pay $10 for a full or half day. Children 4 and under ski free.

Just a few miles north of Tahoe City is **Alpine Meadows,** P.O. Box 5279, Tahoe City, CA 96145 (☎ **916/583-4232,** or toll free **800/441-4423**). Snow School is an active ski program for kids 4–6 with varying levels of experience. A full day of supervision, lessons, equipment, lunch, and snacks costs $57; ask about minimum height and weight requirements. Kids Ski Camp is for children 6–12. Two- and three-hour lessons are offered for all skill levels. Beginners are charged $48, which includes snacks, an all-day lift ticket, and equipment. Or they can take private lessons by appointment.

Family Pak is a package of lift tickets for the entire family, plus a three-hour ski school lesson for children 6–12. The cost for two parents and two children would be $122 (without the package you'd pay $212). The package is at different rates available for all combinations of families. Adult lift tickets cost $42 for a full day, $29 for a half day. Children 7–12 pay $16; kids 6 and under pay $6.

You'll find **Tahoe Donner,** 11509 Northwoods Blvd., Truckee, CA 96161 (☎ **916/587-9444**), two miles west of Truckee, off Donner Pass Road. Tahoe Donner emphasizes its children's ski programs and considers itself the learn-to-ski area in the Tahoe basin. Its Snowflakes Ski School is designed for ages 3–6 who learn skiing skills through both indoor and on-snow activities. Prices include lift, instruction and activities, ski equipment rental and a snack. There are two half-day sessions, each costing $39. A full day, 9am to noon and 1pm to 4, costs $55. The Learn to Ski program for kids 7 years old and older is a group lesson. A lift ticket, lesson, and rental equipment are included in the $22 price.

Standard lift tickets are $26 adults for a full day, $15 half day. Children over age 6 pay $12 full day, $6 half day. Children 6 and under and seniors over 70 ski free.

Tiny Tracks Snow School gives cross-country ski lessons to children ages 5–9 on weekends and holidays. No reservations are needed. Adults can take lessons daily. Ask about lesson prices. Tahoe Donner also offers night skiing on 2.5km of lighted trails. The all-day trail pass is $15 for adults, $9 for children. There are half-day, twilight, and night rates, as well.

There are lodges and plenty of food available in the resort area.

SOUTH SHORE SKI AREAS   About 35 minutes south of Lake Tahoe is the **Kirkwood Ski & Summer Resort,** P.O. Box 1, Kirkwood, CA 95646 (☎ **209/258-6000** for general information, toll free **800/967-7500** for reservations, **209/258-3000** for snow information). Kirkwood has a long ski season, lasting from mid-November into May, because of its high base elevation—in fact, it's the highest in Northern California. Over the 2,000 acres of terrain, there are six triple-chair lifts, four double-chair lifts, and one surface lift. There are plenty of runs for advanced, intermediate, and beginner skiers. The longest run is $2^{1}/_{2}$ miles.

Kirkwood has maintained a good reputation as a family ski resort. Its Mighty Mountain ski school program offers lessons to children 4–12 at all levels of expertise. A children-only lift and enlarged terrain garden help keep things nice and safe. The Mighty Mountain Special is an all-day program, including lessons, lunch, all-day equipment rental, and a small gift, for $50. The half-day package goes for $40. Children can take 90-minute private lessons for $55. "Super Skiers" ages 8–12 who can ski the upper terrain can take a half-day lesson for $15.

Kids 3–6 (out of diapers) will be taken care of in the licensed daycare center. The all-day program, including lunch, runs $35; a half day with lunch, $25. By the hour, with a two-hour minimum, it costs $5, and lunch is another $5.

Standard one-day lift tickets cost adults $39 for a full day, $28 for a half day; children 6–12 pay $5; youths 13–22 pay $29; seniors 60 and up are charged $19; kids under 6 ski free. There are adult and children beginner tickets available on two chair lifts: $22 for adults, $12 for children. Be sure to ask about multiday discounts and the Avid Skier Card. There's also an adult ski school, and equipment rentals are available for adults and children.

Cross-country skiing is big here, too. In addition to standard trail skiing, Kirkwood offers cross-country skating. These skis have no scales on the bottom, making them faster than diagonal stride skis. A family package enables everyone to learn: a trail pass, equipment rental, and lesson costs $30. Junior-size gear is available to fit most kids over 9 years old. Trail passes cost adults $13 for a full day, $10 for a half day. Seniors pay $10 and $8; children 6–12 are charged $5 for a whole day, $3 for a half; kids under 6 ski free. Lessons and equipment are available for adults and children.

You can reserve lodging at Kirkwood in condominiums just steps from the lifts. Some have ski-in/ski-out convenience. When you call for reservations, be sure to ask about the ski packages. A medical center, general store, ski shuttle, and lots of restaurants are all within the ski resort area. The central reservations phone number above can book lodging, lift tickets, lessons, and space in the children's school all in one phone call—what a relief not to have to call a dozen different numbers!

Heavenly, at the corner of Wildwood Ave. and Saddle Rd., South Lake Tahoe (mailing address: P.O. Box 2180, Stateline, NV 89449; ☎ **702/586-7000,** or **916/541-SKII** or **702/586-7000** for ski conditions), is the other south-shore ski area. This full-service ski area, which straddles California and Nevada, has 24 lifts plus three high-speed quads, double and triple chairs, and 79 runs. With a mountain descent over five miles long, it has the longest vertical drop in the basin.

The Ski Explorers program services children 4–12. The full-day session includes lessons, snow play, lift tickets, lunch, equipment rental, and snacks for $58; a half-day session costs $38.

There are also a variety of adult programs, from introductory lessons, daily specials, mini-clinics, and private lessons to snowboard lessons. Rental equipment and repair are available in several locations in the ski area.

Adults pay $42 for full-day lift tickets, $27 for half-day tickets. Children 13 to 15 are charged $30 for a full day, $25 for a half day. Kids 6–12 pay $18 and $12, while children 2–5 ski free. Ask about three- to seven-consecutive-day discounts. If you live in Northern California, check to see if discount promotions with local supermarkets are in effect. Heavenly also has special rates for interchangeable lift tickets.

Heavenly's travel service can arrange lodging, airfare, car rentals, lift tickets, ski lessons, and equipment rentals. Call toll free **800/2-HEAVEN.**

CROSS-COUNTRY SKIING   Lakeview Cross-Country Ski Area (☎ **916/ 583-9353**) is a great place to try cross-country skiing if you've never experienced it. The trails are located just east of Tahoe City, off Calif. 28, six miles west of Kings Beach. Look for the FABIAN WAY sign, which is hard to spot if you're going east, and follow the ski signs to Country Club Road. Some folks who have tried cross-country for the first time never go back to the expense of downhill skiing. This is a rigorous sport, however, but kids 7 and older should do okay. Younger children can often handle very short runs.

At Lakeview there are 36 miles of machine-groomed trails through beautiful countryside: it's ideal for beginners. The Ski School is appropriate for all ages and offers 1$\frac{1}{2}$-hour lessons at 10:30am and 1pm. Kids 3–5 are charged $12; those 5–10, $14. Adult trail fees are $14 for a full day, $11 for a half day. Kids 7–12 pay $5 for a full day, $5 for a half day; juniors 13–17 pay $11 and $8; kids 6 and under are free. Equipment rental is available. Lakeview is open daily, 8am to 6pm, or until dusk.

SKI RENTALS   There are numerous places on each side of the lake from which to rent equipment, in addition to renting from the ski resorts themselves. Here are a few: **Dave's Ski Shops,** 620 N. Lake Blvd., Tahoe City (☎ **916/583-6415**), and 10200 Commercial Row, Truckee (☎ **916/582-0900**), rent alpine and cross-country skis, snowboards, and clothing. Open till May, weekdays from 7:45am to 8pm, to midnight on Friday and Saturday. Ask about multiple-day discounts. **The Ski Renter** can be found at 1093 Ski Run Blvd., South Lake Tahoe (☎ **916/544-2100**), and is open daily from 7:30am to 7:30pm. A basic ski rental package will cost you $17. **Rainbow Mountain Premium Ski Rentals,** 1133 Ski Run Blvd. (☎ **916/541-7470**), in South Lake Tahoe, on the way to Heavenly Valley, rents downhill, snow boarding, and cross-country equipment and clothing for kids and adults. Open daily during ski season from 7:30am to 9pm.

Ice Skating

You may remember seeing a Disney special on television where skaters like Scott Hamilton and Peggy Fleming were skating on top of a mountain. That mountain was in Squaw Valley at the incredible **Olympic Ice Pavilion** (☎ **916/583-6985,** or toll free **800/545-4350;** fax 916/583-8184), the highest artificial ice rink in the world with a magnificent view of Lake Tahoe. The ride up on the cable car, with skating included, is $17 year-round; skate rentals are free. Ice skating lessons are available all year. There are less expensive ride-skate tickets beginning at 5pm: adults $9, kids $6.

Sleigh Rides

No matter where you're from, nothing evokes more nostalgia than the idea of bundling up for a winter ride through a meadow in a horse-drawn sleigh.

Contact **Camp Richardson Corral,** just west of South Lake Tahoe on Emerald Bay Road (Calif. 89) (mailing address: P.O. Box 8335, South Lake Tahoe, CA 96158; ☎ **916/541-3113**), for reservations for the 45-minute ride. It costs $10 for anyone age 4 and older; kids 3 and under ride free; rides are offered daily in winter (beginning December 15—as long as there is snow). Evening sleigh rides with dinner cost $25 for adults, $15 for kids ages 4–8; free for kids 3 and under. Call for reservations.

Borge Sleigh Rides, just next to Caesars Tahoe in Stateline (☎ **702/588-2953**), offers 35-minute rides. These cost $20 for two adults, $5 for children under 12.

Northstar Stables, at Northstar-at-Tahoe, off Calif. 267 between Kings Beach and Truckee (☎ **916/562-1230**) gives 30-minute sleigh rides from 3 to 7pm. Adults pay $12; children under 12 are free. You can also go winter horseback riding at Northstar. The 45-minute trail rides cost $15; 15-minute pony rides are $5.

Snowmobiling and Snow-Play

Snowmobiling Unlimited, on Calif. 267 (mailing address: P.O. Box 1591, Tahoe City, CA 96145) (☎ **916/583-5858**), gives you two options: they offer a personalized guided wilderness tour on the north shore; or you can take the kids for a ride on a circular track in the North Tahoe Regional Park for as short as a half hour. This option is particularly good for children who get cold quickly, or if you have more children than adults. For one to two people on a one-hour ride, the rate is $40 and $60; $60 and $90 for a $1^1/_2$-hour ride. The minimum driving age is 16, with prior experience. Children under 5 with an adult go free. Make reservations. Hours are 8am to 5pm daily in winter.

Snowmobiling Unlimited also rents sleds for $5 per half day to use at **North Tahoe Regional Park,** just off Calif. 28 on National Avenue at the Post Office in Tahoe Vista. There's no fee to use this ideal family winter snow-play area, which has sledding hills, cross-country ski trails, bathrooms, telephones, and playground equipment.

Also contact **Zephyr Cove Snowmobile Center,** 760 U.S. 50, Zephyr Cove, NV 89449 (☎ **702/588-3833**), for information on snowmobile rentals.

WHAT TO SEE AND DO IN SPRING, SUMMER, AND FALL

Each season offers plenty of activities all around the lake. Summer is, of course, one of the most attractive times for family visits. Sometimes the ski season extends itself into spring. Fall is the least crowded time for a visit.

Ski Areas in Summer

Particularly popular with families in summer is **Northstar-at-Tahoe** (mailing address: P.O. Box 129, Truckee, CA 96160) (☎ **916/562-1010**). The list of summer activities goes on and on.

Minors' Camp is the licensed child-care facility at Northstar, open July to Labor Day, Monday through Saturday from 9am to 5pm. You can register the children at a cost of $4 per hour with a two-hour minimum. An additional $3.50 will buy lunch. Occasional weekly outings require an additional charge. Kids must be toilet trained and between ages 2 and 10. The large facility has a ratio of about one adult to every six kids.

Summer activities for the kids might include a creek walk and picnic, gold panning, a trip to Donner State Park and a picnic, a wildflower hike, a fossil hunt, and a visit to the Truckee firehouse. There are big play areas, records, TV, games, toys for all ages, and mats for resting. A large, fenced-in outdoor playground is filled with climbing and swinging equipment.

Summer also means horseback riding at Northstar Stables (☎ **916/562-1230**); children must be age 7 or older to ride; but there are pony rides and lessons in the arena for the little tots: rides cost $5 for 15 minutes; lessons, $20 for 45 minutes. Trail rides with a guide leave on the hour. A 45-minute ride will cost you $15; a $1^1/_2$-hour ride, $28. Half-day and all-day rides run $50 and $100.

An Adventure Challenge course (☎ **916/562-2285**) has been set up at Northstar. We watched families involve themselves in this unique sport which challenges a group to work with cooperation and trust in each other. The ropes and cables are set up in a portion of the pine forest. Children must be at least 10 to participate. The course is open Thursday through Sunday 11am to 4:30pm. Rates run $40 for adults; children 10–17 are charged $30.

Northstar's Mountain Bike Park (☎ **916/562-2248**) is accessible by chair lift for those who don't want to pedal up. Hikers can take the lift, too. The lift runs weekends from Memorial Day weekend to mid-June, and daily from mid-June to mid-September, from 9:30am to 4pm. Adults pay $17; children 12 and under, $13. Mountain bikes can be rented in the village for the whole family. Adult bikes go for

$25 for four hours or less, to $30 for the day. Junior bikes cost $18 and $24, while one-speed children's bikes rent for $10 and $15.

Northstar's 18-hole golf course (☎ 916/562-2490) is open May through October. Also ask about the Junior Golf Clinics for 8- to 15-year-old golfers.

A wonderful recreation center on the property is *the* place to be in summer, but you can use it only if you're staying at Northstar. There's an appealing outdoor junior Olympic swimming pool staffed with lifeguards, a sand-filled tot playground, games room, exercise facilities, saunas, two spas (one for adults only), a snack bar, and all sorts of activities announced daily by the recreation director. There are ten tennis courts, too.

Restaurants are found in the village: The Village Food Company for light food and yummy ice cream; and Timbercreek Restaurant, serving a whole gamut of selections and welcoming children with a large children's menu priced from $2 to $3.50.

If you just want to rest your bones a bit, come for the Sunday-afternoon outdoor jazz programs held in the village. A free shuttle runs throughout the Northstar property; give them a call and they'll come to get you.

Squaw Valley USA (mailing address: P.O. Box 2007, Olympic Valley, CA 96146) (☎ **916/583-6985,** or toll free **800/545-4350;** fax 916/583-8184) has recently expanded its summer offerings. Now visitors can do everything from wall climbing to mountain biking.

You'll know you've found the climbing wall when you enter the cable-car building and spot adults and children attempting the challenge of this very tall, difficult wall. The charge for two hours of climbing is $7 for adults, $10 for children under 14. Shoe rentals are $4.

You might simply want to take the cable-car ride 2,000 feet up to High Camp Bath and Tennis Club for lunch and a breathtaking view of Lake Tahoe. Or you might want to spend more time up there. There are plenty of restaurants and a beautiful bar at the top. The cable-car ride alone, all year, costs $12 for adults, $5 for children 12 and under. Each sports facility at High Camp charges a separate fee, but you can purchase a package. Swimming in the Lagoon and Spa is $17 with the cable car; ice skating on the outdoor rink overlooking the valley and Lake Tahoe is $17 with the cable car. Skate rentals are free, and ice-skating lessons are available all year. Beginning at 5pm, adults can ride the cable car and skate for $9, kids are $6.

The sand volleyball courts are free (you can rent volleyballs). To use the vast mountain bike trails costs $15, which includes a one-way pass on the cable car (most people take it up and ride the bikes down); $25 will give you unlimited rides and biking all day. The bike rentals themselves, available at the base, cost $20 for a full day, $15 for a half day. The price is the same for children. Required helmets cost $5.

You can even go horseback riding at the top. Fees are $17 for a guided 45-minute ride. Children must be at least 7 years old. The stables (☎ 916/583-RIDE) are open from May through mid-September at High Camp. Or you can choose to ride in the valley, where you'll get a one-hour ride for $17.

A popular fun family activity is hiking from the trailhead behind the Olympic Village Inn to Shirley Lake, where you can swim, then hike up to High Camp and take the cable car down. The four-mile hike to the lake takes approximately two hours, and is a fairly comfortable walk with the kids. There are streams along the way for wading and forests for exploring.

Tennis is played all year on one of six courts. Arrange for a court by calling **916/583-6300.** There are even two radiant-heated courts for winter play.

Heavenly ski area operates a tram in summer that travels a mile up. From May to September it leaves every 15 minutes from 10am to 9pm (on Sunday beginning at 9am). In addition to the hiking at the top (see "Hiking," below), lunch and dinner are served at Monument Peak restaurant every day; Sunday brunch is family time at the restaurant. The brunch is offered summers only from 10am to 2pm. Adults pay $19.95, while kids are charged $6.95. Call **916/541-1330**, ext. 6347, for reservations.

Beaches, Parks, and Picnic Areas

NORTH SHORE   If you have questions about beaches or parks on the north shore, give a call to the **North Tahoe Recreation and Parks** office, 8318 N. Lake Blvd., Kings Beach (☎ **916/546-7248**).

Sand Harbor (☎ **702/831-0494**) is considered the nicest, and possibly the most popular, beach in the area. It's located in Nevada State Park, not far from Crystal Bay. With a beach patrol on duty from Memorial Day to Labor Day, a pristine beach, and comfortable picnic spots, Sand Harbor is a great family destination. There's also a natural sand amphitheater at Sand Harbor used for the annual Shakespeare Festival and numerous music festivals. Note that there is limited parking at this beach, so get there early on summer weekends. There is a $5 fee per car.

The beach at **Kings Beach Recreation Area** (☎ **916/546-7248**) is not beautiful, but it's big. This family beach has restrooms and water sports, a playground, and picnic tables. The parking charge is $5 for the day; the beach itself is free. **Lakeside Boat & Sail** (☎ **916/546-5889**) is the official rental concessionaire.

SOUTH SHORE   About three miles from the junction of U.S. 50 and Calif. 89 is **El Dorado Beach,** Lakeview Avenue, the big beach on the south shore. You'll find picnic tables and barbecue pits. **Regan Beach** is just nearby. In addition to picnic facilities, there's a concession stand, playground, and volleyball nets. You'll swim in relative seclusion at **Pope, Baldwin** (☎ **916/544-5994**), and **Tallac Historic Site Beaches** (☎ **916/573-2674**), along the south shore off Calif. 89. There are picnic tables, restrooms, and a parking lot. There's a fee of $3 to enter Pope or Baldwin; Tallac is free.

WEST SHORE   The **D. L. Bliss State Park** (call **916/525-7277** for directions) is a beautiful park with a swimming beach and a hiking trail that leads to Emerald Bay. The Balancing Nature trail is a half-mile long and is perfect for young children. There are picnic areas and campsites. The park's day-use fee is $5 per car. Parking is limited.

Also consider the beaches at **Sugar Pine Point State Park** (see "Hiking," below).

Water-Sports Equipment Rentals and Lessons

There is a plethora of little kiosks, marinas, and stores at which to find equipment rentals and lessons. Here are some:

NORTH LAKE TAHOE   **Tahoe Boat Rentals** (☎ **916/583-3492**) rents speedboats and pontoons. In Tahoe City, **Tahoe Water Adventures** (☎ **916/583-3225**) will rent jet skis and canoes. The jet skis rent for $60–$75 per hour, or $35–$45 per half hour. The minimum age to ski solo is 12.

Goldcrest Resort Water Ski School, in the Goldcrest Motel, 8194 N. Lake Blvd., Kings Beach (☎ **916/546-7412**), gives in-water instruction and will take children as young as 4. Wet suits are supplied. Make reservations; call for current prices.

SOUTH LAKE TAHOE   At **Lakeview Sports,** 3131 U.S. 50, across from El Dorado Campground on the beach side (☎ **916/544-8888** or **541-8405**), you can rent jet skis, mountain bikes, and in-line skates. **Action Watersports** can be found on the beach right next to the Hyatt Hotel (☎ **702/831-4FUN**). They rent jet skis, pedal boats, and canoes, and will take you waterskiing and parasailing.

ZEPHYR COVE   Wet 'n Wild, Zephyr Cove Marina, four miles from Stateline on U.S. 50 (☎ **702/588-3530**), offers jet skis and parasailing (minimum 70 pounds). Call for prices and reservations.

Bicycling

Every other car you see in Lake Tahoe nowadays has a bicycle rack attached to it. There are several trails in the area, some right along the lake, others at the top of the mountains. In addition to the areas mentioned below, see **Sugar Pine Point State Park** in "Hiking," below. **Squaw Valley** and **Northstar-at-Tahoe** also have mountain bike trails you can access via cable car (see "Ski Areas in Summer," above, for information). For more information on bicycling in the area, call the **Tahoe Area Mountain Bicycling Association** (☎ **916/541-7505**).

BICYCLE RENTALS IN SOUTH LAKE TAHOE   With lots of information on trails and anything else to do with bicycling, **Sierra Cycle Works,** 3430 U.S. 50 (☎ **916/541-7505**), rents mountain bikes for adults and children. Open in summer, daily from 10am to 6pm. You can also call **Lakeview Sports,** 3131 U.S. 50, across from the El Dorado Campground on the beach side (☎ **916/544-8888** or **541-8405**), for mountain bike rentals. **Anderson's,** at Calif. 89 and 13th Street, on the lake side (☎ **916/541-0500**), rents bicycles. **Tahoe Cyclery,** 3552 Lake Tahoe Blvd. (☎ **916/541-2726**), also rents bikes for adults and children.

BICYCLE RENTALS IN NORTH LAKE TAHOE   At **Olympic Bike Shop,** 620 N. Lake Blvd. (☎ **916/581-2500**), you can rent bikes or have your own serviced or repaired.

Boat Trips

The family can hop on the *Tahoe Queen,* 970 Ski Run Blvd., at Ski Run Marina, South Lake Tahoe (P.O. Box 14292, South Lake Tahoe, CA 96151; ☎ **916/541-3364,** or toll free **800/23-TAHOE**), for a fun lunch or dinner cruise on a Mississippi paddlewheeler. In summer the boat sails on a 2¹/₂-hour cruise which includes a good look at Emerald Bay. In winter and spring it offers a limited number of lake cruises, and acts as a shuttle service to bus connections on either shore. There is food service and a bar on-board. Reservations on all cruises are highly recommended.

Summer cruises, from June through September, leave every day at 11am, 1:30pm, and 3:55pm. The evening dinner cruise leaves at 7pm. We recommend the daytime cruise for families with young children. Fares are $14 for adults, $5 for children 11 and under. The dinner-dance cruise costs $18 for adults and $9 for children 11 and under. Dinner is an extra $18–$20 per person. In spring and winter, daily cruises of Emerald Bay leave at 12:30pm and 3pm, and the dinner cruise leaves at 6:30pm. Fares are the same as in summer. The ski shuttle leaves Monday through Friday at 8am from the south shore with a buffet breakfast.

North Tahoe Cruises (☎ **916/583-0141,** or toll free **800/218-2464**) offers tours along the north and west shores and Emerald Bay. The *Tahoe Gal* departs from the Lighthouse Marine, 850 N. Lake Blvd. in Tahoe City (behind the Safeway store), daily from June to September. Adults pay $16, children ages 3–12 are charged $6; free for kids under 3. Also inquire about breakfast and dinner cruises.

From Zephyr Cove Pier, you can board a glass-bottom boat, the **Woodwind** (P.O. Box 1375, Zephyr Cove, NV 89448; ☎ **702/588-3000**). The 30-passenger sailboat, with full bar and restrooms, runs cruises from May to October, four times a day between 11:30am and 4pm. The adult fare is $14; children under 12, $7.

At nearby Zephyr Cove Resort, about four miles north of Stateline on Highway 50 (mailing address: P.O. Box 1667, Zephyr Cove, NV 89448), you can hop on the **M.S. Dixie II** for a tour of Emerald Bay. These tours are offered daily, year-round. One of the best cruises for families is the Historic Glenbrook breakfast cruise, offered seasonally. The 1¹/₂ hour tour offers a buffet breakfast and is accompanied by a historian. We recommend that you take the kids on either the Emerald Bay Sightseeing cruise, which has snack-bar service, or on the Emerald Bay Dinner Cruise, but not on the dinner-dance cruise. Fares for the sightseeing cruise are $14 for adults, $5 for children 3–11, free for kids 2 and under. The breakfast tour costs $16.50 for adults, $8 for children and includes the breakfast. The seasonal Dinner Cruise is $24 for adults, $10 for kids, and there is a children's menu. Reservations are strongly recommended on all the cruises.

Hiking

There are so many places to hike in the Lake Tahoe area: Some might be just outside your motel door, others at the top of the mountain. In addition to the hiking trails suggested below, see **D. L. Bliss State Park** in "Beaches, Parks, and Picnic Areas," above. Wherever you take the family to hike, be sure to take along water and snacks, and to layer your clothing in case of abrupt changes in temperature.

Currently, 78 miles of the new 150-mile **Tahoe Rim Trail** (☎ **916/577-0676**), the loop around the top of the ridge that rings the basin has been completed. This has been a community effort to enable hikers to take advantage of the pristine beauty of the wilderness. At this writing, 50 miles of the Pacific Crest Trail are in place. There are currently six major trailheads; call the number above for directions. Remember that the altitude of the trails ranges from 7,000 to 8,500 feet, and the grade is 10%. This means that this probably isn't the hike to take with infants and toddlers, or with anyone who might be altitude sensitive. For those who do want to hike at that altitude, you might consider first taking short hikes with the kids to see how they do.

If you take the tram at the Heavenly ski area, you'll come to **Tahoe Vista Trail,** which has advanced and beginner hiking trails. That trail crests at 9,200 feet.

Emerald Bay (☎ **916/541-3030**) is one of the area's most beautiful sights. You can see it via a boat ride on the *Tahoe Queen* or by driving to Eagle Falls or Inspiration Point off Calif. 89. The hike to Eagle Falls is over rocks, but the view is splendiferous! There's also a main trail which leads to the lakeshore and the Vikingsholm Castle on a more direct route. Parents with infants and toddlers beware—there's no problem taking this trail down, but *up* is another story! The **Vikingsholm Castle,** a summer home built in the Scandinavia Style, can be toured from mid-June to Labor Day, daily from 10am to 4pm. The cost is $2 for adults, $1 for children. Once you reach the shore, there are numerous other trails to hike. You'll also find picnic spots and fishing.

Novice hikers, or folks with small children, will appreciate the nature trails from the **Lake Tahoe Visitor Center** at Taylor Creek, between Fallen Leaf Lake and Lake Tahoe (☎ **916/573-2674**). The visitor center, which is open summer only, daily from 8am to 5pm (weekends only, May 31 to June 21), is the place to begin. Rainbow Trail is the most popular and where you'll discover an underwater look at Taylor Creek from the safety of a glass-covered underground "stream profile chamber." You'll also find out about the **Tallac Historical Site,** one of the historic Tahoe sites and home to the Valhalla Summer Arts Music Festival. Call for information on days of operation and day-use fees.

There are 11 miles of hiking trails in **Sugar Pine Point State Park,** one mile north of Meeks Bay off Calif. 89 (☎ **916/525-7982**). Take along your swimsuit and fishing pole because there's also two miles of beaches. There are plenty of picnic areas, and 100 family campsites available by reservation through MISTIX (☎ toll free **800/444-7275**). The visitor center is the former Ehrman Mansion, a turn-of-the-century former private residence which you might recognize from *Godfather II.* In addition to hiking trails, there are designated trails for mountain biking; in winter, you can use five miles of cross-country ski trails. A Junior Ranger program takes place for kids 6 to 12 daily in summer starting July 1. The day-use fee is $5 per car.

Horseback Riding

We outlined the offerings of **Northstar Stables** (☎ **916/562-1230**) above in "Ski Areas in Summer," above, and "Sleigh Rides" in "What to See and Do in Winter," above. You can also find out about horseback riding at **Squaw Valley** in "Ski Areas in Summer," above.

Guides from **Zephyr Cove Stables,** U.S. 50, Zephyr Cove (across from the **M. S. Dixie II** (☎ **702/588-5664**), will lead you through forest lands on horseback. They offer one- and two-hour rides, and breakfast, lunch, and dinner rides by reservation. Rides, adults' or kids', cost $18 for one hour, $35 for two. Children must be at least 7 years old. Weight maximum is 225 pounds. Open daily 9am to 5pm in summer, 10am to 4pm in spring and fall.

Janey has never forgotten her first horseback riding experience at **Camp Richardson Corral,** along Calif. 89 (Emerald Bay Road) on the south shore (☎ **916/541-3113**); call for directions. Guided tours and extended pack trips are available. Minimum age is 6. The rate is $18 per hour for adults and children. Open June 1 through the end of October, daily from 8am to 5pm. Make reservations one day in advance. Also see "Sleigh Rides" in "What to See and Do in Winter," above.

In S. Lake Tahoe on Hwy. 50, a quarter mile south of the airport, there's horseback riding with or without a guide at **Sunset Ranch** (☎ **916/541-9001**). Hourly rides are given year round. Kids must be at least 5 to ride their own horse; those under 5 can ride double (we don't recommend this). Open daily from 8:30am to 6pm, in winter until dusk. You don't need reservations. The adult rate is $20 for the first hour, $15 for each additional hour, plus a $10 deposit. Children 12 and under pay $15 for the first hour, $10 for every hour thereafter.

Festivals, Games, and Rides

There's more than meets the eye at the **Ponderosa Ranch,** on Calif. 28 just south of Incline Village (☎ **702/831-0691**), where the original *Bonanza* TV series was filmed. Some of you may be too young to remember when the first episode of the series was shown in 1959. In its 13 years on the air it was seen in 86 countries.

Once you get beyond the souvenir shops, the western-themed park gets interesting. There are all sorts of carriages and buggies, ranch implements, and memorabilia from the show on display. We watched a friendly blacksmith turn a piece of iron into a cooking implement. And although he wasn't shoeing a horse, our kids thought it was fascinating. On the way to the ranch house where so much of the show was filmed, there's a petting farm youngsters will enjoy, and Hoss's Mystery Mine, a gravity-defying attraction, not for the faint of heart. Free tours are given of the Cartwrights' ranch house.

Pony rides and a small playground for the children can be found at the bottom of the hill, and there are plenty of food concessions. The favorite activity for children is the all-you-can-eat breakfast hayride to the upper range, offered in summer; call for hours. The charge is $10.50 for adults and includes admission and an all-day stay. Children 5–11 are charged $7.50, and kids under 5, $2.

Regular admission is $8.50 for adults, $5.50 for kids 5–11, and free for kids under 5. Strollers and wheelchairs are provided at the gate. It's a bit of a walk up the hills; those needing assistance are taken up and down in an open-air shuttle. The park is open in summer only.

There are two locations for **Magic Carpet Golf Courses:** in Carnelian Bay, at 5167 N. Lake Blvd. (☎ **916/546-4279**), and in South Lake Tahoe at 2455 Lake Tahoe Blvd. (☎ **916/541-3787**). Weather permitting, they're open in summer, daily from 10am to 10pm; the rest of the year, hours vary. Before 6pm, the 19-hole course will cost you $4; 28 holes, $5.50. After 6, it goes up 50¢.

In little Kings Beach there's **Kings Beach Mini-Golf** (☎ **916/546-3196**), set among the tall pine trees on N. Lake Blvd. just next to the Kentucky Fried Chicken store. From mid-May to mid-September, it opens daily at 10am and the last game can be played at 10:30pm. It will cost you $3 for your first game, $2 for the second.

There's no reason you can't have a little culture with your vacation. July and August signal annual cultural arts festivals. Go with the kids, or get a babysitter and make it Mom and Dad's special night out. In North Lake Tahoe, beautiful Sand Harbor Beach is the site of the annual **Music and Shakespeare at Sand Harbor Festival** in the park's natural amphitheater. Contact the North Tahoe Fine Arts Council (P.O. Box 265, Homewood, CA 96141; ☎ **916/583-9048**) for information and schedules. Also contact the council for information about the **Music at Sand Harbor Festival,** usually held in July.

Lake Tahoe Summer Music Festival, which usually runs July through mid-August, hosts performances at various locations around the lake. A family night brings out picnickers who watch sights such as Daffy Duck and Bugs Bunny conducting a 60-piece orchestra. Contact **916/583-3101** for this year's schedule of events.

For those of you who may be interested, you'll find **video arcades** at Caesars, Harvey's, and Harrah's resorts, all open 24 hours with machines that will definitely tempt your youngsters. The last time we surveyed the scene, we couldn't tell who was having the most fun—the kids or their parents. For more information on Harrah's arcade, see "Where to Stay" later in this chapter.

If there are a few extra dollars burning a hole in your pocket, call **Mountain High Balloons** (☎ **916/587-6922**). We don't recommend that you take children under 5 on a hot-air balloon. **Cal-Vada Aircraft Seaplane Rides** in Homewood (☎ **916/525-7143**) takes scenic flights over the area.

Have you heard of the Donner family who perished in the terrible winter of 1846? There is a museum in memorial to the party at **Donner Memorial State Park,** on I-80 in Truckee (☎ **916/582-7892**). The park itself is a well-used camping, hiking, fishing, and winter Nordic-skiing spot. Admission to the museum is $2 for adults, $1 for kids 6–12, free for kids under 6. It's open Memorial Day to Labor Day, daily from 10am to 5pm, and the rest of the year, daily from 10am to 4pm; closed major holidays. The day-use fee for the park itself is $5. Camping reservations can be made through MISTIX (☎ toll free **800/444-7275**).

WHERE TO STAY

The visitors bureaus of both North and South Lake Tahoe offer free reservations information and services. Contact the **Tahoe North Visitors and Convention Bureau,** P.O. Box 5578, Tahoe City, CA 96145 (☎ **916/583-3494,** or toll free **800/824-6348**). For information and reservations on the south shore, call the **South Lake Tahoe Visitors Authority,** 1156 Ski Run Blvd. South Lake Tahoe, CA 96150 (☎ **916/544-5050,** or toll free **800/288-2463**).

Condominium and house rentals are popular lodging options in Tahoe. There are too many companies that arrange these rentals to list here. Ask the visitors bureaus about their recommendations for this kind of accommodation.

South Lake Tahoe

Embassy Suites, 4130 Lake Tahoe Blvd., South Lake Tahoe, CA 96150 (☎ **916/544-5400,** or toll free **800/EMBASSY;** fax 916/544-4900), just at the border of California and Nevada, is one of this chain's biggest properties with 400 suites. The basic suite concept is the same, but these are possibly the most spacious of the Embassy Suites we have seen. And like many of the other locations in the chain, this one is family oriented. The big lobby is a perfect place for curious kids to explore. The indoor pool is enclosed and is open from 7am to midnight (adults only after 10pm). In summer, you can rent bikes, and in winter, skis, in the sports shop.

Full breakfasts and afternoon drinks and snacks come with the price of your room. You can, however, order from room service as well. There are appropriate children's selections for your youngsters. They'll even send up a frozen microwavable dinner to prepare in your in-room microwave. The hotel restaurants include Pasquale's for pizza, opening at 11am; and Zackary's, open for lunch from 11am to 2pm and dinner from 5pm to 2am. The hotel's restaurants have children's items on all menus.

You may be aware by now that all Embassy Suites locations have thoughtfully come up with Childproof Rooms for your little curiosity-seekers. They have set aside 10% of their rooms to be equipped with electric outlet covers, corner guards, plastic cups, and guards for the hot water handles. Parents must request these units in advance. The Tahoe hotel also has 14 suites equipped for disabled guests.

The living rooms of the suites face the atrium, but they are quite soundproof. Units are furnished in a decor called Old Tahoe, but don't confuse that with western. Dark-wood furniture fills the rooms, and the herringbone wallpapered walls have stenciled borders. A hide-a-bed, reading chair, and table for four, plus a remote-control TV, make up the living room. A wet bar, microwave, coffee maker, refrigerator, and servibar are all nicely to one side. Video machines are found in each room, and children's selections can be rented through room service. They can also access Nintendo on the screens.

The large bedroom comes with a makeup table and chair, an armoire housing the second TV, and a closet. There's a separate sink in the bedroom, clock radio, and the second of two phones. The bathroom is a comfortable size, with a marble-top counter and tub/shower combination. Extra amenities include call waiting and an automated voice-mail message system. One-day dry cleaning and laundry are provided, and there are washing machines and dryers on the eighth and ninth floors. There's even one-day film processing in the hotel's gift shop (which also has a deli menu and ice cream).

All the rooms are the same, and the price difference is based on the season and whether you rent during the week or on weekends. Rooms, based on double occupancy, cost $129–$149 January 3–31, in April, and from November 1 to December 19. The charge is $139–$179 in February, March, May, and June, and from September 8 to October 31. Rates are higher during premium periods: $159–$199 February 14–16 and from July 1 to Labor Day; and $230 and up from December 20 to January 2. Add $20 for each additional adult; kids under 12 are free. Ask about special ski, show, and family packages.

Looking for a spot complete with your own kitchen and space to spread out? The **Lakeland Village Beach and Ski Resort,** at 3535 U.S. 50, Lake Tahoe Boulevard (P.O. Box 1356), South Lake Tahoe, CA 96156 (☎ 916/541-7711, or toll free **800/822-5969;** fax 916/541-6278), is the place. You can't beat the location: it's situated right on the lake with its own private beach, plus three swimming pools, a hot tub, and saunas. If you don't feel like cooking, you're within walking distance of a number of restaurants—Heidi's is just next door. There are also two tennis courts, jet ski and boat rentals, a games room in the summer, and a playground slide.

These individually owned, individually furnished condominiums are comfortable and well worn. You'll feel at ease putting your feet up and relaxing in front of the fireplace or sitting outside on your private deck. A variety of configurations will suit most families' needs. Each condo has a fully equipped kitchen, including a dishwasher and linens, plus cable TV and telephones. There's an on-premises laundry room.

The one-bedroom condominium has 1 1/2 bathrooms and a loft, and can sleep four people. In spring and fall, the charge is $130; in summer and winter, it's $145; at Christmas, $150. Three-story town houses are quite roomy and can sleep 4–10 people. They go from $140 for a one-bedroom/one-bath unit in low season to $400 for a four-bedroom/three-bath lakefront unit in high season. Cribs are free. Ask about family packages, ski packages, and other promotional offers.

Whether or not to stay at a casino-hotel is your choice. **Harrah's,** U.S. 50 (P.O. Box 8), Stateline, NV 89449 (☎ **702/588-6611,** or toll free **800/HARRAHS;** fax 702/586-6606), is one of the most family oriented of the casino-hotels. In addition to the casino, this Mobil four-star and AAA four-diamond hotel has great resort amenities. An indoor pool allows a dip year round; in warm weather, the surrounding glass doors are opened to let in the outdoors. The fitness center is complete with weight machines, massage, sauna and steam, and a Jacuzzi. If you're like us and don't know craps from blackjack, your room TV will solve the problem with on-screen in-room instructions.

While the adults play the slot machines, the older kids can visit the 12,000-square-foot Family Fun Center downstairs, an activity area filled with video games, basketball, skee ball, and air hockey machines, a redemption center for prizes, and a snack area. You'll want to accompany your younger children to the PlayPal located in the Center. This plastic obstacle course is a playland of tunnels, ladders, moonwalks, and ball bins. Admission to the Family Fun Center is free; a charge of $3 is made for the PlayPal.

The folks at Harrah's also attempt to draw the family trade with the G-rated shows they premier in the South Shore Room. Children as young as 5 have attended performances of *Mame,* and each Christmas brings the inevitable *Scrooge* to the stage. If you want to visit the casino or have dinner alone, the concierge can arrange babysitting.

In summer, the hotel offers 1 1/2-hour scheduled yacht cruises, not limited to use by conventioneers or other groups. In winter there is complimentary ski valet service, in-room ski and boot fitting, and overnight ski-waxing service. Free shuttles to various ski areas stop at the hotel. As in most casinos, food is a good value (see "Where to Eat," below). Room service is always available 24 hours daily.

Rooms at Harrah's are grand. They are spacious, clean and very well appointed, with walk-in closets, hairdryers, remote-control TV, reading lights, soundproof walls, and blackout curtains. Each room has two full bathrooms, and each bathroom has its own television in addition to the one in the bedroom. A computerized beverage dispenser holds orange juice in addition to hard liquor, but can be turned off at the front desk. There are no connecting rooms, but two rooms next to each other can be closed off by exterior shared double doors that lock and have their own doorbell.

Based on single or double occupancy, a room with a king-size bed and plenty of space for a rollaway or crib, or one with two double beds costs $119–$159 from November to mid-December, $139–$199 in summer. Weekend rates are higher. Suites are available, including Dignitary Suites with personalized butler service, starting at $450. Children under 15 stay free in their parents' room; additional adults pay $20 per night. Rollaways and cribs are complimentary. Parking is free.

Timber Cove Lodge, a Best Western hotel at 3411 Lake Tahoe Blvd., South Lake Tahoe, CA 95705 (☎ 916/541-6722, or toll free 800/528-1234; fax 916/541-7959), is set on its own sandy beach. Janey's first favorite activity was climbing the huge boulders that decorate the property. Her second was playing hide-and-go-seek among the huge pines and cedars on the beach, observed by a flock of geese that paraded across the grounds once a day. A heated, fenced-in pool provided lots of fun. We strolled along the Timber Cove Marina and Pier, where jet skis and boats are for rent, and watched the fishermen. A bike-rental shop is just across the street, and Heavenly ski area is a five-minute drive.

The hotel's café was a cozy spot for morning coffee. The breakfast buffet proved adequate for Janey's appetite each day. And at $3 for children and $4.95 for adults, you couldn't go wrong. Room service is also available from 7am to 10pm. Within walking distance are numerous restaurants, ice-cream shops, and a big Safeway supermarket.

We suggest staying in lakeview or beachfront rooms on the first floor, so the kids can step right out on the lawn or the beach. Rooms have been recently decorated in burgundy, teal, and green with new bedspreads and bedskirts. Some of the lakeview rooms on upper floors have balconies. Each room has a small table, upholstered chairs, remote-control TV, air conditioning, separate vanities, and coffee makers. And mirrored walls make the rooms look even bigger.

All rates are based on single or double occupancy. In summer, rooms cost $85 weeknights, $95 on Friday and Saturday; other times of the year, $60 weeknights, $75 on Friday and Saturday. Add $10 for lakeview rooms and $20 for beachfront rooms. Base rates are $89 for all rooms during holiday periods, plus the $10 or $20 charge for location. Children under 12 stay free in the same room with their parents; children 12 and over and extra adults are charged $10. Rollaways and cribs are $10.

The **Tahoe Chalet Inn,** 3860 Lake Tahoe Blvd., South Lake Tahoe, CA 96150 (☎ 916/544-3311, or toll free 800/821-2656; fax 916/544-4069), stands out among the many motels that line the boulevard. The lobby is cozy and European: it's a nice place to sit in front of the fire on a cold night, to enjoy the complimentary continental breakfast, or to pause for a cup of coffee anytime during the day. There is a large gated pool that's open in summer. The hot tub is in a more private area, not adjacent to the pool. A sauna, exercise room, and video-games room complete the facilities.

The motel-style rooms are decorated in sort of a European country style. There are mirrored closet doors, individually controlled heating, and remote-control color TV with HBO and pay-per-view movies. If you want a room with air conditioning, request it in advance. If the family suites are not available, there are some adjoining rooms.

Rates are per room, with no extra charge for extra people, and are quite reasonable: rooms with one bed (double, queen-size, or king-size) cost $58–$82 year round; rooms with two double beds are $82, and with two queen-size beds are $88. Rooms with a kitchen cost an additional $12 per night. There are several suites and chalets that sleep up to six for $118 per night. Rates are reduced off-season. There are no rollaways; cribs are free.

The smell of pine needles will greet you at the **Lazy S Lodge,** 609 Emerald Bay Rd., South Lake Tahoe, CA 96150 (☎ **916/541-0230,** or toll free **800/862-8881** from 8am to 10pm; fax 916/541-2503), in a more secluded section of Tahoe's south shore where the cottages and motel-style rooms have their own woodsy backdrop. A fenced-in outdoor pool is a popular spot, and the hot tub is in frequent use. Families can use the picnic tables and barbecues, and can play table tennis, water basketball or maybe throw Frisbees on the wide green lawns. Restaurants and bike and hiking trails aren't far away. Babysitting can be arranged. Your car can be parked just behind your unit.

The owner/managers of this lodge are really nice and helpful. There is a variety of room configurations to suit your needs. All are neat and clean, although the furnishings are not a decorator's dream. Rooms have been updated with wet bars, microwaves, and refrigerators. They all have a coffee maker, TV, and phone. The family-size cottages have small kitchens, dining areas, and fireplaces. Bedrooms are furnished with either a king-size bed or a double and twin bed, plus two hide-a-beds in the living room. A basket of fruit welcomes guests who rent cottages.

In spring and fall, cottages, which can sleep two to six people, cost $69–$79 double; in summer they go for $79–$89. Motel units with optional kitchenettes go for $39–$49 double, off-season, and $49–$59 in summer, with an extra $5 for a kitchenette. The winter rate is between summer and spring rates; ask about special ski packages. Cribs (playpens) and rollaways are complimentary. The extra-person charge is $5.

Along the West Shore

The west shore is one of the prettiest areas of Tahoe. One of the places you might consider staying if you have older children is the **Sunnyside Restaurant & Lodge,** 1850 W. Lake Blvd. (P.O. Box 5969), Tahoe City, CA 96145 (☎ **916/583-7200,** or toll free **800/822-2SKI** in California), which is on the lake. Weekend brunch is wonderful, so whether or not you stay here, you might want to splurge. While you admire a spectacular view from the deck, you can indulge in all sorts of entrees from the all-you-can-eat buffet. Choices run the gamut from the usual egg dishes, breakfast meats, fruits, and salads, to lox and cream cheese, roast beef, and fish. Brunch is offered from 9:30am to 2:30pm on Sunday. The adult price is $14.95; children 8 and under are charged $6.95; under 3 free. The restaurant opens for dinner at 5:30 in winter, 10am in summer.

There are only 23 rooms and suites, and they all have views. Daily continental breakfast buffet and afternoon tea are included in room price. Lodging prices vary depending on the season and are based on single or double occupancy. Lakefront and lakeview rooms in spring and fall are $75–$135; summer rates are $125–$165;

winter rates are $90–$150. Suites go for $115 to $145, depending on the season. There's a charge of $15 for additional adults; children under 3 stay free. Cribs are complimentary.

North Lake Tahoe

The **Hyatt Regency Lake Tahoe Resort & Casino,** Country Club Drive at Lakeshore (P.O. Box 3239), Incline Village, NV 89450 (☎ **702/832-1234,** or toll free **800/233-1234;** fax 702/831-7508), is set in one of the prettiest residential areas on the north shore. Although the first thing you see upon entering is the bright lights of the casino, the games are set off from the lobby so you don't have to walk through them with the kids on the way to restaurants and your room. The resort has an activities desk to make reservations and refer babysitters.

The fitness club can be used by guests ages 13 and older. The fenced-in heated pool area is large and affords wonderful views. Pool service is offered. The Hyatt also has a private beach just across the street complete with lounges, rafts, snack service, volleyball, and beach attendants. There's a big outdoor fire pit, lit at night, and a great play area among the lakeside cottages. Two tennis courts are complimentary, and a large field adjacent to the hotel is perfect for tag and Frisbee.

Camp Hyatt, for kids 3–12, has its own colorful permanent room filled with toys, napping mats, arts and crafts supplies, and a VCR. Along with indoor activities, the agenda includes playtime at the beach, volleyball, and a trip to miniature golf and bowling. Lunch is charged to your room. There are some off-site activities that vary depending on the ages of the children. The club runs daily in summer and during major holidays, plus it's available on weekends throughout the year. In summer and on major holidays, there's also an evening session from 4pm to midnight which adds movies and snacks to the list of activities. In the winter snow-play and indoor activities are held at the hotel. The evening sessions are available on weekends in winter. Kids signed up for Camp Hyatt receive a special room-service menu, a hat, and a frequent-stay passport, which entitles them to a gift after four stays. Camp Hyatt costs $35 for the day session and $25 for the evening program. Make reservations in advance.

There are three restaurants in the hotel. Stetson's (on the lake) and Ciao Mein serve dinner only. You'll find them more comfortable if you leave the kids behind. But the Sierra Café is definitely family appropriate, and is open 24 hours. There are very elaborate buffets in addition to the regular menu, and a children's menu is available. Room service can be contacted 24 hours.

Hyatt rooms are done in rich wine, gold and forest green. Stenciled wall borders and mountain lodge–style furniture makes the rooms cozy. Two oversize double beds or one king-size bed are found in standard rooms. Upholstered reading chairs with ottomans, reading lights, armoires with remote-control TV, Servibars, two-line phones with voice mail, and hairdryers are in all rooms. Rooms have beautiful tiled bathrooms with charming country French wallpaper and new bathroom fixtures. In-room safes cost $3 per day, and refrigerators can be requested. These rooms have space for a crib or rollaway, but not both.

Families like the one-bedroom suites or adjoining rooms the best. The one-bedroom suite consists of a parlor that adjoins a bedroom. A wood dining table with lovely upholstered dining room chairs for six, two full bathrooms, a wet bar, two TVs, and two telephones are all set in a comfortable and roomy environment. If you choose one of these on the Regency Club floor, you'll add continental breakfast, snacks, cocktails, candy, bathrobes, morning newspaper, hairdryers, and extra bathroom amenities to the picture.

If you really want a treat, consider renting one of the Lakeside Cottages, directly across the street. Stone fireplaces, beamed ceilings, wet bars, an ice machine, and a coffee maker are featured in the living room. With the one-bedroom unit, you'll get a total of two TVs and $1^{1}/_{2}$ beautifully decorated bathrooms, plus a king-size bed in the separate bedroom. You can put two rollaways in the living room. In the two-bedroom unit, one of the bedrooms has two double beds and the other has a king-size bed. It's recommended for a maximum of eight people. You can rent a bedroom with two double beds alone, or the whole floor. Private wood decks and a great view of the beach are included.

Room rates depend on the season. During summer, holiday periods, and January 18 to April 15, standard rooms rent for $130–$239. One-bedroom Tower suites are $339 in high season, $255 in low season. Two-bedroom suites cost $439 in high season, $355 in low season. Regency Club guest rooms are $264 in high season, $180 in low season. One-bedroom Lakeside Cottages cost $539 in high season, $355 in low season. Two-bedroom cottages are $639 in high season, $455 in low. Parents of Camp Hyatt kids can reserve an adjoining room for half price off rack rates. Children under 18 stay free in their parents' room; extra adults are charged $15. Cribs and rollaways are complimentary, if available (reserve in advance). Be sure to ask about special packages. Ski storage is free.

The area's largest resort facility is the **Resort at Squaw Creek,** Squaw Valley USA, Olympic Valley, CA 96146 (☎ **916/583-6300,** or toll free **800/3CREEK-3;** fax 916/581-6632). In addition to being a first-class conference resort (with a 33,000-square-foot conference center), Squaw Creek is also going after the family trade. Its location, in one of the most affordable ski areas of Tahoe, is alluring.

The lobby is both spectacular and cozy at the same time. Huge glass windows provide splendid views of the surrounding area, while a massive stone fireplace gives off an inviting glow. Sierra granite, cherrywood, and other natural products were used to complement the surrounding environs. A black glass nine-story building, which actually blends in with the mountains, houses the 405 rooms and suites.

Set among towering pines, boulders, and a waterfall is a water garden. Ideal for children is the beach pool with its artificial sand-filled shore. There's also a plunge pool with a 120-foot water slide and a lap pool heated year round, plus three outdoor spas. A recreation manager is on staff to tell you all about what there is to do in the area. At the Sports Activity Center, you can sign up for winter sports and summer activities such as fly fishing school and golf on the hotel's Robert Trent Jones, Jr., course (Scottish-link style). Two outdoor tennis courts are available for guest use.

Squaw Creek's executive fitness center is equipped with all the latest equipment. You can also reserve spa treatments and attend exercise classes. The resort operates its own chair lift for intermediate skiers, which is always accessible to hotel guests. Beginners are shuttled to Squaw Valley, just minutes away. Each guest is assigned a locker in a special room in the hotel for sports equipment. Skis and boots can be fitted in the sports shop. The outdoor ice-skating rink can be viewed from one of several terraces. A full retail promenade has, in addition to boutiques, a gourmet deli and a small video arcade.

As of this writing, "Mountain Buddies" is the resort's summer family program for ages 3–13. Offered seven days a week, it consists of three sessions, divided into three focuses: Living, Learning, and Leisure. "Living" are sports activities including water basketball and guided hikes; "Learning" are projects like photo tours, kite flights, and fire safety; "Leisure" might include scavenger hunts, dancing, and croquet. The charge for this program is $20 *per session.* Check to see if this program is still in force before planning your vacation around it.

Cascades is the huge all-day-dining restaurant with a glorious buffet. There is a children's menu for kids 3–12, and the little ones under 3 eat free. While the buffet is offered at breakfast, lunch, and dinner, there are also separate, albeit costly, alternatives. Glissandi is the more elegant resort restaurant. Children are welcome, but there is no children's menu. Ristorante Montagna is a great place to stop for lunch. You can ski right to it in the winter, and linger in the warm sun on the patio in the summer. Room service is available.

Rooms are not huge at the resort, but the panoramic picture windows in each one give them a fantastic feel. The small suites have king-size beds and a sofa bed. Bathrooms are standard size with separate vanities topped in beautiful granite. The suites also have wet bars, an honor bar, and some feature kitchenettes. The one-bedroom suite can connect with another bedroom. Double rooms have two queen-size beds, while deluxe rooms have king-size beds. The 14 panoramic suites have fireplaces, wet bars, video service, two TVs, and one bedroom. Be sure to tell the reservationist your needs when you call.

Room rates are $250 for a standard room; suites begin at $325. Children 16 and under stay free in their parents' room; additional adult guests are charged $35. Cribs are free; rollaways cost $20 per night. Ask about special ski, family, and golf packages, when some rates go down to $99 per person.

If it's a condo you're looking for, check out the **Tahoe Marina Lodge,** P.O. Box 92, Tahoe City, CA 96145 (☎ **916/583-2365,** or toll free **800/748-5650**). You'll find it just before—or after, depending what direction you're coming from—Tahoe City's only stop light. The location can't be beat—you can walk to practically anything in Tahoe City from here. This is a small complex of one- and two-bedroom condominiums right on the lake. The sandy beach is swimmable, or if you prefer, there's a gated, heated swimming pool. Big green, grassy areas are great for Frisbees and scrambling toddlers. Two tennis courts are available and there are a limited number of coin-operated washers and dryers.

One-bedroom condos are very small, but would accommodate parents and either one child or a baby. The bedroom comes with a queen-size bed, the bathroom has a shower stall, and the kitchen is really a kitchenette. There's a queen-size hide-a-bed in the living room, but little space for eating. We suggest opting for the two-story, two bedroom versions, which are quite roomy. Each unit has been individually decorated by its owner, but they all come with color TVs, VCRs, phones, private decks or patios, and fireplaces (as do the one-bedroom condos). These offer two bedrooms downstairs, one with twin beds, the other with a queen-size bed. A sofa in the living room upstairs is also queen-size. There's a generous-size, fully equipped kitchen and dining area. Daily maid service can be secured at an extra charge; stays of seven days or longer get midweek cleanings; linens are furnished.

Rates for a one-bedroom garden-view unit in summer run $97–$160, depending on the dates. Two-bedroom lake-view condos go for $118–$189; two-bedroom lakefront units are $131–$211. There's a 5% discount on stays of seven nights or more in the same unit. Winter rates for a one-bedroom are $133; two-bedroom lakeview and lakefront units are $167. Ask about special discounts. Rollaways are not available; cribs are free.

The 12-unit beachfront **Villa Vista Resort,** 6750 N. Lake Blvd. (P.O. Box 47), Tahoe Vista, CA 96148 (☎ **916/546-1550;** fax 916/546-4100), has the well-lived-in comfort and friendliness that keeps the same families coming back year after year. Don't look for snappy furnishings and modern amenities here. Towels are provided and the trash is removed, but linens are supplied only weekly. Limited maid service is available in the kitchen units. The real draw to this owner-operated resort is the swimmable, sandy beach, filled with kids each summer. A wood deck with tables and chairs overlooks the beach and keeps kids within view of Mom and Dad. There's a little pool, but be careful—it's easy for the kids to get in.

Each room has its own wood porch with chairs, and guests have use of several barbecue grills. Three units have a queen-size bed, which can be curtained off from the two twin beds; these rooms come with a small table and chairs and a nice bathroom. One small cottage is perfect for a couple with a baby: it has a small fireplace, one queen-size bed and a fold-out sofa, a refrigerator, a two-burner stove, and a table and chairs. Other units have one bedroom with a queen-size bed and twin beds, plus a sofa bed in the living area and a roomy kitchen. Three large suites provide the most room for large families and are quite comfortable for long stays; these consist of a master bedroom with a queen-size bed. $1^1/2$ bathrooms, an alcove for two twin beds, and a big living room with two fold-out sofas, a fireplace, and a huge kitchen with a dishwasher and an eating area. All rooms have remote-control TVs, reading lights, ceiling fans, and individually controlled heating. Phones can be requested. Only one unit has a lake view.

Motel rooms cost $70–$75; cottages are $95–$145. Weekly rates in summer for the cottages bring the cost down (for example, the $110-per-night accommodation is $660 per week); check for seasonal rates. The extra-person charge is $10 per night. There's no charge for cribs and rollaways, but the owners suggest that you bring your own crib for babies over six months.

The **Red Wolf,** 7630 N. Lake Blvd. (P.O. Box 384), Tahoe Vista, CA 96148 (☎ **916/546-3952;** fax 916/546-7925), is definitely one to put on your list if you're looking for homey, affordable lodgings on the lake. Popular with families, this refurbished lodge is on a beach and within walking distance of jet ski, canoe, kayak, and power boat rentals and the Kings Beach Recreation Area. Two big grassy areas give toddlers a place to run. Guests renting rooms with kitchen facilities can also use the barbecues, and there are several picnic tables at which to enjoy your efforts. The pool area (with a view of the lake) is pretty generous and is gated and protected from wind by glass walls. Morning coffee is served in the Wolf Den, the likes of which we haven't seen before. No doubt your children will enjoy the wolf pictures on the walls. There are some board games in the Den, and equipment for Ping-Pong, tether ball, and volleyball. Management welcomes families and tries to make them comfortable.

The 23 guest rooms vary in size. Standard double-bedded rooms, with wood-paneled walls and natural blue-pine furniture, are charmingly decorated in a country motif and have bathrooms with stall showers, small refrigerators, cable TV with free HBO, and daily maid service. These rooms are not big, but a family of three or four could stay in them. Studios and family suites vary in layout and can sleep two to five people. One has a queen-size bed plus a bedroom with two twin beds, another has double beds in the bedroom and a sofabed in the living room. The lakefront suites are the biggest. There's one that sleeps five; and boasts a fireplace; the other sleeps three. The family units are also furnished in the unusual mountain furniture and come with equipped kitchens, cable TV and HBO, and limited maid service. There are no telephones in any of the rooms.

Standard rooms in summer cost $49–$65 midweek and $59–$70 on weekends and holidays. Studios go for $65–$75 midweek and $70–$85 weekends. Family suites are $85–$140 (for the five-person unit) midweek, and $90–$150 on weekends. Winter rates are just slightly lower. Additional adults pay $10. Rollaways are included in the $10-extra charge, and cribs are an extra $10.

Camping

There's camping on the north side of the lake at **Donner Memorial State Park,** just west of Truckee at Donner Lake. There are 154 campsites. Call MISTIX (☎ toll free **800/444-7275**) for reservations.

On the south shore, **Campground by the Lake** (☎ **916/542-6096** for camping reservations) is a nice campground, on Rufus Allen Boulevard three miles from the junction of U.S. 50 and Calif. 89. It's equipped with 170 sites; no hookups. There are barbecue pits, picnic tables, and showers. It costs $16.50 per night per one vehicle (maximum four people); children under 4 free.

There is also camping at **Camp Richardson,** on Calif. 89 (☎ **916/541-1801**).

On the west shore, campsites are available at **D. L. Bliss State Park** (☎ **800/444-7275**), at **Sugar Pine Point State Park** (☎ **916/525-7982**), and at **Meeks Bay** (☎ **916/544-5994,** or toll free **800/280-2267**).

WHERE TO EAT

It's unlikely you'll drive from one side of the lake to the other for dinner, but you might be on one or the other side of the lake at lunch or breakfast time. Here are some suggestions for family-friendly restaurants.

North Lake Tahoe

We've found what we think are two perfect north-shore restaurants for families. **Rosie's,** at 571 N. Lake Tahoe Blvd. in Tahoe City (☎ **916/583-8504**), is one of them. This place is done up in deer antler fixtures, moose heads, an old buggy, wooden sleds, snowshoes, and other collectibles. The owner has a passion for old bicycles, which are also displayed. The high-ceilinged interior is furnished with wood tables and Bentwood chairs. From the outdoor tables you can watch the local action.

Breakfast is relaxing and the food is yummy. The regular menu offers lots of fancy eggs (around $6.50), omelets ($5.50–$6.25), oatmeal pancakes, French toast, and waffles ($3.95 and $4.95). Lunch is simple: prime rib sandwiches, Philly cheese steak, and Irish dip (warm corned beef on a sourdough roll with Swiss cheese), plus the usual burger, club sandwiches, chicken sandwiches, and salads. Add to that southwestern black-bean chili and jambalaya and you definitely have something for everyone. Lunch prices start at $4 and top out at $8. The many dinner selections include pasta (clams linguine, and seafood pasta, among others), baby back ribs, roast duckling, prawns scampi style, southern fried chicken, several stir-fry meals, sandwiches, and numerous appetizers. Appetizers will run around $6; pastas go for $10–$15; stir-fry is $11–$13; dinner sandwiches run $7–$8; complete entrees with bread, soup and salad, and vegetables are $15–$18. Even more exciting, though, are the specials for which the chef is known. Among the specials the night we were there were jerk ribs and fries for $6.50, cherry-ginger duckling at $14, and a sandwich of soft-shell crab for $10.50. Save room for Mrs. Ed's peanut butter pie, day or night.

The kids' menu, which can be colored and hung on the wall, is limited, but there are lots of choices for the small fry on the adult menu. The 10-and-under crowd can choose eggs, potatoes, and toast, or two pancakes and bacon, for $3.75. Grilled cheese and fries, a burger and fries, fish and chips, or ravioli should hold them over. These go for $4.25 to $5.25. Youngsters under 6 eat free. The staff will provide booster seats and highchairs, and will warm baby food or bottles. There's a full bar and special children's drinks are served. Most of the restaurant is no-smoking.

Rosie's is open daily, including holidays. In summer, breakfast is served from 8am to 2:30pm, lunch is available anytime, and dinner is on from 5:30 to 10pm. Call for seasonal hours. Reservations are accepted at dinner only, and most major credit cards are welcome. Park in front.

Gar Woods, at 5000 N. Lake Blvd., next to the Sierra Boat Company in Carnelian Bay (☎ **916/546-3366** or toll free **800/BY TAHOE**), is the other good restaurant where you can feel comfortable bringing the kids. Its big, wide-open dining room, surrounded by tall glass windows and a good lake view, is most welcoming. Out on the redwood deck, which overlooks the beachfront, Mom and Dad can even watch little Becky play on the sand while they nurse that last cappuccino. One of the four golden retriever dogs at the boat-rental stand next door came by to check up on our kids periodically.

Gar Woods sees lots of families, especially at lunch. The "lunch with a view" menu lists salads (including a warm salmon salad), sandwiches such as lime chicken or fresh crab), and a daily special. There are also cheeseburgers, calamari sauté, and fresh seafood. Lunch prices begin at $6 for a Caesar salad and go up to $12. There are also yummy appetizers.

Dinner is simple: On the seafood side are ocean stir-fry, seafood sauté, scampi, and specials at market price. Or sample citrus chicken, pork tenderloin, prime rib, and New York steak. Dinner entrees cost $14–$18 and come with sourdough bread, vegetables, and either pasta or baby red potatoes. Appetizers include steamed clams, skewered sesame chicken filets, and California roll, and are pegged at $7–$11. Café meals are also available for lighter appetites. These include pasta choices, Thai chicken salad, a cheeseburger, and a couple of other items from the lunch menu ($6–$15).

Kids 12 and under can order from the children's selections: pasta, a quesadilla, a chicken sandwich, and the inevitable cheeseburger, hot cheese dog, and grilled cheese sandwich. Each selection is $5. Drinks are $1.50, and the refills are free. The bartender will also make up a virgin wet woody or fruit daiquiri for $2. The restaurant has booster seats and high chairs. Bottles and baby food will be warmed upon request. There is a split charge for items off the adult menu: $1.50 at lunch, $3 at dinner.

And lest we forget dessert . . . while Grandma and Grandpa munch on apple strudel and mocha crunch ice cream cake, Dad might order white-chocolate Snickers cheesecake, leaving Mom with soft-serve ice cream or Ghirardelli nonfat chocolate yogurt. The kids can have a sundae for $3—or any of Dad's cheesecake.

The Sunday buffet brunch is pretty outrageous. The tables are filled with salads which include beer-steamed prawns, Chinese chicken salad, salmon mousse with bagels, and hot pasta variations, blueberry blintzes stuffed with ricotta cheese, fresh seafood, and chicken, plus lots more. The desserts are decadent—like chocolate fondue with fresh strawberries! For this, adults pay $15 and children 12 and under are charged $8. Kids under 4 eat free.

Saturday breakfast consists of eggs, hot cakes, French toast, and waffles. Prices begin at $4 and top out at $9.

In summer, lunch is served daily from 10:30am to 2pm. Dinner begins at 5pm and ends at 10pm. The Cafe Menu is offered in the bar from 10:30am to 10pm weeknights, and to 10:30pm Friday and Saturday. Saturday breakfast is from 9am to noon; Sunday brunch is served from 9am to 2pm.

In winter, lunch is served on Saturday from 11:30am to 2pm; dinner is offered nightly from 5:30pm to 10pm. The Cafe Menu can be requested Monday through Friday from 4:30pm to 10pm and Saturday and Sunday from 11:30am to 10pm. Saturday breakfast hours are the same; Sunday brunch begins at 10am and goes to 2pm. The entire dining room and patio is designated no-smoking. Reservations and major credit cards are accepted. There's a parking lot, and—are you ready?—valet parking for your boat or dock at the deep water pier.

Tahoe House, 625 W. Lake Blvd. (Calif. 89), just south of the "Y" in Tahoe City (☎ 916/583-1377), will give your children an introduction to Swiss-German cuisine. If you're not a fan of bratwurst, there are also Italian specialties on the menu. The interior is charming brick and pine. It may look fancy, but it's really a casual, family-run restaurant that has been around since 1977. Only dinner is served here. But a full bakery—open 7am to 11pm—offers pizzas, bagels, smoked salmon spread, cookies, brownies, and other typical bakery fare.

For the children, you'll find wienerschnitzel along with pizza, spaghetti, or a small steak. All the dinners are $6.95; a small salad is an extra $2. Highchairs and booster seats are available. Children's drinks can be prepared, and adult entrees can be split for two children.

The adult fare is varied. A number of selections from the grill include Swiss bratwurst, rack of lamb, and grilled chicken or saltimbocca. Or you can choose from the pasta list of linguine con vongole (baby clams in white wine sauce with shallots and mushrooms), vegetable polenta, and several other choices. House specials include schnitzel Cordon Bleu, rahmschnitzel, roast duckling, wienerschnitzel, and veal Tahoe House. Seafood is listed among the daily specials. Salads are extra, but selections do include vegetables and potatoes or spaetzle. Prices range from $6.95–$17.95. Be sure to leave room for the European-style desserts: homemade chocolate truffles, tortes, and other forbidden goodies.

Tahoe house is open every day from 5pm to 10pm. Reservations are accepted. Most credit cards are taken. Park in the lot.

Most kids like pizza, so if yours do, try **Mofo's Pizza,** at 868 Tahoe Blvd., No. 23, in the Christmas Tree Village Shopping Center, Incline Village (☎ 702/831-4999). Mofo's has been around since 1986, and the owners pride themselves on using fresh sauces and vegetables.

One favorite choice is the spinach/garlic pizza, but you can choose the popular pepperoni, sausage, or meatballs if you prefer. The more adventurous in your group might like the Hawaiian version with Canadian bacon, pineapple, and tomatoes, or a Southern-style pie with sun-dried tomatoes, cajun chicken, and artichoke hearts. Pasta selections come with salad bar and garlic bread. The lunch menu includes Italian sandwiches, specials such as a half order of lasagna and the salad bar, mini pizzas, and hamburgers. Lunch prices are quite reasonable starting at $2.75 for a mini-pizza and topping out at $5.75. Regular menu prices are $6–$16.45 for a large pizza.

In the summer, Mofo's is open Monday through Thursday from 11am to 9:30pm, Friday and Saturday to 10pm, and Sunday 4 to 9pm. Winter hours are Monday through Thursday 11am to 2pm and 4:30 to 9pm; Friday and Saturday to 9:30pm, and Sunday 4 to 9pm.

Mexican food is another popular kid-choice. **La Hacienda de la Sierra,** 931 Tahoe Blvd., Incline Village (☎ **702/831-8300**) is a favorite local hangout because it serves consistently good food at reasonable prices.

The menu choices for children 12 and under include, among the six items, a taco, cheese enchilada, or bean burrito and cost $3.50.

Most dinners on the adult menu cost $7.95 for a two-item combo that includes soup and salad. A popular special is the Cortez, a generous turkey burrito ($7.95). Shrimp fajitas will cost you $10.95.

La Hacienda is open in summer for lunch from 11:30am to 4pm daily, and for dinner from 4pm to 10pm. Winter hours are 5pm to 10pm; closed for lunch. Two-for-one dinners are offered if you order between 5 and 6pm. Major credit cards are accepted.

Jasons Saloon & Grille, 8338 N. Lake Blvd., Kings Beach (☎ **916/546-3315**), is not our first choice of a restaurant, but we don't want to judge a place on one or two servers who could be gone the next week. It has a good location overlooking the lake, there is an outdoor patio, and the children's menu is basic. Like many other Tahoe restaurants, the atmosphere is casual.

At lunch the youngsters can have a hamburger, fish and chips, or chicken sticks—all with fries. The salad bar is an extra $1.75 at lunch. Each selection is $4.25 and includes fresh fruit and a cookie. After 5pm, the full children's dinners include a trip to the salad bar, fries, fruit, and a cookie. But the choices are limited to teriyaki chicken dinner or a child's portion of barbecued ribs. Each costs $7.25. Sassy seats and boosters are available. There is a full bar, so children's special drinks can be prepared.

Adults get a huge selection of burgers for lunch ($5.25–$6.50), the salad bar ($5.95), or sandwiches ($5.25–$8.25). At dinnertime, choose between the burgers again or such entrees as baby back ribs, bayou shrimp, prime rib, and a number of other seafood and chicken dishes. Prices for these entrees run $12–$18 and include the salad bar, baked potato, French fries, rice, or a vegetable kebob, and bread. Open daily from 11am to 10pm. Major credit cards are accepted. Park in the lot.

South Lake Tahoe

The **TSR Cafe** is at the Tahoe Seasons Resort, at the corner of Saddle Rd. and Keller Rd., just before the Heavenly Ski Resort (☎ **916/541-6700**). It's off the beaten track, but if you're on your way to Heavenly, it's a nice quiet place in a beautiful resort to stop for breakfast. Mom and Dad can build their own omelet with a base price of $3.55, or order eggs Benedict, steak and eggs, or a continental breakfast. Prices average around $6.

Children can order breakfast menu items at half-price. With this in mind, the kids can choose French toast, Belgian waffles, or pancakes. Breakfast is served from 7 to 11am every day. Hours may change according to the season.

Carlos Murphy's, 3678 Lake Tahoe Blvd. (☎ **916/542-1741**), is a lively, colorful spot to take the kids. The night we got there, a balloon artist was making animals and hats for all the kids—and adults. Balloon artist CC the Clown usually appears nightly from 6 to 9pm. A children's menu (with word games) suggests quesadillas, mini bean burritos, beef tacos, hot dogs, hamburgers, chicken bits, or grilled cheese for $1.95–$2.95. Servers will warm baby bottles and bring special non-alcoholic drinks to the kids. Highchairs and booster seats are available.

There are lots of adult selections. In addition to the typical Mexican dishes, Carlos Murphy's has shrimp burritos, fish tacos, barbecued ribs and chicken, and beef, chicken, and shrimp fajitas. Lunch specialties cost $6–$10, but there are lots of sandwiches, burgers, and Mexican dishes under $5. Dinner prices average $6–$10.

The restaurant is open Sunday through Thursday from 11am to 10pm, on Friday from 11am to 10:30pm, and on Saturday from 11am to 11pm. No reservations are accepted, and weekend evenings can be quite crowded. Major credit cards welcome. A parking lot is available.

Heidi's, located at 3485 U.S. 50, in South Lake Tahoe (☎ **916/544-8113**), is such a cute and pleasant place that Janey insisted on breakfast there every morning. The decor is what you'd expect for a restaurant named after the Swiss book by the same name. The children's menu is for kids 10 and under. They can order Little Folks French toast or Wee Waffles, Little Boy Blue pancakes, cereal, and eggs for $2–$3.50. If they prefer something from the regular menu, the kitchen will split orders. There are stacks of pancakes, in nearly every version you can think of, plus 10 types of Belgian waffles, 18 different omelets, and French toast, muffins, toast, and other goodies. The price for waffles, crêpes, and pancakes ranges from $4.25 to $6.25. Omelets go for $6.50–$10. The family-style breakfast for a minimum of four people costs $7.95 for adults, $4.95 for kids.

Lunch for kids includes junior burgers, corn dogs, grilled-cheese Lemans (means Lake Geneva), plus soup for $2.50–$3.25. There are 16 outrageous burgers, sandwiches, and salads in the $4.50–$9 range. Highchairs, sassy seats, and booster seats are available; there is a non-smoking section.

Breakfast begins at 7am and runs till 2pm. Lunch service starts at 11am. No reservations are accepted. Major credit cards accepted. Park in the lot.

We found an easygoing, fast alternative to McDonalds to stop at on the way back to South Lake Tahoe from the west shore. **Colombo's Burgers A Go Go,** 841 Emerald Bay Dr. (Calif. 89), South Lake Tahoe (☎ **916/541-4646**), has been serving up burgers, and shakes since 1963. This indoor/outdoor self-serve spot has a special children's menu. The Kids Meal comes with curly fries, a beverage, and a prize for $3.60. For that, kids get a junior burger, chicken strips, or a corn dog. A plain junior burger without the extras will cost you a mere $2.

There are plenty of choices for both kids and adults: one-third-pound burgers ($3.50–$4.75), zucchini stix ($3.85), and beer-battered onion rings ($2).

Open daily in summer from 10am to 9pm; in winter, Sunday through Thursday from 10am to 8pm, Friday and Saturday till 9pm. The bathroom is the modular outdoor type. There's a small parking lot.

Casino Dining

Harrah's Forest Buffet, on the 18th floor of the casino-hotel of the same name, on U.S. 50 (☎ **702/588-6611**), is quite a scene. Go early enough for a sunset view of the lake. You'll spot families throughout the large restaurant waiting for the all-you-can-eat breakfast, lunch, and dinner buffets. The dinner buffet, for instance, has something for everyone, from the salad station to the selections of hot entrees and the carver's station. The dessert table gets special attention from the kids.

At breakfast, you pay $7.95 for adults, $5.50 for children 7–10, and $2 for kids 6 and under. At lunch the price is $9.95 for adults, $5.50 for the kids, and $2 for youngsters under 7. Dinner prices range from $11.95 to $19.50 for adults, depending on whether it's the standard buffet, the seafood buffet, or the Saturday-evening special dinner. Kids are charged $7.50, $8.50, or $9.50, and the toddlers, $2. The buffet brunch goes for $10.95 for adults, $6.50 for kids, and $2 for toddlers. The hours here change seasonally, so be sure to call ahead. No reservations are accepted. Major credit cards are welcome.

Café Roma at Caesars Tahoe, on U.S. 50 (☎ **702/588-3515**), will serve the family 24 hours a day. In addition to the usual coffeeshop fare, Café Roma offers a children's menu. Breakfast runs $2.50 and $2.95 for oatmeal and a beverage, pancakes, or eggs. At lunch and dinner, the little tykes can select from hot dogs, hamburgers, chicken fingers, spaghetti, or grilled cheese, each with a beverage ($4–$4.50). Even a before-bed treat of cookies and milk can be ordered for $1.95. There are booster seats and high chairs. Major credit cards are accepted.

You'll also get a good buy for the money across the street at the **Garden Buffet,** in Harvey's Resort, U.S. 50 (☎ **702/588-2411**). Breakfast is "such a deal": it's a hugely popular buffet pegged at $4.50 for adults and children. The breakfast buffet tables are heaped with frittatas (omelets), blintzes, biscuits and gravy, eggs, pancakes, waffles, French toast and breakfast meats, plus fruit, desserts, and beverages.

Dinner buffets are themed; adults pay $7.95–$16.95 depending on the cuisine of the night, while kids are charged $4.95–$9.75. One night might be an Italian theme with pastas, chicken, pizza, soup, bread, and beverages, *plus* the carver's roast, catch of the day, and baked ham.

Breakfast service is Monday through Friday from 8am to 10:30am; brunch is served Monday through Friday from 11am to 2pm, Saturday and Sunday from 8am to 2pm. Dinner runs Sunday through Thursday from 5 to 9pm, and Friday and Saturday from 4 to 10pm (on summer weekends, dinner is served until 11pm). Major credit cards are welcome.

Emergency Numbers

In case of a medical emergency, call **Barton Memorial Hospital,** 2170 South Ave., South Lake Tahoe (☎ **916/541-3420**), 24 hours, or **Stateline Emergency Clinic,** Stateline, Nevada (☎ **702/588-3561**) 8am to 8pm.

The local number for **AAA road service** is **916/541-2430.**

8

Mountain Areas and National Parks

CALIFORNIA'S FAMED MOUNTAINS ARE FAMILY VACATIONS EXTRAORDINAIRE. YOU'LL be amazed how exciting it is to discover nature together. Prepare yourselves for peak experiences—the first time your children see a giant sequoia; their first view of Yosemite; the squeals when they enter an enormous, dark cave; their first meals cooked over an open fire. Imagine the fun of sharing time together on a houseboat, floating down the river on a raft, watching natural bubbling pools rising from the earth. These are treasured memories you create as a family, made even more pleasurable because telephones and televisions don't get in the way.

You'll discover that you remember more about science and nature than you thought. Your senses will be heightened because you're seeing this aspect of the world through young eyes. And when you're in a national park, there are abundant educational opportunities to share. Wherever you turn you'll discover self-guiding trails that describe the terrain and ecology, visitor centers that offer information to hungry minds, and naturalist-led activities for specific interests.

1   Fresno: Gateway to Yosemite, Sequoia and Kings Canyon National Parks

Before we had children, we used to go to Yosemite National Park for weekend excursions. We'd leave Los Angeles at the crack of dawn, making good time through the San Joaquin Valley listening to rock music and suffering through the early-morning radio farm reports. We'd drive right through Fresno and enjoy a leisurely lunch in Wawona before we'd enter the valley. Or we'd stop in one of the small towns along the way and assemble a delectable array of picnic goodies, which we'd enjoy off the road on the way to the park. There were even times when we'd arrive in the valley at dusk and scrounge for a campsite.

We tried to reenact the same experience with our children—after all, having kids wasn't going to change *our* lives! Needless to say, the attempt nearly ruined our entire vacation. Waking two of them up at the crack of dawn was an insane idea—they were exhausted by 10am but wouldn't nap. They didn't want to stop for a leisurely lunch— they just wanted to get there. A delectable picnic to them meant fast food devoured in the backseat of the car. Between the whining and bickering, trash all over the car, and Mom's bout with car sickness from having to face backward a good portion of the trip, we were lucky to make it at all. At least we were intelligent enough to have made reservations in the park in advance!

We learned our lesson. Now we always stop overnight in Fresno, and of course we stop many times along the way (see the "How to Travel with Kids" section in Chapter 1). The next morning after breakfast, we leave for Yosemite (the same applies to excursions to Sequoia or Kings Canyon) full of energy, looking forward to a whole day in the park.

Those of you coming from San Francisco might want to plan to leave early, make lots of stops, perhaps have a picnic, and make it to the park in one day.

ORIENTATION

Fresno, the San Joaquin Valley city of almost 390,000, is the gateway to Yosemite National Park and Sequoia and Kings Canyon National Parks.

Located just off Calif. 99, and serviced by Fresno Air Terminal, Fresno offers a surprising variety of accommodations and activities for families. If you contact the **Fresno City and County Visitors Bureau,** located at 808 M St. (☎ **209/233-0836,** or toll free **800/788-0836;** fax 209/445-0122), they'll be glad to answer any questions.

GETTING AROUND

Fresno sprawls, so it's a good idea to get a map of the area. **Calif. 41** is the main road leading to Yosemite. **Calif. 180** is the road to Sequoia and Kings Canyon. The numerous hotels in the area make it especially convenient for you to stay overnight before leaving for one of the parks. Some families even make Fresno their base in the summer and take day trips to Yosemite, about two hours away.

Children's activities are found throughout the city. The prime attraction, Roeding Park, is located, along with many motels, near Calif. 99. North Fresno, a newer section of town, is where you'll find shopping malls and many good accommodations.

WHAT TO SEE AND DO

Bordered by Olive and Belmont Avenues, **Roeding Park** (☎ 209/498-1551) is a large tree-filled area with activities for the whole family. It boasts the zoo, Storyland, Playland, Lake Washington where you can rent small boats, fishing ponds, and wide-open spaces wonderful for running or Frisbee throwing. There's a nominal entrance fee.

Chaffee Zoological Gardens (☎ 209/498-2671), with its 1,000 animals and large aviary, is open November through February, 10am to 4pm and March through October 9am to 5pm. Don't miss the world's first computerized reptile house. Admission is $4.50 for adults, $3 for seniors, $2 for children 2–11; under 2, free.

Playland (☎ 209/233-3980) is an irresistible treat for the under-7 set. They will squeal with delight on the tiny roller coaster, and have as much fun on the pint-sized Ferris wheel as most teenagers do on giant thrill rides. Open weekdays in summer from 10am–9:30pm; winter only open weekends 11am to dusk. Closed weekdays from October to March. Rides are 30¢–70¢.

Go to **Storyland** (☎ 209/264-2235) next, where the fairytale characters will come alive for the kids as they visit each of the make-believe homes. There are children's plays, a giant beanstalk for climbing, and lots of animals in this tiny land of enchantment. Open daily from 10am to 5pm May through mid-September; open weekends from 10am to 5pm February through April and September through November. Admission is $2.75 for adults, $1.75 for kids 3–14, free for children 2 and under.

Blackbeard's Family Entertainment Center, located at 4055 N. Chestnut Ave. between Ashlan and Dakota Avenues. (**209/292-4554** for recorded information on rates), is another spot that will delight family members of all ages. The facility has three 18-hole miniature golf courses, each with a different theme ($4.75 per person for 18 holes), a six-flume waterslide ($5.00 per person for all day), Slic-Trac Racers ($3.50 per rider), bumper boats ($3.50 per ride), the new Speedway ($3.50 per rider), 9-cage batting range with soft and hardball (20 pitches for 4 tokens—$1.00), snackbars, and video arcade. Cap'n Kids Ride Land and Fun Factory feature the following rides: Pirate Ship, Antique Cars, Planes & Helicopters, Space Train, Carousel, Baby Bumper Boats. The Fun Factory includes a Play Port with ball baths, roller racers, air bounces and much more, a childrens arcade and birthday facilities. (Restrictions apply to some attractions.) Blackbeard's is open every day at 10am.

The **Discovery Center,** 1944 N. Winery Ave. (☎ **209/251-5533,** or **209/251-5531** for a recorded announcement), is billed as *the* science center for the central San Joaquin Valley. Interactive exhibits and hands-on participation make this place delightful for 2-year-olds and seniors alike. Open all year Tuesday through Sunday from 11am to 5pm. Inquire about year-round special events. Admission is $3 for adults, $2 for seniors and children 2–16, free for children under 2.

The **Fresno Metropolitan Museum,** 1515 Van Ness Ave., at Calavers (☎ **209/ 441-1444**), is an important cultural center in downtown Fresno. Exhibits include the San Joaquin Valley's culture and history, quality touring exhibits, and special hands-on activities for families. Call for information on current exhibitions and programs. Open daily 11am to 5pm. Admission is $4 for adults, $2.50 for students, children 4–12 and seniors $3, free for children under 4; $1 for everyone on the first Wednesday of each month.

Additional Activities

Whispering Waters Fishing Lake, 17601 E. Kings Canyon (☎ **209/787-2625**), is just outside Fresno on the way to Sequoia and Kings Canyon. This fishing hole is a great family outing and picnicking spot. No licenses are required, and you can rent everything you need to catch "the big one" right here. There's a fee for each fish caught, based on size. Open on Saturday and Sunday from 9am to 7:30pm. Call for weekday hours. Admission is $2 for adults, $1 for children.

If you're going to make a day of it, you might try swimming or canoeing on the Kings River. **Scott's Canoe Rental,** 17439 E. Kings Canyon, in Sanger (☎ **209/787-3450**), is a place to rent the canoes. The season runs from June through August.

Another way to spend an afternoon is at neighboring **Wild Water Adventures,** 11413 E. Shaw Ave. (☎ **209/297-6500** for hours and special promotions). There are more than 16 different water rides, and lifeguards are on duty. Open mid-May through mid-September, but hours vary, so call for information. Admission is $16.95 for adults $12.95 for kids age 3 and up who are under 48 inches tall, free for children 2 and under. *Don't forget*—water parks require special attention to the kids.

Willow Gardens Nursery and Petting Zoo, 10428 N. Willow Ave., in Clovis (☎ **209/299-5402**), is a treat for the toddlers in the group, but enjoyed by all ages. Little Elizabeth got to meet and pet her first goat, sheep, and burro here. Bring a picnic lunch, then stroll the grounds. Monday through Saturday and on Sunday from both Nursery and zoo are open 9am to 5pm. Admission is 50¢.

Indoor Activities

Although the weather is usually warm here, valley fog or rain can cut short outdoor excursions. But take heart. You might try Fresno's indoor ice-skating rink, **Icelandia,** 2455 N. Marks Ave. (☎ **209/275-1118**), open Wednesday through Friday from 2 to 5pm, plus on Wednesday, from 7 to 9pm Saturday 1pm–3:30pm; Sunday 1:30–4pm. Call for summer hours. Admission is $5 for everyone on weekday afternoons, various prices on weekends and evenings.

Agricultural Tours and Fruit Picking

The San Joaquin Valley is a world supplier of agricultural products. You'll notice vineyards and orchards throughout the area.

At **Bar 20 Dairy Farm,** 4260 W. Madison, in Fresno (☎ **209/264-6583**), kids can see where milk *really* comes from. It's open April through June only; call for an appointment. Admission is free.

For a different kind of taste treat, tour the **Hershey Chocolate Visitor Center & Factory,** at 120 S. Sierra Ave., in Oakdale (☎ **209/848-8126**), two hours north of Fresno. As your mouth waters and your tastebuds come alive, you can watch the making and packaging of chocolate—if you're patient you'll get a taste at the end of the tour. Tours last a half hour and are given Monday through Friday from 8:30am. The visitor center stays open from 10am to 5pm. The whole family is welcome, but the tour is not stroller-accessible. Reservations are required only for groups of 15 or more, and no admission fee is charged. Sign up for tours at the center.

BOOKS AND TOYS

We love to browse in children's bookstores, and the kids enjoy the diversion. One of the most interesting in the Fresno area is **Pegasus Books for Young People,** 349 E. Shaw Ave. in the Mission Village Shopping Center at the southwest corner of Fresno and Shaw Avenues (☎ 209/221-8524).

For toys to keep kids occupied, you may want to stop at **Arthur's Toy Shop,** 4818 E. Tulare Ave. at Chestnut Ave. (☎ 209/252-9365).

ACTIVITIES BY AGE GROUP

The following listings suggest activities divided into specific age brackets. Refer to the individual descriptions for details and any age restrictions.

Teens and Preteens

Agricultural Tours and Fruit Picking
Blackbeard's Family Entertainment Center
Canoe Rentals
Discovery Center
Fresno Metropolitan Museum
Icelandia
Wild Water Adventures

School-age Children

Agricultural Tours and Fruit Picking
Canoe Rentals
Discovery Center
Fresno Metropolitan Museum
Icelandia
Roeding Park (and Zoo, Storyland, Playland)
Whispering Waters Fishing Lake
Wild Water Adventures

Preschoolers and Toddlers

Wild Water Adventures
Roeding Park (and Zoo, Storyland, Playland)
Willow Gardens Nursery and Petting Zoo

WHERE TO STAY

The best bet for your money is the **Hill House Vagabond Inn,** located at 1101 N. Parkway Dr., Fresno, CA 93728 (☎ 209/268-6211; fax 209/268-6211), just off Calif. 99 and near Roeding Park. The management takes great pride in this motel and it shows, making this a great place to stay and an especially good value. A spacious pool area is attractive for kids, and there's a small play area with swings and a slide. Plenty of parking is adjacent to the rooms.

A complimentary continental breakfast is served, and small refrigerators are available in the rooms ($7 per night). There's no dining facility on the premises, but a 24-hour Denny's Restaurant, inexpensive to moderately priced, is next door.

Rooms here are nice-sized, clean, and bright. No-smoking rooms are available. Standard doubles range in price from $45 to $48. But the best bets are the family suites; there are only three available, so request them well in advance. The largest, for $62, is a two-room unit with three queen-size beds and there's still room for a crib or rollaway. The smaller units cost $56 and $50. There's no charge for cribs and $5 for rollaways, and kids under 12 stay free in their parents' room. Extra adults pay $5 per night.

Our recommendation for a first-class all-suite hotel is the **Piccadilly Inn Hotel,** 2305 W. Shaw Ave., Fresno, CA 93711 (☎ **209/226-3850,** or toll free **800/468-3587, 800/468-3522** in California; fax 209/226-2448), in North Fresno. There are three of these four-star Piccadilly suite hotels in Fresno, but most families come to this location. This elegant European-style resort is spread out on $7^{1}/_{2}$ acres and has a beautiful fenced-in pool and spa area with beverage service, and plenty of grassy areas where kids can play. The hotel has 196 elegantly furnished rooms, some even have working fireplaces.

Oliver's Restaurant is a non-smoking restaurant off the lobby bar. It will strike you as formal, yet it caters to children as well as adults for breakfast, lunch, and dinner. Sunday brunch offers special children's selections. Although there is no separate children's menu, the staff will improvise, and they will warm baby bottles and split orders. Selections off the pub menu are child-appropriate. The outside patio is not only pleasant for dining, it is perhaps more comfortable for those with a wandering child. Meal prices range from moderate to expensive. Room service delivers from 6am to 10pm, and fresh perked coffee is available in some rooms.

All the rooms are oversize. A deluxe room comes with a king-size bed and a sitting area. Double rooms are furnished with two queen-size beds. You can also rent a one- or two-bedroom suite. Rates range from $88 single to $98 double for a standard room; are $94 single and $104 double for deluxe rooms and minisuites and from $195 to $240 for suites. Children under 12 stay free in their parents' room and cribs are provided at no charge; children 12 and over are charged $10 per night each.

Another first-class hotel conveniently located on the road to Yosemite is the **Sheraton Smuggler's Inn,** 3737 N. Blackstone Ave. (at Dakota Ave.), Fresno, CA 93726 (☎ **209/226-2200,** or toll free **800/742-1911;** fax 209/222-7147). The Sheraton is possibly in the best location of all the hotels, close to Calif. 41 and I-99 and across from the Manchester Center shopping mall. The pool area at this four-star, four-diamond resortlike hotel will make you want to stay longer. It's large and fenced in and has a Jacuzzi.

The rooms here are oversize, among the largest we've seen, giving you room to spread out with the kids. The newly remodeled rooms are decorated with plush pile carpets and contemporary furniture. Each room has a bar-size refrigerator, coffee maker, hairdryer, an alarm clock radio, a desk, and not one, but three, phones with voice mail are standard. Remote-control color TV with free HBO and ESPN, are provided, but be sure to request that the pay-per-view movies you don't want be turned off at the front desk. Rooms with king-size beds have love seats, some of which are sofa beds, and leather recliners. Some rooms have private patios. You can request connecting rooms and non-smoking units. A guest laundry room has recently been added.

If you do choose to eat in, you'll find friendly, efficient service with a children's menu. Room service can be ordered 7am to 10pm, and you can make arrangements at the front desk for box lunches to take to Yosemite.

Rates are $75–$90 single and $80–$95 double. Children 17 and under stay free in their parents' room; additional adults pay $5 per night. Cribs are free, but rollaways cost $5.

The **Village Inn Best Western** is also on the road to Yosemite, at 3110 N. Blackstone Ave. (at Shields Ave.), Fresno, CA 93703 (☎ 209/226-2110). This hotel has a small gated pool area. Most of the 153 rooms have two queen-size beds, and non-smoking rooms can be requested; there are no suites or adjoining rooms. Complimentary continental breakfast is served. There's a reasonably priced chain restaurant, Denny's, next door. Singles cost $48 and doubles are $54–$58. Children under 12 stay free in their parents' room; additional guests are charged $4 per night each. Cribs are available for a $6 charge; rollaways cost $10.

Another alternative is the **San Joaquin Hotel,** located at 1309 W. Shaw Ave., Fresno, CA 93711 (☎ 209/255-1309, or toll free 800/775-1309; fax 209/225-6021), North Fresno's only suite hotel. Although the furnishings and the quiet atmosphere convey a luxurious adult hotel environment, many families stay here, especially in summer. There are one-, two-, and three-bedroom suites, each with a living room, some with a full kitchen. Continental-plus breakfast is complimentary, or you can order from room service. A small pool and Jacuzzi are in the courtyard, and adults can take advantage of the off-site health club privileges. Room prices include continental-plus breakfast and soft drinks and hors d'oeuvres in the evening.

Rates range from $89 for a one-bedroom unit, which has room for a crib in the bedroom or living room, to $195 for the three-bedroom suites. But add on the extras: The sleeper sofa costs $10 if used, and rollaways are $10 per night. Cribs are free. Ask about weekly, monthly, and winter rates.

Budget-priced and just adequate for an overnight stay is the **Best Western Parkside Inn,** at 1415 W. Olive Ave., Fresno, CA 93728 (☎ 209/237-2086, or toll free 800/442-2284; fax 209/264-9304). Rooms are large but dark, and some adjoining rooms are available. On the good side, there's a heated pool and a children's wading pool; there are many non-smoking rooms, and half the units have refrigerators. Be sure to request a room on the east side, away from the freeway noise. A coffee shop is nearby.

Depending on the season, singles are $50; doubles, $54–$56. Children over 12 and additional adult guests are charged $4 per night. Cribs are $4, and rollaways cost $6 per night.

WHERE TO EAT

A regular stop for us is the **Iron Horse Restaurant,** at 3757 W. Shaw Ave. (☎ 209/276-3757). Our kids insist on a stop here to get their fill of train whistles and clanging bells, and we like the food. The restaurant is designed like an old-fashioned train depot, complete with ticket booth and waiting room. Small electric trains perched high on small shelves chug through the restaurant commanding attention from children and grownups alike. When Junior's order is taken and ready, the train whistle blows, a bell clangs, and servers yell "All aboard." With all that going on, not even the crankiest kid will embarrass you because few others will hear him.

This fun, casual coffee shop has an extensive and marvelous menu for those 10 and under. Our breakfast favorites are the Casey Jones which is pancakes plus an egg and bacon for $3.50, and the Puffing Billy, a two-egg Spanish omelet with hash browns and a biscuit for $3.50. You can order breakfast items until 2pm. At lunch there are great burgers and sandwiches. Adult fare is reasonably priced too.

They have high chairs and boosters, and do not takes reservations—at prime times you may have a wait of approximately 15 minutes. Open for breakfast and lunch daily from 6am to 2pm; Accepts credit cards, parking lot.

The Old Spaghetti Factory, at 2721 Ventura Ave., at R Street (☎ 209/ 442-1066), in downtown Fresno, is traditionally a fun place. Although somewhat out of the way unless you're staying at a downtown Fresno hotel, it's a place where kids can be kids and parents don't have to worry about them making too much noise.

Children's menu selections include spaghetti with tomato sauce ($2.95) or with a meatball ($3.35), and baked lasagne ($3.95), and are served with applesauce, animal cookie, a beverage, and a frozen dessert; and they're even served on just-for-kids plates. A Junior Meal is slightly different: there's no lasagne, but the spaghetti comes with salad, bread, beverage, and spumoni ice cream for $3.75.

Adult entrees are equally inexpensive. For less than $6 you can get a complete dinner which includes spaghetti (choose from a great variety of preparations), salad bread, spumoni ice cream, and coffee, tea, or milk. For $6.75 to $8.10 three combination platters, lasagne and chicken breast, ravioli and spaghetti, or spaghetti with meat sauce or meatballs and a side of sausage and salad, bread, beverage, and spumoni.

Boosters and high chairs are available. Management has provided a "Diaper Deck," a changing table, in the women's restroom. The restaurant is open for dinner only: Monday through Thursday from 5 to 9pm, on Friday and Saturday from 5 to 10pm, and on Sunday from 4 to 9pm. No reservations are accepted, but the average wait on weekends is only 15 minutes. Most major credit cards are accepted.

Williker's Bar and Grill, 1713 E. Shaw Ave. (☎ 209/226-1984), is a local favorite of families. All the children's items are $2.95 and include fries or real mashed potatoes, fruit, and milk or soda. A 4-year-old might go for the chicken strips, but there are other standbys, such as burgers and grilled cheese. Or they'll make whatever your youngsters may want. Special drinks can be ordered. Management lets kids use Etch-a-Sketches while they wait for their food. The adult menu is also extensive, and your choice won't break the bank—most selections are under $10. The favorite— baby back ribs—goes for $8 or $13. The adult bar menu is also unusual. High chairs and boosters are available.

Open Monday through Saturday from 11:30am to 10pm and on Sunday from 11am to 2pm for brunch and until 9pm for dinner. A parking lot is available. All major credit cards accepted.

Picnics

Some people make day trips to the national parks. To meet that need, the following places will pack picnics for you. (Also check with your hotel; many provide the service—if you give one or two days' notice.) Try the **Grape Tray,** 5091 N. Fresno Ave., in Fresno Shaw Plaza (☎ 209/226-6828), and **Moveable Feast,** 736 W. Bullard Ave. (☎ 209/439-3777).

In Case of Emergency

If you're in need of an emergency room, contact the **St. Agnes Medical Center,** 1303 E. Herndon Ave., at the corner of Millbrook Avenue (☎ 209/449-3205) or the **Fresno Community Hospital and Medical Center,** located on Divisadero between Fresno and R Streets (☎ 209/442-3998). Both have 24-hour emergency services.

2 Yosemite National Park

If you have but one national park to visit with your children, it should be Yosemite. Everyone has heard stories about the crowds of people and about traffic problems in the valley (which is true only in summer, anyway), but all of that fades when you enter the park and behold the first grand vista. This is as close to natural perfection as you're ever going to get.

Known for thundering waterfalls and glacier-carved cliffs rising from the valley floor, Yosemite is also meandering rivers, magnificent meadows, spectacular wildflowers, and abundant wildlife. No matter how much you hear about the park before you go, your expectations will not be too high.

Most people think of Yosemite as a summer vacation spot. But off-season it's a gem. Many of the activities are still open, and there are fewer people to contend with. In spring after the snow starts to melt, the waterfalls are full. The change of color in fall is breathtaking. Skiing at Badger Pass and winter activities throughout the area are fun for all family members.

Yosemite, in addition to being a paradise of wild terrain, is a family vacation paradise of hiking, rafting, swimming, picnicking, skiing, and ice skating. (See the "How to Travel with Kids" section in Chapter 1 for specific information about preparing your family for an outdoor vacation.) General information is **209/372-0200.**

GETTING THERE

Four scenic driving routes take you into the park. And while most people don't think of it, you can also get there by public transportation via air, train, or bus.

Public Transportation

By air, fly into Fresno Air Terminal, then take a Gray Line bus or rent a car. **By train** from Los Angeles, you first take a bus to Bakersfield, then the train to Merced and a bus to Yosemite. Amtrak (tel. toll free **800/USA-RAIL**) can arrange the whole package. Amtrak services San Francisco via Emeryville by train to Merced.

California Parlor Car Tours (☎ **415/474-7500** in San Francisco, or toll free **800/227-4250**) offers two- and three-day excursions from San Francisco, daily April through November. Fares include lodging and some meals. Rates range from $175 to $380 for adults from San Francisco. Kids 5–17 are charged $130 for a two-day trip, $280 for a three-day; under-5, free.

By Car

From San Francisco (via Merced), take Calif. 140. From Sacramento (via Manteca, near Stockton), take Calif. 120. From Los Angeles (via Fresno), take Calif. 41. From the east, from locations such as Reno, Lake Tahoe, Bishop, take U.S. 395 to Calif. 120E, also known as Tioga Pass Road. It's a beautiful drive—the highest mountain pass in the Sierras, but open summers only. Check road conditions with **Caltrans Highway Information** if you're concerned about rain, snow, or road closures, or call **800/427-7623.**

The entrance permit costs only $5 per car. If you plan to stay longer than seven days, or wish to or combine this trip with visits to Sequoia—Kings Canyon National Parks and Lassen National Park, it might be worth your while to purchase an annual **Golden Eagle Passport:** for $25 it gives you free entrance to all national parks that charge fees. Or you might want to buy an annual **Yosemite Passport** for $15, which allows you to enter and leave the park at will for the whole year your permit is valid.

As you enter the park, you'll be given a copy of *Yosemite Guide*, a free newsletter describing the season's activities.

An Attraction and a Restaurant En Route

If you take Calif. 41, you'll come to a great little stop before you enter the park proper. **Yosemite Mountain–Sugar Pine Railroad,** just four miles before you reach the park entrance (☎ **209/683-7273**), is an authentic Logger Steam Train that takes you back in history as you ride through magnificent scenery. Kids love the popular open-air Jenny railcars, quaint "Model A"–powered railcars. The giftshop is a mecca for children (and adults) who love train paraphernalia. You'll find a snack bar and clean restrooms. There's a little museum built in 1856, called the Thornberry Museum, which houses all kinds of artifacts from the 1800s. There are logging camp paraphernalia, household items such as old wash basins, and photographs. The museum is open May through October; hours vary.

The Logger Steam Train operates daily from May through September, and on weekends in October; fares are $9.50 for adults, $4.50 for children 3–12, free for children under 3. The Jenny railcars operate daily from April to October; fares are $6.25 for adults, $3.25 for children 3–12, free for children under 3. Call for hours because they change seasonally.

Next door to the Sugar Pine (you'll have to get back on the highway) is a charming restaurant, particularly nice for breakfast and dinner. The **Narrow Gauge Inn Dining Hall,** in the Narrow Gauge Inn, 48571 Calif. 41, Fish Camp (☎ **209/ 683-6446**), offers a splendid view of the High Sierra. The dining room is an eclectic mix of early-19th-century Victorian and western decor. The food is fresh and the portions abundant. Continental breakfast is buffet-style, with plenty of croissants, cinnamon rolls, bagels, cereal, and juices. Prices are reasonable. Regular dinner entrees such as médaillons of beef, lemon-broiled prawns, or New York steak are available in "light" portions for children, seniors, and those with smaller appetites. A separate children's menu lists sesame chicken and fried shrimp, and includes soup or salad and French fries for about $7. There is no extra-plate charge for small children, so you could split your dinner.

Breakfast is served seven days from 7:30 to 9:30am; the continental breakfast is served Monday through Friday. After breakfast or brunch, the restaurant is closed until dinner, which is then served daily from 5:30 to 9pm. The restaurant is open Easter through mid-October. Highchairs and boosters are provided. Reservations are essential; major credit cards accepted. There is a parking lot.

ORIENTATION

Yosemite National Park, on the western slope of the Sierra Nevada range in the central part of the state, attracts about four million visitors each year, many from abroad. There are 800 miles of trails and 196 miles of primary roads to make the park accessible.

Yosemite Valley is the area that comes to most people's minds when they think of Yosemite. Within this area are Bridalveil Fall, Yosemite Falls, exquisite views of El Capitan and Half Dome, beautiful meadows, and the Merced River. There are numerous trails and self-guided walks.

Yosemite Village includes the Village Center store, the Ansel Adams Photography Gallery, the visitor center, a small gift shop, and a theater for evening programs, as well as Degnan's Deli and the Loft Restaurant.

Although the valley is the hub of activities, there are many other areas of the park to visit, including Wawona, Tuolumne Meadows, and Tioga Pass, plus Glacier Point and Badger Pass.

Remember: Don't feed the wild animals, no matter how cute and tame they appear. Not only will they suffer in winter when there's no one to feed them, but you can't be sure just how tame an animal is—after all, these are *wild* animals.

Getting Around the Valley

Once you've arrived in the valley, there's no need to drive. A free **shuttle bus,** complete with overhead windows so you're never far from the sight of the towering mountains, will take you to any of the hotels, and most of the major trailheads and other valley attractions. Shuttle bus hours are 8am to 9pm, with extended hours in summer.

Bus tours also operate every day. There's a year-round two-hour guided tour of the valley, plus several seasonal tours: a one-hour tram tour of the Big Trees, a four-hour tour of Glacier Point, a six-hour guided tour of the Mariposa Grove of Big Trees, a full-day Grand Tour, and a two-hour Moonlight Tour. Fees start at $7 for adults, $3.50 children 4–12, seniors $6.50, children under 4 free. For information and tickets, contact the Tour/Activities desks at Yosemite Lodge, The Ahwahnee, and Curry Village, or the booth next to the Village Store, or call **209/372-1240.**

WHAT TO DO AND HOW TO DO IT IN YOSEMITE VALLEY

Sometimes the beauty and size of the park overwhelm visitors and they don't know where to begin. Although the park is the size of Rhode Island, 80% of the visitors don't venture out of the seven square miles of Yosemite Valley. Here's how to get around that:

When you receive the *Yosemite Guide* at the park entrance, keep it and read it. It gives the lowdown on all that's going on in the area and is your first step in planning what you want to do during your stay. After you've settled in and browsed through the *Guide,* you might want to go to one of the visitor centers, located in Yosemite Village, Big Oak Flat, Wawona, and Tuolumne Meadows. They have a lot of specific information.

Ask the park rangers for suggestions. Just tell them what you want to do and the ages of your children, and they'll come up with loads of ideas. They're also great about giving you the skill level of the various hiking trails and current trail and weather conditions. The people at the tour desks in the hotels are also helpful.

Valley Hiking

The key to enjoyable hiking is to know your limits and the limits of your children, and to come prepared. Many an enjoyable day has been spoiled because of blistered feet and too much walking. Check at the visitor center for details about your hike. Layer your clothes, wear comfortable shoes, bring water and sunscreen (and hats for the little ones), and don't push too hard.

In addition to the many trails you can hike yourselves, there are many ranger-guided walking tours throughout Yosemite Valley. These are detailed in the *Yosemite Guide.* In general, all the hikes in the valley are good for children.

Don't miss the self-guiding tour of the **Yosemite Indian Village** located just behind the visitor center. This short, easy stroll was perfect for Elizabeth's first hiking adventure when she was a toddler, and introduced the rest of us to the Yosemite Miwok tribe. Signs and displays show you how the Native Americans used the natural

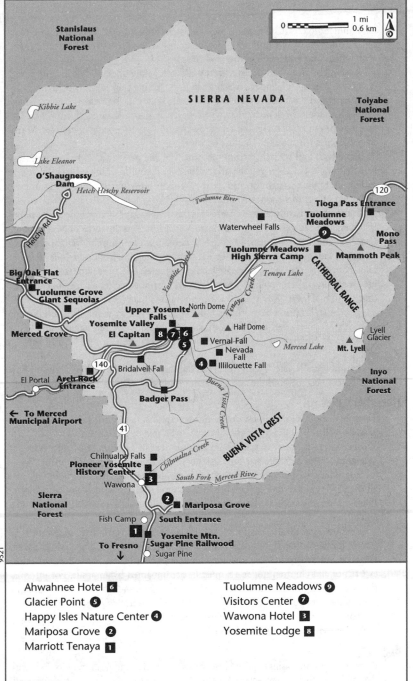

Yosemite National Park

SIERRA NEVADA

Stanislaus
National
Forest

Toiyabe
National
Forest

Kibbie Lake

Lake Eleanor

O'Shaughnessy
Dam

Hetch Hetchy Reservoir

Tuolumne River

Tioga Pass Entrance

120

Tuolumne
Meadows ❾

Waterwheel Falls

Mono
Pass

Mammoth Peak

Tuolumne Meadows
High Sierra Camp

CATHEDRAL RANGE

Tenaya Lake

Big Oak Flat
Entrance

Tuolumne Grove
Giant Sequoias

Merced Grove

Upper Yosemite
Falls

North Dome

Yosemite Valley

El Capitan ❽ ❼ ❻

❺

Vernal Fall

Half Dome

Merced Lake

Lyell
Glacier

Mt. Lyell

Nevada
Fall

❹ Illilouette Fall

140

Bridalveil Fall

Buena Vista Creek

Inyo
National
Forest

El Portal

Arch Rock
Entrance

← To Merced
Municipal Airport

Badger Pass

BUENA VISTA CREST

41

Chilnualpe Falls

Chilnualna Creek

Pioneer Yosemite
History Center

❸

South Fork Merced River

Wawona

Sierra
National
Forest

Fish Camp

❷

Mariposa Grove

South Entrance

❶

Yosemite Mtn.
Sugar Pine Railwood

To Fresno
↓

Sugar Pine

0   1 mi
    0.6 km

N

Ahwahnee Hotel ❻	Tuolumne Meadows ❾
Glacier Point ❺	Visitors Center ❼
Happy Isles Nature Center ❹	Wawona Hotel ❸
Mariposa Grove ❷	Yosemite Lodge ❽
Marriott Tenaya ❶	

environment to create homes and food. Kids can walk into the wooden tepees. During the summer, Native Americans demonstrate basket-weaving, cooking techniques, ceremonial functions, and children love it!

Lower Yosemite Fall is also a great walk with young ones. Only half a mile long, it's easy and beautiful, and it gives little kids the feeling they're actually hiking.

Mirror Lake is approximately a two-hour walk that starts at the Mirror Lake shuttle-bus stop. Check with the rangers if you're in the park during the summer. The lake is in the process of becoming a meadow. As the water evaporates in summer, Mirror Lake becomes Mirror Meadow. It's easy walking.

Bridalveil Fall is reached from the Bridalveil Fall parking area. It, too, is an easy half-mile walk. Go as far as the parking lot even if you don't intend to hike. It's an experience to look straight up and see the water rushing (or trickling, if it's summer) down the side of this enormous mountain.

Happy Isles Family Nature Center is the trailhead for many of the park's popular hikes. You can get there by shuttle bus during the busy months of May through October. The center is especially suited for families with young children. Special programs for kids as young as 8 (Junior Rangers) are ongoing from mid-June to Labor Day. For younger children, there are family programs. There are puppet shows, wildlife programs, and a diorama. Different movies are presented for all ages, but with the tots in mind. This is also a great starting point for a hike to Vernal Fall.

The **Mist Trail** is a beautiful hike that will take you to Vernal Fall and Nevada Falls. It's a leisurely half-day hike, but is *not* for the under-8 set. Parents should use caution with children of any age as there are slippery areas. It's well worth the trip with good hikers.

For more trails, check with the rangers at the visitor center. They'll tell you how steep a trail becomes and the average length of time it takes to hike it with children.

Horseback Riding

Yosemite has one of the largest public riding stables in the world. There are 400 head of stock—all of which carry riders. The stables, located in **Yosemite Valley** near Curry Village, are open Easter to mid-October, and those in **Tuolumne Meadows** and at **Wawona** are open in summer only. All horseback riding is by guided tour.

For older children and adults, there are two-hour ($31), half-day ($44.50), and all-day ($65) guided rides to such places as Yosemite Falls, Nevada Falls, even Glacier Point. Once you arrive in Yosemite, check in at the stables to reserve a space on a guided ride.

Yosemite Stables also has four- and six-day saddle trips to the High Sierra. The camps, located about eight miles apart, are equipped with tents and beds and serve breakfast and dinner. Minimum age is 7; children under 12 must have previous riding experience and children under 18 must be accompanied by an adult. For information, call the High Sierra Reservations Desk (☎ 209/454-2002), or write Yosemite Concession Services Corp., 5410 Home Ave., Fresno CA 93721.

You might also check with Yosemite Trails Park Station in Fish Camp (☎ 209/683-7611 or 209/683-9122).

Bicycling

Bicycling is an increasingly popular way to see the area, and a fun way to do it with the children. When you bicycle in Yosemite, stay on paved bikeways, shuttlebus routes, and one-way roads. Bicycles are not allowed on trails or in the meadows. If you're unsure of the area, ask at the bicycle-rental areas located at Yosemite Lodge Bike Stand

and Curry Village Bike Stand. Rental hours vary according to season and weather. Helmets are available. If you're bike riding in the fall or during cooler weather, bring mittens for yourself and the kids. The weather can be brisk and uncomfortable for a child with exposed hands.

Water Sports

Swimming: The hotels have swimming pools for their guests. The Merced River and Tenaya Lake, especially in the warm, shallow areas near the shore, are also good places to cool down on hot summer days. Usually swimming is good near the campgrounds, but check it out to be sure that you've chosen a safe place. During spring and early summer, rivers and streams run quickly and the water temperatures are low, sometimes too low for safety, and certainly too low for pleasure. One good check is to ask at Curry Village raft rentals. They will only rent river rafts if the water is the right depth and warm enough to be safe. If they are renting rafts in springtime, you can assume it's safe to go swimming; if they're not, don't try it.

One suggested summer outing is to go up to Tuolumne River, bring a picnic, and go on to Tuolumne Meadows Lodge. From there the river is easy to follow. Walk down the river to the shallow pools where the sun warms the granite, making swimming very pleasant.

River Rafting: During June and July (river conditions permitting) there is great rafting on the Merced River. You can rent rafts at Curry Village. All rafters must wear life jackets. While it's not for the tiniest children, it's safe for kids over 4. The recommended age is 6 and older. Don't expect white-water rafting. This is more like a gentle float down the river.

Fishing: Although fishing in the valley isn't the best—the fish are hard to catch—there are good pools up and down the Merced that offer little spots for kids to try for rainbow, brook, and brown trout. The best place is in the high country in out-of-the-way streams. You'll have to bring your own equipment, though, since there are no rentals in the park. Adults and kids over 16 need licenses; they are available at concession facilities in Yosemite Valley and Wawona and at Tuolumne Meadows in summer. Be sure to ask about the exceptions to the open season fishing list.

Tubing: If you bring your own inner tubes, the Merced River offers terrific tubing. Again, if they're not renting rafts, don't go tubing. There may be a problem with the depth and temperature of the water.

Winter Sports

This is a great place for winter sports. There's an outdoor **ice-skating rink** at Camp Curry that's open afternoons, evenings, and weekend mornings and features a warming hut, fire pit, and snack bar. Admission costs $5 for adults, $4.50 for children; skates may be rented for $1.75. It's open mid-November through March, depending on conditions.

Did you know that **Badger Pass Ski Area** (☎ 209/372-1330) is the oldest established ski area in California? Many of us don't think of Yosemite as a winter retreat, but this is particularly good for families. Badger Pass offers cross-country and downhill skiing, and they have family ski packages. Nordic and downhill ski schools teach you and the kids (the little ones have downhill school only; cross-country lessons are for those 7 and older). Skis can be rented right there. Best of all, **Badger Pups,** a program for children 4–6, is $25 per day, including two lessons, learning games, rental equipment, and use of the supervised Badger Den. On the midweek package, the cost is only $25. Children 7 and older take lessons according to ability.

For those of you whose children either don't want to ski or who tire easily in the cold outdoors, the **Badger Pass Babysitting Service** ($4 per hour) will sit for your 3- to 9-year-olds. Games and activities are provided in this group-care facility.

If you're able to take off during the middle of the week, be sure to call Badger Pass and ask about the Midweek Ski Package, which includes lift tickets, lessons, babysitting, and recreational and social activities in one price. (The room charge is not included in the package.) New additions to the package are family-enrichment discovery learning sessions at Yosemite Lodge on Tuesday nights. These are conducted for the Yosemite Concession Services Corp. by the award-winning environmental education school, the Yosemite Institute.

If you're not the sports type, or if your family has had enough of the active life for a while, why not take a **Snowcat Tour?** This one-hour tour from Badger Pass ($5 per person) takes you through the winter wonderland and offers spectacular views of the High Sierra. Or you might try a two-hour **guided sightseeing tour** that explores the valley's awesome sights. Depending on weather conditions in the fall, tours to the Mariposa Grove of Big Trees may also be available. The Valley Floor Tour costs $14.25; the Glacier Point Tour (available June to Thanksgiving) is $17.75; and the Grand Tour (available June to about November 1) is $39.50. You can check with the Tours/Activity desk at your hotel, or call the Winter Hotline (☎ 209/252-4848).

Mountaineering

For brave souls who like to climb mountains, Yosemite is *the* place. Yosemite offers a Mountaineering School and Guide Service. Occasionally there are classes for children: group lessons from 14 years, private lessons from 10 to 13 years, available. If your kids are at all interested in rock climbing, be sure they get some professional training or assistance before they go off on their own. Rock climbing can be dangerous here, as in any park. All inquiries should be sent to: Yosemite Mountaineering School, Bruce Brossman, Director, Yosemite National Park, CA 95389 (☎ **209/372-1244** September through May or **209/372-1335** June through August).

Special Family Programs

No matter what the season, there are special family programs available through the visitor centers. Some can be shared with the whole family; others are ranger-led activities for the kids, independent of Mom and Dad. During the summer, Family Campfires encourage participation from the parents and kids around the fire, and feature songs, skits, and stories. Walks with a ranger and evening programs with slides or a movie explain the plants, wildlife, and history of the park.

Junior Ranger Programs are offered in the summer and winter at Yosemite Valley, and in the summer at Tuolumne Meadows. The interpretive programs are in-depth and cover an aspect of ecology, Native Americans, habitat, or aquatic life. Children 8–12 may sign up to participate in two morning sessions. After completing these programs and attending a ranger-led program anywhere in the park, children receive a special patch. Winter programs might be a snowshoe walk, cross-country ski tour, Junior Snow Ranger scavenger hunt, or nature walk. For more information, write to the Visitor Center, National Park Service, P.O. Box 577, Yosemite, CA 95389.

Evening Programs

During the summer rangers present nightly evening campfire programs. Topics change and will be posted at the visitor center and campgrounds and accommodations. Sometimes you can join a ranger for an early-evening stroll.

What to Do When It Rains or Snows

If it's warm, the two-hour sightseeing tours are a good choice. Enclosed buses are used in the winter. And the Wawona Big Trees tour may be something to do during wet weather.

Or pack up the family and drive up to Glacier Point. It's really something to watch the weather change, because the clouds get hung up on the rocks and swirl through the valley.

Visit the Indian Cultural Center in Yosemite Village.

Walks through the heavily forested areas are nice during the rain. Some areas are so dense you won't even get wet. In the fall the vibrant colors are even prettier when the sky is overcast and dark.

Finally, ice skating and skiing are always ongoing in the winter.

Sometimes the visitor centers will have activities. Call or ask at the front desk of your hotel or check the *Yosemite Guide.*

ACTIVITIES AND SIGHTS OUTSIDE THE VALLEY

Glorious as Yosemite Valley is, there are some attractions of interest in the surrounding area.

Glacier Point

Views and vistas are *the* thing in Yosemite. For two magnificent views, don't miss Washburn Point and Glacier Point. It's difficult to describe the grandeur and beauty from these locations. From both, you can look out to the high country and see a succession of snow-capped granite peaks. From Glacier Point, you have an amazing view of the surrounding peaks, and you can look down into the valley. The views of Half Dome are incredible.

Kids will love to look down to the village and see the miniature cars, swimming pools, and other landmark structures. We took Andrew and Elizabeth to the Ahwahnee first, walked through it, and then drove to Glacier Point. Then we pointed out where they'd just been—this time with a bird's-eye view. It gave them a great sense of just how high up they were.

Wawona

Wawona's **Pioneer Yosemite History Center,** near the Wawona Hotel, is likely to entice kids of all ages. The center consists of historic structures from the late 1800s and early 1900s, and is the setting for a popular summer program in which costumed park volunteers portraying pioneers interpret the pioneer experience in Yosemite. The center is open Wednesday through Sunday from late June through the Sunday of Labor Day weekend. You might even want to take a stagecoach ride. You may schedule a tour of the buildings for Monday or Tuesday. Consult the *Yosemite Guide* at the park for specific schedules.

Not far from Wawona is the **Mariposa Grove of Giant Sequoias** (36 miles south of Yosemite Valley and 2 miles from the south entrance to the park). Be sure to see Grizzly Giant, the oldest tree in the grove. Tram tour and ranger walks are available. Tour rates are $7 for adults, $3.50 for children 5–12, and $6 for seniors. Tour times vary throughout the year, so check with the visitor center.

Yosemite Fire Area

On August 7, 1990, lightning ignited 28 separate fires in the park in the southwestern area of the part, near Calif. 140 and Calif. 41. Although most of these fires were immediately extinguished, several continued to grow. On August 8, high winds fanned the flames and thunderstorms continued. On August 9, 60-mph winds helped the fire consume over 5,000 acres. On August 10, some 15,000 people were evacuated from Yosemite Valley. Finally, on August 14, the fire was almost fully contained after having burned more than 22,000 acres. It gained the distinction of being the largest fire in Yosemite's history.

Spectacular as it was, the fire consumed less than 2% of the park. Although it destroyed much of the town of Foresta and had other negative effects, the aftermath of the fire will afford children positive environmental educational experiences if you choose to discuss the fire with them when you visit the area. The National Park Service has erected informational markers along the highway.

Typically, in an area that has experienced fire, the following spring offers an amazing display of wildflowers and diverse plantlife because of the increased mineral content of the ash in the soil and other environmental factors. After a few years, the forest floor begins to have a carpet of shrubs and grasses. Along with your guidance, your children can have the opportunity to visit the area every few years and watch the regeneration of the forest within their lifetimes.

Tuolumne Meadows and Tioga Road

The highest paved road in the Sierra, Tioga Pass is known for its exquisite beauty. Tuolumne is an enormous sub-alpine meadow. These are wonderful places to venture if you're planning to be in the park for a while. Tuolumne Meadows offers abundant places to have a delightful picnic breakfast or lunch, as well as good easy hikes. One of the real assets of Tuolumne is that it's not as crowded and you're closer to the wilderness areas. In summer the park operates several campgrounds and conducts a full-scale naturalist program. The Valley Visitor Center has information about all these programs.

WHERE TO STAY

Going to Yosemite in the summer requires a bit of advance planning and persistence. For key summer weekends—if you want a hotel room or cottage with a bath—you need to reserve a year and a day in advance. (They won't take your reservation any earlier.)

To make reservations at any of these accommodations, call **Yosemite Reservations** at **209/252-4848,** a central reservations number. Or send a deposit covering one night's lodging by check or money order to **Yosemite Concessions Service Corp.,** 5410 E. Home Ave., Fresno, CA 93727.

All room rates quoted below are approximate and change according to season.

Marriott's Tenaya Lodge at Yosemite, 1122 Calif. 41, Fish Camp, CA 93623 (☎ **209/683-6555,** or toll free **800/635-5807**), is a terrific alternative to lodging inside the park. For one thing, reservations are easier to make, and for another, it's pleasant to stay outside the valley. Located just two miles south of the south entrance, this conveniently situated lodge is a place designed with families in mind. The lobby and other public rooms are open and spacious. Huge ceilings, an enormous stonework fireplace, and large windows contribute to the feeling of expansiveness. It's such a large place that your children can wander and enjoy themselves without your worrying that they may be disturbing others.

The lodge has a wide variety of recreational facilities, including indoor and outdoor swimming pools and Jacuzzis, a fitness center, including saunas and steam rooms.

Camp Tenaya provides children from ages 5–12 with professional care year-round with reservations. Nature walks and Indian lore familiarize the children with special aspects of the Yosemite area. The kids get to "Name a Tree" and participate in a "Jackalope" hunt. Activities range from area native crafts, T-shirt painting, movies, pool play, volleyball, square dancing, alphabet walks, leather crafts, camp songs, face-painting, and more. Each group has no more than 30 children. Meals offered are pre-selected entrees and each child receives a Camp Tenaya T-shirt memento. Special needs and considerations may be arranged. Evening programs cost $25 per child, $40 for two children. Day program costs $35 per child. Camp Tenaya is offered as an option on many packages. In the summer the program is offered seven days a week. Reservations are required 24 hours in advance.

The Sierra Room is open for breakfast and dinner, and the casual Parkside Deli is open from 6:30am until midnight. You'll find sandwiches, burgers, and pizza at the Parkside Deli, along with picnic take-out for those long day trips. Both places have children's menus, highchairs, and boosters. There is also 24-hour room service.

The 242 rooms and suites are quite lovely, and have ample room to spread out. They have cable TV, movies, an honor bar, and the usual amenities you'd expect.

Rooms run $139–$169 from March 30 to mid-June, $189–$209 from mid-June to August 31, $139–$169 from early September to November 1, $89–$139 November 2 to December 31, and $109–$139 January 1 through March. Suites are available. Children under 17 stay free with their parents, and there's no charge for rollaways or cribs. Holiday rates can be quite a bit higher. Ask about the holiday packages.

The **Wawona Hotel,** in Wawona, seven miles inside the south entrance to the park on Calif. 41 (P.O. Box 2005), Yosemite National Park, CA 95389 (☎ 209/252-4848), is a venerable hotel dating back to the 1800s when travelers to Yosemite used it as a stopover for lodging and food. Looking somewhat like a misplaced southern plantation, the Wawona is surrounded by pines and redwoods and visited by small herds of deer. The advantage of staying here, especially in summer, is that it's out of crowded Yosemite Valley, yet near enough to enable you to go back and forth in a reasonable amount of time. It affords you peace and quiet, while still offering gorgeous surroundings.

The large pool, enclosed by a white picket fence, is surrounded by magnificent grounds for children to roam. Golf and tennis are available. For babysitting arrangements, inquire at the front desk.

There are 105 rooms, 50 of which have private baths. The rooms in the Annex building are small, dark, but very clean. Don't expect amenities here. A large family might want to rent two rooms connected by a bathroom. Ask for a corner room in the annex, as they're a little larger. Also inquire about the Little White House and whether it's available. The rooms look spacious and light.

A double room without a bath is $63.25; a double with bath, $86.25. Children under 12 stay free in their parents' room. Cribs are free, and rollaways are included in the additional expense of an extra person. Make summer reservations one year in advance. For spring or fall reservations, call three months ahead. The hotel and restaurant are open from early March to November and weekends during the winter.

Breakfast, lunch, and dinner are served in the restaurant on the premises, but there is no room service. Restaurant selections for kids are limited, but they do exist (southern fried chicken is one possibility, the Wawona burger another). Dinner entrees range from $10 to $17.

The **Ahwahnee Hotel** is one mile east of Yosemite Village on Ahwahnee Drive, Yosemite National Park, CA 95389 (☎ 209/252-4848). Legend has it that in the early 1920s a titled Englishwoman came to visit, and at that time the only hotel in the park was called the Sentinel. She declared that the Sentinel was primitive and classless, and her refusal to stay there caused the director of the National Park Service great consternation. Thus when the two main concessionaires in the park were directed to merge, they had to agree to build a modern luxury hotel, and so the Ahwahnee was born.

Whether or not you stay at the Ahwahnee (if you can even get a reservation during summer season), you must see it. The Great Lounge is decorated in the unlikely combination of Native American and German Gothic. But rare rugs hanging on the walls warm the massive room, and original art is found everywhere.

The view from the huge dining room is picture-postcard-perfect. Breakfast and lunch are served here. Meals here are not cheap. Lunch ranges from $8.20 for soup and half a sandwich to $12.75 for the specialty of the day. Dinner for two adults costs about $50, without drinks or appetizers.

The hotel has a heated pool. There is a giftshop and a sundries shop. Concierge service is available to make all your arrangements, including babysitting.

There are 99 rooms in the main hotel and 24 rooms in seven cottages on the hotel grounds. While each room has its own personality, all cost the same: $201.25 single, $208 double. Children 3–12 stay free in their parents' room; children over 12 and additional adults pay $20 per night. Cottages are ideal for families: They are spacious and comfortable, and have little patios. Some include fireplaces and two pull-out sofas. Separate dressing areas are actually big enough to fit a crib. If you want to stay in the main hotel, explain your needs when you call. Some rooms have two double beds and a balcony, others have a queen-size bed with room for a crib. There are few adjoining rooms in the hotel. The reservationists will attempt to put you in a room appropriate for your needs. As we said earlier, the catch is that you have to make a reservation for summer and holidays one year and one day in advance. But there is availability the rest of the year.

Yosemite Lodge is approximately a mile west of Yosemite Village, on Calif. 140, Yosemite National Park, CA 95389 (☎ 209/252-4848). A tour desk in the lobby lets you make arrangements for horseback riding, mountaineering classes, tours, and transportation. This is also where you'll find out about the myriad activities offered in the park. In addition, the lodge has a full-service post office; giftshops; snacks and sundries; a swimming pool open daily during the summer, weather permitting; showers and changing rooms; an amphitheater used nightly in the summer for slide presentations, movies, and ranger programs; and a bike-rental stand with helmets. The bike rental stand is open daily from April through October, and the rest of the year, weather permitting. The free shuttle service that serves the valley stops outside the lobby. Babysitting arrangements can be made at the front desk.

The Yosemite Lodge Cafeteria is open daily year round, and serves breakfast, lunch, snacks, and dinner. Although it's a typical cafeteria, you'll be surprised at the wide selection, the quality of the food, and the very reasonable prices (75¢ for a cup of coffee!). The Four Seasons Restaurant is great for families. Breakfast is served daily in summer, on weekends only after November 8. Dinner is served during summer and the holiday season, and on weekends off-season, there are appropriate items for kids.

The Mountain Room Broiler serves steaks and lobster at dinner and is open most of the year. Prices here are naturally a bit higher. All dining facilities have no-smoking areas. The Mountain Room Bar has a public big-screen TV and is operated when there's a major sporting event going on. A refreshment stand near the swimming pool is open daily in the summer.

There are 484 rooms to choose from. The spacious Lodge Rooms may remind you of accommodations at a ski resort. Each two-story building houses eight clean and comfortable modern rooms with balconies or patios. Singles or doubles rent for $90.25. Cottage Room accommodations are similar to standard hotel rooms. Singles or doubles with bath are $77, without bath, $61. Cabins—really very small sleeping rooms—go for $63.75, single or double, with bath; $49.50 without bath. Cribs ($5) and rollaways ($6) are available. Kids 3–12 pay $5 per night; under 3, free.

Curry Village, one mile east of Yosemite Village on Calif. 41 and Calif. 140, Yosemite National Park, CA 95389 (☎ **209/252-4848**), formerly called Camp Sequoia, once offered tent cabins at $2 a night. That was in 1899. While you can't get them at quite the same rate, Curry still offers tent cabins at reasonable prices. This rustic Yosemite resort has 180 cabins and 426 tent cabins. There are also a number of standard rooms and loft rooms. The accommodations are quite basic, and the prices are reasonable. Curry Village also has its own tour desk, where you can find out about all the same valley activities and can arrange tours, classes, and horseback riding. Bike rentals with helmets are available daily mid-April to October. Raft rentals are available in summer, as conditions permit. A swimming pool with showers and changing rooms is open daily in summer. There is a giftshop.

Curry Village also houses an amphitheater, the Mountaineering School (offering cross-country skiing instruction and equipment rental November to April, rock-climbing instruction and equipment rental April to June and October to November), the Mountain Sport Shop, and the Ice Rink with skate rentals and instruction (open daily November to March, conditions permitting).

Food is plentiful here too. The Cafeteria is open daily mid-April to October for breakfast, lunch, and dinner. There's also a fast food stand, ice-cream stand, and pizza stand open during that period. Parents often eat outside on the deck while the kids are nearby at one of the stands.

Loft rooms are the best bet here for larger families. There are two double beds downstairs and one double upstairs, with room for a crib, for $77. Tent cabins, especially suitable for families with one older child, are canvas-sided structures and have one double and one single bed; rates are $35 for one or two people, and $5 for each additional person. Standard rooms are small and cute, furnished in pine and calico prints, and have two double beds. These rooms would be cramped with a crib. The rate for these rooms is $77. The cabins with baths are tiny and rather primitive, but can be joined with a second room; they rent for $63.75. The charge for cribs is $5, and rollaways are available. Each additional extra person is charged $7.50 per night. If you're planning to be in Yosemite during summer, make reservations one year in advance (except for tent cabins).

Campgrounds

There are eight campgrounds in the valley, with a total of 828 campsites; Tioga Road and Big Oak Flat Road have nine campgrounds with 913 sites; Glacier Point and Wawona have two with 212 sites. Some sites outside the valley itself are on a first-come, first-served basis. Tuolumne, Hodgdon, and Crane Flat require reservations.

Reservations at the five valley campgrounds with sites for tents and RVs can be made through MISTIX. Advance reservations are taken no more than eight weeks before your stay. In summer especially, it's important to make reservations eight weeks (to the minute) before your planned visit. The valley has a walk-in site for groups and another walk-in site for backpackers. The auto site and the walk-in sites are open year round.

Outside the valley are two auto sites, one to the south and one to the west, that are open year round. In summer the limit on stays is seven days in the valley and 14 days outside the valley; from September 15 through May 31 the limit is 30 days both in the valley and outside. There's a maximum stay of 30 days per year for any one person.

Rates are $3 per person for walk-ins, $12 or $14 per auto, and $6 or $10 per auto site without reservations, with a maximum of six people per site.

WHERE TO EAT

All hotel dining rooms and cafeterias are open to the general public.

In addition, **The Loft Restaurant** is located near the Village center. It serves Mexican-American fare, at lunch and dinner only, at very reasonable prices. Lunch runs $5.45–$6.55. There's also a children's menu. The restaurant is open April through October, closed in winter. Open 11:30am to 10pm daily. No reservations accepted. The average wait at lunch is 10–15 minutes; at dinner, 20 minutes to an hour. The best time to come for dinner is right when they open, at 5:30pm. Highchairs and boosters are available. Major credit cards accepted.

Degnan's Deli, in the same building as the Loft, is the perfect place to pick up food for a picnic. They carry bread, cheeses, cold cuts, wine, soda, and such.

There's also a **market** in the Village center store. No deli food here, but lots of basics.

3 Sequoia and Kings Canyon National Parks

A visit to these two national parks encompasses a full range of climatic zones, from Mediterranean to Arctic. Here is where you'll find some of the most varied terrain in the world. And of course, most people come for a view of the mammoth giant sequoias, the biggest trees on earth. These parks preserve some of the best examples of these trees in the world.

In addition to these big groves of sequoias, Kings Canyon and Sequoia National Parks contain miles of wilderness with an abundance of canyons, lakes, meadows, and spectacular mountain peaks.

GETTING THERE

From the south, take I-5 to Calif. 99N to Fresno. From the north, take I-80 to Calif. 99S to Fresno. Take Calif. 180 from Fresno to the entrance of Kings Canyon and Sequoia National Parks. You can also enter on Calif. 198 via Visalia and Three Rivers, but the road is more difficult to drive.

ORIENTATION

Some people aren't aware that Sequoia is California's oldest national park, and that Sequoia and Kings Canyon are actually two separate parks. If you enter the parks from Fresno, you'll enter Kings Canyon, which puts you within a few miles of Grant Grove. The parks are open all year. However, during winter months, check with the National Park Service (☎ 209/565-3134 or 209/565-3351 for recorded information) for temporary road closures. Visitor centers at Grant Grove, Lodgepole, and Ash Mountain are open all year. Call for hours. During the summer, Cedar Grove and Mineral King also offer visitor information. Check at each visitor center for guided walks offered. (Main telephone switchboard is **209/565-3134**.)

The General's Highway runs through both parks. It meets Calif. 180 at Grant Grove and Calif. 198 at Ash Mountain. This scenic road takes you to many of the important features of the parks and connects the four major visitor areas—Giant Forest, Mineral King, Grant Grove, and Cedar Grove. The main mode of transportation is the automobile. There are no trams or shuttles, and the areas of interest are far enough apart to necessitate driving.

Entrance permits are $5 per car. At the time you enter the parks, ask for a copy of the visitors' newspaper, the *Sequoia Bark.*

WHAT TO SEE AND DO IN KINGS CANYON

The center of activity in Kings Canyon is **Grant Grove Village.** There you'll find the lodge, a full-service restaurant, a giftshop, and the visitor center.

What to See

General Grant Grove is a wonderful introduction to the big trees. The General Grant Tree is the second-largest living thing in the world and has been dubbed "The Nation's Christmas Tree." Make a game of it: As you stand there staring up, ask the kids to imagine it bejeweled with lights and ornaments. Our kids love decorating it in their minds.

Big Stump Trail is located near the park entrance (Calif. 180). This short self-guided trail gives you an idea of the numbers of trees that were logged before the park was created to protect them. This is a great opportunity to talk to the children about ecology.

Roaring River Falls is found approximately $2^1/2$ miles east of the turnoff for the Cedar Grove Ranger Station. From the parking area, walk about 200 yards to a viewpoint of the roaring falls. The surging river is swift and dangerous.

Zumwaldt Meadow, a one-hour loop trail just over a mile long, is one of the most scenic in Kings Canyon. It affords magnificent views of high granite walls, the Kings River, and the meadow. Trailhead parking area is $4^1/2$ miles east of the turnoff to Cedar Grove Village. This is a self-guiding nature trail.

What to Do

During the summer there are **campfire programs.** Check with the visitor center for specific programs and for information on programs offered at other times of the year (☎ **209/565-3341**).

Stables for **horseback riding** are located at Grant Grove and Cedar Grove, and are open June through August. Hour-long, half-day, full-day, and overnight riding is available. Because each stable is privately owned, you'll need to call for rates, locations, and reservations (☎ **209/565-3341**).

Bicycling is best in Cedar Grove because of the flat terrain. Bicycles may not be ridden on hiking trails.

WHAT TO SEE AND DO IN SEQUOIA

The place to congregate in Sequoia is **Giant Forest Village.** It consists of a giftshop, market, tavern, the Village cafeteria, and a studio that is also a giftshop. Nearby **Lodgepole Village** has a market, giftshop, showers, laundry, and quick-food places (open during summer), as well as a visitor center (open year round).

WHAT TO SEE

The **General Sherman Tree** is the largest living thing on earth. Measuring 274 feet tall and weighing about 1,400 tons, it's estimated to be between 2,500 and 3,000 years old (this tree was standing when the pyramids were being built!). It's mind-boggling to see, and even kids are amazed at its size. Ours like to figure out how many people holding hands it would take to encircle it. The **Congress Trail** is a self-guided walk that takes you through this breathtaking forest of giant trees. The trail is easy enough for all children, although you might have to carry the toddlers after a while. Point out to your kids the small sequoia cones from which these giant trees grow.

Hazelwood Nature Trail is an easy, mile-long trail that takes about an hour to walk and is good for the whole family. You'll find the trailhead across the highway from Giant Forest Lodge.

The **Trail for All People,** adjacent to Giant Forest Lodge, a quarter mile north of the village, is a paved, stroller-accessible trail that forms a two-thirds-mile circle around Round Meadow within the sequoia forest. It's a good place to view wildflowers during the summer. Forest and meadow life are described along the pathway.

Moro Rock provides spectacular views of the high country, including the Great Western Divide. Stairs with hand rails provide access to the top of the rock. The climb is quite steep, but the view is worth the effort, even if you only go up part of the way.

On the way to **Crescent Meadow,** a great spot for a picnic, you'll come to **Auto Log**—a novelty that's sure to delight youngsters. This fallen tree has been leveled so cars can drive right on it. Our kids scrambled for pictures of *their* car perched right on top of a giant fallen tree. Nearby is **Tunnel Log,** a fallen tree that cars can drive through.

Children who visit **Crystal Cave** (☎ 209/565-3134) will see fascinating stalagmites and stalactites in various shapes and configurations. The tour is not particularly suitable for infants. Management often recommends that parents take turns babysitting at the entrance while the other one takes the tour. Tours are about one hour long. Bring warm clothing; the cave has a constant 48°F (10°C) temperature. **Note:** The entrance to the cave is half a mile downhill—which means a steep uphill on the way back. It's a long but not horribly difficult walk for people in good health, and there are rest stops along the way. No strollers, backpacks, or tripods allowed in cave. Tickets must be purchased one or two hours in advance at Lodgepole or Foothills Visitor Centers. It's open in summer only. Call for specific times.

Warning

Animal life is abundant. You're likely to see lots of chipmunks, squirrels, marmots, and mule deer. Sequoia and Kings Canyon are *bear country!* These bears are used to people and are not afraid to approach trash cans, coolers, and cars that contain food. *Don't leave food in the car or car trunk.* Many disbelieving tourists have come back to automobiles with broken windows and torn-out backseats. Bears are more afraid of people than people are of them. Usually, if you see a bear, all you have to do is clap your hands and it will run away. But *don't tease the bears with food*—it's very dangerous.

Remember that these are *wild* animals. Don't encourage your children to get close. But that goes for all wildlife.

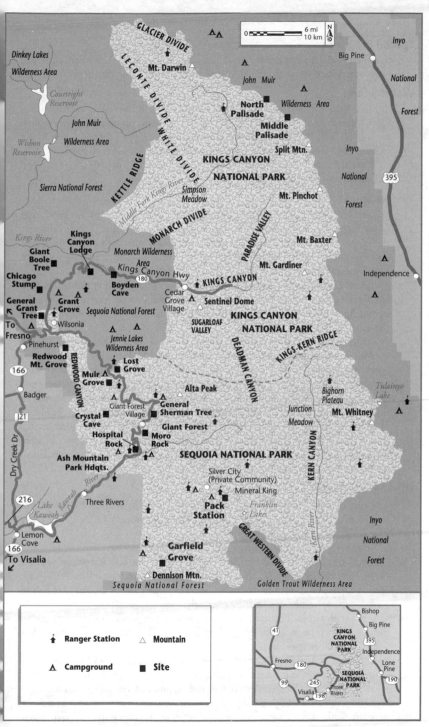

Sequoia and Kings Canyon National Parks

Special Programs

There are evening programs at Giant Forest and Lodgepole. The visitor center will have information about specific times and programs.

Water Sports

Try river **fishing** in the middle fork of the Kaweah River or lake fishing at Hume Lake. (*Don't swim in rivers before checking safety conditions.*) State fishing licenses are required for everyone over 16, and are available at all markets throughout the parks. You'll have to bring your own fishing poles, but tackle and bait are for sale at all markets.

Rafting can be arranged through King's River Expeditions, in Fresno (☎ **209/233-4881**), for rafting the lower end of Kings River.

Winter Sports

Sequoia and Kings Canyon are alive with winter activities. **Wolverton Ski Bowl,** near Giant Forest (☎ **209/565-3381**), is open daily during the season. You can also rent ski equipment here for adults and children. The area is open daily during the season for cross-country skiing. There's a snow play area at Wolverton, but bring your own snow play equipment.

Contact the following centers for information on cross-country skiing: **Sequoia Ski Touring Center** (☎ **209/565-3461**), open from 8am to 5pm mid-November to mid-April; **Grant Grove Ski Touring** (☎ **209/335-2314**), open approximately the same hours and days.

Cross-country ski equipment is also available for rental at Wolverton.

Montecito-Sequoia (☎ toll free **800/227-9900**) is a family resort nestled between Kings Canyon and Sequoia National Parks. This rustic lodge offers family activities year round. Winter activities include campfires, cross-country ski lessons and tours, and ice skating on a private lake. In summer the lake is used for waterskiing, canoeing, sailing, and other water sports. Full camp programs are offered for toddlers to adults, including horseback riding, guided hikes into the parks, guest artists, archery, and swimming. Children and their parents participate together or in separate programs. Room rates vary according to season, meals, and activities included. Open 365 days a year.

WHERE TO STAY

The rates quoted below are for summer (May through October) and holidays. For reservations in both parks, contact **Sequoia Guest Services,** P.O. Box 789, Three Rivers, CA 93271 (☎ **209/561-3314**).

In Kings Canyon, **Grant Grove** offers three types of very basic accommodations. Cabins, two to a unit, run $70.50; they have private baths and little unenclosed porches. Rustic "housekeeping cabins," the only cabins you're allowed to cook in, are $38.50. "Rustic cabins," without private baths, are $32. There's plenty of room for kids to play. A giftshop/minimart offers the essentials.

The Grant Grove Restaurant is perfect for breakfast, lunch, or dinner. Breakfast choices are extensive, priced at $3–$5. Lunch runs $6–$8, and dinner is priced at $6–$12. There's a children's menu.

In Sequoia, **Giant Forest** offers four kinds of accommodations in 245 units. Motel rooms are quite spacious, with two queen-size beds and plenty of room for a crib or rollaway. There are cabins with two double beds, cabins with one double and one single bed, two-room cabins with bed space for seven people, and one cabin with a fireplace. Accommodations run from rustic (no electricity or running water) to comfortable (carpeting, showers, and electricity). Prices range from $35 to $115, single or double. Additional guests pay $6 extra per night. Cribs cost $7 additional.

A dining room is open mid-May to mid-October and serves breakfast, lunch, and dinner. There's a buffet and salad bar at the evening meal. The cafeteria, next door to the giftshop, serves typical cafeteria fare, has plenty of seating, and is open May 1 through October 31. Lodgepole Deli Cafe open year round.

Cedar Grove Lodge in Kings Canyon (☎ 209/561-3314) has an additional 18 units, and **Stony Creek Lodge** in Sequoia has 11 units.

Campgrounds

For further information on the following campgrounds, contact the **National Park Service** (☎ 209/565-3341).

IN SEQUOIA   Nearby **Lodgepole,** with 260 tent/RV spaces, is the only campground for which reservations can be made. The grounds are open all year, but reservations, through Mistix outlets, are taken in summer only, no more than eight weeks to the day in advance; it's open in the winter for snow camping. Stays are limited to 14 days in summer, to 30 days the rest of the year. Rates are $10 per site per night off-season, $12 with reservations in summer.

Two other small campgrounds, with a total of 60 sites at low elevation, are available. **Potwisha** takes tents and RVs; **Buckeye,** tents only. Neither takes reservations, and they're both crowded on weekends. Rates are $10 per night.

There are three more small (73 sites) drive-in grounds available in remote areas off the main road near Mineral King. Pit toilets only. No reservations. Rates: $5 per site per night.

KINGS CANYON   The **Grant Grove** area has three campgrounds, totaling 369 sites for RVs and tents. These are the last grounds to fill up. There are flush toilets. Rates are $8 per site per night; no reservations.

Some 30 miles farther into the canyon off the main road at Cedar Grove are the most popular campsites, which are situated along the Kings River. In these campgrounds there are 314 general sites, with one area for groups. Weekends they get very full. Rates are $8 per site per night; no reservations.

4   Mammoth Lakes

In 1937 Dave McCoy lassoed a Model A Ford truck to a rope tow and a tree, which marked the beginning of Mammoth Mountain's skiing tradition. Some 18 years later the first chair lift was built and more than 2,000 people came to participate. Since then Mammoth has become synonymous with skiing.

Mammoth is the place to be in winter if you like winter sports, crisp alpine fields, fresh air, and plenty of room to explore.

But it's also the place to be in summer, the season that is the area's best-kept secret and the locals' favorite time of year! When the snow melts, Mammoth becomes a summer playground for families who love to experience such outdoor activities as horseback riding over mountain trails, fishing for fat trout in emerald lakes, hiking through rugged wilderness trails, camping out under the stars, picnicking amid wildflowers, bicycling on any of 300 open roads, or playing tennis and golf.

GETTING THERE

From Los Angeles **by car,** take Calif. 14 north to U.S. 395 north through Bishop to Mammoth. The drive takes approximately 5¹/₂ hours. The best way to get to

Mammoth from San Francisco in the winter is to take I-80 to U.S. 395 South. In the summer, take Tioga Pass Road through Yosemite; it's about a 6-hour drive.

Fly into Mammoth/June Lakes Airport via **TW Express** (☎ toll free **800/221-2000**) from Los Angeles.

Greyhound Bus has service twice a day: once northbound, once southbound.

ORIENTATION

Your first activity in Mammoth should be to take a trip on Calif. 203, the main road that leads to Mammoth Mountain, to the **Mammoth Lakes Visitors Bureau,** 3343 Main St. (P.O. Box 48), Mammoth Lakes, CA 93546 (☎ **619/934-2712,** or toll free **800/367-6572**), and gather information on all the activities and festivities. The office is open to visitors daily year-round from 8am to 6pm.

Another "must stop" is the **Forest Service Visitor Center,** also on Calif. 203, right outside town (☎ **619/924-5500**). Here you'll learn everything about Mammoth Lakes and the surrounding areas. The knowledgeable and helpful rangers have information on recreational activities and events, as well as handouts about fishing. You can get wilderness permits here. From July 1 to Labor Day the rangers offer interpretive programs for kids and their parents. Check at the visitor center for scheduled events. Open from the last Friday in June to mid-September, daily from 6am to 5pm; the rest of the year, Monday through Saturday from 8am to 4:30pm.

Other important phone numbers: Parks and Recreation (☎ **619/934-8989,** ext. **222**), 24-hour Mammoth Mountain ski report (☎ **619/934-6166**), June Mountain ski report (☎ **619/934-2224**), road conditions (☎ toll free **800/427-7623** in California), 24-hour weather information (☎ **619/934-7669**), and the U.S. Forest Service (☎ **619/924-5500**).

GETTING AROUND

You really do need a car in Mammoth, especially in the winter. But for daily trips to the slopes, a free shuttle service runs in winter from numerous stops around town. Some condominiums and lodges have complimentary van service to the slopes and into town.

WHAT TO SEE AND DO IN WINTER

Two mountains, Mammoth Mountain and June Mountain, give alpine skiers everything they can possibly imagine, including a season that seems to go on forever. From November to June, Mammoth Mountain is resplendent with an average of 335 inches of packed powder. But what really makes Mammoth Lakes such a perfect family vacation spot is that it offers more than just fabulous alpine skiing during the winter. There are miles of well-groomed cross-country ski tracks on which to discover the beauty and peacefulness of the surrounding wilderness, winter hot-air ballooning over the glacier-carved peaks, snowmobiling through the woods, old-fashioned sleigh rides, exciting dog sledding, and just plain snow fun.

If you're new at downhill or cross-country skiing, learn the ability signs for the trails immediately: A green circle means an easy trail; a blue square means more difficult; a black diamond means most difficult. These are important signs to remember if you get lost and are looking for a trail back. Don't ignore or underestimate these signs—they are for your safety!

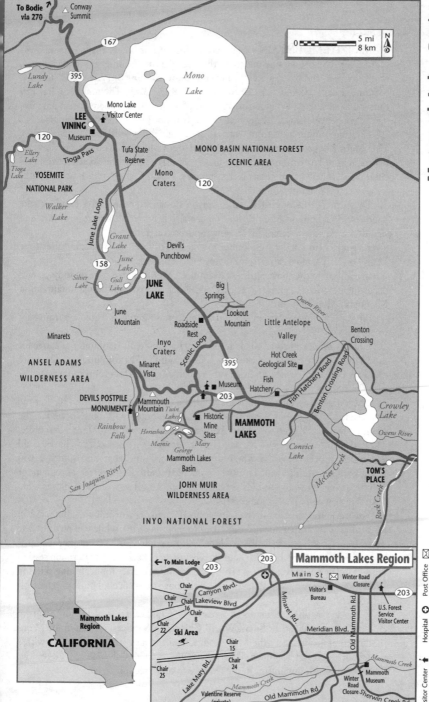

To Bodie via 270

Conway Summit

167

Lundy Lake

395

120

LEE VINING

Museum

Mono Lake Visitor Center

Mono Lake

0   5 mi
    8 km

N

MONO BASIN NATIONAL FOREST
SCENIC AREA

Ellery Lake
Tioga Lake
Tioga Pass

Tufa State Reserve

YOSEMITE NATIONAL PARK

Walker Lake

June Lake Loop

Grant Lake

158

Silver Lake
Gull Lake

June Lake

JUNE LAKE

Devil's Punchbowl

Mono Craters

120

Big Springs

Owens River

Lookout Mountain

Little Antelope Valley

Benton Crossing

Minarets

June Mountain

Roadside Rest

Inyo Craters

Scenic Loop

395

Hot Creek Geological Site

Fish Hatchery

ANSEL ADAMS WILDERNESS AREA

Minaret Vista

Museum

203

Fish Hatchery Road

Benton Crossing Road

DEVILS POSTPILE MONUMENT

Mammouth Mountain

Twin Lakes

Historic Mine Sites

MAMMOTH LAKES

Crowley Lake

Rainbow Falls

Horseshoe

Mamie

George   Mary

Convict Lake

Owens River

San Joaquin River

Mammoth Lakes Basin

McGee Creek

TOM'S PLACE

JOHN MUIR WILDERNESS AREA

INYO NATIONAL FOREST

Rock Creek

Mammoth Lakes Region

CALIFORNIA

Mammoth Lakes Region

← To Main Lodge   203

203

Main St

Chair 7

Chair 17

Chair 16

Chair 8

Chair 22

Ski Area

Canyon Blvd.
Lakeview Blvd

Visitor's Bureau

Winter Road Closure

203

U.S. Forest Service Visitor Center

Minaret Rd.

Old Mammoth Rd.

Meridian Blvd.

Chair 15

Chair 24

Chair 25

Lake Mary Rd.

Valentine Reserve (private)

Mammoth Creek

Old Mammoth Rd

Mammoth Creek

Winter Road Closure

Mammoth Museum

Sherwin Creek Rd.

Visitor Center   Hospital   Post Office

Alpine Skiing

MAMMOTH MOUNTAIN   Mammoth Mountain is one of the largest ski areas in the United States. To find out about the level of a run, facilities at each lodge area, ski instruction, and package rates, contact **Mammoth/June Ski Area,** P.O. Box 24, Mammoth Lakes, CA 93546 (☎ toll free **800/832-7320**). The mountain has 150 runs: 30% advanced, 40% intermediate, and 30% beginner. There are 30 lifts: five quad chairs, seven triples, 14 doubles, one T-bar, one poma, and two gondolas.

There are various areas from which to start your skiing at Mammoth Mountain. The **Main Lodge** is found at Minaret Road and Calif. 203. You can purchase lift tickets, rent or buy equipment, rent a locker, and sign up for the ski school and race clinics here. There's a cafeteria on the premises. Chairs 2 and 15 have ticket booths for easy access to the mountain.

To get to **Warming Hut II,** take Canyon Boulevard off Minaret Road, or take Lakeview Boulevard off Mary Road. You can also get your lift tickets, rent skis, and sign up for ski school here. This section also has a cafeteria.

To get to **Mid-Chalet,** you'll need to take one of seven chair lifts; inquire at the Main Lodge. There's a cafeteria up there, and a sun deck.

In addition to the above facilities, Mammoth Mountain has four ski shops, a race department, lockers, a full-service hotel, and suites, and two additional restaurants at Mammoth Mountain Inn.

Lifts operate midweek from 8:30am to 4pm, on weekends and holidays from 8am to 4pm.

Full-day lift tickets cost $40 for adults, $20 for seniors and children 7–12, free for kids 6 and under. Half-day tickets are $30 for adults, $15 for children. There are multiday packages, and season tickets are available. Sign up for group and private lessons through the ski school. Call for prices.

There are three skiing options for children: They can ski with you (30% of the runs are for beginners) or they can join one of two ski schools, both located at the Main Lodge. The **Woollywood Ski Academy** is recommended for kids 4 and older. There's usually one instructor for each six to eight children here, so if you have a child who has never been on skis, or who is shy or has a hard time separating from you, you might want to start him with a private lesson. **Mammoth Explorers** is a program for kids 4–12. The 4- to 6-year-olds are taken to a roped-off area of the Children's Ski School if they don't have prior experience.

You can enroll the kids for a half day, from 10am to noon or 1:30 to 3:30pm ($25); for a full day, including lunch, from 10am to 3:30pm ($58), while you go off to the slopes feeling confident that they're being well supervised; or let them ski the morning session, meet them for lunch, and then bring them back for the afternoon session ($38). Hot chocolate is supplied. Lift tickets are not necessary for beginning skiers in Woollywood Ski Academy. A-level skiers and above in Ski School must purchase lift tickets.

What do you do with infants to 3-year-olds? Child care is available for infants to children 12 years old at the **Small World Children's Services,** located in the Mammoth Mountain Inn, near the Main Lodge. You can also combine day care with a ski-school lesson and hot lunch. Reservations are essential: Call **619/934-0646.** (See the Mammoth Mountain Inn in the "Where to Stay" section.)

JUNE MOUNTAIN   Just 25 minutes from Mammoth on U.S. 395 and Calif. 158 (☎ **619/648-7733**), June Mountain offers 30 runs, seven chair lifts, and one tram. You can buy lift tickets at the Tram Haus in the parking lot. At the top of the tram is June Meadows Chalet, which has a ski school, race department, rental and repair shop, lockers, restrooms, and a cafeteria. At Lake Haus, at the base of Chair J5, is a day-care facility. There's also a Children's Ski School for ages 4–12 and a snow playground for the kids. Lift tickets between Mammoth and June Mountains are interchangeable. The hours of operation are the same as Mammoth Mountain.

Cross-Country Skiing

Cross-country skiing is a wonderful family outing, but is not recommended for children under 7, except for young children who can ride along on a "pulka" pulled by an adult. At 5, Janey loved the snowy trail and our trek over the open fields, but she was too young to fully maneuver the equipment.

Being such a winter wonderland, Mammoth has lots of trails for this peaceful activity. **Tamarack Cross-Country Ski Center,** on Twin Lakes (☎ **619/934-2442,** or toll free **800/237-6879**), is a beautiful and tranquil setting for experiencing the pleasures of this sport. From town, take Lake Mary Road to Twin Lakes Road all the way up to the top, about a 10-minute trip. Here are 25 miles of meticulously groomed trails for exploring, with at least 10 easy trails. The trails are open from 8am to 5pm. There are some, but not many, restrooms and telephones along the trails.

Full-day trail passes cost $15, $10 for seniors and children, and half-day passes are $10, $7 for seniors; children 10 and under ski free. Full-day rentals cost $15 for adults, $10 for children; half-day rentals, $10 for adults, $7 for children. Twilight skiing from 3 to 5pm costs $7 for adults, $5 for seniors and youths 10–16, free for children under 10; rentals are at the half-day rate. Group and private lessons are available. Make advance reservations for lessons for children 10 and under. Ski Wee Snow School for kids 6–8 is offered at 10am weekends and holidays.

Another wonderful place for cross-country skiing is **Sierra Meadows Ski Touring Center,** Old Mammoth Road, three blocks past Vons (☎ **619/934-6161**), with more than 35 miles of machine-groomed trails, a rental shop, ski school, warming hut, and lunch room. The Meadows occupies a beautiful open field with vistas of snow-capped peaks all around. The friendly and helpful employees will be glad to point out the different mountain ranges to you and explain a little about the history of the area.

Trail passes cost $10; children 7 to 12 pay $5; children under 6 ski free. Full-day rentals are an additional $10 for adults, $8 for children. Private and group lessons are offered daily, and reservations are suggested for private lessons. Trails are open during daylight hours. Office hours for reservations are 8:30am to 5pm daily, weather permitting.

The **Shady Rest/Inyo Craters Trail** system begins behind the Forest Service Center (☎ **619/934-2505**). While not great when it's very cold or icy, it has a nice flat portion beginning at the Shady Rest area that's good for beginners. Trees are marked with trail directions and the level of difficulty. No opening or closing times. No charge.

Dog Sledding

A real treat for kids of all ages is dog sledding (☎ **619/934-6270**). A charming New Zealander named Paul Marvelly runs this dog-sledding operation from the Main Lodge at Mammoth Mountain, and he is extremely knowledgeable and accommodating. Paul is used to kids, because 60% of his business is families. He takes the time to introduce youngsters to his affectionate huskies and lets the kids make friends with them. Then he leads an interesting guided tour of Mammoth while guests recline in comfort on his specially crafted sleds. Kids love the feeling of wind blowing on their faces as they race through the open fields. All dog sledding is subject to weather and trail conditions, so don't show up without calling first or you may be disappointed. Ask about summer rides.

The cost for a two-mile, 25-minute ride is $39 for adults, $19 for children 12 and under, and all ages are welcome. A one-hour ride through Minaret Vista is $65 per adult and $28 per child 12 and under. Inquire about dinner rides. Paul runs the sleds daily. Call for hours, which vary. Reservations are accepted.

Horseback Riding

In winter? What a wonderful idea! Call Sierra **Meadows Ranch,** 1 Sherwin Creek Rd., just off Old Mammoth Rd. (☎ **619/934-6161**) to reserve a time—ride times are flexible. You'll lope over the hills, along a creek, or to the base of the mountains. These are guided tours, and a wonderful family activity. The cost is $25 per hour; children should be at least 7 years old.

Hot-Air Ballooning

Hot-air ballooning is often thought of as a spring or summer adventure. But in Mammoth you can go ballooning all year round. **High Sierra Ballooning** (☎ **619/934-7188,** or **619/873-5838** in Bishop) will take you soaring in the skies. The view over the east side of the Sierra during one of these sunrise flights is unforgettable. Balloon flights are made daily from May through October, wind and weather permitting; reserve in advance. Winter trips can be scheduled. The Sierra Sunrise Brunch trips consist of four hours of fun: an hour or so in the air, off-rode riding, and a scrumptious brunch near a lake or stream. ("Off-rode" riding is a popular sport in the west, in which 4-wheel-drive vehicles are driven in designated off-the-road areas such as undeveloped hilly areas.)

Since hot-air ballooning is not an inexpensive activity, we recommend you think about whether your child will be a happy companion. Adults pay $175; children under 12 are charged half fare. You can try for a standby ride at $100 for adults, half fare for kids. If four or more passengers sign up, there is a $25 per person savings. There is no minimum age requirement, but we recommend this activity for kids over 5. Call for reservations.

Sledding and Tobogganing

Mammoth offers numerous places for sledding and tobogganing. A good spot for adult and teen sledders who like a challenge is the **Crestview-Deadman** area, approximately 10 miles north of Mammoth, just off U.S. 395 (follow the signs). There is no particular place to rent sleds, but you could buy a plastic one at the local Vons market or at one of the many sporting-goods stores. Our little one dragged her sled over to a hill adjacent to our condominium and had a ball going up and down the gentle slope. With very little effort you can find a hill to delight the youngsters.

Sleigh Rides

"Over the meadows and through the woods, to grandmother's house we go. . . . " Is there a more cozy-sounding, nostalgic activity you can think of doing in the snow than taking a sleigh ride? And what a perfect way to go—at night, in the crisp winter air, accompanied by sparkling snowflakes and the shining moon!

Sierra Meadows offers these evening rides at its Ski Tour Center just off Old Mammoth Road, three blocks from Vons (☎ **619/934-6161** for reservations), and all ages participate in this family activity, even babies. Naturally, you should wrap everyone up in very warm gear. The sleigh glides through the meadow for a 30-minute ride, and you are warmed up with hot spiced wine and cider first. A full-course dinner, accompanied by lively guitar or fiddle music, is served in the lodge after the ride during the Christmas holiday period. There are several ride choices, including an afternoon ride at 2pm on Saturday and Sunday. Two rides include a Western supper and live entertainment.

Adults pay $15–$50 depending on the ride; children 3-12 are charged $10–$35; under 3, free. Be sure to call for reservations.

Snowmobiling

One action-filled way to take in the magnificent scenery of Mammoth is to rent a snowmobile and explore the snow-filled forests. We don't recommend this activity for children under 5. Approximately eight minutes from Mammoth, **D.J.'s Snowmobile Rentals,** on U.S. 395 North at Smokey Bear Flat (☎ **619/935-4480,** or **619/937-0123** for reservations), offers guided and self-guided rides for all ages. It's open daily from 9am to 4pm. Call for current prices.

If you seek the freedom to explore the area with a snowmobile in tow, contact **Center Street Rentals,** at P.O. Box 1177, Mammoth Lakes, CA 93546 (☎ **619/934-4020** between 8am and 5pm). They'll hook up a trailer and hitch it to your car at no extra cost. Polaris snowmobiles, clothing, and helmets are for rent. Single riders are charged $40 per hour, with a two-hour minimum. A half day ($3^{1}/_{2}$ hours) costs $80. A full day is $150. Double riders (maximum 270 pounds) pay $90, $160, and $200, respectively. Reservations are accepted by calling in your credit-card number.

WHAT TO SEE AND DO IN SPRING AND SUMMER

In the 1930s Mammoth was strictly a summer resort frequented by those who wanted to get away from city noise and relax in the tranquil setting of crystal lakes, flowering meadows, and alpine mountains. For those in the know, Mammoth is at its best during the summer, when family activities abound and days are warm but never hot. The many lakes surrounding Mammoth make it a haven for water sports. The many alpine fields make hiking a glorious experience. Passes that were closed for the winter linking Mammoth with Yosemite and other park areas reopen in the spring. From April through October the opportunities are endless.

Backpacking and Hiking

An important source for information about these activities is the **U.S. Forest Service,** Mammoth Ranger District, on Calif. 203 (P.O. Box 148), Mammoth Lakes, CA 93546 (☎ **619/924-5500**). Not only can the rangers tell you about the various hiking trails and levels of ability, but they can also explain the free interpretive tours and programs they offer during the summer.

Hiking trails in Mammoth are everywhere. Whether you want to pack your family up for a week or for a few hours, you'll find a trail suited to your needs. The landscapes are beautiful everywhere you look, so you won't be disappointed in any hike you choose. If you're at all concerned that you and the little ones may not have the stamina to make it back, make prior arrangements with **Alpine Adventures**

(☎ 619/934-7188 for Mono County trails, 619/872-2721, or 619/873-5838 for Inyo County; it answers "Greyhound") for its Trailhead Shuttle Service, which will drop you off or pick you up from various trailheads. Call for prices.

The **John Muir and Ansel Adams Wilderness Areas** are magnificent, but they can get congested during the busy summer months. You'll need a wilderness permit for overnight use. Half the daily quotas are on a first-come, first-served basis the day you plan to hike, the rest by advance reservation. Write the U.S. Forest Service at the address above. Reservation requests are accepted with a postmark of March 1 to May 31 only—no phone reservations are accepted. Pick up permits in person at the visitor center. When you stop by, be sure to pick up a copy of "Mammoth Trails," which has maps of the individual hiking trails, as well as levels of ability. This will be your guide to hiking through Mammoth.

Tamarack Lodge Resort, P.O. Box 69, Mammoth Lakes, CA 93546 (☎ 619/934-2442), puts out a short guide to hiking trails in the Tamarack area. It's available to nonguests, and the staff is happy to give you specific information about trails, including those hikes appropriate for young children.

Devils Postpile National Monument, located 14 miles from the Mammoth Visitor Center via Reds Meadow Road, is a fascinating site to visit. It was created 100,000 years ago by lava flowing from the earth's crust. As a result, the formations consist of basaltic rock standing in columns 40–60 feet high. An easy 15-minute hike takes you to these imposing sights, which will fascinate the kids. There are picnic areas and a lovely 1^1/4-mile hike to Rainbow Falls. The rainbow colors of the falls are best seen at midday. From June to September you have to take the shuttle from the Mammoth Mountain Inn. The road is closed in winter, but you can drive yourself in the fall. The shuttle departs daily from 7:30am to 5:30pm. The round-trip fare is $7 per person; $4 for children 5 to 12; children under 5, free. There are 22 campsites available for $8 per site per night.

Another geologic site and an interesting place to hike is **Hot Creek,** three miles south of Mammoth Junction on U.S. 395. A paved trail goes down 250 feet to Hot Creek, a hot spring that heats a cold mountain stream. Open from sunrise to sunset in the summer, Hot Creek is a sanctuary for many interesting mammals and birds, such as great horned owls, bald eagles, and cliff swallows. This is a great place to explore nature, but don't plan to swim here, as the extreme temperatures of the hot spring make swimming inadvisable.

Mono Basin National Forest Scene Area, also located on U.S. 395, 30 miles north of Mammoth, is a haven for thousands of sea gulls. The Lee Vining Ranger Station, Mono Lake Ranger District, is on Calif. 120W (Tioga Pass Road), two miles off U.S. 395 (☎ 619/647-3000). For other information, visit the National Forest Scenic Area Visitor Center, half a mile north of Lee Vining. The Visitor Center (☎ 619/647-3044) has plenty of information about this area, June Lake, and other parts of the district, as well as coloring books, books on fire-prevention for kids, and a book about the area for adults.

The lava-strewn islands of Mono Basin are the result of eruptions hundreds of years ago. The lake is often described as having a lunar landscape effect. This is an interesting area to take the children because it's flat and easy to walk. However, note that stark, rapid climatic changes can occur and the air can change from hot to cold in a matter of minutes, making it tough on youngsters.

If you take Calif. 120E for five miles off U.S. 395, you'll come to the South Tufa Interpretive Site where there is parking and picnic tables. A half-mile self-guiding nature trail begins there. Every day in the summer at 10am and 1pm there are also ranger-guided walks, perfect for kids from age 4 to teens. Walks last one to two hours. Call **619/647-3044** for information on where to meet. The visitor center is open daily in summer from 8am to 7pm; in winter, weekends only.

Hiking trails in the June Lake area are quite steep. Instead, you can take your own driving tour that makes a loop of June Lake. Start 15 miles north of Mammoth on U.S. 395, which begins the southern portion of the loop. It takes you by four of the beautiful mountain lakes—June, Gull, Grant, and Silver—and the village of June Lake. June Lake offers not only beautiful scenery but fishing, hiking, camping, boating, and swimming in an alpine setting.

Mammoth Lakes Basin, carved out of a glacier, contains 13 mountain lakes. Five of them are accessible by car and offer short hikes. Contact the Forest Service for information on what area is appropriate for your family's hiking abilities.

Bicycling

Mountain bikes have become increasingly popular in Mammoth. The difference between them and a standard bike is that they have 18 gears and can climb hills with greater ease. There are 300 miles of open roads to explore in the Mammoth Ranger District. The **U.S. Forest Service** (☎ **619/924-5500**) will be glad to furnish you with information on the best routes to take if you want to ride on your own. If not, there are two companies that provide guided rides. (See below for information on the Mammoth Mountain Bike Park).

Mammoth Adventure Connection, operating from the Mammoth Mountain Inn, P.O. Box 353, Mammoth Lakes, CA 93546 (☎ **619/934-0606**), now offers two- and three-night Mountain Bike Packages & Guided Tours that make a wonderful family trip. The package includes accommodations at the Mammoth Mountain Inn, all breakfasts, unlimited use of a mountain bike and helmet, a guided Kamikaze trail ride, trail map, van support, water bottle, and T-shirt. Trails and tours are available for all ages and ability levels. What a neat way to see the area and spend family time together! Children should be at least 7 years old; day care is provided too, at an additional cost. Prices start at $208 double occupancy; a family of four would pay approximately $180 per person, and there's a discount if you bring your own bike. Tax and tips are included in the price. The package is offered May through October. The trip can be arranged without accommodations.

The folks at Mammoth Adventure Connection can lead you to **Mammoth Mountain Bike Park,** which has 50 miles of single-track trails ranging from flat or gently sloped to a Kamikaze trail that runs from the peak to the base. A BMX track, an obstacle area, and a special area for children can also be found in the park. The park is open from July to September and some weekends in October, weather permitting, and is reached via gondola. There are several entrance fees, depending upon your needs: unlimited access to the gondola and trails costs $18 for adults, $9 for kids 12 and under; one ride on the gondola with a bike costs $10 for adults, $5 for children. Bikes can be rented for adults and children.

Fishing

The fishing season in Mammoth officially opens in April, when the anglers come out to try their luck. There are rainbow, eastern brook, cutthroat, golden, and brown trout in the local lakes and streams. Fishing is a wonderful activity for the whole family, since even the smallest toddler can participate. **Crowley Lake, Lake Mamie, Horseshoe Lake,** and the **Twin Lakes** are just a few of the many places to catch some of the best trout around. Anyone over 16 will need a permit to fish, which is obtained from most sporting-goods stores. For information, call the State Department of Fish and Game (☎ 619/872-1171). Fishing gear can be rented at almost any of the local sporting-goods stores in Mammoth.

Mammoth Adventure Connection, in the Mammoth Mountain Inn, P.O. Box 353, Mammoth Lakes, CA 93546 (☎ 619/934-0606), offers Ultimate Mountain Getaway packages that encompass fly fishing, bike riding in the Bike Park, learning to climb the new climbing wall, horseback riding, and other activities. The package includes two or three nights lodging along with other amenities. Prices start at $114 per person, double occupancy; a family of four can arrange a package for as low as $86. These packages are offered May 1 through October 31. Call for more information.

Hayrides

Morning and evening hayrides are a fun way to experience the area. Call **Sierra Meadows Ranch,** 1 Sherwin Creek Rd., just off Old Mammoth Road (☎ 619/934-6161) to reserve a seat. One hayride adds a cozy campfire complete with marshmallows and hot chocolate. Another revolves around a barbecue dinner. There's live music, as well. Or take a Sunday morning one-hour horseback ride, and return to the ranch for a cowboy-style breakfast. Prices range from $15–$35 for adults, depending on what ride you choose, and $10–$30 for kids under 12. Children 2 and under ride free.

Sierra Meadows runs a wagon through town from Mammoth Shuttle stops. You can get on and off at will. It runs from 4pm to 8pm seven nights a week. Adults pay $3, children $2; toddlers under 38 inches ride free on an adult's lap.

Horseback Riding

Convict Lake Resort, Rte. 1, Box 204, Mammoth Lakes, CA 93546 (☎ 619/934-3800), offers horseback riding for the whole family along scenic Convict Lake and the Sierra. Most popular is the one-hour guided ride, which follows the lake and takes you through gorgeous scenery. The minimum age for children is 7; you can put the younger ones on Walk-and-Lead horses for $9 per half hour. Regular rates for adults and children are $18 for the one-hour ride, $49 for a half-day canyon ride, and $80 for the full-day excursion, which includes lunch and fishing time. Reservations are suggested, especially for any trip over one hour. Open mid-May through mid-October.

Imagine the family riding over rolling hills to enjoy the panorama of the Sierra, the magnificent White Mountains, and Mammoth Mountain. Half-hour to full-day guided tours are conducted by **Sierra Meadows,** Old Mammoth Road, three blocks past the Vons (☎ 619/934-2434 or 619/934-6161). Children should be at least 7 or 8 to participate in this adventure. A half-hour walk-and-lead for little tykes costs $12.50, a one-hour ride is $25. Call for hours.

Bob Tanner, who arranges pack trips, also offers rides. Call **Bob Tanner's Red Meadow Pack Station** (☎ 619/934-2345, or toll free 800/292-7758) for reservations. You can choose a two-hour, half-day, or full-day ride. Adults and children pay $30 for two hours, $45 for a half day, and $65 for the full day. No minimum age requirement for children.

Pack Trips

Pack trips are a unique way of seeing the wilderness area. If you and your family are real horseback riding enthusiasts, you shouldn't miss the chance to explore the mountain trails on horseback and enjoy the camaraderie of eating and singing around an open campfire. Several area companies offer this exciting experience, and some have special parent-child trips regularly scheduled. Most packers provide the horses, food, and other gear, sometimes even tents, while you provide personal items. Contact the packers for brochures which give all trip options as well as lists of necessary gear. Find out which packers make camp at one location and take day trips from there. This is sometimes easier on younger children or first-time packers.

For a complete list of pack stations, contact the **Mammoth Lakes Visitors Bureau,** P.O. Box 48, Mammoth Lakes, CA 93546 (☎ 619/934-2712).

Bob Tanner's Red Meadow Pack Station, P.O. Box 395, Mammoth Lakes, CA 93546 (☎ 619/934-2345, or toll free 800/292-7758), is one such station. Bob Tanner has a variety of trips, ranging from 3 to 7 days. His parent-and-child excursion is a five-day trip designed especially for young buckaroos. You travel at a leisurely pace, and the staff offers special assistance to the novices. They supply the horses, food, cooking, and eating utensils. You supply your own bedroll and tent. Trips are offered in June, July, and August. The price is $495 for adults, $325 for children 14 and under.

In addition to its regular pack trips, **McGee Creek Pack Station,** Rte. 1, Box 162, Mammoth Lakes, CA 93546 (☎ 619/935-4324 in summer, 619/878-2207 in winter; or toll free 800/854-7407 year-round), offers two-, three-, four-, or five-day Family Pack Trip Vacations throughout the summer. A base camp is provided where you'll enjoy family-style meals cooked for you each day. You can ride or hike to explore the High Country. The all-inclusive charge for hikers is $90 per person, per day, for adults, $75 for children. Riders are charged $130 per person per day for adults, $110 for children. There are discounts for two or more children. Call for dates.

Seeing a Ghost Town

For aficionados of the great Old West, **Bodie** (☎ 619/647-6445) is a must-see. It's an easy—and pretty—one-hour drive from Mammoth. Take U.S. 395 north about 60 miles. This ghost town, which had a population of 10,000 in 1879, was a gambling, drinking, and shoot-'em-up mining town. It reportedly saw around $100 million in gold during its heyday years. Preserved as is when it became a state historic park in 1962, 167 buildings remain in various stages of deterioration. Rather than just sitting empty, some still have their contents intact, including the schoolhouse, in which you'll see books and desks and lessons that were written on the blackboard. Kids have a ball reenacting the days of the Old West here. This is the only Gold Rush–era town to be maintained like this; there are no souvenir shops, no T-shirts for sale, no food stands (though there are modern restrooms). Tours are conducted during the spring and summer by the state park system.

The town is open year round: in summer from 9am to 6pm (sometimes later—call ahead), till 4pm the rest of the year; but it's best to visit in spring or summer because of the weather. If you plan a late-fall to early-spring trip, call for road conditions. A $5-per-auto fee is collected.

Swimming

A summer dip is always great entertainment for the kids. Mammoth has a large public facility designed for the whole family, and it's surrounded by breathtaking natural beauty. **Whitmore Pool,** on Whitmore Road (☎ 619/935-4222 or 619/934-8989, ext. **222**), has a kiddie pool, showers, a grassy play area, and a picnic area. The outdoor pool opens in June and closes in September. Recreational Swimming is scheduled from 12:30 to 4pm Monday through Saturday. Lap swimming is scheduled morning and evening. Admission costs $4 for adults 16 and over, $2.50 for youths 7–15, $1.25 for toddlers 1–6; infants, free. Showers are $2. Lessons are also available.

Tennis

Stop by the **Department of Parks and Recreation,** in the Minaret Village Shopping Center, upper level (☎ **619/934-8989,** ext. **222**), for information on the community center public tennis courts.

Indoor Activities

If it's too cold out or you've just had enough outdoor activities, the **Department of Parks and Recreation** (☎ 619/934-8989, ext. 222) offers classes for the family during winter and summer.

For a step back in time, take the family to the **Mammoth Museum** (☎ **619/934-6918**), just off Old Mammoth Road—look for the Equestrian Center. Interpretative displays demonstrate the past and present of the Mammoth area, including the Gold Rush days. The museum is housed in an authentic log cabin built in the 1930s by Emmett Hayden, a mapmaker for the eastern Sierra. Open June through September, daily from 10am to 5pm. Admission is free.

Summer Events

Mammoth offers a wide variety of activities and special events during July and August. Contact the Department of Parks and Recreation for this year's exact dates.

The **Fourth of July** is an exciting time in Mammoth—the locals put on a show that lasts for days. There's a western parade complete with horses, cowboys, and saloon girls, who enact the days of the Old West.

The **NORBA UCI World Cup Cycling Classic** (☎ **619/934-0651**), the mountain bike world's championship event, is in its 10th year. Dates change every year, so call for this year's information. Bike enthusiasts are welcome to join in on the fun, which includes all levels of riding and is open to the public. Fun Day is set aside for all age riders.

The **Sierra Summer Music Festival** (☎ **619/934-2515**) is held in July and August and has workshops for the kids, along with special theater presentations and many concerts.

WHERE TO RENT EQUIPMENT

There are numerous places to rent ski equipment in Mammoth, including locations at the ski areas themselves, and at some hotels. There are also stores that rent summer-activity equipment, such as bikes and camping or backpacking items. As there are so many types of equipment, half- and full-day rates, multiday discounts, children's discounts, etc., we won't list prices here. Inquire when you call.

Kittredge Sports on Main Street (☎ **619/934-7566** or **619/934-9566,** or toll free **800/441-3331** from Southern California), has cross-country and downhill ski equipment for rent. You can also rent bikes, fly-fishing equipment, and camping gear here. Open daily from 7am.

Mammoth/June Ski Resort, in the Main Lodge (☎ **619/934-0670**), in Warming Hut II (☎ **619/934-0770**), and at June Mountain (☎ **619/648-7733**), rents skis, boots, and poles for downhill. The rental shop opens at 7:30am weekends, at 8am weekdays.

Mammoth Sporting Goods is located in the Sierra Centre Mall on Old Mammoth Road (☎ 619/934-3239). In addition to downhill equipment, Mammoth Sporting rents mountain bikes in summer. Open daily from 7am to 10pm in winter, 8am to 7pm in summer.

WHERE TO STAY

Because Mammoth is a world-class winter resort, you'll have an abundance of condominiums and motels to choose from when booking your accommodations. Be sure to ask about midweek and holiday rates and minimum length of stay when you call or write for reservations. Each establishment has its own policy.

One of the most luxurious condominium rentals in Mammoth is **Snowcreek Resort,** situated on Mammoth Creek in town. Write to Snowcreek Property Management, P.O. Box 1647, Mammoth Lakes, CA 93546 (☎ 619/934-3333, or toll free 800/544-6007; fax 619/934-1619). Snowcreek offers every kind of convenience for families, including indoor recreational facilities at the Snowcreek Athletic Club. During the winter months a shuttle transports guests to and from the ski area at Mammoth Mountain, a ten-minute ride, or to various bus stops in town. In the summer, hiking trails, lakes, and nature walks are close by. The resort is entirely surrounded by picturesque mountains, and the stream that runs through the complex even provides trout fishing for the youngsters. There are plenty of open spaces for kids to run around and play. In the winter the kids can sled on the nearby hills—the first thing we did when we arrived. The geese, ducks, and dogs that roam the wooded area provide hours of entertainment.

The adjacent Snowcreek Athletic Club (☎ 619/934-8511) is free to guests and offers hours of activities après-ski, when you don't want to ski, and in the summer. Racquetball and tennis, an indoor lap pool and outdoor pool, a full-size gym for team sports, weight rooms, steam, and spas are just some of the facilities you can use. The club also has a day-care center, which charges $2 per child per hour when using the club. Snowcreek's nine-hole golf course is available for guest use.

All condominium units have fireplaces and are completely furnished with towels, linens, and kitchen appliances. The open lofts and beam ceilings create a feeling of spaciousness and warmth. There are one-, two-, three-, and four-bedroom town houses with lofts available. A one-bedroom unit can sleep up to five people; three bedrooms can sleep ten. There is no daily maid service; if you stay more than seven days, there's a midweek cleaning. Fresh towels can be picked up daily.

Rates are $105–$350 in winter, $100–$230 in summer. There are some cribs available at no charge; be sure to request them ahead of time. No rollaways. The extra-person charge is $10 per night. Children 5 and under sleep free. Winter reservations are taken beginning October 1. Make weekend reservations at least one month in advance. There's a two-night minimum.

Another lovely condominium complex right next to Warming Hut II at Mammoth Mountain is the **1849 Condominiums,** P.O. Box 835, Mammoth Lakes, CA 93546 (☎ 619/934-7525, or toll free 800/421-1849; fax 619/934-6501). There's an assortment of layouts here, depending on your needs, ranging from one to four bedrooms.

This complex offers three spas and a pool outdoors, an indoor sauna, showers and exercise equipment, as well as a big-screen TV and table tennis. You can buy your lift tickets here. There are no restaurants on the premises, but Mammoth Mountain Inn, with two restaurants, is just up the road.

All the units have fireplaces, fully-equipped kitchens, TVs, video recorders, stereos, and daybeds. The condos come equipped with linens and towels, and maid service is provided the second day of your stay. Fresh towels are given daily. For an extra charge, daily maid service is available upon request. There are coin-operated laundry facilities on the premises. Van service is offered to the airport and shops.

Weekday winter rates start at $160 for a one-bedroom unit (which sleeps four) and go up to $345 for a four-bedroom condo, which sleeps ten. Weekend winter rates are $195–$400. Summer rates are $80–$150 (beginning May 1). Inquire about midweek specials in the winter; six-night specials in summer. Cribs are available at no charge.

Mammoth Mountain Inn, at 1 Minaret Rd. (P.O. Box 353), Mammoth Lakes, CA 93546 (☎ 619/934-2581, or toll free **800/228-4947;** fax 619/934-0700), offers the convenience and full service of a hotel within walking distance of the Main Lodge. During the ski season, just walk across the street to the ski lifts; in the summer, the inn offers mountain bike tours, fishing, hiking, a climbing wall, ropes course, and horseback riding. It also provides year-round complimentary shuttle service to the village and airport.

The inn offers the excellent Small World Care Center (☎ 619/934-0646) run by Donna Fleming. The day-care program is open seven days a week from 8am to 5pm, and in the winter reservations are recommended eight weeks in advance. The center programs are divided by age, beginning with newborns and going up to age 12. Snacks and meals are provided, and they'll even take your kids skiing if you sign them up for the program. Half-day rates are $30 for all ages; full-day rates are $45 for newborns and toddlers, and $40 for all other ages. There is a discount for two or more children from one family. Packages are available for day care/ski school, beginning at $60. Ski rentals cost $8. Summer programs are offered and include hiking, picnicking, and ecological studies.

There are two restaurants, the Mountainside Grill and the Yodler Restaurant (see the "Where to Eat" section for more information). The Chili Dog's Arcade snack bar/ games room in the basement sells sandwiches, hot dogs, pizza bread, chili, sodas, and candy, and has a video arcade open from 5 to 10pm daily. Although room service is available for breakfast and dinner, there aren't many selections for young children, and this service is provided only in the Main Building. The inn also has three cocktail lounges, three indoor spas, a giftshop, and a sport shop.

The inn offers standard hotel rooms, suites, and condominiums. Because there are so many configurations of accommodations, be sure to explain your needs to the reservationist. All rooms come with color television. Condos have kitchenettes and phones, and the two-bedroom units have two bathrooms. There are suites with queen-size beds in the lofts, outdoor decks, and refrigerators.

In winter, hotel rooms rent for $80–$150, single or double, in midweek, and $95–$175 on weekends and holidays. Suites and condominiums run $120–$325 midweek and $145–$365 on weekends and holidays. Summer rates are $76–$99 for a hotel room and $88–$155 for a suite or condominium. Special winter and summer packages are available. In summer, children 12 and under stay free in their parents' room; in winter, children 2 and under. No charge for cribs or rollaways.

The **Tamarack Lodge Resort,** P.O. Box 69, Mammoth Lakes, CA 93546 (☎ 619/934-2442, or toll free **800/237-6879;** fax 619/934-2281), is a small retreat high up in the mountains surrounded by lakes and beautiful trails. There are 11 rooms in the lodge and 25 newly renovated cabins clustered around it on six wooded acres.

The grounds are beautiful and overlook a sparkling alpine lake. In the winter you can rest in front of a blazing fire after a day of cross-country skiing while your children play checkers, cards, or any of the numerous games available in the main room. In the summer, listen to Mozart on the stereo system and put your feet up after a hike through the mountain trails. The Lakefront Restaurant, on the premises, serves fresh home-made goodies for breakfast seven days a week. In summer they'll pack a lunch to eat on the trail; in winter we warmed up with soup and chili by the fireplace. Dinner is served nightly year round. There's a children's dinner ($9), or you can order smaller portions of grownup entrees.

Five of the lodge rooms have private baths; the others have sinks and mirrors but share toilet and bath facilities. There's a lovely two-bedroom suite on the third floor with living room, dining room, kitchenette, and private bath, but it's reserved for adults. The clean cabins all have kitchens and bathrooms, and some have fireplaces. No daily maid service in the cabins, but towel and linen exchange is available daily.

Weekday winter rates, single or double occupancy, are $60 for a lodge room with a shared bath, $70–$100 for a lodge room with a private bath. The upstairs suite is $130 for two to three people. Remodeled cabins vary from $85 for a studio cabin, which sleeps two, to $270 for a three-bedroom cabin, which sleeps 10. There are all sorts of configurations in the middle. Weekend rates are higher.

In the summer, lodge rooms are $45–$80; cabins rent for $75–$270. There are porta-cribs for a one-time charge of $10. No rollaways. No charge for kids under 2. The extra-person charge is $15 per night. **Note:** There's a no-smoking policy in effect throughout the lodge.

The **Alpenhof Lodge** is a charming chalet-style lodge on Minaret Road (P.O. Box 1157), Mammoth Lakes, CA 93546 (☎ **619/934-6330** or **619/934-8558;** fax 619/ 934-7614), three miles from the main ski area and half a mile from Warming Hut II. This is an excellent choice for moderately priced accommodations. The Alpenhof has a cozy, old-world feeling. The hotel has a recreation room, an inside therapy pool, and an outdoor pool open in summer only. Kids love the forestlike setting that sur-rounds the hotel. There are picnic tables and a barbecue. A laundry room is for guest use. The charming Matterhorn Restaurant, adjacent to the hotel, is open for break-fast and dinner.

Some units have fireplaces, some have kitchenettes, and all have color TV, HBO, and direct-dial phones. Rooms are clean, and most have lovely views.

Winter midweek rates are $64–$85 for standard singles or doubles, $78–$95 for a room with a queen-size bed and a fireplace, $115 for a mini-suite. Cottages are $135. Weekend rates are approximately $12 higher per room. Several ski packages are avail-able in midweek, which include lift tickets and shuttle passes. Summer rates are $51–$65. The cost of a suite is $85; cottages run $90. There is no charge for cribs or kids under 12 in their parents' room; those 12 and over are charged $7. The fee for rollaways is $7.

The **EconoLodge Wildwood Inn,** on Calif. 203 (P.O. Box 568), Mammoth Lakes, CA 93546 (☎ **619/934-6855,** or toll free **800/424-4777;** fax 619/934-5165), halfway between town and the Main Lodge, offers a swimming pool in the summer and a Jacuzzi year round. A free in-room continental breakfast is offered, and coffee, tea, and hot chocolate are served all day in the lobby. There's no restaurant on the premises, but the Wildwood is within walking distance of many eateries.

The 32 rooms are clean and utilitarian and come with cable color TV with HBO, phone, and in-room coffee. The rooms with two queen-size beds are quite large, with plenty of room for the kids to play. Some units have refrigerators and microwaves as well. Winter midweek rates are $59 for a room with one queen-size bed and $79 with two queen-size beds. Weekend rates are $79 and $89 respectively. Summer rates are reduced (call for new summer rates). There's no charge for children 18 and under in the same room with their parents. Cribs are also free. Rollaways cost $10 per night.

For the truly budget-minded, Mammoth Lakes offers a **Motel 6** right on the main highway at 473372 Main St. (P.O. Box 1260), Mammoth Lakes, CA 93546 (☎ **619/934-6660;** fax 619/934-6989). Reservations are essential at this 150-room motel, especially in the winter. Some rooms face the enclosed pool, which is open in summer only. Local calls are free, and there are free in-room movies. There's no restaurant on the premises, but there are vending machines for soft drinks, juice, and candy. A ski shuttle to all lifts stops in front of the motel every 15 minutes.

Rates Sunday through Thursday evenings are $35.99 for one person. Add $6 for the first additional person, $2 for each person after that. The weekend and holiday rate is $39.99 for one. No charge for children under 18 staying in their parents' room. Cribs are free (reserve in advance); there are no rollaways.

A Bed-and-Breakfast Inn

Located right off Calif. 203, the **Snow Goose Inn,** 57 Forest Trail (P.O. Box 946), Mammoth Lakes, CA 93546 (☎ **619/934-2660,** or toll free **800/874-7368;** fax 619/934-5655), is Mammoth's quaint bed-and-breakfast home away from home. Unlike some bed-and-breakfast establishments that shy away from renting to children, owners Bob and Carol Roster have 13 grandchildren and a closet stocked with games for all ages.

Modeled after a European country inn, the Snow Goose offers 18 rooms with private bath, phone, and color TV. A full complimentary breakfast is served daily in the main room, featuring homemade baked goods. An appetizer party is held from 5 to 6pm, and coffee and tea are available all day. There's also a hot tub to relax those sore muscles.

Winter midweek rates are $78 for standard rooms; kitchenette rooms rent for $88, double occupancy. Suites rent for $148 for four people midweek and $168 on weekends. Ask about midweek ski packages. After May 1, rates are $58, $68, and $88, midweek or weekends. Children under 3 stay free; those 4 and over are charged $10 extra.

Camping

This is a great way to experience the open meadows and rustic beauty of Mammoth. There are 14 family and 4 group campgrounds in just the mammoth Ranger District, ranging from 10 to 95 sites in the family campgrounds. We strongly suggest that first you go to the **Ranger Station** on Calif. 203 (☎ **619/924-5500**) to obtain current information. Family campgrounds are all first-come, first-served, except Sherwin Creek, where half of the sites are available by reservation. Family campgrounds range in price from $8 to $11 per night. Make reservations by calling toll free **800/280-2267.** Follow the instructions on the Fee Board at the campground entrance when paying for a first-come, first served family campsite. Overnight camping in the wilderness areas require a Wilderness Permit.

WHERE TO EAT

The **Mountainside Grill,** located inside Mammoth Mountain Inn, across from the Main Lodge (☎ **619/934-0601**), serves breakfast, lunch, and dinner in a typical lodge setting of wooden rafters and high ceilings. Breakfast features lots of choices for adults and kids alike, including omelets ($5 and up), pancakes ($4, $3.45 for short stacks), huevos rancheros ($6.95), "The Demon" (three scrambled eggs with Italian sausage, spinach, mushrooms, onions, and cheese for $6.45), cereals, French toast, and Belgian waffles. The lunch menu includes sandwiches, salads, fresh fish, chicken, and burgers; prices range from $4.95 to $8.50. At dinner, adults can choose from seafood specialties, pastas, steaks, lamb, fresh fish, and three kinds of chicken. The house specialty, camarones flores, is delicious: jumbo shrimp wrapped in bacon and served with a jalapeño-hollandaise sauce ($18.50). Dinners include soup or salad, a fresh vegetable, potato or rice, and bread, and cost between $11 and $18. (Leave room for the homemade desserts.) The wine list is extensive with numerous California labels.

A children's menu is offered at all three meals. For breakfast, there's eggs, pancakes, cereal, or French toast ($2.45–$3.25). At lunch and dinner, kids 10 and under can order a hamburger, grilled cheese sandwich, fish sticks, peanut butter and jelly, or a grilled chicken breast. Entrees are $2.25–$6. Servers will supply you with a highchair or booster seat and will split dinner in the kitchen.

Meals are served daily: breakfast from 7 to 11am, lunch from 11am to 2pm, and dinner from 5:30 to 9:30pm. Reservations are preferred on weekends for dinner. All major credit cards accepted. Parking lot.

The **Yodler Restaurant,** adjacent to the main building of Mammoth Mountain Inn (☎ 619/934-2581, ext. 2236), serves lunch and dinner only in a casual setting, and it's a real draw for families. This Swiss-style chalet, built in Switzerland and reassembled in 1959 on its present site, has high ceilings, beautiful hand-carved wood designs, and a lovely view of the mountains. Soups, salads, burgers, barbecued ribs, chicken, fish, steak, and pasta are served here. The portions are large and very filling. Lunch and dinner prices range from $5.50 to $12.50; specials average around $15.

A children's menu consists of the standard fare: grilled cheese, burgers, spaghetti, or barbecued chicken, priced at $3.50–$4.75. Boosters and highchairs are available. The best time to bring kids is between 5 and 7pm.

Many families take advantage of the Yodler's take-out service. Call first and your food will be ready when you get there. The restaurant, including take-out service, is open daily for lunch from 11am to 2pm and for dinner from 5 to 9:30pm. In summer, dinner only 5 to 9:30pm. No reservations; major credit cards are accepted. There's a parking lot.

For a special night out, **Whiskey Creek,** located at the corner of Calif. 203 and Minaret Road, near the town and the slopes (☎ 619/934-2555), is the ultimate in sophisticated family dining. Whiskey Creek may be the most popular restaurant in town. Inside you'll find big, comfortable booths, polished wood beams, stone fireplaces, and a California-chic atmosphere.

Adults are offered some very interesting menu selections, such as Bangkok pork chops ($11.95), shrimp and scallops, and other fish, pasta, chicken, and meat items ($11.25–$17). There are also daily specials. All entrees include freshly baked breads, and two fresh vegetable. The house salads are also excellent. Be sure to save room for the desserts, which are wonderful.

Children have their choice of teriyaki chicken, hamburger, pasta, or barbecued ribs, along with freshly baked bread ($3.25–$5.95). Highchairs and boosters are available, and the staff will happily warm bottles or baby food. Special nonalcoholic drinks can be ordered.

Open daily from 5 to 10pm. Reservations are an absolute must on weekends and are recommended on weekdays. Bring the kids for an early dinner or you could have a long wait in store. Major credit cards accepted. Parking in front.

A great place to take the whole family for breakfast, lunch, or dinner is the **Swiss Café,** on Old Mammoth Road north of Meridian Boulevard, in the center of town (☎ 619/934-6196). This charming lodge-style room with an inviting fireplace is cozy in the winter. Kids love the carved wooden reindeer in the middle of the room, as well as the beautiful view of the mountains from the big windows. In summer, you'll enjoy sitting on the lovely wooden deck outside, where you watch the sun rise or set over the mountains. As soon as you are seated, your children will be brought crayons and a children's menu to color. This will keep them amused while you choose your meal and relax. The service is quick and efficient, and the staff manages to keep kids happy and entertained throughout the meal. There are highchairs, new and hand-carved, and boosters.

The children's menu features pancakes ($1.75), oatmeal ($1.50), egg with bacon or sausage ($2.50), or French toast ($1.75), all served with milk or orange juice. For lunch and dinner, the kids can choose from a hamburger or hot dog with fresh fruit ($2.50 and $2.95), fish and chips ($3), chicken served with potatoes, vegetables, and a drink ($3.25), or a grilled-cheese sandwich ($1.75). The regular menu offers lots of selections for breakfast, including omelets, pancakes, French toast, and assorted other goodies. The prices range from $3.50 to $9.

For lunch you might want bratwurst ($7.95), fish and chips ($5.75), hot or cold sandwiches ($5-$6.50), hamburgers or salads ($3.95-$6.95). The dinner menu has delicious bratwurst ($9.25), smoked pork chops ($10.90), or American specialties ranging from broiled chicken breast ($7.50), pasta ($6.95), to a New York steak ($11.75). Soups, which come with the dinners, are wonderful, as is the fresh-baked bread.

The Swiss Café is open daily from 6:30am to 9pm. Owners Steve and Patti Rooks will be happy to accommodate you, and suggest that you make reservations on weekends during the busy meal times. Major credit cards are accepted. A parking lot is available.

Also located in town, in Minaret Mall at the corner of Meridian Boulevard and Old Mammoth Road, is **O'Kelly and Dunn Co.** (☎ 619/934-9316). Owner Nancy O'Kelly serves breakfast, lunch, and dinner in this country-style café, which resembles a country inn, with lace curtains, fresh flowers, homemade jams, and a small boutique in the front of the restaurant selling beautiful and unusual imported items.

Portions are large, and everything is fresh and appealing. Although there is no children's menu, the kitchen will prepare scaled-down portions for the little ones. When they see families with young children, the staff is sure to ask how they can best accommodate them. They supply highchairs and boosters.

At breakfast, the oatmeal, served with butter, honey, brown sugar, and raisins, is delectable ($2.95) and too much for one person to finish. The omelets and special egg dishes, served with Irish spuds and choice of toast or muffins, are well prepared and delicious. Prices range from $2.95-$6.95 for a complete breakfast. The grilled-cheese sandwiches and hamburgers are the most popular luncheon choices for kids ($5-$6.25). Adults go for the Cobb salad or open-face beef brisket sandwich. Lunch averages $6. Dinner choices can be as simple as a hamburger, sandwich, or meatloaf, or as interesting as chicken Divan, pasta, or chili ($5.50-$11.50). Children can order breaded shrimp, meatloaf, pasta, fish and chips, or a hamburger off their own menu ($4.95-$5.95).

The restaurant is open daily from 6:30am to 9pm. The busiest breakfast time is 8 to 10am, and at lunch from noon to 1:15pm. Reservations are welcomed, especially on weekends and for large groups. Major credit cards are accepted. Parking is in the shopping center lot.

Another popular breakfast spot in town is **The Stove,** at 644 Old Mammoth Rd. (☎ 619/934-2821). Named after a big, old-fashioned pot-bellied stove, the restaurant is a 20-year-old tradition in town. It serves breakfast, lunch, and dinner in a rustic, country-style atmosphere. Breakfast offers a range of specialties, including oversize pancakes, original-recipe cinnamon toast, and four-egg omelets. Prices start at $3.25 and go up to $6.45. At lunch there are huge original and traditional sandwiches, burgers, Mexican selections, fresh fish, or soup and salad. Lunch is in the $5–$6 range. For dinner, there's old-fashioned pot pies, lasagne, meatloaf with brown sauce, steak, chicken, and homemade soups and bread. You'll pay $6.25–$12.95 for dinner entrees. Save room for the Stove's famous deep-dish fruit cobblers à la mode.

There's no children's menu at breakfast and lunch, but they will serve half orders for little eaters. At dinner a short children's menu offers a hamburger, fried chicken, lasagne, or a grilled-cheese sandwich with french fries and milk for $5.45. Highchairs and booster seats are available, and the staff will warm baby food and bottles.

Monday through Friday, breakfast is served from 6:30am to 2pm, lunch from 10am to 2pm, and dinner from 5 to 9pm. On weekends and holidays the Stove is open straight through from 6:30am to 9pm. Expect a long wait if you come on a busy weekend. Reservations are accepted for dinner, and major credit cards are honored. There's a parking lot.

For the best hamburger around, try **Berger's Restaurant,** on Minaret Road (☎ 619/934-6622). This very busy place, located near the slopes, is quite popular with families. The portions are enormous and the service is efficient. The Berger's burger is a quarter pound of charcoal-broiled beef served on a toasted bun with tomato, pickle, lettuce, and special sauce for $3.50. An order of chili fries is enough for four people to split, and consists of french fries loaded with chili for $4.95. They also offer salads ($3.50–$6.95), half a chicken with garlic bread and choice of salad or potatoes ($8.95), beef or pork rib dinners ($11 and $13). Fresh fish (at market price) and wonderful hot sandwiches served with french fries (starting at $4.95) are also available. Berger's does a big take-out business, with brisket, chicken, soup, chili, and ribs available to go. You can call ahead to order.

A children's menu for folks under 12 is brief: a hamburger, grilled-cheese sandwich, and hot dog are offered at $3.50–$4.50. They have highchairs and boosters, and will split meals at no charge.

Open daily in winter from 11am to 10pm. Reservations (same-day only) are essential for dinner. Some credit cards are accepted, and there's plenty of parking.

In an Emergency

The emergency number here is **911.** There is emergency-room service at **Centinelia-Mammoth Hospital,** 85 Sierra Park Rd. (☎ **619/934-3311**).

Another popular place for take-out or dining in is **Angel's Restaurant,** Main Street at Sierra Road (☎ **619/934-RIBS**), halfway between town and the ski slopes, next to Motel 6. Known for its barbecued ribs and chicken, Angel's also serves soups and salads, an assortment of sandwiches ($5.25 and up), hamburgers ($4.75–$5.95), and complete dinners after 4pm, with such specialties as chicken pot pie, vegetable lasagne, and chicken Chimayo. Lunch prices average $7; dinner, $4.50–$13. The children's menu offers such items as grilled-cheese sandwiches, hamburgers, ribs, and chicken, all served with french fries. Prices run $3–$5. Boosters and highchairs are available.

Angel's has a busy bar area for après-ski lounging, so an early dinner to avoid the crowds is recommended. Take-out is another possibility.

Open Monday through Friday from 11:30am to 10pm; on Saturday and Sunday for dinner only, from 5 to 10pm. No reservations accepted, but major credit cards are welcome. Parking is in a lot.

SHOPPING

For everything you need for kids, visit **Munchkins,** located in the Sierra Center Mall on Old Mammoth Road (☎ **619/934-7337**). You'll find children's clothes, toys, books, stuffed animals, dinosaurs in all sizes and shapes, games, baby things, and anything else your child could want. The staff is very helpful. Open daily year-round; call for hours.

The Central Coast

9

Many people think of the Monterey Bay area as romantic—leisurely strolls near Lover's Point overlooking Monterey Bay, a cozy room warmed by a fireplace, or gallery-hopping in the quaint village of Carmel. But the Monterey Peninsula has much to offer families too. For example, instead of setting your sights on shopping in Carmel, think about tidepooling in Pacific Grove. Instead of limiting yourself to excursions along the exquisite Seventeen Mile Drive, ride the gilded carousel in Cannery Row or visit the Monterey Bay Aquarium, highlights of any trip to the area.

South of Carmel is the breathtaking Big Sur coast, one of the most beautiful stretches of coastline in the world. Famous in the past as a haven for artists and hippies, Big Sur is now a family's delight, replete with hiking, camping, and outdoor adventures galore.

From San Francisco, take Calif. 1 south. From Los Angeles, you have two choices: You can take U.S. 101 north to Salinas and then take Calif. 68 west to Monterey. Or if you prefer to drive the coast, take U.S. 101 to San Luis Obispo and then take Calif. 1 north to Monterey.

Farther south you'll come to beautiful San Luis Obispo County, a region of green rolling hills dotted with cattle and occasional ranches. Edged by an exquisite, rugged coastline that gives way to high sand dunes, this part of the central coast is the transition from Northern California seascape to Southern California beaches.

San Luis Obispo County is an undiscovered jewel for traveling families. The towns of San Luis Obispo and San Simeon offer the historical and cultural riches of the Mission and Hearst Castle, while the beach towns of Pismo, Avila, and Morro Bay have all kinds of outdoor gems. Cambria adds artistic flavor to the mix.

The county is small, so you can choose to stay at one end and visit the other, and since it's located midway between San Francisco and Los Angeles, it's a perfect place to spend a few days on a trek from one big city to the other.

From San Francisco, you can choose to take either U.S. 101 South or Calif. 1, the coast route. To get to San Luis Obispo County from Los Angeles, just take U.S. 101 North. (You'll have to take Calif. 1 to Morro Bay, Cambria, and San Simeon.)

Greyhound Bus Lines also services this area (☎ **805/543-2121** for information; call **800/555-1212** for the local toll-free number). **Amtrak** offers daily service on the *Coast Starlight* (☎ **805/541-0505**, or toll free **800/USA-RAIL**). Three airlines service the county: American Eagle, United Express, and Skywest.

Before you start, contact the friendly folks at the **San Luis Obispo County Visitors and Conference Bureau,** at 1041 Chorro St., Suite E, San Luis Obispo, CA 93401 (☎ **805/541-8000,** or toll free **800/634-1414**). They have an enormous array of information about the country.

1 Monterey

Situated at the southern end of crescent-shaped Monterey Bay, Monterey is 120 miles south of San Francisco and 320 miles north of Los Angeles.

Rich in historical significance, Monterey is a charming seaside town that still feels very much like a working fishing village. Until recently the canneries were a major part of city life, and even today the wharf bustles with fishing activity.

Monterey was the capital of Alta California long before it was part of the United States. First discovered by Portuguese explorer Juan Rodríguez Cabrillo, who was searching for riches, it wasn't until 1602 that the Spanish began to colonize the area,

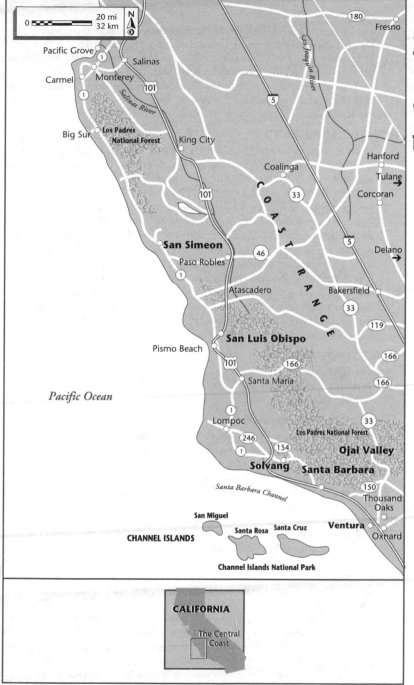

0   20 mi
     32 km
N

180
Fresno

Pacific Grove
Carmel
Monterey
Salinas
1
101

Big Sur
Los Padres
National Forest
Salinas River
King City

101

Hanford
Tulane →
Corcoran
Coalinga
33
5

San Simeon
46
Delano →
Paso Robles
1
Atascadero
Bakersfield
33
119

C O A S T   R A N G E
San Joaquin River
5

San Luis Obispo

Pismo Beach
101
166
166

Santa Maria
166

Pacific Ocean

1
Lompoc
33
Los Padres National Forest

246
1
154
Ojai Valley

Solvang
Santa Barbara
150

Santa Barbara Channel
Thousand
Oaks

San Miguel
Ventura
Oxnard

Santa Rosa
Santa Cruz

CHANNEL ISLANDS

Channel Islands National Park

CALIFORNIA

The Central
Coast

and on June 3, 1770, it became the capital under Fr. Junípero Serra (who was the head of the California missions). It remained under Mexican and Spanish rule until 1846, when Commodore John Drake Sloat raised the United States flag over the Custom House. In 1850 California became a state.

You can still see the Spanish and Mexican heritage in the delightful early California architecture. Many Spanish-style adobe buildings built around patios are still standing. It's an interesting mix with the maritime influence.

HOW TO GET ORIENTED

The main areas of town are located along the waterfront (Cannery Row, Fisherman's Wharf, the Monterey Bay Aquarium) and near downtown (Alvarado Street). A stop at the **Monterey County Visitors & Convention Bureau,** 380 Alvarado St. (P.O. Box 1770), Monterey, CA 93942 (☎ **408/649-1770**), will be very helpful in getting you started. Pick up the walking-tour brochure, called "Historic Monterey: Path of History Walking Tour." It details all the sights of historical significance. Since most children have less interest than their parents in this aspect of travel, we have designed a mini-walk with just a few historical sites we think the kids will appreciate, so that you can enjoy them too. Those of you with exceptionally attentive, historically minded kids can refer to the brochure for additional sites to explore. It costs $2 and can be purchased at Pacific House, Colton Hall, and Cooper Store. In addition, a 112-page "Visitors Guide" is available to visitors by calling, writing, or stopping by the office. You can also visit the Monterey Visitors Center at 401 Camino El Estero. Call the Visitors & Convention Bureau for hours.

WHAT TO SEE AND DO

The highlights for children in this area are, without question, the Monterey Bay Aquarium, Cannery Row, and Fisherman's Wharf. We head there first. Here's how we make a day of it.

The Monterey Bay Aquarium

Monterey Bay has now become the nation's 11th and largest protected marine area. The Monterey Bay National Marine Sanctuary extends along more than 400 miles of coast from San Francisco's Golden Gate, through Big Sur, to San Simeon and San Luis Obispo, an area of 5,312 square miles—1 1/2 times the size of the largest national park in the continental United States. The Aquarium is a testimony and exploration of much of that sea life.

The aquarium, located at the west end of Cannery Row at no. 886 (☎ **408/648-4888**), is not to be missed and will probably be the high spot of your trip, especially if you have children over 4.

Go ahead, "ooooh and ahhhh" as you enter the tremendous, cavernous building designed to reflect the atmosphere of the huge cannery that used to be here. Looking up, you'll see the **Marine Mammals Gallery,** a procession of life-size replicas of killer whales, dolphins, gray whales, and other mammals that hang from the ceiling.

This is one of the largest aquarium in the country, with more than 6,500 creatures and 100 exhibits, many of them interactive. Don't expect marine life in simple fish tanks though. What makes this aquarium unique is that it gives you an "undersea tour" of Monterey Bay and the rich marine life that inhabits the region. Children may not grasp the superb nature of this place at first. It will help if you inform them beforehand that it's not like Sea World or Marine World. This is marine life in its natural habitat, not a collection of performing animals.

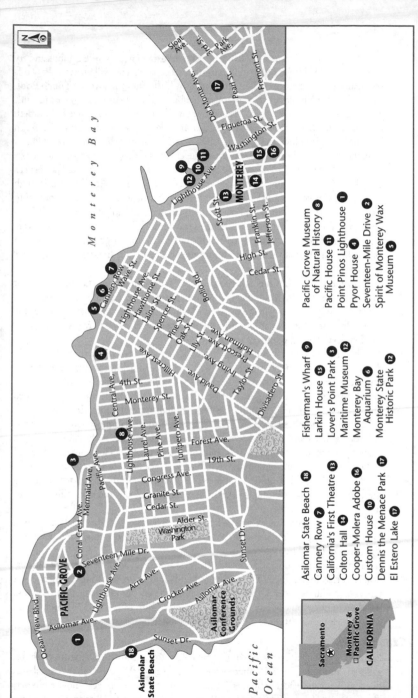

Monterey & Pacific Grove

Asilomar State Beach 18
Cannery Row 7
California's First Theatre 13
Colton Hall 14
Cooper-Molera Adobe 16
Custom House 10
Dennis the Menace Park 17
El Estero Lake 17

Fisherman's Wharf 9
Larkin House 15
Lover's Point Park 3
Maritime Museum 12
Monterey Bay Aquarium 6
Monterey State Historic Park 12

Pacific Grove Museum of Natural History 8
Pacific House 11
Point Pinos Lighthouse 11
Pryor House 4
Seventeen-Mile Drive 2
Spirit of Monterey Wax Museum 5

CALIFORNIA
Sacramento
Monterey & Pacific Grove

It's a place you'll return to again and again, to experience favorite exhibits and try new ones as the kids get older and their interests expand. You will want to allow different amounts of time for kids of different ages. Little ones will love the **Touch Pool,** where they can handle sea stars, decorator crabs, and sea cucumbers under the guidance of patient volunteer instructors who show them what to do. At age 8, Elizabeth talks about the first time she held a starfish. It makes quite an impression. Kids also love the bat ray pool, where they can watch—and pet—the fish. Plan to spend lots of time there. Teens will appreciate most of the exhibits if they don't expect gimmicks.

Don't miss the **Kelp Forest,** a diver's-eye view of a towering forest of California's giant kelp. One of the most impressive exhibits of the aquarium, it's three stories high and can be viewed from different levels. Amazingly, the giant plant can grow up to ten inches a day! Show the kids how the light changes depending on how far it is filtered from the surface. And don't miss the **sea otters.** California's 2,000 sea otters are found mainly along the central coast. This two-story exhibit gives kids a chance to watch these animals at play, in and out of the water. And feeding time for the otters is an event you won't want to miss.

Monterey Bay Habitats is a spectacular 90-foot-long hourglass-shaped exhibit that re-creates the environment of the bay. It's what you would see if you went scuba-diving in the area—in the order in which you would see it. That is, you see the habitat from the deepest part of the bay to the shallowest, from the reef and the sandy sea floor to the wood pilings of the wharf.

The **Sandy Shore** is an open-air bird sanctuary that re-creates the shoreline. As the waves come in, you can watch the fish that swim just below the surface. You enter this aviary via a revolving door which helps to confine the birds. Strollers are not allowed through the revolving door. Elsewhere there's an exhibit featuring live video broadcasts from a research submarine deep in the Monterey submarine canyon.

The **Watching the Bay** exhibit highlights the resources of the sanctuary. It incorporates a video about regional weather and a weather station with real information about the temperature, tides, winds, and currents in the bay. The sanctuary is visited by 26 species of marine mammals, including seals, sea lions, sea otters, and a variety of whales and dolphins. Some 94 species of sea birds are in the sanctuary, including the California brown pelican, the American peregrine falcon, and the California least tern.

You might want to snack or lunch at the Portola Café open from 10am to 5pm. We were surprised at the pleasant café, the varied menu, and a children's menu too. There is a gift- and bookstore.

The aquarium is open daily from 10am to 6pm, except Christmas Day. Admission is $11.25 for adults, $7.25 for students and seniors over 65, $5 for children 3–12 years old; children under 3, free. The aquarium is a very popular attraction. To avoid standing in line, you can buy tickets by phone (in Calif. **800/756-3737**) before you arrive in Monterey, or purchase them at your hotel.

Cannery Row

Next on your outing, walk down Cannery Row toward town. A mixture of shops, galleries, and restaurants, Cannery Row was until recently a bustling industrial area filled with sardine-packing houses, immortalized by John Steinbeck's novels *Cannery Row* (1945) and *Sweet Thursday* (1954). At its peak there were 18 canneries that processed almost a quarter million tons of sardines. The sardines disappeared in the late

1940s, and with them went the people who worked at the canneries by day and partied at Cannery Row in taverns and bars by night. These lively, raucous characters are the ones who peopled Steinbeck's novels and gave the Row its reputation. Now, after years of neglect, it has become a colorful, inviting spot to visit—sans the sardines.

For many years after the loss of the sardines, the famous author and his haunts kept tourists coming. This later prompted developers to restore the decaying buildings that were once canneries and warehouses. As you look around, you can almost hear the din of long ago.

Children and parents both love to wander through the renovated canneries, but you'll have to ask about stroller-access in some of the buildings. Don't miss **700 Cannery Row,** which houses several delightful places for children of all ages. The building houses **Steinbeck's Spirit of Monterey Wax Museum** (☎ **408/375-3770**), which tells the story of old Monterey. Open from 9am to 9pm. Admission is $5.95 for adults, $2.95 for children 7–12, $4.95 for students and seniors; under 7, free.

Don't miss the **Edgewater Packing Company,** 640 Wave St. (☎ **408/649-1899**), up one block from the main Cannery area. Billed as a family fun center, it has an arcade, a favorite of kids over 5, plus a toy store, an ice-cream shop, and a candy store. The main attraction for us, though, is the fabulous antique carousel built in 1905. It has 34 hand-carved horses, two zebras, and two chariots, as well as 940 lights! One word of caution, though—this is a very crowded area that attracts a lot of teenagers. Be careful to hold little hands and be sure you don't get separated from each other. The Edgewater Packing Company is open daily from 11am.

When you're finished with your activities at Cannery Row for the day, walk to Fisherman's Wharf. Just take the pathway and head back toward the town of Monterey. It's an easy walk along the waterway. It takes about 25 minutes and is fine for strollers.

Fisherman's Wharf

The recently opened **Maritime Museum of Monterey and History Center at the Stanton Center,** at 5 Custom House Plaza (☎ **408/373-2469**), near Fisherman's Wharf, presents priceless maritime artifacts. It recalls the seafaring heritage of this region where galleons and tall ships once sailed. The varied exhibits include "Discovery and Development," which explores the voyage of the Spaniards settling Monterey Bay by Father Serra; "Flags over Monterey," which shows Monterey's ties with the United States military community; and "Charts and Navigation," which has some wonderful instruments and artifacts. "Commerce and Trade" shows re-creations of life at sea; there's a life-size captain's quarters that shows the way that people traveled, complete with a wooden bed in the wall and a wash basin. The huge Fresnel lens that came from the Point Sur Lighthouse is a beautiful sight to behold. The museum is open daily from 10am to 5pm. Admission is $5 for adults, $3 for children 13–18, $2 for children 6–12, and free for kids under 6.

Fisherman's Wharf was once a pier for trading schooners to unload their wares when Monterey was the major port on the Pacific. Today, although it's still a working pier, it's where you'll find excursions for sport fishing, sightseeing, and whale-watching. The wharf is lined with giftshops, restaurants, and fresh seafood stands in an authentic atmosphere. The commercial fishing fleet is now at the Municipal Pier, Wharf 2, where there's a lot more activity, and you can walk there, too.

The wharf is a great place to watch the sea lions. You won't miss them—their loud barks give them away. You can't miss the **Carousel Candy Shop,** either. You'll recognize it by the giant ice-cream cone outside and the clown inside the window. They have specialty candies and very good ice cream. There's also a second branch in the Doubletree Plaza.

Other Sights Around Town

Lake El Estero is a pretty little lake in a pretty park bordered by Fremont, Del Monte, Camino Aguajito, and Camino El Estero Streets. Our children love watching the ducks or taking out a paddleboat on the lake. Call **408/375-1484,** as hours and rates change frequently.

Dennis the Menace Park, located at Lake El Estero, was designed by cartoonist Hank Ketcham, creator of Dennis the Menace. We've spent many hours here, the kids playing on the steam locomotive, the roller slide, and the spaceshiplike structure, while we simply took advantage of the fresh air and beauty of nearby Lake El Estero. Open every day from 10am to dusk. For information call **408/646-3866.**

Monterey State Historic Park (☎ **408/649-7118**) is a group of historically important adobes and other buildings located in Monterey. The buildings, owned by the state, are open to the public for viewing, and many have guided tours. The **Path of History,** mentioned at the beginning of this section, is a delightful walking tour of those buildings as well as many others in the area that are owned by foundations, societies, and individuals. You can pick up a brochure which details the 45 historic landmarks on the path at the visitors center, or at the park's offices at 20 Custom House Plaza. You can begin your tour at any location. If you plan to go to several of the sites in the state park, you can buy a 2-day pass ($5 for adults, $2 for children 6–12). Single-building admissions are $2 for adults and $1.50 for kids. Call ahead to check hours.

Our kids are not up to a long walk of historic buildings yet. We've found this to be true of many children, regardless of age so we'll recommend a few highlights of this tour. Many people like to start with the **Custom House** centrally located near Fisherman's Wharf. It's the oldest government building in California, and the place where the United States flag was raised in 1846. The museum is open daily from 10am to 5pm June through August, till 4pm the rest of the year. Nearby, in Custom House Plaza, is **Pacific House;** an historic landmark built in 1847, it also houses a museum of Native American and early California history. Admission is free, and it's open the same hours as the Custom House.

Colton Hall, at 522 Pacific St., between Madison and Jefferson Streets (open daily from 10am to 5pm), is where the first Constitutional Congress of California met, the place where the California Constitution was written and the Great Seal designed. This is a delightful place to visit, almost like living history without the people. Tables are set up as if the people who were in the process of creating the constitution were still at work and just got up for a break. Glasses of water, pens and paper, hats on the back of chairs bring history to life. Operating as the first town hall and public school of Monterey, it now houses a historical museum.

The **Cooper-Molera Adobe,** near Munras and Polk Streets, is a good example of Monterey colonial architecture. It houses a small maritime museum and sits on two acres of grounds. Open daily except Monday. Tours are given at 10am and 11am and in summer also at 12pm. Another architecturally interesting house nearby is the **Larkin House,** at Jefferson Street and Calle Principal. Built in the New England style, it's considered an architectural treasure. Open daily except Tuesday and Thursday. Tours are given at 1pm, 2pm, and 3pm, and in summer at 2, 3 and 4. Tours are $2 for adults, $1.50 for children 13–17, $1 for children 6–12.

California's First Theatre, located at the corner of Scott and Pacific Streets (☎ 408/375-4916), has staged productions since the 1840s. During the day you can walk through the empty theater if you'd like, but at night the place comes alive with old-fashioned melodramas. Throughout the year, performances are held on Friday and Saturday nights at 8pm. During July and August there are performances Wednesday through Saturday at 8pm. The cost is $8 for adults, $6 for seniors (over 60) and teens 13–19, $5 for children under 12. Call for program information.

An Early-Morning Walk

On those mornings when your little ones are up especially early and you want to let the others sleep, you can treat yourself to a **walk on the Wharf at sunrise.**

We left at about 6:30am, stroller filled and heavy jackets on. Take the path next to the Doubletree Inn (on Alvarado and Del Monte) and through the Doubletree Plaza. The area is quiet and deserted except for an occasional jogger or a hearty bicyclist. The air is chilly, and if you're lucky there will be some mist to add atmosphere. You'll pass the **Pacific House** (see above). Our children enjoyed simply roaming around the large plaza area where the house sits. Next, you'll approach the **Custom House** (see above) and its plaza (with tables for a morning picnic breakfast of muffins and coffee).

As we got closer to the Wharf, we watched the fishermen get ready for the day's work, cups of steaming coffee in their hands. We could hear the barking of the nearby sea lions. It's a special time to be on the Wharf.

If you want a quick cup of coffee or a bite to eat, you might try the **Cove Restaurant,** at 46 Fisherman's Wharf (☎ 408/373-6969). Booster and sassy seats are available. Dinners range from $7.95 to $14.95. Open for breakfast and lunch Monday through Friday from 6:30am to 5pm and on Saturday and Sunday from 6am to 5pm; dinner is served daily from 5 to 9pm (closed for dinner Monday and Tuesday in winter).

Another good possibility is **Pino's Italian Café,** 221 Alvarado St. (☎ 408/649-1930), a great little place to get Italian ice cream and yogurt, cappuccino, espresso, caffé latte (coffee with milk), sandwiches, and homemade muffins. It's open daily from 5am to 6pm.

ACTIVITIES IN THE SURROUNDING AREA

Since the communities of Monterey, Pacific Grove, and Carmel are so close together, there are many activities that you can do in the general area. For example, you can rent bicycles in one town and go for a bike ride in another.

Beaches

Caution! Beaches in Monterey, Pacific Grove, Carmel, and Big Sur may look inviting, but swimming can be quite hazardous. Riptides and cross currents make some areas extremely dangerous, and the water is very cold. Check to see if there are lifeguards on duty, and if so, heed any warning signs. Children have been lost off the rocks in heavy surf, and they can easily be caught in the strong crosscurrents.

The following beaches may be of interest: **Carmel Beach** (see the "What to See and Do" section in Carmel), **Carmel River State Beach** (see the "What to See and

Do" section in Carmel), and **Lover's Point** (see the "What to See and Do" section in Pacific Grove).

Asilomar State Beach, in Pacific Grove, is a wonderful place for exploring dunes and tidepools. You'll find comfortable picnic spots sheltered from the wind, but don't attempt to swim. Take Ocean View Drive as it follows the ocean.

Tidepooling

Look for good tidepools along the rocky areas between Point Pinos and Asilomar Beach in Pacific Grove during low tide.

Caution! Remember that the ocean waves can be unpredictable and may surprise you. Always be careful. Remember, too, that the area is slippery.

Here are some tips for tidepooling (courtesy of the Monterey County Visitors and Convention Bureau):

1. Remain with your group—don't go off alone.
2. Don't fool around on the rocks.
3. Walk slowly and carefully, since the rocks are very slippery.
4. Wear tennis shoes.
5. Don't get trapped by the rising tide.
6. Waves can knock you down, so always watch for them.
7. Don't take glass containers in the tidepool areas.
8. Don't pry animals from the rocks.
9. Return animals to the same area from which you removed them.
10. Return each rock to the exact spot you took it from.
11. Sea animals don't like being stepped on or having fingers poked at them.
12. Leave empty shells on the beach—they may be some animal's future home.
13. Remember that all tidepool life is protected by law.

Bicycling

Bicycling in the area is wonderful. You have a choice of scenery and terrain. You can either stay on designated bike paths or ride in lovely residential areas. One of the most scenic paths is the **Shoreline Bike Path** from Lover's Point in Pacific Grove to Fisherman's Wharf. This path is also good heading south, where you ride along the shore of the Seventeen Mile Drive, an easy six-mile ride.

Adventures by the Sea (☎ 408/372-1807) is a full-service bicycle-rental company that has free pickup and delivery, as well as package rates and preplanned tours. They have mountain bikes, beach cruisers, and tandem bikes, plus helmets and locks. They also have children's bikes, and bicycles with training wheels and toddler-carrier seats. Half-day rates are for four hours, a full day means eight hours of rental, and there are overnight and multiday rates as well. They also rent other outdoor equipment. They include carrier seats, daypacks, locks, helmets, and delivery. Delivery is not included in half-day rentals, and there are also delivery restrictions that apply in Carmel, Carmel Valley, Monterey, and Pacific Grove. You might want to rent a child's trailer for $5 per hour. They also rent kayaks at $20 per day, which includes instruction and dry clothes; no experience is necessary. In-line skates can be rented for a two-hour minimum at $10, or $20 for all day; all safety gear is included. Adventures by the Sea is open daily from sunrise to sunset.

Bay Bikes, 640 Wave St. (☎ 408/646-9090), is located on the Shoreline Bike Path on Cannery Row, one block from the aquarium. They rent 21-speed mountain bikes, ten-speeds, tandems, and children's bikes. They also have quadricycle/surreys that will hold three adults sitting next to each other, with a basket in front that holds two children up to age 6. Helmets, safety wear, in-line skates, locks, cables, and packs are included in the rental price. Riding from 9am to 5:30pm (a full day), starts at $18, and there are also hourly rates. There's a repair stand in the shop for people who bring their own bikes. The delivery charge for each bike is $2 (for drop-off or pickup); reserve ahead. Surreys are also available.

Horseback Riding

Group rides are available at the **Pebble Beach Equestrian Center,** on the corner of Portola Road and Alva Lane (☎ **408/624-2756**). Escorted trail rides are offered twice daily. And they offer two different rides: a 50-minute forest ride for $30 and a 75-minute beach and forest ride for $45. These rides are by reservation only. Groups must be no more than six people, unless your own group is larger; and children must be at least 12 years old.

Fishing

Your kids can **pier fish** at the Monterey Municipal Pier, Wharf 2 (☎ **408/646-3950**).

Randy's Fishing Trips, 66 Fisherman's Wharf (☎ **408/372-7440**), is open daily from 5:30am to 5pm (kids don't need fishing licenses, but adults do). They offer group-charter boats for deep-sea and salmon fishing daily out of Monterey. Whale-watching trips are offered December through March; call for reservations.

Chris's Fishing Trips, 48 Fisherman's Wharf (☎ **408/375-5951**), offers deep-sea fishing trips. The charge is $24 weekdays and $27 on weekends; children under 12 are charged $15 both weekdays and weekends. There's no minimum age as long as you're willing to keep track of your own kids. Trips are from 7:30am to 2:30pm weekdays and from 6:30am to 2:30pm on weekends.

Indoor Activities (for Rainy, Foggy Days)

In Monterey, you might enjoy a second visit to the **Monterey Bay Aquarium** (☎ **408/648-4800**); see above for details.

There's also the **Del Monte Gardens Roller Rink,** 2020 Del Monte Ave. (☎ **408/375-3202**). It's open Wednesday through Sunday evenings from 7:30 to 10pm, with late sessions on Friday and Saturday nights from 9:30 to 11:30pm. Daytime sessions are only on Saturday, Sunday, and holidays from 2 to 4pm. Fees are $3.50 for matinee sessions, $4 for evening sessions, and $3 for late-night sessions. If you attend the full Friday- and Saturday-night sessions (7:30 to 11:30pm), the cost is $6.50.

For bowling, try **Lincoln Lanes,** at 2161 N. Fremont St. (☎ **408/373-1553**).

In Pacific Grove, you might try the **Pacific Grove Museum of Natural History** (☎ **408/648-3116**); see "What to See and Do" in Pacific Grove for details.

Seasonal Events and Festivals

The **Monterey County Fair** (five days in mid-August) is a county fair par excellence. The kids will love the livestock exhibitions and the carnival rides. This event brings you back to the flavor of an old-fashioned county fair. It's held at the Monterey Fairgrounds, 2004 Fairground Rd., Monterey (☎ **408/372-1000** for information).

Monarch Butterfly Festival and Parade (October) is a time-honored and fun event in Pacific Grove. All the elementary schoolchildren of Pacific Grove welcome the monarch in this colorful parade, which features 900 children in costume.

Whale-watching (mid-December to March) is the chance to see the yearly migration of whales down the California coast. **Randy's Fishing Trips** (☎ 408/372-7440) and **Sam's Fishing Fleet** (☎ 408/372-0577) offer excursions.

Custom Tours

Otter-Mobile Tours and Charters (☎ 408/625-9762) and **Seacoast Safaris** (☎ 408/372-1288) offer personalized tours.

WHERE TO STAY

You won't have any trouble finding the kind of accommodation that fits your needs and pocketbook. Here are a few that we like.

Expensive

The **Doubletree Hotel at Fisherman's Wharf,** Two Portola Plaza, Monterey, CA 93940 (☎ 408/649-4511), is a full-service hotel in a great location. Almost everything is within walking distance. The lobby is a large, open-air atrium, a combination indoor/outdoor area with shops, restaurant and a bar. Boats, in-line skates, and bicyclists are just outside your window.

Dine at the Plazatree Café, which offers a wide array of foods. It's open daily from 6am to 2pm and 5 to 10pm (to 11pm on weekends). A children's menu is offered at breakfast, lunch, and dinner. Kids can choose from such goodies as shortstack pancakes with sausage, boxed cereals with milk, sandwiches of peanut butter and jelly or grilled cheese, hot dogs, and spaghetti.

Room service is available from 6am to 11pm. Other facilities include the Brass Tree Lounge, a rooftop nightclub overlooking the bay; the lobby lounge, with a big-screen TV; and a heated pool and Jacuzzi, open from 7am to 10pm. The rooms are large, with plenty of space for an additional crib when needed. Room rates are $125–$225.

One of the nice places to stay in Monterey is the **Monterey Marriott,** 350 Calle Principal, Monterey, CA 93940 (☎ 408/649-4234). One of the tallest structures in Monterey, this ten-story building offers panoramic views of Monterey Bay from many of the rooms. The two-story atrium lobby absorbs much of the tumult and noise from the kids while serving as a comfortable and popular gathering spot. We saw dozens of young-uns, many of whom were rambunctious, and the style of the lobby accommodated them well.

The hotel has an outdoor swimming pool and Jacuzzi that are sheltered from the wind on three sides. The pool is very large and quite inviting when the weather is warm enough. There is also a health club (for guests over 18) with exercise equipment, weights, and bicycles, a beauty salon and barbershop, and a giftshop.

Services and amenities include a full concierge staff, room service (from 6am to 11pm) and, if you give housekeeping a call, nightly turn-down service. The nightly turn-down service is the closest you'll get to a fairy godmother. Andrew and Elizabeth left toys scattered over the bed when we rushed out to dinner one night. When we returned, the toys were piled neatly on the chaise longue and the clothes were folded at the foot of the bed!

The concierge staff is concerned that your stay be pleasant. They will make reservations for you, arrange babysitting, and do all manner of things.

The Three Flags Café, a family-style restaurant, is open for breakfast. The Characters Sports Bar and Grill is open from 11am to 2am and has entertainment nightly.

Highchairs and booster seats are available at both these restaurants. Ferrante's, located on the 10th floor, is an Italian restaurant and bar with a spectacular view. Even if you don't eat here with the kids, take them up here at sunset to see the view.

The 344 rooms have refrigerators, game tables and chairs, and dressing rooms with vanity areas. Connecting rooms are available, and there are a wide variety of suites. All rooms are spacious and airy, and there's plenty of room for kids to play with blocks and puzzles on the floor. You can request a room with two double beds or a king-size bed, and many rooms have a sofa or love seat. Rates range from $185 to $225, depending on the floor, the view, and the room set-up. Suites vary from $225 to $850. Children under 17 stay free in their parents' room if no additional beds are needed. No charge for cribs which are some of the nicest around, but rollaways cost $20. Ask about seasonal, weekend, and family special rates.

The **Monterey Plaza,** 400 Cannery Row, Monterey, CA 93940 (☎ **408/ 646-1700,** or toll free **800/631-1339, 800/334-3999** in California), a Waterfront Hotel that describes itself as "where the ocean greets you at the door," has beautiful rooms with breathtaking views. Many of the 285 deluxe rooms are built over the bay, affording an unparalleled view of Monterey and the curving coastline of the bay. This is indeed elegance. But if you have young children, be alert near the windows since they open wide. The lobby is quiet, but there is a large outdoor plaza area where kids can wander. Rooms are beautifully decorated and come with luxurious amenities, including hairdryers. There's an honor bar/refrigerator, cable television, and pay movies. Room service is available from 6:30am to midnight. Babysitting can be arranged by the concierge. Rooms are $149–$225, single or double. Additional adults are $20. Children under 12 stay free. Cribs are free, and rollaways are $20. Valet parking $10 per night or street parking.

The **Best Western Monterey Beach Hotel,** at 2600 Sand Dunes Dr., Monterey, CA 93940 (☎ **408/394-3321,** or toll free **800/242-8627**), is off Calif. 1, on Monterey State Beach, and has been recommended to us by locals. The hotel features a heated pool and Jacuzzi and cable color TV. There's a full-service restaurant on the premises with a panoramic view of Monterey Bay, and it has a children's menu. The Monterey Beach has 195 guest rooms, and these rent for $99–$179 per night for one to five people, depending on the season. Suites go for $200–$300. Children under 18 stay free in their parents' room. There is no charge for cribs or rollaways. Ask about special packages.

Moderate

If you're looking for moderate and inexpensive motels, you might try driving down "motel row," which is located on Fremont and Munras Avenues. Another option is to check out the recommendations in Pacific Grove, which is adjacent to Monterey. These accommodations are equally close to most sightseeing attractions as those listed below.

We really liked the **Holiday Inn Resort Monterey,** 1000 Aguajito Rd. (at Calif. 1), Monterey, CA 93940 (☎ **408/373-6141**). This modest resort offers a heated swimming pool, shuffleboard, a putting green, Jacuzzi, and sauna, and a location that's perfect if you're planning activities in Carmel and Big Sur as well as in Monterey and Pacific Grove. Babysitting can be arranged.

The Monterey Rose restaurant is open from 6:30am to 10pm, and has boosters and highchairs. Room service is available for breakfast, lunch, and dinner, with hamburgers and fried chicken on the menu.

Ask for a room facing the pool or garden. Room rates are $105–$180 single or double. Children under 18 stay free in their parents' room. Cribs are free, but rollaways and additional adults are $15.

A good motel in Monterey is **Casa Munras Garden Hotel,** 700 Munras Ave., Monterey, CA 93940 (☎ **408/375-2411,** or toll free **800/222-2558, 800/222-2446** in California). Originally built in 1824 as the official residence of the last Spanish ambassador to the state of California, Casa Munras is set on 3 ½ acres of landscaped, flowering gardens. There is an outdoor heated pool with a large shallow area for children. Babysitting is arranged through a referral service.

Although there's no room service, the Casa Café and Bar is on the premises. It's open Monday through Friday from 7am to 2pm and 5 to 9pm, and on Saturday and Sunday from 7am to 1pm. Boosters and highchairs are available, and there is a children's menu. Prices range from $2.50 for French toast, hotcakes, or waffles for breakfast, to $13 for a full prime rib dinner, including soup and salad, garlic bread, and fresh vegetable.

Rooms at Casa Munras are good-sized, with plenty of space for a crib and toys for kids. Extra care is shown in the decor; for example, brass beds and comforters are part of the standard room. Rates run $71–$350 (for a room with a king-size bed, sofa-sleeper, and fireplace). Children under 12 stay free in their parents' room if no extra beds are needed. No charge for cribs; rollaways cost $12 per night. Some connecting rooms are available.

Budget

A reasonably priced inn is the **Sand Dollar Inn,** 755 Abrego St., Monterey, CA 93940 (☎ **408/372-7551,** or toll free **800/982-1986;** fax 408/373-0916). There is a heated swimming pool, Jacuzzi, and guest laundry. Accommodations vary from rooms with queen-size beds and fireplaces to suites with two queen-size beds. Some rooms have only showers while others have shower/bath combinations; some even have honor bars and private balconies. All rooms have TV and telephone, but no air conditioning. Prices range from $64–$74 (for the smallest room) to $94–$104 (for the largest), depending on the season. Children under 12 stay free in the same room with their parents. Additional people 12 or over pay $5. Cribs are free. There's a Denny's restaurant next door.

The **Best Western Steinbeck Lodge,** at 1300 Munras Ave., Monterey, CA 93940 (☎ **408/373-3203**), is a modest little motel of 32 rooms. The quoted rate includes a continental breakfast of danish pastry and coffee. Room prices range from $49 to $159 single, $59 to $159 double, depending on the season and kind of room. Rollaways and cribs, $10.

WHERE TO EAT

The Monterey Bay area towns of Monterey, Pacific Grove, and Carmel are so small and close to each other that it's easy to have breakfast in Pacific Grove, lunch in Carmel, and dinner in Monterey. We list restaurants by their city, but don't forget to check the other areas for ideas before making your choice.

Expensive

We couldn't believe it when we were told that the famous **Whaling Station Inn,** 763 Wave St., Cannery Row (☎ **408/373-3778**), loved kids and catered to families. Nestled one block above Cannery Row, this gem of a restaurant is the perfect place to spend a relaxed evening with or without children. Don't let the candles and elaborate dessert table fool you. While the ambience of this legendary restaurant is quiet and elegant, the service is gracious and helpful to parents. Managers, waiters, busboys, even the parking valets have an appreciation for a dining experience with children, and even more important, a sense of humor and camaraderie with the parents. "It happens all the time" is the response to a spilled Shirley Temple drink. Management says "We don't want the ambience to scare away any family." Fussy infants are greeted with little goldfish crackers and warm bread. Adults sit down to the artichoke appetizers that come as part of the meal. There is a children's menu or they'll gladly serve half portions of the pasta dishes, or split fish or steak dinners between two children. Of course, they have highchairs and boosters here, and they'll warm bottles and baby food. Prices range from $13.50 for sautéed chicken to $44 for fresh abalone and filet and lobster tail. Complete dinners include artichoke for two, fresh vegetables, and fresh, warm bread. The children's menu includes pasta, fish and chips, and more for $5.95.

The restaurant is open Sunday through Thursday from 5 to 9:30pm, on Friday and Saturday till 10pm. Reservations are recommended for weekends. Major credit cards accepted. Valet parking.

The **Abalonetti Seafood Trattoria,** 57 Fisherman's Wharf (☎ **408/373-1851**), is owned by the same people as the Whaling Station Inn. It is a large restaurant with open-planked ceilings that look out onto the bay and recreation path. What a perfect location, and so very airy—the epitome of Monterey! And there's great seafood, too! The specialty is calamari: baked calamari with eggplant and marinara sauce, calamari filets fried with lemon butter, and calamari stuffed with cheese and sausage served over pasta. Dinner, including salad and bread, costs $11.95–$13.95. You might prefer pasta, pizza, or one of the house specialties such as breast of chicken, cioppino, or New York steak ($7.95–$16.95). Lunch includes a wide range of calamari dishes, fish and chips, pizza, and pasta, or sandwiches and burgers ($6.95–$12.95). The children's menu includes spaghetti, pizza, burgers, fish, and calamari at $4.95–$5.95. They serve half orders, warm bottles and baby food, and make children's drinks. They provide boosters and highchairs and give every child a coloring book. Open daily from 11am to 10pm. Reservations are accepted and recommended. There's a parking lot nearby.

An institution in Monterey, the **Old Fisherman's Grotto,** 39 Wharf No. 1, (☎ **408/375-4604**), overlooks Monterey Bay. It is known for great seafood and a very congenial atmosphere. Fisherman's Grotto offers shellfish, such as crab, scallops, clams, mussels, oysters, lobster, and fresh fish, including snapper, sandabs, mahi mahi, calamari, and salmon. If you'd prefer pasta, meat, or poultry, you can get those too. Lunch prices range from $7.50 to $8.95; dinner, from $8.95 to $15.95. The children's menu offers hamburgers, fish and chips, spaghetti, and fried shrimp, all served with clam chowder and fresh fruit ($4.95–$5.50). They will split adult portions in the kitchen for two children, warm bottles and baby food, and also make special drinks. They provide crayons and paper, and boosters and highchairs are available.

Open daily from 11am to 9:30pm. During the summer and on holidays reservations are accepted only for parties of eight or more, so expect a 10- to 15-minute wait. This is an all no-smoking restaurant.

Mark Thomas Outrigger, 700 Cannery Row (☎ **408/372-8543**), is a moderately priced seafood and steak restaurant. Set on the water, this is a fine spot to enjoy a leisurely meal while watching the seals and pelicans. Ask for a window seat and your children are likely to spend their time fascinated by the activity on the water: By day there's a wealth of boats and fishing vessels; near sunset, they can watch small fields of floating kelp and the ever-changing colors on the distant shoreline of Seaside and Santa Cruz. Or you may want to request seating in the back dining room, which is bright and spacious for obtrusive highchairs and wandering children, rather than in the main dining room.

This is the kind of place where you can order a petite filet with béarnaise or an Australian lobster tail while your son or daughter munches on a hamburger. Adult dinners range from $6 to $30. The children's menu $4.75 caters to a variety of sophisticated palates and includes a kid's shrimp Louie, deep-fried calamari, and fish and chips. The kiddie menu also has a drink list that includes a nonalcoholic daiquiri (banana, coconut, strawberry, etc.) and piña colada, along with the more traditional Shirley Temple and Roy Rogers. They will warm bottles and baby food. Highchairs and boosters are available. Open daily from 11:30am to 10pm. Reservations are accepted for parties of six or more, but if you have to wait, there's a little beach area next to the restaurant that keeps the kids occupied. Be careful of the rocks, though. Some credit cards accepted. Street Parking is available.

Moderate to Inexpensive

You may be surprised at how many great places in the Monterey Bay area welcome children.

The **Old Monterey Café,** 489 Alvarado St. (☎ **408/646-1021**), is where the locals go for breakfast and lunch. Centrally located, it's a good place to try during a walk downtown, if you're doing part of the Adobe Tour, or after a jaunt in Dennis the Menace Park. The food is fabulous, and the menu varied and unusual. Omelet lovers can choose from such exotic combinations as avocado, bacon, and onions ($5), or artichoke hearts, bacon, and Jack cheese ($6); or you can invent your own omelet filling, which might include broccoli, pineapple, or Italian sausage as well as the more usual fixings. And all omelets are made with four eggs. The old-fashioned hash browns and the homemade muffins are well worth the trip. Breakfast is served until 2:30pm. Lunch offers the same kind of variety in sandwiches, half-pound burgers, salads, and homemade soups. There's no children's menu, but they'll serve a child's portion, and will warm bottles and baby food. Highchairs and boosters are available. Open daily except Tuesday from 7am to 2:30pm. No reservations, but credit cards are accepted. There's validated parking.

Another obvious favorite is **Marie Callender's,** 1200 Del Monte Shopping Center (☎ **408/375-9500**). For anyone unfamiliar with Marie Callender's restaurants, these are generally good places for breakfast, lunch, and dinner. While some have children's menus and others don't, you can feel certain that your meal will be a step above coffeeshop fare. They serve a surprising variety of entrees and have many specialties. The chain is known for their excellent fruit pies (20–30 kinds daily) and heartland pot pies, and they also serve very good soup and chili. This branch also has good lasagne, and quiche. The array of pot pies includes chicken pot pie and chicken divan pot pie, as well as the standard turkey. Cornbread is another of their specialties. The kids' menu offers a variety, from hamburgers and fries and spaghetti to soup and children's salad bar.

This location, decorated in a San Francisco saloon motif like most other Marie Callender's, is a comfortable place to take a child. The noise level is sufficiently loud to muffle the antics of the crankiest child. Marie Callender's restaurants tend to be very popular, so you may have to wait for a table at prime time. It's a good idea to go early for lunch or dinner. If you have to wait, there's WaldenKids and Toys, Etcetera nearby. Highchairs and boosters are available. Reservations are accepted, and major credit cards are welcome. Parking is in the shopping center lot.

Don't miss our favorite place. It has wonderful Italian food to eat in or take out, and it's a great place to come after a walk through the aquarium or a visit to Cannery Row. **Gianni's Pizza,** at 725 Lighthouse Ave. (☎ **408/649-1500**), an inexpensive, family-owned restaurant, has a pasta bar, a cocktail bar, a dessert bar, and a coffee bar. While the artichoke fritatta and fresh breadsticks are a find, Gianni's specializes in traditional Italian pizzas. There's no children's menu, but pizza and pasta are made for sharing. Pizzas take about 20 minutes to prepare, and at peak hours on Friday, Saturday, and Sunday (from 5:30 to 9pm) you may have to wait 10 minutes to get a table. Boosters and highchairs are available. Gianni's is open Monday through Thursday from 4 to 11pm, on Friday and Saturday from 11:30am to midnight, and on Sunday from 11:30am to 10pm. No credit cards accepted. There is both street and lot parking.

Step into downtown **Rosine's Restaurant,** 434 Alvarado St. (☎ **408/375-1400**), and it's like you're entering an early California outdoor plaza. If there's such a thing as "faux outdoor early California," this is it. The walls are painted to look as if you're sitting in an outdoor plaza, complete with blue shutters painted on the walls that "open" into the restaurant. Breakfast, lunch, and dinner are served. There are highchairs and boosters, but no children menu, plus there's a charge for splitting food. However, at dinner one pasta dish for children is offered. And some of the menu items, like a half sandwich with soup or salad or a bagel with cream cheese and soup or salad, are fine for small appetites. Breakfast is served all day. For more grownup tastes, there are Reuben, Philly, and calamari sandwiches, as well as full dinners served after 5pm. Open Monday through Friday mornings at 7:30am and on Sunday at 8am; closing hours vary. Reservations are not necessary. Major credit cards accepted. Street parking is available.

Nick's Oceanside Café, 700 Cannery Row (☎ **408/649-1430**), is a gem of a place for breakfast, lunch, and dinner. It has good food, you can't beat the prices, and you'll never have a wait. Located on the ground floor of the Old Cannery that now houses the Paul Masson Winery, Nick's is a favorite of many locals, especially when they're looking for something simple. The specialties are simply prepared seafood, though you can also get pasta, chicken, and beef. Complete dinners, including soup or salad and potato, are usually less than $10. Highchairs are available and the servers will warm baby food and bottles. Open Monday through Thursday from 7:30am to 5pm, to 8pm on Friday, Saturday, and Sunday. Some major credit cards are accepted. Parking is in a nearby lot.

For more terrific restaurants, see the "Where to Eat" sections in Pacific Grove and Carmel.

For picnic lunch provisions, there's a **Lucky Supermarket** at the Del Monte Shopping Center (☎ **408/372-3634**).

In an Emergency

The **Community Hospital of the Monterey Peninsula,** 23625 Holman Hwy. in Monterey (☎ **408/624-5311**), has the only 24-hour emergency room in the area. There is also a 24-hour pharmacy.

2 Pacific Grove

Just next door to Monterey is the picturesque town of Pacific Grove. Also known as Butterfly Town, U.S.A., because the monarch butterflies return here in droves every year, Pacific Grove is a place you'll remember fondly. The kids especially love to wander around here. A drive down Ocean View Boulevard to Lover's Point is surely one of the most beautiful excursions you'll take. Or walk through the quaint streets downtown and you'll feel as if you're back at the turn of the century.

WHAT TO SEE AND DO

The best place to start is beautiful **Lover's Point,** near Ocean View Boulevard, a bluff overlooking the crashing water. It offers a spectacular view of the bay, and is not to be missed. There are stairs down to the beach, but swimming is not suggested.

Point Pinos Lighthouse, at the end of Lighthouse Avenue, at Asilomar Boulevard (☎ 408/648-3116), is the oldest continuously working lighthouse on the West Coast. The grownups in our group were more excited about it than the kids (whose great pleasure was counting the number of steps up to the top). If your group has never seen a lighthouse before, take them to this one—the kids will enjoy it in their own way, and you don't need to spend much time there. There's a small museum downstairs. Open on Saturday and Sunday (except holidays) from 1 to 4pm. Admission is free.

Pacific Grove Museum of Natural History, at Forest and Central Avenues (☎ 408/648-3116), is a small museum where you can learn about the natural history of Monterey County and the monarch butterflies' annual winter return to Pacific Grove. Open Tuesday through Sunday from 10am to 5pm. Admission is free.

The **Recreation Trail or Walkway to Fisherman's Wharf** begins at Lover's Point and 17th Avenue and continues on to Cannery Row and Fisherman's Wharf and beyond. It would take a family approximately one hour to walk, and it's a wonderful way to get the flavor of the area.

Touted as "the slowest way between Carmel and Monterey," the **Seventeen Mile Drive** meanders through exquisite coastal scenery. Many people love this route. Others with kids who are poor car travelers aren't so sure. If your kids will cooperate, you'll love it. If you go, begin the drive from the Calif. 1 Gate (Munras Avenue to Calif. 1). Although there are three gates to take you to the drive, this one is the most convenient. At the toll gate, you'll receive a guide map that shows the highlights you'll be passing. During your drive, you'll enter the Del Monte Forest and Pebble Beach, home of the Lone Cypress tree and Seal Rock. Be sure to stop to enjoy the exquisite views. You'll also pass several picnic areas, championship golf courses, and the famous Lodge at Pebble Beach. A stop at Lone Pine or Seal or Bird Rock will give you a glimpse of thousands of sea birds and lots of seals and sea lions. The toll is $6 per car.

You might choose to bicycle in the area. We suggest the wonderful bike path, a continuation of the one that goes to Monterey's Fisherman's Wharf. This one goes in the other direction, continuing on Ocean View Boulevard, and changes to Sunset Boulevard. The path, which is on the road, follows the coast, is relatively flat, and is free. (For suggestions about bicycle rentals, see "Other Activities in the Monterey Bay Area," in Monterey.)

WHERE TO STAY

Pacific Grove has a good selection of mid-priced hostelries.

The **Beachcomber Inn,** 1996 Sunset Dr., Pacific Grove, CA 93950 (☎ **408/373-4769,** or toll free **800/634-4769** in California), at Asilomar State Beach, is a small 25-room inn that's basic but very clean. It's the last property before the beach. The rooms are small, but adjoining rooms can be rented. Refrigerators are in every room. The outdoor swimming pool is heated year round. There are some adult bikes for guests' free use. In winter, rates start at $49.50 (for a room with a queen- or king-size bed) and go up to $100. In summer, the prices run $69.50–$119.50. There's a complimentary continental breakfast. The Fishwife restaurant (see "Where to Eat" for details) is on the premises.

The **Pacific Gardens Inn,** 701 Asilomar Blvd., Pacific Grove, CA 93950 (☎ **408/646-9414,** or toll free **800/262-1566**), across the street from Asilomar State Park and Beach, is another good choice. Nestled in the trees and lovely gardens, this cozy, rustic motel has 28 units, most of which have fireplaces. There are two hot tubs on the property. Kitchen units and adjoining rooms are available upon request. All rooms have refrigerators. We loved the fresh popcorn we could make at night with the popcorn maker that comes with each room. Rates include complimentary continental breakfast, and wine and cheese in the evening. Rooms come with one or two queen-size beds or a king-size bed, and range in price from $70 to $98. One- and two-bedroom suites range from $105 to $150. No charge for cribs. Children under 12 stay free in their parents' room if additional beds are not needed; children over 12 are charged $5 each per night.

Bed-and-Breakfast Inns

Yes, even families can partake of the hospitality of a bed-and-breakfast. You just have to know if the inns accept children. The following two accommodations welcome families. (See the Carmel accommodations section for a third bed-and-breakfast inn.) Please, remember that in such close quarters you can usually hear *everything*. Fussy babies and poorly behaved kids don't belong in B&Bs. Refer to the section in Chapter 1 for advice on staying with children in bed-and-breakfast accommodations.

The **Green Gables Inn,** 104 5th St., Pacific Grove, CA 93950 (☎ **408/375-2095**), is a Queen Anne–style mansion located on a breathtaking section of the Monterey Bay coastline. You'll be amazed as you first step into the high-ceilinged living room, elegantly decorated with antiques, and face the sea through large, bay-windowed alcoves. The view is spectacular! Across the street is a lovely public beach and a trail for jogging or strolling. Afternoon tea, sherry, and wine are served with hors d'oeuvres in the parlor and a full breakfast is served in the English-style dining room. Complimentary beverages are available throughout the day. The guest accommodations in the main house are furnished with antiques and have shared bathrooms, so they're not advisable for kids. Instead, the Carriage House has five separate accommodations with queen-size beds, fireplaces, sitting rooms, and private baths. These are the rooms to request. There are no TVs, air conditioning, or telephones. The rates for Carriage House rooms are $160, single or double, including breakfast, beverages and afternoon refreshments. Cribs are available at no charge. Children over 2 pay $15 extra per night. Major credit cards are accepted.

With older children, you might consider the **Gosby House Inn,** 643 Lighthouse Ave., Pacific Grove, CA 93950 (☎ **408/375-1287**), in picturesque downtown Pacific Grove, owned by the same chain as Green Gables. Inspired by European country inns, this bed-and-breakfast has been in operation since 1887, and was placed in the National Register of Historic Places in 1980. It's considered an excellent example of authentic Quxeen Anne architecture, with bay windows and a rounded corner tower reminiscent of a turret. This charming inn is a two-story wooden building painted yellow with white trim. Light, airy and cheerful, this is a wonderful place for children who are quiet and self-restrained. Carriage house rooms and outside rooms are good for children. Over 2¹/₂ years old or pre-walking are the best ages. Girls (and adults too) will delight in the antique doll collection located in the parlor. And the small garden is a perfect place for reading and breakfast.

Some 20 of the 22 rooms have bathrooms. If you're an antiques buff, ask for a room with a clawfoot tub. Amenities include concierge service, nightly turn-down, and breakfast in bed (on request). You can have the staff fix a picnic basket of fruit and cheese (and wine at an extra charge) so that you won't have to stop at a restaurant. Breakfast and afternoon tea, sherry, and hors d'oeuvres are included in the room price. Rates range from $85 to $150, single or double. Children over 2 and additional adults are charged $15 per night (for food). Major credit cards accepted. There's a no-smoking policy at the inn.

The 31 beautifully decorated suites of the **Lighthouse Lodge Resort,** 1249 Lighthouse Ave., Pacific Grove, CA 93950 (☎ **408/655-2111,** or toll free **800/858-1249**), are the ultimate when staying in Pacific Grove. Near golf courses and beaches, the resort is a quaint, cozy, charming place to stay. Some rooms have ocean views, and all of them are beautifully located. Rooms have fireplaces, Jacuzzis, bathtubs, kitchens with microwaves, and wet bars. Complimentary wine and hors d'oeuvres are offered, and breakfast is made to order. Suites range from $185 to $350, single or double. Children stay free with their parents, but there's a $10 charge for every additional person.

WHERE TO EAT

Although these restaurants are in Pacific Grove, they're very close to Monterey and can easily be a choice for a meal from either location.

Moderate

We love the **Tinnery at the Beach,** on Lover's Point in Pacific Grove (☎ **408/646-1040**). This is the place to go for a spectacular view of Monterey Bay. The restaurant is situated on the point so it looks out onto the curve of the bay. The contemporary chrome-trimmed interior compliments the stunning view outside.

Billed as "creative and contemporary dining," there is a good children's menu for breakfast, lunch, and dinner. Kids' dinners are $4.99 with salad, fresh vegetables, fries, beverage, and ice-cream cone. Highchairs and boosters are available, and the staff will warm bottles and baby food. Adult dinners can be light or full continental cuisine meals, including bread, salad, and fresh vegetable, and range from $9 to $17 (for lobster, scallop, and prawn kebab). And there are good burgers and salads at lunch ($5–$10).

Rather than making reservations, management suggests that you call a half hour before you plan to arrive to put your name on the waiting list; that way there's usually only a 15-minute wait. They will, however, take reservations for parties of six or more.

If you have to wait, take advantage of the park across the street and walk around Lover's Point. The Tinnery is open daily from 8am to 1am; dinner ends at 11pm and the bar closes at 1am. Most major credit cards are accepted. Street parking.

Inexpensive

Our favorite restaurant in Pacific Grove is **The First Awakenings,** 125 Ocean View Blvd. (☎ 408/372-1125). The great atmosphere, plentiful portions of good food, and low prices make this a perfect breakfast or lunch place before or after a visit to the Monterey Bay Aquarium. On the border of Monterey and Pacific Grove, it's a short two-block walk along the waterfront from the aquarium to the restaurant and surrounding shops. It's housed in the old American Tin Cannery building, where the rough concrete-and-brick walls and huge two-story windows draw you back into the time when sardine canning was the big industry in Monterey.

The homey atmosphere even comes across in the menu. Children can order gourmet pancakes or luscious French toast by the number they think they can eat. Unique breakfast items include raisin-walnut pancakes and fresh vegetable frittatas. Breakfast items range from $2.75 to $6.75. Salads and sandwiches are served too, with prices from $4.25 (for fresh fruit crêpes) to $5.25 (for a classic Reuben). Complimentary coffee is served if you have to wait. Highchairs and boosters are available. Open daily from 7am to 2:30pm. Most major credit cards are accepted, and parking is provided in a lot across the street.

You won't find a more beautiful setting than **Fishwife,** located at 1996 ¹/₂ Sunset Dr., at Asilomar Boulevard (☎ 408/375-7107). This moderately inexpensive restaurant offers consistently good California cuisine and is off the beaten track so you don't have to compete with all the other tourists. However, the food is so good that locals flock to this place. If you go for Sunday brunch, lunch, or an early dinner, you'll have the beauty of Asilomar Beach to enjoy.

This restaurant really cares about food being healthy and nutritious, and offers special dishes to accommodate weight watchers, as well as low-sugar and low-salt dieters. And the kids will love the crayons and paper on the table. Lunches can be golden-fried calamari or red snapper sandwiches, omelets, salads, and pastas, with prices from $4 to $6. Dinners include fresh vegetables, French bread, and rice or potatoes, ranging in price from $6.75 to $11.95. You can choose from prawns Belize and calamari abalone style to New York steak with cracked peppercorns, as well as many of the salad and pasta selections also available at lunch. The child's plate is served with potatoes and fresh vegetables, and costs $4–$4.50 for chicken or fish entrees. They'll gladly warm bottles and baby food, and split adult entrees for kids. Highchairs and booster seats are provided. Open every day except Tuesday from 11am to 10pm. Reservations are accepted. Some major credit cards welcome. There's parking nearby.

Located downtown, **Toasties Café,** 702 Lighthouse Ave. (☎ 408/373-7543), is a wonderful home-style American café that's very accommodating to children. It has an extensive children's menu with prices from $1.30 to $4.25. They'll warm baby food and split adult portions. There are highchairs and booster seats, coloring books and crayons, and even 20 hand-held water toys to borrow.

This homey café boasts great country specialties made from scratch. The corned-beef hash and Philly steak are favorites, and the pancakes, waffles, and French toast are specialties of the house. Try San Francisco Joe's Omelette (ground beef, onions, spinach, and cheese) served with country potatoes, toast, or pancakes for $5.95.

They'll even make omelets without egg yolks for people watching their cholesterol intake. We had delicious French toast with blueberries, and Baby Cakes (dollar-size pancakes) at 35¢ each.

Reservations are accepted only for dinner. For an after-meal treat, try the little park one short block away on Caledonia and Central Avenues, which has a play area and basketball net. Toasties is open for breakfast and lunch Monday through Saturday from 6am to 3pm and on Sunday from 7am to 2pm; and for dinner Tuesday through Saturday from 5 to 9pm. Some credit cards accepted. There is street parking.

3 Carmel and Carmel Valley

Carmel-by-the-Sea, or Carmel, is known worldwide as a lovers' getaway and an artists' colony. Tiny shops and outdoor cafés give Carmel its European flavor. Nestled among the Monterey cypress and other pines, with grand vistas of white-washed beaches and sapphire-colored ocean, this village is a place you'll long remember. But it is primarily a town for romantic getaways, fabulous shopping, and gallery-hopping. Although there are places for kids to go and things for kids to do, don't plan extended days in town. Lodging and restaurants that welcome families are abundant—and so are cars in summer!

For information in advance, including a 128-page *Guide to Carmel,* with listings of inns and hotels, restaurants, art galleries, recreational opportunities, and shops, contact the Carmel Business Association, P.O. Box 4444, Carmel, CA 93921 (☎ 408/624-2522) or stop by while in town. It's located in the Eastwood Building on San Carlos Avenue between 5th and 6th, next door to Hog's Breath Inn.

The **Monterey Visitors and Convention Bureau,** 380 Alvarado St. (P.O. Box 1770), Monterey, CA 93940 (☎ 408/649-1770), will also send you material.

WHAT TO SEE AND DO

Beautiful stores and boutiques line Ocean Avenue and the surrounding streets of **Downtown Carmel.** While you may be more interested in art galleries and gift stores, your youngsters will enjoy **Thinker Toys,** at San Carlos and 7th Streets (☎ 408/624-0441). Kids are welcome to play in the store while parents browse through the array of European-made Brio toys, mobiles, model trains, radio-controlled cars, and the like. Open Monday through Saturday from 9:30am to 9pm and on Sunday from 10am to 5:30pm. The **Game Gallery,** Ocean Avenue east of San Carlos Street (☎ 408/625-4263), is "just for fun." It has fantasy games, two-person strategy games, manipulative jigsaw puzzles, and family board games. It's open daily from 10am to 5pm (open later in summer). **Books, Inc.,** on Ocean Avenue (☎ 408/625-2550), is open daily from 10am to 9:45pm.

When the kids get tired of shopping, one of the adults can take them to the lovely pocket park across the street from Carmel Plaza on Ocean Avenue. **One note of caution:** This area can be very crowded at peak tourist times. You may want to consider going on a weekday, or very early in the day if you have young kids.

Carmel Mission (Mission San Carlos Borromeo del Rio Carmel), located at Rio Road and Calif. 1 (☎ 408/624-3600), was the second mission founded by Fr. Junípero Serra in 1770. Set on lovely grounds, its Moorish-style tower and sandstone exterior make it one of the prettiest missions in the state. This was Fray Serra's headquarters as he continued to establish missions throughout California, and the place he chose to be buried. You can walk through and see the spartan rooms in which Fray

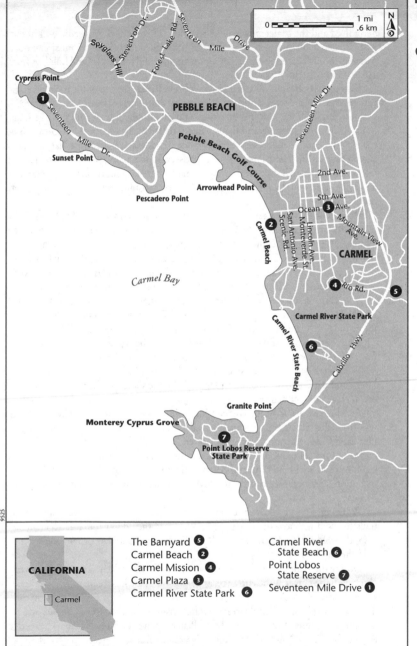

N

0   1 mi
     .6 km

Cypress Point

Spyglass Hill

Stevenson Dr.

Forest Lake Rd.

Seventeen Mile Drive

PEBBLE BEACH

Seventeen Mile Dr.

Seventeen Mile Dr.

Sunset Point

Pebble Beach Golf Course

Arrowhead Point

2nd Ave.

5th Ave.

Ocean Ave.

Pescadero Point

Mountain View Ave.

San Antonio Ave.

Scenic Rd.

Carmel Beach

Monteverde St.

Lincoln Ave.

CARMEL

Carmel Bay

Rio Rd.

Carmel River State Park

Carmel River State Beach

Cabrillo Hwy.

Granite Point

Monterey Cyprus Grove

Point Lobos Reserve State Park

9525

Serra lived and the cemetery where he's buried. There is also a museum and library with displays of interesting relics of the California mission period. The mission is open Monday through Saturday from 9:30am to 4:30pm and on Sunday and holidays from 10:30am to 4:30pm. A donation of $1 is suggested.

Carmel City Beach and **Carmel River State Beach** are two of the most magnificent beaches in California. Exotic gnarled cypress and Torrey pines grace the stretches of white sand. Although it can be chilly, and downright cold at times, we've spent hours building sand castles and flying kites at these beaches. Carmel City Beach is at the end of Ocean Avenue. Carmel River State Beach is a 106-acre area that also has a lagoon for frolicking and a marshy area that's a bird sanctuary, plus picnic tables and restrooms. To get to it if you're coming from Monterey, go south on Calif. 1 and take a right on Rio Road, then take a left after Carmel Mission, and continue making left turns until you're there.

Point Lobos State Reserve, three miles south of Carmel on Calif. 1 (☎ 408/624-4909), is referred to as the Crown Jewel of the California state park system. It's a spectacular living museum where flocks of pelicans, gulls, and cormorants, as well as 250 other animal species and over 300 plant types, can be seen on the fantastic granite rock formations in the little coves and in the rolling meadows. The ocean is wonderfully wild here, and if you look closely, you'll notice sea otters floating offshore.

Two-thirds of the reserve is an **underwater refuge** protecting the rich and varied sea life. Diving restrictions apply, but you can visit six different areas: the sea lion area, the cypress grove, the pine wood, Bird Island, North Shore Trail, and Whaler's Cove. This is a simply wonderful spot for children over 6, who will love everything about it, from the vividly colored wild mushrooms to the thick, lush ferns.

We always love the **Cypress Grove Trail,** a 30-minute walk starting at the Sea Lion Point parking area, which wanders through the stand of Monterey cypress. The ocean views are spectacular.

Another favorite of the kids is **Sea Lion Point.** You get there on an easy 30-minute trail from the same starting point that takes you to the barking sea lions and past Headland Cove, where you can see sea otters. Bring binoculars, so you can get a better look at the sea lions. There are wooden steps that lead to an overlook of Devil's Cauldron and Sea Lion Point, and if you're lucky enough to be there during the whale migration, you might see enormous blow sprays and the huge flapping tails of a gray whale.

Warning! Poison oak is abundant in the reserve. Have your children stay on the trails to avoid it. Show them what it looks like so they don't touch it accidentally. Also, the wild surf and dangerous cliffs make the reserve a place where you want to hold the hands of any young child.

During the summer there are guided nature walks twice a day. The rest of the year, check with the ranger at the entrance, as guided walks are less frequent. On weekends when the weather is clear, you can see cars lined up waiting for admittance. Go early if you want to get in. When the reserve is full, visitors are asked to wait in line and are permitted in one at a time as others leave. Plan to spend at least half a day. The reserve is open daily from 9am to 5pm, slightly later in summer. The entrance fee is $6 per vehicle, but you can also park outside the reserve and walk in.

The Barnyard shopping complex is located at the entrance to Carmel Valley on Calif. 1, off Carmel Valley Road (☎ 408/624-8886), and has seven restaurants and more than 55 shops. What's most appealing, however, is its setting: Flowers, trees, walkways, and terraces create a ranchlike atmosphere. The Barnyard was born years ago with the **Thunderbird Bookshop Café** (see the "Where to Eat" section for details). When the owners decided to expand, they retained the natural feeling of a ranch and built authentic-looking barn structures to house the new shops. You won't want to miss taking the kids to the Thunderbird Bookshop. If you have time, your kids will also enjoy **Thunderbird for Kids** bookstore.

WHERE TO STAY

There are a variety of choices in Carmel.

Expensive

We like **La Playa Hotel,** Camino Real at 8th Street (P.O. Box 900), Carmel, CA 93921 (☎ **408/624-6476,** or toll free **800/582-8900**), located two blocks from the beach and four blocks from the central village area of Carmel. The only full-service hotel in town, it's an elegant old Mediterranean-style villa with exquisite formal gardens. It was built in 1904 and grew into a hotel. Each of the 75 rooms and five storybook cottages has a view of the ocean, garden, residential Carmel, or the red-tiled patio area. The one- to three-bedroom cottages are perfect for families; all have full kitchens or wet bar, fireplace, and outdoor patio or lawn area.

There's a lawn area for kids to play on, a beautiful outdoor swimming pool, and free parking for guests. Golf and tennis can be arranged. Other services include nightly turn-down, a concierge desk, valet parking, and same-day laundry service on weekdays. Room service, available from 7am to 11pm, has tasty items for kids, including burgers and sandwiches. The Terrace Grill (☎ **408/624-4010**) serves breakfast, lunch, dinner, and Sunday brunch. Breakfast prices average $5–$12, lunch runs $6–$15, and dinner prices are from $14–$45. Sunday brunch costs $19.50 per person; children under 12 pay $10.50.

The rooms carry out the Mediterranean motif. Decorated in light, airy colors, they have hand-carved furniture, refrigerators, and hair-dryers. Room rates range from $95 to $210, single or double; suites run $210–$495. Children under 12 stay free in their parents' room; no charge for cribs. Children 12 and over and additional adults pay $15 per night.

Moderate

Located at the entrance to Carmel Valley at Calif. 1 and Rio Road, the **Carmel Mission Inn,** 3665 Rio Rd., Carmel, CA 93923 (☎ **408/624-1841,** or toll free **800/348-9090**), enjoys the warmer weather and beauty of Carmel Valley. Surrounded by sculptured gardens and winding walkways, the inn has an outdoor heated pool and Jacuzzi. Because it's located near the Barnyard shopping area, we found it convenient to wander over there when the kids wanted something to do but wanted to stay close to the hotel. Babysitting can be arranged.

Sassy's Bar and Grill is open for breakfast and dinner and serves American and continental cuisine. For breakfast, try the yummy waffles, pancakes, omelets, even eggs Benedict. For dinner there's fresh fish, fresh pasta, Kansas City baby back ribs, and sinful desserts. Room service is available, offering such children's favorites as waffles, grilled cheese, pizza, and peanut butter sandwiches. Poolside food service is available.

The 165 recently remodeled rooms are spacious and well maintained, and open onto hallways, not parking areas. Refrigerators are available upon request and there are free in-room movies. Connecting rooms and suites are available. Room rates range from $99 to $149. Suites start at $189. There's no charge for cribs, and children under 12 stay free if additional beds are not needed. Ask for seasonal and holiday special rates.

A real find if you like rustic ranch-style living is **Mission Ranch,** 26270 Dolores St., Carmel, CA 93923 (☎ **408/624-6436** or toll free **800/538-8221**), near the Carmel Mission at the end of Dolores Street. Originally a working dairy farm, the grounds are spacious and dotted with 100-year-old Monterey cypress trees and even older redwoods. The ranch looks out onto a meadow, Point Lobos, and the Pacific Ocean. Clint Eastwood bought, restored, and renovated it. It occupies 20 acres and is dotted with grazing sheep and huge eucalyptus trees. It's wonderful for children, in fact, the ambience is such that many families come back year after year. It's located between the Old Mission and a school, and the management is used to having kids move through the property. On weekends and during the summer, children can use the playground equipment at the school next door. If you need a babysitter, the staff will provide referrals.

Mission Ranch (☎ **408/625-9040**), the restaurant on the property, began serving meals in 1937. It's a funky old ranchhouse with a sing-along piano bar. Most of the tables look out onto the sheep pastures. A casual, comfortable place where the locals go to eat, it's surrounded by the grassy play area that is the ranch. The restaurant serves American cuisine and specializes in prime rib, but also serves lamb, back ribs, chicken, and fish. Prices for full dinners, which include relishes, bread, soup or salad, vegetables, and potato, are $10.75–$22.95. The children's dinner costs $7 and includes soup, fries or rice, choice of entree, vegetable, dessert, and milk. Open for dinner every day. Major credit cards accepted.

Several kinds of accommodations are available at this ranch. Meadow- and ocean-view cottages include kitchens/kitchenettes and televisions, and some have living rooms and two bedrooms. These are perfect for families and range in price from $195–$225. There are also motel units, which range from $95–$150. Finally, there are rooms in the Farmhouse, but these are set up for couples. Children under 16 are discouraged from staying in this area. The Bunkhouse is a complete cottage, with a living room, dining room, bedrooms, and a full kitchen, for $195. There's no charge for cribs. Included in the room price is a continental breakfast of cereal, croissants, fruit, juice, and beverage.

Tucked away in a quiet residential area one block from Carmel Beach, the **Colonial Terrace Inn,** on San Antonio Avenue between 12th and 13th Streets (P.O. Box 1375), Carmel, CA 93921 (☎ **408/624-2741** or toll free **800/345-1818**), doesn't even look like a hotel. All rooms look out at manicured gardens or quiet courtyards, and there are grassy play areas for energetic kids. Each of the 25 rooms is uniquely furnished. All have fireplaces and refrigerators. Connecting rooms are available. Because each room is different, rates vary widely. Tell the reservationist what you need when you call. Here are some sample rates: rooms with one queen-size bed, $85; with a queen-size bed and a hide-a-bed, or single, $150, with two queen-size beds, $145; with a queen-size bed and a double bed (with two baths), $190. No charge for cribs. Rates include a complimentary continental breakfast served in the lobby.

The **Wayside Inn,** at Mission and 7th Streets (P.O. Box 1990), Carmel, CA 93920 (☎ **408/624-5336** or toll free **800/433-4732**), is a small, colonial-style inn. Most rooms are mini-suites with queen-size sofa beds in the living room; most have full kitchens and fireplaces. Free continental breakfast is delivered to your room. Rates range from $99 to $149; family units cost $190–$225. The Wayside Inn is one of several inns managed by Inns by the Sea, some of which have swimming pools. Ask about the other inns in Carmel and Monterey.

Bed-and-Breakfast

If you like the bed-and-breakfast concept, you'll love the **Cobblestone Inn,** at Junipero Avenue and 8th Street (P.O. Box 3185), Carmel, CA 93921 (☎ **408/625-5222**). Each of the 24 guest rooms has its own entrance, and is decorated with antiques, a fireplace, telephone, color television, private bath, and fresh flowers. A refrigerator, bathrobes, and complimentary toiletries are provided in each accommodation. Other amenities not often thought of as part of a bed-and-breakfast inn, such as concierge service, nightly turn-down, and morning newspaper are provided. Many rooms open onto a U-shaped courtyard. But remember that this, like other older hotels, doesn't have the level of soundproofing that newer hotels might have. Cross the courtyard to the living room with a fireplace, where the complimentary breakfast and afternoon sherry, wine, tea, and hors d'oeuvres are served. Guests can dine inside or at tables outside for breakfast in the summer. This is great for kids because they are able to get up from breakfast and run around. Complimentary beverages are available all day.

A room with a queen-size bed and shower rents for $95–$125; one with a king-size bed, shower, and wet bar, $145–$160. A two-room suite with a king-size bed, shower, and sitting room costs $175, while the suite with the king-size bed and tub/shower combination goes for $175. All rates are single or double occupancy. Cribs are free. Children over 2 and additional adults are charged $15 each per night.

WHERE TO EAT

Known for good food and restaurants with ambience, Carmel is a sure winner almost anywhere you go. But meals can be pricey.

Expensive

We love the **Clam Box Restaurant,** on Mission Street between Fifth and Sixth Avenues (☎ **408/624-8597**), a lively, fast-moving place that serves excellent seafood and caters to families. The atmosphere is casual and the tables are close together, but it all adds to the geniality of the place. The service is fast—soup, bread, and butter are delivered immediately. There are not only highchairs and boosters, but our kids were given crayons to while away the time. We've heard talk that storybooks often make their appearance as well.

There is a huge selection of seafood, and dinners start with both homemade soup and salad. Dine on tender abalone (market price), broiled filet of salmon ($15.75), and broiled lobster tails ($24.50), and enjoy. For the under-8 set there's a choice of filet of sole, old-fashioned ham, or hamburger with fries, plus soup or salad, for $6.50.

With all of this going for it, you'd expect a line: and that's what you'll get if you come after 6pm; waits can be up to an hour long. No reservations are taken, but if you get there before 6pm, it's easy to get a table. If you do have to wait, take a leisurely stroll on the nearby streets, and don't miss the park, where your kids can run off any excess energy before they sit down. Open for lunch Tuesday through Saturday, 11:30am to 2:30pm; for dinner Tuesday through Sunday from 4:30 to 9pm. Street parking.

Most people go to the **Hog's Breath Inn** (yes, that's the name of the restaurant), located in central Carmel on San Carlos Street between Fifth and Sixth Avenues

(☎ 408/625-1044), because Clint Eastwood owns it and is often seen there. Eastwood and his friend Walter Becker opened this unusual place 20 years ago. Most impressive is its outdoor patio, where you can lunch surrounded by trees, five fireplaces (and warming heaters), wood burl tables, and sculptures of hogs—an experience, indeed.

You'll love the menu. The Dirty Harry burger is a favorite, or there's the Eiger sandwich, and Sudden Impact (Polish sausage with jalapeño peppers on a French roll). The dinner menu offers: Coogan's Bluff (a 12-ounce steak); For a Few Dollars More (you guessed it—this is a 16-ounce steak); and High Plains Rancher (a large cut of prime rib). There are daily specials as well. Anything on the menu is available in a child's portion at a smaller price. Booster seats, but no highchairs, are available.

Be prepared to wait because they do a booming business and don't take reservations. The lunch wait may be 15 minutes; dinner, from 30 minutes to 1½ hours. We suggest that you go for a drink and people-watching. It's noisy, and the staff welcomes children. So take a rest from a day's wandering, order a hot chocolate for the kids and peppermint tea (or libations from the full bar) for the adults, and enjoy. Open daily from 11:30am to 3pm for lunch, from 5 to 10pm for dinner. The bar is open until 2am. Most major credit cards accepted. Street parking.

Moderate

A Carmel landmark, the **Thunderbird Bookshop Café,** in the Barnyard, 3600 The Barnyard (☎ 408/624-8103), is unique. Have your meal while you're surrounded by 40,000 books. You can dine year round in the Solarium Patio that has a retractable glass roof. Wooden tables and a blazing fire in the fire pit make this casual, rustic-style place a real pleasure. It's open daily for lunch from 11am to 3:30pm and serves soups, sandwiches, and salads ($4–$8). Open daily from 10am to 9pm and serves pasta and prawns, three different steak and chicken dinners, as well as angel-hair pasta and linguine Alfredo. Highchairs and boosters are provided. Reservations are accepted and major credit cards are welcome. Parking is available in the Barnyard parking lot.

Country charm and excellent food are what you find at **Katy's Place,** on Mission Street between Fifth and Sixth Avenues (☎ 408/624-0199). They are famous for their eggs Benedict—they have seven different kinds, including crab, salmon, and vegetarian, starting at $6. We luxuriate in the eggs while our kids order silver-dollar pancakes (each under $1), all while sitting at the counter and watching the chefs. While there is no children's menu, a regular-size breakfast easily feeds two or three children, and the side orders (bacon, cereal, fruit, waffles) will satisfy any picky eater. Portions are enormous. If you like home fries, go off your diet for the home-fried red potatoes here. There are sassy seats and boosters. The service is generally very fast. The outside patio is lovely, a wonderful place to sit on sunny days.

Open daily from 7am to 2pm. No credit cards are accepted.

The **Fabulous Tootz Lagoon,** at Dolores Street and Seventh Avenue, Carmel (☎ 408/625-1915), looks like a turn-of-the-century San Francisco saloon, but it's even more eclectic than that. There's polished redwood, ceiling fans, music, and sports on TV. It's a good place for ribs, chicken, steak, salad, pasta, and pizza. Children's menu includes pizza, spaghetti, hotdogs, grilled cheese and chicken strips for $4.95–$5.95. There are sassy seats and boosters, and the staff will warm bottles and baby food, and will also make specialty drinks such as Shirley Temples or Fruit Seltzers. Open daily from 11:30am to 11pm. Reservations are accepted. Most credit cards accepted. Park in the street.

In an Emergency

In a medical emergency, the **Community Hospital of the Monterey Peninsula,** 23625 Holman Hwy. (☎ **408/624-5311**), has the only 24-hour emergency room in the area. It also has a 24-hour pharmacy.

If you like Mexican and southwestern cuisine, don't miss **Cactus Jack's,** on San Carlos Street between Fifth and Sixth Avenues (☎ **408/626-0909**). You should go here just to see the decor: bright reds and greens, and a charming outdoor patio with a mural—complete with a full moon, cactus, and a howling wolf—which transports you to Santa Fe. The menu features buckets of Mississippi fried chicken, which includes cornbread and jalapeños; appetizers such as quesadillas; and full Mexican or southwestern dinners. For Mexican food, choose an enchilada, beef tamale, or burritos; from the southwestern grill you might choose smoked baby back ribs, chicken fried steak, or grilled talapia filet. Prices range from $3.75 to $16.95. Highchairs and boosters are available. Open Monday through Thursday, 4:30pm to 10pm, Friday through Sunday 12pm to 10pm. Reservations and credit cards accepted.

The food is great and the service is superb at **Em Lee's,** on Dolores Street between Fifth and Sixth Avenues (☎ **408/625-6780**). The scrumptious French toast is served only until 11am (till 12pm on Sunday). Breakfasts and lunches are ample and range in price from $1.75 to $7. For kids there are eggs, bacon, pancakes, and burgers, even though there isn't a children's menu. Sassy seats and boosters are provided, and they'll gladly warm bottles and baby food. Open daily from 6:30am to 3pm. No reservations are taken, and you'll have to wait on weekends. Cash only. Parking is on the street.

Picnic Supplies

Get a picnic basket full of goodies from the **Mediterranean Market,** at the corner of Ocean Avenue and Mission Street (☎ **408/624-2022**), open daily from 9am to 6pm. You'll find yummy treats here.

The **Village Market** is located at the corner of Dolores Street and Eighth Avenue (☎ **408/624-3476**).

4 Big Sur

Without doubt, Big Sur has to be 90 miles of nature's most incredible coastline. To the west, the crashing sea meets steep cliffs that jut out of the sand. Small coves of vibrant aquamarine- and sapphire-colored water greet you on many turns. Huge jagged black rocks that have tumbled into the sea are hosts to gulls and otters. To the east are pine forests and redwoods that create a veil for the wanderer in the woods and provide astonishing backdrops for hiking and camping.

Calif. 1 on the Big Sur coast, also known as Cabrillo Highway and the Coast Highway, can be some of the most treacherous driving in California. While the road is well maintained, a healthy respect for Calif. 1 is good, and caution is necessary, especially if you're not used to winding roads. Drive defensively, and never drive it if you have had anything to drink, or if you are fighting sleep. Also, check weather conditions, because dense fog or heavy rains can make the highway difficult, if not impossible, to drive.

The drive from Monterey to Big Sur Village takes from 45 minutes to an hour. As you head south past Point Lobos, the coastline gets increasingly rugged. There are plenty of turnouts where you will undoubtedly want to stop and take pictures.

Warning! Because of the makeup of the terrain, it's easy to lose your footing. Little ones must be held by the hand. Exquisite as the vistas are, it's important to wait until you get to a big turnout or vista point where you can park.

Although the beaches are breathtakingly beautiful, don't be fooled. There are few approachable beaches, and swimming is *not* safe along the coast because of riptides and treacherous currents.

WHAT TO SEE AND DO

Probably the one Big Sur landmark that most people recognize is **Bixby Bridge.** This often-photographed bridge, with its huge arch, was built in 1932, and was considered a spectacular engineering feat. The bridge spans Bixby Canyon, where Little Bixby Creek runs. There's a turnout on the north end of the bridge.

Although there's no hiking here to recommend for families, you can drive the South Coast Road, a dirt road that winds through Bixby Canyon across the Little Sur, and comes out at Andrew Molera State Park. You travel through redwoods and high meadows, and the drive affords sensational views of the ocean.

Andrew Molera State Park, about 21 miles south of Carmel (☎ 408/667-2315), is a lovely beach and walk-in campground. Enter the park via a short driveway off Calif. 1 that leads you to the parking lot. You'll have to walk to the park; it's one-quarter mile distance on flat ground. From the camp to the beach is about half a mile. There is a river, equestrian trails, firepits, pit toilets, and no water. This is a great place to hike. The Bluffs Trail is an easy two-mile trail that goes along the ocean to the bluff. The Headlands Trail is about a one-mile hike that takes you to the Headlands above the mouth of Big Sur River as it flows into the ocean. You get a beautiful view of the river, the ocean, and the canyon. The Bobcat Trail is about two miles long, taking you through the redwoods along the Big Sur River. There's a $6 charge for day use of the park, or $3 per person per night if you are camping.

Nason Ranch/Molera Big Sur Trail Rides is located here (☎ 408/625-8664). All rides are four hours long and go to the beach. Open daily from March through November. Rides are offered at 9am, 1:30pm, and four hours before sunset. These half-day trips cost $50 per rider. Minimum age is 7. There are horses for advanced, intermediate, and beginner riders. Reservations recommended.

As you travel south from Andrew Molera State Park, you enter **Big Sur Village,** the place many consider the heart of Big Sur. This is where you can get something to eat, find a place to stay overnight, and gas up the car. (For details, check the "Where to Stay" and "Where to Eat" sections, below.)

Fabulous hiking and picnicking among the redwoods and thick forests are in store at **Pfeiffer–Big Sur State Park,** about 26 miles south of Carmel (☎ 408/667-2315). Even if you're not camping you'll enjoy a day here. There's no beach access in this 852-acre forest, but the Big Sur River runs through the park.

As you enter the park, on the east side of the highway the park aids in the Information Booth, which operates like a visitor center, will sell you detailed maps and let you know if there are any current restrictions on hiking, picnicking, and camping. There's a $6 day-use fee. A Nature Center is located near the Pfeiffer Falls trailhead. The center has displays of natural history and cultural history of the area. Ask about the ranger guided walks.

The most popular hike for families with young kids is the easy half-mile trek that goes up to Pfeiffer Falls. Another one is the $1^1/4$-mile-long Oak Grove Trail, which takes off from the Pfeiffer Falls trailhead. The Valley View Trail takes off from the falls and goes up from there (the climb is 400 feet in a distance of a half mile). The quarter-mile trail takes you to a high point that gives you a view of the entire Big Sur Valley and Point Sur.

Farther south, **Julia Pfeiffer Burns State Park** (☎ 408/667-2315) is an 1,800-acre wooded day-use park with a $6 day-use fee. There is no camping. In addition to telephones, restrooms, and a picnic area with fire grills, there are several trails, some of them suitable for novice hikers. One easy trail, a third of a mile long, runs from the parking lot to McWay Cove, where you'll get a wonderful view of McWay Falls as it drops 50 feet into the ocean.

Farther down the coast is the **Coast Gallery** (☎ 408/667-2301), a craft and art gallery which has a large selection of fine art, wood items, and ceramic pieces. There's a permanent exhibit of watercolors done by author Henry Miller, who once lived in Big Sur. The grounds on which the gallery sits has many varieties of succulents and flowering plants. This is also a good place to buy original gift items. Open daily from 9am to 5pm in winter, till 6pm in summer. The Coast Cafe serves a light lunch of homemade sandwiches, salads, soups, and baked goods. There is a great ocean view from the upper deck.

WHERE TO STAY

If you're lucky enough to get a room, **Big Sur Lodge,** on Calif. 1 (P.O. Box 190), Big Sur, CA 93920 (☎ 408/667-2171), is a wonderful place to experience the redwood forest while having some of the comforts of home. Located within Pfeiffer–Big Sur State Park, it's only a short distance from the park entrance, which means that you and your family can enjoy the evening activities, or take sunset hikes, without having to drive anywhere afterward. Tucked in among the pines and redwoods, the guest cottages are on a hill surrounded by the mountains and the Big Sur countryside. Surprisingly, there's an outdoor heated swimming pool, but even when it's too cool to swim, the large grassy areas beckon children to play Frisbee and tag. Open year round, the lodge has a grocery store, giftshop, and restaurant. For those who are just looking around, the lodge also has one of the few public restrooms in Big Sur.

Big Sur Lodge Restaurant serves breakfast, lunch, and dinner in a lovely glassed-in little dining room that makes you think you're eating among the redwoods. With a child's menu that has everything from fettuccini to fried chicken for $4.95 ($2.95 for breakfast), your kids will find something appealing, and you'll be delighted with the place too. It's open from 8 to 11:30am for breakfast, from noon to 2pm for lunch, and from 5 to 9pm for dinner. Highchairs and boosters are provided, and some credit cards are accepted.

Some rooms have kitchenettes (but without cooking equipment), and refrigerators are available upon request. Some units accommodate up to six people, but no cribs are available. Rates are based on the number of beds and whether or not there's a kitchen or fireplace. Summer rates start at a base of $95 for two people (one queen-size bed), and winter rates start at $89 for two people. If you want a kitchen or second bedroom, add $20 for each, and if you want a fireplace, add $20. Continental breakfast is included. Reservations are a necessity, especially in summer.

Camping

You can camp at **Andrew Molera State Park** (see the "What to See and Do" section). This is a walk-in campground with 50 sites and a fee of 50¢ per person per night.

There is also wonderful camping at **Pfeiffer–Big Sur State Park,** Big Sur, CA 93920 (☎ 408/667-2315), which offers camping along the Big Sur River with terrain that varies from redwoods to oak groves. There's great hiking. The 218 developed sites, each with a table and campfire ring, run through the canyon, but most campsites are less than 300 yards away from the river. Flush toilets and showers are nearby. The sites can accommodate trailers up to 27 feet and motor homes up to 31 feet. In summer there are interpretive ranger programs that include guided walks and campfire programs. The fees are $14–$16 per campsite and $6 per extra vehicle. Reserve through MISTIX (☎ 619/452-1950, or toll free 800/444-7275 in California).

Another place to camp is the privately owned **Ventana Campground,** Calif. 1, Big Sur, CA 93920 (☎ 408/667-2688). Located on Calif. 1 just two miles south of Pfeiffer–Big Sur, Ventana has 60 campsites set in among the redwoods. Each site has a fireplace, drinking water, and a table, and there are bathrooms with hot showers nearby. The fees start at $20 per night for two adults and one vehicle per campsite—no facilities for RVs/or campers over 22 feet. Reserve in advance.

WHERE TO EAT

The world-renowned, **Nepenthe,** on Calif. 1, three miles south of Big Sur State Park (☎ 408/667-2345), sits perched high over the pounding sea and looks out onto redwoods and oaks. Magic surrounds the place. The story goes that Orson Welles bought the little house on the property for his then-new bride Rita Hayworth. She kept the place after their divorce and sold it to the family who opened Nepenthe in 1949. Movies have been filmed here, and it remains a favorite spot of some of the area's celebrities. Few restaurants evoke such vivid memories after you return home, whether you have a startlingly beautiful, clear day or a foggy, cold, damp one.

The walk to the restaurant takes you up steps that follow a little fern-lined stream. It's as if you're walking deeper into the forest. You're met at the top with a breathtaking view of Big Sur (if it's not foggy). You'll see the large fire pit that rages every evening that dinner is served outdoors. If you dine on the terrace at night amid the candlelight with the huge fire pit blazing, you'll agree that it's one of the most romantic places on earth. Maybe it's the feeling of being quiet and tucked away from the rest of the world, almost as if hiding its inhabitants. Maybe it's the open-air feeling inside the restaurant or the expanse of beauty surrounding you if you sit on the patio or veranda that encircles the restaurant. Quiet and inviting, it is many things to many people. Plan to spend time there.

During the day it's a fabulous place to while away time having a coffee or good lunch with your family. The patio area is especially inviting for wandering children. Large tables make family seating easy, and the wide-open spaces make it great for accommodating families with young children. Because the place is so famous, the owners are used to children trekking in and out. Crackers are brought to the table right away, and they'll bring hungry kids carrots to munch on. If the wait is long, explore the area around the restaurant or visit the famous Phoenix giftshop downstairs. You'll see it as you drive up.

For dinner or lunch, try the famous Ambrosiaburger, a delicious ground-steak sandwich on a French roll ($10) or the wonderful French dip ($10). Also available are soup and salad ($9.25), steak sandwich ($19.25) and Holly's crustless quiche ($9.75). There is no children's menu, but they will split adult portions into halves or thirds. Boosters and highchairs are provided.

Open daily (except Christmas and Thanksgiving nights and a few days in the winter—it's good to call ahead) from 11:30am to 4:30pm for lunch, and from 5 to 10pm for dinner. No reservations accepted. Major credit cards welcome.

While the Nepenthe is one slice of Big Sur Life, the **River Inn,** south of Big Sur Village (☎ **408/625-5255**), is another. The restaurant is very modest, almost rough, and serves breakfast, lunch, and dinner at moderate prices. Go for the outdoor treat as well. Where else can you find a river, the Sur, with a rock sculpture garden? Where else would you see people with table and chairs *in* the river enjoying the morning sun? As you enter, get your food and walk outside to the chairs on one of the two wooden decks or sit on the grass looking out to the river. If it's warm, the kids can play in the shallow water, or they can swim in the inn's swimming pool. The changing room/ bathroom area is adequate for changing into swimsuits.

Local musicians perform nightly from 7:30pm; there's jazz on Saturday and Sunday. Open daily from 8am to 9pm. Highchairs, children's menu, and boosters are provided. Credit cards accepted. Reservations suggested.

5 San Simeon/Cambria

Located in the northern part of San Luis Obispo County, the town of San Simeon straddles Calif. 1 and is divided into two sections: One is near the entrance to Hearst Castle; the other is a few miles south and has lodging and a few restaurants. The main attraction, of course, is Hearst Castle, that palatial structure created by William Randolph Hearst. You may be surprised that it is a trip you can take with children who are over the age of 6, and infants who will sleep through it.

Cambria is a tiny artists' colony tucked into the rolling hills that snuggle up to the coastline just a few minutes south of San Simeon. After the bustle of city sightseeing, a few hours roaming Cambria Village or wandering in the surrounding hills and on the coast is like taking a deep breath of relaxation. This is a special family town, located on Calif. 1, known by the slogan, "Where the pines meet the sea."

Because the towns are so close together, you can easily stay in a motel in San Simeon and have your meals in Cambria.

WHAT TO SEE AND DO IN SAN SIMEON

Most people stop in San Simeon because they want to see **Hearst Castle,** located off Calif. 1 just north of Cambria. The castle is an impressive monument, begun in 1919 and built over the course of 28 years by publishing magnate William Randolph Hearst. Our kids are usually excited when we tell them they're going to see a castle, and, indeed, even 6-year-olds can appreciate the wealth that was needed to create this fantastic dwelling. The castle looks like a Mediterranean-style cathedral with towers, walkways, pools, and incredibly beautiful gardens, and sits on 127 acres known as La Cuesta Encantada, "The Enchanted Hill."

The buildings are only part of the treat. The castle has more than 100 rooms that serve as museum space for the eclectic treasures that Hearst collected during his lifetime. There are priceless antiques, rich tapestries, beautiful Oriental rugs, and all kinds of unusual art objects.

We love to talk with our kids about how it would feel to live in the castle. They always respond that they'd get lost! But the question gets them to look at the art objects a little more closely, if even for a brief period. The kids seem impressed by the sheer size and numbers of things they see around them, whether they deem them valuable or not.

Our children's favorite part of the tour is the indoor pool with the 22-karat-gold inlaid tile. The room is dimly lit and the spectacular pool is still and looks as if it's filled with liquid glass. They even appreciate the gardens, although they have to stay on the walkways and remain with the group.

We recommend this sightseeing attraction for families with children 6 and older, but even 6- and 7-year-olds need to be fairly sophisticated to really appreciate the surroundings for $1^3/4$ hours. The 15-minute bus ride up the hill from the visitor center parking to the castle, and then back down again, adds more time that children must sit still. Some people carry a few little toys to give the kids as their interest wanes and they become impatient to leave. This really isn't the place for pre-schoolers, and strollers are not allowed. All tours are considered walking tours. They tell people that they must be able to walk at least a half mile and climb 150 stairs. There's a separate tour for handicapped visitors.

There are several different tours of the castle. Tour 1 is the one you should take on your first visit as it gives you an overview. You'll see one of the guesthouses, a beautiful section of the garden, the first floor of the castle including the movie theater (always a shocker for the kids), the Neptune Pool, and the indoor Roman Pool. There are 150 stair steps in this tour.

Tour 2 is limited to a small group, and includes some of Hearst's personal rooms as well as the library and kitchen. You'll also see two pools. There are 377 stair steps.

Tour 3, also a small-group tour, takes you through the north wing of La Casa Grande, which has more than 30 bedrooms, sitting rooms, and bathrooms, and includes a video about the construction of the castle. There are 316 stair steps.

Tour 4, yet another small-group tour, covers the wine cellar, the largest guesthouse, and acres of gardens and walkways. There are 306 stair steps.

In the spring and fall, a night tour is offered. This tour, limited to 18 people, focuses on life during the 1920s and '30s. It includes both swimming pools, one guesthouse, the library and Gothic study, the assembly room, kitchen, refectory, billiards room, and the theater. One thrill is the "living history" people in period dress that are positioned throughout the castle and grounds during this tour. You might see gentlemen playing billiards or a butler polishing the silver. This tour lasts approximately two hours. The cost of this tour is higher than the others: $25 for adults, $13 for children 6–12.

Hearst Castle is open daily except New Year's, Thanksgiving, and Christmas Days. The ticket office is open from 8am to 4pm, and tours are scheduled at least every hour from 8:20am to 3pm in winter and more frequently during holidays and summer. Tickets cost $14 for adults, $8 for children 6–12; children under 6 are free. You should make reservations before you leave home. MISTIX is the place to call (toll free **800/444-4445**). The office is open daily from 8am to 5pm.

Believe it or not, there are other attractions in San Simeon. **Sebastian's General Store,** across from the castle entrance at 442 San Simeon Rd. (☎ **805/927-4217**), is a State Historical Landmark. Don't be surprised if you have the urge to "tie up your horse" out front. Built in 1852, the store offers a potpourri of knickknacks, toys, kid's books, drinks, and snacks. There are old whale guns, harpoons, and whaling memorabilia on display and, of course, lots of Hearst Castle souvenirs. There is a snackbar/ outdoor café that's open daily from 8:30am to 6pm.

We also like **Bleschyu Golf Park,** 9255 Hearst Dr. between Hearst Castle and Cambria (☎ **805/927-4221**), an 18-hole miniature golf course. A round of miniature golf will cost $4 for adults, $3 for kids 11 and under. The kids will also love the video arcade, and teens will enjoy the pool tables. Open daily from noon to 10pm in summer, weekends from noon to 10pm and weekdays from 3 to 10pm in winter.

William Randolph Hearst Memorial State Beach in San Simeon is a day-use area. You can see the castle off on the hill while you enjoy the sandy beach. This is where the **San Simeon Pier** is located. This 700-foot-long wooden pier offers pier fishing and is the starting point for fishing excursions and whale-watching tours.

San Simeon Landing/George's Tackle Shop, Old Calif. 1 (☎ **805/927-1777,** or toll free **800/ROCKCOD**), will rent pier poles and other equipment. Summer hours are 5am to 5pm; during other times of the year, call ahead. San Simeon Landing offers harbor tours and half-day, full-day, and "long-range" trips for cod fishing. Call ahead for reservations because some trips don't run every day.

WHAT TO SEE AND DO IN CAMBRIA

The tiny neighbor just a bit south, **Cambria Village** is actually two little stretches of shops, galleries, and restaurants, one is called East Village or Old Town, and the other is West Village. Main Street connects both parts of the quaint village. Plan to spend part of the day meandering through the village shops. Even though some kids don't enjoy shopping, the surrounding area offers lots of places for them to play, and there are a few shops they'll love.

Two of these shops we think of as highpoints of any trip to the area. **The Soldier Factory,** 789 Main St. (☎ 805/927-3804), is a factory and museum of miniature soldiers from every era, starting from medieval times to World War II. There are little plastic soldiers, tin soldiers, porcelain soldiers, soldiers on horseback, and battle-posed soldiers. Jack Scruby started the factory when he began to cast and paint soldiers himself and became completely engrossed in the hobby. He continued to make soldiers and began selling the miniatures via mail order. There are other miniature figures, such as the Scarecrow from *The Wizard of Oz* and Merlin the Magician from *King Arthur.* The factory is open daily from 10am to 5pm; closed Thanksgiving and Christmas Days.

Nearby is a wonderful little shop, **McKinney's Gems and Mineral Store,** 777 Main St. (☎ 805/927-4742). Not only is there an exciting collection of rocks for the kids to peruse, but the owner loves to talk with children about his collection. There are rocks for sale, some for as little as 50¢. Open daily from 10am to 5pm.

Kids can start their own rock collection at **Moonstone Beach and Shamel Park,** on Moonstone Beach Drive. The beach is beautiful, and great for rock collecting. You can find moonstones, quartz, and petrified wood. But be careful not to swim here— the water is too cold and the undertow too strong for safe swimming. Adjacent Shamel Park has a complete playground, huge grassy area, barbecue pits, and bathrooms with changing areas for sandy children.

By bicycle or on foot, **Santa Rosa Creek Road** makes a great all-family activity. This peaceful rural road winds through a beautiful little farm valley where we enjoy looking at cattle ranches, farms, and orchards. You can also enjoy the drive in your car. Start at Santa Rosa Creek Road where it intersects Main Street. While the road is narrow, locals know to watch out for bicyclists. But be advised anyway. As we travel through the pass, we stop at **Linn's Fruit Bin,** five miles east of Main Street on Santa Rosa Creek Road (☎ **805/927-8134**). In days past we actually picked berries at Linn's, but the Linn family now offers fresh fruit, fresh-baked pies, and beverages instead. Take your goodies and enjoy the shade while the kids play on the homemade rope swing. Open in winter, daily from 10am to 4pm, 5pm Saturday and Sunday; in summer, on weekends from 9am to 5pm.

Bicycle Rentals

Overland Adventures offers free delivery of bicycles to area hotels, motels, and campgrounds. Rentals start at $22 for 24 hours. In Cambria and San Simeon, call **805/927-5885.**

WHERE TO STAY

The only oceanfront motel in the area is the **Best Western Cavalier Inn,** 9415 Hearst Dr. (Calif. 1), San Simeon, CA 93452 (☎ **805/927-4688,** or toll free **800/826-8168**).

All rooms have VCR, remote control TV, stocked minibar and refrigerator, hair dryer and full combination bath. There are two restaurants, two outdoor heated pools, spa, Nautilus-equipped exercise room, guest laundry, shopping center with unique shops, California Wood Carver's Gallery, and video arcade.

Ocean-view front rooms with king-size bed, wood-burning fireplace, private patio overlooking the ocean $95–$135. Family accommodations with two queen-size beds are $71–$99. Additional persons are $6 each. Rollaways are $10; cribs are free.

Just a short walk from the ocean, the **Sands Motel,** 9355 Hearst Dr., San Simeon, CA 93452 (☎ **805/927-3243**), is a pleasant 33-room place to stay. The motel has a real luxury: an indoor swimming pool that's heated and warm enough to keep even the most finicky child comfortable. The pool has a gate with a high latch so toddlers can't wander off, and a nice three-foot shallow area. At the beach, the winds are great, and there is plenty of room for flying kites, but the beach isn't good for swimming. This is "rock heaven," so let those little rock collectors go to it.

The rooms are average size and most have tub/shower combinations. Some rooms have two queen-size beds, and there's still room for a crib or rollaway. All rooms have a color TV with free HBO and coffee makers. A free continental breakfast is served each morning in the office. The friendly managers will be glad to warm bottles or baby food. Rates are $45–$65 single, $55–$75 double; adjoining rooms are available. Cribs and rollaways cost $6 per night.

WHERE TO EAT

The **Brambles Dinner House,** 4005 Burton Dr., two blocks off Main Street in Cambria (☎ **805/927-4716**) is one of the most famous restaurants on the coast. The colorful cottage has an old-world ambience and is adorned with antique plates and a fabulous clock collection. The fireplace and candlelight give the restaurant a quiet, cozy warmth. The Brambles was built in 1874 as a family home and was converted to a restaurant in 1965. There are several dining rooms, each with its own mood.

Hot bread is set on the table as soon as you're seated. The restaurant is known for great prime rib served with traditional Yorkshire pudding; they also serve steak, seafood, chicken, and ribs. New additions include vegetarian and pasta dishes. The delicious dinners are sizable and include soup or salad, baked potato, and peas: prices range from $10 to $18.

There are not only highchairs and boosters, but "junior chairs" for children in-between. The children's menu is extensive and is priced at $4–$7; or they'll split an adult portion for two kids and add $5 for extra salad and potato. With a full bar, they're able to fix all kinds of special drinks for the kids. Open for dinner only, Sunday through Friday from 4 to 9:30pm and on Saturday from 4 to 10pm with early-bird dinners. Reservations are advised. Major credit cards accepted. Parking in the lot.

The **Chuck Wagon Restaurant,** at Moonstone Beach Drive and Calif. 1 in Cambria (☎ 805/927-4644), offers an all-you-can-eat buffet for lunch and dinner. Choose from the complete salad bar, plus fried chicken, fried fish, ham, ribs, or turkey and dressing and vegetables. Lunch costs $6; dinner, $8. Don't expect anything fancy, but the home-style cooking is good and plenty. Children's prices are about $2.50 for ages 2–5, $3.50 for ages 6–9, and $5.50 for ages 10 and 11. Highchairs and boosters are available. Open daily: from 11am to 8:30pm in winter, from 6:30am to 9pm in summer. Credit cards accepted. There's a large parking lot, and buses are welcome.

For breakfast you might try the **Cambria Village Bakery,** 2214 Main St., Cambria (☎ 805/927-8227), for homemade specialties. There are fresh fruit/yogurt muffins and carrot/apple bran muffins, croissants, vegetable soup, cream of asparagus soup, and Cornish meat pasties. Prices of individual items range from 75¢ to $2.50. European and French roast coffee and teas are served. There are boosters, but no highchairs, in this tiny tea room. Open Tuesday through Saturday from 6:30am to 6pm and on Sunday from 6:30am to 2pm. No reservations or credit cards accepted. Parking lot.

Another great place for breakfast, lunch, and dinner that locals love is **Linn's Fruit Bin,** 2277 Main St., downtown (☎ 805/927-0371). Highchairs are available. Open Sunday through Friday from 8am to 9pm and on Saturday from 8am to 10:30pm. No reservations, but credit cards are accepted.

6 Morro Bay/San Luis Obispo/Pismo Beach

The towns in southern San Luis Obispo County are clustered together in a small area. Surrounding them are wide open spaces. We'll start at Morro Bay, then go to the towns of San Luis Obispo and Pismo Beach.

Morro Bay

This sleepy little seaside village of fewer than 10,000 residents is the place to go when you want to slow down and relax. Named for Morro Rock, the "Gibraltar of the Pacific", a 576-foot monolith that is one of seven extinct volcanoes in the area, Morro Bay offers lots of outdoor family fun.

There is a long peninsula of sand dunes that separates Morro Bay from the ocean. These dunes, called **Morro Bay Sandspit,** can be as high as 85 feet, providing lots of roaming area.

Morro Bay has been designated a bird sanctuary, and you can see more than 100 kinds of birds in the nearby estuary in Morro Bay State Park. Take your binoculars and watch for egrets, kingfishers, pelicans, and herons. Morro Bay also hosts monarch butterflies. In October the orange-and-black beauties migrate to the area, seeking warmth in the stands of eucalyptus that are throughout the region.

For further information, contact the **Morro Bay Chamber of Commerce,** 895 Napa (P.O. Box 876), Morro Bay, CA 93442 (☎ 805/772-4467, or toll free 800/231-0592). The **San Luis Obispo County Visitors and Conference Bureau,** at 1041 Chorro St., Suite E, San Luis Obispo, CA 93401 (☎ **805/541-8000,** or toll free **800/634-1414**), is also helpful.

WHAT TO SEE AND DO

The **Embarcadero** is the place to get the true flavor of this fishing village. This ocean-front strip, loaded with gift stores, restaurants, and fish markets, is where you'll get great views of Morro Rock and the sand dunes, and enjoy the sea with its otters, sea gulls, and fresh ocean breezes. You can watch fishermen preparing for the day or unloading their catch.

The **Morro Bay Aquarium,** 595 Embarcadero (☎ **805/772-7647**), is a very small place, but one you'll want to stop at with the family. The owners take in injured and abandoned sea otters and seals and nurse them back to health. Working with the Department of Fish and Game, they release the recovered animals back to the sea. You can see the ones they're doctoring as well as 300 other saltwater specimens. Open daily in summer from 9am to 6pm, to 5pm in winter; closed major holidays. The admission fee is $1 for adults, 50¢ for children 5–11, free for children under 5.

Many families enjoy a one-hour cruise on the paddlewheeler *Tiger's Folly II,* 1205 Embarcadero, departing from the Harbor Hut restaurant dock (☎ **805/772-2257** or **805/772-2255**). The cruise stays within the calm waters of Morro Bay. Tickets cost $6 for adults, $3 for children. Call for the cruise schedule. Note that Sunday brunch cruises depart at 10am and 12:30pm.

A really fun place to go with the kids is the **Giant Chess Board,** located on Centennial Pkwy. (☎ **805/772-6278**). These life-size wooden chess pieces were carved by the music director of the high school, and are used to . . . yes, play "life-size" games of chess. It's fun to watch, even if you don't understand the game. Anyone can play, as long as you have a reservation. Make them at the Recreation and Parks Department at 1001 Kennedy Way. Open from Monday through Friday from 8am to 8pm. The fee is $13.75.

How about a tour of a **Coast Guard cutter?** The boats are docked at the Embarcadero, and the public can tour them on weekends when they're not out on patrol. Call the day you want to tour (☎ **805/772-2167**) or just show up. Kids delight in exploring the Coast Guard patrol boats—the bridge, the search-and-rescue equipment, and the hold. There's no admission fee.

You can also drive to **Morro Rock.** Take Embarcadero north till it turns toward the Rock and continue to follow it. You'll pass little Coleman Park on the way, with its smattering of playground equipment. But be sure to get all the way to the Rock. The views looking north are exquisite. With the Rock and breakwater, huge waves file in, giving you a strong sense of the power of the ocean. You'll see surfers and sunbathers as you look north toward Atascadero and Morro Strand State Beaches.

Morro Bay Marina, 699 Embarcadero (☎ **805/772-8085**), offers "taxi" service across the bay to the **Morro Bay Sand Dunes.** Taxi service is available daily in summer, and Thursday through Monday in the winter. Round-trip fares are $7 for adults, $4 one-way trip and you need to make reservations ahead of time. They also rent one and two-man kayaks.

Virg's Fish'N, 1215 Embarcadero (☎ **805/772-1222**), offers full-day and half-day sportfishing trips for rock cod. Full-day trips are from 7am to 3pm and cost $29 for adults and $25 for children 12 and under and seniors. Rod rental is $5–$7. The half-day trips are from 8am to noon and 1 to 5pm and 3:30pm and 7:30pm May through

September and cost $20 for adults and $18 for children and seniors. Rod rental is $4. Bait is included with all rentals. There are also 2¹/₂-hour whale-watching trips between December 26 and mid-March. Dates for trips vary, so call ahead for information and reservations. Boats leave at 11am and 2pm. Rates are $15 for adults, $10 for children and seniors. You can also rent pier poles here at $3 for 24 hours; an additional deposit is required. Virg's Fish'N is open daily from 5:30am to 6pm, sometimes later depending on scheduled trips. There are also kayak and motor boat rental.

This entire area is a great place for kite flying, and you'll find a terrific selection at **Kites Galore,** at the corner of Embarcadero and Beach Street (☎ **805/772-8322**). They also rent four-wheel pedal carriages at $10 per hour. They are open daily from 9am to 6pm, to 9pm during the summer.

For inside fun, **Flippo's Surfside Skate Harbor,** 220 Atascadero Rd. (☎ **805/772-7851**) is a great roller-skating rink. It's open daily, but call ahead because the schedule varies depending on the day and what events are taking place at the rink. Admission fees vary depending upon the time.

State Parks and Beaches

Lovely **Morro Bay State Park** is a pretty state park with Monterey pines, eucalyptus, and a large marshy area that's home to more than 250 species of birds. The marsh serves as a bird reserve. In the park on State Park Road is the **Morro Bay Museum of Natural History** (☎ **805/772-2694**). Don't miss it, even if just to take in the view alone. At White Point, a rocky point that rises above the bay, kids can easily climb the trail to the top to see where the Native Americans used to grind their acorns. The museum has displays that explain the natural history of the area: Morro Rock, the lagoon, the large numbers of birds, and the local Chumash tribe. There's a telescope for viewing the shoreline. Call ahead to see if they have any special docent-led family programs scheduled. Open daily from 10am to 5pm. Closed New Year's, Thanksgiving, and Christmas Days. Admission is $2 for adults, $1 for children 6–12, free for kids under 6.

Montana de Oro State Park is located along the coast just 11 miles south of Morro Bay. To get to the park, take the Los Osos/Baywood Park exit off Calif. 1. Montana de Oro literally means Mountain of Gold and many people refer to this 7,000-acre area as "petite Big Sur," with its rugged terrain and stony cliffs. Spooner's Cove is a secluded little swimming area of aquamarine-colored water that your family will love. You'll find lots of wonderful hikes in this area that offer splendid views of the coastal bluff or forest streams, and colorful wildflowers in season. Many of the hikes are great with the little ones. Kids will love watching the sea otters at play in the area.

If you have the stamina, one of the great walks in the region starts at the trail called Hazard Reef. This short walk goes through a eucalyptus grove to the beach, where there are tidepools, and continues on to the Morro Bay Sandspit area of high dunes. Don't expect to do a lot because walking in the dunes is hard work, but worth the effort.

The campground here is tucked in among the trees, across from the beach. There are 46 tent or motorhome sites, but no hookups. There are barbecue pits for picnickers. For more information, contact the rangers c/o Montana de Oro State Park, Pecho Valley Road, Los Osos, CA 93402 (☎ **805/528-0513** or **805/772-7434**). Reservations can be made in the summer through MISTIX outlets or call for a registration form (☎ **619/452-1920**, or toll free **800/444-7275** in California).

Atascadero State Beach, just north of Morro Rock, is a popular beach because the waves are gentle here and the location is lovely. It's a good place for kids. Restrooms, showers, and dressing rooms are available.

Morro Strand State Beach is north of Atascadero State Beach. This is a long, sandy beach, with usually gentle waves. Restrooms and picnic tables are available.

WHERE TO STAY

There are lots of little motels in this nautical town. But if you plan to come during the summer, book your room far ahead, at least a month.

We like the **Embarcadero Inn,** 456 Embarcadero, Morro Bay, CA 93442 (☎ 805/772-2700, or toll free 800/292-ROCK), a tastefully decorated motor inn located on the waterfront. The inn is quite comfortable and has nice large rooms that offer lovely views of Morro Rock and the bay it rests in. We enjoyed sunset on the balcony, watching the white-capped water shimmer in the dimming light. There are two Jacuzzis on the premises. This little 32-room inn has lots of nice touches, including a free continental breakfast in your room. All rooms face the bay, and 30 have balconies. Every room has a refrigerator, remote-control color TV, and VCR (cassettes are on loan at the office or bring your own). There are fireplaces, fresh-perked coffee, and an amenity basket. Some rooms have fireplaces. The rooms are generously sized, with plenty of space for cribs and rollaways. Rates vary, based on room location and number of beds. Single or double, they cost $60 to $130 in winter and $70–$170 in summer. Suites feature living rooms with wet bars, fireplaces, and refrigerators, and they range in price from $95 to $170. Children 11 and under stay free in their parents' room; each additional person over 11 pays $10 per night. Cribs cost $5; rollaways, $10.

The **Best Western San Marcos Inn,** 250 Pacific St., Morro Bay, CA 93442 (☎ 805/772-2248, or toll free 800/528-1234), only a block from the waterfront restaurants and shops, is another good choice. With a Jacuzzi, free deluxe continental breakfast, nightly there is free apple cider, wine, and cheese and crackers, color television with free HBO, a refrigerator, and an elevator, this reasonably priced inn is a pleasing place. Rates range from $46–$94 for a room with a king-size bed to $46–$109 for a room with two queen-size beds. Additional guests pay $5. There's no charge for cribs, but a rollaway costs $10.

The **Sunset Travelodge,** 1080 Market Ave., Morro Bay, CA 93442 (☎ 805/772-1259, or toll free 800/578-7878), is another budget alternative. Within walking distance of the Embarcadero, this newly renovated 31-room motel has a nice heated pool and an inviting glassed-in sun deck. The lovely deck has tables, chairs, and lounges, just perfect for Mom and Dad to bask while the kids play nearby. All rooms have remote-control TVs with free HBO, separate vanity areas, and coffee makers. Some have a refrigerator, microwave, and wet bar. Some have tub/shower combinations (request these when you reserve your room). Rates vary greatly and range from $39 to $78, single or double. Each additional person pays $6—except in winter when children stay free. Suites rent for $56–$95. Cribs are free; rollaways cost $6. Higher rates are in effect during special events.

Camping

You'll find a lot of good camping in this area. **Morro Bay State Park** has 115 developed campsites with tables and stoves, and restrooms with showers. Trailers or motor homes up to 31 feet long can be accommodated. There are 20 sites with water and electricity hookups, and a sanitation station is available.

Morro Strand State Beach has 104 developed campsites, but no showers. The sites can accommodate trailers and motor homes up to 24 feet long.

For information about the above campgrounds, write c/o Morro Bay State Park, Morro Bay, CA 93442 (☎ 805/772-2560), or make reservations through MISTIX (☎ toll free 800/444-7275).

For information about **Montana de Oro State Park,** see the "What to See and Do" section, above.

WHERE TO EAT

You'll enjoy a meal at **Dorn's, the Original Breakers Café,** 801 Market St. (☎ 805/772-4415). It sits on a hill overlooking the Embarcadero and the bay, and commands a beautiful view—Morro Rock is directly ahead.

This seafood restaurant is moderately priced and offers good fresh food for breakfast, lunch, and dinner. It's famous for its buttermilk pancakes, waffles, and omelets at breakfast, and for its delicious fresh fish at lunch and dinner. The marinated seafood salad is one of the best; it has large chunks of shrimp, crab, calamari, and lobster mixed in among the tossed greens ($13.50). Breakfast is served from 7am to 2pm and prices range from $5 to $9.50. Lunch is served from 11am to 4pm and prices range from $5.50 to $10.50. Dinner is served from 4 to 10pm and prices range from $11 to $30. Order the generous shrimp cocktail appetizer for $5.

There are highchairs, children's menus, and booster seats. The waiter brought fresh fruit for our baby, so she could have something while we were all eating. The service is friendly and fast. Open daily from 7am to 10pm. You need reservations, but there can still be a wait during peak hours. It's so beautiful, though, you can just take a walk. Some credit cards accepted. There's a parking lot across the street.

Another choice is the **Galley Restaurant,** 899 Embarcadero (☎ 805/772-2806). This family-owned restaurant serves up a delicious selection of seafood, sandwiches, steaks, and salads. The bay shrimp salad is a favorite, and the fish and chips are crispy but not oily. Lunches range from $4.25 to $8.75. Dinners include chowder, salad, bread, potatoes or rice, beverage, and dessert, and range $11.25–$23. A la carte entrees (including bread and potato or rice) cost $8.25–$29. The children's dinner special is $7.50 for a choice of fish or ground beef, and the only difference from the adult meal (besides portion size) is a choice of soup or salad. Highchairs and boosters are available, and the waiter will bring crackers to the table right away. Open daily for lunch and dinner from 11am to 8:30pm in winter, till 9:30pm in summer; closed from Thanksgiving to December 26. Reservations are advised and honored. Some credit cards accepted. Street parking is available.

Margie's Diner, 1698 N. Main St. (☎ 805/772-2510), located just south of Calif. 41, claims to be the home of the world's best burger. Margie's is open for breakfast, lunch, and dinner, with a menu that features real home-style cooking. Eggs and omelets are served up with home-fried potatoes, a choice of toast, biscuits, or English muffins. Prices are $3.95–$7.95 (for a six-ounce top sirloin). Burgers are $4.95–$6.95; sandwiches range from $4.25 (for a grilled cheese) to $7.50. Full dinners served after 4pm, include soup or salad, rolls, vegetable, and potatoes. Barbecued chicken ($8.95), ground round steak ($9.95), and top sirloin ($10.95) are just some of the favorites. Don't miss the yummy malted milkshakes ($3.50–$3.95). Boosters and highchairs are available. Open daily from 6:30am to 9pm. No credit cards or reservations are accepted. There is another location in San Luis Obispo at 1575 Calle Joaquin (at Los Osos Valley Road and U.S. 101; ☎ 805/541-2940).

San Luis Obispo

Nestled in the hills of the Santa Lucia mountain range, San Luis Obispo is a small, charming city with an eclectic mixture of early California buildings and Victorian-style frame houses. Its population is about 35,000. Originally established in 1772 with the founding of San Luis Obispo Mission by Fr. Junipero Serra, it's the cultural and historical center of the county. It has two colleges (California Polytechnic and Cuesta College), a Mozart festival, and a symphony orchestra. For maps, a calendar of events, and information on attractions, contact the **San Luis Obispo Chamber of Commerce,** 1039 Chorro St., San Luis Obispo, CA 93401 (☎ 805/781-2777), open seven days a week. The **San Luis Obispo County Visitors and Conference Bureau,** at 1041 Chorro St., Suite E, San Luis Obispo, CA 93401 (☎ **805/541-8000,** or toll free **800/634-1414**), is also helpful.

WHAT TO SEE AND DO

Probably the first place to start your visit is at **Mission San Luis Obispo de Tolosa,** at Chorro and Monterey Streets (☎ **805/543-6850**). Founded in 1772 by Fray Serra and José Cavaller, and named for the French saint, Louis, bishop of Toulouse, the mission was the fifth of the 21 missions in the state. It is simple and small, but has a charming little garden where you'll want to spend some time wandering. Inside, notice the hand-painted stenciled walls, the simple windows, the huge wood-beamed ceilings, and the wooden pews. The Mission Museum has artifacts from the local Chumash tribe, and it offers a glimpse into the lifestyles of the Spanish settlers. It specializes in Native North American books and unique and hard-to-find religious articles. Open daily from 9am to 4pm (to 5pm in summer). A donation of $1 is requested. Closed New Year's, Easter, Thanksgiving, and Christmas Days.

Bordering the mission is **Mission Plaza,** at Monterey and Chorro Streets, a tree-filled area with the San Luis Creek running through. This town square offers many shady places to stop for a picnic lunch, just to rest, or to let the kids run around. It serves as a gathering area for townsfolk and visitors alike. If you're lucky, you may happen upon a concert in the park. You can walk through Mission Plaza to the downtown shopping area of Higuera Street, part of which borders the plaza.

If you want to browse or shop, lots of specialty store that are located on Higuera Street back up to San Luis Creek and have entrances creekside. The best shopping is between Chorro and Broad Streets.

Across from the plaza is the **San Luis Obispo County Historical Museum,** 696 Monterey St. (☎ **805/543-0638**), which displays photographs and interesting exhibits depicting life in the county from the time of the Chumash tribes to the present day. Open Wednesday through Sunday from 10am to 4pm; closed major holidays. No admission charge.

Your kids might like one of the **Heritage Walks** of San Luis Obispo. The four walks include different highlights of the town: Downtown, the Historic Core, Old Town Residential, and an Adobe–Railroad District Walk. You can pick up a map at the above-mentioned visitor center and begin your tour at Mission Plaza.

The new **San Luis Obispo Children's Museum,** 1010 Nipoma St. (☎ **805/544-KIDS**), is a place for children of all ages, especially toddlers through elementary school. Kids enjoy putting on a play in the Chumash tribal cave where they can create their own drawings on the cave walls. They can pass through the lens of the "Living Camera," be an ant in a giant ant maze, zip down the dinosaur slide, and play educational games on computers. For toddlers, there's a playhouse of Duplo blocks, koosh balls, and other playthings. Open in summer daily except Wednesday from 10am to 5pm; the rest of the year, on Thursday and Friday from 1 to 5pm, and on Saturday and Sunday from 10am to 5pm. Admission $3 for those 2 and older, under 2 is free.

Every Thursday night beginning at 6pm you can join the activities at the **Farmer's Market.** Higuera Street is closed to automobiles and several blocks are filled with tables laden with freshly harvested produce to be sold by local farmers. It's more like a fiesta than a market, with local talent performing. Outdoor tables are set up by neighboring restaurants so you can enjoy a picnic-style supper. People partake of the ribs, barbecued chicken, hot dogs, and other goodies offered. Even if you're not buying, it's fun to stroll through and enjoy the entertainment and small-town camaraderie.

California Polytechnic State University, affectionately called Cal Poly, is located in central San Luis Obispo (☎ 805/756-1111 or 805/756-2417). The university is known for its agriculture, engineering, architecture, and computer-technology degree programs. Guided campus tours are available each Monday, Wednesday, and Friday year round, except on academic and other holidays. Tours begin at 10am and 2pm. Families can also wander through the campus and look at horses, pigs, and other livestock, but call the information clerk first to find out what's open for viewing during your visit.

Many kids enjoy poking through a little shop at 1033 Chorro St. called **Burris Saddlery** (☎ 805/543-4101). It has saddles, saddlebags, and horse and pack equipment. We love this little store, and our city kids find it hard to believe that it's the real thing. Open Monday through Saturday from 9:30 to 11:45am and 12:45 to 5:15pm.

Avila Beach

The tiny area called Avila Beach is a friendly little community, host to Port San Luis Harbor. The beach area is small and the short drive through the oaks and sycamores from U.S. 101 through See Canyon is beautiful. Avila Beach is great for families, with playground equipment at Front and San Francisco Streets. There are picnic tables and lifeguards in summer. There's fishing from Avila Pier. The little town of Avila offers ample places for food and drinks. You can drive to the jetty and watch the boats being repaired in dry dock, or observe the fishermen at work.

If you're looking for something really unusual, you might stop at **Sycamore Mineral Springs,** located at 1215 Avila Beach Dr. (☎ 805/595-7302, or toll free 800/234-5831), for a stint in a mineral bath. Children are welcome. Sycamore Springs is really a motel (with 27 units, each with its own balcony and hot tub), but we prefer stopping here for a fun daytime excursion. The big attractions are the 22 private redwood hot tubs (all emptied and scrubbed daily) and the other amenities of a mineral springs, such as massage for Mom and Dad. With the hourly rental of the hot tub comes the use of the facilities, including a heated swimming pool and two volleyball courts. Children 3–12 pay $5 per hour and adults are charged $10 per hour for use of the hot tubs; an all-day pool pass is included. Or you can get just a pool pass: $6 for adults, $5 for children. Hot tubs are open 24 hours; the swimming pool is open from 9am to 6pm. A restaurant on site, called the Gardens of Avila, offers California cuisine and the menu changes daily. Dinners range from $9 to $17.

WHERE TO STAY

In San Luis Obispo there are several places to choose from. The **Apple Farm Inn and Restaurant,** 2015 Monterey St., San Luis Obispo, CA 93401 (☎ **805/544-2040,** or toll free **800/255-2040** in California), is unique and fun. This new inn, which has already received a four-diamond rating from the Automobile Club of Southern California, is a replica of a 19th-century Victorian inn. These rooms have the bonus of modern soundproofing and private baths in addition to the traditional accoutrements of the 1800s, such as four-poster beds, fireplaces, and wingback chairs. There is also a swimming pool and Victorian gardens in which you and the kids can stroll. This delightful inn, which is near the banks of the San Luis Creek, has an authentically reproduced Mill House, a picnic area, a gift store, bakery, and restaurant. The Apple Farm Restaurant is wonderful, and serves home-style American breakfasts, lunches, and dinners (for a complete description, see "Where to Eat," below).

Amenities include complimentary wake-up coffee delivered to the rooms, complimentary newspapers, and fresh flowers. Ask about the "Breakfast in Bed" service. Rooms cost $75–$225, single or double, depending on size, view, and special details. Children under 18 stay free when they share their parents' room. Additional adults pay $15 each per night. There is no charge for cribs.

The **Quality Suites,** 1631 Monterey St., San Luis Obispo, CA 93401 (☎ **805/541-5001,** or toll free **800/221-2222**), is a wonderful moderately priced choice for families. Built to look like an early California villa, the airy lobby, terra-cotta tile floors, and large ceiling fans set off the two-story ceilings. There are inviting conversation areas and a little room off the lobby called the Library. But you'll love the landscaped outdoor area best of all. One courtyard has a fenced and gated pool area, complete with a one-foot wading pool and Jacuzzi. Another courtyard features a fountain and grassy area.

Included in the room rates are cooked-to-order breakfasts, served Monday through Friday from 6:30 to 9:30am and on Saturday and Sunday from 7 to 10am; evening chips, salsa, and nonalcoholic drinks, and free newspapers. This location has a giftshop and sundry store, with microwave items available. There is a coin-operated laundry for guest use.

The 138 two-room suites have two remote-control televisions, with VCR and AM/FM stereo cassette player, wet bar, honor bar, refrigerator, microwave oven, and two phones. The living room has a large queen-size sofa sleeper and a dining table. The sleeping room has two double beds or one king-size bed and an enormous vanity area. The bathroom includes a tub/shower combination and toiletries. Rates are $93 single and $103 double in winter, $115 single and $125 double in summer. Kids under 18 are free if they use existing beds; each additional adult is charged $10 in winter, $10 in summer. Cribs are provided free of charge, but there are no rollaways.

Another moderately priced accommodation is **La Cuesta Motor Inn,** 2074 Monterey St., San Luis Obispo, CA 93401 (☎ **805/543-2777,** or toll free **800/543-2777;** fax 805/544-0696). This is a tastefully decorated motor inn with a definite southwestern flair. The lobby has an inviting area for sitting and chatting, a place where you can enjoy the complimentary continental breakfast and afternoon tea-and-cookie service. The large pool is heated year round and is fenced and gated. There's also a Jacuzzi. Extra touches, such as flowers and paintings in the guest hallways, make this an attractive place. Rooms are good-size and new. Some have pretty views of the mountains. All have cable television with free HBO, tub/shower combinations, game tables, and chairs. Some rooms even have refrigerators. Rates are the same for single and double occupancy: $64–$95.

And of course there's the ever-famous, ever-astonishing **Madonna Inn,** 100 Madonna Rd., San Luis Obispo, CA 93405 (☎ **805/543-3000,** or toll free **800/543-9666** in California). You'll recognize the Madonna Inn as soon as you begin your approach—pink lightposts line the drive up to the multistory gingerbread-style abode. Inside, you'll see pink and red all around you, from the banquettes and napkins to the little cupids. While this is really more of a couples' hideaway, it's so famous you really must stop by. We're including it as a possible place to stay, but we usually "do" the Madonna Inn as a sightseeing attraction. We stop for a snack or lunch and roam the property. The kids love the wildly colorful coffee shop (open daily from 7am to 10pm; breakfast prices run $5–$10, and lunch or dinner costs $9–$18). Don't let the kids miss the swinging doll in the restaurant lobby. And then, of course, there's the big tourist attraction—the rushing waterfall urinal in the men's bathroom. You'll also find a giftshop, bakery, boutique, a gourmet and wine-tasting shop, and beautifully landscaped grounds which you can admire but not romp through. There is a formal dining room featuring continental dinners for $15.95–$22.95 with a child-priced portion.

If you arrive between noon and 2pm, you can go to the front desk and ask which rooms are in the process of being cleaned. You're welcome to poke your head in those unoccupied rooms as long as a housekeeper is inside. It's pot luck, but you might be able to see some of the famous rooms. Among the most interesting are the Cave Man Room, with rock ceiling, walls, floors, and a waterfall in the bathroom; the Round Room, which is bright green with a merry-go-round motif; and the kids' favorite, the Pony Room, which has barn-type paneling painted red and is decorated with pony ornaments.

If you choose to stay in this fairyland, expect to pay from $72 (for one person) to $180 (for four people), depending on the room configuration and types of beds. Suites range from $130 to $180, and can accommodate up to eight or nine people. Cribs and rollaways are free. Visa and Mastercard cards are accepted at the inn.

WHERE TO EAT

In San Luis Obispo don't miss the **Apple Farm Restaurant,** at 2015 Monterey St. (☎ **805/544-6100**). The food is Americana, and it's absolutely delicious! Try the hot apple dumplings served with hot cinnamon sauce and ice cream; they make their dumplings and pies from scratch using local apples. The decor of the place is especially endearing. The Apple Farm opened in 1977 as a small restaurant and it continues to expand. The gift store and the main area of the restaurant were originally a Victorian house. You'll see Victorian architecture with turrets and towers, and lots of leaded-glass panels, Tiffany glass, crate-label art of the early 1900s, and patchwork quilts. The apple theme is carried throughout with apple-crate labels decorating the walls and apple souvenirs in the giftshop. There's also a toy shop. Owner Bob Davis, who has traveled extensively with his own family, decided to create a restaurant that would both capture the American imagination and cater to families.

Be sure to see the Quilt Room, a dining room where antique quilts line the walls. Another dining room overlooks the outdoor gazebo and waterwheel of the inn. There's also a patio waiting area where coffee is served. The service is friendly and the food is great. There's a large breakfast menu with a price range of $3.75–$7.50. Lunches can be a simple soup-and-sandwich combination or meatloaf, roast beef, or turkey sandwiches, priced at $5.95–$6.95. For dinner you can have old-fashioned chicken and dumplings or roast turkey and gravy, among other choices. All dinners include soup or salad, cornbread, fresh vegetables, and potatoes, and cost $7.50–$14.95. Children have similar appetizing treats for $2.45–$3.75. There's an adorable children's menu, and highchairs and booster seats are available.

Open weekdays from 7am to 9:30pm, till 10pm on weekends. Major credit cards accepted. You can park in the lot.

Another fun place is **Hudson's Grill,** at 1005 Monterey St. (☎ **805/541-5999**). This American grill has simply fabulous burgers, and milkshakes so rich and thick that you can't use a straw. The jukebox and neon lights add a certain '50s touch, but the old Hudson automobile coming out of the wall is classic '40s-era stuff! The menu includes specialty salads, sandwiches, Mexican food, and pasta; prices are in the $3.95–$7 range. The kids' coloring book–menu includes burgers, hot dogs and grilled cheese. Prices range from $2 to $3.95. Our kids couldn't wait for the bill to arrive, because it comes with a Tootsie Roll pop for each person. There are highchairs and booster seats, and the staff will warm bottles and baby food.

Open daily from 7am to midnight. No reservations accepted. Most major credit cards welcome. Parking is in the street.

Margie's Diner also has a branch here (see "Where to Eat" in the Morro Bay section).

Pismo Beach

This seaside village is a surfer's paradise and a beach lover's mecca. Located about 11 miles south of San Luis Obispo via U.S. 101, Pismo has lots of surfers and would-be surfers. You'll have a great time here, especially if you have teens. This is also the place to see dunes. You can even drive your car on the beach. Pismo used to be known for its clams and clam digging. A recent boom in the clam population has resurrected this sport, which was nearly wiped out by overclamming in the 1960s and '70s. You'll love clam digging, but find out first about regulations; adults will need fishing licenses.

Stop by the **Pismo Beach Chamber of Commerce,** 581 Dolliver St. (☎ **805/773-4382;** or toll free **800/443-7778** in California), for information about local attractions, events and clamming instructions for the novice. The office is open weekdays from 9am to 5pm, on Saturday from 10am to 4pm, and on Sunday from noon to 4pm.

WHAT TO SEE AND DO

The **Pismo Beach Pier** is the center of this village town. The beach stretches for miles both north and south, enticing sunbathers, swimmers, surfers, and Frisbee throwers alike. Kids and parents can also fish from the pier. There are public restrooms.

Pismo State Beach is a 20-mile strip of sand dunes, part of which is open only to all-terrain-vehicles, often called off-highway vehicles. Some of the areas with hard-packed sand are open to automobiles. A "ride on the sand" will cost you $4 per vehicle. **Pismo Dunes State Vehicular Recreation Area** is the spot if you and your family are aficionados of off-road-vehicle sporting. Or you can enjoy watching the others in their treks up and down the dunes. The recreation area is located at the southern tip of Pismo State Beach.

Another way to enjoy the spectacular scenery is to ride on horseback to Pismo Beach. The **Livery Stable,** 1207 Silver Spur Place, in Oceano, about three miles south of Pismo Beach (☎ **805/489-8100**), has horses for advanced, intermediate, and beginning riders. During the summer the stable is open daily from 8am to 5pm, in winter till 4pm (closed Tuesday during the winter). No reservations are taken. Rates are $15 per hour for adults and children, plus a deposit per horse. Children between 2 and 8 must ride on a horse with an adult, but they ride free.

For a simply fabulous sunset view of the coast north and the dunes to the south, get a snack or cool drink at the **Sea Venture Restaurant,** located on the sand at Pismo Beach at 100 Ocean View (☎ **805/773-4994**). They serve little Spanish appetizers (tapas). You can munch on fajitas, tempura, fish and chips ($5–$7) while enjoying a beverage and the view. Full dinners are served too. Boosters and highchairs are available. It's open from 4 to 10pm.

You may discover that you need some sand toys or beach paraphernalia. You can get them at **Beach Gear and More,** in the mall at 175 Pomeroy Ave. (☎ **805/773-1999**). They sell pails, boogie boards, splash balls, even beach chairs. Open daily from 10am to 6pm.

WHERE TO STAY

There may be more motels and inns in Pismo Beach than in any other town in the county.

The **Quality Suites,** 651 Five Cities Dr., Pismo Beach, CA 93449 (☎ **805/773-3773**), is our choice here. Located just off U.S. 101 at 4th Street, this accommodation is quite similar to its sister motor hotel in San Luis Obispo, and is a perfect place for families. This all-suite hostelry offers a complimentary made-to-order full breakfast, and the suites are quite lovely (see the description of the Quality Suites hotel in the San Luis Obispo section). In addition to the heated swimming pool, wading pool, and Jacuzzi, this location has a quiet courtyard and a putting green.

Like the other Quality Suites, all 133 two-room accommodations have two remote-control color TVs, two phones, a VCR, AM/FM stereo cassette player, a microwave, and a mini-refrigerator.

From mid-June to late September, rates are $79–$109 single, $89–$118 double; the rates are lower the rest of the year. Children under 18 stay free. Those over 18 and additional adults pay $9 each per night. No charge for cribs; no rollaways available.

The **Edgewater Motel on the Beach,** 280 Wadsworth Ave., Pismo Beach, CA 93449 (☎ **805/773-4811**, or toll free **800/634-5858**), is a budget accommodation located on the waterfront with access to the beach. Although the sound of the pounding surf and the sight of white beaches beckon, this motel also has a glassed-in outdoor heated swimming pool and Jacuzzi. There is a coin-operated laundry. The office has a small adjacent reception room in which free continental breakfast is served from 7 to 10am.

All rooms have refrigerators, cable color TVs, tables, and tub/shower combinations. Some have double sinks. Rooms with king-size beds and ocean views have Jacuzzi jets in the bathtub. There are also rooms with queen-size beds and others with two double beds. Connecting rooms are available. Cribs and rollaways cost $7 per night.

Rates vary considerably, depending on the room, the number of people, and the time of year. They run from $60 to $85 for one or two people. Family rooms, with two double or two queen-size beds, run $70–$135. Some have fully equipped kitchens.

Camping

As in the Morro Bay area, you'll find good camping here. **Pismo State Beach** has three separate campgrounds. North Beach is developed and has space for 31-foot trailers and campers ($16 fee), Oceano is developed and has space for 18-foot trailers and 31-foot campers ($16 fee), and Oceano (hookup) has spaces for 31-foot trailers and 36-foot campers ($20 fee). **Pismo Dunes Vehicular Recreation Area** has 500 primitive sites with pit toilets.

For more information on these campsites, contact Pismo State Beach, Pier Avenue, Oceano, CA 93445 (☎ **805/489-2684**). You can make reservations for state parks at a **MISTIX** outlet or you can call for registration forms (☎ **619/452-1950**, or toll free **800/444-7275** in California).

WHERE TO EAT

There is one all-time favorite in Pismo Beach for dinner. It is **F. McLintocks Saloon & Dining House,** 750 Mattie Rd. (take the Shell Beach exit off U.S. 101) (☎ **805/773-1892**), one of the top-10 grossing restaurants in all of California. Why? The managers answer that question with "Good food, good prices, and a great show." This lively down-home place, where your busboy may stand on a chair to pour your water and waiters yell to each other across the large dining room, has a real cowboy atmosphere. They say, "Bring the kids and you'll all have a great time."

They serve 1,200 meals a day in August, and can do 1,000 meals on any hopping Saturday night. What people keep coming back for is the superb service and the great steaks and seafood. They serve aged meat hand-cut on the premises and cooked over oakwood. Dinners include 14 different kinds of steak entrees, and fish and seafood like halibut, scampi, lobster, seafood combinations, and calamari. All dinners include onion rings, fresh spinach, house Caesar, or tossed green salad, beans, salsa, garlic bread, ranch fried potatoes, and an after-dinner liqueur or sherbet. Most prices for dinner range from $16 to $25 (for a 28-ounce T-bone steak!).

This family place has highchairs, boosters, a wide variety of children's drinks, and a nice children's menu of ground steak, fresh fish, steak, or ribs. A complete dinner and dessert (plus a prize from the saddlebags) runs from $1.95 to $3.25 for kids under 12. Open Monday through Friday from 4pm to 10pm, Saturday 3pm to 10:30pm, and Sunday 2pm to 9:30pm. The Sunday ranch breakfast is served from 9am to 1:30pm, and Sunday dinner from 2 till 9:30pm. With the waits being so long, try to make reservations (not accepted on Friday and Saturday). The best time is 5pm for dinner. In the summer, Friday and Saturday nights are busy—and no reservations are taken. They accept credit cards.

MORE AREA ACTIVITIES

When you find yourself trapped in the fog on the coast, you can drive into San Luis Obispo and see if the sun appears. If not and you'd like to try some indoor activities, here are a few suggestions.

Go bowling at **Laurel Bowl,** 1234 Laurel Lane, San Luis Obispo (☎ **805/543-2711**), open daily from 11am to 10pm (until midnight on Saturday and Sunday). Prices are $2.60 per game per person, $1 for shoe rentals. Children 12 and under pay only $2 per game.

Pismo Bowl, 277 Pomeroy Ave., Pismo Beach (☎ **805/773-2482**), is open from noon till midnight—but check for open lanes because they have a lot of leagues. Fees are $2.50 per game per adult and children, plus $1 for shoes.

Mann Festival Cinemas (☎ 805/481-7553), just south of Pismo Beach off U.S. 101, has ten movie theaters.

Picking Fruit and Vegetables

San Luis Obispo County is ripe with agricultural products for the picking. One place to try is **Kaminaka U-Pick Farms,** 945 Pomeroy Rd. in Nipomo, about 15 miles south of Pismo Beach (☎ 805/929-1374). This family farm has been in operation for more than 35 years and has allowed the public to pick crops for at least 21 years. You can pick strawberries and vegetables such as carrots, beets, beans, cabbage, tomatoes, and peppers. Fruits and vegetables picked from the fields are usually priced per pound. If you're lucky, and arrange it ahead of time, you can get a tour of the farm by the owners. There's also a complete farm stand if you don't wish to pick your own. Open April through November 15 daily from 8am to 6pm; closed December to April.

If You're Leaving for Points South

You might want to try a brief stop if you're traveling all the way to Los Angeles or Santa Barbara. **Pea Soup Andersen's California Highway Center,** at 376 Avenue of the Flags in Buellton (☎ 805/688-5581), is a good place to get out and stretch, and enjoy some of Andersen's great pea soup. Pea Soup Andersen's is close to Solvang, and completely embraces the Danish motif. The complex consists of a large gift shop and tasting room. But people come for the soup—it's that good! The Traveler's Special includes all the soup you can eat, yummy Danish onion-cheese or Danish pumpernickel bread, and a beverage (even a milkshake) for $4.95—and you can get it to go. There are also good salads, sandwiches, burgers, and hot entrees such as pot roast, veal cutlets, prime rib, New York steak, calves' liver, or filet of sole. You can order à la carte or a full dinner, which includes all the soup or salad you want, bread and butter, and beverage. Prices range from $4.95 to $15.25. The children's menu is a small coloring/game book. All items cost $2.25 and kids can choose from three breakfast items, and a large variety of lunch and dinner items: peanut butter sandwich, soup and a sandwich, chicken nuggets, or a hot dog. The service is friendly and crackers are put on the table as soon as you sit down, but the wait can be long, especially during mealtimes when everyone on the road decides to stop here. We usually call ahead when we know our approximate arrival time and make a reservation. With a set-up expressly for travelers, they have highchairs and boosters. The women's bathroom has a large vanity area that's good for diaper changing. Open daily from 6:30am to 10pm. Parking lot. They accept some major credit cards.

Area Festivals and Annual Events

You'll find many local events and festivals all year long in the central coast area. Here are some of the ones we enjoyed:

La Fiesta de San Luis Obispo (May) takes place at Mission Plaza. This is a lively festival with music, dancing, costumes, and a parade. Call **805/543-1710** for information.

The Renaissance Pleasure Faire (July) takes place at the El Chorro Regional Park in San Luis Obispo (☎ 805/481-4894). This event is a lively affair with participants wearing period costumes. There's entertainment, food, and crafts hearkening back to the days of old.

The **California Mid-State Fair** (August) in Paso Robles (☎ 805/238-3565) is an extraordinary state fair, drawing over 400,000 people in two weeks' time. The fair is on the National Rodeo circuit, and has tractor pulls, food exhibits and competitions, and an old-fashioned midway. Kids from all over the country bring their pigs, lambs, and goats to exhibit and sell. Top entertainment has included Bill Cosby, Dolly Parton, Kenny Loggins, and Glen Campbell.

Morro Bay Harbor Festival (October) in Morro Bay (☎ 805/772-4467) is one of the county's highlights. The festival has a carnival, a beach treasure hunt, and a parade of boats. The giant chessboard is used, with people dressed in costumes. A "live chess match" takes place.

Pismo Beach Clam Festival (October) at Pismo Beach pier (☎ 805/773-4382), includes a clam chowder cook-off, carnival, and clam-digging contest.

Morro Bay Lighted Boat Parade (December) in Morro Bay.

Whale-Watching (December through mid-March), all along the coast.

In an Emergency

Should a medical emergency occur during your stay, the following hospitals in San Luis Obispo have emergency room service: **Sierra Vista Hospital,** 1010 Murray Ave. (☎ 805/546-7600); **French Hospital,** 1911 Johnson Ave. (☎ 805/543-5353); and **General Hospital,** 2180 Johnson Ave. (☎ 805/781-4800).

If your family needs immediate medical care, but it's not an emergency, you might consider using **Med Stop,** 283 Madonna Rd., Suite B, San Luis Obispo (☎ 805/549-8880). There's a physician on duty at all times and no appointment is necessary. Open daily from 8am to 8pm.

Santa Barbara
and Vicinity

Tｈｉｓ ＣＨＡＰＴＥＲ WILL INTRODUCE YOU TO THE SPANISH/MEDITERRANEAN CHARM OF Santa Barbara, harbor adventures in Oxnard and Ventura, and the rural landscape and tranquil hills of Ojai.

Each town has something different to offer a family in terms of activities, climate, and location. In just a few days you could visit all of them. You might rent a boat in Ventura, loaf on a beach in Santa Barbara, or just drive down a country road in Ojai.

1 Santa Barbara

Santa Barbara is the epitome of a great beach town. It has fantastic, wide beaches and a wonderful, long bike path. It's in a gorgeous setting, with the ocean on one side and the Santa Ynez Mountains on the other. The temperatures are near perfect, and it offers activities for every season. Its Andalusian-like look of red-tile roofs and white Spanish buildings complements the calm, laid-back attitude of its inhabitants. In a nutshell, Santa Barbara is nearly perfect.

Its history goes all the way back to 1542, when the Portuguese explorer Juan Rodriguez Cabrillo discovered the channel. He didn't stay, and so the region was not named until much later—December 4, 1602, to be precise. On that date, St. Barbara's Day, Sebastian Vizcaino, a Spanish conquistador, entered the channel and named it after the saint. By the late 1700s Santa Barbara was a Spanish stronghold. The Europeans followed, ripping down the simple Spanish buildings and in their place putting up a hodgepodge of uninspired post-Victorian buildings. Ironically, it was with the help of an earthquake in 1925 that the city was able to get rid of the nondescript architecture and implement an order that all new structures had to be in the Mediterranean style. What a relief!

GETTING THERE

Just 90 miles north of Los Angeles and 330 miles south of San Francisco, Santa Barbara is reached **by car** via Calif. 1 or U.S. 101. **Santa Barbara Airport** is served by a number of local and national carriers. The Santa Barbara Airbus will whisk you to and from Los Angeles International Airport (☎ **805/964-7759,** or toll free **800/733-6354, 800/423-1618** in Southern California). Major rental-car companies are located at the airport and in town; check the *Yellow Pages* for local addresses and phone numbers. **Amtrak** (☎ toll free **800/USA-RAIL**) serves Santa Barbara direct from Los Angeles, San Diego, and San Francisco. But make your reservations a month in advance; this is the same train that travels up the coast and it books up quickly. There is also the **Greyhound Bus** service (☎ toll free **800/231-2222**) linking major cities with Santa Barbara.

ORIENTATION

There's more to do in Santa Barbara than meets the eye. To get information before your visit, contact the **Santa Barbara Conference and Visitors Bureau,** 510A State St., Santa Barbara, CA 93101 (☎ **805/966-9222;** or toll free **800/927-4688**). When in town, stop by the **Santa Barbara Visitor Information Center,** at 1 Santa Barbara St., Santa Barbara, CA 93103 (☎ **805/965-3021**), to get all the facts you need. The office is open daily from 9am to 5pm. Also, the **Santa Barbara Chamber of Commerce,** 504 State St. (☎ **805/965-3021**) stays open Monday through Friday from 9am to 5pm, to offer assistance and information.

Outlying Montecito to the south and Hope Ranch to the north are two of the most exclusive residential areas of Santa Barbara. The visitor center has mapped out a scenic drive that encompasses these and other points of interest.

Another spot that can help you with arrangements in town is **Hot Spot,** an accommodation service at 36 State St. (☎ **805/564-1637;** or toll free **800/793-7666**). This cappuccino/espresso bar-cum–information service can book hotels for your next trip and show you menus from a variety of restaurants. Ask about the free coupon book with discounts for a variety of local restaurants and stores. Hot Spot stays open year round, daily 24 hours each day.

State Street is one of the main shopping streets in town, with the hub between Victoria Street and the ocean. State Street is lined with boutiques, cafés, and snack shops, bookstores, Mexican import shops, and numerous stores that will appeal to kids and teenagers. On Brinkerhoff Avenue you'll find a large number of antiques stores.

Where State Street and Cabrillo Boulevard meet is the point at which **Stearns Wharf** begins and the Santa Barbara Trolley stops (you'll find more information in "What to See and Do," below). This is where you'll find the statue of the dolphin. It's a good point to use as a meeting place if the family separates to do different things. It's also a good place to catch the free electric shuttle that will take you downtown or around the waterfront (see below).

The main streets downtown are one way, running east and west. Santa Barbara is a dream to get around. There are signs to important points of interest. **Cabrillo Boulevard** leads you to most of the important streets.

A superb way to get around town is via the **Downtown/Waterfront Electric Shuttle** (☎ **805/683-3702**). This open-air shuttle follows two local routes: one running along the waterfront itself, from the harbor to the zoo, every half hour; and the other running up and down State Street as far as Sola Street, about every 10 to 15 minutes. The earliest service begins at 10am; waterfront service stops at 5pm, and State Street service ends at 6pm weekdays and 8pm on weekends. Summer hours are longer. Just stand under one of the round blue signs with the ship emblem and the shuttle will stop for you. A ride will cost you 25¢.

WHAT TO SEE AND DO

Santa Barbara lends itself to doing things leisurely, whether it's a slow ride along the bike path or a visit to the Santa Barbara Mission. This is a place to take your time, never feel rushed, and never feel you have to do "everything."

Bicycling

It seems that everyone in Santa Barbara has a bicycle, and bicycles here get plenty of use. Just about everywhere you look there are families pedaling those Italian Pedalinas, cute red four-wheel cycles with canvas tops. Junior (up to 50 pounds) sits in the front and Mom and Dad do all the work pedaling. But the Pedalinas aren't just limited to family fun. Teenagers like to rent them too, and go tooling down the beach with their friends.

A $3^1/_3$-mile two-lane bikeway, beginning on Cabrillo Boulevard, is easy to navigate and leads you through the beaches, crossing the boulevard at Milpas Street. Heading east, you'll come to the **Andree Clark Bird Refuge,** at 1400 E. Cabrillo Blvd., a 42-acre preserve of ducks and other waterfowl, and little islands dotting the lagoon. We like to spend an hour or so walking through the preserve on the footpath. On our way back, we sometimes ride to the Santa Barbara Zoo, but only when we've rented standard bikes rather than the Pedalinas. You can also ride up Stearns Wharf, the Fisherman's Wharf of Santa Barbara; but don't try it with the Pedalinas.

Bicycles are easy to rent in Santa Barbara. Stop at **Cycles-4-Rent,** 101 State St., one block from the dolphin statue at State Street and Cabrillo Boulevard (☎ **805/652-0462**). You can rent 1- and 6-speed beach cruisers and 21-speed mountain bikes. Beach cruisers rent for $4 and $6 per hour, and mountain bikes go for $7. Sixteen- and 18-speed tandems rent for $8, and Pedalinas are $10 an hour. Be sure to ask about half-day, full-day, and weekly rates. Bike locks, seatbelts for the front of the Pedalina, and child helmets come free. Additionally, Cycles-4-Rent has in-line skates, bike racks for autos, Joggettes, and Recumbent Triykes. Also ask about special winter weekday rates.

Open daily, 9am to 6pm weekdays, 8am to 8pm weekends. No reservations are accepted, but there's hardly ever a wait, even on summer weekends.

Cycles-4-Rent also operates out of Fess Parker's Red Lion Inn, from the Radisson Hotel, and at Lake Casitas. Bring ID (driver's license or passport) to expedite your rental.

Beach Rentals is located directly across the street from Stearns Wharf at 8 W. Cabrillo Blvd. (☎ **805/963-2524**). Besides 21-speed mountain bikes, Pedalinas, beach cruisers, and tandems, children's bikes, children's helmets, and child carriers for adult bikes are available here. Roller skates and in-line skates, in children's sizes too, may be rented. Bicycles run from $5 per hour for children's bikes to $7 and $8 an hour for the other bikes. Child seats are available on the $5 bikes. Skates cost $5 per hour. Delivery can be arranged for a minimum charge, but there are no reservations. Beach Rentals is open daily from 8am to 9pm in summer and 8am to 8pm in winter. Again, remember to bring ID.

Beaches

If you traveled from Los Angeles, you passed through Carpinteria. Just a few minutes outside Santa Barbara, the beach at **Carpinteria** (☎ **805/684-2811**) bills itself as the world's safest, and it's considered a wonderful family beach because of the calm waters and lack of riptides. There are concession stands and restrooms, and you can camp here (call MISTIX at **800/444-7275**). Parking is $5. Would-be surfers should get to **Rincon Point,** just south of Carpinteria Beach, famous for having perfect waves, and the best winter waves for surfers. As you continue north through Montecito, you'll come to **East Beach,** our favorite. Here you'll find dozens of volleyball nets and fun playground equipment. At the Cabrillo Bath House at East Beach (you can't miss it), you can rent just about anything you need for a day in the sun, including beach chairs, umbrellas, volleyballs, and boogie boards. A parking lot is adjacent, and there's a nice playground, food service, and restrooms. You'll see **Chase Palm Park** before you get to the pier, with its grassy areas perfect for playing Frisbee and having picnics. Just past the pier is **West Beach,** considered the best spot for windsurfing; parking and restrooms are available. Then comes **Leadbetter Beach,** with a parking lot, picnic areas, and restrooms. The Sea Cove Café, on the beach, is good for an outdoor snack. If you continue farther north, you'll come to **Arroyo Beach,** one of the nicest beaches in the area, with parking, picnic areas, and restrooms. You can surf here too.

Boating, Fishing, and Cruising

Harbor cruises are less available in Santa Barbara than elsewhere on the coast, but they are possible. **Captain Don's Harbour Cruises** (☎ **805/969-5217**) offers a fully narrated tour on the *Harbour Queen*. It's docked at Stearns Wharf across from Moby Dick's

Restaurant and offers a 40-minute cruise along the waterfront. The boat leaves daily in summer (June through October); weekends and holidays the rest of the year, weather permitting. It sails on the hour, from 11am to 6pm. The fare is $7 for adults, $5 for children of any age. Reservations aren't necessary.

Sailing is a wonderful activity to pursue in Santa Barbara, and you can partake of it even if you've never sailed before. **Navigators Channel Island Cruise,** 1621 Posilipo Lane (☎ **805/969-2393**), which meets at the Breakwater in front of the Yacht Club on Cabrillo Boulevard, will customize your sailing trip. Generally, they recommend either a midmorning luncheon sail or a midafternoon cocktail trip. The charge is $40 for adults, $20 for children under 12. There's a minimum of two people, a maximum of six, and an overall minimum charge of $100. They sail year round, depending on the weather, and reservations are necessary.

Windsurfing is another popular Santa Barbara sport. You can rent everything you need, or take lessons, from **Sundance Ocean Sport,** 2026 Cliff Dr. (☎ **805/966-2474**). Group lessons, given at West Beach Wednesday through Saturday, Easter through September, cost $40 per person for three hours; one-hour private lessons are $40. Call for reservations. Children must weigh at least 80 pounds and be 10 years or older. They also rent boogie boards, surfboards, and wetsuits for children and adults. Open daily from 10am to 6pm.

Santa Barbara Sailing Center, at the Breakwater (☎ **805/962-2826,** or toll free **800/350-9090**), rents sailboats from 21 to 50 feet. The fee is $20–$90 per hour with a minimum of two hours. Skippered charters can be arranged on a 30- or 50-foot sailboat. Call for prices. If you plan to stay in town at least a week, ask about signing up for sailing lessons ($35 per hour). Slick-looking jet boats for four can also be rented.

The 50-foot *Double Dolphin* catamaran sails afternoons on weekdays and weekends and costs $14.95 per person. Call for hours. Sunset cruises go out weekends from 6 to 8pm and cost $20 for adults, $12 for children. Call for reservations. A dinner cruise will cost $30 for adults, $21.95 for children. Open daily from 9am to 6pm, year-round.

Sail off into the Santa Barbara sunset on **Sunset Kidd's** 25-foot sailboat, on the Breakwater (☎ **805/962-8222**). The boat only takes six people at a time, so you'll get a very personal look at the area. One-hour cruises are only $12.50 per person; kids 9 or younger pay $10. The favorite is the two-hour trip at $22 per person, $20 for kids. There's also a sunset cruise available for a charge of $20 per person, adult or child. Bring along refreshments or nibbles on any of the trips. There's also a one-night/two-day trip to Santa Cruz Island which includes food and costs $85 each, based on four passengers. Life jackets in all sizes are provided on all trips. Reservations are required. The staff begins answering the phone daily at 7:30am.

Sea Landing, at Cabrillo Boulevard and Bath Street (☎ **805/963-3564**), offers a number of other possibilities appropriate for the whole family. You can arrange a half day of sportfishing, which is a fun thing to do with children. You'll take off on the 50-foot *Hornet* and stay within view of the coastline. Who knows what you'll catch, but they'll clean and package it for a small fee. There's even a galley on board with soft drinks and beer. Tackle is for sale. When you make your reservation, inquire about adult fishing licenses; children under 16 don't need one. Summers and weekends, your trip will be from 7am to noon or 12:30 to 5:30pm. Winter hours are 10am to 3pm. The half-day rates are $25 for adults, $20 for children under 12 and seniors (senior price weekdays only). Call for reservations.

If you're seeking yet an even more challenging excursion, Sea Landing will put you on the 65-foot *Seahawk*. You'll join a crew that goes out fishing for bass year round, or for yellowtail, albacore, and halibut in season. The *Seahawk* has a full galley serving food and drinks. Departures are daily, depending on the weather, and trips last from 7am to 3pm. Join the twilight fishing trip June through September from 5:30 to 10pm. The three-quarter-day trip costs $34.50 for adults, $29 for children under 12. The twilight trip costs $20 for adults, $15 for kids. Call for reservations.

The 88-foot *Condor* will whisk you away on one- and two-day island excursions to Santa Cruz, Santa Rosa, and San Miguel Islands. Visitors may only have time for the one-day trips. Call for dates. Adults are charged $65; children 12 and under pay $35. (See whale-watching information below.)

Those who scuba-dive will love it around Santa Barbara. Some companies go out to the Channel Islands from here. **Truth Aquatics,** at Sea Landing, is one. Write or call for information on the various packages which can run from one to five days: Truth Aquatics, Inc., Sea Landing, Breakwater, Santa Barbara, CA 93109 (☎ 805/962-1127).

Whale-Watching

Whale-watching is a Southern California obsession. Join the **Santa Barbara Museum of Natural History,** 2559 Puesta del Sol Rd., Santa Barbara, CA 93105 (☎ 805/682-4711), on its selected excursions in February and March. You can't make phone reservations, but call in advance to find out this year's dates and to request a form for a mail-in reservation. These are special trips, led by naturalists and museum docents, and they fill up early. On the vessel are hands-on displays of sea lion and otter pelts, barnacles, a killer whale tooth, and other items which will be discussed during the trip.

You'll leave on the *Condor* from Sea Landing at 9am, and the trip lasts 2^1/2 hours. Adults pay $22; children 12 and under, $12. These trips are appropriate for kids over 5.

The *Condor* also goes out on whale-watching trips not sponsored by the Museum of Natural History. Prices are the same. These trips (☎ 805/963-3564), sailing from the Sea Landing, Breakwater, are available from February to May 1, daily during the height of the season. There are three departures: at 9am, noon, and 3pm. The trips also last 2^1/2 hours.

Santa Barbara Zoo

The Santa Barbara Zoological Gardens, 500 Niños Dr., off Cabrillo Boulevard (☎ 805/962-5339, or 805/962-6310 for recorded information), is one of those places we return to again and again, not so much to see the animals, but because we like the atmosphere and because it's such a nice place to let the kids wander and play. In fact, one of the most delightful aspects of the zoo is the intricate, yet small, play area with equipment designed for children 3–10. We usually picnic on the sprawling grassy area and find it a relaxing experience.

The miniature train ride ($1 for adults, 50¢ for children) and the Discovery Area are especially popular with the young ones, who love to climb, crawl, and explore.

In the rest of the zoo, you will see wallabies, anteaters, pumas, toucans, sea lions, monkeys, elephants, giraffes, and many endangered species.

The zoo reflects the change in philosophy toward zoo animals. Sitting on 41 land-scaped acres, exhibits are designed to incorporate the natural habitat and enhance the outdoor feeling. Instead of chain-link fences and bars, the Santa Barbara Zoo uses moats

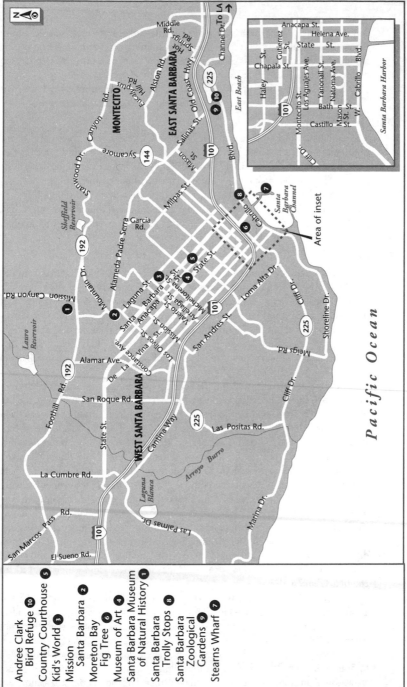

Santa Barbara

Andree Clark Bird Refuge 10
Country Courthouse 5
Kid's World 3
Mission Santa Barbara 2
Moreton Bay Fig Tree 6
Museum of Art 4
Santa Barbara Museum of Natural History 1
Santa Barbara Trolly Stops 8
Santa Barbara Zoological Gardens 9
Stearns Wharf 7

Pacific Ocean

and other more natural means to keep the animals apart from each other and from the people. We like to visit during the special training demonstrations held during the summer and on weekends. If you're lucky, you'll see them teach the elephants to do their routines. The zoo has a snack bar and a gift shop.

The zoo is open daily from 10am to 5pm (9am to 6pm in summer). Admission is $5 for those over 12, $3 for seniors and children 2–12; under 2, it's free.

Mission Santa Barbara

The tenth of the 21 Franciscan missions built in California, this "Queen of the Missions" was founded in 1786. You'll find it at the upper end of Laguna Street at East Los Olivos Street (☎ 805/682-4713 or 805/682-4715). Set in a striking locale overlooking the city, the mission is a beautiful structure built of Spanish, Moorish, and neoclassical elements, and its gardens are exceptionally lovely and tranquil. It's the only one of the 21 missions to be in continuous use as a parish church. The little rooms, gardens, chapel, and cemetery don't take long to see. Open daily from 9am to 5pm. You can take a self-guided tour for $2; children under 16 are free.

Museums

A visit to the **Santa Barbara Museum of Natural History,** 2559 Puesta del Sol Rd. (☎ 805/682-4711), set in lush Mission Canyon, is one way to get the kids out of the sun. Outside is a fascinating 72-foot touchable blue-whale skeleton, a sight that never fails to elicit "oohs" and "aahs" from our group. The museum houses information and displays about the Chumash tribe, prominent in these parts, a planetarium with programs every Saturday and Sunday, not appropriate for kids under 7; and many other permanent and changing exhibits, most of which focus on the Santa Barbara area.

The museum will take you from the beginnings of time to the future with its new Astronomy Center. The center is filled with the latest high-tech equipment, including touch screens and computer stations. Interpreters mingle with the visitors to help them sort out the hard-to-understand. "Star Games and Stories" is a lesson in constellations and how other cultures see them; "Journey to the Planets" puts space travelers on one of four planets to explore the differences; the "Time Tunnel" lets you know what other cultures saw in the skies at different periods of time. Kids get to walk through the inside of a telescope and can play with the images the astronomers work with in "Space Link." They can examine the skies at three computer stations, and even have their pictures taken in a cut-out of a real space suit on the moon. The Astronomy Center is open daily from noon to 4pm; admission is free with museum admission.

The museum is open Monday through Saturday from 9am to 5pm and on Sunday and holidays (except Christmas, Thanksgiving, and New Year's Days, and Fiesta) from 10am to 5pm. Admission is $4 for adults, $3 for teens and seniors, and $2 for children 12 and under.

The **Santa Barbara Museum of Art** is located in the heart of Santa Barbara at 1130 State St. (☎ 805/963-4364). This small, bright museum hosts a good collection of photographs, American and European paintings, ancient sculpture, and Asian art. Take the kids for an hour or two as a nice break in the day.

It's open Tuesday through Saturday from 11am to 5pm and on Sunday from noon to 5pm. On Thursday it stays open until 9pm, making it a possible after-dinner attraction. Admission is free on Thursday. Other days, adults pay $4; seniors $3; students and children $2.50; children under 6, free. Call for information about occasional Family Days and Sunday Family Fundays.

Santa Barbara Trolley Company

Trolleys are fun ways to see a city or get from one point to another. The **Santa Barbara Trolley** is no exception. Catch it at the dolphin statue, State Street and Cabrillo Boulevard (☎ 805/965-0353). The 90-minute narrated tours take you (not in this order) through Montecito, past the Court House, up State Street, and by the Botanic Gardens, make a stop at the Mission, and end back at Stearns Wharf. If your flock gets antsy, you can get on or off the trolley at any time along the route. Tours leave every 90 minutes beginning at 10am. Adults pay $4, while children 12 and under are charged $2, for an all-day pass. Don't confuse this with the free electric shuttles, which are strictly for transportation.

Festivals

For five days in early August each year, it's fiesta time in Santa Barbara. **Old Spanish Days in Santa Barbara** is an exciting community celebration created to preserve and perpetuate the city's heritage, which began with its Spanish roots. One of Santa Barbara's important fiestas was the 1820 celebration of the dedication of the Santa Barbara Mission—that's how far back these fiestas go. During the five-day celebration, there are two parades, including the Children's Parade with more than 2,000 children participating; a children's variety show; free performances; and a rodeo. Two special marketplaces are set up, and dancing goes on in the streets into the night. Contact the office of Old Spanish Days in Santa Barbara, 15 E. De La Guerra St. Mailing address: P.O. Box 21557, Santa Barbara, CA 93121-0557 (☎ 805/962-8101), for the dates of this year's fiesta. And if you plan to stay over during the fiesta, make reservations as far in advance as possible because the town gets booked up 100%.

The **Summer Solstice Celebration** takes place annually in June on the Saturday closest to the summer solstice. Consisting of a parade without advertisements, written words, motorized vehicles, or live animals, the parade moves downtown, then turns into a party at Alameda Park with dance, mimes, music, and theater performances.

Parks

A fine place to run off energy is **Kid's World,** at the corner of Micheltorena and Garden Streets in Alameda Park. More than 4,000 local volunteers helped build this delightful playground. Kids were asked what their dream playland would be, and many of their wishes were fulfilled. Suspension bridges, a tree house, mazes, and tunnels are all part of the fun. There's something for almost any age child. Park on the street.

Tours, Shops, and Gardens

There's still lots more to do here, some of which has to do with the striking architecture and mission history of the town. Visit the **Santa Barbara County Courthouse,** at 1100 Anacapa Street (☎ 805/962-6464), and ride up the 85-foot clocktower to the observation deck. Kids love to do this. The view from the top is absolutely exquisite. This unusually beautiful Spanish-Moorish courthouse was constructed in 1927–29 after the 1925 earthquake destroyed the original building. You can get a free guided tour of the courthouse Monday through Saturday at 2pm; on Wednesday and Friday there's an additional tour at 10:30am. Or visit the courthouse weekdays from 8am to 5pm, and on Saturday, Sunday, and holidays from 9am to 5pm. Admission is free.

If the kids are game, take them on the **Red Tile Walking Tour,** a 12-block tour of Santa Barbara historical landmarks. A map is available from the Visitor Information Center. Or after dinner, ride up to the parking lot of the Santa Barbara Mission. While the children play near the gurgling fountain, relax and watch the sun set over the city below you.

While you're downtown, take a stroll through **El Paseo,** the grand Spanish-style shopping arcade with entrances at 812-814 State St. and 813 Anacapa St. (☎ 805/ 962-8978). El Paseo is built around an actual adobe home of a prominent Santa Barbara family who lived there in 1827. The home is being renovated and will be open to the public. El Paseo was one of the nation's first shopping centers. At number 15-16 El Paseo you'll find the **Santa Barbara Toy & Craft Museum** (☎ 805/899-1231) with its displays of toys and collectibles from 1900 to 1990. Your entrance donation will go to the Pediatric AIDS Foundation. The museum is open daily from 10am to 6pm. While exploring El Paseo, you might stop for lunch at **El Paseo Restaurant,** which has been serving up Mexican dishes since 1922.

Just across the street from El Paseo is **Paseo Nuevo** (☎ 805/963-2202), on State Street between Canon Perdido and Ortega Streets, a two-block complex of shops, restaurants, cinema, and live theater. Nordstrom and the Broadway are the anchor department stores. For kids and teens there's The Gap, The Limited Too, and The Nature Company. Rudy's is great for take-out Mexican food, or you can sit down and be served at California Pizza Kitchen. The stores are open Monday through Friday from 10am to 9pm, Saturday until 7pm, and Sunday from 11am to 6pm. Parking is available in the parking structure.

State Street itself is overflowing with shops. Be sure to make a pilgrimage to the **Earthling Bookshop,** at 1137 State St. (☎ 805/965-0926). Along with scheduled children's events, there's a marvelous children's section where the kids can just plop themselves down and examine the latest books. While classical music plays in the background, Mom and Dad can sit near the fireplace for a five-minute look at this week's bestsellers, or grab a cup of coffee (or breakfast, lunch, or dinner) from the in-store café. Open Sunday through Thursday from 9am to 11pm, till midnight on Friday and Saturday.

Take a hike through the **Santa Barbara Botanic Garden,** 1212 Mission Canyon Rd. (☎ 805/682-4726). There are five miles of easy-to-walk self-guided nature trails to choose from. Lead the children through a wildflower meadow and cactus gardens to a canyon filled with coastal redwoods. You can cross a dam that dates back to 1806 and was built by Chumash Indians under the direction of the Mission padres. In fact, the Mission Creek was once a vital source of water to the Santa Barbara Mission. Bring along a picnic lunch.

Open daily from March to October on weekdays from 9am to 5pm, weekends to 6pm. The rest of the year, closing is one hour earlier. Admission is $3 for adults, $2 for teens 13–17 and seniors 55 and over, $1 for children 5–12; under 5, free. A trail map and children's activity book are available at the Admissions desk or in the Garden Shop. Docent-guided tours are offered daily at 2pm and also on Thursday, Saturday, and Sunday at 10:30am.

Drive over to Chapala and Montecito Streets to see what's considered the Northern Hemisphere's largest **Moreton Bay fig tree.** It is said that 10,000 people could stand in the shade of its branches at noon. The kids might find it interesting to know that it was planted as a seedling by a little girl in 1876 and it now has a branch spread of 160 feet.

If you're in town between June and September, take the family to an **outdoor concert** at the Alameda Park Bandstand, near the corner of Micheltorena and Santa Barbara Streets (☎ 805/963-0611). These family-oriented concerts make a lovely way to spend an hour. They are held on Sunday afternoon between 3 and 4pm. Free admission.

Stick around for the traditional Sunday **arts and crafts show** on Cabrillo Boulevard, which has been going on since 1966. More than 300 local artists in all media display their wares for sale from 10am until dusk.

After you've looked around, take a walk up **Stearns Wharf,** a three-block extension of State Street, a Santa Barbara landmark built in 1872, once used as a dock from which passengers were ferried to gambling boats. You might get an ice-cream cone at the **Great Pacific Ice Cream Company,** or have your palm read. Visit the **Sea Center** (☎ 805/962-0885) to view displays of the marine life of the Santa Barbara Channel. This joint project of the Natural History Museum and the Channel Islands National Marine Sanctuary intrigues children with sea specimens they can hold at the outdoor Touch Tank, which is open daily except Wednesday from noon to 4pm. The center is open daily from 10am to 5pm. Admission is $2 for adults, $1.50 for seniors, $1 for children 3–17; under 3, free. Or stop for fantastically fresh seafood at the **Santa Barbara Shellfish Co.** at the end of the wharf, where there are live shellfish tanks from which to choose crab and lobster. It opens at 10am. Watch the fog roll out from a window at **Moby Dick's,** or stop for a souvenir from one of the many shops on the wharf.

One of the best things to do at the wharf is to rent tackle at **Mike's Bait & Tackle,** next to the Shellfish Co., and spend the morning reeling "them" in at the end of the pier. We watched greedy pelicans line up for the fishermen's rejects, and kids who were somehow able to get the ubiquitous pigeons to perch on their arms.

Wharf parking is $2 per hour, or free for two hours with a validation.

WHERE TO STAY

As distances are not a problem in Santa Barbara, you'll pick your hotel based on cost and amenities. We've given you two or three good choices in each price category.

Deluxe

The **Four Seasons Biltmore,** 1260 Channel Dr., Santa Barbara, CA 93108 (☎ 805/969-2261, or toll free **800/332-3442;** fax 805/969-4212), is one of the best and certainly one of the most beautiful places in the deluxe category to stay with a family. Built as a private residence in the early 1900s, the Biltmore sits on 21 lush acres, with views of both the ocean and the Santa Ynez Mountains. The hacienda-style main building, the clusters of smaller individual cottages, the extraordinary gardens and walkways, the grand lobby, and Patio dining room are painstakingly maintained. Just walking through the gardens of fuchsias, roses, impatiens, tropical trees, and other plants, which you can tell have been here for years, brings a sense of serenity and is actually a perfect activity with a young child.

The hotel is very much geared toward families, as is evident by the young, energetic staff and the activities and amenities offered. On the grounds are tennis courts, shuffleboard, croquet, badminton, and a putting green, which may be used more by the kids than by the grownups. Bikes are available at no charge, starting with ones sized for 12-year-olds. A few child carriers and helmets are available.

Appropriately named "Kids for All Seasons," the Biltmore's complimentary summer children's program, for ages 5–12, is a great success. The program is offered daily throughout the summer months, and weekends the rest of the year with extended week-long activities during holidays. Kids under 5 are welcome if a parent stays with them. When the kids arrive, they receive their own registration packet and wrist-bracelet identification. Run by a fun-loving, energetic staff, the program combines water sports, arts and crafts, movies, and games, tailoring the program to the ages and desires of the children. Each week has a theme, such as Little Mermaid Beach Party or Teenage Mutant Ninja Turtles. A bright, spanking-clean activities room enables the kids to bake with the pastry chef, create masterpieces at the easels, and critique the latest movies.

There's also a supervised Star Fish program for children 5–12, which is often combined with the "Kids For All Seasons," but which focuses more on swimming. For this there are eight one-week sessions; kids can sign up for one day, a week, or the entire session. The program includes Red Cross swimming lessons, day trips, arts and crafts, tidepooling, beach games, and lunch. It runs weekdays from 10am to 3pm. The charge is $30 a day, or $125 a week.

At the press of a telephone button, you can secure many family amenities. A limited number of strollers are available, so when you reserve your room, let them know you'll need one. When you make your reservation, ask for a child's bathrobe to be included along with your standard terrycloth robe. The concierge will get you baby bottles, blankets, lotion, oil, powder, diapers, and shampoo. They'll also supply highchairs and playpens. Forget the toys? They have tons of toys, ranging from infants' playthings to board games, cards, children's videos, and a Nintendo system. Naturally, they can arrange babysitting.

In addition to a fenced-in pool on the hotel grounds, guests of the Biltmore can use the facilities at the refurbished Coral Casino across the street, which is also a private club. There's an Olympic-size swimming pool, actually one meter longer than Olympic regulations, and built that way to ensure that no events are ever held there, a sun deck, spas, and access to the beach. Choose from poolside food service, or takeout from the Raft, which features sandwiches and light meals.

The hotel's Patio restaurant is a pleasant dining room to share with the children. Set in a glass-enclosed courtyard with a retractable ceiling, the Patio is sunny and pleasant. Al fresco dining is available when weather permits. Adults can order salads, full entrees, and a few sandwiches. Some entrees, indicated by an asterisk, are calorie-, sodium-, and cholesterol-controlled. The children's menu is fun and has plenty of choices. How about French toast ($3.50)? "Tummy Ticklers" and "Hot Schtuff" include soup, chicken nuggets, pasta, and other usual offerings. Prices range from $1.50 for soup to $6.50 for grilled chicken breast, mashed potatoes, and vegetables. The Sunday brunch, an incredible spread in itself, has a special station just for the children. Room service is available 24 hours a day. Ask for children's selections.

If adults want a special night out alone, the elegant La Marina restaurant features nouvelle cuisine and a lovely panoramic view of the ocean.

Rooms at the Biltmore are generous in proportion and feel tropical and cool in the summer, warm and cozy in the winter. Standard poolside rooms are roomy and come with double or king-size beds, plantation shutters, ceiling fans, and an armoire containing the remote-control TV with cable and in-room movies. Waiting for every young arriving guest is a giant chocolate-chip cookie for munching, a famous Four Seasons trademark, and a glass of milk. Stocked minibars, terrycloth robes, full-length mirrors, hand-held hairdryers, makeup mirrors, and two telephones are additional amenities. The bathrooms have marble-top vanities. Downstairs poolside rooms have small brick patios designed to feel as though you have your own private garden. Upstairs rooms have balconies and cathedral ceilings. None of the rooms has air conditioning, but electric blankets, VCRs, and almost any other amenity you can think of are available. Cottages are popular with large families (but pricey). There are several configurations, and you can get up to a five-bedroom unit. They are bright and spacious, with lots of windows, huge walk-in closets, hide-a-beds, a full bathroom in the parlor unit, fireplaces, and patios with tables and chairs.

Standard rooms start at $295 for a garden view and go up to $350 for an ocean view. Cottage rooms without parlor are $325. Junior suites are $425, suites in the main building are $650, and cottage suites with a parlor are $695. Large suites go for $730–$1,700. (Prices for suites are based on one bedroom and a parlor.) There is no charge for an extra person or for children under 18. Cribs and rollaways are supplied free. Ask about special packages.

We hesitate to recommend the **San Ysidro Ranch,** 900 San Ysidro Lane (off U.S. 101), Montecito, CA 93108 (☎ **805/969-5046,** or toll free **800/368-6798;** fax 805/565-1995), as a family resort because it's such a wonderful romantic retreat. But not only do parents bring their children, some families hold reunions here. If your children don't need much entertaining, and you want to get away for a relaxing vacation, this is the place to go.

As you drive the winding roads to San Ysidro Lane, all city stress begins to disappear. This residential area of Montecito is glorious! Private homes are set behind tall hedges or fences on narrow countrylike lanes. The magnificent trees and flowers of Santa Barbara are at their most plentiful, and all you hear is the quiet. Then you pass stables and finally reach the ranch, which is really just ten minutes off the highway but seems like 30. There's a small lobby and a lounge, perfect for a game of billiards or for curling up with a good book. Original art and framed reprints line the walls, with stories about the celebrities who have stayed here, such as Vivien Leigh and Laurence Olivier, whose wedding was held at the ranch practically minutes after they received divorces from their former spouses. The resort has been a member of Relais & Châteaux since 1988.

When children check in at the Ranch, they get a personalized welcoming cookie, while parents get the family name branded on wood and placed on their cottage. But the children's amenities don't stop there: a child-size bathrobe is provided, bubble bath and toys can be requested, as can children's videos. Some cottages have pull-out couches, and rollaways are provided, each made up with themed sheets and blankets.

You'll discover that the grounds are for walking and exploring, and the parklike grassy areas are for playing. If you've brought your pet, which you can do, it may never want to leave. Trails leading through the mountains make good walks, or you can go on horseback with a guide. There are gardens everywhere, always blooming with bright purple, red, yellow, and white. Some of the plants are even taller than your toddler! The herb and vegetable garden used by the chef is in full view, and there's a little lawn-bowling area. The playground area includes a clubhouse, ladders, swings, and other play equipment.

It will be hard to keep your mind on tennis at one of the two courts, because each has a pretty good view of the ocean. Better to take the kids to the heated pool, which has a very small wading area for little children, but a glorious ocean view on a clear day. At the pool is a health club facility, a massage room, and a par course. There's poolside food service and drinks, and the children's menu is posted.

San Ysidro's Camp SYR runs daily in summer and during major holidays. The complimentary program runs from 9am to 3pm. Days are filled with pony rides and basic riding instruction, plus hiking, roping, and panning for gold in a nearby creek. Kids learn about the Chumash Indians and their ways of communication, swim, and have lunch.

In keeping with the Ranch's Hollywood history, young versions of Orson Welles learn to write, direct, and shoot their own films on video. They then get to reap their rewards at a mini-Oscar ceremony in the hacienda.

If they still need more activity, they can visit the petting zoo at the horse stables, where chickens, rabbits, a dwarf goat, and a pot-bellied pig reside.

The resort's Stonehouse Restaurant is known far beyond Santa Barbara for its great food. It's open for breakfast, lunch, and dinner, and has an outdoor patio for warm-weather dining. The award-winning American regional cuisine offers up a variety of selections for adult tastes.

The Plow and Angel Pub features more informal dining but the menu is the same as the Stonehouse. This eatery is open every night from 5pm. On those nights you have a babysitter, this is a good place to go for live jazz on Thursday and Friday from 8 to 11pm.

The children benefit, too, from the gourmet kitchen with special entrees served on tin dishes in portions perfect for their size. Selections are available in both restaurants, at the pool, and via room service.

No matter which restaurant you choose, be sure to leave room for the truly tummy-pleasing desserts like baked custard with burnt-sugar crust, hot apple brown Betty with maple cream, or peanut butter ice-cream sundae with hot fudge.

The cottages at the San Ysidro Ranch are not glitzy; rather, they're quietly elegant in that sort of "old money" way, decorated in an understated casual country decor. The 21 cottages offer 44 guest rooms and suites and come in all sorts of configurations. Some are totally private; some are attached to others. All have wood-burning fireplaces and private decks, color TV with cable HBO and VCRs. You can use the hotel movies or bring your own. Refrigerators are found in each room. Bathrooms have been updated. Thirteen cottages have private Jacuzzis. One sumptuous cottage has a deck the full length of the cottage, overlooking a small canyon and bubbling creek; plus it has a huge living room with a massive fireplace, a dining area, a wet bar, and a large bedroom with a king-size bed. Still another has a wonderful ocean view from the deck, and the Jacuzzi is hidden behind high doors.

A standard room would be fine for a couple with an infant—there's plenty of room for a crib, which must be arranged for in advance. Your best bet is a one-bedroom suite, but they do offer rollaways if one isn't available. Standard rooms without Jacuzzis are priced at $195. Deluxe cottage rooms cost $365. One-bedroom suites cost $450–$625; two-bedroom units, $525–$730. Cottages with private Jacuzzis start at $425. There's no charge for children or extra adults. A two-night minimum applies on weekends.

Moderate

Fess Parker's Red Lion Resort, 633 E. Cabrillo Blvd., Santa Barbara, CA 93103 (☎ **805/564-4333,** or toll free **800/879-2929** or **800/RED-LION;** fax 805/962-8198), one of the newest of Santa Barbara hotels. You can't miss it as you drive up Cabrillo Boulevard—it's the one painted that gorgeous pink with the huge rotunda in front. Set across the street from the beach and minutes from the zoo and town, the Red Lion is a most convenient place to stay. A nearby Scolari's market on Milpas, open 24 hours, is stocked with everything you might need for the children or for a picnic.

There are no children's programs here, but there is a big, heated, fenced-in pool and spa open from 7am to 11pm and a small game room with video and pinball machines. Poolside barbecues are held on the weekends, and Pedalinas, standard bikes, and in-line skates are available for rent poolside. The three night-lighted tennis courts cost $8 per hour (lessons available for a nominal charge). Adults can use the health club and saunas. There's also a putting green, shuffleboard court, and full-court basketball. Call the concierge to arrange fishing trips, golf, whale-watching, or sailing. Babysitting can be arranged.

The place to take the family to eat is Café Los Arcos, the big open-air restaurant adjacent to the lobby. The children's selections are limited, but adequate. An egg, cereal, or chocolate-chip pancakes are offered for breakfast ($2.25–$3.50). Lunch and dinner choices consist of fish and chips, the ubiquitous burger, a broiled chicken breast, or peanut butter and jelly. Prices start at $2.25 and go to $4.25. The adults in the group can pick from a number of standard offerings. The restaurant is open from 6am to 11pm, to midnight on weekends. Room service has similar hours.

The standard rooms at the Red Lion are oversize. With two queen-size beds or a king-size one, there's still plenty of room for a crib and for moving around. An armoire holds a minibar and the remote-control color TV, which comes with cable, the Family Channel, and HBO, as well as pay-per-view movies. There are double vanities in every room, and tub/shower combinations. The bathtubs are the tiniest we've ever seen, making it more of a shower-only bathroom. But what a perfect size for bathing a baby! If you're on the second or third floor with a toddler, request a stuccoed balcony or no balcony. The ones with wrought-iron fences are too dangerous! There are 335 rooms and 25 suites in this hotel, so you shouldn't have a problem getting what you request.

Deluxe rooms with two queen-size beds or a king-size bed are even more spacious and include a small sitting area with love seat and reading chair. The bathrooms in these rooms are huge, and the tub could accommodate two people easily. If you're traveling with a large family, or need the space to spread out, definitely request a deluxe room (the difference in price isn't that great). There are also studio, parlor, and executive suites available. All units are air-conditioned and soundproof, and there is same-day laundry and dry-cleaning service.

Rates (single or double occupancy) for standard rooms with two queen-size beds or one king-size bed are $189, $219, and $269, depending on view; deluxe rooms with two queen-size beds or a king-size bed cost $239 and $289; suites run $345–$700. Children under 18 stay free in their parents' room; additional adults pay $15. Rollaways cost $15 per night; cribs are free. Ask about package plans.

The mission–style **Radisson Santa Barbara Hotel,** 1111 E. Cabrillo Blvd., Santa Barbara, CA 93103 (☎ **805/963-0744,** or toll free **800/325-3535;** fax 805/962-0985), is decorated in soft desert hues and outfitted with casual wood furniture. If you're traveling with the family, you can't beat the location: across from East Beach and the beach's playground equipment, down the street from the beach's great volleyball nets, and within walking distance of the Santa Barbara Zoo.

There's a small fenced-in, heated pool at the hotel, and an excercise room for guests over 16. Bike rentals are available on the property on weekends.

Room service runs from 6:30am to 10pm, and there's poolside food service. Zack's at the Beach is the hotel's restaurant, open from 6:30am to 10pm. The breakfast menu is extensive and includes a breakfast buffet. There's a children's menu at breakfast, lunch, and dinner. Mom and Dad get to pick from various American regional cuisine offerings. For early risers there's complimentary coffee service in the lobby from 6 to 9am.

Rooms at the Radisson vary in size, and all have queen- or king-size beds. If you need a larger room, indicate this when you make your reservations. Remember the wrought-iron-fenced balconies are not safe for very young children. Patio rooms are available upon request. And we suggest that if you or the kids are light sleepers, request a room away from the parking lot.

The room with a king-size bed is not very big, although it can fit a rollaway or a crib. Double-bedded rooms will accommodate a family of three or four. Large families should know that there are lots of connecting rooms, as well as two suites of different sizes, including one with a kitchenette. The rooms are light and bright with adobelike walls, and come with an armoire housing the TV and juice-stocked minibar, full-length mirrors, clock radios, and Spectravision. The Radisson is one of the few area hotels with air conditioning. No-smoking rooms can be requested.

Room rates from the end of April to the end of June are $139–$199, single or double; from July 1 to the end of October, $149–$219; the remainder of the year, $129–$179. Suites are $420 and $650. Children under 17 stay free in their parents' room; those 17 and over, and extra adults, pay $20 each per night. Cribs are free, but rollaways cost $20. Ask about special package rates.

The Radisson also owns a 24-unit budget hotel called the **Parkside Inn**, a two-minute walk from the Radisson. Guests there have full use of the main hotel amenities, including room service. Reservations for the Parkside are made through the local Radisson number. Standard rooms are small, with double beds, TVs, balconies, and small bathrooms. A mini-suite offers a separate bedroom with a queen-size bed and a small living area with a hide-a-bed. Rates run $89–$124, depending on the season.

If you plan to be in Santa Barbara for a lengthy stay, ask the Radisson reservationist about the five apartments that can be rented, for a minimum stay of one month. These four one-bedroom units and one two-bedroom unit are fully furnished and come with twice-weekly maid service.

You'll find the **Harbor View Inn** directly across the street from Stearns Wharf, at 28 W. Cabrillo Blvd., Santa Barbara, CA 93101 (☎ **805/963-0780** or toll free **800/755-0222;** fax 805/963-7967), within walking distance of restaurants, bicycle-rental shops, and the beach.

The Harbor View has a lovely pool area, very comfortable for families. A large grassy area tempts Frisbee players, or your most energetic toddlers. The heated pool and spa are fenced in and surrounded by glass for protection from ocean winds. Complimentary wine, cheese, and lemonade are served in the afternoon, and a pot of coffee is always perking in the lobby. Even newspapers are complimentary each morning. Vending machines offer lots of snacks, and there's even a fruit-juice machine. There's no room service. Besides the restaurants within walking distance, Eladio's, the hotel's restaurant, is just next door and serves breakfast, lunch, and dinner. Hotel guests receive their complimentary continental breakfast at Eladio's in addition to a 10% discount on any food purchases.

No matter what hotel wing you choose, you'll find immaculate rooms. In the motel-style west wing of the hotel the rooms are small, but the light-wood furniture and the pastel furnishings make them very comfortable. Two-bedded rooms are available, and there are adjoining accommodations. There's no air conditioning in this wing, something rarely needed with the ocean breezes coming from just across the street. If you can afford it, request the partial ocean-view room, which has a king-size bed, a seating area with room for a crib, and a little refrigerator. Rooms in the west wing cost $85–$100; those with an ocean view go for $135.

In the three-story east wing, the air-conditioned rooms are larger and open to wide, quiet hallways. These rooms have in-room safes and small refrigerators. Third floor rooms have cathedral ceilings, and some offer wet bars, or sunken tubs. Desks, love seats, and comfortable upholstered reading chairs complete the picture. Ocean-view rooms are luxurious and spacious. In the east wing you'll pay $150–$165; ocean-view units are $200–$215.

Rooms at the Harbor View have king-, queen- or double-size beds, direct-dial phones, and color TVs. One-day laundry service is available. Babysitting is by referral. There are no rollaways; cribs are free. Each additional person over age 5 is charged $15. Parking is free.

For years, families have been heading for the blue-tiled roofs of the **Miramar Hotel,** U.S. 101 at San Ysidro Road (P.O. Box M), Santa Barbara, CA 93102 (☎ **805/ 969-2203** or toll free **800/322-6983;** fax 805/969-3163); take Calif. 1 to the San Ysidro turnoff. The two pools, rooms right on the beach, grassy play areas, and roomy cottages have created its popularity, and the location of the Miramar can't be beat. The rooms have been refurbished, but the decor is nothing to shout about. Soon the lobby will go through a major renovation.

In addition to the two pools, in summer the hotel anchors a raft off the beach for guest use. You can get beach umbrellas, backrests, and mats from the ever-present lifeguard. You can also rent bikes and play tennis, paddle tennis, table tennis, or shuffleboard.

Your children will love the authentic railcar that sits near the tennis courts, and has been turned into a diner. It's a good place for hamburgers, shakes, sandwiches, and salads. Eat there or take your food out to the beach. There's also a full-service dining room (The Terrace), open for breakfast, lunch, and dinner right next to the lobby; and a lobby bar. Room service is available from 7am to 1:45pm and from 6 to 9:45pm.

You can choose from poolside rooms, downstairs with one double bed and one twin bed or upstairs with two double beds. All have color TV and standard cable, a small desk and a dressing area, table and chairs, and tub/shower combinations. There's definitely room for a crib or rollaway. Lanai rooms have sliding glass doors that look out to the ocean. Oceanfront rooms are big, with two double beds, a rattan desk, and deck chairs on the outside patio. Not only is there room for a crib, but these units can connect with a parlor that sleeps two and has a full kitchen. This could then connect to yet another bedroom, making it a full suite that could sleep ten. The two-story oceanfront buildings are fronted by a big old wooden boardwalk that was originally an actual pier.

Cottages come in various configurations. You can get a one-bedroom cottage, with a king-size bed in the bedroom and a living room with a fireplace, or one with a partitioned semiprivate bedroom. A small kitchenette is equipped with a refrigerator and stove. This could also connect to two more bedrooms, making it a three-bedroom cottage. Most cottages have small wood decks. Parking is available for one car per cottage.

Light sleepers should note that a train comes through the grounds in the middle of the night. Request a room away from the tracks if you think you'll wake up from it.

Rates for singles or doubles are $70–$135. One-, two-, and three-bedroom cottages are $115–$285. Children 12 and under stay free in their parents' rooms; those over 12, and additional adults, pay $8 each per night. Cribs cost $8; some rollaways are available. There's a two-night minimum on weekends May to October, three nights on holidays.

The **Casa del Mar** (formerly the Sandman at the Beach), 18 Bath St., Santa Barbara, CA 93101 (☎ 805/963-4418, or toll free 800/433-3097; fax 805/966-4240), is a real find. Newly refurbished, the whole place is now brighter and airier. There's no pool, but the beach is a block away. A fenced-in spa is the centerpiece of the courtyard, which is filled with flowers and tropical plants.

The newly decorated lobby offers a generous space with tables for the complimentary "extended" continental breakfast of cereal, muffins, bagels, and juices. Wine and cheese are served in the evening, and the coffee is perking all day.

From the outside it looks small, but inside you'll find a variety of room configurations to fit most families. The rooms here aren't fancy, but they are clean and well priced. Room choices include five rooms with queen-size beds, two rooms with either a king-size and a queen-size bed or with two queen-size beds, and three rooms with king-size beds and hide-a-beds. Other choices are: seven rooms with a king-size bed, six also with kitchens; and three two-room suites, one with one bathroom and two with two bathrooms.

Our favorite room is no. 38, a second-story, two-room suite fronting the courtyard. The furniture is modern bamboo. The main room is quite large, with a king-size bed, a sofa that converts to a double bed, a big walk-in closet, fireplace, TV, and two reading chairs. The second room comes with a queen-size bed, making ample sleeping room for six. A big advantage for families is the full-size kitchen. Color TVs, a special AT&T phone system enabling calls to come directly to your room, wall heaters, and clock radios are standard. There's a covered parking area and a small parking lot near the courtyard.

Room rates in summer, double occupancy, run $104–$179 (for two rooms with two baths). In winter, rooms go for $59–$149. Holiday rates are slightly higher. Kitchens are free. Children 12 and under stay free; those over 12 and additional adults pay $10 per night. Weekends are almost always booked, so call in advance. If you're planning a weekday visit, ask whether special rates are in effect. There are also weekly and monthly rates. The inn participates in the city's "free nights" program.

Budget

Just across the street from Casa del Mar is the **Eagle Inn,** 232 Natoma Ave., Santa Barbara, CA 93101 (☎ 805/965-3586, or toll free 800/767-0300; fax 805/966-1218), a Spanish-colonial apartment building converted into a hotel, where the rooms have remained the size of small apartments. These spacious vacation apartments are a good buy, especially for large families. There's no pool, but you get free use of an athletic club a 10-minute walk away. The inn is also within walking distance of the beach, and has its own parking lot. A complimentary breakfast is served every morning.

Only two of the suites are without kitchens, but those have refrigerators. The rest offer a full-size, fully equipped kitchen with an eating area. Units are varied: Some have small separate bedrooms and living areas with sofa beds; others have a queen-size bed and one or two twin beds in one large room. They all come with direct-dial phones and cable TV with a free movie channel. Because there's no elevator, the rooms are not really handicapped-accessible.

Rates in winter are $60–$115; in summer, $70–$130, or $490–$665 per week.

The **Motel 6** in Santa Barbara, 443 Corona del Mar, Santa Barbara, CA 93103 (☎ **805/564-1392** or **505/891-6161;** fax 805/963-4687), has as its claim to fame the distinction of being the first Motel 6 ever built. Because of its wonderful location, within walking distance of the beach and behind the Radisson Santa Barbara, it's always booked, so you must make reservations far in advance. There's a small, gated, heated pool near the parking lot, and lots of vending machines.

This 30 plus-year-old motel has 51 rooms, five of which are designated no-smoking. Upstairs are some connecting rooms (a single connects with a double) and a few with partial ocean views. Singles have room for a crib; it would be a tight squeeze in a double; you'd be better off to get connecting rooms. Some rooms are handicapped accessible. There are color TVs with a movie channel, phones with free local calls, and little dressing areas. Shower stalls are standard. The rooms are clean and tidy, and the maids even use a room-deodorizing spray after each stay, eliminating most of that "motel smell."

You can't beat these rates anywhere: $47.99 single and double. Children under 17 sleep free in the same room as their parents. Cribs, when available, are free.

An Alternative

A unique stay in Santa Barbara is offered through the **University of California at Santa Barbara Vacation Center,** University of California, Santa Barbara, CA 93106 (☎ **805/893-3123;** fax 805/893-4918). You don't have to be an alum of UCSB to sign up for this "family camp." For a week at a time, usually in July and August, families can enjoy tennis, golfing, swimming, a fitness program, entertainment, even faculty seminars and educational programs geared to all ages. It's a chance to participate together as a family: The program offers hikes, carnivals, campfire sing-alongs, talent shows, and other family programs. A fully equipped crafts center offers free instruction daily. Mom and Dad also get wine tasting, casino nights, and tours. With the package comes tennis, golf, and swimming instruction, plus aerobics and aquacize. If these activities aren't enough, there are 21 weekly tournaments from backgammon to tennis.

An extensive childcare program accommodates infants through teens, generally from 9am to 9pm. The counselors, many of whom are students of education and child development at the university, are selected from hundreds of applicants and usually spend several summers working at the center.

Families stay in one of several residential complexes. Each family is assigned its own suite, which contains two to four bedrooms, a private bath, living room, and refrigerator. Some of the units have ocean or mountain views. Three meals a day, with choice of entree and unlimited second helpings, and daily maid service are included.

Weekly rates are $560 for alums, $590 for non-alum/adults, $465 for kids 6–11, $395 for children 2–5, and $260 for infants age 1–23 months. The daily rate for one to three days is $75 per day for adults, $50 for kids.

A Little Bit Far Away but Worth It

Two miles south of Solvang lies **The Alisal Guest Ranch,** 1054 Alisal Rd, Solvang, CA 93463 (☎ **805/688-6411,** or toll free **800/425-4725;** fax 805/688-2510), a 10,000-acre guest ranch/resort set within sight of the Santa Ynez Mountains.

Families can enjoy golf, tennis, horseback riding (kids need to be at least 7 to ride), sailing, swimming and fishing on the stocked lake. All the equipment necessary for fishing and watersports can be rented. Youngsters can play around the large pool and Jacuzzi, and there's a wide-screen TV and Ping-Pong and pool tables nearby.

Seasonal children's programs include junior golf school, horseback riding, arts and crafts and lake programs. Some of the most popular activities are the Kid's mini–lakeside dinners and breakfast rides. In the evening, talent shows, movies, bingo, and other programs are scheduled. Babysitting can be arranged.

The Alisal is on the Modified American Plan (MAP), meaning that breakfast and dinner are included in the room charge. Men must wear jackets to dinner, but lunch is a more casual affair at the snackbar near the pool.

Immaculate, comfortable bungalows come with wood-burning fireplaces, refrigerators, and coffee makers, but you won't find TVs or telephones. Perfect family accommodations are the two-room lofts that sleep four and have a king-size bed and two studio beds, plus $1^1/2$ baths. A three-room bungalow with a youth room is furnished with a king-size bed, four twin beds, one youth bed, two baths, a front porch, and a wet bar.

The rates for a studio are $245 single and $285 double. Two room suites cost $325 double. Each additional person between ages 3–5 is charged $40 per night, age 6 and older, $65 per night. The price includes meals. Cribs are complimentary. Reserve rooms well in advance for summer and holiday stays. Remember: Recreational activities like trail rides and greens fees cost extra. Ask about special all-inclusive packages available from September through May.

WHERE TO EAT

Many of the restaurants in town, especially those lining State Street, post their menus outside so that you can decide for yourself whether there is something appropriate for the whole family.

We discovered **Piatti,** 516 San Ysidro Rd. in Montecito (☎ **805/969-7520**), quite by accident; look for it at the end of the little shopping center. It's trendy, suburban, rustic, and contemporary all rolled into one. The cuisine is Italian trattoria style. There's indoor and al fresco dining, a small open-air kitchen which fascinated Janey, and a young, extremely professional serving staff. Booster seats are provided.

The food is delicious and fresh. There are familiar choices, such as angel-hair pasta with fresh tomatoes, basic, garlic, and olive oil ($8.95), and ravioli filled with spinach and ricotta ($9.50), as well as many specialties: cannelloni ($11.75), a rotisseried chicken ($11.95), fresh mussels and clams in a tomato broth ($13.50), and lasagne al pesto made with grilled zucchini, tomato pasta, sun-dried tomatoes, pine nuts, and assorted cheeses, at $11.25. Salads are enticing; there's a nice selection of antipasti, and several pizza and calzone selections are baked in their special oven. These range in price from $7.50 to $9.75. Prices are lower at lunch.

Children often split the pizza, salad, or spaghetti, we're told. The restaurant serves lots of kids at Saturday and Sunday lunch; for dinner, the best time to come with kids is usually between 5 and 7pm.

Piatti is open for lunch seven days from 11:30am to 4:30pm. Dinner is Sunday through Thursday from 5 to 10pm, on Friday and Saturday until 11pm. Reservations are accepted. Major credit cards are honored. There is a parking lot.

You'll find **Tony Roma's,** 26 W. Anapamu St. (☎ **805/963-3278**), a good choice for a family dinner. A statement on the menu reads, "Children are our special guests at Tony Roma's, too. That's why we have a special menu just for kids." Can't get more welcoming than that, can you?

If you've been to a Tony Roma's in another city, you'll recognize the menu selections. Regular menu offerings list lunch and dinner portions of the famous ribs, barbecued chicken, salads, sandwiches, and fish. Dinner is much of the same. Prices are moderate. Salads are $7, ribs average $8 for a lunch portion, $11.95 for the dinner size. Other dinner items range from $6 to $14. There is a full bar and an extensive wine list.

The kid's choices are simple: chicken fingers, a hamburger, child's portion of ribs, or chicken in a basket—all with fries, and priced between $2.95 and $4.95. Kid-style drinks can be ordered, too. They're all made with a mix of juice and soda or cream. Little ones get entertained with crayons and little table toys.

The Santa Barbara location also offers a barbecue Sunday brunch with complimentary champagne. It comes with made-to-order omelets, salads, fish, French toast, breakfast meats and potatoes, a variety of appetizers, and just-baked breads and desserts. Adults are charged $9.95; kids under 10, $3.95.

Servers will warm bottles and baby food. Highchairs and booster seats are available. Seating is indoors or out.

The restaurant is open Sunday through Thursday from 11am to 10pm. Sunday brunch is served from 10:30am to 2:30pm. On Friday and Saturday the restaurant stays open till 11pm. Reservations are accepted. When you call, ask about weekly specials. When we were last there, they had an all-you-can-eat rib night for $12.99. Take-out and delivery are also options. Major credit cards are honored. Park on the street or in City Lot No. 5 behind the restaurant.

Woody's Beach Club & Cantina may be a little off the beaten path at 229 W. Montecito St. (☎ **805/963-9326**), but it's lively, fun, and the price is right! Sawdust covers the floor, red-and-white checked plastic tablecloths cover the tables, and there's a big-screen TV for entertainment. Walls are lined with old skis and license plates, pails, signs, and more. There's plenty for little eyes to look at while you stand in line to place your order.

The Kids' menu for little buddies under 12, includes a turkey dog, a kidburger, Dino ribs, or quesadilla ($1.95–$2.95). Kids' choices come with a soft drink and fries.

There are lots of selections for grownups: ribs, chicken, barbecued beef, turkey, tri-tip, hamburgers, pizza, pasta and salads, fries and bread. Woody's prices are anywhere from $4.25 to $20. Beer (including microbrew beers) and wine are served.

Highchairs are plastic wrapped! There are also booster seats. They will warm bottles and baby food, and will even deliver to your hotel.

Woody's is open Monday through Saturday from 11am to 11pm and on Sunday from 11am to 10pm; closed Christmas Day. During Fiesta, check the hours. You can make reservations on weeknights only. Most major credit cards accepted. Street parking, or park in the car lot across the street after 5pm.

The **Harbor Restaurant,** 210 Stearns Wharf (☎ **805/963-3311**), is the wharf's not-too-nautical restaurant. It's really quite comfortable, with booths and tables overlooking the water. A children's menu, for youngsters 12 and under, offers the usual hamburger, grilled cheese, and peanut butter and jelly sandwiches ($1.95–$3.95). But it also has fried shrimp, chicken tenders, and fish and chips ($3.95–$6.95). For adults, lunch selections include soups and salads, pasta, sandwiches, and fish. You'll pay anywhere from $5.95 for a salad to $19.95 for a complete meal featuring sirloin steak.

Dinner prices are quite dear. Paella is pegged at $24.95, and other specials and regular dishes of chicken, steak, or seafood run $14.95–$25.95.

The casual, upstairs **Longboard's Grill** features lighter fare like fish and chips, burgers, salads, and sandwiches, plus the children's menu. Eat inside or outside. Highchairs and booster seats are provided.

The Harbor is open for lunch Monday through Saturday from 11:30am to 2:30pm. Sunday brunch is offered from 10:30am to 2:30pm. Dinner service Monday through Thursday is from 5:30 to 10pm, on Friday and Saturday to 11pm. Longboard's is open Monday through Thursday from 11:30am to 11pm, on Friday and Saturday from 11:30am to midnight (to 2am nightly for cocktails), and on Saturday and Sunday for breakfast from 8 to 11:30am. Major credit cards are accepted. Complimentary valet parking is available on the wharf.

Moby Dick's (☎ 805/965-0549) is Stearns Wharf's answer to the nautical coffee shop. This casual seaside restaurant, with its rough wood floors, wood beams, and uncomplicated menu, located near the end of Stearns Wharf, affords a great view. Breakfast, which is served until 11am, offers pigs in a blanket served with applesauce, Belgian waffles, omelets, eggs, pancakes, French toast, and hot cereal with brown sugar, raisins, and cream. You can even get yogurt with fresh fruit, honey, and wheat granola. Prices start at $1.75 and go to $16 for steak and eggs.

For lunch there are hot and cold sandwiches, salads, fried seafood, and hamburgers ($4–$11). At dinner you can get full entrees served with soup or salad, rolls, and baked potato, rice, or french fries. Entrees include sweet-and-sour shrimp, stuffed sole, grilled Maryland crab cakes, and grilled salmon, halibut, or swordfish. Or you can get seafood linguine with Alfredo sauce or with a marinara topping, a New York steak, or fried chicken, as well as fried seafood ($8.50–$16). The kids can have any of those entrees, if they can finish them, or order from the children's menu for youngsters under 12. That menu includes a four-ounce chopped steak, fried shrimp, or fish and chips, all served with french fries, sliced tomatoes, milk or a soft drink, and frozen yogurt; entrees are $4.25 and $4.50.

There are sassy seats, boosters, and highchairs. Baby bottles can be warmed.

Open daily from 7am to 8:30pm. Reservations are accepted. Major credit cards welcome. Park on the wharf and get a validation at the front desk.

Get ready for a stroll down memory lane when you visit **Be Bop Burgers,** 111 State St. (☎ 805/966-1956) a block from Stearns Wharf. Be Bop is sort of an indoor drive-in from the '50s, and it's perfect for *all* your children, from infants to teens. Rather than pulling in and ordering food from your car, though, you'll pull into parking spaces labeled with names from the past—you might park in Elvis's spot, or maybe Chuck Berry's or one of the Beatles'.

Here, '50s-style booths, set up like record listening booths with tables in the shape of 45s, line the walls. When it's crowded or if there's a private party, table hop service is provided in the back by servers on roller skates. On weekends, a live DJ takes requests and MC's trivia, Hula Hoop, and bubble gum bubble–blowing contests. A wall of top hits of the "golden age" of rock 'n' roll will test your memory while the kids eye the classic car on display. Got your camera? A Surfin U.S.A. scene offers a photo opportunity. When you place your order you don't get a number for your pickup, you get a name. Ours was "teen queen" one day, "Be Bop baby" on the next visit.

Now for the food—read "cheap!" You can get your before-beach breakfast here starting at 7am. Eggs, bacon, and pancakes will cost you only $1.95, while French toast, an egg, and bacon is only $2.40. Other choices include omelets, pancakes, ham and eggs, and a burger breakfast. Lunch and dinner offer typical drive-in picks: The Great Pretender's Chicken Tenders ($3.95), It's My Party Patty Melt ($3.25), tons of burgers (none over $4.70), turkey and veggie burgers (a bow to the '90s), salads, and finger foods. A large order of more Fun Fries costs $2.50 and comes in a Be Bop Blaster (megaphone) for keeping. Surprisingly, there's also a "Smaller Appetites" (children's) menu. Grilled cheese and Howdy Doody peanut butter and jelly, corn dog, and hot dog (with fries) are priced no higher than $1.95.

Now, are you ready for desserts? Have the kids try to say this five times before they get to order it: banana fanna moe manna banana split! Shakes are pretty outrageous: pick from those made with banana, Oreo cookies, or pineapple, plus regular flavors. And there are plenty more to make this a place to stop for a snack. Sassy seats and booster seats are available. This is a no-smoking restaurant.

Be Bop Burgers is open weekdays from 7am to 10pm, on weekends until 11pm. Breakfast is available until 11am. Some major credit cards are accepted. Parking is free in the lot.

La Super-Rica, 622 N. Milpas St. (☎ 805/963-4940), has been around for a while, but we just discovered it on a recent trip. Look for it at the corner of Cota and Milpas Streets—it's where you'll see the people lining up to order. Place your order at the window, then grab a wooden table and wait to be called. This tiny, fast-food-style taco stand serves up some of the best tacos we've ever tasted. Forget those store-bought crispy shells—these soft tacos are fresh and homemade.

A taco on two corn tortillas will cost you $2.10. One is enough for a young child; adults might want to order two or more. Lomito suizo, marinated pork with melted cheese and two corn tortillas, goes for $2.90. The most expensive thing on the menu is the Super-Rica Special: roasted chile pasilla with cheese combined with charcoal-broiled marinated pork and three tortillas; this runs $5.10. A daily special might be enchiladas del plaza: corn tortillas filled with potatoes, mushrooms, red chile sauce, and avocado. Mexican and domestic beer is available; sodas are 95¢.

Open daily from 11am to 9:30pm. The parking lot is quite small, but there is street parking—be sure to check the parking restriction signs.

In Summerland

The **Big Yellow House,** 108 Pierpont Ave., Summerland (if traveling south, take the Summerland exit off U.S. 101; north, take Evans Ave.) (☎ 805/969-4140), is a good choice for breakfast, lunch, or dinner, and is only a few minutes from Montecito. The service is efficient and friendly. The house itself, which is more than 100 years old, has an interesting history. Read all about it on the menu. In fact, read the story aloud to the kids.

Besides the standard French toast and buttermilk pancakes for breakfast, there are also design-your-own omelets, homemade corned beef hash, huevos rancheros, and standard egg dishes. Breakfast prices run $3–$9 (omelets average $6).

In an Emergency

If a medical emergency should arise during your stay in Santa Barbara, there's a 24-hour emergency room at **St. Francis Hospital,** 601 E. Micheltorena St. (☎ 805/568-5711 or 805/962-7661).

At lunchtime, kids can dig into burgers with chips for $3.50, grilled cheese ($3.25), or a hot dog on a stick for $2.95. Or order salads, standard-size hamburgers, home-made chili, hot and cold sandwiches, or fish and chips off the main menu. At lunch, salads cost around $7, while other items are $5–$7.50.

Dinner is also fun for the family. Adults get broiled steak, the restaurant's famous fried chicken, old-fashioned pot roast, or Teriyaki chicken, all with soup or salad, a fresh vegetable, and choice of rice or potato. These complete dinners will cost you $9 to $12. The restaurant also offers a Lite menu with selections such as steamed clams or mussels, salads, fish and chips, or simple cheeseburgers, all well-priced at $6–$7.

Kids aren't forgotten at dinner either: a fresh fruit plate, fried chicken, hot dog on a stick, or a hamburger is served with a vegetable, french fries, and a scoop of sherbet for $3 to $5.50. Special drinks can be made for the kids, and there are booster seats and highchairs available. Baby bottles and baby food can be warmed.

Open Sunday through Thursday, 7:30am to 9pm, Friday and Saturday to 10pm. Reservations are accepted at dinner only. Major credit cards are welcomed. Park in the lot.

The **Summerland Beach Café,** 2294 Lillie Ave., Summerland (☎ **805/ 969-1019**), down the street from the Big Yellow House, is an alternative stop. Only breakfast and lunch are served in this turn-of-the-century-style restaurant decorated with wooden benches and booths, stained-glass windows, stenciled wall decorations, and hanging plants and ceiling fans. Portions are large and could be split, but there's a children's menu for the 12-and-under set. Junior French toast or eggs, each coming with fresh fruit, sausage or bacon costs $2–$3. Grilled cheese, peanut butter, or a tur-key "samwich" are the luncheon items ($2 to $2.95).

The regular menu lists ten versions of omelets, which include skillet potatoes, an English muffin, and fresh fruit, and are priced quite reasonably at $4.95. Or there's oatmeal, eggs, pancakes, real Belgian waffles served with or without a fruit topping ($3.25 or $4.25), and French toast for $3.25. Lunch consists of lots of sandwiches, including a chicken breast with mushrooms, spinach, and Swiss cheese, innovative salads, and hamburgers from the traditional to turkey burgers, to specialties like the burger with peanut butter, bacon, and Jack cheese ($4.45–$6.25).

Sassy seats and booster seats are available. Servers will bring extra plates for split-ting meals at no charge. Baby bottles can be warmed.

Open weekdays from 7am to 3pm. On weekends they stay open until 4pm. No reservations are accepted, but the wait usually isn't more than 20 minutes on busy mornings. Major credit cards accepted. There's a parking lot and street parking.

2 Ventura/Oxnard

The Ventura/Oxnard area is within easy driving distance of Los Angeles and Santa Barbara. From Los Angeles, take the Ventura Freeway (U.S. 101) north to the Rose exit going west. Go right on Gonzalez, and take that all the way to Harbor Boulevard. Make a right to Ventura, a left to Oxnard. Some people make Oxnard or Ventura their base; others just visit for the day. Ventura and Oxnard are only about 10 or 15 minutes apart on Harbor Boulevard.

Ventura

Located just off the coast of Ventura is one of the area's main attractions. The Chan-nel Islands are a group of eight islands off the California coast, five of which comprise **Channel Islands National Park.** You'll want to start out at the visitor center, which is at the end of Spinnaker Drive (no. 1901) in Ventura, CA 93001 (☎ **805/658-5730**). Not only will you get information on the islands, plus maps and brochures, but the children will also enjoy the little museum. The museum of marine life includes an indoor tidepool (tidepool talks are given Saturday and Sunday at 11am), with glass windows enabling the little kids to see, and displays of Chumash Indian artifacts. Special weekend programs provide interesting facts about the animals and birds that inhabit the area. These programs are conducted by park rangers and are most appropriate for youngsters over 6. Ask about the fascinating live Underwater Video program presented Tuesday and Thursday at 2pm in summer. A free 25-minute film about the islands is also shown on the hour, and some children will enjoy this. It's a lovely place to just sit by the ocean and watch the harbor boats. Open summer from 8am to 5:30pm from Memorial Day to Labor Day, from 8:30am to 4:30pm the rest of the year.

Next door to the visitor center is **Island Packers,** 1867 Spinnaker Dr., Ventura, CA 93001 (☎ **805/642-1393** for reservations or **805/642-7688** for information), the official park concessionaire. This is where you'll get information and make reservations to tour the islands. Island Packers run boats to Santa Cruz, Anacapa, and Santa Barbara islands regularly during spring and summer and at scheduled times the rest of the year. They take small groups to the islands on basic, open boats to capture the feel of the environment. You won't be embarking on plush cruise boats: There are restrooms on board but no food service. There's a deli/snack shop near the embarkation point.

The islands are virtually unsullied by development; their natural state has been and is being maintained. These rugged islands are wonderful fun for boys and girls who love to explore. Come prepared. Wear layered clothing for warmth, and shoes with good gripping soles for walking. If you intend to hike, be prepared to carry young children. Tell the kids they'll be seeing some very precious sea and land mammals, plants, endangered brown pelicans, and exquisite wildflowers. Because the islands are so undisturbed, the sea life is abundant. The kids are fascinated by the teeming life in the tidepools. Interesting rock formations, giant sea caves, and steep cliffs vary at the different islands, and some can be seen as the boat gets closer to the islands. Happily, there are no souvenir shops on the islands and no stores. On some of the islands there's not even fresh water, so you will have to fill your own canteens ahead of time.

Anacapa is the island closest to the mainland. It's the one you will most likely visit the first time, as it has the shortest crossing and the easiest landing. But it does have its drawbacks. The cruise to Anacapa takes $1^1/_2$ hours. In winter the water conditions vary; be prepared for rough landings! While you can explore it with very young children, there are very sheer cliffs and no guardrails to protect those who run off on their own. When you land on the east side, you must walk up 153 steps to reach the top, where there's a tiny visitor center and the beginning of a $1^1/_2$-mile self-guiding trail. The landing cove is 20–30 feet deep and calm enough for summer swimming.

From November through May, Island Packers docks on the west side at Frenchy's Cove, which is noted for its fine tidepools. You're given time to explore the sea life, and are then taken on a narrated cruise around the rugged coastline, where you'll also be treated to views of sea lions, seals, and birds. From June through October, special swim and snorkel days are designated for just relaxing on the small beach. There's no fresh water on the island, and very little protection from the sun. Remember to bring your own water, food, and sunscreen. To see the wildflowers, you should visit in the spring, from January to April, but the weather is not predictable then. For calmer weather, visit from June through August (which is also the heaviest tourist time). September through October is considered the best time to go; but it's cooler. Island Packers also offers half-day nonlanding tours to Anacapa.

Ask for specific information about **Santa Barbara, Santa Rosa,** and **San Miguel Islands.**

Camping on Anacapa (year round) and Santa Barbara (Memorial Day through Labor Day) is restricted to 30 people on each island. From July through September, it's okay to camp on San Miguel Island. Reservations and permits are necessary: Call or write the National Park Service, Channel Islands National Park (☎ **805/644-8262;** mailing address, 1901 Spinnaker Dr., Ventura, CA 93001).

Call for rates; half-day, full-day, and two-day excursions can be reserved, as well as camper transportation and kayaking tours. Reservations are necessary most times of the year, but especially on weekends. In summer, reserve two to four weeks in advance by phone. Vessels carry 25–100 passengers. The stay on the islands is $2^1/_2$–$3^1/_2$ hours.

Once you're back on the mainland, you will want to visit **Ventura Harbor Village,** at 1559 Spinnaker Dr., off Harbor Boulevard, in Ventura Harbor (☎ **805/644-0169**), a quaint village of shops selling souvenirs and gifts. Of particular interest to the kids are the shells, kites, and nautical items. Adjacent to the Ventura Yacht Club and overlooking the harbor, it's a charming spot for an afternoon stroll. There are lots of restaurants and free live entertainment each weekend. Keep your eyes open for the **Carousel Market,** which has an indoor carousel and a very small video arcade. Look for boat rentals along Spinnaker. The Village gets crowded on weekends, and parking, even in the lot, can try your patience. Stores are open daily from 10am to 6pm. Restaurant hours vary, so check ahead. Checkout the always-busy **Village Kite & Toy Store.**

Theatre-By-The-Sea, located inside the center below Hornblowers, features Saturday shows for children, which may intrigue your youngster. Call **805/645-5624** for schedules and prices. The box office is closed weekdays in winter.

Forty-minute cruises of Ventura Harbor are available every hour on the hour on the *Bay Queen,* which is docked at 1567 Spinnaker Dr. in Ventura Harbor Village, adjacent to the Coastal Cone Co. (☎ **805/642-7753**). Tours depart in the winter and summer on Saturday and Sunday from noon to 4pm. Fares are $5 for adults, $3 for children. While you're there, you can also rent one of the four-seat pedalboats; rentals cost $10 an hour, with a $20 deposit necessary. Kayaks rent for $10 per hour per person.

WHERE TO EAT

There are a variety of restaurants in this vicinity.

Christy's, 1559 Spinnaker Dr., in Ventura Harbor Village (☎ **805/642-3116**), is one good choice. Open for breakfast and lunch, this bright and cheerful sit-down restaurant serves eggs, omelets, sandwiches, salads, and burgers (prices average $5). There's no harbor view or children's menu, but the food is good. They keep a stock of children's books to entertain the kids. Boosters and highchairs are available. Open daily from 7am to 3pm. Credit cards accepted. Park in the village lot.

For an even faster food stop, try **Fayro's Famous Hot Dogs,** a short distance from the *Bay Queen.* You can chow down on the $2 dogs at an outdoor picnic table, or try **A. J. Burgers** next door. **Andria's Seafood & Restaurant,** near the end of the village, is good for family style orders of fish and chips.

The primary connection between Ventura and Oxnard is Harbor Boulevard, a 4-mile stretch with a well-marked bike trail on each side of the road. Off this route is the entrance to **McGrath State Park and Beach.** The beach is a 10-minute walk from the parking lot. Pretty and peaceful, and equipped with barbecue pits and picnic tables for campers (and restrooms), McGrath is a day-use park and has a campground. The public beach makes a great morning or afternoon stop. There is a nature trail and other hiking areas in the park. Request a map of the nature trail and information on birdwatching and the summer programs from the park rangers.

Day use is $5 per car; overnight, $16; walk-in camping, $3. Seniors pay $4 for day use and $14 to camp. Make campsite reservations for the 174 developed sites through MISTIX (☎ toll free **800/444-PARK**).

Oxnard

Oxnard's **Channel Islands Harbor** is its main waterfront recreation area. There are seven miles of uncrowded beaches just north of the harbor, and slips for more than 2,500 pleasure boats. From Pacific Coast Highway, follow the signs to Channel Islands Harbor (west). Sportfishing boats and boat rentals are plentiful at South Victoria Avenue, Channel Islands Landing. At the south end of Victoria Avenue is a protected children's beach. The small visitor center can give you maps and special event information. It's located at 3600 S. Harbor Blvd., in the Marine Emporium, Suite 234, Oxnard, CA 93035 (☎ **805/985-4852**).

When you spot the mock lighthouse, you will have found **Fisherman's Wharf,** a small New England–style shopping area at the corner of Channel Islands Boulevard and Victoria Avenue. The children can watch the boats unload their catch of the day nearby. While many of the shops cater to tourists, you might want to stop by **Shell World** (☎ **805/985-3030**), which has a wonderful selection of both inexpensive and very rare and costly shells. Another interesting establishment is the **Oxnard Fisherman's Wharf Seafood Company,** at the end of the block of stores (☎ **805/382-8171**). The menu is on the wall, and you can introduce the kids to a wide assortment of seafood at the counter to take home or to eat on the large outdoor courtyard set with tables. Select from all sorts of fish (including shark) and shellfish, with lots of side orders. Prices run $5–$10. Kids love to look at the live lobster and crab bins outside. Open daily from 10am to 7pm.

Your older children might enjoy a peek into the world of tall ships at the **Maritime Museum,** 2731 S. Victoria Ave., in Fisherman's Wharf (☎ **805/984-6260**). Not only is this a fascinating look at history, but the displays of model ships are like nothing else anywhere. Docents can walk you through if you wish and explain all the details. The models, all made by professional modelers, display the rigging of all sorts of ships. Some of the models are more than 200 years old—one was made by a French prisoner of war. The Ed Marple models reveal his fantastic attention to detail. On his *Royal George* model, the figurehead alone took almost 600 hours to complete. Open Thursday through Monday from 11am to 5pm. The suggested adult donation is $3; children 5–12, $1. The docent-led tours are free. The museum is stroller- and wheelchair-accessible.

Another nearby themed shopping center is **Harbor Landing,** located on South Harbor Boulevard. In addition to its retail shops, the enclosed Spanish-style courtyard is surrounded by a number of quick-service restaurants offering fish, barbecued dishes, frozen yogurt, and pizza. In good weather you can sit outdoors overlooking the harbor.

If you plan to be here in the spring, allow time for the annual **Strawberry Festival,** a two-day event held the third weekend in May that attracts more than 50,000 people. Everything revolves around that tasty fruit, including strawberry-shortcake-eating contests and the judging of the outstanding strawberry blonde (there's one of these contests for 5- to 12-year-olds too). There are bands, dances, arts and crafts displays, and tons of strawberry products for sale. Contact the **Oxnard Visitors Bureau,** 711 S. A St., Heritage Square, Oxnard, CA 93030 (☎ 805/385-7545), for this year's exact dates, and for information on other events.

Gull Wings Children's Museum, 418 W. 4th St. (☎ 805/483-3005), is in downtown Oxnard. Children can let their imaginations run wild in this small, but full, hands-on museum. Geared for kids ages 2 and older, the museum has a section just for toddlers. The older children can pretend to be doctors or geologists, or they can pretend to go camping.

Gull Wings is open Wednesday through Friday and Sunday from 1 to 5pm, and on Saturday from 10am to 5pm. It is closed on major holidays. Adult admission is $3; children 2–12, $2; free for children under 2. Street parking.

WHERE TO EAT

While there are many quick-food establishments scattered throughout the area, you might want to stop for more substantial fare. Or you may want to visit this area just for brunch and a view of the harbor. Here are several selections.

The Whale's Tale, 3950 Bluefin Circle, Channel Island Harbor (just off S. Harbor Boulevard), Oxnard (☎ 805/985-2511), is an excellent restaurant with a superb view of the marina. The choices here are mainly seafood and beef, and there's a great salad bar set up in a replica of a fishing boat. The portions are large and the food is good.

Young travelers will be kept busy while you wait for your food with the crayons and mini-coloring books provided by the restaurant. Children can order from their own menu, which features pasta, quesadillas, pizza, a hamburger, or fried shrimp. Meals include a trip to the salad bar or a cup of clam chowder. Prices range from $5 to $8. For Sunday brunch, your young tykes under 12 get to choose between French toast, waffles, eggs, grilled cheese, and the salad bar. Items are $4; children under 5 eat free. Servers will split orders for kids, warm bottles and baby food, make special children's drinks, and provide boosters and highchairs.

Adults have loads of choices for lunch and dinner. Besides the salad boat, generous salads include the seafood Cobb, a cold chicken and pasta salad, and the Whale Boat, a seafood salad. There are basic ham-and-cheese sandwiches, crab melts, crab and bacon double-deckers, and a marina salad sandwich, among others. Daily specials and pasta and hamburgers can also be selected. Lunch prices range from $4 to $10. Dinner has more seafood selections, including baked sole, Gold Coast cioppino, beer-batter-fried shrimp, and steak and lobster stir fry. There's also lobster tail, prime rib, pasta, chicken, and combinations. Dinners are substantially higher, starting at $12 and going up to $29.

Upstairs in the Whale's Tale is a shellfish bar for light eating. Another great view awaits you there. You can easily make a lunch or dinner from selections such as shellfish, sandwiches, salads, burgers, and daily specials. Prices range from $6 to $10.

The Whale's Tale is open for lunch Monday through Saturday from 11:15am to 2:30pm. The Sunday brunch is offered from 10:30am to 2:30pm. Dinner is Monday through Thursday from 5 to 10:30pm on Friday and Saturday from 5pm to 11pm, and on Sunday from 4 to 10:30pm. Reservations are accepted (you can *request* a window table). The Shellfish Bar serves food Monday through Thursday from 11am to 11pm. On Friday and Saturday it stays open to 11pm. Sunday hours are 10:30am to 11pm. Major credit cards welcome. Parking nearby.

The best bet for a moderately priced breakfast, lunch, or dinner is **Tugs,** 3600 S. Harbor Blvd., Channel Islands Harbor (☎ **805/985-TUGS**). It doesn't have a children's menu, but most kids will be satisfied with the selections. It's comfortably casual, there's outdoor seating, and the view of the harbor is great.

For breakfast, youngsters can have pancakes, waffles, or French toast, while you can choose corned-beef hash and eggs, omelets, or steak and eggs. Breakfast runs $2.75–$7.95. Lunch includes chowder, salads, fried seafood entrees, sandwiches, and burgers ($5–$10). Dinner includes some steak, prime rib, pasta, and chicken choices, but is mostly seafood and fish dishes ($7.50–$16). On Sunday they present an abbreviated breakfast menu with some special items—variations of eggs Benedict, pasta, egg burritos, design-your-own omelets, and huevos rancheros ($4.25–$8).

Highchairs and boosters are provided. The servers will split any entree for two children, and will warm bottles and baby food in the kitchen.

Open daily from 8am to 9pm. Reservations accepted only for parties of six or more. The wait's not too long, and the view keeps most children occupied. Some major credit cards accepted. Parking is nearby.

WHERE TO STAY

Many Los Angelenos choose Oxnard as a weekend family retreat. The **Mandalay Beach Resort and Conference Hotel,** 2101 Mandalay Beach Rd., Oxnard, CA 93035 (☎ **805/984-2500,** or toll free **800/433-4600,** fax 805/984-8339), is the hotel of choice. This all-suite hotel is located on a swimmable beach, but it also has a large heated free-form pool and two huge spas set in secluded, plant-filled areas. Lush foliage, waterfalls, and streams give the Spanish-style buildings a tropical feel. And the lobby, with its three-story-high ceiling, makes a pleasant place to wander with restless toddlers.

Two night-lit tennis courts are on the premises, and there are public courts nearby. Single bikes for adults and children, with child carriers and helmets, as well as tandem bikes, mountain bikes, and four-wheel Pedalinas, can be rented every day in the summer, and weekends year round, at the poolside rental office. Boogie boards—even giant squirt guns—can also be rented. The Mandalay also offers video games and a Ping-Pong table.

Beach Buddies is the name of the Mandalay's children's program for kids 5–12. It runs on Friday and Saturday in summer from 11am to 4pm, and we are assured it runs no matter how many children sign up. In addition to activities scheduled in the Beach Buddies' own bungalow, there are outdoor activities at the beach, art projects with a recycling theme, shell decorating, and nature walks. The charge is $20 per day and includes lunch and snacks.

A *separate* Movie Night is offered on Friday and Saturday nights from 6 to 9pm in summer. For a charge of $15, the 5- to 12-year-olds get pizza, a movie, and art projects. Contact the concierge about other special children's activities which might be scheduled during your stay. The concierge can also refer babysitters.

Full complimentary breakfast is served every morning. A separate kids' corner has been set up so that young children can have their own tables. On the summer weekends a barbecue lunch is fixed poolside, although it's not complimentary.

The Capistrano Restaurant is a beautiful spot for lunch and dinner. The children's menu is limited but adequate, and there are booster seats and highchairs. A hot dog, grilled cheese, or peanut butter and jelly sandwich will run $3–$3.50. Adults can select sandwiches and salads ($8.95 and up) as well as full entrees of pasta, chicken, fish, beef, and lamb ($10–$17). The lounge will serve snacks and entrees all day. There is evening entertainment. Room service is available from 11am to 11pm, with two or three selections the kids will like.

Each suite comes with two full bathrooms, a living room with a queen-size hide-a-bed, two color TVs, multiline phones, a small dining area, and a kitchenette with a compact microwave and a small refrigerator. You'll find coffee in the room, and you can request microwavable dishes. The marble bathrooms are nice-sized. First-floor patio rooms open to the courtyard, the beach, or a grassy area. Second-floor rooms have patios with open-slatted balconies, great for relaxing but best for over-toddler-age kids. Upper-floor terraces are large enough to play on and are safe for curious toddlers and infants. Make your request and the hotel will try to honor it. The first two levels are furnished with king-size beds; the upper floor, with two queen-size beds. Six two-bedroom apartments can be reserved, and there are no-smoking rooms.

In summer, rooms cost $129–$259 single, $144–$259 double. Suites are $350–$400. In winter, singles go for $99–$179 and doubles are $114–$179 (these double rates are based on a family of four). Honeymoon suites rent for $249–$299. Children under 12 stay free in their parents' room; those 12 and over, and additional adults, pay $15 each per night. Cribs are available for children weighing less than 20 pounds at $15 per night. There are no rollaways. Ask about the two-, four-, and seven-night packages. The underground parking is free.

The **Casa Sirena Resort,** located at 3605 Peninsula Rd., Channel Islands Harbor, Oxnard, CA 93035 (☎ **805/985-6311;** fax 805/985-4329), is a more moderately priced establishment, good for families who don't want to spend lots of money but still want to be near the water and have things for the kids to do. There's a small pool and two whirlpools (room service is available poolside), a fully equipped exercise room, three tennis courts (two public and one private), a putting green, and bicycle rentals. An under-equipped game room offers a pool table and video machine. A beautiful city park in the middle of the resort overlooks the harbor and makes a great area for children to play, with slides, a merry-go-round, and other playground equipment built into a giant sandbox. Five minutes away are clean public beaches.

The resort's restaurant, the Lobster Trap, is open for lunch and dinner. There's no children's menu, but they will accommodate little appetites with small portions at smaller prices. The Trampita Coffee Shop serves breakfast and lunch; surprisingly, there's no children's menu here either. Room service is available from 6am to 2pm and 5 to 10pm from the Lobster Trap, and from 6:30am to 2pm from the coffee shop.

The rooms here come with double or king-size beds; some have gas fireplaces, and all have small refrigerators and separate vanities. There are lots of adjoining rooms. Family suites are perfect for two adults and two children. There's a separate bedroom, and the living room has a hide-a-bed. The kitchen comes with a four-burner stove, a full-size refrigerator, and a sink. The bright family suites overlook the marina, with triple-window sliding doors leading out to a balcony with high railings. Larger suites are also available. Clock radios and TVs are standard in all rooms.

Rooms at Casa Sirena rent for $79–$89 single and $89–$99 double. Family suites with kitchen cost $139 single, $149 double; specialty suites, which have a large living room and separate bedroom, cost $169–$275. Children under 12 stay free in their parents' room; those 12 and over, and additional adults, pay $10 each per night. Cribs are free; rollaways cost $12. Ask about package plans.

3 The Ojai Valley

Ojai, pronounced "*O*-high," was named by the Chumash tribe many, many years ago. It means "the nest," which is really quite appropriate, since the town's quiet, pastoral character and its valley setting make it such a comfortable retreat.

Ojai is the place to spend the day bicycle riding, hiking, or taking leisurely drives on picture-perfect backcountry roads. It's a town of art galleries, artists' studios, antique stores, and alternative-living centers.

It's a day trip from Los Angeles, or part of a day from Santa Barbara or Oxnard. The 85-mile drive from Los Angeles is an easy one. The exit off U.S. 101 is about ten minutes outside Oxnard. The two-lane highway to Ojai passes through little picturesque towns. Or incorporate a visit here with one to Ventura and Oxnard, 14 miles away. Santa Barbara is 20 miles north.

You can't miss the Spanish mission-style architecture of the **Arcade,** the main shopping area in town. Stop by the **Ojai Valley Chamber of Commerce,** 338 E. Ojai Ave. (Calif. 150), Ojai, CA 93023 (☎ **805/646-8126**), for a free copy of *The Visitor's Guide to the Ojai Valley.* The chamber has detailed lists of bike and hiking trails and campgrounds as well. The office is open weekdays from 9:30am to 4:30pm and on Saturday and Sunday from 10am to 4pm.

WHAT TO SEE AND DO

There's nice **shopping** in and around the Arcade. **Libbey Park** is across from the center of the Arcade on Ojai Avenue. This is where you'll want to picnic if you've come just for the afternoon. It's a charming park with lots of oak trees, a nice picnic area, and a children's playground. Libbey Bowl is the site of many of Ojai's cultural events, including the old-fashioned **band concerts** offered every Wednesday night in the summer. Summer also is the time for Ojai's outdoor **Shakespeare Festival.** The rustic outdoor theater is set in the wooded back end of the park.

The little **Ojai Valley Historical Society and Museum,** 109 S. Montgomery St. (☎ **805/646-2290**), was a real surprise to us. It's a compact look at the history of the local Chumash Indians and the town of Ojai itself. Janey enjoyed the display of the school artifacts from the early 1900s. One exhibit showed what the kids were doing then—the same things they do now—jacks and marbles. Donations are accepted. The museum is open Wednesday through Monday from 1 to 4pm.

Bicycling is one of the most popular activities in town. There are a number of roads for pedaling, including the paved bike trail that begins at Fox Street and continues for 9¹/₂ miles. The tree-filled neighborhoods and groves of eucalyptus trees make a perfect setting for a family ride. If you don't have bikes, join the rest of the people who use this as a walking trail. You can also take an easy ride through orange and avocado groves by taking Ojai Avenue east and making an easy loop around the east side of town. This is a very popular route for biking because of the flat, paved road and the surrounding perfume of oranges. Soule Park, on Boardman, just south of Ojai Avenue, east of town, is a good place to stop for a picnic during a ride.

Rent a bike from **The Bicycle Doctor,** 212 Fox St., two blocks from the Arcade (☎ **805/646-7554**), who rents cruisers for folks age 12 and over. Open daily except

Wednesday and Sunday from 9am to 5pm. Bikes rent by the hour or day and can be reserved in advance.

Besides the nearby Los Padres National Forest, there are other places for day hikes in the area. One is **Matilija Lake,** about six miles from Ojai. Take Calif. 33 north toward Taft to Country Campground No. 1. Take the quarter-mile hike to the lake from the old road at the end of the campground. There are plenty of rest stops along the way, which also make great places to picnic.

If you don't feel like walking, jogging, or bicycling, or if you want a look at the whole town, grab a ride on the **Ojai Trolley** (☎ 805/646-8126). It runs seven days a week. Pick up a schedule at City Hall, the post office, the library, or the visitors center. Adults and children 5 and older are charged 25¢; seniors over 75 and kids under 5 ride free.

Plan to spend the entire day at **Lake Casitas Recreation Area,** 11311 Santa Ana Rd., Ventura (☎ 805/649-2233), just five miles from Ojai. Take Calif. 33 south to Calif. 150. Turn right and go 3 miles to the entrance. Set on 6,200 beautiful acres in the Ojai Valley, Lake Casitas is used as a reservoir. There is no swimming or waterskiing allowed, but you can camp, fish, hike, and picnic here. There are more than 400 camp-sites available on a first-come, first-served basis and 60 hookups available by reserva-tion (☎ 805/649-1122). Ask for current fees. Coin-operated showers and restrooms are plentiful, and you'll find a park store, a snack bar, a first-aid station, pay phones, and fish-cleaning sinks on the grounds. If you aren't camping out, come just for a picnic or a hike. There are lots of picnic tables, easy hiking, and several areas with playground equipment. The recreation area is open year round. Day use is $5 per vehicle, or park at the entrance and walk the half mile for free.

Fishing licenses and bait are available inside the park at the **Boat, Bait & Tackle Shop** (☎ 805/649-2043), where you can also rent boats. Janey loved being the cap-tain of the little motorboat. There are rowboats, a 10-passenger patio deck boat, and motorboats of varying sizes and horsepower, suitable for fishing or just a leisurely ride around the lake. Rentals are by the hour, two to five hours, or the day. You can reserve a boat ahead of time for a full-day rental by mailing in a full-day's deposit. Contact **Casitas Boat Rentals,** 11311 Santa Ana Rd., Ventura, CA 93001 (☎ 805/649-2043), for current rates and deposit information.

WHERE TO EAT

There are several places to eat in town, and they range from the super-relaxed casual to the "dressed-up casual." The **Ojai Valley Inn** restaurant is on the dressed-up casual side (see the "Where to Stay" section).

Roger Keller's, 331 E. Ojai Ave. (☎ 805/646-7266), qualifies in the mid-casual range. Old brick, changing art by California artists, and ceiling fans decorate this one-room restaurant, which also has a full bar.

The California cuisine is light, yet varied. For lunch, you might want to try a Cobb salad, Black Forest ham croissant, or several varieties of burgers, including chicken. A starter of bruschetta might entice you in the evening, followed by blackened filet of beef or poached salmon. Lunch prices range from $5.50 to $9.95, while dinner will cost you between $6.75 to $16.95.

Although the children's menu seems limited, don't let that stop you from trying the restaurant. Children are very welcome at Roger Keller's. Their own menu comes with crayons, kids are gladly fed first, if that's your request, and servers make sure the chef knows youngsters are at the table so food preparation time can be gauged. The menu offers grilled-cheese sandwiches on whole-wheat bread, spaghetti, or a hot dog, each $2.50. They can order a hamburger at any time for $4.75. Roger and his staff will make almost anything you want for the kids. They can have a half order of something, or the chef will prepare something two or three kids can split. Servers will happily warm bottles and baby food. Booster seats and highchairs are available.

The restaurant is open for lunch Monday through Friday from 11:30am to 2:30pm, Saturday and Sunday from 11:30am to 3pm. Dinner is Sunday through Thursday 5 to 10pm, Friday and Saturday to 10:30pm. Reservations are accepted but not necessary (the wait depends on what's going on in town that day). All major credit cards are accepted. There is street parking.

Around the corner from the Arcade is a cute, casual place for a quick bite and a soda or sundae—or Chinese food. What a combination! **Soda Bar & Grill,** 219 E. Matilija St. (☎ 805/646-7632), has a jukebox in the center of the room and a few video games to keep everyone occupied. Sit at the counter or in one of the '50s-style booths. "Mitey Bites," little hamburgers with everything, are perfect for little appetites; buy them for 85¢ each. There are also quarter-pound burgers, sandwiches, hot dogs, croissant sandwiches, chicken and chips, and salads ($2–$5). Save room for the mini- and full-size banana splits and sundaes, plus shakes, floats, pies, and fudge brownies.

And as for the Chinese food—at dinner, you can try curry rice, kabobs, rice and shrimp or Tean Su Uk (fried beef and sweet and sour sauce) for $6.95 to $10.95.

Highchairs and booster seats are provided. Bottles and baby food can be warmed. Open daily from 11am to 9pm. No reservations accepted. Cash only; no credit cards honored. Park on the street or in the lot behind the Arcade.

Another quick-stop restaurant, and also a great place for take-out picnic food, is **Pederson's Ojai Kitchen,** 328 E. Ojai Ave., in the Arcade (☎ 805/646-0207), a favorite with locals. There are plenty of kid-appropriate choices at this super-casual place. At breakfast there's a huge selection of omelets ($4.40–$5.80) as well as full breakfasts. For the toddlers, you can get a side order of pancakes for $2.25. There are also eight kinds of bagels plus three flavors of cream cheese to eat here or to go. At lunch there are hot and cold sandwiches in full or half sizes, hamburgers, and Mexican food. Little tykes might like Mitey Bites—two miniature burgers for $1.99, or spaghetti with salad and garlic bread for $3.29. There's nothing over $6.50 on the menu. Open Monday through Saturday from 7am to 7pm and on Sunday from 7am to 5pm. Highchairs and boosters are provided. Cash or checks only. Park in the Arcade lot.

WHERE TO STAY

Ojai is such a serene town to visit, it would be a shame not to stay overnight. The **Ojai Valley Inn,** Ojai, CA 93023 (☎ 805/646-5511, or toll free 800/422-OJAI; fax 805/646-7969), is the perfect choice. Its setting is one of the most beautiful in California. In fact, the surrounding valley and Topa Topa mountain range are what attracted director Frank Capra for his 1937 film *Lost Horizon.* To him, this really was "Shangri-La."

The inn graces 220 acres of verdant lawns, mature trees, and brilliant flowers. An award-winning par-70 golf course, considered one of the prettiest in the state, eight tennis courts (four night-lit), sauna, spa, and fitness center are all first-class. The adjacent Ojai Trail we talked about earlier is often used by inn guests for jogging or bicycling. Complimentary bicycles, including some for children, can be checked out near the lobby.

The pool area is gorgeous, and there were plenty of children around for Janey to play with. A lap pool is available for serious swimmers, while the other pool is big enough for everyone. Food service, a spa, a fitness center, and a Ping-Pong table surround this informal setting.

The inn's brochure claims that "Children of all ages are always welcome at the Inn . . ." It's true, as is shown by the number of repeat families over the years. A big playground, located at the inn's recreation field, is where the kids engage in all kinds of activities. A sand volleyball court, jungle gym, and a shaded picnic area are set in a wonderfully wooded, green area. Camp Ojai, for kids 3–14, offers sessions during Thanksgiving, Christmas/New Year's, and Easter/spring vacations, and in summer from mid-June through Labor Day. From 9am to 5pm daily, the schedule includes everything from field games, swimming, tennis lessons, table tennis, arts and crafts, and face painting. The kids also get to have ice-cream socials and make cookies. Even clowns and mimes are brought in for entertainment.

The children meet in one of the inn's suites where parents must sign them in and out. The inn attempts to keep a ratio of about one counselor to two children. The day's program is usually customized to the ages of the children. This program runs no matter how many kids sign up. New to the Inn is the Children's Farm at Rancho Dos Rios where kids can ride a pony or go on an old fashioned hayride. The fee is $25 per day. The children can have their lunch with counselors, and meals, program fees, pony- and hayrides can be billed to your room.

A separate Saturday-night program in the summer and during holidays gives the kids something to do from 6 to 10pm while Mom and Dad get a night out. Pizza, movies, storytelling, and arts and crafts are on that schedule.

Speaking of eating, the inn's policy is that children 4–12 order off the regular menus for half the price, and those 3 and under eat free. There is also a well-priced children's menu. There are two dining rooms to choose from. Janey was comfortable and treated well in both, but we'd suggest the Oak Grill and Terrace if you have young children. Outdoor dining during nice weather is a real treat. Room service, which is available 24 hours, also has a children's menu or the kids can order off the regular menu at the discount mentioned above.

The rambling resort has all sorts of rooms. Some have mountain views; some face the fairway or are set on the fairway. Some have fireplaces, terraces, or patios. There are two-bedroom cottages, one-bedroom suites, connecting rooms, and units with sofa beds. Your best bet is to explain your family's needs when you make your reservation and let them put you in the most appropriate of the 207 rooms and suites. Accommodations are roomy and are equipped with king- or double queen-size beds. Hairdryers, robes, color television, stocked minibars, brewed coffee, and air conditioning are standard.

Rates for standard rooms, single or double occupancy, range from $195 to $240. A deluxe room will cost $260, and a junior suite (with a fireplace) is $345, as is a one-bedroom with parlor. There's even a one bedroom with parlor and two fire-places for a charge of $395. Cottages with two bedrooms, a parlor, and a fireplace run $600; three bedrooms, $850. Children of any age sleep free when sharing their parents' room. Extra adults are charged $25. Ask about the special summer family packages and holiday packages. Cribs and rollaways are complimentary. Parking is free.

Los Angeles

ONE OF THE MOST POPULAR TOURIST DESTINATIONS IN THE UNITED STATES, LOS Angeles attracts nearly 50 million visitors a year. It's no surprise to native and transplanted Angelenos that visitors flock to this tourist mecca. The glamour, the weather, and the vast number of things to do bring travelers back again and again.

People once joked about the "sleepy little town," founded in 1769 by Gaspar de Portolá's expedition party but not colonized until 1781 by a Spanish party sent from Mexico and named El Pueblo del Río de Nuestra Señora la Reina de los Angeles (the Town of the River of Our Lady, Queen of the Angels). But today, as the second-largest city in the country and leader of the Pacific Rim, Los Angeles is no joke. That "sleepy little town" comprises 467 square miles, boasts almost $3^{1}/_{2}$ million residents, has some 525 miles of freeway, and copes with more than 6 million registered vehicles! Los Angeles County is over 4,000 square miles and has almost $8^{1}/_{2}$ million residents.

So what does all this mean to you when you're traveling with your family? While Los Angeles has become a leader in business, it still has its "laid-back" attitude. This city of youth-lovers and fun-seekers is an outdoor culture where people place importance on sports and leisure activities. Children fit right in. And there's more to do than you could ever fit into one or two or even three vacations. In the Greater Los Angeles area you can swim and surf off miles of beaches, see movies being shot right on the streets, visit major movie studios, tour renowned museums (including two just for children), attend concerts, watch professional sports, stroll through the spacious shopping malls, and spend days at theme parks.

And much to the delight of your kids, almost every hotel, even motels, will have a swimming pool. Eating out won't be a problem, as there are numerous restaurants perfect for the whole family.

And of course, the climate is wonderful. People talk about smog, and it is a consideration on a bad day, especially if you want to do something very active. But most people don't talk about the pleasure, the ease of a reliably pleasant 70°–85° day with low humidity. Angelenos take it for granted. Rain throws them into a tizzy. They're so spoiled by delightful, predictable weather that even night and morning low clouds, so common in the late spring and early summer, are met with grumbles by natives. There are few activities that must be canceled or postponed because of weather. Sun worshippers should know, though, that May and June bring hazy, foggy mornings, and it's not until afternoon that the sun breaks through. L.A.'s real summer is July through September.

1 Getting There

BY CAR

To get to Los Angeles from San Francisco, take I-580 to I-5 south through the San Joaquin Valley. You can also take the Coast Route (Calif. 1, the Pacific Coast Hwy.) and U.S. 101 from parts north. From Sacramento and San Joaquin Valley towns, just get onto I-5 south and follow the signs. If you're coming from San Diego, take either I-5 or I-405 north.

A Stop Along the Way

If you travel I-5 through the San Joaquin Valley, you're taking the fast route, but it's truly boring and doesn't have many good places to stop. We find that the kids need a break every few hours. We stop at least twice: once at **Harris Ranch** (☎ **209/ 935-0717,** or toll free **800/942-2333**), which is midway between Los Angeles and San Francisco on I-5, and once near the town of Buttonwillow (about 110 miles north of Los Angeles at the juncture of I-5 and Calif. 58).

If you're taking U.S. 101, you might want to try **Pea Soup Andersen's California Highway Center,** at 376 Avenue of the Flags in Buellton (☎ **805/688-5581**) (see Chapter 9, under "Pismo Beach," in "The Central Coast," for details). We stop again in Santa Barbara.

BY TRAIN

The train is an exciting way to travel. **Amtrak,** with its terminal at 800 N. Alameda in Los Angeles (☎ **213/624-0171,** or toll free **800/USA-RAIL**), is the way to go. Amtrak's *Coast Starlight,* originating in Los Angeles, runs the length of California, Oregon, and Washington.

If you're coming from out of state, check Chapter 1, "Traveling to California," for details.

BY BUS

The major transcontinental bus line that services Los Angeles is **Greyhound/Trailways Bus Lines,** with its main terminal at 1716 E. 7th St., one block east of Alameda Street (☎ **800/231-2222**).

BY AIR

Los Angeles is a major air transportation hub for the West Coast, with several area airports and many airlines providing scheduled service.

The Airports

The major airport servicing Los Angeles is **Los Angeles International Airport (LAX)** (☎ **310/646-5252**). However, depending on your travel plans, you may prefer to fly into the other smaller airports servicing the area. **Burbank-Glendale-Pasadena Airport** (☎ **818/840-8847**), **Long Beach Municipal Airport** (☎ **310/421-8293**), and **Ontario International Airport** (☎ **909/988-2700**) are possibilities that are often more convenient than LAX. If you're planning to start your trip in Orange County, you might consider landing at **John Wayne Airport** in Santa Ana (☎ **714/252-5006**).

Airlines

Some of the airlines that fly into Los Angeles International Airport include: Aero México (☎ toll free **800/237-6639**), Air Canada (☎ toll free **800/776-3000**), Air France (☎ toll free **800/237-2747**), Air New Zealand (☎ toll free **800/262-1234**), Alaska Airlines (☎ toll free **800/426-0333**), Alitalia (☎ toll free **800/223-5730**), American Airlines (☎ toll free **800/433-7300**), America West (☎ toll free **800/235-9292**), British Airways (☎ toll free **800/247-9297**), Canadian Airlines International (☎ toll free **800/426-7000**), Cathay Pacific Airways (☎ toll free **800/233-2742**), China Airlines (☎ toll free **800/227-5118**), Continental Airlines (☎ toll free **800/435-0040**), Delta Airlines (☎ toll free **800/221-1212**), El Al Israel (☎ toll free **800/223-6700**), Finnair (☎ toll free **800/950-5000**), Hawaiian

Airlines (☎ toll free **800/367-5320**), Japan Air Lines (☎ toll free **800/525-3663**), KLM (☎ toll free **800/374-7747**), Korean Airlines (☎ toll free **800/438-5000**), Lufthansa (☎ toll free **800/645-3880**), Mexicana Airlines (☎ toll free **800/531-7921**), Northwest (☎ toll free **800/225-2525**), Philippine Airlines (☎ toll free **800/435-9725**), Qantas Airlines (☎ toll free **800/227-4500**), Scandinavian Airlines System (SAS) (☎ toll free **800/221-2350**), Singapore Airlines (☎ toll free **800/742-3333**), Skywest (☎ toll free **800/453-9417**), Southwest Airlines (☎ toll free **800/435-9792**), TWA (☎ toll free **800/221-2000**), United Airlines and United Express (☎ toll free **800/241-6522**), and USAir (☎ toll free **800/428-4322**).

There are also charters that fly into LAX.

Ground Transportation to the City

It's a given that Los Angeles is a huge city. Therefore your choice of ground transportation depends on the airport you use and your destination. Taxi service can be very expensive, so be sure you know how much the tab will run before you tell the driver to go ahead. You can get a taxi at the airport. The average taxi fare between LAX and downtown Los Angeles is about $30. From LAX to Beverly Hills is about $35. Confirm the cost first, however. Should you want to call a taxi, you might try **United Independent Cab Co.** (☎ 310/558-8294), **Beverly Hills Cab Co.** (☎ 310/273-6611), or **Celebrity Cab Co.** (☎ 310/278-2500).

All major car-rental companies are located in Los Angeles. You might want to try **Avis Rent-A-Car** (☎ 310/646-5600, or toll free **800/331-1212**), **Budget Rent-A-Car** (☎ 310/645-4500, or toll free **800/527-0700**), **Dollar Rent-A-Car** (☎ 310/645-9333, or toll free **800/800-4000**), **Hertz Rent-A-Car** (☎ toll free **800/654-3131**), or **Thrifty Rent-A-Car** (☎ 310/645-1880, or toll free **800/367-2277**). Most have counters at the airports and offices throughout the Greater Los Angeles area.

Also, check with the hotel where you will be staying. Those near the airport usually have complimentary shuttle service.

2 Getting Your Bearings

Los Angeles lies in a basin. Ringed by mountains, the city grew up between them and the Santa Monica Bay. The Santa Monica Mountains run east to west and divide the city from the San Fernando Valley.

We suggest that you write to the **Los Angeles Visitor Information Center,** 685 S. Figueroa St., Los Angeles, CA 90017, for maps and brochures. Or, when you get to L.A., contact them directly (☎ 213/689-8822); open Monday through Friday from 8am to 5pm and on Saturday from 8:30am to 5pm. There is also another **information center** in Hollywood at the Janes House, Janes House Square, 6541 Hollywood Blvd., near Vine Street (☎ 213/461-4213), open Monday through Saturday from 9am to 5pm.

The centers will help make your visit a memorable experience. And they've had lots of practice. Over 25 million guests visited the Greater Los Angeles area. The tourist bureau staff know that Los Angeles is a sprawling metropolis that at first impression seems impossible to master. You'll find them very helpful.

SECTIONS OF TOWN

Yes, Los Angeles has a **downtown.** This is the central part of the city. We include the area surrounding the Civic Center and East Wilshire, as well as Little Tokyo and Chinatown, when we refer to downtown. Most people now think **Hollywood** is a state of mind. But there still is a Hollywood, long known as the world's glamour and film capital, and it's a place everyone seems to need to make a pilgrimage to.

The area loosely bordered by Doheny Drive to the west, La Brea Avenue to the east, Santa Monica Boulevard to the north, and Wilshire Boulevard to the south is called many things. It takes in the **West Hollywood, Mid-Wilshire, Fairfax, and Melrose** areas, and throws together the older European population with artists, designers, and other trendsetters. It's a section of town burgeoning with coffeehouses, smart boutiques, unusual shops, and many ethnic restaurants.

The **Westside,** which includes Beverly Hills, Century City, Westwood, and Brentwood, is alive with shopping, restaurants, and delightful places for the family. Beverly Hills still draws thousands of people to its golden streets, while Century City pulsates with the energy of everyday business combined with professional theater, cinema, and shopping. Westwood is the fun, youthful village of first-run movie theaters, clothing shops for the college set, and good, informal restaurants.

The **Coastal Region** includes Santa Monica, Marina del Rey, and the airport, areas where almost every traveler spends some time. Beautiful beaches are everywhere and Marina del Rey and Santa Monica are fun places to explore with the kids. This is the part of town where the family can get out and roller skate, ride bikes, and simply enjoy Los Angeles.

Universal City and Burbank are part of the **San Fernando Valley.** This is where many films are now being produced.

MAIN STREETS

The major east-west streets in "town" are Wilshire, Sunset, Pico, and Olympic Boulevards. Major north-south streets are Lincoln Boulevard, Sepulveda Boulevard, La Cienega Boulevard, La Brea Avenue, and Vermont Avenue.

Santa Monica Boulevard is one of the more confusing streets, at one point running parallel to Wilshire Boulevard, then crossing it in Beverly Hills. There's a short portion of street beginning at Rexford Drive in Beverly Hills and continuing to Sepulveda Boulevard in West Los Angeles; its street signs say "Santa Monica Boulevard," but it's usually referred to as "little" Santa Monica. It's the next street parallel to "big" Santa Monica.

In the San Fernando Valley, Ventura Boulevard is the main east-west thoroughfare.

TELEPHONE AREA CODES

Unlike most other major American metropolitan areas, Los Angeles has five area codes. Parts of Los Angeles can be reached using the 213 area code, while other parts require 310; the valleys are 818. Occasionally, you'll even find a 714 or 909 number. If you get the wrong area code, an operator will remind you. Sometimes tourist and leisure activities have more than one number and area code.

3 Getting Around

Okay, so we all know that Los Angeles is synonymous with freeways. If you have a car (and you'd probably be better off with one), you'll want to understand the freeway system. You don't have to be an expert, but if you have a good map, you can get anywhere. Try the visitors bureau, the Southern California Automobile Club, Gousha maps, or the *Thomas Brothers Map Guide* for suitable maps. And don't be shy—you can ask for directions.

DRIVING TIPS

Remember always to wear your seatbelts—this is required by California law! Children 40 pounds and under or 4 years and under must be in an approved car seat. If you're driving to Los Angeles from out of state, be sure to bring one. If you plan to rent a car, ask your rental agency to secure one for you. Before you get behind the wheel, be sure you're familiar with all California driving regulations, as some of them may be different from those in your home state.

Freeway driving can be pleasant, or it can be a harrowing experience. Be sure you allow plenty of time to get to your destination. Know where you're going, and if you get confused, it's a good idea to exit the freeway and stop to read your map so you can get your bearings rather than drive uncertainly on the freeway.

If you can, stay off the freeways between 6 and 9am and 4 and 7pm—you'll be better off. We often keep water or juice for the kids inside the car (not in the trunk). There have been many times when the freeway has been jammed, making a ten-minute jaunt into a 25-minute ordeal with thirsty, uncomfortable kids.

If you need assistance, the **Automobile Club of Southern California** (☎ 213/741-3111) is extremely helpful to its members with emergency service, travel advice, and other services. AAA members in other states are automatically covered here. Call for information.

For information on **road conditions,** call the California Department of Transportation (CALTRANS) (☎ 213/897-3656). Or listen to either of two radio news stations (KFWB-AM at 980 on the dial, or KNX-AM at 1070) for frequent traffic reports that will help you bypass the jams.

BUSES

Los Angeles isn't known for its exceptionally good rapid transit. Don't expect the frequency and choice that many other major cities offer. However, if you need to use public transportation, there are three major rapid-transit companies to call:

The **Los Angeles County Metropolitan Transit Authority (MTA)** (☎ 310/626-4455 or toll free 800/COMMUTE) covers all of Greater Los Angeles, **Culver City Municipal Bus Lines** (☎ 310/202-5731, 310/559-8310 on weekends) has service between Culver City and Santa Monica and West L.A., and **Santa Monica Municipal Bus Lines** (☎ 310/451-5444) operates coaches to Westwood, Culver City, Century City, and Marina del Rey. Call for exact route information.

The City of Los Angeles Department of Transportation runs **DASH,** a series of natural gas–powered community shuttles (☎ toll free 800/2LA-RIDE). These inexpensive rides are only 25¢, and separate shuttles run in Westwood Village, Hollywood, downtown Los Angeles, the Fairfax district, and Pacific Palisades. Call for hours and exact routes.

Visitors can also get RTD route information and schedules, and can create individual bus itineraries by using a hotline phone hooked up to the RTD and available at the **Visitor Information Center,** at 7th and Figueroa Streets in downtown Los Angeles.

Tours

We rarely take our children on bus tours, but if you have older children who you believe would enjoy this kind of experience, you might try **Advantage Tours & Charter** (Mailing address: P.O. Box 1192, Beverly Hills, CA 90213; ☎ **310/823-0321**), which offers day tours to some of the most popular sightseeing attractions in Southern California, including stars' homes. Tours originate downtown, in Hollywood, in Santa Monica, at the Farmers Market, and from a variety of local hotels. Special rates for children are available. You might also try **Oskar J's** (☎ **818/785-4039**), which also offers children's rates.

4 Where to Stay

Los Angeles is such a large city that one of your main considerations will probably be location. Wherever possible, we've provided the name and address of a market for your convenience, and the name and location of a park so you can take the kids out to run off some energy.

BEVERLY HILLS

Needing no introduction, the city of Beverly Hills has its own atmosphere. While you might not actually see movie stars all around you, the glamour of the city makes you think you're about to discover someone any minute.

For those who stay in Beverly Hills and environs, there is a Pavilions Market at 9467 W. Olympic Blvd. (☎ **310/553-5734**) open from 6am to midnight; and a 24-hour Hughes Market at 9040 Beverly Blvd. (☎ **310/278-1351**). A fabulous neighborhood playground is Roxbury Park (see "Neighborhood Parks" under "Outdoor Activities" in "What to See and Do," below, for details).

Deluxe

A combination of first-class European luxury and American friendliness awaits families at the **Four Seasons Hotel at Beverly Hills,** 300 S. Doheny Dr., Los Angeles, CA 90048 (☎ **310/273-2222,** or toll free **800/332-3442**), the only five-star hotel in the greater L.A. area. Opened in 1987, and located adjacent to residential Beverly Hills, the Four Seasons combines the richness of a European manor with the easygoing ambience of Southern California. Antiques, marble floors, accent pieces, and fresh flowers and plants indoors give way to lush, manicured gardens and courtyards with Mexican fan palms and jacaranda trees. The indoor-outdoor atmosphere is heightened by the extensive use of windows and French doors. It's a lovely place to be.

Elegant as the hotel is, the staff is so family-oriented that you need not feel worried about your children. The staff is trained to be welcoming and helpful, and to anticipate guests' needs, including those of children. And attitude has much to do with it. Many of the staff have children and talk about what it's like to see life from a 2½-foot perspective. There's a brochure of children's services and family amenities offered by the hotel. On hand, and without charge, you can get a baby bathtub, disposable bottles, baby shampoo, pacifiers, playpens, and vaporizers. Car seats and strollers are available for guests' use. Older kids are welcome to board games, pool toys, and playing cards, and if the need arises, hot-water bottles and thermometers can be provided.

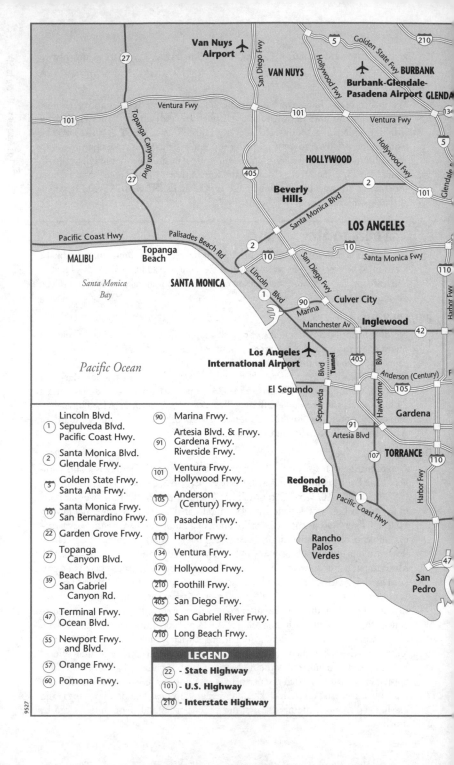

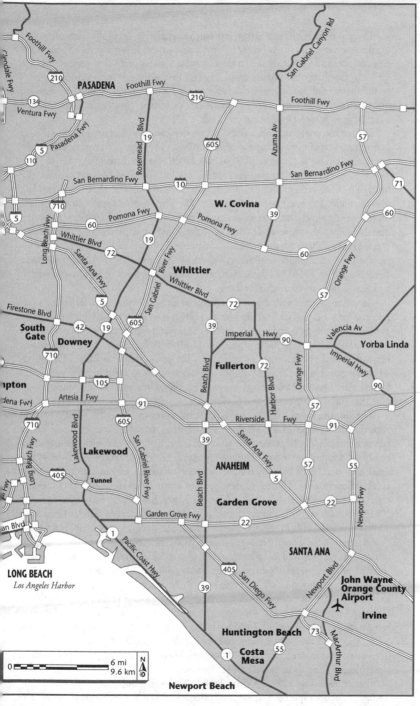

Los Angeles Freeway System

There's concierge service, which pays such attention to detail that they often personally interview babysitters before recommending them to hotel guests. Other hotel services include 24-hour room service, complete laundry and valet services, complimentary shoeshine, twice-daily maid service (certainly a gift from someone's fairy godmother), valet parking, exercise facilities, and a wide range of business services. You can rent cars and limousines at the hotel. In addition, courtesy limousine service is available to Rodeo Drive in Beverly Hills.

The rooftop pool area is open and spacious, designed to make guests feel as if they're part of the surrounding residential neighborhood. The large pool has a nice shallow area for kids. This is a favorite place to have lunch with the little ones.

Of course you'll want to visit area restaurants, but you also have your choice at the hotel. The Café is very informal, and is open for breakfast, lunch, dinner, and late into the night. Prices range from $15–$25. The Windows Lounge is more sophisticated, offering appetizers, afternoon tea, and cocktails. Gardens Restaurant is the fine dining room on the premises. It offers breakfast, lunch, and dinner. The international menu averages about $8 for breakfast and about $15 for lunch. Dinner entrees include such treats as cherry-smoked sea scallops, grilled swordfish, and New York steak. Prices range from $16–$30. Alternative menus for those on low-calorie, low-cholesterol, and low-sodium diets are also available.

An extensive children's menu is available at all hotel restaurants. There's a separate one for room service as well. The kids can choose from peanut butter and jelly sandwiches, fresh fruit and yogurt, grilled-cheese sandwiches, chicken fingers, pasta, small sirloin steaks, and more. Prices are $5.50–$10. Ice-cream floats, cheesecake, hot-fudge sundaes, and brownies are among the other goodies available. Of course, whenever possible, the servers will bring small portions of adult items if your child prefers that. There are even mugs with two handles to make it easier for little hands. Need we add that highchairs and boosters are available?

The ultimate kid-pleaser, though, is the Sunday brunch. We've been to lots of them with the kids (Father's Day, Mother's Day, Easter), but this is the only one with a genuine children's buffet table. The table is 2^{1}/$_{2}$ feet high, covered with a tablecloth of colorful dinosaurs and robots. The centerpieces are stuffed animals—teddy bears and unicorns—and beach balls. The buffet selection includes such children's favorites as chicken fingers, peanut butter sandwiches, and pizza. There are alphabet cookies and chocolate beyond belief—M&Ms, Hershey's Kisses, brownies. The children's buffet is $19 for children 5–11, and no charge for children 5 and under. Sunday brunch for adults costs $39, with its seafood (oysters, clams, crab legs, smoked tuna, and Nova Scotia salmon), fresh fruit, peppered sirloin, pastry-wrapped veal and loin of lamb, as well as omelets prepared to order by a chef who will indulge any fantasy. Of course, there's fresh fruit, vegetables, and a huge pastry table and other desserts.

The 285 plush rooms are large and beautifully decorated. Each has French doors that lead to a step-out balcony where you have a lovely view of either Beverly Hills or Century City and West Los Angeles. The rooms have remote-control color TVs, refrigerator/minibars, multiline phones (at least two in a room), hairdryers, terrycloth robes, and a full line of bathroom amenities. We like the Four Seasons rooms best. They have a parlor area that can be closed off. These have an additional television in the parlor, making them perfect for families.

Regular rooms are $295–$355 single and $325–$385 double; suites rent for $400–$3,000. Ask about specials and weekend rates, which can be much less expensive. The

Four Seasons Family Plan means that if two rooms (usually connecting) are used, each is charged at the single-occupancy rate. Children stay free. There's no charge for cribs; rollaways are free for kids, $25 per night for additional adults. Valet parking is $15 per night and self-parking is free.

Who hasn't heard of the **Beverly Hills Hotel and Bungalows,** 9641 Sunset Blvd., Beverly Hills, CA 90210 (☎ **310/276-2251**), the pink stucco California mission-style legend that embodies early Hollywood? It's located in residential Beverly Hills amid other mansions, on acres of fabulously manicured gardens with palm trees and abundant plantlife. Unfortunately, the hotel will be closed for renovation through part of 1995.

Expensive

Conrad Hilton opened the famed **Beverly Hilton,** 9876 Wilshire Blvd. (at Santa Monica Boulevard), Beverly Hills, CA 90210 (☎ **310/274-7777,** or toll free **800/HILTONS**), in 1955 to a throng of guests that included stars and tycoons. But regular folk have always been catered to as well. Today, after a $35-million renovation of its public areas, 581 guest rooms and suites, and restaurants, the Hilton is even more inviting. Its welcome policy for families has been in existence for many years (even before it was fashionable—and profitable), and is still somewhat more generous than many other hostelries. The Family Plan means that there is no charge for children—*regardless of age*—occupying the same room as their parents. And if you take two rooms for the family, you get charged the single rate for each room.

Services abound. The full-time concierge and multilingual staff will help with babysitting arrangements as well as other travel or sightseeing needs. Room service is available 24 hours a day. In addition, there are car-rental and airline offices, a full-service beauty salon, barbershop, currency exchange, airport shuttle service, boutiques, and a complete fitness center with Lifecycles (kids under 16 are admitted with a parent). The Hilton also has a very large giftshop with lots of sundries and an extensive assortment of gifts. You can also arrange for complimentary Lincoln Town Car service that will take you within a two-mile radius (which includes such local sights as Beverly Hills, Century City, and Westwood).

There are two outdoor heated swimming pools. One is Olympic size with a shallow end and an equally large garden area surrounding. The other, a circular pool with a fountain in the center, is five feet deep in all spots, but the enclosed patio surrounding it is perfect for playing children because it's quieter than the area around the larger pool.

In addition, there are two restaurants, a coffee shop and a lounge. Trader Vic's offers Polynesian cuisine, and although a bit on the pricey side, it's a treat for the kids with its festive decor. The Mr. H Restaurant has a tempting array of buffets as well as an à la carte menu for breakfast, lunch, and dinner. This appealing garden-style restaurant sits poolside. Café Beverly is a coffee shop serving breakfast, lunch, and dinner, and offers a children's menu. Both restaurants and the café have highchairs and boosters. For evening adult entertainment, there are two cocktail lounges.

Guest rooms are located in one of three buildings. All rooms have either one king-size bed or two double beds. Rooms with king-size beds feature love seats; rooms with two double beds have two overstuffed chairs and an end table, and may have a balcony and a view of Century City. All rooms have a desk, a mini-refrigerator/honor bar, two telephones, and remote-control television with free HBO, ESPN, and CNN. Bathrooms have marble floors and counters, tub/shower combinations, and bathroom amenities. Bathrobes are provided in most rooms.

The main building has rooms with balconies, all large enough to accommodate lounge chairs. Most rooms here have an inviting view, so they are generally priced higher than in the other two locations.

Garden lanai rooms are around the main pool. These rooms are very large, accommodating two double beds, a desk, and a table and chairs. The rooms downstairs open onto the pool area. Poolside lanai rooms are $280; poolside cabaña rooms, $280.

The Palm Court building, is a low, four-floor structure adjacent to the fountain pool. The junior suites have a king-size bed, a sofa bed, and two baths. One- and two-bedroom suites have two baths and two entrances, one of which goes directly into the bedroom. Junior suites cost $280; one- and two-bedroom suites range from $300 to $800.

Children stay free regardless of age when occupying the same room as their parents; cribs and rollaways are also free. The charge for an extra adult is $25 per night. The Hiltons frequently have specials that can run as low as half the regular rate. Be sure to ask if there are any special packages when calling for a reservation. Parking costs $15 per day.

Moderate

The **Ramada Hotel Beverly Hills,** 1150 S. Beverly Dr. (at Pico Boulevard), Los Angeles, CA 90035 (☎ **310/553-6561**, or toll free **800/2-RAMADA**), is close to central Beverly Hills and world-famous Rodeo Drive, and is as good a location as you can get in the city.

The Ramada has an outdoor heated swimming pool which gets sun all afternoon. Guests may request privileges at a nearby fitness club, which features a class for children. For babysitting, the front desk staff will refer you to an agency. Room service is available from 6am to 10pm.

Summerfield's, a small, gardenlike restaurant, serves breakfast, lunch, and dinner. Prices range from $2.75 (breakfast) to $15 (dinner). You'll find boosters and highchairs, and an ingenious little children's menu that has colorful animals and a game that will keep most youngsters occupied for a few minutes. Kids can choose from spaghetti, chicken, hamburgers, hot dogs, and a turkey sandwich. Prices run $1.75–$2.25.

The 260 attractively decorated rooms have either oak or cherrywood furniture, a game table and desk, and a color television in the armoire, with free cable and pay-per-view movies. All rooms have tub/shower combinations with bathroom amenities, and all rooms above the fourth floor have views. Suites come with king-size beds, and a living room with a large sofa, a refrigerator, and a sink.

Room rates are $115–$125 for singles, $130–$140 for doubles, $175 for suites. But weekend rates can be about a third less. For additional people, the charge is $10 per night. Cribs are free; rollaways cost $10. Children under 12 stay free in the same room as their parents. The Family Plan means that adults and their children (up to four people) stay in a room for $115–$125, depending on location. Parking costs $5.

WESTSIDE REGION

The Westside, comprised of Westwood, Brentwood, Century City, and West Los Angeles, includes some of the most beautiful residential areas of the city. Close to Santa Monica beaches and to Beverly Hills, the Westside is pricey, but a favorite of traveling families because of its convenient location. If you're staying in West Los Angeles, the Westward Ho Market, 1515 Westwood Blvd. (☎ **310/479-6702**), and Pavilions Market, 11750 Wilshire Blvd. (☎ **310/479-5294**), are fairly close to you. If you're looking for a park where the kids can roam, you might try Cheviot Hills

Recreation Area (see "Neighborhood Parks" under "Outdoor Activities" in "What to See and Do," below, for details) or Westwood Park, located just south of Wilshire Boulevard on Veteran Ave.

Deluxe

Exquisite and gracious, the **Century Plaza Hotel & Tower,** 2025 Avenue of the Stars (off Santa Monica Boulevard), Los Angeles, CA 90067 (☎ **310/277-2000,** or toll free **800/228-3000**), is a beautiful hotel that actively courts family and leisure travelers. Located in the heart of Century City, the Century Plaza Hotel is a uniquely attractive, curving 20-story structure set on 14 acres of tropical gardens, interlaced with reflecting pools and fountains. The setting makes for wonderful walks around the grounds.

In 1961 Twentieth Century Fox Studios sold off more than 200 acres of land. Century City had begun. Celebrated Japanese architect Minoru Yamasaki was commissioned to design a hotel with a resortlike atmosphere that would also fit well with the bustling, connected shopping arcades, numerous restaurants, and nightclubs, while offering space for the city's grand social events. The doors of the Century Plaza opened on June 1, 1966, and in 1984 the $85-million **Tower at Century Plaza** was added.

Since 1966 the Century Plaza has played host to the wealthy and powerful and every U.S. president since the hotel opened, including President Reagan, who resided in the famed Plaza Suite whenever he was in town. Presidents Ford, Carter, Nixon, Johnson, and Bush have also visited. And you're as likely to see a television or movie "shoot" in one of the patio areas as you once were able to spot stars on Hollywood Boulevard.

Plush furnishings, inlaid marble floors, and an exceptional collection of fine art and rare antique pieces grace the colonnaded lobbies and richly decorated public areas. A pianist plays lovely melodies in the grand lobby during the afternoon. Lest you think this is all too grand for your little ones, the hotel staff is accommodating and friendly to children. The Century Plaza's Westin Kids' Club program is a fabulous, comprehensive package. Not only do children receive a welcome pack—including coloring kits, a sports bottle, and baseball cap, but children under three also receive tippy cups, baby shampoos, powder, teething rings, etc. If you so desire, you can have a safety kit for the room that includes electrical outlet covers, child's ID bracelet, night-lights, and Band-Aids.

Cookies and milk at bedtime are also part of the treat. You can also have a highchair, stroller, bottle warmer, step stool, and all the necessary accessories. You'll also find toys and games galore for your room, if you want, as well as children's menus at hotel restaurants and a concierge staff that will be glad to help with zoo tickets, Disneyland trips, and the like. Little candy lovers might find jars of jelly bellies awaiting them at night in the room.

Regular hotel services include complete concierge staff (who will assist you with babysitting), multilingual staff, twice-daily maid service, complimentary shoeshine (at the Tower only), and same-day laundry and valet. There's also a complete business center. A large shopping arcade within the hotel has a camera store, convenience shop, travel agency, beauty center, florist, and men's and women's clothing store.

You and the kids will want to sample some of the delights in the Century Square Shopping Center and in the underground ABC Entertainment Complex, but you'll also have a choice of five restaurants within the Century Plaza Hotel and the Tower. The Café Plaza is an informal restaurant, reminiscent of a sidewalk café in Paris—and just perfect for families. Prices for breakfast, lunch, and dinner range from $10 to $15. It's open from 6am to midnight, and the kids will love the freshly baked breads and pastries. We've often purchased a box lunch here to take with us on outings. The Terrace Restaurant, in the Tower, is open daily for lunch ($7–$14) and Monday through Saturday for dinner ($20–$25). This restaurant has huge windows that open onto strikingly beautiful gardens, accentuating a breezy, indoor/outdoor feeling. You may be surprised to learn that these restaurants all have highchairs and boosters, and will provide children's portions. The 24-hour room service has children's items on the menu.

For fine dining, the Tower at Century Plaza has one of the city's acclaimed restaurants, La Chaumière. (Leave the kids with a sitter when you dine here.) The restaurant alone is worth the experience. With the ambience of a European club, amid alderwood paneling, upholstered burled-elm chairs, and five enormous 18th-century French paintings, guests dine on classic French and nouvelle California cuisine. Monday through Thursday at 5pm there's a pianist entertaining. Open for both lunch and dinner, with prices ranging from $11 to $16 and $16 to $35, respectively.

The Century Plaza has 750 guest rooms; the Tower has 322 guest rooms. Every room is soundproofed, which we find to be an enormous advantage. We didn't worry about disturbing guests, even when little Elizabeth would waken.

Rates for the Century Plaza: $165–$202 single, $190–$235 double; one- and two-bedroom suites are $300–$1,025. The Tower rates are from $220 single, from $245 double. Ask about weekend rates, when many of the Century Plaza rooms are 50% less. Children 18 years and under are free when they stay in their parents' room. No fee for cribs; rollaways are free for children, but cost $25 for adults. The charge for an additional adult is $25. Valet parking costs $15 per day; self-parking, $8.

Moderate

BEST BET FOR THE MONEY The **Century Wilshire Hotel,** 10776 Wilshire Blvd. (between Malcolm and Selby Avenues), Los Angeles, CA 90024 (☎ **310/ 474-4506,** or toll free **800/421-7223** outside California), is a charming small hotel in the European tradition, with only 99 rooms. Thus the staff is able to get to know the guests (some of whom stay for weeks and even months at a time), and takes pleasure in helping them. The hotel draws an eclectic mix: staffs of consulates who stay at the hotel while looking for homes to rent, traveling businesspeople, and families.

The hotel is decorated with traditional-style furnishings, and exudes a homey ambience, inviting for families. There is a multilingual staff, free parking, valet service, and staff on the premises who love to babysit.

Wonderfully situated on Wilshire Boulevard just outside Westwood Village, the hotel is built around a garden courtyard, where guests can partake of their continental breakfast while basking in the sun and enjoying the lovely little fountain. Or they may also use the breakfast room that opens on to the garden. The continental breakfast is not a meager offering, but a full repast of fresh fruit, toast or muffins, cereal, and beverage.

Another lovely feature of the Century Wilshire is the large pool area, also in a gardenlike setting with palm and banana trees. There are plenty of chaises longues and tables with umbrellas. The pool (heated fall through spring) is good for lap swimming, but also has a nice shallow area for the kids.

The attractive rooms are clean and airy, with lace curtains and comfortably worn furniture. Some have balconies with poolside views. All have stall showers, and some have good old-fashioned bathtubs next to the stall showers. All rooms have color television. Rooms with two double beds are spacious. Junior suites and one-bedroom suites have fully equipped kitchens that will meet your basic needs, even if you stay for an extended period of time—but don't expect a dishwasher. These suites have full dining areas and plenty of storage space. The junior suites are perfect for traveling families, and the one-bedroom suites are like apartment units.

Room rates start at $65 single, $75 double. Junior suites start at $80; and one-bedroom suites at $125. Cribs are $10 per night, as are rollaways (but the fee can be negotiated depending on the length of your stay). Additional guests per room are charged at $10 each above the double-occupancy rate.

OTHER MODERATELY PRICED CHOICES   Although more expensive than the Century Wilshire, the **Holiday Inn Westwood Plaza Hotel,** 10740 Wilshire Blvd. (at Selby Avenue), Los Angeles, CA 90024 (☎ **310/475-8711,** or toll free **800/472-8556**), is a nice hotel in a fabulous location. Within walking distance of Westwood Village and very close to Beverly Hills, Brentwood, and the San Diego Freeway (I-405), the hotel also provides complimentary transportation within a $2^{1}/_{2}$-mile radius, which includes Century City, Beverly Hills, UCLA, and Brentwood. The traditional-style hotel has 19 floors and 300 newly refurbished rooms.

The ground-level promenade arcade that leads to the pool and spa features a giftshop, video-game room, and an exercise room (children under 14 may use the exercise room when accompanied by an adult). The pool is heated year round and has a shallow end for the younger children.

A concierge staff, available every day from 8am to 8pm, will help with babysitting arrangements.

Café Le Dome serves breakfast and lunch from 6:30am to 2pm and dinner from 4 to 10:30pm. It features an extensive children's menu with prices ranging from $1.25 to $3.50. Room service is offered from 6:30am to 2:30pm and 5 to 10pm.

Standard rooms have two double beds and Queen Anne–style furniture: side chairs, a game table, and a desk. You can choose a room with one queen-size bed and a small sofa. Suites come with one or two baths and, depending on the suite, may have a large living room with a sofa, desk, and comfortable chairs. All rooms have a color TV with free 36-channel cable.

Rooms are priced at $84–$120 single and $84–$120 double. Suites go for $200. Cribs are free; rollaways cost $10 each. Children under 19 stay free in their parents' room. There's free covered parking.

Located in the heart of Westwood Village is the **Royal Palace Westwood Hotel,** 1052 Tiverton Ave., Los Angeles, CA 90024 (☎ **310/208-6677,** or toll free **800/631-0100**), a newly renovated small motor inn with 35 recently redecorated rooms. Expect a very simple place, but one with advantages. You're paying for an ideal location that's within walking distance of more than 80 restaurants, 20 first-run movie theaters, and shops and department stores, as well as UCLA. You're also on one of the few convenient major bus routes that will take you to the beach, Century City, and Beverly Hills.

There's a small office area and limited free parking—a rarity in Westwood. They don't handle babysitting.

Each room has a small but complete kitchenette with an eating area. The standard rooms with one queen-size bed are on the small side if you have to bring in a crib. Go for a room with two queen-size beds, since these rooms are much larger and accommodate a crib, and they don't cost that much more. The suites feature a queen-size sofa bed with a very small bedroom in which a king-size bed and dresser just fit. The closet space is very large. The suites also have a complete kitchen and nice bathroom. HBO, CNN, and ESPN are available in all rooms. Complimentary breakfast is served. Rates are $67 single and $73 double in a room with a queen-size bed and kitchen, $70 single and $76 double in a room with two queen-size beds and kitchen. A mini-suite (with a king-size bed and a sofa bed, or a queen-size bed and queen-size sofa bed) with a kitchen rents for $75 single and $81 double; a one-bedroom suite (with a king-size bed and a queen-size sofa bed) costs $90 single and $96 double. Cribs and rollaways are $6 per night. Children under 12 stay free in their parents' room. Additional adults over double occupancy are charged $6 per night each.

Budget

If you're looking for a less expensive place to stay, the **TraveLodge Los Angeles West,** at 10740 Santa Monica Blvd., Los Angeles, CA 90025 (☎ **310/474-4576,** or toll free **800/255-3050**), is a clean little two-story motel unit of 55 rooms about one mile from Westwood Boulevard. It looks onto the lovely Los Angeles Mormon Temple with its imposing statue and vast lawn. The small heated pool is gated and locked.

The rooms are comfortable, newly remodeled and about what you'd expect from a budget motel in pricey West Los Angeles. Rooms have game tables, refrigerators, color TVs, instant coffee makers, radios, and showers. Some have tub/shower combinations.

Rooms with a queen-size bed cost $57 single and $64 double, rooms with a king-size bed are $63 single and $68 double, rooms with two twin beds run $68 double, rooms with a queen-size bed and two twin beds rent for $68–$72, and rooms with two queen-size beds are $75–$79. The Family Plan means that one or two children under 17 are free in their parents' room if additional beds are not needed. Cribs are free; rollaways cost $7. Connecting rooms are available.

THE COASTAL REGION

If you're looking for cool climate and beautiful surroundings, the beach areas are for you. Santa Monica and Marina del Rey have many more family accommodations than you might think. If you're in need of a market, you'll find a Vons Market at 1311 Wilshire Blvd. (☎ **310/394-1414**) in Santa Monica and another Vons at 4365 Glencoe Ave. (☎ **310/821-7208**) in Marina del Rey.

If you're looking for a park in Santa Monica, don't miss Douglas Park (see "Neighborhood Parks" in "Outdoor Activities" under "What to See and Do" for details). In Marina del Rey, you can let the kids roam at Burton Chace Park, which is at the west end of Mindanao Way.

Loews Santa Monica Beach Hotel, 1700 Ocean Ave., Santa Monica, CA 90401 (☎ **310/458-6700,** or toll free **800/223-0888** outside California), is a relatively new arrival on the L.A. scene, and is the only 4-star/4-diamond hotel in Los Angeles that's on the beach. Overlooking the Pacific, this airy, lavish hotel is just two blocks south of the Santa Monica Pier.

The hotel offers a complete children's program during the summer, called the Splash Club, designed for children between 4 and 12. The club operates Friday night through Saturday night and costs $25 per child per session, including lunch and snack. The Splash Club takes kids to the Santa Monica beach and then to play in the hotel's private playground and swimming pools. The hotel offers arts and crafts, puppet shows, treasure hunts, and kite flying. Call for information, and be sure to reserve beforehand to avoid disappointment.

The hotel has two restaurants and a poolside snack bar. It also has a 3,200-square-foot fitness center with steam and saunas, an indoor/outdoor swimming pool, and Jacuzzi. You can rent bikes, boogie boards, in-line skates, and roller skates. Other services include twice-daily maid service, 24-hour room service, dry cleaning, and shoeshine and beauty salon services. Babysitting is arranged through the concierge.

Each of the 329 rooms and 31 suites has a minibar, two televisions, and three phones with two phone lines (a reminder of home for those of you with preteens and teens). Rooms have either a king-size bed or two double beds.

Rates are $195–$355 single and $215–$355 double, depending on location and type of room. Suites start at $300. Children under 18 are free when they stay with their parents; additional adults pay $20 per day. Cribs are free. Valet parking $14 per day; self-parking $12 per day.

Expensive

Ah, to be so close to the city and yet feel far away . . . that is the **Marina Del Rey Hotel,** 13534 Bali Way (at Admiralty Way), Marina del Rey, CA 90292 (☎ **310/301-1000,** or toll free **800/862-7462**), the only hotel in the marina that's on the water. As you drive to the end of Bali Way, you're encircled by masts of sailboats and yachts. At the end sits the three-story white stucco building with royal-blue awnings and a rather grand entryway. It's set on the main canal of the Marina del Rey harbor. The grounds are beautifully planted with bougainvillea. The hotel has views from almost every room. It sits on a private road for the boat owners who rent slips, which keeps the access to the hotel limited.

You can sit by the swimming pool (with a large shallow area and lots of room to play), surrounded by water, and watch the boats move in and out of their slips. It's a gorgeous sight, and the atmosphere is like a resort. There's also a putting green. The small three-story atrium lobby gives the upper floors a sense of openness and continuity. There's a seating area on each floor that serves as a mini-lobby. It has sofas, tables, and a patio.

The Crystal Seahorse is a waterfront terrace restaurant that offers breakfast, lunch, and dinner. Prices range from an intimate $4.50 to $19.50. The restaurant has highchairs and boosters.

Other hotel amenities include room service, valet service, free parking, and car rental service. In fact, you can even have the Marina cruise line pick you up at the hotel. The hotel offers free shuttle service to and from the airport. Ice machines are located on each floor.

All 160 rooms have cable color television (including free Select TV) with remote control, pay movies (with locks so children can't use movie channels without your consent), and AM/FM radios. Most rooms have balconies with chairs and a table so you can enjoy the sea breeze; many have spectacular views. The rooms have nice bathrooms done in marble with tub/shower combinations, separate vanity areas, and bathroom amenities. You can also request refrigerators, irons, and hairdryers at no extra charge.

Rooms are good-sized and comfortably done. Those with two double beds have enough space for the kids and their toys; the room with a king-size bed has adequate space for a crib or rollaway. Suites are available and can connect to rooms with two double beds.

Singles cost $125–$190; doubles, $145–$210; and suites, $350–$400. There's no charge for children under 18 in their parents' room if additional beds are not needed. Cribs are free; rollaways cost $15. Free parking.

The **Miramar Sheraton Hotel,** 101 Wilshire Blvd. (at 2nd Street), Santa Monica, CA 90401 (☎ **310/394-3731,** or toll free **800/325-3535**), sits on the bluff across the street from Palisades Park. Close to the Santa Monica Pier and all the Santa Monica beaches, this garden hotel has a perfect location.

The hotel's rich history began over 100 years ago, when United States Sen. John P. Jones built a private mansion on the spot and called it Miramar (literally, "view of the sea"). Jones, a prosperous politician, struck it rich in the silver mines. Looking for a place to build a railroad and harbor so he could carry his silver to be minted in San Francisco, he chose Santa Monica Bay as the port for his endeavor. With his partner, Col. Robert Baker, he founded the city of Santa Monica.

Jones bought the land on which the Miramar sits for $1, and completed building in 1889. Political figures and other luminaries have come and gone, including Susan B. Anthony, Mark Twain, Greta Garbo, Susan Hayward, Eleanor Roosevelt, and John and Jacqueline Kennedy, all drawn to the ocean view and the hotel's lovely tropical gardens. In fact, the story goes that Betty Grable was "discovered" at the hotel bar. The hotel grounds, swimming pool, and bungalows have also served as the location for television shows and movies. The hotel has had a $33 million renovation.

Hotel amenities include concierge service, 24-hour room service, complimentary newspaper, laundry and valet service, nightly turn-down, limousine and car rentals, airline desk, hair salons for men and women, boutiques and giftshops, a heated outdoor swimming pool, a lounge, and two restaurants.

The Café is open from 6:30am to 11:30pm, offering casual breakfast, lunch, and dinner dining. The kid's menu offers breakfast for $1.50–$2, and lunch and dinner entrees run $2–$2.25. The little menu includes games and mazes to keep the kids occupied.

Of the 303 guest rooms, 60 are suites. You can choose from two different towers or the small garden bungalows. The hotel's Ocean Tower and Palisades rooms come in two styles—traditional with dark woods and elaborate moldings, and light pastels with rattan, bleached-wood furniture, and polished brass fixtures. You can choose rooms with a king-size bed or with two double beds. Each room has an honor bar/refrigerator, coffee makers, two-line phones, voice mail, game table, color television, and bathroom amenities. Most have tub/shower combinations, but request one specifically if it's important to you. All rooms have remote-control television and in-room safes.

Rates are for single or double occupancy. Poolside Lanai rooms are $275, Palisades rooms cost $185, Ocean Tower rooms run $195, and Palisades suites (one-bedroom suites) rent for $275. Ocean Tower suites start at $375. Children 18 and under stay free in their parents' room if additional beds are not necessary. Additional adults pay $20 per night. Cribs are free. Parking is $5 per day.

Moderate

One of our favorite hotels is the **Marina International Hotel and Bungalows,** 4200 Admiralty Way (at Palawan Way), Marina del Rey, CA 90292 (☎ **310/301-2000,** or toll free **800/529-2525**). This smallish hostelry of 135 rooms in a pleasant garden setting is just perfect for families. Believe it or not, while it's pricey, it's probably the best value in the moderate price range if you want something near the water.

There is a main building and garden bungalows that give you a choice of the kind of accommodation you'd like for your family. Furthermore, it's across the street from a sandy beach with gentle, lapping water instead of waves. You also have your choice of dining experiences here, with loads of restaurants nearby.

The two-story lobby resembles a large cheery sitting room or enclosed patio. There's a huge skylight and plants that continue the outdoor effect. There are small conversation groups with tables and chairs at which you and the kids can enjoy the happy-hour appetizers served in the adjacent lounge.

The hotel offers free parking, and shuttle service to and from the airport. Other hotel amenities include 24-hour room service, vending and ice machines on each floor, and a very pretty pool area that has a large shallow area and is tucked away so that you don't have to worry about the children. Above the pool is a nice area for sitting. There is a laundrette and shopping center within easy walking distance. Babysitting can be arranged through the front desk.

The Crystal Fountain Restaurant is open for breakfast, lunch, and dinner. They have highchairs and boosters, but no children's menu. Prices range from $4.75 to $7.50, for breakfast and $6.50 to $7.50 for lunch.

The very large rooms are done in a sunny Southwest motif that adds to the life and verve of the place. They're bright, with large white shutters filtering the light and providing privacy. All rooms have balconies and come complete with free remote-control cable television, including Select TV, and pay movies (the channels are locked so parents can keep kids from watching X-rated movies). There are game tables and chairs, desks, and AM/FM clock radios. Bathrooms come with tub/shower combinations.

Bungalows are set up in a charming, flower-filled courtyard where there's ample space for kids to wander. The ones on the ground floor have balconies that are cordoned off by planters so that even toddlers won't wander off. Our kids usually spend time sitting outside playing jacks and pick-up-sticks on the cobblestone ground. Bungalows are split-level rooms with a loft, cathedral ceilings, and large windows. There are huge closets, two televisions, two telephones, a double bed, and a sofa bed.

Rates are $110–$160 for singles, $125–$180 for doubles (two doubles or one queen-size or king-size bed). Bungalows and suites in the main building range from $198 to $288. Junior suites with a queen-size bed and a sofa bed that pulls out to a double bed are $180 double occupancy. Children under 16 stay for free when sharing a room with their parents if additional beds are not needed. Cribs are free; there's no charge for rollaways for children under 16, but there's a $15-per-night charge for additional adults. Connecting rooms are available. Free parking. Always ask if there are any special discount packages available, which can be as much as 30% lower.

Apartmentlike accommodations and a great location make the **Hotel Shangri-La,** 1301 Ocean Ave., Santa Monica, CA 90401 (☎ **310/394-2791,** or toll free **800/345-STAY;** fax 310/451-3351), a good family choice. The hotel is located directly across the street from Palisades Park overlooking the ocean, and it's within walking distance of the Third Street Promenade, the new "place to be." You aren't far from the beach or the Santa Monica Pier. The free parking makes it even easier to go back and forth to these sites without worrying about finding a space to park.

A large outdoor courtyard makes a perfect place to have your coffee and watch the kids play, although there's no pool or playground equipment.

The streamlined art deco building houses studio rooms, and one- and two-bedroom suites with fully equipped kitchens. The little "apartments" are bright and clean. A one-bedroom suite has plenty of room for a family of four. In addition to the kitchen, there's a color TV and pay movies. Two-bedroom suites have two bathrooms, a living room, dining room, and the kitchen. The second bedroom is furnished with two single beds, and there's room in the living room for two to three rollaways.

A studio room with a living room/bedroom combination rents for $80–$160; single or double; suites $200 to $250. Cribs are free; rollaway is an extra $10. Children under 17 free in same room with adults; maximum four occupants per room.

The **Pacific Shore Hotel,** 1819 Ocean Ave. (at Pico Boulevard), Santa Monica, CA 90401 (☎ **310/451-8711,** or toll free **800/622-8711**), is a pleasant eight-story, 168-room hotel with a breezy, seasidelike atmosphere. Its big attraction, though, is its proximity to the beach, which is across the street. The swimming pool and spa area is quite spacious, and the shallow end of the pool can be cordoned off to keep little swimmers out of the deep end.

Very much a family-oriented place, the hotel has a guest laundry, same-day valet service, free parking, a giftshop, and a complimentary continental breakfast of coffee, croissants, and jam. Babysitting is handled through a referral agency. A refrigerator is $25 per day (request one when you make your reservation). Room service, which includes a children's menu, is available from 7am to 10pm.

A Baker's Square restaurant is adjacent to the hotel. If you're unfamiliar with this chain, they are nice coffee shops with lunch and dinner prices ranging from $4.25 to $7.25. In essence, you're paying coffee shop prices, *not* hotel restaurant prices.

The newly renovated rooms all have remote-control cable color televisions, pay-per-view movies, AM/FM radios, small desks, tub/shower combinations, and bathroom toiletries. The best family rooms are those with two double beds, but there are also rooms with king-size beds. Connecting rooms can have a king-size bed and two double beds. In fact, you can connect three rooms with two doubles on either side and a king in the middle.

Rates range from $95–$120 single, $100–$130 double. Children 12 and under stay free when sharing a parent's room. Cribs are free; rollaways are $10 per night, and an extra person is charged $10 per night. Free parking.

Also within walking distance from Venice Beach is the **BayView Plaza Holiday Inn,** 530 Pico Blvd. (at 6th Street), Santa Monica, CA 90405 (☎ **310/399-9344,** or toll free **800/HOLIDAY**). The attractive four-story atrium-style lobby is done in California contemporary style. Large enough to feel spacious and allow you to let your kids walk around, it's small enough that you don't have to worry about their getting lost. This full-service hotel has two outdoor, heated swimming pools (one has a good shallow area) and two Jacuzzis, an exercise room, giftshop, beauty salon, complimentary parking, and a free shuttle to LAX. Other amenities include room service from 6:30am to 11pm, coin-operated laundry, and a lobby lounge.

The Bay View Café serves breakfast, lunch, and dinner, offering such American standards as hotcakes, burgers, and seafood. Breakfast costs $4.25–$12, or all-you-can-eat buffet for $9, lunch is $6–$20, and dinner runs $5–$21.99. The café has highchairs, boosters, and a children's menu.

The hotel has over 309 attractive rooms. The rooms are standard size, and most of them have balconies; four rooms even have their own outdoor Jacuzzis. Each has a remote-control cable color TV with pay movies, minibar/refrigerator, bathroom amenities, and nice views. Some rooms also have sofa beds; some have two bathroom sinks and vanities.

Room rates depend on location and view. Singles range from $80 to $133; doubles, from $80 to $143. Suites rent for $250. Cribs are free; rollaways cost $10. Children 18 and under are free in the same room with an adult. Free parking.

Budget

An excellent choice for the money is the well-kept **Comfort Inn,** 2815 Santa Monica Blvd., Santa Monica, CA 90404 (☎ **310/828-5517,** or toll free **800/228-5150**). Although it isn't within walking distance of the beach (it's actually about ten minutes away), this is a good West Los Angeles/Santa Monica location, just minutes (by car) from Westwood, Brentwood, and downtown Santa Monica. You can't beat it for value. The swimming pool is quite large, with a good-size shallow area. You can lie around the pool using the lounge chairs provided, or sit on the outdoor patios on the first and second floors. There's plenty of room for kids to wander or play quiet games on these patios, and tables are provided so you can enjoy the outdoors. The staff is friendly and used to families. Indeed, so successful is this little motor inn that a large percentage of their business is repeat customers.

The 100 rooms are tidy and surprisingly good-sized. All have tub/shower combinations, individual air conditioning, instant coffee makers, oversize closets, game tables, and color TV. Complimentary continental breakfast is served 6:15am to 10am. Rooms with two double beds are especially large and have plenty of room for a crib. The rooms with king-size beds also feature a small love seat.

Rates are $55–$75 single and $65–$85 double. Children 18 and under stay free when sharing the same room as their parents. Cribs and rollaways are $10 per night. Adjoining rooms (usually two doubles connect to a room with a king-size bed) are available. Free parking.

THE AIRPORT AREA

Most people who stay near Los Angeles International Airport stay here because they want the convenience. If you need a supermarket in this area, your best bet is to ask someone at the front desk.

Expensive

The **Los Angeles Airport Hilton & Towers,** 5711 W. Century Blvd., Los Angeles, CA 90045 (☎ **310/410-4000,** or toll free **800/HILTONS;** fax 310/410-6250), the largest airport hotel in the world, has more than 1,200 rooms to choose from and a complimentary airport shuttle runs 24 hours a day. Don't be put off by the formal-looking lobby. Children are welcome at this hotel. The Hilton features an outdoor pool surrounded by four spas and a self-service eating area. There are also three garden terraces at which room service is available and where children can entertain themselves. Mom and Dad can work out, play racquetball, or get a massage at the Family Fitness Center, which costs $5 per stay and provides child care for $1 per hour (kids must be six months or older). Or contact the concierge staff, which can arrange babysitting through an outside agency.

There are several restaurants at the Hilton, but the best one for families is The Café on the lobby level. It is open for breakfast, lunch, and dinner and supplies a children's menu. Or order from room service 24 hours daily. If you still need other choices, the Bistro stays open 24 hours. The self-service eatery offers pizza, sandwiches, salads, and other simple choices.

As a full-service hotel, the Hilton provides same-day laundry and dry cleaning service and coin-operated washers and dryers for guest use. There's also free shuttle service to the airport as well as to the Manhattan Beach Village Mall.

The clean, nicely lighted rooms come with remote-control TV and free cable. Refrigerators are available for $15 per night. Rooms with king-size beds can fit a rollaway and a crib, while rooms with two double beds could take one or the other. Features include mirrored closet doors, sleek and clean bathrooms with tub/shower combinations, clock radios, and two-line phones with voice mail. A parlor is a good choice for large families. It's quite roomy and has a sofa bed, refrigerator, table, chairs, and desk. Some are equipped with wet bars. It can connect to one or two sleeping rooms, affording you extra space in the daytime. Handicapped-accessible and no-smoking rooms can be reserved.

You can request a Lanai room with doors that open directly to the garden area. Rooms on the 14th floor are geared toward the business traveler; they come equipped with dataports, fax machines, irons, and ironing boards. A number of two-room Executive suites are designed with European-style furnishings, a living area and separate bedroom, two TVs, two bathrooms, and two closets. On the Tower Floors, guests have use of a private lounge where they can check in and out. Complimentary breakfast, evening drinks, and hors d'oeuvres are served.

Because this is such a large hotel, you might want to request rooms close to the elevators if you are *schlepping* water wings, backpacks, and baby bottles. Single rooms are priced $99–$149; a double room runs $119–$169. Tower rooms are $119–$169 single, and $139–$189 double. Executive suites run $144–$194 single; $164–$214 double. Parlors start at $175. Suite prices start at $305. Children sleep free in their parents' room regardless of age. An extra adult is charged $20 per night. Cribs and rollaways are complimentary. Ask about special weekend packages when continental breakfast is included, and about special summer rates (which are often less expensive than the rest of the year because this is a business person's hotel). Self-parking is $8 per day, with in-and-out privileges. Valet parking is also available at $12 per day.

Also close to the airport and freeways is the **Embassy Suites,** 9801 Airport Blvd., Los Angeles, CA 90045 (☎ **310/215-1000,** or toll free **800/EMBASSY;** fax 310/215-1952).

Like most Embassy Suites, this one has an atrium lobby in which the cooked-to-order complimentary breakfasts, and afternoon snacks and drinks, are served. In addition, there is the Century Cafe & Lounge, which is open for lunch and dinner and offers a children's menu.

A small indoor pool and spa, plus the exercise room are entered from the lobby. Each suite is spacious, and some have one king-size bed in the bedroom, while others have two double beds. There's a pull-out sofa in the living room, plus a dining table with four chairs. Two TVs (one with Nintendo) and two telephones (with voice mail) are found in every suite along with a coffee maker and microwave. Microwavable snacks can be purchased in the hotel's gift shop.

Babysitting can be arranged at the front desk. The hotel provides a coin-operated laundry for guest use, a complimentary morning newspaper, and underground parking ($7.70 daily with in-and-out privileges).

Suites rent for $125–$145. Each additional person 12 and over is charged $15. Cribs are complimentary; there are no rollaways. There is 24-hour complimentary airport transportation.

Moderate/Budget

Two clean and well-priced chains fit this description: The **Quality Inn,** 5249 W. Century Blvd., Los Angeles, CA 90045 (☎ **310/645-2200,** or toll free **800/266-2200** or **800/228-5151;** fax 310/641-8214) is one. Singles are $85, doubles cost $95; suites are $135. But there are many summer family specials at lower rates. Kids 18 and under stay free in their parents' room. Extra adults are charged $10. Cribs are complimentary, rollaways $10. Parking is $6. The nearby **Motel 6,** 5101 Century Blvd., Los Angeles, CA 90304 (☎ **310/419-1234;** fax 310/677-7871) is the other. Singles rent for $39.99, and doubles are $45.99. A third and fourth person in the room is another $3 each. Kids 17 and under sleep free in their parent's room. Cribs, free, rollaways $10. Free parking.

HOLLYWOOD

This area draws scores of travelers because of its romantic history. While we would not advise taking an evening stroll in dark areas, it's well patrolled and safe for sightseeing during the day. Universal City is just over the hill from Hollywood, and is a city unto itself. People stay there to be close to the studios and the freeway. Ask the staff at the front desk for the names and addresses of markets in the area.

Business leaders in Hollywood are going to great lengths to spruce up this historic town and make it safe. To this end, a significant number of police patrol the area on bicycles. As is the case with any major metropolitan area, Hollywood has its safety problems; we don't recommend wandering too far off Hollywood Boulevard.

Expensive

The **Radisson Hollywood Roosevelt Hotel,** 7000 Hollywood Blvd., Hollywood, CA 90028 (☎ **213/466-7000,** or toll free **800/950-7667;** fax 213/462-8056), epitomizes Tinsel Town when it was in its heyday. This deluxe hotel, which was the site of the first Academy Awards presentation in 1929, was renovated in 1985 and carefully restored to its original glory. The hotel is located diagonally across from Mann's Chinese Theatre and within easy access of a major freeway, downtown, and Beverly Hills.

When you enter the Hollywood Roosevelt, you'll feel as if you've just stepped back in time. (See "Hollywood" in "What to See and Do," below, for information on the hotel's mini historical museum.)

The two-story lobby with its hand-painted ceilings and Spanish wrought-iron grillwork remains. It's a large lobby with lots of seating for good people-watching. Be sure to take a walk by the Olympic-size pool to see the David Hockney painting on the bottom. There's plenty of room for lounging around the pool, but only a tiny grassy area for wandering toddlers. Poolside food service is available. For those who can't rest, an exercise room is adjacent. The concierge can arrange babysitting.

Theodore's is the hotel restaurant, which, unfortunately, doesn't have a children's menu; prices are reasonable. The adjacent Teddy's Lounge serves snacks all day in the lobby area. Room service can be ordered; the chef will cater to special requests.

The rooms are done in soft, relaxing colors; some have art deco touches. Standard accommodations have room for a rollaway or crib. Request either two double beds or a king-size bed. Some Tower rooms have connecting doors. The more expensive cabaña rooms have small private balconies or open to the outside gardens (keep this in mind if you're traveling with young wanderers). Remote-control TVs and Spectra Vision, clock radios, and room safes are standard. The oversize room with king-size bed is your best bet. The large living area features a sofa bed, and there's plenty of space to spread out. You could even fit a rollaway and crib in here. The three-room Star Suites have great deco furniture. The two-room Hollywood Suites are furnished in country French, and the three-story Gable/Lombard Suite rents for $1,500 a night.

Tower rooms cost $105–$115 single, $125–$135 double. Cabaña rooms run $125 single, $145 double. There are Executive Level rooms that rent for $150–$170. Suites cost $275–$350. Children of any age stay free in their parents' room. Extra adults are charged $20. Cribs are complimentary; rollaways cost $15. Valet parking is only $8 per night.

Located in the heart of Hollywood, not far from the Hollywood Roosevelt, the **Holiday Inn Hollywood,** 1755 N. Highland Ave., Hollywood, CA 90028 (☎ **213/462-7181,** or toll free **800/465-4329;** fax 213/466-9072), is appropriate for families who want to stay in a moderately priced hotel centrally located to many southland attractions. You'll recognize the hotel by its revolving top floor. The hotel offers a small heated outdoor pool area. Babysitting can be arranged with an outside agency through the housekeeping department.

The Show Biz Restaurant is the place to take the family for breakfast (beginning at 6am), lunch and dinner (with reasonably priced hamburgers and sandwiches). Children's menus are provided. Windows on Hollywood is a more formal restaurant on the revolving top floor, and only sophisticated taste buds need attend. But the Sunday brunch is fine if your kids like jazz (kids pay $9.95 for brunch). Room service is available with a "For Kids Only" section.

The modern rooms are simple and compact. All come with two double beds or a king-size bed, and all have room for a crib or rollaway. Some rooms with king-size beds are furnished with either sofa beds or reading chairs. Remote-control cable TV (with free Showtime) and in-room movies are standard features as are in-room safes ($4 per day). Hairdryers and extra phones are available upon request. There are adjoining rooms suitable for large families. Or rent one bedroom and an adjoining mini-suite, which has a bedroom and a seating area. Bathrooms are small, and all have tub/shower combinations.

Single occupancy costs $105–$125; double occupancy is $115–$135. Mini-suites with kitchenettes rent for $125–$149. Children under 18 sleep free in their parents' room; those 18 and over are charged $10. Cribs are free; rollaways cost $10. If you're traveling in the summer, ask about special rates. Parking costs $5.50 per day, and there's room for motorhomes in the lot.

UNIVERSAL CITY

The **Sheraton Universal,** 333 Universal Terrace Pkwy., Universal City, CA 91608 (☎ **818/980-1212,** or toll free **800/325-3535**), is located on the lot of Universal Studios, perched high above the San Fernando Valley floor. Many of the rooms literally overlook the famous studio, and others have views of the Hollywood Hills. If you want to be close to Hollywood, downtown Los Angeles, and Burbank, you can't beat this location.

The hotel's 446 rooms are in a 20-story tower and in the two-story poolside lanai buildings. The enchanting outdoor pool area is surrounded by clusters of tall palm trees and umbrellas, offering shade to outdoor diners and a wonderful area for sun worshippers. The pool has a large shallow area and lots of space to laze the day away if you and the kids are so inclined.

Hotel amenities include concierge service, 24-hour room service, laundry and valet service Monday through Saturday, a giftshop, and complimentary shuttle service to Universal Studios Tours.

In addition to being within walking distance of Universal's City Walk, Fung Lum's, Tony Roma's and Victoria Station (see the "Where to Eat" section for details), the hotel's restaurant, Californias, serves breakfast, lunch, and dinner. Breakfast prices run $3.50–$12.75 lunch is $7.25–$11, and dinners average around $16. Kids can ask for a hot dog or hamburger ($3).

The hotel rooms are bright, set off with pastels and light-wood furniture. You can choose rooms with king-size beds and a comfortable, overstuffed chair, rooms with two double beds, or parlor suites that have king-size beds with full-size sectional couches. Deluxe suites have a sleeping room that closes off and a parlor.

All rooms have a fancy phone system with call waiting, direct-dial to hotel service, and phone jacks that allow you to move the phone around the room. Remote-control television comes with free HBO and video checkout, and pay Spectra Vision. All bathrooms have tub/shower combinations and complimentary toiletries.

Rooms are $175–$195 single and $195–$215 double. Suites cost $210 and up. Connecting rooms are available. Cribs are free; rollaways cost $20. Children 17 and under are free if they share their parents' room and additional beds are not needed. Parking is $9.50 per day.

WEST HOLLYWOOD

This area can be trendy and exciting, if somewhat on the expensive side. Many families prefer this part of town because of its location near Hollywood, Beverly Hills and the mid-Wilshire District. You'll find a 24-hour Hughes market at 9040 Beverly Blvd. (☎ 310/278-1351), and at Santa Monica and Robertson Boulevards is a 24-hour Pavilion Place (☎ 310/273-0977) containing a pharmacy (☎ 310/273-5126) that's open weekdays until 9pm. The West Hollywood Park, with some children's equipment and a big sandbox, is between Melrose Avenue and Santa Monica Boulevard, and Robertson and San Vicente Boulevards.

Expensive

Set in a quiet residential neighborhood, **Le Parc Hotel,** 733 N. West Knoll Dr., West Hollywood, CA 90069 (☎ **310/855-8888,** or toll free **800/578-4837**; fax 310/659-7812), is convenient to Beverly Hills, downtown, and many local attractions.

This all-suite hotel, actually a converted apartment building, hides a small outdoor pool, sun deck, spa, and tennis court on the roof. The restaurant, Café Le Parc, is open only to guests. Even though there's no children's menu, breakfast here is no problem because the standard choices will appeal to most children. Lunch, with a French menu, also offers the ever-faithful cheeseburger. Dinner at Le Parc is only for the sophisticated—and rich! There are highchairs here, but no boosters. A plus, though, is that you'll find all sorts of snacks and soft drinks in the cocktail cabinet in your generous-size kitchenette. Management will supply toasters, cookware, and dishes at your request (room service will do the dishes). Occasionally, complimentary hors d'oeuvres are served in the restaurant.

The warm, comfortable rooms come with gas fireplaces, two phone lines, and nice-size closets. In the standard executive suites, and the slightly larger deluxe suites, the bedrooms with their king-size beds are a step up from the living room (separated by a curtain). A separate dressing area contains a hairdryer and makeup mirror. There is room for a crib and a rollaway. All units have two cable TVs and videocassette players, and movies (for kids, too) are available at the front desk. The one-bedroom suites have completely private bedrooms, but instead of a sofa bed in the living room, you must request a crib or rollaway. There's plenty of room for the kids in these accommodations. You can request a room with a hide-a-bed; if you need a larger refrigerator or a room with a stove, request it in advance.

Rates are based on single or double occupancy: Executive suites (both standard and deluxe) rent for $165–$245; a one-bedroom corner suite, $185–$265. Each additional person is charged $30, but children under 17 sleep free in their parents' room. Cribs and rollaways are available at no charge. Be sure to ask if special discount rates are in effect, especially for the standard executive suites (the furnishings are not quite as plush, but the suite can be rented for a very reasonable rate). Also ask about the special weekend rate of $115. Babysitting can be arranged through an agency. Parking is $8, with in-and-out privileges.

You may wonder why we're recommending yet another all-suite hotel in the same general neighborhood. The advantages of **Summerfield Suites Hotel,** 1000 Westmount Drive, West Hollywood, CA 90069 (☎ **310/657-7400,** or toll free **800/833-4353;** fax 310/854-6744) are that it is centrally located in a quiet residential area, is a fairly small hotel, and offers apartment-like accommodations that are very comfortable and affordable, especially for long stays.

A pool, spa, and garden are found on the rooftop and provide good views. Guests with children will appreciate the coin-operated laundry facilities, 24-hour convenience store in the lobby, and daily valet service.

A complimentary buffet breakfast is offered each morning and can be enjoyed either in the small dining room, on the patio, or back in your room. There is even a Japanese-style breakfast provided. Although there is no room service, meals can be ordered from a list of restaurants provided in each room, then charged to your hotel bill. The hotel staff will even do your grocery shopping for you.

Each suite is a converted apartment, making accommodations pretty roomy and comfortable. The smaller junior suite features a step-up sleeping area with a queen-size bed, divided from the living area with a curtain. The living area itself is furnished like a small apartment, with a sofa, chairs, and small table. In the room are a microwave, coffeemaker, a refrigerator, and dishes. This unit would work for a small family. The executive suite also has the step-up sleeping area, but is a larger unit with a sofa sleeper and a full kitchen with a dishwasher, refrigerator, and a two-burner stove. The one-bedroom guest room is again larger, with a full kitchen, separate bedroom, and large bathroom. All the accommodations have separate vanity areas, TVs, hairdryers, two two-line telephones, balconies, gas fireplaces, and mirrored-closets. There are handicap accessible and no-smoking rooms available.

Room rates, single or double, are $139 for the junior suite, $159 for the executive suite, and $189 for the one-bedroom. Children under 12 stay free in their parents' room. Additional guests pay $25; cribs are free, rollaways cost $10. Ask about special weekend rates and discounts. Parking in the underground garage is $6 daily with in-and-out privileges.

MID-WILSHIRE/MIRACLE MILE AREA

You'll find good value for your money in this part of town. Located south of Hollywood, east of Beverly Hills, and bordering on chic West Hollywood, this area is full of attractions. If you choose to stay in the vicinity, you can find a 24-hour Ralph's Market at 6350 W. 3rd St., at Fairfax Avenue (☎ 213/930-1023), and another 24-hour Ralph's nearby in the Beverly Connection, at West 3rd Street and La Cienega Boulevard (☎ 213/655-6226). Pan Pacific Park, located between Beverly Boulevard and West 3rd Street, is a big park with a children's play area on the bottom level, and one for very young children above, at the Gardner Avenue entrance.

Moderate

The location of the **Beverly Plaza,** 8384 W. 3rd St., Los Angeles, CA 90048 (☎ **213/658-6600,** or toll free **800/62-HOTEL;** fax 213/653-3464), makes it a good choice for travelers. It's within walking distance of the huge Beverly Center shopping mall, five minutes' driving distance from Beverly Hills, 15 minutes from Century City, 25 minutes to the beach, and 20 minutes from downtown. Complimentary taxi service shuttles you to and from anywhere within a five-mile radius.

You won't find many recreational facilities in this small 98-room European-style hotel, but don't let that stop you from staying here. Families are definitely welcome. There is a tiny heated wading pool perfect for young children (it's three feet deep) set on a very small patio on the second floor. The pool area is furnished with lounge chairs and umbrella tables, and poolside food service is provided. The hotel also has a small health club, sauna, private trainer, and massage therapist (on call).

Cava is the hotel's restaurant and it serves breakfast, lunch, and dinner. Most children should be able to find something they like at breakfast; you may choose to venture elsewhere for lunch and dinner. In addition to the excellent small neighborhood restaurants, several within walking distance of the hotel, nearby Jerry's Deli delivers free right to your room, and the check can be charged to your hotel bill. Room service is available 24 hours daily. There is coffee and tea in the lobby each morning.

Most of the rooms at the Beverly Plaza will have been refurbished by the time you read this and are decorated in soft, relaxing colors and furnished with natural linens, robes, and towels—no synthetics. Even the soaps and shampoos are environmentally correct.

Accommodations can be requested with either a king- or two queen-size beds. A room with one queen-size bed has a sitting area and can fit a crib and a rollaway. A king-size bed room with large sitting area also has a hide-a-bed. The room with two beds and two wingback chairs can add either a rollaway or crib. Large families can rent a double queen-size room that connects to a king-size room. Each unit is equipped with remote-control cable TV, a minibar, two telephones, hairdryers, clock radios, and writing desks. There are no-smoking units, as well.

Standard rooms with two queen-size beds rent for $128 single or double. A luxury unit with one queen or one king-size bed and a sitting area rent for $168 single or double. Children under 12 stay free in their parents' room; those 12 and over are charged $10. Cribs are complimentary and rollaways cost $10. A special weekend and holiday rate of $92, single or double occupancy, is offered year-round on a space-available basis; it includes a continental breakfast. Parking costs $8 overnight, with in-and-out, privileges; valet parking is available.

Budget

The old saying "Don't judge a book by its cover" applies to the **Farmer's Daughter Motel,** 115 S. Fairfax Ave., Los Angeles, CA 90036 (☎ **213/937-3930,** or toll free **800/334-1658**). Although it's not much on the outside, the refurbished rooms are clean and pleasant, making this a fine budget choice. Because of its location and rates, the motel is often sold out. It's across the street from the Farmers Market and CBS, and within walking distance of restaurants and a first-run movie theater. Two tour-bus companies stop at the motel, and reservations can be made at the front desk.

There's a very small pool on the premises, fenced in and surrounded by a few chaise longues, chairs, and umbrella tables. Overlooking the pool on the second floor is a small outdoor patio with an umbrella table, chairs, and a chaise. It's perfect for a rest and a snack with the kids. The motel has plenty of ice (free), soda, candy, and other food-vending machines. Parking is plentiful and convenient to the rooms.

The small accommodations are furnished with either one queen-size bed or two double beds, and are wallpapered and decorated with new whitewashed furniture and rich green carpeting and bedspreads. Rooms with one bed have space for a rollaway (in rooms with two beds it would be tight). Each unit is the same: There are reading lights, color TV, a table and two chairs, coffee maker, separate vanity, and tub/shower combinations.

From January through mid-June and September through December, a room rents for $58, single or double. From mid-June through August, rooms cost $65. The extra-person charge is $3, child or adult. There are no cribs; rollaways are free.

DOWNTOWN

Downtown Los Angeles offers elegant accommodations. Ask at the front desk if you need to find a market nearby for diapers, formula, or snacks.

Deluxe

The **Westin Bonaventure,** 404 S. Figueroa St. (between 4th and 5th Streets), Los Angeles, CA 90071 (☎ **213/624-1000,** or toll free **800/228-3000;** fax 213/612-4800), is known for its round mirrored towers, huge atrium lobby, and exterior glass elevators, visible to the eye almost anywhere in the downtown area. But remember that staying at the Bonaventure is like staying in a small city: There are nearly 1,400 guest rooms, 20 restaurants, and three lounges, and more than 30 retail shops. There's always something to look at and someplace to wander. A large Starbucks Coffee lounge is new to the lobby. It lists children's drinks, too.

The shopping gallery hosts jewelry stores, art galleries, book and card shops, and clothing stores. The lobby itself is a six-level atrium with six reflection pools. There's a large fenced-in outdoor pool and patio on the fourth level with room to romp. For guests who miss their exercise, there's a state-of-the-art fitness center accessible via a skybridge for a charge of $7.50 daily.

The Westin Hotels' increased attention to the family market is obvious at this location, too. Like the other Westin properties, this one offers preferred restaurant reservations for guests with children; guests can call ahead to order meals at the hotel's Sidewalk Cafe; when families reserve rooms and indicate their children's ages, there will be bottle warmers, potty seats, highchairs, bed rails, and/or cribs in the room upon check-in (cribs are even made up with special Westin Kids Club sheets); there are special prices for children's laundry.

Kids have their own check-in card that lists special items and services that can be requested. Special age-appropriate packages give the kids tippy cups (for toddlers) or sports bottles, plus other items such as a Westin Kids Club hat, a safety kit of electric outlet covers, a night-light, Band-Aids, a laundry bag, baby shampoo, and other items. Kids get unlimited free drinks in their cups.

The Bonaventure has three of its own restaurants, including the Sidewalk Cafe, which is perfect for families and, of course, has its own children's menu. The bountiful breakfast buffet costs $10.95 for adults and $1 per year of each child up to age 10. An International Brunch, with the foods of many countries served at individual food stations, is available on Sunday. The evening Happy Hour is a great deal: Beer, wine, and other drinks, plus all appetizers, cost $2.50. Children's selections are also available through room service.

All of the Bonaventure's rooms are fitted with custom-made armoires that house a minibar and remote-control television. In the standard rooms, the headboard provides one convenient spot for the phone, lights, and music. A mirrored wall adds space, while mirrored closets make finding those lost toys much easier. Bathrooms are of generous size and have tub/shower combinations. Connecting rooms and no-smoking rooms can be requested, and queen or king-size beds are available.

The new Tower Suite rooms are an alternative that families should consider. There's a separate bedroom with either a king-size or two queen-size beds, and a full bathroom. The adjoining living area houses a powder room, wet bar, microwave oven, coffee maker and refrigerator, plus a large sleeper-sofa, and a second television and telephone. On the Executive Club Floor, add to that a complimentary continental breakfast and a lounge with food and beverage service. If you need even more space and privacy, the Hollywood suite is a larger one-bedroom unit with a spacious connecting living room and full bathroom. The hotel prides itself on the fact that no room is more than seven doors from an elevator—an important fact when you're dragging teddy bears, infant seats, 16 Tonka trucks, and the kids.

Rates at the Bonaventure are: standard rooms, $157 single, $175 double. Tower suites cost $177 single, $195 double; the Hollywood suite runs $190 single or double; a standard room on the Executive Club floor will run you $167 single, $185 double. Children 18 and younger sleep free in the same room with their parents. Rollaways cost $25 and cribs are free. Parking costs $18.15 weekdays, 50% less on weekends, and there are in-and-out privileges. Be sure to ask about packages and weekend rates.

The **Hyatt Regency Los Angeles,** 711 S. Hope St. (at 7th Street), Los Angeles, CA 90017 (☎ **213/683-1234,** or toll free **800/233-1234;** fax 213/629-3230), offers advance check-in from anywhere in the world by calling toll free **800/CHECK IN.** Although this is primarily a business person's hotel, the rooms here are quite lovely, and the hotel is centrally located. It's connected to the Broadway Plaza Shopping Center, a welcome treat for parents always in search of fast food and interesting adventures for their tots. The shopping center is open daily. Hold on tight to your teenagers when you exit the lobby, as Judy's boutique across from the entrance is quite "the thing," carrying the latest in styles for that age group.

The hotel's well-equipped gym is geared toward adults, and the sun deck adjacent to it is very limited in size. The spa is extremely small and is better suited to aching muscles than to rambunctious children. Babysitting can be arranged.

The Brasserie restaurant, on the lobby level, is definitely appropriate for families. Featuring American bistro-style cooking, it's open for breakfast and lunch; boosters and highchairs are provided. The Camp Hyatt children's menu is provided, or the standard menu offers "smaller portions for children under 12 at half the price." Room service is available seven days a week.

The rooms at this Hyatt are spacious and recently furnished with mahogany armoires and brass accents. Roomy bathrooms have been redone in marble. Remote-control TVs with complimentary cable stations are standard; VCRs can be rented. There's also a dataport for a PC hookup, and call-waiting and voice-mail service. Beds are automatically triple-sheeted. Additionally, the hotel offers one-day valet service.

A big surprise for a downtown hotel is that the guest-room windows open! But they open at the bottom only, and although the space isn't big enough for a child to crawl through, you should be careful with very small, curious, crawling infants. No room is more than six doors from the elevator—great news when your arms are full and you have little Megan in tow!

Rooms with king-size beds have space for a crib, or a rollaway. Most families, we're told, rent either the corner rooms—which are half again as big as a normal room with a king-size bed and come with a refrigerator—or rooms with two queen-size beds. There are connecting rooms available for even larger families. Suites are lovely and feature a bedroom and sitting alcove, plus a living room and dining room, wet bar, refrigerator, stereo, and half-bath. Some suites seat six in the dining rooms. Hairdryers and refrigerators can be requested.

Standard and corner rooms begin at $189 single, $209 double. Suites range from $225 to $600. Children under 18 stay free in their parents' room. Rollaways and cribs are complimentary. Adults 18 and over are charged $25 each per night. Be sure to ask about special weekend and holiday rates, which are usually good deals. Parking in the 2,800-space lot is $15 per night, with unlimited in-and-out privileges.

Elegance still prevails at the **Biltmore,** 506 S. Grand Ave. (between 5th and 6th Streets), Los Angeles, CA 90071 (☎ **213/624-1011,** or toll free **800/245-8673;** fax 213/612-1545). Built in the 1920s, the Biltmore was a showpiece of the grand style, with lavish ceilings and Italian wall paintings. Expanded in 1928, and modernized in 1987, the hotel went through a multi-million-dollar restoration to preserve the incredible beauty of its original design. Now while its 700 rooms are somewhat contemporary, the rest of the hotel hasn't lost its elegant Spanish-Italian Renaissance design.

Although the Biltmore is not exactly your typical family hotel, the management has embarked on a program to make it easier for you to enjoy the benefits of the Biltmore with your children in tow. The hotel's concierge is equipped with a "Kid's Sheet" of toy and clothing stores and ice-cream parlors, and will suggest those within walking distance reachable via the hotel's complimentary weekend shuttle service. He will also give you coloring books and crayons, refer babysitters, and arrange for the use of car seats and strollers. The hotel's spectacular indoor pool has special family hours, and kickboards can be borrowed. Parents can indulge themselves at the full-service health club.

The Biltmore has two restaurants: Smeraldi's, and the award-winning Bernard's. Smeraldi's offers food service from 6:30am to 11pm and has a children's menu. Kids shouldn't have any trouble choosing something to eat here, and highchairs are available. The Biltmore also has a pastry shop and three bars, including the Grand Avenue Bar. Room service, available 24 hours daily, also has a children's menu.

Rooms come in 26 different configurations and are furnished in contemporary colors with French provincial furniture. Jim Dine engravings decorate every room. Everything is fresh and clean, lighting is custom-designed, and shuttered windows add an unusual touch. Standard rooms and rooms with king-size beds come with a comfortable reading chair, desk, and armoire. Bathrooms have full-length mirrors and separate vanities, tub/shower combinations with extra-deep tubs, and elegant pedestal sinks. Club Floor accommodations include minibars, complimentary continental breakfast, and late checkout. Parlors, which can connect with sleeping rooms, have big sitting and dining areas, a sofa and love seats, a small refrigerator, and a liquor cabinet. Junior suites, larger than the regular suites, come with two remote-control TVs and king-size beds.

Rates in standard rooms are $185–$215 single, $205–$215 double. Club Floor rooms rent for $275, single or double. Executive suites are available at $325; one-bedroom suites start at $400. Children under 18 sleep free in their parents' room; extra adults are charged $30 per night. Rollaways and cribs are available at no charge. Inquire about the special weekened rates. Parking is $17 per night, with in-and-out privileges.

5 Where to Eat

Los Angeles restaurants have become world renowned for the quality of their chefs. While you probably won't be taking your family to the more elegant of these, you won't have a problem finding good, accommodating places to feed your brood.

BEVERLY HILLS

There are lots of eateries in Beverly Hills perfect for the family. And many of them are surprisingly affordable.

Expensive

Benihana of Tokyo, 38 N. La Cienega Blvd., just north of Wilshire Boulevard (☎ **310/659-1511**), is a place where the kids will enjoy the show as much as the food. The building itself is authentic, with wood beams and mammoth stones that were once part of a Japanese farmhouse. A koi pond and arched bridge will intrigue the kids as well.

We know families who take their children here for special occasions. Featuring teppanyaki/hibachi-style cooking, chefs prepare and serve the food in front of you with style and a flourish. Kids are caught up in the dramatic way the chefs cook and juggle the food.

All food is cooked at your table. For lunch, there is hibachi chicken (with fresh mushrooms, onions, and bean sprouts) and four kinds of steak to choose from. The Benihana Special is a combination of the chicken and New York steak with fresh vegetables. All luncheons include salad, shrimp, rice, and tea. Prices range $7.50–$11.

For dinner, you have a slightly larger selection. In addition to hibachi chicken, sukiyaki steak, hibachi steak, filet mignon, and steak teriyaki, you can have lobster or scallops. Again, all entrees include a shrimp appetizer, soup, salad, rice, and tea. Prices range $15–$22.

Benihana is used to accommodating families. It has highchairs and boosters, makes Shirley Temple cocktails, and accepts reservations. While there isn't a children's menu, kids can split meals.

Open for lunch Monday through Friday from 11:30am to 2pm, and for dinner Monday through Thursday from 5:30 to 10pm, on Friday and Saturday from 5:30 to 11pm, and on Sunday from 4:30 to 10pm. Valet parking is available. Most major credit cards are accepted. There's another branch at 14160 Panay Way, in Marina del Rey (☎ **310/821-0888**).

If you're a family of prime rib lovers and your children are able to enjoy a leisurely dining experience, **Lawry's the Prime Rib,** located in the heart of Beverly Hills' Restaurant Row at 100 N. La Cienega Blvd., half a block north of Wilshire Boulevard (☎ **310/652-2827**), is a treat you don't want to miss. Walking into Lawry's is like entering an Edwardian manor house. Decorated on a grand scale with plush carpets, traditional English paintings, and candelabra-style chandeliers, the restaurant is divided into several dining areas. Huge silver serving carts are brought to your table so that chefs can carve your meat to your specifications. This means that the aisles are very wide.

We usually request one of the booths, which are ornately upholstered and well padded, offering privacy from neighboring diners and allowing us greater peace of mind when the kids get a tad noisier than we wish. Tables are comfortable too, complete with padded high-back chairs.

Lawry's secret to success is that it serves only one entree—prime rib. For 54 years Lawry's has served standing rib roasts that have been dry-aged for two to three weeks. You can choose between English and Lawry cuts, a California cut (for light eaters) or a Diamond Jim Brady cut (extra thick with a bone) for $18.95–$25.95. With each dinner comes the house salad, mashed potatoes, traditional Yorkshire pudding, and creamed horseradish. The children's portion ($12.95), which also includes a beverage and dessert, is almost the same as the California cut adult portion. There's a full bar that offers non-alcoholic drinks as well as standard cocktails.

We have only one caution about bringing youngsters here. You must be prepared for a leisurely meal. A 2-year-old may do fine for an hour, but even the best-natured toddler may get restless or even troublesome when it extends beyond that. Also, there are no highchairs here, but booster seats are available.

Lawry's is open Monday through Thursday from 5 to 10pm, on Friday and Saturday from 4:30pm to 11pm, and on Sunday from 3 to 10pm. Reservations are advised, and most major credit cards are accepted. Valet parking is available.

RJ's, the Rib Joint, 252 N. Beverly Dr., between Dayton Way and Wilshire Boulevard (☎ 310/274-RIBS), is one of those fun spots that you remember as much for the experience as for the food, although the food is very good and the portions are very generous. Everything at RJ's is done on a grand scale. The exposed-brick saloon-style main dining room opens to an enormous bar with a floor-to-ceiling display of more than 500 brands of bottles. Here customers may wait for tables while they munch on peanuts in the shell. Lots of wood tables and booths line the room, and the walls are decorated with black-and-white celebrity photos and large back-lit stained-glass hangings.

This is where you'll find RJ's famous Green Grocery salad bar, a truly extraordinary assortment of salad fixings, presented among a symphony of fresh fruits and vegetables. The last time they counted, there were over 80 items, including such yummy treats for kids as fruit compote, dates, grated coconut, and fresh fruit, as well as more unusual goodies for adults—hearts of palm, artichoke hearts, sliced avocado, and two soups. The salad bar can easily make a meal in itself. Otherwise you can choose one of the full meals, which includes the salad bar as well. Portions are large and most people walk out of the restaurant with a whimsical aluminum-foil creation that holds their leftovers. Known for hickory-wood smoked ribs, RJ's offers pork back ribs and beef ribs or a combination. Rattlesnake chicken is the number-one seller: chicken breasts cut into strips covered with a hot spicy barbecue sauce, served with rice and beans and coleslaw and blue-corn chips. If you prefer something else, there are other chicken dishes; steaks, including one smothered in chili; and fresh seafood, including scampi and swordfish. Menu prices range $5.95–$25.

We were especially impressed with the friendly servers and the large number of them. Even during the more crowded dinner hours, smiles were given all around, and the staff never seemed harassed: "We'll do everything for kids but change their diapers."

Children are treated to smaller portions off the menu for $4–$5, and they can munch these salad-bar items before the main course arrives so you won't have whining youngsters on your hands. Sassy seats and boosters are available, and the immense bar makes one think that bartenders here can make any non-alcoholic creation your children can come up with. On Friday night a strolling magician performs his magic.

RJ's is open Monday through Thursday from 11:30am to 10pm and on Friday and Saturday from 11:30am to 11pm. On Sunday, brunch is served from 10:30am to

2:30pm, and dinner from 4 to 10pm. Reservations are advised. If you don't want to wait—either for a table or in a line at the Green Grocery—try to come early, between 5 and 7pm. Most major credit cards are accepted. Valet parking is available after 6pm; or if you prefer, there's a Beverly Hills municipal parking lot just a few doors south, which offers free parking for two hours.

Moderate

The **Cheesecake Factory** has four convenient locations: at 364 N. Beverly Dr., in Beverly Hills (☎ **310/278-7270**); 4142 Via Marina, in Marina del Rey (☎ **310/306-3344**); 11647 San Vicente Blvd., in Brentwood (☎ **310/826-7111**); and 605 N. Harbor Dr., in Redondo Beach (☎ **310/376-0466**). There's also a Valley location at 6324 Canoga Ave., in Woodland Hills (☎ **818/883-9900**). The Beverly Hills location has lots of action and interesting conversation going on among this mostly Beverly Hills crowd. The Marina del Rey spot is large and features a patio overlooking the marina; the Redondo Beach address is also on the water at Kings Harbor.

"We are happy to serve families with kids, and kids love us!" they say, and our kids agree. But sadly, they have no separate children's menu, although they've added more and more kid favorites to the menu.

The extensive menu offers American, Chinese, Mexican, and Italian specialties. You might go for coconut beer-fried shrimp ($14.95), Thai chicken pasta ($13.95), or a sandwich, hamburger, omelet, or salad. Prices bounce all over the place from $4.95 to $15.95. "Lite Lunches" are served daily, with a selection of luncheon-size portions of pasta, salads, and house specialties ($7 or $8). They are very accommodating to such special requests as low-salt or low-fat meals.

The grilled-cheese sandwich ($5.50) is big enough for small kids to split, and it's served with french fries. Or they can have a half sandwich and cup of soup, hamburgers, a simple pasta marinara, or individual pizzas (served evenings only). All locations except Beverly Hills has "mini roadside sliders," which are tiny hamburgers, taquitos, and mini-quesadillas, any of which might be perfect for your child.

Sunday brunch offers not only egg dishes, but a breakfast pasta, a breakfast burrito, stuffed French toast, and lox, onions, and eggs. Prices begin at $7.95 and go to $8.95. For an extra $4.25 you can add your beverage, fresh fruit, and a cocktail or juice. A separate Children's Brunch, priced at $4.95, includes a small order of French toast, a cup of fruit, one scrambled egg, and two strips of bacon.

And then there's dessert. If you can choose among the 35 different cheesecake concoctions, you're better than we are! If you can't make up your mind, try the fudge cake, mud pie, banana split, or one of the other tempting, fattening, and wonderful desserts.

All locations have booster seats and highchairs, and they will split orders and warm bottles and baby food. Each restaurant has a full bar, and food can be packed to go.

Except for Beverly Hills, the restaurants are open Monday through Thursday from 11:30am to 11:30pm, on Friday and Saturday to 12:30am, and on Sunday from 10am to 11pm. Beverly Hills is open a half hour earlier and closes a half hour earlier weekdays. There are no reservations except for large groups, early in the evening and at lunch, and the wait can be 20–45 minutes during rush hours. Major credit cards welcome. In Beverly Hills there is street parking and a city lot nearby with two hours' free parking. The Marina has valet parking; in Redondo Beach there's a lot; in Woodland Hills there's valet parking or a parking structure; in Brentwood there is valet parking.

There seems to be a **Louise's Trattoria** popping up nearly everywhere in Los Angeles. The Beverly Hills location can be found at 342 N. Beverly Dr. (☎ 310/274-4271). The restaurants are unpretentious open rooms, the food is satisfying, and the prices are reasonable.

One nice thing about these neighborhood trattorias is that in addition to having an individual slice of pizza, kids 12 and under can order off the children's menu. Selections come in three categories: Mini-pizzas cost $2.75 and come with either tomato and cheese or barbecued chicken. Full entrees include wagonwheel pasta with Alfredo sauce or with butter and cheese, spaghetti and meatballs, or cheese mini-ravioli for $3.95. Kids' beverages cost a mere 50¢, and desserts are $1.50.

While the kids make their decision, adults can choose Louise's original pizza or a California version like roasted Tuscan vegetables with sun-dried tomatoes and goat cheese. There are sandwiches too, such as grilled eggplant, or chicken parmigiana; plus calzones, pasta, risotto, ravioli, lasagne, and chicken and seafood entrees. Some of these selections are designed to be lower in fat and salt. Traditional pizzas range from $10.50–$17. Gourmet pizza versions, and the other entrees, go for $6–$13; sandwiches and salads average around $6.50. A slice of pizza costs $1.75. Fresh-made desserts from Old Town Bakery in Pasadena are in demand. After-dinner cappuccino, espresso, and specialty teas can be ordered.

All locations have booster seats, highchairs, or Sassy seats, and all are convenient to sightseeing venues or the beaches. The Beverly Hills restaurant is open Monday through Thursday from 11:30am to 10pm, on Friday and Saturday from 11am to 11pm, and on Sunday from 11am to 10pm. Take-out and delivery service are available. No reservations, but some major credit cards are accepted. Street parking.

Other locations are in Larchmont at 232 N. Larchmont Blvd. (☎ 213/962-9510), in West Hollywood at 7505 Melrose Ave. (☎ 213/651-3880), in Santa Monica at 1008 Montana Ave. (☎ 310/394-8888), in West Los Angeles at 10645 Pico Blvd. (☎ 310/475-6084), in Brentwood at 264 26th St. (☎ 310/451-5001) and at 11645 San Vicente Blvd. (☎ 310/826-2000). Hours at all locations are similar to those at the Beverly Hills branch.

Tony Roma's A Place for Ribs, 50 N. La Cienega Blvd. (☎ 310/659-7427), reopened in Beverly Hills in 1992. As is the case with most Tony Roma's restaurants, this one is a pleasant place for the whole family. Deep, rich colors, dark wood, brick walls, and ceiling fans give it a subdued ambience, but it's a lively, busy place.

Lunch offerings include the ever-popular baby back ribs, barbecued chicken and shrimp, and grilled fish. There are also different daily specials and sandwiches, soups and salads. Lunch prices are $3.99–$8.99. Combination plates of ribs and chicken or shrimp go for $7.59–$13. Dinner is a selection of three types of ribs, grilled chicken, steak, or fish, barbecued chicken or shrimp, burgers, salads, and the famous Tony Roma's loaf (and half loaf) of fried onions. Prices start at $5.99 and go up to $13.

The children's menu has all sorts of games and is usually the same at all Tony Roma's branches: chicken strips, ribs, pizza, a grilled-cheese sandwich, or a burger, each served with french fries or fruit, a vegetable appetizer, and dessert and ranging $2.99–$4.99 in price. Booster seats and highchairs are provided, and servers will warm bottles and baby food. Take-out is available.

The restaurant is open Sunday through Thursday from 11am to 10pm and on Friday and Saturday from 11am to 11pm. Reservations accepted only for parties of eight or more. Major credit cards are honored. Valet and validated self-parking are available for a nominal charge.

For other locations, see Universal City/Burbank/San Fernando Valley.

Nate'n Al Delicatessen, 414 N. Beverly Dr. (☎ 310/274-0101), is an atypical East Coast deli restaurant. No one yells and screams at the counter. But Mom and Dad will love it because the food is good and the people-watching is even better. While most families come here on the weekends, you'll sometimes find a local grandpa or mom or dad here with junior before school. You'll also see some of the "old guard" Hollywood types on weekday mornings.

You and the kids have to be able to wait on weekends, because they don't take reservations. Get your name on the waiting list, smile nicely at the hostess, then take a walk for 20–30 minutes—it's a great area for strolling. Once you sit down you'll be able to get crackers or a bagel right away for the kids. Service is quick and friendly.

There's no children's menu, but they're willing to split most items. Lots of youngsters go straight for the chicken soup. Cottage cheese and potato pancakes are popular items, too. You can get peanut butter or grilled-cheese sandwiches and hot dogs and hamburgers here as well. Adults can choose typical deli items, including cream cheese and lox, blintzes, and pastrami and roast beef sandwiches. Prices range from $4 to $14. Breakfast is served all day. There are specials for dinner, but take the kids here for breakfast or lunch. Pound cake lovers should save room for the marble pound cake.

Highchairs and boosters are available. The kitchen will split orders and warm baby food and bottles. There's also counter service for take-out items: order there or call ahead.

Nate'n Al's is open every day of the year except Yom Kippur, nightly from 7:30am to 8:45pm. There is street parking, or park in the city lot half a block north (free for two hours—no validation necessary). Credit cards are accepted, but not reservations.

If you're in a hurry or can't get a booth at Nate'n Al's, try **The Nosh of Beverly Hills,** just a few blocks away at 9689 Santa Monica Blvd. (☎ 310/271-3730). It's a simple room with plenty of windows so the kids can watch the passing cars. The breakfast menu provides omelets, eggs and lox or salmon, or whitefish, matzoh brei, French toast, pancakes, bagels, and smoked-fish platters. Breakfast will run $3.95–$10.50. Lunch choices include the usual deli sandwiches, deluxe sandwiches, grilled Reubens, knockwurst, and patty melts, plus salads. Lunch costs $4.95–$9.95.

Kids don't seem to have a problem choosing something to eat in a deli. However, there is a children's menu for youngsters 12 and under. Silver-dollar pancakes should get them interested. Or there's cereal, eggs and bagels, hot dogs, peanut butter and jelly, a hamburger, grilled cheese, or soup. Prices on the kids' menu are $1.95–$3.95. There are highchairs and booster seats. Take-out and delivery are available. Open daily from 7am to 5pm. No reservations. All major credit cards are accepted. Street parking or park in the city lot.

Larry Parker's Beverly Hills Diner, 206 S. Beverly Dr. (☎ 310/274-5655), is a Beverly Hills institution. Do you ever have trouble making a decision? You will at Larry Parker's. You can get almost anything you want to eat from the 29-page menu. This diner epitomizes the fun and diversity of Los Angeles. Mom may order lox, eggs, onions, and a bagel; Dad may select a meatloaf sandwich or a stuffed croissant; Gramps might choose one of the 35 burgers; Gram may eat soft tacos or Szechuan shrimp, and Uncle David may go for one of the vegetarian entrees. And the list of salads (over 40 of them) is truly amazing. The children's menu includes macaroni and cheese and "pisquetti" (spaghetti) at $3–$3.50.

Yet the food is only part of the experience. This is a small restaurant that was built in 1947. Not your flash-in-the-pan trendy diner, this 24-hour restaurant claims to have served more than four million people. People come for the food, yes, but they also come for the fun. Helium balloons with hanging strings bob on the ceiling, a jukebox plays constantly (and each table has its own selection box as well), neon signs and old pictures line the walls, and old-fashioned pink bubblegum comes with the check.

Read the signs: "If you really were a good customer, you'd order more!" "Dancing in the aisles only." "Help keep Beverly Hills clean. Wipe your feet before you leave." With this sense of humor here, you're not going to feel inhibited with your kids.

Highchairs and boosters are available, and they'll warm bottles and baby food and give the kids balloons. They may charge $2 extra for splitting orders, though, and they take reservations only for parties of six or more. One Hollywood-style amenity is the free limousine service (for five or more) provided to and from the restaurant Monday through Friday from 10am to 3pm. Another only-in-Los Angeles trademark are the telephones at each table.

Open 24 hours daily. Most major credit cards accepted. Free parking at a nearby municipal lot for two hours or metered street parking available.

Inexpensive

The American short order is alive and well at **Ed Debevic's Short Orders/Deluxe,** 134 N. La Cienega Blvd., on Restaurant Row (☎ **310/659-1952**). To eat here is to take a trip back to the 1950s! True to its L.A. location, it's filled with plenty of music and theatrics. It's a great place to go with the children—the noise level is perfect. The vinyl booths are nostalgic, the many signs on the walls will keep the kids busy, the servers are a riot, and the really low menu prices will keep you happy. But, so you shouldn't think you're *really* back at the Homesick Diner in Talooca, Illinois, in 1952 (after which this is modeled), there's that Beverly Hills touch—valet parking.

The hamburgers are what many people come for, and there are eight different kinds ($4.75–$5.65) plus a turkey burger. But there are also sandwiches, including 1950s meatloaf sandwiches; plus chili, hot dogs, a salad bar, side orders of cheese fries, and fries with gravy or chili. Of course, a dinner wouldn't be complete without such deluxe plates as chicken fried steak, chicken pot pie, and a roast turkey dinner ($5.35–$6.95).

Janey orders the world's smallest hot-fudge sundae for an exorbitant 59¢ (who can resist?). If you dare, try old-fashioned devil's food cake, Linda C's fudge brownies, or banana cream pie, to name just a few of the decadent dessert selections.

Boosters and highchairs are available. Baby food and bottles can be warmed. Also, an unbelievable find in a restaurant bathroom—a sign telling you to turn a switch to signal an attendant if the bathroom isn't clean!

Open weekdays from 11:30am to 11pm, on weekends until 1am. Reservations are accepted only for weekday lunch. Major credit cards accepted. Valet parking.

Jeremiah P. Throckmorton Grille, 255 S. Beverly Dr. (☎ **310/550-7111**), is quick; it's nice, it's comfortable, and it's convenient. Pick a Hebrew National hot dog, a burger, or hot and cold sandwiches. Sit at the counter and watch them make the food. The kids from Beverly Hills High School love to hang out here. Prices run $2–$4.65. Open Monday through Saturday from 11:30am to 8:30pm and on Sunday from noon to 5pm. Cash only. Take-out service. Park on the street.

WESTSIDE

The Westside is a fashionable and trendy and pricey part of town. It includes Century City, Westwood, Brentwood, Rancho Park, and West Los Angeles. It's certainly an area you'll visit frequently because of the many, many visitors' attractions and restaurants.

Moderate

Anna's Italian Restaurant, 10929 W. Pico Blvd. (☎ **310/474-0102**), is like walking into a little Italian villa. It has red-checked tablecloths, big red-leather booths, and old chandeliers. It's a favorite with neighborhood families as well as those who come from miles away, so there's always a lot of activity here. This is not your romantic candlelit Italian restaurant, so bring the kids and relax.

We've actually taken a sleeping infant here and kept him in the stroller while we enjoyed our dinner. The waiters weren't crazy about having to serve around the stroller, but they were gracious and accommodating, and even our then-4-year-old Elizabeth put them through their paces.

If you like marinara salad, this is the place to order it. Anna's version has large chunks of seafood tucked into the well-dressed greens. But, then, everything here is very good.

The lunch menu offers pizza, pasta, salads, sandwiches, omelets, veal, and fish for $5–$11, as well as weekday specials that include soup or salad at $5.25. Anna's dinners come with soup or salad, spaghetti, and vegetable. Choose from steaks, poultry, seafood, and 11 styles of veal. There are also pizzas, pasta dishes, and large salads. The dinner specials, served Monday through Thursday, cost $9.95. Dinner items range in price from $6.95 (for pizza) to $20.

Highchairs and boosters are available, but there is no children's menu here. We usually share our food with the little ones, or order pizza to split for older kids. The folks at Anna's will warm bottles and baby food, give the kids a lollipop, and make special children's drinks.

Open Monday through Thursday from 11:30am to 11pm, on Friday from 11:30am to midnight, on Saturday from 4pm to midnight, and on Sunday from 4 to 11pm. Reservations are advised if you don't want to wait. Most major credit cards are accepted. Street parking is available during lunch hours; free valet parking is available during dinner.

How about a place that serves two million eggs a year? Or almost two tons of coffee a month? Not only is the food fresh, but the cuisine at **Junior's Deli,** 2379 Westwood Blvd., West L.A. (☎ **310/475-5771**), is delicious and the waitresses are fantastic with the kids. All their fish is flown in from New York (whitefish, Nova Scotia lox, smoked salmon, and cod) and the brie comes from France. It's a gourmet deli.

We admit it—we're regulars there. And why not? Just a mention, in passing, to the hostess that it's Elizabeth's birthday, and much to our surprise, a singing trio presents her with a cupcake and best wishes. And for everyday needs, they have the usual highchairs, sassy seats, and boosters; a very good kid's menu (grilled cheese, peanut butter and jelly, hot dog, and pancakes for around $3–$4); and they'll gladly let you split and share adult portions. Maybe the greatest draw for the kids, and for the sugar-loving adults in our family, is the cinnamon-bread French toast. The bread is baked with thick rings of cinnamon and sugar so that when it's dipped in the egg and grilled, it melts into a sinful goody ($6.25 for a regular order, $5.25 for a petite).

This is a real family place. The owner, Marvin Saul, says he developed the children's menu in response to his regular customers who said they couldn't bring their children because it became too costly to feed three kids from the regular menu. He asked other customers what they'd like to see on the menu and then created it.

Junior's serves breakfast, lunch, and dinner. Everyone in the family will enjoy something on the 300+-item menu. There's old-fashioned "like Grandma used to make" roast brisket of beef, knockwurst with beans or sauerkraut, and chicken-in-the-pot. Not to ignore the health-conscious, there are low-cholesterol items, such as roast turkey drumstick (with kasha and coleslaw) and fresh steamed vegetables.

Deli standbys such as corned beef, roast beef, and pastrami sandwiches plus burgers, salads, cold fish platters, soups, and dairy dishes round out the menu. For a treat, try the bananas and strawberries in sour cream. Breakfast items including three-egg omelets, matzoh brei, kippers, and eggs are served all day long. Breakfast prices range from $2.25 to $10.25 (for Nova Scotia lox and eggs). Lunches and brunches range from $5 to $15 (for a sturgeon platter, with two bagels). Dinner between $6 and $10.

Open Sunday through Thursday from 6am to 11pm and on Friday and Saturday from 6:30am to 12:30am. Unfortunately, they don't take reservations for parties of fewer than six, which means that you'll have to wait for at least 15 minutes during the busy times. We always try to arrive between 7 and 9:30am for Saturday or Sunday breakfast. It's crowded at dinner just as it gets dark, so plan accordingly. Once seated, the turnover is fast. Some major credit cards are accepted. There's a parking lot adjacent and limited street parking.

Lotus West, 10974 W. Pico Blvd. (☎ **310/475-9597**), is one of the places our kids ask to return to again and again. This pleasant neighborhood eatery has white linen cloths and a more subdued atmosphere than the typical Chinese-style restaurant. On Sunday nights you'll see a many families enjoying the Mandarin, Shanghai, and Szechuan cuisine. It's no wonder. In such a family-loving place, you'll certainly find highchairs and booster seats and lots of chopsticks to replace the ones that fall on the floor. The staff will do just about anything to keep your family happy.

We're particularly fond of the lemon chicken (large slices of chicken with a wonderfully tangy flavor), and the kids are crazy for the beef with broccoli and the eggroll. You might be interested in some of the more unusual dishes, such as walnut beef, hot spiced sliced fish, or spicy chicken chunks with pine nuts. Entree prices $6.95 to $19.95.

Open weekdays and Saturday for lunch from 11:30am to 3pm, and weekdays for dinner from 5 to 10pm. Saturday dinner is served from 5 to 10:30pm. Open Sunday from noon to 10pm for dinner. Reservations and most major credit cards are accepted. There is an adjacent parking lot.

Mario's Italian Restaurant, 1001 Broxton Ave., Westwood (☎ **310/208-7077**), is an institution in Westwood Village. Located at the corner of Broxton and Weyburn Avenues in the center of Westwood, Mario's has seen nearly three decades of students, professors, tourists, and families come through "the Village."

Traditional red-and-white-checked tablecloths and a festive atmosphere greet you. This family place has highchairs and booster seats, and while they don't have a children's menu, they gladly do half-orders of pasta. Children love the mini-size pizzas and the hamburger entree as well. They can also have half-orders.

Mom and Dad might want to try the house specialties, linguine Sorrento (with langostino, shrimp, and clams cooked in a bag) served with soup or salad for $18.95, or farfalle ("bow tie" pasta) with pesto and sun-dried tomatoes for $12.95. Dinners include minestrone soup or salad, pasta, and vegetable (pasta entrees include soup or salad and bread). Prices are $11.25–$22.95. Pizzas start at $6.95. Lunches are $7.25–$13.50.

Open Monday through Thursday from 11:30am to 11pm, on Friday from 11:30am to 12:30am, on Saturday from noon to 12:30am, and on Sunday from noon to 11:30pm. Reservations are accepted, as are most major credit cards. There are pay parking lots nearby. There's another location at 1445 3rd St. Promenade, in Santa Monica (☎ **310/576-7799**).

Rosie's Barbecue Grillery, 11845 W. Olympic Blvd. (near Bundy), in the Westside Towers office building (☎ **310/473-8533**) is the best place that both 8-year-old Elizabeth and 14-year-old Andrew agree is the best . . . for dinner or lunch. The all-you-can-eat salad bar is enormous (50 items), and is sure to please everyone.

The treat here is the scrumptious barbecue—any way you like it—ribs, chicken, or sandwiches. For lunch, ribs and chicken cost $6–$10, hamburgers are $5.95, and the sandwich-and-salad bar is $6.95. For dinner, chicken and ribs range from $5.95–$15.95, including salad bar. Try the tri-tip dinner, a treat at $11.95. There are also burgers and other entrees for dinner.

While you wait for your order to arrive, the kids busy themselves with the elaborate coloring/activity book that comes with the children's menu. Prices for children's meals range from $2.95 to $5.95 and include a drink and ice cream.

Open Monday through Friday from 11am to 9:30pm; Saturday and Sunday from 4pm, boosters and highchairs are available. There are early-bird specials from 4 to 6pm. Reservations for parties of six or more and major credit cards are accepted.

Inexpensive

Some of our family's favorite pizza comes from **Earth, Wind & Flour,** 1776 Westwood Blvd., at Santa Monica Boulevard, in Westwood (☎ **310/470-2499**). The menu is simple, the service is fast, and the food is good. In addition to wonderful Boston-style pizza, six different pasta types with eight different sauces, chicken, salads, and a sampling of sandwiches and burgers are all tempting.

Very casual, this is a place with sawdust on the floors and a rustic cabinlike interior of rough-wood walls and lots of hanging plants. Great for a Sunday quick bite. Prices range from $3.50 to $15.45 (for a large pizza with five toppings). A family of four can easily have dinner for under $20. Highchairs and boosters are available.

Open Monday through Thursday from 11:30am to 11pm, on Friday and Saturday till midnight, and on Sunday from 4 to 10pm. No reservations accepted. Major credit cards are honored. There's an adjacent parking lot.

Other branches are at 2222 Wilshire Blvd., at 23rd Street, Santa Monica (☎ **310/829-7829**), and 17644 Ventura Blvd., near White Oak, Encino (☎ **818/986-0772**).

Islands, 10948 W. Pico Blvd., West L.A. (☎ **310/474-1144**), is a fun and lively eatery that boasts gourmet hamburgers, soft tacos, chicken sandwiches, and great salads. This restaurant is a favorite of the kids, and one we love too, because we can all find something here we enjoy. It's really a bit of Southern California "camp," capitalizing on every Southern Californian's dream of lazing on an island, riding the surf. Islands comes complete with tropical atmosphere: Ceramic parrots hang overhead, servers wear island clothes, and photographs of surfers riding the great waves line the walls.

The food is good, with many unusual burger combinations: Try the Maui which has guacamole, lettuce, tomato, Swiss, and bacon or the Makaha with chili, cheese, and sautéed onions. We also like the five kinds of chicken-breast sandwiches and five kinds of salads. And everybody just has to have at least one side order of Islands fries. The portions are large and can easily be split between two children, but little surfers age 12 and under may choose from the Gremmie menu, which features a small burger, grilled cheese, or hot dog for $2.45. There's a full bar, so Shirley Temples can be had for the asking. Adult items range from $3.95 to $6.50.

Highchairs and boosters are available, and the servers will warm bottles and baby food.

Open daily at 11:30am for lunch, and open for dinner and snacks as well, Monday through Thursday until 11pm, on Friday and Saturday until 11:30pm, and on Sunday until 10pm. Reservations are not accepted, which means that at peak lunchtime hours you might have to wait at least 15 minutes for seating. For dinner it's best to come before 7pm (5:30pm on Sunday) if you want to avoid a 20- to 25-minute wait. Once you're seated, though, you'll be served quickly. Major credit cards are accepted.

There is limited street parking before 5pm and valet parking afterward.

There are other branches at 404 Washington St., in Marina del Rey (☎ 310/822-3939); 350 S. Beverly Dr., Beverly Hills (☎ 310/556-1624); and 3200 Sepulveda Blvd., in Manhattan Beach (☎ 310/546-4456).

THE COASTAL REGION (SANTA MONICA AND MARINA DEL REY)

The Coastal Region offers good dining possibilities, oftentimes with a view of the Pacific. These restaurants tend to be more casual than in many other parts of the city.

Expensive

Gladstone's 4-Fish, 17300 Pacific Coast Hwy. (☎ 310/GL4-FISH), is one of the most popular restaurants on the beach. With sawdust on the floors, large wooden booths with benches, and a passageway to the beach just outside, this is a terrific place for families. And everyone in town agrees—so there's usually a wait. For a detailed description, see "Where to Eat in Malibu" in "The Beach Communities" in Chapter 12. Open Sunday through Thursday from 7am to 11pm and on Friday and Saturday from 7am to midnight. Children's menu prices are $2.95–$4.95. Booster and sassy seats are available, but no highchairs. Reservations are advised, and most credit cards are accepted. Valet parking.

Moderate

"Enough of this California cuisine," you say? Then make a stop at **Aunt Kizzy's Back Porch,** 4325 Glencoe Ave., in the Villa Marina Shopping Center, Marina del Rey (☎ 310/578-1005), for some real down-home cookin'. It's not easy to find at first, but it's worth it. The restaurant is warm and charming. Red-checked cloths top the tables, and the walls are covered with photos of African-American history and important people. The emphasis here is on food—good southern food, based on recipes handed down from friends and relatives. Daily lunch specials (which come with two fresh vegetables, rice and gravy, or cornbread dressing and gravy) might be smothered pork chops on Monday, smothered steak on Tuesday, meatloaf on Wednesday, chicken and dumplings on Thursday. Get the picture? Fried chicken is a daily special. Lunch specials cost $6.95. At dinner, you might sample chicken and sausage jambalaya, or red beans and rice and hot links. These come with vegetables, too—but not your basic broccoli. You'll get black-eyed peas, creamy red beans, fresh collard greens, and others. Dinner runs $10.95–$11.95. Be sure to order the fresh lemonade served in a Mason jar. The desserts are homemade and rich: sweet-potato pie, pineapple-coconut cake, and sweet peach cobbler are a few examples.

Kids can have the macaroni and cheese, or a child's portion of anything on the regular menu for $5.95. There's a $3 charge for splitting an order at lunch, $5 at dinner.

One good way to sample lots of this filling food is at Sunday brunch, served buffet style. There are breakfast items such as grits and grilled country potatoes with onions; and fried chicken, barbecued beef ribs, smothered pork chops, and lots of their good vegetables. Most children will love the buttery, sugary candied yams they serve at an additional price. Brunch also includes dessert and beverage, and costs $11.95, $5.95 for kids.

Boosters and highchairs are provided.

Open for lunch Monday through Saturday from 11am to 4pm and for Sunday brunch from 11am to 3pm. Dinner is served Sunday through Thursday from 4 to 10pm, on Friday and Saturday till 11pm. No reservations or credit cards accepted. Parking is in the shopping center lot.

Fama, 1416 4th St., Santa Monica (☎ **310/451-8633**), is one of those new, fun places to take the kids. Mediterranean in style, it offers sandwiches, homemade pastas and luscious main courses. Prices are $6.75–$14.50. As trendy as the adult menu may be, the children's menu will please your kids: Mini cheese-and-tomato pizza, spaghetti, and macaroni and cheese are a few of the choices. Prices run $4.50–$5. Of course, there are highchairs and boosters, and the staff will be glad to warm baby bottles.

Open Tuesday through Friday from 11:30am to 2:30pm and 6 to 10pm, on Saturday from 5:30 to 11pm, and on Sunday from 5:30 to 9:30pm. Reservations and most credit cards accepted.

Yankee Doodles, 1410 3rd St. Promenade, Santa Monica (☎ **310/394-4632**), is no ordinary place. It offers billiards, and is really fun to go to with the kids. With big picture windows that look out onto the Promenade, Yankee Doodles will give you one hour of free billiards during lunch from 11am to 3pm. The menu is eclectic, with south-of-the-border, Cajun, and all-American selections. There's a Cajun shrimp, and several pasta selections, plus chicken, ribs, burgers, steaks, and fish—prices at $3.95–$11.25. The children's menu, called "little shooters," has prices from $3 to $5. Highchairs are available.

Open Monday through Saturday from 11am to 2am and on Sunday from 11am to 2am. Most credit cards accepted.

If your kids like seafood, **The Fish Co.,** at 174 Kinney St., a block west of Main Street, south of Ocean Park Boulevard and north of Rose Avenue, in Santa Monica (☎ **310/392-8366**), is a great place to go. The staff at this casual, airy restaurant with high wood ceilings, wood floors, and tasteful nautical decorations is perfectly comfortable with children. There are two glassed-in kitchen areas where kids can watch the cooks. There's also a small plant-filled patio.

The children's menu has coloring activities and consists of charcoal-broiled shrimp or whitefish, chicken strips, or a quarter-pound cheeseburger, each for $4.95. The lunch menu offers items from the oyster bar, lots of seafood salads, and a few sandwiches. Mesquite-broiled fresh fish and chicken teriyaki, calamari, steaks, Caesar salads, and a good ole hamburger are other tempting choices. At dinner you can get much of the same, plus lobster, scampi, cioppino, seafood fettuccine, a healthy-heart plate, and a light eater's plate, consisting of choice pieces of fish. There are plenty of desserts here, or stroll down Main Street after dinner and have a treat at one of the ice-cream shops.

Lunch prices average $7; dinner costs between $7 and $18. Boosters and highchairs are available. The servers will split orders for children, warm baby bottles and food, and make special children's drinks.

Open for lunch Monday through Friday from 11:30am to 4pm, on Saturday and Sunday to 3pm. Dinner is served Monday through Thursday from 4 to 10pm, on

Friday till 11pm, on Saturday from 3 to 11pm, and on Sunday from 3 to 10pm. Reservations accepted. Major credit cards are accepted. Park on the street or get validated parking for one hour in a lot one block south.

Fromin's Restaurant, 1832 Wilshire Blvd., Santa Monica (☎ **310/829-5443**), is one of those kosher-style delis that's perfect on a Sunday morning when you're craving bagels and cream cheese. For some reason, there's less of a crowd at breakfast than at lunch or dinner, so that's when we come here most often.

The children's menu is extensive, with breakfast, lunch, and dinner items at $2.35–$4.25. The adult portions are ample, and they split orders. They'll bring the kids a bagel on request (or pickles in the afternoon and evening). For omelet lovers, there are 20+ varieties like ham and cheese, bologna, pastrami, and Reuben. If that doesn't suffice, they'll let you create your own extravaganza from 17 different ingredients. Omelets start at $5.45.

There are also traditional breakfast offerings, deli platters with lox, whitefish and bagels, soups, 14 different salads, burgers, and a huge assortment of sandwiches, from typical deli fare (salami, sardine, cold roast beef) to triple-decker and hot creations. Prices range from $6.45 to $9.45. At night you can order à la carte, or a complete dinner with soup or salad; potato, coleslaw, or vegetable; and bread and butter; plus dessert and beverage. Choose from such entrees as sweet-and-sour rolled cabbage, corned beef and cabbage, chicken in a pot, fish, or boiled beef. Dinners range from $9.45 to $11; à la carte entrees run $6.95–$9.

Highchairs and boosters are available, and if you're bringing tiny ones, your server will be glad to warm bottles or baby food.

Open weekdays from 6:30am to 10pm and on weekends from 7am to 10pm. Best times to come are before noon on weekdays and between 5 and 6pm weekdays and weekends. Early-bird and senior citizens dinners available. Some major credit cards accepted. Parking lot. There's another branch at 17615 Ventura Blvd., in Encino (☎ **818/990-6346**).

Most people will agree that Southern California is one of the best places to eat Mexican food. Fortunately, Mexican restaurants generally welcome children. **Tampico & Tilly's,** 1025 Wilshire Blvd., in Santa Monica (☎ **310/451-1769**), is one. The Wilshire branch is inviting, and makes you think you've entered a home south of the border, with high ceilings, tile floors, and lace curtains. Both tables and booths are available, and there are several dining areas from which you can choose. The library in the back is particularly quaint, but when we're with the kids we choose the main room because there is lots of activity here. Our kids virtually dive into the bowl of tortilla chips that comes to the table as soon as you sit down.

The menu is especially diverse, offering an assortment of tame Mexican food. We like the Monterey salad (with crabmeat, shrimp, and avocado) and the fabulous burritos. There are scads of other delightful dishes, including tostadas, tacos, fajitas, and enchiladas. They even offer Mexican omelets. Lunches are priced at $4.95–$10. For dinner, you can enjoy many of the same entrees as at lunch, but with larger portions and including soup or salad, rice, and beans. You may also choose from several steak, seafood, and other dishes. Prices range from $5.25 to $12.75. For children under 12 there's a separate menu of four items: taco, cheese enchilada, hamburger, and grilled-cheese sandwich for $4.50-$4.75.

Highchairs and boosters are available, and they'll warm bottles and baby food. There's a full bar, with music and dancing on Friday and Saturday nights.

Open Monday through Thursday from 11:30am to 10pm, on Friday and Saturday from 11:30am to 11pm, and on Sunday from 10am (for brunch) to 10pm. The bar is open later. Most major credit cards are accepted and there is valet parking.

Inexpensive

Even many locals are not familiar with the **Brentwood Country Mart,** at 26th Street and San Vicente Boulevard in Santa Monica (☎ 310/395-6714). But once you find out about it, you'll return again and again. It attracts people of all ages—neighborhood preteens out for lunch with friends, grandparents with their toddler charges, and whole families. A mini-marketplace of 30 shops (the kids will enjoy browsing through Brentwood Toys and the nearby Candy Alley) and eateries, the Country Mart is housed in a red barn structure that surrounds an open-air plaza complete with outdoor firepit.

Not only is it a delightful place to take the family for lunch and shopping, but the ride down San Vicente Boulevard, going either east or west, is lovely. Here unusual Coral trees with their odd-shaped branches line the wide boulevard strip where joggers make their daily treks down to Palisades Park. As you drive along San Vicente, you'll see some of Brentwood's most impressive homes.

The Country Mart has a wide variety of gourmet fast-food restaurants: choose deli or chicken or fruit-and-yogurt creations. Our favorite is **Reddi Chick,** whose succulent rotisserie chicken is a winner with everyone. The chicken wing basket (six wings for $4.25) is a wing-lover's dream, and the teriyaki steak sandwich costs only $5.05. To shop for your own picnic, there's a full market with great produce.

Don't miss the small side patio where two kiddie rides keep preschoolers entertained long enough for adults to enjoy a leisurely lunch. (It's generally less crowded than the central patio too.) After lunch, don't miss a walk through Taste of Chocolate, a fabulous gourmet candy store featuring stuffed dried fruits, hand-dipped chocolates, and even low-calorie, salt-free goodies.

Stores and restaurants are generally open daily from 9am to 6pm, but call before you go because hours can vary.

Now if it's back to the '50s and '60s you want, come home to what almost became an extinct art form—the American diner. **Edie's Diner,** at 4211 Admiralty Way, Marina del Rey (☎ 310/823-5339), has lots of windows and a small outside patio overlooking the boats. Inside, the black-and-white-tile floor, stainless-steel mixers, red cushioned booths, and long, low counter will put you back in another era. You can impress your wide-eyed children as you find you can suddenly remember all the words to "Itsy-Bitsy, Teeny-Weeny, Yellow Polka Dot Bikini" and can sing along with practically every song on the table-attached jukeboxes.

When you get down to the real job of eating, you're sure to find something on the four-page menu, such as Edie's special waffles or hot dogs for $4.95; blue-plate specials (before *our* time) of southern fried chicken, vegetable, mashed potatoes and gravy, soup, and roll and butter for $6.85; meatloaf with gravy for $6.45; chicken pot pie, vegetables, potatoes and gravy, soup, and roll and butter for $6.90; plus chili burgers and regular hamburgers (in the $5 range), and sandwiches (priced reasonably).

For the small appetites of kids 12 and under, there's a limited but well-priced selection: hot dog, miniburger, and grilled cheese with fries (each $1.95), and fried chicken (at $2.75). Highchairs and booster seats are provided. Management is willing to warm bottles and baby food.

Insomniacs and parents of children who don't sleep will be happy to learn that Edie's is open from 6:30am to 2:30am Sunday through Thursday, and 24 hours on

Friday and Saturday. No reservations except for very large parties. The wait averages 20 minutes. Major credit cards are accepted. There's self-parking in the restaurant lot.

The small, quaint **Ocean Park Omelette Parlor,** 2732 Main St., Santa Monica (☎ 310/399-7892), is a satisfying choice for breakfast or lunch. It serves good old-fashioned breakfasts, salads, sandwiches, and an array of omelets. Almost everyone will find something to enjoy. It's hard to find better prices: three-egg omelets (including potatoes and muffin) cost $5.95 and salads are in the $5–$6 range. Sandwiches are a great bargain at about $5–$5.50.

Open daily from 6am to 3pm. No reservations, but booster and sassy seats are available. Dining can be enjoyed on the outdoor patio. Some major credit cards are accepted. You can park on the street or in the metered parking lot behind the restaurant.

THE AIRPORT/WESTCHESTER AREA

We define this area as the small confines around Los Angeles International Airport, bordered roughly on the east by Sepulveda Boulevard, and running from Culver Boulevard in the north to Century Boulevard in the south. These restaurants are particularly good when you're going to or from LAX.

Dinah's Family Restaurant, 6521 S. Sepulveda Blvd., near Centinela, Westchester (☎ 310/645-0456), is a basic all-American home-style coffee shop with hard-to-beat prices. With families accounting for over half its business, Dinah's has sassy seats, boosters, and a children's menu with spaghetti, fried chicken, and fish and chips for about $3.50. The staff will warm bottles and baby food.

The restaurant is known for its original-recipe fried chicken and its large selection of pancakes (be sure to try their specialty, the German and apple pancakes). Breakfasts start at $2 (for buttermilk pancakes) and go up to $7.25 (for steak and eggs). Lunch and dinner items are equally inexpensive. Salads, sandwiches, and burgers range from $3.95 to $5.65. A complete fried-chicken dinner with soup or salad, whipped potatoes and gravy, vegetable, and beverage is $8.35. You can also get spaghetti, fish, chicken fried steak, and the like. Weekdays there are all-you-can-eat specials available.

Open daily from 6am to 10pm. No reservations accepted. Between 4 and 6pm is the best time to come for quick service, but expect a 15-minute wait for weekend breakfasts. Credit cards accepted. There's plenty of parking.

HOLLYWOOD/MID-WILSHIRE/WEST HOLLYWOOD

These areas are rich with neighborhood-style restaurants. New eateries are always opening.

Expensive

It didn't take long for the **Daily Grill,** 100 N. La Cienega Blvd., West Hollywood (☎ 310/659-3100), to catch on with the 30- and 40-something crowd of parents, many of whom were already familiar with the fashionable, upscale Grill in the Alley in Beverly Hills, from which these more casual and less expensive restaurants were spun off. White-and-black tile floors, wooden booths, Venetian blinds, and deco-like hanging lamps contribute to the traditional look of the place. Butcher paper on the tables allows busy hands to draw. Come any time between 6 and 8pm and you will see families with children of all ages. Families like the fact that the service is excellent, the wait is usually no more than 15 or 20 minutes, and the food is consistently good. Booster seats and highchairs are provided; servers can warm baby food and bottles, and prepare drinks like a Shirley Temple or a Roy Rogers.

To accommodate the large numbers of families dining at the Daily Grill, management came up with an extensive children's menu. Kids age 11 and younger can order the usual burgers (including chicken), grilled cheese, and peanut butter and jelly sandwich, plus meatloaf or turkey steak with mashed potatoes, spaghetti with meatballs, panfried chicken, bacon and eggs, a tuna melt, or a BLT. Prices are $1.75–$5.50. Side orders of soup or salad are on the menu, and yummy desserts include a fudge brownie and ice cream, rice pudding, or a fruit cobbler ($1.50–$2.50).

The regular menu is also extensive, and includes such hearty standard grill fare as steaks, chops, seafood, and five varieties of chicken, including great broiled chicken. Hamburgers are thick and satisfying, and salads come in small and main-course sizes. Daily specials include chicken hash, meatloaf with mashed potatoes, calves' liver, bacon and onions, a steamed vegetable plate, and Joe's special—a traditional San Francisco dish of ground beef, spinach, and eggs. Vegetables and potatoes are à la carte, but you get a giant order of broccoli with most entrees. Share a plate of fried potatoes and onions (for two to four people) while you wait for your order. Leave room for dessert—our favorite is the hot fudge cheesecake. The price range is wide: from $6.95 for a simple hamburger to $17.75 for swordfish. Wine, beer, and champagne are served.

The West Hollywood location is open Monday through Thursday from 11:30am to 11pm, on Friday and Saturday from 11:30am to midnight, and on Sunday from 11am to 11pm. No reservations are taken. Major credit cards are accepted. Take-out and delivery are available. Validated parking in the lot.

Other Daily Grill locations can be found in Brentwood at 11677 San Vicente Blvd. (☎ 310/442-0044), in Newport Beach at Fashion Island (☎ 714/644-2223), in Encino at 16101 Ventura Blvd. (☎ 818/986-4111), and in Studio City at 12050 Ventura Boulevard (☎ 818/769-6336).

Prices at **Genghis Cohen,** 740 N. Fairfax Ave., West Hollywood (☎ 213/653-0640), are a bit steep, but the food is worth it. Just half a block north of trendy Melrose Avenue, Genghis Cohen gets its share of music studio people, Melrose wanderers, and the Westside chic. The dining room is lovely and subdued, and the service is prompt and helpful. Most families visit on Sunday.

There's no children's menu, but most dishes are suitable for sharing. If you like duck, try the half a crispy duck. Or sample the candied garlic shrimp, crackerjack shrimp, spicy garlic lamb, or orange-peel chicken. Or order triple kung pao, platters of shellfish, or the three-flavor mu shu (which they call their famous Oriental fajitas!). They will make your Szechuan choices as hot as you want, and they don't use MSG in anything. Entrees range from $9 to $16.50. Duck and seafood specialties go for $17.50–$27.50. Highchairs, boosters, and Shirley Temples are available.

Open for lunch Monday and Friday from noon to 3pm, and for dinner Monday through Saturday from 5 to 11pm, on Sunday till 10pm. Reservations are accepted, as are most major credit cards. There's a small parking lot or try for street parking.

Moderate

The story of **El Cholo,** 1121 S. Western Ave., between Olympic and Pico Boulevards (☎ 213/734-2773), goes back to 1927, when it opened across the street from its present location with six booths and a counter. Somehow it survived the Depression, and in 1931 it moved into a bungalow at its current address. The front room and bedrooms became dining rooms. What you see was the actual house, now decorated in the style of a Spanish hacienda. The various dining rooms are named after employees who stayed with El Cholo more than 30 years. The bar is separate from the dining rooms, and has inviting chairs and sofas perfect for waiting for your table. There are also tabletop video games and a big-screen TV. The lively dining rooms are comfortable for children, and on Mondays you can listen to the mariachis serenade the whole family.

El Cholo has won a Restaurant Writers of Southern California award and is famous for its margaritas and green-corn tamales. In addition to the usual Mexican appetizer selections, you can get five crab taquitos or five beef taquitos ($5.50–$6.50 per order). Entrees include fajitas (try the house specialty, shrimp fajitas); combination plates with enchiladas, tamales, tacos, and chile rellenos; the special Sonora-style enchilada (topped with olives and a fried egg), first served there in 1927; green-corn tamales (served June through September only); tostadas; tacos of the day; and a chimichanga. Entree prices range from $7.45 to $11.25.

There is no written children's menu, but if your child is under 12, tell your server you want the children's-priced items. They'll make a taco, cheese enchilada, chile relleno, or tamale with rice, beans, or french fries. Each selection is $6.25. There are highchairs and boosters. Servers will split adult portions for children at no charge, and will warm baby food and bottles. Special children's drinks are available.

Open Monday through Thursday from 11am to 10pm, on Friday and Saturday till 11pm, and on Sunday till 9pm. Reservations are recommended; on weekends (including Sunday) the wait can be up to an hour without them, 40 minutes on weeknights. Major credit cards are accepted. Valet parking, or park in the lot across the street, or at meters.

If you're traveling with teenagers, you'll have to make a pilgrimage to the **Hard Rock Café,** 8600 Beverly Blvd., street level of the Beverly Center, West Hollywood (☎ 310/276-7605). It's one of L.A.'s most popular casual restaurants, and teens love it! We're convinced that people don't just *go* to the Hard Rock, they make a pilgrimage here. The green Cadillac plunging through the roof, and the digital countdown of destroyed rain forests and new births, make the Hard Rock hard to miss. Inside you'll be met by loud rock music and rock 'n' roll decor everywhere. (This is not a place for noise-sensitive infants and toddlers.) In fact, management has seen fit to produce a pamphlet to guide you through the maze of memorabilia. Once you get a table—and that can be a very long wait on weekends and at prime dining hours— you'll be doing so much looking around at the eclectic crowd the restaurant attracts that it will be hard to concentrate on the meal. We let the kids decide on their dinner and then let them walk around to look at the displays. During one of the few quiet times, the waiter gave them a personally conducted tour. There is ample opportunity to choose a Hard Rock–logo'd item from the "boutique."

The kids' menu at Hard Rock is simple and to the point: grilled cheese, a Hard Rock burger, and lime barbecued chicken, at $2.95–$3.95. There's ice cream for dessert and shakes priced at a hefty $3. Coloring books and crayons are given out. Highchairs are available and special drinks can be ordered.

Adult appetites are satisfied with good-size salads, fish, fajitas, hamburgers or turkey burgers, and sandwiches. The big attractions are the lime barbecued chicken with fries and a salad and the baby rock watermelon ribs—or get a combination of both. Finish off the meal with a scrumptious hot-fudge sundae or an old-fashioned banana split. Food costs begin at $5.95 and top out at $13 for steak. The house specials are $8.95–$11.50.

Open Sunday through Thursday from 11:30am to 11:30pm, on Friday and Saturday from 11:30am to midnight. No reservations are accepted (remember that anytime after 5:30pm you'll have a wait). Most major credit cards are accepted. Valet and self-parking are available at the Beverly Center.

Chinese restaurants make great family eating experiences, and **Hunan Taste,** 6031 W. San Vicente Blvd., at the crossroads of Fairfax Avenue and Olympic and San Vicente Boulevards, in the mid-Wilshire District (☎ **213/936-5621** or **213/936-6133**), is no exception. This friendly neighborhood restaurant, where you see the same faces again and again, is perfect for a Sunday-night or any night dinner. Unlike some Chinese restaurants that never quite got decorated, Hunan Taste is bright and cheerful, with linen-covered tables set far apart and a comfortable atmosphere. Our 11-year-old, who practically grew up on the wonton soup served here, convinced the staff of the need to bring crispy noodles as soon as a child is seated.

Owner/chef Tommy Yan, a veteran of three well-known L.A. Chinese restaurants, is known for his velvet shrimp Peking style and hot-and-sour soup, but kids seem to like almost everything here. Some are partial to the three-ingredients dish; others, to almond chicken. Dishes are prepared Hunan style, so be sure to specify if you want milder versions of spicy dishes. Your waiter can suggest combinations of orders for the best sharing. Make one of your selections a house special. A few good choices are Hunan whole fish (priced seasonally), Hunan lamb ($9.50), and slippery shrimp ($10.95). Ask about weekly specials. Dinner entrees average $9.

We've made Hunan a lunch stop before the Los Angeles County Museum of Art and Page Museum, but you may want to try it on your way downtown from the Westside. Such lunch specials as beef with broccoli, chicken lo mein, hot braised shrimp, and other Hunan-style dishes come with soup, appetizer, and fried rice, and cost $4.75–$5.75. Or you can order off the regular menu.

Boosters and highchairs are available, and the staff will warm bottles and baby food. Shirley Temples are cheerfully provided. If you're staying in the area, you might consider ordering take-out. Open daily from 11:30am to 10pm. Reservations accepted. Major credit cards welcome. Park in the lot.

Inexpensive

Canter's, at 419 N. Fairfax Ave., near CBS and the Farmer's Market (☎ **213/651-2030**), one of Los Angeles's oldest delis, is a find because it's open 24 hours a day. You'll usually find an eclectic crowd at Cantor's—families, local would-be celebrities, neighborhood residents, and tourists. Eat in the dining room, where tables are far apart and booths are roomy, or in the original room at a booth or counter. You can have meats, cheeses, sandwiches, and baked goods wrapped to take back to your hotel or to the beach. Don't take the surly waitresses too seriously—some have been there for years. Ask for a "We Love Kids" balloon on the way out.

In addition to oatmeal, egg dishes, Belgian waffles, and matzoh brei, there's Canter's fresh baked goods (a slice of their pumpernickel-raisin bread can't be beat). Hot corned beef and pastrami are first on the list of sandwiches, followed by the standards: chopped liver, brisket, salami, bologna, and cheese. There are also hot sandwiches, lots of soups, fish dishes, hot dogs, hamburgers, steak sandwiches, and even pasta. A plate of lox, bagels, and cream cheese is the most expensive item on the menu at $11.50. Most sandwich selections range around $6.40.

They will split orders for two children, warm bottles and baby food, and make special children's drinks. Highchairs and boosters are available.

Open 24 hours daily. The bar serves from 10am to 1:40am. Reservations for parties of seven or more; some major credit cards accepted. There's validated parking in Canter's parking lot, two doors away.

No matter what the time of day or night, **Jerry's Famous Deli,** seems to be filled with pastrami lovers of all ages (8701 Beverly Blvd., West Hollywood; ☎ 310/289-1811). The noise level is usually perfect for hiding your most boisterous 3-year-old. Tables here and there are always topped with infant carriers, right amid the movie and TV-industry types seated in the booths and at the tables. The place is cavernous; there's an outdoor area in front and a patio.

The menu takes forever to read. The "regular" sandwiches are huge; I always end up taking the other half home, but half-sandwiches are available. There are also numerous salads, full and light platters, triple-decker sandwiches, hamburgers, soups, and full entrees. Breakfast is served all day and night. With so much on the menu, prices jump around; suffice it to say that a whole pastrami sandwich will run you $8.25, while boiled chicken in the pot goes for $13.25. Most menu items fall in the $7–$9 range.

A separate children's menu for youngsters 10 and under offers up an egg and pancakes with sausage and bacon for $5.25, a hot dog and fries at $4.25, and macaroni and cheese for $5.50. There are at least six other items on that menu, and each comes with a beverage.

There are booster seats and highchairs here.

Jerry's is open every day, 24 hours each day. No reservations. Major credit cards are accepted. There is valet parking, or park on the street. There are other locations at 12655 Ventura Blvd., Studio City (☎ 818/980-4245), and at 13181 Mindanao Way, Marina del Rey (☎ 310/821-6626).

Your kids will like **Carneys Express Limited,** 8351 Sunset Blvd., Hollywood (☎ 213/654-8300). They serve what most children love in a place where children feel comfortable—an authentic Union Pacific railway car set on train tracks. There are outside tables too, but most youngsters prefer to eat in the train car. The fare is simple here, and all self-service. There are good old cheeseburgers and double burgers served with chili, hot dogs, tuna melts, chicken sandwiches, soft tacos, veggie sandwiches, and pasta salad. Prices start at $1.65 for a simple hot dog, and go up to $4.25 for a half-pound cheeseburger. There's ice-cream or orange-juice bars and huge frozen chocolate-dipped bananas for dessert.

Owner Bill Wolf and his staff will do much to accommodate families, including warming bottles and baby food. There is only one highchair here, and no booster seats. Open daily from 11am to midnight. No reservations or credit cards accepted. Park in the lot behind the train car. There is another Carneys at 12601 Ventura Blvd., Studio City (☎ 818/761-8300).

Du-Par's Restaurant, at 3rd Street and Fairfax Avenue in the Farmers Market (☎ 213/933-8446), has been an institution for more than 50 years. While there are two other locations in Los Angeles and Studio City, this one seems to be the most popular. You'll sit in booths or at the counter and wonder when they plan to redo the interior. Boosters and highchairs are available, and balloons are given to all kids. Breakfast is the best time to go. The pancakes are outstanding and the coffee is good and strong. The short order of pancakes is plenty for one child, or split it between two light eaters. You can also choose omelets, French toast (which comes in short-order size too), cereals, or eggs, and freshly made bakery goods. Prices range from $4.55 to $7.95 for full breakfasts.

Open daily from 6am to 10:30pm. No reservations are taken, but the wait isn't more than 10–20 minutes, even on Sunday morning. Major credit cards are accepted. There's a parking lot available.

Family owned and run, **Lucy's Café El Adobe,** 5536 Melrose Ave., Hollywood (☎ 213/462-9421), is a 30-year-old Los Angeles tradition, a homey neighborhood restaurant now serving the second and third generations of its customers. Thrown into the limelight when Jerry Brown was California's governor, Lucy's is still visited by recognizable celebrities. It's just across the street from Paramount Studios.

The food is simple and good, the margaritas are great. House specialties include arroz con pollo (chicken and Spanish rice), chile Colorado (fresh chopped beef with red chile sauce), ropa vieja (shredded beef in sauce), gallina en mole (breast of chicken in mole sauce), and carne seca con huevo (beef jerky with scrambled eggs). Specialties come with soup, salad, rice, beans, tortillas, and butter, and average around $9. Enchilada dinners come in seven variations and run $8–$9.50. There are also tostadas, taco combinations, and steak dinners. Janey warns that the salsa is pretty hot!

Children can get the "under 12" choices of a taco or enchilada with rice, beans, soup, or salad, or a chicken, beef, or bean burrito with rice, soup or salad, each meal $6, or they can order off the à la carte menu for about $2.75.

Only booster seats are available. Bottles and baby food will be warmed, and special children's drinks can be made.

Open Monday through Saturday from 11:30am to 11:30pm; closed Sunday. Reservations for groups of six or more; the average wait is 10 minutes. Some major credit cards accepted. Parking on the side and in back.

The **Old Spaghetti Factory,** 5939 Sunset Blvd., Hollywood (☎ 213/469-7149), is like a turn-of-the-century museum. A mammoth chandelier greets you in the foyer, and stained-glass windows from 1900s Chicago decorate the restaurant, along with one-of-a-kind light fixtures, hand-carved doorways, and antique tables. Children will have a ball looking at all the ornate decorations; all love the 1918 trolley car, which actually ran in Seattle and was lowered into the restaurant because it was too big to get through the door. You can even request a table inside it.

What is served here is obvious. Lunch and dinner feature many of the same items—only the price is different. Spaghetti comes with mushroom sauce, clam sauce, meat sauce, tomato sauce, meatballs, sausage, or browned butter and mizithra cheese. Or you have your choice of fettuccine Alfredo, spinach tortellini with Alfredo sauce, pasta salad, sausage or meatball sandwich, and soup. Prices range from $3.35 to $5.35. Complete dinners, including salad, bread, beverage, and spumoni, cost $4.25–$7.75.

An under-12 dinner for kids consists of spaghetti with meat or tomato sauce, salad, bread, a beverage, and dessert for $3.75. The little kids get smaller meals served on a special dinosaur plate for $2.95 or $3.35. Boosters and highchairs are provided. Baby food and bottles will be warmed upon request.

Open for lunch Monday through Friday from 11:30am to 2pm, and for dinner Monday through Thursday from 5 to 10pm, on Friday and Saturday from 5 to 11pm, and on Sunday from noon to 10pm. No reservations; during busy times the wait is 15–30 minutes, and on weekends it can be 30–45 minutes. Come early so as not to wait. Some credit cards accepted. Park in the lot.

Roscoe's House of Chicken and Waffles, 1514 N. Gower St. (☎ **213/466-7453** or **213/466-9329**), is an interesting place to stop if you're in the Hollywood area. The name reflects their specialties, and both are served in many ways. From delicious chicken smothered with gravy and onions, accompanied by grits and biscuits, to fresh chicken livers, a special-batter waffle, potato salad or fries, you'll find large portions at reasonable prices. You can get waffles alone (two for $4.50) or combine them with a southern-style chicken dish ($6.80–$8.60). There's also a chicken burger and chicken sandwiches ($4.10–$5.20). These dishes are served all day. They'll split orders for two kids, warm bottles and baby food, and provide boosters and highchairs.

Open Sunday through Thursday from 8:30am to midnight and on Friday and Saturday from 8:30am to 4am. No reservations (busiest time is 11:30am to noon). All major credit cards accepted. Street parking only. There's another branch at 5006 W. Pico Blvd., near La Brea Avenue (☎ 213/934-4405 or 213/936-3730).

Johnny Rocket's, 7507 Melrose Ave. (☎ 213/651-3361), is where to find 1950s nostalgia L.A.-style, complete with juicy burgers and creamy malts. Probably the hippest diner of its kind in town, Rocket's is a great place to sit at the counter and watch the chefs cook up chili fries for you and fix peanut butter and jelly for the kids. There's nothing on the menu over $4.55. Some locations, including this one, have outdoor tables. Be prepared for a wait during peak hours.

Open Sunday through Thursday from 11am to midnight, on Friday and Saturday to 2am. Major credit cards are honored. Park on the street. There are Johnny Rocket's branches at 10959 Weyburn Blvd., in Westwood (☎ 310/824-5656); 10250 Santa Monica Blvd., in the Century City Shopping Center, West Los Angeles (☎ 310/788-9020); 474 N. Beverly Dr., in Beverly Hills (☎ 310/271-2222); and 100 N. La Cienega Blvd., in the Beverly Connection (☎ 310/657-6073). Hours vary.

The **Souplantation,** 8491 W. 3rd St., in the Beverly Connection (☎ 213/655-0381), is a good choice for budget family dining, especially with a big family. See the description of the Pasadena location in Chapter 12 for details about food and hours.

UNIVERSAL CITY/BURBANK/SAN FERNANDO VALLEY

Officially part of the San Fernando Valley, Universal City and Burbank are part of the Hollywood state-of-mind. You'll find yourself spending at least one day (and maybe more) in this general area close to Hollywood and downtown Los Angeles.

Make **Fung Lum Restaurant,** 222 Universal Terrace Pkwy. (☎ 818/763-7888), a must on your list of interesting restaurants to visit. Set on the side of the hill leading up to Universal Studios, the restaurant looks like an Oriental palace. The palatial look is continued in the interior, which you enter through ornate hand-carved doors. Moongates (arched entryways) lead to exquisite gardens, and inside are embroidered silk decorations and panels inlaid with coral and ivory. But don't let the formality of the decor discourage you. This restaurant is a fine place to take the family. The main dining room seats 500 people comfortably.

Cantonese is the primary Chinese cuisine served here, although Hunan and Szechuan dishes are also prepared. Since Chinese food is made to share, you won't find a children's menu here. But there are dozens of things that will please the kids, such as chicken chow mein, fried rice, and moo shu chicken. For lunch there is dim sum and an abbreviated version of the large dinner menu. Lunch prices run $5.40–$9.50 for main courses.

At dinner there are many duck entrees, 11 kinds of soup, and a huge list of seafood, vegetable, chicken, beef, and pork dishes. You could come back again and again and still not taste everything on the menu. Dinner prices range from $8.50 to $24 (for Maine lobster baked with ginger and scallions). For $35 you can have the celebrated shark's-fin soup with shredded chicken, or whole winter-melon soup, which has to be ordered in advance and serves 10 people. Don't wait for fortune cookies here, though. We're told that they are not authentic Chinese desserts, so Fung Lum won't serve them. Instead there is ice cream, lichee nuts, and Fung Lum pudding.

Sunday brunch features a buffet and nonstop champagne. Adults are charged $11.95; children, half price.

There are booster seats and highchairs available. The staff will warm bottles and baby food, and will prepare special children's drinks.

Open for lunch Monday through Saturday from 11:30am to 2:30pm, and for dinner Monday through Thursday from 5 to 9:30pm, on Friday and Saturday from 5 to 10:30pm, and on Sunday from 3 to 9:30pm. A Sunday brunch is served from 11am to 3pm. Reservations are accepted. Major credit cards accepted. Valet parking.

Victoria Station, 100 Universal Terrace Parkway, atop the hill at Universal Studios (☎ 818/622-8180), is located next to the Universal Studios tours. While that intrigues the adults and older kids in our party, the younger ones are delighted that they're eating inside a replica of a famous train depot. Victoria Station re-creates the ambience of the London railroad station. In fact, you can eat inside one of the original Flying Scotsman fleet of British railway cars.

Specializing in carved-to-order prime rib and continental cuisine, Victoria Station caters to families. For adults, there are steak entrees, fresh seafood, pasta, and chicken selections. Dinners include salad bar or soup du jour, and baked potato, fries, mashed potatoes, or saffron rice. Prices range $3.95–$22.95. Lunch offerings, costing $3.95–$11.95, include such items as top sirloin, honey-grilled chicken, chicken stir-fry, and Caesar salad. There are quiche and burgers as well.

Highchairs and boosters are available, and children's non-alcoholic drinks can be ordered. The server will warm bottles or baby food, and will bring crackers to the table if your kids are hungry. Open Monday through Thursday from 11:30am to 10pm, on Friday and Saturday from 11:30am to 11pm, and on Sunday for dinner only, from 11:30am to 10pm. Reservations are suggested. Most major credit cards are accepted. Valet parking is available in addition to parking in a nearby lot ($6).

Tony Roma's A Place for Ribs, 1000 Universal Center Drive, Universal City (☎ 818/763-7662), is always a good bet for consistent quality, fast service, and a welcoming attitude toward kids. Probably the most attractive setting of the Tony Roma's branches in Los Angeles, this one in Universal City has a perfect location, in the Citywalk, near the Universal Studios entrance. With large picture windows, it offers a lovely view on clear days.

The menu has the usual mouth-watering assortment of barbecued ribs and chicken, and a few other grilled entrees. Dinners include coleslaw and tangy ranch-style beans, baked potato, or fries, and range in price from $8.95 to $14.95. Lunches include the same choices (without the potato), priced at $3.95–$12. The terrific little children's menu doubles as a page to color, and offers burgers, chicken fingers, hot dogs, grilled cheese, and rib, all with fries and ice cream, for $2.99–4.95. Highchairs and boosters are available. Your server will be glad to let you split adult portions, and will warm bottles and baby food.

Open Sunday through Thursday from 11am to 10pm and on Friday and Saturday from 11am to 11pm. Reservations are not accepted, but most major credit cards are. The large parking lot for Universal Studios is nearby. There are other branches at The Westside Pavilion in West Los Angeles (☎ 310/470-0737); 319 Santa Monica Blvd., in Santa Monica (☎ 310/393-0139); 20720 S. Avalon Blvd., Redondo Beach (☎ 310/329-5723); and 50 N. La Cienega Blvd., in Beverly Hills (☎ 310/659-7427). Hours vary.

DOWNTOWN

The following restaurants are good choices if you are staying in a downtown hotel or are visiting Olvera Street, the Children's Museum, the Museum of Contemporary Art, or Chinatown and Little Tokyo.

Expensive

Weekend breakfast time is when you'll find the most families with children dining at the **Pacific Dining Car,** 1310 W. 6th St. (☎ **213/483-6000**). Although it's open 24 hours a day, don't expect a coffee shop—the ambience is more luxurious, and the prices are quite high. Weekdays, L.A.'s major powerbrokers spend their breakfasts here making major deals.

Set in an enlarged replica of a real railway dining car, this restaurant has been serving food in this location since 1923. Through the years it became famous for its aged meats. While the coffee is no longer 10¢ and you can't get a sirloin for 65¢ anymore, it still draws a loyal crowd of diners for breakfast, lunch, dinner, and aftertheater supper. The rooms are handsome and the atmosphere subdued. We like to sit in the area near the entrance, the original railwaylike car, with windows on one side.

Breakfast features mostly egg dishes such as fresh avocado scramble, Swiss eggs, and omelets. There are lots of specials and low-calorie options, too. Our kids love the pancakes and the homemade blueberry and bran muffins. You can also get a bowl of granola or Familia muesli. Breakfast prices start at $6.50 and go up to $14.50.

Lunch and dinner feature seafood, steaks, and veal. Lunch will cost you $13 to $25. Dinner selections include chicken, shrimp diavolo, and a T-bone steak. Hefty dinner prices are $20 to $35. Entrees come with a potato, but vegetables are à la carte.

Boosters and sassy seats are provided. The staff will warm bottles and baby food, and prepare special children's drinks. The chef will split orders.

Breakfast is served Monday through Friday from 11pm to 11am, and on Saturday and Sunday until 4pm. Lunch is served Monday through Friday from 11am to 4pm, afternoon tea may be ordered daily from 3 to 5:30pm, and dinner is served 24 hours every day. Almost anything on the menu is available whenever you want it. Reservations, and some credit cards, are accepted. Valet parking.

There's another Pacific Dining Car at 2700 Wilshire Blvd., in Santa Monica (☎ **310/453-4000**).

Moderate

Not too many Los Angeles restaurants can claim more than 68 years of business without having closed their doors once. But **The Original Pantry,** at 877 S. Figueroa St. (☎ **213/972-9279**), can. Walking into this place is like entering a time warp circa the 1930s. It's not diner style, mind you, but there's real linoleum on the floors and Formica on the tables. Waiters in white shirts, aprons, and black bow ties know their business, which is to serve generous portions of real American food. Locals know that the Pantry's hallmark is the line out the door. The best time to come for the shortest wait is between 2:30 and 5pm.

While in line, you might want to amuse your children with some fun trivia about the restaurant. For instance, it takes a harvest of more than 20,000 coffee trees to supply the $10^1/_2$ *tons* of coffee used by the Pantry annually. Or the fact that more than 2,400 eggs are used in the restaurant—every day. On the average, the restaurant buys 46,000 bottles of catsup, 15 tons of sugar, and 2,190 gallons of syrup each year. To make the yummy pancakes served here, the Pantry consumes eight tons of flour, 1,946 gallons of milk, and 2,000 dozen eggs every year.

The menu changes daily, but basically you'll get hearty breakfasts, plus hamburgers, steaks, short ribs, ham hocks and beans, rib roast, pork, soup, and salads. Prices are quite reasonable: breakfast averages $4; lunch, $6.50; and dinner, $8. There's no children's menu here, but they'll gladly split orders. Highchairs and booster seats are available.

Next door to the Pantry is the **Pantry Bake & Sandwich Shoppe,** 875 S. Figueroa St. (☎ **213/627-6879**). With the same feel of the 1930s, the Bake Shoppe has a large quick-service counter area for snacks and fast meals. The main feature of the Bake Shoppe is that it serves a lighter lunch than its neighbor, with such fare as sandwiches; breakfast and dinner items are the same at both places. Hamburgers here run $3.10–$4.95; sandwiches cost $2.60–$4.45. There are also daily specials and rotisserie chicken for $6.20.

The Original Pantry is open 24 hours daily—and there's usually always a line. As far as waiting goes, approach this restaurant with a sense of humor—after all, it's an L.A. landmark. The Bake Shoppe is open weekdays from 6am to 3pm, on weekends to 9pm. No reservations at either establishment. No credit cards accepted at either restaurant, but traveler's checks are welcome with identification. Parking is across the street and is $1 with a validation.

IN CHINATOWN   In the heart of Chinatown is **Ocean Seafood,** 750 N. Hill St. (☎ **213/687-3088**). Big windows run the length of the two spacious dining rooms. The white tablecloths and burgundy lacquered chairs lend elegance. But don't let that stop you from bringing the children. This is a good place to introduce children to Chinese food; there are many selections and the waiters here are familiar with serving children because so many of the customers are Asian families.

Ocean Seafood prepares more than 300 dishes in the gourmet Cantonese style of Hong Kong. This is not your usual chop suey Cantonese restaurant. Breakfast consists of many fresh dim sum selections ($1.60 each), a clever way to show kids the Chinese version of the American roll-and-coffee breakfast. Lunch might be anything from sticky rice in lotus leaf to braised E-Fu noodles with crabmeat. If all else fails to tempt them, the Chinese chicken noodles in soup will probably be a hit. Lunch prices are $2.40–$10.

Dinner is a cornucopia of exotic selections, and you will get to watch dishes being prepared tableside. In addition to such familiar dishes as Peking duck ($20), lemon chicken ($8 for a half order, $15 for a full order), and sweet-and-sour pork ($5), the restaurant prepares braised sea cucumber with preserved shrimp eggs ($10), pan-fried lobster with ginger and green onions (priced seasonally), geoduck clam Japanese style ($15), and squab steamed with wine sauce ($9.50). There are several desserts you may never have heard of, like almond Jell-O, coconut and bird's nest, and sweetened red-bean soup with lotus.

There are boosters and highchairs, and bottles and baby food will be warmed upon request.

Open daily from 8:30am to 10pm. Reservations are accepted at dinner only. Major credit cards honored. Valet parking.

Inexpensive

If you're downtown at the Children's Museum, or have enough Mexican food on Olvera Street, be sure to take the kids to **Philippe the Original,** 1001 N. Alameda St. (☎ **213/628-3781**). Like the Pantry, Philippe's is an L.A. tradition, this one dating back to 1908.

The setting is informal, the tables are long and to be shared, and the floors are covered with sawdust. The restaurant draws a clientele that ranges from Westside attorneys, Pasadena accountants, and Los Angeles celebrities to downtown blue-collar workers. Self-serve is the word here. Pay and order at the counter and choose eggs, French toast, or fresh baked goods for breakfast (35¢–$4.25), or the famous Philippe's French-dip sandwiches for lunch or dinner. French-dip pork, beef, ham, lamb, or turkey, and tuna sandwiches are scrumptious and reasonably priced at $3.55. Adults will want to have a cup of Philippe's coffee, still Depression-priced at 10¢! Don't miss the candy counter!

There are highchairs only here.

Open daily from 6am to 10pm; closed Thanksgiving and Christmas Days. No reservations or credit cards accepted. Free parking in the back or in the lot on Ord Street.

RESTAURANTS BY CUISINE

Because we know that children can be finicky eaters, and because Los Angeles can be overwhelming in the number of its restaurants, we've divided these establishments by cuisine.

American

Brentwood Country Mart, 26th Street and San Vicente Boulevard, Brentwood (p. 431).

Carneys Express Limited, 8351 Sunset Blvd., Hollywood (p. 436). Other location: 12601 Ventura Blvd., Studio City.

Cheesecake Factory, 364 N. Beverly Dr., Beverly Hills (p. 421). Other locations: 4142 Via Marina, Marina del Rey; 605 N. Harbor Dr., Redondo Beach; 11647 San Vicente Blvd., Brentwood; and 6324 Canoga Ave., Woodland Hills.

Daily Grill, 100 N. La Cienega Blvd., West Hollywood (p. 432). Other locations: 11677 San Vicente Blvd., Brentwood ; 16101 Ventura Blvd., Encino; at Fashion Island in Newport Beach and at 12050 Ventura Blvd., Studio City.

Dinah's Family Restaurant, 6521 S. Sepulveda Blvd., near Centinela, Westchester (p. 432).

Du-Par's Restaurant, 3rd Street and Fairfax Avenue, in the Farmers Market, L.A. (p. 436).

Ed Debevic's Short Orders/Deluxe, 134 N. La Cienega Blvd., Beverly Hills (p. 424).

Edie's Diner, 4211 Admiralty Way, Marina del Rey (p. 431).

Hard Rock Café, 8600 Beverly Blvd., in Beverly Center, West Hollywood (p. 434).

Islands, 10948 W. Pico Blvd., West L.A. (p. 427). Other locations: 404 Washington St., Marina del Rey; 350 S. Beverly Dr., Beverly Hills; and 3200 Sepulveda Blvd., Manhattan Beach.

Jeremiah P. Throckmorton Grille, 255 S. Beverly Dr., Beverly Hills (p. 424).

Johnny Rocket's, 7507 Melrose Ave., West Hollywood (p. 438). Other locations: 10959 Weyburn Blvd., Westwood; 10250 Santa Monica Blvd., in the Century City

Shopping Center, West L.A.; 474 N. Beverly Dr., Beverly Hills; and 100 N. La Cienega Blvd., in the Beverly Connection.

Larry Parker's Beverly Hills Diner, 206 S. Beverly Dr., Beverly Hills (p. 423).

Lawry's the Prime Rib, 100 N. La Cienega Blvd., Beverly Hills (p. 419).

Ocean Park Omelette Parlor, 2732 Main St., Santa Monica (p. 432).

The Original Pantry, 877 S. Figueroa St., L.A. (p. 440), and the **Pantry Bake & Sandwich Shoppe,** 875 S. Figueroa St., L.A. (p. 441).

Pacific Dining Car, 1310 W. 6th St., L.A. (p. 430). Other location: 2700 Wilshire Blvd., Santa Monica.

Philippe's the Original, 1001 N. Alameda St., L.A. (p. 441).

RJ's the Rib Joint, 252 N. Beverly Dr., between Dayton Way and Wilshire Boulevard, Beverly Hills (p. 420).

Roscoe's House of Chicken and Waffles, 1514 N. Gower St., Hollywood (p. 437). Other location: 5006 W. Pico Blvd., L.A.

Rosie's Barbecue Grillery, 11845 W. Olympic Blvd., West L. A. (p. 427).

Souplantation, 8491 W. 3rd St., in the Beverly Connection, West Hollywood (p. 438). Other location: 201 S. Lake Ave., Pasadena.

Tony Roma's A Place for Ribs, 1000 Universal Center Drive, Universal City (p. 439). Other locations: The Westside Pavilion; 319 Santa Monica Blvd., Santa Monica; 50 N. La Cienega Blvd., Beverly Hills; and 20720 S. Avalon Blvd., Redondo Beach.

Victoria Station, 100 Universal Terrace Pkwy., Universal City (p. 439).

Yankee Doodles, 1410 3rd St. Promenade, Santa Monica (p. 429).

Chinese

Fung Lum, 222 Universal Terrace Pkwy., Universal City (p. 438).

Genghis Cohen, 740 N. Fairfax Ave., West Hollywood (p. 433).

Hunan Taste, 6031 W. San Vicente Blvd., L.A. (p. 435).

Lotus West, 10974 W. Pico Blvd., West L.A. (p. 426).

Ocean Seafood, 750 N. Hill St., Chinatown (p. 441).

Delicatessens

Canter's, 419 N. Fairfax Ave., West Hollywood (p. 435).

Fromin's Restaurant, 1832 Wilshire Blvd., Santa Monica (p. 430). Other location: 17615 Ventura Blvd., Encino.

Jerry's Famous Deli, 8701 Beverly Blvd., W. Hollywood (p. 436). Other locations: 13181 Mindanao Way, Marina del Rey; and 12655 Ventura Blvd., Studio City.

Junior's Deli, 2379 Westwood Blvd., West L.A. (p. 425).

Nate'n Al, 414 N. Beverly Dr., Beverly Hills (p. 423).

Nosh of Beverly Hills, 9689 Santa Monica Blvd., Beverly Hills (p. 423).

Italian

Anna's Italian Restaurant, 10929 W. Pico Blvd., West L.A. (p. 425).

Earth, Wind & Flour, 1776 Westwood Blvd., Westwood (p. 427). Other locations: 2222 Wilshire Blvd., at 23rd Street, Santa Monica; and 17644 Ventura Blvd., Encino.

Louise's Trattoria, 342 N. Beverly Dr., Beverly Hills (p. 422). Other locations: 232 N. Larchmont Blvd., L.A.; 7505 Melrose Ave., West Hollywood; 1008 Montana Ave., Santa Monica; 264 26th St., Brentwood; 10645 Pico Blvd., West L.A.; and 11645 San Vincente Blvd.

Mario's Italian Restaurant, 1001 Broxton Ave., Westwood (p. 426). Other location: 1445 3rd St. Promenade, Santa Monica.

Old Spaghetti Factory, 5939 Sunset Blvd., Hollywood (p. 437).

Mexican

El Cholo, 1121 S. Western Ave., between Olympic and Pico Boulevards, L.A. (p. 433).

Lucy's Cafe El Adobe, 5536 Melrose Ave., Hollywood (p. 437).

Tampico & Tilly's, 1025 Wilshire Blvd., Santa Monica (p. 430).

Seafood

The Fish Co., 174 Kinney St., Santa Monica (p. 429).

Gladstone's 4-Fish, 17300 Pacific Coast Hwy., Santa Monica (p. 428).

Other Types of Cuisine

Aunt Kizzy's Back Porch, 4325 Glencoe Ave., in the Villa Marina Shopping Center, Marina del Rey (p. 428). Southern food.

Benihana of Tokyo, 38 N. La Cienega Blvd., Beverly Hills (p. 419). Japanese. Other location: 14160 Panay Way, Marina del Rey.

Fama, 1416 4th St., Santa Monica (p. 429). International.

6   What to See and Do

Los Angeles is many things to many people. It's a place so well suited to children that you almost don't have to think about where to take them—you just take them. The wide-open spaces and the good weather make it easy and simple to do almost anything with kids.

Because you'll be driving to so many activities, we have clustered them, roughly, according to their location. We will begin with downtown Los Angeles and work our way west to the beaches.

DOWNTOWN

Downtown L.A. is a culturally and historically rich section of the city. Let's start with the oldest section of town.

Old Los Angeles

Even this super-modern metropolis has its historical roots. **El Pueblo de Los Angeles State Historic Monument,** gives a flavor of the Los Angeles of days past. Nothing remains of the original cluster of earth-and-willow huts, circa 1780, that constituted the first incarnation of Los Angeles. However, on the spot of those original huts sits this park, a collection of 27 historic buildings that date from 1818 to 1926. Plan to spend several hours wandering around.

We like to start with the excitement of **Olvera Street,** a colorful Mexican-style marketplace. For kids, this street is definitely the highlight of the tour. In a city with such strong Hispanic ties, this area gives children a more visual and sensual awareness of the city's roots. Over 85 giftshops and stalls offer authentic Mexican goods, such as sombreros, piñatas, and leather goods. Children especially like to watch the craftspeople at work: glassblowers, silversmiths, candlemakers, and leather makers.

Our kids are always ready to sample the local tasty treats—sugary churros are one such specialty. You probably won't be able to keep your kids away from the other colorful Mexican candies for sale. If you can bargain with them to have lunch first, you'll find a bounty of choices here, from casual food stalls to sidewalk cafés and full-scale restaurants. The most historic choice is **La Golondrina Restaurant,** housed in the **Pelanconi House.** Built in the mid-19th century as a private residence, it was one of the earliest buildings in Los Angeles made of fired brick. The food served there is very traditional Mexican fare. **El Paseo** is another choice nearby.

Olvera Street is often host to special events, so write ahead for exact dates of events to the **Visitor Center,** 125 Paseo de la Plaza, Suite 400, Los Angeles, CA 90012 (☎ 213/628-1274). The Cinco de Mayo (May 1–5) and Mexican Independence Day (September 16–18) celebrations are especially fun.

Perhaps the most kids-oriented of these events is the Blessing of the Animals in mid-April, in which local residents dress up their animals, parade them down the street, and have them blessed by the local Catholic bishop. Kids of all ages are delighted by the animals, which range from cats in hats, dogs on fancy leashes, cows in bonnets, birds in colorful cages, to even goldfish. The blessing is meant to acknowledge the loyal affection that animals have for their human owners.

At the center of Olvera Street is the historic **Sepulveda House,** built in 1887, which houses the park's visitor center. Here, if your kids are historically inclined, an 18-minute film on Los Angeles's past can be viewed on request. You can also buy the walking self-tour brochure for 50¢ and see the rest of the historic park on your own. Also sold here are children's books and gifts.

If you prefer **guided tours,** walk to the Docent Office, 130 Paseo de la Plaza, next to the Old Plaza Firehouse at 501 N. Los Angeles St. The tours last 45 minutes, are free, and are conducted Tuesday through Saturday at 11am, noon, and 1pm. At this office, you can also sign up for two-hour guided bus tours of the central city, which are given the first and third Wednesdays of the month. Reservations are required (☎ 213/628-1274). The visitor center is open Monday through Saturday from 10am to 4:30pm.

Beyond Olvera Street it takes a parent's knowledge to determine which sights will interest kids. **Firehouse Number 1,** which displays fire-fighting memorabilia from the 19th century, is often a favorite. The **Avila Adobe,** the oldest existing residence in Los Angeles, gives kids a sense of what everyday life was like for wealthy California ranchers in the 1840s. And since kids are often intrigued by statues, you might show them the **Felipe de Neve Statue** (the Spanish governor of California who was responsible for founding El Pueblo del Río de Nuestra Señora la Reina de Los Angeles in 1781) and the **Fray Junipero Serra Statue** (the Franciscan padre who founded the first nine of California's 21 missions).

The majority of the park is stroller-accessible. There are a number of bathrooms, most equipped with changing tables. Open in summer, daily from 10am to 10pm;

the rest of the year, on weekdays from 10am to 7pm and on weekends from 10am to 9pm. Monument buildings are open Tuesday through Friday from 10am to 3pm, on Saturday and Sunday till 4:30pm. Parking is available on Main Street between Hope and Arcadia Streets for $1.50 for each 20 minutes or about $7.50 for the full day. Or park at 615 N. Main St.

The Civic Center

With young kids in tow, these destinations are best reached by car. This is where Los Angeles city government is centered. The 28-story **City Hall,** 200 N. Spring St., the seat of city government, was for many years mandated by law to be the tallest building in the city, because of earthquake fears. However, that ended in 1957 when architectural techniques improved.

The **Music Center,** 135 N. Grand Ave. (☎ **213/972-7211**), is the modernistic $35-million complex of performing-arts theaters, consisting of the **Dorothy Chandler Pavilion,** the **Ahmanson Theater,** and the **Mark Taper Forum.** This is where you'll find the Los Angeles Philharmonic, Symphonies for Youth, the Master Chorale, and the Los Angeles Music Center Opera. There are daytime tours available year round (☎ **213/972-7483**), but it's probably best viewed at night when the lights of the complex accent the unusual architecture. At anytime, though, a walk through the plaza and some time spent around the fountains, is pleasant.

Museum of Contemporary Art (MOCA)

If you want to show arts-oriented kids what's really new, come to MOCA, at California Plaza, 250 S. Grand Ave. (☎ **213/626-6222**). This museum, which opened in 1983, is dedicated to exhibiting only contemporary art created from 1940 to the present. Today, MOCA's permanent collection numbers about 2,000 paintings, sculptures, prints, photographs, drawings, and mixed-media works. This is challenging artwork.

MOCA wants kids to see and experience the collection. To this end, they provide visitors with a booklet entitled "Together at MOCA: A Guide for Families," which offers excellent tips on how to enjoy the museum with children. It's published in English and Spanish.

Although it's a rather sophisticated adult environment, quiet and subdued, kids are encouraged to ask questions, even to sit on the floor and contemplate a sculpture. Tuesday through Sunday, "Gallery educators" are on hand at 1 and 2pm to answer questions and talk about what's on view.

The museum is fully accessible to strollers and wheelchairs, and the museum provides them at no charge. Regular admission is $6 for adults, $4 for students with ID or seniors over 65, free for children under 12.

The museum is open Tuesday through Sunday from 11am to 5pm, and also on Thursday from 11am to 8pm. From 5 to 8 pm on Thursday, admission is free for everyone. Closed Mondays, New Year's, Thanksgiving, and Christmas Days. Parking is available at the Music Center Garage for $6 per car for four hours (pay a $14 deposit and receive an $8 refund with a validation), and beneath the California Plaza at the California Plaza Garage for $24.75 maximum weekdays, or a $4.40 flat rate after 5pm and on weekends.

Los Angeles Children's Museum

Located at 310 N. Main St., in the Los Angeles Mall (☎ **213/687-8800** for 24-hour information), this museum is a place that kids always want to visit. The interactive exhibits are fun and educational at the same time. Children love the fact that parents don't have to say "no" to anything—they can participate in everything. The museum is geared to kids 2–10, but adults will thoroughly enjoy the experience. Our first-grade cousin enjoyed dressing up in a fireman's costume and playing with giant foam-filled and Velcro-edged blocks, acting as a television anchorwoman on a videotape of a nightly newscast, and making music on jug-band instruments such as lids, rubberbands, and jugs. His preschool sister got to apply face paints and drive the once-active city bus, and she was proud of her accomplishments at the drop-in arts and crafts sessions.

Especially educational is the ongoing Ethnic L.A. exhibit, which teaches kids, in an interactive way, about various Los Angeles ethnic cultures. On one visit, the Japanese-American culture was featured, and our first-grader was taught how to make elaborate Japanese paper dolls. Another permanent exhibit, the Louis B. Mayer Performance Space, provides a stage for mimes, actors, and storytellers. Theatrical games and music and dance workshops are also featured. There are 17 other permanent hands-on exhibits.

In summer the museum is open to the public Tuesday through Friday from 11:30am to 5pm and on Saturday and Sunday from 10am to 5pm. The rest of the year it's open to the public on weekends only from 10am to 5pm. Call about special holiday tours. Admission is $5; children under 2 are admitted free. Not stroller-accessible, but accessible to the disabled. Fast food available downstairs in the L.A. Mall, except Sunday.

Park in the L.A. Mall garage (the entrance is on Los Angeles Street), at Municipal Lot 7 (on the corner of Temple and San Pedro Streets), at Union Station on Alameda Street, or in the Olvera Street lots (two blocks north). Street parking is also available on weekends.

Little Tokyo

A walk through Little Tokyo is like stepping through a portal into the Far East. Los Angeles has traditionally had many Japanese residents. Little Tokyo, located between Alameda and Los Angeles Streets and 1st and 3rd Streets, is where Japanese traditions crystallize. The area is a collection of Japanese shops and restaurants.

A walk around **Japanese Village Plaza,** on 1st and 2nd Streets between San Pedro Street and Central Ave. (☎ **213/620-8861**), is a pleasant way to spend an hour. The plaza area features authentic Japanese shops (as well as American ones) in a distinctly Japanese setting. You might want to make a special stop at **Mikawaya Sweet Shop.**

The **New Otani Hotel & Garden,** 120 S. Los Angeles St., at 1st Street (☎ **213/629-1200,** or toll free **800/421-8795, 800/273-2294** in California), is the most dazzling building here. The garden walkways are especially beautiful. If you have a chance, go to the rooftop garden for a peaceful few moments.

Of special interest are Nisei Week and Children's Day in Little Tokyo, during which time there are crafts fairs, performances for children, and fun-runs for kids. For specific information about Children's Day, contact the **Japanese-American Cultural and Community Center** (☎ **213/628-2725**); for general information and Nisei Week information, call **213/687-7193.** For general questions about the area, contact the **Little Tokyo Business Association,** 244 S. San Pedro St., Room 501, Los Angeles, CA 90012 (☎ **213/620-0570**).

The **Japanese American National Museum,** 369 E. 1st St. (☎ **213/625-0414**), is the first museum in America to highlight the Japanese-American experience. The museum offers a variety of programs—exhibitions, educational programs, films, and publications—to detail the cultural heritage of these Americans. Open on Tuesday, Thursday, Saturday, and Sunday from 10am to 5pm and on Friday from 11am to

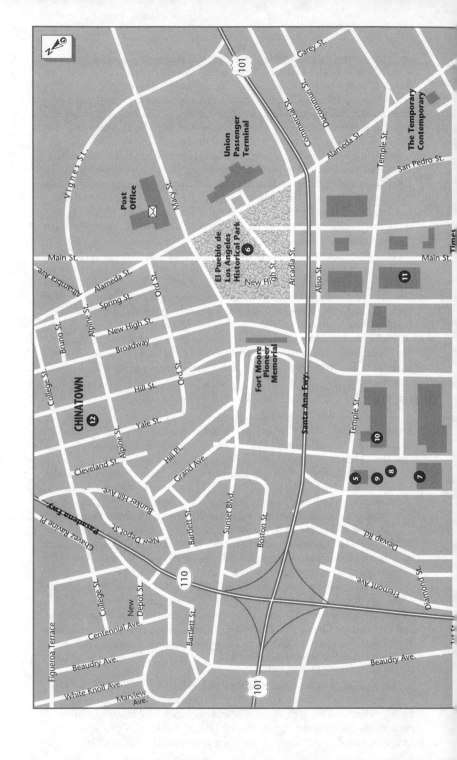

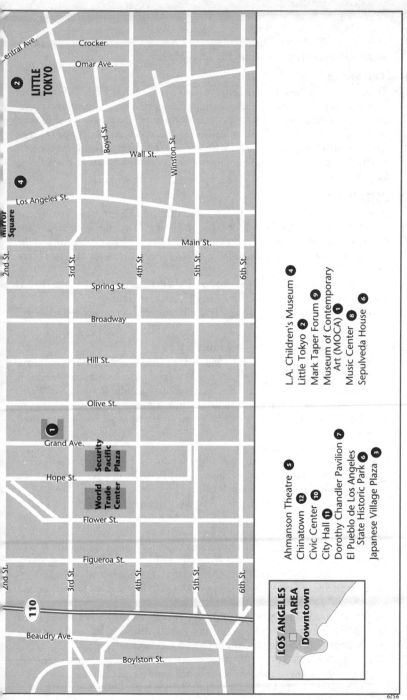

Downtown Los Angeles Attractions

Ahmanson Theatre ❺
Chinatown ⓬
Civic Center ❿
City Hall ⓫
Dorothy Chandler Pavilion ❼
El Pueblo de Los Angeles
  State Historic Park ❻
Japanese Village Plaza ❸

L.A. Children's Museum ❹
Little Tokyo ❷
Mark Taper Forum ❾
Museum of Contemporary
  Art (MOCA) ❶
Music Center ❽
Sepulveda House ❻

LOS ANGELES
AREA
☐ Downtown

Post Office ⊠

9529

8pm; closed New Year's, Thanksgiving, and Christmas Days. Admission is $4 for adults, $3 for seniors and students, free for children under 5.

New Chinatown

This Asian cultural center is neither as modern nor as clean as Little Tokyo, nor as impressive as its San Francisco counterpart. If things Chinese are important to you, however, just remember that it's a congested, small area. The section is bounded by North Broadway, North Hill Street, Bernard Street, and Sunset Boulevard. The centerpiece is **Mandarin Plaza,** 970 N. Broadway. For seasonal festivals and events, contact the **Chinese Chamber of Commerce,** 977 N. Broadway, Suite E, Los Angeles, CA 90012 (☎ **213/617-0396**).

EXPOSITION PARK

Exposition Park is a culturally and recreationally rich area. The site of the Los Angeles Memorial Coliseum, the Los Angeles Memorial Sports Arena, the Rose Garden, the California Museum of Science and Industry, the Natural History Museum, and the California African-American Museum, it's a place you'll want to spend quite a bit of time.

To get to Exposition Park, take the Santa Monica Freeway (I-10) to the Harbor Freeway (I-110) south and follow the exit signs to the museums.

Currently the museum is undergoing major reconstruction, which will result in a new complex by 1997.

California Museum of Science and Industry

Most people don't know that the California Museum of Science and Industry, 700 State Dr. (☎ **213/744-7400**), is the second-largest science/technology museum compound in the United States. The largest is the Smithsonian Institution in Washington, D.C. But you won't be surprised by that fact once you see the complex of buildings. This is a lively place where kids will want to spend time learning and experimenting.

The museum, with its many exhibit halls, gives new meaning to the word "interactive." Here kids and adults can "talk" with the exhibits, go inside them, move them around, even create with them. And there are so many different kinds of exhibits that each family member is sure to find something that strikes a responsive chord.

As you wander through Exposition Park, you'll see an F-104 Starfighter plane suspended on the outside of one structure. This is **Aerospace Hall.** School-age children just love this place because they can almost touch many of the aircraft and satellites suspended in the air. You can see the actual *Gemini 11* spacecraft and replicas of *Explorer 1, Sputnik 1, Pioneer 1,* and *Pioneer 5* satellites and the Mars lander–*Viking* spacecraft. In addition to satellites and spacecraft, it has many actual and model airplanes, including the 1911 Wright Brothers Model B aircraft, an air force T-38, and a Northrop F-20 Tiger Shark.

Watch the kids at the interactive exhibits. They love them. There's one in which the children maneuver a model rocket, and another where the kids pull levers and push buttons to experience concepts such as lift and thrust.

Aerospace Hall has a wonderful gift store that has many unique items for children and adults interested in astronomy, aircraft, and space paraphernalia.

Don't miss the nearby **Corwin D. Denney Air and Space Garden,** where a full-size DC-8 and a DC-3 are majestically placed for all to view.

Science South (a temporary structure) offers "Our Urban Environment: Eggciting Beginnings," with a chick hatchery and a new exhibit on chemistry called "Molecules in Motion."

Technology Hall houses the **Earthquake Exhibit,** where a realistic simulation of a large-magnitude earthquake gives you the feel of what a real temblor is like. There are actually three parts to the exhibit, but this one never fails to dramatize the point. You step up several stairs into a model living room complete with television set, bookcases, and the like. The television is tuned to a local broadcast where a popular weatherman is discussing the climate when he (and you) are interrupted by a large tremor. The platform on which you're standing rocks. Simulated newscasts of the destruction are interrupted by power failures and more small jolts. While the exhibit is realistic enough to bring home reality to the adults, children have a lot of fun but are startled when they feel the first shaking. It's best to warn your little children of what's to come.

The two other sections of the exhibit deal with earthquake preparedness and survival information, and geological information explaining earthquakes and how they happen.

Other delights are three popular, not-to-be-missed displays: **Mathematica,** the **Bicycle Company,** and **Invisible Forces/Electricity and Magnetism.**

Kinsey Hall of Health offers exhibits on "Lifestyle Choices" with information on drugs, "Health for Life" and "Your Insides Out" and live plays at the Bijou Theater.

Another important exhibit deals with AIDS, providing information in a clear and understandable way for all ages. The museum does a good job of presenting this difficult material.

Don't leave Exposition Park without seeing the **IMAX Theater.** The IMAX shows live-action movies on a huge screen, which are shot in such a way that you feel you're almost experiencing the real thing. The surround-sound system intensifies the experience. It's incredible, and the movies are usually educational to boot. Young children, although welcome, may not do well. The sound effects are quite loud and can be overwhelming to a 3-year-old. For theater information, call **213/744-2014.**

The California Museum of Science and Industry runs children's science workshops throughout the year (although the summer workshops are each a week long). Registration is by mail only, but you can get on the mailing list or find out about openings by calling **213/744-7440.** Open daily (except New Year's, Thanksgiving, and Christmas Days) from 10am to 5pm.

(If you don't want to pack a lunch, there is a McDonald's—with an exhibit—next to the main building.)

California African-American Museum

Once part of the Museum of Science and Industry, the CAAM is now located in its own modernistic building (with several exhibit halls and a gift store) at 600 State Dr. (☎ **213/744-7432**) in Exposition Park.

Although the museum is small, it's worth wandering through because it is one of the few museums that focuses on the talents and contributions of African-Americans in the fields of the arts, humanities, sciences, sports, and so forth. The atrium court sculpture garden is a place where children can feel comfortable speaking in normal tones and wandering through the sculptures by African American artists.

Special, hands-on, very involving workshops are available. Call for details. The museum is open Tuesday through Sunday from 10am to 5pm. Admission is free.

Natural History Museum of Los Angeles County

You'll find the Natural History Museum at 900 Exposition Blvd. (☎ 213/744-3466 or 213/744-3414). The museum's permanent collections include a megamouth shark, the only one on exhibit in the world and the second one ever found, and an exhibit entitled "Chaparral: A Story of Life from Fire." You are taught the importance of chaparral through a fascinating multimedia display. Dinosaurs, most every child's favorite thing "ever," are well represented here, as are "younger" North American and African mammals.

An American History gallery and Gem and Mineral Hall will appeal to youngsters above toddler age. But don't leave the little ones at home, because one of the best things about the museum is the **Ralph M. Parsons Discovery Center,** a multisensory space for children 2 years old and up.

Finally there is a place where children can touch, examine, smell, and manipulate the things that are so often behind glass in a museum. Once in the Discovery Center, our kids can't wait to check out a "discovery box." Different boxes offer different educational activities, such as challenging a child to identify sounds made with assorted objects with eyes closed, and allowing a youngster to create a turtle from skeletal bones. Our children also love to try on the costumes from around the world, then touch the taxidermic wild animals, which suddenly look so gentle. This is one of the few places that children can actually touch fossils or the teeth of a full-size polar bear. They get to listen to the ocean through sea shells, use a magnifying glass for a better look at butterflies, and make crayon rubbings of fossils which are embedded in a rocklike wall.

Dung scarabs, Malaysian dead leaf mantids, hairy scorpions, and Madagascan hissing cockroaches. Sound dreadful? Well, you won't necessarily get close up and personal with these new residents at the museum. The **Ralph M. Parsons Live Insect Zoo** is situated upstairs from the Discovery Center, and the displays are behind glass. Kids love to get good looks at these creepy crawlers, and the exhibit does make them interesting. A bioscanner, a viewer-operated video camera, allows you to really get a good look at an insect's home—without the insect residents getting mad at you.

The museum is open Tuesday through Sunday from 10am to 5pm. The Discovery Center is open to 3pm. Admission to the museum is $5 for adults, $3.50 for children 12–17 and seniors, $2 for children 5–12; under 5, free. The first Tuesday of every month admission is free. Admission to the Discovery Center is free with museum admission. Cafe B.C. is a well-priced cafeteria in the museum open during museum hours. Park on the street or in the lot off Menlo for $2 (quarters only). During Coliseum events, parking is $10. For parking information call **213/744-3414.**

GRIFFITH PARK

Griffith Park is 4,100 acres of wooded park area tucked into the Hollywood Hills. The largest park within the boundaries of any U.S. city, it is over three times as large as San Francisco's Golden Gate Park. The park was given to the city of Los Angeles in 1896 by Col. Griffith J. Griffith, and its natural state is largely preserved today. The terrain is diverse. Dry foothills, shady little valleys, and wooded areas cover the park that ranges in elevation from 384 feet to 1,600 feet above sea level. Like Los Angeles, Griffith Park is huge and sprawling.

Among its abundant recreational facilities it has something for everyone, including the Griffith Observatory, the Laserium, the Los Angeles Zoo, the Greek Theater, Travel Town, and myriad other delights. Don't even bother to try to see a lot of it in one day, because you can't make a dent in it. There are over 53 miles of hiking trails and bridle paths, four golf courses, and two overnight camps. In fact, the park is so large that many Los Angeles locals who visit the park regularly are surprised to learn that it has a municipal swimming pool.

Griffith Observatory and Planetarium

Located at 2800 E. Observatory Rd. (☎ **213/664-1191** for recorded information, or **213/664-1181** for further information), the observatory and planetarium are a highlight of any trip to Los Angeles. Fascinating and educational at the same time, the **planetarium theater** with its 75-foot domed ceiling re-creates the skies, taking kids and adults on journeys through space. Serious stargazers and awestruck children alike watch as the enormous domed ceiling is transformed from nothing to astral heavens with thousands of stars. Your narrator takes you on voyages through these stars to different planets and different eras.

This is best for children over 5. While children 5 and over delight as the room gets dark (complete with sunset over the mountains) and the "sky" gets jet-black, setting the stage for the evening stars and a lesson in astronomy, younger ones tend to get scared by the darkness.

When Elizabeth was 2, she couldn't quite decide whether or not she liked it. She would be content for a while, and then, when the music rose or the sky changed in a dramatic way, she'd start to cry and one of us would have to stand with her near the exit where there was more light. There is one performance each Saturday and Sunday at 1:30pm where children under 5 are admitted. These shows are a little shorter and a little more general. We found the major difference to be that young children are in abundance so we didn't have to worry so much about disturbing other people who may be serious about their astronomy education.

The shows last one hour, with several different presentations offered during the year.

Planetarium shows are given in summer Monday through Friday at 1:30, 3, and 7:30pm; and on Saturday and Sunday at 1:30, 3, 4:30, and 7:30pm. In winter shows are given Tuesday through Friday at 3 and 7:30pm; and on Saturday and Sunday at 1:30, 3, 4:30, and 7:30pm; closed Monday. Admission is $4 for adults, $3 for seniors, $2 for children 5–12, free for children under 5 (who are admitted only to the 1:30pm children's show or other special shows on Saturday and Sunday).

The **Hall of Science** has displays as well as interactive exhibits about physical science, astronomy, and geology. The Foucault Pendulum is one of the most fascinating exhibits you're likely to see. You watch as the earth's rotation allows the pendulum to knock down little pegs as it swings. There's also a solar telescope, six-foot globes of the earth and moon, and a working seismograph. (Watch the kids jump in an effort to get the needle to register.) There's also a large telescope you can use on clear evenings from sunset to 9:45pm when the hall is open.

The Hall of Science is open in summer every day from 12:30 to 10pm. In winter it's open Tuesday through Friday from 2 to 10pm, on Saturday and Sunday from 12:30pm; closed Monday. Admittance to the Hall of Science is free. Don't miss the bookstore, one of the best for astronomical slides, book starfinders, and souvenirs.

The **Laserium, The Laser Show** (☎ **818/997-3624**) is presented at the Observatory. This fantastic light-and-music extravaganza is a favorite of teens and adults who like bold, pulsating music. The performer projects laser imagery on the domed planetarium ceiling (five stories high at the top) to accompany and accentuate the

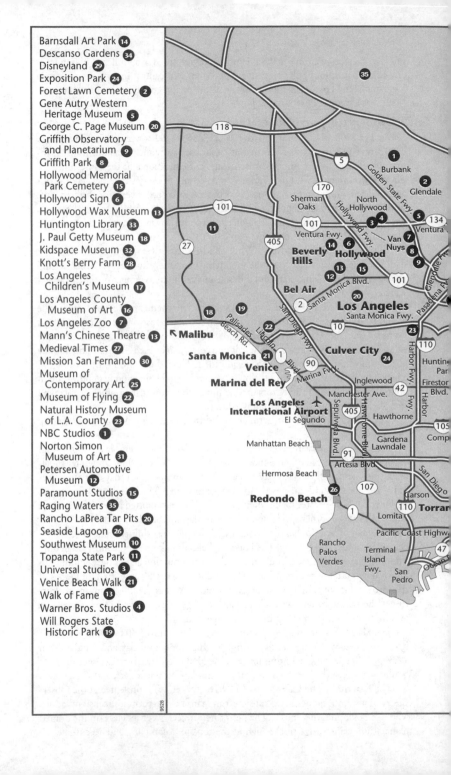

9528

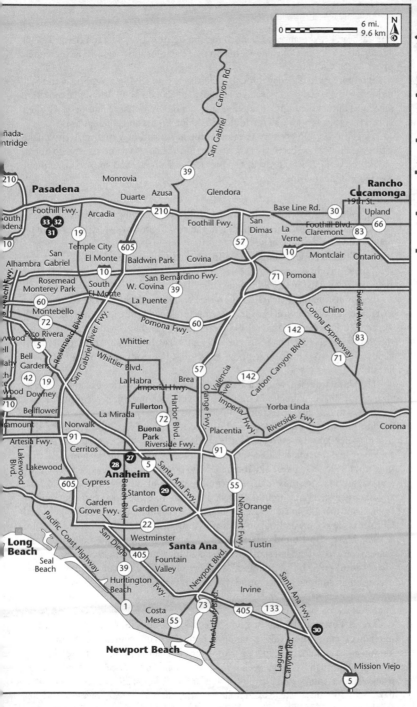

Los Angeles Area Attractions

musical beat. Performances are done to rock music, new age music, and classical. (Call ahead and ask for the schedule.) This isn't an event for little ones. In fact, children under 5 aren't admitted.

Shows are given Tuesday through Thursday at 6 and 8:45pm; on Friday and Saturday at 6, 8:45, and 9:45pm; and on Sunday at 6 and 8:45pm. Additional shows are scheduled during the summer and holidays. Get there well ahead of time as it's often crowded. Tickets cost $6.50 for adults, $5.50 for seniors and children 5–12.

To get to the Observatory, located at the north end of Vermont Avenue, take either the Hollywood Freeway (U.S. 101) to the Vermont Avenue exit and go north, or take the Golden State Freeway (I-5) to the Los Feliz exit and go west to Vermont Avenue and then north.

The Rides

Young children love spending the day in Griffith Park enjoying the ponies and riding on the miniature train, the carousel, and the new Simulator, which gives them an opportunity to show how brave they are.

The **Griffith Park & Southern Railroad,** the Simulator, and the pony and wagon rides are located in the park on the east side of Crystal Springs Drive, near Los Feliz Boulevard (☎ **213/664-6788** for the railroad and Simulator).

The miniature open-air train runs on a 1¹/₂-mile track through an environment that makes junior riders feel like they are actually taking a little trip. It runs year round, weekdays from 10am to 5pm (4:30pm on Monday) and weekends from 10am "till the crowds leave." In winter, rides close 45 minutes earlier. Adults are charged $1.75; children under 13, $1.25; those under 19 months, free. Kids under 5 must ride with an adult.

The **Simulator** takes you on a 5-minute ride that imitates a ride on a roller coaster, then an airplane. Children must be over 2 years old, and those under 5 must ride with an adult. Same hours as the train. All tickets cost $1.25.

The **pony rides** (☎ **213/664-3266**), located at Los Feliz and Riverside Drive, provide something for everyone. Little children ride in a circle on ponies tied to a stationary hookup. Older kids can ride around a separate track on their own. All children must be at least 1 year old and under 100 pounds to ride the ponies. There are also wagon rides, for those kids not yet too keen about riding horses, that take the children on a short ride around a track. The pony rides are open year round, daily from 10am to 4:30pm but closed Monday (except on Monday holidays). Closed Christmas Day. Pony and wagon rides are $1.50 per child.

The **Merry-Go-Round** is far enough away from the miniature train that you'll want to drive to it. Find it just off Griffith Park Drive, near the main concession stand (☎ **213/665-3051**). Our young children love to ride this antique carousel over and over again. In summer it runs weekdays from 11am to 5pm, till 6pm on weekends. In winter it's open weekends and all Los Angeles Public School holidays, from 11am to 5pm. Rides are 75¢ for everyone.

Travel Town, at the end of Zoo Drive (☎ **213/662-5874**), is a small outdoor museum of trains. There's also a stationary pony ride, a miniature train ride that takes kids on a five-minute ride, and a narrow-gauge model train exhibit. Travel Town is open April through October, weekdays 10am to 6pm, and on weekends and holidays from 10am to 5pm. From November to March, the hours are 10am to 4pm weekdays, until 5pm on weekends and holidays. Admission to Travel Town is free. Fares for the miniature train ride are $1.75 for adults, $1 for seniors, $1.25 for children 2–13; under 19 months, free.

Other Activities

The **Griffith Park Recreation Center** has a **swimming pool** that's open from mid-June through mid-September. Call for hours and fees (☎ **213/665-4372** for pool information, **213/666-2703** for the Recreation Center).

For information about the **tennis courts,** call **213/661-5318** for the Riverside Drive courts, and **213/664-3521** for the Vermont Avenue courts. For reservations, call **213/520-1010.**

For information about **golf courses,** call **213/663-2555** for the Wilson/Harding Starters office, **213/665-2011** for the Roosevelt course, and **213/663-7758** for the Los Feliz course.

Los Angeles Zoo

Actually located within Griffith Park, the Los Angeles Zoo, 5333 Zoo Dr., at the junction of the Ventura and Golden State Freeways (☎ **213/666-4090**), has over 1,500 different mammals, birds, and reptiles of about 500 different species. Sitting on 113 acres, the zoo is divided "zoogeographically." This means that the animals are divided into the five continents on which they live. With a zoo this large and hilly, it's a good idea first to sit down with the zoo map and chart out what you want to see. During the summer, get an early start because the zoo tends to get hot and smoggy. Plan to spend at least half a day here, probably more with older children.

This is Southern California, remember, and the zoo is not to be outdone by all the theme parks and attractions surrounding it. It, too, has special shows: "Animals and You," and "Wild in the City." It's a good idea to plan around those events when mapping out your day. During the weekends and daily during the summer, you can hear the keepers talk about their orangutans, gorillas, rhinoceros, chimpanzees, bears, kangaroos, and tigers. It's a treat!

If your time is limited, you might want to hop on the Safari Shuttle, which will transport you around the perimeter of the zoo. There are six well-marked stops along the way, and you can get on and off at any of them. This is not a guided tour, but the driver gives general information about the zoo. Tickets cost $3 for adults, $1 for children 2–12 and seniors; under 2, free. The shuttle runs the same hours as the zoo and is stroller- and wheelchair-accessible.

Adventure Island is the children's zoo. The focus is on the wildlife of the southwestern U.S.: the shoreline, the cave, the desert, the meadow, the mountain, the hacienda barnyard, and the nursery. Throughout Adventure Island, interactive devices allow curious visitors to see through the eyes of a prairie dog, compare their sense of smell to a bear's, hatch a variety of eggs, and much more. If you're around in summer, ask about the "Music at the Zoo" evenings.

Open daily (except Christmas Day) from 10am to 5pm. Admission is $8.25 for adults (13 and over), $5.25 for seniors, $3.25 for children 2–12, and free for children under 2. Stroller rentals are $2.

Gene Autry Museum

Want some real ole' Western fun? The **Gene Autry Western Heritage Museum,** 4700 Zoo Dr., Griffith Park (☎ **213/667-2000**), is one place you're sure to find it, pardner! This museum captures the spirit of the West and communicates it to children, instantly. This place is fun!

Murals, movies, and interactive exhibits tell the story of the West in a way that few other museums have been able to do so far. One of the world's most comprehensive repositories of American West history, its collections include firearms, common tools, clothing, toys, games, and furnishings of many of the famous and not-so-famous people of that era. Allow enough time to meander through the entire space with time to wander outside and also spend some time in the museum store. Both grownups who loved western movies growing up, those who want to learn more about the Old West, and children who simply delight in this period of our country's history will love this place.

Be sure to make a stop at the *Los Angeles Times* Children's Discovery Gallery, which replicates the home of an American Southwest family. Visitors can touch the items, try on the period clothing, and read the diaries and journals. It's a particularly personal perspective on a real western family. Ask about special movie presentations and activities which are offered with some regularity. The Golden Spur Café is a self-service restaurant on the premises.

Open Tuesday through Sunday from 10am to 5pm. Admission for adults is $7; for seniors and students, $5; for children 2–12, $3. Parking is free. The museum is stroller-accessible.

HOLLYWOOD

Entertainment capital of the world! Glitter capital of the world! Hollywood is a state of mind, where dreams come true. You've probably heard all the clichés, and now you want to see the real thing. Well, the Hollywood of your dreams is no more. It is slowly getting cleaned up, but it's still not the place for a late-evening stroll with the family. Everyone who comes to Los Angeles must see Hollywood, however, so put on your blinders, ignore the shabby parts, and take a daytime stroll down Hollywood Boulevard.

Beginning at Hollywood Boulevard and La Brea Avenue and walking east, you'll come to **Mann's Chinese Theatre,** 6925 Hollywood Blvd. (☎ 213/464-8111 for movie information), where Mary Pickford and Douglas Fairbanks initiated the footprint ceremony in 1927, the year the theater was built by Sid Grauman. From then on, whenever a movie premiered there, the stars embedded their foot and handprints in the concrete. One of the most ornate movie palaces of the time, the building was decorated with rare Chinese artifacts, authentic temple bells, and pagodas. Kids love to try to match their footprints with those of the stars.

On the other side of the street is the **Radisson Hollywood Roosevelt Hotel,** at 7000 Hollywood Blvd. (☎ 213/466-7000), a museum in itself, from the bronze statue of Charlie Chaplin sitting on a lobby bench to the Gable/Lombard Suite that was regularly visited by those two superstars. The hotel's ballroom was the site of the first Academy Awards presentation. On the mezzanine level is a mini-museum chronicling Hollywood's history in pictures. It's open to the public, and worth a visit.

Next, you can't miss the **El Capitan Theatre,** at 6838 Hollywood Blvd. (☎ 213/467-7674), which in 1926 opened as a house for song-and-dance revues. In 1942 the ornate interior was covered over when it was turned into a movie house. Luckily it was salvaged, and in 1989 turned back to a "prince" by Disney and Pacific Theatres. Even in this incarnation it serves as a first-run movie house.

Continue east to the **Hollywood Wax Museum,** at 6767 Hollywood Blvd. (☎ 213/462-8860). If you don't see a live celebrity on your trip, at least you can see your favorites duplicated in wax. The museum is open on Friday and Saturday from 10am to 2am, and Sunday through Thursday till midnight. Admission is $8.95 for adults, $7.50 for seniors, $6.95 for children 6–12; under 6, free.

The Max Factor Building, 1666 N. Highland Ave. (☎ 213/463-6668), houses the **Max Factor Museum,** which opened in 1935. What more perfect place for a beauty museum than Hollywood? Stars such as Judy Garland, Claudette Colbert, Rita Hayworth, and Marlene Dietrich attended the museum's opening. If your girls have just discovered makeup they'll enjoy seeing how it was used on the stars of the '20s and '30s. The museum is open Monday through Saturday from 10am to 4pm; admission is free.

Walk across the street about a half a block and you'll see the arch identifying the **Janes House,** where you'll find an office of the **Los Angeles Convention and Visitors Bureau** in the Queen Anne Victorian home in the rear, at 6541 Hollywood Blvd., Los Angeles, CA 90028 (☎ **213/689-8822**). The Janes House was a one-owner private residence from 1903 until its restoration in 1985. The Janeses made it into a schoolhouse for a time, and educated the children of such motion-picture pioneers as Douglas Fairbanks, Jesse Lasky, and Noah Berry. Now you'll find helpful brochures, maps, and even complimentary tickets to various TV shows. Open Monday through Saturday from 9am to 5pm.

Across the street is **Hollywood Toys & Costumes, Inc.,** 6562 Hollywood Blvd. (☎ **213/465-3119**), a treasure trove of children's costumes, wigs, masks, and toys. Backtrack one block west to **Larry Edmunds Bookshop,** 6644 Hollywood Blvd. (☎ **213/463-3273**), where you'll discover one of the most comprehensive collections of movie- and theater-related books and posters.

If you stand at the corner of Hollywood and Vine, just a few blocks east, and look north, you'll spot the **Capitol Records Building,** at 1750 N. Vine St. (☎ **213/462-6252**), completed in 1956 in the shape of a stack of 45-rpm records—remember those? In the lobby (open weekdays from 9am to 6pm) you'll see displays of gold records. As you're looking up this way, you can't help but see the famous **Hollywood sign,** which has gone through so many transformations since it was put up in 1923 to advertise Hollywoodland, a real estate development.

Back on Hollywood Boulevard, a little east of Vine Street, is the **Pantages Theater.** Pop your head in, if you can, to see the magnificent art deco interior. Currently a legitimate theater, the Pantages was originally built as a movie theater and was host to the Academy Awards from 1949 to 1959.

Hollywood has also given us **Roscoe's House of Chicken and Waffles,** 1514 N. Gower St. (☎ **213/466-7453**), a Hollywood institution serving nothing but those two dishes; **C. C. Brown's,** 7007 Hollywood Blvd. (☎ **213/464-7062**), which, although more than 75 years old, still serves the hot-fudge sundae it first created; and **Musso and Frank's,** Hollywood's oldest restaurant, at 6667 Hollywood Blvd. (☎ **213/467-7788**), where Hollywood's famous writers used to gather, and where important people still stop for a bite to eat.

If you're going to be in town during the winter season, watch for the **Hollywood Christmas Parade,** originally called the Santa Claus Lane Parade in the early 1920s. Held the Sunday after Thanksgiving, it has evolved into one of the grandest city parades and is seen on TV all over the world.

As you've been walking down the boulevard, you couldn't help but notice the pink and charcoal terrazzo stars imbedded in the sidewalk on both sides of Hollywood Boulevard between Sycamore and Gower Streets, and on Vine Street between Sunset Boulevard and Yucca Street. Nearly every month since 1961 the Hollywood Chamber of Commerce has honored a movie star on the **Walk of Fame** with a ceremony dedicating his or her star. Call **213/469-8311** for information on the next ceremony.

A short ride in the car will take you to the other sights Hollywood claims as its own. **Paramount Studios,** for instance, is located at 5555 Melrose Ave. at Gower. This famous studio, in business as Paramount since the 1920s, is still producing movies, making it the longest continuously operating film studio in Los Angeles. (See "Studio Tours/TV Tickets" below for tour information.)

Hollywood also claims the **Barnsdall Art Park,** 4800 Hollywood Blvd. (☎ 213/485-4581), which houses the **Los Angeles Municipal Art Gallery.** If the kids aren't satisfied with those exhibits, walk a few yards away to the **Junior Art Gallery,** where there's always something of interest on display. Both galleries are open Tuesday through Sunday from 12:30 to 5pm. Entrance to the Municipal Gallery is $1 for adults, free for children under 13. Admission to the Junior Arts Gallery is free. If you're around on a Sunday, you're invited to Sunday Open Sunday (☎ 213/485-4474), Barnsdall's Junior Arts Center free family art workshops, where the sessions (most Sundays from 2 to 4pm) are open to all age groups.

STUDIO TOURS/TV TICKETS

One of the reasons people come to Southern California is to see the stars. And one way to do it is by attending an audience-participation TV show. Some shows allow children; some do not. Another way is by taking a studio tour, all of which allow children, but there are age restrictions for some. Tickets to TV tapings are free.

In addition to the ticket information to follow, the Los Angeles Convention and Visitors Bureau prepares a free listing of TV tapings with show names, taping dates, locations, and phone numbers. The list is updated monthly. Send a self-addressed, stamped business-size envelope to **Los Angeles Convention and Visitors Bureau,** c/o TV Tapings, 633 W. 5th St., Suite 6000, Los Angeles, CA 90071.

Tickets for more than 30 network shows and specials are available through **Audiences Unlimited** (☎ 818/506-0067 for recorded information). You can pick up tickets at the Fox Television Center, 5746 Sunset Blvd., Hollywood, on the Van Ness side of the street, off the Hollywood Freeway (U.S. 101) at the Sunset Boulevard exit. Tickets are on a first-come, first-served basis, and are available on Wednesday for the following week. The box office is open weekdays from 8:30am to 6pm and on Saturday and Sunday from noon to 5pm.

To order tickets by mail for future shows, or to receive a monthly schedule send a self-addressed, stamped envelope to Audiences Unlimited, 100 Universal City Plaza, Bldg. 153, Universal City, CA 91608. Expect a two- to three-week response. All tickets are complimentary.

The **Warner Bros. VIP Tour** is a technical/educational behind-the-scenes look at how a studio operates. It's located at 4000 Warner Blvd., Burbank, CA 91522 (☎ 818/954-1744). The tour office is found at Hollywood Way and Olive Ave., Gate 4. Tours are limited to 14 people, and children under 10 are not permitted. This tour is more suited to serious production buffs. You never know what you're going to see when you sign up, as guides depend on daily production schedules and the whims of various directors. You might see backlot sets, art and prop areas, set construction, post-production or sound stages.

Two-hour tours are offered daily, Monday through Friday. Tickets are by reservation only. It's best to call one week in advance, but reservations can be arranged up to 60 days ahead. (Don't hesitate to try for last-minute reservations.) Tickets are $27 per person, adult or child.

CBS-TV tickets are available at 7800 Beverly Blvd., Los Angeles, CA 90036 (☎ 213/852-2624). Mail your request with the name of the show, the number of tickets, and the date(s) you prefer. Enclose a stamped, self-addressed envelope. Tickets are sent within a 125-mile radius of CBS. Others receive a Guest Card, which

N

Western
Garfield
Gramercy Pl.
Wilton Pl.
Taft Ave.
Van Ness Ave.
Canyon
Carlton Way
Harold Way
Delongpre Ave.
St. Andrews Pl.
La Mirada
Lexington Ave.
Virginia
Sierra Vista
Wilton Pl.
Ridgewood
Maplewood
Elmwood Ave.

Capitol Records Building
Hollywood Blvd.
Sunset Blvd.
Fernwood Ave.
Bronson Ave.
Tamarind Ave.
Gordon St.
Beachwood Dr.
Gower St.
Lod Pl.
El Centro Ave.
Santa Monica Blvd.
Hollywood Memorial Park Cemetery
Paramount Studios ❾
Barton Ave.
Eleanor Ave.
Gregory Ave.
Camerford Ave.
Melrose Ave.
Clinton St.
Rosewood Ave.
Desilu Studios

Argyle Ave. ❻
Ivar ❼
Cosmo
Cahuenga Blvd.
Morningside
Leland Way
Delongpre Ave.
Afton Pl.
Homewood Ave.
Delongpre Park
Vine St.
Lillian Way
Cahuenga Blvd.
Cole Ave.
Wilcox Ave.
Hudson Ave.
Seward St.

Grace Ave.
Whitley Ave.
Yucca St.
Hudson Ave. ❺
Cassil Ave.
Selma Ave.
June St.
Cherokee Ave.
Cherokee Ave.
Las Palmas Ave.

Emmet Tr.
❽
❶ ❷ ❸ ❹
Chinese Theatre
McCadden Pl.
Highland Ave.
Citrus Ave.
Mansfield Ave.
Orange Dr.
Sycamore Ave.
La Brea Ave.

Sycamore Ave.
La Brea Ave.
Yucca St.
Leland Way
Delongpre Ave.
Lexington Ave.
Santa Monica Blvd.
Samuel Goldwyn Studios
Detroit St.
Formosa Ave.
Poinsettia Rec. Center

Alta Vista
Poinsettia Pl.
Palmero Camino
Franklin
Hollywood Blvd.
Hawthorn Ave.
Martel Ave.
Vista St.
Gardner St.
Sierra Bonita Ave.
Curson Ave.
Stanley Ave.
Courtney Ave.
Genesee Ave.
Poinsettia Dr.
Greenacre
Fuller
Plummer Park
Romaine St.
Fountain Ave.
Spalding Ave.
Gardner St.
Poinsettia Dr.
Willoughby Ave.
Waring Ave.
Melrose Ave.
Clinton St.
Rosewood Ave.
Oakwood Ave.

9531

is redeemable for tickets, if available, when you turn it in at the Television City Information Window. Age minimums are printed on the face of each ticket. You can also pick up tickets in person from 9am to 5pm Monday through Friday (on weekends if shows are taping). Your ticket does not guarantee admission to the show.

Fox TV tickets can be ordered through Audiences Unlimited, 100 Universal City Plaza, Building 153, Universal City, CA 91608 (☎ **818/506-0067**). Enclose a self-addressed stamped envelope for tickets, and expect a two- to three-week response. Tickets are free.

KCET-TV, at 4401 Sunset Blvd., Hollywood, CA 90027 (☎ **213/953-5242**), is Los Angeles's public television station. This technical tour lasts 1 1/2 hours, and includes a visit to production areas and a look at lighting, cameras, stages, technical operations, and the master control room. Guides tell you about the history of the lot, which is the old Allied Artists studio, but you won't see shows being filmed. This tour requires children to be a minimum of 11 years old. Call for your reservations one week in advance. There is no charge for the tour, which is offered on selected Tuesdays and Thursdays, usually at 10am.

The **NBC Studio Tour** is located at 3000 W. Alameda Ave., Burbank, CA 91523 (☎ **818/840-3537**). The 1 1/2-hour tour takes you to sound-effects studios, makeup, wardrobe, and set construction. Visitors may also see the satellite-transmission equipment. What some folks like the best is the stop at "The Tonight Show," where they might get a peek at a rehearsal and see the famous stage.

There are only 15 people on each tour, there are no age restrictions, and the tour is stroller-accessible. No reservations are necessary. Tours leave weekdays, on the hour, from 9am to 3pm. The charge is $6 for adults, $3.75 for kids under 12; under 5, free.

To obtain tickets to NBC television shows, you can write two to three weeks in advance to the address above. Be sure to include a stamped, self addressed envelope. Tickets for "The Tonight Show" are available in person only on the day of the show. Holding a ticket guarantees a place in line; it does not guarantee admission to a show. Be sure to arrive early for seating. The ticket office is open weekdays from 8am to 5pm.

Paramount Studios, 860 N. Gower St., Hollywood (☎ **213/956-5575**), has TV tickets as well as a studio tour. Tickets are available here not only for Paramount Studios' shows, but for other programs as well. Call for recorded information. Tickets can be picked up five days in advance of the show you are interested in. The office is open weekdays 8am to 4pm. A ticket to any of the shows does not guarantee entrance to the show. Be at the ticket office by 8am.

Paramount's walking tour takes you on a two-hour visit to the working studio. There are no guarantees that you will see any production activity; the tour is subject to the daily production schedules. The guide gives out lots of history and information. Children under 10 are not allowed. The charge is $15 for adults or children, and credit cards and checks are *not* accepted. Tours are available on a first-come, first-served basis only, and depart on the hour from 9am to 2pm Monday through Friday.

UNIVERSAL STUDIOS

The world's largest and busiest motion-picture and television studio is Universal Studios Hollywood, at 100 Universal City Plaza, located off the Hollywood Freeway (U.S. 101) at either the Universal Center or Lankershim Boulevard exit (☎ **818/508-9600**). Quintessential Hollywood, and now bigger and better after a multi-million-dollar expansion, Universal Studios Hollywood thrills nearly everyone over the age of 4. Step onto this studio lot and you're stepping into Hollywood behind-the-scenes.

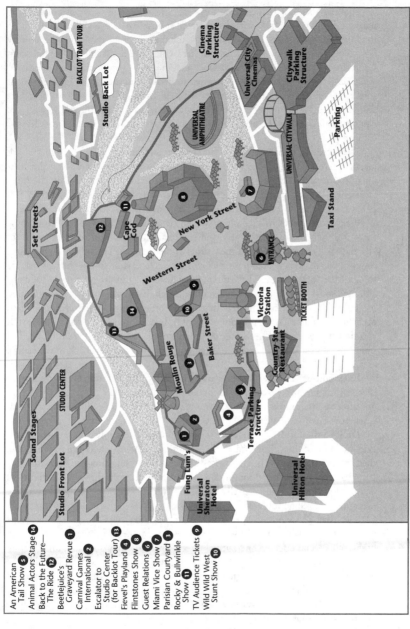

Universal Studios Hollywood

9536

An American
Tail Show **5**

Animal Actors Stage **14**

Back to the Future—
The Ride **12**

Beetlejuice's
Graveyard Revue **1**

Carnival Games
International **2**

Escalator to
Studio Center
(for Backlot Tour) **13**

Fievel's Playland **4**

Flintstones Show **8**

Guest Relations **6**

Miami Vice Show **7**

Parisian Courtyard **3**

Rocky & Bullwinkle
Show **11**

TV Audience Tickets **9**

Wild Wild West
Stunt Show **10**

Like all sightseeing venues, there are certain tricks that make your visit much more pleasant. If this is your first visit, plan to spend at least five to seven hours. We've been to Universal many times, and several of them have been in extremes of weather: very hot, smoggy summer days, and days that were windy and bone-chilling (for Southern California). At night, even in the summer, expect it to be very cool. So consider what you'll need to make yourself comfortable. In the summer, be sure to bring plenty of sunscreen, sun visors, and little hats for the kids. In the winter, bring warm jackets and layer clothes. It may only be 60º, but the wind on the hill really picks up. Approximately 70 of the attractions are outdoors, so you'll want to be dressed comfortably.

The **Guided Tram Tour** is a 45-minute open-air tram excursion through the back lots of Universal Studios. Not only do you get backstage knowledge about the making of movies and television, but visitors are also treated to an array of special-effects creations. The tram travels through the 420-acre back lot that has more than 500 outdoor sets. You'll see facades from *The Sting, Psycho,* and "Murder, She Wrote."

Visitors are treated to encounters with the enormous 30,000-pound King Kong, the world's largest animated figure, and Jaws; and they also experience the terror of "Earthquake, the Big One" and the parting of the Red Sea. This adventurous tour is certainly worth the time, but it's difficult to predict how your youngsters may react to some of the special effects. Enormous King Kong may be frightening to toddlers, although some very young kids love it; others might get scared by Jaws. The spinning Ice Tunnel is another special effect that alarms some young children. Most children over the age of 5 or 6 delight in almost all of it. In addition, if part way into the tour you find that your child is having too much trouble, talk with the tour guide. The tram can be stopped at any time and standby vans will take you back to the central area.

Entertainment Center is the unguided portion of the tour that offers live amphitheater shows. All shows are 15–20 minutes in length and are timed so you can see one after another. On crowded days you may have to line up early, so consider when you try to schedule viewing the shows.

Back to the Future—The Ride is something you certainly don't want to miss. Engulfed in a cool fog, you and the kids board an eight-passenger time vehicle, and then careen through time in a whirlwind of three-dimensional images. After colliding with glaciers, thundering through exploding volcanoes, even through the mouth of *Tyrannosaurus rex*, you'll finally enter the future—circa 2015. This is a ride extraordinaire. Good for kids 6 and older.

The **Miami Vice Action Spectacular** is a live-action show set in an elaborate scene in the Caribbean where doubles for Crockett and Tubbs perform amazing stunts amid high-tech special effects. The special effects are truly amazing, including aerial, underwater, and pyrotechnic tricks. While Elizabeth (when she was 2) didn't like the noise, the fact that the show is in a large open-air theater diminishes the intensity of the stunts and allows parents with fearful tots to get up and stand on the side so as not to disturb other spectators. We always try to take seats on the aisle, just in case a little one needs to be taken out or comforted.

The Flintstones Show is a 30-minute live musical attraction.

Young kids love the **Animal Actors Stage,** where trainers show how they get animals to perform. **The Wild, Wild West Stunt Act** is the new stunt show that's fun and good for the whole family.

There are several other new attractions at Universal. To begin with, don't miss the extraordinary special effects you'll see at **Backdraft,** a re-creation of the motion picture. The sound stage becomes "engulfed" in flames, and spectators can watch fuel lines rupture and metal melting. Of course, this is all controlled and, we're assured, quite safe. **The E.T. Adventure** is another one that children love. Studio guests climb aboard skyward-bound bicycles and feel what E.T. and his little human friend must have "felt" in the movie. And there's the **Rocky & Bullwinkle Show,** a fun extravaganza which will delight children and adult Rocky and Bullwinkle lovers. And for the little ones, there's **An American Tail: Fievel Goes West.** Based on the sequel to *An American Tail,* this attraction takes kids on a rousing journey to visit with Fievel in the Wild West. This is an interactive attraction, with a 15-foot-high banana peel (really a giant slide), a 12-foot brown boot (a massive playhouse), and an 11-foot slice of Swiss cheese (a maze of tunnels).

Don't miss **Streets of the World,** actual shooting sets used in some of the all-time great movies. See Baker Street (from Sherlock Holmes), the Moulin Rouge, Mel's Diner (from *American Graffiti*) and Faber College (from *Animal House*).

Don't be surprised to see cartoon and famous Hollywood personalities strolling around the park. They'll gladly sign autographs.

Outdoor eating areas abound and offer a choice of Italian, Mexican, and American goodies. If you want regular restaurant fare and would prefer to eat indoors, you can choose from **Tony Roma's** (barbecued ribs, chicken, and sandwiches), **Victoria Station** (prime rib, fish, sandwiches, and salad bar), and **Fung Lum** (Chinese cuisine) (see the "Where to Eat" section, above, for details).

Universal Studios Hollywood operates daily except Thanksgiving and Christmas Days. Summer and holiday hours are 8am to 5pm; the rest of the year, 9:30am to 3:30pm on weekdays and 9:30am to 3:30pm on weekends. Admission is $31 for adults (including children over 11), $24.95 for children 3–11 and seniors; children under 3 are free. A celebrity season pass (unlimited visits for one year) costs $15 over the one-time admission fee. Parking is $6. Your admission price entitles you to see all the shows in the Entertainment Center and to the 45-minute Tram Tour.

MID-WILSHIRE/FAIRFAX/MELROSE AVENUE

These areas, roughly bordered by Wilshire Boulevard to the south, Melrose Avenue to the north, La Cienega Boulevard to the west, and La Brea Avenue to the east, are seeing many of the new boutiques, restaurants, and hotels which have been going up at breakneck speed. **Mid-Wilshire,** home to the County Museum of Art, the Craft and Folk Art Museum, and the La Brea Tar Pits, was once a very important retail center of town. It is beginning its renaissance. The **Fairfax** area, where you'll find the CBS Studios and the Farmers Market, is also home to much of L.A.'s older Eastern European population. While Fairfax Avenue between Beverly Boulevard and Melrose Avenue has been spruced up with new storefronts and a giant mural, it still retains its open-air fish and fruit stands, Hungarian and Israeli restaurants, kosher meat markets, and numerous bakeries. **Melrose Avenue,** an exciting place for a walk with the kids, has been written up in newspapers all over the country as Los Angeles's trendiest section of town. Preteens and teenagers will love this street. Small live-performance theaters, clothing boutiques, casual and chic restaurants, funky stores, and antique shops line the avenue from just east of La Brea, west to La Cienega.

Los Angeles County Museum of Art

Located at 5905 Wilshire Blvd. in the Mid-Wilshire District (☎ 213/857-6000), the Los Angeles County Museum complex, adjacent Hancock Park, and the La Brea Tar Pits/George C. Page Museum make for a day of excitement and culture.

We usually go to a museum gallery, have a snack, let the kids romp in the park, or watch the mimes and musicians, and then spend another hour at the Page.

Let's back up a bit. Opened in 1965 with three buildings, the Los Angeles County Museum of Art has almost doubled in size. Today it is the largest art museum in the west. The original structure is the **Ahmanson Building,** which houses the permanent art collection that includes American and European paintings and sculpture, decorative arts, costumes and textiles, and Far Eastern, Indian, and Southeast Asian art. The new **Robert O. Anderson Building** is the place for modern and contemporary art. The **Pavilion for Japanese Art** has screens and scrolls and paintings. The **Frances and Armand Hammer Building** has special exhibitions. And the **Times-Mirror Central Court** is a cool, partially covered plaza with a most unusual fountain that the children adore. The new outdoor sculpture garden is a lovely place to stroll. There are two cafés where you can lunch or snack.

Family programs are offered the last Sunday of each summer month for children 5–12 and their parents. There are programs for younger children as well. Call **213/857-6108** for details.

Open Wednesday through Friday from 10am to 5pm, on Saturday and Sunday, 11am to 6pm; closed Monday, Tuesday and New Year's, Thanksgiving, and Christmas Days. Admission is $6 for adults, $4 for students with ID and senior citizens over 62, and $1 for children ages 6–17; museum members and children under 6 admitted free. The second Wednesday of each month is free for everyone.

To get to the museum, take the Santa Monica Freeway (I-10) to Fairfax Avenue. Go north to Wilshire Boulevard and then go right. Or take the Hollywood Freeway (U.S. 101) to the Santa Monica Boulevard exit and go west to Fairfax Avenue. Take a left on Wilshire Boulevard. From Beverly Hills and West L.A., go east on Wilshire. It's just east of Fairfax Avenue. Parking is at meters on the street or in nearby lots.

George C. Page Museum of La Brea Discoveries

One of our favorite attractions, the **George C. Page Museum,** 5801 Wilshire Blvd. (☎ **213/857-6311,** or **213/936-2230** for a recording), and the **La Brea Tar Pits** has one of the largest deposits of Ice Age mammals and birds in the world. Kids can see displays where optical illusions "change" the skeleton of a mammal into a huge ferocious saber-tooth cat, and another skeleton, the "La Brea Woman," seems to come to life before their eyes. They experience the sticky substance the mammals were trapped in by trying to pull large poles out of the asphalt and they see close up just how large a Columbian Mammoth was.

Over the last 40,000 years, animals became trapped in what is now called the La Brea Tar Pits. These pits were found by the first people who wandered this part of the world, and again by the first overland explorers in 1769, who saw bubbling pools of asphalt. Two movies explain various aspects of the museum and paleontology.

But the first American who owned the land, Henry Hancock, didn't think too much about the bones he found when he was quarrying the area. He thought they were just cows and local animals. Later, paleontologists realized these were Ice Age animals. In 1912 George Allen Hancock, Henry's son, gave the Museum of Natural History the rights and jurisdiction over the digging and excavation of the bones. In 1918 he deeded the 23-acre park to the county of Los Angeles. Some 60 years later George C. Page built the museum so the animals "could have a home," and gave the museum to the county. The Page is still a working museum.

Even today you'll see ponds of the bubbling material. There is a major dig in the middle of the park called Pit 91, where paleontologists have recovered thousands of specimens over the years. Watch them work from a viewing station (hours vary).

Free one-hour park tours for the general public are given Wednesday through Sunday at 1pm, weather permitting. Call for times and meeting place. There is also a general museum tour Tuesday through Sunday at 2pm. Call for special tours (☎ 213/857-6306 after 1pm).

The museum is open Tuesday through Sunday from 10am to 5pm. Admission is $5 for adults, $3.50 for students and seniors over 62, $2 for children 5–10; those 4 and under get in free with their parents. Tours and museum are fine for strollers. Wheelchairs are available at no charge.

Petersen Automotive Museum

What would the land of the automobile be without an automobile museum? The creators of this museum at 6060 Wilshire Blvd. (corner of Wilshire and Fairfax), L.A. (☎ 213/930-2277) have created a four-story, 300,000-square-foot space to educate visitors on the role the automobile has had in our culture. Where else to put a museum of this nature than in the car capital of the world?

Visitors can walk through historical dioramas with the first stop at Carl Breer's 1902 steam-driven car. They can see autos used in movies, cars from France, coffin cars, and future cars; they can watch car movies, sit in a NB5000, and even take classes. The beautiful museum also houses a huge retail store. The museum is open Saturday through Thursday, 10am to 6pm; Friday to 9pm. Admission is $7 adults, $5 seniors over 62, $3 for children ages 5–12; under 5 free. Park in the museum's garage for $4 all day; enter on Fairfax.

The Craft and Folk Art Museum

The Craft and Folk Art Museum (☎ 213/937-5544) is due to reopen in its original building at 5800 Wilshire Blvd., in the Miracle Mile area, in March 1995. The museum pays tribute to the rich ethnic diversity of Los Angeles and Southern California with rotating exhibits of international folk art and contemporary crafts. When it does reopen (be sure to call first), hours will be Tuesday through Saturday from 10am to 5pm, Sunday from 11am to 5pm.

If you're in town around mid-October, the amazing Festival of Masks, sponsored by the museum, will be in full swing at Hancock Park. Held at the corner of Curson Avenue and Wilshire Boulevard, the free family event celebrates Los Angeles' ethnic diversity. The weekend event spotlights performances of mask dance and theater, mask-making workshops, mask vendors, and international music and cuisine. The spectacular Parade of Masks travels down Miracle Mile, beginning at Cochran Avenue and winding down at Hancock Park.

Farmers Market

It's hard to believe that 3rd Street and Fairfax Avenue, home to the Los Angeles Farmers Market (☎ 213/933-9211), was once a vacant field on the *edge* of Los Angeles. But that was the case in 1934 when 18 farmers set up their stalls to try to make a living during the Depression.

Today the Farmers Market is made up of more than 125 individually owned businesses. You can take the children here and walk through the various food stalls and stores. Visitors go crazy over the fresh fruit and vegetables displayed in the stands. This is also a popular place to get gift-wrapped packages of dried fruits and nuts. Many visitors send oranges, grapefruit, and other seasonal fruit back to their homes from here.

There's even a good-sized supermarket, the **Farmers Market Grocery,** Stall 150 (☎ 213/936-2596), for diapers and other necessary items to take back to the hotel. Most of the retail stores here are tourist stops. But **Kip's Toyland,** Stall 150-2 (☎ 213/939-8334), is a small toy store with some nice selections for those playthings you left at home; there's a **B. Dalton,** Stall 156 (☎ 213/936-7266), for adult and children's books; and the **Paper Shop,** Stall 150-5 (☎ 213/935-4938), is a great store for postcards, stationery, and stickers for the kids. No doubt you won't be able to keep the kids away from **Just For Fun,** Stall 710 (☎ 213/931-6781), for all sorts of Mickey Mouse–inspired clothes and accessories. There's also a small post office located around the corner from the Sports Section.

Locals love to eat in the open-air dining area, where you can choose from all types of ethnic food for breakfast, lunch, or early dinner from more than 25 kitchens. It's also a good spot just to stop and have a sundae or other afternoon treat. If you go in the morning, don't miss **Bob's Coffee & Donuts,** Stall 450 (☎ 213/933-8929), for possibly the best donuts in town. You'll also find **Du-Par's** here for indoor, sit-down dining (see the "Where to Eat" section, above, for details). In summer the Farmers Market is open Monday through Saturday from 9am to 7pm and on Sunday from 10am to 6pm; in winter, Monday through Saturday from 9am to 6:30pm and on Sunday from 10am to 6pm. Parking is free, and there's no charge for walking around.

BEVERLY HILLS

In the 1880s Beverly Hills was a series of bean fields—lima beans, to be exact. But instead of beans or underground diamond mines it was water that made Beverly Hills come alive. Burton E. Green was the man who founded the water company and created the residential community in the early 1900s. The city's growth did not happen all at once, however. Although business tycoons had mansions in the area that now surrounds the Beverly Hills Hotel, few others lived there. It wasn't until the 1920s, when Mary Pickford and Douglas Fairbanks moved in, that Beverly Hills really became a popular place to live for the movie industry crowd.

Today you'll find a Beverly Hills where stars live, work, and dine, and are regularly seen. Household income is one of the highest in the country; property values are astronomical and mansions are common. In fact, the most business licenses given out in Beverly Hills are to gardeners! Even the high school is famous for its underground oil wells. The city also has what is possibly the most expensive jogging track in the world, based on land values, located on the parkway that runs parallel to Santa Monica Boulevard.

The Beverly Hills **Golden Triangle** is the business district bordered by Canon Drive, and Santa Monica and Wilshire Boulevards. The streets are lined with shops sporting price tags often beyond the reach of the average consumer. But there are also good family restaurants (see the "Where to Eat" section, above) and stores with reasonable prices. Christmas is a great time to walk the streets of Beverly Hills. You're likely to spot a celebrity running in to his or her favorite store to stock up on presents. You can't help but want to peek into the ever-present limousines to see who might be sitting there. At other times you'll find an almost constant promenade up and down the streets, day or night. In fact, no matter where your family has dinner, Rodeo Drive (pronounced "Ro-*day*-oh") is a great place to walk it off in the evening. Take the kids

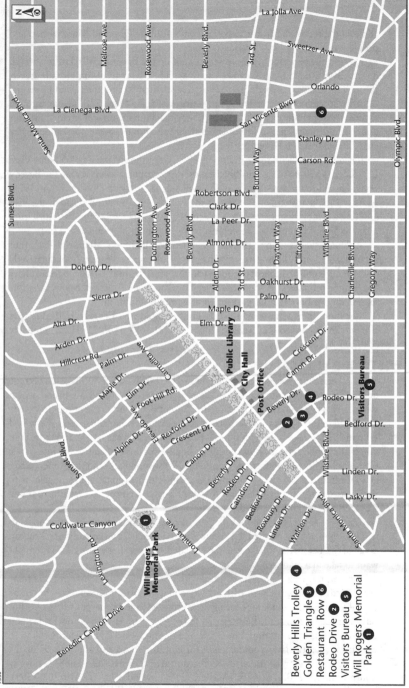

Beverly Hills

Beverly Hills Trolley ④
Golden Triangle ③
Restaurant Row ⑥
Rodeo Drive ②
Visitors Bureau ⑤
Will Rogers Memorial Park ①

9530

and join the rest of the crowd, especially on Saturday night, and window-shop and people-watch to your heart's content.

Possibly the best tour deal in town is found on the **Beverly Hills Trolley,** which departs from Rodeo Drive and Dayton Way. The narrated 30-minute ride travels through the Golden Triangle past boutiques, restaurants, and hotels, and by several celebrity homes in the nearby residential area. Catch a ride for $2, Tuesday through Saturday, except rainy days and holidays, every half hour from 10:30am to 5pm. Kids under 12 ride free. The Trolley operates from July through September, and the day after Thanksgiving to December 31.

There are other sights to see in Beverly Hills. **Greystone Mansion,** 905 Loma Vista Dr. (☎ 310/550-4654), is possibly the most extravagant mansion ever built in Beverly Hills. This 55-room mansion was built by oil magnate Edward Doheny, Sr., in 1928. Although the mansion is not open to the public, you can stroll through the lush grounds, a part of what was once a 428-acre estate. Open October through April from 10am to 5pm; May through September it is open till 6pm. Admission is free.

Although there's no playground equipment, **Will Rogers Memorial Park** (not to be confused with Will Rogers State Historical Park), across the street from the Beverly Hills Hotel, is one of the most beautiful parks in which to push a stroller or relax under the gigantic palm trees. (Also see the "Neighborhood Parks" section, below, for information on two Beverly Hills parks with playground equipment.)

For more information on Beverly Hills, contact the **Beverly Hills Visitors Bureau,** 239 S. Beverly Dr., Beverly Hills, CA 90212 (☎ 310/271-8174, or toll free 800/345-2210).

WESTWOOD VILLAGE

With its beginnings as a college town, home of UCLA, Westwood Village has become one of the hottest communities in Los Angeles. The area now called Westwood, which is bordered by Pico Boulevard to the south, Sunset Boulevard to the north, Sepulveda Boulevard to the west, and Beverly Hills to the east was originally named Westwood Hills in 1923. It now has over 5,000 shops and services, several hotels, and more than 500 eating establishments. It has within its boundaries one golf course and four parks: Cheviot Hills Recreation Center, Palms Park, Westwood Park, and the Stoner Recreation Center. It is generally recognized to be the cinema capital of Los Angeles with its dozens of first-run movie theaters. Not surprisingly, Westwood is a favorite of young teenagers and the college crowd.

One way to see Westwood Village is to take the kids in the late afternoon to window-shop or walk on the UCLA campus, and then have an early dinner. You can do all of this before the Village gets too crowded with evening visitors. Or you might want to take in a matinee.

One caution: The Village is jammed with people, many of them teens, on Friday and Saturday nights. It's alive with activity and a fun place to people-watch, but be careful to hold onto your kids. During these crowded times we never use a stroller but carry our toddlers instead. Be prepared for potential street closings on Friday and Saturday nights in the summer, holidays, and during special events. Hours will vary.

This is a particularly popular place for clothing shops and shoe stores for the under-30 set. Don't miss **Aahs!,** 1083 Broxton Ave. (☎ 310/824-1688), a novelty store par excellence; **B. Dalton Bookseller,** 904 Westwood Blvd. (☎ 310/208-7395), is a full-service bookstore with a line of children's books; and **Tower Records,** 1028 Westwood Blvd. (☎ 310/208-3061), has a large, unusual selection of classical, rock 'n' roll, and jazz records, tapes, and compact discs. **Häagen-Dazs Ice Cream,** 10878 Kinross (☎ **310/208-7405**), and **Mrs. Field's Cookies,** 907 Westwood Blvd. (☎ **310/208-0096**), are great snack places.

UCLA

The world-famous University of California at Los Angeles (UCLA), 405 Hilgard Ave. (☎ **310/825-4321**), has more than 30,000 full-time students. The beautiful hilly campus of more than 400 acres is set between Westwood Village and Bel Air. If you need information or would like to take a tour, contact the **Community Relations/ Visitors Center,** 1417 Ueberroth Bldg., 405 Hilgard Ave., Los Angeles, CA 90024 (☎ **310/206-8147**).

If you prefer to simply wander around, a walk on campus during the quieter week-ends is delightful and gives the kids an opportunity to rollick in the open grassy areas while you witness an amazing mix of architectural styles.

Don't miss Royce Hall and "the Quad," the spiritual heart of the campus. From there, wander to the **Franklin D. Murphy Sculpture Garden,** north of Royce Hall, near the University Research Library, where green lawns dotted with trees are home to more than 50-sculptures. Originally conceived as a place to bring art to the outdoors where students could enjoy it as they studied, visited, and relaxed, the Sculpture Garden is a welcome retreat for families. You'll see lots of kids playing tag, reading, picnicking with their parents.

If your family likes botanical gardens, you might enjoy a stroll through the **Mildred E. Mathias Botanical Garden** (☎ **310/825-3620**), located at the southeastern part of the campus. Enter at Le Conte and Hilgard Avenues. This compact garden features 4,000 species of plants in 225 families, and specializes in subtropical and tropi-cal plants that aren't grown in other parts of the U.S. except in greenhouses.

It's open Monday through Friday from 8am to 5pm and on Saturday and Sunday from 8am to 4:30pm; closed university holidays. Admission is free.

SANTA MONICA

Close your eyes and conjure up the images you have when you hear the words "Santa Monica." Palm trees lining the boulevards, miles and miles of ocean, children build-ing sand castles, and almost perfect weather are the fantasies that most people have. Surprisingly, the fantasy is reality.

Hugging the coastline of Santa Monica Bay, the city of Santa Monica is a family wonderland. It has 13 miles of wide, white-sand beaches with endless year-round activities, the historic Santa Monica Pier, beautiful Palisades Park, bike paths, board-walks for roller skating, and terrific people-watching opportunities. Add to that several wonderful shopping areas, and you have the makings of a sightseer's delight.

You'll probably want to contact or stop at the **Santa Monica Visitors Information Center,** 1400 Ocean Ave., Santa Monica, CA 90401, in Palisades Park (☎ **310/393-7593**), open daily from 10am to 4pm.

Santa Monica Pier

The famous Santa Monica Pier, at the end of Colorado Boulevard and Ocean Avenue (☎ **310/458-8900**), the oldest pleasure pier on the West Coast, was built in 1908. At that time, it was one of several piers in the area built to house amusement parks and fun zones, probably the most popular one being Lawrence Welk's Aragon Ball-room. Today, the pier is host to arcades, shops, restaurants, and kiddie rides.

Fun Zone, at the Santa Monica Pier, is a seasonal mini-midway of rides for young children. From April to Labor Day, you can spot the Ferris wheel near the carousel. Kiddie rides are $1; the Ferris wheel is $1.50. Open daily during summer; in April and May, weekends only. Hours vary.

The beautiful carousel, with its hand-painted wooden horses, is open Tuesday through Sunday in summer from 10am to 9pm, and on winter weekends from 10am to 5pm. Rides cost 50¢ for adults, 25¢ for children 12 and under.

You can rent bikes and roller skates near the pier too. **Sea Mist Skate and Bike Rental,** 1619 Ocean Front Walk, across from the carousel (☎ **310/395-7076**), rents kids' and adult bikes at $5 for the first hour, $4 for each additional hour. Tandems rent for $9 for the first hour and $5 for each additional hour. Child carriers, socks, helmets, and locks are free. Kid carts and roller skates, for kids and adults, are $4 for the first hour, $3 for each additional hour.

Open daily in summer from 9am to 8pm on weekdays and on weekends; the rest of the year, from 10am to 4:30pm on weekdays and 9am to 6pm on weekends. Parking lot.

Palisades Park

One of the most famous places in Santa Monica, Palisades Park is a favorite one-mile stretch. Perched on the bluffs overlooking the ocean, palm-tree-studded Palisades Park is 26 acres of walkways and lawns. The views are unparalleled, and it's a wonderful place for tykes on trikes.

You'll find the park on Ocean Avenue. Its southern border is Colorado Boulevard, but the farther north you go, the prettier it is. There is metered street parking.

Main Street

A walk along Santa Monica's Main Street is a pleasant way to spend an hour or so. Trendy shops, art galleries, one-of-a-kind novelty stores, and restaurants line Main Street from Pico Boulevard to Rose Avenue, but the main cluster of shops is from Ocean Park Avenue to Pier Avenue.

Third Street Promenade is touted as a festive marketplace, and it offers a wonderful opportunity for you to stroll amid the artwork and fountains while the kids romp. There are numerous specialty bookstores and wonderful cafés. Each week there's an outdoor farmer's market.

The Museum of Flying, 2772 Donald Douglas Loop N. (at the Santa Monica Airport) (☎ **310/392-8822**) is a celebration of the history and achievement of aviation. It houses an amazing display of vintage aircraft, including the Douglas World Cruiser (the first to circle the globe—in 1924), the P-51 Mustang, the Spitfire Mark IX, and many others.

The museum is open Tuesday through Sunday from 10am to 5pm. Admission is $5 for adults, $4 for seniors, $3 for kids 3 to 17.

Angel's Attic

This restored Victorian home at 516 Colorado Ave. (☎ **310/394-8331**) is now a delightful museum. Especially captivating for children from 5 to 95 who love dollhouses, dolls, and miniatures, the museum also has a collection of stuffed animals and toys.

You can buy miniature dollhouses, dolls, and books. It is a nonprofit museum and contributes to the support of the Brentwood Center for Educational Therapy. It's a fun place for a tea party with your favorite little girls. Open Thursday through Sunday from 12:30 to 4:30pm; closed major holidays. Admission is $4 for adults, $3 for seniors 65 and over, $2 for children under 12. Metered street parking.

Venice Beach Ocean Front Walk

If you take the San Diego Freeway (I-405), north or south, exit at Venice Boulevard. Go west on Venice and you'll run right into Venice Beach. There's parking on the southeast corner of Venice and Pacific for $5 all day; or find a spot on the street, which is more difficult on summer weekends. Or you can take the Pacific Coast Hwy. (Calif. 1) to Venice Boulevard.

The key words to remember when visiting Venice Beach's Ocean Front Walk are "experience" and "keep an open mind." Strolling down this boardwalk is truly an experience, and one in which parents need to keep an open mind. On a Sunday afternoon you'll see a cornucopia of L.A.'s most eclectic population. Some are scantily clothed; some have blue hair, some yellow; a few come decked-out in chains; one or two are covered with cloth from head to toe. But there are "normal" people here too, including the archetypal Southern California man and woman. It's an inexpensive and fun way to spend a Saturday or Sunday afternoon.

You can take children of any age on this walk, but be forewarned about some raunchy language used in some of the street acts. It's also quite crowded on weekends, the best time to come for prime people-watching, so hold onto those little hands.

There are a couple of **children's playgrounds** on the beach, one half a block north of Ocean Front Walk and Paloma, the other about two blocks north of Venice Boulevard and Ocean Front Walk. We don't recommend Venice Beach as a swimming beach because there are riptides, and it's not considered a particularly safe beach. But for playing and picnicking, the sand is fine.

If you've wanted to find a California souvenir, you should be able to find one on Ocean Front Walk: thousands of T-shirts are for sale, hats of every description, sandals, sunglasses, jewelry, clothes, bathing suits . . . and much more. You'll probably be surprised when you catch a glimpse of the Venice police who are always patrolling the area—in their shorts.

There are lots of fast-food stands serving up hot dogs, sandwiches, ice cream, frozen yogurt, pizza, hamburgers, and popcorn. Rest your weary feet by having lunch on the beach, or stop by one of three sit-down restaurants: **Sidewalk Café,** 1401 Ocean Front Walk (☎ 310/399-5547), open for breakfast, lunch, or dinner, with an extensive menu and prices ranging from $2.95 to $12; **Figtree Café,** 429 Ocean Front Walk (☎ 310/392-4937), specializes in natural foods, serving breakfast items, salads, fish, pizzas, and lots of vegetarian specialties, priced at $2.75–$12.

Not only can you walk the boardwalk, but you can ride bikes, roller skate, or skateboard your way along. In fact, you can ride all the way from the Venice Beach boardwalk past the Santa Monica Pier. Everything is for rent. **Spokes 'n Stuff,** in the Jamaica Bay Inn parking lot, 4175 Admiralty Way, Marina del Rey (☎ 310/306-3332), rents 10-speeds, children's bikes, bikes with baby seats, tandems, mountain bikes, and adult tricycles, as well as roller skates and in-line skates. Rates start at $3.50 per hour for children's bikes and go up to $8 for tandems, and $4 per hour for skates. They also rent boogie boards, for $4 per hour. Prices are better the longer you rent. Open summer daily from 10am to 5pm and weekends from 9:30 to 6pm. Call for winter hours.

Venice Pier Bike Shop, 21 Washington Blvd. (☎ 310/301-4011), has children's bikes for rent as well as beach cruisers, 6-speeds, and mountain bikes, 3-, 6-, 10-, and

18-speeds, tandems, bikes with baby seats, and helmets for children. Rates begin at $2 per hour. Rent your boogie boards, roller skates, and in-line skates here, too. Open summer weekdays from 9am and weekends from 8:30am. Call for closing hours and winter hours.

MARINA DEL REY

Just five minutes north of Los Angeles International Airport is Marina del Rey, a pocket of blue water, sailboats, and yachts. Although just minutes out of the city, the Marina makes you feel as if you've been transported to a European seaside village.

Marina del Rey is the largest artificial pleasurecraft harbor in the world. Bounded by Lincoln Boulevard, Washington Street, and the Pacific Ocean, the Marina is home to more than 6,000 boats, myriad shops, pricey condos and apartments, movie theaters, night spots, and a huge array of restaurants.

Here you can rent boats, cruise the marina, sunbathe, swim, fish, windsurf, roller skate, fly kites, walk, and ride your bikes. One of our favorite pastimes is to take breakfast to the **North Jetty** between Via Marina and Pacific Avenue, find a spot, and enjoy our meal while we watch the boats as they pass through the main channel of the Marina. For more information, the Marina has its own visitor center. Contact the **Marina del Rey Visitors Information Center,** 4701 Admiralty Way, Marina del Rey, CA 90292 (☎ **310/305-9545**).

Bike Rentals

One place to try is the **Jamaica Bay Inn Beach Hut,** 4175 Admiralty Way (☎ **310/306-3332**). The Beach Hut rents beach cruisers and 10-speeds at $3.50 for the first hour, $10.50 for four hours, $14 for the day (10:30am to 6:30pm). Mountain bikes are $5.50 for the first hour, $16.50 for four hours, $22 for the day. Tandem bikes are $8 for the first hour, $18 for four hours, and $24 for the day. Children's bicycles are available, as are baby carriers and helmets. They also rent rollerskates and in-line skates. Open daily from 10:30am to 6pm in the summer; closed Monday and Tuesday in the winter.

Boat Rentals

Rent-A-Sail, 13719 Fiji Way (☎ **310/822-1868**), rents sailboats, powerboats, canoes, and catamarans. Rates range from $10 to $34 per hour, depending on the boat, and sailing lessons are available. Open daily from 10am to dusk. **California Sailing Academy,** 14025 Panay Way (☎. **310/821-3433**), rents sailboats. Hours vary.

Roller-Skate Rentals

Rent skates at **Skatey's,** 102 Washington St. (☎ **310/823-7971**). Open weekdays from 10am to 6pm and weekends from 9am to 7pm in summer.

Fishing

For those of you who want to fish, you can try **Marina del Rey Sportfishing,** 13759 Fiji Way (☎ **310/822-3625**). You can also go dock-fishing at Fisherman's Village, 13763 Fiji Way.

Some Parks and a Shopping Center

If you're just looking for a nice place to let the kids run around, **Burton Chace Park** is a nine-acre waterfront park at the western end of Mindanao Way with picnic areas, a fishing dock, and views of the boats.

Admiralty Park is on Admiralty Way between Palawan and Bali Ways, near the bird sanctuary.

Serious shopping in the Marina is best at the **Villa Marina Center** at Mindanao and the Marina freeway. Here you'll find 20 restaurants, first-run movie theaters, a Vons supermarket, a Savon/Osco drugstore, a video arcade, and other necessities.

Fisherman's Village

Fisherman's Village, located at 13755 Fiji Way (☎ 310/823-5411), looks like a little fishing village, and it's a delightful place to walk and relax with the family for an afternoon. As you stroll along the boardwalk on a sunny weekend day, you'll see hundreds of pleasure boats in all sizes. You, too, can cruise the harbor on a 45-minute tour. **Hornblower Dining Yachts** (☎ 310/301-6000), located right at the village, has boats that leave daily, every hour on the hour from 11am to 5pm every day in the summer, on Saturday and Sunday the rest of the year. The fare is $7 for adults, $4 for seniors and children 2–12; children under 2, free. Or you can rent your own sailboat from **Rent-A-Sail** (☎ 310/822-1868). Rental prices range from $10 to $34 per hour, with a two-hour minimum, depending on which boat you choose, and there's a $20 deposit required (cash only accepted). Rent-A-Sail is open daily from 10am to sundown.

In the village there are art, souvenir, and jewelry stores; an import shop; a kite and toy store; and a T-shirt shop all housed in little cottages. Four sit-down restaurants serve Mexican food, pizza and pasta, seafood, and steaks. For outdoor snacks on the boardwalk, there are cookies, ice cream, hamburgers, candy, sandwiches, and fish and chips. On Saturday and Sunday, weather permitting, you can hear free live jazz concerts from 1 to 4pm in the center of the village.

Most of the shops and restaurants are open from 10am to 10pm on Friday and Saturday; Sunday through Thursday, open from 10am to 9pm. Parking is free.

OUTDOOR ACTIVITIES

You've just read about outdoor activities near the beach areas. Los Angeles offers even more. Take your pick. There's hiking, swimming, boating, windsurfing, surfing, jogging, roller skating, bicycling, walking, horseback riding, and probably scads of other outdoor ventures you'll dream up.

Let's start with the Santa Monica Mountains, a range that offers delightful outdoor adventures for the active, and even the not-so-active, family.

Hiking

For specific hikes and other information, you'll want to contact the **Santa Monica Mountains National Recreation Area Visitor Center,** 30401 Agoura Rd., Suite 100, Agoura Hills, CA 91301 (☎ 818/597-9192). The offices are open daily from 8am to 5pm. Concerts, ranger-led programs, hiking, horseback riding, swimming, birdwatching, camping, tidepooling, bicycling, picnicking, whale-watching, scenic drives, and special events can be enjoyed.

Franklin Canyon Ranch is in the hills above Beverly Hills where Beverly Drive meets Coldwater Canyon Drive. Call for directions (☎ 310/858-3834 and 818/597-9192). Here you can enjoy self-guided trails, hiking, picnicking, and jogging.

Topanga State Park, located off Topanga Canyon Boulevard at Entrada Road (☎ 310/455-2465), is a wooded area with self-guided nature trails and 32 miles of hiking trails. Open daily from 8am to 7pm from the beginning of April through October, to 5pm November to April. Fee for parking.

Will Rogers State Historic Park, 14253 Sunset Blvd., between Amalfi Drive and Brooktree Road, about eight miles inland from Calif. 1, the Pacific Coast Highway (☎ 310/454-8212), is a wonderful place that's easy to take kids of all ages. Everyone enjoys the self-guided audio tours of Will Rogers's Ranch House, and there are two enormous fields for picnicking and romping. One is a polo ground where polo matches take place Saturday afternoon and Sunday morning (call for specific hours). The trails are relatively easy and offer splendid views of the ocean and city on clear days. The park is open daily from 8am to 6pm, to 7pm in the summertime. Fee is $5 for parking.

This is where the **William O. Douglas Outdoor Classroom** is located, which offers a variety of **public walks,** most of which are designed for families. Walks are geared to such varied topics as the food chain, ecology, photography, and wildflower exploration. Two to three times a week they offer **Babes in the Woods Walks** for children 3 months to 3 years and their parents. And on the weekends, they also offer **Tykes on Hikes** for children 4–6 years old and their parents.

On these sensory-oriented nature walks, children smell, touch, look, and listen to nature. Kids sit under the trees and the docent uses puppets to tell stories. The big hit is to feed the ducks. They'll feel soft sycamore leaves, listen to the birds, look for little mosquito fish in the pond and scoop them up to study them. The program also offers **Adventure Quest,** designed for teens; teens walk with peers while the family goes on another walk. There's a **Full-Moon Hike** monthly.

Guided hikes for young children are free but are by reservation only; contact the William O. Douglas Outdoor Classroom, P.O. Box 2488, Beverly Hills, CA 90213 (☎ 310/858-3834). All other hikes do not need reservations. All hikes are free.

Coldwater Canyon Park is located at the east side of the intersection between Coldwater Canyon and Mulholland Drive (☎ 818/753-4600). This is the home of Treepeople, 12601 Mulholland Dr., a nonprofit environmental group. The park is open daily from 9am to dusk. On Tuesday and Saturday from 2 to 4pm, adults and children can get involved by volunteering to plant and nurture tree seedlings in the TreePeople's nursery. Park visitors can also walk along the five miles of hiking trails and visit the recycling and composting displays. Guided tours are available by appointment.

Nursery Walks

A group of volunteers, sponsored by the **Palisades-Malibu YMCA** at 821 Via de la Paz, Pacific Palisades (☎ 310/454-5591), leads nature walks for infants and preschoolers and their parents. To help families develop a love for nature, they offer walks of about two hours duration and about half a mile in length. About halfway, they take a break.

Using all the senses, they get the tots involved with their surroundings by having them pretend to be Native Americans, use flowers to make soap, or smell leaves. The walks are held at Leo Carrillo State Beach, Malibu Lagoon State Beach, Topanga State Park, Will Rogers State Park, Griffith Park, and several others.

Older sisters and brothers are welcome. Reservations are required—usually a month in advance. A donation of $4 is requested.

Swimming Beaches

We'll start at the north and work south. (Check Chapter 12 on the Greater L.A. area for beaches north and south of these.) Unless indicated otherwise, all parking lots charge a fee, usually $5–$8. In some cases, you can find street parking as well.

Will Rogers State Beach (☎ 310/394-3266) is a nice clean family beach with two designated surfing areas. Located just north of Santa Monica Beach, starting at Chautauqua Boulevard and going for three miles to Topanga Canyon, this lovely beach has parking, restrooms, showers, a snack bar, volleyball courts, and lifeguard stations. It has a few playgrounds, one near lifeguard Tower 8, near Temescal Canyon.

Santa Monica State Beach (☎ 310/394-3266) is the 3.3-mile-long stretch of beach below the bluffs of Palisades Park. This very wide sandy beach has just about all the facilities you could hope for, and the crowds to go with them. Divided by the Santa Monica Pier, it's a tourist-oriented beach with an abundance of parking. (If you want fewer crowds, drive farther north and you'll be rewarded.) Most activity centers around the pier. You might want to stay north of the pier, where the ocean is much safer than on the south side. Just south of the pier, you'll find gymnastics equipment and volleyball courts. Both north and south of the pier, you find restrooms and outdoor showers. There are ample snack bars and concessions.

Peninsula Beach (☎ 310/394-3266) is in Marina del Rey at the end of Washington Street near the breakwater. South of the pier is a very nice part of the beach. Parking is difficult, which keeps the beach less crowded. There are restrooms and a smattering of little restaurants at the foot of Washington Street. This is more of an adult beach than a kids' beach, but it's lovely.

Neighborhood Parks

With so much land in Los Angeles, neighborhood parks are not too difficult to find. Here are a few we find special:

Douglas Park, 1155 Chelsea Ave., near Wilshire Boulevard and 20th Street in Santa Monica (☎ 310/458-8311), is a charming little park complete with a duck pond, a wading pool which doubles as a tricycle demolition racetrack when it's dry, and fabulous wooden play structures. The equipment offers amusement for older kids as well as the younger ones. Picnic facilities, barbecue stands, restrooms, and tennis courts complete the picture.

Cheviot Hills Recreation Area is a large well-known park. Located at 2551 Motor Ave. in West Los Angeles (☎ 310/837-5186), the large park has playground equipment, basketball courts, baseball diamonds, tennis courts, picnic and barbecue facilities, and a large municipal swimming pool (☎ 310/836-3365). The recreation center offers a wide variety of activities as well.

One beautiful in-town place to run off some excess energy is at **Roxbury Park** in Beverly Hills, 471 S. Roxbury Dr., at Olympic Boulevard (☎ 310/550-4761). Besides paths for walking, a softball field, tennis and basketball courts, lawn bowling, and croquet greens, there are two large play areas for children in the back of the park. Nearby are picnic tables and barbecue grills, which are available by advance reservation, with priority given to Beverly Hills residents. Park in the metered spaces in back of the park if you intend to stay by the playground equipment. Restrooms and soda machines are nearby.

La Cienega Park, 8400 Gregory Way, between Gregory, Olympic, and La Cienega Boulevards, Beverly Hills (☎ 310/550-4625), has play equipment, tennis courts, a softball field, picnic tables, and restrooms. Parking is at a premium; park in the lot across the street.

Bike Paths

In Santa Monica, the **South Bay Bicycle Trail,** 22 miles altogether, runs along Ocean Avenue. Although it's quite scenic, there can be a lot of traffic.

In Marina del Rey, you can start your bicycle ride at the Bird Sanctuary near the Marina International Hotel, at Palawan and Admiralty Ways, for an approximately two-mile ride to Fisherman's Village. There's a county parking lot where you can park for $1 in quarters during the winter and $5 during the summer (sometimes the machine requires exact change). Your ride will take you across Admiralty Way past the huge pleasure boats in drydock on your way to Fisherman's Village. Beware of a couple of unmarked crossings across busy streets. From Fisherman's Village you can ride along the **Ballona Creek Bike Trail,** located at the end of the **South Bay Bike Trail** (see Chapter 12, on Greater Los Angeles, for details). The trail winds along Ballona Creek from Fisherman's Village all the way to Culver City.

Horseback Riding

J. P. Horseback Riding Stables, 914 S. Mariposa, Burbank, located at the northeast corner of Griffith Park, just south of Riverside Drive (☎ **818/843-9890**), offers guide-led horseback rides through Griffith Park. Your family may have a guide of its own, or you may share with other people. The fees are $14 for the first hour, $11 for each additional; there's an $11 deposit on each horse. Fees are in cash only. The minimum age is 6 years old. Horses are available on a first-come, first-served basis. Open daily year round from 8am to 4pm.

Miniature Golf

Sherman Oaks Castle Miniature Golf, 4989 Sepulveda Blvd., in Sherman Oaks (☎ **818/385-1739**), is a miniature golf lover's dream. Three attractively designed golf courses with an abundance of fountains, ponds, and greenery delight children. There are also batting cages, a huge video arcade, and a snack bar. The facility is open daily from 10am to 11pm; midnight on Friday and Saturday. Adults pay $5; kids 13 and under, $4.

AMUSEMENT AND WATER PARKS

Outdoor activities are not limited to adventures in nature. L.A. also has its share of hair-raising adventure.

Six Flags Magic Mountain

Ah, but the kids enjoy this place! Located in Valencia (take the Magic Mountain Parkway exit off I-5) about 25 minutes north of Hollywood (☎ **818/367-5965** or **805/255-4111**), Magic Mountain's 260 acres offers family fun for every age. There are 100 rides in all, plus live shows, a dance club, petting zoo, and a year-round crafts village. Always popular with thrill-seeking teens and preteens who delight in the stupendous roller coasters and water adventures, Magic Mountain has added several attractions to entertain the younger set.

Magic Mountain is best known for its electrifying roller-coaster rides. **Viper,** the world's tallest and fastest steel-looping roller coaster, is 188 feet above the ground, and it plunges down a 55° drop. **Ninja,** the black belt of roller coasters, is the fastest suspended roller coaster. Traveling at speeds of up to 55 m.p.h. on a half-mile route through the surrounding forest, this coaster is suspended from an overhead track. There's nothing underneath riders as they go through steep drops and side-to-side swings of up to 110°. **Colossus** is the gargantuan double-track wooden roller coaster that is invariably rated in the top 10 in America. **Revolution** was the world's first coaster with a 360° vertical loop, and has the distinction of being one of the world's largest steel coasters. **Flashback** is a hairpin-drop roller coaster with six 180° turns.

Magic Mountain was one of the first to have water flume rides. **Log Jammer** takes its riders in hollowed-out logs through a winding, twisting voyage that plunges through the water. In **Jet Stream,** riders in speedboats plummet down a 52-foot drop. **Tidal Wave** is a ride that takes 20-passenger boats on a plunge over a 50-foot waterfall.

The newest adventure here is **Gotham City Backlot,** a six-acre themed area that transports you to Bruce Wayne's city, complete with eerie underground tunnels. Don't miss the batcave. **Batman—The Ride** is a state-of-the-art thriller that combines high-speed technology and hairpin turns with Batman movie magic. It is truly heart-throbbing fun.

Little kids enjoy **Bugs Bunny World,** a six-acre area especially designed for them. Little squeals of excitement can be heard from the **Wile E. Coyote** roller coaster, a scaled-down version of the bigger item. After the young ones have had their share of rides, meander to **Wile E. Coyote Critter Canyon.** Here, they can see 55 different kinds of animals, including miniature horses, and touch many of them.

When we need a break, we hightail it over to **Spillikin Handcrafter's Junction,** an 1800s-style crafts village where we find some shade and just relax.

Show highlights change from season to season.

Here are some tips for doing the park. Arrive early in the day. If you have very young kids, you might want to bring a stash of juice. Many a time we've been hard-pressed to find a vending machine or snack bar that has anything other than soft drinks and milk. But if your kids are like ours, they'll want to try all the goodies and sweets they see, so expect to be reaching in your pockets often. Valencia, like many other spots, can be quite warm on summer days. Be sure to bring sunscreen, hats, and a change of clothes (there are lots of water rides) if you'll be visiting during the summer. Rental strollers and coin lockers are available. You can find diapers at the Pamper Baby Care Center, located near Bugs Bunny World. Open daily at 10am from Memorial Day through Labor Day, on weekends and school holidays the rest of the year. Call ahead for specific dates and closing times. General admission (which entitles you to unlimited use of all rides, shows, and attractions) is $28; children under four feet tall, $15; seniors 55 and older is $18; children under age 2 free. Parking is $6.

Raging Waters

Have you ever been to a water theme park? Get ready, because this is an experience—a day of sun, wet thrills, and throngs of excited, screaming children! Situated on 44 acres in the 2,200-acre Frank G. Bonelli Regional Park in San Dimas, Raging Waters makes you feel as if you've entered a beach town designed for the young and daring. Raging Waters is located at 111 Raging Waters Dr. (☎ **909/592-8181,** or **909/592-6453** for recorded information), 30 minutes east of downtown Los Angeles, 20 minutes north of Anaheim, where I-10 and Calif. 210 meet. Exit at Raging Waters Drive.

Large sandy areas, where lotion-covered moms and dads watch swimming youngsters, surround enormous sandy-bottomed swimming holes, where school-age kids and preteens enjoy small water slides, water swings, a lily-pad walk, and rope nets above the water. An area called **Wavecove** is the closest you'll come to bodysurfing in this neck of the woods. Waves as high as three feet give even the meekest among us the chance to experience an oceanlike ride.

But this is not a place for the faint of heart. Teens, preteens, and others who believe they're invincible are the ones who probably enjoy it the most. Billing itself as the largest water theme park west of the Mississippi, Raging Waters has four speed slides, four flume rides, and a water rapids. The **Dropout** is a free-fall experience where adventure seekers descend seven stories in four seconds at speeds of up to 40 m.p.h.— straight down! **Rampage** is a ride on a hydro-sled from a tower four stories high. **Raging Rocket** and **Screamer** are slides with eight-story descents that take you up to 25 m.p.h.

The flumes **Demon's Drop, Thunder Run, Tree-Top Twisters,** and **Canyon Chute** have more than 400 feet of curves and dips, ending in a refreshing splash down pool. **Raging Rivers** is the longest artificial inner-tube rapids; this quarter-mile waterway has rapids, whirlpools, and waterfalls. For the littlest tots, **Little Dipper** is a grassy area with pools only one foot deep. Not to be outdone, this area has its own fountains and mini-water slides. Children over 8 aren't even allowed in these pools. And Raging Waters has an entire **playground** for little kids.

A Note of Caution: While there are lifeguards and trained slide operators, we're always super-cautious when there are lots of kids in the water. For the rapids, flumes, and steep slides, the park has its own rules, which should be strictly adhered to. And at this kind of park, more than almost anywhere else, remember the sunscreen and sunblock, since the kids will be baking in the sun all day.

Dressing rooms and coin-operated lockers are available. Life vests are provided free, and you can rent rafts and inner tubes for $5 ($2 is refunded when you return the item). You will find a variety of food, from Mexican to Italian, at the snack stands. There are picnic areas also.

Raging Waters is open from April through the beginning of October, but call ahead for specific dates and times as these vary greatly. For the smallest crowds, be sure to get there when the park opens. Admission prices are based on height: General admission, for anyone over 48 inches, is $19.99; children 42–48 inches and seniors pay $11.99, under 42 inches, admitted free. Parking costs $4.

PERFORMING ARTS

No doubt many of you and your teenagers have heard of Los Angeles's outdoor concert venues where some of the world's most popular groups perform. And the Roxy and the Troubador, clubs made popular in the '60s and '70s, are still in full swing with today's newest groups. An **Events Hotline** (☎ 213/689-8822) offers 24-hour information on L.A. events in several languages.

Concert Sites

The famed **Greek Theater,** 2700 N. Vermont Ave., Los Angeles (☎ 213/665-1927), is an outdoor amphitheater nestled in the woods of Griffith Park offering a wide range of musical fare. The season runs from late May to October. Tickets are available through TicketMaster (☎ 213/480-3232). You can also purchase them at the box office daily from noon to 6pm and to 9pm on performance days.

The **Universal Amphitheater** (☎ 818/980-9421) is an indoor theater on the Universal Studios lot, located off the Hollywood Freeway (U.S. 101) in Universal City. Take the Lankershim Boulevard exit and follow the signs. Tickets are available through TicketMaster (☎ 213/480-3232), local Robinson/May Company stores, and Music Plus stores. The Amphitheater box office is located in the parking lot of the site, above the entrance to the Registry Hotel. It's open Tuesday through Saturday from 1 to 9pm.

Clubs

The **Roxy** is at 9009 Sunset Blvd., West Hollywood, east of Doheny Drive (☎ 310/276-2222 or 310/278-9457). All the shows in this club are geared to teenagers and young adults, but call ahead to find out who is playing. Featured artists might be local unknowns or superstars such as David Bowie. There's no age minimum, but there is a minimum drinking age in California, which naturally the Roxy adheres to. Tickets are available only at the door before the shows, but call ahead because selected show tickets are available through TicketMaster (☎ 213/480-3232).

All ages are also allowed at **Doug Weston's Troubador,** 9081 Santa Monica Blvd., West Hollywood, corner of Santa Monica Boulevard and Doheny Drive (☎ 310/276-1158). Food is available here, and performances are appropriate for teenagers.

The Groundlings, 7307 Melrose Ave. (☎ 213/934-9700), is one of the city's best-known improvisational theaters. Adults and teenagers will appreciate it. Call for show times.

Music and Theater

The **Music Center,** 135 N. Grand Ave., at 1st Street, downtown (☎ 213/972-7211), is Los Angeles's grand complex of three theaters—the **Dorothy Chandler Pavilion,** the **Ahmanson Theatre,** and the **Mark Taper Forum** (☎ 213/972-7353). The theaters present a mix of the Los Angeles Philharmonic, Los Angeles Opera, Broadway theater, experimental theater, ballet, and other live performances. From the Pasadena Freeway (Calif. 110), exit at Hill Avenue to Temple Avenue and make a right, then a left on Grand Avenue. From the Harbor Freeway (I-110), exit at 4th Street to Olive Street, then turn left on Olive, left on 1st Street, and right on Grand Avenue. From the Hollywood Freeway South (U.S. 101), exit at Temple Avenue and make a left, then a right on Grand Avenue. If you're coming north on the Hollywood Freeway, exit at Grand Avenue and turn right.

To get tickets by mail for any of the theaters, write two weeks in advance to the Box Office, 135 N. Grand Ave., Los Angeles, CA 90012. The Dorothy Chandler Pavilion box office hours depend on who is on stage. It's best to get tickets through TicketMaster (☎ 213/480-3232 or 365-3500). The Mark Taper Forum box office is open Tuesday through Saturday from 10am to 8pm, and on Sunday from noon to 7:30pm. Or you can get tickets through TicketMaster (☎ 213/480-3232 or 365-3500). The Ahmanson Theatre box office is open on Monday from 10am to 6pm, Tuesday through Saturday from 10am to 8:30pm, and on Sunday from noon to 6pm. Or order through TicketMaster.

PRO SPORTS

Angelenos are crazy about sports and about their teams! With league-leading crews like the Lakers and the Dodgers, sporting events rank right up there with fun-in-the-sun and good food.

The **Dodgers** play baseball at Dodger Stadium, 1000 Elysian Park Ave., Los Angeles (☎ 213/224-1500), from April through October. There are numerous family-oriented special event dates scheduled during the season. Tickets are available by calling the Dodger Ticket Order Line (☎ 213/224-1-HIT), or at the Dodger Advance Ticket Office, 1750 Stadium Way. Both are open Monday through Saturday from 8:30am to 5:30pm beginning in mid-March. Or purchase from TicketMaster (☎ 213/480-3232). Purchase tickets by mail from Dodger Ticket Office, P.O. Box

51100, Los Angeles, CA 90051. Box seats cost $11, reserved seats are $8, and top deck and Pavilion tickets cost $6. General admission tickets are discounted to $3 for children 12 and under when purchased at the stadium 1 1/2 hours before game time.

The **Los Angeles Raiders** play football at the L.A. Memorial Coliseum, 3911 S. Figueroa St. (☎ 213/747-7111). The football season runs from August through December. For tickets, send a self-addressed, stamped envelope with a money order as early as possible to: Raiders Tickets, 332 Center St., El Segundo, CA 90245 (☎ **310/322-5901**). Call for ticket prices. You can purchase them in person at the El Segundo office. You can also get tickets through TicketMaster (☎ **213/480-3232**), and at the Sports Arena, 3939 S. Figueroa St. (☎ **213/748-6136**).

The National Hockey League **Los Angeles Kings,** the **Los Angeles Lakers** of the National Basketball Association, and the **Los Angeles Strings** of Team Tennis, all play at the Great Western Forum, 3900 W. Manchester Blvd., Inglewood (☎ **213/419-3182** for ticket information). The Forum box office is open daily from 10am to 6pm.

Currently, the **NBA L.A. Clippers** play basketball at the Sports Arena, 3939 S. Figueroa St. (☎ **213/748-6136**). Tickets can be purchased at the gate or through TicketMaster (☎ **213/480-3232**).

INDOOR ACTIVITIES

It *never* rains in Southern California, but should you experience a little dampness or fog during your stay or should you prefer an indoor activity, here are a few things you can see or do indoors.

The **Southwest Museum,** 234 Museum Dr., at Marmion Way, Highland Park (☎ **213/221-2164**), Los Angeles's oldest museum, is devoted to the study of Native American cultures from Alaska to South America. It has one of the finest collections of Native American art and artifacts in the country.

Children who have studied Native Americans love the romance that surrounds the stories they hear. At the museum they get to see many of the things they've read about, such as an authentic tepee, baskets, pottery and jewelry made by various tribes, and items used for carrying and clothing babies and small children many years ago.

If you plan to be in town a while, check with the museum to see if any special family programs are scheduled. Past events have included storytelling by a Navajo Storyteller, paper cutting and piñata-making during a Mexican Traditions festival, and a craft workshop on making a simple Native American toy.

Although the Southwest Museum is not near many other attractions and does take some time to get to, it's a special little museum for those people interested in the arts and artifacts of the Americas. It's not too far from Pasadena. Call for directions. The museum is open Tuesday through Sunday from 11am to 5pm. Admission is $5 for adults, $3 for students and seniors, $2 for youths 7–18, and free for children under 7.

Ice Skating

The **Culver City Skating Rink,** 4545 Sepulveda Blvd. (☎ **310/398-5719**), is a good place to take a break on sizzling August days. Open Monday through Friday from 10am to 5pm and on Saturday and Sunday from 9:30am to 1pm, and 1:30 to 5pm, as well as evenings Wednesday through Sunday from 8 to 10:30pm. Call ahead because they close the rink when the Los Angeles Kings practice here.

Admission is $5.25 for adults, $4.75 for children 12 and under. Skate rentals are $1.75, and children's sizes are available.

Located in Burbank, the **Pickwick Ice Center,** 1001 Riverside Dr. (☎ 818/846-0032), is a place where the staff believes that any child, any age, can skate. Open on Monday, Wednesday, and Friday from 1:15 to 5:30pm; on Wednesday from 8:30 to 10pm; on Friday from 1:15 to 5:30pm; on Saturday and Sunday from 2:30 to 4:30pm and Saturday night 8pm to 10:30pm; and on Sunday from 2:30 to 4:30pm. Admission is $6 for adults, $5 for seniors and children to age 17 ($2 off for the short Tuesday-afternoon session). Skate rentals are $3.

Shopping Malls and Children's Stores

The **Beverly Center,** 8500 Beverly Blvd. (☎ 310/854-0070), with 900,000 square feet of retail space, one of Los Angeles's largest fully enclosed shopping complexes, is a good place for shopping, people-watching, or as a change of pace for wound-up little travelers. We can spend a couple of hours just walking from one end of the mall to the other, peeking into stores, visiting the animals in the pet shop, riding the glass-enclosed elevators, and stopping for a piece of pizza and some ice cream on the top floor. It's a particularly nice diversion on a hot smoggy day.

Its two flagship stores are The Broadway and Bullock's. Between them are approximately 200 shops and restaurants. On the sixth floor, the first retail floor, look for F.A.O. Schwarz, the New York–based fantasy toyland; the pet store, with puppies, kittens, and birds on display; GapKids and Baby Gap; Friends for "in" girls' clothes fitting infants on up; Brooks Stride Rite Shoes with popularly priced kids' shoes; and the first Warner Bros. Studio Store.

The Beverly Center houses Brentano's bookstores and Learning-smith. The 13-and-up visitors in your group will love to shop for clothes at Judy's, Express, and The Gap, or Benetton, Rampage, and Laura Ashley. On the eighth floor is the 13-screen Cineplex Odeon movie theater, offering first-run films, fast-food stands, and sit-down restaurants. A 15,000-square-foot Sam Goody's has a huge selection of CDs, tapes, and videos.

On the street level, there's the popular Hard Rock Café, California Pizza Kitchen, and Gaucho Grill.

Strollers and wheelchairs are available at the information booth, located on the sixth floor under the middle escalators. Parking entrances are on La Cienega, San Vicente, and Beverly Boulevards. Valet parking is available at the Beverly or La Cienega Boulevard entrance. There is a charge of $1 for three hours of parking.

The center shops are open Monday through Friday from 10am to 9pm, on Saturday till 8pm, and on Sunday from 11am to 6pm. The theaters and restaurants are open after shopping hours.

Century City Shopping Center & Marketplace, 10250 Santa Monica Blvd. (☎ 310/277-3898), is between "little" Santa Monica Boulevard and Constellation, and Century Park West and the Avenue of the Stars, on what was once the back lot of Twentieth Century Fox Studios. Since 1964 this center has been a favorite Westside open-air shopping center. Although it is more than 770,000 square feet and has more than 140 shops, it doesn't feel too large. It has always been a good place to keep energetic kids entertained and a safe place for an evening walk with tireless toddlers. Access to elevators for parents with strollers is not easy. There is an elevator from the parking lot to The Broadway department store, two in the Marketplace, and one in the parking garage. Steel structures shade the hot sun. A 14-theater complex shows first-run films.

There are lots of outdoor places to sit and watch the world go by while chomping on a hot dog from a bright-red cart. In addition to the outdoor specialty carts selling hot pretzels, popcorn, and hot dogs, in the international food hall, there are vendors specializing in ethnic foods, and there are several sit-down restaurants surrounding them. **DIVE!** is the latest addition, a 300-seat sub-sandwich spot simulating a submarine.

Toy stores such as Toy's International and Imaginarium are necessary stops, and the Disney Store, Stamp Stamp Stamp, and the Nature Company have special appeal. Gap Kids, Half Pint, Mille Petites Fleurs, and Petit Jardin are appealing for youngsters clothes. Judy's, Laura Ashley, and The Limited will appeal to the slightly older girls in your group. The Broadway and Bullock's are the two major department stores.

Parking is plentiful, and there's even that priceless Southern California phenomenon, valet parking, near the Little Santa Monica Boulevard entrance. Other parking entrances are on Constellation and Century Park West. Free parking is available with validation. The information booth is near The Broadway. No strollers are available. Open Monday through Friday from 10am to 9pm, on Saturday 11am to 8pm, and on Sunday from 11am to 7pm. Restaurants and theaters are open longer hours.

Santa Monica Place is another good mall. Completely renovated, it is located between Colorado Avenue and Broadway, between 2nd and 4th Streets (☎ 310/394-5451), Santa Monica Place has more than 160 shops and restaurants, including Robinson's on the west end and The Broadway at the east end. The three-story mall is completely covered with a glass skylight, giving it a bright, open feeling, very appropriate for Santa Monica. If you have time, don't miss the Public Ocean View Terrace on the third floor, where you'll see the huge expanse of the Pacific before you.

The highlight of the mall is located on the ground-floor level, where you will find a wishing pond with a waterfall. This is a great place to let the kids spend some time while you sit and relax.

After that, we start our excursion with a visit to Kids in Motion and KCET Store of Knowledge. Next, we're off to the Imaginarium and Toys International, and then on to the San Rios Surprises and Warner Bros. Studio Store.

The other stores of interest are Gap Kids, Baby Gap, Cotton Kids, and Gymboree. The food court is on the ground floor and gives you a great variety of fast food and other choices. You might also want to try the Panda Inn, a sit-down Mandarin-style restaurant (☎ 310/393-6557), Tilly's Terrace restaurant (☎ 310/393-1404), or the Avanti Trattoria (☎ 310/393-1655). Santa Monica Place is open Monday through Saturday from 10am to 9pm and on Sunday from 11am to 6pm. There's lots of parking.

The **Westside Pavilion,** 10800 W. Pico Blvd., West Los Angeles (☎ 310/474-6255), is a modernistic mall located between Westwood Boulevard and Overland Avenue. It has one of the best food courts in the city, offering almost anything you could want to eat. With Nordstrom and Robinson-May as the anchor stores located on either end of the shopping mall, the shops in the Westside Pavilion run the gamut in price.

Our all-time favorite is Walden Kids. This store has an area in which the kids can play on the floor to try out some of the goodies before Mom or Dad purchases them. It has a good selection of educational toys, computer software, and cassette tapes. Although it's a small shop, we've always found it to have a great collection of books.

Other shops of interest are GapKids, Brooks Shoes, Bergstrom's, Records West, and Mr. G's Toys. For older kids and computer buffs, check out the Electronics Boutique.

And a treat for everyone is Pet Headquarters, located in the expansion. You'll also find the Samuel Goldwyn Pavilion Cinemas here. There are four theaters. Mall hours are Monday through Friday from 10am to 9pm, on Saturday from 10am to 7pm, and on Sunday from 11am to 6pm. There is a Pavilions Market (☎ **310/470-2284**) located below ground level. Free parking. Rooftop parking is good for stroller access.

Children's Book World, 10580¹/₂ W. Pico Blvd., West Los Angeles (☎ **310/559-2665**), offers an extensive selection of books, educational aids, CDs, records, and cassettes for infants up to high schoolers. They carry a large selection of videos and foreign-language books. The staff is very helpful and loves to help adults and children find just that right book. Kids feel at home here, browsing and buying, then settling down for a good "read" on the children's couch while Mom and Dad make their purchases. There are storytelling sessions and author visits. Open Monday through Friday from 10am to 5:30pm and on Saturday till 5pm.

Lakeshore Learning Materials Store, 8888 Venice Blvd., Los Angeles (☎ **310/559-9630**), has a fabulous variety of educational books, toys, workbooks, records, and arts and crafts supplies. There are lots of materials here you can't find in most children's book or toy stores. Open Monday through Friday from 9am to 6:30pm, Saturday till 5pm, and on Sunday from 11am to 5pm.

FESTIVALS AND SEASONAL ACTIVITIES

While Los Angeles doesn't have a parade for every holiday and a festival for every event, it does have its fair share of exciting seasonal activities.

Renaissance Pleasure Faire

The traditional spring rite that takes place on weekends from mid-April to mid-June, the Renaissance Faire is a taste of Elizabethan England in southern California. The Faire is located at the Glen Helen Regional Park in San Bernardino, 55 minutes from downtown. Take the I-10 east to I-15 north; exit at Devore, at the intersection of I-215, if you're coming from the other direction (like Palm Springs).

Like opening a door to the past, visitors to the Faire often dress in costume and join the over 3,000 Elizabethans, from washerwoman and wench to jousting knight and nobleman in the centuries-old tradition of English rural faire.

The Faire is a *must-see* for children and adults of all ages. Here actors help you believe that you've stepped into Elizabethan England complete with 16th-century marketplace, authentic foods, and crafts. If you're in the mood, you can have quail, shepherd's pie, Cornish pasties, or sausages, not to mention the Southern California favorites of falafel and churros. But you'll not find hamburgers or hot dogs. If your kids are finicky eaters, plan accordingly and pack something for them. Adults pay $16.50; seniors and students 11–16, $13.50; children 3–11, $7.50; kids under 3, free. You can purchase tickets at the gate, or by phone (☎ toll free **800/52-FAIRE**). It's $2 less per ticket if you order by telephone.

Los Angeles County Fair

The Los Angeles County Fair goes on from September through the beginning of October. Far from being a rural town fair, most people are surprised to find out that the Los Angeles County Fair is the largest county fair in the world. In 1991 over 1.6 million people attended! Not a tiny event, to be sure.

Since 1922 the event has taken place in Pomona at the Los Angeles County Fair and Exposition Center, 1101 W. McKinley Ave. (☎ 714/623-3111), approximately 30 miles east of Los Angeles, two blocks north of I-10 (exit at Fairplex, White, or Garey Avenues). Today the fair is on 487 acres, with an astonishing variety of exhibits. Not only are there livestock and dairy exhibits, but there is fine art, photography, gems and minerals, even wines. Add to this 12 acres of carnival grounds, and you've got a kid's delight in the making.

A Note of Caution: It can be extremely hot and smoggy during the fair. Go early in the day, bring sunscreen, and wear hats and light clothing.

Admission costs $8 for adults, $6 for seniors, $4 for children 6–12; free for children under 6. Open Monday through Friday at 11am and on Saturday and Sunday at 10am. Buildings remain open until 10pm, except on Friday and Saturday, when they're open until 11pm. Call for this year's dates.

Other Annual Events

The **Tournament of Roses Parade** (January 1) in Pasadena (☎ 818/449-ROSE, a 24-hour, year-round hotline for parade and game information), held each New Year's Day.

Kite Flying Festivals (March) on Santa Monica Pier, Santa Monica (☎ 310/458-8900). Also occurs at other times during the year.

Blessing of the Animals (the day before Easter), on Olvera Street, downtown (☎ 213/628-7833).

Festival of Masks (October), Hancock Park (☎ 213/937-5544).

Renaissance Pleasure Faire (April—see above for details).

Cinco de Mayo (May 5), on Olvera Street, downtown (☎ 213/625-5045).

Children's Day (in May), in Little Tokyo, downtown (☎ 213/628-2725).

The **Hollywood Bowl** (the season begins in July and runs to September); tickets are usually available (☎ 213/850-2000).

Sports and Arts Festival (August and September) in Santa Monica (☎ 310/458-8311).

Nisei Week, Japanese Festival (August and September) in Little Tokyo, downtown (☎ 213/687-7193). Nisei Week is when Little Tokyo comes alive with carnivals, parades, and crafts.

Los Angeles County Fair (September and October—see above for details).

Marina del Rey Christmas Boat Parade (December) (☎ 310/821-0555).

Hollywood Christmas Parade (Sunday after Thanksgiving) (☎ 213/469-2337 or 213/461-4213).

ACTIVITIES BY AGE GROUPS

The following listings suggest activities divided into specific age brackets. Refer back to the individual descriptions for details and any age descriptions. Be sure to also check Chapter 12 on Greater Los Angeles for additional activities.

Teens and Preteens

Audience Participation Shows (Paramount Studios)
Barnsdall Art Park

Beverly Hills Trolley
California African-American Museum
California Museum of Science and Industry (Aerospace Hall, Technology Hall)
Chinatown
Craft and Folk Art Museum
Culver City Skating Rink
Doug Weston's Troubador
Farmers Market
Fisherman's Village
Gene Autry Western Heritage Museum
George C. Page Museum of La Brea Discoveries
Greek Theater
Griffith Park Laserium (The Laser Show)
Griffith Park Observatory and Planetarium
Griffith Park Travel Town
The Groundlings
Hollywood (Mann's Chinese Theatre, Hollywood Wax Museum)
J. Paul Getty Museum
J.P. Stables
Japanese American National Museum
La Brea Tar Pits (George C. Page Museum)
Little Tokyo
Live Insect Zoo (at Ralph M. Parsons Discovery Center)
Los Angeles County Fair
Los Angeles County Museum of Art (Ahmanson and Anderson Buildings)
Los Angeles Zoo
Museum of Contemporary Art
Museum of Flying
Museum of Natural History
The Music Center (Dorothy Chandler Pavilion, Ahmanson Theater, Mark Taper Forum)
Olvera Street
Pickwick Ice Center
Petersen Automotive Museum
Pro Sports
Raging Waters (speed slides, flume rides, and water rapids)
Renaissance Pleasure Faire
The Roxy
Santa Monica Pier
Sherman Oaks Castle Miniature Golf
Six Flags Magic Mountain (roller coasters and water flumes)
Southwest Museum
Studio Tours (Paramount Studios, Warner Bros., NBC Studio)
UCLA
Universal Amphitheater
Universal Studios
Venice Beach Ocean Front Walk
Westwood Village

School-Age Children

Angel's Attic
Barnsdall Art Park
Beverly Hills Trolley
California African-American Museum
California Museum of Science and Industry (Aerospace Hall, Technology Hall)
Chinatown
Craft and Folk Art Museum
Culver City Skating Rink
Farmers Market
Fisherman's Village
Fun Zone (Santa Monica Pier)
Gene Autry Western Heritage Museum
George C. Page Museum
Griffith Park Merry-Go-Round
Griffith Park Observatory and Planetarium
Griffith Park Travel Town
Hollywood (Mann's Chinese Theatre, Hollywood Wax Museum)
J. Paul Getty Museum
J.P. Stables
Japanese American National Museum
La Brea Tar Pits (George C. Page Museum)
Little Tokyo
Los Angeles Children's Museum (Ethnic L.A. exhibit)
Los Angeles County Fair
Los Angeles County Museum of Art (Ahmanson and Anderson Buildings, Central Court)
Los Angeles Zoo
Museum of Contemporary Art
Museum of Flying
Museum of Natural History
Olvera Street
Petersen Automotive Museum
Pickwick Ice Center
Pro Sports
Raging Waters (Little Dipper, playground, and water rides)
Ralph M. Parsons Discovery Center and Live Insect Zoo (Museum of Natural History)
Renaissance Pleasure Faire
Santa Monica Pier
Sherman Oaks Castle Miniature Golf
Six Flags Magic Mountain (Bugs Bunny World and rides)
Southwest Museum
Studio Tours (Paramount Studios, Warner Bros., NBC Studio)
UCLA
Universal Studios
Venice Beach Ocean Front Walk

Preschoolers and Toddlers

Barnsdall Art Park
Culver City Skating Rink
Farmers Market
Fisherman's Village
Fun Zone (Santa Monica Pier)
Gene Autry Western Heritage Museum
George C. Page Museum
Griffith Park Carousel
Griffith Park Miniature Train, Pony Rides, Simulator
Los Angeles Children's Museum
Los Angeles County Fair
Los Angeles Zoo
Museum of Natural History
Olvera Street
Pickwick Ice Center
Ralph M. Parsons Discovery Center and Live Insect Zoo (Museum
   of Natural History)
Renaissance Pleasure Faire
UCLA
Sherman Oaks Castle Miniature Golf

In Case of Emergency

Should a life-or-death emergency arise during your visit to Los Angeles, call **911** for the police or fire department, or an ambulance. In addition, there are a number of hospitals and pharmacies with extended hours available to you.

HOSPITALS   The following hospitals have 24-hour emergency rooms: **Cedars-Sinai Medical Center,** 8700 Beverly Blvd., Los Angeles (☎ **310/855-5000,** or **310/855-6517** for the emergency room); **Queen of Angels Hollywood Presbyterian Medical Center,** 1300 N. Vermont Ave., Los Angeles (☎ **213/413-3000,** or **213/913-4896** for the emergency room); and the **Glendale Adventist Medical Center,** 1509 Wilson Terrace, Glendale (☎ **818/409-8000,** or **818/409-8202** for the emergency room).

PHARMACIES WITH EXTENDED HOURS   The following Los Angeles pharmacies offer extended-hour services: **Horton & Converse,** 11600 Wilshire Blvd., West L.A. (☎ **310/478-0801**); open until 2am; **Thrifty Drugs Store,** 300 N. Cañon Dr., Beverly Hills (☎ **310/273-7293**), open 24 hours, and **Thrifty Drugs Store,** 4633 Santa Monica Blvd., Hollywood (☎ **213/666-6126**), open daily from 8am to 10pm.

In Van Nuys in the San Fernando Valley: **Horton & Converse,** 6625 Van Nuys Blvd. (☎ **818/782-6251**), open daily from 8:30am to 2am.

12

Greater Los Angeles

GREATER LOS ANGELES SPRAWLS FROM THE SAN GABRIEL MOUNTAINS TO THE SEA, from Malibu south to Long Beach. The communities surrounding L.A. don't have to be in the city proper to be part of the Los Angeles scene. And lucky for us. Greater Los Angeles offers so many family activities that you'll have difficulty deciding what to do.

You can visit the island of Catalina, with its tiny town of Avalon and vast wilderness. The kids can don Sunday clothes and you can head to Pasadena, the grand dame of the area and haven of artistic masterpieces.

And if you just want to experience the idyllic Southern California lifestyle, there are miles of sandy white beaches on which you and the kids can swim, surf, boogie board—and just soak up the sun. Children can play; teens can people-watch.

We start with a day in L.A.—the beaches, that is.

1   The Beach Communities—Malibu, Manhattan, Redondo, and San Pedro

Malibu is world famous as a haven for movie stars and celebrities, but its recreational possibilities for families are less widely known.

The drive on the Pacific Coast Highway (Calif. 1) through Malibu is part of the experience. The 27 miles of shoreline front shimmering emerald seas. Eroded cliffs and chaparral-covered rolling hills border the Pacific Coast Highway. Tile-roofed Spanish-style villas and homes with huge picture windows line the beach for miles at a stretch. Then, as you get farther up the coast, Malibu becomes more rural. Homes dot the hillsides of the Santa Monica Mountains, and kennels and boarding stables appear. The best beaches are here.

While restaurant prices in this affluent community are higher than in many other parts of Los Angeles County, there are many fast-food favorites—and you can picnic at the beach or in the parks.

This part of the Santa Monica Bay coastline runs east and west. When people say they're going "up" the coast to Malibu, it's because here Malibu is actually west of Santa Monica. The coastline starts to curve north near the Los Angeles–Ventura County line. Note that the Pacific Coast Hwy. (PCH, as it is affectionately known) becomes clogged with beach-going traffic on weekends and every day in summer. Plan for this in your schedule and bring things for the kids to do in the car if you should get hopelessly stuck in traffic.

Before you start out, you might want to contact the **Malibu Chamber of Commerce,** 23805 Stuart Ranch Rd., no. 100, Malibu, CA 90265 (☎ **310/456-9025**).

WHAT TO SEE AND DO IN MALIBU

Here are a few recreational activities for your family to enjoy.

J. Paul Getty Museum

Set on a hill overlooking the Malibu shores is the **J. Paul Getty Museum,** 17985 Pacific Coast Hwy., at Coastline (☎ **310/458-2003** for information and reservations). The building that houses the museum is in itself worth the trip. A re-creation of an Italian villa, complete with fountains and ornate pools, the building and the surrounding complex are very impressive.

The Getty has a very positive attitude toward children. Gallery teachers routinely take groups of elementary-school children through the collections and express delight when children bubble with enthusiasm and questions. Kids are encouraged (both individually and in groups) to look closely. Parents of young children are not admonished if their children are noisy, but instead are invited to take a break with the kids in the lovely gardens.

Parents who have taken their kids to the Getty Museum think it's best to keep the visits very short. On an outing with then 7-year-old Andrew, we found that he was completely enchanted by the statues of the mythological gods and the ornate antique furniture but his attention waned after viewing only a few paintings. Even so, he loves to return again and again.

Gallery teachers think that most of the exhibits are good for families, including the Decorative Arts Collection, paintings from the 12th century to the early 20th century, and the Antiquities Collection (artifacts from ancient life). Their attitude is that children are never too young to start appreciating fine art. Children will enjoy the experience if their parents don't expect too much of them.

The Getty hosts an excellent and extensive series of programs expressly for families. Each month, small groups of children with their parents would delve into one aspect of the art that is presented in the museum. For example, one workshop was on mythology. The gallery instructor took them through the appropriate collection of art and statues, and when they finished viewing, they were told to talk with their parents and create a myth about their families or their lives. Other workshops might cover portraiture, or animals on puzzling pots. If you want to participate, you must sign up in advance. Call or write for more information about these special family programs.

Because there are limited parking facilities, you must also make a (free) parking reservation 7–10 days in advance (by mail or telephone). You cannot park on the streets near the museum. Since there is no walk-in traffic permitted, you may enter the museum grounds only by bicycle, motorcycle, taxi, or MTA bus (no. 434—get a museum pass from the driver).

The Getty Museum is open Tuesday through Saturday from 10am to 5pm. There is no admission charge.

Swimming Beaches

Malibu beaches vary from rocky caves and little pocket beaches to long white sandy stretches. Let's begin at the western tip of Malibu.

Leo Carillo State Beach (☎ 818/706-1310) is a 1,600-acre beach and campground that offers a wonderful day in the sun and salt air. Leo Carillo has a nature trail, tidepools, even sea caves, in addition to good swimming and surfing. The caves remind us of the home of the dragon in the movie *Pete's Dragon*. The waves splash up through the tunnel-like caves, taunting us to get wet. We jump to avoid them, but of course, that's all part of the fun since we're in swimsuits anyway.

Although exploring the caves is a wondrous experience for most kids, be prepared to carry the younger children. One 4-year-old boy we saw seemed scared to explore the twisting caves, but enjoyed them when his mother carried him. The beach has restrooms, lifeguards, firepits, and a parking lot. (See the "Where to Stay" section below, for details about the campground.)

Nicolas Canyon County Beach (☎ 310/457-9891) is a delightful, small beach that's hidden from the road by eroded cliffs that rise out of the sand. It's about one mile east of Leo Carillo (across from the Malibu Riding and Tennis Club) and about five miles west of Zuma. Parking is available above the beach. There are stairs and a ramp down.

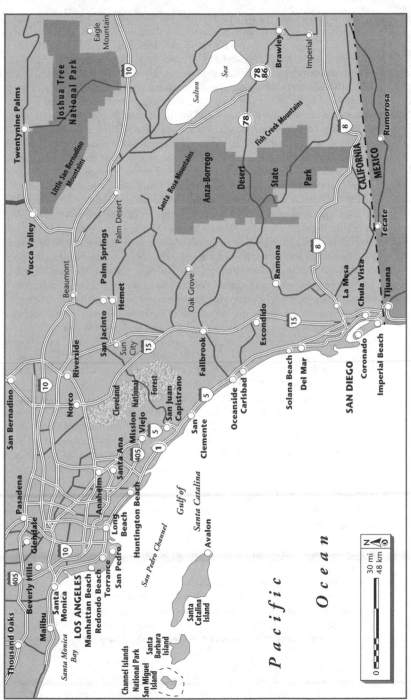

The Southern Coast

Zuma Beach County Park (☎ 310/457-9891 or 310/457-2527) is a large, sandy beach with playground equipment, snack bar, restrooms, lifeguards, and lots of parking space. During spring break and summer vacations, San Fernando Valley children and teens flock to this long, wide stretch of beach for sunbathing, surfing, and ogling.

If you continue to walk southeast from Zuma, you'll come to **Westward Beach** (☎ 310/457-9891). This long, narrow beach has good swimming, boogie boarding, and surfing. Edged by cliffs that give a secluded atmosphere, Westward Beach is a good choice for families. Restrooms and parking are available; lifeguards are on duty.

Malibu Lagoon State Beach and the adjacent **Surfrider Beach** (☎ 310/456-9497) are perfect for little kids and for teens, too. Youngsters can watch as wet-suited surfers ride the waves. Until recently, this picturesque beach also offered lagoon wading as well; pollution has taken its toll on that recreation. But the lagoon is still home to ducks and birds, and its banks afford wonderful wandering. Picnic tables, restrooms, and parking are available; lifeguards are on duty.

Zuma Jay Surfboards, 22775 Pacific Coast Hwy. (☎ 310/456-8044), is the place to rent surfboards ($20 a day), boogie boards ($6 a day) and wet suits ($5 a day). Hydrobikes—you sit and peddle in the ocean—rent for $50 a day, $35 for a half day.

You need to reserve months in advance for the once-a-month nature walks sponsored by the William O. Douglas Outdoor Classroom. **Babes at the Beach** is a sensory nature walk, led by a naturalist, designed especially for children 3 months to 6 years and their parents. The group explores the estuary and tidepool habitats; the nature guide points out the various marine animals in the intertidal zone. They actually go out on the rocks and explore the tidepools and look at the starfish, sea urchins, and anemones that live there. It's free, but be sure to tell the reservationist that you're coming from out of town—extra effort will be made to try to fit you in. Call or write for a specific date and time to the William O. Douglas Outdoor Classroom, P.O. Box 2488, Beverly Hills, CA 90213 (☎ 310/858-3834).

If you're interested in the local culture, there is a little-known treasure adjacent to the lagoon that you can tour. The **Malibu Lagoon Museum and Historic Adamson House,** 23200 Pacific Coast Hwy. (☎ 310/456-8432), is reminiscent of Hearst Castle on a tiny scale. The home was built for Rhoda Rindge Adamson, daughter of May and Frederick Rindge, who were the last owners of the Rancho Malibu Spanish land grant. One of the family businesses was the Malibu Potteries, which produced exquisitely colored ceramic tiles. To our knowledge, the Malibu Pier was built before the Malibu Potteries was founded in 1926, to service the Rindge Cattle Ranch and to bring supplies to build the Rindge railroad. The use of the decorative tile throughout the house and gardens is fantastic. There are rare, beautiful fountains, hand-carved doors, and filigreed wrought iron. The small museum gives a chronology of Malibu's history—from its Chumash Native American origins through its growth as a most desired small rural seaside community. In addition, this is one of the most spectacular views of the ocean, Malibu Pier, and the lagoon.

The museum and house are open for tours Wednesday through Saturday from 11am to 3pm. Reservations are made for large groups to tour on Tuesday. Admission is $2. The gardens are open from dawn to dusk. Parking is on the Pacific Coast Hwy. or in the adjacent Los Angeles County parking lot for $5 during the summer months.

Parks in the Santa Monica Mountains

The Santa Monica Mountains, which run east and west along the coast, offer many beautiful places to explore, from deep canyons to hilltop vista points, and they provide miles of hiking trails and splendid picnicking.

Malibu Creek State Park (☎ 818/880-0350 or 818/706-1310) is located in the mountains halfway between Malibu and the San Fernando Valley about 100 yards south of Mulholland Hwy. on Las Virgenes/Malibu Canyon Road. The park has over 30 miles of hiking trails, canyons, a lake, and waterfalls. The main trail, Crags Road, will take you past the spot where television's "M*A*S*H" was filmed. The trail has one hill—the rest is level—and the round-trip is about five miles, with good picnicking en route. Ask at the visitor center about other good trails. The visitor center is open weekends only, from noon to 4pm. The parking fee is $5.

Tapia County Park (☎ 310/457-7247) is a smaller park located near Malibu Creek State Park, five miles south of Calif. 101 (Ventura Freeway) on Las Virgenes/Malibu Canyon Road. The park has hiking trails and good picnic areas.

The **Peter Strauss Ranch** at Lake Encanto (☎ 818/888-3770) is actually in Agoura on Mulholland Hwy. If you're coming from U.S. 101, exit at Kanan Road, go south to Troutdale, and turn left onto Mulholland Highway. If you're coming from Malibu, go up to Kanan Road to Troutdale, then take a right onto Mulholland Highway. There are a few good trails and a nature walk, plus special children's events, including music festivals and ranger-led hikes. Call for more information.

Topanga State Park (☎ 310/455-2465 or 818/706-1310) has a self-guided nature trail in addition to 35 miles of trails. It's located off Topanga Canyon Road at 20825 Entrada Rd., Topanga Canyon. The park is open daily: April through October from 8am to 7pm, November through March from 8am to 5pm.

For information about other parks in the Santa Monica Mountains, see "Outdoor Activities" under "What to See and Do" in Chapter 11.

Nursery Walks

If you hesitate to take your little ones on nature hikes . . . don't. **Nursery Walks,** sponsored by the Palisades-Malibu YMCA, 821 Via de la Paz, Pacific Palisades, CA 90272 (☎ 310/964-3955), is an organization of volunteers who lead nature walks for infants, toddlers, and preschoolers. Their goal is to develop an appreciation and love for the out-of-doors, so that as children get older, they will have a healthy respect for the environment. The walks are two hours long, and about half a mile in length. About halfway, they take a break.

Leaders get the children to try and use all the senses—they do a lot of looking, listening, and touching. For example, they'll pretend to be Native Americans so they learn to be quiet and listen to the sounds in the quiet. They'll do such activities as using flowers to make soap, matching rocks to their environment, smelling leaves, and talking about their purposes. During the summer, most of the walks are either along the coast or during the evenings when they're paired with a picnic dinner (each family brings their own).

If you have older kids also, they're welcome. Although the programs are geared for younger kids, leaders attempt to involve the older ones in the activities as well. Call **213/964-3955** for reservations. It's best to try to make them ten days to two weeks in advance. A donation of $4 is requested.

The nursery walks in this area are conducted at Leo Carillo, Malibu Lagoon, and Topanga State Park. Phone for reservations a month in advance.

WHERE TO STAY IN MALIBU

The choices for overnight stays are limited. We suggest that you take a room in nearby Santa Monica (see "Where to Stay" in Chapter 11) or camp out.

If you prefer a motel in pricey Malibu, we recommend the **Casa Malibu Inn on the Beach,** 22752 Pacific Coast Hwy. (Calif. 1), Malibu, CA 90265 (☎ **310/ 456-2219** or toll free **800/831-0858**). This garden motel, opened in the late 1940s, is clean, newly renovated and well kept; it has a tidy little garden that opens onto a large patio with an ocean view. Steps lead down to a quiet little beach, and sand chairs, towels and showers are provided. Each room of the motel is shaped differently and accommodates a different number of people.

The motel has its share of older families and prefers quiet, well-behaved children or teens. The ocean-view rooms (some are just above the sand) have one king-size bed or two double beds and decks with lounge chairs; other rooms have a garden view. All rooms have coffee makers, color TVs, telephones, and small refrigerators.

The rates are the same for single or double occupancy: $95–$155. Rooms with kitchens can be rented for an extra $10 per day (three-day minimum rental). Each additional person beyond double occupancy, including children, is charged $10 per day. Cribs and rollaways are available. Reserve early for summer.

Camping

The best camping in the area is at **Leo Carillo State Beach,** 35000 Pacific Coast Hwy. (Calif. 1) (☎ **818/880-0350**), where a 134-site campground nestles into the canyon near the beach.

There is a 31-foot limit for RVs or trailers. There are no hookups, but they do have a dump station. There are restrooms, hot showers, and a camp convenience store open from 7am to 7pm daily in summer.

The nightly fee is $14 per campsite (eight-person maximum per site). There are ranger-led nature walks on Sunday and campfire programs on Saturday nights. You may reserve a campsite through MISTIX (☎ toll free **800/444-PARK**).

WHERE TO EAT IN MALIBU

The ultimate in California casual is **Gladstone's 4-Fish,** 17300 Pacific Coast Hwy. (☎ **310/GL4-FISH**), located on the beach where Sunset Boulevard meets the ocean. A local favorite, Gladstone's has sawdust on the floor, large wooden booths with benches, and glass panels throughout. Views through the large windows look out at the sandy beach and the blue water.

People go for the view, the atmosphere, and the seafood. On Saturday and Sunday mornings the place is brimming with families who get an early start for breakfast and spend the rest of the day at the beach. This popularity means that the place can get noisy, and there's sometimes a wait for a table even with reservations. But this shouldn't be a problem, because there's a little ramp to the beach where you can go for a stroll while you wait.

The kitchen states they'll prepare anything on the menu from 7am on— including seafood—but we prefer our fish for lunch or dinner. Traditional breakfasts range from $5.95 to $11.95.

We love the seafood. The huge assortment of fish and shellfish will delight seafood lovers. Entrees can be simple (mesquite-broiled fresh sea bass) or more elaborate (fresh salmon steamed in parchment with tomatoes, onions, mushrooms, and scallions). There are clams, shrimp, oysters, mussels, crab, and lobster, too. The six seafood salads are heavenly. Steak and burgers are also available. Dinners include chowder or salad, bread, and potato or vegetable. Main-dish prices range from $7.95 to market-price lobster.

Gladstone's is open Sunday through Thursday from 7am to 11pm and on Friday and Saturday from 7am to midnight. There are booster seats, but no highchairs. Reservations are recommended and major credit cards are welcome. Valet parking.

Carlos and Pepe's Seafood Grill, at 22706 W. Pacific Coast Hwy. (☎ 310/456-3105), graciously welcomes children. This south-of-the-border lookalike has terracotta floors, artificial palm trees, and parrots all around—but the real kid pleaser is the aquarium filled with tropical fish.

Every seat has an ocean view and there is a path to the beach adjacent to the restaurant. Some parents select a table by the windows and let older kids play outside while they have their meal. There's also outside seating on the deck and, in summer time, tables right on the sand.

Typical Mexican fare, seafood, hamburgers, sandwiches, and salads are served here. Our kids gobble down the chips and mild salsa and pretend to be very sophisticated when drinking the non-alcoholic margaritas in huge glasses with straws. Adult dinners range from $8.50 to $14.75; seafood items are higher. Open Monday through Saturday from 11:30am to 11pm and on Sunday from 11am to 11pm. There are booster seats and highchairs. No reservations are accepted, so expect to wait. Come before 6pm if you don't want to linger for 1–1½ hours in the waiting area. If you have a short wait, you can always wander out onto the beach. Valet parking.

For standard, moderately priced American food, the **Malibu Inn and Restaurant,** 22969 Pacific Coast Hwy. (☎ 310/456-6106), is a good place to try. It's like stepping into a Victorian-style greenhouse. Saloon doors, wood floors, carved posts, and celebrity photographs on the walls comprise the eclectic interior.

Lunch and dinner items include creative sandwiches and salads, eggs, and omelets priced at $3–$6. For dinner there's seafood, chowder, oyster stew, fish and chips, chicken or shrimp fajitas, and terriyaki chicken at prices ranging from $7 to $13.

Booster seats are available. Open Sunday through Thursday from 6:30am to 10pm, on Friday and Saturday till 11pm. No reservations accepted (on weekends the wait is about 20 minutes to an hour; avoid the wait on weekends and eat before 9am or after 2pm). Some major credit cards welcome. Parking is available.

WHAT TO SEE AND DO IN MANHATTAN BEACH AND REDONDO BEACH

If Malibu is a rustic retreat for the rich and famous, the South Bay beach towns of Manhattan and Redondo are the suburban havens for the upwardly mobile. Charming beachfront cottages, multilevel condominiums, and high-priced apartments line the beaches. On busy weekends the beaches teem with families carrying ice coolers, Frisbees, and exotic sand toys. Bicyclists pedal their way along the shorefront bike path, recognized as one of the best in Southern California. Well-built singles roller skate or lounge on the beach, eyeing each other and checking out the action.

You, too, can play volleyball, roller skate, bicycle, surf, and swim in these sandy sanctuaries. And while the beaches may be more crowded than those in Malibu, they're less crowded than those of their northern neighbor, Santa Monica. Parking, though, is tough.

Redondo Beach is probably the best-known town in the area. It boasts a colorful history. In 1890 well-known entrepreneur Henry Huntington opened the Hotel Redondo on a bluff overlooking the Pacific. In 1907 during a vacation in Hawaii, Huntington saw a young Polynesian man ride the ocean waves using planks of wood. Huntington invited the young man, George Freeth, to do surfing exhibitions at his new Hotel Redondo as a way to advertise the property. In 1909 a plunge was built, and Freeth trained lifeguards to protect the thousands of weekly bathers. Freeth, called the Father of Surfing, is acclaimed as the first American lifeguard, and even won congressional medals for his rescues.

Contact the **Manhattan Beach Chamber of Commerce,** P.O. Box 3007, Manhattan Beach, CA 90266 (☎ **310/545-5313**), and the **Redondo Beach Chamber of Commerce,** 1215 N. Catalina Ave., Redondo Beach, CA 90277 (☎ **310/376-6913**), for information.

Beaches

One of the first features you'll notice about South Bay beaches are their width. Some are incredibly wide stretches of sand (and unbearably hot on bare feet after the sand has baked in the sun).

Manhattan State Beach is a large beach with a playground, restrooms, outdoor showers, and volleyball courts. Parking is difficult; try to come early to get a spot. The South Bay Bicycle Trail runs along the edge of the sand. The adjacent 900-foot **Manhattan Beach Pier,** located at the foot of Manhattan Beach Boulevard, is a lovely place to stroll. This is also the area to find food and sundries.

The **Seaside Lagoon** (☎ **310/318-0682**) is located in Redondo Beach at the southwest corner of Harbor Drive and Portofino Way. This large heated saltwater lagoon has a wading area and diving boards; it's a wonderful swimming area for children of all ages. There's a sandy beach, lifeguards, playground equipment, volleyball courts, restrooms, hot showers, and a snack bar. Open from Memorial Day to early September, daily from 10am to 5:45pm. Adults pay $2.50; children 2-17, $1.25.

Redondo State Beach is a very wide beach located below the bluffs. It has lifeguards, restrooms, and parking. The South Bay Bicycle Trail follows the coast here.

If you're here during August, check out the **International Surf Festival.** Teens will love the lifeguard competition; younger kids will love the sandcastle-design contests. It's one of more than 20 fun events. For information, call **310/318-0680**.

The place to rent boogie boards or wet suits is **Dive 'n Surf,** 504 N. Broadway, next to the Sheraton in Redondo Beach (☎ **310/372-8423**). Boogie boards rent for $8.50 for first day, $4 per day thereafter; wet suits cost $12.50 per day, and short or spring wet suits are $9 per day. All items are half price for each additional day.

Bike Path

The **South Bay Bicycle Trail** is part of a longer trail that extends north and south. This bike path is over 22 miles long, if you take it all the way from Will Rogers Beach in the north to Torrance Beach in the south. This is probably the most popular bike path in the Los Angeles area, which means it's best to do it early or late in the day to avoid the crowds. It's even better if you can do it off-season. In fact, we prefer the bike path during the spring, fall, and winter because the air is crisp, making it more comfortable to ride long distances. We also find that the kids do it better when there aren't so many other riders stacked up.

The wide path (with markers indicating the direction of traffic) follows the beach, making for enjoyable watching as well as easy riding. We usually start at Fisherman's Village in Marina del Rey (see "What to See and Do" in Chapter 11) and head south. If you choose to go all the way south, you'll ride 12 miles from this point. Or you may choose to drive to any parking area near the beach and pick up the bike path there. There are restrooms and telephones along the way.

Also along the way, you may stop at Manhattan Beach Pier, Hermosa Beach Pier, or Redondo's King Harbor.

Bicycle Rentals

To rent bicycles, try the **Hermosa Cyclery,** 20 13th St., Hermosa Beach (one block north of the Hermosa Pier) (☎ **310/376-2720**). They rent children's bicycles for $5 per hour or $15 per day; adult bikes are $6–$10 per hour or $18–$36 per day, depending on the type of bike. Carriers and helmets are free with bike rental. They also rent roller skates or rollerblades for $5–$6 per hour or $15–$18 per day. Children's skates are available.

Open daily from 8am to 9pm in summer, 8am to 8pm in winter. Reservations are not accepted, so it's best to get there before 10am in summer and on weekends.

Fun Bunns Beach Rentals, 1116 Manhattan Ave., Manhattan Beach (☎ **310/ 372-8500**), one block from the beach, rents adult and children's bikes, toddler carriers, and roller skates (children's size 4 to men's size 13). Helmets, knee guards, blade skates, mountain bikes, and wrist guards are available. Rates are $6.50–$8.50 per hour per bike; tandem bikes cost $12 per hour; skates are $5.50 and $6.50 per hour. Open daily from 10am to dusk.

King Harbor and Redondo Beach Pier

King Harbor and Redondo Beach Municipal Pier, at the foot of Torrance Boulevard (☎ **310/318-0630** or **310/318-0631**), offer restaurants, fast-food eateries, shopping, pier fishing, fish markets, and a fun zone, all within view of sailboats and yachts. The **International Boardwalk,** located just north of the pier, has shops and casual eateries; it's open 365 days a year. The **Redondo Fun Factory** (☎ **310/379-8510**) is a 30,000-square-foot indoor "carnival" with hundreds of video-pinball games and rides; it's open daily from noon to 10pm.

Redondo Sport Fishing Pier, located at 233 Harbor Dr. (☎ **310/372-2111** or **213/772-2064**), offers sport fishing and pier fishing. They have a barge that is good for children because there is less motion. You may go for an hour at a time. The barge is open daily from 7am to 4:30pm, and in summer also from 6pm to midnight. The barge is closed from December to Easter vacation. Half-day trips aboard sports fishing boats (4^1/$_2$ hours) are $19 for adults and $14 for children under 12. Eight-hour trips are $28 for adults and $10 for children. Full-day trips (from midnight to 6pm) cost $47 for adults and $42 for children; full day rates include bait, bunk, and parking. Pier poles rent for $7. Live bait is available. The pier is open 24 hours a day.

Whale-watching cruises start at the end of December and continue through April.

WHAT TO SEE AND DO IN SAN PEDRO

Pack up the kids for a journey to the seaside area of San Pedro. San Pedro Bay is home to one of the world's largest artificial harbors—Los Angeles Harbor. But San Pedro offers more than cargo and freighters; it has two enchanting areas you'll want to explore.

Cabrillo Marine Aquarium

Children and parents will delight in an excursion to the Cabrillo Marine Aquarium. It's a marvelous place to spend at least a half day and for children of all ages to see marine life of Southern California. Located within a stone's throw of the ocean, at 3720 Stephen White Dr. (☎ **310/548-7562**), the Cabrillo Marine Museum has 35 seawater aquaria that are home to hundreds of marine species and plantlife. The elaborate displays—kelp forests, rocky shores, and sandy habitats—are arranged especially for children and can be viewed from all sides. Skilled docents explain the exhibits at children's level. The high point of our trip was the touching pool where the children got to hold anemones, sea stars, and sea cucumbers.

You may want to take a tour, then go back and browse more leisurely through the exhibits. There is also a variety of fascinating children's programs, ranging from one-day workshops to week-long sessions. Call for reservations and information.

There is no admission charge, but there is a $6.60-per-car charge for parking. Open Tuesday through Friday from noon to 5pm and on Saturday and Sunday from 10am to 5pm; closed Thanksgiving and Christmas Days. The last touch tank hour is 3:30pm and the giftshop closes at 3:30pm also. To get to the Cabrillo Marine Aquarium, take the Harbor Freeway (I-110) south to the end, turn left onto Gaffey Street, left onto 22nd Street, right onto Pacific Avenue, then left onto 36th Street.

Across the parking lot from the aquarium is a grassy area and a wonderful beach. **Cabrillo Beach** (☎ **310/832-1179**) has very gentle waves because it's inside the breakwater that protects the harbor. It offers perfect swimming for children, yet has enough action to let them dodge the low-breaking waves. Check the tide tables and try to be there during low tide so you can wander through the tidepools on the rocks. **Careful, though, it's slippery.** Take water shoes or old sneakers for the rocks.

Ports O' Call Village, Whaler's Wharf, and Fisherman's Village

Spend a few pleasant hours at Ports O' Call Village (☎ **310/831-0287**), Whaler's Wharf, and Fisherman's Village, located at Berth 77 on the main channel of Los Angeles Harbor. Cobblestone streets and waterfront dining make you feel as if you've suddenly landed in an old New England seaport town. There are three villages, each with its own flavor. One has huge fresh fish markets and open-air barbecues where you can have the fish cooked to order. Many visitors buy drinks and enjoy the delectable fish on the open-air decks.

Altogether the villages have 15 eateries (including better restaurants, light-fare places, and fast-food stops), 75 shops, and boathouses for harbor cruises and whale-watching trips. Our favorite stop is **Candy Town** (☎ **310/514-2669**). This emporium offers everything from imported chocolates to sweet dinosaur eggs.

Strolling through villages are musicians and clowns. But the real treat is watching the traffic in the harbor. We saw tugboats, huge freighters, cruise ships, and sailboats. Kids squeal when they see a pelican, and hungry seagulls are part of the fun.

Open daily from 11am to 9pm in summer, until 7pm the rest of the year. There's plenty of free parking. To get to Ports O' Call, take the Harbor Freeway (I-110) south to Harbor Boulevard, exit in San Pedro, and turn right onto Harbor Boulevard; then turn left at 6th Street and follow the signs.

To really get a sense of the harbor, take the **Los Angeles Harbor Cruise** (☎ **310/ 831-0996**). This one-hour trip goes all around the harbor, passing the Vincent Thomas Bridge, Terminal Island Federal Prison, and Angel's Gate Lighthouse. Television lovers will enjoy seeing the home of "The Love Boat." Our (then) 7-year-old especially liked the supertankers and freighters that we saw. School-age children do well for half the trip; after that, it's a bit of a struggle to keep them entertained. We brought snacks and trinkets for them.

2 Catalina

"Twenty-six miles across the sea. . . ." Actually, it's 22 miles across the sea to Santa Catalina Island, the island of romance.

First discovered by Juan Cabrillo in 1542, it wasn't until 1892 that the island was purchased and turned into the Santa Catalina Island Company for the purpose of becoming a pleasure resort. The island has been the home to the Catalina Native Americans and to sea otters, both of which were wiped out by the Russians and their accompanying tribes of fierce Aleut and Kodiak Indians. It was also home to pirates, cattle- and sheepherders, fur traders, and miners.

The year 1919 marked the beginning of its prime development phase when William Wrigley, Jr., bought controlling interest in the company. He was instrumental in preserving the island's wilderness. The Santa Catalina Island Conservancy was organized in the early 1970s to preserve and protect the more than 42,000 acres of wilderness areas.

It was the Wrigleys who really made the island a popular vacation spot. Although a great place to spend a romantic weekend, Catalina is not just for twosomes. The activities are numerous, and there's something for everyone in the family. You can enjoy Catalina as a day trip from Los Angeles.

GETTING THERE

There are several ways to get to Catalina Island.

By Boat

From Los Angeles, you can choose Catalina Express or Catalina Cruises. Rough waters, of course, can cause seasickness, in which case, liquid Dramamine, extra plastic bags, and a change of clothes come in handy even for a day trip.

Catalina Express, which leaves from Berth 95, Port of Los Angeles Harbor (Catalina Sea and Air Terminal) in San Pedro, or Catalina Express Port/Queen Mary Landing in Long Beach (☎ **310/519-1212, 310/510-1212** on the island, or toll free **800/995-4386**), whisks you to Avalon from San Pedro and Long Beach in one hour. Two new state-of-the-art boats now make the San Pedro to Avalon run shorter and smoother. Catalina Express is the boat service we recommend. It has airline-style seats, cabin-attendant service, and refreshments. The open upper deck is great on a sunny day or mild evening. Boats travel to Avalon and Two Harbors year-round. In summer there are as many as 22 departures daily; in winter, as many as 16. Reservations are required; call for specific times. Tickets can be purchased by calling **310/519-1212** or through TicketMaster (☎ **213/480-3232;** ask for the Catalina line). With TicketMaster, a $4 service charge is added to each round trip ticket. Round-trip fares from San Pedro and Long Beach are $35 for adults, $32 for seniors, $26 for children 2-11, $2 for children under 2.

Catalina Cruises boasts three 700-passenger triple-deck vessels that leave from downtown Long Beach, 320 Golden Shore. Take the Long Beach Freeway (I-710) to the downtown Long Beach Golden Shore exit. The trip to Catalina takes 1³/₄ hours. On board are snack bars, beverage counters, and table seating. Reservations are not necessary on weekdays, including summer. For weekend and holiday reservations, call toll free **800/CATALINA.** Tickets may be purchased through TicketMaster (☎ **213/480-3232**). Round-trip fares are $21 for adults and seniors, $19 for children 2–11, and $2 for children under 2.

From Orange County you leave from Balboa Pavilion in Newport Beach. The catamaran *Catalina Flyer*, operated by **Catalina Passenger Service** (☎ **714/673-5245**), holds 500 passengers and has three decks, snack service, and a full bar. The trip takes 1¹/₄ hours; there is one round-trip scheduled per day, leaving at 9am and returning at 4:30pm. Call ahead for reservations. Round-trip fares are $32.50 for adults, $16.50 for children 3–12, $2 for children under 2.

By Air

Island Express (☎ **310/510-2525**) is a jet helicopter service that leaves from San Pedro and Long Beach (from a helipad near the *Queen Mary*). Call for reservations and directions to the helipad. Fares are $110 round-trip for anyone over age 2.

ORIENTATION

Welcome to Avalon, Santa Catalina's main and only town. Avalon's year-round population of a little over 3,000 swells in summer to 6,000 on weekdays and 10,000 on weekends. Avalon boasts 267 days of sunshine, and an average high temperature of 76° and an average low of 58.4° June through October. Mid-October and mid-April are its wet months. Summers rarely get above 80°; winters, rarely below 50°.

Avalon itself is only about one square mile in size. The island is 21 miles long and 8 miles wide. The interior of the island is wild, beautiful, and pristine—and off-limits to private vehicles, and hikers and campers without permits. Protected by the Catalina Conservancy, whose job is to preserve it for posterity, it is accessible by tour bus or permit.

Get maps, brochures, and information on island activities in advance from the **Catalina Island Chamber of Commerce and Visitors Bureau,** P.O. Box 217, Avalon, CA 90704 (☎ **310/510-1520**). The very useful 88-page "Visitors Guide" about the area is offered free. Once you've arrived, stop by the **Discovery Tours Center,** located in the center of town. From this location you can purchase tour passes for Santa Catalina Island Discovery Tours.

Two Harbors, on the other side of the island at the Isthmus, is a remote, peaceful location for camping, hiking, and water activities. Its **Visitor Services** is in Two Harbors (☎ **310/510-0303**).

You'll find that addresses aren't used much here. Instead, directions are given according to certain landmarks and piers. The natives are friendly and are glad to point you in the right direction.

GETTING AROUND

Most hotels have complimentary taxis to take guests to and from the boat dock, airport, or heliport. Autos are not allowed on the island except by special permit held by residents. Reasonably priced taxis are always available through **Catalina Cab Co.**

(☎ 310/510-0025). Bikes can be rented (see Brown's Bikes under "Land Activities," in "What to See and Do," below). Many families with kids are seen in gasoline-powered golf-cart-type vehicles rented from **Cartopia Cart Rentals,** located at 615 Crescent Ave. (☎ 310/510-2493). Drivers 25 years old and up can rent these four-passenger vehicles for $30 per hour plus a $30 deposit (rentals by the hour only) all year round. Open daily during the season from 9am to 5pm and off-season from 9am to 5pm. No advance reservations accepted. Only cash or traveler's checks accepted.

Finally, Avalon is an easy place to get around on foot. Depending on the time you spend there, you probably won't need to rent anything.

WHAT TO SEE AND DO

When you arrive in Avalon, your first stop should be the **Discovery Tours Center** (☎ 310/510-2000), located on Crescent Avenue across from the Green Pleasure Pier. This is where you'll find information on land and water tours, and you can purchase tickets for different tours at one time. The Tour Center is open daily from 8am to 5pm, year-round.

Tours leave a minimum of twice a day, some, 10 to 12 times a day on weekends. There's no need for reservations except for the Inland Motor tour, which departs daily at 9am (hours are extended in summer). Tickets for other tours can be purchased at all Discovery Tour ticket booths. Booths can be found in four locations on the island, and three mainland sites, at the Long Beach offices of Catalina Cruises and Catalina Express, and the San Pedro office of Catalina Express.

The Tour Center suggests a half-day outing combining the Glass-Bottom Boat Tour, the Avalon Scenic Tour, and the Coastal Cruise to Seal Rocks. You'll have to decide whether your children can handle all that in half a day (we spread it out over two days). Children over 5 could certainly handle all the water tours in one day, but it would be too much to do in just half a day. Inquire about special prices for combination tours.

Land Tours

For the land tours, the Tour Center staff will direct you to the bus terminal, which is a short walk past the center. You can leave your strollers at the terminal. Soft drinks and sandwiches are available at the terminal, but you can't take the snacks on the buses. There are restrooms at the terminal.

The **Avalon Scenic Tour** shows you some of the highlights of Avalon. This 50-minute tour is taken in an open-air tram-style bus, and is fine for a sleeping infant or child who can sit still for an hour. But there are no stops during the tour. The fee is $7.50 for adults, $6.50 for seniors, $3.75 for children 2–11, and free for children under 2.

Children over 7 will enjoy the **Skyline Drive Tour** because they can catch a glimpse of the buffalo and other animals that roam the 42,000 acres of the Conservancy. A guide narrates the two-hour tour, outlines the history of the island, and explains which rare plants and trees you are seeing. The tour takes you ten miles into the Conservancy, which is accessible only by tour or by hiking. The road to the top is quite scary and kids love it! We all held our breaths looking down over the sheer cliffs while the driver negotiated the car-width turns with the huge bus. There was cheering after each successful maneuver. About 40 minutes into the tour, there's a stop at the **Airport-in-the-Sky,** Catalina's commercial and private airport for a visit to Catalina's Nature Center. The charge is $14 for adults, $12.25 for seniors, $8 for children 2–11, and free for children under 2.

Because cars are prohibited in the backcountry, a good way to see the remote wilderness and herds of buffalo is by taking the **Inland Motor Tour.** During the half-day tour, you visit El Rancho Escondido where you'll be treated to a horse show by the Arabian horses that are raised there, and you'll also stop at the Airport-in-the-Sky; there are several restroom stops. The tour costs $24.50 for adults, $22 for seniors, $13 for children 2-11, and free for children under 2. Reservations are necessary for this tour. Call **310/510-2500.**

Water Tours

Water tours leave the Green Pleasure Pier directly across from the Discovery Tour Center, where there are food stands and restrooms. Strollers cannot be taken aboard the boats.

The **Coastal Cruise to Seal Rocks** is a one-hour boat trip that cruises close to shore. Sea lions return to the area from May through September and the boat is able to reach their sunning area—we watched one come right up to the boat. This tour is fine for toddlers and children, but teens may find it boring. Use restrooms on the dock as there are none on board. Fares are $7.50 for adults, $6.50 for seniors, $3.75 for children 2–11, free for children under 2.

The **Glass Bottom Boat Trip** is a 40-minute ride, just perfect for short attention spans. The waters off Catalina are so clear that you'll have no trouble spotting the various sea creatures. A guide explains and points out special marine life. Adults pay $7.50 for daytime and $8 for evening trips, seniors pay $6.50 day, $7 evening, children 2–11 pay $3.75 for day trips and $4 for evening, free for children under 2.

The **Flying Fish Boat Tour** fascinates and draws many families. The boat shines a 40-million-candlepower searchlight on the water, attracting the flying fish to sail through the air. This 55-minute evening tour runs from mid-May through September. Dress warmly; by September it gets chilly in the evenings, and the water spray makes it even colder on the open boat. No restrooms on board. Fares are $8.50 for adults, $7 for seniors, $4.25 for children 2–11, free for children under 2.

For an up-close look at life under water, there's the **Undersea Tour** aboard the *Starlight,* the only semi-submersible vessel in Southern California. The cabin lies under the water's surface and offers a submarine-style view of Catalina's Undersea Gardens, a sight previously available only to divers. The narrated, 40-minute tour costs $18 for adults, $16.50 for seniors and for children 2 to 12; kids under 2 are free.

Water Activities

Beach lovers only have two choices on the Avalon side of the island. While hordes of tourists enjoy the beach on either side of the Green Pleasure Pier on summer weekends, we prefer the **Descanso Beach Club,** on the other side of the casino (☎ 310/510-2780). You can bicycle there pretty easily. You will spend your day at a private beach where you can rent towels and a beach chair. Outdoor showers and changing rooms are available. Rafts, snorkels, and kick boards can be rented, and you can play volleyball. There are also family cookouts during the summer. Descanso provides the condiments, baked potato, salad bar, and rolls; you bring the entree and grill it in their barbeque pit (make reservations). There is also a sidewalk café and an open-air bar.

Admission to the beach is $1.50 for adults, 50¢ for children under 12. Cookout prices are $7.95 for adults, $4 for children.

Brave souls who want to stay at the beach by the Green Pleasure Pier have various beach-supply rentals available to the right of the pier. Sand chairs, umbrellas, mats, tubes, floats, and even beach towls can be rented, summers only, from 9am.

Many kids will love the idea of renting your own boat. Visit **Joe's Rent-A-Boat,** on the Green Pleasure Pier (☎ **310/510-0455**). Rowboats, pedalboats, 16-foot runabouts, and 15-hp sportsters are available. Paddleboards, which are also available, are a favorite with the teens.

Joe's doesn't take reservations, but the wait is usually no more than half an hour on a busy summer weekend. Open from the weekend before Easter Sunday through the month of October, daily from 6am to 7pm; closed for the rest of the year.

Hourly rates are $5 for paddleboards, $10 for rowboats, $22–$25 for runabouts, $30 for a sportster, and $10 for pedalboats.

Boatstand Charters (☎ **310/510-2274**) on the pier has boats available for fishing, diving, and sightseeing.

Wave runners are available at **Catalina Jet Ski,** at Hamilton Cove (☎ **310/510-0791**). Go to Joe's Rent-a-Boat on the Green Pleasure Pier for tickets. Kids must be a minimum of 13 years old for the wave runners and must have a parent's signed authorization. Wave runners rent for $45 per half hour, $65 per hour. Open April through October, daily from 8am to 6pm.

Another water-sports rental facility is **Wet Spot Rentals,** just after the boat terminal, on the bay side on the way into town (☎ **310/510-2229**). At this kiosk, you can rent pedalboats for $10 per hour and kayaks (kids must be 10 or older to go alone) for $10 per hour. Masks, snorkels, and fins cost $10 for the day (four hours).

If you're interested in diving in Catalina's beautiful waters, there are three places to check: **Argo Diving Service** (☎ **310/510-2208**), **Island Charters** (☎ **310/510-0600,** or toll free **800/262-DIVE**), and **Catalina Diver's Supply** (☎ **310/510-0330**).

The older kids in our group loved the raft trip with **Catalina Ocean Rafting,** 103 Pebbly Beach Rd. (P.O. Box 2075), Avalon, CA 90704 (☎ **310/510-0211**). Children ages 5–9 can try this four-hour voyage, which is offered twice a day in summer, and costs $65 per person for adults, $49 for kids.

Are you ready for parasailing? It's not as scary as it looks. You decide—they say it's safe enough even for 4-year-olds. Contact **Island Cruzers,** 107 Pebbly Beach Rd. (☎ **310/510-1777**). The boats take six people per hour, every hour. The parasailing itself lasts 8–10 minutes. There is no age minimum, but children must be at least 100 pounds to go up. The charge per ride for adults and children alike is $38.

Land Activities

After you've gotten your bearings, visit **Brown's Bikes,** right under the Holly Hill House (☎ **310/510-0986**), where you can rent bikes by the hour or day. A limited number of child carriers and helmets is available. Be sure to take the bike map provided. Lockers store your bulky items. Reservations are accepted, although there isn't much of a wait for regular bikes, even on summer weekends. Brown's is open daily in summer from 9am to 5pm and in winter from 10am to 4pm.

Hourly rates are $5 for one-speeds, $6 for six-speeds, $9 for mountain bikes, $10 for tandems, $12 for six-speed tandems, and $5 for single-speed children's bikes, $6 for six-speed bikes; strollers and wheelchairs cost $10 per day.

There is an 18-hole miniature golf course, perfect for the whole family, located one block from the beach in the Island Plaza. **Golf Gardens** (☎ **310/510-1200**) is open daily from Easter to mid-June; daily and evenings from mid-June to mid-September; daily from mid-September through October; and winter weekends and holidays, weather permitting. Since hours vary, call first or check the sign out front.

Hiking in Catalina is best for families in good condition, or as part of a camping experience. In the island's interior, routes follow existing roads and Jeep trails. From Avalon into the interior, the trail gains 1,450 feet of elevation in less than three miles. From Two Harbors, it climbs only 800 feet in two miles, but the route is longer.

To hike on the island, contact **Doug Bombard Ent. (☎ 310/510-2800)**. The Two Harbors office is open daily from 7:30am to 6pm. Free permits are required for hiking. Ask the staff about the accessibility of certain trails for children. The same office will provide camping and lodging information.

If you decide to hike, be aware that the temperatures change drastically during certain times of the year—it may be extremely hot in the interior, but only 60° at the beach. Bring layers of clothing and sunscreen, and don't forget to bring water.

Another way to see the island is on horseback. **Catalina Stables,** on Avalon Canyon Rd., six blocks from the ocean (☎ **310/510-0478**), offers 1- and 1¹/₂-hour guided rides into the mountains behind the golf course. You'll cover five miles of beautiful Catalina scenery. The group limit is eight people and no one under 8 years old may ride. Although children do not need prior riding experience, the owner will interview them to determine if they are strong enough to handle the horses. Although the horses are gentle and well trained, the five-mile ride covers some difficult terrain. There's also a maximum weight limit of approximately 200 pounds; and you must wear closed-toe shoes, not sandals. Reservations must be made in person, and only on the day before or day of the ride. The stables are open daily: in summer from 9am to 3pm, in winter from 10am to 3pm, weather permitting. Rates are $25 to $35 per person, adult or child.

The **Wrigley Memorial and Botanical Gardens,** located at the head of Avalon Canyon (☎ **310/510-2288**), is a nice walk for the family if you have lots of time. You can even walk there from the center of town via Avalon Canyon Road—it's a 1.7-mile walk uphill. Once there, you'll wander through 38 acres of plants native to Catalina, mostly cacti, succulents, and flowering shrubs. It's a memorial to William Wrigley, Jr., who worked so hard to protect Catalina Island. The actual memorial is built of material indigenous to Catalina. Open year-round, admission is free.

. . . and a Natural Area

Two Harbors is a secluded natural area located on the other side of the island. The **Visitor Services** phone number is **310/510-0303.** Catalina Express from San Pedro (☎ **310/519-1212,** or toll free **800/995-4386**) and Catalina Cruises from Long Beach (☎ **213/235-9800;** or toll free **800/CATALINA**) can take you directly to Two Harbors. Or you can take the twice-daily summer shuttle from Avalon on Catalina Express. Catalina Safari Bus (☎ **213/510-2800**) will take you there from Avalon or they can transport you to one of two campgrounds (see "Camping" in "Where to Stay," below). Round-trip bus fares to and from Avalon are $28.30 for adults, $20.40 for children 2–11. The same phone number will give you information about Catalina Safari Tours. Select snorkeling trips by boat from Two Harbors or naturalist-led hikes and short walks—both great ways to introduce children to the natural side of the island.

Once in Two Harbors, you'll find nearly empty beaches. You can snorkel, dive, kayak, hike, even camp.

This side of the island is a place to relax—there are no sights except the natural ones you'll see while hiking or snorkeling. There's a general store open daily from 8am to 5pm and a snack bar open from 8am to 3pm. A restaurant is open for dinner from mid-February through Thanksgiving.

Avalon Extras

If you've forgotten those important sand toys, visit the **Island Toy Store,** 119 Clarissa Ave. (☎ **310/510-1869**). There are toys for all ages, plenty of beach toys, and books as well. In summer it's open daily from 10am to 4pm. Call for winter hours.

Have some extra time? There's a tiny **park** with swings and climbers between the Cartopia stand and the Catharine Hotel.

WHERE TO STAY

The **Pavilion Lodge,** at 513 Crescent Ave. (P.O. Box 737), Avalon, CA 90704 (☎ **310/510-2500,** or toll free **800/4-AVALON** in California; fax 310/510-7254), is just steps away from the beach. A large interior-court garden with lawn chairs is an inviting spot to relax while the kids play, and two resident youngsters are always seeking playmates. The hotel is within easy walking distance of many eateries (there's no on-premises restaurant). There is courtesy baggage service to and from the Avalon terminal. Babysitting can be arranged through the front desk.

The bright, light, newly remodeled rooms have air conditioning, plantation shutters, refrigerators, and coffee makers. Remote-control color TVs offer free Showtime and Disney Channel cable service. Rooms are furnished with one king-size bed, or two queen-size or double beds; some rooms have sleeper sofas.

Rates are $49–$158, single or double occupancy. Special packages include island tours. Minimum stay is required on all summer weekends. No charge for children under 12 or cribs, but rollaways cost $12 in season, $8 off-season. Each additional person is charged $12.

Catalina Canyon Hotel, 888 Country Club Dr. (P.O. Box 736), Avalon, CA 90704 (☎ **310/510-0325,** or toll free **800/253-9361** in California; fax 310/510-0900), is off the beaten track, accessible by the hotel's courtesy shuttle or by taxi. You can walk to town, but it's not a short hike. The hotel has a small, fenced-in heated pool, a sauna, and a Jacuzzi. The on-premises restaurant is open for breakfast, lunch, and dinner; a snack bar is open on weekends, with longer hours in summer. The rooms are not large, but a family of four can make it work; accommodations with one king-size bed can better fit a crib. Or you can opt for adjoining rooms. Units on the fifth floor offer glass sliding doors, which make the rooms seem more open. All (but one) rooms have patios overlooking the gardens, air conditioning, heat, and color TVs.

Rooms in summer cost $135 double occupancy on weekends, $109 midweek. From November through May, rooms are $95 on weekends, $75 weekdays. Children 16 and under stay free in their parents' room; additional adults are charged $20. Cribs and rollaways cost $20. Ask about special packages.

Camping

There are five campgrounds on the island. The first is in Avalon, two are in the interior, and the other two are in the Two Harbors area.

Hermit Gulch (☎ **310/510-TENT**) is the closest campground to town. It accommodates 230 people and has water, toilets, hot showers, vending machines, and picnic tables. Sites are $7.50 per person per night.

Call **Catalina Camping Reservations** (☎ **310/510-2800**) for information about the next four campgrounds. **Blackjack** campground is approximately 2¹/₂ miles from the airport, at a 1,500-foot elevation. Some 75 campers can stay here, and there are chemical toilets, water, and picnic tables. Reservations are $6.50 per person per night. **Little Harbor** is on the south shore on the beach. There are 150 sites, with chemical toilets, picnic tables, and cold showers. Reservations are $7.50 per night per person; children under 6 are free.

Two Harbors Camping is a quarter mile from the Two Harbors pier and accommodates 250 campers. Sites have barbecue pits, picnic tables, water, rinse-off showers, and chemical toilets. Reservations cost $7.50–$8.50 per person per night; kids under 4 are free. **Parson's Landing,** seven miles west of Two Harbors, is more primitive and accessible only by foot or boat. It has room for 48 campers. There are chemical toilets. Stoves and lanterns can be rented in Two Harbors. Firewood and bottled water are provided. Reservations are $15 for one camper, $5 for each additional person; kids under 4 are free.

WHERE TO EAT

For outdoor breakfast in a nautical and casual atmosphere, visit **The Busy Bee,** at 306 Crescent Ave. (☎ **310/510-1983**), directly across from the Southern California Bank of Catalina. While you sit outside, kids can occupy themselves watching the harbor and sneaking food to the pushy seagulls that congregate beneath the dock. Breakfast selections include lots of omelets, eggs, and pancakes, priced at $4.50–$10. For lunch or dinner, there are Mexican entrees, a large selection of salads and hamburgers, hot sandwiches, and health foods; prices average $7.50. There are lots of homemade desserts. Breakfast, lunch, and dinner are served all day. A few selections for kids: hot dog, grilled cheese sandwich, or spaghetti at $3.50. Highchairs and booster seats are provided.

Open daily in summer from 8am to 10pm; winter hours are 9am to 4pm weekdays (depending on the weather) and 8am to 9pm on weekends. Reservations are not accepted and major credit cards are welcome.

The Channel House, 205 Crescent Ave. (☎ **310/510-1617**), conveniently located on the main street, is a big, friendly place. Choose either the gardenlike open-air room in front or the inside dining room.

Lunch offerings include hamburgers, salads, and sandwiches, at prices ranging from $5.75 to $9. Adults can sample pasta, seafood, steak, or duck à l'orange, the house specialty at dinner. Soup and salad are included. Prices start at $13 and top out at $24 (for the duck). At dinner there's a children's menu featuring chicken nuggets, a fishburger, or a burger and french fries ($7).

Special children's beverages will be made, baby food will be warmed, adult portions will be split (for a charge), and highchairs and booster seats are available.

Lunch is served in summer only (beginning July 1), daily from 11am to 2pm. Dinner is served in winter, Wednesday through Sunday from 5pm. In summer, dinner is offered nightly. Reservations accepted. Major credit cards are welcome. In summer it gets quite busy. Without a reservation, it's best to get there between 5 and 6pm.

In an Emergency

In case of a medical emergency during your visit to Catalina, there's 24-hour service at the **Avalon Municipal Hospital,** 100 Falls Canyon Rd. (☎ **310/510-0700**).

Café Prego is a darling little bistro-type restaurant, near the beginning of town at 603 Crescent Ave. (☎ **310/510-1218**). Café Prego is a three-time winner of the Southern California Restaurant Writers Association Silver Award for food, service, ambience, and an appropriate wine list.

Management welcomes children with their own menu, priced from $4.95 to $5.95. Children under 10 can order spaghetti four ways, each with soup or salad, or they can choose manicotti or lasagne. Adult pasta dinners, with soup, salad, and bread, cost $10–$14. Dinner seafood specials, such as red snapper parmigiano cost $13–$24. Steak, chicken, and veal selections, which come with soup, salad, and spaghetti, are priced at $14–$17. House specialties, such as steak, scampi, or a platter of various pastas, run $14–$38. Early bird specials can be ordered from 5 to 5:30pm. Open for lunch (summer only) from 11am to 2pm, and daily for dinner from 5pm; closing time changes with the seasons. Reservations and credit cards accepted.

Can't make a decision? Try **Mi Casita,** located at 111 Clarissa Ave. (☎ **310/510-1772**). The menu for children under 12 includes such Mexican selections as a taco, enchilada, tamale, or flauta (priced at $4.90–$5.90), as well as hamburger and fries ($5.20). Grownups can try burritos, enchiladas, tacos, flautas, Mexican pizza, combinations, and dinner specialties. Lunch prices average $5; dinner specials cost $8.80–$13; or you can order from the à la carte menu.

Highchairs and booster seats are available. Baby food and bottles can be warmed. Special children's drinks can be ordered from the bar.

Open April through October, weekdays from 11:30am to 9pm, on weekends from 11am to 10pm; in winter, Wednesday through Sunday only from 11:30am to 9pm. No reservations accepted—the average wait is 15 minutes.

To put your picnic together, stop at **Fred & Sally's Market,** 117 Catalina Ave. (☎ **310/510-1199**). And pick up your dessert across the street at the **Avalon Bake Shop** (☎ **310/510-0361**), which opens at 5:30am.

3   Pasadena/Glendale

Pasadena is Los Angeles's bulwark of tradition. Originally founded in 1886 as a resort community called the Indiana Colony, Pasadena was a sunny sanctuary of industrialists and other members of the classes who came from points east to spend their winters. In fact, the area on South Orange Grove Boulevard near the Rose Bowl used to be called Millionaire's Row because of the many gorgeous mansions there.

In decades past, Los Angeles society was centered exclusively in Pasadena. There's still a lot of wealth in Pasadena, although there are now other pockets of society living in this metropolis.

In appreciation of the beauty of its once-splendid downtown buildings, Pasadena has restored a ten-block section called Old Pasadena to a facsimile of its original glory. The area is bordered by Pasadena Avenue, Arroyo Parkway, Holly Street/Union Street, and Del Mar Boulevard. The historic buildings are not only interesting for their architecture and interiors, but they now house an eclectic group of cafés, boutiques, and art galleries. It's a nice place to walk on a Saturday or Sunday. Be sure to check out the back alleys for hidden stores and street entertainment. This is where you'll find The Gap, J. Crew, and other stores appropriate for kids and teens. For a quick burger, there's a Johnny Rockets, hidden behind A.B.S., and across from it, a multiscreen movie theater. You can sample a chocolate-chip bagel at Goldstein's Bagel Bakery,

86 W. Colorado Blvd. An ice-cream cone or frozen yogurt is a must—try the Pasadena Creamery at 50 W. Colorado Blvd., then stop in at Sticky Fingers Candy Store, next door at 54 W. Colorado, where the candy is self-selected and sold by weight. If you're a fudge-lover, search for Heminger's Fudge & Chocolate Co., tucked away down the street at 42 E. Colorado Blvd.

WHAT TO SEE AND DO

Pasadena is well known for its museums, gardens, theater, and music. Two of its most famous attractions are the Huntington Library and the Norton Simon Museum, both of which are known worldwide. But what most people think of when they hear of Pasadena is the Rose Bowl and Parade, officially known as the Tournament of Roses.

The Tournament of Roses

The Tournament of Roses (☎ 818/449-ROSE, a 24-hour, year-round hotline for parade and game information) has been held each New Year's Day since 1890, at which time Pasadena streets are filled with the colors of millions of flowers covering lavishly decorated floats. Each year the parade attracts gorgeous floats, marching bands, and high-stepping equestrians, and is watched by more than a million curbside spectators and more than 450 million television viewers worldwide. Besides colorful floats, you see the Rose Queen and her Court (seven beautiful young women chosen from a field of about 1,000 students of the Pasadena Area Community College District) and various celebrities riding on the floats. The parade's grand marshals of the past have tended to be celebrities, too.

Many people, kids especially, love to camp out for curbside viewing of the parade. Thousands of people flock to the parade route the night before, secure a good viewing spot, talk with other hardy campers, catch a few winks in a sleeping bag, and then wake up to New Year's Day excitement. (If New Year's Day falls on a Sunday, the parade and game are held the next day, Monday, January 2.) If a hotel room sounds more comfortable, reserve both your hotel room and grandstand seat far in advance. Expect a three- to five-night minimum stay, payable in advance, for hotel rooms in Pasadena at this time. Contact the **Pasadena Convention and Visitors Bureau,** 171 S. Los Robles Ave., Pasadena, CA 91101 (☎ 818/795-9311), or the **Pasadena Chamber of Commerce,** 117 E. Colorado Blvd., Suite 100, Pasadena, CA 91105 (☎ 818/795-3355), for information about area accommodations.

The parade starts at 8am and ends at 10:30am. Tickets for grandstand seats can be purchased for $24–$40 from the **Sharp Seating Co.,** P.O. Box 68, Pasadena, CA 91102-0068 (☎ 818/795-4171), or for a substantially higher price from various ticket agencies. Tickets go on sale February 1 for the next year, and the good seats tend to sell out by early summer. Parking is an additional $15. To avoid the driving mayhem, you can take a chartered bus from **Santa Monica Bus Lines** (☎ 310/458-1975), **Gardena Bus Lines** (☎ 213/321-0165), or **Long Beach Public Transportation** (☎ 213/591-8753); call at least two months in advance for reservations. If you do drive, be sure to park by 6:30am to get to your seats.

The parade has substantial RV accommodations, available through Sharp Seating (see above). The **Good Sam RV Club** (☎ 805/389-0300) sells packages to RV users.

The Rose Bowl college football game, played after the parade, pits the winner of the Pacific-10 (on the West Coast) against the winner of the Big Ten Conference (in the Midwest), a tradition that started in 1902.

Tickets to the game are distributed primarily to loyal fans of the universities involved, but you can participate in a drawing for the sale of 4,500 end-zone seats by mailing a postcard with your name and address to **Rose Bowl Ticket Drawing,** P.O. Box 91386, Pasadena, CA 91109. Postcards must be postmarked between September 1 and October 1 for the November drawing.

If you wish to view the festivities closer, you can take the kids for a look at the floats after the parade at Sierra Madre Boulevard between Washington Boulevard and Sierra Madre Villa Avenue, and on Washington Boulevard between Sierra Madre and Woodlyn Road. Viewing takes place on the afternoon of the parade from 1:30 to 4pm and the next day from 9am to 4pm. Write or call the association at 391 S. Orange Grove Blvd., Pasadena, CA 91184 (☎ 818/449-4100).

If you do go to the game, you're better off waiting until the next day for viewing. Park on nearby residential streets.

Huntington Library, Art Collections, and Botanical Gardens

There are essentially three major parts to the **Huntington Library,** 1151 Oxford Rd., San Marino (☎ 818/405-2141), each worth a separate visit: the library, the art galleries, and the botanical gardens.

Older children who know just a bit about art and literature will appreciate the Huntington Library more than younger ones, who may get bored here. Before embarking on this cultural wonderland, pick up the short, self-guiding tour booklets.

The Huntington Library is an institution devoted entirely to the study of British and American history and literature. It contains 600,000 reference and rare books, many thousands of photographs, prints, and microfilms, and nearly 2.5 million valuable individual manuscripts. Many of the things your kids are studying in school come alive for them in this wonderful library. Even the 14-year-old with us was fascinated by the most reliable manuscript in existence of Chaucer's *Canterbury Tales,* circa 1410; the Gutenberg Bible, one of only three animal-skin copies still in existence in America, circa 1455; and Shakespeare's *Comedies, Histories, and Tragedies* (the First Folio) printed in 1623. There are also documents by Benjamin Franklin, George Washington, Euclid, Milton, Galileo, Thomas Paine, Abraham Lincoln, Robert Frost, James Joyce, W. B. Yeats—even a draft of the U.S. Constitution (1787).

The art collections are equally prized. The **Huntington Art Gallery** is devoted primarily to British art of the 18th and early 19th centuries, and houses a multitude of masterpieces. Kids seem to love Gainsborough's *Blue Boy* and Lawrence's *Pinkie,* which face each other. But there are other notable drawings of children as well, because the artists of this period showed a tender concern for children. Particularly touching is Greuze's *Young Knitter Asleep,* and so are the two children posing in elaborate period dress in *The Young Fortune Teller.* This gallery also features furniture, decorative objects, and sculpture from the same period.

The **Virginia Steele Scott Gallery** displays American paintings from the 1730s to the 1930s including works by artists Stuart, Copley, Bingham, and Cassatt. Renaissance paintings and 18th-century French sculpture, tapestries, porcelain, and furniture are found in the Arabella Huntington Memorial Collection, housed in the west wing of the main library building.

The **Huntington Botanical Gardens** are just as impressive. They occupy about 130 acres and consist of one wondrous garden after another. There's the Rose Garden with its 2,000 varieties arranged historically from circa A.D. 1000. There are various international gardens—the Australian Garden, the Subtropical Garden, the Desert

Garden, and the Palm Garden (a must-see because this is, after all, Los Angeles). Our romantic 14-year-old friend still occasionally mentions the 18th-century French stone Temple of Love, in which she saw a statue entitled *Love, the Captive of Youth*.

There is restaurant service from 1 to 4pm and an elegant English tea service certain days of the week; call **818/683-8131** for tea room reservations. Picnics are not allowed. Pets are not permitted. The Huntington is stroller-accessible.

The museum and grounds are open Tuesday through Friday from 1 to 4:30pm and on Saturday and Sunday from 10:30am to 4:30pm; closed Mondays and major holidays. Admission is free, but a donation of $5 per adult and $3 per child is suggested.

The Norton Simon Museum

The Norton Simon Museum is located at Colorado Boulevard and Orange Grove (☎ **818/449-6840**), at the intersection of the Foothill Freeway (I-210) and the Ventura Freeway (Calif. 134). This museum is a wonderful opportunity for your child to view a large collection of rare masterpieces, some contemporary but mostly classical: Matisse, Picasso, Raphael, and Rembrandt, among many others. There are 30 galleries and a sculpture garden—about 1,000 works of art altogether. Children over 7 will enjoy this museum. The sixth-grader in our group liked the sculpture the best, especially the three rooms of Degas miniature *modèles*. We break up the viewing by spending time in the outdoor sculpture garden, a tranquil spot for the kids to roam if they get restless. You may be surprised at how much culture they can soak up just by walking among the statues.

There are no eating facilities, but you may leave and return on one admission. The museum is wheelchair- and stroller-accessible. Note that there are no changing tables in the restrooms. There is ample parking.

The museum is open Thursday through Sunday from noon to 6pm. Admission is $4 for adults, $2 for seniors and students with ID, free for children under 12 accompanied by an adult.

Other Museums and Attractions

Kidspace Museum, 390 El Molino Ave. (☎ **818/449-9143**), is a small participatory museum geared to spark the curiosity of children from 1 to 12. Kids feel comfortable in this casual museum, which has special programs and workshops throughout the year, as well as permanent exhibits. Plan to spend a couple of hours here.

The Television Studio and The Disc Jockey Booth are permanent exhibits that enable kids to experience the world of communications. They feel uninhibited enough to just start dancing to the music coming from the booth. Or they take turns recording their own messages.

Critter Caverns is a three-level environmental exhibit that allows children to explore life above and below ground and at ground level. Kids can wiggle their toes in the sand and explore Pacific marine life in The Beach and investigate the stars and the sky in The Planetarium. Back Stage encourages kids to explore the world of theater and drama. The little toddlers have their own space in Toddler Territory.

There are grassy areas and picnic tables. Street parking. Open September through June, on Wednesday from 2 to 5pm and on Saturday and Sunday from 12:30 to 5pm; June to September, Tuesday through Friday from 1 to 5pm and on Saturday and Sunday from 12:30 to 5pm. Call to confirm the schedule and to learn what special workshops, programs, and performances will be offered. Admission is $5 for adults,

$3.50 for seniors, $5 for children over 2, $2.50 for 1- and 2-year-olds, and free for children under 1.

The **Pacific Asia Museum,** 46 N. Los Robles Ave. (☎ **818/449-2742**), is a gem of a museum devoted to past and present Asian and Pacific art and culture. The museum, built in 1929 in the Chinese Imperial Palace courtyard style, is listed in the National Register of Historic Places. Be sure to mention to your children that the garden they'll see at the museum is an authentic Chinese courtyard garden, one of only two such gardens in the United States.

The museum has a special Student's Gallery with displays designed especially to interest many age levels. Besides special exhibitions and changing displays, there are hands-on experiences and workshops. Family Free Days are sponsored on the third Saturday of every month; these free programs may include dance performances, arts or crafts demonstrations such as origami or fan-making, or other programs featuring the cultural arts of the many different Asian and Pacific countries.

The museum is open Wednesday through Sunday from 10am to 5pm. Docent tours are available at 2pm on Sunday. Adults pay $3; seniors and students with ID, $1.50; free for children under 12.

Descanso Gardens is located at 1418 Descanso Dr., in LaCanada–Flintridge (☎ **818/952-4400**), at the junction of the Glendale Freeway (Calif. 2) and the Foothill Freeway (I-210). Call for recorded directions.

The garden's name says it all—translated it means a place of rest. Set on 165 acres in the San Raphael Hills northeast of Los Angeles (55 cultivated acres are open to the public), Descanso is the home of the largest camellia collection in the world. Above it towers a 30-acre parasol of California live oaks. There is also a lilac grove and a wide selection of azaleas.

Experience Descanso two ways: on foot or by tram. Short walking trails enable you to see the plants close up and invite you to take your time meandering through the area. A stream flows through the Live Oak Forest and birds are everywhere. You can hike to the Bird Observation Station to get the best view of the different land and water birds.

The 45-minute narrated tram ride will take you through the camellia forest, rose gardens, and California Native Plant Gardens, and up into the hills, stopping at the Hospitality House where there's an Art Gallery. Afterward visit the Japanese Tea House set in the tranquility of pools, waterfalls, ornamental stones, and azalea beds. Whether you're a garden buff or just enjoying a restful stop in the midst of touring fast-track Los Angeles, you'll be happy you stopped here while in Pasadena.

Food service is available at the entrance to the gardens daily, or bring a picnic lunch. There are picnic grounds adjacent to the parking lot.

Descanso Gardens is open daily (except Christmas Day) from 9am to 4:30pm. Guided tram tours are given Wednesday through Friday at 1, 2, and 3pm, and on Saturday and Sunday at 11am and 1, 2, and 3pm. Tram charge is $1.50 for both adults and children. Admission to the gardens is $5 for adults, $3 for seniors 60 and older and students with ID, 75¢ for children 5–12, free for children under 5. On the third Tuesday of the month, admission is free. Parking is free.

WHERE TO EAT

If your children have sophisticated palates, they'll love the **Parkway Grill,** located at 510 S. Arroyo Pkwy. (☎ **818/795-1001**). The ambience is completely charming.

Originally a warehouse, it still has bare brick walls and a wood-beamed ceiling that attest to its heritage. There are stained-glass windows, fresh flowers and plants galore, even a fireplace in the dining room.

The Parkway Grill serves regional American cuisine and uses only fresh ingredients of high quality. Appetizers include blue-corn tortilla tostada ($9) and cocoa crêpe stuffed with lobster ($8.50). Out-of-the-ordinary pizzas and pasta, and grilled meats and fish, comprise the large assortment of offerings. Lunch prices are $9–$14; dinners run $10–$24. The very friendly and helpful servers will delight children with all kinds of non-alcoholic drinks, split adult portions, warm baby food and bottles, and they provide booster seats.

Open for lunch Monday through Friday from 11:30am to 2:30pm and on Sunday from 11am to 2:30pm. Dinner is served Monday through Thursday from 5:30 to 10pm, on Friday and Saturday from 5 to 11pm, and on Sunday from 5 to 10pm. Reservations are advised. Credit cards are accepted. There is complimentary valet parking.

A charming place that invites you to an outdoor area for dining or just sitting, is the **Green Street Café,** located in the heart of downtown Pasadena at 146 Shopper's Lane (☎ **818/577-7170**). Inside, this large restaurant is attractively decorated with modern artworks and partitions create areas unto themselves. Green Street offers an extensive menu of American food for breakfast, lunch, and dinner. Omelets, eggs, French toast, and pancakes cost $4–$7.75. Sandwiches, burgers, and salads go for $4.75–$8. Complete meals with steak, chicken, or fresh vegetable platter plus fries and fresh fruit included cost $8–$9.50.

The children's menu was diligently researched and developed by a number of children for whom the dishes are named. At breakfast, there's Marc's buttermilk pancakes, Andy's pancake with sausage or bacon, Anthony's English muffin with peanut butter, and Adam's cinnamon toast; prices are $1–$3.25. The lunch and dinner offerings include Annemarie's spaghetti, Kelly's macaroni and cheese, and Molly's hot dog, in addition to standard fare; prices are reasonable at $3.50–$4.50. Servers will bring crackers and split portions. Sassy seats and boosters are provided.

Green Street is open Monday through Thursday from 6:30am to 9pm, on Friday and Saturday from 6:30am to 10pm, and on Sunday from 8am to 9pm. Reservations accepted for groups of five or more. Credit cards are welcome.

Ever see a salad bar nearly a mile long? **The Souplantation,** 201 S. Lake Ave., in the Union Bank building at Cordova and Lake Avenue (☎ **818/577-4797**), offers such a salad bar and it includes fresh foods with all the fixings from greens to pasta. Try Chinese sesame chicken salad, tortellini basil, bow tie pesto, or tuna tarragon. There are over 14 kinds of salad dressings, including such unusual ones as no-oil honey mustard, low-calorie New Orleans French, and fat-free Italian.

Where does the name come from? Souplantation offers five different soups plus home-style chili which you can smother with onions and cheddar cheese. Warm cornbread is yummy with chili. They offer an assortment of fresh muffins. From the Dessert Shoppe you may select nonfat frozen yogurt, soft ice cream, or fresh fruit among other choices. The adult price for soup and salad bar is $7.20; for just soup or salad it's $6.60.

The self-serve Souplantation welcomes families. There's no children's menu, but children's portions are priced less. For children under 12, the charge is $4. There are highchairs and booster seats.

The restaurant is open Sunday through Thursday from 11am to 9pm and on Friday and Saturday from 11am to 10pm. Reservations are accepted only for large parties during nonpeak hours; however, the line moves quickly and the wait usually isn't longer than 10 minutes. Credit cards are honored. There is validated parking under the building (enter on Cordova). There's is also another branch located at the Beverly Connection, 8491 W. 3rd St., in the West Hollywood/Mid-Wilshire area (☎ 213/655-0381), which is open daily from 11am to 10pm.

Know any restaurant that dedicates its menu to "everybody who can't wait until tomorrow because they get better looking every day"? **Robin's** does. This fine family restaurant is located a bit off the sightseeing path at 395 N. Rosemead Blvd. (☎ 818/351-8885). There's something friendly for everyone here: special prizes for kids, complimentary jar of baby food for infants, discounts for senior citizens, family nights, special theme nights, children's selections for breakfast, lunch, and dinner, and, of course, boosters and highchairs.

Robin's menu presents build-your-own omelets, baby back ribs, several stir-fry dishes, plus salads, burgers, and sandwiches. Prices are $4.45–$9.95. Nightly until 10pm (except Saturday) is family night with all-you-can-eat specials: barbecue on Monday, Turkey on Tuesday, beer-batter fish fry on Wednesday and Friday, and chicken fajitas and fried chicken on Sunday.

The 12 and under crowd can order individual pizzas, mini-nachos with cheese, and fish fry, besides the usual popular children's dishes. There are Shirley Templeses and Roy Rogerses, plus REO Speed Wagons (an ice cream, chocolate, and Oreo shake) and gooey chocolate sundaes. Kids' menu prices are $1.30–$3.90. Robin's is open Sunday through Thursday from 7am to 11pm and on Friday and Saturday from 7am to midnight. No reservations, but credit cards are accepted. Parking is free.

13

Weekend Trips from Los Angeles

WITHIN THREE HOURS OF DOWNTOWN LOS ANGELES SIT THE HIGHEST MOUNTAINS in Southern California and the low desert of Palm Springs. Family travelers will find alpine skiing, mountain hiking, hot-air ballooning, fruit picking, and perfect swimming within the wonderland that surrounds the Los Angeles Basin.

1 Palm Springs and the Desert Communities

To sun worshipers, tennis lovers, and golf aficionados, the Palm Springs area needs no introduction. For families who have never visited before, it does.

Palm Springs has been called the Playground of the Stars and the Golf Capital of the World. Although you might still see a star or two, that's not its main attraction anymore. And while Palm Springs is a popular retirement spot, it is also a fun—and relaxing—place to bring the kids. The desert communities offer great weather, plenty of ways to relax, and lots of outdoor activities. Combine those qualities with an abundance of restaurants and a casual atmosphere, and you have the consummate resort.

GETTING THERE

Getting to Palm Springs is easy. It's 107 miles southeast of L.A., about a two-hour drive **by car** via I-10 East (the San Bernardino Freeway). It is about three hours from San Diego, taking I-15 North to I-60 East (the Pomona Freeway) to I-10 East.

The **Palm Springs Regional Airport** is served by numerous major airlines, including United, Alaska, Delta (not in summer), and American. Ontario is nearby, and its airport is also served by major airlines.

The nearest **Amtrak** depot is in Indio, 20 miles from Palm Springs (☎ toll free **800/USA-RAIL** for schedules and information). **Greyhound Bus** service is available to Palm Springs. Check with your local Greyhound office for connections.

ORIENTATION

When people refer to Palm Springs, they usually mean all the desert communities—Palm Springs, Cathedral City, Rancho Mirage, Palm Desert, Indian Wells, La Quinta, and Indio. Although the towns are set one right after the other along Calif. 111, each has its own identity.

Calif. 111, the main thoroughfare between towns, becomes a big-city nightmare during rush hour. Thus, getting from Palm Springs to Palm Desert during prime time can take over a half hour. For alternative routes and detailed maps—and other visitor information services—visit the **Palm Springs Desert Resorts Convention and Visitors Bureau,** located at The Atrium, 69-930 Calif. 111, Suite 201, Rancho Mirage, CA 92270 (☎ **619/770-9000** or toll free **800/417-3529**). The office is open weekdays only, from 8:30am to 5pm. For the 24-hour Information Line, phone **619/770-1992.** Or drop by the **Palm Desert Chamber of Commerce,** 72-990 Calif. 111, at Monterey, in Palm Desert (☎ **619/346-6111**), open Monday through Saturday from 9:30am to 4:30pm.

The climate is the area's greatest draw, and the more than 7,000 swimming pools are proof of that near-perfect weather. This is desert climate, Colorado Desert climate to be exact. Days are mostly warm, sunny, and dry, although the addition of thousands of swimming pools to the area has increased the humidity over what it was 10 years ago. Evenings are comfortable, but can get cold in the winter months. The "season" is really October through May. The warmest fall and winter months are October and November, and March and April in the spring, when daytime temperatures average 86°. Summer, when family rates are popular, can be extremely hot, with temperatures reaching 108° in July. But air conditioning and Micro Mist, an outdoor air conditioning system, make it bearable.

If you plan to visit during the winter, come with warm-weather clothes, but throw in something for unpredictable rains and cold nights. Visitors from the Midwest and East Coast might think we're nuts, but we Californians bring down vests or parkas to Palm Springs during December and January to combat those cold desert nights.

For summer fun, be sure to bring hats and/or visors and lots of sunscreen. If you golf or play tennis, make your plans for the cooler morning hours, or play on night-lighted tennis courts. Bicycling and hiking should be planned for mornings too. The desert sun is not deceiving at all—it burns!

GETTING AROUND

The major car-rental agencies have service desks at the airport, and there are several **taxi companies** in town (check the *Yellow Pages* for listings). Most visitors drive their own car or a rental car when visiting the area. Call **Budget** (☎ toll free **800/527-0700**), **Hertz** (☎ toll free **800/654-3131**), or **Avis** (☎ toll free **800/331-1212**).

A shuttle bus called **Sunline** (☎ **619/343-3451**) runs year round through the entire Coachella Valley from Desert Hot Springs to Indio.

WHERE TO STAY

The desert cities offer a multitude of hotels and condominiums in a number of price ranges.

Be sure to ask questions before you choose your accommodations: What's the best price I can get? Are two connecting rooms a better deal than a suite? If I come another weekend instead of this weekend, is there a better price? Are you having any specials? Is there a special family rate? In any case, you're better off calling these hotels directly rather than going through the chain's reservation number. The hotel reservationists can meet your family's needs much better, and they are knowledgeable about current packages. Also check on minimum-stay requirements. Some establishments demand a three- or even four-night minimum on holiday weekends. Be sure to ask.

Hotel and condominium rates are based on three seasons. Winter rates are the highest, shoulder rates in the middle, and summer rates the lowest. To simplify, we will list only winter and summer rates. Also, there are packages galore to choose from, including weekend specials, holiday packages, and summer packages.

Below are the basic cutoff dates for each season. But sure to double-check at the hotel you choose. Its season cutoff could be a few days before or after the following dates, changing the price of your room substantially.

Summer is June 1 through September 12.

Shoulder is September 13 through December 19.

Winter is December 20 through Memorial Day.

Staying in Palm Springs

Staying in hotel-style condominiums is one convenient way to have the best of both worlds: family-style accommodations with all the services of a full-scale hotel; and your visit needn't be for a month at a time to make it worthwhile.

One such hotel-condominium is the **Oasis Villa Hotel,** at 4190 E. Palm Canyon Dr., Palm Springs, CA 92264 (☎ **619/328-1499,** or toll free **800/247-4664;** fax 619/324-8659). It's located across the street from the Gene Autry Hotel. There's a mini-mart/liquor store across the highway for emergency milk or other supplies,

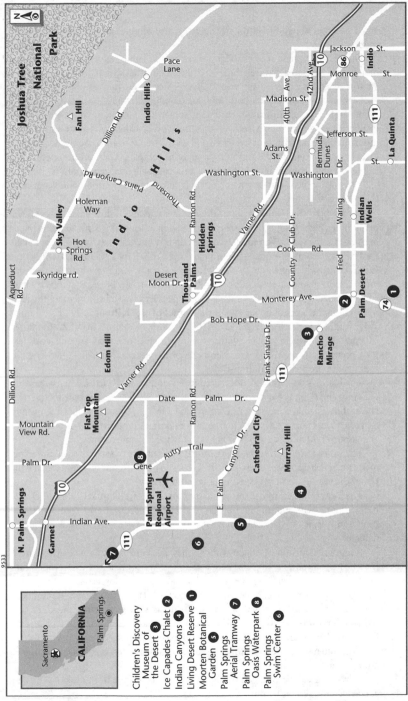

Palm Springs

Children's Discovery
Museum of
the Desert **3**

Ice Capades Chalet **2**

Indian Canyons **4**

Living Desert Reserve **1**

Moorten Botanical
Garden **5**

Palm Springs
Aerial Tramway **7**

Palm Springs
Oasis Waterpark **8**

Palm Springs
Swim Center **6**

9533

and a 24-hour Vons Market on the highway, five minutes east by car, for grocery shopping.

For the price, these accommodations are a good family value. Each is furnished individually and has a private garage; they are all outfitted with patio furniture and a gas barbecue, and a private washer and dryer. Kitchens are fully equipped with dishwashers, microwaves, dishes, pots, and pans. Some villas have breakfast nooks *and* dining areas. We found maintenance to be somewhat uneven, so you might inquire in advance whether the unit has been properly cleaned. The grounds are set up like a miniature suburban community, gated and with 24-hour security. Some guests bring bikes from home and let the kids ride through the complex. There are also eight pools to keep them occupied, nine hot spas, and five night-lighted tennis courts. Bicycles and other equipment can be rented. There is complimentary airport and water-park shuttle service.

For the best value, inquire about the summer packages, when villas start at $179 per unit per night (don't forget that you can sleep at least six people to a unit) with free passes to the Oasis Waterpark (same owners). Winter rates start at $259 for a standard two-bedroom 960-square-foot unit and rise to $329 for a 1,375-square-foot unit (sleeps eight), which includes two bedrooms, two baths, and a den with a queen-size sofa. Rates are based on six adults per unit, and include daily breakfast. Cribs are free. There are many special holiday and week-long packages available throughout the year.

Right in the heart of downtown is the **Palm Springs Hilton**, at 400 E. Tahquitz Way, Palm Springs, CA 92262 (☎ **619/320-6868**, or toll free **800/522-6900;** fax 619/320-2126), where you'll be within walking distance of Palm Canyon Drive, near the Convention Center, and within minutes of the airport. The hotel offers complimentary airport pickup and drop-off.

The Hilton's pool, though not fenced in, encompasses $1^{1}/_{2}$ acres. There are plenty of lounge chairs, and the pool bar is equipped with Micro Mist. Poolside food service is available. The hotel has six tennis courts and a full pro shop, as well as a tennis pro on staff. Court charges are $12 per hour per court. Arrangements can be made for golf at one of 40 nearby courses. There's a small videogame room.

The Body Spa (our favorite spot) affords you a choice of services such as waxing, massages, saunas, and cellulite wraps. It stays open on weekends in summer, daily the rest of the year. A small fitness room is complimentary.

The Terrace Restaurant is the casual spot for well-priced breakfast, lunch, or dinner selections, with indoor and outdoor seating. In addition to the continental and American cuisine, there is a children's menu. Room service is available beginning at 6:30am.

Junior suites are quite popular with families. Each one is like a small apartment. A large bedroom houses a king-size bed, and an L-shaped sofa in the living room pulls out into a sleeper. There's a large-screen TV and plenty of closet space. A room with two queen-size beds has enough space to add two rollaway beds, and it is filled with drawers. A standard room with a king-size bed has a love seat, table and chair, and full-length mirrors, and is also roomy. All the units have plantation shutters, reading lights, minibars, hairdryers, vanity areas with makeup lights, and remote-control TV with in-room movies. Refrigerators are standard only in suites. If you need one, they'll arrange it for a $5 charge.

Babysitting can be arranged through the concierge or the front desk. Note that a concierge is on duty only during season.

Room charges are for single or double occupancy. Winter room rates run $195–$225; junior suites are $255 and $285; full suites let for $315–$695. In summer, the rates drop—$80–$100 is charged for standard rooms, $115 and $130 for junior suites; and $125–$390 for full suites. Children 18 and under stay free in their parents' room. Those over 18 and extra adults are charged $20 per night. Rollaways are $20, and cribs are complimentary. Be sure to ask about special packages and promotions.

It may be off the beaten path, but many families have discovered that the **Doubletree Resort Palm Springs** makes a good family destination. It's located at Vista Chino at Landau Blvd. (P.O. Box 1644), Palm Springs, CA 92263 (☎ 619/322-7000, or toll free **800/637-0577**; fax 619/322-6853).

The fenced-in pool area is very large, with graduated steps at one side of the pool where all the little tykes like to play. We enjoyed being able to "chat" with the resident ducks who live in the pond near the golf course. Janey was able to convince them to watch her cartwheels, which she performed on the spacious grassy lawn next to the pool. Even in August there were lots of kids bobbing around in the pool, and pool toys were available for rent. On weekends, snacks can be purchased poolside.

The Doubletree has a tennis and fitness club, in addition to a volleyball net, 27 holes of golf, 10 tennis courts, and two indoor racquetball courts at the adjacent Desert Princess Country Club. Bike rentals can be arranged.

Families will feel most comfortable in the open-air Promenade Café (open at 6:30am), where breakfast, lunch, and dinner are served. The children's menu covers all tastes and is reasonably priced at $3–$4 for all choices. Standard coffeeshop fare is available for Mom and Dad. There are often specials, buffets, and specially priced menus during the summer months. Room service hours are 6:30am to 11pm. (Hours vary in summer.) For children's items—they're not on the menu.

All the rooms have balconies or patios and desert or mountain views. You can get a room with a king-size bed or two double beds and there's still space for a rollaway or crib. Bathrooms are roomy and all have double sinks, tub/shower combinations, and hairdryers. Each unit has a complimentary refrigerator and an individual safe. For a bedtime snack, everyone gets a package of special chocolate-chip cookies on their first night's stay.

Winter room rates are $215–245; summer rates run $105–125. There are numerous summer specials each year, so ask about them when you make your reservations. Also inquire about special golf packages. Children under 18 sleep free in their parents' room; extra adults pay $15. Cribs are free; rollaways cost $15. Inquire about discounts that apply to extended stays.

The hotel has 100 one- and two-bedroom condominiums, some with dens, also available, for rents ranging from $225 to $300 in the winter, and $115 to $160 in the summer. Discounts are also applicable to condominiums.

The spruced-up **Quality Inn** is located at 1269 E. Palm Canyon Dr., Palm Springs, CA 92264 (☎ 619/323-2775, or toll free **800/472-4339**; fax 619/323-4234). Rooms are cheerful and spotless with whitewashed furniture and fresh bed covers and upholstery. The small deck area and pool, plus a children's wading pool and Jacuzzi, are quite popular. A barbecue and gazebo are available for guest use. Sometimes you'll see families picnicking on the hotel's 2½-acre park just in back of the property. Coin-operated washers and dryers are provided.

There's no hotel restaurant, but a Carrow's (open 24 hours) and Jeremiah's (serving dinner and nightly entertainment) are steps away and offer hotel charge privileges. Jeremiah's will give hotel guests a discount.

The family suites are very popular. There are only 8 available, so reserve one well in advance. Each one consists of two connecting rooms, one with a king-size bed, the other made into a small living room with a sleeper sofa. Each suite has two full bathrooms, two TVs, and two phones, plus a refrigerator and a small microwave. Like all the hotel accommodations, the family suites have cable TV and pay movies, a small table and chairs, and a coffee maker. The new phone system includes PC and FAX hook ups. Double rooms are small but have two queen-size beds, while single-bedded rooms are available with a queen- or king-size bed. Standard rooms have space for either a rollaway or a crib, but not both. Some rooms have refrigerators and microwaves.

In the winter, on weeknights a room will cost $69–$119; on weekend evenings, $79–$149. Summer rates are $39–$69 weeknights; $44–$89 weekend nights. Room charges are based on single or double occupancy. There are a limited number of rollaways at $5 per night in summer, $10 in winter. Cribs are free. Children 18 and younger stay free in their parents' room. Additional guests are charged $5 per night in summer, $10 in winter. Parking is usually very close to the room.

The **Hampton Inn,** 2000 N. Palm Canyon Dr., Palm Springs, CA 92263 (☎ **619/320-0555,** or toll free **800/732-7755,** fax 619/320-2261), is a pleasant surprise. Located close to the Palm Springs Aerial Tramway, yet away from the hustle and bustle of downtown Palm Springs, it provides an affordable way to enjoy the desert.

The heated outdoor pool and spa are fenced in. The pool area, though small, has plenty of shady areas with umbrella tables and chaise longues.

There's no full-service restaurant on the premises, but the pool bar provides a limited menu and stays open until 7pm. There are also two barbecues near the pool available for guest use. A free California buffet breakfast is served every day in the hotel lobby.

Rooms aren't huge, but they are clean and newly spruced up. The "king study" has a king-size bed and a sleeper sofa, plus a separate vanity, small bathroom, full-length mirrors, and a coffeemaker. All king studies have refrigerators. The standard room with a king-size bed comes with a recliner, and there's room for a crib. A room with two double beds affords you space for four people and room for a crib. Amenities include remote-control TVs with free movie stations, radios, and same-day valet service. Rooms equipped for the handicapped and no-smoking rooms are available. Poolside rooms can be noisy, so we'd suggest units away from the pool.

In the winter, rooms cost $64–$79 single or double. In the summer, those rooms go for $32–$54. Add an extra $10 to each room on Friday, Saturday, and holiday nights. Children 18 and younger stay free in a room with their parents. There is no charge for a third and fourth extra adult. Cribs are complimentary; rollaways are $10. Parking is, in most cases, close to the room. Ask about special packages.

For a budget hotel, check out the **TraveLodge,** at 333 E. Palm Canyon Dr., Palm Springs, CA 92264 (☎ **619/327-1211,** or toll free **800/578-7878;** fax 619/320-4672). The hotel is centrally located and features two heated pools (not fenced in), a Jacuzzi, and a small games area and a volleyball net.

Rooms are motel style (parking is close to each room), with tiny patios and sliding glass doors. Request rooms with a balcony or patio for the most sunlight. A unit with two double beds still has room for a crib. Two of the buildings have rooms with queen-size beds. There is cable TV with movie channels. Refrigerators are available upon request at $3 per day and you can request a microwave for $5. Most accommodations have shower stalls, so if you need to bathe a baby in a bathtub, be sure to request such a room in advance. No-smoking rooms are available. There is a laundry for guest use.

In winter, rooms run $55–$75, single or double; the highest rates are charged on weekends. In summer, rates run $35–$45. There is no charge for cribs or rollaways. Children under 17 stay free in the same room with their parents. Each additional person pays $10 per night. Poolside rooms cost $10 extra. Be sure to inquire about packages which offer discounts to area activities.

Rancho Mirage

A true service-oriented, first-class hotel in Rancho Mirage is **The Ritz-Carlton,** 68-900 Frank Sinatra Dr., Rancho Mirage, CA 92270 (☎ **619/321-8282,** or toll free **800/241-3333;** fax 619/321-6928). Nestled in the foothills of the Santa Rosa Mountains in Rancho Mirage, it is neighbor to a herd of rare bighorn sheep, whose protected reserve is just behind the resort. The hotel's formality might put you off at first, but you'll discover it's a very friendly resort with comfortable rooms and fine service.

Even the Ritz has adapted itself to the family market. There's practically nothing the staff won't do to accommodate the kids—other than sending them to college! For your youngest tots, the hotel can provide anything from car seats and walkers, to strollers and stuffed animals. One call to the gift or sundry shop can get you baby lotion, pacifiers, bottles, or anything else you might need. Our late-night request for cough medicine was handled pleasantly and efficiently. Cookies and milk are delivered if they know in advance you're coming, and repeat guests are given a surprise amenity.

Both the Café and the Mirada restaurants have a children's menu, which is also available through room service. And kids 10 and under eat free off the children's menu when accompanied by an adult. There are tons of board games and children's videos available from the concierge, and you can even get children's books and coloring books if you left yours at home.

The Ritz Kids children's program makes every attempt to incorporate nature activities in the schedule. In addition to nature walks, kids create collages using unusual desert plants and rocks; learn how to prepare healthy, natural snacks; and learn about Native American folklore. The Ritz Kids Center is filled with Little Tykes toys, books, and board games. Kids also get to participate in relay races, water games, T-shirt painting, origami, miniature golf, volleyball, and lots more. A biologist from the Bighorn Sheep Institute visits to speak with the youngsters. Only 5- to 12-year-olds can join the program, which meets daily, year-round, from 9am to 4pm. The program runs no matter how many children sign up. During peak periods it's best to reserve a place in advance, although the staff will make every attempt to honor last-minute requests. The program charge is $45 for the day (which includes a T-shirt), or $25 for a half day.

The tiny tot program accommodates 4- and 5-year-olds. Their day includes storytelling, sing-alongs, and snacks, and costs $20. With advance notice, the concierge can make arrangements for babysitters.

An evening program called Kids Night Out gives the children a chance to have dinner together and watch a G-rated movie while Mom and Dad have dinner out. That weekend and holiday program costs $25 and runs from 6 to 9pm. (There must be a minimum of four children.) Holidays are special too. In addition to themed programs, the annual Teddy Bear Tea (at $5.75 per child) has become a tradition for lots of families. Have little Penny or Jeremy bring along their favorite teddy, and treat them to hot cocoa and other snacks at this adorable little tea.

While the kids are busy, you can just relax by the pool or utilize any of the hotel's recreational facilities. The Ritz maintains a hiking and running trail through the mountains, and while it's not much to look at, it will surely get your heart pumping. A stop first at the Fitness Center will secure a guide for the trail walk, complete with warmup exercises. Or there are exercise machines in the small club, and personalized weight and exercise consultations can be arranged, as well as in-room or in-club massage. Have the concierge arrange for a babysitter if necessary, then reserve a court at the Tennis Club, one of the hotel's biggest draws. Tom Gorman, coach of the U.S. Davis Team and the U.S. Olympic tennis team, is the on-premises director, and two teaching pros are on staff. The club has ten courts lit for night play and a full-service restaurant. Golf lovers aren't left out either. The Ritz-Carlton has reciprocal agreements with several courses in the area.

The Mirada is the hotel's casual cliffside al fresco café adjacent to the pool. You can order continental breakfast on weekends, or lunch and dinner every day. We found that the Café, despite its formal decor, was perfectly comfortable with the family. It's open for breakfast, lunch, and dinner. The Club Grill, open for dinner only, is more appropriate for adults (men are required to wear jackets). Room service can be ordered 24 hours.

If you stay on the Club Floor, a private concierge will painstakingly explain the complimentary continental breakfast, afternoon tea, hors d'oeuvres, and after-dinner treats displayed each day in the exclusive lounge.

Accommodations in the hotel are quite spacious and comfortable, are decorated traditionally, and have huge, luxurious bathrooms. All the room amenities of a first-class hotel are offered, including maid service twice a day and valet service daily. Rooms are defined as minimum, superior, and deluxe. The difference is in the view: the first offers a view of the Santa Rosa foothills; the next gives you the choice of the Santa Rosa Mountains or the valley below; in a deluxe room there is the possibility of a pool, courtyard and valley, or mountain view.

In high season, standard rooms cost $260–$350. On the Club Floor you'll pay $395; suites go for $650–$2,000. From July to September, standard rooms let for $89–$109; Club rooms cost $179; suites range from $350–$800. Ask about special packages. Cribs and rollaways are available at no charge. Children under 18 sleep free in their parents' room; adults 18 and over are charged $25 per night. Valet parking costs $12 per day.

When you reach the shimmering blue-tile dome and soothing Moorish architecture of **The Westin Mission Hills Resort,** Dinah Shore and Bob Hope Drives, Rancho Mirage, CA 92270 (☎ **619/328-5955;** fax 619/770-2199), you'll have arrived at an oasis of sorts. But as romantic and expensive as it may first appear, this 360-acre Westin resort is a popular destination for repeat family visitors. In addition to offering plenty of rooms with two queen-size beds and special family promotions, the attitude here is very welcoming to families.

Westin has increased its commitment to families by creating an all-around awareness of family needs. Now not only do children receive a welcome package when checking in (geared to their age), but they get a beverage container that can be refilled at every meal for no charge. Here's a sample of just some of the hotel's efforts: families get preferred restaurant reservations and express meal service (at the Bella Vista); special laundry prices are charged for children's items; bottle warmers and emergency diapers and wipes are given upon request; in-room refrigerators, jogging strollers, children's bathrobes, and even potty seats and step stools are provided!

The Cactus Kids Club, the resort's youth program, is structured to the ages of the participating children, but is open to kids 4–12 from 8am to 5pm daily, year round, no matter how many kids register. You can sign up the children by the hour ($4 per) or all day ($25). An evening program is offered when there's a big enough request. The program is set in its own special clubhouse equipped with toys, games, arts and crafts supplies, a VCR, bathroom, and a limited amount of outdoor equipment. Almost every outdoor activity is close to the club, except for the main pool where the children are taken for swimming. Counselors are not water-safety trained, but there are two lifeguards at the pool. Counselors go in the water with the kids and provide water-wings for the nonswimming children if you wish. Be sure to let them know if you don't want your kids to participate in water activities. Children also get to play tennis, shuffleboard, and croquet, and can use the putting green. And ask about Cactus Tennis Register your kids in advance, because the program is limited to 20 children, and be prepared for a lengthy registration form.

The El Chiquito Café next door to the Club is where they go for lunch, and the charge is added to your room. Take it from our experience: Let the counselors know what your child can or can't order in advance so that you're not surprised by a very hefty restaurant charge at the end of your stay! When you are dining as a family, you'll be pleasantly surprised to discover that kids eat for free.

While the children are being entertained and making new friends, you can sample the rest of the hotel's recreational offerings. The Reed Anderson Tennis School, rated one of the top five in the country (by *Town & Country* magazine), has come to the Westin with week-long, midweek, and weekend tennis programs, as well as daily instruction. A tee-off time can be reserved on one of the two 18-hole championship golf courses designed by Pete Dye and Gary Player. There are also three practice putting greens and two driving ranges. The Westin has three swimming pools and four spas, and each has poolside food and beverage service. The free-form Las Brisas pool is designed with waterfalls and a 60-foot waterslide that drops into a separate pool. If you still can't sit still, there are bicycle rentals, horseshoes, badminton, and a regulation sand volleyball court.

Soothe those aching muscles in the Health Club's steam room. There's also massage, fitness equipment and weights, and plenty of aerobics and yoga classes. The Aida Grey Institût de Beauté is on the premises, as is a hair salon. Ask about the numerous salon packages.

The gorgeous Bella Vista restaurant is the most appropriate of the two hotel dining spots for families with young children. You can eat indoors in the dramatic dining room, or on the outdoor patio. Food is served from 6:30am to 10pm. A separate children's menu offers lots of breakfast, lunch, and dinner selections. If you're ready for a special adult night out, La Concha is a stunning restaurant offering Pacific Rim Cuisine. Asian flavors and Pacific ingredients are blended with European techniques. One night we caught the sunset from the patio of the Lobby Lounge where you can have drinks and bar snacks. Room service can be ordered 24 hours. There's even a complete children's menu available through room service for kids 12 and under.

Resort and deluxe rooms (the difference is the view) are terrifically spacious and furnished with either two queen-size beds or one king-size bed. The furnishings are contemporary whitewash with faux stone tables, interesting table lamps, and Berber carpets. Amenities include a comfy chair and reading lamp, voice mail, digital clock radio, remote-control with cable color TV in-room movies, and minibar. Bathrooms have double sinks, and a separate vanity area with a coffee maker and wall safe. Upstairs rooms have cathedral ceilings.

If you need a crib only, you might consider a room in the "23-series." These have a semiprivate seating area, two overstuffed chairs, a king-size bed, and a TV that swivels from the seating area (where you could put a crib) to the bedroom. Spacious junior suites are in high demand. Each has three patios, two TVs, a bedroom with a king-size bed, a hide-a-bed, table and chairs, and a bathroom with a double vanity. A more expensive room in the Royal Oasis Club entitles you to complimentary limousine service to and from the airport; personalized check-in in the Club; private concierge; daily newspaper; complimentary continental breakfast, hors d'oeuvres, and cocktails; complimentary use of the health club; and preferred reservations for golf, tennis, and dining.

In winter, resort rooms rent for $199, deluxe rooms go for $229, the Royal Oasis Club is $259, and suites begin at $330. In summer, resort rooms cost $119, deluxe units are $149, rooms in the Royal Oasis Club are $179, and suites begin at $210. Rates are double or single occupancy. Children 18 and under stay free in their parents' room; additional adults are charged $25. Cribs are complimentary; roll aways cost $10. Make sure you inquire about the special summer promotional rate of $79 based on availability. Also, from June to September, Sunday through Thursday, when you reserve a room for two nights, you get the third night free. There are also numerous promotions throughout the year, including holiday packages with special children's programs. Parking is free.

The pace at **Marriott's Rancho Las Palmas Resort,** 41000 Bob Hope Dr., Rancho Mirage, CA 92270 (☎ **619/568-2727,** or toll free **800/458-8786;** fax 619/568-5845), is leisurely, but the service is first class. Your first encounter with this four-star resort is like a step back into old California. First you see gorgeous early California architecture framed in brilliant bougainvillea and surrounded by lush landscaping. Then you enter a lobby designed in the authentic decor of that era.

Weekends and holidays you can expect both adult and children's activities. Based on a theme, the programs offer family Bingo, movies, aerobics, scavenger hunts, carnivals, and ice-cream socials.

During the summer, children 5–12 can participate in Kactus Kids Kamp, from 9:30am to noon. Swimming, crafts, games, cookie-making, and lunch are included for a charge of $20 per child the first day, $10 per day thereafter. (There must be a minimum of two kids signed up for the program to run.)

The resort has three swimming pools (with food and beverage service), a golf course, tennis courts (junior tennis is regularly scheduled), a clubhouse, and lots of green grassy areas. Adult and children's bikes are for rent. The pool at the country club (available free to guests) has a wading pool and small playground area.

There are four restaurants in the hotel, but the Fountain Court is the best choice for families with young children. It offers a children's menu (crayons included) for breakfast, lunch, and dinner at quite reasonable prices. And 24-hour room service is available.

The newly refurbished rooms are not fancy, but they are certainly deluxe. Double rooms come with small sofas, some of which pull out to make an extra bed, and comfortable reading chairs with ottomans. There's just barely room for a crib. Patios have a chaise longue and table. All rooms have coffee makers and remote-control TV (you can even check out via TV) with "on-command video," allowing you to pick from hundreds of movies to watch whenever you want. Bathrooms are small. Most rooms can connect; there are numerous non-smoking accommodations. Parents of toddlers note: when requesting ground-floor accommodations, be sure to avoid the rooms that open up to the little ponds, which are not fenced off.

During high season, rooms are at four-star rates. If these are too steep, come during the summer when the rates drop substantially—but the service doesn't. In winter, rates are $235–$280, single or double; suites cost $475–$1,000. In summer the rooms run $59–$125; suites, $250–$500. There are American Plan (AP) packages, Modified American Plan (MAP) packages, and golf packages. Check to see if any of these meet your family's needs. And be sure to ask about special promotions.

Staying in Palm Desert

When you step into the lobby of **Marriott's Desert Springs Resort & Spa,** 74855 Country Club Dr., Palm Desert, CA 92260 (☎ **619/341-2211,** or toll free **800/228-9290;** fax 619/341-1872), you immediately feel the energy. This is a hotel designed for activity. The sound of waterfalls flowing into the hotel's lagoon greets you first. Look up and you'll see the gigantic eight-story atrium lobby; look down and you'll see an oasis in the middle of the desert. Mini-tour boats greet guests at the lagoon dock for a boat tour of the hotel grounds. It will even drop you off at the Tuscany or the Mikado, two of the hotel restaurants. Kids love the boats, and the drivers are usually responsive to the hundreds of questions and requests for boat driving.

This 895-room hotel boasts numerous activities for adults and children alike. Children ages 5–12 can join The Kids Klub, which provides supervised activities such as fish feeding, indoor and outdoor games, movies, and arts and crafts. The program runs daily year-round from 10am to 5pm as long as a minimum of three children have signed up by 9pm the preceding evening. You can pay either by the whole day ($25 includes lunch), or pay $5 per activity. The hourly rate allows you to spend time with the kids, then perhaps take off the morning or afternoon for golf or the spa. Babysitters can be arranged for children under five. During holidays, special activities are scheduled to include the entire family, as well as individual recreation for the children. Be sure to pre-register for these days.

There are two 18-hole championship golf courses on the property, as well as The Greens, a putting course available for $10 per play ($5 for children). Fifteen hard-surface tennis courts (six lighted) can be reserved, and the spa offers a 22-station gym, exercise pool, plunge pools, and jogging paths. Three pools, including one remarkable one surrounded by an artificial sandy beach, offer a variety of places to meet new friends. At one pool, a cafeteria-style snack bar makes it easy to have lunch at the pool without having to change clothes first.

There are numerous restaurants and lounges on the premises. All the restaurants have children's menus, including the Mikado, a Japanese restaurant that serves teppanyaki tableside, and they are all no-smoking. The Colonnade of Shops is quite impressive and features a children's clothing shop.

There are a variety of rooms to choose from, all decorated in the ubiquitous desert pastels. Units with two double beds, individually or connecting to a room with a king-size bed, are quite popular with families. And the one-bedroom suites are in high demand. The sleeping rooms are roomy enough for a crib, and have digital clock radios, upholstered reading chairs or hide-a-beds, minibars, free wall safes, remote-control TVs with in-house movies that can be turned off at the front desk, and patios with chairs. Refrigerators can be requested at no charge. The large bathrooms have separate showers and lots of personal-care amenities.

In winter, standard rooms run $250–$310, single or double; suites, $600–$2,100. In summer, rates are $105–$165, single or double, and suites run $375–$1,400. Children sleep free in their parents' room, and there's no charge for a crib or rollaway. Ask about special packages. The busy time for the Desert Springs is summer weekends (for which you should make reservations at least three weeks in advance) and the Memorial Day and Labor Day weekends (for which reservations should be made at least one month in advance).

If your love is tennis, or if you want to learn, the **Shadow Mountain Resort & Racquet Club,** 45-750 San Luis Rey, Palm Desert, CA 92260 (☎ **619/346-6123** collect, or toll free **800/472-3713** in California; fax 619/346-6518), is the place to stay. Not only has *Tennis* magazine named it one of the top 50 tennis resorts in the country for 17 consecutive years, but Shadow Mountain also offers spacious condominiums at affordable prices, with the comforts of a full-service hotel. There are 16 courts (4 night-lit), and four swimming pools, one a huge figure-eight near the lobby. Reciprocal golf privileges are arranged at nearby courses. On the property are two paddle-tennis courts, two grass volleyball courts, basketball courts, and bicycle rentals (some children's bikes are available). Even tennis court fees are included in the nightly rate, although there's a nominal charge for the clinics. And there are tennis clinics even for teens.

This is a friendly, residential-style site, where families gather around the big pool, toddlers play on the grassy area, and kids bicycle through the gated/guarded grounds. A poolside restaurant serves breakfast, lunch, and cocktails, and barbecue grills are available for guest use.

There are usually a variety of activities going on at the complex. Sometimes it's water aerobics, another time Bingo by the pool. The Little Lizards Kidz Kamp is a fairly unstructured children's program which meets on Saturday and Sunday (also during the week in winter). The program is for ages 5–12 and runs for a limited number of hours in the morning. The cost per child is $8, $15 including lunch. On Saturday nights, Mom and Dad can take off while the Coyote Club takes over. This evening program of games, movies, arts and crafts, pizza, and refreshments costs $15 per child for the full evening session (from 6 to 10pm). Babysitting can be arranged with advance notice.

There are numerous accommodations to choose from; your best bet is to describe your family's needs to the reservationist. Basically, there are four types of units: guest rooms, studios, villas, and condominiums. All the accommodations are privately owned, so furnishings and decor vary, but all come fully equipped with kitchenware, linens, and beach towels, and there is daily maid service. Guest rooms and studios are basically very large rooms with kitchenettes, some nearly the size of a small home kitchen. Villas and condos have one to three bedrooms; these large apartments have

In Case of Emergency

Desert Hospital, 1150 N. Indian Canyon Ave., Palm Springs (☎ **619/323-6511**) has 24-hour emergency-room service.

comfortable living rooms with sleeper-sofas, dining room furniture, fully stocked kitchens, and good-sized bathrooms. VCRs and current movies are available for rent. All units have air conditioning, cable color TV (with the Disney Channel), and direct-dial phones with message waiting. Some first-floor condos have sliding glass patio doors opening directly to large grassy areas, or even a creek, so that kids can just walk out and play. Coin-operated laundries are available.

Rates for summer weekends are: guest rooms and studios, $80–$95; one-bedroom condos, $140–$160; two bedrooms, $190–$205; three bedrooms, $225–$245. On weekends the rest of the year, guest rooms and studios cost $104–$170; one-bedroom condos, $180–$240; two bedrooms, $225–$340; three bedrooms, $270–$440. Add $15 for a two- or three-bedroom villa. There are good savings or long-term rentals. Midweek rates in all categories are about $15–$20 cheaper each night. Daily rates for guest rooms and studios include continental breakfast. Children 18 and under sleep free in their parents' room; additional adults are charged $15 per night. Cribs and rollaways are available with advance notice for $15 per night.

If you are familiar with the **Embassy Suites,** 74-700 Highway 111, Palm Desert (**☎ 619/340-6600,** or toll free **800/633-2834;** fax 619/340-9519), you know they offer one-bedroom suites with a separate living room complete with hide-a-bed. This one is no exception.

The property itself has an 18-hole putting green, six lighted tennis courts, and a very small exercise room. The pool, although small, is pleasant and fenced in.

Rooms are small and somewhat dark, but cool. The living room holds a queen sleeper sofa, coffee maker, and refrigerator. Microwaves are available by request at no charge. Each suite has two televisions and two telephones. Some come with two double beds in the bedroom, others with one king-size bed.

Like all the Embassy Suites, this one serves up a made-to-order complimentary breakfast and afternoon drinks and snacks. If you choose room service for lunch or dinner, a children's menu is provided.

In winter, room rates are $164–$184 weeknights, $189–$230 weekends. In summer, the rates are $79–$89 weekdays, $89–$99 weekends. Children under 12 are free; those over 12 and adults are charged $15 each night. No rollaways are available; cribs are complimentary. Be sure to inquire about minimum-stay requirements on holidays.

Indian Wells

"A touch of Europe . . . " is what everyone said when the **Hyatt Grand Champions Resort** opened in 1986 at 44-600 Indian Wells Lane, Indian Wells, CA 92210 (**☎ 619/341-1000,** or toll free **800/233-1234;** fax 619/568-2236). Because it had that tag of luxury and formality, some families weren't so eager to bring little Johnny. Announcement: You *can* bring little Johnny and feel comfortable in this elegant resort hotel. While the appointments are decidedly European and luxurious, and the lobby is grand, the hotel will welcome your children and the staff will treat them with care.

The Camp Hyatt program for children 3–13 operates daily from 9am to 4pm, year round, and will operate even if only one child signs up. The indoor group activities include challenging craft projects, Nintendo, movies, games, and a supply of toys; the outdoor activities include swimming, volleyball, croquet, tennis, and a playground facility that keeps kids busy. Parents can sign up their children for the whole day at a cost of $35, or a half day for $21. Lunch is $6.50 extra. An evening program is charged by the hour. Dinner can be ordered for $6.50.

For teens, 13–17, the Rock Hyatt program offers some off-property trips during holiday periods.

While your little ones enjoy meeting and playing with other kids, you can check out the Hyatt facilities, such as the Health & Fitness Club. Spa treatments, massage, and aerobics classes, as well as an indoor spa, sauna, and steam room, are part of the services. Bicycle rentals for you alone or with the family can be arranged in the club. Two 18-hole championship golf courses, plus 12 tennis courts (including a sunken celebrity court and a 10,500-seat stadium for special events), four pools, and two Jacuzzis round out the recreational offerings.

The hotel has both fine dining rooms and casual eating places. Austin's is a steakhouse, open for dinner only. Trattoria California is where you and the kids will feel the most comfortable, whether dining al fresco or indoors; it's open for breakfast, lunch, and dinner, and provides children's portions at lower prices. Pianissimo is a lounge with live entertainment and a dance floor. Charlie's is a separate restaurant located near the Tennis Club, open for dinner. Poolside food service is available, and room service runs 24 hours.

There are 336 all-suite rooms at the Hyatt, each decorated in pale, soft colors, European in ambience, but not stuffy. The standard parlor suites are split-level accommodations facing the mountains, pool, or golf course. The marble bathrooms are spacious, and each one has an individual deep tub and glass-enclosed shower. A small serving bar and minibar are adjacent to the sleeping alcove, which is furnished with either two double beds or one king-size bed. The step-down living area contains a sofa, chair and writing desk. In some rooms the sofa converts to a bed. Balconies with table and chairs are comfortable. Robes, hairdryers, two telephones, full-length mirrors, coffeemakers, remote-control TV, and pay movies are all standard.

One step up in accommodations is the Regency Club, offering guests concierge service, complimentary continental breakfast, cocktails, and hors d'oeuvres. The rooms on this floor are also parlor suites with prime pool views. Penthouse suites have separate bedrooms, a sitting room, $1^1/2$ baths, large terraces, stereo cassette players, and other amenities.

The villas are something else! The one- and two-bedroom accommodations are in a separate building, each with a private courtyard and Jacuzzi. Every villa is decorated differently, but all have large living rooms and dining areas, skylights, Roman shades, and a step-up bath. They even have wood-burning fireplaces, two-line phones, and stereo cassette players. But best of all, they come with a 24-hour European-trained butler who fills your culinary needs!

Concierge service is expert and complete. The Business Center is equipped with computers, copiers, and fax machines. Babysitting and anything else you may need can be arranged.

In winter, rates are $240–$285 for standard parlor suites, $325 in the Regency Club, $375 for Penthouse suites, and $725–$925 for a villa. Summers are more affordable. Parlor suites rent for $119–$139, the Regency Club costs $179. Penthouse suites are rented at $210, and villas run $350–$450. Children under 18 are free when sharing a parent's room. An adjoining room can be reserved at 50% off when you pay the regular price on the first room. Those over 18 are charged $25 per night. There are cribs and rollaways available at no charge. Ask about special packages. Self-parking is free and valet parking costs $8 per night.

The management of the **Stouffer Esmeralda Resort,** 44-400 Indian Wells Lane, Indian Wells (☎ 619/773-4444, or toll free **800/552-4386;** fax 619/346-9308) is absorbed with details, details, details—from the emery boards in the bathrooms to the welcome carpet in the elevator, which is changed daily to reflect the day of the week.

The lobby is grand and while the kids might be tempted to sail down the bannister of the elegant African oak staircase to the multicolored stone floor below, we'd strongly discourage it. A clubby, cool lounge with lots of sofas and overstuffed pillows looks out at a mountain view. Sirocco, the hotel's smartly appointed dining room, has an excellent reputation. Charisma is the all-day dining room with indoor and outdoor seating. The children's menu opens like a storybook and is accompanied by an actual paperback story, "The Legend of Esmeralda." Breakfast, lunch, and dinner choices included everything from the ubiquitous chicken nuggets to a five-ounce filet. Room service can be requested 24 hours daily.

The property is lush, and the staff is family-friendly. The pool area, filled with chaises longues and umbrellas, not only includes several shallow pools and two spas, but also a sandy beach decorated with plastic beach toys for the toddlers. There's a one-foot wading pool and waterfalls, all bordered by an artificial lake. A pool bar serves snacks and drinks.

Seven lighted tennis courts, a tennis pro who schedules clinics, and 36 holes of golf are on the sports menu, along with an on-property basketball court, sand volleyball court, and croquet. Items necessary to play these games, as well as bike rentals, can be arranged at the Logo Shop. Tired muscles aren't forgotten at the full-service health spa where guests will find a workout area, massage, facials, steam rooms, and other beauty services.

The Kids Beach Club tailors the day's program depending on the number and ages of the children signed up. Generally, the activities range from water-balloon toss, Ping-Pong, arts and crafts, to relays, treasure hunts, and movies. Be sure to sign up a day in advance, and note that the program runs only if a minimum of three children are registered. Half-day sessions, including lunch, cost $20. A full day, also with lunch, will cost $35. On holidays and certain special nights, the hotel offers an evening program for kids.

Standard Esmeralda rooms are furnished with either two queen-size beds or one king-size bed, remote control TV plus a small TV in the bathroom, mini-bar, hairdryer, three phones, ironing board and iron, bathrobes, and a reading chair. There are also in-room movies and a computer/fax port in the telephone. These accommodations have room for a rollaway or a crib. Spacious corner rooms with sitting areas and a king-size bed offer two closets. The only caveat: the property is quite large. If you plan to spend much time at the pool and are traveling with small children and all their pool paraphernalia, we'd strongly suggest requesting a room near either the pool elevator or the main bank of elevators.

The room rates in winter are $275–$375 single or double, suites rent for $600; in summer the price is $145–$195, and suites let for $320. There are a number of packages to consider. A Family package includes vouchers for children's meals, two vouchers per child up to age 11 each night, for up to two children, plus the room for: winter weeknights $189, Friday and Saturday $209. In summer, that rate falls to $89 midweek, $109 weekends. Children under 18 sleep free in their parents' room. Additional adults pay $25 per night. Cribs are complimentary; rollaways cost $15 per night.

La Quinta

It's well worth the extra drive past Palm Springs to stay at **La Quinta Hotel Golf & Tennis Resort,** 49-499 Eisenhower Dr. (P.O. Box 69), La Quinta, CA 92253 (☎ **619/564-4111,** or toll free **800/854-1271, 800/472-4316** in California; fax 619/564-5718). The desert's oldest resort hotel originally opened its doors in 1926 with 56 casitas. Today 640 guest casitas cover the grounds, but you'd never know it. Low, whitewashed, adobe-style "pods," with red-tile roofs and bright-blue doors, are spread throughout the flower-filled grounds. The warm, rich hacienda-style lobby is inviting, and opens to two salons. It's as if you are visiting a private ranch. The fire-places in the Santa Rosa Room wait to be lit on a cool desert evening. Returning guests have donated a collection of favorite teapots, and new guests can pick the one they want to use for afternoon tea.

The plaza looks as if it has been there from the beginning. Janey and her friend Joey spent at least an hour traversing the saltillo-tile pathways which led past colorful tile aqueducts, fountains, and antique lampposts. Two floors of retail shops and two of the hotel restaurants are found through the graceful arches. In addition to the bou-tiques, the wine shop (with the only wine-tasting bar in the desert), and the flower store, there is a fabulous-looking art deco beauty parlor, a children's store, and a fit-ness center.

Of the three main hotel restaurants, Morgans and the Adobe Grill are the most comfortable for families.

Morgans is a 1920s-style café with an open kitchen. It's open for breakfast, lunch, and dinner, and features "blue-plate" specials in addition to its other offerings. For lunch and dinner, there is a children's menu priced under $6.50. It might be a good idea to let the hostess know you're not interested in a leisurely meal. We experienced very slow service—not a pleasant thing with two energetic children.

The Adobe Grill puts you right in the mood for regional Mexican cooking. It's cool and open and beautifully decorated. A limited children's menu offers a taco, quesadilla, or burrito, each $4.75. Room service is available 24 hours.

With 25 pools and 35 spas, none of which is too far from your front door, it's not too difficult to find a place to light with the kids. There's also 90 holes of golf includ-ing PGA West's TPC Stadium and Jack Nicklaus Resort courses; Tennis is offered on 30 courts (no charge), and you have a choice of grass, hard, or Har-Tru clay. A tennis pro shop, pool and spa, and another dining room are nearby.

Camp La Quinta is offered on summer weekends and certain holidays with super-vised activities for children 3–11. The daytime program runs from 10am to 3pm and includes lunch, the evening program is from 6 to 10:30pm and includes dinner. The holiday programs are priced separately: $12.50 for the day with lunch, and $25 for an evening of activities and dinner. There are all sorts of indoor and outdoor games and crafts on the schedule, but no swimming.

The original casita rooms are cool and private, all with small private patios. Some rooms are connecting; you can even get one with a screened-in porch or a fireplace. All have lovely bathrooms with big deep tubs, a separate shower, and double sinks. There are two phones, remote-control TV with in-room movies, full-length mirrors, and overstuffed chairs. Twice-daily maid service, a refrigerator or ice maker, and terrycloth bathrobes are also included.

Other rooms open to swimming pools. These have a king-size bed or two double beds, a comfy reading chair, and a large bathroom with separate shower stall and double sinks. Deluxe units are a little larger and have oversize bathrooms. Some also have fireplaces. Others have a separate little alcove with a counter, glasses, and refrigerator. Each room is a little different, but all deluxe units have space for both a crib *and* a rollaway bed.

A big surprise at the resort are the six specially decorated rooms furnished with families in mind. In the lovely double-bedded cottage is a separate alcove furnished with a brightly decorated junior bed giving a child the feeling of his/her own private space. The rooms are away from the pools but have private patios and plenty of adjacent green grass to play on. A little child's chair is parked in front of the fireplace. The bathrooms are large and have separate dressing areas.

Attention to detail is the norm at La Quinta Hotel, so it wasn't surprising to see a sign on the gates leading to these newer rooms which read "Please close the gates to protect our little guests." If you see a big yellow ribbon on the door of a room, it's for a returning guest.

During the high season, from January through April, room rates range from $200 to $290, and suites range from $600 to $2,100. In the summer, from June through September, rooms rent for $80–$150 and suites cost $300–$1,200. Cribs are complimentary and rollaways cost $15 extra. Children, regardless of age, stay free in their parents' room, and there is no extra-person charge. Parking is also free.

Condominiums in Palm Desert and Palm Springs

The advantages to staying in a condominium or rental home are obvious. For longer stays, the comfort of having separate sleeping quarters, a place to cook, a washer and dryer, a living room, and a private pool (in rental homes) is important to many people. And the rates are usually quite reasonable, especially for long stays. While most of these rentals do not include daily maid service, arrangements can be made separately for those services. There are many folks who visit the area for several weeks or a month at a time, and these accommodations are perfect for them. Some rentals are in country clubs that offer golf and tennis privileges. If you call the following companies and state your family's needs, they'll try to locate the right accommodation for you. There's usually a minimum length of stay, especially for private homes. Rates vary so drastically between accommodations that they will not be listed here.

Frontier Vacation Villas, at 222 N. Calle El Segundo, Palm Springs, CA 92262 (☎ toll free **800/284-5527**) will afford you a great location, two super pool areas, and spacious, comfortable accommodations at reasonable rates. The condos are located in the 102-unit Plaza Villas complex in downtown Palm Springs. The two-story buildings are in walking distance of the Convention Center and Palm Canyon Drive.

Each one- or two-bedroom apartment has a dining room, a fully equipped kitchen the size of many home kitchens, washer and dryer, color TV, phones, air conditioning, and a private patio. Sheets, towels, dishes, and cooking utensils are provided; maid service can be arranged for a charge. The master bedroom has a king-size bed and private bathroom. The second bedroom comes with two twin-size beds, and there's a second full bathroom. The "super" two-bedroom unit is furnished with a hide-a-bed in the living room, making it large enough for six people. Cribs are available; no rollaways or highchairs.

Call for rates and be sure to ask about summer, weekend, and holiday weekend packages. Longer stays mean lower rates.

Sunrise Company Rental Division, 76-300 Country Club Dr., Palm Desert, CA 92260 (☎ **619/345-5695,** or toll free **800/869-1130**), specializes in renting condominiums located within prestigious country clubs such as Rancho Las Palmas, the Lakes, Monterey, Palm Valley, and PGA West at La Quinta. All these clubs include tennis and golf facilities as well as pools and spas.

The Rental Connection, 170 E. Palm Canyon Dr., Palm Springs, CA 92264 (☎ **619/320-7336,** or toll free **800/462-7256;** fax 619/320-3521), can provide you with condos or private homes. They'll set you up in one of more than 40 locations throughout Palm Springs. Call with your specific needs.

WHERE TO EAT

There are some fine eating establishments in the area that cater to adults, but you don't need to feel that you are depriving your child of a good meal by going to one of the chain restaurants located throughout the desert communities. Following are some restaurants that either have a big family clientele or have children's menus. And don't forget the restaurants at the hotels we've mentioned. Several have children's menus, and all welcome little diners.

Palm Springs

Billy Reed's, 1800 N. Palm Canyon Dr. (☎ **619/325-1946**), close to the Aerial Tramway, has a large selection of traditional food and a children's menu. Breakfast, lunch, and dinner choices are served anytime. The usual egg, pancake, and cereal breakfast selections are available. All the pastries are made on the premises ($1.95–$2.45)—be sure to try the cinnamon roll or pecan roll.

Lunch selections include lots of hamburgers, sandwiches, casseroles, and salads. Prices range from $4.95 to $13. At dinner, there is country fried steak, pot roast, ground steak, and shrimp. Full dinners run $10–$17. Desserts are sumptuous, and there are lots of choices.

Kids can order pancakes, waffles, cereal, pig-in-a-blanket, or eggs at breakfast for $2–$3. Lunch choices are the ubiquitous burger, hot dog, grilled cheese, peanut butter and jelly, or Mickey Rooney and cheese. Lunch costs $3. Dinner comes with kid-size soup or salad and there's meatloaf, a hot beef sandwich (with "non-yuk vegetables"), fish sticks, and chicken drumsticks. Dinners go for $4–$5. Highchairs and boosters are available. Servers will split adult portions for two kids, and will warm baby bottles.

Open daily from 7am to 11pm. There is live entertainment on weekends. A no-smoking section is provided. Call ahead to find out how long the wait is—weekends can be very busy. All major credit cards are welcome, and parking is available.

The Las Casuelas group of restaurants, each individually owned and run, have been around the desert for years. **Las Casuelas Restaurant,** at 368 N. Palm Canyon Dr. (☎ **619/325-3213**) is the original, which opened in 1958. Small and dark, with rows of booths, it serves up burritos, tostados, tacos, machaca, steak, and combination plates of enchiladas, chile rellenos, and tamales with gusto, using family recipes from five generations back. There's nothing on the menu higher in price than $11.75, and that's for steak. Combination plates average $7, complete dinners go up to $9.50, and the other offerings range from $1.85 (for a taco) to $6.95 (for New Mexico enchiladas). Beer is the only alcoholic beverage served.

You'll see lots of children here. The child's plate (for kids under 12) offers a hamburger patty, one taco, or one egg with beans and rice, and bread or tortillas for $4.25. Or kids will find plenty to choose from in the à la carte column of the menu. For an extra dollar, adult portions can be split. Highchairs and booster seats are available. Baby food and bottles are no problem to warm in the kitchen.

The restaurant is open Sunday through Thursday from 10:30am to 10pm and on Friday and Saturday from 10:30am to 11pm. Reservations are accepted and major credit cards are honored. There's a parking lot in the back off Indian Avenue.

Las Casuelas Terraza, 222 S. Palm Canyon Dr. (☎ **619/325-2794**), in downtown Palm Springs, is owned by a Delgado family member, and is a landmark to most visitors and residents. Most everyone has walked by its outdoor vine-covered terrace at one time or another—probably getting a spritz of the Micro Mist used to cool the patio in summer. This restaurant offers plenty of atmosphere along with its menu selections. Lots of small alcoves with intimate booths and high ceilings decorated with piñatas and ceiling fans in the large dining room, and of course the terrace, give it charm and character. The beautifully costumed servers are sensitive to children's needs, and bring crackers along with highchairs.

At lunch or dinner, youngsters 7 and under can order a small quesadilla, burrito, hamburger, or nachos for $3. Special nonalcoholic "cocktails" can be ordered. Lunch on the regular menu features several varieties of quesadillas and combination plates, as well as such house specials as shrimp enchiladas ($9.75), fajitas ($8.95), and a burrito ranchero ($6.95). There are hamburgers and salads, as well as several brunch offerings, all featuring eggs. Additional full dinner choices feature steak, chicken, and machaca, all served Mexican style ($11.95–$13.50), including soup or salad, tortillas, rice, and beans. There are also *especiales del mar,* specialties of the sea, that are complete dinners. You might choose a white fish in a spicy sauce or in a wine-and-butter sauce, or prawns fixed three different ways ($11.95–$12.95). At either meal, you can treat yourselves and the kids to deep-fried ice cream, flan, or an empanada (a Mexican apple pie).

Baby food and bottles can be warmed, and booster seats and highchairs are available. Nightly entertainment varies.

The restaurant opens at 11am Monday through Saturday, and at 10am on Sunday; closing time depends on the crowd. Reservations are definitely needed during the season, and they try to honor them within 15 minutes. Up to 5:30pm it won't be hard to get in; after that, it's at least a one-hour wait weeknights, and two hours on weekends, without a reservation. Major credit cards are honored. There's a parking lot or street parking.

The familiar black, yellow, and white of the **California Pizza Kitchen** is found in two desert locations: at the Palm Desert Fashion Plaza, 123 N. Palm Canyon Dr., Palm Springs (☎ **619/322-6075**), and at 73-080 El Paseo, Palm Desert (☎ **619/776-5036**). These roomy, casual restaurants are well known to parents who like the well-priced, unusual pizzas and pastas such as Peking Duck pizza with breast of duck, the wonton fettuccine and mushrooms, or ginger black-bean sauce pasta (angel hair or spaghetti) with chicken or shrimp, broccoli, scallions, and garlic-ginger black-bean sauce. For the timid, there are simple salads, sandwiches on pizza buns, and popular mushroom/pepperoni/sausage pizzas, or spaghetti bolognese. Items on the regular menu never top $10. There are also daily lunch specials.

Children have basic choices such as a cheese or pepperoni pizza or pasta. We've seen many children order the Hawaiian pizza and the original barbecue chicken pizza. Prices on this menu run $3.25–$4.75. A single scoop of Häagen Dazs ice cream in a kids' sundae costs $1.95. Children are given crayons and coloring books. Booster seats and highchairs are provided.

Each location is open Sunday through Thursday, 11:30am to 10pm; Friday and Saturday until 11pm. No reservations are accepted. At high season and on holidays, the wait at prime times can be an hour or more. Unless your children like to take walks, it's best to arrive before the usual dinner hour. Major credit cards are welcomed. Parking for both locations is either on the street or in adjacent parking lots.

Here's a restaurant the kids may find unusual. **Wok in the Desert,** in downtown Palm Springs at 246 S. Palm Canyon Dr. (☎ **619/778-1728**), makes ordering food simple. At this tiny eatery you select your own combination of vegetables, meats, and sauces at the counter. With each entree comes rice or lo mein noodles. Everything is quickly cooked in a wok then eaten at either the small indoor tables or on the outdoor patio. Depending on what protein you choose (tofu, chicken, steak, shrimp, or vegetables-only), your meal will cost $4.75 to $7.95.

The restaurant is open Monday through Wednesday from 11:30am to 9pm, Thursday and Friday to 10pm, and Saturday from noon to 10pm. We spotted one highchair, no booster seats. There are no reservations; major credit cards are accepted. Park on the street or in nearby lots.

For breakfast especially, be sure to try **Elmer's Pancake and Steak House,** 1030 E. Palm Canyon Dr. (☎ **619/327-8419**). On our recent visit, it was full of kids. There's a children's menu with little games that offers varied selections for breakfast ($2.95), lunch ($2.25), and dinner ($3.25). Adult selections are extensive and very moderately priced. There are 15 varieties of pancakes and waffles alone! Highchairs and booster seats are provided.

Open Sunday through Thursday from 6am to 9pm, on Friday and Saturday till 10pm. They don't take reservations, and during the high season the wait can be pretty long. Elmer's is particularly popular on Sunday mornings, but call ahead and they'll put your name on a waiting list. Major credit cards are accepted. There's a convenient parking lot.

Cathedral City

If your kids are tall enough to play the video games, and if you're in the mood for pizza in a nice super-casual setting, head for **Nicolino's,** at 35325 Date Palm Dr. (☎ **619/324-0411**). Here, kids can play the video machines in the next room and the noise of the games won't be right on top of you while you wait for your order. There's a large choice of Italian entrees of veal, seafood, chicken, and pasta for dinner ($7.95–$13). Pizza comes in three sizes with lots of toppings. Lunch offerings include pasta, sandwiches, and Italian salads. Kids 12 and under can have pasta, pizza, or fried chicken, for $3.95 and $4.25.

Highchairs and boosters are available. There's a $3 charge for splitting entrees, and they'll gladly warm baby bottles in the kitchen. There's a full bar.

Open Monday through Saturday from 11am to 9pm; closed Sunday and late July and all of August. Reservations are accepted for groups of eight or more. This spot is very popular, so come early. Credit cards are welcomed. A parking lot is available.

When there's a 30-minute wait at one restaurant and a 45-minute wait at another, and you have hungry children with you, try this little hidden spot. The **Red Bird Diner,** in the Lucky's Plaza Center, 35955 Date Palm Dr. (☎ **619/324-7707**), is a simple, good choice, especially for breakfast. Authentic 45s and LPs decorate the walls along with posters of James Dean and American Bandstand regulars. There are the requisite jukeboxes and soda-shop chairs.

Not to be beat by McDonald's, the Red Bird serves a grilled English muffin with scrambled egg, cheese, and sausage for $2.25. Tots might be happy with a short stack (two) of pancakes for the same price. There are eggs, cholesterol-free egg beaters, omelets, lox, bagel and cream cheese, and other side orders. Breakfast prices are $2.25–$5.85. Dinners come with potato, vegetable, soup, salad, and bread. Home-style beef liver and onions, country fried steak and gravy, baked lamb shank and gravy, and deep-fried shrimp are some choices. Dinners run $7–$13. Kids 12 and under can order a ground-chuck meat patty, chicken drumettes, meatloaf, or spaghetti, with soup or salad and milk, for $4.25–$5. There are booster seats and highchairs.

The Red Bird is open daily from 7am to 8:30pm. Most credit cards are accepted. Park in the Lucky's lot.

Rancho Mirage

A walk through the entrance of **Las Casuelas Nuevas,** 70050 Calif. 111 (☎ 619/328-8844), will give you an immediate feeling of being in Old Mexico. Although it's the largest independently owned restaurant in the Coachella Valley, it's more like a retreat than a huge dining establishment. Canteras stone sculptures, terracotta tile, and Mexican wrought-iron chairs decorate the shady outdoor patio. Children will be tempted to throw coins into the five fountains gracing the patio. Indoors the mood varies from room to room. We like the middle room with its huge skylight.

Families are encouraged to dine here and are always made welcome. The Sunday brunch buffet, with its many choices is a good time to introduce the children to Mexican cuisine. Besides the typical Mexican dishes, there are omelets and fajitas. The kids will love to make their own sundaes at the ice-cream bar. Adults pay $15.95, while children 10 and under are charged $10.95.

At lunchtime you have your pick of salads, a salad bar, house specialties such as steak picado ($10.25) or fajitas ($9.25). A chimichanga is $6.95, and a tostada suprema is $7.25. You can create your own combination plate, too. What you pay depends on how many items you choose. Your under-10 guests get either two deep fried burritos, or a mini-taco, cheese enchilada, quesadilla, bean burrito, or taquito, for $5. There is also an all-American hamburger for the timid ($6.25).

The dinner menu has several more choices: Lobster Ensenada brings in the heftiest charge at $22.95. Or you can get several other Mexican seafood and fish entrees, priced at $14.25–$16.95. Chicken in mole is special here ($14.25), or try machaca (seasoned shredded beef combined with egg, onion, and peppers) for $13.25. The Mexican plates and combinations from the lunch menu are offered at dinner as well.

The full bar prepares everything from a margarita del rey (Grand Marnier, Cuervo 1800 Tequila, and Cointreau) for adults, to virgin drinks of any sort for the kids. Booster seats and highchairs are available; servers will gladly warm baby food and bottles.

Las Casuelas is open Monday through Thursday from 11am to 10pm, Friday and Saturday 11am to 11pm, and on Sunday from 10am to 10pm. Reservations are strongly suggested, and they attempt to honor them within 10 or 15 minutes. All major credit cards are accepted. There is a parking lot or valet parking.

Coco's Bakery Restaurant, 42560 Bob Hope Dr. (☎ 619/568-5050), is a chain restaurant with a family-friendly attitude, a convenient location right off Calif. 111 between Palm Springs and Palm Desert, and an extensive menu. There are lots of breakfast specialties, such as breakfast quesadilla and chicken fried steak and eggs; traditional favorites, such as omelets; combinations, such as cinnamon French toast and eggs and bacon; and healthy starters, such as multigrain pancakes. Breakfast prices are about $3.50–$6. Our favorite is the $4 multiple-choice breakfast offered weekdays only; you pick one choice from each of four categories: eggs or cereal, bakery or griddle, bacon or sausage, fruit or potatoes. Lunch and dinner offer salads, soups and chili, sandwiches, hamburgers, seafood, chicken, beef, pasta, and healthy foods. There are lots of special pies, including sugar-free, and other desserts. Lunch and dinner prices begin at $5 and go up to $10, with most items around $6. Breakfast, lunch, and dinner also provide specially priced selections for "youngsters" 55 years old and over: $5–$6.50 at lunch and dinner, $2.50–$4 at breakfast.

The extensive children's menu provides games, stories, and coloring pages in addition to its list of special meals for kids 10 and under. Breakfast is served all day and prices average about $2.50. Lunch of burgers, corn dogs, chicken fingers, or pizza goes for $2.19 to $2.79 and includes french fries. Dinner comes with soup or salad plus a chocolate sundae or Jell-O Jigglers. To the lunch choices add fish and chips, chicken fried steak, macaroni and cheese, spaghetti, shrimp, and broiled chicken. Dinner will cost between $3.19 and $3.69.

The staff will warm baby food and bottles. Highchairs and booster seats are provided. There's no bar, but plenty of beverage selections. A no-smoking section is provided.

The restaurant is open daily during the season from 7am to 10pm; hours vary slightly in summer. No reservations. Major credit cards are accepted. Park in the lot. There are other locations, in Palm Desert at 73397 Calif. 111 (☎ **619/346-5563**), and in Palm Springs at 1901 E. Palm Canyon Dr. (☎ **619/327-2666**).

Palm Desert

The **Daily Grill,** 73-061 El Paseo, Palm Desert (☎ **619/779-9911**) is a welcome sight. The food is consistently fresh and well prepared, and the servers are well trained. Like its other locations, this one has a nice casual but upscale feel to it. Sit at tables and booths or on the outdoor patio.

Children 11 years old and younger can pick sandwiches (including a tuna melt, burgers, grilled cheese, and Canadian bacon) or specials such as pan-fried chicken, turkey steak with mashed potatoes, spaghetti and meatballs, or meatloaf. There are also kid-sized soups and salads, and yummy hot fudge sundaes, rice pudding, and fruit cobbler. These choices run from $1.75 for peanut butter and jelly to a whopping $5.50 for pan-fried chicken.

The regular menu is quite extensive. There's char-broiled fish and meat, seafood, pasta, salads in two sizes, sandwiches, chicken, and lots of potatoes and vegetables that can be ordered as side dishes. You always know you can get Daily Grill specials like chicken Marsala, steak tartar, Joe's Special (a kind of hash dish), and chicken potpie. They don't scrimp on desserts on this menu either. There are also daily Blue Plate specials that include soup and salad, and senior portions at reduced prices. Prices begin at $6 and go to $19 for a 16-ounce T-bone steak. You'll get potatoes and the Grill's signature serving of emerald-green broccoli with almost every entree.

Servers will prepare special drinks for the kids, and they'll bring you a highchair or booster seat. Bottles and baby food can be warmed.

The Daily Grill is open Monday through Thursday and Sunday from 11am to 10pm, Friday and Saturday to 11pm. Reservations only for six or more; be prepared for a wait during prime times. Major credit cards are honored. Park either on the street or in the lot behind the restaurant.

Whimsical elephants and funky safari gear adorn the walls of the **Elephant Bar,** 73833 Calif. 111 (☎ **619/340-0456**). This large, comfortable restaurant offers indoor and outdoor seating. A skylight in the middle of the room lightens the rich wood-paneled walls and forest-green carpet and upholstery. Pictures of Babar the Elephant line the wall along the route to the restrooms. Tables are spread out, and banquettes are roomy. A big-screen TV in the bar area can be viewed from some of the tables.

The food is strictly American here, not British, as you might expect, and the place is popular with families. Hamburgers and sandwiches are reasonably priced at $4.25–$6.95. Salads are filling and range from $4 to $7.50. There are also pasta dishes and favorites like Cajun fried shrimp, Hawaiian chicken, and fajitas with price tags of $6–$13.95. If you're still hungry, there are plenty of appetizers, side dishes, and desserts.

Boys and girls 10 and under have their own menu and Adventure Book. Kids' menu selections include a hamburger, grilled-cheese sandwich, chicken tenders, a corn dog, chicken quesadilla, or spaghetti for $2.95. Each choice comes with french fries (except spaghetti and the quesadilla), milk or a soft drink (in a cute animal-foot mug), and a scoop of ice cream. A full bar serves non-alcoholic specialty drinks.

Servers will split adult portions. Booster seats and highchairs are provided; baby food and bottles will be warmed in the kitchen. Youngsters will get crayons and balloons. Senior citizens can get discounts, too.

Elephant Bar is open Monday through Thursday from 11am to 10pm, on Friday and Saturday from 11am to 11pm, and on Sunday from 10am to 10pm; summer hours vary. No reservations; with hungry youngsters, come before 6pm during high season. Major credit cards are honored. There is street and lot parking.

Children are made to feel welcome at **TGI Friday's,** 72-620 El Paseo (☎ **619/568-2280**). Distinctively dressed servers greet them with balloons and a coloring-book menu and crayons. If one of your brood is celebrating a birthday, the staff will sing special songs and provide a complimentary dessert and a bouquet of balloons.

It's hard to believe that you won't find something you want on this menu. There are more than ten salads, plus combinations of salads, soups, and sandwiches; sandwich selections ranging from French dip and charcoal-grilled turkey to fajita steak baguettes; hamburgers designed for every day of the week, plus a make-your-own burger list; pasta and pizza and Southwestern selections. Add steak and rib choices, chicken dishes, and seafood, and you have the world's biggest menu selection! And the prices aren't out of line; there are only a few things on the menu over $10.50.

The children's menu offers choices most appropriate to very young tots, especially since there's so much to choose from on the adult menu. At lunch or dinner, they can have chicken fingers, a hamburger, hot dog, or grilled-cheese sandwich, or pepperoni pizza on baguette bread, for under $3. Sunday brunch choices cost around the same. There are several yummy desserts and special drinks. Servers will split adult items for two kids and will warm baby food and bottles. Highchairs or booster seats are provided.

Open daily, year round, from 11am to 2am. Sunday brunch is served from 11am to 3pm. No reservations are accepted (management says they're not necessary and that, except on rare occasions, you'll be seated immediately). All major credit cards are honored. Park in the lot.

There are two branches of **Tony Roma's.** In Palm Desert it's at 73155 Calif. 111 (☎ **619/568-9911**); the Palm Springs location is at 450 S. Palm Canyon Dr.

(☎ 619/320-4297). Both have a full bar and the same menu selections for lunch and dinner: ribs, barbecued chicken, salads, fish, and sandwiches. At lunch, ribs cost $7.99; other selections range up to $13. Dinner prices are higher, with ribs starting at $7.99 for a half-slab and going up to $14 for full slabs. Shrimp, chicken, fish, steak, etc. go for $8–$11. Entrees come with coleslaw and a potato or beans.

As in all Tony Roma restaurants, children have their own menu from which they can choose ribs, burgers, chicken strips, pizza or a grilled-cheese sandwich ($2–$4). The price includes a vegetable appetizer and dessert. Booster seats and highchairs are plentiful.

During the season, both places are open weekdays from 11am to 10pm and on Friday and Saturday from 11am to 11pm. Instead of reservations, they offer "preferred seating." Call in before 5pm, tell them what time you want to come, and, when you arrive, your name will be put at the top of the waiting list. If you can't call, we suggest arriving by 5pm with children, for less of a wait. Take-out is another option. The entire restaurant and patio areas are no-smoking. Major credit cards are honored. Park in the lot or on the street.

If you find yourself in or around the Palm Desert Town Center, you may want to try the **Marie Callender's** restaurant, 72840 Calif. 111 (☎ **619/773-4PIE**). Its indoor patio is a good spot from which to watch the action in the mall.

The Marie Callender's chain of restaurants serve home-style American food. The regular menu features pot pies (a specialty), meatloaf sandwiches, chicken broccoli fettuccine, and fresh vegetable platters ($5.95–$11). There are also full dinners which change nightly, and include top sirloin, fresh fish, and lemon or terriyaki chicken ($8.95–$12.95). You can get hamburgers and large salads, too ($5.50–$7.95). Marie Callender's is famous for its pies, and this location is no exception: There are more than 40 varieties, including offerings such as chocolate satin crunch and mile-high Boston cream pie.

The children's menu comes with crayons and a balloon, and is reserved for kids under 12. Spaghetti, chicken fingers, ham or lasagna, grilled cheese, hamburgers, or a junior turkey dinner can be ordered any time of the day. Children's meals cost $2.49 for ages 10–12, and $1.99 for kids under 10, and these include soup and salad and a bakery treat. Breakfasts include a "happy face pancake" or a waffle with scrambled eggs and bacon or sausage for $2. A Shirley Temple or Roy Rogers costs 50¢. If you visit Tuesday or Wednesday, you can take advantage of the "Kids Eat Free" program: one free kid's meal from the children's menu for children 12 and under per paid adult entree. Servers will warm baby food or bottles, and provide highchairs and boosters.

Marie Callender's is open Sunday through Thursday from 9am to 9pm, on Friday and Saturday till 10pm. Reservations will be taken for parties of eight or more. Major credit cards are honored. Park in the mall's parking lot.

There is another location at 698340 Calif. 111, Rancho Mirage (☎ **619/328-0844**).

WHAT TO SEE AND DO

There are things to do in the desert all year round. Just remember that summers can be brutal, and if you choose an activity that takes some physical effort, you're better off doing it in the morning or late afternoon.

Want something to do with the toddlers in the early morning? Drive to the corner of Gerald Ford Drive and Da-Vall Road (Mission Hills Country Club) in Rancho

Mirage. There you'll find a large pond filled with ducks and geese. These beautiful birds love to be fed by visitors. To the squealing delight of little children, the birds come right up on the grass and waddle up to the person with the most bread. We've seen families with entire loaves of fresh bread spending an hour with their feathered friends. It's a great diversion for restless kids.

Ballooning

Hot-air ballooning is usually not recommended for children under 5, because very young children are often frightened by the loud noise of the burners used to pump the balloons. If you have the time, it's a good idea to bring the kids by to judge their reaction before you decide to take them up. Know your child before you decide to spend this kind of money. Ballooning is an exhilarating experience, and one you'll all remember forever. But once you're up there with a group of people, you can't get away from a frightened, screaming child.

John Zimmer's **Desert Balloon Charters,** P.O. Box 2713, Palm Desert, CA 92261 (☎ 619/346-8575), will fly you over the desert for an hour and 15 minutes. Make reservations for your ride, which is available mid-September through May. Adults are charged $125; children under 14 pay $95.

Sunrise Balloons, P.O. Box 891360, Temecula, CA 92589 (☎ toll free **800/548-9912**), has been making desert flights since 1976. It has its own balloon park at the El Dorado Polo Club, 50950 Madison St. in Indio. Sunrise suggests that pregnant women and children under 10 not fly. Rates are $100–$160 per person, and there are family discounts.

Also contact **Fantasy Balloon Flights** (☎ **619/568-0997**, or toll free **800/GO-ABOVE**) or the **American Balloon Charters** (☎ **619/327-8544**).

Bicycling

If you're coming by car, you're best off bringing your own bikes, carriers, and helmets to the desert, because most of the bicycle-rental locations don't have child carriers.

Canyon Bicycle Rentals Etc. is at 305 E. Arenas Rd., Palm Springs (☎ **619/327-7688**). Beach cruisers, three-speeds, and mountain bikes are available for adults. There are smaller bikes and tricycles for the kids, as well as helmets. Rentals are by the hour, half day, full day, week or month. Open daily from 9am to 5pm. Call for summer hours.

Mac's Bike Rentals is located at 70-053 Calif. 111 (in Desert Cyclery), Palm Desert (☎ **619/321-9444**). All bike sizes and varieties for kids and adults can be rented, and bikes will be delivered if you rent for a minimum of one day. Open year-round, Monday through Saturday from 9:30am to 5:30pm and on Sunday from noon to 5pm. Call for current rates.

For those teenagers in the family, try **Palm Springs Cyclery,** 611 S. Palm Canyon Dr., Palm Springs (☎ **619/325-9319**); or 73-360 Calif. 111, Palm Desert (☎ **619/341-7823**). Only adult bikes are available at these two locations. Call for current rates.

There are bike paths all over town, including some within various hotel or condominium properties (for guest use only). The **Palm Springs Recreation Department** has bike-path maps of the Palm Springs area; they are located at 401 S. Pavilion Way in Palm Springs (☎ **619/323-8272**). Or purchase a book on hiking, biking, and equestrian activities from Rancho Mirage City Hall, 69-825 Calif. 111 (☎ **619/324-4511**).

Note: Don't let your kids ride along Calif. 111. It's much too busy, and there are many prettier places to ride. A sidewalk bike trail begins at Cook Street in Palm Desert and runs east alongside Calif. 111. It's even lighted at night.

Bowling

Should the heat get you down, or should you be looking for an evening activity, try bowling a few lines at the **Palm Springs Lanes,** 68-051 Ramon Rd., Ramon at Landau, Cathedral City (☎ **619/324-8204**). If your children have never tried bowling before, you might start them off with bumper bowling. Call in advance for that. There are children-size balls and shoes (down to children's size 6). Snacks can be purchased.

The lanes are open Sunday through Thursday from 9am to 1am, and Friday and Saturday until 2:30am (until 4:30am in winter!). From 9am to 5pm, it will cost you $2 per game; after 5pm, you'll be charged $2.75.

Family Concerts

Call about free **Fall Concerts in the Park** at Sunrise Plaza, 1901 E. Baristo Rd., one block north of Ramon Road between Sunrise and Farrell (☎ **619/323-8272**). These popular concerts are held outdoors on the lawn on various evenings.

Hiking

The entrance to the **Indian Canyons** can be found at the end of South Palm Canyon Drive. You may not know that the Palm Springs area was originally settled by the Agua Caliente Cahuilla tribe. Much of the land in the area is still owned by Native Americans, and many hotels and homes sit on that land, their owners paying rent on 99-year leases. The Cahuillas created their communities within five canyons, three of which are open to the public, one of which you need a permit to hike in, and the last, Chino, where you'll find the Aerial Tramway. Still part of the reservation, the canyons are maintained by the Agua Caliente Cahuillas.

Palm Canyon is a good place to start. This is where you'll find the Trading Post, which sells hiking maps, snacks, and Native American art and artifacts from 10 different tribes. There is a paved footpath near the post that leads down into the canyon. You can hike from this point, or just bring a picnic lunch and sit by the stream. The paths aren't too steep for young children. The native palms, the *Washingtonia filifera,* are in abundance here. In fact this canyon is known to have the most palm trees in the world, and is listed on the National Register of Historic Places.

There is a pretty easy $1/4$-mile hike in **Andreas Canyon** and a foot trail through the canyon and picnic tables along the way. Be sure to check at the tollgate whether the grade is too steep for your kids (or yourself!).

Murray Canyon, entered to the left of Andreas, is less accessible, but if you are determined to see it, you can hike there from Andreas. The hiking path within the canyon runs for five miles. If you're lucky, the children will spot some of the abundant wildlife.

Admission to the canyons is $5 for adults, $1 for children 6–12, $3.50 for students, $2.50 for seniors, free for children under 6. If you're on horseback, it costs $6. Open daily September through June from 8am to 5pm.

The **Palm Springs Aerial Tramway** is located at Calif. 111 (north) and Tramway Road, in Palm Springs (☎ **619/325-1391**). The best thing about the tramway is what you find when you get to the top of Mount San Jacinto. As you travel the 18-minute 12,800-foot distance in the 80-passenger cable car, you will see the same range of varieties of flora and fauna you would see if you drove from Sonora, Mexico, to the Arctic Circle. Be sure to take layers of clothing with you, as the temperature drops greatly at the top. If you aren't prepared, a giftshop at the entrance sells mittens, sweatshirts, hats, and other warm clothing.

Once you get to the top, you'll be in **Mount San Jacinto State Park.** Even if you never make it to one hiking trail, you'll still enjoy the immediate area outside the tram station. Janey loved her first attempt at "mountain climbing." There's a great hill after you pass the first curve of the concrete hand-railed path. It's an easy climb for older kids, a bit of work for the toddler set. The giant flat-topped boulder is perfect for their first goal. We sat on the top of it watching the people below, the glorious pine trees, and the sun changing position. Just beyond that boulder is a cave, clean and quite open. Someone about three feet tall can just about stand up straight in it. There's a narrow crawlspace through the cave to an opening on the other side leading to a trail. It's big enough for an adult, but we wouldn't let the toddlers go through by themselves. We spent nearly two hours on that one hill, our 4-year-old friend climbing part of the way up alone, over and over again. We found all sorts of rocks, big walking sticks, and giant pine cones. Explain to the kids that the natural things they find in a state park cannot be removed. There's even a depository for "found" pine cones right before you leave the park, to remind people not to take them home.

If you do continue down the winding concrete path to the park itself, you enter 54 miles of campgrounds, hiking trails, and a ranger station. A sign at the end of the path illustrates where the three-quarter-mile self-guiding **Nature Loop Trail** begins and shows you where the ranger station is in nearby Long Valley (walking distance). Check at the station for maps and information on guided nature hikes. Camping is permitted in the wilderness with a permit, available at the ranger station. If you don't feel like hoofing it, a guided mule-back **Wilderness Trail Ride** is available during the hot summer months. The ride is 20 minutes long. Signs at the tram station will lead you to the mules.

During hot desert summers, a visit to the top is a welcome relief. In spring there's an Easter egg hunt for young children. Before Halloween, those under 12 can join in a pumpkin-decorating contest. Winter is also lively in the park. (See "Winter Activities," below, for ski information.)

Each tram station (coming and going) has a snack bar, giftshop, observation areas, and restrooms. A Ride 'n' Dine package (the restaurant is cafeteria-style) is available for those who want to have dinner at the top. The round-trip fare and dinner is $19.95 for adults, $12.95 for children 12 and under. The fare alone is $15.95 for adults, $9.95 for children 12 and under.

Cars run at least every 30 minutes. The tramway opens during daylight saving time Monday through Friday at 10am, on Saturday and Sunday at 8am. The last tram up is at 8pm; the last tram comes down at 10pm. During the rest of the year, the last car goes up at 7pm and comes down at 9pm. The tram closes the first two weeks in August for maintenance. Check ahead. During holidays the wait for a tram up can be anywhere from a half hour to two hours. There is ample parking, with shuttle service from the parking lots available during weekends and holidays. The tram is not stroller-accessible.

Horseback Riding

Horseback riding is one way to really experience the desert the way the pioneers did. **Ranch of the 7th Range,** Avenue 58 behind PGA West, La Quinta

(☎ 619/777-7777), rents horses and ponies by the hour, with a guide. They allow children 4 and under to ride double with a parent, but we don't recommend this. The cost is $27 per person per hour, guide included. Pony leads are $8. Open in summer, 7 to 10am, and closed Sunday. In winter, hours are 8am to 5pm every day.

Smoketree Stables, 2500 Toledo Ave., Palm Springs (☎ 619/327-1372) schedules guided one-hour rides on the hour. Adults and children pay $25. A two-hour ride to the Indian reservation costs $50, including admission to the canyon. Longer rides can be scheduled by reservation only. Children should be at least 5 to ride their own horses; little kids can take a 15-minute pony ride for $10. The stables are open daily, year-round: summer, 8am to noon (call for afternoon arrangements); in winter, 8am to dusk. Arrive about 15 minutes before the hour.

Indoor Activities

The **Ice Capades Chalet,** Palm Desert Town Center Mall, 72840 Calif. 111, Palm Desert (☎ 619/340-4412), is an anomaly in the middle of the desert. It's great fun all year round, but an especially welcome relief in the summer. Public skating is offered daily year round at various times, day and evening. Call for the schedule. For those not staying long enough to get into a class, Director Nalani Philipson offers private lessons at $13 for 15 minutes, $26 for half an hour. Call in advance. Skate rental is available for ages $2^{1}/_{2}$ through adult ($2.25). Tuesday is family night. A family of four or more pays $19 for admission and skate rental. Admission to the rink is $5.25.

Jeep Tour

Kids 6 and over get a kick out of taking the Jeep tours run by **Desert Adventures,** 611 S. Palm Canyon Dr., Suite 7445, Palm Springs, CA 92262 (☎ 619/864-6530). On the Santa Rosa tour, you'll travel 4,000 feet to the Bighorn Reserve, where rock formations and animal life are abundant. The guides explain why certain birds make nests in cactus and why you shouldn't get near some of those cactus needles! The guides also colorfully describe how the Agua Calienta Cahuilla tribe used the yucca tree and how they hunted. (Descendants of the tribe are now some of the wealthiest landowners in Southern California because of the land they lease to residents and hotel owners in the Palm Springs area.)

The Mystery Canyon Adventure is a tour that runs along the San Andreas earthquake fault, California's dubious claim to fame. Intricate rock formations appear throughout the canyons and ravines. You'll get an earful of the story of the Coachella Valley. The Indian Canyon Tour visits the largest natural palm oasis in the world, an area with abundant pools, waterfalls, and wildlife, which has been home to the Cahuilla people for hundreds of years. The area offers excellent nature walks and hikes, unusual rock formations, Cahuilla rock art, and an actual grinding hole used for preparing food.

You can arrange for one-, two-, or four-hour tours. We found the morning departure better because it's cooler. Complimentary hotel pickup, continental breakfast in the morning, and beverages and snacks for the afternoon departure are included in the four-hour tours. It's fun to bring a picnic lunch, or with advance notice, the Jeep company will provide one. Take a hat, sunscreen, and a jacket in the winter months. A two-and-a-half hour summer tour is taken via a jeep equipped with Micro-Mist ($49). Children under 5 are not permitted unless you arrange for a private tour (minimum of five people). This activity is best suited to children over 7.

Adults are charged $65 for the two-hour tour, $99 for the four-hour tour. Children 12 and under pay $60 and $95, respectively.

Miniature Golf

Camelot Park, 67-770 East Palm Canyon Drive, Cathedral City (☎ **619/321-9893**), will provide several hours of family entertainment. Outdoors, there is a miniature golf course, go-carts, and action bumper boats, as well as batting cages featuring slow and medium softball, and slow, medium, fast, and very fast baseball. There's no shade outdoors, so in summer you may want to stay indoors in the video arcade. There are a few games for young children, a small snack bar, and skeeball machines. During holidays the wait to get on the golf course can be long.

Camelot is open Monday through Thursday from 10am to 11pm, Fridays until 1am, Saturday 9am to 1am, and Sunday 9am to 11am.

Museums and Gardens

The **Children's Discovery Museum of the Desert,** 42-501 Rancho Mirage Lane, in Rancho Mirage (☎ **619/346-2900**), is a gem of a small-town museum. Temporarily set in what was a dentist's offices, the museum has separate little rooms with individual themes. The museum stresses professions and vocations, so you'll find a dentist's office, of course, and one for a doctor and an artist. Local architects donated and designed the architect's office, where kids can learn to draw in perspective and create model buildings with an abundant supply of wooden blocks. Outdoors is a garden for budding botanists and for those who have never seen a carrot pulled from the ground or how a watermelon is grown. A docent leads you through the museum your first time around, describing what there is to do and offering suggestions. Local volunteers give their time to teach special subjects, such as origami. Lots of art activities are done outside, where plenty of recycled "stuff" is available for creative projects. A special toddler room is safe and nonthreatening, but small. A separate room is set aside for thespians with a small stage, costumes, and folding chairs for the audience. Kids have been known to gather up other children visiting the museum to put on impromptu performances.

The museum is especially appropriate for children 12 and under. It is stroller-accessible; parking is in the small lot or on the street. Don't plan to just drop off the kids and leave—this is a place you'll want to experience with your children. Lemonade, cold water, and graham crackers are always available for snacks. The building is air-conditioned, and there are misters outside.

The museum is open to the public September through June Saturdays from 9am to 3pm, June and July Fridays and Sundays, noon to 4pm, Saturday 10am to 3pm. It is closed the entire month of August. Nonmember children pay $2; adults are free.

The **Living Desert,** 47-900 Portola Ave., Palm Desert, 1¹/₂ miles south of Calif. 111 (☎ **619/346-5694**), should not be missed. Janey has been introduced to many new birds, animals, and insects at the wildlife park's special "critter closeup." Allot one to two hours for this family activity, which is perfect for all ages.

Numerous animal species live here in naturalistic habitats—many we've never heard of! As you walk from setting to setting, you travel through botanical gardens made up of 10 desert regions. Fascinating plants, even prehistoric species, Native American exhibits, biking trails, an animal nursery, and a gift shop are all on the grounds. In addition to the critter close-ups, a weekend Discover Room and special nature walks are featured. Kids can view mountain lions and naked mole rats among the 30-plus species in the new Eagle Canyon exhibit.

Restrooms, water fountains, and soft-drink machines are conveniently located. Although there are shaded areas throughout the grounds, you might want to bring extra drinks, hats, and sunscreen. Make a day of it and bring a picnic lunch to enjoy at the park's shaded picnic area. The Meerkat Cafe offers sandwiches, hot dogs, salads, and desserts.

The reserve is stroller-accessible, and there are strollers and wheelchairs available for use.

The wildlife park is open from September 1 to June 15, daily from 9am to 5pm. Closed mid-June to September 1. Parking is free. Adults pay $7, seniors 62 and over, $6, children 3–12, $3.50; free for children under 3.

On a nice desert day a beautiful spot for a picnic lunch is at **La Quinta Sculpture Park,** 67-325 Madison St., La Quinta (☎ **619/564-6464**). Within the 20-acre park is a lake and more than 100 sculptures by well-known and up-and-coming artists. A snack bar is on the grounds, as are picnic areas and a theater-in-the-round. The park is open daily from 9am to 5pm; closed June 16 through August 31. Adults pay $4.50, seniors, $3.75, and children 3–15, $2.50.

Moorten Botanical Gardens, 1701 S. Palm Canyon Dr., Palm Springs (☎ **619/327-6555**), is a nice place to take the family on a morning walk. There are more than 2,000 varieties of desert plants, including hundreds of kinds of cactus. Open Monday through Saturday from 9am to 4:30pm and on Sunday from 10am to 4pm. Admission is $1.50.

The **Palm Springs Desert Museum** is at the foot of a mountain in the San Jacinto range, at 101 Museum Dr., Palm Springs (☎ **619/325-0189**). A visit to this museum is a delightful indoor activity, especially on a hot (or cold) day.

The museum houses fine art and exhibitions of classic western, American, and contemporary California art. Natural-science exhibits and special programs offer something for everyone. Recently, for instance, the museum had dinosaur and snake exhibits in the natural-science wing, along with special programs to complement them, including a family day. Check the museum schedule for events that might be interesting to your family, such as hikes in the canyons.

The museum is open Tuesday through Thursday, and Saturday and Sunday, from 10am to 4pm. Friday hours are 1 to 8pm. Closed Monday. The museum season is September through May, closed major holidays. Admission is $5 for adults, $4 for seniors, $2 for children 6–17 and students with ID, free for children under 6.

Tennis

If your hotel courts are tied up, there are public courts at **DeMuth Park,** 4365 Mesquite Ave. (four courts); **Ruth Hardy Park,** 700 Tamarisk Rd. (eight courts); and the **Palm Springs High School,** 2248 Ramon Rd. (six courts). The **Palm Springs Tennis Center,** 1300 E. Baristo Rd. (☎ **619/320-0020** for more information), has nine night-lighted courts open to the public for a small fee.

The **Reed Anderson Tennis School,** located at the **Westin Mission Hills Resort,** Dinah Shore & Bob Hope Drive, Rancho Mirage (☎ **619/770-2148,** or toll free **800/288-1171**), offers a number of tennis packages to suit most needs. Call for rates.

Water Activities

The **Palm Springs Oasis Waterpark,** at 1500 Gene Autry Trail, Palm Springs (☎ **619/325-SURF**), is just that—an oasis in the middle of the desert. On a hot summer day in the desert, there's no better place to be. Every age group is represented here.

For your youngest ball of energy there is Creature Fantasy, with an oversize Froggy, Whale and Shipwreck Waterslides, a giant climb-on alligator and sea monster, and a splashy pool. There's a slide area just for toddlers, and another was recently added for children 30 to 40 inches tall. Whitewater River was just our speed. The slow-moving inner-tube ride was set in 3¹/₂ feet of water. Lots of 6-year-olds were in it alone, and lifeguards were stationed all along the 600-foot loop. There's also a pair of family slides so Junior can travel down to the 80° water with Mom or Dad on an inner tube. Even the young kids can surf on the 3¹/₂-foot waves in the wave pool. Surf- and bodyboards can be rented. Although lifeguards are on duty, this is a huge pool, so we suggest that you accompany your young children. Altogether there are seven "adult" slides: four slides are for riders at least 48 inches tall and three others are geared for kids 40 inches and up. Two are seven stories high and you (not us!) travel at speeds up to 40 m.p.h.!

Day passes to the Oasis Health Club can be purchased. It offers a private spa and fitness center with a whirlpool, aerobics, steam, sauna, and a wide array of cardiovascular and weight-training equipment. Mist-cooled private cabanas with food service start at $65 for four people on the weekend, $50 on weekdays. At the water park there are three food stands, lockers, changing rooms, and showers. Come early on weekends for shade or lounge chairs.

The water park is open daily mid-March through Labor Day and on weekends through October. It opens at 11am, closing at 5:30pm through May and in September and October, and at 7pm from June through Labor Day. Adults pay $16.99; children 4–11 are charged $11.50; under 4, free. Families who stay at the Oasis Villa Hotel earn several free passes (see "Where to Stay," above). Self-parking is $2; valet parking is available.

The **Palm Springs Swim Center,** 405 S. Pavilion Way, at the corner of Sunrise Way and Ramon Road in Sunrise Park, Palm Springs (☎ **619/323-8278**), has an outdoor Olympic-size pool open to the public, with lifeguards year round. There's a diving board and a separate shallow area of the pool roped off for children. Private swimming lessons cost $41 for five 30-minute classes for anyone age 6 months and older. It's open daily, year round. Call for current hours. During the hot summers the pool is open for night swimming. Admission for adults (age 13 and up) is $3; children 4–12, $2; under 4, free.

If you're willing to make about a 25-mile round-trip, you can go fishing at **Whitewater Trout Fishing,** Whitewater exit off I-10 West (☎ **619/325-5570**). After Dad (or Mom) has caught "the big one," you can grill and eat it right there. Or the staff will clean and wrap your catch. It's open year round, Tuesday through Sunday from 9am to 5pm (last fishing time is 4:15pm). The entrance fee is 50¢ per person for anyone over the age of 2, and a $2.50 fee for tackle, bait, bucket, towel and cleaning, plus $2.56 for each pound of fish caught. Fish range from one to five pounds. It's closed the first two weeks of December.

Winter Activities

Believe it or not, people really do ski in Palm Springs. Cross-country ski lessons are available at the **Palm Springs Nordic Ski Center,** at the top of the tram (☎ **619/327-6002**). When you reach the end of the concrete trail outside the station, you'll see signs leading you to the center.

If you bring your own equipment and don't need lessons, there's no charge to ski in the park. Lessons, for both adults and children (the director suggests a minimum age of 5), last 1–1¹/₂ hours ($15 per person). Lessons can be taken on weekends at 10am, noon, or 2pm. For a weekday lesson, call to make arrangements.

Equipment can be rented. Adults pay $7 per hour or $16 per day; children, $4 per hour or $10 per day. Snowshoes and snowboots can also be rented. There is no need to make reservations for weekend lessons, but the center does close weekdays if business is slow, so call ahead. The tram is an additional charge (☎ 619/325-1391).

It is open from mid-November until mid-April, snow permitting: weekdays from 10:30am to 5pm, and weekends and holidays from 8am to 5pm.

Fairs, Festivals, and Seasonal Activities

Visitors to the area in the middle of February like to take the family to the **Date Festival and Riverside County Fair** in Indio (☎ 619/863-8247). Stay on Calif. 111 east until you get to Indio; signs will direct you to the festival. For 10 days there is special entertainment, displays, camel and ostrich races, a livestock show, art exhibits, and more. Watch the local papers for the schedule of events.

Memorial Day weekend is **Cherry Festival** time in nearby Beaumont, 27 miles west of Palm Springs on I-10 (take the Beaumont Avenue exit to the festivities). For five days, visitors can see a carnival, attend an old-fashioned pancake breakfast, watch a parade, and attend a horse show. For information on this year's festival, contact the Beaumont Chamber of Commerce, P.O. Box 637, Beaumont, CA 92223 (☎ 909/845-9541).

Cherry-picking season usually runs from the end of May to the first of July. There are signs directing you to public cherry-picking orchards in Beaumont and nearby Cherry Valley. For specific information on cherry orchards open to the public for picking, stop at the Cherry Festival Association Information Booth at the corner of Cherry Valley Boulevard and Beaumont Avenue (2¹/₂ miles north of Beaumont). Or call the president of the Cherry Grower's Association (☎ 909/845-3628). Be sure to tell her you have children in the group, as they are not allowed at certain orchards.

Apple-picking adventures are abundant in the area. This is a fun activity to do as a family. Not only do you all get outdoors, but the children get to eat what they actually pick. Oak Glen is a veritable mecca for apple picking and cider making, as well as just a nice place to visit. To get there, take I-10 west from Palm Springs to the Beaumont Avenue exit and go north six or seven miles to Oak Glen.

There are orchards open to the public that allow you to pick your own apples, then pay for them by the pound (signs along Oak Glen Road will lead you right to them): **Riley's Log Cabin Farm & Orchard,** for you-pick apples and pears, and you-press cider (☎ 909/790-2364); **Los Rios Rancho,** for apples and cider, bakery, and snacks (☎ 909/797-1005); **Johnny Appleseed Orchard,** for apples (☎ 909/797-7575); **High Country Orchards** (☎ 909/797-4249); **Mr. Laws** (☎ 909/797-3130); **Wood Acres** (☎ 909/797-8500); **Wilshire's Apple Shed**

In Case of Emergency

If a medical emergency should arise during your visit to Palm Springs, there is 24-hour emergency-room treatment available at **Desert Hospital,** 1150 N. Indian Canyon Ave., Palm Springs (☎ 619/323-6511).

(☎ 909/797-8731); and **Snowline Ranch** (☎ 909/797-3415). Orchards are open at various times, but apple season is generally September through December; call the individual orchard for information or contact the Oak Glen Information (☎ 909/797-6833). Some of these orchards also have raspberry picking in late summer. There are also apple sheds at ranches along Oak Glen Road selling all sorts of apple products. **Parrish Pioneer Ranch** (☎ 909/797-1753) and Riley's (above) are open all year.

For those of you *not* escaping the Midwest and East Coast snowstorms, **Oak Glen** is a place to visit from January to March to introduce the family to snow. Or come mid-April through mid-May to see the gorgeous apple blossoms bloom. In the summer it's a place to escape a day of searing heat in Palm Springs, as the temperatures in Oak Glen are at least 10°–15° cooler.

Call the Yucaipa Valley Chamber of Commerce (☎ 909/790-1841) for information on the area.

2   Lake Arrowhead and Big Bear Lake

Lake Arrowhead and Big Bear Lake are the two most popular mountain communities in the San Bernardino Mountains. Located about 1^1/$_2$ hours from Los Angeles, and 30 miles from each other, both are considered year-round resorts, and offer winter and summer activities galore. To get to Lake Arrowhead and Big Bear Lake from Los Angeles, take I-10 east to Calif. 215 north, go four miles to the Mountain Resorts turnoff, and continue to Waterman Avenue, which is Calif. 18 (Rim of the World Drive); turn left and proceed to Lake Arrowhead and Big Bear.

Lake Arrowhead ───────────────────────────

Lake Arrowhead is actually seven tiny communities surrounding the lake. Its 14-mile shoreline, all of which is privately owned, offers myriad summer delights. You might want to contact the **Lake Arrowhead Communities Chamber of Commerce,** P.O. Box 219, Lake Arrowhead, CA 92352 (☎ 909/337-3715), for further information.

ACTIVITIES ON AND AROUND THE LAKE

Alpine-style **Lake Arrowhead Village** is the hub of activities in the area. With over 60 shops and restaurants located on the banks of the lake, the village is a good place to spend a little time. It has a swimming beach and marina (open Memorial Day through Labor Day).

Located at Lake Arrowhead Village Waterfront (☎ 909/336-6992), the recently refurbished *Arrowhead Queen* paddlewheeler tours the lake year round. The narrated cruises are offered hourly. Open Monday through Thursday 11am to 5pm, Friday 11am to 6pm, and Saturday and Sunday 10am to 6pm. Adults pay $9.50, seniors pay $8.50, and children under 12 pay $6.50; group rates for 10 or more, $7.50 per person. Tickets are available at Le Roy's Sports, or call to reserve tickets.

OTHER ACTIVITIES

One mile from Arrowhead Village, in the little hamlet of Blue Jay, you and the kids can enjoy hours of ice skating, even on a hot summer day, at **Blue Jay Ice Castle Skating Rink,** 27307 Calif. 189 (☎ 909/336-2111). Ice Castle is a completely covered rink that opens on the sides so that you feel as if you're skating in the forest. Children as young as 2 years old grace the ice. Ice hockey matches and private skating lessons are given, so the hours for public skating vary. Call ahead. Admission is $7 per person and skates are included in the admission price. If you bring your own skates, admission is $6 per person.

Another enchanting place is **Santa's Village** (☎ 909/337-2481), located just a few miles from Lake Arrowhead in Skyforest. It is especially designed for young children, who enjoy the elves, the miniature rides, and the little petting farm that even includes reindeer. There's an Antique Auto Ride, Cinderella's Pumpkin Coach Ride, and the Magic Train Ride. Of course, since this is Santa's Village, there is a toy shop, a candy store, and a bakery. Open daily from 10am to 5pm mid-June through mid-September and mid-November through December; weekends and holidays in January, February, late May, early June, September, and October; closed March, April, and most of May. Admission is $10 for children 3 years old through adults; children under 2, free.

Snow Valley Ski Area (☎ 909/867-2751) is a 235-acre area that offers both natural and artificially made snow. Located five miles east of Running Springs on Calif. 18 (between Lake Arrowhead and Big Bear Lake, 85 miles from Los Angeles), Snow Valley has 13 chair lifts and a handle tow for the children's Adventure Ski Area. There are 35 runs, a complete rental service, and night skiing five nights a week. The ski school offers half-day and full-day group lessons, and private lessons by the hour. The Ski Wee program is for kids 5–11, and offers classes and activities from 9am to 4pm. A full- and half-time ski school costs between $35 and $55, depending on the length of time and if you rent equipment.

Lift tickets cost $39 for adults, $22 for children and seniors, and there are lower prices for night skiing, and half-day and late-day skiing (from 12:30 to 9pm). Open daily for day and night skiing, Snow Valley limits the number of tickets it sells. Ask about packages that include lift tickets, lessons, and equipment rentals. For current snow conditions, call **909/867-5151** or **800/680-SNOW**.

Trails and Forests

There are loads of hiking trails in the area, ranging from easy to difficult. Contact the **Arrowhead Ranger District,** 28104 Hwy. 18 in Skyforest (mailing address: P.O. Box 350, Skyforest, CA 92385) (☎ 909/337-2444), for specific trail information. Send $1.08 and they'll mail you a hiking and trail map.

The **National Children's Forest** is one small 20-acre area in the San Bernardino National Forest. It was developed so that children—including those in wheelchairs and the visually impaired—could enjoy nature. The origins of the National Children's Forest date back to 1970, when one of the worst fires started in San Bernardino National Forest. After 3,000 firefighters worked for six days, it was finally over, but 53,000 acres had been blackened.

The slopes couldn't be left bare. Thousands of trees were needed to restart the forest and protect the topsoil. In the same year, across the country, five million acres of forest were destroyed. Hunt-Wesson Foods, Inc., began to help the National Forest Service in the huge job of replanting. This started the idea of getting children involved. A National Children's Forest was created to show humankind's interest in nature and desire to help. Many children have participated in the replanting of the forest. Three National Children's Forests were chosen, and San Bernardino was one of them. As in other regions of this national forest, the Ponderosa pine is abundant. You'll also see lovely dogwood trees. To get there from Lake Arrowhead, take Calif. 330 to Calif. 18 east and pass Deer Lick station; when you reach a road marked IN96, make a right and go three miles. The road is opened in late May.

Trail of the Phoenix starts at the entrance to the Children's Forest. On the half-mile paved nature trail you see pine and oak trees and manzanita bushes. Have the kids watch for animals and birds such as ground squirrels, hawks, and blue jays. During the summer, be on the lookout for rattlesnakes—it's not likely that you'll see them, but they are there. The trail is stroller-accessible.

Ten miles from the Children's Forest, near the town of Blue Jay, the **Enchanted Loop Trail** is another easy trail that will take about half an hour to walk. This trail is in the Dogwood Campground, not far from the lake, where the Sequoia and Fir loops meet. **Heaps Peak Arboretum Trail** is another easy walk. Located half a mile east of Santa's Village on the north side of Calif. 18, the trail winds through a grove of redwoods.

WHERE TO STAY IN LAKE ARROWHEAD

The only full-service resort is **Lake Arrowhead Resort and Village,** P.O. Box 1699, Lake Arrowhead, CA 92352 (☎ **909/336-1511** or toll free **800/800-6792**). The Resort offers a variety of family activities in a picturesque setting; it sits on the edge of the lake, commanding exquisite views. The two-story lobby is very open and spacious with a bridge connecting the third-floor wings, overlooking the fireplace sitting area. The mountain ambience is evident as you enter the "alpine" chalet with high ceilings, blazing fires, lush greenery, and light wood accents.

A special feature of this resort is its children's program, the Kids Club, which offers fully supervised activities seven days a week during the summer, and on weekends and holidays in winter. It's a wonderland of things to do and see, presented in a way that allows youngsters to enjoy these things in their own way. They fish, build sandcastles, go on nature hikes, and ice skate. Day activities are planned from 7am to 4:30pm with lunch included. The evening program, is available on weekends from 6 to 10pm and features roasting hot dogs and marshmallows on the resort's private beach, playing volleyball, and watching movies. Special programs are planned for New Year's Day, Easter, and Christmas. Reservations are recommended for Kid's Club programs. For the younger children, the concierge can arrange babysitting.

Other features of the resort are video games, and a lending desk where kids can check out cards, checkers, horseshoes, table tennis equipment, and other games. In-room movies are available, and you can even order pizza from room service.

Adults can enjoy the world-class health club (for $5 per person), racquetball and tennis courts, pool and spa, and private beach.

The Lobby Cafe has a children's menu that includes pizza, peanut butter and jelly, grilled cheese, spaghetti, grilled chicken, and pasta. The waitresses are friendly and helpful, providing highchairs and boosters if needed. Prices run $1.95–$3.95, and hours of operation are 7am–10pm.

The rooms at the resort are large, with a game table and chairs, sofa, and some have a balcony. Rates vary, depending on the room type and view, from $99 to $299. Kitchen units start at $199 and include a kitchen, loft, 1 1/2 baths, and living room. Children stay free in the same room as their parents, and there is no charge for cribs. Rollaways are available for $10.

Note: When you book your room, be sure to tell the reservationist the number of kids you have and if you'll need a crib. If the crib isn't in your room when you arrive, ask for it immediately. We spent a few hours with a cranky baby while we waited for the crib so she could take her nap.

Big Bear Lake

The vacation area known as Big Bear centers around Big Bear Lake and the alpine forest surrounding it. At 6,700 feet in elevation, Big Bear Lake offers a multitude of activities in winter, spring, summer, and fall. Contact the **Big Bear Chamber of Commerce,** 630 Bartlett Rd, (P.O. Box 2860), Big Bear, CA 92315 (☎ **909/866-4608**), for complete information if you're going to be spending more than a few days.

WINTER ACTIVITIES

It's hard to believe that less than two hours from the Palm Springs desert (and Los Angeles) is one of Southern California's major ski areas. **Snow Summit** (☎ **909/866-5766,** or **909/866-5841** for credit-card reservations) is one of the most popular ski resorts in the area. There are 12 chair lifts and 35 runs offering day and night skiing. The ski school gives a wide range of group and private lessons. You'll be surprised at the extent of the family programs: for children 5–12, full- and half-day lessons are offered. For children 2–7, Little Bear Care Center provides a comfortable environment that will entertain your child while you ski. Space is limited, so reservations are recommended.

Lift tickets cost $41 for adults, $19.75 for children 12 and under. Be sure to inquire about the family discount; it offers substantial savings to families with children 18 and under. Snow Summit limits ticket sales in an effort to shorten lift lines. Ticket reservations are recommended, and can be made through the Snow Summit credit-card reservations service (there's a $2 charge).

Another good ski area is **Bear Mountain Ski Resort,** P.O. Box 6812, Big Bear Lake, CA 92315 (☎ **909/585-2519** for information and a snow report). Bear Mountain is another of the Southern California ski areas that has the capacity to produce snow on all its trails. The 11 lifts (including a high-speed quad chair), a complete ski school, and a rental and repair shop, as well as restaurant and snack facilities, make this area one of the most popular in the San Bernardino Mountains.

Ski instruction includes the children's Junior Ski School, for kids 4–12. Offering half- and full-day programs, the Junior Ski School is open daily from 10am to 3pm. Children can be checked in as early as 8am. The half-day session is from 1 to 3pm and costs $35; the full-day rate (including lunch) is $50. Rentals cost $10. Lift tickets cost $38 for adults for a full day, $24 for a half day. Junior (12 and under) lift tickets are $21 for a full day, $16 for a half day. Adult group lessons cost $21 for a half-day (two-hour) session; private lessons run $50 per hour. Adult (age 13 and over) beginner packages for beginner runs (with snowboarding) include a two-hour group session, lift ticket, and equipment rental, and cost $39.

OTHER ACTIVITIES

Big Bear offers a wide array of active family entertainment.

The **Alpine Slide at the Magic Mountain Recreation Area** (☎ **909/866-4626**) is a child's delight. This playland, located on Big Bear Boulevard, offers year-round recreation. The Alpine Slide whizzes you down the track on a specially constructed sled that has levers to control the speed. It's open daily, mid-June to mid-September, from 10am to 6pm; 10am–9pm on weekends and holidays year round, weather permitting. Admission is $3 for a single ride, $12 for a five-ride book. Children under 48 inches tall or between 2 and 6 years old ride free with an adult.

Magic Mountain also has a **water slide** and horseback riding, video games, and a snack bar. An all-day pass on the water slide costs $10. A 10-ride ticket book costs $7; a single ride is $1. Children under 5 ride free when accompanied by an adult. The water slide is open mid-June to mid-September, daily from 10am to 5pm.

There are **snowplay** areas, where kids can ride down with inner-tubes. Admission to these areas is $10 per person for a full day, including use of a tube. If you have your own tube, the fee is $8. Children 6 and under go free with an adult. The snowplay areas are open daily during the winter season from 10am to dusk as long snow conditions exist.

The **Moonridge Animal Park/Zoo,** at 43285 Moonridge Rd., in Moonridge (909/866-0183), is a 2.2-acre park with such animals as endangered wood bison, cougars, wolves, racoons, coyote, fox, and numerous birds of prey, including a bald eagle. The park is open from mid-May to October 31, daily from 10am to 4:30pm, depending on the weather. Admission is $2 for adults, $1 for children 5–10, and free for kids under 5. Tours are available for an additional fee; contact the district office (909/866-0130).

Boating

This is a treat on Big Bear Lake. Boat rentals are available at **Big Bear Marina,** located at the corner of Pane and Lakeview about a quarter mile west of Big Bear Village (909/866-3218). You can rent motorboats at $12 per hour, $20 for 2 hours, and $50 for a full day. Pontoon boats rent for $35–$45 per hour, $95–$120 for a half day, and $140–$170 for a full day. Deposits are required. The marina is open May through October, daily from 6am to 6:30 or 8pm.

Other boat-rental places you may want to try are **Pine Knot Landing** (909/866-2628), **Gray's Landing** (909/866-2443), and **Holloway's Marina** (909/866-5706). All the marinas are closed during winter months.

Fishing

Want to guarantee that the kids will catch fish? The **Alpine Trout Lakes,** 440 Catalina Rd., one long block off Calif. 18 (909/866-4532), is as good as a guarantee. This lake is stocked with trout, so kids can always catch something. Not only are there picnic and barbecue facilities, but all the fixings for cooking your fish are available at a little store. A snack bar is available for drinks and desserts. It costs just $3.50 for the entire family to fish, but you must pay for what you catch at $4.87 per pound. Fishing equipment rents for $3.50 per pole. Open daily from March to mid-November. Call for hours during the year.

Hiking

If your family enjoys the outdoors, the San Bernardino Mountains offer lots of different trails to choose from. For specific trail information, contact the **Big Bear Ranger District,** P.O. Box 290, Fawnskin, CA 92333 (909/866-3437).

We like the **Champion Lodgepole Trail** (less than half a mile long) and the connecting **Bluff Mesa Trail** (also half a mile long). These short family hikes take you through lodgepole and Jeffrey pine trees. In fact, the Champion Lodgepole Trail takes you past one of the largest lodgepoles in the entire state. Another easy trail is the **Pacific Crest National Scenic Trail,** which starts near Calif. 38 at Onyx Summit and ends 39 miles away at Holcomb Creek. You can walk as far as you want and see beautiful vistas along the way.

Horseback Riding

You can go riding at **Magic Mountain Stables,** next to the Alpine Slide (☎ **909/878-4677**). One-hour guided rides through the forests cost $15 per hour. Children must be 8 years old to ride alone. The stables are open daily from 10am to 5pm weekdays and 9am to 6pm weekends. Closed January 1 through May 1. Open year round, **Baldwin Lake Stables** (☎ **909/585-6482**) is another place to rent horses. Call for rates and hours as they vary during the seasons.

Miniature Golf

You'll find this sport at **Putt'N Around,** next door to the Alpine Slide (☎ **909/866-4626**). It's open from 9am to 9pm on weekends, and daily during summer.

Swimming

You can go lake swimming at **McDill Swim Beach,** in Meadow Park at the corner of Knight and Park Avenues (☎ **909/866-0135**). It's a cordoned-off beach area on Big Bear Lake with lifeguards, snack bar, restrooms, and parking lot. The beach is open mid-June through Labor Day from noon to 5pm. Ages 11 and over pay $2.50; children 5 to 10, $2; under 4, free. Children 10 and under must be accompanied by an adult.

ANNUAL EVENTS

Old Miner's Days (July and August) are ten days when the Old West visits Big Bear. There are log-rolling and rafting contests, donkey rides and races, and a carnival. The event culminates in a terrific parade.

Big Bear Rodeo (September) has bronco riding and roping competitions, and other rodeo events.

Oktoberfest (September 1 through October) is a celebration with German food, dancing, and music; weekends only.

WHERE TO STAY IN BIG BEAR LAKE

Big Bear offers a very unusual service. The **Big Bear Lake Resort Association** (☎ **909/866-7000**), will help you make reservations at cabins, condominiums, bed-and-breakfasts, homes, motels, and hotels. They will try to take your specifications and meet your particular needs.

Marina Riviera Resort, 40770 Lakeview Dr., Big Bear Lake, CA 92315 (☎ **909/866-7545**), is a luxury lakefront property that has table tennis, volleyball, horseshoes, and a lovely lakeside grassy area for barbecuing and picnics. It's a great place to stay where you can watch the kids play for hours at the water's edge while you sit and enjoy the sandy shore. Of course, there's a pool and spa.

Adjoining rooms are available. Some rooms have Jacuzzi tubs, some have refrigerators, and a few have full kitchens. Prices range from $120 to $175, depending on the amenities.

The **Smoketree Lodge,** 40210 Big Bear Blvd. (P.O. Box 2801), Big Bear Lake, CA 92315 (☎ **909/866-2415,** or toll free **800/352-8581**), is a very basic, quaint lodge composed of cabins and motel units. Kids love it—and vice versa. Management calls this place "The Lodge That Loves Kids." Kids are wild about the heated swimming pool with its water slide. The lodge has a Jacuzzi, volleyball, Ping-Pong, basketball and shuffleboard courts, and a children's playground.

Most units have wood-burning fireplaces and coffee makers. Some cabins have cooking facilities and are equipped with all you need for basic cooking. Prices vary considerably, since the rooms are very different. They run from a low of $39–$120 in the off-season to $75–$150 in peak season. Cribs and rollaways are $10.

Camping

Six campgrounds are located in the Big Bear Ranger District. **Big Pine Flats** has 17 sites with water and pit toilets, and charges $8 per night, on a first-come first-served basis. **Serrano** has 132 sites, water, flush toilets, showers, and charges $12 per night. It also has RV sites with hookups and dump stations, and charges $20 per night. Half of the camps are first-come, first-served, or you can make reservations (☎ 800/280-CAMP). **Hanna Flats** has 88 sites with water and flush toilets, and costs $12 per night. **Holcomb Valley,** with 19 sites, has pit toilets but no water—no charge. **Pine Knot** has 48 sites with water and flush toilets, and charges $11 per night. Open mid-May until November 1, but call ahead.

WHERE TO EAT

The **Cowboy Steakhouse,** 40433 Lakeview Dr. (☎ **909/866-1486**), is a very popular place, and boasts the world's tiniest sundae—for only 45¢. The specialty is steak, and boy, do they serve 'em up! There's a full-pound Porterhouse for $16.95, a choice top sirloin for $12.95, and a flank steak for two for $17.95. But wait—even if you're not a steak lover, there's pork and beef ribs and scrumptious chicken. Food is served with fresh garden salad and beans or potatoes. The chuck wagon biscuits and honey butter are just out of this world! The children's menu offers burgers and chicken strips, as well as ribs, including a drink and world's smallest sundae, priced at $2.99.

Open Sunday through Thursday, 4:30pm to 9pm, Friday and Saturday, 4:30pm to 10pm, and Sunday 9:30 to 2:30pm for brunch. Boosters and highchairs are available. Credit cards are accepted.

Hansel's, 40701 Big Bear Blvd. (☎ **909/866-9497**), open for breakfast, lunch, and dinner, is a European-style restaurant with a varied menu. Two eggs with bacon, potatoes, and toast is $3.95; omelets are $4.95–$5.95. Lunches consist of burgers and sandwiches ($4.75–$7.95), and dinners include bread, soup or salad, rice or potatoes, and vegetables. Try the sesami chicken salad ($6.95) or a hot entree such as Atlantic white fish, a German sausage platter, or the Hansel burger combo ($6.95–$15.95). There's a children's menu, and highchairs and boosters are available.

Hansel's is open Monday through Friday from 8am to 3pm and 5 to 9pm, and on Saturday and Sunday from 7am to 3pm and 5 to 9pm. Most credit cards are accepted.

The **Log Cabin Restaurant,** 39976 Big Bear Blvd. (☎ **909/866-3667**), is geared to family dining. Specialties include German-American food, such as sauerbraten and potato pancakes, but they also have steaks, ribs, and other good American food. They have boosters and highchairs, and a children's menu. Breakfast averages $4, lunch runs $6, and dinner goes for $9. They split adult portions in the kitchen and warm baby food or bottles. They accept reservations Sunday through Thursday (daily if your party is larger than nine people), and some major credit cards are honored. There's a very large parking lot.

Teddy Bear Restaurant, 583 Pine Knot Ave., in the village (☎ **909/866-5415**), is a nice coffee shop that serves a wide variety of food. For breakfast, there are home-style buttermilk pancakes, Belgian waffles, eggs, and omelets (priced at $1.75–$6). For lunch and dinner, you can choose from burgers, sandwiches, salads, and a health bar, which has natural-style foods; prices are $3.75–$6.95. Full dinners (served after 5pm) of steak, chicken, ham, or fish cost $6.75–$9.75. The children's menu consists of chicken strips or shrimp with soup of fruit or salad and fries ($1.95–$3.50). Highchairs and booster seats are available. The restaurant is open every day—from 6am to midnight Sunday through Thursday, and 2 to 3am on Friday and Saturday. There is parking, and they honor some major credit cards.

While you're there, stroll over to **Teddy Bear Miniatures and Dolls,** next door (☎ **909/866-2811**). This little store is a treasure chest of stuffed animals and miniatures. Open daily from 10am to 5pm.

Orange County

14

T HE NAME ORANGE COUNTY CONJURES UP IMAGES OF FAMILY OUTINGS AND vacation fun. For most of us, Orange County made it on the map in 1955 when Disneyland opened its gates. At that time orange groves graced the roadsides and the area's famous beach cities were almost unknown.

Today, with a population of over 2 million, Orange County boasts more than 39 million visitors a year, making it one of the country's premier vacation destinations. And people aren't coming just to see Disneyland. They are also interested in Knott's Berry Farm, the Movieland Wax Museum, and the San Juan Capistrano Mission. They travel to see the Los Angeles Rams and the California Angels. They come to play on the beaches and stroll through the tidepools of the fabulous 42-mile coastline that is now being called the Côte d'Orange.

HOW TO GET THERE

Most people come from Los Angeles (via **Los Angeles International Airport**), but a growing number are flying directly into **John Wayne/Orange County Airport,** 19051 Airport Way No., Anaheim (☎ **714/252-5006**). From both, there are five major companies that offer ground transportation to and from the airport.

Orange County is also serviced by **Greyhound** (☎ **714/635-5060**), and **Amtrak** (☎ toll free **800/USA-RAIL** for reservations, or **714/385-1448** for recorded information). They make stops in Anaheim, San Juan Capistrano, and several other locations in the area.

Although this is Southern California, you can do passably well without a car since most of the hotels offer shuttle service to the major sightseeing attractions. Sightseeing tour buses also operate in the area. **Pacific Coast Gray Line** (☎ **714/978-8858,** or toll free **800/828-6699**) is a very popular one. You can also try **Valen Tours** (☎ **714/956-2252**).

If you want a car for a day or two, all major **car-rental companies** have locations in Orange County; consult the *Yellow Pages* for local numbers. If you're driving to the area, see the specific sections in this chapter for directions.

For complete information about the area, contact the **Anaheim Area Visitor and Convention Bureau,** 800 W. Katella Ave., Anaheim, CA 92803 (☎ **714/999-8999**). These folks know a lot about Orange County, and if there's anything they don't know, they'll find out for you.

1 Theme Parks—Anaheim and Buena Park

Anaheim is the largest city in Orange County, and contrary to many people's perception, it is *not* a suburb of Los Angeles. In fact, if you're talking with a native, be sure you remember that Anaheim is the home of Disneyland not the other way around! Because of Disneyland and the enormous Anaheim Convention Center, it offers services and hotels that will please even the most discriminating family members. Buena Park is its neighbor, and home to several sightseeing attractions as well.

The easiest way to get to Anaheim by car is via I-5, the Santa Ana Freeway. If you're coming from either Los Angeles or San Diego, exit at Harbor Boulevard. To get to Buena Park, exit at Beach Boulevard south.

DISNEYLAND

The granddaddy of all the theme parks, Disneyland is still a world of magic and wonderment, even when compared to the dozens of other parks that have sprung up in recent years. Many of us remember Disneyland in its infancy, when orange groves and walnut trees surrounded the park, when you could see the Matterhorn from miles away, when the Jungle Cruise ride was state-of-the-art fun. Disneyland has matured from 18 attractions to more than 60, but it still maintains the Disney hallmarks that make it special. For us, the Disney magic is as much the friendliness and helpfulness of the people who work there as the rides. The streets and walkways are so clean, you never think twice about sitting on the curb to watch a parade.

Disneyland is the place where fantasy is elevated to a classic art form, where the outside world seems less real than the heightened reality inside the park. One family we know tells the tale of visiting Santa Fe, New Mexico, only to have the youngsters exclaim that it looked just like Frontierland. Indeed, a sort of Disneyland reality takes over. For example, Star Tours not only takes you on a fantastic space voyage, but even while you're waiting in line to get a seat on the ride, equipment and videos simulate a space station—complete with aliens and exotic locations.

The "happiest place on earth," Disneyland is located off I-5, the Santa Ana Freeway (take the Harbor Boulevard exit), about 27 miles south of Los Angeles. The story goes that Walt Disney happened upon the idea of a "magical little park" when he was watching his young daughters enjoy themselves at local amusement parks. He originally envisioned a little two-acre park next to the Disney Studios in Burbank, but quickly discovered that his ideas needed more space in which to flourish.

Never the one to do things on a small scale, Disney turned to Stanford University's Research Institute to determine the perfect location. He found it in 1953 and broke ground on July 21, 1954. He risked everything and invested $17 million in a park that everyone else thought would be a dismal failure. But genius and vision prevailed. Only seven weeks after the doors opened in 1955, the one-millionth visitor walked through the gates.

Disney originated the theme-land concept, where movies come to life and animation is made real. Today there are eight theme areas. They radiate out from a central hub at the end of Main Street, U.S.A. The park is situated on 80 acres with another 100 acres just for parking.

Main Street, U.S.A.

Main Street is the entry to the park. It sets the mood for your excursion into this world of fantasy. In fact, Main Street is like walking through the lens of a camera into a cinematic world.

Modeled on small-town turn-of-the-century America, Main Street has a lot to offer. Here you can rent strollers, get a locker to store bring-along items, and tell the children where to meet if they get separated from you. For parents of infants, the **Baby Center** is an area where you can prepare formula, warm bottles, and change diapers (although many restrooms throughout the park have these facilities).

There are some intriguing one-of-a-kind shops here. Our favorites are **Main Street Magic Shop** and the **Silhouette Studio.**

Adventureland

The theme here is the exotic regions of Asia, Africa, and the South Pacific. You'll find the **Jungle Cruise** ride, **Swiss Family Treehouse,** and the **Enchanted Tiki Room.**

The **Indiana Jones Adventure** is the newest attraction. An expedition through ancient temple ruins, this ride has action and thrills around every corner. You board well-worn World War II transports for what appears to be a standard archaeological tour to search for Indy. But the amazing vehicles rock and roll through clouds of smoke, fire, bubbling lava pits, ominous steam vents, a crumbling ceiling, and an encounter

 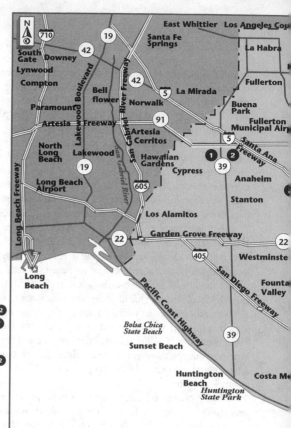
9534

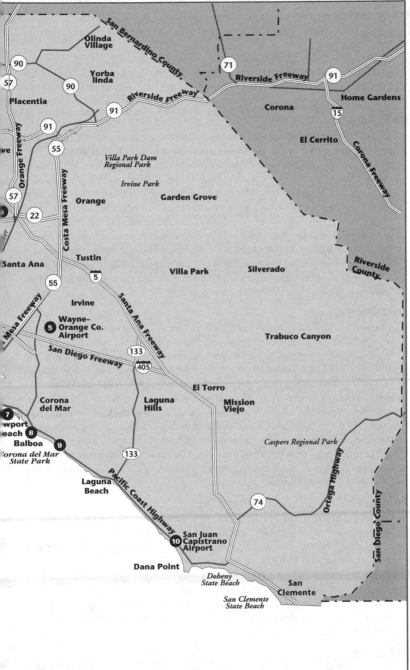

90
Olinda Village
57
Yorba linda
90
Placentia
91
91
55
57
22
Santa Ana

Orange Freeway

Costa Mesa Freeway

San Bernardino County

Riverside Freeway

71

Riverside Freeway **91**

Home Gardens

Corona

15

El Cerrito

Corona Freeway

Villa Park Dam Regional Park

Irvine Park

Orange

Garden Grove

Tustin

5

Villa Park

Silverado

Riverside County

Irvine

55

Wayne– Orange Co. Airport

5

San Diego Freeway

133

405

Santa Ana Freeway

Trabuco Canyon

Mesa Freeway

El Torro

Corona del Mar

Laguna Hills

Mission Viejo

7
wport each
8
Balboa
9
orona del Mar State Park

Caspers Regional Park

133

Laguna Beach

Pacific Coast Highway

Ortega Highway

74

San Diego County

10
San Juan Capistrano Airport

Dana Point

Doheny State Beach

San Clemente

San Clemente State Beach

with a temple diety. Explorers discover more surprises around every bend in this sub-terranean world.

Two tips for families with young children. We have noted that some very young ones are afraid of the special effects, so warn them that they're not real, and prepare them for gunshots and other sudden noises. The Enchanted Tiki Room is a great place to sit and rest in a cool spot. However, the show may be a bit long for toddlers.

New Orleans Square

The home of pirates and ghosts, this quaint area is a wonderful place to rest and people-watch. Park favorites **Pirates of the Caribbean** and **Haunted Mansion,** with its 999 ghosts, are located here. **Note:** While neither ride is scary for children over 6, younger kids may have a little trouble; there are two lose-your-stomach water slides, and some loud gunshots. The Mansion is one ride we think might best be left for school-agers and older. With ghostly cries and darkened rooms, little ones may find it too frightening.

If you can time it right, a meal at **Blue Bayou Restaurant** is a treat. Where else could you eat by the cool moonlight to the sound of crickets in the middle of a warm Southern California day? **Pieces of Eight** giftshop with its treasure chest of goodies is a favorite of our little pirates. Both 4- and 10-year-olds inevitably chime in together requesting trinkets from the pirates' pots of gold.

Critter Country

The down-home backwoods is the theme here. One of Disney's newest attractions—and one that's completely worth the wait in line—is **Splash Mountain.** Try to see it while others are waiting to see the parades. This water-slide ride is based on the movie *Song of the South,* where delightful characters give you a lively rendition of "Zip-a-Dee-Doo-Dah" as you zip along in your boat. The thrill ride has a flume that drops 52 feet, and more than 100 AudioAnimatronic characters, including Br'er Rabbit, Br'er Bear, and Br'er Fox. We loved it as much as **Pirates of the Carribean** and **Star Tours.** We didn't take Elizabeth on this ride until she was 6 because she's uneasy about the water slide. However, other parents of preschoolers do. Again, each child reacts differently. Popular with the littlest ones is the **Country Bear Playhouse,** where they can sing along with the animated stuffed animals. Older children enjoy **Davy Crockett's Explorer Canoes.**

Frontierland

Back to the days of the pioneers and the Old West where shoot-'em-ups happened at the town square and riverboats coursed the waters. **Big Thunder Mountain Railroad** is a huge hit with kids over 7 and even brave little ones. **Big Thunder Ranch,** a two-acre replica of an 1880s homestead, is a hit with the smallest children. There is a petting barnyard here (closes at dusk) and a walk-through model of an antique pioneer log cabin. **Tom Sawyer Island** is the original "run-around play area" for children with lots of energy. It has caves, a rope bridge, and balancing rocks. And if you're there in the morning, don't miss the Mickey Mouse–shaped pancakes at River Belle Terrace, overlooking New Orleans Square.

Fantasyland

Ah, Fantasyland. If there ever was a land of fairytales—but one where dreams do come true—it's this one. This is a place where little eyes grow huge as they spot the **Sleeping Beauty Castle** and cross the bridge to Pinocchio, Mr. Toad, and Peter Pan.

Larger-than-life Cinderellas, Snow Whites, and Seven Dwarfs greet little ones with big hugs on the castle drawbridge.

The storybook kingdom has more than 17 attractions. Gentle, nonfrightening rides are the **King Arthur Carousel, Dumbo the Flying Elephant, Casey Jr. Circus Train, Motor Boat Cruise, Storybook Land Canal Boats,** and **Fantasyland Autopia. It's a Small World** may well be the favorite of the under-6 set—small boats cruise through a wonderland of singing and dancing dolls that serenade you with the well-known catchy tune with a world brotherhood theme.

Many of the other adventure rides (often in the spooky dark) may be best for children 4 and older, and children under 7 must be accompanied by an adult. **Alice in Wonderland, Peter Pan's Flight, Snow White's Scary Adventures,** and **Mr. Toad's Wild Ride** may frighten very young children. **Pinocchio's Daring Journey** isn't very daring, and children of almost any age love to point out all the characters they recognize.

The one problem with rides in Fantasyland is that they are low capacity, so lines move slowly. If you can't avoid the crowds, it's best to come up with a strategy where one adult wanders with the kids for a time while the other one waits in line.

But Fantasyland is not relegated exclusively to tiny tots. This is also the home of the **Matterhorn Bobsleds,** a thrilling ride through the snow-capped park landmark, the Matterhorn. While older kids and teens love this, don't subject your little tykes to it. Although it is open-air and not darkened, the bobsleds move very quickly, encountering the Abominable Snowman along the way.

Tomorrowland

The dynamic, vibrant world of tomorrow is what you'll find here. **Space Mountain, Rocket Jets, Submarine Voyage, Captain EO** (the 3-D movie featuring Michael Jackson), and **Star Tours** are located here. These are among the most popular attractions in the park. **Note:** Although *Captain EO* is one of our all-time favorite attractions, the sound is so loud that it scares some toddlers. Instead, we take the toddlers to **Skyway to Fantasyland.** A trip on the **Disneyland Monorail** is always a thrill.

There will be a very long line for Star Tours, sometimes over $1^1/2$ hours. Surprising as it may seem, the long wait is worth it. Here you see what happened when the genius of George Lucas met Disney craftsmen. The result was state-of-the-art ride technology. You'll come away feeling as if you've just been on a journey in space.

Mickey's Toontown

Mickey's Toontown is almost a suburb of Fantasyland, and although you might think it's for the little ones, adults—and even teenagers—find its tongue-in-cheek antics hysterically funny.

The area is an animated downtown and suburban neighborhood where Disney cartoon characters live. The buildings are whimsical—none of the homes or "city" landmarks are what you'd expect. And, believe us, even the wait in line to get into the attractions is fun. Not only will you be able to interact with Mickey, Minnie, Donald, Goofy, and Roger Rabbit, you'll also be able to have a conversation with a fire hydrant. Head here early in the day if you can. It gets very crowded later, and there are parades galore that you don't want to miss.

Disneyland Shows

Disney's extravaganzas are known for their magnificence. The **Main Street Electrical Parade** and **Fantasy in the Sky** have long been favorites. Now Disney steps into

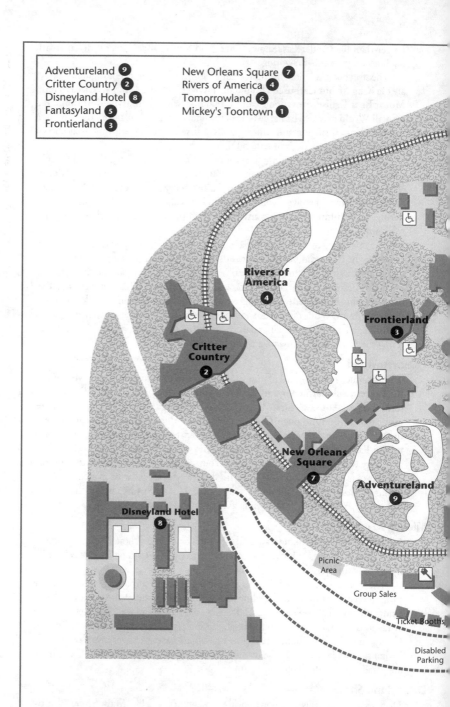

Adventureland **9**
Critter Country **2**
Disneyland Hotel **8**
Fantasyland **5**
Frontierland **3**

New Orleans Square **7**
Rivers of America **4**
Tomorrowland **6**
Mickey's Toontown **1**

Rivers of America **4**

Frontierland **3**

Critter Country **2**

New Orleans Square **7**

Adventureland **9**

Disneyland Hotel **8**

Picnic Area

Group Sales

Ticket Booths

Disabled Parking

9106

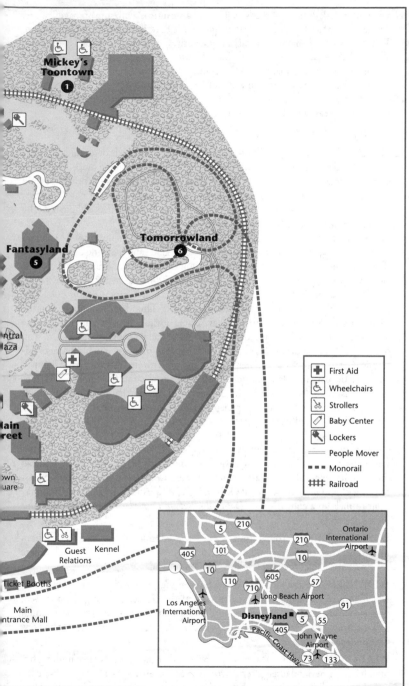

Disneyland

Mickey's
Toontown ❶

Fantasyland ❺

Tomorrowland ❻

ntral
aza

ain
reet

own
uare

Guest   Kennel
Relations

Ticket Booths

Main
ntrance Mall

	First Aid
	Wheelchairs
	Strollers
	Baby Center
	Lockers
	People Mover
	Monorail
	Railroad

Los Angeles
International
Airport

Long Beach Airport

Disneyland

John Wayne
Airport

Ontario
International
Airport

Pacific Coast Hwy.

5   210   210   10   101   405   1   10   110   710   605   57   91   5   55   405   73   133

a new after-dark dimension that's really hot. **Fantasmic** is a mixture of magic, music, live performers, and special effects that light up the Rivers of America in Frontierland. The story includes many of the Disney favorites, as well as villains Ursula from *The Little Mermaid* and Maleficent from *Sleeping Beauty*. Pyrotechnics, lasers, mist screens, and other imaginative techniques interact with the huge cast of performers to make this a really spectacular show. Be sure to to find a spot early so you can view the extravaganza comfortably. We waited two hours and it was worth the wait! There's a new show—**Beauty and the Beast–Live.**

Tips on How to "Do" the Park

SOME FACTS   Disneyland's off-season is mid-September through mid-June, except for holiday periods such as Thanksgiving, Christmas, and spring break. Off-season is the best time to come. But, obviously, most people come during the peak times. No matter what season you plan to be there, Saturday is the busiest day. Surprise, surprise—during the summer, Friday and Sunday are less crowded, although not by much. Weekdays are the lightest during the rest of the year.

Peak hours are noon to 5pm. A lot of people leave after sunset; in the summer another large group leaves after the first Electrical Parade and fireworks at about 9pm. If you have older kids who can stay up late, you can do a lot of rides when everyone else is watching the first parade, and catch the second parade at 11pm.

Try to do the most popular attractions, such as Star Tours, *Captain EO*, Space Mountain, the Matterhorn, Splash Mountain, Big Thunder Mountain, Haunted Mansion, and Pirates of the Caribbean, as early as possible. This goes for many of the low-capacity rides in Fantasyland as well. If you're lucky enough to have more than one day at Disneyland, you might consider doing what many veteran Disneyland visitors do. Get to the park early. When it gets extremely crowded, get your hand stamped and leave the park until late afternoon. You can return in time for dinner—and thinner crowds. If you're coming in the summer, you can purchase your tickets in advance and arrive at 8am, when the park opens, to get a headstart on the crowds. If you can't do that, park officials suggest that you get there at 7:30am because the ticket lines can be long.

As soon as you get your *Souvenir Guide,* take time to plan your day so you don't waste time backtracking. If you've never been to the park before, you can write ahead for the guide to decide which attractions you want to see most. Address your request to Disneyland Guest Relations, P.O. Box 3232, Anaheim, CA 92803. Or you may want to pick up a copy of *The Unofficial Guide to Disneyland* (Macmillan) at your local bookstore.

LOST CHILDREN   Young strays can be retrieved from the Lost Children Station, located next to Central First Aid, near Main Street. Or you can go to City Hall, where the staff will contact the Lost Children Station for you.

BABY NEEDS   Baby food is available both in the Market House on Main Street, which also stocks medium-size diapers, and at the Gerber changing room as well. Diapers are also available at the Emporium on Main Street at the women's counter, in Tomorrowland at Star Traders at the camera counter, and at the Hat Shop in New Orleans Square.

HEALTHIER FOODS   Many people believe that theme parks offer nothing but junk food. Disneyland offers alternatives, even at the fast-food service lines. Here is a sampling; check the back pages of the *Disneyland Souvenir Guide* for a complete listing; *Main Street U.S.A.*—Carnation Ice Cream Parlor (boneless breast of chicken);

Town Square Café (chef's salad and seafood Louis), Plaza Inn (fresh fish), Plaza Pavilion (spaghetti with meatless sauce, lemon herb chicken); *Adventureland*—Tahitian Terrace (chicken sandwich, vegetable stir-fry); *New Orleans Square*—Blue Bayou Restaurant (chicken breast, angel-hair pasta primavera, fresh fish), Café Orleans (Cajun chicken, tuna salad sandwich); French Market Restaurant (trout, spinach tortellini); *Critter Country*—Hungry Bear Restaurant (fresh fruit salad), Harbour Galley (tuna sandwich with cholesterol-free mayonnaise); *Frontierland*—Casa Mexicana (fresh fruit), River Belle Terrace (fresh fruit), Big Thunder Barbecue (trout); *Fantasyland*—Village House Restaurant (fresh fruit salad, fresh vegetable salad); and *Tomorrowland*—Tomorrowland Terrace (frozen yogurt, muffins for breakfast, chef's salad), Space Place (garden salad and tuna sandwich with cholesterol-free mayonnaise).

HOURS   The park is open daily, all year. From Memorial Day through Labor Day, the extended hours vary. From September through May, the park is open weekdays from 10am to 6pm and on Saturday and Sunday from 9am to midnight. There are special hours during holidays. It's best to check hours in advance (☎ **714/999-4565,** or **213/626-8605,** ext. 4565).

ADMISSION   Adults pay $33 for a one-day pass, $57 for a two-day pass, and $79 for a three-day pass. Children 3–11 are charged $25 for a one-day pass, $42 for a two-day pass, and $57 for a three-day pass. Children under 3 are free.

KNOTT'S BERRY FARM

Don't expect glamour and glitter when you visit Knott's Berry Farm, 8039 Beach Blvd. in Buena Park (☎ **714/220-5200**), two miles south of the Santa Ana Freeway on Calif. 39. Knott's is still a pretty down-to-earth theme park, and it can be visited in one day. Knott's has its own charm, mostly because of its small size and the rustic Old West theme that prevails over even the most modern sections.

Knott's began as a real farm, and owner Walter Knott cultivated the first boysenberry here. Mrs. Knott (Cordelia) began selling her boysenberry pies and chicken dinners to make money during the Depression. Her famous dinners and pies are still a roaring success at the **Chicken Dinner Restaurant** in the Marketplace.

But what will the kids find most interesting? If you have young children, you'll probably want to start with **Camp Snoopy,** where they'll meet up with Lucy, Snoopy, and Charlie Brown. There are over six acres of rides in Camp Snoopy, tailor made for youngsters. In fact, some of the toddler-appropriate rides are extremely short and very gentle. The staff takes longer than necessary to get kids ready for a ride (even with short lines), so be prepared. Beary Tales Playhouse was undoubtedly our (then) 4-year-old's favorite Camp Snoopy activity. She reported that going through the bears' tree house was scary and fun at the same time. In front of some of the bear scenes along the way are narrow semi-enclosed "trails" for the toddlers to crawl through. They are dark and can be claustrophobic. While we were there, several youngsters needed to be pulled out by their parents midway along the trail.

Fiesta Village, next along the road, is where you'll find Montezooma's Revenge. Sure to cause inexplicable excitement in preteens and teens, this roller coaster goes not only in a loop, but backward too! Brave souls can move on to the **Roaring '20s,** home of the Sky Tower, a parachute jump that deposits you 20 stories down at free-fall speed. Not for the faint of heart.

Calmer experiences can be found in **Ghost Town,** an authentic 1880s Old West Gold Rush town and the original section of the amusement park. Kids love the ride on the authentic stagecoach. Be aware that there are always long lines here. The steam engine fascinates children of all ages. Even if they don't take the ride, kids love to stand close to this monstrous iron horse and just see how it's put together.

Kingdom of the Dinosaurs is a star in Knott's world. We can honestly say that the "monsters" are extremely realistic and were quite frightening to Elizabeth (then 4)—and her mother as well. Older kids, however, love it. In this age of dinosaur-mania, it's a perfect thrill ride for ages 7 and up. As you exit this ride, you'll come to a huge arcade of games with something for every age.

Mystery Lodge is a new, multisensory journey deep into the Native North American West.

The **Wild Water Wilderness Area** features an exhilarating ride down the longest man-made white-water rapids.

Altogether, there are over 165 rides, attractions, live shows, restaurants, and shops at Knott's, so there will be something to appeal to all ages.

BABY NEEDS   Near the exit of Beary Tales in Camp Snoopy, there's a baby station with changing tables and a microwave for heating bottles. There's another one in the Marketplace at the First Aid Station. Stroller rentals are available here.

HOURS   In summer, Knott's is open Sunday through Friday from 9am to midnight and on Saturday from 9am to 1am; in winter, Monday through Friday from 10am to 6pm, on Saturday from 10am to 10pm, and on Sunday from 10am to 7pm. The park and Marketplace are open all holidays except Christmas. If you plan to go on another holiday, call first for hours. Hours vary.

ADMISSION   Adults 12 and older pay $28.50; children 3–11, $18.50; handicapped, expectant mothers, and seniors 60 and over, $18.50; children 2 and under are free. Holidays often mean special rates, so call first. Off-season, there's sometimes a "Kids Are Free" promotion, during which time one child is admitted free per paid adult; call for details.

OTHER THINGS TO SEE AND DO IN THE AREA

Although the kids know Disneyland and Knott's Berry Farm the best, there are other places to visit in Anaheim and Buena Park.

Movieland Wax Museum

Probably one of the best wax museums in the country, Movieland Wax Museum, at 7711 Beach Blvd., just one block north of Knott's Berry Farm (☎ 714/522-1155), is a place that movie buffs shouldn't miss. We wonder how many of the 240 movie stars exhibited children recognize, but even 6-year-olds appreciate the craft that goes into creating these life-size replicas of celebrities in their most famous roles. The exhibits are staged with realistic props and authentic costumes that re-create famous movie and television scenes.

While your children may not have seen *Dr. Zhivago* or *Gone with the Wind,* they'll surely appreciate the bridge of Star Trek Starship *Enterprise,* manned by Captain Kirk, Mr. Spock, and the rest of the crew. You can be sure they'll marvel as you join Superman in the walk-through Fortress of Solitude from a scene in the movie. Superman stands in the center of ice crystals while a cool breeze blows to simulate the icy atmosphere. It's a cool, dimly lit alcove where Superman music finishes the mood.

And there's Michael Jackson with background vocal, Mr. T, and Sylvester Stallone as *Rocky.* Even though our kids had never seen footage of *The Wizard of Oz* and the Our Gang comedies, they were fascinated by the sets and realism of the wax figures. Kids are amazed at Our Gang's Alfalfa, whose tooth is being pulled. "Doesn't he look real?" they ask.

Much to our delight, the Chambers of Horrors is set off by itself and can easily be avoided. In addition to lots of movie-star memorabilia, you can watch old-fashioned moving picture machines, such as mutoscopes and biographs. These are a real treat and also give our video-generation kids a chance to see some of the development of the medium.

Allow about one to two hours for the self-guided tour. The museum is completely stroller-accessible. The wax museum is open Sunday through Thursday from 9am to 7pm and on Friday and Saturday from 9am to 8pm; the box office closes 1$^{1}/_{2}$ hours before. Admission is $12.95 for adults, $10.55 for seniors, $6.95 for children 4–11, and free for children under 4.

Medieval Times

As kids, many of us daydreamed about castles and kings, knights and chivalry. Perhaps your children do too. Medieval Times, 7662 Beach Blvd., right near the wax museum (☎ **714/521-4740,** or toll free **800/899-6600**), takes you back to 11th-century Europe. You are the guests—the nobility—at the castle of Count of Perelada and his countess, where you partake in a four-course feast and watch the tournament of knights.

Each guest, young and old alike, is given a colored paper crown as he enters the castle. Your colors are the colors of the knight you are to cheer on to victory during the games. Guests enter the Hall of Arms, where there are authentic medieval artifacts and lots of souvenir vendors. Hold on to your wallets, though, because souvenir vendors and picture-taking minstrels hail you on a regular basis. One of them will even research your family's coat-of-arms and motto, for an extra fee, and present you with a sketch of it.

The kids really get into the spirit of it, skipping happily through the grand halls wearing their crowns and waving their colored banners in anticipation of the show.

The real production is inside the 1,000-seat main arena, where you and the kids sit at long tables surrounding the open central arena. Serfs and wenches in medieval attire serve you fresh vegetable appetizers, soup, chicken, ribs, potatoes, and dessert tarts—all of which you must eat with your fingers as they did in the 11th century, or you'll be thrown in the dungeon. As you eat, the show goes on.

Trumpeters herald the entrance of the knights of the realm, and the show begins. During the two-hour performance, the knights parade on horseback, show how their Arabian stallions were trained, joust, and compete in games on horseback. There is even swordplay.

While you could take children 4 and older here, it requires a considerable attention span to really enjoy it.

Show times vary. Admission prices are $33.75 for adults, $19.95 for children 12 and under. The 6:30pm Saturday show is $37.75 for adults and children. Major credit cards are accepted. Reservations are required—make them as far in advance as possible, since Medieval Times is a very popular year-round attraction. Parking lot available.

Wild Bill's Wild West Dinner Extravaganza

A trip to the Old West awaits you at Wild Bill's Wild West Dinner Extravaganza, 7600 Beach Blvd., Buena Park, near Medieval Times (☎ **714/522-6414**). Your evening includes a four-course western banquet (stew, salad, chicken and ribs, baked beans, baked potato, corn on the cob, and old-fashioned apple pie and ice cream), beer or wine and soft drinks, coffee or tea, and a variety show with western music, cowboys, Indians, and singers and dancers. Call for show times. Reservations are suggested. Admission for adults is $32.27 Monday through Thursday, $34.43 on Friday and Saturday, $29.04 for Saturday and Sunday matinees; for children, $21.50 (ages 3–11) for all performances.

Hobby City

A planned 15-minute visit to Hobby City, 1238 S. Beach Blvd., Anaheim (☎ 714/527-2323), turned into a two-hour stay. The kids liked this low-key center with its teeny park in the middle because there was nothing glitzy or showy about it.

Moms and grandmas will likely love the **Doll and Toy Museum** as much as the kids. Behind the doll and toy shop, which is housed in a half-scale model of the White House, is a doll museum filled to the rafters with Barbie and Ken dolls. Barbie's sister, Skipper, is also there, along with ancient and antique dolls, and dolls made out of almost any material you can think of. Over 50 years of collecting went into this display of more than 3,000 dolls and toys, many exhibited at a child's-eye level. It takes no more than a half hour to go through it. The store itself sells and repairs antique and modern dolls. The doll accessories and clothes are truly unbelievable. Admission to the museum is $1 for adults, 50¢ for children under 12.

Also at Hobby City is the **Hobby City Choo Choo,** which will appeal to your littlest ones. It's not an exciting ride, but the kids love this tiny, repainted, open-air train, maybe because it's so close to their size, and because they see real things, rather than the make-believe of the amusement parks. There are a couple of picnic tables and a snack bar adjacent to the tracks.

The **Cabbage Patch Adoption Center** is staffed with salespeople dressed like doctors and nurses. There's a small room with an incubator and a doctor's office for preemie Cabbage Patch dolls. Naturally, there are lots of dolls and accessories for sale. Right across the street is the **Bear Tree,** stocked with stuffed animals from around the world, all housed in a replicated tree.

Hobbyists have a choice of shops from stamps and coins, rocks, gems, arts and crafts, and yarn goods to miniatures, aquarium goods, driftwood, and candles. There is also a small restaurant next door to the Doll Museum.

Hobby City is open every day from 10am to 6pm. Parking is plentiful. Welcome one and all.

Ripley's Believe It or Not!

Ripley's Believe It or Not! is located one block north of Knott's Berry Farm on Beach Blvd., across from Movieland Wax Museum (☎ 714/522-7045). Adults pay $8.95; children 4–11, $5.25; under 4, free. Open Sunday through Thursday from 10am to 7:30pm, on Friday and Saturday till 8:30pm. The box office closes 1¹/₂ hours before closing.

Crystal Cathedral

Have you ever seen a building made completely of glass? The unique Crystal Cathedral, 12141 Lewis St. in Garden Grove (☎ 714/971-4000), home of television's Rev. Robert Schuller, is made of 10,000 panes of glass! Free half-hour walking tours of the grounds, arboretum, and cathedral are conducted daily. The cathedral is open Monday through Saturday from 9am to 3:30pm and on Sunday there is one tour at 12pm. Worship hours are Sunday 8:30, 9:30, and 11am and 7pm. Childcare available.

Other Activities

The sports fans in your group might enjoy taking in a ballgame while you're vacationing here. The **California Angels** play baseball from April through October at Anaheim Stadium, 2000 Gene Autry Way, Anaheim (☎ 714/634-2000). The **Los Angeles Rams** play football at the stadium from August through December (☎ 714/937-6767).

Kids who love baseball and football enjoy the **Anaheim Stadium Tour** (☎ 714/254-3120). You'll see the 70,000-seat stadium as you've never seen it before, including a locker room and the press boxes. Tours are scheduled daily from 11am to 2pm except when there's a day game. Adults pay $3; children 6–16, $2; under 5, free. Reservations are required for groups of 10 or more.

Golf-'N-Stuff Miniature Golf Course (☎ 714/778-4100) is an 18-hole course and video arcade located across from Disneyland. It opens daily at 9am and closes at 10pm Sunday through Thursday and at midnight on Friday and Saturday. Admission is $5.50 for adults and children 6–12, free for children under 6.

Fountain Valley Golf and Recreation Center, 16800 Magnolia St. (☎ 714/842-1011), has bumper-boats, go-karts, and batting cages, as well as two 18-hole miniature golf courses and a game arcade. It opens daily at 10am. Closing times vary, so call when you're planning to go. To play miniature golf, adults pay $5; children 12 and under are charged $3.50.

Even in the Southern California sun, you can ice skate at **Ice Chalet,** 2701 Harbor Blvd. (☎ 714/979-8880). Children as young as 2 can rent skates here. Afternoon sessions are on Monday from 3 to 5pm, Tuesday through Friday from 1 to 5pm, and on Saturday and Sunday from 1 to 4pm. Evening sessions are on Wednesday and Thursday nights from 7:30 to 10pm and on Friday and Saturday nights from 8 to 10pm. Admission is $5.50 for adults and children. Skate rental is $2.50.

Evening Entertainment

Don't miss the **Neon Cactus Country Western Saloon** at the Disneyland Hotel (☎ 714/778-6600) (see "Where to Stay," below, for details).

For top musical performances, try the **Irvine Meadows Amphitheater** in Irvine (☎ 714/855-6111). There is lawn and reserved seating.

The **Orange County Performing Arts Center,** 600 Town Center Dr., in Costa Mesa (☎ 714/556-ARTS), is a 3,000-seat theater that presents nationally and internationally acclaimed productions. There are children's performances as well. Kids and parents are invited to take a tour of the center on Monday and Wednesday at 10 and 11am and the first Saturday of the month at 10 and 11am. Call for further information (☎ 714/556-2122, ext. 833).

WHERE TO STAY

Expensive

Let's start with the hotel whose very name produces a smile on the lips and crinkles around the eyes.

Does the **Disneyland Hotel** really need any introduction, though? It's one hotel that you should save your nickels and dimes for so you can experience it once. Known as the official hotel of the Magic Kingdom, the magical aura of Disneyland permeates this family recreation complex. The only stop on the Monorail ride, this hotel is located at 1150 W. Cerritos Ave., Anaheim, CA 92802 (☎ 714/778-6600, or 213/636-3251 in Los Angeles). With three swimming pools, a fitness center, a spa, ten tennis courts, volleyball, a white sand beach, a small marina, 11 restaurants, free family entertainment, 20 shops and boutiques, and fun for children this 60-acre resort has enough going on that we sometimes find ourselves neglecting other activities in Anaheim and Buena Park.

The complex, which includes three towers, villas, and a convention area, has 1,132 guest rooms and is built around a lovely mini-marina. It recently underwent a two-year renewal. The marina is called Seaports of the Pacific and it's a child's delight. Here's where you'll find a miniature replica of the *Queen Mary* with tiny remote-control tugboats that scurry around her. There are also two-seater pedalboats. There are also free family shows. Probably the most unusual is the Fantasy Waters Show, in which water lights, and music create a dazzling effect. These shows are presented twice nightly. Nearby a state-of-the art video game center houses 64 games; an adult favorite (much to the chagrin of the kids waiting in line) is the off-road raceway with remote-control miniature cars.

And would it be the Disneyland Hotel if you couldn't meet some of the Disney characters? The Disney Character meals (in Goofy's Kitchen) give little ones the chance to meet the likes of Minnie Mouse and Goofy. The breakfast buffet is offered daily from 7 to 11:30am; dinner is served Friday through Sunday from 5 to 9pm. For breakfast, adults pay $12.50; children are charged $7.95. Dinner prices are $17.50 for adults and $8.50 for children. Reservations are not required.

With 11 restaurants and lounges on the premises, you're sure to find plenty to satisfy your appetite. All restaurants have Mickey highchairs and booster seats. All the lounges except two are geared to children, featuring Shirley Temples and Roy Rogerses drinks.

The Neon Cactus Saloon is a country-western nightspot suitable for the kids. There are shows nightly Wednesday through Sunday; call for exact times. Finger food is served and there is no cover charge. There are karaoke-style sing-alongs on Monday and Tuesday. Children allowed until 8pm.

All rooms have balconies or patios, most with a view of Disneyland, the gardens, or the hotel marina. All rooms have color TV with the Disney Channel, plus bath amenities and a stocked honor bar (which cannot be used as a refrigerator). Standard rooms are good-sized. Most come with two double beds, though some king- and queen-size beds are available. Some rooms in the Oriental Gardens sleep six. Parlor rooms and junior suites vary in size. Most suites have refrigerators and wet bars. Hotel amenities include room service with selections good for kids, laundry and dry cleaning, car rentals, photo processing, and babysitting referrals.

Room rates run $150–$170, single or double. Suites start at $300. Cribs are free (only one per room), but rollaways cost $15. Refrigerators are complimentary upon request.

The **Anaheim Hilton Hotel and Towers,** 777 Convention Way, Anaheim, CA 92802 (☎ **714/750-4321;** toll free **800/222-9904** or **800/233-6904**), is in a perfect location—across the street from the Convention Center, two minutes from Disneyland (there's complimentary shuttle service), and only 15 minutes from Knott's Berry Farm. This is a huge hotel with 1,600 rooms and a three-story atrium lobby with a reflection pool in the middle. There's a lovely recreation area on the fifth floor with a huge fenced-in pool and four Jacuzzis, open year round. There is food service and showers nearby. Rooftop gardens and sun decks give you many options for a before-dinner walk. A game center houses video games and pool tables.

Most interesting for families is the Hilton's Vacation Station, a program in effect from June through Labor Day. When you check in, your little ones get to go to their own registration desk. They'll get a membership button to this exclusive club, which entitles them to free Disney movies every day complete with popcorn and punch. They can also check in at the Vacation Station Clubhouse to enjoy arts and crafts or sports programs and to meet other kids. There are also tours of the hotel, and other special things just for kids. Children must be between 5 and 12.

The hotel features three restaurants, a sushi bar, a nightclub, and three lounges. The Café Oasis is especially pleasant for families and is open 18 hours. Breakfasts range in price from $2.75 to $8.75, lunches are $5–$8.50, and dinners cost $7.75–$12.50. Hasting's Grill serves continental cuisine for lunch (prices start at $7.25) and dinner (with prices from $15.50). Pavia has northern Italian food, with dinners starting at $14.50. Room service is available until 2am. At breakfast, certain items can be ordered as a child's portion and you'll be charged half price. For lunch and dinner there's a special children's menu. Room service is extremely fast.

Accommodations are comfortable and roomy. Rooms with two double beds have space for a crib or rollaway. Bathrooms are small, with tub/shower combinations. Rooms have remote-control TV and complimentary cable. On the lanai level, rooms open out to the garden; but watch this with the toddlers—there are no screens. Rooms aren't soundproof, so be sure to request that you're not assigned a room over one of the ballrooms. Because the hotel is so big, it can be a long way from your room to the elevators; if your children are at the carrying age, you might want to request a room closer to the elevators.

Singles run $89–$235; doubles, $89–$255. Suites range from $550 to $1,200. Children, no matter what age, sleep free in the same room with their parents. Rollaways and cribs will be provided at no charge. Extra adults pay $20 each per night. Check out the "Magic of Disneyland" package. It includes breakfasts, tickets to Disneyland, and of course, accommodations (two adults and two children for $199).

Quite plush and completely renovated, the **Anaheim Marriott,** 700 W. Convention Way, Anaheim, CA 92802 (☎ **714/750-8000,** or toll free **800/228-9290**), is located only two blocks from Disneyland. With 1,033 rooms and its location adjacent to the Convention Center, this large hotel gets many convention guests. Because it's so busy, children's noises and activities get absorbed into the general hubbub.

The highlights of the hotel for families, are its complete game room with more than 20 video and pinball machines, and the two lovely heated swimming pools. The pools have large shallow areas, allowing lots of swimming space for even the tiniest child, although there's room for lap swimming as well. One of the beautifully landscaped pools is partially covered with a skylight-type ceiling that creates an indoor effect while remaining very open and airy. There are also two spas, a fitness center that can be used by children over 14, a giftshop, dry cleaning, and a laundry.

Other amenities include a concierge desk, concierge floor, and shuttle service to and from Disneyland via the Marriott's cute little green-and-white trolley. Room service is available from 6am to 1am. A refrigerator costs $5 per night.

Several restaurants offer a wide variety of dining. La Plaza is an early-California–style restaurant that serves breakfast, lunch, and dinner. It has a "Just for Kids" menu that includes standards as well as unusual fare such as beef tostada and prime rib. Prices range from $2 to $3.75. Adult dishes run about $5.50 for sandwiches, $7–$16.50 for dinner entrees. JW's, an elegant restaurant serving continental cuisine, has been voted one of the three best restaurants in Southern California. Both have highchairs and boosters. There's also a Pizza Hut restaurant—just great for families (it's also available through room service).

The guest rooms are decorated in light, airy colors and are standard size. Tell them you're bringing your family so they'll give you one of the larger rooms. All rooms have two telephones, cable TV with free HBO and Disney Channel, "on-command" video movies, and express video checkout. All have tub/shower combinations; most have balconies.

In addition to rooms with king-size and double beds, the hotel has 53 suites. Many of the parlor suites have a Murphy bed, so the room can be used as a living room during the day. Other suites are more traditional, with living rooms that contain a dining table, a love seat, two chairs, wet bars, and refrigerators.

Room rates vary greatly, but whatever the season, children under 18 stay free in their parents' room. There's no charge for cribs, but rollaways cost $15 per stay. There are many special packages, so ask just as soon as you get the reservationist on the line.

Rooms range from $89 to $182, but some Saturday and Sunday specials include rooms for $79. Suites range from $250 to $625 and up. If you get two rooms for your family, each will be charged at the single-occupancy rate. Be sure to ask about the "Special to Disneyland" package. For $169 per night, it includes a room for a family of up to five people, free self-parking, buffet breakfast, and two adult tickets to one of five favorite theme parks (including Disneyland and Knott's Berry Farm).

You'll know this hotel as soon as you see it from the freeway. The **Sheraton-Anaheim Hotel,** 1015 W. Ball Rd., Anaheim, CA 92802 (☎ **714/ 778-1700,** or toll free **800/325-3535**), which recently underwent an extensive renovation, is designed to resemble a medieval castle inside and out. The outdoor areas are large, complete with grassy, flower-filled courtyards, a rose garden, a little pond with a bridge, and inviting sitting areas.

While parents are more impressed with the complete concierge service which also helps arrange for babysitters and room service which is available from 6am to 11pm, kids fancy the video-game room. There's also a large heated swimming pool, health club and shuttle service to and from Disneyland.

The Garden Court Bistro, a moderately priced coffee shop, has a children's menu with prices from $2.95 to $5. A sandwich, salad, or burger here is about $6; full meals start at $6.25. There's also a quick-serve deli. Classy Adrienne's restaurant serves continental cuisine, and entrees start at $11. Highchairs and boosters are available in all the restaurants. The Spaghetti Station is located across the street (see "Where to Eat," below, for details).

Some rooms open out onto the swimming pool, while others open onto the grassy areas or indoor hallways. The 490 guest rooms are generously sized and tastefully decorated. Connecting rooms and suites are available. In-room amenities include cable color TV, in-room pay movies, and complimentary toiletries.

Rooms rent for $125 single and $140 double. Suites start at $275. Children under 18 stay free in their parents' room. Cribs are free, but rollaways cost $15.

Across from the Disneyland entrance, the **Anaheim Plaza Resort Hotel,** 1700 S. Harbor Blvd., Anaheim, CA 92802 (☎ **714/772-5900,** or toll free **800/228-1357**), is simply a favorite with the kids. The gardens and grounds are spacious, the Olympic-size swimming pool area is lovely, and the 300 recently renovated rooms are extremely pleasant and large. And it's moderately priced for this location.

Another jewel is the video-game room. Babysitting service is available through the front desk. Other amenities include complimentary shuttle to and from Disneyland, a Disney specialty giftshop, complimentary cable TV including the Disney Channel, air conditioning, telephone, in-room coffee/tea maker, and a coin-operated laundry. The hotel's Palm Court café serves breakfast, lunch, and dinner, and has highchairs for the littlest ones.

Rooms are $69–$110 single and $79–$110 double; suites are $250–$375. Children under 18 stay free in their parents' room; each additional person 18 or over pays $10. Rollaway beds are $10.

The **Hyatt Regency Alicante** is at Harbor and Chapman (P.O. Box 4669), Anaheim, CA 92803 (☎ **714/750-1234,** or toll free **800/972-2929;** fax 714/740-0465). You'll arrive at the door of this 400-room Hyatt via a dramatic black-and-white-tiled driveway bordered by tall palms. The entrance centerpiece is a magnificent fountain surrounded by gigantic faux pink flamingos. The 17-story atrium, typical of the Hyatt chain of hotels, is made of glass and steel. The lobby is surprisingly small for such a striking entry; instead they leave the roominess for the rooms.

The hotel, located only a mile from Disneyland, has complimentary shuttle service back and forth every half hour all year round. In addition, Guest Services will arrange tours to Universal Studios, the San Diego Zoo, and other attractions. Tour fees are individually priced.

From Memorial Day through Labor Day, Camp Hyatt operates on Friday and Saturday evenings from 6 to 10pm for children ages 3–15. Many parents will be happy to use this service after a long day at Disneyland or Knott's Berry Farm. Understand that Camp Hyatt is more or less a babysitting service: Kids are supervised and kept occupied with Nintendo games, board games, movies, coloring, and such, and they all get milk and cookies for an evening snack. The groups are usually small, so there's one adult for approximately eight children. The fee is $4 per hour per child. At all times, children can register at their own desk and receive the Hyatt Passports and induction into the Frequent Stay Program wherein kids get a free Camp Hyatt Backpack after four stays. At check-in they receive a Camp Hyatt cap and a squeeze bottle.

The third-floor pool area is wide open and airy—and not fenced in. The heated pool itself is small and is only $3^1/2$ feet deep. Also on that floor are outdoor tennis courts, a games room with video machines, and a fitness center. There's no snack bar, but food can be ordered from room service.

There are two restaurants in the Alicante. You may want to save Papa Geppetto's for that evening alone. It offers Italian food Tuesday through Sunday from 5 to 10pm. In addition to gourmet pizza, the menu lists risotto and pasta ($10–$14), veal and other main dishes ($10.50–$20), and three three-course, calorie-conscious meals at $20. Hours may vary.

Café Alicante is the open-air lobby coffee shop. Children have their own menu of moderately priced items; the adult menu offers everything from sandwiches to full-course dinners, and there's also a special *cuisine naturelle* menu with a small number of natural food selections. The café is open from 6:30am to midnight daily. Room service can be ordered until midnight, and children can have a smaller portion of regular selections at smaller prices. Hours may vary.

The accommodations at the Alicante are roomy, and very clean. Closets are small. All rooms include direct-dial telephones, clock radios, hairdryers, and remote-control television with complimentary HBO, ESPN, CNN, and, of course, the Disney

Channel; pay movies can be turned off at the front desk. Many families choose adjoining rooms—one with a king-size bed, the other with two double beds. The room with a king-size bed has a love seat and room for a crib. Double-bedded rooms are quite comfortable for a family of three or four, and you can squeeze in a rollaway or a crib. If you're very sound conscious, request a "Disney view" room (you don't really get much of a view of Mickey, but you're not over the atrium where you may pick up the sounds of the more boisterous visitors). For those who can afford it, suites are available with wet bars, dining for six, two bathrooms, and a big living area.

Regular rates are $79–$135 single, $79–$155 double (king-size bed or two double beds). Children up to age 18 stay free in the same room with their parents; extra adults pay $25 per day. Rooms on the Gold Passport floors (14–17) include complimentary coffee and juice in the mornings. Cribs, rollaways, and refrigerators are available at no charge.

The Hyatt offers family packages, too: For $99 you can have a deluxe room, with a second room for the children at half price, plus breakfast for two in the Café Alicante. The Disney package can be customized for families of any size and basically includes deluxe rooms and Disney tickets for two adults (additional Disney tickets can be purchased). The package starts at $149. Valet parking is $6 per night; self-parking costs $4. Airport transportation is arranged at a small fee.

Moderate

Located on four acres of grounds, **The Anaheim Inn at the Park,** 1855 S. Harbor Blvd., Anaheim, CA 92802 (☎ 714/750-1811), is a large hotel with 500 rooms, 400 of which have two double or two queen-size beds; 9 are suites. This is an attractive hostelry, with a friendly attitude toward kids. The nicely landscaped pool area has a large patio with lots of chaise longues and a pretty little gazebo for shade. The kids also enjoy the video-game room. Other amenities include room service from 7am to 11pm, free shuttle to and from Disneyland, a giftshop with Disney memorabilia, and help with arrangements for babysitting.

For dinner, the Overland Stage Steak and Seafood Restaurant looks like it was lifted out of Disney's Frontierland, complete with antique prints of the Old West, hanging lanterns, rich velveteen tapestries, and a lovely grandfather clock. The dinner menu consists of steaks, chops, lobster, and prime rib. The inn's moderately priced coffee shop serves breakfast, lunch, and dinner.

Every room has a balcony, with a view of either the gardens or Disneyland. During the summer we request a room facing Disneyland and enjoy the summer fireworks that don't start until after the toddlers have gone to sleep. Each room has remote-control TV and in-room pay movies, plus a game table with chairs. There are a variety of suites, all with refrigerators and sofa beds. Or you can connect three regular guest rooms (and have three baths).

Rooms rent for $110–$140 single and $120–$150 double, with packages as low as $59 per room. A mini-suite costs $150; one- or two-bedroom suites cost $330. Children under 18 stay free in their parents' room. There's no charge for cribs, but rollaways cost $15 per night.

The **Quality Hotel Maingate,** 616 Convention Way, Anaheim, CA 92802 (☎ 714/750-3131, or toll free 800/231-6215), is an excellent choice in the moderate range. Although it's only a few blocks from Disneyland, the hotel has shuttle service. There's a large heated pool, lots of lounge chairs, and a video-game/vending-machine area for the kids. Babysitting can be arranged.

There are two restaurants: the Tivoli Gardens Café, which serves breakfast and lunch, and Greenhorn's Gourmet restaurant. Both have highchairs and boosters. Both have a children's menu, and there is room service from 6:30am to 10pm.

Many of the 284 rooms have balconies, some facing Disneyland (so you can see the fireworks). Rooms also have a color TV, and a free refrigerator upon request (on a first-come, first-served basis). Two-bedded rooms have just enough space to add a crib. There are studio suites with two double beds and a sofa bed, microwave and refrigerator included. Connecting rooms are available. Several floors have a guest laundry.

Rates range from $62 to $90, single or double, depending on the season and the studio. Suites begin at $99. Children 18 and under stay free in their parents' room; additional guests over 18 are charged $5 each per night. Cribs are free, but rollaways cost $10 per night. *Shuttle $99 2 Queen*

Located close to Disneyland, the **Holiday Inn Anaheim at the Park,** 1221 S. Harbor Blvd., Anaheim, CA 92805 (☎ **714/758-0900,** or toll free **800/545-PARK**), is an attractive, sprawling hostelry that combines early California style with a tropical motif. The inviting lobby has tile floors and lots of palm trees. The tropical ambience continues outside to the manicured grounds, including a large lawn area with palm and banana trees. The large pool has two shallow ends and is open 24 hours. There's deck space to walk on, and a grassy area ideal for playing. Babysitting can be arranged through the front desk, and to the delight of the kids, there's a small games area located by the pool, also open 24 hours. Other niceties include a giftshop, valet laundry, and complimentary shuttle service to and from Disneyland and Anaheim's airport and bus terminals.

The hotel restaurant is Poppy's Café, which serves a wide variety of foods, from light snacks to full meals. Breakfast prices are $3.50–$6, lunch costs $4–$7, and dinner is priced at $6–$14. Highchairs and booster seats are provided. The café is open daily from 6:30am to 10pm. Poppy Pub open daily 5pm to 12am. Room service is available the same hours.

Each of the 254 rooms has either king- or queen-size beds, color TV with Cablevision and pay channels, table and chairs, and double-paned windows to drown out freeway noise. Some rooms have a partition separating the sofa bed from the queen bed next to it.

Rates June through August run $79 single and $89 double. The rest of the year, prices drop to $69 single and $79 double. Children under 19 stay free in their parents' room; no charge for cribs. Children 18 and over and additional adults pay $10 each per night.

Budget-Priced Hotels *AAA $69.00 20 $99 Suite $P9.00*

The best bet for your money is **Best Western Raffles Inn & Suites,** 2040 S. Harbor Blvd., Anaheim, CA 92802 (☎ **714/750-6100** or toll free **800/654-0196**), a small, well-kept motor inn with prices you can't beat. A complimentary continental breakfast is served in a charming little parlor room off the swimming pool area. Newly renovated, Best Western Raffles has Disneyland packages available. All rooms and suites have coffeemakers, and the front desk staff will help you arrange everything from tours to babysitting. There is also a gift shop on the premises.

The 122 rooms are very clean. Family suites can sleep six people. They have large living rooms with sofa sleepers and lots of room, enough even for two rollaways. The master bedrooms have king-size beds, plus sinks and vanity areas. Kitchenettes are

Tour to University $65 Adult $52 child

outfitted with the basics. Mini-suites have small parlor rooms with sofa sleepers and refrigerators, and the bedrooms have either king or queen-sized beds.

Rates for deluxe rooms with two queen-size beds range from $44 to $64, from one to four persons. Mini-suites cost $59–$79, and family suites $125–$145. Children under 18 sleep free in their parents' room. Rollaways beds are $5 per night, and cribs are free.

Another alternative is **Best Western Stovall's Inn,** 1110 W. Katella Ave., Anaheim, CA 92802 (☎ **714/778-1880**). Located near Disneyland, Stovall's is a large, basic motor inn with such nice touches as topiary gardens surrounding much of the property—there are even sculpted Disney characters. The inn has 290 rooms, two swimming pools, two whirlpools, and a small wading pool. Catering to the traveling family, the inn offers same-day photo processing at the giftshop; assistance with sightseeing tours, car rental, and babysitting; free shuttle to and from Disneyland; and a VCR-rental facility. There is both valet service and coin-operated laundry machines. There's no restaurant on the premises, but the inexpensive Coco's Coffeeshop is next door.

Rooms have double, king-size, or queen-size beds, and cost $65–$90 in high season, $55–$75 in low season. Two-room suites run $110–$150. Children under 18 stay free in their parents' room. No charge for cribs.

Another good budget hotel is the **Comfort Inn,** 2200 S. Harbor Blvd., Anaheim, CA 92802 (☎ **714/750-5211,** or toll free **800/479-5210**). This motel offers a few nice touches. There's a complimentary continental breakfast in the lobby for guests, and a complimentary shuttle bus to and from Disneyland (three blocks away). The swimming pool has a shallow end that extends over half the area of the pool. The clean, attractive rooms are nicely appointed, with large dressing areas. Some have king-size, queen-size, or double beds. All have a table and chairs and a color TV with cable movies (VCRs and in-room movies can be rented at the office).

Rates run $44–$55 single and $48–$65 double. Adjoining rooms and mini-suites (with king-size beds) are available. Children under 18 stay free in their parents' room. There's a $5 charge for cribs and rollaways.

The **Anaheim Travelodge Park South,** 2171 S. Harbor Blvd., Anaheim, CA 92802 (☎ **714/750-3100,** or toll free **800/578-7878** in California), is a basic motel with 128 rooms. The fenced-in pool area has a small heated swimming pool, spa, and bathroom. Free continental breakfast and in-room movies are included in the nightly price. Complimentary shuttle service is offered to Disneyland and the bus depot. The motel has coin-operated laundry facilities. All rooms have TV, and table and chairs, and come with either queen-size or king-size beds. Two-room/two-bath family suites are available.

Rates range from $39 to $59, depending on the season and the room. Family suites, with four beds, two baths, and two TVs, run $99. Children under 17 sleep free in their parents' room. There is no charge for cribs, but rollaways cost $5 per day.

WHERE TO EAT

Your kids may want to spend all their waking hours at the theme parks and fast-food parlors. While Knott's Berry Farm is known for its food and Disneyland has fine fare, the adults in our group sometimes yearn for another dining choice.

Let's start with **Mr. Stox,** 1105 E. Katella Ave. (☎ **714/634-2994**), a well-regarded restaurant in Orange County. Put on the Mary Janes for this lovely restaurant that offers very grown-up selections for children. The contemporary California cuisine served here is created with extra care; for example, they grow their own fresh herbs. The wine list is recognized as one of the best in the country.

The restaurant is so close to Disneyland that the staff handles children of all ages with ease. Of course, they'll make Shirley Temples and Roy Rogerses for young visitors. Booster seats are available. Selections for children include shrimp scampi priced between $6.95 and $9.95, fresh halibut, and mesquite-broiled chicken breast. Adults can choose from a lunch menu that changes daily and includes fresh seafood, a large variety of salads, and homemade pastas. Prices range from $6 to $12. At dinner, the emphasis is on fresh seafood, pasta, veal, and rack of lamb, with entrees from $12 to $23.95. Open for lunch Monday through Friday from 11:30am to 2:30pm and for dinner Monday through Saturday from 5:30 to 10pm and on Sunday from 5 to 9pm. Reservations are advised. Most major credit cards accepted. Valet parking.

A more casual place, **Tony Roma's** is at 1640 S. Harbor Blvd., across from Disneyland (☎ 714/520-0200). This large restaurant boasts the same terrific food that the other locations have. All dinner entrees come with coleslaw and a choice of beans, french fries, rice, or baked potato. Choose from ribs and chicken ($11.95), grilled shrimp, marinated breasts of chicken, New York steak, barbecued beef, or an old-fashioned burger ($5.99–$14.95). A la carte entrees and full-size salads are also available. For lunch, choose from an array of soups and sandwiches, and other items ($3.95–$9.95). The adorable children's menu offers your kids chicken fingers, burgers, ribs, or chicken with fries and slaw for $2.95–$4.95. Highchairs and boosters are available.

Open Sunday through Thursday from 11:30am to 11pm and on Friday and Saturday from 11:30am to 12pm. Reservations are not accepted, but most major credit cards are. It's best to come before 6pm to avoid the 15- to 45-minute wait. There's a large parking lot.

Peppers Restaurant, 12361 Chapman Ave., at Harbor Boulevard, in Plaza Alicante, Garden Grove (☎ 714/740-1333), is a perfect example of an adult restaurant where you can comfortably include the kids. It's lively and fun, charming and sophisticated. Potted plants and ceiling fans complement the soft-pink and blue decor. A large noisy bar is on the other side of the reception area, out of the way of the diners.

Tortilla chips are brought immediately, and the service is prompt and efficient, even at the busiest hours. The children's menu items offer hamburgers, hot dogs, grilled cheese, cheese enchilada, burrito, or taco for $2.95, which include a beverage and ice cream in the price.

Mom and Dad get to choose from an array of dishes, including enchiladas, burritos, chimichangas, and such specials as filet mignon, camarones Mérida, or fajitas. Dinner prices range from $5.50 to $19. Lunch has many of the same selections, plus tostadas, and salads. Prices range from $3.75 to $9. Be sure to leave room for something indecently rich on the dessert menu, like deep-fried ice cream, Kahlúa mousse, or cheesecake. The "all you can eat" Sunday brunch costs $12.95 for adults, $6 for kids 10 and under.

The kids love the complimentary shuttle that picks them up from their hotel and takes them back after dinner. When Janey was 4 years old, she felt she was riding in her own private coach. There are boosters and highchairs here. Baby bottles and food will be warmed in the kitchen upon request.

Open for lunch Monday through Saturday from 11am to 4pm. Dinner is served Monday through Thursday from 4 to 10pm, on Friday and Saturday till 11pm.

Sunday brunch hours are 10am to 2pm. Reservations and major credit cards are accepted. There is a large parking lot.

Just across the street from the Hyatt Alicante Hotel is the **Belisles,** 12001 Harbor Blvd., Garden Grove (☎ 714/750-6560). This restaurant is a hodgepodge of Victorian, country French, and early American furniture and decorations. Everything seems to be red! And huge.

The prices are high, but the portions are fit for the giant at the top of the beanstalk. Breakfast is really delicious: lots of fresh fruits, omelets, homemade biscuits and gravy, hotcakes, and waffles. The more modest selections run $4.95–$18.95. Try the heavenly pecan rolls and muffins.

Children 12 and under have three breakfast selections of hotcakes, eggs, or French toast with bacon, plus milk, for $3.95–$4.95. The rest of the day, youngsters can order hamburgers with mashed potatoes and gravy, spaghetti, fish and chips, barbecued beef ribs, or roast turkey, with prices averaging $10. These dinners include soup or salad, a vegetable, dessert, and milk. Servers will split adult portions for two kids, and will warm bottles or baby food. Booster seats and highchairs are provided. Of course there are sandwiches, burgers, salads, and complete dinners for adults. You'll pay anywhere from $5.95 (for grilled cheese) to $18.95 (for broiled teriyaki steak). The restaurant is open Sunday through Thursday, 7am to 12pm; Friday through Sunday, until 2am. No reservations, but credit cards are accepted. There's free parking in the lot.

The Old West comes alive at the **Spaghetti Station** restaurant and saloon, 999 W. Ball Rd. (☎ 714/956-3250) with its "Welcome Pardner" sign and lifelike statues of cowboys, horses, and buffalo. Surrounded by the decor of the American West, including antique mining carts, desert plants, stagecoach wheels, and chest luggage, the Old West Museum/Eatery has more to offer inside its rustic wood building.

For very little wampum, you can feast on 14 different home-style spaghetti dinners, pony pizzas for young'uns and cowboy pizzas for adults, and specials like lasagna, shrimp scampi, chicken Alfredo, barbecue ribs, and chicken with fries. For lunch, from $3.75–8.75, you can have the pasta and pizza selections plus sandwiches or salads, chicken, and fresh fruit salad. Adult dinners run $6.50 for pasta with tomato sauce, to a $14.50 steak and pasta meal called Sitting Bull. For youngsters under 12 there's Sugarfoot Sal spaghetti dinner with tomato sauce for $4.75 or Billy the Kid with meat sauce for $5.25. All lunch and dinner entrees come with salad and piping hot sourdough bread and garlic butter.

Highchairs and booster seats are provided. In the evenings, kids will have fun with the clown or balloon artist. Everyone is welcome to sing at the Sit n'Bull Saloon Karaoke nights, Thursday through Sunday from 8pm.

Reservations taken only for parties of eight or more. In the evening, be prepared for a 20- to 30-minute wait if you come between 6:30 and 8:30pm on a Friday or Saturday. Best to come before 6, or after 8pm. Open for lunch Monday through Friday from 11am to 2pm, Saturdays and Sundays from 12am to 2pm, and for dinner Monday through Friday from 4:30pm to 10pm and on Saturdays and Sundays from 2 to 11pm. Most credit cards accepted. There's a large parking lot.

If the kids are just dying for a good old-fashioned hamburger, **Flakey Jake's,** 101 E. Katella Ave. (☎ 714/535-1446), is the place to go. Here's where you'll find huge hamburgers, grilled-chicken sandwiches, baked potatoes, and taco salads for adults, and Jake's Junior menus for the kids. Jake's Junior meals offer burgers, fish sandwiches, and hot dogs, and include fries and a beverage with free refills for $2.50–$3. There are also great pizza lunch deals and a breakfast buffet daily. Best of all, the food is as fresh as you'll find anywhere. If you're not familiar with Flakey Jake's, be forewarned that there is no table service. But the kids love the place, and they occupy themselves during the wait for food in the small video arcade. Highchairs and boosters are provided.

Open daily from 7:30am to 10pm, on Friday and Saturday until 11pm. No reservations accepted.

2 Newport Beach and Environs

Of late, the coast from Huntington Beach to San Clemente has been called the American Riviera. That swath of beautiful sandy beach is excellent for swimming, surfing, sunbathing, and boating. In Newport, there are ecological reserves, harbors, and coves waiting to be explored. Newport and its companion, Balboa Island, have been family-resort towns (albeit for the very rich) for many years. Even today, families flock to this sun-drenched area for weeks of relaxation and play.

One of the first things you'll want to do is to contact the **Newport Beach Conference and Visitors Bureau,** 366 San Miguel Dr., Newport Beach, CA 92660 (☎ 714/644-1190).

WHAT TO SEE AND DO

The main attractions of the area are the wonderful wide sandy beaches and the harbor with its yachts and sailboats. The other activities of greatest interest for families are concentrated in a small area along the shore.

Balboa Peninsula and Balboa Island

Balboa Peninsula creates a gentle bay where eight small islands sit, old-fashioned auto ferries run, and children play in the warm sand. Homes on the peninsula and on Balboa Island remind you of New England. Indeed, like Cape Cod, since the 1930s Newport Beach, and Balboa in particular, has been a summer-resort town where well-to-do families rent clapboard cottages for a month at a time.

Let's start with **Balboa Pier,** a 919-foot-long structure that is lined with fishermen of all ages. At the foot of the pier you'll find a nice public beach with play equipment, showers, and restrooms. At the end of the pier is **Ruby's Diner** (see the "Where to Eat" section for details). To get to the pier after you're on Balboa Peninsula, go to Palm Street and turn right to the public parking lot.

The boardwalk is a terrific place to skate or bicycle, and enchanting little Main Street offers places to stop and grab a quick snack. You can rent bikes and roller skates at **Ocean Front Wheel Works,** at 105 Main St., just before you get to the pier (☎ 714/723-6510). They rent adult bicycles, bikes with child carriers, children's bikes, and three-wheel bikes. Three-wheel bikes, however, are not allowed on the sidewalks. Both adult and child's bike rentals are $5 for the first hour, $4 to $6 for the second, and $3 for the third; fourth hour is $2 and additional hours are free. Adult and child roller skates cost $5. Beach items are also available. Chairs, umbrellas, and boogie boards rent for $8 a day. Open weekdays from 10am to 6pm and on weekends from 10am to 8pm (times vary according to season).

Only a few blocks away on the harbor side of the peninsula is the historic **Balboa Pavilion,** an ornate Victorian structure that today houses a restaurant and giftshop, and is the terminus for harbor excursions, whale-watching trips, and Catalina Island transportation. It's considered the hub of Newport Harbor. This registered historic landmark was built as a bathhouse and originally served as a terminal for the electric

Red Car. The pavilion was also the place where many of the Big Band greats played— Benny Goodman and Count Basie among them.

At the pavilion, you can book a cruise on the double-decker **Pavilion Queen** (☎ 714/673-5245), which has regularly scheduled tours of the harbor. During the summer, tours depart on the hour from 11am to 7pm; during the winter, they leave at 11am, noon, and 1, 2, and 3pm. Call to verify schedule. The 45-minute cruises cost $6 for adults, $1 for children, and free for kids 5 and under; 90-minute cruises are $8 for adults, $1 for children, free for kids 5 and under. The *Catalina Flyer* departs from Newport daily at 9am for Catalina Island and departs the island at 4:30pm; the crossing takes 1¼ hours. Adults pay $32; children 12 and under are charged $16.50. Reservations are required.

Davey's Locker at Balboa Pavilion, 400 Main St. (☎ 714/673-1434), offers fishing expeditions and all-day fishing trips to Catalina Island. The fishing trips leave at 11am, return at 5pm, and cost $55 for adults and $40 for children ages 15 and under (includes a bunk). Half-day boat trips go from 6am to noon or 12:30 to 5pm, and these fish locally from Huntington Beach to south of Laguna. The rates are $22 for adults and $14 for kids 15 and under. From December through mid-March there are whale-watching cruises. You can buy a license here, and also rent fishing poles ($7). Davey's Locker is open daily from 5am to 6pm. Other fishing trips available.

The **Fun Zone** is a small area along the waterfront near the Balboa Pavilion that's specifically geared to children of all ages. Kids can spend hours here riding the Ferris wheel and the merry-go-round, and playing in the video arcades. A book of five merry-go-round tickets costs $5. Fast-food stands dot the little strip. Pedalboats and pontoons can be rented, and harbor cruises sail from here.

You can catch the **Balboa Island Ferry** (☎ 714/673-1070) here too. This short, delightful ride transports only a few vehicles at a time across to Balboa Island, but it's a treat—one the kids will remember. Ferry service runs from 6:30am to midnight on weekdays, till 2am on weekends (one leaves every three to four minutes), and costs 90¢ for a car with one passenger and 25¢ for each additional passenger, 40¢ for a bicycle, and 25¢ for pedestrians; children 5–11 are charged 10¢, free for children under 5.

You can also drive onto the island via Jamboree Road, but parking is atrocious on the island, so we suggest that you park at the public lot near Balboa Pier and ferry across without your car.

Balboa Island is a tiny, picturesque village with homes placed so close together that windowboxes and miniature gardens replace the more usual Southern California front and side lawns. Its size is perfect for walking. Marine Avenue is the place to go for gifts, restaurants, and ice-cream shop. You can see the island in 45 minutes, allowing you to get back to the peninsula and the better beaches.

Newport Beach and Pier

Each morning about 6am, the **Dory Fishing Fleet** sets out to sea from McFadden's Pier. Some fishermen go as far as Catalina Island. At about 8am they return, set up their weighing scales on the boats, and sell their catch on the beach. It's a taste of a dying lifestyle. The boardwalk area is vintage 1940s. The beach is just over five miles long, with volleyball nets, outdoor showers, and restrooms. Pier fishing is a popular sport here, and no state license is required to fish from the pier.

Baldy's Tackle, 100 McFadden Place, at the foot of the pier (☎ 714/673-4150), rents a variety of items: fishing equipment, beach cruisers, children's bikes, bodyboards, beach chairs, and umbrellas. Rods, reels, hooks, and sinkers are $2 per hour, $7.50 for all day. Children's bikes rent for $4 per hour, $20 for all day (you leave your driver's license as a deposit). Baldy's is open in summer daily from 6am to 8pm; in winter, Sunday through Thursday from 7:30am to 5:30pm and on Friday 7:30am to 6pm; and Saturday from 6am to 6pm.

Upper Newport Bay Ecological Reserve

For some truly wonderful outdoor experiences, you'll enjoy this 700-acre state ecological reserve, home to all kinds of wildlife and birds. Get the kids out here on bicycles or on foot, and savor the quiet, natural setting. Take Backbay Drive to the reserve.

Newport Dunes Resort

Newport Dunes Resort, a family beach and park located on a 15-acre lagoon at 1131 Backbay Dr., Newport Beach (☎ 714/729-DUNE), is a place where kids can build sandcastles to their hearts' content and swim in the calm water. At the beach you can rent paddleboats, sailboats, windsurfers, and kayaks, and also take lessons. There is also a boat launch. The park is equipped with a playground, café, shower, and barbecues, and there's also a boat launch. There are lifeguards and first-aid stations from June 15 to Labor Day. The kids love the floating whales that mark the cordoned-off children's swim areas.

There's a restaurant, a grocery store, and firepits for barbecues. For day use, it costs $5 per car, $20 per van.

There are also campsites for tents, RVs, trailers, and boats. They begin to take reservations for the summer on January 1. Call for rates because they vary depending on the site and the length of stay.

Other Area Beaches and Tidepools

The protected coves of **Corona Del Mar Marine Life Refuge** (☎ 714/644-3047) are teeming with sea life. To get to the tidepools, park your car where Poppy and Ocean Boulevard meet and walk down the asphalt pathway. You can walk on the rocks when the tide is low, and help the kids spot sea urchins and other wonders. Remember to replace everything you pick up, exactly where you took it from. For tide tables, call **714/675-8420.** Most bait-and-tackle stores can also tell you when low tide occurs. Tours are given by park rangers, but call ahead.

According to people in the know, the best beach in the area for families may be **Corona Del Mar State Beach,** better known as **Big Corona,** off Ocean Boulevard and Iris. The large beach is sheltered so that wave action is usually gentler than at other areas. There are barbecue pits, showers, a snack bar, and restrooms. The beach is open daily from 6am to 10pm.

Adjacent to Huntington Pier, off the Pacific Coast Highway (Calif. 1) **Huntington City Beach** (three miles north of Newport) has lifeguards, volleyball nets, and concession stands.

Huntington State Beach is just south of there. With three miles of shoreline, lifeguards, snack stands (seasonal), showers, and restrooms, it is very popular.

Surfing

Huntington Beach may be the most popular surfing beach around. In fact, some say that Huntington Beach epitomizes the ever-famous California surf scene. However, this popular sport is allowed at most beaches, with certain restrictions during the summer. Call before you go. **Huntington State Beach** (☎ 714/536-1455),

Huntington City Beach (☎ 714/536-5281), **Newport** (☎ 714/673-3371 for a surf report), and **Corona Del Mar** (☎ 714/644-3047) are places to try.

Surfing buffs will enjoy the **Huntington Beach International Surfing Museum,** 411 Olive St. in downtown Huntington Beach (☎ 714/960-3483). Open Wednesday through Sunday from noon to 5pm, it chronicles the history of surfing in this surf-famous town with old surfboards, photographs, and memorabilia. Many of you will remember Dick Dale—whose surf guitar is on display.

Bike Paths

There is a wonderful bike path that extends from the north at Bolsa Chica State Beach south along the shoreline into Newport Beach.

In Newport Beach, you can take the **Backbay Drive** bike path that winds through the Ecological Reserve. This path climbs gradually up the hill, past the Backbay, offering bicyclists the chance to see all kinds of birds.

The Anaheim Area Visitors and Convention Bureau suggests the following bike tour through Newport Beach and Balboa. Start at the Balboa Pier and head south to the "wedge." This picturesque stop is very popular with body surfers, and the kids will love watching them. Double-back toward the Balboa Pavilion and take the Balboa Auto Ferry to Balboa Island. Take any of the streets on the island and you'll ride past close-set, quaint cottages. You might want to stop at Marine for a snack. Then head back via the ferry and ride north to McFadden's Pier (Newport Pier). The ride is level, with wonderful views throughout the entire trip. Call the Department of Parks and Recreation for information (☎ 714/644-3151).

In addition to **Ocean Front Wheel Works** and **Baldy's Tackle** (see above), you can rent bikes at **Pedal Pusher Bikes,** 404 32nd St. (☎ 714/675-2570), open from 11am to 5pm daily.

Shopping

Newport Beach and nearby Costa Mesa have some wonderful shopping malls. **Fashion Island,** at Newport Center (☎ 714/721-2000), is an exclusive shopping district with more than 200 shops and services, including Neiman-Marcus and I. Magnin. Open Monday through Friday from 10am to 9pm, on Saturday from 10am to 6pm, and on Sunday from noon to 6pm. The Atrium Court features the Farmer's Market, a gourmet grocery experience, and other eateries.

Located in Costa Mesa, **South Coast Plaza** (☎ 714/435-2000) is one of the most interesting malls in Southern California. With about 300 shops such as Nordstrom, Saks Fifth Avenue, Bullock's, Laura Ashley, and Ann Taylor, you know the plaza is upscale. It's a beautiful mall with a stained-glass dome, and there's concierge service, valet parking, and a carousel for the kids. Shops you won't want to miss with the kids are F.A.O. Schwarz, Toys International, the Disney Store, Sesame Street, and Gamesmanship. The mall is open Monday through Friday from 10am to 9pm, on Saturday from 10am to 7pm, and on Sunday from 11am to 6:30pm.

Another addition is **Planet Hollywood** (☎ 714/434-STAR), located in South Coast Plaza Village, across the street from the South Coast Plaza shopping mall. This fun restaurant has California cuisine and is a real Hollywood experience, housing some of the most famous film memorabilia.

A DAY TRIP OUT OF NEWPORT

You can spend all day at the 20-acre **Wild Rivers Waterpark,** located at 8770 Irvine Center Dr. (☎ 714/768-WILD). With over 40 water rides and other attractions,

Wild Rivers is a big hit with the kids. The park has an African theme and boasts Southern California's largest man-made earth mountain, which offers 19 water rides. Wild Rivers Mountain offers white-water inner-tubing, super-speed rides down a slide the size of a football field, and a jet-speed ride through a dark tunnel.

Some of the rides at Wild Rivers Mountain have been scaled down for children. Our little ones loved Pygmy Pond—less than a foot deep, with swings and slides. We loved the Safari River Expedition, an inner-tube float. And Explorers' Island is designed for families. Thunder Cove has two side-by-side wave-action pools in which all ages can bodyboard and surf. Board rentals are available. **Note:** As with all water parks, utmost caution should be taken with the kids so that accidents are avoided. Children 9 and under should be accompanied by an adult.

The park is open from mid-June through the beginning of September, daily from 10am to 8pm; from mid-May to mid-June and mid-September to October, on weekends and holidays from 11am to 5pm. Schedules change, so check before you go. General admission is $16.95 for everyone over age 10; junior admission (ages 3–9) is $12.95. Children under 3 are free. Season passes and group rates are available. Parking $3. To get to Wild Rivers, take the San Diego Freeway (I-405) to Irvine Center Drive, which is adjacent to the Irvine Meadows Amphitheater.

WHERE TO STAY

First-class hotels are easy to find in this wealthy city—moderate ones are difficult.

Expensive

The **Newporter Hyatt,** 1107 Jamboree Rd., Newport Beach, CA 92660 (☎ **714/729-1234,** or toll free **800/233-1234**), is the quintessential Southern California luxury resort hotel. Even the sunny rose-colored buildings invite you to share the good life . . . and to our surprise, you can do it with your kids. The lobby is California-design, bright and airy, with countless doors opening onto the patio, and inviting you to relax in the sun. The 410 guest rooms, suites, and villas sprawl on 26 beautifully landscaped acres.

Facilities include three large swimming pools, one especially for children. All have patio areas for dining and sunning as well as grassy slopes for playing, an exercise spa, three Jacuzzis, tennis (for a reasonable court fee), shuffleboard, Ping-Pong, bicycle rentals, and a nine-hole par-three golf course. The full concierge service includes an activity director during the summer who oversees such daily activities as Ping-Pong tournaments for adults and kids, volleyball, and hula-hoop contests. Other services include free airport shuttle to and from Orange County/John Wayne Airport, same-day laundry and valet, and room service (available from 6am to 12:30am). Babysitting can be arranged.

Not only is the hotel enchanting, but the location is superb. We love to rent bikes and ride the bike path along Newport's Backbay where the wildlife sanctuary is located, or cross the street and let the kids enjoy the sand and water sports at Newport Dunes Resort (see "What to See and Do," above, for details). Ask the concierge for a pamphlet that lists children's activities; you may pick up some other ideas. Camp Hyatt is available on weekends for ages 3–15.

There is indoor/outdoor dining at the Jamboree Café. Prices range from $4.75 to $8.75 for breakfast, $6 to $16 for lunch, and $6.50 to $25 for dinner. For parents who have the energy at night to enjoy live entertainment, there is Duke's Country Western nightclub, where cocktails and appetizers are served.

The rooms are large, light, and pretty, much as you'd expect from the rambling villa-type architecture. They look out onto the golf course, gardens, or pool areas. All rooms have either a king-size bed or two double beds, remote-control cable TV with free HBO and in-room pay movies. Some of the larger rooms have small sofas and coffee tables; all have game tables and chairs. All rooms feature tub/shower combinations with separate vanity areas and small refrigerators. Connecting rooms and suites are available. Rooms rent for $99–$174, single or double, the higher rate for the better views. Suites run $275–$395. Children 12 and under stay free in their parents' room. There's no charge for cribs, but rollaways cost $15 per night. Be sure to ask about specials.

The **Four Seasons Hotel, Newport Beach,** 690 Newport Center Dr., Newport Beach, CA 92660 (☎ **714/759-0808,** or toll free **800/332-3442**), is a gracious, elegant hotel. The lobby, done in quiet tones, has highly polished marble floors, comfortable sofas and chairs in conversation groupings, sculptured carpeting, and elaborate fresh flower arrangements throughout.

But can an ultra-luxurious hotel welcome families? At the time you make your reservation, the reservationist will ask the ages and names of your children and inquire as to any special needs or services. From the moment the young guests arrive they will feel at home at the Four Seasons Hotel Newport Beach. Delivered to their room upon arrival . . . a kid-sized Four Seasons terry bathrobe and a special "goodie bag" that includes 3-D glasses with 3-D book, crayons, balloons, gummie bears, fresh-baked cookies, and juice.

The concierge has lots to offer the younger traveler . . . board games, coloring books and crayons, croquet sets, table tennis, jumping ropes, children's furniture, VCR with movies, Supernintendo, Nintendo, and more! At your request, the concierge will also provide you with a list of local activities geared especially for children.

For your infants the hotel is happy to supply stock baby bottles, specific baby foods and formula, diapers and any other items you may need. And you'll be delighted to learn that the cribs come with bumper guards—a feature you won't find often elsewhere. Strollers and car seats are available as well as babysitting services provided upon request.

There are two hotel restaurants. Pavilion Restaurant serves breakfast, lunch, and dinner daily. Breakfast in the Pavilion ranges from $9 to $14.50; lunch $6.50 to $13.50; dinner $15 to $25. Dress is California leisure. The Conservatory Lounge offers lunch and dinner daily ranging in price from $7–$13.50. Also offered is a varied menu of hors d'oeuvres, lite fare and burgers as well as a savory "pizza bar" and afternoon tea. Children receive their own dinosaur-theme menu (that comes with crayons and doubles as a coloring book) in the Pavilion, Conservatory, or when ordering from room service. It includes such favorites as chicken nuggets, corn dogs, and grilled cheese sandwiches, and their order arrives in a custom box replica of a '57 Chevy Convertible. Another feature standard to Four Seasons Hotel is their alternative menus—they will prepare low-calorie, low-cholesterol, and low-sodium dishes. When holiday brunches are offered, children can enjoy the Kiddies Korner Buffet—a two-foot-high buffet, decorated with toys and stuffed animals, that features favorites of the younger diner, including silver-dollar pancakes.

All 285 oversize rooms have balconies with beautiful views. Rooms come equipped with remote-control color TV, bathrobes, hairdryers, lighted makeup mirrors, several telephones, refrigerator/minibars, even a small television in the bathroom. Some of the rooms have stall showers in addition to the tub/shower combinations.

A standard room with a king-size bed has an overstuffed chair, an ottoman, and a large desk, with plenty of room for a crib or rollaway. Most families stay in the Four Seasons rooms. These L-shaped accommodations have two rooms. You enter a good-size sitting or living room that has a table and chairs, couch, chair, coffee table, and television. The bedroom has doors that shut it off completely from the living-room area. There is a small deck with chairs and table that overlook the surrounding area. This unit has a very large dressing area, separate bath, and shower rooms.

Rates for moderate to deluxe rooms are $205–$275 for singles and $235–$275 for doubles. Four Seasons rooms cost $305. One-bedroom suites start at $330; two-bedroom suites, at $535. Ask about summer, weekend, and golf packages.

The **Newport Beach Marriott Hotel and Tennis Club,** located across from Fashion Island at 900 Newport Center Dr., Newport Beach, CA 92660 (☎ **714/ 640-4000,** or toll free **800/228-9290**), is a fine hotel where you'll feel quite comfortable with your kids, even at their crankiest moments. The hotel staff exudes a warmth and delight with children, while maintaining an appreciation that not all guests want to have the room next door to such a group.

The recently renovated hotel is built as a series of towers connected by covered passageways centered around a large outdoor pool and lovely atrium courtyard. The atrium court has an enormous fountain two stories high, flanked by colorful flowers and greenery. Guests are welcome to sit in the atrium when private parties are not using it.

The hotel has two swimming pools, two whirlpools, eight lighted tennis courts, a pro shop, a full health club, and a giftshop. The Newport Beach Country Club is a lush 18-hole golf course located next door. Full concierge service is available, and room service offers children's items (and adult fixings too) from 6am to 1am. Babysitting can be arranged through the front desk. There is same-day and overnight laundry service, as well as coin-operated washers and dryers.

The pool areas are palm-edged gardens, nice places to sit. The main pool is freeform in shape, with a great shallow end for the kids. It has ample lounge chairs as well as tables with umbrellas. The smaller pool is much quieter, almost as if guests are unaware it exists. This is a great place to come with the kids.

The hotel has several restaurants. J. W.'s California Grill is casual dining, open daily for breakfast, lunch, and dinner. Breakfast and lunch prices start at around $5; dinners start at $5.25 (for sandwiches) and climb on up. Most selections on the extensive children's menu are around $3. Highchairs and boosters are provided. The View Lounge on the north tower's 16th floor offers snacks and dancing for adults. Food service is available at poolside as well.

Set up on a bluff, many of the 600 rooms have a view of the golf course or ocean. Decorated in California casual, with floral bedspreads, pale walls in peach tones and slate blues, every room has a balcony or patio, free HBO, remote-control color TV, pay movies, tub/shower combinations, and a complimentary basket of toiletries. There is nightly turn-down service, and Ghirardelli chocolate squares will be left on your pillow to beckon sweet dreams. The rooms in the north tower are quite spacious. Some have a king-size bed, a couch, easy chair, and coffee table. Others have two double beds. All have adequate space to accommodate a crib.

Basic rates for singles and doubles range from $139 to $169; the concierge-level rooms rent for $145–$165, and the one- and two-bedroom suites range from $500 to $800. Cribs and rollaways are free. Children under 12 stay free in their parents' room (but double-check if you get a special rate). Older children and additional adults pay a $15-per-night supplement. Be sure to ask about their frequent special packages.

Moderate

Nothing fancy, the **Best Western Bay Shores Inn,** 1800 W. Balboa Blvd., Newport Beach, CA 92663 (☎ **714/675-3463,** or toll free **800/222-6675**), is in a wonderful location, one block from the bay and one block from the ocean. This plain but well-kept motor inn has 20 rooms, most of them small. The rooms with two double beds are adequate for four; the suites, which have full kitchens, dining rooms, and separate bedrooms, are large enough to sleep seven.

This is straight motel style—no pool, no large lobby (just an office)—but a free continental breakfast (brioche or blueberry muffins, fresh fruit, and coffee or tea) is included in the price. There are some other nice touches here. A number of the rooms have ocean views. Each unit has a videocassette player (there are free films in the lobby), a hairdryer, a basket of amenities, and a tub/shower unit. A free newspaper is delivered to the door each day, and there is a coin-operated washer/dryer on the premises.

Rates are $85–$92 single and $92–$109 double. Some of the units have one king-size bed (a crib will just fit) and others have two double beds. Suites are available for $129–$209. Children under 12 stay free in their parents' room. Those 12 and over and additional adults pay $7 each per night. Cribs are free, but there are no rollaways. Check for lower rates out of season (October to April).

Home or Apartment Rentals

When you consider the price of rooms in Newport Beach, it's not surprising that many families simply rent homes or apartments for a week at a time or longer. The prices are more reasonable, and although you won't have maid service, this is an excellent alternative to consider in this pricey neighborhood. Rental agents will find an accommodation that fits your needs and your budget. Some typical rentals are two-bedroom oceanfront properties ($750–$3,000 per week) and beach cottages or duplexes ($500–$1,400 per week). Most properties are within a few blocks of the beach. Whenever possible, it's a good idea to preview the property before you rent it. Ask how the realtor handles that. If you're planning to be in Newport during the summer, you should begin to make your arrangements at least six months in advance. Be prepared for a refundable cleaning and breakage deposit, and a 9% bed tax.

Three local rental agents are **Prudential Realty,** 3377 via Lido, Newport Beach, CA 92663 (☎ 714/673-1900); **Beach and Bay Rental Company,** 603 E. Balboa Blvd., Balboa, CA 92661 (☎ 714/673-7368); and **Burr White Realtors,** 2901 Newport Blvd., Newport Beach, CA 92663 (☎ 714/675-4630).

Camping

Camping facilities are available at a number of beaches. **Huntington City Beach** offers RV camping (but no hookups) from mid-September through May. For reservations, contact City of Huntington Beach-Sunset Vista, P.O. Box 190, Huntington Beach, CA 92648 (☎ 714/969-5621).

For details on **Newport Dunes Resort,** see "What to See and Do," above.

Doheny State Beach, 25300 Dana Point Harbor Dr., Dana Point, CA 92629 (☎ 714/496-6172), has over 100 campsites, and you can make reservations through MISTIX (☎ toll free **800/950-7275** in California).

San Clemente State Beach, 3030 Avenida Del Presidente, San Clemente, CA 92672 (☎ 714/492-3156), has sites with hookups for RVs. Make your reservations through MISTIX (at the number above).

WHERE TO EAT

The restaurants on the Orange coast span a wide price range.

Expensive

One of our favorite places in Newport is on the harbor. **Villa Nova,** 3131 Pacific Coast Hwy. (☎ 714/642-7880), is a little Italian villa look-alike that even has a bit of honest-to-goodness history: it was created to resemble the owner's ancestral home in Venice, complete with a mini-tugboat docked outside. The restaurant was established over 50 years ago on the Sunset Strip in Los Angeles, where it was the watering hole for many a celebrity during the Strip's heyday. In 1967 the family moved it to Newport. Inside, wall murals continue the theme of waterfront Venetian dining. The piano bar will keep you humming.

They want to help youngsters appreciate fine dining. You'll be surprised at some of the kids' menu selections such as scampi and scaloppine piccata (veal sautéed in lemon butter). Children's plates cost $6.95–$8.95. The extensive adult menu includes many different kinds of pastas (spaghetti, ravioli, fettuccine, mostaccioli, manicotti, lasagne, and on and on) plus more than a dozen veal dishes, and chicken, beef, and seafood. Prices range from $9.50 to $24.

The kids can start on breadsticks (already on the table), while they wait for their Shirley Temples or nonalcoholic piña coladas. Boosters are available, and of course, bottles and baby food will be warmed. There are window seats that offer a view of the gondolas. The best hours for kids are before 9pm, and you can tell your server if you want a leisurely or fast-paced meal. Open daily from 5pm to 1am. All major credit cards are accepted. Valet parking.

Another waterfront restaurant is **The Cannery,** 3010 Lafayette Ave. (☎ 714/675-5777). Housed in the historical landmark building that was a fish cannery from 1920 to 1966, the restaurant is adorned with loads of canning artifacts, which make the rooms interesting to look at and maintain the flavor of the building's original use. One wall is lined with huge cans; machinery and equipment are all around. Our kids found the old boiler in the center of the restaurant to be the most interesting.

This is a lively place—great for lively kids. You can also dine on the patio beneath heat lamps. The patio decks sit just above the water at a boat turnaround area, so kids can watch the boats. Highchairs and boosters are available.

Children's items on the menu include fish, chicken, and hamburger ($9.95). The lobsters are huge (ask the waitress if they're big enough to split between two adults) and the abalone is delectable. Interestingly, the swordfish is speared, not caught in the usual way—and it did taste delicious! Dinners come with soup or salad, rice or potato, fresh vegetable, and bread. Prices range from $15 to $35 (for lobster or abalone). The Sunday champagne brunch is $8.95–$12.75; children pay $4.95.

For a different kind of treat, the Cannery hosts two-hour harbor cruises for dinner and Sunday brunch. The Sunday brunch cruises, which are the best for kids, are held at 10am and 1:30pm, year round. Adults pay $30; children, $20.

Open Monday through Saturday from 11:30am to 2am and on Sunday from 10am to 2am. Happily, this restaurant takes reservations, which are advised since the wait can be an hour during the season. Major credit cards accepted.

For another innovative place to eat on the waterfront, we like **Charley Brown's,** 151 E. Pacific Coast Hwy. (☎ 714/675-5910). Built in 1963 to re-create a Mississippi riverboat, the *Reuben E. Lee,* the floating restaurant is 190 feet long and 52 feet wide and actually moves slightly on the water. This is a genuine treat for kids, who are always excited to experience something unusual—and indeed this is different! It's like walking onto a Louisiana riverboat. Wooden planks surround the showboat so you can view the harbor from all vantage points. The interior is enchanting too. It's done in antebellum southern decor, with small-print wallpaper, mirrors, bas-style walls, and a huge grand staircase that takes diners up to the top deck and dining rooms.

The menu specializes in seafood and prime rib, and the portions are large and very tasty. For lunch, prices range from $6 to $10; for dinner, prices range from $10 to $20, including soup and salad. The children's menu offers eight entrees for $3–$6, including prime rib, shrimp, grilled cheese, and a cheeseburger. There are highchairs and boosters available, and loads of nonalcoholic creations for young patrons.

Open Monday through Thursday from 11:30am to 9pm, on Friday and Saturday from 11:30am to 11pm, and on Sunday from 9:30am to 9pm. Reservations and all major credit cards are accepted. Valet and self-parking are available.

Moderate

The branch of **Tony Roma's** at 2530 W. Pacific Coast Hwy. (☎ 714/642-9070) offers the same menu as at other locations: tasty barbecued ribs, chicken, and steak, as well as salads and burgers. Adult prices range from $4 to $13 at lunch and $5 to $14 at dinner, and all include coleslaw, beans, potato, or rice, corn, or mixed vegetables. Highchairs and boosters are provided, and a children's menu is available. Open for lunch daily from 11am to 4pm, and for dinner Sunday through Thursday from 4 to 10pm and on Friday and Saturday from 4 to 11pm. The no-reservations policy can mean a long wait (come for dinner between 4:30 and 5:30pm if you don't want to wait). All major credit cards are accepted. They'll deliver (even to your hotel if it's within their delivery area). Valet parking.

The Cheesecake Factory, 1141 Newport Center Dr. (☎ 714/720-8333), has great California-style cuisine. The choice of food is more than you can imagine, and is quite reasonably priced. (For a detailed description of food and prices, see "Where to Eat" in Chapter 11 on Los Angeles.) The place feels very open and is visually interesting with high ceilings, tile floors, lots of glass and mirrors. They have boosters and highchairs, and a complimentary baby plate. As soon as waiters see a baby or toddler, they cut up bananas or slice an orange or some sourdough bread, and bring it to the table. Open daily from 11:30am to 11:30pm. Credit cards are accepted.

If your children are fish lovers, the **Crab Cooker,** 2200 Newport Blvd. (☎ 714/ 673-0100), is a small hole-in-the-wall you'll want to check out. The throngs of people waiting on benches outside this seafood grill should be enough to tell you that the food is good, and the prices are probably the best in all of Newport Beach.

But don't expect anything fancy. Linoleum floors, heavy-duty paper plates, and plastic silverware is what you'll get here. The main dining room also houses the glassed-in grill area where you can watch chefs cook the seafood. We usually put our name on the waiting list, buy a small bowl of the tasty Manhattan clam chowder, and wander the streets enjoying the town.

A combination plate with shrimp, scallops, and choice cuts of fish broiled on a skewer is $9.70 at lunch and dinner. Charcoal-broiled oysters cost $7.25 at lunch and $9.40 at dinner, and charcoal-broiled lobsters are $17.60 lunch and $23.50 dinner.

The child's plate (broiled fish on a skewer) can also be ordered by adult "light eaters," and costs $4.95 for a filling meal. All plates come with potatoes or rice and coleslaw or tomatoes. Highchairs and booster seats are available. Open Sunday through Thursday from 11am to 9pm, on Friday and Saturday till 10pm. No credit cards or reservations accepted. Street parking.

Inexpensive

When you're near Balboa Pier, **Ruby's,** at the end of the pier (☎ **714/675-7829**), is a great little place to grab breakfast, lunch, or dinner. You can order from an outside window and eat on the pier, or wait for a table inside the restaurant. Either way, plan to spend time watching the fishermen reel in their catches. Ruby's is an authentic '40's diner, fun, and small with an energetic staff. It has four long booths and three long tables that can accommodate families. With windows all around, you feel as if you're on the water (and on clear days, you can see Catalina Island). The setting is beautiful. The tables and walls are white Formica; the napkins and food baskets are bright red.

Chili cheeseburgers with fries are great! And the shakes and malts finish off the meal perfectly. If that sounds a bit heavy for you, you might try the roast turkey sandwich or tuna melt or the original Rubyburger. There are also salads, chowder, and chili. For breakfast, you can have omelets, eggs, and other breakfast specialties. Prices range from $4 to $4.85. The children's menu includes such favorites as miniburgers, corn dogs, and more. They come with fries and a drink for $3 and are served in your choice of a cardboard Rubymobile, boat, or a Frisbee (a dollar extra). Sassy seats are provided. **Note:** There are *no* restrooms here or at this end of the pier—so proceed with caution. Paper and plastic tableware is used here.

Open for breakfast every day from 7 to 11am; for lunch and dinner, Sunday through Thursday from 11am to 9pm, and on Friday and Saturday until 10pm. No reservations are taken, so you can expect a long wait for breakfast or dinner on weekends and during the summer if you want to eat inside. Major credit cards accepted. Parking lot at the pier entrance.

B.J.'s Chicago Pizzeria, 106 Main St., Balboa Peninsula (☎ **714/675-7560**), less than half a block from Balboa Pier and beach, is a lively pizza house that's a great place after a day at the beach. Very basic wood tables and booths set the mood for this inexpensive eatery. Medium deep-dish pizzas cost $9.35–$14.35. You can also choose from a selection of pastas and sandwiches as well as a large salad bar. There is a children's menu which includes 6-inch cheese or pepperoni pizza, spaghetti ravioli, or submarine sandwich. Highchairs and boosters are available, and they'll warm bottles and baby food.

Open from 11:30am to 11pm weekdays, until midnight on Friday and Saturday. There can be a long wait during peak hours, but you can order your pizza ahead of time so it will be almost ready when you sit down. No reservations are accepted. Some major credit cards honored. There is a public parking lot.

For good standard fare for breakfast or lunch, which can sometimes be difficult to find, we suggest **Coco's,** at 151 Newport Center Dr. (☎ **714/644-1571**), open daily from 6:30am to 11pm, Friday and Saturday from 7am to midnight.

3 Laguna Beach and San Juan Capistrano

While Laguna Beach and San Juan Capistrano are not far from the other Orange Coast towns, they make excellent day trips from Los Angeles, San Diego, and Anaheim.

Laguna Beach

Some say that Laguna Beach is the most beautiful beach town in Southern California. True or not, Laguna is unlike other nearby coastal towns. It prides itself on its artistic core, galleries, and art festivals. It is cultured with a distinctive seaside flair. This delightful upscale village is centered where the Pacific Coast Highway meets Broadway. On one side you have Main Beach; on the other, little streets filled with boutiques, restaurants, and novelty stores radiate eastward toward the hills. And for blocks along the Pacific Coast Highway you'll find galleries and craft shops.

Summertime is festival time in Laguna. The world-famous Pageant of the Masters, the Festivals of Arts, and the Sawdust Festival draw an international crowd. Laguna is essentially not a child's town, but because of the famous art festivals and the beauty of the setting, it's a place adults enjoy—and one that kids can enjoy for a few hours. The coves of Laguna Beach are well-known play areas for families.

For information about Laguna, contact the **Laguna Beach Chamber of Commerce,** at 357 Glenneyre St., underneath the library (P.O. Box 396), Laguna Beach, CA 92652 (☎ 714/494-1018).

WHAT TO DO

Parks and Beaches

Centrally located **Main Beach** is said to be one of the best-planned beaches around. Indeed, it's a beach that integrates the town and the sand. Although it gets a bit too crowded for our taste, Main Beach has lots of goodies. There is elaborate wooden play equipment, lawn areas, showers, and volleyball nets. A lifeguard tends the beach area. The park and adjacent beach back up to some of the local shops, making it extremely convenient if you need any supplies or kiddie treats.

Heisler Park (☎ 714/497-0716), north of Main Beach, is a large park perched on a bluff overlooking the ocean. This is a wonderful place for a picnic or barbecue lunch or dinner. There is a large grassy area, picnic tables, restrooms, and shuffleboard nearby. Take the stairs to get down to the beach. It's located off Jasmine or Myrtle Street, which intersect Pacific Coast Highway.

These same streets (Jasmine and Myrtle) will take you down to beaches with tidepools. There is **Picnic Cove,** which has a ramp, and **Diver's Cove.** Lucky children may see sea urchins, starfish, mussels, even baby octopus. And you'll find great shells. But remember that this is a preserve, so leave everything just where you found it.

Festivals

During the months of July and August, Laguna hosts its annual **Festival of Arts,** a time when recognized artists display their works in the outdoor setting of Irvine Bowl. Spread over six acres are paintings, sculpture, wood crafts, ceramics, and more. Free art workshops are conducted throughout the day for kids of all ages. Varied types of live entertainment are featured on weekends.

Probably the most famous part of the festival is the unique **Pageant of the Masters.** This two-hour pageant, held in an open-air amphitheater, presents life-size re-creations of famous works of art in which people play the central roles. As the lights come up, a painting, statue, or tapestry comes to life as actors take their positions and remain posed for about 90 seconds. These are, indeed, "living pictures." The sight is quite amazing, and is popular with older children (10 and above), especially with teens who have even the slightest interest in art.

The pageant is staged nightly at 8:30pm, but you must buy tickets far in advance. Contact the Festival of Arts, P.O. Box 1659, Laguna Beach, CA 92652 (☎ 800/487-3378). Tickets run $15–$40.

Although they are sponsored by separate groups, the **Sawdust Festival** occurs in conjunction with the Festival of Arts. Located at 935 Laguna Canyon Rd., down the street from Irvine Bowl, the Sawdust Festival attracts artists and craftspeople who will discuss or demonstrate their work. Kids are intrigued by the glassblowers and the potters throwing pots on their wheels. There's even a children's booth with free materials for budding artists. For information, call **714/494-3030.**

WHERE TO STAY

The **Surf & Sand Hotel,** 1555 S. Coast Hwy., Laguna Beach, CA 92651 (☎ 714/497-4477, or toll free 800/524-8621), sits on the beach overlooking the magnificent coastline in this part of southern Orange County. Resembling a small Mediterranean villa, the hotel is open and airy, taking full advantage of its proximity to the ocean and its spectacular view. The hotel has two restaurants, Splashes and Towers. The ambience at Splashes is quite wonderful, a great place to begin the day or stop for lunch. It sits just 25 feet above the water, and is so intimate that it gives the sense of being in someone's private villa. Towers Restaurant is known for its dinners.

Rooms are large and comfortable, all with private balconies overlooking the ocean. All rooms are newly remodeled and include stocked honor bars. Rates vary depending upon the room, location, and season—single and double occupancy cost the same.

Room prices are $165–$295; suites and penthouses start at $475 and go up to $700. Additional adults and children are $10 per person. When you make reservations, check if the hotel is offering its kids' cooking school during your stay—it's a real treat.

WHERE TO EAT

We love **The Cottage** restaurant, at 308 N. Pacific Coast Hwy. (☎ 714/494-3023), and make it a point to go there whenever we're in Laguna or nearby Newport. The Cottage is a turn-of-the-century home that was a residence until 1938, when it became a café; the current restaurant opened in 1964. Beautiful antiques grace the rooms, and there is a fabulous photographic exhibit in the waiting area. The dining areas were once living areas and are wonderfully restored with solid oak and colored leaded glass.

The Cottage serves home-style food for breakfast, lunch, and dinner. Items on the breakfast menu include such favorites as buckwheat and cranberry-orange pancakes or eggs with ham, sausage, or top sirloin. Prices range from $2.75 to $8.75. The junior breakfast of bacon, eggs, and pancakes costs $3.35. Lunch offers such entrees as lasagne and Swiss steak, and a lighter fare of salads and sandwiches. Lunch prices range from $4.95 to $8.25. Dinner entrees offer many meat dishes (braised sirloin tips, Swiss steak), poultry, fish, and pastas, as well as two chef's specials each day. Dinners are priced at $8.95–$14.95. Most dinners include soup or salad, fresh vegetables, and rolls. The children's menu ranges from $3.50 to $4.50. Highchairs and booster seats are available.

The Cottage is open Sunday through Thursday from 7am to 9:30pm, Friday and Saturday until 11pm. Reservations are advised. Some major credit cards are accepted. Street parking available.

Mission San Juan Capistrano

Glorified in song, romanticized in stories, Mission San Juan Capistrano is known as the "Jewel of the Missions." This gem takes you back over 200 years to the beginnings of California history when Fr. Junípero Serra was making his way up the California coast on his mission quest.

The mission was actually founded twice. The first undertaking, in 1775, came to an abrupt end when news was received of a native attack at nearby Mission San Diego. The missionaries buried the chapel bells and headed south. The next year (1776) Fray Serra, called by some "The Father of California," returned to the site to establish Mission San Juan Capistrano. Later in that century an elaborate church was built. By its completion in 1806 it was considered the most beautiful mission in the California chain. Unfortunately, it was severely damaged in 1812 when an earthquake felled much of it, leaving only Serra Chapel (the only chapel left in which Serra actually presided) intact. The rest is in ruins.

In the long history of Mission San Juan Capistrano, the annual return of the swallows is a relatively new event. For over 50 years the swallows have faithfully returned to Capistrano on St. Joseph's Day, March 19, to stay until mid-October when they leave for their home in the south (or so the story goes). No one can explain why they choose the mission.

Missions were supposed to serve as outposts of Spanish civilization, with educational, health, and housing facilities for the natives as well as religious services. As you walk through San Juan Capistrano, you'll see the breadth of its contributions to the early community it spawned.

Children enjoy wandering through the mission. Its elaborate gardens, contained by graceful archways and time-worn stone and brick walls, are a restful, rejuvenating place to spend time. The four mission bells, flanked by ancient walls, ignite the imagination, and carefully constructed displays such as bread ovens and ceramic kilns educate the youngsters. We've seen older children linger in Serra Chapel, intrigued by the detailed altar that came from Barcelona, Spain.

The mission staff is dedicated to helping children appreciate the historical significance of the structure. A "children's touching table" is set up on one of the walkways. Kids are invited to handle Native American and Spanish artifacts—rawhide, tools, even petrified wood. In addition, the mission museum holds special days for children, called Saturday at the Mission. Children learn about mission life through skits, crafts, and other hands-on activities. They may play Native American games or make headbands.

A GREAT RESORT

Dana Point is a gem of a place to visit between Orange County and San Diego. We go there for long weekends knowing we don't have to spend time lining up for sightseeing attractions. If we feel like it, we roam the small harbor, or make our way on foot to Doheny State Beach. The Orange County Marine Institute, and its adjacent tidepools, can keep us occupied for hours. We haven't tried the whale-watching trips or parasailing yet, but they are available.

The **Dana Point Resort,** 25135 Park Lantern, Dana Point, CA 92629 (☎ **714/661-5000,** or toll free **800/533-9748**), sits atop a cliff overlooking the yacht harbor in all its Cape Cod refinement. We like to stay here because the two pool areas are so large and comfortable, and are bordered by a spacious lawn where the kids can play. The resort abuts a perfect-size, emerald-green park where we fly kites and play tag.

When Janey was little we'd walk to the nearby playground which is outfitted with pint-sized equipment. There are also bikes to rent through the guest services, but bring your own for kids under 6. A bike path leads to San Juan Capistrano—coming back *up* the hill to the resort at the end of the ride is something else! Tennis buffs get match-play service, and can participate in tennis clinics and private lessons (racquet rentals are available). The resort has a health club, three spas, and Nautilus equipment and steepers. Just outside the grounds are a basketball court, a parcourse, and jogging trails. If you still need activity, guest services can arrange everything from windsurfing and jet skiing to boogie board and snorkeling equipment rentals.

Club Cowabunga, for kids 5–12, offers a day program, which includes lunch and costs $35, and an evening program with dinner, which costs $20. Each morning your children will get a chance to decode the "secret message" slipped under your door, telling where Club Cowabunga will meet for that day. Tidepool exploring, picnics, tennis lessons, swimming, arts and crafts projects—and even some local history—are on the agenda. During the school year, Club Cowabunga is offered weekends. From Memorial Day Weekend on, it runs daily through Labor Day. Be sure to check ahead— there must be a minimum of three children signed up 24 hours in advance for the program to commence.

At Watercolors, the resort's large restaurant, Janey found her children's menu printed on a coloring book she could keep. But she wanted a selection off the adult menu; we found the chef most accommodating each time we made a special request. Service is geared more to adult-style dining (remember when you could finish a sandwich *and* a conversation?), so warn the kids they may have a wait. Food is served poolside, and room service is available from 6am to 2am. There are also numerous family-friendly restaurants near the harbor.

Rooms are comfortable, but not large, except for those on the concierge floor. On that floor, we could get a breakfast in the morning, snacks and soft drinks in the afternoon, full bar and hors d'oeuvres and late-night snacks. Remote-control TVs, two telephones, and lounging robes are included in all the rooms. Room rates, single or double occupancy, range from $170 to $280, depending on the location, view, number of beds, and room configuration. We found it to be an adventure to take the train in the morning, spend a few hours at the mission, eat lunch, and take the train back.

The Depot serves steaks, prime rib, chicken, daily fresh fish, and Mexican food, and prices range from $4.95 to $10.95 for lunch, $5 to $18 for dinner. There are highchairs and boosters, and they'll make half orders for kids.

Open Monday through Saturday for lunch from 11:30am to 2:30pm, and on Sunday for brunch from 10am to 3pm. Dinners are served daily from 5 to 10pm. Reservations are accepted, as are most major credit cards. Should you be driving, there is a parking lot.

FESTIVALS AND ANNUAL EVENTS IN ORANGE COUNTY

Whale-Watching (January and February) off the coast of Newport (☎ 714/675-9881).

Festival of Whales, at Dana Point (☎ 714/496-1094 or 714/496-1555). There are lectures, films, and activities.

The Glory of Easter (March and April), at the Crystal Cathedral in Garden Grove (☎ 714/54-GLORY).

Fiesta de las Golondrinas (Return of the Swallows to Capistrano), at Mission San Juan Capistrano (☎ 714/248-2048). There are parades and special programs.

Strawberry Festival (Labor Day weekend), in Garden Grove. There are arts, crafts, pie-eating contests, and food booths. Contact P.O. Box 2287, Garden Grove, CA 92640 (☎ 714/638-0981), for information.

Laguna Festival of Arts, Pageant of Masters, and the **Sawdust Festival** (July and August). See the "Festivals" section in Laguna Beach for details.

Character Boat Parade (July or August), in Newport Beach (☎ 714/673-5070). Festive, decorated boats travel through Newport Harbor.

Annual Surf Championship (July and August), at Huntington Beach (☎ 714/536-5486). Watch top surfers from around the world compete.

Sand Castle Competitions, in Corona del Mar (☎ 714/673-4050). Everyone gets into the act at this delightful, extraordinary event. Kids are welcome to try their hand at creating a master sandcastle.

The Glory of Christmas (November and December), at the Crystal Cathedral in Garden Grove (☎ 714/54-GLORY).

Parade of Christmas Boats (December), in Newport Harbor (☎ 714/644-8211). This is a fabulous parade of lights. Make reservations early.

ACTIVITIES BY AGE IN ORANGE COUNTY

For your quick reference, here's a synopsis of what attractions are most suitable and best enjoyed by children of different ages.

Teens and Preteens

Anaheim Stadium Tour
Balboa Island Ferry
Balboa Peninsula and Balboa Island
Balboa Pier
California Angels
Corona del Mar Marine Life Refuge
Crystal Cathedral
Disneyland
Fountain Valley Golf and Recreation Center
Fun Zone
Knott's Berry Farm
Ice Chalet
Irvine Meadows Amphitheater
Laguna Beach
Laguna's Pageant of the Masters, Festival of Arts, and Sawdust Festival
Los Angeles Rams
Medieval Times
Mission San Juan Capistrano
Movieland Wax Museum
Newport Beach and Pier
Orange County Performing Arts Center
Ripley's Believe It or Not!
Upper Newport Bay Ecological Reserve
Wild Bill's Wild West Dinner Extravaganza
Wild Rivers Waterpark

School-Age Kids

Anaheim Stadium Tour
Balboa Island Ferry
Balboa Peninsula and Balboa Island
Balboa Pier
Cabbage Patch Adoption Center
California Angels
Corona del Mar Marine Life Refuge
Disneyland
Doll and Toy Museum
Fountain Valley Golf and Recreation Center
Fun Zone
Golf-'N-Stuff Miniature Golf Course

Hobby City
Ice Chalet
Irvine Meadows Amphitheater
Knott's Berry Farm
Laguna Beach
Laguna's Sawdust Festival
Medieval Times
Mission San Juan Capistrano
Movieland Wax Museum
Newport Beach and Pier
Newport Dunes Resort
Orange County Performing Arts
  Center
Ripley's Believe It or Not!
Upper Newport Bay Ecological
  Reserve

Wild Bill's Wild West Dinner
  Extravaganza
Wild Rivers Waterpark

Preschoolers
Balboa Island Ferry
Cabbage Patch Adoption Center
Corona del Mar Marine Life Refuge
Disneyland
Doll and Toy Museum
Fun Zone
Hobby City Choo Choo
Knott's Berry Farm
Newport Dunes Resort
Upper Newport Bay Ecological
  Reserve

In an Emergency

If an emergency should occur during your visit in Orange County, you'll find 24-hour emergency room at **Anaheim Memorial Hospital,** 1111 W. La Palma Ave., near Harbor Boulevard, in Anaheim (☎ **714/774-1450**); and at **Hoag Memorial Hospital,** 301 Newport Blvd., in Newport Beach (☎ **714/645-8600**).

15

San Diego and Vicinity

THOSE OF YOU WHO THINK THAT THE SAN DIEGO AREA IS SEA WORLD, THE ZOO, and the Wild Animal Park, hold onto your hats. You're about to embark on a journey that offers so many possibilities that it will have you coming back again and again.

San Diego is a perfect family vacation destination. It consistently has one of the finest climates in the nation—daytime temperatures average 70°, and it rarely rains. From the heart of San Diego, you can be in the desert or the mountains, at the ocean, in flower fields, and even in another country in a short time. Whether you stay in San Diego, La Jolla, Coronado, or even Tijuana, you are within 10–30 minutes of any major attraction. And speaking of attractions, there's something for everyone here. Even those attractions geared for children are done so nicely that adults can't help enjoying them too. In addition to the commercial attractions, there are gracious historical sites, outdoor activities galore, and some of the most beautiful beaches in the world.

1 Greater San Diego

California history began in San Diego with the arrival of Portuguese explorer Juan Rodriguez Cabrillo in 1542. Later Fr. Junipero Serra established the first mission of the historic El Camino Real here. And Old Town is the site of the first European settlement on California land. It wasn't until 1846 that San Diego came under American rule.

GETTING THERE

Driving to San Diego is simple from most major California cities. From Los Angeles **by car,** take I-5 south for the 2$^{1}/_{2}$-hour, 125-mile trip. Also take I-5 south from Orange County—it's 1$^{1}/_{2}$ hours, 90 miles. From Palm Springs, take Calif. 74 to Calif. 215 south, which becomes I-15 and runs right into town, a 3-hour, 139-mile trip.

Amtrak (☎ toll free **800/USA-RAIL** for information and reservations) services San Diego from many cities both within California and across the nation. It stops at the Santa Fe Depot in downtown San Diego.

Most of the major airlines, and some minor ones, fly into San Diego's **Lindbergh Field** (also known as **San Diego International Airport**), three miles northwest of downtown (☎ **619/231-7361**). For information and reservations, call Alaska Airlines (☎ toll free **800/426-0333**), American Airlines (☎ toll free **800/433-7300**), Continental (☎ **619/232-9155**, or toll free **800/525-0280**), Delta (☎ toll free **800/221-1212**), Northwest (☎ toll free **800/225-2525**), Southwest (☎ toll free **800/531-5601**), TWA (☎ **619/295-7009**, or toll free **800/221-2000**), or United (☎ toll free **800/241-6522**).

Major car-rental companies can be found at the airport and throughout San Diego: **Avis** (☎ toll free **800/331-1212**), **Budget** (☎ toll free **800/527-0700**), and **Hertz** (☎ toll free **800/654-3131**).

Greyhound services San Diego; its downtown terminal is at 120 W. Broadway (☎ toll free **800/231-2222**).

2 Getting Around

The best way to see San Diego is by car. Unobtrusive signs point out routes to major attractions. Convenient freeways make it simple to get around. Most hotels have maps or helpful printed directions indicating routes to various attractions from that

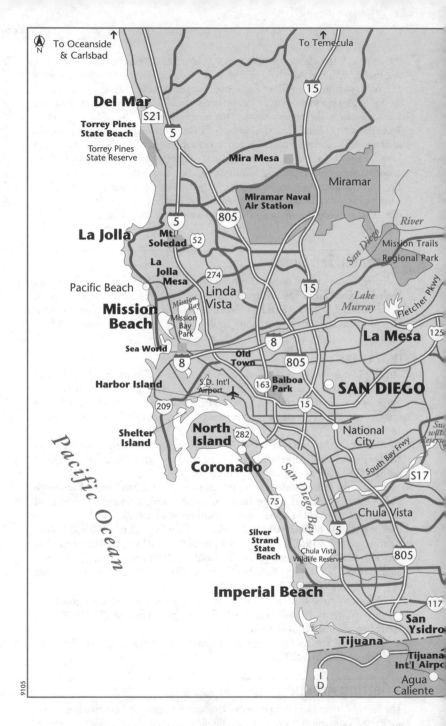

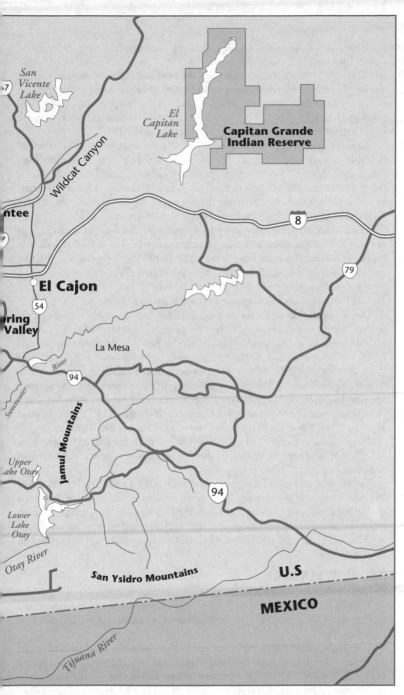

particular hotel. You can also get maps from the International Visitors Information Center (see "Getting Your Bearings," below).

Although the easiest way to get around the San Diego area is with a car, you can also use the region's **Metropolitan Transit System (MTS)** bus and trolley routes.

To get around through the downtown area, you can take a bus or a trolley. Call the **San Diego Trolley** (☎ **619/231-8549** for a recorded announcement or **619/233-3004** for information on all public transit services).

The East Line Trolley stops at the Gaslamp Quarter and Convention Center and at Seaport Village, originating at Centre City. It runs daily every 15 minutes from 5am to 8pm, then every 30 minutes on weekends till 10pm. Trolley fares are $1–$1.75, depending on the distance you travel. Tickets can be purchased from vendomats located in every station. Be sure to take the kids out of their strollers before you try to get on; the trolley waits less than half a minute at each stop.

The South Line Trolley runs every 10–15 minutes from Centre City San Diego to the U.S. border, a 40-minute ride. Once at the border, you can either walk into Mexico or board a Mexicoach bus (☎ **619/232-5049**), which departs every 30 minutes from 9am to 9pm; the fare is $1. The South Line runs daily, every 15 minutes, from 5am to 9pm, then every 30 minutes till midnight.

Call the information number above for specific station stops.

Day Tripper Transit Passes are good deals for families planning to use public transportation. In addition to the trolley, the passes are good for unlimited rides on all MTS buses and the Coronado Ferry. A one-day pass costs $5 and a four-day pass is $15; children 5 and under ride free. Passes can be ordered by mail, but expect a wait of 10 days for delivery. Add 50¢ to cover postage and handling, and be sure to include the dates you need them. You can also purchase passes on the day of travel from the Transit Store, 449 Broadway at the corner of Fifth Avenue, at the San Diego Ferry ticket booths at the Convention Center, or at the Santa Fe Depot's Railroad Museum office. **Note:** Your pass entitles you to a discount to Sea World.

Bus service is available to all major visitor attractions. Ask for the free brochure "The Best of San Diego by Bus and Trolley," which outlines the routes. Call, write, or pick one up at the Transit Store.

Yet another method of transportation is the **Old Town Trolley** (☎ **619/ 298-8687**), the orange-and-green "bus" you'll see zipping around town. It offers a two-hour narrated tour covering Old Town, the Embarcadero, the Gaslamp District, and Coronado. You can get on and off at will. Call for boarding information. Adults pay $16, kids 6–12 are charged $7, and kids under 6 ride free. It runs daily except on major holidays.

GETTING YOUR BEARINGS

Several communities comprise Greater San Diego.

La Jolla is a village of stunning beaches, international shops, and restaurants, and a town lucky enough to have both the Salk Institute and the Scripps Institution of Oceanography.

Coronado, called the Crown City, has its share of sandy beaches. And its del Coronado is one of the most famous hotels in the world for both its architectural beauty and for the royal families and movie stars who have stayed there.

Mission Valley is home to Hotel Circle North and South, where many of the city's hostelries are located. **Harbor and Shelter Islands** are not really islands but artificially created playgrounds for boating and fishing enthusiasts. They also have many parks, beaches, and hotels.

Mission Bay is a mecca of aquatic activity. Its 4,600 acres include Sea World, resort hotels, and restaurants. This is also one of the best family spots for swimming, bicycling, roller skating, windsurfing, and almost all other forms of outdoor recreation.

Ocean Beach and **Pacific Beach** are popular beach communities. Ocean Beach was home to the hippies of the '60s, while Pacific Beach was a quiet community. Now they are more trendy and upscale than in their former lives.

For the most complete tourist information on San Diego and its environs, contact the **International Visitors Information Center** (a part of the San Diego Convention and Visitors Bureau), 11 Horton Plaza (First Avenue and F Street), San Diego, CA 92101 (☎ 619/236-1212). The multilingual staff can provide you with brochures, maps, and other information. The office is open Monday through Saturday from 8:30am to 5pm and on Sunday from 11am to 5pm (June through August only). You can also write to the main office of the **San Diego Convention and Visitors Bureau,** at 401 B St., Suite 1400 Dept. 700, San Diego, CA 92101.

3 Where to Stay

In addition to the following hotels, there are accommodations in La Jolla and Coronado; see those sections for suggestions.

MISSION BAY/MISSION BEACH

The **San Diego Hilton Beach and Tennis Resort,** 1775 E. Mission Bay Dr., San Diego, CA 92109 (☎ 619/276-4010, or toll free 800/445-8667; fax 619/275-7992), is about as family-appropriate as a hotel can be. It's located directly on a half mile of beach and has a private dock with sailboat, catamaran, windsurfer, and Aqua-Cycle rentals. Adults and children can learn to scuba dive in the pool with SCUBA San Diego. Those age 12 and over can then take their knowledge out for an ocean dive with experts from SSD.

Kid-size bicycles (even a couple with training wheels), baby carriers, and helmets can be rented, along with adult bicycles. There are five tennis courts and a free exercise room with a Jacuzzi and a sauna. The huge pool area is a parent's dream: a separate baby wading pool is surrounded by lots of chaise longues; the regular pool, large enough for everyone's swimming styles, has a roped-off shallow section. In the summer there are pool toys and snorkeling equipment for rent, a nearby video game room, and a strategically located snack and ice-cream bar keep everyone happy. Add to all of this a supervised children's program, a small playground, family and adult activities, and three putting greens, and you have an ideal destination.

The complimentary Kids Klub Vacation Station runs daily from Memorial Day to Labor Day, and on weekends the rest of the year. Although you must sign permission agreements, and parents of youngsters under 6 must stay with them for each activity, it's an informal program in which children can participate one hour at a time, depending on the activity. One hour-long activity may feature making balloon animals, another hour of cartoons. There are theme days, pool parties, sports days, and even kids' aerobics. A family movie is shown each evening in summer. The program stresses that it's not a babysitting service, rather "an opportunity to enhance the experience of your entire family's visit."

Summer also means *family* programs. There's usually a western-style barbecue along with live country entertainment and a mexican fiesta night, plus other evening activities which change each season.

Seating is either indoors or outdoors at the Garden Lanai Café. The children's menus, for kids 12 years and under, is priced fairly, and there are games on the menus to keep them occupied. Room service is available from 7am to 11pm, and there are appropriate children's selections at half the adult price.

The Hilton has gone through a massive renovation inside and out. If you haven't visited lately, you may be surprised by the decidedly Mediterranean flavor of the architecture, and the cool florals and light woods of the room interiors. The Tower Rooms are still quite comfortable and large enough to add a crib or a rollaway. They have added ceiling fans in the bedrooms, and Italian marble in the bathrooms. We like the various garden rooms for the sliding glass doors that open directly to very large grassy areas or to the beach. From these rooms you don't have far to go with pails, shovels, and the diaper bag. Even the bathrooms have been enlarged in these rooms. The pyramid-topped Garden Court rooms still have private patios or balconies and the private court with Jacuzzi in the middle. All accommodations are furnished with minibars, ironing boards and irons, small refrigerators and coffee makers (with ceramic cups!), plus remote-control TV with free HBO, Disney, and pay movies.

Room rates range from $145–$225 single or double. Suites rent for $375–$650. Prices differ according to location of the room. Children of any age sleep free in the same room with their parents. Extra adults are charged $20. Cribs and rollaways are free. Parking is free, as is airport transportation. Be sure to inquire about special promotions.

The **Catamaran Resort Hotel,** 3999 Mission Blvd., San Diego, CA 92109 (☎ **619/488-1081,** or toll free **800/288-0770, 800/233-8172** in Canada; fax 619/488-1081), is a South Seas paradise complete with palm trees swaying in the ocean breeze, rolling lawns, and rock-lined ponds. The oversize pool is enclosed with a bamboo-pole fence, and there's a large exercise room nearby for adults. A lifeguard is on duty in summer and food is available poolside. Mission Bay is just a few steps away, and the Pacific Ocean is a short block away. The hotel has its own sailboats, catamarans, pedalboats, and sailboards for rent, and you can take sailing lessons here, too. Landlubbers can rent bicycles, roller skates, and rollerblades.

Be sure to inquire whether the new children's program has been implemented when you visit.

The lobby makes a good walk with the children, as they can look at the waterfall, live orchids, and black rock. A cockatoo perches on a branch in the pond and will happily engage in a yelling contest with youngsters. Rich mahogany is abundant, the furniture is caned, and the finishing touch is a catamaran suspended from the ceiling.

The spacious Atoll restaurant serves breakfast, lunch, and dinner. On a warm day, you will especially enjoy lunch on the patio, just yards from the bay. The dinner menu features innovative continental entrees. Youngsters can choose from six selections, plus dessert and a soda, for $3.95. The room service menu has children's selections and is available from 6:30am daily. The hotel's cabaret-style Cannibal Bar rocks with nightly entertainment, at no cover charge for guests (adults only).

This family-owned and -run hotel has great family accommodations. Standard garden rooms with two double beds are sizable and comfortable. Our favorite room is a bay-view lanai room with a king-size bed, a hide-a-bed, the wet bar, a coffee table, desk, swivel TV, and double-sink vanity.

Bayfront suites house up to six guests and come with all the same amenities, plus a spacious living room with a hide-a-bed, a separate bedroom with two double beds, and two TVs—and there's plenty of room to spread out. Both these bayfront suites and the garden rooms are perfect for families because you can walk right out your sliding glass door to the beach (double locks keep curious toddlers from wandering out).

It may be hard to decide between the garden and bayfront accommodations and the soundproof Tower rooms. Most Tower rooms have large, well-equipped kitchenettes and breakfast bars. Extra touches like wallpaper in the bathrooms, makeup lights, and good reading lights add to the comfort. There's also a large Tower studio which offers a family more space. It has two double beds, a sofa, coffee table, and kitchenette. There are also one-bedroom suites for up to four people.

Rates are based on room location. A room with a king-size bed or two double beds rents for $140–$195. The one-bedroom bayside suites are $265. In the Tower, the studio rents for $150–$195 and one-bedroom suites go for $265–$295. Children under 12 stay free in their parents' room; anyone 12 and over is charged $15 each per night. Cribs are free, but rollaways cost $15. Secured parking costs $5 per day. Ask about special packages and promotions, and seasonal rate changes. You can purchase discounted tickets for Sea World or the Zoo at the hotel's front desk.

Mission Bay is also home to the **Hyatt Islandia,** 1441 Quivira Rd., San Diego, CA 92109-7898 (☎ **619/224-1234,** or toll free **800/233-1234;** fax 619/221-4880). The cool lobby opens to a path leading to a small pond filled with koi fish. When we were there, the young children seemed to meet there every afternoon to climb around the rocks and watch the fish. They also loved the big, fenced-in heated pool and large Jacuzzi. There's no beach access here, but you can walk across the street and picnic on the cliff overlooking the bay. It's a favorite fishing spot, and we spent several hours one evening watching the locals reel in sand sharks and other "exotic" sea creatures. Bonita Cove, with plenty of playground equipment, is a short drive over the bridge. Ask the concierge for croquet, volleyball, or paddleball equipment.

The Camp Hyatt program, for kids 3–15, runs from Memorial Day through Labor Day on weekend evenings only, from 4 to 10pm. No advance reservations are necessary. Usually, there's a ratio of one counselor to every four children. Swimming, kite flying, board games, movies, and barbecues are often the activities of choice. The charge is $5 per hour for the first child and $2.50 per hour for your other children. Dinner is extra.

Baja Café is casual and comfortable for all ages. Adults can order the usual breakfast selections, or try such house specialties as fresh chicken hash, raisin-bread French toast, or smoked-salmon omelet. A special *cuisine naturelle* menu has been added, offering healthy gourmet entrees. The Camp Hyatt menu is fairly extensive and the prices are very reasonable: French toast with all-fruit syrup costs $2, and crispy fish sticks with mashed potatoes are $3. There's room service from 6am to midnight, and you can request children's portions.

The most popular rooms for families seem to be the Marina suites in a low-rise building adjacent to the tower. Decorated with bamboo furnishings, each small suite has a balcony, separate bedroom with a king-size bed or two queen-size beds, a living area with a pull-out sectional sofa, a large bathroom (with a hairdryer), an upholstered reading chair, dressing table, full-length mirror, a table and chairs, coffee maker, wet bar, and two phones and TVs.

Garden rooms are priced well and are perfectly comfortable for a small family. These rooms are furnished with two double beds, a reading chair, small table and chairs, armoire, and full-length mirrors. Ask for a ground-level room and you'll have sliding glass doors leading to a courtyard. Tower rooms afford great views from the nice-sized balconies. The accommodations are equally comfortable here.

All rooms offer Guest Choice, a video selection of 80 movies that can be watched at your own time schedule. Refrigerators can be requested at no charge. The concierge can arrange babysitting.

Room rates are based on single or double occupancy and vary just slightly on weekends. Marina rooms cost $159, garden rooms are $109, and Tower rooms cost $145. Regency Club rooms, with a separate elevator key and complimentary breakfast, rent for $170. The weekend breakfast package is a good deal. For $15 extra per room—except in the Regency Club—a family of two adults and one child can have a full American breakfast. Children 18 and under are not charged when sharing a room with their parents. An adjoining room for kids is 50% off the rate. Each additional adult is charged $25. Cribs and rollaways are complimentary. Parking is free. Ask about 21-day advance rates, and discounted Sea World and Zoo tickets.

Set on 14 acres on a private peninsula surrounded by Mission Bay, the **Bahia Hotel,** 998 W. Mission Bay Dr., San Diego, CA 92109 (☎ **619/488-0551,** or toll free **800/288-0770;** fax 619/488-1512), is the Catamaran's sister hotel.

This is a good family resort for several reasons. There's a private beach, where you can rent sailboats, catamarans, or paddleboats. If you choose to come by boat, the Bahia has a slip awaiting you. The resort has an Olympic-size pool and a helpful attendant who doubles as a lifeguard. The pool has a roped-off shallow area for the kids. Poolside snacks and beverages are available. A large pond, home to a family of seals, will delight you with their antics, and a family of ducks takes the stage in one of the several ponds.

The Bahia's sternwheeler, the *Bahia Belle,* also services guests from the Catamaran. Cocktails and dancing delight the adults. Families can take advantage of the Family Hours, when a strolling banjo player, free balloons, and a beverage menu for the kids are featured on board.

The Bahia also boasts the Comedy Isle, one of only three comedy clubs in San Diego. The cabaret-style room seats 190 for stand-up comics fresh from shows such as "The Comedy Club Network."

Breakfast is served on the patio of the Bahia Café, which opens for the early riser at 6am. There is a children's menu for all three meals, and prices average $4. Room service begins at 6:30am and runs to 10pm.

There are various types of rooms at the resort, and many have been newly renovated. Some open directly to the beach, others to a lush garden area with ponds, a little bridge, and a narrow walkway. The beach-view rooms in the one-story buildings are quite popular with families. The garden-view rooms, which are a good bargain, have their front entries angled to give the appearance of individual front yards. The deluxe bayside suites are designed in a Mediterranean style with a large bank of sliding doors that look out at the bay. These spacious suites come with one king-size bed or two double beds, plus a sleeper sofa and a stocked kitchenette. There are refrigerators in most rooms. The entire property has been made handicapped accessible including the pool and access to telephones.

Rates are the same for single or double occupancy and vary according to the view and the season. A room with a queen-size bed or two double beds rents for

$105–$135. A studio goes for $120–$150, and the bayside suite is $175–$250. Children under 18 stay free in their parents' room; those 18 and over and additional adults pay $15 each per night. Cribs are free and rollaways cost $15. Free parking.

The **Dana Inn,** 1710 W. Mission Bay Dr., San Diego, CA 92109 (☎ **619/ 222-6440,** or toll free **800/445-3339;** fax 619/222-5916), is also a good choice for folks on a budget. It has its own marina, bayside park, paddleboats, bicycle and boat rentals, and tennis courts, and it's right next door to Sea World. A large patio surrounds the heated pool and spa. Snacks and drinks are served poolside in the summer, and you and the kids can play tennis, Ping-Pong, and shuffleboard.

Breakfast, lunch, and dinner are served at the Red Hen Country Kitchen, a cozy restaurant ideal for informal family meals. Or have them pack you a picnic lunch for the beach. A children's menu offers old-fashioned French toast with sausage for $3.45, as well as junior beef stew, fried chicken, and other good choices priced between $2 and $4. The restaurant is open from 7am to 10pm. Room service is also available.

The inn has 196 rooms and suites, many with bayside views. All are comfortably furnished, and have good reading lights, radios, in-room coffee, and satellite TV with free HBO and Disney Channel; refrigerators are available free on request. Most of the rooms have showers only, so if you prefer a tub, be sure to request one in advance.

Room rates are based on location: Bay-view units are the most expensive and poolside rooms are moderate. In winter, singles cost $54–$109; doubles, $59–$119. In summer, singles rent for $69–$119 and doubles cost $79–$129. Children under 18 stay free in their parents' room; those 18 and over and additional adults pay $10 each per night. Cribs are free, but rollaways cost $10. During busy summer weekends, a two-night minimum stay may apply; ask when you reserve. There's a two- or three-night minimum on holidays. Ask about special packages and promotions. Free parking.

SHELTER AND HARBOR ISLANDS

The **Sheraton Harbor Island,** 1380 and 1590 Harbor Island Dr., San Diego, CA 92101 (☎ **619/291-2900,** or toll free **800/325-3535;** fax 619/296-5297), is a sprawling two-tower complex and marina in an incomparable setting. The buildings are connected by a 300-yard marina walkway. Although the hotel is near the airport, you'll have the feeling you are getting away from it all as soon as you cross the bridge to Harbor Island.

If you plan to stay on Harbor Island, the Sheraton makes a good place to stay with the family. Although there is no organized children's program, kids can play at the small sanded beach area, swim in the "fantasy" pools (pools decorated with waterfalls and fountains), stop by the video game room, bike ride, and play Ping-Pong, tennis, or volleyball.

We suggest staying in the East Tower if you're traveling with small children, because the wading and swimming pool, and the playground area and video arcade are in this area.

This full-service resort also offers tennis on lighted courts ($5 per person) and lessons from the resident pro at $50 per hour. Rackets can be rented. A paved walkway around the island affords joggers and cyclers a panoramic view. While the kids play, you can visit the spa and fitness center which is complete with a salon, treatment rooms, and fully supplied locker rooms. The fitness center costs $6 a day or $10 per entire stay at the resort.

Harbor's Edge is the beautifully redone restaurant in the East Tower with wide windows opening onto the bay. All the hotel's restaurants have special kids' menus.

The Bakery is a food-lovers delight, stocked as it is with desserts and deli items. Quinn's Bar overlooks the harbor and features live music in the evenings. Waterworks is a special favorite. Located adjacent to the pool, Waterworks serves youngsters on hubcaps, hot rocks, marble slabs, in colanders, and other nontraditional ways.

In the West Tower, Spencer's offers a breathtaking view of the harbor, with indoor and al fresco seating. Children are welcome and a children's menu, highchairs, and boosters are made available.

Rooms in the East Tower have either two double beds or one king-size bed. The very small balconies are double-railed (so no one can escape!). The furnishings are nicely done in dark wood and faux stone and headboards are padded. Each room is equipped with reading lights, remote-control TV, full-length mirror, a coffee maker and ceramic mugs, two telephones equipped with voice mail, a minibar, an ironing board and iron, and a digital clock radio. The granite-topped bathroom has a mini-TV and a hairdryer. Complimentary newspapers are delivered to your door. The West Tower rooms share many of the same amenities, but the rooms are a bit larger and the furnishings are contemporary. Rooms with a king-size bed have hide-a-beds and small sitting areas. This building is a quieter, more adult-oriented location.

Rates at the Sheraton are the same in both towers. Rooms cost $200 single or double. Rooms on the Club Level cost $220 and include daily continental breakfast. Children under 17 stay free in their parents' room; additional adults pay $20. Cribs are complimentary; rollaways and refrigerators cost $20. Ask about seasonal promotions. Self-parking is $8.

At **Humphrey's Half Moon Inn,** 2303 Shelter Island Dr., San Diego, CA 92106 (☎ **619/224-3411,** or toll free **800/542-7400;** fax 619/224-3478), you can choose a harbor, marina, or courtyard pool view from your balcony or patio. Fresh flowers decorate the grassy areas around the heated pool and spa, where youngsters can romp and grownups can soak up the sun. The service is friendly, and the staff makes you feel at home. Walks along the marina or through the gardens (residence to a family of ducks) are popular. There are free bicycles in all sizes, including ones for children, and lawn games such as a putting green, badminton, croquet, and a Ping-Pong table on the grounds.

The hotel's restaurant, Humphrey's, is well known locally for its outdoor "Concerts by the Bay," held on the lawn from May through September (see "What to See and Do," below). The restaurant is open for breakfast, lunch, dinner, and Sunday brunch, and there is a limited children's menu. Prices average $8.50 at lunch, $15.50 at dinner. Boosters and highchairs are provided. Room service is available.

Accommodations at the resort are pleasantly decorated, some with wood-framed woven-straw headboards and beamed ceilings to carry out the hotel's Polynesian look. The rooms have plenty of floor space for a crib or rollaway, even with two queen-size beds. The 23 junior suites and seven executive suites have full kitchens. Each room has in-room coffee, complimentary newspapers, full-length mirrors, color TVs, refrigerators, and free 24-hour in-room movies. There are rooms with and without balconies. If you get a ground-floor room, note that the sliding doors open directly to the hotel grounds. The steep stairs to the upper floor and the landings have middle cutouts, so watch those tiny tots.

Babysitting can be arranged. When you reserve your room, ask whether the summer concert series is in effect, then decide whether you want a room close to the music.

Rates for standard rooms vary according to location. Singles are $89–$139, doubles, $99–$149. Suites with kitchens can be rented for $109–$249. Children 18 and younger stay free in their parents' room; those over 18 pay $10 per night. No charge for cribs, but rollaways cost $10. Ask about seasonal and package specials. Free parking.

PACIFIC BEACH

Just steps from the beach is the **Best Western Blue Sea Lodge,** 707 Pacific Beach Dr., San Diego, CA 92109 (☎ **619/488-4700,** or toll free **800/BLUESEA;** fax 619/ 270-1129). This is a most appropriate hotel for families because of the beach location. There's also a small pool (not fenced in) and the fenced-in whirlpool and sun deck. A complimentary continental breakfast is served daily, and there are at least a dozen eateries within a four-block radius. A special service delivers from nearby restaurants; an in-room directory lists the choices. Also, there are charge privileges at the World Famous restaurant next door (be sure to get a card from the front desk). Coffee, hot chocolate, and tea are available all day in the lobby. Management can arrange babysitting. There is a laundry for guest use. Just behind the hotel is Aquarius Surf & Skate which gives discounts on skates, boogie boards, and other sports equipment to hotel guests.

Rooms at this Best Western have been newly refurbished to reflect a tropical theme. Light oak furniture, seashell lamps, and the tropical colors of the new upholstery and bedding all fit nicely with the beach location. If you're traveling on business, ask for the corporate traveler rooms which have a desk and chair and computer/modem hookups.

There are rooms of various sizes. All have patios and all are outfitted with color TVs with free HBO, air conditioning, and heat. Units may be furnished with two double beds, or a king-size bed. Most of the units have well-equipped kitchenettes and breakfast bars. Our favorite is the oceanfront deluxe room with one double-size bed and a sofa bed, plus a tub/shower combination and the kitchenette. You can book adjacent rooms with one private door leading to both rooms. Suites are marvelously spacious. Some units have shower stalls only.

Rates are based on location. In summer, rooms run $116–$131 single and $126–$141 double. A room with two double beds goes for $136–$156. Suites run $195–$280. In fall and winter, those rates drop $10–$15. Children under 18 sleep free in their parents' room. Cribs are free; rollaways cost $15. Inquire about discounts for AAA members and senior citizens, and special weekly and monthly off-season rates.

The **Beach Cottages,** at 4255 Ocean Blvd., San Diego, CA 92109 (☎ **619/ 483-7440;** fax 619/270-8819), offers cottages and motel-style accommodations. A family-owned and -operated establishment for more than 40 years, it gives the feeling that you are visiting the home of close friends who go all-out for your comfort. You can play Ping-Pong and shuffleboard, build castles in the sand, take a dip in the ocean, then cook up a barbecue dinner on the patio. In addition to beach activities, the major San Diego attractions are not far away by car. Within walking distance are shops and restaurants offering everything from fast food to gourmet waterfront dining. On the premises is a giftshop stocked with lots of Mickey Mouse items and fascinating toys. The staff will refer babysitters.

There are several choices of accommodations here. The recently remodeled original cottages have kept their beach-cottage feel. Each is appointed with sand-blasted white wood walls and ceilings, hardwood floors, and simple, rugged furniture upholstered in country prints, and each has a semiprivate furnished patio. There is a fully stocked, nice-size kitchen, eating area, living room with a small hide-a-bed, and one small bedroom with a double bed.

The standard motel rooms in the older, two-story building are quite small, so I'd opt for the rooms in the newer three-story building. These modern accommodations with their blond furniture and pastel colors are quite comfortable. Hidden away are a wet bar, microwave, and coffee maker. The two-bedroom suites are as big as small apartments and come with a full kitchen, gas barbecue, breakfast bar, table and chairs, three bathrooms, and two bedrooms, one with a very large dressing area.

The cottages cost $85–$165, depending on number of guests and location. A standard motel room will run you $55–$90 single, $70–$110 double. Studios are $75–$115. Suites go for $175–$240. Prices differ depending on the season and location of the room. Each extra person of any age is charged $7. Cribs and rollaways cost $7. Parking is free. Because of the popularity of this place, you should make reservations well in advance.

OLD TOWN

The **Hacienda Hotel Old Town,** 4041 Harney St., San Diego, CA 92110 (☎ **619/ 298-4707,** or toll free **800/888-1991;** fax 619/298-4707), combines the charm of the old-world hacienda lifestyle with all the modern amenities. Located in the center of Old Town, this new hotel is fashioned after the rambling old ranches that once occupied this area. The red-roofed white stucco hotel is made up of 150 suites, each unique in design. It is built on a hill away from busy streets, giving guests privacy and quiet, but is within walking distance of the Bazaar del Mundo. The hotel provides complimentary shuttle service to and from the airport and the Amtrak station. There are spacious patio areas on several levels, with plenty of room to relax and soak up the sun. Videotapes are available at the front desk if your youngsters become restless.

A buffet breakfast is served in the hotel's Acapulco Restaurant, located at the top of the hotel's property, with a beautiful vista of San Diego and the bay. A complimentary Manager's Social is offered Monday through Thursday evenings. There's a children's menu in the restaurant, and room service offers kids' portions too. The hotel also provides gas barbecue grills near the pool for guest use. Ask about charge privileges at nearby restaurants.

All accommodations here are suites, each with a sleeping area and a very small sitting area. The rooms are decorated with well-worn Santa Fe–style furnishings, and have ceiling fans, shutters, new carpeting and bedding, and mirrored wardrobe doors. Refrigerators, microwaves, and coffee makers are provided in each suite, as are TVs and VCRs (complete with popcorn); some rooms have double sinks. Some units have private balconies; others open onto the courtyard. Every suite has a sofa bed, and bedrooms contain one or two queen-size beds. These suites can sleep up to five people, depending on which layout you choose, and there are a few connecting rooms for larger families. No-smoking and handicapped-accessible units are also available.

In winter, accommodations rent for $99 single and $109 double. In summer (June through August), singles cost $109; doubles, $119. Children under 16 stay free in their parents' room, but anyone 16 and over pays $10 each per night. Cribs are free, but rollaways cost $10. Ask about seasonal and promotional packages. There is free covered off-street parking.

Built on the site of the Gila House Hotel, one of Old Town's grandest structures from the 1850s, the **Ramada Hotel Old Town,** 2435 Jefferson St., San Diego, CA 92110 (☎ **619/260-8500,** or toll free **800/255-3544;** fax 619/297-2078), is a modern version of Old Southwest charm. The exterior has the look of an elegant hacienda, and the lobby and rooms are decorated Native American–style. The effect is restful and welcoming. Although the hotel is off the beaten path of Old Town by just a block or two, you can take advantage of Old Town's shops and restaurants. Within a five-minute drive are Sea World, the San Diego Zoo, downtown, and the beaches.

The fenced-in heated pool is small, and there is a Jacuzzi. The Gila House restaurant provides poolside service and is open for breakfast, lunch, and dinner. There are plenty of choices for children. Room service is available from 6:30am to 1:30pm, and from 5 to 10pm. Complimentary full buffet breakfast and cocktails are served, and box lunches for a picnic can be ordered. Babysitting can be arranged by the front desk.

Choose from 151 clean and well-maintained rooms and suites. Some have two queen-size beds or a king-size bed and a twin sofa bed, ideal for giving families maximum living space. Double queen-bedded units are fine for three or four, but they're too small to fit a rollaway or crib. All rooms are decorated with Native American–design bedspreads and drapes. Attractive armoires house the remote-control TV and in-room movies. Bathrooms have tubs, and there are separate vanities. Some refrigerators are available. Large families should consider the suite that sleeps six and rents for $189, or the slightly smaller suite with one king-size bed and a hide-a-bed, plus room for a crib or rollaway ($159).

Travelers on a budget can request to be put up at the Ramada's Western Inn next door. Rooms are small, but the building is quiet, and the facilities at the Ramada (and the complimentary breakfasts) can be used by guests staying at the Western Inn. Some rooms have a microwave and small refrigerator. Rooms here rent from $79 to $109. There's also a junior suite with a separate bedroom and TV and a living room with a TV, wet bar, microwave, refrigerator, sofa, and desk which lets for $109.

Single-occupancy rooms go for $109; doubles are $119. The 12 different styles of suites range in price from $129 to $189. Children under 16 stay free in their parents' room; those 18 and over pay $10 each per night. There's no charge for cribs, but rollaways cost $10. Free covered parking and airport transportation. Call the chain's office (☎ toll free **800/2-RAMADA**) to ask about special promotions and packages before you call the hotel.

HOTEL CIRCLE/MISSION VALLEY

Expensive

Town & Country Hotel, 500 Hotel Circle North, San Diego, CA 92108 (☎ **619/ 291-7131,** or toll free **800/77-ATLAS;** fax 619/291-3584) is a surprise. From the outside it appears to be a large, impersonal hotel, and with its attached convention center it hardly seems to be a family destination. But inside are some charming rooms, four swimming pools, and four restaurants. While it does cater to the business traveler, its location just off the freeway may appeal to your family.

The Lanai Coffee Shop, Cafe Potpourri (not always open), The Gourmet Room, and Kelly's all have children's menus and health-conscious items. There is also room service from 6:30am to 11pm. A men's and women's salon plus two giftshops are also on the property. A van is available by request to take guests to the nearby Fashion Island Shopping Center or to area attractions.

The West Tower is a good choice for families because the rooms are larger here than in the East Tower, and all the rooms sport balconies. There is plenty of room for a rollaway or crib, especially in the king-bed rooms. But the poolside garden rooms are quite charming, surrounded by flowers and opening right to the pool (which is not fenced in). Here you'll find two queen-sized beds, a mirrored closet, sloping bright white ceilings and blue and white wallpaper. All of the Town & Country rooms are furnished in rich blue and rose and have dark colonial furniture. While accommodations are furnished nicely, they are short on amenities. There is remote control color TV with in-room movies and valet service.

Standard room prices start at $95 and go up to $140. Children under 18 sleep free in a parent's room; extra adults are charged $10. There is no charge for cribs; rollaways are $10. Be sure to ask about the special family package which includes breakfast for four and tickets to the zoo or Sea World. Parking is free.

Moderate/Budget

This area has two budget hotel chain options to consider: **Days Inn-Hotel Circle,** 543 Hotel Circle S., San Diego, CA 92108 (☎ **619/297-8800,** or toll free **800/ 227-4743;** fax 619/298-6029) charges $50 to $79 single; $56 to $85 double. Children 17 years old and under stay free in their parents' room. The extra-adult charge is $10. Cribs are free, and rollaways cost $10. Parking is free. There is a pool; a restaurant is next door. Some rooms have kitchenette and rent for $67–$86. **Budget Motel of America,** 641 Camino del Rio S. (Mission Valley), San Diego, CA 92108 (☎ **619/ 295-6886,** or toll free **800/624-1257;** fax 619/296-9661) rents rooms for $34–$42 singles; $39–$47 doubles; suites $85. Children under 18 years old stay free. Cribs are complimentary, rollaways are $10. Add a refrigerator for $4. Free parking.

DOWNTOWN

You can walk to Seaport Village from the **Embassy Suites Hotel,** 601 Pacific Coast Hwy., San Diego, CA 92101 (☎ **619/239-2400,** or toll free **800/EMBASSY;** fax 619/239-1520), and you're very close to the Embarcadero and downtown San Diego. Like most Embassy Suites, this one has a dramatic atrium lobby where guests gather for complimentary, cooked-to-order breakfasts, and free afternoon cocktails and soft drinks. An indoor pool sits in a pretty, plant-filled tiled room, and there is a small outdoor Jacuzzi. The exercise machines are in a bright room complete with TV and sauna.

A number of Embassy Suites rooms have been made child-safe with electrical outlet covers and the like.

Barnetts Grand Café is a lovely, colorful restaurant serving pasta, seafood, and other health-conscious selections for lunch and dinner. The children's menu is adequate for most youngsters' tastes. You can also enjoy snacks and sandwiches in the bar, indoors or on the outdoor patio.

The newly refurbished suites offer a separate bedroom with two double beds or one king-size bed, and have plenty of space for a family of four (even six if you opt for two beds in the bedroom). The living areas are furnished with a fold-out bed, a small refrigerator, microwave, coffee maker, and a wet bar. The hotel will provide plates upon request, and the giftshop stocks microwavable snacks. Two two-line phones with voice mail are standard. The wallpapered bathrooms are nice-sized, and there's a separate extra sink in the bedroom. Two remote-control cable TVs give you plenty of choices, along with free Showtime and in-room pay movies. Closet space is limited. Request a corner unit if you need more room, but it won't have a balcony. Coin-operated washers and dryers are on the 12th floor, and valet service is available.

Rates vary from $119 to $159, depending on the season and the number of occupants. Children 12 and under stay free in their parents' room; those over 12 and additional adults are charged $15. Cribs are available. There's a charge for parking, whether self- or valet parking. Airport transportation is free.

Holiday Inn on the Bay, 1355 N. Harbor Dr., San Diego 92101 (☎ **619/ 232-3861,** or toll free **800/4-Bayside;** fax 619/232-4924) has 600 rooms to choose from and is conveniently located just across the street from the *Star of India* and harbor cruises. If you've got the energy, you can even walk to Seaport Village from here.

The hotel keeps a table tennis game and Foosball table near its outdoor pool, and features live entertainment and poolside barbecues in summer (hamburgers and hot dogs cost a whopping $1). There is also a small game room equipped with video machines, and board games can be checked out at the front desk. Outdoors is a tiny sand-filled play area for toddlers and adjacent picnic tables.

Adults won't have to forego their exercise routine, as the hotel has an equipped exercise room free to guests.

In addition to the hotel restaurant and room service (both which offer children's menus), there's a food court next door featuring a deli, Ruth Chris' Steak House, and fast food eateries. Kids ages 12 and under eat free in the hotel restaurant.

Double-bed rooms at the Holiday Inn are adequately sized for a family of three. You might even consider the king-bed room which also has a sofabed. Larger families should either request adjoining rooms, or ask for a large king room which has space for both a crib and a rollaway and is all-around larger (these are available only by calling the hotel directly).

All accommodations have remote control color TV and on-command videos. Phones have computer/modem hookups and voice mail message capability. AM/FM clock radios, hairdryers, and ironing boards and irons are standard in all units. The vanity and sink area is separate from the shower/toilet room. Same-day valet service is provided, or there are coin-operated laundry machines for guest use.

Accommodations cost $135 single, $165 double. There is an extra $20 charge for a bayview room. Kids 18 and under sleep free; extra adults are charged $10. Cribs and rollaways are complimentary. Be sure to ask about special packages and promotions, some of which incorporate Seaworld tickets or cruises to Ensenada. Parking at the hotel is $10 daily with in and out privileges.

The **Best Western Bayside Inn,** 555 W. Ash St., San Diego, CA 92101 (☎ **619/ 233-7500,** or toll free **800/341-1818;** fax 619/239-8060), is a high-rise hotel conveniently located at the hub of San Diego's tourist activities and is within walking distance of the San Diego Trolley and the Convention and Performing Arts Centers. One side of the hotel looks out onto the bay, the other onto downtown San Diego, and either view can fascinate you for hours. But if you're traveling with a toddler, you may want to ask for the first floor and forgo the upper-floor rooms, all of which have balconies. The hotel has a small outdoor pool and a Jacuzzi. Inquire about bike rentals.

Complimentary breakfast is served from 6:30 to 11am in the adjacent Bayside Bar & Grill. The restaurant also serves lunch and dinner. Kids can order from the limited "Children's Corner" selections. Room service is available during restaurant hours. Coffee and tea are available all day in the lobby.

The clean contemporary rooms typically come with one or two queen-size beds, but a few rooms with king-size beds are available. Ask for one if you desire lots of living space, or ask about adjoining rooms. Units are nicely decorated and have in-room movies, individually controlled heat and air conditioning, and full-length mirrors. Bathrooms are small but adequate.

Summer rates (July to September) are $80 for a single, $86 for a double. In winter, singles cost $70; doubles, $76. A room with a harbor view is $8 extra anytime.

Children under 12 stay free in their parents' room; anyone 12 and over is charged $6 per night. Cribs are free; rollaways, $12. Ask about special packages. There is free covered parking, and a complimentary airport shuttle.

A LITTLE FAR AWAY BUT WORTH IT

For those who enjoy the sporting life, the **Rancho Bernardo Inn,** 17550 Bernardo Oaks Dr., San Diego, CA 92128 (☎ **619/487-1611;** fax 619/673-0311), is a paradise. The inn is located 30 miles from San Diego near the Wild Animal Park. Set amid rolling green hills on 265 acres of a former California ranch, this golf and tennis retreat offers all you'd expect from a contemporary luxury resort in an atmosphere of plush early California. Antique tables, chairs, and chests furnish the spacious lobby, and the rough-hewn beamed ceiling and area rugs add warmth and character.

The inn is famed for its tennis camp and golf courses, and it also has two swimming pools, Jacuzzis, volleyball, badminton, and Ping-Pong. The lobby's music room includes a great jigsaw-puzzle table. Children will enjoy the Spanish fountains that decorate the grounds. Take them to the charming wishing well at the end of the lobby walkway. When you want to take the kids sightseeing in San Diego, rental cars are available on the premises.

Family-oriented activities are held at the inn over holiday weekends, as well as three weeks in August, a week at Easter, and during the December holidays when the inn celebrates with a Holiday Festival Program, which includes a Children's Holiday Camp for kids 5–17. Young guests play miniature golf and tennis, swim, construct kites, go on scavenger hunts, and make ice cream.

Camp RBI is held for children of the same age group during Easter week and throughout August. Summer programs add such seasonal activities as cookouts, campfires, and luaus. Sports activities include swimming, soccer, basketball, hockey, softball, and track meets. A Saturday Cartoon Breakfast (breakfast and cartoons) is offered, along with field trips, carnivals, and movies. Youngsters can participate in any or all of the activities. For teenagers, the programs are structured to meet individual interests.

There is a charge of $20 for the full-day children's program, from 9am to 9pm, and $15 for a half day, 9am to 3pm.

A Tennis College is held at the inn with packages ranging from two to five days, and the rate includes instruction, accommodations, meals, and social activities. The cost varies with the length of your stay and the time of year.

The Golf Holiday Package includes your room, greens fees, dinner on arrival day, breakfast and dinner other days, and breakfast on departure day.

Parents will enjoy dining at the gourmet restaurant, El Bizcocho. Here elegant French cuisine is served as patrons take in the panoramic view of the golf course. The wine list features more than 600 selections. The restaurant is open daily for dinner, and on Sunday for brunch. Jackets required for gentlemen.

The less formal Veranda Room is open for breakfast, lunch, and dinner, and is suited for families. Seating is indoors or outdoors overlooking the golf course. Mission-style arches and turn-of-the-century furniture set the early-California atmosphere. This is the place for a lazy breakfast on a sunny morning. Highchairs are available. Ask for children's food items not included with the printed menu. This restaurant also provides 24-hour room service.

The 287 rooms come in a variety of shapes and sizes, all with patios or balconies. Pots of plants and colorful flowers will make you feel welcome. Earth tones and heavy wood furniture carry out the early-California theme. The rooms are all spacious enough for a crib. Large closets and a wooden vanity are standard. Upper-floor rooms have beamed ceilings. A room with two queen-size beds will give you a separate vanity. Parlor suites have a sofa bed in the living area and come with two bathrooms and a large closet. Remote-control TV, honor bars, and hairdryers are standard amenities.

Summer rates for standard rooms are $135–$185, single or double. October through March, rates range from $185–$215. Executive suites rent for $180–$250, one- and two-bedroom suites cost $245–$500, and the two VIP suites are $450–$600. The rates for suites remain the same year round. Children 12 and under stay free in their parents' room. The extra-person charge is $15. There is no charge for cribs; no rollaways available. Free parking.

CONDOMINIUMS

Capri by the Sea Rental Management, 4767 Ocean Blvd., Pacific Beach (mailing address: P.O. Box 9473, San Diego, CA 92169) (☎ **619/483-6110,** or toll free **800/248-5262** outside California; fax 619/483-9141), offers condominium rentals, a comfortable alternative to a hotel stay. This beachfront high-rise features fully equipped, large one-, two-, and three-bedroom units, all with ocean views. Maid service is available at an additional charge; towels and linens are provided. Comfortable living rooms are furnished with cable TV, telephones, and stereo units. The adjoining eating area has a table and chairs. Highchairs and cribs can be rented for $35 per week. The constant ocean breezes eliminate any need for air conditioning. Note that sliding glass doors lead to narrow balconies; parents often bring along baby gates to block them off.

In addition to the immediate beach access, the building has a heated pool, spa, sauna, and rooftop lanai with barbecues. Although many of the units are occupied by year-round tenants, there is a front desk to tend to the needs of tourists. There you can arrange for babysitting through an agency. Free parking is available, either underground or in the outdoor parking lot. Coin-operated washers and dryers are located on each floor.

One other nice thing about Capri is that you can rent units for as short as a three-night stay, or for as long as you want. A hefty $200 security fee is required, which is reimbursed 10 days after departure, and you must pay in full 30 days before your arrival.

One-bedroom accommodations, which are approximately 900 square feet, sleep four comfortably, plus you can add a rollaway and/or a crib (which rent for $35 each per week). Two-bedroom units sleep six to eight. There are penthouse units available with one to three bedrooms. The extra-person charge is $10 per night.

Rates are seasonal but do not increase for holidays and special events. Generally, the charge for a one-bedroom condo starts at $600 per week in the fall and month of May, $750 per week from December through June, and $1,000 per week from July to Labor Day. Two-bedroom units go from $800 to $950 to $1,600 for the same periods. Two-bedroom corner condos and penthouse accommodations are a little more expensive. Inquire about three-night rates and special discounts.

Don't let the name scare you: **Beach Bum Rentals,** 747¹/₂ San Fernando Place, Mission Beach (mailing address: P.O. Box 9216, San Diego, CA 92109) (☎ **619/488-3100;** fax 619/488-6820), has been in business renting cottages, apartments, and condominiums for 20 years. A variety of accommodations, many ocean- or bayfront, are available fully equipped. Some have towels and linens; if not, that can be arranged for separately.

Advance rentals require a one-week stay. Daily rentals are sometimes available, but only at the last minute. Those rates vary greatly. A security deposit of $200–$500 will be asked of you, refundable 14 days after your stay, and a deposit of 50% of the rent is due when the reservation form is returned. The balance and tax is due 30 days before arrival.

Weekly rents range from $300 to $3,000, depending on your needs. As an example, an oceanfront condominium on Mission Beach runs $1,800 per week. The two-story condo has two bedrooms, a den, 2^{1}/2 baths, a Jacuzzi, fireplace, and TV. It sleeps six people, and linen is provided.

CAMPING

Campsites in the area are numerous and the terrain is varied—from mountains to desert to beaches to city. Contact the following places for specific information on campsites:

For Local Camping in County Parks

Write or call the **San Diego County Department of Parks and Recreation,** 5201 Ruffin Rd., Suite P, San Diego, CA 92123 (☎ **619/694-3049** for information, **619/565-3600** for reservations). Reservations are not required but are recommended. Sites run from $10 to $16.

For State Parks

Make reservations through **MISTIX** (☎ toll free **800/444-7275**). There is no main phone number for camping in state parks. Other areas should be contacted individually.

For information about camping at San Elijo and South Carlsbad State Beaches, try the **San Diego Coast District,** 3990 Old Town Ave., Suite 300C, San Diego, CA 92110 (☎ **619/220-5400;** fax 619/296-5539).

For mountain camping at Cuyamaca Rancho State Park or Palomar Mountain State Park, contact the **Montane Section,** 12551 Calif. 79, Descanso, CA 91916 (☎ **619/765-0755**).

For desert camping, the contact is the **Anza-Borrego Desert State Park,** P.O. Box 299, Borrego Springs, CA 92004 (☎ **619/767-5311**).

For Camping in the National Forest

Campsites are available on a first-come, first-served basis in the Cleveland National Forest. Contact the **United States Forest Service,** Cleveland National Forest Headquarters, 10845 Rancho Bernardo Rd., San Diego, CA 92127 (☎ **619/673-6180**); the Palomar Ranger District, 1634 Black Canyon Rd., Ramona, CA 92065 (☎ **619/788-0250**); or the Descanso Ranger District, 3348 Alpine Blvd., Alpine, CA 91901 (☎ **619/445-6235**).

4 Where to Eat

San Diego is full of restaurants that are suitable for families with children of various ages. Don't forget to check the La Jolla dining section also, as those restaurants are only about 15 minutes away from downtown San Diego.

HARBOR ISLAND

Once Coast Guard Beacon No. 9, **Tom Ham's Lighthouse,** 2150 Harbor Island Dr. (☎ **619/291-9110**), sits on the picturesque point of Harbor Island with water on three sides. The panoramic view is beautiful after dark, and you may want to time your dinner so that you can watch the sun set over the bay. The children will be pleasantly surprised to discover that the restaurant is also a museum. The whole family will enjoy the framed ship's charts and other seagoing artifacts that decorate the restaurant.

The delicious lunch buffet is served from a large rowboat and includes salads and tasty enchiladas. Seafood entrees include lobster and scampi, and beef is also a specialty. The daily lunch buffet costs $6.95. Or you can order sandwiches, salads, and such house specialties as fried shrimp and salmon, enchiladas, and hamburgers. A la carte lunch items run $5.25–$10.95.

Dinners are pricey and range from $14.95 (for halibut) to $29.95 (for lobster tails and prime rib or filet mignon). There is a variety of beef, seafood, and pasta selections, all of which come with soup or salad. Carne asada is a specialty, as is Lighthouse Newburg and scampi. A children's dinner menu is available for ages 12 and under, with prices from $5.50 to $9 for fried shrimp, prime rib, sirloin steak, fish and chips, a hamburger with french fries, or sautéed chicken breast and rice, and these include soup or salad.

Early Bird menu items cost $9.95 and feature pasta with chicken and shrimp, an 8-ounce prime rib, seafood brochette, and other chicken, fish, or beef items. Each comes with bread and soup or salad. Sunday Brunch is a family affair with prices of $10.50 for adults, $5.75 for kids ages 7 to 12, and $4.85 for tykes 6 and under.

Booster seats and highchairs are provided. The servers will warm baby bottles and baby food in the kitchen, and Shirley Temples and other children's drinks can be ordered from the bar.

Lunch is served Monday through Friday from 11:15am to 3:30pm (the buffet closes at 2:30); the Sunday buffet hours are 10am to 2pm. Dinner is available Monday through Thursday from 5 to 10pm, on Friday from 5 to 11pm, Saturday 4:30 to 11pm and on Sunday from 4 to 10pm. The Sunday champagne brunch begins at 10am. Early Bird Specials are featured Monday through Friday from 5 to 6pm, and Sunday from 4pm to 6pm. Reservations are recommended. Major credit cards are honored. Free parking in the lot.

El Torito on the Island, 1590 Harbor Island Dr. (☎ **619/299-3464**) is a lively spot for a family dinner. The big, airy dining room has a bay view and is furnished with many banquettes and tables.

An activity book and crayons keep youngsters busy with connect-the-chilies, mazes, and word games. The under-12 set eat for $2.99. Their choices include a taco, burger, quesadilla, chicken fingers, a burrito, or an enchilada, and drink refills are free. Entrees come with a sundae and mini-nachos, plus a choice of either French fries or rice and beans.

On Wednesdays, kids 12 and under can eat free off the children's menu. Each child must be accompanied by a paying adult.

The lunch and dinner menus don't vary too much, although dinner prices are higher. In addition to the combination plates, tacos, enchiladas, burritos, and fajitas, there are vegetarian creations and lunch specials such as a Santa Fe enchilada ($5.99) and sea bass tacos ($6.45). Lunch prices range from $5.50 to $8.50. Dinner specials add marinated pork carnitas ($8.95), sea bass fajitas ($10.95), and a delicious twice-grilled BBQ burrito ($7.99), among other evening specials. The standard menu prices go from $6.95–$12. À la carte choices can also be ordered.

An all-you-can-eat Sunday buffet brunch is a real bargain. For this adults are charged $8.95, while kids pay $2.99.

Highchairs and boosters are provided.

El Torito is open Monday through Friday from 11am to 10pm, to 11pm on Saturday. Sunday Brunch is served from 9am to 2pm, lunch and dinner can be ordered until 10pm. Reservations are accepted. Major credit cards are welcome. Parking is free; valet parking is provided weekend evenings.

PACIFIC BEACH

The **Tony Roma's** branch in Pacific Beach, at 4110 Mission Blvd. (☎ 619/ 272-7427), is a nice large establishment perfect for all age groups. Any day or night, kids automatically get crayons and an activity book as they sit down. If you bring them here on Saturday evening in summer, they'll enjoy the entertainer who creates balloon animals and figures. Kids can order off their own menu. Choices include chicken fingers, hamburgers, ribs, and pizza, each served with french fries or fruit, a vegetable appetizer, and a dessert. ($3–$6). Soft drinks, milk, or juice are extra. Highchairs and booster seats are provided.

Adults can order Tony Roma's great standards—ribs, barbecued chicken, or burgers—or one of its meal-size salads or fish. Dinners run $6.25—$15.50. And take-out is available.

The restaurant is open Sunday through Thursday from 11am to 9pm, on Friday and Saturday to 11pm (to 10pm in winter). No reservations accepted. Weekend nights are the busiest, so come early (your best bet is to come before 6pm or after 8pm). Major credit cards are welcome. There's validated parking in the underground garage.

Chicagoans especially will recognize the name **Pizzeria Uno,** 4465 Mission Blvd. (☎ 619/483-4143), an institution in Chicago since 1943. The deep-dish pizza takes anywhere from 14 to 20 minutes to prepare (depending on your selection), but it's well worth waiting for. You may want to order the pizzettas—thin-crust pizzas available in individual sizes or larger. Pizzas cost $5.25–$13. If you're not in the mood for pizza, there are salads, burgers, sandwiches, and pastas priced at a reasonable $4–$10. And we always choose Chicago cheesecake for dessert.

Kids aren't left out at Uno's. The under-12 set can order their own cheese or pepperoni pizza, "taters & fraters" (chunks of hot dogs with fries), spaghetti, or "chix & stix" (chicken "thumbs" and fries), priced at $2–$3. All soft drinks, for kids and adults, come with free refills. They carry a long list of Epic beers, some exclusive to Uno's.

Choose indoor seating or an ocean view from the upstairs outdoor patio. Highchairs and booster seats are available. Servers will split adult portions and warm baby food or bottles. There's a full bar, and they will prepare children's drinks upon request. Take-out is available.

Open everyday 11am to 2am. Reservations are accepted only for 8 or more. The wait can be anywhere from 20 minutes to an hour on summer weekends. During the summer months, and weekends especially, get there before 7pm. Credit cards are accepted. There is a parking lot.

For one of the best-priced breakfasts in town, try the **Café Broken Yolk,** 1851 Garnet St. (☎ 619/270-0045). A step up from a coffee shop, this cute, bright, casual restaurant draws an eclectic Pacific Beach crowd. The breakfast specialty is omelets: There are 24 varieties listed, or you can custom-order one to your taste. Besides traditional choices, there are lots of vegetarian and Mexican omelets. You can split these large portions at no extra charge. You'll also find banana, blueberry, and buttermilk pancakes, plus waffles, biscuits and gravy, quiche, eggs, and many side dishes. Breakfast prices range from $3 to $7. For lunch, choose from 10 different hamburgers, five variations of a grilled-cheese sandwich, or four types of BLTs. There are also other sandwiches and salads. Prices average $5.

Youngsters have their own choices: eggs prepared various ways, pancakes, French toast, or cereal, plus a beverage, for $2.25. Lunch choices are cheese quesadillas, grilled cheese, peanut butter and jelly, or a hamburger for the same price. The servers will split orders, warm baby food and bottles, and provide boosters and highchairs.

Open daily except Thanksgiving and Christmas Days from 6am to 3pm. No reservations are accepted, and the usual weekend wait is 10–15 minutes. There is parking on the street and in the lot out back. Major credit cards are welcome. There is another Café Broken Yolk branch at 3350 Sports Arena, Point Loma (☎ 619/226-0442). Call for hours.

EMBARCADERO/SEAPORT VILLAGE

Anthony's Fish Grotto, 1360 N. Harbor Dr. (☎ 619/232-5103), is one of those places where prices are terrific, food is good, and the view is wonderful. But the wait is very long. Because it's perched over the water, our kids love to watch the boats, airplanes, and ocean liners (when we're lucky) as they parade past the large glass windows.

This is strictly a seafood restaurant, and, surprisingly, it is almost completely filled with families in the earlier hours. Lunch choices off the regular menu include seafood salads, fried shrimp and fried clams, and such sandwiches as grilled crab and cheese, shrimp salad, and tuna and cheese. Lunch prices range from $4 to $7.95. At dinner, some of the selections are Hawaiian tuna, trout, mahi mahi, and albacore. Those prices start at $6.75 and go to $19.95 for lobster thermidor.

The children's menu has a number of choices. There's grilled cheese, fish and chips (in two sizes), Pacific red snapper, shrimp nuggets, tuna sandwich, noodles and sauce, a fish taco, and chicken breast. These selections cost $2.50–$4.95, and come with salad or coleslaw and french fries. "We do everything to make it convenient for our customers to come here," says the management. The staff will bring crackers to the table for the little ones, and the children's menu is a connect-the-dots game. They'll split adult portions, warm bottles and baby food, make special children's drinks, and provide highchairs and booster seats.

Open daily except major holidays from 11:30am to 8:30pm. No reservations are accepted. Major credit cards are honored. Street parking.

Anthony's Star of the Sea Room (coat required) is at 1360 N. Harbor Dr. (☎ 619/232-7408). Dining here is leisurely and prices are high. **Anthony's of La Jolla** is at 4120 La Jolla Village Dr. (☎ 619/457-5008).

The **San Diego Pier Café,** 885 W. Harbor Dr., Seaport Village (☎ 619/239-3968), attracts lots of families—and no wonder. Situated on its own pier, with wood-planked floors and a great view, it's a comfortable, casual spot for breakfast, lunch, or dinner. Children have their own menu at lunch and dinner, which features shrimp or fish and chips, chicken and chips, grilled cheese, and cheeseburgers ($4.95 each). It's the same menu at dinner. Some breakfasts come with a muffin, so toddlers can nibble on yours. Or there are pancakes, omelets, waffles, and side dishes, plus heuvos rancheros, breakfast burritos, and three versions of eggs Benedict. Prices are $2.50 to $9. Highchairs and boosters are available.

Adult dinner selections consist of lots of seafood entrees, such as Cajun-style barbecue shrimp, fish and chips, steak and garlic, shrimp and at least 10 other entrees. All entrees come with rice or potatoes, vegetables, and sourdough bread, and start at $9 and go up to $18.

Lunch off the regular menu runs $6–$13 for seafood fettuccine. Or there's fish, chicken, beef burgers, calamari sandwiches, and full lunches of seafood chili, sauteed scallops, fish tacos, a vegetable plate, or lots of salads.

Open weekdays from 7am to 9pm (to 10pm in summer) and on weekends from 7am to 10pm (to 11pm in summer). No reservations are accepted except for six or more. In summer the wait can be up to an hour; come before 7pm to avoid the lines, or put your name on the waiting list and walk around the village. Major credit cards are welcome. Parking in the village lot is validated.

Another Seaport Village restaurant draws lots of families. **The Jolly Roger,** 807 W. Harbor Dr., Seaport Village (☎ **619/233-4300**), is a chain restaurant featuring simple, reasonably priced food for breakfast, lunch, and dinner.

In addition to traditional breakfast fare, the menu lists Lite Breakfasts (with yogurt, egg substitutes, etc.), and hearty recipes such as frittata ranchera (an open-face omelet topped with all sorts of goodies). Full breakfasts run $3–$7.50. Kids 10 and under are served eggs, cereal, French toast fingers, or pancakes with a beverage included for around $2.

Lunch and dinner selections will satisfy almost everyone's taste. There are lots of appetizers, salads, sandwiches, and special dishes, such as chicken pot pie at lunch and barbecue baby back ribs at dinner. Nothing on the lunch menu is over $7.75. At dinner, you entree can run $6–$14.45. The combination dinners are a good deal at $10.95, and you can combine two entrees from a list that includes tempura shrimp, ribs, New York steak skewer, and red snapper. Junior can order the usual burgers, grilled cheese, fried chicken strips, turkey, or a cheese quesadilla. Lunch or dinner, with french fries and a beverage, runs $2–$3. Children also get a free sundae if they finish coloring their menu.

A happy hour each night provides free hors d'oeuvres from 4 to 7pm. In addition the standard drinks, more exotic libations are served, including special alcohol-free drinks for the kids.

Servers will provide highchairs and booster seats, and will warm baby food and bottles. There is a separate no-smoking section.

The Jolly Roger is open seven days a week: from 7am to 11pm weekdays, until midnight on weekends. Reservations are accepted, and senior citizens are given a discount. Major credit cards welcomed. Validated parking.

The Fish Market, 750 N. Harbor Dr., next door to Seaport Village (☎ **619/232-3474**), is an excellent family choice—as long as everyone likes fish. The large, pleasant restaurant seems to have its fair share of families with kids of all ages. The Fish Market folks own their own fishing boats ensuring a fresh catch for their restaurant customers. They also own part of an oyster farm in Washington, producing hybrid Westcott Bay oysters in pollution free water.

Children 12 and under eat for $3.95 and have choices such as shrimp or fish and chips, a Fish Market pizza, or pasta marinara. Their selection comes with ice cream and a beverage.

At lunch and dinner there are chowders and salads, numerous appetizer selections such as smoked fish, raw oysters and clams, and baked or steamed shellfish. Entrees include potatoes or rice, coleslaw, and bread. All the fish is fresh and can even be viewed first at the retail counter in the front of the restaurant. Items such as Alaskan Troll Chinook salmon, Hawaiian Ono, California Thresher shark (plus numerous other varieties of fish) come mesquite char-broiled, skewered, or grilled. For non-fish eaters there is a rib eye steak or chicken. Oyster bar selections are quick and delicious. Our favorite was seafood marinara with pasta—delicate red snapper in a mildly spicy marinara sauce over linguine. Wine and beer (and micro brews) are served. The dessert special is baked Alaska. Prices will always vary slightly, but standard entree prices at lunch are around $8 to $29 (for Maine lobster); portions at dinner are approximately two ounces larger and $2 to $4 more per entree. At dinner time, Oyster Bar items range $7.85–$19.35 for the restaurant's popular Dungeness crab cioppino.

Servers will provide highchairs and booster seats, and baby food and baby bottles can be warmed.

The restaurant is open daily from 11am to 10pm. The wait on Friday and Saturday in summer after 6:30 can be 45 minutes to an hour and a half. (In a hurry? Try for a seat at the Oyster Bar with the kids.) Weeknights aren't quite so busy. Reservations are accepted for 8 or more. Major credit cards are honored. There is metered parking in the lot (free after 6pm) and valet parking.

OLD TOWN AREA

Just outside of Bazaar del Mundo, at the end of Twiggs Street and under the arch leading to Casa de Lopez, is **Carlos Murphy's,** 3890 Twiggs St. (☎ **619/260-0305**). This big, open-air Mexican restaurant (with heating lamps) was built in 1835 for the family of Don Francisco de Lopez, one of the oldest Spanish families in the area. Carlos Murphy's is a chain of restaurants featuring satisfying Mexican choices such as chile rellenos, grilled fish tacos, super quesadillas, and shark, shrimp, and beef and chicken fajitas. There are also the standard combos which are served with rice and beans. Dinner choices average around $7, while lunch items can be had for under $5. Margaritas are taken seriously, and there are nonalcoholic special drinks, as well. There's a full bar and a Happy Hour.

Children are always provided for at Carlos Murphy's. A balloon artist arrives weekend evenings to create the puppies, hats, and snakes that make kids squeal. And on Sunday through Thursday evenings, children are charged one cent per pound of their weight for items ordered off the children's menu (12 years old and under). Their menu includes quesadillas, hot dogs, mini bean burritos, hamburgers, and tacos. Beverages are refilled for free. There's nothing over $3 on the children's menu.

Servers will warm baby bottles and baby food, and there are booster seats and highchairs. Be sure to make reservations, as the wait can be at least 45 minutes at prime times without them.

The restaurant is open Sunday through Thursday from 11am to 10pm, and Friday and Saturday food is served to 11pm. The parking is free, and major credit cards are welcome.

The **Guadalajara Grill,** 4105 Taylor St. (☎ **619/295-5111**), sister of the Tijuana restaurant of the same name, is a charming eatery in Old Town that offers Mexican food with a difference. Recipes are from the southern part of Mexico and require more ingredients and more complicated preparation than dishes from farther north. Extra care was given to the renovation of the building. A hand-painted mural lines one wall, and colorful plates and trays, along with stained-glass windows, liven the neutrals of the tile floors and adobe walls. There's a patio for outdoor dining.

Begin your meal with an appetizer of ceviche Acapulco or fried cilantro cheese ($6). A sizzling grill is brought to your table when you order chicken, beef, or shrimp fajitas or a combination. The meal includes soup or salad, beans, and tortillas, and costs $9–$14. Chef's specialties offer you something from a beef, pork, or chicken selection. If you like spicy, try the sabana arriera—beef filet cut thin and sautéed with olive oil, garlic, green onions, spices, and dry pasilla. Fish may be covered with cilantro butter sauce or simply steamed Veracruz style. There are also quesadillas, combination plates, and even vegetarian specialities. Food will cost you anywhere from $6 to $15. Finally a Mexican restaurant with something other than just flan for dessert! We can't resist the bunuelo, which is a deep-fried flour tortilla topped with vanilla ice cream, caramel, sugar, and cinnamon.

If you have youngsters 10 and under, you can order from a limited children's menu of a bean burrito, cheese quesadillas, a beef taco, or a cheese enchilada with rice and beans, for $3.50. Boosters and highchairs are provided. They will warm baby bottles and food in the kitchen. Special children's drinks can be ordered from the bar.

The Guadalajara Grill is open for lunch Monday through Friday from 11:30am to 4:30pm. Dinner is served Sunday through Thursday from 4:30 to 8:30pm and on Friday and Saturday to 2am. Sunday brunch is offered from 9am to 2pm. Reservations are accepted. Major credit cards are honored. There is free parking.

Can you wait? If so, put your name on the list for a seat at **Old Town Mexican Café y Cantina,** 2489 San Diego Ave., in Old Town (☎ **619/297-4330**). People line up at this lively, colorful Old Town tradition for a taste of fresh homemade tortillas, frosty margaritas, and familiar dishes like tacos, enchiladas, tostadas, and chiles rellenos. Dinner also adds chicken verde enchiladas, carne asada, and steak picado. A la carte items are in abundance. House specialties include carnitas (quite tasty), Mexican-style ribs, Old Town pollo (Mexican-style rotisserie chicken), and fajitas. A la carte items cost $2.35–$5.75, while the more complete dinners range from $5.25 to $11 for shrimp. Brunch will wake you up for sure. Chilaquiles are corn tortillas in hot chile sauce served with fried eggs and beans. Breakfast averages $5.50.

Kids 12 and under get more traditional offerings, all accompanied by tortillas. For the kids, lunch or dinner is a quesadilla, burger, bean burrito, or beef tacos at $1.75–$2.75. They can order breakfast for about $2. They can also spend time watching the ladies make the fresh tortillas in the front of the restaurant. We couldn't stop eating our tortillas.

Highchairs and booster seats are available, and specialty children's drinks can be ordered. There is a full and lively bar.

Open daily from 7am to 11pm. No reservations, but credit cards are accepted. Park on the street, in an Old Town parking lot, or in the restaurant's limited parking lot.

Rancho el Nopal Restaurant & Cantina, Bazaar del Mundo at 4016 Wallace St. (☎ **619/295-0584**), was formerly Hamburguesa Restaurant and Cantina. The kids still love the lively decorations and south-of-the-border colors. There's always something to draw their attention. Now the charming restaurant has a pleasant, spacious outdoor patio from which to enjoy a warm San Diego night.

The kids 12 and under still have their own selections such as a cheese enchilada, quesadilla, taco, cheese dog, burrito, or hamburger, each at $3.

The rest of the family can choose from a varied menu that includes Mexican favorites of enchiladas Suizas, chimichangas, and carne asada tacos. These choices run $6–$8. House specials include fajitas, chiles poblanos, Senor Wong chicken, and chicken tamales and cost $6–$9. Health-conscious travelers have a list of items ranging from chicken and black bean tostadas, fiesta fajitas, and enchiladas verdes de pollo. Each dish has an ingredient analysis as do the sides of black beans, rice, and guacamole. The special items are $4.50–$7. If these choices aren't enough, you can order salads, soups, hamburgers, or egg dishes, too.

Boosters and highchairs are available. Full bar.

The restaurant is open daily from 11am to 10pm. Reservations are accepted as are major credit cards. Park in Bazaar del Mundo.

El Indio Shop, 3695 India St. (☎ **619/299-0333**), is a 50-year-old San Diego institution known for its authentic, homemade tortillas. This location is convenient to Old Town, downtown San Diego, and the airport. It's the perfect spot for a quick, delicious meal to eat in, to take back to your hotel room, or to enjoy at the beach or park.

The cheese enchiladas are especially tasty, and go well with the crisp flavored chips. One enchilada with rice is $2.15. Orders such as the chicken burrito plate come with beans, rice, and chips for $4.20. Breakfast is also served, with items such as huevos rancheros and Mexican bakery goods.

A new Natural Choice menu offers items cooked with or from vegetables and seeds. For instance, you can order a vegetarian tamale made with seven fresh vegetables, or an enchilada filled with zucchini, chilies, tomato, onion, and spices. Prices for these selections don't exceed $3.

The children's selections are a well-priced $1.99. A burrito, taquito, quesadilla, or mini-enchiladas come with beans, French fries, chips, and an 8-ounce drink.

El Indio opens daily at 8am. Lunch and dinner are served until 9pm. No reservations are accepted. Some credit cards are honored. Park in the lot or on the street. Other locations include one in Pacific Beach at 4120 Mission Blvd., second floor (☎ **619/272-8226**), and another in San Ysidro at 115 W. Olive St. (☎ **619/690-1122**). A downtown location is at 409 F St. (☎ **619/239-8151**).

HOTEL CIRCLE/MISSION VALLEY

Looking like a rustic cabin set amid the pines, the **Hungry Hunter,** 2445 Hotel Circle (☎ **619/291-8074**), offers a relaxed ambience accented by brass lanterns, stone planters, and a hunter's green color scheme. It's down a slight hill, so look for the sign and the cabinlike building. Young children will enjoy the resident fireplace moosehead, nicknamed Bullwinkle. Families are welcome, and the staff has even been known to walk a crying child around the restaurant, allowing Mom and Dad to enjoy their meal.

A complete breakfast menu includes a selection of omelets and griddle favorites, plus hearty breakfasts that pair eggs with ham or prime rib or steak. Breakfasts run $3–$7.25. A "Just for Kids" selection consists of eggs or a short stack of pancakes, bacon or sausage, and milk or juice for $2.95. The lunch menu lists salads, sandwiches, and chicken and steak. A whiskey-peppercorn top sirloin steak is served with salad and fries for $7.95. Salads and sandwiches run $5–$7. Dinners feature seafood and steak, and come with a steaming cup of home-style soup and a lazy-Susan-style salad bar served right at your table. The steak, served several different ways, is priced $13.50–$19. Tempura shrimp costs $14.45, and a prime rib and Alaskan king crab combination dinner is pegged at $18. The house specialty is prime rib, which is offered in several serving sizes. From 4:30 to 5pm Monday through Thursday, menu entrees can be ordered at half price.

No children's menu is available at lunch, though the staff will be happy to split orders in the kitchen. At dinner, though, they can order prime rib and tempura shrimp at $6.95, with soup and salad and potatoes. Or there are thin-sliced ribs, a hamburger, or a grilled cheese for $3.95–$5.95. Booster seats and highchairs are provided. The staff will warm baby food and bottles. There are unlimited children's drinks (such as a Shirley Temple or Roy Rogers).

The Hungry Hunter is open for breakfast Monday through Friday from 7 to 10:30am, on Saturday from 8 to 11am, and on Sunday from 8am to 1:30pm. Lunch is served Monday through Friday from 11am to 2:30pm and on Saturday from 11:30am to 2pm. Dinner is served Monday through Thursday from 4:30 to 10pm, on Friday and Saturday 4 till 11pm. Reservations recommended. Major credit cards accepted. There's a parking lot adjacent.

D.W. Ranch Family Restaurant, 2438 Hotel Circle N. (☎ **619/297-3393**) can be found just across the street from the Hungry Hunter. Look for the sign for the River Valley Sports Center. This very casual coffee shop–style restaurant serves breakfast, lunch, and dinner.

Children 12 and under are charged $3.25 for either an egg, cottage fries, and toast; French toast; or hot cakes, each with milk or juice. At either lunch or dinner they have a number of items to choose from included a soft taco, grilled cheese, chicken nuggets, a burger, or fish and chips, each with french fries and a drink for $3.95.

All the usual breakfast items are offered on the regular menu, plus Mexican beef chorizo and eggs, a chicken fajita omelet, and breakfast burritos. Breakfasts range from $3 to $6 for eggs benedict. Lunch and dinner offerings are the same. The menu is fairly large. Here's a sampling: omelets, 11 different burgers, steaks, chicken, seafood, salads, sandwiches, and full dinners of short ribs, liver, and pork chops. You'll pay anywhere from $4.40 for a hamburger to $12 for steak and shrimp.

The restaurant's servers will warm baby bottles and baby food. Highchairs and booster seats are provided.

The restaurant is open every day from 6:30am to 9pm (later in summer). There are no reservations accepted, and the wait can be about 20 minutes during busy periods in summer. The kids can play on the grass near the golf course outside, and you can take them to the stream that runs through it. Parking is free. Visa and MasterCard are accepted.

HILLCREST

Not far from downtown San Diego and the Embarcadero is the **Corvette Diner,** 3946 Fifth Ave. (☎ **619/542-1001**). One step inside will take *some* of you back to the '50s and '60s, and the menu will remind you of when "he" used to say "made in the shade" and "she" used to say "what a fake-out." A real Corvette, of course, neon lights, and turquoise-colored booths create the atmosphere. There's plenty of loud music to drown out kvetchy kids, and lots of food choices to make your life easy. DJs spin your requests and take dedications seven nights a week. And a magician or other performer provides entertainment tableside on Tuesday, Wednesday, and Friday through Sunday.

The 12-and-under set can have spaghetti and a meatball, a baby burger and fries, a peanut butter and jelly, a corn dog and fries, chicken fingers, or a grilled cheese, plus a soft drink or milk and dessert for $3.95. The older ones can have salads, sandwiches, hamburgers, major entrees, and "blue plate" specials. Because you won't go broke here, reward yourselves with one of the decadent desserts ("Choco-peppermint smoothie" is one) or a real old-fashioned malted milk.

Booster seats and highchairs are available, and baby food and bottles can be warmed.

The restaurant is open Sunday through Thursday from 7am to 11pm and on Friday and Saturday from 8am to midnight. Since they don't accept reservations, you'd better get there by 5pm, or try it at lunchtime. Some major credit cards accepted. Valet and street parking.

---

5   What to See and Do

One of the reasons families keep coming back to San Diego again and again is that there's so much to see and do. Every time the children get a year older, there's always a new way to appreciate an old familiar sight.

BALBOA PARK

Every city in America should have a Balboa Park. Put a trip to this wonderful 1,400-acre park near the top of your list of places to visit. Known as the cultural hub of the city, it's a park that has something to offer everyone.

Most of the buildings in the park today were built for the Panama–California Exposition of 1915–16 and the California Pacific International Exposition of 1935–36. The first thing that will strike you is the beauty of the buildings, then the expansive layout of the park with its bountiful gardens, green lawns, and stately trees. We like to visit off-season when it's not so crowded, but the summer weekend crowds lend a festive air to the surroundings. You can eat at **Cafe del Rey Morro** or the **Sculpture Garden Cafe,** both in the park. This is the home of the famous **Old Globe Theater,** where you may find some performances quite suitable for your entire family. Although there are 11 buildings dedicated to the arts and museums, not all of them will appeal to children.

First-time visitors should make their initial stop the **Balboa Park Visitor Center** (☎ **619/239-0512**). Take Sixth Avenue to Laurel and turn into the park down El Prado. If you park in the Plaza de Panama lot, you'll find the visitor center nearby. Be sure to ask about the Passport, a good discount ticket that will save adults money on admission to museums (it's not much of a savings on children's tickets, though).

Don't plan to do everything in one day, there's just too much. Be sure to leave some time to just wander.

We like to visit the **San Diego Museum of Man** (☎ **619/239-2001**), which features exhibits describing human and cultural development over the ages. The kids love to linger in front of the exhibits devoted to Native Americans and their crafts and tools, as well as the other interesting displays. Our daughter was fascinated, and a little frightened, by "Lucy," a cast of the oldest human ancestor (only 11 other museums in the world have this cast). Wednesday through Sunday, there are special live exhibits, such as tortilla making—we not only watched this, but were able to sample the result. We also watched as a Native American artist carefully wove brightly colored yarn into a blanket on a loom.

The museum is open daily from 10am to 4:30pm. Admission is $4 for adults, $2 for children 13–18, $1 for children 6–12; under 6, free.

Airplane lovers really appreciate the **Aerospace Museum and International Aerospace Hall of Fame,** 2001 Pan American Plaza (☎ **619/234-8291** and **619/232-8322**). World War II fighter planes, including those of our former enemies, are everywhere—some hang from the ceiling as if they are really in flight. There are even planes from World War I, exhibits honoring early space exploration, and a room devoted to the accomplishments of women in space and aviation. Open daily from 10am to 4:30pm. Adults pay $4 admission; children under 18, $1; under 6, free.

An absolute must-see for school-age children is the **Reuben H. Fleet Space Theater and Science Center,** located right near the huge fountain (☎ 619/238-1233). In the Space Theater, the OMNIMAX films are projected onto a 76-foot dome, which seems to lift you out of your seats and right into outer space. Several different films alternate daily. Youngsters always want to return to the Science Center, where more than 60 hands-on exhibits let them become actively involved in learning science firsthand.

The sand pendulum lets them make interesting and often unpredictable designs with sand from a free-swinging pendulum. The Bernoulli ball demonstrates an aerodynamic principle with a colorful beach ball that floats over a stream of air.

Open Sunday through Thursday from 9:30am to 9pm, and on Friday and Saturday till 10:30pm. Science Center admission is $2.50 for adults, $1.25 for ages 5–15; children 4 and under, free. Tickets for the OMNIMAX Space Theater (which includes admission to the Science Center, too) are $6 for adults, $4.50 for seniors, and $3.50 for kids 5–15; children 4 and under are free. The price of tickets to the laser show varies.

Most children love natural history museums, and Balboa Park's **Natural History Museum,** located at the east end of El Prado (☎ 619/232-3821), is no exception. Complete with a few resident dinosaurs, the museum focuses on the geology, plants, and animals of the Southwest. The museum is open daily in winter from 9:30am to 4:30pm (until 5:30pm in summer); there are later hours on Thursday. Admission is $6 for adults, $5 for seniors, $2 for children 6–17, under 6, free.

Sports fans get a kick out of the **Hall of Champions** (☎ 619/234-2544), which chronicles the exploits of San Diego's finest athletes, who represent more than 40 sports. There are videotapes of various important sports events, as well as jerseys, shoes, photos, and other items that will keep fans busy for a long time.

Open daily from 10am to 4:30pm. Admission is $3 for adults, $1 for children 6–17; under 6, free.

We also visit the **Marie Hitchcock Puppet Theater** (☎ 619/466-7128), located in Pan American Plaza, next to the Automotive Museum. The short shows have been entertaining three generations of children (since 1948). They give very young children their own activity for the day. We've seen youngsters jump into the aisles to participate, and they love to sing along when the puppeteer gives the word. Show times are irregular, so call ahead. There are special Easter, Halloween, and Christmas shows. Admission is $2 for adults, $1.50 for children 2–14; free for children under 2.

You mustn't forget the **Model Railroad Museum,** in the Casa de Balboa, on the south side of El Prado, west of the fountain and the Reuben H. Fleet Space Theater (☎ 619/696-0199). Look for the two-story semaphore that flags the museum's downstairs entrance. (Pushing a stroller? Take the elevator east of the stairs.) Friendly, grandfatherly hobbyists wearing blue-and-white-striped caps loom giantlike over miniature mountains and rock-strewn desert gorges. With a sound like rushing water, tiny trains glide past turn-of-the-century stations and villages, cross high trestles, and emerge from mouse-size tunnels. A large LGB toy train, called "The Big Train," has been added, and the Lionel Lines layout has been expanded and several more "industries" have

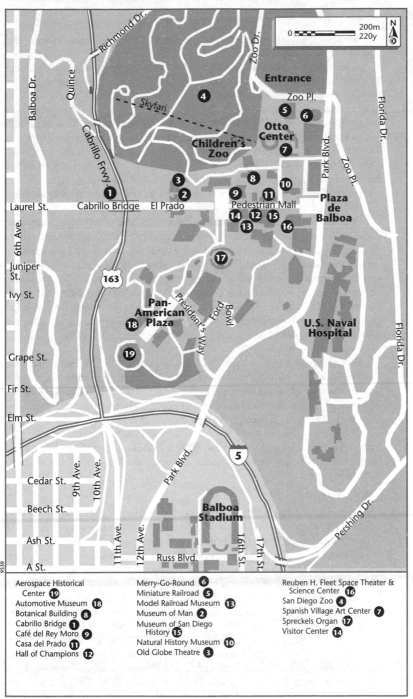

Balboa Park

Aerospace Historical Center **19**
Automotive Museum **18**
Botanical Building **8**
Cabrillo Bridge **1**
Café del Rey Moro **9**
Casa del Prado **11**
Hall of Champions **12**

Merry-Go-Round **6**
Miniature Railroad **5**
Model Railroad Museum **13**
Museum of Man **2**
Museum of San Diego History **15**
Natural History Museum **10**
Old Globe Theatre **3**

Reuben H. Fleet Space Theater & Science Center **16**
San Diego Zoo **4**
Spanish Village Art Center **7**
Spreckels Organ **17**
Visitor Center **14**

been attached. Visitors view the half-dozen exhibits through Plexiglas. Viewing plat-forms have been added for the kids.

The museum is open the first Tuesday of the month, and every Wednesday through Friday, from 11am to 4pm. On Saturday and Sunday, it stays open until 5pm. Admission is $5 for adults; children 15 and under are free.

There are even more diversions at this magnificent park. Take the kids for a walk to the **Spreckels Organ Pavilion,** between Pan American Plaza and Plaza de Panama. It's a wonderful old outdoor concert area, and on Sunday there are free organ con-certs. Or visit the **Lily Pond** near the Botanical Building and the Casa del Prado Build-ing (☎ **619/234-8901**). Its surprisingly peaceful even on the busiest days. Watch out, though: Your toddlers will want to catch the squirmy goldfish. Some children have never seen lily ponds before, and these are wondrous natural sights to introduce them to. It's open Tuesday through Sunday, from 10am to 4pm.

Walk up to the huge fountain at the **Plaza de Balboa.** Usually there's some sort of street entertainment going on—a mime, perhaps, or the exquisitely scary painted tribe members we watched doing their native dances. Even on winter weekends you might see the balloon maker who forms those skittish pieces of plastic into magical animals in front of the adoring eyes of boys and girls who can stand there for as long as an hour waiting for theirs. Then walk over to **Spanish Village** (☎ **619/233-9050**) to watch artists at work in one of more than 35 studios. You might see a sculpture being crafted, a pot being thrown, or a piece of jewelry being created, as well as dis-plays by the Mineral and Gem Society and the Enamel Guild. The village is open daily from 11am to 4pm.

If you've made it through Spanish Village, you won't be too far from the **carousel** and the **miniature train** rides adjacent to the zoo entrance. The carousel ride is open daily in summer, on winter weekends, and on legal holidays (except Thanksgiving and Christmas), from 11am to 5pm, and costs $1 per ride. The train will take you through five acres of the park. It operates the same hours as the carousel.

If you didn't notice it yourself, your children will probably have discovered it on their own—it's the huge **Moreton Bay fig tree** located near the village. The colossal roots and fantastic way in which nature created this setting make this a terrific con-versation piece.

SAN DIEGO ZOO

Located in Balboa Park off Park Boulevard, the San Diego Zoo (☎ **619/234-3153** or **619/231-1515**) is a must-see for all ages. Included in the vast array of animals in open-air settings here (more than 4,000 animals of 800 species) are a surprising num-ber of rare, exotic, and endangered species. The zoo is also famous for having the larg-est number of parrots and parrotlike birds ever assembled. Covering 100 acres, the zoo is set in a remarkable botanical garden—be sure to look around at the bountiful plants that have been growing here for about 75 years. Known as one of the finest zoos in the world for its innovative design, the zoo has a three-acre simulated ecosys-tem called **Tiger River.** This unique exhibit sets up an experience: Instead of walking from cage to cage, or from enclosure to enclosure, visitors walk along pathways that lead to groups of animals and plants coexisting as they would in their natural habitat. Predators are separated from their natural prey, but it's done so subtly you hardly know it. As you go through this tropical rain forest, complete with humidity and mist, you feel as if you're actually visiting an exotic natural environment. It's educational for the children—and parents too.

If you haven't been to the zoo lately, you'll be pleased to learn there are two new exhibits: **Meerkat Manor** and **Australian Outback.** The meerkats (African mongooses) rent space to some funny-named enjoyable animals such as Kenyan dik-diks and bat-eared foxes, while in the Australian Outback, wallabies, wallaroos, and emus play hosts.

The San Diego Zoo also has a well-known **Children's Petting Zoo,** which is geared to 4-year-olds, but can be enjoyed by any age. Most youngsters never want to leave the animals. They enjoy petting them, watching eggs being hatched, and viewing the animal nursery where the little newborns are fed and taken care of. Admission is free.

Besides walking, there are two more ways to see this large zoo. A 40-minute narrated **bus tour** covers three miles of the zoo's interior. The open-sided double-decker buses leave every few minutes from the zoo station, to the right of the Flamingo Lagoon, just inside the entrance. This is a good way to see the zoo if you don't have much time to spend. The tour covers a good 80% of the grounds. But be sure your child can sit through 40 minutes on a bus! The bus leaves daily from 9am to 4pm. Adults pay $3; children 3–15, $2.50; free for kids 2 and under.

Another way to go, and one that's fun just for itself, is the **Skyfari Aerial Tramway,** which travels over the zoo from one side to the other—170 feet in the air. You'll find the eastern cable lift at the Reptile House, at the left of the entrance, and the western lift at Horn and Hoof Mesa. The tram runs daily from 10am. The eastern terminal closes at 4pm; the western, at 4:15pm. Round-trip fares are free. And people movers are placed strategically throughout the zoo to help you get around.

There are several free animal shows too. The performances and schedules change, so check at the entrance for current information. Plan to spend the whole day at the zoo, but even then don't expect to see everything. Figure that if you've seen some of the main highlights and the Children's Zoo, you've been successful. If at all possible, plan to view the animal exhibits when the park is least full—early morning or late in the day. That's also usually the time when the animals are the most active.

People-food is available at a variety of places, including the new Treehouse, a four-story marketplace of giftshops, a café, and outdoor concessions. Stroller and wheelchair rentals are available near the entrance. You can also purchase disposable diapers there, or buy diapers and baby wipes near the exit in the Jungle Bazaar Gift Shop. Baby-changing facilities are located in the men's and women's restrooms.

From July to Labor Day the hours are 9am to 5pm daily. Between Labor Day and the end of June the zoo closes at 4pm daily. General zoo admission is $13 for adults, $6 for children 3–15; kids 2 and under, free. Check at your hotel about discount tickets.

SAN DIEGO WILD ANIMAL PARK

The animals run free—but the visitors don't—at the San Diego Wild Animal Park (☎ 619/480-0100 or 619/747-8702). Take I-15 north to Via Rancho Parkway (45 minutes from downtown San Diego) and follow the signs. Opened in 1972, this 2,200 acre wildlife preserve is home to more than 3,000 wild animals.

You enter the park through **Nairobi Village,** an area that includes shops, restaurants, animal enclosures, and a walk-through aviary. Half a dozen animal shows are performed in various places throughout the park. Children enjoy petting gentle deer and sheep in the **Petting Kraal** (note that the baby animals visit the Kraal from 9 to 11am daily) and viewing the **Animal Care Center,** where baby animals are kept and fed. **Hawk Talks** give an opportunity to see rare birds close up and learn all sorts of information about them from their trainers.

A narrated five-mile **monorail safari** glides along the periphery of four ecological regions: the swamps and highlands of Asia, the South African veldt, the North African mountains, and the East African savanna. For best viewing, sit on the right side of the monorail and bring a pair of binoculars. The animals sleep in the heat of midday (which can get up to 100° in late summer), so plan to go in the morning or early evening.

Infants and toddlers may find the 50-minute ride tiring, but children over the age of 5 will delight in discovering that those gray boulders ("See? Over there, under that tree, near the muddy pond . . .") are really rhinos. They'll also spot wild horses, tigers, cheetahs, giraffes, zebras, impalas, gnus, mountain goats, ostriches, and others. A special treat, particularly in late spring and early summer, are the many animal babies. The park is proud of its success in breeding endangered species.

All areas are stroller-accessible, and strollers may be rented. Women's restrooms have diaper-changing facilities. A nursing room is provided in the restroom near the monorail. You can purchase disposable diapers in the giftshop.

From June 19 through Labor Day, the park is open daily from 9am to 6pm; the rest of the year the park closes at 4pm. Admission prices are $17.45 for adults, $10.45 for children 3–11, free for children under 2. All tickets include the monorail. Parking costs $3.

SEA WORLD

San Diego's Sea World has so many small experiences to savor that people sometimes forget that there's more to the park than Baby Shamu. Sea World is located at 1720 S. Shores Rd., Mission Bay (☎ **619/226-3901**). To get to the park, exit west off I-5 onto Sea World Drive. Although we devote only one day to Sea World each time we visit, you could easily spend two days there (especially with youngsters who tire easily). Families return year after year—either to see their favorite exhibits again, or to see the ones they missed the last time.

Sea World is a theme park dedicated to the creatures of the sea and the sea itself. And though there are a great many things to see and do, we will just highlight some of the best.

Rocky Point Preserve is the former Dolphin Pool where visitors relished the chance to feed and—when they were lucky—touch the docile dolphins. You can still buy those fish and feed one of the world's favorite animals. But the pool has been redesigned to show more of the dolphins' natural habitat and has added some educational information. Be sure to hold on to that smelly fish food so the sea gulls don't swoop down and grab it out of your hand! We've lost many a "plate" of fish to those fast gulls.

The newest park exhibit/ride is **Mission: Bermuda Triangle,** a motion-based theater which gives you the sensation of diving aboard a submersible craft. The idea here is to explore the mysterious Bermuda Triangle joining scientists as they conduct experiments and research into the unknown area of ocean where supposedly thousands of lives and hundreds of ships and planes have disappeared.

The **California tidepools** is a most wonderful exhibit, and it educates children without their even knowing it. Park guides explain the wonders you see, including spiny lobsters and sea anemones. We touched our very first starfish here, and were able to gently examine it and feel it before we returned it to its natural habitat living quarters.

The **Penguin Encounter** is another special exhibit. It's set up so beautifully that you can see nearly all of these comical, overdressed birds as they strut around their 5,000-square-foot re-created Antarctic environment. Once we were lucky to be there at feeding time, and were fascinated by the interaction between the humans and these now-dependent polar birds.

The beautiful black-and-white **killer whales** are the biggest draw, and the show has gotten better now that the trainers are allowed to get back in the water with these mammals. A multimedia show has been added, too. Baby Shamu is a real "ham." Be sure you don't sit in the bottom rows, although the kids love to get splashed when the whales perform. There's also a dolphin and whale show and a hysterically funny sea lion and otter show.

The **Forbidden Reef** is a two-part exhibit which includes a display of the largest collection of California moray eels anywhere. A hands-on exhibit allows guests to touch and feed bat rays. We finally got up the courage to touch and were amazed at how velvety they feel. Be sure to let the kids feed the rays—it's okay because their stingers have been removed.

The **Shark Encounter** is probably more frightening for adults than for children. The 8- and 10-year-olds we talked to thought it was great fun. The younger children didn't really understand what they were seeing. A 60-foot submerged viewing tube allows you to "walk" through shark-infested waters.

Cap'n Kid's World, with its two acres of climbing and bouncing paraphernalia, and **Cap'n Kid's Boardwalk,** a game and video arcade, are two areas we save for the end of our visit. If the kids still have some energy left, this is a good place to let them get rid of it!

There are many more shows, aquaria, and exhibits. In the summer, when the park remains open until 11pm, there are lots of evening special events. Strollers and wheelchairs can be rented just within the entrance. Women's bathrooms have separate diaper-changing facilities. Disposable diapers can be bought at Cap'n Kids World, not far from the entrance. There's one main first-aid station and three satellites (in the summer, nine nurses are on staff full time). Outdoor food stands are everywhere. Harborside Café is the sit-down restaurant near the lagoon.

Sea World is open daily from 9am to dusk. In the summer, including July 4, it's open from 9am to 11pm. Adults pay $27.95 admission; children 3–11, $19.95; under 3, free. Ask at your hotel about discounted tickets for Sea World. Parking is $5, and the lot is huge.

THE EMBARCADERO

A hundred years ago, most people who visited San Diego arrived by ship. They came ashore at what is now the Embarcadero on Harbor Drive, just north of Seaport Village, between Market and Hawthorne Streets. Today the area has restaurants, a bayside boardwalk, a three-ship maritime museum, and plenty to explore.

Unless one of the big white Love Boat cruise ships is in town, the most prominent ship you'll see is the *Star of India,* a restored 1863 merchant sailing vessel and one of the three ships that make up the **Maritime Museum,** located at 1306 N. Harbor Dr. (☎ **619/234-9153**). Park your strollers with the ticket taker and turn your tots loose in the 19th century. They'll climb on coiled ropes as thick as boa constrictors, play pirate on the poop deck, and ask you what a chamber pot was used for. In the children's cabin they see toys and a small rocking horse. The ship was used to transport emigrants from London to New Zealand.

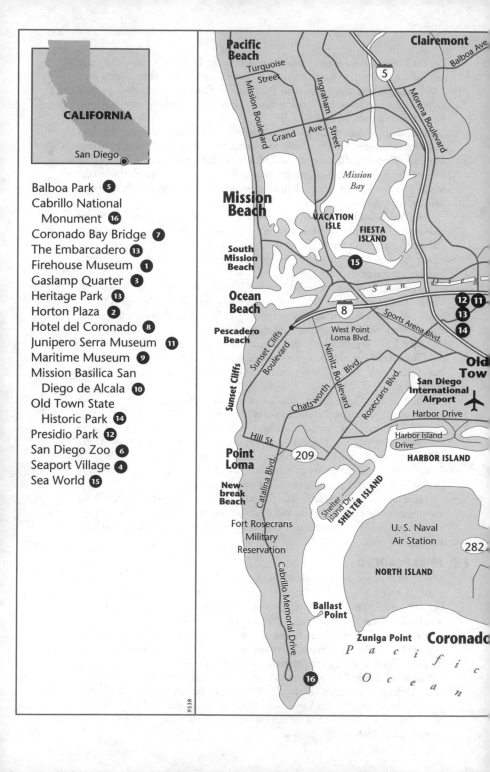

CALIFORNIA

San Diego

Balboa Park **5**
Cabrillo National
    Monument **16**
Coronado Bay Bridge **7**
The Embarcadero **13**
Firehouse Museum **1**
Gaslamp Quarter **3**
Heritage Park **13**
Horton Plaza **2**
Hotel del Coronado **8**
Junipero Serra Museum **11**
Maritime Museum **9**
Mission Basilica San
    Diego de Alcala **10**
Old Town State
    Historic Park **14**
Presidio Park **12**
San Diego Zoo **6**
Seaport Village **4**
Sea World **15**

Date Street

Upis Street

①

Cedar Street

Beech Street

Ash Street

Drive

Highway

Columbia Street

A Street

B Street

4th Ave.

5th Ave.

6th Ave.

7th Ave.

8th Ave.

9th Ave.

10th Ave.

11th Ave.

C Street

Broadway

②

Harbor

Pacific

E Street

F Street

③

G Street

State Street

Market Street

Union Street

Front Street

1st Ave.

2nd Ave.

3rd Ave.

④

DOWNTOWN

Harbor Drive

Island Avenue

J Street

K Street

Vista Rd.

Linda

Friars Rd.

River

⑩

8

0   2 mi
2.4 km

N

⑤

Balboa Park

⑥

Pacific Hwy.

5

1st Ave.

1st

See inset

Ash Street

Broadway

Market Street

SAN DIEGO

805

⑨

S   a   n

3rd St.

4th St.

Orange Ave.

⑦

San Diego-Coronado Bay Bridge (Toll)

D   i   e   g   o

B   a   y

National Ave.

Logan Ave.

Euclid Ave.

National City

Division St.

8th St.

⑧

Coronado Beach

Silver Strand

75

5

18th St.

805

Youngsters 7 and older will enjoy the miniature ships in bottles and maritime miscellany on board the 1898 ferryboat *Berkeley,* as well as running across the gang-plank to the 1904 luxury yacht *Medea.*

The Maritime Museum is open daily from 9am to 8pm. A boarding pass good for all three ships costs $6 for adults, $4 for children 13–16, $2 for children 6–12; under 5, free.

If you visit the Embarcadero on a weekend, by all means attend a **navy ship's open house**—perhaps a submarine, aircraft carrier, or destroyer will be in port. Kids love the ladderlike stairways that go through holes in the deck, playing captain on the bridge, and asking questions of the hospitable crew. Visit between 1 and 4pm. The treat is free, but there may be up to an hour's wait.

See the city from the bay via one of the harbor tours. The **San Diego Harbor Excursion,** at the foot of Broadway at Harbor Drive (☎ 619/234-4111, or toll free 800/44-CRUISE) runs tours daily. There are one- and two-hour excursions that go under the Coronado Bay Bridge on the way to view navy ships. The shorter trip is best for smaller children; it's fine to take strollers aboard. Bring sweaters or windbreakers even if the weather seems warm. The one-hour tour costs $10 for adults, $8 for seniors. The two-hour excursion runs $15 for adults, $13 for seniors. Children 3–12 are charged half price. Under-3s are free at any time.

The **San Diego Bay Ferry** (same address and phone number as the Harbor Excursion, above) takes you to and from Coronado in 15 minutes. The ferry leaves daily, on the hour, from 9am to 9pm weekdays, on Friday and Saturday till 10pm. It lands at the Ferry Landing Marketplace in Coronado and returns every hour on the half hour, beginning at 9:30am. The fare is $2 each way, 50¢ for bicycles (or an all-day pass for $4). Purchase tickets at the San Diego Harbor Excursion's ticket booth. In Coronado, pick them up at the Coronado Ferry Co. at the Ferry Landing Marketplace. Once you're in Coronado, you won't have any trouble getting around. You can walk or rent a bike. The Electric Shuttle makes its way up and down Orange Avenue.

The ships of **Hornblower Invader Cruises** leave from 1066 N. Harbor Dr. (☎ 619/234-8687) on one- and two-hour tours that sail past the Pacific Fleet, under the Coronado Bay Bridge, and through the San Diego Harbor. Cruises leave daily, with nightly dinner cruises available. There are four one-hour cruises per day, and one departure for the two-hour trip. Adults pay $10 for the one-hour tour, $15 for two hours. Children 12 and under pay half price for all cruises. Call for dinner cruise prices. There's also a Sunday Brunch cruise from 10:30am to 1pm. Adults pay $29.95, seniors $27.95, children $17.

You can't miss the colorful building of the **Children's Museum of San Diego,** 200 W. Island Ave. (☎ 619/233-KIDS) near Seaport Village and the Convention Center. Inside is art-making in the Art Zone and Incunabula, where toddlers under 3½ can play. There are also experiential and interactive exhibits and a stage for impromptu plays. Much can be done here on a large scale, as the interior of this old warehouse is huge.

The museum is open Tuesday through Saturday from 10am to 4:30pm, and Sunday from 11am to 4:30pm. Closed Monday. Admission for adults and children 2 and older is $4, seniors are $2, kids under 2 are free. Park on the street.

HISTORIC SIGHTS

Despite San Diego's venerable status as the birthplace of California, the number of historic sights found here isn't overwhelming. The ones that follow will be enjoyed by young and old alike. Most have vast outdoor areas surrounding them, good for strolling, picnicking, or playing.

Old Town/Bazaar del Mundo

Old Town San Diego State Historic Park is the site of San Diego's roots. From the north, take I-5 south to the Old Town Avenue exit. From downtown, take I-5 northwest to the Old Town Avenue exit. From Mission Valley, take I-8 west to the Taylor Street exit, follow Taylor south, cross the railroad tracks, then turn left into the parking lot. The Old Town trolley will shuttle you to Old Town. From Harbor Island, take Rosecrans Street east across Pacific Hwy. right into Old Town.

Only six square blocks in size, Old Town makes a short but interesting walking tour for the whole family. Stop by the **Park Headquarters** at 4002 Wallace St., San Diego, CA 92110 (☎ 619/220-5423), for a map of a self-guided walking tour ($2).

As the first European settlement in California, Old Town was the hub of San Diego's life from 1821 to 1872. Original buildings from the city's Mexican period still stand, as well as some from its early American period. The oldest is an adobe building dating from 1827. You'll see where the first American flag was raised. Your children will enjoy looking at the old one-room Mason Street schoolhouse, and will have a good time poking through the Seeley Stables, where they will find a fascinating collection of stagecoaches and other horse-drawn vehicles and a wonderful collection of western memorabilia. An 18-minute slide show about the history of transportation in Old Town is just short enough to hold kids' attention. It's shown daily, every hour on the hour, from 11am to 4pm, and is free with admission to the stables (adults pay $2; children 6–17, $1; under 6, free).

There are other historical buildings on and off the tour that you might want to see. It depends on the stamina of your children. **La Casa de Estudillo** is one that won't take long to tour. The one-story adobe house dating from 1827 will stimulate conversation as you view what life was like in those days.

The nice thing about Old Town is that it makes a pleasant place to spend the day. Just walking around the park and enjoying the outdoor scenery will entice you to pop your head into buildings along your path—not a bad way to sightsee. And there's a free one-hour guided walking tour that leaves daily (except Thanksgiving and Christmas Days) at 2pm from the Park Headquarters next door to the Rancho Nogal Restaurant.

You'll find public restrooms across from the stables on Calhoun Street and behind Racine and Laramie's Tobacco Store. A third one can be found at Park Headquarters. The park is stroller-accessible. Parking in the park itself is quite limited. There are parking lots on the outskirts, but be prepared to walk. There's one between San Diego Avenue and Twiggs Street and one on Taylor Street near Pacific Hwy.

Bazaar del Mundo, located on Juan Street, is a lively marketplace of shops and food-to-go and sit-down restaurants, most with a Mexican flavor. Set within courtyards and surrounded by lush trees, red-tile roofs, festive gardens, and fountains, it's a fun place to take the family. Our kids love to stop for a sugary-sweet churro (long rolls of dough fried and dipped in sugar) and then accompany us into the little boutiques and art shops. We stop to watch a lady preparing tortillas by hand right near Casa del Pico restaurant. Sometimes there's entertainment going on and we stop for a look. (For information on the sit-down restaurants, see "Where to Eat," above.)

Several other small retail areas in Old Town beckon curious shoppers. At **Squibob Square,** adjacent to the visitor center at San Diego Avenue and Twiggs Street, costumed craftspeople purvey their wares. **Old Town Mercado** has a number of import shops on Congress Street, across from Casa de Machado y Stewart. **Old Town Esplanade** is not only a Mexican marketplace, it's where art shows, craft demonstrations, and strolling musicians gather on weekends. It's located near Conde Street, San Diego Avenue, and Congress Street. If your children have never seen or heard a mariachi band, this is the place to take them—no doubt they'll think the instruments are interesting. Park in the Old Town State Park lot, and walk three blocks.

Serra Museum and Presidio Park

On the top of a hill east of Old Town State Historic Park, overlooking Mission Valley, is the **Serra Museum,** part of lushly landscaped **Presidio Park** (☎ 619/297-3258).

The museum looks so much like a mission that many people assume it is one. Actually, what's left of the original structures—a mission and presidio, or walled city—are under grass-covered mounds on the hillside below the museum. This is the birthplace of California, the home of the first Spanish settlers, founded in 1769 by Fr. Junipero Serra. Early San Diegans began moving into the area that is now Old Town in the 1820s. The museum and park were completed in 1929.

Museum exhibits of early mission and Native American artifacts will interest children of the fourth-grade level and up. Kids of all ages pretend they're soldiers in the Spanish garrison as they climb the tower's steep stairs and peer out narrow windows set in thick walls. Pictures of the old San Diego can be compared to today's sites.

Grassy slopes below the museum are steep enough in places for a good roll (lie on your side, arms over your head, and kick off!). Plan a picnic, walk the trails, and enjoy the views.

Museum hours are Tuesday through Saturday from 10am to 4:30pm and on Sunday from noon to 4:30pm; closed major holidays. The park is free; museum admission is $3 for adults, but children under 12 are free.

Mission San Diego de Alcala

California's first mission, founded by Fray Serra on Presidio Hill in 1769, was moved to its present Mission Valley location in 1774. It's located just east of the stadium at 10818 San Diego Mission Rd. (☎ 619/281-8449). The restored church echoes history in its thick adobe walls, decorated alcoves, and tiled archways. There is a small museum of artifacts, a bell tower, a garden, and a courtyard.

Children 7 and older will enjoy the tote-a-tape tour. For $1.50, you can rent a portable tape recorder that provides a narrated tour of the mission and details the lifestyle of the early Native American and Franciscan inhabitants.

Because this is a popular place for weddings and funerals, and masses are hourly all day Sunday, the best time to visit is during the week. No snacks or refreshments are available, and because of the many stairs, stroller access is limited.

Open daily from 9am to 5pm; closed Thanksgiving and Christmas days. Admission is $2 for adults; $1 for students and seniors; 50¢ for children under 12.

Cabrillo National Monument/Point Loma Lighthouse

Cabrillo National Monument (☎ 619/557-5450) sits atop the southern tip of Point Loma, a peninsula that forms the west side of San Diego Bay. Take I-8 to the Rosecrans Street exit. Go west toward the beaches and turn right on Canon Street, then go up Canon, make a left on Catalina Boulevard, and drive all the way to the end. The main attraction is also a local landmark: the restored 1855 **Old Point Loma Lighthouse.**

Older children can imagine living there 100 years ago. Would they have created ornate picture frames from seashells, like the ones in the lighthouse parlor?

Films geared to school-age children are shown in the auditorium near the visitor center. They describe how Portuguese explorer Juan Rodriguez Cabrillo discovered San Diego Bay in 1542; another explains the migration of the gray whales, which can be viewed from the point from December through February.

Often-overlooked areas include the bayside trail and the tidepools. Look for the signs or ask directions at the visitor center. These side trips are ideal for children 7 and older; younger children won't enjoy hiking back up the steep trail, and you'll worry about them climbing slippery rocks. Inquire at the visitor center for current schedules.

The **Visitor Information Center** is located at the east end of the parking lot and is open during park hours. It and the lighthouse are easily stroller-accessible. Restrooms have diaper-changing facilities. Vending machines provide snacks.

Summer hours are 9am to sunset daily; fall through spring, it's open from 9am to 5:15pm daily. Admission is $4 per car.

OUTDOOR ACTIVITIES

There are beaches for every purpose in San Diego and the surrounding areas. The 70 miles of sand and varied water conditions enable the town to specialize. The 53 county parks offer unlimited choices.

Beaches and Parks

The green lawns, wide paved walkways, playgrounds, and sandy beaches of man-made **Mission Bay Park** encompass seven square miles of San Diego Bay. The park entrance can be found at 2688 E. Mission Bay Dr., off I-5 just north of I-8—take the Clairemont Drive exit (☎ **619/221-8901**). Dotted around the bay are resort hotels, marinas, sportfishing docks, restaurants, campgrounds, and numerous picnic tables and fire rings. On the south side is Sea World. There is no admission charge. Parking is plentiful; you can get to the many lots from East Mission Bay Drive, a frontage road that runs between Calif. 5 along the east edge of the bay. The area is crowded only during summer and holiday weekends.

Check with the **Mission Bay Visitor Information Center** (☎ **619/276-8200**) for information on San Diego area attractions. The staff can also make hotel reservations, often with a 10%–50% discount. This is a private facility not affiliated with Mission Bay Park itself. The office is right at the park entrance.

Right near the Hilton Hotel (between Fiesta Island and the Hilton) is the new **Tecolote Shores Play Area,** an outdoor sand-filled playground with colorful climbing "things" and playground equipment.

In addition to renting sailboards, sailboats (including Hobie Cats), waterskis, kayaks, and powerboats from the **Mission Bay SportCenter,** 1010 Santa Clara Place (☎ **619/488-1004**), you can sign up your kids for the center's summer youth camp. For 12- to 15-year-olds, one-week sessions in basic and intermediate sailing and surfing cost $115. Lessons in racing, windsurfing, and sailing catamarans runs $120, while one week of waterski instruction will cost $140. A session for children 6–8 includes a variety of water sports, including kayaking and sailing. There are two sessions per day, each lasting three hours.

Instructors are certified in CPR, first aid, and advanced lifesaving, and waterski instructors have Coast Guard licensing. Children must pass a swim test. Sessions begin in June and end in August. Advance reservations are suggested.

The SportCenter is open in summer, daily from 10am to 6pm; in winter, daily except Tuesday and Wednesday from 11am to 4:30pm. Youth camp begins at 9am. Next to the SportCenter is a children's playground and public basketball court.

The shoreline of La Jolla is one of San Diego's loveliest. There are parks, inlets for swimming and diving, and caves to explore. The Côte d'Azur ambience is enhanced by resorts, hotels, winding cliffside streets, and Mediterranean-style homes.

Parking can be a problem, except early in the morning. Expect to do some walking. Leave your car along the south end of Prospect Street, near the La Jolla Museum of Contemporary Art, and walk one block west to the ocean.

Your first stop will be the **Children's Pool Beach,** at the foot of Jenner Street, where you easily could spend the day. This sandy beach, sheltered by a crescent-shaped concrete breakwater, is guarded by a lifeguard in a glass-enclosed tower. Showers and restrooms are handy. There are rocks to climb and a cave to explore—all ideal for children over 7. Younger ones should be watched carefully—the water gets deep quickly and the rocks can be slippery. Be sure to walk along the top of the breakwater. It has a sturdy guard rail, and children of all ages enjoy looking out to sea and watching waves foam, crash, and recede on rocks and tidepools a few feet below. This is considered the most popular family beach, and the scuba-diving and skindiving are considered unparalleled here.

From the Children's Pool, stroll northeast along the coast past the wide green lawns and tall, slender palms of **Ellen Scripps Park** (a good place to picnic). Continue up Coast Boulevard, past the beach at the cove. As you do so, look over the edge of the concrete retaining wall; we watched pelicans cruise the cliffs, squirrels scurry, and a seagull guard a nest that contained two brown-speckled chicks. The ocean below is home to the **San Diego–La Jolla Underwater Park,** a haven for divers and snorkelers.

Your walk up the steep hill will be rewarded by a well-stocked shell shop, **La Jolla Cave and Shell Shop,** in a cottage at 1325 Coast Blvd. Children will be thrilled to discover stairs that lead to a beach cave—right in the middle of the shop! **Sunny Jim's Cave** is open Monday through Saturday from 10am to 5pm and on Sunday from 11am to 5pm. Admission is $1.25 for adults, 50¢ for children 3–11, free for kids under 3. The opening in the cliffs at the end of 145 steps frames a view of ocean and coastline. The tunnel is steep and narrow, but perfectly safe. You'll have to decide whether your child can handle the walk back up—for some kids it might be too much. Also, remember that you might have to carry a very small child back up those 145 steps. Other kids may enjoy the opportunity to pretend they're pirates or explorers.

La Jolla Shores is popular for surfing and scuba-diving. Boating, fishing, and sailing go on just north of the pier. Also on the north side of the pier are tidepools, a wonderful sight to show the children. Lifeguards are always on duty. There are picnic areas and restrooms aplenty here.

La Jolla's **Windansea Beach** (take La Jolla Boulevard to Nautilus Street) is considered the best place for surfing. Let your surfers out and take a walk along the beach.

Pacific Beach and its boardwalk are popular draws for locals and tourists (take the Grand Avenue exit off I-5 and go west to Mission Boulevard). Families congregate near **Crystal Pier.** And there are roller skates and surfboards for rent near the roller coaster. If you keep following the boardwalk south, you'll eventually reach **South Mission Beach** (but it's not really within walking distance). On the bay side is a nice family beach.

Whale-Watching

A popular California sport, whale-watching usually takes place between December and March, when the whales are on their 10,000-mile journey from Alaska's Bering Sea to the breeding grounds in the warm bays of Baja California, Mexico. It is suggested that you make reservations for a cruise as far in advance as possible with any of the companies listed below. Landlubbers can get a great view of the whales from Cabrillo National Monument (take Chatsworth Street west to Point Loma). On a good day during peak season, you can sometimes spot as many as 60 or 70 of these beautiful grays.

Even if you've escaped winter on the East Coast or in the Midwest, you'll need to wear layers of clothing on these boat trips—it can get pretty chilly out at sea at this time of year. Rubber-soled shoes are most appropriate.

San Diego Harbor Excursion, at the foot of Broadway at Harbor Drive (☎ 619/234-4111, or toll free 800/442-7847), offers narrated cruises, lasting about three hours, daily from mid-December through the end of the migratory season (usually March). Refreshments are available on board. Cruises leave at 10am and 1:30pm. Call for current fees. Reservations are recommended.

At **Fisherman's Landing,** 2838 Garrison St. (☎ 619/222-0391), you can board the 65-foot *Apollo* for 3-hour whale-watching cruises. There's a snack bar on board. Cruises leave from mid-December through mid-March, daily at 10am and 1:30pm. Call for current rates.

Point Loma Sportfishing, 1403 Scott St., Point Loma (☎ 619/223-1627), will take you whale-watching weekdays at 1pm. On Saturday and Sunday, departure times are 9am and 1pm, and trips last approximately three hours. Call for current rates. No age minimum. Point Loma also has sportfishing boats for private charter and offers half- and three-quarter-day fishing trips.

H & M Landing, 2803 Emerson St., Point Loma (☎ 619/222-1144), will take you whale-watching December through March, on three- or five-hour cruises. Adult fares are $15; children under 17, $10 for the three-hour cruises.

Another way to go is via the classic luxury yacht, *Lord Hornblower,* 1066 N. Harbor Dr., at the Embarcadero next to the San Diego Cruise Ship Terminal (☎ 619/234-8687), takes you out on the 151-foot company flagship for a 3½-hour whale-watching trip. The ship, which holds 750 people, serves snacks and beverages. It sails twice daily from mid-December through mid-March, at 9:30am and 1:30pm. Call for current rates.

Boat Rentals/Sailing/Deep-Sea Fishing

Ever dreamed of sailing on the San Diego Bay? You can sail on it with the **San Diego Sailing Club and School,** located at Marina Cortez, 1880 Harbor Island Dr., San Diego, CA 92101 (☎ 619/298-6623). The staff can give you sailing lessons, rent sailboats, or take you sailing with a captain. On your own, you'll pay from $75 for four hours on a Catalina-22. Take along a captain for $20 per hour. Private basic sailing lessons for nonmembers ages 12 and up are $125 for eight hours. Ask about specials and discounts for more than one student.

Seaforth Boat Rentals, at 1715 Strand Way, Coronado, CA 92118 (☎ 619/437-1514), is on a calm, sheltered bay. This branch has a large fleet of paddleboats, and the sailing lessons are geared to children as well as adults. In addition, there are lots of ducks around to feed. Food and snacks are available at the boat-rental shop, and you can picnic nearby at any of the grassy areas. In addition to lessons, sailboats, fishing boats, ski boats, speedboats, and private charter boats for deep-sea fishing can be rented. Sailing lessons cost $10 per half hour and waterskiing is $70. They are open daily from 9am to 5pm.

The other branches are located at 1641 Quivira Rd., Mission Bay, San Diego, CA 92109 (☎ **619/223-1681**), which also rents bicycles (open on weekdays from 8am to 6pm and on weekends from 7am to 7pm).

H & M Landing, 2803 Emerson St., Point Loma, San Diego, CA 92106 (☎ **619/222-1144**), will take you saltwater fishing year round. Available every day are half-day, three-quarter-day, full-day, and multiday trips. Call for prices. Tackle rental is available.

Islandia Sportfishing, 1551 W. Mission Bay Dr., San Diego, CA 92109 (☎ **619/222-1164**), takes off on half-day and three-quarter-day fishing trips. Twilight departures are offered, as well as nighttime shark fishing and whale watching. Call for prices.

The **Harbor Island Sailing Club,** 2040 Harbor Island Dr., Suite 104, San Diego, CA 92101 (☎ **619/291-9568,** or toll free **800/854-6625** outside California), rents and charters sailboats. If you're already a member of a sailing club, check whether you have reciprocal privileges with Harbor Island. Public rentals, without a skipper, begin at $70 for four hours on a 19-foot Rhodes; a skipper is $20 per hour extra. Reservations must be made in advance for extended charters.

You can rent jet skis, ski boats, sailboards, catamarans, and sailboats from **C.P. Watersports,** at the San Diego Hilton (☎ **619/276-4010**) and the Dana Inn hotels (☎ **619/226-8611**). For kids and adults both there are also kayaks and aqua cycles, and you can get sailing and windsurfing lessons. Call about one-hour, half-day, and full-day prices.

Bicycling

Rent bicycles from **Rent A Bike,** at the San Diego Hilton, East Mission Bay Drive, which delivers and picks up free anywhere in San Diego (☎ **619/275-1512**). You can rent 1- and 5-speeds ($8 per hour), tandems ($12 per hour), cruisers ($7 per hour), children's bikes ($6 per hour), and bikes with baby seats ($10 with a cruiser). Helmets and locks are free. Maps are available.

Hamel's Action Sports Center, 704 Ventura Place (in Mission Beach near the roller-coaster) (☎ **619/488-5050**), also rents bicycles. You can get adult bikes, beach cruisers, tandems, and children's bikes, all at $5 per hour, $20 per day. You can also rent boogie boards, surfboards, in-line skates, and roller skates. Child carriers are free, as are helmets and pads. No reservations are necessary; they do not pick up or deliver. Hamel's is open daily in summer from 9am to 8pm; in winter, from 10am to 6pm.

Horseback Riding

When you have the time to spend and want more than just "a schlepp through the woods on a horse," you'd do well to visit **Holidays on Horseback,** 24928 Viejas Blvd. (P.O. Box 474), Descanso, CA 91916 (☎ **619/445-3997**). Liz and Earl Hammond offer a multitude of possibilities for getting away to the desert or the mountains. And they are only about 42 miles from San Diego. The Hammonds feel that their trips are well suited to families because they provide a complete wilderness experience. And indeed these are not ordinary one-hour horse rentals. Guides point out the local flora and how it is used by the mountain and desert people; you'll stop to watch the wildlife and talk about the history of the areas you ride through. They offer guided day trips, two-day, three-day, and all sorts of other rides.

Call or write them and tell them your riding experience and what you'd like to do, and they'll figure out which trip is best for you. They take children 6 and up. Prices are the same for kids and adults; they'll give a 10% discount for families of five or more. Prices start at $22 for a 1^1/$_2$-hour ride (weekdays only) and go up from there.

SPECTATOR SPORTS

The **San Diego Padres** (baseball) and the **San Diego Chargers** (football) play at Jack Murphy Stadium, 9449 Friars Rd., off I15 west, San Diego. To get tickets to the Padres' games, write at least two weeks in advance to the San Diego Padres Ticket Office, P.O. Box 129000, San Diego, CA 92112-9000 (☎ **619/283-4494**). To charge by phone, call TicketMaster (☎ **619/297-2373**). Or you can purchase tickets on the north side of the stadium at Advance Window C anytime before or during the game.

The best way to get San Diego Chargers tickets is by requesting an order form from the Chargers Ticket Office, P.O. Box 609100, San Diego, CA 92160 (☎ **619/280-2121**).

The **Del Mar Race Track,** at the Del Mar Fairgrounds west of Calif. 5, Del Mar (☎ **619/755-1141** for information, **619/792-4242** for the ticket office), is open late July through mid-September for thoroughbred horse racing. It's a beautiful racetrack with a new Spanish-style grandstand. When the Del Mar meet is over, there's wagering on Thoroughbreds, quarter horses, and harness racing from other tracks at the Satellite Wagering Facility at the fairgrounds.

SPECIALTY SHOPPING

San Diego combines its shopping areas and centers with sightseeing attractions.

Seaport Village

San Diego's wonderful harbors make strolling and watching boats a natural form of recreation. After you've visited the Embarcadero and its harbor sights, make a stop at Seaport Village, West Harbor Drive and Kettner Boulevard (☎ **619/235-4014**). Although first and foremost a shopping center, it does have its appeal as a place to visit with the family. Designed to look somewhat like a California fishing village, it's set on 14 acres in three adjacent plazas, each with shops and restaurants. A boardwalk along the oceanfront ties them all together.

The children will be charmed by the circa-1900 **carousel,** restored to its original glory after being sold piecemeal to musicians around the country and then purchased in toto by Seaport Village. A 12-piece brass band plays regularly, and you might see other entertainers. Usually on Sunday at 1pm in the West Plaza, there's a 45-minute program of mime and puppetry called **Kazoo's Kids Show,** performed by Kazoo, the village mime. The audience participates and the children each get a kazoo at the end of the show.

The children will also enjoy the **Time-Out Family Amusement Center** (☎ 619/233-5277). It features video games, pinball machines, and other amusements.

Cinderella Carriage stops near the Harbor House Restaurant. For $30 per half hour you can be transported through parts of San Diego in the old-fashioned elegance of a horse-drawn carriage. Rides are available from 11:30am to 11pm daily.

There are 75 shops, 13 specialty or themed restaurants, and four traditional restaurants. There are crafts shops; clothing boutiques; kite, poster, and souvenir shops; and jewelry, wooden toy, and music box specialty shops. The shops are open daily from 10am to 10pm in summer, 10am to 9pm September through May. Restaurants have longer hours. Parking is free for two hours with a validation.

Horton Plaza

Located right in the heart of downtown San Diego, the Horton Plaza Shopping Center, between Broadway and G Street, and First and Fourth Avenues (☎ 619/238-1596), is an interesting place to spend some time after you've exhausted all the sightseeing venues in town. Built on the site of San Diego's first park, it is modeled after European urban centers. Storefronts are varied, and the layout is elaborate. It's not very easy to get around Horton Plaza (and especially not easy with a stroller). It has more than 140 shops and restaurants, with specialty stores such as Imaginarium, the Disney Store, Horton Toy & Doll, men's and women's clothing and shoe shops, three department stores, and sports apparel and equipment stores. There are a number of fast-food spots, including Mrs. Fields Cookies, La Salsa, and Pogo Pizza. Frogg Lane, Galaxie Grill, Marie Callender's, and the Panda Inn are good sit-down restaurants.

On the street level, exterior, at First Avenue and F Street (11 Horton Plaza), is the **International Visitor Information Center** (☎ 619/236-1212). Open (except Thanksgiving, Christmas and New Year's Days), Monday through Saturday from 8:30am to 5pm and on Sunday from 11am to 5pm in June, July, and August.

Enter the parking garage at 2nd or 3rd and G Streets, or at 4th and F Street. Stores are open Monday through Friday from 10am to 9pm, on Saturday from 10am to 6pm, and on Sunday from 11am to 6pm. Summer hours are longer. Restaurants, theaters, and some shops have extended hours.

Gaslamp Quarter

Between Fourth and Sixth Avenues and Broadway and L Street in downtown San Diego is a 16-block area of specialty shops, restaurants, and art galleries called the Gaslamp Quarter. Once the site of the town's red-light district, it is now a National Historical District. Baroque revival and Victorian buildings have been restored to their original spirit. Two-hour walking tours are offered by the foundation; contact it for meeting places and times. A better bet for families is the 45-minute self-guided audio tour (adults $5, children $3). The Gaslamp Quarter Foundation is at 410 Island Ave. (☎ 619/233-4692; or 233-4691 for recorded information).

Belmont Park

Located in Mission Beach at 3126 Mission Blvd. (☎ 619/488-0668, or 619/488-1549 for ride information) is an interesting combination of new and old. Belmont Park has been restored to reflect its early amusement park days, while adding modern shops and restaurants. The 67-year-old **Giant Dipper** roller coaster is its focal point. Now a National Historic Landmark, it was restored at a cost of more than $1 million. Originally the centerpiece of the 33-acre Mission Beach Amusement Center built by John D. Spreckels in the '20s, the roller coaster joins the **Liberty Carousel,** reproduced in the fashion of those machines of the "Golden Age" of carousels, and **The Plunge,** once considered the "largest indoor saltwater pool in the world," as major points of interest in Belmont Park. You can ride the Dipper for $2.50, the carousel for $1, and bumper cars for $2.

The Plunge should be seen, whether you use the facilities or not. It's a stunning deco restoration which maintained the original tile lining, the "island" in the shallow end, and other historical parts of the original. It's open to the public on a short-term basis. Pool admission is $2.25 for adults; children 6 months to 17 years and seniors pay $2. Or purchase a one-day pass to the adjoining fitness center for $8, which includes the use of the pool and water exercises.

There are also remote control boats, ride simulators, restaurants, snack shops, and specialty and clothing shops at Belmont Park. With its location right on the boardwalk and with easy beach access, Belmont Park makes a good place for a beach picnic. If you want to explore on in-line skates, **Volley World** (☎ 619/488-1992) rents them. Parking is free.

Joining Belmont Park is the not-just-for-kids **Pirate's Cove** (☎ 619/539-7474), a play center of soft, modular mazes, obstacle courses, cargo-net climbs, colorful ball crawls, and a four-story spiral slide. Two buildings are connected by an underground "tunnel" the kids will love. There are different sections appropriate for different age groups, and parents are encouraged to participate with the kids (they'll even lend you knee pads if your knobby ones aren't used to crawling around!). There's a small video arcade for youngsters under 44 inches tall—the video machines are harmless and just their size. The older kids in the family can visit one of two other arcades in the park.

Pirate's Cove also has a snack bar, and there's a fun pizza-maker right out of the "Jetsons." You'll see what we mean when you watch the pizzas drift along a conveyor belt and the toppings are released from overhead canisters. Admission to the playland is $6.50 all day in summer for kids 2–12. Parents pay $2.50. Beginning in September, non-weekend days or holidays cost $4.50. Those under 2 and over 65 are free. Open Monday through Thursday 11am to 8pm, Friday to 9pm, Saturday 10am to 9pm, Sunday 10am to 7pm.

FAIRS/FESTIVALS/SEASONAL EVENTS

The **Del Mar Fair** is held for 20 days from mid-June through early July at the Del Mar Fairgrounds, 20 miles north of San Diego. Take I-5 to the Villa de la Valle exit. Call **619/755-1161** or **619/793-5555** for current dates and schedules of events. Midway rides, carnival games, art shows, agricultural displays, home arts and floral exhibits, and daily grandstand shows with name performers are among the offerings.

Are you with an infant who sleeps through all sorts of music? Or with a teenager who will listen to all sorts of music? Then **Humphrey's Concerts by the Bay** are for you. These outdoor evening concerts overlook Shelter Island Marina at Humphrey's Half Moon Inn, 2241 Shelter Island Dr., and feature pop and jazz stars. Chairs are set up on the lawn, and the atmosphere is festive and informal. Most of us will recognize the performers—Ray Charles, David Sanborn, and Dianne Schur are just some of the names. Performances run May through October. Call **619/523-1010** for schedule information. Tickets are available through TicketMaster (☎ **619/278-8497**) or at Humphrey's Restaurant (Tuesday through Saturday from 11am to 6pm). Show times and ticket prices vary (tickets run between $20 and $50).

Throughout the summer there are **Twilight in the Park Concerts** at the Organ Pavilion in Balboa Park (☎ **619/239-0512** until 4pm). Concerts range from jazz to rock to performances by the navy band. The free performances are held June through August on Tuesday, Wednesday, and Thursday evenings from 6:15 to 7:15pm.

Each fall, all of San Diego participates in a weekend celebration, the **Cabrillo Festival,** to honor Juan Rodriguez Cabrillo's landing in San Diego Harbor. It also marks him as the first European to set foot on what is now the west coast of the United States. Most of the activity is held at the Cabrillo National Monument; the events include an open house, dancing, music, and foods from Portugal, Spain, Mexico, and the United

States. A reenactment of the landing of Cabrillo's ship is the highlight of the final day of celebrations. Write or call for a schedule of events: **Cabrillo National Monument,** P.O. Box 6670, San Diego, CA 92166-0670 (☎ **619/557-5450**).

May signals the **Cinco de Mayo Festival** in Old Town. In December, two Sundays before Christmas, is the **Parade of Lights** on the San Diego Bay, a breathtaking sight of small boats—yachts, fishing boats, other little boats—adorned with Christmas lights, reindeer, Santa Clauses, and other decorations, hooked together and parading from Harbor and Shelter Islands to Seaport Village past the Embarcadero. Call the Visitor Information Center for information (☎ **619/276-2071**).

TOURS

Old Town Trolley Tours (☎ **619/298-8687** or **298-1014**) is a fun way to see the sites and get around town. Red and green trolley cars follow a continuous loop while "conductors" give a continuous narration describing the interesting sites along the two-hour tour. Passengers can get on and off at any of ten stops along the way and reboard later to return to the original embarkation point. The trolleys cover Coronado, the harbor area, downtown San Diego, parts of Old Town, and Balboa Park. Generally, tours run daily except major holidays; they begin at 9am and run every 30 minutes until 6pm. City Tours gives you a handy day-planner that offers suggestions on how long it will take to visit the attractions along the way. Tours cost $16 for adults, $7 for children 6 to 12, and free for kids 5 and under. Call for trolley stops and schedules.

In addition to its popular city tours, **Old Town Trolley Tours** now takes visitors to local **military bases** for a look at what goes on in the largest military complex in the world. On Thursdays, visit Naval Station San Diego and Naval Medical Center for a look at our country's destroyers, amphibious landing ships, and frigates. After a half-hour stop for souvenirs and refreshments at Club Metro on the base, the tour takes you to the Medical Center, which is the largest military hospital complex in the U.S. This is a fully narrated three-hour tour.

On Fridays, the trolley travels to North Island NAS for a look at the historic airfield where the first Army and Navy aviators learned to fly. This Coronado base is filled with aircraft carriers, deep sea submersible units, helicopter squadrons, and high tech repair facilities. There is also a half-hour "pit" stop.

Anyone who saw the movie *Top Gun* will recognize Miramar Naval Air Station. This visit will give you an up-close look at the Top Gun School, various jet-testing and pilot-training facilities. You may see a take-off or landing of an F-14, an F/A-18, or an E-2.

History buffs will appreciate this one. Pending is a Sunday Marine Corps Recruit Depot walking tour through the command museum, along with a drive through the parade grounds, obstacle courses, and buildings of the Naval Submarine Base.

Military base tours leave from Old Town State Park. Unlike the City Tour, you must make reservations in advance by calling toll free **800/NAVY TOUR.** Tours run once a day, Monday, Thursday and Friday (Sunday is pending). Be sure your child can sit still for the time before and after the rest stops. The cost is $20 adults, $7 ages 5–12; under 5 free; military affiliation, $16. You can also purchase a package of the City Tour and the Military Tour. The package costs $30 for adults, $14 for children. You can split up the two tours and take them on any day.

Other Activities

If you're still looking for things to do, you can take the kids to the movies on Tuesday, when it's dollar day, or visit the downtown **San Diego Library,** at 820 E St., between 8th and 9th Streets (☎ **619/236-5838**), which offers story hours, magic shows, puppet shows, films, and arts and crafts. All programs are free.

Take a 1¹/₂-hour drive to the Gold Rush mountain town of **Julian** via Calif. 79 through Descanso Junction, or Calif. 78 outside Ramona. In the winter, there's snow; in the spring, wildflowers. Autumn is harvest time, when apples are plentiful. Julian was built in the 1870s, but its Gold Rush era lasted only 10 years. The town kept itself going with its abundant apple orchards. Autumn weekends are crowded with people hunting for apple products. Contact the Julian Chamber of Commerce, P.O. Box 413, Julian, CA 92036 (☎ **619/765-1857**), for information on what to do while in town. Business hours are Friday through Monday, 10am to 4pm.

Another nice drive is to **Palomar Observatory,** atop Palomar Mountain, 66 miles north of San Diego, via County Road S6, one hour from Escondido (☎ **619/ 742-2119**). Show the kids the country's largest Hale telescope (200 inches), with an optical range of nearly one billion light-years. In addition to the telescope there is an exhibit hall of pictures taken through the Palomar and other telescopes, and a movie which explains how the research is done. The telescope and exhibit hall can be visited daily from 9am to 4pm. There is no admission charge.

Take a drive through **North County,** which begins in Del Mar, 20 miles north of downtown San Diego, and extends to the Orange County border. North of Del Mar, home of the Del Mar Thoroughbred Club racetrack, is **Encinitas.** From May through September you'll see ribbons of color throughout the town because Encinitas is one of the capitals of flower-growing. Encinitas and its neighbor, Leucadia, are the world's leading growers of poinsettias. Some of the companies will let you look in at the greenhouses. But even driving down the roads you'll see acres of these red, yellow, and white Christmas flowers. Farther north is **Oceanside,** where you'll discover the West Coast's longest municipal pier.

ACTIVITIES BY AGE GROUP

The following listings suggest activities divided into specific age brackets. Refer back to the individual description for details and any age restrictions.

Teens and Preteens

Balboa Park (including the Museum of Man, Aerospace Museum,
    Reuben H. Fleet Space Center, Natural History Museum, Hall of Champions,
    Model Railroad Museum, Spanish Village)
Beaches
Belmont Park (including the Giant Dipper roller coaster, The Plunge,
    the video arcade, the beach)
Bicycling
Boating, sailing, fishing
Cabrillo Festival
Cabrillo National Monument
Cinco de Mayo Festival
Del Mar Annual Regional Fair
Harbor Excursion
Horseback riding

Humphrey's Concerts by the Bay
Julian
Maritime Museum
Mingei International Museum of World Folk Art
Mission Bay Park
Mission San Diego de Alcala
Old Town State Historic Park
Old Town Trolley tours
Pro sports
San Diego Bay Ferry
San Diego Wild Animal Park
San Diego Zoo
Seaport Village (including Time-Out Family Amusement Center, horse-drawn carriage rides)
Sea World
Serra Museum
Spreckels Park concerts—Coronado
Stephen Birch Aquarium
Surfing
Twilight in the Park concerts
Whale-watching

School-Age Kids

Balboa Park (including the Museum of Man, Aerospace Museum, Reuben H. Fleet Space Center, Natural History Museum, Hall of Champions, Model Railroad Museum, Spanish Village)
Beaches
Belmont Park (including Giant Dipper roller coaster, the Liberty Carousel, The Plunge, the video arcade, the beach, Pirate's Cove)
Bicycling
Boating, sailing, fishing
Cabrillo Festival
Cabrillo National Monument
Children's Museum of San Diego
Cinco de Mayo Festival
Del Mar Annual Regional Fair
Harbor Excursion
Horseback riding
Julian
Maritime Museum
Mingei International Museum of World Folk Art
Mission Bay Park
Mission San Diego de Alcala
Old Town State Historic Park
Old Town Trolley tours
Palomar Observatory
Pro sports
San Diego Bay Ferry
San Diego Library

San Diego Wild Animal Park
San Diego Zoo
Seaport Village (including mime/puppet shows, Time-Out Family
    Amusement Center, horse-drawn carriage rides)
Sea World
Serra Museum
Spreckels Park concerts—Coronado
Stephen Birch Aquarium
Twilight in the Park concerts
Whale-watching

Preschoolers

Balboa Park (especially the Marie Hitchcock Puppet Theater,
    lily pond, carousel, miniature train)
Beaches
Belmont Park (including the Liberty Carousel, The Plunge, the beach,
    Pirate's Cove)
Cabrillo Festival
Children's Museum of San Diego
Cinco de Mayo Festival
Del Mar Annual Regional Fair
Julian
Mission Bay Park
Old Town State Historic Park
Palomar Observatory
San Diego Library
San Diego Wild Animal Park
San Diego Zoo (especially the Children's Petting Zoo)
Seaport Village (especially mime/puppet shows, horse-drawn carriage rides)
Sea World
Spreckels Park concerts—Coronado
Stephen Birch Aquarium
Twilight in the Park concerts

In Case of Emergency

Should a life-or-death emergency arise during your visit to San Diego, call **911** for the police or fire department, or an ambulance. In addition, there are a number of hospitals and a pharmacy with extended hours available to you.

Hospitals   The following hospitals have 24-hour emergency rooms: **Scripps Memorial Hospital,** 9888 Genesee Ave., La Jolla (☎ **619/457-4123**); **Coronado Hospital,** 250 Prospect Place, Coronado (☎ **619/435-6251**); **University Hospital, University of California Medical Center,** 200 W. Arbor Dr., San Diego (☎ **619/543-6222**); and **Mercy Hospital and Medical Center,** 4077 Fifth Ave., San Diego (☎ **619/294-8111**).

A Pharmacy with Extended Hours   The following San Diego pharmacy offers extended-hour services: **University City Pharmacy,** 3338 Governor Dr., San Diego (☎ **619/453-4455**); open Monday through Friday from 9am to 9pm, on Saturday from 9am to 8pm, and on Sunday from 10am to 7pm.

6 La Jolla

Long known as the Jewel of the Pacific, La Jolla (pronounced La Hoya) is a perfect place to walk with the family. Whether you choose to walk in the village along Prospect Street and Girard Avenue, or along Coast Boulevard, which parallels the ocean, you'll have lots to look at. The village bursts with boutiques carrying imported clothing, jewelry shops, art galleries, and other specialty shops. Restaurants are everywhere, and there are lots of ice-cream shops to assuage a small child's hunger. A walk above the cliffs is breathtaking. You'll see La Jolla's famous beaches; the magnificent homes you've probably heard about, with their gardens exploding in color; rocky cliffs; and ocean-carved caves.

La Jolla is just 15 minutes from the heart of San Diego. Even if you don't stay overnight here, you can spend the day at a beach or an afternoon in the village. Or come for an early dinner and a stroll afterward. Parking is not easy on busy summer weekends, so plan on walking. Park wherever you can, and be sure to bring that Snuggly or stroller for your youngsters.

WHERE TO STAY

Walk into the **Embassy Suites Hotel,** 4550 La Jolla Village Dr., San Diego, CA 92122 (☎ **619/453-0400,** or toll free **800/EMBASSY;** fax 619/453-4226), and you enter a 12-story atrium courtyard with plants hanging from balconies and a pond filled with koi fish. The glass roof gives an open-air feeling, and four glass elevators carry guests through this lush paradise. The pool is indoors and the Jacuzzi is outdoors, surrounded by chaises for sun worshippers. There's a small exercise room with showers and lockers. Older children can hang out in the lobby area, where they'll find a billiards table and Pac-Man. Babysitting can be arranged through the front desk.

Included in your room price is a complimentary breakfast and complimentary evening cocktails and soft drinks. The lobby restaurant, the Coast Café, cooks breakfast to order and also serves lunch and dinner (till 11pm). A deli adjacent to the restaurant is ideal for snacks and quick meals. Room service is available from 11am to 11pm.

Every unit here is a nicely decorated suite. Most have a bedroom with its own vanity and sink, and two double beds or a king-size bed. All the suites have a living area with a fold-out sofa bed, microwave, small refrigerator, coffee maker, and dining table and chairs, plus TVs and two telephones. A few larger suites are available, including a two-bedroom/two-bath suite with a larger living area and a formal dining table. All accommodations open overlooking the courtyard, so you can avoid dark hallways and stairways. A large number of suites are designated no-smoking.

Suites rent for $149–$179. Two-bedroom suites cost $250–$325 double. Children under 12 stay free in their parents' room; those 12 and over and additional adults pay $10 each per night. There is no charge for cribs; rollaways cost $15. Ask about special promotions and packages. Parking is free.

In the heart of La Jolla's picturesque village, the **Colonial Inn,** 910 Prospect St., La Jolla, CA 92037 (☎ **619/454-2181,** or toll free **800/832-5525, 800/826-1278** in California; fax 619/454-5679), offers the ambience of a small European hotel. Built in 1913, the inn is set on a hill overlooking a cove and beach. The lobby looks like an elegant living room, complete with grand piano, chandeliers, and a fire crackling in the fireplace. The emphasis here is on service, and accordingly the staff will do whatever it can to assist you.

Guests can play tennis at nearby public courts at no extra charge, and can use a nearby health club at a discount. In summer, there is poolside food service. The unusual round hotel pool is ideal for the children, because it's no deeper than four feet anywhere. You are also within walking distance of the area's best family beach, the Children's Pool (see "What to See and Do" in San Diego, above). A nearby recreation center, just across from the San Diego Museum of Art, has a public playground. La Jolla Walking Tours (☎ 619/450-6825 or 619/453-8219) operates 1¹/₂-hour guided walking tours of La Jolla departing from the hotel. Only you know if your child will get through a tour of buildings, shops, and restaurants.

Just off the lobby is Putnam's Restaurant and Bar on the site of what was the original pharmacy and soda fountain. This lovely restaurant serves breakfast, lunch, and dinner, and provides room service for guests. Continental cuisine is the norm here. The atmosphere is elegant and subdued; if you have young children, a better bet is to choose a more informal restaurant in the village. You're within walking distance of numerous casual eateries (see "Where to Eat in La Jolla," below), and there's a McDonald's just up the street.

Every one of the 75 guest rooms and suites in the Colonial Inn is unique in configuration. Deluxe accommodations are actually large mini-suites furnished with a king-size bed and a spacious living area. Other rooms have two double beds or one king-size bed. If you have a large family, consider two ocean-view double-bedded rooms that can be connected, giving you 500 square feet of room. All accommodations have large windows and are appointed with floral drapes and bedspreads and old-world furniture. Bathrooms are small, but there are separate dressing areas in most units. Because many rooms are heated by old-fashioned radiators that are controlled at the front desk, you may want to request a room with electric heat if you fear your toddler may get too close to the radiator.

Requests for evening turn-down service, complimentary use of refrigerators, robes, hairdryers, irons and ironing boards, and babysitting arrangements can be made at the front desk. Guests are given complimentary continental breakfast (not available with special weekend rates) and a daily newspaper, and a bottle of mineral water is provided in each room. Even the valet parking is free—a real plus in La Jolla.

Rooms at the Colonial Inn rent for $150–$210, single or double, depending on the view. Suites will run you $230–$250. There is no extra charge for a third person, or for cribs or rollaways. Ask about holiday programs and special promotional rates.

Beach lovers and budget-conscious families will enjoy staying at the **La Jolla Beach TraveLodge,** 6750 La Jolla Blvd., La Jolla, CA 92037 (☎ 619/454-0716, or toll free **800/255-3050;** fax 619/454-1075). This recently remodeled motel is only a block from the famous Windansea Beach, where you can swim and surf to your heart's content. A heated pool in the hotel is suited to play and lap swimming. Although there is no restaurant in the hotel, four are within a block and Su Casa is right across the street (see "Where to Eat in La Jolla," below).

Rooms are not fancy, but are clean and comfortable and large enough for a crib or rollaway. Some rooms with two double beds have a small kitchenette that can be closed off by a folding door. Color TV and free cable stations are included. If you need a bathtub, request it ahead of time. You'll find coffee makers in all the rooms. Suites are available with a separate living area furnished with fold-out sofas. The motel has no adjoining rooms. The suite kitchenettes are stocked with coffee makers, stoves, refrigerators, and utensils, and there is a kitchen table and chairs. No-smoking rooms can be requested.

Room rates vary seasonally, ranging from $35 to $74 weekdays, and $39 to $79 weekends, for a single. Off-season, add another $5 per double room. Suites with kitchens are an extra $30 per week (kitchen units are not available on a one-night basis). Inquire about holiday minimums. Parking is free.

WHERE TO EAT

Su Casa, 6738 La Jolla Blvd. (☎ 619/454-0369), one block from the beach, is a Mexican restaurant specializing in fresh seafood. Booths and tables, subdued lighting, hanging plants, and a nautical theme all contribute to the warm and inviting feeling.

The Mexican lunch selections include tamales, fajitas, tostadas, and specials of fresh mojarrita (a freshwater fish), chile relleno poblano, or Mexican pizza. Lunch prices are $5–$10. Dinnertime offers special Mexican combinations of Su Casa spinach crêpes or enchiladas verdes, tampico (a chicken enchilada and chile relleno), or Mexican pizza ($5.50–$8). Seafood choices include fresh steamed lobster tail, camarones al chipotle (jumbo shrimp marinated in chipotle sauce), Mexican bouillabaisse, a seafood tamale, and other fresh fish; these cost $12–$13. You can order fajitas, chicken dishes, and meat entrees, and create your own tacos; prices range from $9 to $13. Sunday brunch is an all-you-can-eat affair with omelets, Belgian waffles, a carving station, and more. Adults are charged $8.95, seniors $6.95, kids $3.95. At Su Casa, food is prepared with canola oil—no lard is used. There are lots of special coffee drinks and desserts.

For kids under 12, there are hamburgers, fish and chips, tacos, enchiladas, flautas, or quesadillas, each served with rice, beans, or french fries, and costing $3.95. The bartender will prepare special kiddie drinks. Servers will warm baby food and bottles, and supply highchairs and booster seats.

Su Casa is open Monday through Thursday from 11:30am to 10pm and on Friday and Saturday from 11:30am to 11pm. Sunday brunch is served from 10am to 2pm, dinner until 10pm. Reservations and major credit cards are accepted. Park in the lot.

In downtown La Jolla, stop at **The Spot,** 1005 Prospect St. (☎ 619/459-0800), for lunch or dinner. Here you can sit back and enjoy the lively decor: surfboards and skis hang on the walls, copper kettles adorn the used-brick fireplace, and light rock music sets the tone. Service is fast and friendly, and the menu lists a wide variety of choices. A favorite for lunch is the Cobb salad: chunks of roast turkey, bacon, tomato, avocado, and crumbled bleu cheese on a bed of crisp greens, served with the house vinaigrette dressing and a grilled English muffin ($6.95). For dinner, try the full slab of ribs, prepared from an original Chicago recipe more than 30 years old, served with french fries, garlic bread, and coleslaw ($15.95). Another specialty here is pizza—it's delicious, but be prepared for a 30-minute wait. Sandwiches, salads, and hamburgers run around $6.50. You can also order steaks and grilled salmon for $12 and up. Lunch and dinner specials are well priced.

For children, adult portions can be split in the kitchen, you can split a pizza, or order a grilled-cheese sandwich or a hamburger. Special children's drinks can be ordered from the bar. Boosters and highchairs are available, and the servers will warm baby food and bottles.

The Spot is open every day of the year. Lunch is served from 11am to 4pm and dinner is from 4pm to 1am. Breakfast is served on Saturday and Sunday only. Reservations are accepted only for parties of eight or more. Major credit cards welcome. Street parking.

To Del Mar ↑
(3 miles)

To Los Angeles ↑
(110 miles)

N

Pacific Ocean

Torrey Pines Rd.

Miramar

Genesee Ave.

La Jolla
Village Dr.

Ylla La Jolla Dr.
Gilman Dr.

Nobel Ave.

Scripps Pier

Scripps Beach

La Jolla Cove

La Jolla Caves

La Jolla Shores Dr.

La Jolla Scenic Dr.

Regents Rd.

Boomer Beach

Shell Beach

Children's Pool Beach

Av. de la Playa

Ardath Rd.

Coast Blvd.

Jenner

Rosalyn Lane

Wall St.

Cave St.

Prospect Pl.

Exchange Place

Hidden Valley Rd.

Via Capri

Casa Beach

Silverado St.

Herschel Ave.

Ivanhoe Ave.

Torrey Pines Rd.

San Clemente Canyon Rd.

Wipeout Beach

Coast Blvd. South

Girard Ave.

Fay Ave.

Kline St.

Eads Ave.

Pearl St.

Country Club Dr.

5

Marine Street Beach

Draper Ave.

La Jolla Blvd.

Genter St.

West Muirlands Dr.

La Jolla Country Club

La Jolla Scenic Dr. South

Wind "N" Sea Beach

Post Office ⊠

Sacramento
★

☐ Bay Area

CALIFORNIA

The **Hard Rock Café,** a fixture in many cities here and in Europe, can also be found in downtown La Jolla at 909 Prospect St. (☎ **619/454-5101**). We watched the teen crowd capturing the atmosphere with their cameras, while the parents lined up to purchase the famous Hard Rock T-shirts in the Promo Room (which opens a half hour earlier than the restaurant).

One thing the Hard Rock is famous for is its extensive, hand-picked, museum-quality collection of rock memorabilia. In fact, ask for the pamphlet that will guide you in detail through the collection.

Once you settle down indoors or outdoors on the small patio, you'll find the selections are simple: salads ($5.95 and $6.95), sandwiches and hamburgers ($5–$8), and Hard Rock specialties such as lime barbecued chicken ($8.95) and watermelon ribs, a favorite ($11.95). Dessert choices are plentiful. If you have children with you aged 12 and under, they can choose from grilled cheese, hamburgers, or the special lime barbecued chicken for $2.95 and $3.95.

The Hard Rock is known for not using additives or preservatives, and for management's commitment to recycling. Both highchairs and booster seats are provided. Baby food or bottles can be warmed.

The Hard Rock is open Sunday through Thursday from 11:30am to 11pm, and on Friday and Saturday to midnight. The bar stays open longer. Since no reservations are taken, get there early if you're with hungry children. On weekends, especially in summer, it's best to arrive before 7pm. There is street parking or validated valet parking. Major credit cards are honored.

Just a couple of blocks away is the popular **Johnny Rockets,** 7863 Girard St. (☎ **619/456-4001**), tucked away on the bottom floor of the Wall Street Plaza. This small lively diner has two counters and a couple of red leather booths plus outdoor patio seating. It's simple and fun, and the kids love it. If you're not familiar with Johnny Rockets, you may be surprised by the simplicity of the menu—hamburgers, a few sandwiches, fries, and chili. And of course you can order flavored Cokes, plus malts and shakes. Apple pie—à la mode or with cheese—is dessert. You won't pay over $4.75 for anything on the menu (unless you add every single "extra" to your hamburger).

Even with this reasonably priced menu, there's another menu for children under age 10. For $1.65 to $2.15 they can choose grilled cheese, egg salad sandwich, a hamburger or peanut butter and jelly. All sandwiches are half-size and come with French fries. There are highchairs and booster seats.

Open Sunday through Thursday from 11am to 10pm, on weekends until 11pm. You're likely to have a wait between noon and 2pm and 5:30 to 7pm. Reservations are not accepted. Major credit cards are accepted. Street parking.

El Torito, 8910 Villa La Jolla Dr. (☎ **619/453-4115**), near the University and not far from the Stephen Birch Aquarium, is a perfect family restaurant. Mom, Dad, and all the kids are welcome here, and the food is mild enough for even the most finicky eater. The Old Mexico–style interior is pleasant and large. On a cold winter night, you may want to request a table or booth near the big fireplace.

Sunday brunch is a feast of make-your-own omelets, carnitas, Mexican pastries, a waffle bar and hot American and Mexican entrees (adults $8.95, kids 12 and under $3).

Niños and niñas can order off their own menu, which is full of games and things to color. Here, $3 will buy a choice of a quesadilla, burrito, enchilada, taco, chicken fingers, or hamburger with mini-nachos; a choice of french fries, rice and beans; and an ice-cream sundae. Special kids' drinks, including a special collector's cup, can be ordered, too. Best of all, kids under 12 eat absolutely free from the children's menu on any Wednesday, lunch or dinner, as long as there is one paying adult per child. Servers will warm baby food and bottles, and provide boosters and highchairs.

Dinnertime choices for adults include the reliable combination plates, enchiladas, burritos and chimichangas, fajitas, and classic entrees of carne asada, arroz con pollo, and taquitos rancheros. A few things can be ordered à la carte. Dinner prices are reasonable at $6.95–$12, with most choices around $7 or $8.

El Torito is open for lunch Monday through Saturday from 11am to 3pm. Dinner is served Sunday through Thursday from 3 to 10pm, and on Friday and Saturday from 3 to 11pm. Sunday brunch is served from 9am until 2pm (but starting at 1pm you can order off the regular dinner menu). Reservations are accepted. Major credit cards are welcome. There is a large free parking lot.

Just next door you'll find a totally different atmosphere at the safari-themed **Elephant Bar & Restaurant,** 8980 Villa La Jolla Dr. (☎ **619/587-1993**), where the tables and booths are spread out. Weeknights it's a combination of young and old diners; weekends it's filled with college folks. Diners have a vast choice of nonjungle fare. House specialties include kona barbequed shrimp, St. Louis spareribs, and charcoal-broiled fish tacos. These and the other specialties cost $8–$10. The Elephant BBQ Platter provides a feast of barbecued spareribs, beef, and barbecued chicken breast for $12.95. You can also order prime rib, chicken, pastas, hamburgers, or sandwiches. Prices range from $4.95 to $13.

Appetizers are plentiful, and can be ordered for the kids. Or, a little coloring-book menu offers kids 10 and under a burger, chicken tenders, grilled cheese, a corn dog, spaghetti, or a chicken quesadilla for $3. Included is a glass of milk or soda and a small ice-cream sundae. Kids' drinks are served in cute animal-foot cups. Save room for the Kooky Cookie ($3.50), two giant chocolate cookies stuffed with vanilla ice cream and covered with caramel fudge and whipped cream! There are other "conservative" choices, too. Special nonalcoholic drinks can be ordered from the bar. Booster seats and wrapped highchairs are provided, and baby food and bottles can be warmed.

The Elephant Bar is open Sunday through Thursday from 11am to 10pm and on Friday and Saturday from 11am to 11pm. Reservations accepted. Credit cards are accepted. Free parking in the lot.

WHAT TO SEE AND DO

We've separated La Jolla's sightseeing attractions from those in San Diego only because you might want to spend a couple of days doing things just in this area. Don't forget the beaches—they're wonderful. See the "Outdoor Activities" section in "What to See and Do" in the San Diego section for information on La Jolla's beaches.

Every room of **John Cole's Book Shop,** 780 Prospect St. (☎ **619/454-4766**), an early La Jolla beach cottage, overflows with books. You'll find it two doors north of the museum, toward the village. The children's room has a small table and chairs and a view of the sea through lead-paned windows. Children are welcome to play with the wooden trains and ride the rocking horses. In addition to English, there's a large section of foreign-language books for kids. Open Monday through Saturday from 9:30am to 5:30pm.

If your kids are oozing energy and you need a break, turn them loose at the playground of **La Jolla Park and Recreation Center,** across from the museum on Prospect Street, between Culver and Draper Streets. There's plenty of playground equipment for them to use.

Stephen Birch Aquarium-Museum

There has been a Scripps Aquarium around since 1903. Now, a new and larger complex has been opened not far from the UCSD campus. The **Stephen Birch Aquarium-Museum,** 2300 Expedition Way, La Jolla (☎ **619/534-3474**), houses just over 30 well-lit tanks exhibiting colorful fish from the cold waters of the Pacific Northwest to the warm waters of Mexico. We were fascinated by the giant kelp forest, which can be viewed from a small gallery, and we loved the little seahorses and the exquisite Living Coral Reef. When the Aquarium is crowded, it's a bit difficult to get up close, but it's worth the wait.

"Exploring the Blue Planet" is the unique museum exhibit designed to introduce people to the history of oceanography, as well as current research, and what's in store for the future. Remember, this is an interpretive center where displays are described in depth. Some interactive displays teach children about tides, weather, and earthquakes. The Ocean Supermarket is an interesting opportunity to tie together our everyday lives with products identified with the ocean.

The Submersible Deep Diver took us through a simulated deep-sea dive. The "submersible" is equipped with remote cameras panning the ocean's floor. The 15-minute experience should be left for children over 3, as the darkness and noise may unnerve the tots. Plus, it takes a while to get through the initial screened presentation and then the submersible itself. This is not something impatient children will want to do; peak periods often mean long waits. But for those willing to wait, it's an interesting way to travel to the ocean's floor to see what we'd see if we were really there. The outdoor Tidepool Plaza is sometimes staffed with docents who explain the fragile creatures to the children.

Plan to spend about two hours here. The museum is stroller- and wheelchair-accessible. A snack bar and picnic tables are located outside. Open every day except Thanksgiving day and Christmas Day from 9am to 5pm. Ask your hotel concierge about possible shuttle service to the Aquarium. Admission is $6.50 for adults, $5.50 for seniors, $4.50 for juniors 13–17, $3.50 for children 3–12, and free for kids under 3. Parking is $2.50.

Mingei International Museum of World Folk Art

On the north side of one of San Diego's largest shopping centers, University Towne Centre (inland from La Jolla at 4405 La Jolla Village Dr.), is the Mingei International Museum of World Folk Art (☎ **619/453-5300**). Mingei means "arts of the people"; it was coined 50 years ago by a Japanese scholar.

Exhibition items, which range from textiles, folk toys, and weather vanes to pottery and musical instruments from all over the world, are always colorful and imaginative. Because the museum offers an ideal introduction to art for children, it's a popular destination for school field trips.

Open Tuesday through Saturday from 11am to 5pm and on Sunday from 2 to 5pm; closed national holidays. Admission is $3 for adults; $1 for children; under 6, free. Park near Nordstrom.

7   Coronado

Coronado's roots go back to 1885, when two midwesterners decided to build "the finest watering spot on the Pacific Coast." Elisha Babcock, Jr., and Hampton L. Story bought the peninsula for a mere $110,000 (big money at that time) and went to work looking for investors. John D. Spreckels, the sugar baron from San Francisco, was a big investor and eventually bought out most of the original people and led the town's development.

Today, like a winding silver-blue ribbon, the Coronado Bay Bridge ties Coronado to San Diego. A slice of beach called the Silver Strand was and still is the land connection between the two, but taking the toll bridge is the easiest way to make the 2.2-mile drive to the peninsula.

Although you'll feel you are on your own small island in Coronado, you are actually only a short drive from San Diego's main attractions. If you're not staying in Coronado, plan to spend part of a day touring this quaint town with its interesting shops and restaurants. It makes a nice walk with the children. You can stop by, write, or call the **Coronado Visitor Information Bureau,** 1111 Orange Ave., Suite A, Coronado, CA 92118 (☎ 619/437-8788, or toll free **800/622-8300**), for information on the peninsula. The office is open weekdays from 9am to 5pm, and on Saturday and Sunday from 10am to 4pm.

It's simple to get there even if you don't drive. Take the San Diego Bay Ferry over from the Broadway Pier in San Diego to the Ferry Landing for $2 each way. It runs weekdays from San Diego, leaving on the hour beginning at 7am to 10pm, on weekends till 11pm. From Coronado it leaves every hour on the half hour, beginning at 9am.

The **Ferry Landing Marketplace,** 1201 First Ave., at B Street (☎ 619/435-6195), is one of the newest of the Coronado sightseeing attractions. It's a pleasant place to walk and spend an afternoon. You can fish from the pier, rent a bicycle, browse in specialty shops, and have a bite to eat from a fast-food cart or at a sit-down restaurant. The shops are open daily from 10am to 6pm.

The **Electric Shuttle** will take you from the Ferry Landing along Orange Avenue (the main shopping area) to the Meridien Hotel and back, or you can stop and get off anywhere along the way. A mere 50¢ gives you a ride.

Bring a bicycle on the ferry from San Diego, or rent bikes at **Hollands Bicycle Shop,** 977 Orange Ave., two blocks from the Hotel del Coronado (☎ 619/435-3153), and pedal around town. Children's bikes and adult beach cruisers cost $3 per hour; tandems are $8; children's buggies, $4. Helmets are available. Open weekdays from 10am to 6:30pm, on Saturday from 9am to 5pm, and on Sunday from 10am to 4pm. Another store, called **Bikes & Beyond,** can be found at Ferry Landing Marketplace (☎ 619/435-7180).

Bike Coronado, 137 Orange Ave. (☎ 619/437-4888, or toll free **800/431-4888**), has more than 70 bikes for rent. Cruisers and children's bikes cost $5 per hour; tandems, $10; child carriers, free; carts (attached to the bike for kids too big for child carriers but too small for their own bike), $2. There are also half-day, full-day, and weekly rates. Helmets, locks, and baskets are free. Open daily from 9am until dark year round. Call to reserve in summer and holiday weekends.

Both bike shops have maps of the bike trails. The Silver Strand bike trail is an eight-mile flat route that will take you along the Silver Strand beach.

Summer Sundays, June through September, are delightful in **Spreckels Park,** on Orange Avenue between 6th and 7th Streets (☎ 619/435-9260), which is Coronado's largest park. At 6pm, free band concerts entertain families with a different performance each week.

Whether or not you decide to stay overnight in Coronado, you must visit the Hotel del Coronado. Although there's a self-guided walking-tour audiotape you can purchase in the lobby giftshop for $3, children might find the 45-minute walk tedious. Instead, walk around by yourselves—the staff doesn't mind.

It was when the peninsula was made up of acres of sagebrush in the 1880s that construction began on the **Hotel del Coronado,** 1500 Orange Ave., Coronado, CA 92118 (☎ **619/522-8000;** fax 619/522-8262), and it opened in February 1888. Thomas Edison himself designed the electrical system and returned to the hotel in 1904 to flip the switch on the West Coast's first electrically lit, live outdoor Christmas tree. The tree still flourishes on the grounds, outside the Crown Room restaurant.

Through the first 100 years of the hotel's life, it has housed such notables as Presidents Woodrow Wilson, Franklin D. Roosevelt, Jimmy Carter, and Ronald Reagan. Charles Lindbergh celebrated his historic flight at a hotel dinner in his honor in 1927. It is rumored that the hotel was the site of the first meeting of Wallis Simpson and the Prince of Wales. The hotel served as a backdrop in Marilyn Monroe's classic *Some Like It Hot* in 1958. Astronaut Scott Carpenter was honored here with a rocket-shaped cake. John Wayne, Frank Sinatra, and other Hollywood figures have found the "Del" a quiet getaway.

Designated a National Historic Landmark in 1977, the Hotel del Coronado, under the direction of its sixth set of owners, has recently been renovated to emphasize its Victorian architectural tradition.

The hotel originally consisted of nearly 400 rooms. Two buildings of contemporary-style rooms were added in the 1970s, bringing the total close to 700. The lobby of the original building is a delightful place to sit and take in the atmosphere. Victorian "lamps" provide soft lighting, and columns of Illinois oak and colorful brocade chairs add to the luxury. A cagelike elevator takes guests to the upper floors.

At Christmastime the lobby is transformed into a holiday wonderland. Each year the hotel staff decorates a tree that is two stories tall. A different theme is chosen each year for the decorations. The tree has been hung with hundreds of teddy bears, dolls, and characters from the Land of Oz. The breathtaking finished product is a treat for all ages.

The lower lobby arcade is filled with shops that are sightseeing attractions in themselves. Make a beeline to the candy shop for caramel apples and taffy.

The "Del" is situated on the longest strip of white sandy beach in Southern California, and it's perfect for swimming, picnicking, and playing Frisbee. If you prefer warmer water, the hotel has two huge pools, complete with poolside snack service.

A highly professional staff of counselors led by an equally professional activities director, organizes programs for children and adults. The summer youth program is broken down into three categories. Children 4–6 attend Camp Oz and are led on scavenger hunts, crafts, swimming, and games. The 7- to 12-year-olds get involved with more water-oriented sports including group sailing, paddleboats, and swimming in Camp Breaker. A swim test is required for this group. These programs run from 1 to 4pm daily from July through August, and the charge is $17 per child. Teenagers conquer the wind challenging their skills in Wind Riders, the program that teaches windsurfing and sailing skills. This is a morning program, and the fee is $18. Landlubbers 7–15 can opt for the Youth Tennis Program lead by Master Pro Ben Press and his staff, and offered daily for one hour. Even kids 3 to 6 can play tennis. Teeny Tennis puts them through their paces using Frisbees, balloons, and other items to teach them fundamentals.

The myriad adult programs take you behind the scenes of this historic hotel; introduce you to the hotel's chefs as you learn about and sample their tasty goodies; or teach you all about sailing in the "First Tack" sailing clinic where, in one lesson, you'll learn to sail your own boat. Or try Tennisize, power walks, and fitness classes. Some programs are complimentary; others have a charge. Reserve a spot with the resident botanist for a nature walk through the hotel grounds and on the beach. This free activity is offered in summer. For anyone who has ever dreamed of hangin' ten on a surfboard, now's the time. Surfing lessons are taught by skilled instructors.

It's nice to know there are family activities, too. The kids can go along with their parents on the "Coronado on Wheels" bike trip through town (with a stop for frozen yogurt; $17 per person), or play croquet with them. "Discover Diving" gives everyone a chance to experience this fascinating sport in the comfort of the hotel pool. When you feel brave, you can sign up for ocean dives. Possibly the most popular family activity in the entire hotel is the Monday and Thursday evening Sunset Marshmallow Roast, where everyone gets together for an early evening of marshmallows and hot chocolate; the kids meet other kids and the adults mingle, too.

Kids Jamboree is an evening program available in summer and holidays (on Tuesday, Wednesday, Friday, and Saturday) for ages 6–12. From 6:30 to 9:30pm children are supervised through refreshments, a movie, and games. The cost is $12 per child.

During the Christmas and Easter holidays, the daytime children's programs are suspended, except for Youth Tennis and the Kids Jamboree. Many of the family and adult activities are still held.

Check with the concierge to make arrangements for a jog along a prescribed course. There are six tennis courts, and court time and lessons are available at an extra charge. The health club has an exercise room ($10 a visit), lockers, showers, a steam room, sauna, and therapy pool; massage can be reserved for a fee. Bikes can be rented (helmets and child carriers are available), golf can be arranged through the concierge, and boogie boards, paddleball, and volleyball equipment can be rented.

There are plenty of dining possibilities, too. The Crown/Coronet Room, with its crown chandeliers and paneled walls, is a popular spot for breakfast, lunch, or dinner. The Sunday brunch is an outstanding array of edibles. The Ocean Terrace is open seasonally for outdoor lunches and snacks, and for hors d'oeuvres and entrees from 4 to 9pm. Prices are quite reasonable—and the pastrami is great!—at Del Deli, located in the lower lobby, where you can order sandwiches, salads, breakfast items, and late-night snacks until 2am. The Lobby Bar serves daily from 6am and features live piano music in the evening. It's a great spot for people-watching and a cup of tea. Room service can be ordered around the clock, and there is a children's menu.

Rooms in the main Victorian building are all unique in size, shape, and decor. There are spacious rooms and cozy rooms; some rooms have balconies. Some have large walk-in closets and pedestal sinks. All are full of charm with their Victorian furniture, ceiling fans, and skirted beds; choose two double beds or a king-size bed. There are remote-control TVs, separate vanities, in-room safes, and digital clocks in each room.

The new complex, built in the 1970s, has traditional first-class accommodations. You can choose from units with a king-size bed or with two double or queen-size beds. Rooms are spacious, and the decor tends to be contemporary. Accommodations are roomy enough for a crib or rollaway, and bathrooms have standard modern fixtures.

Rates in the main building vary according to the view. They range from $154 to $269, single or double. Oceanfront lanai rooms rent for $359, and suites cost

$399–$750. Rates in the new complex are also based on view and start at $189 and go up to $299, single or double. Suites cost $499–$1,275. Children $15 and under stay free in their parents' room. Those over 15 and additional adults pay $25 each per night. No charge for cribs or rollaways. There is a minimum two-night stay on weekends. Parking costs $10 per day.

The lure of the **Loews Coronado Bay Resort,** 4000 Coronado Bay Rd., Coronado, CA 92118 (☎ **619/424-4000,** or toll free **800/815-6397**; fax 619/424-4400), is its private location in Coronado. You'll think you've reached the end of the peninsula. A weekend here will make you feel that you've managed to "get away from it all"—with the kids in tow.

There are myriad recreation opportunities to choose from. Three pools and a Jacuzzi are situated adjacent to one another in a lush and lovely setting. Although it's not formally designated as such, one pool is often suggested for the kids, so that they can all play together and meet one another (and so adults can maintain some quiet and privacy at the other pools). During summer and holiday periods the poolside Astra Bar & Grill serves light fare from 11am to dusk. Or you can order from room service.

Right close by is the health and fitness center. Use of the state-of-the-art exercise equipment, sauna, steam, and showers, power walks, and aerobics classes is $6 per day, and massage is available by appointment. Five lighted tennis courts can be reserved, and racquets can be rented. Private tennis instruction for adults or children can be booked. Facilities for docking your own private boat are available. Recreational boat rentals, sailing lessons, and waterskiing can be arranged through the hotel. Our family enjoyed being able to sail under the Coronado Bridge alongside some of the massive navy boats anchored in the bay. Silver Strand Beach is within walking distance. The concierge can arrange the rental of bicycles, in-line skates, and skateboards.

The hotel also offers shuttle service to Fashion Valley and Horton Plaza, as well as transportation on Saturdays to the Mexican border. A Sunday farmer's market in summer is a mini country fair with fresh produce, cooking demonstrations, and yummy food treats.

Designed and run by an outside service, the hotel's Commodore Kids Club schedules a variety of themed activities in half-day, full-day, or evening programs. The only caveat is that there must be at least two children signed up for any program to take place, but it does run daily year-round. Children must be signed up by 6pm the night before. At that time, the concierge will let you know whether other kids have registered. The club accepts children 4–12; if your child is too young, or if there aren't enough kids signed up, the concierge can arrange babysitting. There are the usual arts and crafts supplies, VCRs, toys for younger children, board games, and books all housed in two bright and clean rooms permanently assigned to the program. Older kids might enjoy the video game room next door.

Each daytime program revolves around a particular theme. Treasure Island day includes pirate expeditions, hunts for buried treasure at the beach, a movie, pirate-themed arts and crafts, and lunch at the beach. A tennis day offers a tennis clinic with pro Terry Addison. The full-day program, from 9am to 5pm, costs $30 per child; a half day costs $17. Lunch and two snacks, plus a stocked beach bucket, are included in the cost of the program. In summer, you can sign up by the hour ($5 per hour).

The evening programs, offered Thursday through Saturday from 6:30 to 9:30pm, consist of dinner, arts and crafts, and a movie and popcorn, plus a bag of goodies; the evening session costs $12.

A special holiday program for children features a reading of *How the Grinch Stole Christmas,* by a Dr. Seuss character, perfect to set the holiday mood.

Breakfast, lunch, and dinner are served in RRR's Café, where you can dine indoors or out. Sunday champagne brunch is served from 10:30am to 2:30pm. Adults pay $21.95; children 12 and under, $10.95. A children's menu is available. If you have the time, request a seat on RRR's Sunset Terrace for an afternoon cocktail and a great view of the setting sun.

One of the most innovative hotel "shops" we've ever seen is the RRR's Market, a gourmet market/giftshop/coffee bar. Little café tables and chairs make it a comfortable spot for a light snack—order espresso or cappuccino, or a picnic basket for the beach. The best southwestern chips we've ever tasted are sold here.

A night out *without* the kids might include dinner at the upstairs Azzura Point Restaurant overlooking the bay. While it's billed as a casual seafood specialty restaurant, it's upscale and special, cozy and intimate. Not that you can't bring the kids— but we suggest it for a private night out. The server will allow the youngsters to order off the RRR Café menu, if necessary.

There are five wings to this large hotel, each connected to each other and to the lobby. Standard double rooms have all the amenities you would expect from this class of hotel. Accommodations are winsomely decorated with padded headboards and flower-skirted beds, and the breakfast table is skirted and fitted with upholstered armchairs. Charming wallpaper and prints decorate the walls, and rattan and white-washed wood are used in the desk, chair, and armoire which houses the minibar and remote-control color TV. You have your choice of a room with one king-size bed, which will have room for a crib (or secure an adjoining room), or a room with two double beds. We were delighted with the large marble-and-tile bathrooms. There's an ultra-deep bathtub (with a ledge to set out all the bath toys!) and a separate glass-enclosed shower. The usual bathroom sundries are supplied, in addition to robes, plush towels, makeup mirror, and a phone in the bathroom.

The hotel provides twice-daily maid service, in-room movies, a furnished patio or balcony, and a clock radio. Room service can be ordered 24 hours, and a separate children's menu is offered.

Rooms at Loews cost $175–$225 single or double, depending on the location. Suites rent for $375–$1,500. Children under 18 stay free when sleeping in their parents' room; additional adults are charged $20. Cribs and rollaways are free. Be sure to ask about special promotions and packages. Valet and self-parking are available.

Your introduction to **Le Meridien,** 2000 2nd St., Coronado, CA 92118 (☎ **619/ 435-3000,** or toll free **800/543-4300;** fax 619/435-3032), is flamingos bathing in a pond. This elegant hotel is designed so that wherever you wander on the 16-acre property, you always have a view of water and sky. Twelve specially made lagoons complement the bay, and the walkways between rooms and buildings are open to the stars.

The Meridien is equally suited to adult and family travelers. Although there is no organized children's program, supervised activities for children of any age are available upon advance request during the summer and on holidays. Depending on their ages and desires, children can join in pool games, arts and crafts, and reading. There is no charge. Or the hotel can arrange babysitting for you.

The whole family can swim together in one of three pools, rent bicycles (no baby carriers or bikes for small kids), visit with the resident ducks, hop on the Electric Shuttle ($1 takes you all over Coronado), or take the free hotel shuttle to Horton Plaza in San Diego, which runs six times a day.

For adults, the hotel has a full-time activity staff to coordinate sports such as jogging, yoga, water volleyball, and all kinds of workouts. Facilities include the Le Meridien Spa and Clarins Institût de Beauté, plus six lighted tennis courts. And bring along your golf clubs—an 18-hole course is adjacent to the hotel (the greens fee is $14).

L'Escale Restaurant serves breakfast, lunch, and dinner indoors and outdoors; it opens at 6:30am. There is a limited children's menu, but prices are steep. Marius serves fine gourmet food and its atmosphere and prices are more suited to adult dining.

Meridien rooms have balconies or patios, upholstered reading chairs and lights, separate showers and deep tubs, makeup lights, and full-length mirrors. Amenities include a stocked minibar, remote-control color TV, a radio, bathroom scale, and bathroom telephone. Rooms have space for a crib or rollaway.

There are seven one-bedroom executive suites in addition to the standard rooms. Families may want to request a studio and an adjoining one-bedroom suite, and spread out in style.

One area of the property houses 28 villas. These condominiumlike accommodations are studios or one-bedroom suites with kitchenettes and patios. The villas are named after French impressionist artists such as Gauguin, and are decorated with the art of their respective namesakes. The decor is country French—even the bathrooms have French doors. You'll find extra amenities in the villas and suites such as Jacuzzis in the tubs.

Rates are the same for single or double occupancy, and vary according to room location. Standard rooms rent for $165–$225. Executive suites cost $475. A one-bedroom villa rents for $475, while a two-bedroom villa costs $625. Studio villas are available for $190 and $375. Children 12 and under stay free in their parents' room; those over 12 and additional adults pay $15 each per night. Inquire about "Kids Stay Free"—you pay for one room at the regular price and get an adjacent or connecting room free (when available). There's no charge for cribs or rollaways. Parking costs $7 per day.

8 Tijuana

Tijuana loves to bill itself as the most visited city in Mexico, and indeed it might be. In 1990 more than 70 million people crossed the border here. While in the past most of the reservations made for accommodations in Tijuana and the rest of Baja were for singles or couples, in the last couple of years the tourist bureau has found that many of their requests have been from families.

Before leaving for Tijuana, stop by or call the **Tijuana and Baja Office of Tourism,** 7860 Mission Center Court, Suite 202, San Diego, CA 92108 (☎ **619/299-8518** or **619/298-4105;** toll free **800/225-2786** or **800/522-1516** in California, Arizona, and Nevada). This office also has a Central Reservations System to make your hotel reservations. Just past the border is a tourist information center as well.

The **International Visitors Information Center** at Horton Plaza in San Diego (☎ **619/236-1212**) will also provide you with general information on Tijuana attractions.

GETTING THERE

There are three ways to get to Tijuana. You can **drive over the border,** but prepare for long lines returning to the United States, especially in the early evening on weekends. There are signs marked "Centro" that will lead you to downtown Tijuana.

You'll find guarded lots near Avenida Revolución, and there is street parking. Or you can park your car on the U.S. side and walk across the border. Taxis wait there all the time to take you into town. Once in Tijuana, you can walk to most places, or grab a taxi or rental car.

Another way to get to the border is via the **San Diego Trolley** (☎ 619/233-3004). The big red trolleys depart from the corner of Kettner Boulevard and C Street in San Diego, across the street from the Amtrak station, every 15 minutes from 5am to 7pm, and every 30 minutes thereafter, with the last trolley returning from the border at 1am. The trip to the border takes 40 minutes depending on the station you leave from, and once at the border you'll need a taxi to get to downtown Tijuana, about $5.

What You Need to Know About Travel to Mexico

Although United States citizens do not need a visa or a passport to enter Mexico as long as they remain within 100 miles of the border and stay in Mexico less than 72 hours, U.S. Customs and Immigration officers can be less than accommodating when you try to return. You might find it easier to leave your baggage in San Diego rather than possibly undergo a thorough U.S. Customs inspection upon your return from Mexico. (If you're planning to stay more than 24 hours, or if any of your traveling companions are naturalized citizens or resident aliens, check the current border regulations at a Mexican Consulate or Tourism Office before you enter Mexico. You can get two helpful booklets, "Know Before You Go" and "Travelers' Tips," free of charge from your nearest U.S. Customs Service office.)

Even if all members of your family are U.S. citizens or legal residents of the U.S., bring along birth certificates or other **proof of U.S. citizenship or permanent residence** for each member of your family. (Resident aliens must carry their alien registration cards; naturalized citizens should carry their naturalization certificates.)

If minors are traveling into Mexico with adults other than their parents (grandparents, for instance), it is imperative that a notarized letter signed by both parents be carried by the accompanying adults, even if they are part of the extended family. Minors are not allowed to travel to Mexico without an adult supervisor.

If you drive into Tijuana, be sure to have a valid driver's license, and arrange for car insurance before crossing the border. **American auto insurance is not valid in Mexico.** If you have a rental car, ask the rental agent whether you can get insurance for Mexico. Offices for Mexican auto insurance can be found all over San Diego and close to the border. The International Visitors Information Center (☎ 619/236-1212) or the San Diego *Yellow Pages* are sources for these offices.

There are a number of **money-changing services** in San Ysidro, the town right before the border. The value of the peso has been fluctuating on a daily basis, so check the rates on the day you decide to go to Tijuana. The American dollar is accepted almost anywhere in Tijuana, Rosarita Beach, and Ensenada.

Each adult can bring back up to $400 worth of **duty-free goods** into the United States, and one quart of liquor.

Most merchants and restaurant employees speak English. But if you should need assistance, you can contact: the **U.S. Consulate** (☎ 817-400 in Tijuana) and the **Office for Tourism Assistance** (☎ 880-555 in Tijuana, **63-686** in Ensenada).

Finally, you can visit on an **organized tour,** but we don't recommend this for children.

WHAT TO SEE AND DO

Those of you who visited Tijuana years ago will remember it as kind of tacky and rough—the place where sailors and teenagers went to avoid the drinking-age limit in San Diego. Efforts have been made to spruce up the city. Lucky for us, though, it hasn't lost its Latin flavor and the traditional touches that still make visiting there an adventure.

Tijuana is a place you can safely take the whole family for the day, evening, or overnight. As a whole, the Mexican people love children and they make it comfortable for you to take your kids nearly everywhere with you. Many restaurants in Tijuana will greet your children warmly. We like to go late in the afternoon (the stores stay open late), walk around, visit the Cultural Center or Mexitlán, bargain for merchandise in some of the small shops, have a lively dinner, and return to San Diego at 10pm or so.

A visit to **Mexitlán** (☎ 619/531-1112 in the U.S., or 38-4101 in Mexico) is a unique way to introduce the children to the wonders of Mexico. It's three blocks from Avenida Revolución, and half a mile from the border. Look for a giant glass piñata in front of "Mercado de Artesanías."

This open-air rooftop park re-creates the important buildings, monuments, and archeological sites of Mexico in miniature. Children love to stand next to the replicas and gauge their height in comparison to the "giant" cathedrals and pyramids. If you can go on Saturday or Sunday you can watch the folkloric dancers, mariachis, and ballet dancers perform traditional and contemporary Mexican music and dances. At dusk there's a sound-and-light show, and in summer, miniature fireworks. Entertainment is presented approximately every four hours.

Shops, fast-food emporiums, a buffet, and a sit-down restaurant are located in the complex. You can make reservations to have guides lead you through the displays by calling in advance. It is open Tuesday through Friday from 10am to 6pm, Saturday and Sunday noon to 8pm; closed Monday; from the end of October through the end of December, and during the month of February, the closing time is 8pm. Mexitlán costs $3.25 for adults and children over 12; children under 12 are free. Covered, free parking.

The **Tijuana Cultural Center,** the city's proud accomplishment, is located at Paseo de los Héroes y Ave. Mina at the Río Tijuana Zone, less than a mile from the border (☎ 841-132). In addition to a museum and exhibit halls, there is an OMNIMAX Space Theater and a Performing Arts Center. The Space Theater has a 180° screen to wrap you inside the presentation. The daily "People of the Sun" show is a dramatic view of such beautiful sights as Copper Canyon, Cancún, and the Mayan and Aztec pyramids. It's shown in English daily at 2pm. Admission is $4.50 for adults, $2.25 for children 12 and under.

The exhibit halls act as an art museum, often displaying the works of local and internationally acclaimed Mexican artists. The museum is open daily from 11am to 7pm. Admission is $1 for adults and children.

Sports are big draws to Tijuana. You and the older children might enjoy watching **Greyhound racing** at **Agua Caliente Racetrack,** Blvd. Agua Caliente (☎ 619/231-1910, or 817-811 in Tijuana). Races are scheduled nightly at 7:45pm; Saturday and Sunday there's an additional 2pm race.

Jai alai is a fascinating game that your older kids might enjoy seeing. The only places you can see it in the United States are in Florida and Connecticut. In Tijuana it's played at **Fronton Palacio Jai Alai,** Calle 7 and Avenida Revolución (☎ 619/ 231-1910, or 852-524 in Tijuana). A Basque game similar to handball or racquetball, jai alai originated in 18th-century Spain. The ball is called the *pelota,* and the basketlike net that catches it is called the *cesta.* It's an extremely fast game (the ball can travel at more than 160 m.p.h.) and is played with singles or doubles. Pari-mutuel wagering on the games is offered. The Palacio is open every night except Wednesday at 7pm (closed throughout the Christmas and New Year holidays). The first game is at 8pm. Admission varies from $3 to $5.

Avenida Revolución is the original main shopping thoroughfare, and a part of the city's modernization efforts. Now it sports outdoor cafés and trees and flowers. Most of the stores here carry the finer jewelry, clothing, and artwork of Mexico. These aren't the shops to bargain in. Do that in the souvenir shops on the side streets; in the better boutiques and jewelry stores, they won't accept it. Although the street has been modernized, the ubiquitous photographer and his trusty donkey are still there to snap your souvenir picture. Since Tijuana is a duty-free spot, you'll also want to visit the **Río Tijuana Shopping Plaza,** next to the Cultural Center, to find French perfume, English cashmere, and Baccarat crystal.

If you want to continue farther down the peninsula, you can stop at the **Rosarito Beach Hotel** in Rosarito Beach, about 20 miles south of Tijuana. Built in the 1930s, the hotel was once the haunt of movie stars and visiting royalty. Local restaurants offer very reasonably priced fresh lobster lunches. Contact the **Rosarito Convention & Visitor Bureau** (☎ toll free **800/962-BAJA**) for a complimentary guide to the area. Or continue farther south to **Ensenada,** only 70 miles south of Tijuana. It's an easy and pretty ride on a four-lane toll road. Once you get there, you can walk around town and visit the shops or stroll closer to the water and stop for great food, including fresh lobster, at incredibly low prices. Nearby (you have to drive) is the **Bufadora,** a water spout that shoots spray high into the air when the tide rises. If you're there in May, you may be in time for the international **San Diego–Ensenada yacht race.**

Index

Now Save Money On All Your Travels By Joining
FROMMER'S™ TRAVEL BOOK CLUB
The World's Best Travel Guides
At Membership Prices!

Frommer's Travel Book Club is your ticket to successful travel! Open up a world of travel information and simplify your travel planning when you join ranks with thousands of value-conscious travelers who are members of the Frommer's *Travel Book Club.* Join today and you'll be entitled to all the privileges that come from belonging to the club that offers you travel guides for less to more than 100 destinations worldwide. **Annual membership is only $25.00 (U.S.) or $35.00 (Canada/Foreign).**

The Advantages of Membership:

1. Your choice of **three free** books (any **two** Frommer's Comprehensive Guides, Frommer's $-A-Day Guides, Frommer's Walking Tours or Frommer's Family Guides—plus **one** Frommer's City Guide, Frommer's City $-A-Day Guide or Frommer's Touring Guide).

2. Your own subscription to the **TRIPS & TRAVEL** quarterly newsletter.

3. You're entitled to a **30% discount** on your order of any additional books offered by the club.

4. You're offered (at a small additional fee) our **Domestic Trip-Routing Kits.**

Our **Trips & Travel** quarterly newsletter offers practical information on the best buys in travel, the "hottest" vacation spots, the latest travel trends, world-class events and much, much more.

Our **Domestic Trip-Routing Kits** are available for any North American destination. We'll send you a detailed map highlighting the best route to take to your destination—you can request direct or scenic routes.

Here's all you have to do to join:

Send in your membership fee of $25.00 ($35.00 Canada/Foreign) with your name and address on the form below along with your selections as part of your membership package to the address listed below. Remember to check off your three free books.

If you would like to order additional books, please select the books you would like and send a check for the total amount (please add sales tax in the states noted below), plus $2.00 per book for shipping and handling ($3.00 Canada/ Foreign) to the address listed below.

FROMMER'S TRAVEL BOOK CLUB
P.O. Box 473
Mt. Morris, IL 61054-0473
(815) 734-1104

[ ] **YES!** I want to take advantage of this opportunity to join Frommer's Travel Book Club.

[ ] My check is enclosed. Dollar amount enclosed_____*

(all payments in U.S. funds only)

Name _____

Address _____

City _____ State _____ Zip _____

Phone ( ) _____ (In case we have a question regarding your order).

All orders must be prepaid.

To ensure that all orders are processed efficiently, please apply sales tax in the following areas: CA, CT, FL, IL, IN, NJ, NY, PA, TN, WA and CANADA.

*With membership, shipping & handling will be paid by Frommer's Travel Book Club for the three FREE books you select as part of your membership. Please add $2.00 per book for shipping & handling for any additional books purchased ($3.00 Canada/Foreign).

Allow 4-6 weeks for delivery for all items. Prices of books, membership fee, and publication dates are subject to change without notice. All orders are subject to acceptance and availability.

Please send me the books checked below:

FROMMER'S COMPREHENSIVE GUIDES

*(Guides listing facilities from budget to deluxe,
with emphasis on the medium-priced)*

	Retail Price	Code			Retail Price	Code
☐ Acapulco/Ixtapa/Taxco, 2nd Edition	$13.95	C157		☐ Jamaica/Barbados, 2nd Edition	$15.00	C149
☐ Alaska '94-'95	$17.00	C131		☐ Japan '94-'95	$19.00	C144
☐ Arizona '95 (Avail. 3/95)	$14.95	C166		☐ Maui, 1st Edition	$14.00	C153
☐ Australia '94'-'95	$18.00	C147		☐ Nepal, 2nd Edition	$18.00	C126
☐ Austria, 6th Edition	$16.95	C162		☐ New England '95	$16.95	C165
☐ Bahamas '94-'95	$17.00	C121		☐ New Mexico, 3rd Edition (Avail. 3/95)	$14.95	C167
☐ Belgium/Holland/ Luxembourg '93-'94	$18.00	C106		☐ New York State '94-'95	$19.00	C133
☐ Bermuda '94-'95	$15.00	C122		☐ Northwest, 5th Edition	$17.00	C140
☐ Brazil, 3rd Edition	$20.00	C111		☐ Portugal '94-'95	$17.00	C141
☐ California '95	$16.95	C164		☐ Puerto Rico '95-'96	$14.00	C151
☐ Canada '94-'95	$19.00	C145		☐ Puerto Vallarta/ Manzanillo/Guadalajara		
☐ Caribbean '95	$18.00	C148		'94-'95	$14.00	C135
☐ Carolinas/Georgia, 2nd Edition	$17.00	C128		☐ Scandinavia, 16th Edition (Avail. 3/95)	$19.95	C169
☐ Colorado, 2nd Edition	$16.00	C143		☐ Scotland '94-'95	$17.00	C146
☐ Costa Rica '95	$13.95	C161		☐ South Pacific '94-'95	$20.00	C138
☐ Cruises '95-'96	$19.00	C150		☐ Spain, 16th Edition	$16.95	C163
☐ Delaware/Maryland '94-'95	$15.00	C136		☐ Switzerland/ Liechtenstein '94-'95	$19.00	C139
☐ England '95	$17.95	C159		☐ Thailand, 2nd Edition	$17.95	C154
☐ Florida '95	$18.00	C152		☐ U.S.A., 4th Edition	$18.95	C156
☐ France '94-'95	$20.00	C132		☐ Virgin Islands '94-'95	$13.00	C127
☐ Germany '95	$18.95	C158		☐ Virginia '94-'95	$14.00	C142
☐ Ireland, 1st Edition (Avail. 3/95)	$16.95	C168		☐ Yucatan, 2nd Edition	$13.95	C155
☐ Italy '95	$18.95	C160				

FROMMER'S $-A-DAY GUIDES

(Guides to low-cost tourist accommodations and facilities)

	Retail Price	Code			Retail Price	Code
☐ Australia on $45 '95-'96	$18.00	D122		☐ Israel on $45, 15th Edition	$16.95	D130
☐ Costa Rica/Guatemala/ Belize on $35, 3rd Edition	$15.95	D126		☐ Mexico on $45 '95	$16.95	D125
☐ Eastern Europe on $30, 5th Edition	$16.95	D129		☐ New York on $70 '94-'95	$16.00	D121
☐ England on $60 '95	$17.95	D128		☐ New Zealand on $45 '93-'94	$18.00	D103
☐ Europe on $50 '95	$17.95	D127		☐ South America on $40, 16th Edition	$18.95	D123
☐ Greece on $45 '93-'94	$19.00	D100		☐ Washington, D.C. on $50 '94-'95	$17.00	D120
☐ Hawaii on $75 '95	$16.95	D124				
☐ Ireland on $45 '94-'95	$17.00	D118				

FROMMER'S CITY $-A-DAY GUIDES

	Retail Price	Code		Retail Price	Code
☐ Berlin on $40 '94-'95	$12.00	D111	☐ Madrid on $50 '94-'95	$13.00	D119
☐ London on $45 '94-'95	$12.00	D114	☐ Paris on $50 '94-'95	$12.00	D117

FROMMER'S FAMILY GUIDES
(Guides listing information on kid-friendly
hotels, restaurants, activities and attractions)

	Retail Price	Code		Retail Price	Code
☐ California with Kids	$18.00	F100	☐ San Francisco with Kids	$17.00	F104
☐ Los Angeles with Kids	$17.00	F103	☐ Washington, D.C. with Kids	$17.00	F102
☐ New York City with Kids	$18.00	F101			

FROMMER'S CITY GUIDES
(Pocket-size guides to sightseeing and tourist
accommodations and facilities in all price ranges)

	Retail Price	Code		Retail Price	Code
☐ Amsterdam '93-'94	$13.00	S110	☐ Montreal/Quebec City '95	$11.95	S166
☐ Athens, 10th Edition (Avail. 3/95)	$12.95	S174	☐ Nashville/Memphis, 1st Edition	$13.00	S141
☐ Atlanta '95	$12.95	S161	☐ New Orleans '95	$12.95	S148
☐ Atlantic City/Cape May, 5th Edition	$13.00	S130	☐ New York '95	$12.95	S152
☐ Bangkok, 2nd Edition	$12.95	S147	☐ Orlando '95	$13.00	S145
☐ Barcelona '93-'94	$13.00	S115	☐ Paris '95	$12.95	S150
☐ Berlin, 3rd Edition	$12.95	S162	☐ Philadelphia, 8th Edition	$12.95	S167
☐ Boston '95	$12.95	S160	☐ Prague '94-'95	$13.00	S143
☐ Budapest, 1st Edition	$13.00	S139	☐ Rome, 10th Edition	$12.95	S168
☐ Chicago '95	$12.95	S169	☐ St. Louis/Kansas City, 2nd Edition	$13.00	S127
☐ Denver/Boulder/Colorado Springs, 3rd Edition	$12.95	S154	☐ San Diego '95	$12.95	S158
☐ Dublin, 2nd Edition	$12.95	S157	☐ San Francisco '95	$12.95	S155
☐ Hong Kong '94-'95	$13.00	S140	☐ Santa Fe/Taos/ Albuquerque '95 (Avail. 2/95)	$12.95	S172
☐ Honolulu/Oahu '95	$12.95	S151	☐ Seattle/Portland '94-'95	$13.00	S137
☐ Las Vegas '95	$12.95	S163	☐ Sydney, 4th Edition	$12.95	S171
☐ London '95	$12.95	S156	☐ Tampa/St. Petersburg, 3rd Edition	$13.00	S146
☐ Los Angeles '95	$12.95	S164	☐ Tokyo '94-'95	$13.00	S144
☐ Madrid/Costa del Sol, 2nd Edition	$12.95	S165	☐ Toronto '95 (Avail. 3/95)	$12.95	S173
☐ Mexico City, 1st Edition	$12.95	S170	☐ Vancouver/Victoria '94-'95	$13.00	S142
☐ Miami '95-'96	$12.95	S149	☐ Washington, D.C. '95	$12.95	S153
☐ Minneapolis/St. Paul, 4th Edition	$12.95	S159			

FROMMER'S WALKING TOURS
(Companion guides that point out the places
and pleasures that make a city unique)

	Retail Price	Code		Retail Price	Code
☐ Berlin	$12.00	W100	☐ New York	$12.00	W102
☐ Chicago	$12.00	W107	☐ Paris	$12.00	W103
☐ England's Favorite Cities	$12.00	W108	☐ San Francisco	$12.00	W104
☐ London	$12.00	W101	☐ Washington, D.C.	$12.00	W105
☐ Montreal/Quebec City	$12.00	W106			

SPECIAL EDITIONS

	Retail Price	Code		Retail Price	Code
☐ Bed & Breakfast Southwest	$16.00	P100	☐ National Park Guide, 29th Edition	$17.00	P106
☐ Bed & Breakfast Great American Cities	$16.00	P104	☐ Where to Stay U.S.A., 11th Edition	$15.00	P102
☐ Caribbean Hideaways	$16.00	P103			

FROMMER'S TOURING GUIDES
(Color-illustrated guides that include walking tours,
cultural and historic sites, and practical information)

	Retail Price	Code		Retail Price	Code
☐ Amsterdam	$11.00	T001	☐ New York	$11.00	T008
☐ Barcelona	$14.00	T015	☐ Rome	$11.00	T010
☐ Brazil	$11.00	T003	☐ Tokyo	$15.00	T016
☐ Hong Kong/Singapore/ Macau	$11.00	T006	☐ Turkey	$11.00	T013
☐ London	$13.00	T007	☐ Venice	$ 9.00	T014

Please note: If the availability of a book is several months away, we may
have back issues of guides to that particular destination.
Call customer service at (815) 734-1104.